The Longman Anthology of World Literature

◆━━◆≍◈≍◆━━◆

VOLUME E

THE NINETEENTH CENTURY

David Damrosch
COLUMBIA UNIVERSITY
The Ancient Near East; Mesoamerica

April Alliston
PRINCETON UNIVERSITY
The Age of the Enlightenment

Marshall Brown
UNIVERSITY OF WASHINGTON
The Nineteenth Century

Page duBois
UNIVERSITY OF CALIFORNIA, SAN DIEGO
Classical Greece

Sabry Hafez
UNIVERSITY OF LONDON
Arabic and Islamic Literature

Ursula K. Heise
COLUMBIA UNIVERSITY
The Twentieth Century

Djelal Kadir
PENNSYLVANIA STATE UNIVERSITY
The Twentieth Century

David L. Pike
AMERICAN UNIVERSITY
Rome and the Roman Empire; Medieval Europe

Sheldon Pollock
UNIVERSITY OF CHICAGO
South Asia

Bruce Robbins
COLUMBIA UNIVERSITY
The Nineteenth Century

Haruo Shirane
COLUMBIA UNIVERSITY
Japan

Jane Tylus
NEW YORK UNIVERSITY
Early Modern Europe

Pauline Yu
AMERICAN COUNCIL OF LEARNED SOCIETIES
China

The Longman Anthology of World Literature

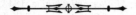

David Damrosch

General Editor

VOLUME E

THE NINETEENTH CENTURY

Marshall Brown

Bruce Robbins

with contributions by

April Alliston, David Damrosch,

David L. Pike, Sheldon Pollock, and Pauline Yu

PEARSON
Longman

New York   San Francisco   Boston
London   Toronto   Sydney   Tokyo   Singapore   Madrid
Mexico City   Munich   Paris   Cape Town   Hong Kong   Montreal

Vice President and Editor-in-Chief: *Joseph Terry*
Development Manager: *Janet Lanphier*
Development Editor: *Adam Beroud*
Senior Marketing Manager: *Melanie Craig*
Senior Supplements Editor: *Donna Campion*
Media Supplements Editor: *Nancy Garcia*
Production Manager: *Douglas Bell*
Project Coordination, Text Design, and Page Makeup: *Elm Street Publishing Services, Inc.*
Senior Design Manager/Cover Designer: *Nancy Danahy*
On the Cover: Detail from *Cowlitz Mother and Child,* c. 1848, oil on canvas, by Paul Kane
    Caw-Wacham. Montreal Museum of Fine Arts, purchased with William Gilman Cheney
    Bequest. Photo by Denis Farley, The Montreal Museum of Fine Arts.
Photo Research: *Photosearch, Inc.*
Manufacturing Buyer: *Lucy Hebard*
Printer and Binder: *Quebecor-World/Taunton*
Cover Printer: *The Lehigh Press, Inc.*

For permission to use copyrighted material, grateful acknowledgment is made to the copyright
holders on pages 969–971, which are hereby made part of this copyright page.

Library of Congress Cataloging-in-Publication Data

The Longman anthology of world literature / David Damrosch, general editor.—1st ed.
    v.   cm.
    Includes bibliographical references and index.
    Contents: v. A. The ancient world—v. B. The medieval era—v. C. The early
modern period—v. D. The seventeenth and eighteenth centuries—v. E. The
nineteenth century—v. F. The twentieth century.
    ISBN 0-321-05533-0 (v. A).—ISBN 0-321-16978-6 (v. B).— 0-321-16979-4
    (v. C).— 0-321-16980-8 (v. D).— 0-321-17306-6 (v. E).— 0-321-05536-5 (v. F)
    1. Literature—Collections.   2. Literature—History and criticism.
I. Damrosch, David.
PN6013.L66   2004
                                                          2003061890

Please visit us at http://www.ablongman.com/damrosch.

To place your order, please use the following ISBN numbers:

ISBN Volume One Package *The Ancient World to The Early Modern Period*
(includes Volumes A, B, and C): **0-321-20238-4**

ISBN Volume Two Package *The Seventeenth Century to The Twentieth Century*
(includes Volumes D, E, and F): **0-321-20237-6**

Or, to order individual volumes, please use the following ISBN numbers:

ISBN Volume A, *The Ancient World*: 0-321-05533-0
ISBN Volume B, *The Medieval Era*: 0-321-16978-6
ISBN Volume C, *The Early Modern Period*: 0-321-16979-4
ISBN Volume D, *The Seventeenth and Eighteenth Centuries*: 0-321-16980-8
ISBN Volume E, *The Nineteenth Century*: 0-321-17306-6
ISBN Volume F, *The Twentieth Century*: 0-321-05536-5

1 2 3 4 5 6 7 8 9 10—QWT—06 05 04 03

CONTENTS

⇒ PERSPECTIVES ⇐
On the Colonial Frontier   374

THE ROMANTIC FANTASTIC   425

SAMUEL TAYLOR COLERIDGE (1772–1834)   426

LUDWIG TIECK (1773–1853)   444

HONORÉ DE BALZAC (1799–1850)   455

LEO TOLSTOY (1828–1910)   593

FYODOR DOSTOEVSKY (1822–1881)   600

OTHER AMERICAS   680

HATHALI NEZ AND WASHINGTON MATTHEWS
(1843–1905)   680

HERMAN MELVILLE (1819–1891)   711

FREDERICK DOUGLASS (1818–1895)   735

HARRIET JACOBS (1813–1897)   788

EMILY DICKINSON (1830–1886)   810

LIST OF ILLUSTRATIONS

Maps

On the Cover

Detail from *Cowlitz Mother and Child,* c. 1848, oil on canvas, by Paul Kane Caw-Wacham. This striking image of a native Canadian woman and her child is both a portrait of wilderness nobility and an ethnographic study of native customs. The mother has her child firmly bound in a frame that presses on its forehead to create a flattened and elongated profile—the kind of profile that the mother herself displays, a mark of distinction and beauty among her tribe. The board would be progressively tightened with its rawhide cord to produce the desired effect. As foreign as this practice is to Euro-American eyes, the figures in the painting already begin to show the effects of contact with the settlers' culture: the baby wears a necklace of European beads along with a handmade native necklace.

PREFACE

Our world today is both expanding and growing smaller at the same time. Expanding, through a tremendous increase in the range of cultures that actively engage with each other; and yet growing smaller as well, as people and products surge across borders in the process known as globalization. This double movement creates remarkable opportunities for cross-cultural understanding, as well as new kinds of tensions, miscommunications, and uncertainties. Both the opportunities and the uncertainties are amply illustrated in the changing shape of world literature. A generation ago, when the term "world literature" was used in North America, it largely meant masterworks by European writers from Homer onward, together with a few favored North American writers, heirs to the Europeans. Today, however, it is generally recognized that Europe is only part of the story of the world's literatures, and only part of the story of North America's cultural heritage. An extraordinary range of exciting material is now in view, from the earliest Sumerian lyrics inscribed on clay tablets to the latest Kashmiri poetry circulated on the Internet. Many new worlds—and newly visible *older* worlds of classical traditions around the globe—await us today.

How can we best approach such varied materials from so many cultures? Can we deal with this embarrassment of riches without being overwhelmed by it, and without merely giving a glancing regard to less familiar traditions? This anthology has been designed to help readers successfully navigate "the sea of stories"—as Salman Rushdie has described the world's literary heritage. This preface will outline the ways we've gone about this challenging, fascinating task.

CONNECTING DISTINCTIVE TRADITIONS

Works of world literature engage in a double conversation: with their culture of origin and with the varied contexts into which they travel away from home. To look broadly at world literature is therefore to see patterns of difference as well as points of contact and commonality. The world's disparate traditions have developed very distinct kinds of literature, even very different ideas as to what should be called "literature" at all. This anthology uses a variety of means to showcase what is most distinctive and also what is commonly shared among the world's literatures. Throughout the anthology, we employ three kinds of grouping:

☞ **CROSSCURRENTS: A major grouping at the beginning of each volume, bringing together literary responses to worldwide developments.**

☞ **PERSPECTIVES: Groupings that provide cultural context for major works, illuminating issues of broad importance.**

☞ **RESONANCES: Sources for a specific text or responses to it, often from a different time and place.**

The "Crosscurrents" sections that open our six volumes highlight overarching issues or developments that many cultures have faced, often in conversation with neighboring cultures and more distant ones too. "Creation Myths and Social Realities" in antiquity, for example, brings together creation stories that circulated throughout the ancient Near East, westward to Greece, and eastward to India. "The Folk and Their Tales" in the nineteenth century shows the interplay of folk traditions between India and Europe, Africa and the Americas, Native Americans and Euro-Americans.

Regional divisions predominate in our Volumes A through C, reflecting the distinctive development of the world's major literary traditions over the centuries before the modern period. For each of these volumes, the Crosscurrents provide an initial, cross-cutting overview of a major issue, giving a reminder that there have been important contacts across cultures as far back as we know—and showing too how different cultures can independently address matters of common human concern. In our more globally organized later volumes D through F (mid-seventeenth century to the present), the Crosscurrents demonstrate the increasing interconnectedness of the world's literary traditions.

Throughout the anthology, our many "Perspectives" sections provide cultural context for the major works around them, giving insight into such issues as the representation of death and immortality (in the ancient Near East); the meeting of Christians, Muslims, and Jews in medieval Iberia; the idea of the national poet in the nineteenth century; and "modernist memory" in the twentieth. Perspectives sections also provide an opportunity for focused regional groupings within our globally structured later volumes, with "Other Americas" in the nineteenth century, for example, and "Modernism and Revolution in Russia" in the twentieth. Perspectives sections give a range of voices and views, strategies and styles, in highly readable textual groupings. The Perspectives groupings serve a major pedagogical as well as intellectual purpose in making these selections accessible and useful within the time constraints of a survey course.

Finally, our "Resonances" perform the crucial function of linking works across time as well as space. For Homer's *Iliad,* a Resonance shows oral composition as it is still practiced today north of Greece, while for the *Odyssey* we have Resonances giving modern responses to Homer by Franz Kafka, Derek Walcott, and the Greek poet George Seferis. Accompanying the traditional Navajo "Story of the Emergence" (Volume E) is an extended selection from *Black Elk Speaks* which shows how ancient imagery infused the dream visions of the Sioux healer and warrior Nicholas Black Elk, helping him deal with the crises of lost land and independence that his people were facing. Resonances for Conrad's *Heart of Darkness* (Volume F) give selections from Conrad's diary of his own journey upriver in the Congo, and a speech by Henry Morton Stanley, the explorer-journalist who was serving as publicist for King Leopold's exploitation of his colony in the years just before Conrad went there. Stanley's surreal speech—in which he calculates how much money the Manchester weavers can make providing wedding dresses and burial clothes for the Congolese— gives a vivid instance of the outlook, and the rhetoric, that Conrad grimly parodies in Mr. Kurtz and his associates.

PRINCIPLES OF SELECTION

Beyond our immediate groupings, our overall selections have been made with an eye to fostering connections across time and space: a Perspectives section on "Courtly Women" in medieval Japan (Volume B) introduces themes that can be followed up in

"Court Culture and Female Authorship" in Enlightenment-era Europe (Volume D), while the ancient Mediterranean and South Asian creation myths at the start of Volume A find echoes in later cosmic-creation narratives from Iceland (Volume B), Mesoamerica (Volume C), and indigenous peoples today (Volume E). Altogether, we have worked to create an exceptionally coherent and well-integrated presentation of an extraordinary variety of works from around the globe, from the dawn of writing to the present.

Recognizing that different sorts of works have counted as literature in differing times and places, we take an inclusive approach, centering on poems, plays, and fictional narratives but also including selections from rich historical, religious, and philosophical texts like Plato's *Republic* and the Qur'an that have been important for much later literary work, even though they weren't conceived as literature themselves. We present many complete masterworks, including *The Epic of Gilgamesh* (in a beautiful verse translation), Homer's *Odyssey,* Dante's *Inferno,* and Chinua Achebe's *Things Fall Apart,* and we have extensive, teachable selections from such long works as *The Tale of Genji, Don Quixote,* and both parts of Goethe's *Faust.*

Along with these major selections we present a great array of shorter works, some of which have been known only to specialists and only now are entering into world literature. It is our experience as readers and as teachers that the established classics themselves can best be understood when they're set in a varied literary landscape. Nothing is included here, though, simply to make a point: whether world-renowned or recently rediscovered, these are compelling works to read. Throughout our work on this book, we've tried to be highly inclusive in principle and yet carefully selective in practice, avoiding tokenism and also its inverse, the piling up of an unmanageable array of heterogeneous material. If we've succeeded as we hope, the result will be coherent as well as capacious, substantive as well as stimulating.

LITERATURE, ART, AND MUSIC

One important way to understand literary works in context is to read them in conjunction with the broader social and artistic culture in which they were created. Literature has often had a particularly close relation to visual art and to music. Different as the arts are in their specific resources and techniques, a culture's artistic expressions often share certain family resemblances, common traits that can be seen across different media—and that may even come out more clearly in visual or musical form than in translations of literature itself. This anthology includes dozens of black-and-white illustrations and a suite of color illustrations in each volume, chosen to work in close conjunction with our literary selections. Some of these images directly illustrate literary works, while others show important aspects of a culture's aesthetic sensibility. Often, writing actually appears on paintings and sculptures, with represented people and places sharing the space with beautifully rendered Mayan hieroglyphs, Arabic calligraphy, or Chinese brushstrokes.

Music too has been a close companion of literary creation and performance. Our very term "lyric" refers to the lyres or harps with which the Greeks accompanied poems as they were sung. In China, the first major literary work is the *Book of Songs.* In Europe too, until quite recent times poetry was often sung and even prose was usually read aloud. We have created two audio CDs to accompany the anthology, one for Volumes A through C and one for volumes D through F. These CDs give a wealth of poetry and music from the cultures we feature in the anthology; they are both a valuable teaching resource and also a pure pleasure to listen to.

AIDS TO UNDERSTANDING

A major emphasis of our work has been to introduce each culture and each work to best effect. Each major period and section of the anthology, each grouping of works, and each individual author has an introduction by a member of our editorial team. Our goal has been to write introductions informed by deep knowledge worn lightly. Neither talking down to our readers nor overwhelming them with masses of unassimilable information, our introductions don't seek to "cover" the material but instead try to uncover it, to provide ways in and connections outward. Similarly, our footnotes and glosses are concise and informative, rather than massive or interpretive. Time lines for each volume, and maps and pronunciation guides throughout the anthology, all aim to foster an informed and pleasurable reading of the works.

GOING FURTHER

The Longman Anthology of World Literature makes connections beyond its covers as well as within them. Bibliographies at the end of each volume point the way to historical and critical readings for students wishing to go into greater depth for term papers. The Companion Website we've developed for the course (www.ablongman.com/worldlit) gives a wealth of links to excellent Web resources on all our major texts and many related historical and cultural movements and events. The Web site includes an audio version of our printed pronunciation guides: you can simply click on a name to hear it pronounced. Finally, the Web site includes readings of works in the original and in translation, with accompanying texts, giving extensive exposure to the aural dimension of many of the languages represented in the anthology.

For instructors, we have also created an extensive, two-volume instructor's manual, *Teaching World Literature*—written directly by the editors themselves, drawing on our years of experience in teaching these materials.

TRANSLATION ACROSS CULTURES

The circulation of world literature is always an exercise in cultural translation, and one way to define works of world literature is that they are the works that gain in translation. Some great texts remain so intimately tied to their point of origin that they never read well abroad; they may have an abiding importance at home, but don't play a role in the wider world. Other works, though, gain in resonance as they move out into new contexts, new conjunctions. Edgar Allan Poe found his first really serious readers in France, rather than in the United States. *The Thousand and One Nights,* long a marginal work in Arabic traditions oriented toward poetry rather than popular prose, gained new readers and new influence abroad, and Scheherazade's intricately nested tales now help us in turn to read the European tales of Boccaccio and Marguerite de Navarre with new attention and appreciation. A Perspectives section on *"The Thousand and One Nights* in the Twentieth Century" (Volume F) brings together a range of Arab, European, and American writers who have continued to plumb its riches to this day.

As important as cultural translation in general is the issue of actual translation from one language to another. We have sought out compelling translations for all our foreign-language works, and periodically we offer our readers the opportunity to think directly about the issue of translation. Sometimes we offer distinctively different translations of differing works from a single author or source: for the Bible, for example, we give Genesis 1–11 in Robert Alter's lively, oral-style translation, while we give selected psalms in the magnificent King James Version and the Joseph story in the lucid New International Version. Our selections from Homer's *Iliad* appear in Richmond Lattimore's stately older translation, while Homer's *Odyssey* is given in Robert Fagles's eloquent new version.

At other times, we give alternative translations of a single work. So we have Chinese lyrics translated by the modernist poet Ezra Pound, by the scholar-aesthete Arthur Waley, and by the contemporary poet and novelist Vikram Seth; and we have Petrarch sonnets translated by the Renaissance English poet Thomas Wyatt and also by contemporary translators. These juxtapositions can show some of the varied ways in which translators over the centuries have sought to carry works over from one time and place to another—not so much by mirroring and reflecting an unchanged meaning, as by refracting it, in a prismatic process that can add new highlights and reveal new facets in a classic text. At times, when we haven't found a translation that really satisfies us, we've translated the work ourselves—an activity we recommend to all who wish to come to know a work from the inside.

We hope that the results of our years of work on this project will be as enjoyable to use as the book has been to create. We welcome you now inside our pages.

David Damrosch

ACKNOWLEDGMENTS

In the extended process of planning and preparing this anthology, the editors have been fortunate to have the support, advice, and assistance of many people. Our editor, Joe Terry, and our publisher, Roth Wilkovsky, have supported our project in every possible way and some seemingly impossible ones as well, helping us produce the best possible book despite all challenges to budgets and well-laid plans in a rapidly evolving field. Their associates Janet Lanphier and Melanie Craig have shown unwavering enthusiasm and constant creativity in developing the book and its related Web site and audio CDs and in introducing the results to the world. Our development editors, first Mark Getlein and then Adam Beroud, have shown a compelling blend of literary acuity and quiet diplomacy in guiding thirteen far-flung editors through the many stages of work. Peter Meyers brought great energy and creativity to work on our CDs. Donna Campion and Dianne Hall worked diligently to complete the instructor's manual. Celeste Parker-Bates cleared hundreds and hundreds of text permissions from publishers in many countries, and Sherri Zuckerman at Photosearch, Inc., cleared our many photo permissions.

Once the manuscript was complete, Doug Bell, the production manager, oversaw the simultaneous production of six massive books on a tight and shifting schedule. Valerie Zaborski, managing editor in production, also helped and, along the way, developed a taste for the good-humored fatalism of Icelandic literature. Our lead copyeditor, Stephanie Magean, and her associates Martha Beyerlein, Elizabeth Jahaske, and Marcia LaBrenz marvelously integrated everyone's writing, and then Amber Allen and her colleagues at Elm Street Publishing Services worked overtime to produce beautiful books accurate down to the last exotic accent.

We are specifically grateful for the guidance of the many reviewers who advised us on the creation of this book: Roberta Adams (Fitchburg State College); Adetutu Abatan (Floyd College); Magda al-Nowaihi (Columbia University); Nancy Applegate (Floyd College); Susan Atefat-Peckham (Georgia College and State University); Evan Balkan (CCBC-Catonsville); Michelle Barnett (University of Alabama, Birmingham); Colonel Bedell (Virginia Military Institute); Thomas Beebee (Pennsylvania State University); Paula Berggren (Baruch College); Mark Bernier (Blinn College); Ronald Bogue (University of Georgia); Terre Burton (Dixie State College); Patricia Cearley (South Plains College); Raj Chekuri (Laredo Community College); Sandra Clark (University of Wyoming); Thomas F. Connolly (Suffolk University); Vilashini Cooppan (Yale University); Bradford Crain (College of the Ozarks); Robert W. Croft (Gainesville College); Frank Day (Clemson University); Michael Delahoyde (Washington State University); Elizabeth Otten Delmonico (Truman State University); Jo Devine (University of Alaska Southeast); Gene Doty (University of Missouri—Rolla); James Earle (University of Oregon); R. Steve Eberly (Western Carolina University); Walter Evans (Augusta State University); Fidel Fajardo-Acosta (Creighton University); Mike Felker (South Plains College); Janice Gable (Valley Forge Christian College); Stanley Galloway (Bridgewater College); Doris Gardenshire (Trinity Valley Community College); Jonathan Glenn (University of Central Arkansas); Dean Hall (Kansas State University); Dorothy Hardman (Fort Valley State University); Elissa Heil (University of the Ozarks); David Hesla (Emory University);

Susan Hillabold (Purdue University North Central); Karen Hodges (Texas Wesleyan); David Hoegberg (Indiana University-Purdue University—Indianapolis); Sheri Hoem (Xavier University); Michael Hutcheson (Landmark College); Mary Anne Hutchinson (Utica College); Raymond Ide (Lancaster Bible College); James Ivory (Appalachian State University); Craig Kallendorf (Texas A & M University); Bridget Keegan (Creighton University); Steven Kellman (University of Texas—San Antonio); Roxanne Kent-Drury (Northern Kentucky University); Susan Kroeg (Eastern Kentucky University); Tamara Kuzmenkov (Tacoma Community College); Robert Lorenzi (Camden County College—Blackwood); Mark Mazzone (Tennessee State University); David McCracken (Coker College); George Mitrenski (Auburn University); James Nicholl (Western Carolina University); Roger Osterholm (Embry-Riddle University); Joe Pellegrino (Eastern Kentucky University); Linda Lang-Peralta (Metropolitan State College of Denver); Sandra Petree (University of Arkansas); David E. Phillips (Charleston Southern University); Terry Reilly (University of Alaska); Constance Relihan (Auburn University); Nelljean Rice (Coastal Carolina University); Colleen Richmond (George Fox University); Gretchen Ronnow (Wayne State University); John Rothfork (West Texas A & M University); Elise Salem-Manganaro (Fairleigh Dickinson University); Asha Sen (University of Wisconsin Eau Claire); Richard Sha (American University); Edward Shaw (University of Central Florida); Jack Shreve (Allegany College of Maryland); Jimmy Dean Smith (Union College); Floyd C. Stuart (Norwich University); Eleanor Sumpter-Latham (Central Oregon Community College); Ron Swigger (Albuquerque Technical Vocational Institute); Barry Tharaud (Mesa State College); Theresa Thompson (Valdosta State College); Teresa Thonney (Columbia Basin College); Charles Tita (Shaw University); Scott D. Vander Ploeg (Madisonville Community College); Marian Wernicke (Pensacola Junior College); Sallie Wolf (Arapahoe Community College); and Dede Yow (Kennesaw State University).

   We also wish to express our gratitude to the reviewers who gave us additional advice on the book's companion Web site: Nancy Applegate (Floyd College); James Earl (University of Oregon); David McCracken (Coker College); Linda Lang-Peralta (Metropolitan State College of Denver); Asha Sen (University of Wisconsin—Eau Claire); Jimmy Dean Smith (Union College); Floyd Stuart (Norwich University); and Marian Wernicke (Pensacola Junior College).

   The editors were assisted in tracking down texts and information by wonderfully able research assistants: Kerry Bystrom, Julie Lapiski, Katalin Lovasz, Joseph Ortiz, Laura B. Sayre, and Lauren Simonetti. April Alliston wishes to thank Brandon Lafving for his invaluable comments on her drafts and Gregory Maertz for his knowledge and support. Marshall Brown would like to thank his research assistant Françoise Belot for her help and Jane K. Brown for writing the Goethe introduction. Sheldon Pollock would like to thank Whitney Cox, Rajeev Kinra, Susanne Mrozik, and Guriqbal Sahota for their assistance and Haruo Shirane thanks Michael Brownstein for writing the introduction to Hozumi Ikan, and Akiko Takeuchi for writing the introductions to the Noh drama.

   It has been a great pleasure to work with all these colleagues both at Longman and at schools around the country. This book exists for its readers, whose reactions and suggestions we warmly welcome, as *The Longman Anthology of World Literature* moves out into the world.

ABOUT THE EDITORS

David Damrosch (Columbia University). His books include *The Narrative Covenant: Transformations of Genre in the Growth of Biblical Literature* (1987), *Meetings of the Mind* (2000), and *What Is World Literature?* (2003). He has been president of the American Comparative Literature Association (2001–2003) and is general editor of *The Longman Anthology of British Literature* (1998; second edition, 2002).

April Alliston (Princeton University). Author of *Virtue's Faults: Correspondence in Eighteenth-Century British and French Women's Fiction* (1996), and editor of Sophia Lee's *The Recess* (2000). Her book on concepts of character, gender, and plausibility in Enlightenment historical narratives is forthcoming.

Marshall Brown (University of Washington). Author of *The Shape of German Romanticism* (1979), *Preromanticism* (1991), *Turning Points: Essays in the History of Cultural Expressions* (1997), and, forthcoming, *The Gothic Text.* Editor of *Modern Language Quarterly: A Journal of Literary History,* and the *Cambridge History of Literary Criticism,* Vol. 5: Romanticism.

Page duBois (University of California, San Diego). Her books include *Centaurs and Amazons* (1982), *Sowing the Body* (1988), *Torture and Truth* (1991), *Sappho Is Burning* (1995), *Trojan Horses* (2001), and *Slaves and Other Objects* (2003).

Sabry Hafez (University of London). His books include *The Genesis of Arabic Narrative Discourse* (1993) and the edited volumes *A Reader of Modern Arabic Short Stories* and *Mahmoud Darwish.*

Ursula K. Heise (Columbia University). Author of *Chronoschisms: Time, Narrative, and Postmodernism* (1997) and of the forthcoming *World Wide Webs: Global Ecology and the Cultural Imagination.*

Djelal Kadir (Pennsylvania State University). His books include *Columbus and the Ends of the Earth* (1992), *The Other Writing: Postcolonial Essays in Latin America's Writing Culture* (1993), and *Other Modernisms in an Age of Globalizations* (2002). He served in the 1990s as editor of *World Literature Today* and is coeditor of the *Comparative History of Latin America's Literary Cultures* (2004). He is the founding president of the International American Studies Association.

David L. Pike (American University). Author of *Passage Through Hell: Modernist Descents, Medieval Underworlds* (1997) and *Subterranean Cities: Subways, Sewers, Cemeteries and the Culture of Paris and London* (forthcoming), and of articles on topics ranging from medieval otherworlds and underground Paris, London, and New York to Canadian cinema.

Sheldon Pollock (University of Chicago). His books include *The Ramayana of Valmiki* Volume 3 (1991) and *The Language of the Gods in the World of Men* (forthcoming). He recently edited *Literary Cultures in History: Reconstructions from South Asia* (2003), and (with Homi Bhabha et al.) *Cosmopolitanism* (2002).

Bruce Robbins (Columbia University). His books include *The Servant's Hand: English Fiction from Below* (1986), *Secular Vocations* (1993), *Feeling Global: Internationalism in Distress* (1999), and a forthcoming study of upward mobility narratives in the nineteenth and twentieth centuries. Edited volumes include *Cosmopolitics: Thinking and Feeling Beyond the Nation* (1998).

Haruo Shirane (Columbia University). Author of *The Bridge of Dreams: A Poetics of "The Tale of Genji"* (1987) and of *Traces of Dreams: Landscape, Cultural Memory, and the Poetry of Bashō* (1998). He is coeditor of *Inventing the Classics: Modernity, National Identity, and Japanese Literature* (2000) and has recently edited *Early Modern Japanese Literature: An Anthology 1600–1900*.

Jane Tylus (New York University). Author of *Writing and Vulnerability in the Late Renaissance* (1993), coeditor of *Epic Traditions in the Contemporary World* (1999), and editor and translator of Lucrezia Tornabuoni de' Medici's *Sacred Narratives* (2001). Her study on late medieval female spirituality and the origins of humanism is forthcoming.

Pauline Yu (American Council of Learned Societies). President of the American Council of Learned Societies, she is the author of *The Poetry of Wang Wei* and *The Reading of Imagery in the Chinese Poetic Tradition*, the editor of *Voices of the Song Lyric in China*, and coeditor of *Culture and State in Chinese History* and *Ways with Words: Writing about Reading Texts from Early China*.

The Pilgrim's Vision. Frontispiece to Matt. Twain, The Innocents Abroad, 1869

The Pilgrim's Vision. Frontispiece to Mark Twain, *The Innocents Abroad*, 1869.

The Nineteenth Century

Toward the end of the eighteenth century things heated up in and around Europe. Not in terms of the climate—cold weather and bad harvests in the 1780s and 1790s contributed to the anguish of the French Revolution—but socially and politically. After the many political and religious upheavals of the seventeenth century, the century that followed saw long, stable reigns in England and France as well as the rapidly westernizing Russia and the self-isolated Spain, punctuated by relatively local, short-lived conflicts and accompanied by fairly steady economic progress. Under the surface, however, discontent grew as early industrial development increased the gap between the rich and the working poor and as increasing literacy, especially among crafts workers and laborers, raised expectations and hopes. The ringing words that open Rousseau's *Social Contract* fired a flame that spread across the continents and through the century: "Man is born free, and everywhere he is in chains."

The term *revolution* itself originally meant rotation. It first came to mean rebellion in 1688 when the "Glorious Revolution" drove the crypto-Catholic James II off the English throne. After that there were no comparable events until the Americans revolted in 1776. The century that followed was strongly marked by turmoil and warfare around Europe, lasting from the fall of the Bastille in 1789 through the definitive fall of Napoleon in 1815, the Greek War of Independence (1821–1828), the Revolution of 1830 in France that replaced the restored Bourbon monarchy with the "Citizen King" Louis-Philippe, the continent-wide revolutions of 1848 that mostly failed but left strong democratic and even communist movements in their wake while overthrowing the French monarchy for good, and the blitzkrieg Franco-Prussian War of 1870, an early salvo in nearly a century of German expansionism.

Meanwhile, the New World was struggling to shake off the yoke of the old, with Haiti rising up soon after the United States, followed by all the major mainland Spanish possessions and, late in the century, trailed peacefully by Canada and violently by Cuba. There had never before been a mass war such as Napoleon led, but then the American Civil War of 1861–1865 and the Paris Commune of 1871 broke out with unprecedented internecine violence. Clearly a whole new kind of energy was on the loose, accompanied and symbolized by the power of steam and the speed of railroads, and reflected, steered, and resisted by the influential and imaginative writers of the era.

ROMANTICISM

"The three great tendencies of the age are The French Revolution, Fichte's *Doctrine of Knowledge,* and Wilhelm Meister." So wrote Friedrich Schlegel in 1798 (in a collection of so-called "Fragments" in his journal *Athenaeum*), one of the cluster of incandescent intellectuals who drove German culture to unprecedented heights around 1800. Schlegel is as responsible as any individual for the label that we attach to the culture and writing of the early decades of the century, and unpacking his utterances can give us a way to organize the multifariousness of the period. Willfully, Schlegel

1

aligns the mass political outburst in France with the latest philosophical blockbuster and the title figure of a massive new novel by Goethe. In the middle of things it was hard to see what was really happening, and indeed modern scholars continue to differ radically about the thrust of the French Revolution, its chronological limits, and even its outcome. Schlegel's brilliance was to see the revolution not as a thing—whether a political event or a social manifestation—but as a "tendency," an ongoing process, escaping definition. As such, it works through events, not just in them. And, as Schlegel suggests, books can work on us as powerfully as external actions, if not as dramatically. Johann Gottlieb Fichte was the first great successor to Immanuel Kant's "Copernican revolution" in philosophy; in abstract treatises and fiery moral and political lectures Fichte preached a doctrine of the absolute primacy of the self, which must, however, strive for self-fulfillment through the most demanding individual and community discipline. "Tendency" is just the term to capture the perpetual unrest driving a philosopher whose emotions radiated through Thomas Carlyle and Ralph Waldo Emerson into the Victorian soul and through Ludwig Feuerbach and Karl Marx into the social thought of central and eastern Europe.

Schlegel's third "tendency" refers to Goethe's novel *Wilhelm Meister's Apprenticeship.* The title is ironic, since "Meister" means "master," while Wilhelm is in fact just an overprotected bourgeois adolescent. (Adolescence was itself a new category, penetratingly portrayed in female guise a few years later by Jane Austen and a decade further on in Mary Shelley's precocious but immature scientist Victor Frankenstein and the unloved monster to whom he gives birth.) Goethe's novel reflects a focus on individual development; it begins with childhood infatuations as few novels before Rousseau had (but many later ones by Dickens, Flaubert, Joyce, and countless others), and it proceeds to tell of Wilhelm's unfinished development toward becoming a functioning member of a far-flung society. Individual psychology is thus discovered to be as crucial as mass movements to the destinies of civilization. Like most educated German speakers in subsequent generations, Sigmund Freud was a passionate admirer of Goethe, and his studies in infantile sexuality and his writings on culture stand at the end of tendencies originating in the Romantic period. Schlegel's aphorism implies a recognition that mass movements and individual ideals are inseparably connected.

Romantic striving takes many forms, all of them intense but not all noisy. "Near is / And hard to grasp / The god," writes the great German mythic poet Friedrich Hölderlin at the start of his ode "Patmos" (1803), using the simplest words in typically contorted grammar to express everyman's struggle toward comprehension. John Keats and Percy Bysshe Shelley wrote poems to nightingale and skylark, dreaming of flying in the age that invented hot-air balloons: "Hail to thee, blithe spirit! / Bird thou never wert," as Shelley wrote in "To a Sky-Lark," with exuberant disrespect for his addressee's identity. Wordsworth counseled humane alertness to the quietest signs of life—the hermit's smoke of "Tintern Abbey," or the quiet play of lights in the late sonnet, "Mark the Concent'red Hazels." William Blake, meanwhile, wrote massive epics of social and sexual struggle, confronting private and public demons such as those imaged in the fearful symmetry of "The Tyger."

Parallels can be found in the other arts. Beethoven was composing some of the loudest music yet heard on the face of the earth, to be performed by huge orchestras and choruses in front of vast audiences, and explicitly preaching heroism (*Eroica* Symphony), liberation from tyranny (the opera *Fidelio*) and brotherhood (the choral setting of Friedrich Schiller's poem "Ode to Joy" in the Ninth Symphony). At the same time, Romantic exaltation finds quiet expression in Franz Schubert's many hundreds of art-songs (a new musical form), in William Constable's many paintings of the heaven-directed, pastorally sited spire of Salisbury Cathedral and in the natural cathedrals of Caspar David Friedrich's sublime landscapes (see page 97). Some modern readers complain of too much self-assertion in one kind of Romanticism, others of too much complacency in alternative kinds. But the various moods are best considered to be a dialogue reflecting different attempts to confront the spirit of the age—its vital forces, its electricity (another newly discovered phenomenon). "Spirit of the age" is itself a Romantic idea, the notion that a hidden inner force rather than a rational ideal or external guide permeates and motivates individuals and groups. They share an innovative awareness even where they may disagree about responses.

In another pithy formula, Schlegel called Romanticism "a progressive universal poetry." What did he mean by this? Colonial expansion had been in progress for centuries by then, and not even Goethe's *Faust* could be more cosmic than Dante's *Divine Comedy,* Shakespeare's *King Lear,* or Milton's *Paradise Lost.* But universal doesn't mean overwhelming—an ambition that would be inconsistent with the open-ended striving of Romanticism. Goethe's Faust is a highly educated old man; unlike Renaissance versions of the legend, he wants to know and experience everything, not to have ultimate power, and he dies after a fit of blind philanthropy. Even in the demonic forms of the French Revolution at its worst, universality implies an ideal of brotherhood—a universal embrace rather than a world order.

The word *Romanticism* itself has universal overtones in this sense. In its derivation from Rome it evokes the grand world-empire of the classical past, and more broadly the glories of thought and imagination of the classical world. But romances (as then conceived) were medieval tales of knighthood and adventure and ballads of the common people. Romance in this sense evokes national histories and traditions, preserved in unschooled writings and obsolete dialects, and in the rural folktales and folk songs that were gradually collected starting in the mid-eighteenth century. Romances suggest the aura of mystery and magic that is part of the transhuman universality of Romanticism, and they also suggest the nation mystically rooted not in political and military history but in the essence of a popular spirit. Then, at an individual level, romance means love. To the eighteenth century, physical love tended to seem irrational (in novels of uncontrolled passion) or ridiculous (as in Lemuel Gulliver's scornful horror at the different kinds of affection he encounters in his various voyages), if not straightforwardly animalistic, as in the many casual marriages of Daniel Defoe's *Moll Flanders.* To the nineteenth century, love was a magical and spiritual passion like that of Wagner's Tristan and Isolde, edifying or terrifying (or both at once, as in much of Baudelaire's poetry), but always a force implicated in moral good or evil, at times even transcending both. Finally, in German as in French, Italian, and Russian, "Roman" or its near equivalent is the word for what English and Spanish call a "novel." Hence the quintessentially "Romantic" form of progressive universal poetry is the novel understood as the story of the new. The great Russian writer Pushkin subtitled *Eugene Onegin* a "Novel in Verse," while the great Russian comic writer Nikolai Gogol subtitled his comic novel *Dead Souls* a "Poem." Novels are detailed stories based in the everyday world, and Romantic writers prepared the way for the

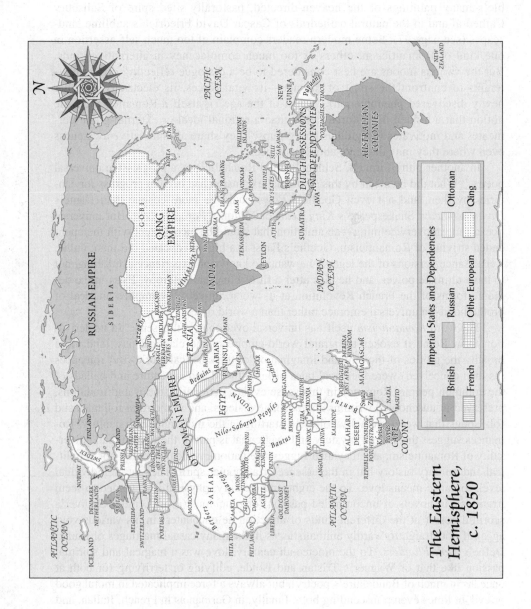

The Eastern Hemisphere, c. 1850

Imperial States and Dependencies

British

French

Russian

Other European

Ottoman

Qing

ATLANTIC OCEAN

ICELAND

NORWAY

SWEDEN

FINLAND

DENMARK
NETHERLANDS

BELGIUM

BRITAIN

SWITZERLAND

FRANCE

PRUSSIA

POLAND

AUSTRIAN EMPIRE

KINGDOM OF THE TWO SICILIES

SERBIA
WALLACHIA
MOLDAVIA

SPAIN

PORTUGAL

MOROCCO

SAHARA

Berbers

Tuaregs

FUTA TORO

KAARTA

MOSSI

Segu KINGDOM

FUTA JALON

ALGERIANS
TUNIS

OTTOMAN EMPIRE

EGYPT

SUDAN

Nilo-Saharan Peoples

Beduins

ARABIAN
PENINSULA

YEMEN

BAHRAIN
OMAN

PERSIA

BALUCHISTAN

AFGHANISTAN

Kazakhs

KHIVA

SMALL STATES

BUKHARA

BALKH

TURKMEN

KOKAND

BADAKSHAN

KUNDUZ

RUSSIAN EMPIRE

SIBERIA

GOBI

QING
EMPIRE

HIMALAYA NEPAL

INDIA

MANIPUR

BURMA

TENASSERIM

CEYLON

SIAM

LUANG PRABANG

ANNAM

CAMBODIA

AUTEN

MALAY STATES

SULU

SARAWAK

BRUNEI

BORNEO

PHILIPPINE ISLANDS

KOREA

JAPAN

PACIFIC OCEAN

SUMATRA

JAVA AND DEPENDENCIES

DUTCH POSSESSIONS
AND DEPENDENCIES

PORTUGUESE TIMOR

Papuans

NEW GUINEA

NEW ZEALAND

AUSTRALIAN COLONIES

INDIAN OCEAN

LIBERIA

GOLD COAST

DAHOMEY

ASANTE

DAGOMBA

BORGU KINGDOMS

BENIN

NIGERIANS

BORNU

Bantus

ANGOLA

RONGHI KINGDOMS

ETHIOPIA

DARFUR

Cushites

BUNYORO

BUGANDA

RWANDA

BURUNDI

SUKONA

KAZEMBE

LUNDA

KUBA

LUBA

KANIOK

KHOSAN

KALAHARI DESERT

REPUBLIC OF WINBURG

POTCHEFSTROOM

Zulu

SWAZI

NATAL

BASUTO

CAPE COLONY

PORTUGUESE EAST AFRICA

MADAGASCAR

MERINA KINGDOM

ATLANTIC OCEAN

N

great realistic novels that dominated literary production in the second half of the nineteenth century. Often drawing their inspiration from the comprehensive social vision of Shakespeare, who was just then being rediscovered and translated on the Continent, Romantic writers wanted to bring all things to all people, linking the past with the present, the individual with the nation, Europe with the rest of humanity, the soul with the body, nature with culture. These linkages are the subjects of the Perspectives sections in this volume.

A WORLD WITHIN THE WORLD

Another typical genius in this age of geniuses was Wilhelm von Humboldt—brother of the great explorer and naturalist Alexander von Humboldt after whom the Humboldt Current in the Pacific Ocean and Humboldt County in California are named. Wilhelm wrote on aesthetics, politics, anthropology, and classical civilization, composed and translated poetry, served as Prussian ambassador to Rome, and founded the University of Berlin that now bears his name and that established the model for university education to the present day. Of course, every age has its universal intellects. But Wilhelm von Humboldt's greatest passion was distinctive to his age, for he made himself into the founder of modern linguistic study. Linguists from the later eighteenth century had been discovering the seemingly universal relationships of human languages and hence of human cultures. Goethe (who read at least seven languages and explored the literatures of many others) coined the term *world literature;* Friedrich Schlegel (poet, literary critic, philosopher, historian of culture, theologian) studied Sanskrit, the oldest relic of the Indo-European language family, and wrote an influential book on the language and wisdom of the Indians. Thoreau, another devotee of Eastern cultures, trod the same paths, as when he writes in the "Reading" chapter of *Walden:* "The oldest Egyptian or Hindoo philosopher raised a corner of the veil from the statue of the divinity; and still the trembling robe remains raised, and I gaze upon as fresh a glory as he did, since it was I in him that was then so bold, and it is he in me that now reviews the vision." But Humboldt's striving for universality outdid them all. He went into unrelated territory, learning well over a hundred languages including the most exotic that could be investigated—Basque, American Indian languages, and the Kavi language of what is now Indonesia.

When the globe was opened on this scale, it was no longer possible to comprehend the commonality of humankind, and that was not Humboldt's goal. Rather he (like his close friend Goethe) sought to understand the differences among cultures. Respect for difference was as much a part of Romantic striving as global ambition. It extended even to new kinds of reverence for the animal and plant worlds, familial pets and ecological treasures such as Wordsworth and Dickinson celebrated in verse and Rousseau and Thoreau studied in their intensive botanizing.

For Humboldt, as for many others, however, social difference was crucial, and above all the difference among societies that arise from linguistic difference. Humboldt famously referred to language as a "world within the world": the language that you speak governs all of your perceptions. Kant had earlier argued that there are no "things in themselves" accessible to our awareness, but only subjective perceptions of things, and Humboldt asserted that there aren't even perceptions in themselves, but only the words we give to them, and these vary radically among languages, as do the grammatical structures that create meaning. Modern linguistics continues to split sharply between Humboldtians who believe in linguistic relativity and anti-Humboldtians (including artificial intelligence specialists) who believe in a common basis for language that allows for an ideal of perfect equivalence and translation among them. For a Humboldtian, progress then comes to mean either learning and understanding more and more different linguistic and cultural worlds, or else, as in some of the more notorious projects for colonial education, suppressing difference in favor of English (or Spanish or French) as a universal medium of communication and civilization.

Through Humboldt we can see how Romanticism develops into the kind of mystical nationalism that first emerged in the later stages of the French Revolution. A country isn't just where you happen to live, not just family and community, but a spiritual essence that grounds your whole being. It becomes a compelling Truth and leads fanatics to strive to impose their truths on all other people around. ("Fanatic" earlier just meant a madman; during the Romantic period it came to mean the impulsive devotee of a cause.) If language is a world within the world, for fanatics the nation becomes an identity inseparable from the self. In 1847, on the threshold of a new revolutionary movement that he avidly supported, Jules Michelet prefaced his great history of the French Revolution with these words: "The Revolution is inside us, in our souls; it has no external monument. Living spirit of France, where shall I seize thee, if not within myself?" Such a spirit can seem noble, or it can seem tyrannical. The first great English historian of the French Revolution, the "Victorian sage" Thomas Carlyle, writes of its "tendencies" with equal mysticism but accompanied with horror; he imagines, in a powerful series of questions:

> that, as no external force, Royal or other, now remains which could control this Movement, the Movement will follow a course of its own; probably a very original one? Further, that whatsoever man or men can best interpret the inward tendencies it has, and give them voice and activity, will obtain the lead of it? For the rest, that as a thing *without* order, . . . it must work and welter, not as a Regularity but as a Chaos; destructive and self-destructive; always till something that *has* order arise, strong enough to bind it into subjection again? Which something, we may further conjecture, will not be a Formula, with philosophical propositions and forensic eloquence; but a Reality, probably with a sword in its hand!

Thus the great writers of the nineteenth century are united only in confronting a problem. The electric tendencies of self, nature, language, and national culture no longer seemed masterable in a comprehensive formula such as many had imagined in the eighteenth-century age of Enlightenment. Karl Marx's greatness as an economic theorist, for instance, was to understand economic relations as mysteriously spiritual forces—describing prices, for example, as "wooing glances cast at money by commodities." And at the end of the century, Freud's *Interpretation of Dreams* (1900) finally codified countless imaginative insights into the language of the unconscious. National and individual destinies tied to national and idiosyncratic languages are the topic of Walter Scott's novels, which determined how nineteenth-century Europeans conceived of cooperation or dissension in constructing their polities. Americans explored similar issues via James Fenimore Cooper's fascination with Indian speech. The rousing choruses of Verdi's operas *Nabucco* and *Il Trovatore* caught the pulse of a people and stirred them to action toward Italian independence. Hopeful visionaries like Emerson or Nietzsche looked forward toward a reconstructed humanity; pessimists like

Plate 1 Ilya Repin, *Alexander Pushkin at Tsarskoe Selo*, Russia, 1911. Painted in the tumultuous period of agitation for and against reform in the years before the Russian Revolution of 1917, this large canvas portrays a lithe young Pushkin dramatically declaiming his poetry to the Czar's court. The scene testifies to Pushkin's enduring importance as a national icon, a figure of forward-looking youthful skepticism and energy, implicitly challenging the aged, hidebound aristocrats who strain to hear his words. (*State Russian Museum, St. Petersburg, Russia / The Bridgeman Art Library.*)

Plate 2 John Constable, *Salisbury Cathedral from the Meadows*, 1831. One of Constable's many views of this scene, this painting puts pastoral nature in the foreground, human settlement in the distance and a dramatic living stump at the right, while a cathedral spire framed by trees and rainbow in the very center points to the sky. The Gothic architecture of Salisbury Cathedral suggests an obscure parallel between the truths of history and of nature. (*Private collection / The Bridgeman Art Library.*)

Plate 3 George Caleb Bingham, *Fur Traders Descending the Missouri*, United States, 1845. The romance of the American frontier is dramatized in this luminous painting of French traders taking their goods to market in St. Louis. The river is both peaceful and dangerous, with submerged logs able at any moment to send the boat to the bottom. The traders' own effect on nature is in turn indicated by the dark figure of the bear cub tied to the boat's prow, probably taken captive after its mother was caught and killed for her fur. *(The Metropolitan Museum of Art, Morris K. Jesup Fund, 1933 [33.61]; photograph © 1992 The Metropolitan Museum of Art.)*

Plate 4 George Catlin, *Going and Returning from Washington,* United States, 1837–1839. Born in Pennsylvania in 1796, Catlin began traveling through the American West in 1832, becoming famous for his detailed, sympathetic paintings of Native Americans in the Western territories. This unusually comic image shows a native chief in full regalia visiting the White House, then coming home to his village sporting all the latest fashions, including a ladies' fan as well as a man's umbrella, smoking a jaunty cigarette in place of his peace pipe. *(Smithsonian American Art Museum, Washington / Art Resource, New York.)*

Plate 5 Alfred Morgan, *One of the People*, England, 1885. William Ewart Gladstone, head of Britain's Liberal Party for decades, pressed for social and governmental reform during four terms as prime minister. This painting shows him forgoing the private carriage used by the gentleman who can be seen through the window. Instead, Gladstone takes public transportation—a horse-drawn omnibus crowded with women, children, and a middle-class man. It's hard to say whether the painter is celebrating Gladstone's democratic impulse or hinting that he is out of place among his carriagemates, who sit in awkward silence around him. *(Christie's Images, London, UK / The Bridgeman Art Library.)*

Plate 6 *Ladies at the piano,* Japan, late 19th century. Japanese artists began producing elaborately detailed and colored woodblock prints in the 18th century, emphasizing scenes of everyday life known as *ukiyo-e,* "images of the floating world." This print was made during the Meiji era (1867–1912), when Japan opened to Western influences. Dressed in Victorian garb, including modern hats atop their traditional hairdos, these women enjoy the pleasures of the newly imported spinet. Their changing world is shown behind them in the form of a Western-style building, looming much larger than the traditional structure tucked away under the pine tree in the distance. *(Published by Omori Kakutaro. Photo courtesy of Laurie Platt Winfrey, Inc.)*

Plate 7   Paul Gauguin, *When Are You to Be Married?* Tahiti, 1892. Profoundly dissatisfied with life in France, Gauguin abandoned a career as a stockbroker at age 35 to devote himself to painting and moved to Tahiti in 1891 in search of a more primal style and subject-matter. There he created mysterious paintings using flat planes and bright, unnaturalistic colors. Although Gauguin's Tahiti is often a largely imagined place untouched by Western civilization, in this painting the woman in the background is wearing a European dress, perhaps foreshadowing the future of her companion, the flower at her left ear signaling her unmarried state. *(Rudolph Staechelin Family Foundation, Basel, Switzerland / The Bridgeman Art Library.)*

Plate 8 Édouard Manet, *Bar at the Folies-Bergère*, France, 1881–1882. A master of emotionally charged realism, Manet regularly shocked his viewers by his boldly unsentimental portrayals of women, whether the commercial sexuality of prostitutes or (as in this painting) the disillusioned weariness of a barmaid. Behind her is a large mirror, which reflects the scene in front of her: the happy crowd drinking and evidently watching one of the extravagant floor shows, featuring scantily clad women, for which the Folies-Bergère was famous. Over at the far left can be seen the barmaid's own reflection and the image of a customer, who may be seeking a date rather than a drink. This gentleman must, in fact, be standing precisely where the viewer is located—rather like Baudelaire's "hypocrite reader"—ironically detached from the melancholy scene. (*Courtauld Institute Gallery, Somerset House, London / The Bridgeman Art Library.*)

Leopardi and (sometimes) Melville looked down a tunnel into darkness. Meanwhile, rapid material progress in a century that opened with coaches and ended with telephones and automobiles put the question of the Real with ever-increasing urgency.

REALISM

It has been argued that realism came into being when Walter Scott wrote his ambivalent novels about the downfall of feudalism in the Scottish Highlands and its replacement by humdrum Anglo-Scottish commercialism. Scott's loyalties were divided between the generously heroic, doomed figures of the old aristocratic order and the rational but mean-spirited representatives of modernity, which promised both greater democracy and a lower, narrowly self-interested view of human motives and aspirations. Realism didn't result, as one might think, from a sudden and unprecedented desire to see the world clearly and accurately. Nor did it represent a major break with Romanticism. Rather, it emerged from a conviction (shared with the Romantics) that the social world itself had been set irrevocably in motion. Realists saw that historical change was powered by social contradictions such as those between feudalism and capitalism, and they understood that these contradictions didn't just affect society's leaders but worked themselves out in everyday feelings and relationships. Unlike previous stories of the rise and fall of kings, history now reached down deep into the lives of ordinary people. Thus the ethical meaning of ordinary lives—increasingly the subject literature took for itself—was now hard to agree upon. This uncertainty is reflected in the period's characteristic literary modes. When we speak of the narrators of Dostoevsky's *Notes from Underground* and Melville's "Bartleby the Scrivener" as "unreliable," for example, we imply that the official moral standard of the time has lost much of its authority. This loss is also reflected in the distinctive narrative technique known as "free indirect discourse," in which the voice of the narrator appears to become contaminated with the voice or perspective of the character being described. It is hard to know, therefore, whether the narrator is being ironic at the character's expense or whether the character's subjectivity has briefly slipped free from narrative judgment, appealing to the values of the reader (or the future) over the head of the narrator and his time.

Honoré de Balzac, who sought to understand the passage from an aristocratic to a bourgeois order in France after the fall of Napoleon, was one of many writers inspired by Scott's example. Examining the moral and emotional meaning of this immense transformation, Balzac gave his own loyalty to the reactionaries calling for a return to the old monarchy and its tried-and-true values. But as Friedrich Engels wrote in a famous letter, Balzac's distaste for the direction history was taking didn't stop him from becoming a brilliant chronicler of its contradictions—far more useful, Engels went on, than the well-intentioned but heavy-handed socialism of his successor Emile Zola. Like many other observers, Engels disliked Zola's dark determinism. The coal miners of Zola's novel *Germinal* are innocent victims, but they are also *passive* victims, caught up and inevitably destroyed by huge, obscure forces that seem beyond anyone's control. Naturalism, the more pessimistic variant of realism that was gaining force in the second half of the nineteenth century, was in part an accommodation to the rising authority of natural science, in part a delayed reaction to the general sense of helplessness that followed the failure of the 1848 revolutions.

Walter Crane, *The Vampire,* 1885.

Revolutions had indeed broken out in 1848 all across Europe and beyond, a "springtime of peoples" seeming to promise that the world could at last be remade in the name of the democratic ideals of 1789. But they also expressed the specific discontent of the new industrial working class, and that is why in early 1848 Alexis de Tocqueville told the Chamber of Deputies, "We are sleeping on a volcano." Both the sense of hope and the threat to private property that made so many property-holders draw back from this eruption are captured in the *Communist Manifesto,* which came out the same year. This was the key moment for Gustave Flaubert, who narrates the Paris street fighting in his *Sentimental Education* (1870), as well as for Elizabeth Gaskell, whose novel *Mary Barton* (1848) describes industrial conflict with serious and unprecedented sympathy for the workers. More indirectly, in Charles Dickens's *Bleak House* (1851–1852) a revolution that doesn't happen is displaced onto plague, murder, and "spontaneous combustion."

SCIENCE AND TECHNOLOGY

The political upheavals of midcentury were matched by a revolutionary ferment in natural science. The period of Charles Darwin's treatise *On the Origin of Species by*

Means of Natural Selection (1859) also saw the development of antiseptics by Lister and pasteurization by Pasteur as well as Clerk Maxwell's electromagnetic theory of light (1862), Mendeleyev's presentation of the periodic table of the elements in 1869, and many other breakthroughs of almost incalculable importance. It was perhaps inevitable that such advances would generate a certain overconfidence. The celebrated physicist Lord Kelvin announced, somewhat prematurely, that all the basic problems of physics had been solved. Though scientific advances and their technological applications were gradually responsible for improving the lives of ordinary people in numerous ways, especially in health, transportation, and communication, Antonio Machado's "The Psychiatrist" and Charlotte Perkins Gilman's "The Yellow Wallpaper" testify to a growing awareness of the danger that the authority attributed to science might easily be abused. Though Darwin himself was cautiously modest about the social implications of his discovery, others like Hebert Spencer (1820–1903) hastened to seize his authority on behalf of so-called "Social Darwinism," the belief that competition for survival was as natural in human society as it was among animal species and that, if not meddled with by governments, it would lead to the evolutionary progress of humankind. This political philosophy preexisted Darwin—it had inspired British authorities to let the victims of the Irish famine starve in the 1840s—but with new support from the theory of evolution it became a widespread tool of imperial expansion, generating convenient contempt for peoples held to be below or behind on the evolutionary ladder.

AN AGE OF EMPIRE

A period of relative European stability followed the crushing of the 1848 revolutions, felt by many artists and writers as the defeat of creativity by conformity and philistinism. This calm at home coincided with, and was perhaps made possible by, an enormous expansion of European control over the non-European world. More and more, the social disparities and conflicts that had led to 1848 could in effect be exported to the colonies. Algeria, the first Arabic-speaking country to be conquered, fell to France in 1847. The rest of Africa was swiftly divided up by the various powers, and soon Ethiopia was the only African country that remained unconquered. Colonialism extended across the Pacific as well, and after the Opium War of 1840–1842 (the result of China's refusal to buy English opium imported from India), China was forced to cede Hong Kong to England and to open itself to European traders. Britain took over official control of India after the so-called Mutiny of 1857–1859, better described perhaps as the first Indian war of independence. By the end of the century, Britain alone controlled a quarter of the earth's land area. (See the inside front cover for an exuberant imperial map.) Between 1804 and 1827, Russia defeated Iran in three wars, thus annexing Georgia and Azerbaijan, and Russian troops were still fighting for control over the mountain tribes of the Caucasus in the late 1830s when the novelist Lermontov's unit was posted there. Russia expanded eastward through Central Asia toward the Pacific, which was soon all that separated it from the westward-expanding United States. In the 1860s slavery ended in the United States (see the texts by Frederick Douglass and Harriet Jacobs) and serfdom ended in Russia, but neither society worried too much about the racially different natives it was subjugating or exterminating. Meanwhile the

A Scene on the Shores of Lake Nyassa.

settler colonies of Latin America, which had won their independence in the first half of the century, likewise continued their campaigns to seize land from their remaining indigenous populations and make it commercially profitable. From a global perspective, nineteenth-century Europe was distinguished not only by its proud scientific and technological achievements, but even more by the fact that it made most of the surface of the earth into colonies, protectorates, and spheres of influence for European states or European settlers. It was, and was seen to be, an age of empire.

The consolidation and clashing of nations and empires came at a high cost even for the Europeans themselves. In the Crimean War (1854–1856), Russia's territorial aspirations ran up against British interests in India and the Middle East, leading to its confrontation with an alliance of British, French, and Ottoman armies in the Crimea—to nineteenth-century Russians, a zone of the mysterious Orient. The war is best known to students of English literature for Alfred Lord Tennyson's "The Charge of the Light Brigade"—a poem about military courage in the face of mismanagement and, perhaps, the meaninglessness of one's own cause—"Their's not to reason why, / Their's but to do and die." On the Russian side, the combatants included Count Leo Tolstoy. One can perhaps guess his reflections on "the reason why" from the story "After the Ball." In the midst of the war, the great poet and patriot Adam Mickiewicz traveled to Istanbul to organize Polish and Jewish troops to fight with the Ottomans on behalf of his fellow Poles, who remained subject to Russia. Mickiewicz died there of cholera in 1855. As soldiers in the Crimea died like flies, more from disease than from enemy fire, the nurse Florence Nightingale became famous for her struggles on behalf of rational sanitation, thus striking as well a blow on behalf of professional careers for middle-class women. This brief and inconclusive war resulted in approximately 600,000 casualties, about the same as the American Civil War and many more than the fierce battles for the unification of Germany and Italy that were happening during the same period.

A journey around the world in eighty days, as imagined by Jules Verne, would have been impossible in 1848. With few railways in operation and steamships a novelty, the journey would have taken at least eleven months. By 1872, however, railways had connected huge tracts of territory (their intrusion is marked even in Ohiyesa's narrative of his childhood in "Perspectives: On the Colonial Frontier," below), and a round-the-world journey in eleven weeks had become quite feasible. Yet the cultural consequences of this new global interconnectedness were complex and often difficult to ascertain. Better informed about other regions than they had ever been, thanks to such inventions as the steamship, the telegraph, and the camera, European readers were not thereby prevented from embracing Rudyard Kipling's assertion of absolute civilizational difference: "East is East and West is West." Imperialist enjoyment of the exotic became an increasing part of everyday European consciousness via the mass market success of boys' adventure novels such as those of the Englishman H. Rider Haggard and the German Karl May, and Oriental stereotypes such as Sax Rohmer's Dr. Fu Manchu, and Buffalo Bill's Wild West Show. And it was possible for the English realist novels of the 1840s to ignore completely the catastrophic Potato Famine in Ireland, a colony only a stone's throw away.

On the other hand, some British writers identified with aspirations to national independence even at the expense of Britain's allies. Tennyson's sonnet "Montenegro" (1877)—repeatedly translated into Serbian—glorified the struggles of the Montenegrins, friends of the Russians and enemies of the Ottomans. English became the official language of instruction of India in 1835, replacing Sanskrit, Arabic, and Persian. The intention was to form an English-educated native class through whom much of the administration could be handled. But the results would include an extraordinary cultural flowering, as for example in the bilingual and multicultural writing of Rabindranath Tagore. Now that science fiction and utopian visionaries could more easily imagine the earth as a whole, the trend seemed to be paradoxically toward dystopias, visions of a future in which things were worse rather than better. Nature, which the Romantics had by and large seen in a positive light and which indeed had served as an impetus to social revolution, now suffered from its embroilment in the demystifying efforts of science, the effort to justify competitive capitalism through "social Darwinism," and the appropriative efforts of imperialism, which tended to identify the landscape with the brutality of local inhabitants who resisted the improving advance of enlightenment. The global triumph of European culture was not a cause for universal celebration even in Europe.

Even as nation-states unified themselves, their literary cultures were becoming more and more varied, and writers took inspiration across regions and borders alike. Emerson and his fellow American Transcendentalists were inspired by the new interpretations of Hinduism coming out of British-occupied India; in Paris, Adam Mickiewicz lent his copy of Emerson's *Nature* to his fellow republican Edgar Quinet; Parisian modernism revealed itself to Rubén Darío when he was given Lautréamont's poetry to read on a visit to El Salvador. Even in the century that saw the world shrink so dramatically, it is of course impossible to trace any single line through all of the world's literatures. Industrialization in Britain and political revolutions in France, beginning in 1789 and continuing throughout the century, were world-historical events, like imperialism itself. Unprecedented anywhere in the world, they were extraordinarily and inevitably influential almost everywhere in the world. And so were their cultural sequels. Romanticism, a product of both industrial and political revolution, moved through the world's literatures in waves, arriving earlier in some places, later in others. The Byronic hero of Pushkin and Lermontov, the democratic Transcendentalism of Emerson and

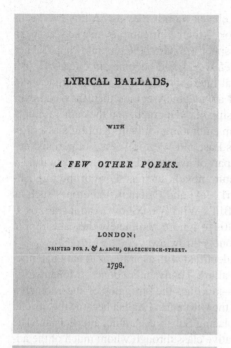

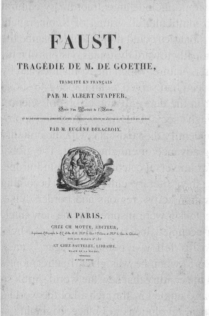

Like book jackets today, title pages promoted and advertised older books, which were sold unbound. Earlier title pages were typically illustrated and typographically lavish, often containing epigraphs and lengthy descriptions of their contents. Spare title pages like that reproduced on the upper left give only the title, author's name (and not even always that), genre, and publisher. They illustrate how books had become ordinary objects of commerce rather than valuable possessions and were intended for private reading of the contents more than for fashion or display. *Sense and Sensibility* and *Walden,* typical of a later day, illustrate a simple, rather bourgeois nostalgia for earlier modes of book production.

Tagore are unthinkable without their English, French, German, and Indian predecessors. In its turn to popular songs, ballads, folktales, and the notion of national revival, Romanticism is also tied to nationalism, which again moved around the world in waves. For better and for worse, Romanticism often stages a scene in which educated elites construct and mobilize an image of profound and desirable continuity with the folk. This is one reason why nineteenth-century culture is often so politicized, and why culture continues to be of intense and immediate significance in Third World countries that follow comparable paths at a later point.

But it would be a mistake to think of literary schools and fashions as simply emanating out from a center in Europe. Many South American countries became independent before some of the European states that carried out the project of imperialism, and their literatures are thus on a different timetable. There was a Latin American turn to the folk as well—including a celebration of the same natives they were still in the process of subduing and assimilating—in order to define a positive national identity distinct from that of the European motherland. There was also a Latin American tendency (for example, in the Argentine writers Esteban Echevarría and Domingo Sarmiento) to be more enthusiastic about modernizing thought like the positivism of Auguste Comte (1798–1857). The same might be said about the energetic upsurge of thinking in the nineteenth-century Arab world, which was pondering both its Ottoman and its European masters in relation to its Muslim heritage, and in Asia, particularly in China, though there much of the new thought came through Japan. Warnings against the Romantic illusions of national continuity came from the Frenchman Renan and the German Nietzsche but also (later) from the Martiniquan Frantz Fanon. When Mahatma Gandhi read the Victorian art critic John Ruskin, he assimilated him to Hindu thought, which went back centuries and was undergoing a recent renaissance. The self-educated Brazilian writer Machado de Assis quoted many and various European authors but dug deep into Brazilian popular culture for the prime resources of his fiction. There is no precedent in European literature for José Rizal's extraordinarily powerful fusion of satire and national melodrama in the Philippines.

CITIES, WOMEN, ARTISTS

Among the common threads that do run through the world literature of the nineteenth century, one of the foremost is the tension between the country and the city. On every continent, an abyss opened up between the modernizing tendencies of the capital and the traditional culture of the hinterland. Sometimes colonialism widened this abyss from both ends. In Africa, for example, whose artistic traditions of live oral performance do not lend themselves easily to textual reproduction, the colonizers often selected and exaggerated aspects of rural native culture for the purpose of ruling indirectly through surrogates. The sparkling coastal cosmopolitanism of cities like Alexandria and Beirut didn't always resonate with small farmers in the interior. The Petersburg of Gogol and Dostoevsky, the New York of Melville and Whitman, the Paris of Baudelaire, would have seemed to many of their compatriots as foreign as European cities seemed to the Muslim travelers of the age.

In trying to make sense of urban life, nineteenth-century writers were also trying to make sense of their writerly vocation. The century's second half sees Romantic nature poetry succeeded in part by a new poetry of the city. To Baudelaire and his successors,

Paris is as mysterious, inviting, dangerous, and sublime as Romantic nature. Yet its buildings and crowds, its novel rhythms of companionship and perception, also remind the poet of his or her own mode of artistic shaping. The same insight made a home for itself in fiction. "Oh for a good spirit who would take the housetops off," Dickens appealed in *Dombey and Son*. The city should be made to reveal the hidden, often sordid interconnections that held society in place, a society that seen from the urban perspective was clearly produced by people and could be changed by them, as Dickens observed in "Vice and Fever," through "the social retributions which are ever pouring down, and ever coming thicker." The spiritlike narrators and complicated plots of Dickens's own novels could be seen as an answer to this appeal, especially when they anticipate the urban detective story genre that would find its most famous expression in Conan Doyle's Sherlock Holmes. As urbanization inches closer to becoming a social norm for the first time in history, the poet and the novelist become two of its heroic figures.

As does the new independent woman. One would never guess it from the novels of Emily and Charlotte Brontë, set as they are on the wild Yorkshire heath, but the nineteenth-century rise in literary and political attention to the condition of women has much to do with the rise of cities. In cities children were less of an economic asset to their families than they had been on the farm, in part because of compulsory schooling, in part because of a new separation of the workplace from the place of residence. One result was lower birth rates and the emancipation of at least some women from the burdensome tasks of continual child rearing. Most women in Europe and elsewhere remained subject both to the will of men and to double labor, but for increasing numbers, there was new leisure and new access to education. Thus the emancipation of women could be imagined with new energy and, increasingly, acted upon in movements for women's suffrage. In literature, the throwing into question of assumptions about women's proper place, feelings, and aspirations is expressed in stories of adultery, one of nineteenth-century fiction's greatest themes, as in *Madame Bovary* and *Anna Karenina*, as well as such revolutionary texts as Emily Dickinson's poetry, Charlotte Perkins Gilman's "The Yellow Wallpaper," and Henrik Ibsen's *A Doll's House*.

It was also in the city that the artist's new and reluctant submission to market forces was most visible. Angry reactions to the increasing dominance of mass production and the profit-motive in the cultural sphere included the Arts and Crafts movement, as represented for example by William Morris, and an artistic avant-garde, reacting against a perceived cheapening of art, that turned in the direction of "art for art's sake." For the first time in history, perhaps, artists began to boast of their *lack* of popular success. These were tendencies out of which would develop today's literary studies. By the *fin de siècle*, many of Europe's artists, more and more hostile to a mass public they saw as incapable of understanding them, were becoming interested in the exotic civilizations of the East and the "primitive" art of Africa and Oceania, which reinforced their sense of distance from the status quo at home. The global awareness that Goethe foresaw when he coined the term "world literature" in 1832 was becoming a marked feature of literature at the century's end.

THE NINETEENTH CENTURY

YEAR	THE WORLD	LITERATURE
1770		
		1774, 1786 J. W. Goethe, *Werther*
1780		**1781, 1788, 1790** Immanuel Kant, *Critique of Pure Reason, Critique of Practical Reason, Critique of Judgment*
		1782, 1789 J. J. Rousseau, *Confessions, Reveries*
	1783 First balloon flight	
	1789 Fall of the Bastille (beginning of the French Revolution)	**1789, 1794** William Blake, *Songs of Innocence, Songs of Experience*
1790	**1792** Discovery of electromagnetism	
	1793 Execution of the king and queen of France	
		1795–1796 Goethe, *Wilhelm Meister's Apprenticeship*
		1796 Ludwig Tieck, "Fair Eckbert"
		1798–1799 Friedrich Schiller, *Wallenstein* (translated by Coleridge in 1800)
		1798 Wordsworth and Coleridge, *Lyrical Ballads*
1800	**1800** Volta's invention of the electric battery	
	1803 Louisiana Purchase	
	1804 Haitian declaration of independence	**1804** Ludwig von Beethoven, *Eroica Symphony*
	1806 Mungo Park expedition to the Niger River	**1805** Wordsworth, first version of *Prelude* completed (published, much revised, in 1850)
	1806 Dissolution of the Holy Roman Empire	
	1807 Fulton sails a steamboat on the Hudson River	**1807** G. W. F. Hegel, *Phenomenology of Mind*
	1809–1825 Independence movements in South America	**1808** Goethe, *Faust, Part 1*
1810		**1810** Madame de Staël, *On Germany*
		1812, 1815 J. and W. Grimm, *Fairy Tales*
		1813–1822 E. T. A. Hoffmann's tales published in various collections
	1815 Final defeat of Napoleon; restoration of the Bourbon monarchy in France	**1814** Walter Scott, *Waverley*
		1819–1824 Lord Byron, *Don Juan*
1820		**1820** John Keats, *Lamia, Isabella, The Eve of St. Agnes, and Other Poems*
	1825 Failed "Decembrist" Revolution in Russia	
	1825 First scheduled railroad	
1830	**1830** Revolution of 1830 in France ; Louis-Philippe become the "Citizen King"	
	1830 France seizes Algiers: beginning of French colonization of North Africa	
		1831 Stendhal (Henri Beyle), *The Red and the Black: A Chronicle of 1830*
		1831 Honoré de Balzac, *The Wild Ass's Skin* (first work designed as part of the collective *Human Comedy*)
		1832 Goethe, *Faust, Part 2*

YEAR	THE WORLD	LITERATURE
	1832 Death of Goethe; death of Scott; English Reform Bill	
	1832 Greek Independence achieved after war of 1821–1828	
	1833 Abolition of slavery in Britain's colonies	1833 Alexander Pushkin, *Eugene Onegin*
	1838 Slave mutiny aboard the *Amistad*	1836 Ralph Waldo Emerson, *Nature*
	1839–1842 Opium War in China	
1840		
		1840 Mikhail Lermontov, *A Hero of Our Time*
		1842 Nikolai Gogol, "The Overcoat"
		1845 Edgar Allan Poe, "The Raven"
	1848 Revolutions throughout Europe, mostly suppressed, but leading to the end of the French monarchy	
	1848 War between United States and Mexico	
1850		
	1850–1864 Taiping Uprising in China, eventually put down with Western intervention	
	1851 Sojourner Truth delivers her "And Ain't I a Woman Speech" at the Woman's Rights Convention in Akron, Ohio	1851 Herman Melville, *Moby Dick;* first issue of *New York Times*
		1852 Harriet Beecher Stowe, *Uncle Tom's Cabin*
	1853–1856 Crimean War	1854 Alfred Tennyson, "The Charge of the Light Brigade"
		1854 Henry Orvid Thoreau, *Walden*
		1855 Walt Whitman, *Leaves of Grass*
	1856–1857 British-Persian War	1856 Elizabeth Barrett Browning, *Aurora Leigh*
	1857 Indian revolt known as "Mutiny"	1857 Gustave Flaubert, *Madame Bovary*
	1858 Chinese ports opened to Western trade	1859 Charles Darwin, *On the Origin of Species by Natural Selection*
	1859–1861 Wars of national unification in Italy	
1860		
	1860 Anglo-French troops occupy Beijing and burn Summer Palace	
	1861 Emancipation of serfs in Russia; outbreak of Civil War in United States	
	1862 Richard Gatling patents machine-gun	
	1863 French troops occupy Mexico City	1864 Leo Tolstoy, *War and Peace*
	1868 Meiji restoration in Japan, abolition of Shogunate	1866 Fyodor Dostoevsky, *Crime and Punishment*
		1867 Marx, *Das Kapital,* vol 1
1870		
	1870–1871 Franco-Prussian War, Paris Commune	1871–1872 George Eliot, *Middlemarch*
	1873 Ashanti tribes fight British in West Africa	1872 Jules Verne, *Around the World in 80 Days*
	1874 Iceland becomes independent from Denmark	
	1875 Korea becomes independent from China	

YEAR	THE WORLD	LITERATURE
	1876 Schliemann excavates Mycenae in Greece; massacre of Bulgarians by Turkish troops; General Custer defeated by Sioux at Little Big Horn	**1876** George Sand, *Marianne*
	1877 Samurai revolt suppressed in Japan	
	1879 Edison invents electric light bulb; Britain invades Afghanistan; Chile defeats Bolivia and Peru in "Nitrate War"	
1880		
	1880 France annexes Tahiti	**1882** Henrik Ibsen, *An Enemy of the People*
		1883 Friedrich Nietzsche, *Thus Spake Zarathustra*
		1884 Mark Twain, *Huckleberry Finn*
		1885 Emile Zola, *Germinal*
	1886 First meeting of Indian National Congress	
1890		
	1890 New Zealand is the first nation to give women suffrage	**1890** Knut Hamsun, *Hunger*
	1894–1895 War between China and Japan; China loses Formosa and Port Arthur	
	1895 Cuban revolution against Spanish rule	**1895** Oscar Wilde, *The Importance of Being Earnest*
	1896 Italy is defeated in war with Abyssinia and withdraws	**1896** Anton Chekhov, *The Seagull*
	1897 First Zionist congress, Basel, Switzerland	
	1898 Spanish-American War	
		1899 Joseph Conrad, *Heart of Darkness*
1900		
		1900 Sigmund Freud, *The Interpretation of Dreams*

⌘ CROSSCURRENTS ⌘
The Folk and Their Tales

Folk song, folktale, folkways, folk legend, folk belief, folk saying, folk wisdom. These have existed, of course, ever since there were people to share them. But only in the later eighteenth century did Europeans feel enough distance from "the folk" to stand back and admire. Indeed, it was only then that these very phrases were coined and entered our language. The first modern collection of folk songs was Thomas Percy's *Reliques of Ancient Poetry* (1765), which mixed popular ballads with well-known poems from the last three centuries. In England Percy was followed notably by the young Walter Scott's *Minstrelsy of the Scottish Border* (1802–1803), which pursued the association of folk writing with rural and regional cultures. But it was especially in the politically fragmented and culturally backward Germany that the search for roots and commonalities fueled a compelling interest in folk materials. In 1778 and 1779 Johann Gottfried Herder, a friend of Goethe's and a prolific literary critic, philosopher, world historian, preacher, theologian, educator, poet, and translator, issued *Folksongs,* a collection with the newly minted word as its title and with a novel arrangement by regions and cultural groups, mostly European but ending with a section entitled "Songs of the Savages." For Herder, folk literature was the authentic expression of original cultures. "It cannot be doubted that poetry and especially song were originally entirely *popular* ["volksartig"], i.e., light, simple, from objects and in the language of the crowd as well as of nature's richness and universal feeling. Song loves the crowd, the concord of many.... The whole world and its languages, particularly the oldest, gray orient, provides a host of traces of this origin."

Other popular traditions long preceded folk songs. From antiquity came beast fables, and the magical tales of *The Thousand and One Nights* were translated into French in the seventeenth century, riding a wave of fascination with the Near and Far East. All these currents came together in another German collection that has surely become one of the most widely read of books, the *Children's and Domestic Tales* of the brothers Jacob and Wilhelm Grimm (1812, 1815), more often known by some version of the title *German Folktales.* The Grimms collected their tales from informants, then adapted them into a distinctive mix of sentimental propriety with a sometimes gory notion of primitive purity. An essay written in 1816 by Wilhelm Grimm reflects the idealization of folkways that emerged out of the combined interests in ballad, magic, and exoticism:

> A good angel is granted to man from his homeland and accompanies him on his journey through life as a companion; he who does not feel the benefits that he reaps thereby may well feel them when he crosses the borders of his fatherland, where the angel abandons him. This benevolent companionship is the inexhaustible reward of fairy tales, legends, and story, which, together, strive to bring us ever after into proximity with the fresh and enlivening spirit of primitive times.

Especially in its German form (*Volk,* pronounced "follk" with an audible *l*), the term "folk" has sometimes been corrupted by modern racism and genocide. But a fruit may be wholesome before it rots. The fables of Aesop and their French imitations were long used as school texts on account of their accessible simplicity, their palatable morality, and (in La Fontaine's case) their wry humor. After Herder and Grimm, literature for children came to be understood as the literature of childhood, representing both individual development and the early stages of society. A new interest in different cultures and different stages of life made folk documents into powerful sources of inspiration and understanding. Some degree of condescension toward "primitives" and "savages" remained and was inseparable from the dawning apprehension of their contributions to humanity; it is hard to learn from children, to respect them, and to teach them all at the same time, and the complexity increases when it becomes an issue of regional cultures, alien civilizations, and the dark reaches of the psyche. In the tales and in their telling it is worth the effort of sorting out and understanding all these intricate motivations beneath the fascinating surface.

·→· ·⊠◊⊠· ·←·

Aesop's Fables
c. 6th century B.C.E.

Aesop's fables were popular in ancient Athens. Their author and exact nature remain a mystery. The name Aesop is attached to a sixth century B.C.E. slave. It is said that he was very ugly and that the citizens of Delphi threw him off a cliff for nonpayment of a charity; the gods punished them with a plague. Written fables survive only from centuries after the time of the supposed author, originally in prose, later in verse. The best-known collection consists of ninety-seven fables in easy but not childish Latin verse written by a freed slave named Phaedrus in the first century B.C.E. These were perennially used as introductory readings for students learning Latin, as all educated European men (but few women) did throughout the nineteenth century. Given here are several fables in an anonymous prose translation typical of the more childlike versions of the nineteenth century, in which the fables are both charming in style and pointed in their conclusions.

The Wolf and the Lamb

Once upon a time a Wolf was lapping at a spring on a hillside, when, looking up, what should he see but a Lamb just beginning to drink a little lower down. "There's my supper," thought he, "if only I can find some excuse to seize it." Then he called out to the Lamb, "How dare you muddle the water from which I am drinking?"

"Nay, master, nay," said the Lamb; "if the water be muddy up there, I cannot be the cause of it, for it runs down from you to me."

"Well, then," said the Wolf, "why did you call me bad names this time last year?"

"That cannot be," said the Lamb; "I am only six months old."

"I don't care," snarled the Wolf; "if it wasn't you it was your father;" and with that he rushed upon the poor little Lamb and—

WARRA WARRA WARRA WARRA WARRA—

ate her all up. But before she died she gasped out—

"ANY EXCUSE WILL SERVE A TYRANT."

The Lion's Share

The Lion went once a-hunting along with the Fox, the Jackal, and the Wolf. They hunted and they hunted till at last they surprised a Stag, and soon took its life. Then came the question how the spoil should be divided. "Quarter me this Stag," roared the Lion; so the other animals skinned it and cut it into four parts. Then the Lion took his stand in front of the carcass and pronounced judgment: "The first quarter is for me in my capacity as King of Beasts; the second is mine as arbiter; another share comes to me for my part in the chase; and as for the fourth quarter, well, as for that, I should like to see which of you will dare to lay a paw upon it."

"Humph," grumbled the Fox as he walked away with his tail between his legs; but he spoke in a low growl—

"YOU MAY SHARE THE LABOURS OF THE GREAT, BUT YOU WILL NOT SHARE THE SPOIL."

The Town Mouse and the Country Mouse

Now you must know that a Town Mouse once upon a time went on a visit to his cousin in the country. He was rough and ready, this cousin, but he loved his town friend and made him heartily welcome. Beans and bacon, cheese and bread, were all he had to offer, but he offered them freely. The Town Mouse rather turned up his long nose at this country fare, and said: "I cannot understand, Cousin, how you can put up with such poor food as this, but of course you cannot expect anything better in the country; come you with me and I will show you how to live. When you have been in town a week you will wonder how you could ever have stood a country life." No sooner said than done: the two mice set off for the town and arrived at the Town Mouse's residence late at night. "You will want some refreshment after our long journey," said the polite Town Mouse, and took his friend into the grand dining-room. There they found the remains of a fine feast, and soon the two mice were eating up jellies and cakes and all that was nice. Suddenly they heard growling and barking. "What is that?" said the Country Mouse. "It is only the dogs of the house," answered the other. "Only!" said the Country Mouse. "I don't like that music at my dinner." Just at that moment the door flew open, in came two huge mastiffs, and the two mice had to scamper down and run off. "Good-bye, Cousin," said the Country Mouse. "What! going so soon?" said the other. "Yes," he replied—

"BETTER BEANS AND BACON IN PEACE THAN CAKES AND ALE IN FEAR."

The Fox and the Crow

A Fox once saw a Crow fly off with a piece of cheese in its beak and settle on a branch of a tree. "That's for me, as I am a Fox," said Master Reynard, and he walked up to the foot of the tree. "Good-day, Mistress Crow," he cried. "How well you are looking to-day: how glossy your feathers; how bright your eye. I feel sure your voice must surpass that of other birds, just as your figure does; let me hear but one song from you that I may greet you as the Queen of Birds." The Crow lifted up her head and began to caw her best, but the moment she opened her mouth the piece of cheese fell to the ground, only to be snapped up by Master Fox. "That will do," said he. "That was all I wanted. In exchange for your cheese I'll give you a piece of advice for the future—

"DO NOT TRUST FLATTERERS."

The Frogs Desiring a King

The Frogs were living as happy as could be in a marshy swamp that just suited them; they went splashing about caring for nobody and nobody troubling with them. But some of them thought that this was not right, that they should have a king and a proper constitution, so they determined to send up a petition to Jove to give them what they wanted. "Mighty Jove," they cried, "send us a king that will rule over us and keep us in order." Jove laughed at their croaking, and threw down into the swamp a huge Log, which came down—*kerplash*—into the swamp. The Frogs were frightened out of their lives by the commotion made in their midst, and all rushed to the bank to look at the horrible monster; but after a time, seeing that it didn't move, one or two of the boldest of them ventured out towards the Log, and even dared to touch it: still it didn't move. Then the greatest hero of the Frogs jumped upon the Log and commenced dancing up and down upon it, whereupon all the Frogs came and did the same; and for some time the Frogs went about their business every day without taking the slightest notice of their new King Log lying in their midst. But this didn't suit them, so they sent another petition to Jove, and said to him, "We want a real king; one that will really rule over us." Now this made Jove angry, so he sent among them a big Stork that soon set to work gobbling them all up. Then the Frogs repented when too late.

"BETTER NO RULE THAN CRUEL RULE."

The Hare and the Tortoise

The Hare was once boasting of his speed before the other animals. "I have never yet been beaten," said he, "when I put forth my full speed. I challenge anyone here to race with me."

The Tortoise said quietly, "I accept your challenge."

"That's a good joke," said the Hare; "I could dance round you all the way."

"Keep your boasting till you've beaten me," answered the Tortoise. "Shall we race?"

So a course was fixed and a start was made. The Hare darted almost out of sight at once, but soon stopped and, to show his contempt for the Tortoise, lay down to have a nap. The Tortoise plodded on and plodded on, and when the Hare awoke from his nap, he saw the Tortoise just near the winning-post and could not run up in time to save the race. Then said the Tortoise:

"SLOW AND STEADY WINS THE RACE."

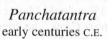

Panchatantra
early centuries C.E.

Sometime in the sixth century C.E., so legend has it, Nushirvan, the enlightened King of Persia, sought to acquire a celebrated Indian text on political wisdom:

> Having heard that there existed in India a book containing every kind of instruction, Nushirvan directed his vizir to find a man acquainted with the Indian and Persian languages. Barzoye, a scholar who had earlier traveled to India to extend his knowledge of medicine and chemistry, was given the task of procuring the book, supposed to be in the library of the king of India. After great difficulties, Barzoye at last obtained not only the book he was seeking but also other works of great value. He labored day and night translating the book into Persian, fearing that the king of India might ask for it back. That done, he returned home. A large assembly was convened, and the book was read aloud, to universal acclaim.

We shouldn't let the romance aspect of this tale obscure its factuality. We know that the Sanskrit *Panchatantra,* the text at issue here, was indeed translated into Middle Persian (Pahlavi) in around the sixth century. Thus began a long journey that would bring the work to Paris in the seventeenth century.

The *Panchatantra* (Five Principles, or Books), ascribed to a legendary figure named Vishnusharma, is the most celebrated book of social wisdom in South Asian history. Framed as a series of discourses for the education of princes, the *Panchatantra,* like the Greek Aesopian tradition, uses the rather odd motif of talking animals—and it is rather odd that animals should speak, and speak wisdom!—to explore such core ethical problems of human existence as the nature of trust or the limits of risk.

PRONUNCIATION
Panchatantra: PUHN-chuh-TUHN-truh

from PANCHATANTRA
The Turtle and the Geese[1]

Along a certain seashore there once lived a pair of sandpipers. One day the lady sandpiper, as she was close to laying eggs, said to her husband: "My lord, find some place suitable for laying eggs."

Sandpiper: "Don't you think that this very place has many advantages? Why don't you lay your eggs right here?"

Lady sandpiper: "I don't want even to hear about this place; it's too dangerous! The high tide may well flood it and wash away my children."

Sandpiper: "The ocean, my dear lady, is too weak to engage in a fight like that with me."

Lady sandpiper, laughing: "Look at the great disparity in strength between you and the sea! Can't you even recognize your own strengths and weaknesses? For it is said:

> To measure oneself is an uphill task,
> 'Am I up to this task or am I not?'
> When a man has the skill to make this call,
> He will not fail even when times are hard.

"And further,

> When a man does not heed the words of friends
> who only wish him well,
> He will perish like the foolish turtle
> who fell down from the stick."

The sandpiper asked: "How did that happen?"

The lady sandpiper narrated this story:

In a certain lake there once lived a turtle named Kambugrīva, the Shell-neck. He had two friends, a couple of geese named Saṃkaṭa, the Slim, and Vikaṭa, the Stout. In the course of time, the region was struck by a twelve-year drought. So the geese reflected: "This lake has lost most of its water. Let us go to another lake. But let us first say good-bye to our dear friend Kambugrīva, whom we have known for so long."

When they did so, the turtle said to them: "Why are you saying good-bye to me? If you love me, you should rescue me also from these jaws of death. And here's the reason. When the water level of this lake goes way down, the most you will suffer, after all, is some scarcity of food; for me, on the other hand, it means death. So think, what is worse? Loss of food or loss of life?"

The geese: "What you say is true, and your point is well taken. You know what is appropriate—we will take you with us; but don't be stupid enough to say anything on the way."

The turtle: "I won't."

1. Translated by Patrick Olivelle.

The pair of geese brought a stick and said to the turtle: "Now, hold on to the middle of this stick firmly with your teeth. We will then take hold of the ends and carry you through the air to a large lake far away."

So they did this, and as the turtle was being flown over a town near that lake, the town's people saw this and caused a commotion, shouting: "What is that pair of birds carrying in the air? It looks like a cartwheel."

When the turtle, whose end was near, heard this, he let go of the stick and asked: "What is the commotion?"

The words were no sooner out of his mouth than he lost his grip on the stick, fell to the ground, and was killed. As soon as he fell down, people eager for his flesh cut him up into pieces with sharp knives.

The lady sandpiper continued: "Therefore I say:

When a man does not heed the words of friends . . ."

•→ ☖◊☗ →•

Jean de La Fontaine
1621–1695

The French poet and dramatist Jean de La Fontaine made his career in Paris, where he was supported by noble patrons who were charmed by his wit even though they were often unsettled by his religious skepticism and easy-going morality. The raciness of some of his tales drew the disapproval of King Louis XIV, but the purity and grace of his style led to his election to the Académie Française, the group of forty leading writers charged with protecting and perfecting the French language. La Fontaine is best know for his witty, ambiguous *Fables,* published in several series between 1668 and 1692. The first series was modeled on Aesop, but then La Fontaine turned to oriental sources. He knew the *Panchatantra's* tales from a French translation of a Persian or Arabic translation ascribed to Pilpay (the name derives ultimately from the Indian sobriquet, Vidyapati, "Lord of knowledge") of the Sanskrit original. That La Fontaine should have found the work so pertinent to the perilous world of Absolutist France, with which he was intimately familiar as a client of the courtly nobility, is testament not only to the enduring value of a good story but also to the enduring need for understanding the small ways of getting ahead, or getting away—knowing how to use your wits and, above all, when to bite your tongue.

The Turtle and the Two Ducks[1]

> A turtle, none too quick of mind,
> And tiring of her hole, was quite inclined
> To roam the world and visit lands far-flung.
> (A common wish, especially among
> 5   The lame, or slow of limb, confined
>   To lodgings that they come to hate,
> Such as our tortoise friend.) At any rate,
> Two ducks she prattled to of her ambition
> Assured her they could bring it to fruition:

---

1. Translated by N. R. Shapiro.

Two Geese Carrying the Tortoise, illustration from *Kalila wa Dimma,*
c. 14th century.

10   "Our highway is the sky, and we
        Can take you where you've never been.
      We'll fly you to America! You'll see
      Kingdoms, republics, peoples never seen.
      Imagine what you'll learn. You'll be
15   Just like Ulysses, traveling far and near."
      (Ulysses? Who would think to find him here!)
        No sooner does she answer "Yes!"
        Than, there and then, the ducks prepare
        Their transport for our pilgrimess—

20   A simple stick. Each bites one end: "Now, there!"
      They say. "You bite the middle." She complies.
          The ducks advise: "Hold tight! Take care!"
          And up they rise, high in the air,
          Much to the wonder and surprise
25   Of those below, who see her, house and all,
      Hanging between two ducks! "Come look!" they call.
      "A miracle! The Turtle Queen is flying
      Heavenward!" "Queen!" she boasts. "There's no denying . . ."
      Those words would be her last. Poor fool! She should
30   Have kept her big mouth shut! Instead,
      She opened it, and now it's shut for good,
      As she lies—dashed to pieces—proud, but dead.

      A babbling tongue, vain curiosity,
          And witlessness: one family!
35   All of a kind, all kith and kin—
      And all of them, in time, will do you in.

The Pali Jatakas
early centuries B.C.E.

It is not easy to conceive of two worlds more distant from each other in time, space, and mentality than that of the Buddhists of India in the last centuries B.C.E., and of African-American slaves of the antebellum South. Yet, in an even more remarkable episode in the global circulation of stories than the one just noted, some connections between them seem possible to trace. In the early stages of their discipline, folklorists vigorously debated whether an identical folk motif can be independently invented in several places (what is called *polygenesis*), or whether a motif is invented once only and disseminated from its place of origin (*monogenesis,* or diffusion theory). Often the peculiarity of the motif—and a sticky adversary is certainly peculiar—was thought to be significant for a judgment of monogenesis, and the next task was to figure out the exact route of diffusion.

The tale of Prince Five-Weapons is preserved in a story collection in the Pali Canon of Buddhist scripture, containing several hundred *jatakas*—stories told by the Buddha of his former births in the course of the vast cycle of transmigration. In each birth-story the Bodhisattva, or future Buddha, exemplifies some moral attainment of the Middle Path. Like the *Panchatantra,* the tale of Prince Five-Weapons along with other birth stories was translated into Persian and from Persian into Arabic. Arabs may then have passed along the stories to Africans who came within their ambit in the course of the Atlantic slave trade.

Two broader implications can be drawn from studying this kind of circulation. What is so often represented as the unique genius of a given folk and their authentic cultural property—everything from tales to musical motifs to textile patterns—often turns out to have been borrowed from another folk, who borrowed it from yet another, and so on indefinitely. Identifying any link in the chain as the ultimate source is therefore only to admit that historical research can take us no further; in fact, culture can be seen to flow through the world like water or air. That said, however, different folk clearly make different uses of the pieces of culture they acquire. For the early Buddhists the tale of the sticky adversary would afford an opportunity to reflect on the need to overcome, and the possibility of overcoming through knowledge, all attachments—quite literally!—even to life, and all violence, which only condemns us to further transmigration. For the slaves of the American south, the tale was an opportunity to reflect on the dynamics of race and morality and the dangers of life in a social world of unjust force and unequal power.

PRONUNCIATION.

Jatakas: JAH-tuh-kuhs
Bodhisatta: BHOH-dee-SUH-tuh

from THE PALI JATAKAS[1]
Prince Five-Weapons (*Panchavudha Jataka*)

"*When no Attachment.*"—This story was told by the Master[2] while at Jetavana,[3] about a Brother who had given up all earnest effort.

Said the Master to him, "Is the report true, Brother, that you are a backslider?"

"Yes, Blessed One."

"In bygone days, Brother," said the Master, "the wise and good won a throne by their dauntless perseverance in the hour of need."

And so saying, he told this story of the past.

Once on a time when Brahmadatta was reigning in Benares, it was as his queen's child that the Bodhisatta[4] came to life once more. On the day when he was to be named, the parents enquired as to their child's destiny from eight hundred brahmins, to whom they gave their hearts' desire in all pleasures of sense. Marking the promise which he shewed of a glorious destiny, these clever soothsaying brahmins foretold that, coming to the throne at the king's death, the child should be a mighty king endowed with every virtue; famed and renowned for his exploits with five weapons, he should stand peerless in all Jambudīpa.[5] And because of this prophecy of the brahmins, the parents named their son Prince Five-Weapons.

Now, when the prince was come to years of discretion, and was sixteen years old, the king bade him go away and study.

"With whom, sire, am I to study?" asked the prince.

"With the world-famed teacher in the town of Takkasilā in the Gandhāra[6] country. Here is his fee," said the king, handing his son a thousand pieces.

So the prince went to Takkasilā and was taught there. When he was leaving, his master gave him a set of five weapons, armed with which, after bidding adieu to his old master, the prince set out from Takkasilā for Benares.

On his way he came to a forest haunted by an ogre named Hairy-grip; and, at the entrance to the forest, men who met him tried to stop him, saying:—"Young brahmin, do not go through that forest; it is the haunt of the ogre Hairy-grip, and he kills every one he meets." But, bold as a lion, the self-reliant Bodhisatta pressed on, till in the heart of the forest he came on the ogre. The monster made himself appear in stature as

---

1. Translated by Robert Chalmers.
2. The Buddha.
3. The site of a famous monastery.
4. Future Buddha.

5. The "Rose-apple Island," a name for the inhabited world.
6. In the northeast of present-day Afghanistan.

tall as a palm-tree, with a head as big as an arbour and huge eyes like bowls, with two tusks like turnips and the beak of a hawk; his belly was blotched with purple; and the palms of his hands and the soles of his feet were blue-black! "Whither away!" cried the monster. "Halt! you are my prey." "Ogre," answered the Bodhisatta, "I knew what I was doing when entering this forest. You will be ill-advised to come near me. For with a poisoned arrow I will slay you where you stand." And with this defiance, he fitted to his bow an arrow dipped in deadliest poison and shot it at the ogre. But it only stuck on to the monster's shaggy coat. Then he shot another and another, till fifty were spent, all of which merely stuck on to the ogre's shaggy coat. Hereon the ogre, shaking the arrows off so that they fell at his feet, came at the Bodhisatta; and the latter, again shouting defiance, drew his sword and struck at the ogre. But, like the arrows, his sword, which was thirty-three inches long, merely stuck fast in the shaggy hair. Next the Bodhisatta hurled his spear, and that stuck fast also. Seeing this, he smote the ogre with his club; but, like his other weapons, that too stuck fast. And thereupon the Bodhisatta shouted, "Ogre, you never heard yet of me, Prince Five-Weapons. When I ventured into this forest, I put my trust not in my bow and other weapons, but in myself! Now will I strike you a blow which shall crush you into dust." So saying, the Bodhisatta smote the ogre with his right hand; but the hand stuck fast upon the hair. Then, in turn, with his left hand and with his right and left feet, he struck at the monster, but hand and feet alike clave to the hide. Again shouting "I will crush you into dust!" he butted the ogre with his head, and that too stuck fast.

Yet even when thus caught and snared in fivefold wise, the Bodhisatta, as he hung upon the ogre, was still fearless, still undaunted. And the monster thought to himself, "This is a very lion among men, a hero without a peer, and no mere man. Though he is caught in the clutches of an ogre like me, yet not so much as a tremor will he exhibit. Never, since I first took to slaying travellers upon this road, have I seen a man to equal him. How comes it that he is not frightened?" Not daring to devour the Bodhisatta offhand, he said, "How is it, young brahmin, that you have no fear of death?"

"Why should I?" answered the Bodhisatta. "Each life must surely have its destined death. Moreover, within my body is a sword of adamant, which you will never digest, if you eat me. It will chop your inwards into mincemeat, and my death will involve yours too. Therefore it is that I have no fear." (By this, it is said, the Bodhisatta meant the Sword of Knowledge, which was within him.)

Hereon, the ogre fell a-thinking. "This young brahmin is speaking the truth and nothing but the truth," thought he. "Not a morsel so big as a pea could I digest of such a hero. I'll let him go." And so, in fear of his life, he let the Bodhisatta go free, saying, "Young brahmin, you are a lion among men; I will not eat you. Go forth from my hand, even as the moon from the jaws of Rāhu[7] and return to gladden the hearts of your kinsfolk, your friends, and your country."

"As for myself, ogre," answered the Bodhisatta, "I will go. As for you, it was your sins in bygone days that caused you to be reborn a ravening, murderous, flesh-eating ogre; and, if you continue in sin in this existence, you will go on from darkness to darkness. But, having seen me, you will be unable thenceforth to sin any more. Know that to destroy life is to ensure re-birth either in hell or as a brute or as a ghost or among the fallen spirits. Or, if the re-birth be into the world of men, then such sin cuts short the days of a man's life."

---

7. Eclipse, personified as a demon.

In this and other ways the Bodhisatta showed the evil consequences of the five bad courses, and the blessing that comes of the five good courses; and so wrought in divers ways upon that ogre's fears that by his teaching he converted the monster, imbuing him with self-denial and establishing him in the Five Commandments.[8] Then making the ogre the fairy of that forest, with a right to levy dues, and charging him to remain steadfast, the Bodhisatta went his way, making known the change in the ogre's mood as he issued from the forest. And in the end he came, armed with the five weapons, to the city of Benares, and presented himself before his parents. In later days, when king, he was a righteous ruler; and after a life spent in charity and other good works he passed away to fare thereafter according to his deserts.

This lesson ended, the Master, as Buddha, recited this stanza:—

> When no attachment hampers heart or mind,
> When righteousness is practised peace to win,
> He who so walks, shall gain the victory
> And all the Fetters utterly destroy.

When he had thus led his teaching up to Arahatship[9] as its crowning point, the Master went on to preach the Four Truths,[1] at the close whereof that Brother won Arahatship. Also, the Master showed the connexion, and identified the Birth by saying, "Angulimāla[2] was the ogre of those days, and I myself Prince Five-Weapons."

Joel Chandler Harris
1848–1908

Joel Chandler Harris grew up in rural Georgia, where he worked as a reporter for local newspapers. Fascinated with the rhythms and dialects of rural African-American speech, Harris began writing humorous sketches in African-American dialect, and these began to reach a wider audience after he was hired by the *Atlanta Constitution* in 1876. He published his most famous dialect story, "The Tar-Baby," in 1879, one of a series he wrote in the voice of a wise old former slave, Uncle Remus, who tells animal tales to the son of his plantation's owner. In many of these, the wily Brer Rabbit escapes the clutches of the hungry Brer Fox, in a pattern that recalls Native American "trickster tales" as well as the African and Asian traditions brought to America by the freed slaves' ancestors. Harris always claimed that his stories came directly from plantation workers he knew: "Not one of them is cooked," he declared, "and not one of them nor any part of one is an invention of mine."

The Wonderful Tar-Baby

"Didn't the fox *never* catch the rabbit, Uncle Remus?" asked the little boy the next evening.

"He come mighty nigh it, honey, sho's you born— Brer Fox did. One day atter Brer Rabbit fool 'im wid dat calamus root,[1] Brer Fox went ter wuk en got 'im some

---

8. The "five bad courses" are killing, taking what is not given, sexual misconduct, telling lies, and taking intoxicants. The "five good courses" are abstention from these acts. The Five Commandments refer to these abstentions.
9. The "state of being a 'worthy one,'" or a disciple who has attained the final stage of spiritual development.
1. The truths concerning suffering, the arising of suffering, the ending of suffering, and the path that leads to the

ending of suffering.
2. A notorious brigand so named because he wore a "necklace made of the fingers" of his victims. He was converted by the Buddha.
1. Brer Rabbit was invited to dinner by Brer Fox; when on arriving he became suspicious, he made his escape, claiming he needed calamus root to season the meat to be served for dinner.

tar, en mix it wid some turkentime, en fix up a contrapshun wat he call a Tar-Baby, en he tuck dish yer Tar-Baby en he sot 'er in de big road, en den he lay off in de bushes fer to see wat de news wuz gwineter be. En he didn't hatter wait long, nudder, kaze bimeby here come Brer Rabbit pacin' down de road—lippity-clippity, clippity-lippity—dez ez sassy ez a jay-bird. Brer Fox, he lay low. Brer Rabbit come prancin' 'long twel he spy de Tar-Baby, en den he fotch up on his behime legs like he wuz 'stonished. De Tar-Baby, she sot dar, she did, en Brer Fox, he lay low.

" 'Mawnin'!' sez Brer Rabbit, sezee—'nice wedder dis mawnin',' sezee.

"Tar-Baby ain't sayin' nothin', en Brer Fox, he lay low.

" 'How duz yo' sym'tums seem ter segashuate?'[2] sez Brer Rabbit, sezee.

"Brer Fox, he wink his eye slow, en lay low, en de Tar-Baby, she ain't sayin' nothin'.

" 'How you come on, den? Is you deaf?' sez Brer Rabbit, sezee. 'Kaze if you is, I kin holler louder,' sezee.

"Tar-Baby stay still, en Brer Fox, he lay low.

" 'Youer stuck up, dat's w'at you is,' says Brer Rabbit, sezee, 'en I'm gwineter kyore you, dat's w'at I'm a gwineter do,' sezee.

"Brer Fox, he sorter chuckle in his stummuck, he did, but Tar-Baby ain't sayin' nothin'.

" 'I'm gwineter larn you howter talk ter 'specttubble fokes ef hit's de las' ack,' sez Brer Rabbit, sezee. 'Ef you don't take off dat hat en tell me howdy, I'm gwineter bus' you wide open,' sezee.

"Tar-Baby stay still, en Brer Fox, he lay low.

"Brer Rabbit keep on axin' 'im, en de Tar-Baby, she keep on sayin' nothin', twel present'y Brer Rabbit draw back wid his fis', he did, en blip he tuck 'er side er de head. Right dar's whar he broke his merlasses jug. His fis' stuck, en he can't pull loose. De tar hilt 'im. But Tar-Baby, she stay still, en Brer Fox, he lay low.

" 'Ef you don't lemme loose, I'll knock you agin,' sez Brer Rabbit, sezee, en wid dat he fotch 'er a wipe wid de udder han', en dat stuck. Tar-Baby, she ain't sayin' nothin', en Brer Fox, he lay low.

" 'Tu'n me loose, fo' I kick de natal stuffin' outen you,' sez Brer Rabbit, sezee, but de Tar-Baby, she ain't sayin' nothin'. She des hilt on, en den Brer Rabbit lose de use er his feet in de same way. Brer Fox, he lay low. Den Brer Rabbit squall out dat ef de Tar-Baby don't tu'n 'im loose he butt'er cranksided. En den he butted, en his head got stuck. Den Brer Fox, he sa'ntered fort', lookin' des ez innercent ez one er yo' mammy's mockin'-birds.

" 'Howdy, Brer Rabbit,' sez Brer Fox, sezee. 'You look sorter stuck up dis mawnin',' sezee, en den he rolled on de groun', en laughed en laughed twel he couldn't laugh no mo'. 'I speck you'll take dinner wid me dis time, Brer Rabbit. I done laid in some calamus root, en I ain't gwineter take no skuse,' sez Brer Fox, sezee."

Here Uncle Remus paused, and drew a two-pound yam out of the ashes.

"Did the fox eat the rabbit?" asked the little boy to whom the story had been told.

"Dat's all de fur de tale goes," replied the old man. "He mout, en den agin he moutent. Some say Jedge B'ar come 'long en loosed 'im—some say he didn't. I hear Miss Sally callin'. You better run 'long."

2. Properly spelled *sagaciate,* meaning "to thrive and prosper."

Charles Perrault
1628–1703

Charles Perrault belonged to one of the best connected bourgeois families in France. After working as a lawyer for a few years, he took up a post with few duties attached as secretary to his brother, the Paris tax collector, which allowed him time to write. His career as a poet took a turn for the better when, in 1660, he started writing poems in praise of Louis XIV. Three years later he was promoted to the post of secretary for the king's powerful finance minister, Jean-Baptiste Colbert, which he held for twenty years. The years 1671 and 1672 were most eventful for Perrault. During that time he was put in charge of the royal buildings, elected to the Académie Française, and married to Marie Guichon. In the first of these capacities he influenced the design of the royal palaces of the Louvre and Versailles. In the last, he fathered three sons, whom he educated himself after their mother died in giving birth to the youngest in 1678. He is best known, however, for his contributions—direct and indirect—to the literary debates of the Academy.

Perrault retired from public life on a generous pension after the death of Colbert in 1683, and within a few years had ignited the already smoldering *quérelle des anciens et modernes* (battle of ancients and moderns), whose consequences dominated literary aesthetics for the following century. The quarrel was between those who insisted on following classical models and rules of composition, and those who favored greater freedom of style and subject matter. Although the Sun King himself officially ended the dispute in favor of the conservative "ancients" in 1697, and Jonathan Swift reinforced the French king's judgment in *The Battle of the Books* in Britain the same year, Perrault was not to be silenced. That very year he published his still beloved collection of *Tales of Past Times, with Morals,* which he soon retitled *Mother Goose Tales.* Although he could no longer argue openly in favor of the moderns, he could publish a model of modern writing under a pseudonym. Literary fairy tales, not intended as children's literature, were already a favorite genre of many "modern," mainly female, writers. "Donkey-Skin," less well-known than "Cinderella" and others, is one in which Perrault more directly addresses the condition of women. Its "moral" typifies his playfully ironic approach: "Pure water and brown bread are enough nourishment for young women, so long as they have beautiful clothes." Although the Grimms' treatment of similar European folk material in "All-Kinds-of-Fur" (page 54) is earnest and nationalist by comparison with Perrault's urbanely ironic style, they and the rest of the Romantic movement are clearly the heirs of the "moderns" he championed.

Donkey–Skin[1]

Once upon a time lived the most powerful king in the world. Gentle in peace, terrifying in war, he was incomparable in all ways. His neighbors feared him while his subjects were content. Throughout his realm the fine arts and civility flourished under his protection. His better half, his constant companion, was charming and beautiful. Such was her sweet and good nature that he was less happy as king and more happy as her husband. Out of their tender, pure wedlock a daughter was born, and she had so many virtues that she consoled them for their inability to have more children.[2]

Everything was magnificent in their huge palace. They had an ample group of courtiers and servants all around them. In his stables the king had large and small horses of every kind, which were adorned with beautiful trappings, gold braids, and

1. Translated by Jack Zipes.
2. Louis XIV is clearly recognizable in this description of the king. Louis had many mistresses, making "pure wedlock" ironic.

embroidery. But what surprised everyone on entering the stables was a master donkey in the place of honor. This discrepancy may be surprising, but if you knew the superb virtues of this donkey, you would probably agree that there was no honor too great for him. Nature had formed him in such a way that he never emitted an odor. Instead he generated heaps of beautiful gold coins that were gathered from the stable litter every morning at sunrise.

Now, heaven, which always mixes the good with the bad, just as rain may come in good weather, permitted a nasty illness to attack the queen suddenly. Help was sought everywhere, but neither the learned physicians nor the charlatans who appeared were able to arrest the fever, which increased day by day. When her last hour arrived, the queen said to her husband, "Before I die, you must promise me one thing, and that is, if you should desire to remarry when I am gone—"

"Ah!" said the king, "your concern is superfluous. I'd never think of doing such a thing. You can rest assured about that."

"I believe you," replied the queen, "if your ardent love is any proof. But to make me more certain, I want you to swear that you'll give your pledge to another woman only if she is more beautiful, more accomplished, and wiser than I."

Her confidence in her qualities and her cleverness were such that she knew he would regard his promise as an oath never to remarry. With his eyes bathed in tears, he swore to do everything the queen desired. Then she died in his arms.

Never did a king make such a commotion. Day and night he could be heard sobbing, and many believed that he could not keep mourning so bitterly for long. Indeed, some said he wept about his deceased wife like a man who wanted to end the matter in haste.

In truth, this was the case. At the end of several months he wanted to move on with his life and choose a new queen. But this was not easy to do. He had to keep his word, and his new wife had to have more charms and grace than his dead one, who had become immortalized. Neither the court, with its great quantity of beautiful women, nor the city, the country, nor foreign kingdoms, where the rounds were made, could provide the king with such a woman.

The only one more beautiful was his daughter. In truth, she even possessed certain attractive qualities that her deceased mother had not had. The king himself noticed this, and he fell so ardently in love with her that he became mad. He convinced himself that this love was reason enough for him to marry her. He even found a casuist who argued logically that a case could be made for such a marriage. But the young princess was greatly troubled to hear him talk of such love and grieved night and day.

Thus the princess sought out her godmother, who lived at some distance from the castle in a grotto of coral and pearls. She was a remarkable fairy, far superior to any of her kind. There is no need to tell you what a fairy was like in those most happy of times, for I am certain that your mother has told you about them when you were very young.

Upon seeing the princess, the fairy said, "I know why you've come. I know your heart is filled with sadness. But there's no need to worry, for I am with you. If you follow my advice, there's nothing that can harm you. It's true that your father wants to marry you, and if you were to listen to his insane request, it would be a grave mistake. However, there's a way to refuse him without contradicting him. Tell him that before you'd be willing to abandon your heart to him, he must grant your wishes and give you a dress the color of the sky. In spite of all his power and wealth and the favorable signs of the stars, he'll never be able to fulfill your request."

So the princess departed right away, and trembling, went to her amorous father. He immediately summoned his tailors and ordered them to make a dress the color of the sky without delay. "Or else, be assured I will hang you all."

The sun was just dawning the next day when they brought the desired dress, the most beautiful blue of the firmament. There was not a color more like the sky, and it was encircled by large clouds of gold. Though the princess desired it, she was caught between joy and pain. She did not know how to respond or get out of her promise. Then her godmother said to her in a low voice, "Princess, ask for a more radiant dress. Ask for one the color of the moon. He'll never be able to give that to you."

No sooner did the princess make the request than the king said to his embroiderer, "I want a dress that will outshine the star of night, and I want it without fail in four days."

The splendid dress was ready by the deadline set by the king. Up in the night sky the luster of the moon's illumination makes the stars appear pale, mere scullions in her court. Despite this, the glistening moon was less radiant than this dress of silver.

Admiring this marvelous dress, the princess was almost ready to give her consent to her father, but urged on by her godmother, she said to the amorous king, "I can't be content until I have an even more radiant dress. I want one the color of the sun."

Since the king loved her with an ardor that could not be matched anywhere, he immediately summoned a rich jeweler and ordered him to make a superb garment of gold and diamonds. "And if you fail to satisfy us, you will be tortured to death."

Yet it was not necessary for the king to punish the jeweler, for the industrious man brought him the precious dress by the end of the week. It was so beautiful and radiant that the blond lover of Clymene,[3] when he drove his chariot of gold on the arch of heaven, would have been dazzled by its brilliant rays.

The princess was so confused by these gifts that she did not know what to say. At that moment her godmother took her by the hand and whispered in her ear, "There's no need to pursue this path anymore. There's a greater marvel than all the gifts you have received. I mean that donkey who constantly fills your father's purse with gold coins. Ask him for the donkey skin. Since this rare donkey is the major source of his money, he won't give it to you, unless I'm badly mistaken."

Now this fairy was very clever, and yet she did not realize that passionate love counts more than money or gold, provided that the prospects for its fulfillment are good. So the forfeit was gallantly granted the moment the princess requested it.

When the skin was brought to her, she was terribly frightened. As she began to complain bitterly about her fate, her godmother arrived. She explained, "If you do your best, there's no need to fear." The princess had to let the king think that she was ready to place herself at his disposal and marry him while preparing at the same time to disguise herself and flee alone to some distant country in order to avoid the impending, evil marriage.

"Here's a large chest," the fairy continued. "You can put your clothes, mirror, toilet articles, diamonds, and rubies in it. I'm going to give you my magic wand. Whenever you hold it in your hand, the chest will always follow your path beneath the ground. And whenever you want to open it, you merely have to touch the ground with my wand, and the chest will appear before you. We'll use the donkey's skin to make you unrecognizable. It's such a perfect disguise and so horrible that once you

---

3. Wife of Helios, the sun god in Greek myth. It is significant also that Louis XIV was known as the "Sun King."

conceal yourself inside, nobody will ever believe that it adorns anyone so beautiful as you."

Thus disguised, the princess departed from the abode of the wise fairy the next morning as the dew began to drop. When the king started preparations for the marriage celebration, he learned to his horror that his bride-to-be had taken flight. All the houses, roads, and avenues were promptly searched, but in vain. No one could conceive of what had happened to her. Sadness and sorrow spread throughout the realm. There would be no marriage, no feast, no tarts, no sugar-almonds. The ladies at the court were quite disappointed not to be able to dine, but the priest was most saddened, for he had been expecting a heavy donation at the end of the ceremony as well as a hearty meal.

Meanwhile the princess continued her flight, dirtying her face with mud. When she extended her hands to people she met, begging for a place to work, they noticed how much she smelled and how disagreeable she looked, and did not want to have anything to do with such a dirty creature, even though they themselves were hardly less vulgar and mean. Farther and farther she traveled and farther still until she finally arrived at a farm where they needed a scullion to wash the dishclothes and clean out the pig troughs. She was put in a corner of the kitchen, where the servants, insolent and nasty creatures all, ridiculed, contradicted, and mocked her. They kept playing mean tricks on her and harassed her at every chance they had. Indeed, she was the butt of all their jokes.

On Sundays she had a little time to rest. After finishing her morning chores, she went into her room, closed the door, and washed herself. Then she opened the chest and carefully arranged her toilet articles in their little jars in front of her large mirror. Satisfied and happy, she tried on her moon dress, then the one that shone like the sun, and finally the beautiful blue dress that even the sky could not match in brilliance. Her only regret was that she did not have enough room to spread out the trains of the dresses on the floor. Still, she loved to see herself young, fresh as a rose, and a thousand times more elegant than she had ever been. Such sweet pleasure kept her going from one Sunday to the next.

I forgot to mention that there was a large aviary on this farm that belonged to a powerful and magnificent king. All sorts of strange fowls were kept there: chickens from Barbary, rails, guinea fowls, cormorants, musical birds, quacking ducks, and a thousand other kinds, which were the match of ten other courts put together. The king's son often stopped at this charming spot on his return from the hunt to rest and enjoy a cool drink. He was more handsome than Cephalus[4] and had a regal and martial appearance that made the proudest batallions tremble. From a distance Donkey-Skin admired him with a tender look. Thanks to her courage, she realized that she still had the heart of a princess beneath her dirt and rags.

"What a grand manner he has!" she said, even though he paid no attention to her. "How gracious he is, and how happy must be the woman who has captured his heart! If he were to honor me with the plainest dress imaginable, I'd feel more decorated than in any of those I have."

One Sunday the young prince was wandering adventurously from courtyard to courtyard, and he passed through an obscure hallway, where Donkey-Skin had her humble room. He chanced to peek through the keyhole, and since it was a holiday,

---

4. Beautiful mortal man beloved by Aurora, Roman goddess of the dawn.

she had dressed herself up as richly as possible in her dress of gold and diamonds that shone like the sun. Succumbing to fascination, the prince kept peeking at her, scarcely breathing because he was filled with such pleasure. Her magnificent dress, her beautiful face, her lovely manner, her fine traits, and her young freshness moved him a thousand times over. But most of all, he was captivated by the air of grandeur mingled with modest reserve that bore witness to the beauty of her soul.

Three times he was on the verge of entering her room because of the ardor that overwhelmed him, but three times he refrained out of respect for the seemingly divine creature he was beholding.

Returning to the palace, he became pensive. Day and night he sighed, refusing to attend any of the balls even though it was Carnival. He began to hate hunting and attending the theater. He lost his appetite, and everything saddened his heart. At the root of his malady was a deadly melancholy.

He inquired about the remarkable nymph who lived in one of the lower courtyards at the end of the dingy alley where it remained dark even in broad daylight.

"You mean Donkey-Skin," he was told. "But there's nothing nymphlike or beautiful about her. She's called Donkey-Skin because of the skin that she wears on her back. She's the ideal remedy for anyone in love. That beast is almost uglier than a wolf."

All this was said in vain, for he did not believe it. Love had left its mark and could not be effaced. However, his mother, whose only child he was, pleaded with him to tell her what was wrong, yet she pressured him in vain. He moaned, wept, and sighed. He said nothing, except that he wanted Donkey-Skin to make him a cake with her own hands. And so, his mother could only repeat what her son desired.

"Oh, heavens, madam!" the servants said to her. "This Donkey-Skin is a black drab, uglier and dirtier than the most wretched scullion."

"It doesn't matter," the queen said. "Fulfilling his request is the only thing that concerns us." His mother loved him so much that she would have served him anything on a golden platter.

Meanwhile, Donkey-Skin took some ground flour, salt, butter, and fresh eggs in order to make the dough especially fine. Then she locked herself alone in her room to make the cake. She washed her hands, arms, and face and put on a silver smock in honor of the task that she was about to undertake. It is said that in working a bit too hastily, a precious ring happened to fall from Donkey-Skin's finger into the batter. But some claim that she dropped the ring on purpose. As for me, quite frankly, I can believe it because when the prince had stopped at the door and looked through the keyhole, she must have seen him. Women are so alert that nothing escapes their notice. Indeed, I pledge my word on it that she was convinced her young lover would gratefully receive her ring.

There was never a cake kneaded so daintily as this one, and the prince found it so good that he immediately began ravishing it and almost swallowed the ring. However, when he saw the remarkable emerald and the narrow band of gold, his heart was ignited by an inexpressible joy. At once he put the ring under his pillow. Yet that did not cure his malady. Upon seeing him grow worse day by day, the doctors, wise with experience, used their great science to come to the conclusion that he was sick with love.

Whatever else one may say about marriage, it is a perfect remedy for love sickness. So it was decided that the prince should marry. After he deliberated for some time, he finally said. "I'll be glad to get married provided that I marry only the person whose finger fits this ring."

This strange demand surprised the king and queen very much, but he was so sick that they did not dare to say anything that might upset him. Now a search began for the person whose finger might fit the ring, no matter what class or lineage. The only requirement was that the woman be ready to come and show her finger to claim her due.

A rumor was spread throughout the realm that to claim the prince, one had to have a very slender finger. Consequently, every charlatan, eager to make a name for himself, pretended that he possessed the secret of making a finger slender. Following such capricious advice, one woman scraped her finger like a turnip. Another cut a little piece off. Still another used some liquid to remove the skin from her finger and reduce its size. All sorts of plans imaginable were concocted by women to make their fingers fit the ring.

The selection was begun with the young princesses, marquesses, and duchesses, but no matter how delicate their fingers were, they were too large for the ring. Then the countesses, baronesses, and all the rest of the nobility took their turns and presented their hands in vain. Next came well-proportioned working girls who had pretty and slender fingers. Finally, it was necessary to turn to the servants, kitchen help, minor servants, and poultry keepers, in short, to all the trash who with their reddened or blackened hands hoped for a happy fate just as much as those with delicate hands. Many girls presented themselves with large and thick fingers, but trying the prince's ring on their fingers was like trying to thread the eye of a needle with a rope.

Everyone thought that they had reached the end because the only one remaining was Donkey-Skin in the corner of the kitchen. And who could ever believe that the heavens had ordained that she might become queen?

"Why not?" said the prince. "Let her try."

Everyone began laughing and exclaimed aloud, "Do you mean to say that you want that dirty wretch to enter here?"

But when she drew a little hand as white as ivory and of royal blood from under the dirty skin, the destined ring fit perfectly around her finger. The members of the court were astonished. So delirious were they that they wanted to march her to the king right away, but she requested that she be given some time to change her clothes before she appeared before her lord and master. In truth, the people could hardly keep from laughing because of the clothes she was wearing.

Finally, she arrived at the palace and passed through all the halls in the blue dress whose radiance could not be matched. Her blonde hair glistened with diamonds. Her blue eyes, so large and sweet, whose gaze always pleased and never hurt, were filled with a proud majesty. Her waist was so slender that two hands could have encircled it. All the charms and ornaments of the ladies of the court dwindled in comparison. Despite the rejoicing and commotion of the gathering, the good king did not fail to notice the many charms of his future daughter-in-law, and the queen was also terribly delighted. The prince, her dear lover, could hardly bear the excitement of his rapture.

Preparations for the wedding were begun at once. The monarch invited all the kings of the surrounding countries, who left their lands to attend the grand event, all radiant in their different attire. Those from the East were mounted on huge elephants. The Moors arriving from distant shores were so black and ugly that they frightened the little children. People embarked from all the corners of the world and descended on the court in great numbers. But neither prince nor king seemed as splendid as the bride's father, who had purified the criminal and odious fires that had ignited his spirit in the past. The flame that was left in his soul had been transformed into devoted paternal love. When he saw her, he said, "May heaven be blessed for allowing me to see you again, my dear child."

Weeping with joy, he embraced her tenderly. Everyone wanted to share in his happiness, and the future husband was delighted to learn that he was to become the son-in-law of such a powerful king. At that moment the godmother arrived and told the entire story of how everything had happened and culminated in Donkey-Skin's glory.

Evidently, the moral of this tale implies it is better for a child to expose herself to hardships than to neglect her duty.

Indeed, virtue may sometimes seem ill-fated, but it is always crowned with success. Of course, strongest reason is a weak dike against mad love and ardent ecstasy, especially if a lover is not afraid to squander rich treasures.

Finally, we must take into account that clear water and brown bread are sufficient nourishment for all young women provided that they have beautiful clothes, and that there is not a damsel under the skies who does not imagine herself beautiful and somehow carrying off the honors in the famous beauty contest between Hera, Aphrodite, and Athena.[5]

> The tale of Donkey-Skin is hard to believe,
> But as long as there are children on this earth,
> With mothers and grandmothers who continue to give birth,
> This tale will always be told and surely well received.

⊷ ⊷⧫⊷ ⊶

Benedikte Naubert
1756–1818

Christiane Benedikte Eugénie Hebenstreit was born in Leipzig to parents whose families were both associated with the university there. Her father died when she was small, and her mother proved incapable of bringing her up. Like most educated women of the period, Benedikte was introduced by male relatives—her brother and stepbrother—to academic subjects such as classical languages, history, and philosophy, from which girls were normally excluded. She also learned French, English, and Italian, and studied music. When her brothers died, she had to support her mother and sisters, and in her late twenties she began writing at a furious rate. In all she published fifty original works of fiction, mostly historical novels and fairy tales, and thirty translations from English. Until the last year of her life, she published everything under what she called her "Vestal veil" of anonymity, for it preserved her domestic feminine modesty. At forty-one she married a wealthy vintner who died not long afterwards. A few years later, at forty-six, she married Johann Georg Naubert, mainly so he could tend the vineyards she had inherited from her previous husband. Having suffered from periodic blindness, she went back to Leipzig in 1818 for eye surgery, but instead died of pneumonia.

Like Madame de Lafayette in France and Sophia Lee in England, Naubert innovated the technique of weaving romance plots, told partly in personal letters, into well-researched histories. Sir Walter Scott acknowledged her influence in his adoption of the historical novel. Naubert was equally important in the development of the literary fairy tale. A few years after the appearance of Johann Musäus's *German Folk Tales* (1782–1786)—but long before the publication of

---

5. This contest is usually called the Judgment of Paris. The son of King Priam of Troy, Paris was chosen by three goddesses to judge their beauty. Aphrodite, the goddess of love, won by promising him possession of Helen, the most beautiful woman in the world. In fulfillment of this promise Paris later abducted Helen, sparking the Trojan War.

the Grimms' tales (1812–1815)—Naubert published *New German Folk Tales* in five volumes
between 1789–1792. Less rationalist than those of Musäus, and less overtly nationalist than
those of the Grimms, her tales show more strongly the French influence of Perrault and seventeenth-century women writers. The Grimms interviewed Naubert when putting together their
own collection—along with twenty-four other women, the majority of whom were women of
letters rather than simple peasants. There are notable similarities between Naubert's novella *The
Cloak* and the Grimm stories "Dame Holle" and "All-Kinds-of-Fur" (page 54) among others.
Ludwig Tieck borrowed from *The Cloak* in his famous tale, "Fair-haired Eckbert" (page 445),
and the fantastic tales of E. T. A. Hoffman also owe much to Naubert's work. *The Cloak* itself
incorporates elements of medieval romance, as well as folk material.

from The Cloak[1]

The Britons, time out of mind, have fabled so much of their King Arthur that a portion of these wonderful tales have echoed across the sea, and been repeated by the
neighboring people. Of course, the legends, when told by such various tongues, have
not always remained the same: here, something has been added; there, something has
been omitted; hence the many variations of the old English legends, and hence so
many romances, the fruit of British soil, to which posterity has given the name of a
Gallic or German hero.

The Emperor Charles the Great was particularly fortunate, in that the fabulous
histories of King Arthur were so frequently set down to his account. Like him a hero,
like him a friend to love, and like him a member of the society of Saint Gangolph,[2]
most of those wonderful adventures fitted him very passably; and, were it not for our
conscientious honesty, we might aptly enough, in compliance with the German tradition, set down this legend, which really belongs to the court of the old Briton, as having happened under the eyes of the son of the great Majordomo.[3] But to show you,
gentle reader, that you may rely upon our word, we freely confess it is not Charles the
Great and his countless wives or mistresses, but King Arthur and his lady Guinevere
that are the hero and heroine who are to figure here.

The court at Carlisle had, besides the Queen, many a blooming, and many a fading beauty, who still maintained their rank on the score of seniority. Some of these we
must name to you, as they have their parts to play in the course of the story. The
loveliest amongst them was Iselda, the beloved of the brave Hector; who for fifteen
long years had let her knight sigh for her love, without having as yet granted him any
other favor than the liberty sometimes of kissing the hem of her veil. After her came
Rosalia and Isabella, the wives of Sir Gawain—whose name cannot be unknown to
you—and of the bold Iwain, the King's son; these ladies were sisters, and while the
one had adopted Pride as the guardian of her honor, the other one took up Piety as her
watchman. Next on the list is Sir Ydier's bride, the Lady Agnes, who, notwithstanding her sleepy watery blue eyes and her rather stupid dove-like looks, yet maintained
her rank amongst the British goddesses. The wild Britomarte follows, who used to
punish with one or two years' banishment every presumptuous glance of her knight,
the bashful Girflet. Below in charms, but, according to age and their own estimation,
in the very first place, come the lusty wife of Sir Guy the Seneschal, and Lady

---

1. Translated by Jeannine Blackwell.
2. The patron saint of all cuckolded husbands [Naubert's
note].
3. The reference is to Charles the Great or Charlemagne
(742–814), son of Pépin the Short (715–768), king of the

Franks. Pépin was himself descended from a long line of
Frankish lords of the same name, some of whom bore the
title "Majordomo." Naubert is conflating these earlier ancestors with Charlemagne's father.

Eleanor, the wife of Peter the Holy, Count of Brittany, who herself was itching for a halo and in the meantime neglected nothing to maintain that rank in the British court which she expected one day to hold in the court of Heaven.

Two beauties we have omitted to mention—the one because she could in no respect be said to belong to the court of Queen Guinevere, being mortally hated by her—the other, because it was only from her extreme loveliness that she was placed upon a level with the rest, for neither by birth nor by property had she any title to rank amongst the high court-ladies.

The first of these two as yet unnamed beauties was the Princess Morgana, the sister of King Arthur. The second was little Genelas from Wales, who came to court an orphan, and made the Queen an indifferent return for her kindness by completely eclipsing with her simple loveliness all the splendor of the royal beauty. The little maiden, however, should be forgiven; she did not desire any of the admiration which was lavished upon her; but one must have been blind not to have preferred Genelas, unadorned, to the proud British Queen in the splendor of her diadem—especially after taking into account innocence, simplicity, and goodness, of which Queen Guinevere possessed very little.

Although we have coupled Genelas and Morgana together, the reader must not imagine that they were of the same stamp; as little inequality as there was in their beauty, yet they differed a whole world in manners and thinking, and not less so in wealth and rank. The Princess sought for conquests, pleased, loved, and was beloved; the little Welsh girl knew nothing of conquests—after which she did not strive— pleased without wishing it, and was beloved without replying to it, or even being aware of it. Morgana was a wise and deeply learned lady, well versed in all the mysteries of nature, a pupil of the great Merlin, and, to say all in one sentence, an enchantress of the second rank. Genelas, on the contrary, knew no magic but that of her needle and spindle, which she was skillful in using, notwithstanding she was a court-lady. Besides, she willingly remained within the narrow limits then prescribed to female knowledge and was on that account so much the sweeter.

The Princess was on the point of bringing to a conclusion her seven-and-twentieth love affair, while it was only within the few last days that Genelas had gained a dim awareness of her first. Sir Carados—surnamed the Armbreaker, because this sort of damage was the least with which his opponents could normally reckon—a hero, as mild in peace as bold in war, had at the last court-festival passed over all the other ladies, and led her out to dance; at parting too he had tenderly squeezed her hand, a point which she did not clearly comprehend, and yet which her heart told her was not without meaning.

Amongst all the inequalities between the two ladies whom we have thus coupled were also the causes of the low esteem in which they both were held by Queen Guinevere—that is, Genelas, on account of her humble manners, was despised; and Morgana, on account of her arrogance, detested.

We have often observed that the sisters of married men stand at best on a footing with stepmothers. These good creatures are always peculiarly jealous of their dear brothers' honor, strict censurers and inexorable judges of every error of those whom love has converted into their relations; and if they happen to be young and handsome enough to rival their sister-in-law in their conquests, then war at once is declared, and not unfrequently they proceed to open hostilities.

Through all these circumstances King Arthur's sister was destined to be Guinevere's enemy; the scenes of overdone courtesy and friendship, which are generally used in the commencement of such hostilities as the cover of real feelings, had long ago been played out between them, and they had got to the second act, namely, that of conscious avoidance and occasional little sarcasms, which often degenerated into earnest, and led people to anticipate the conclusion of the tragedy, a public rift.

* * *

A peep into the great book of the stars would no doubt have shown Morgana the snare laid for her, and she would then have found the means of avoiding it; but at present she read in no book but the eyes of her twenty-seventh lover; nothing existed for her in the world except him; for his sake she sank into the weakness of a common mortal, and, to confess the truth, after so many intrigues, behaved in the whole affair very like a little girl who, for the first time, hears from a young man's lips that she is a sweet little thing.

Oh, how Queen Guinevere rejoiced at the way in which her enemy laid herself open! She pretended to be blind to the love of Morgana and Guiomar, to make them the more secure, watched all their motions in silence, and looked forward to the moment when it would be in her power to expose the weakness of the enamored damsel to the whole court, and by this striking proof of his sister's moral laxness either persuade the King to be deaf forever to her covert slanders, or else to make him banish from the court a hated informer, whose watchfulness laid such hard restraints on the Queen's private pleasures.

That she not let this desired moment slip by, strict injunctions were given to the female courtiers of the third order; all were to seek, to peek, to creep, to sneak, and to repeat, that the slippery forelock of Occasion might not elude their grasp, and all were ready enough for such an occupation. By nature light, crafty, supple, and inclined to little malicious tricks, they found pleasure in that which was imposed upon them as a duty; Genelas had always behaved so very awkwardly in such matters the few times she had an inkling of the subterfuge, that she was now left alone, and the development of the catastrophe was reserved for her, either as a punishment for her dullness, or to put the truth in so much more striking a light through the mouth of simplicity.

That which made the little Welsh girl so stupid now—particularly now—in one of the most fashionable points of female education, was not so much her own pious simplicity, not so much the modest lessons instilled into her from childhood by her nurse, as—a love affair of her own. At the last court-festival Sir Carados had again led her out alone to the dance, had again squeezed her hand, met her for several days after at various times as if by chance, and latterly, when she was surprised by a storm as she traveled on the Queen's affairs, had wrapped her up in his cloak and brought her safely home. So many sweet speeches had passed in these short journeys that no one but a naive girl like Genelas could have doubted the knight's real intentions; she, however, was so astonished, so confounded, that she scarcely knew what she said, or what she heard, and that—that—we can scarcely write it without blushing—that she not only received a kiss from Sir Carados, given in the dark, but even returned it.

Genelas was beside herself at her own recklessness; she wept her eyes red, expected the contempt of her lover for this breach of maidenly manners, and endeavored to regain his respect by assuming prudery and diligently avoiding his company altogether. But all this found her inexperienced heart with so much employment, that she had no senses for anything else, committed a thousand blunders in her duties, and, above all, showed very little inclination to interfere in Morgana's matters.

As the court had no lack of other, more effective, agents, the time came on without her aid for the catastrophe of the tragedy in which Morgana and Sir Guiomar were to play the principal parts. Queen Guinevere had assembled her privy council, in which all the above-named ladies had a seat and voice, and opened the sitting with the question—"What should be done to her who watches with an eye of censure over the actions of others, and at the same time abandons herself in secret to the grossest excesses?"—and all had unanimously voted for death or a public exposure.

* * *

Eleanor and Isabella vaunted that they could annihilate all Morgana's magic with a single Ave, while Iselda and Rosalie doubted altogether the Princess's possessing any such knowledge; but the Queen, who feared the loss of the favorable moment, paid no attention to the advice of her councillors; she ordered little Genelas to be called, and, feigning a desperate hurry, dispatched her to Morgana, desiring her not to be stopped by anything, but to press on into Morgana's chamber, and if she found that princess not in a state to comply with the Queen's request of coming to her, that then she should steal away quietly, and bring back an exact account of the condition in which she had seen her.

Guinevere had taken care to stage things so that, immediately upon the dismissal of Genelas, the King with his nobles should be in her chamber, so that he might be present at her return, and witness the unmasking of his sister.

King Arthur knowing nothing of all this, had, as usual, not the foggiest notion, and came into the room at this moment, only because it was the customary time for his visit, which, as a very punctual gentleman, he never missed.

"My dear lord," said the Queen, approaching him with that respect which artful women ever use to conceal from their husbands that they in fact command them, "my dear lord, you find us all assembled here to beguile the remainder of the day in play or dance at your pleasure. Two persons only are wanting to our circle, whom we cannot do without; I mean your noble sister and the hero Guiomar. I have sent after the first myself, and to the latter you will be pleased to dispatch a messenger."

The King had already turned round to the Seneschal to give him the commission requested by the Queen, when little Genelas, half out of breath and blushing like Aurora, entered the room, and quietly took her place.

"Have you executed my commission?" said the Queen.

"No," replied Genelas, blushing still more deeply.

"Did you not find the Princess then?"

"Yes—no—yes," stammered the maiden.

"Oh!" said Lady Seneschal, "I will lay anything that our absent little maiden forgot your message along the way, and now does not know how to extricate herself from her embarrassment. Recollect, my child; you were to request the Princess to grace this company with her presence, and you have not spoken to her?"

"No, indeed."

"And why not?"

"I think she was in the bath."

"And where?"

"In truth I do not know; I listened through the trees, and saw—saw that her maidens were around her, amusing her with dance and song."

"What nonsense the child is chattering!" exclaimed the Queen; "she looked, and knows not where, saw, and knows not what."

"Allow me, your highness," said Britomarte, "to go and fetch you more accurate information. The bath scene is probably in the Princess's garden."

"That is not necessary," said Guinevere; "we will all go and see whether Genelas has told us the truth."

"Indeed, indeed," said the maiden, "I think I have not lied; that much at least is certain: the garden was closed, and, had I not been ordered to press on without stopping, I should hardly have forced my way through the bushes to see what I saw."

"Fool!" cried the Queen; "you know not what you say; you contradict yourself at every word. Come, my lord; we will go and see ourselves."

"But only consider," said Genelas, throwing herself at the Queen's feet, "the Princess is in the bath."

"Very well," replied the Queen, "we will go, and you shall be our guide."

The fat Lady Seneschal here seized the weeping Genelas by the arm, pulled her up, and dragged her along the well-known way to Morgana's garden, the whole court following them.

Morgana availed herself of her magic only to enjoy the pleasures of life in full measure. By means of that her palace was the most splendid, her attendants the most numerous, and her gardens comprised all that the earth has most alluring; and even her own beauty, as her enviers maintained, was so irresistible only through the power of magic. "All deceit and vapor!" Guinevere would often say in a philosophical mood, "born from a breath, and just as easily destroyed again by a breath; a void, as it was formed by the Creator."

Adorned with all the attractions of a goddess, the Princess would often give splendid festivals in her magic gardens to King Arthur's court; but her most splendid celebrations were in the arms of a confidential friend, surrounded by no other witnesses than a part of her own court, who owed their existence to her wand, and at a touch from it would again melt into vapor; these of course were the zealous servants of her will as long as she left them life and, as may be supposed, silent, unimportant witnesses of her secret pleasures. It was in this circle that the innocent Genelas saw the fair enchantress; she had found, as she told them, the palace empty, the garden closed, and had made a way for herself through the bushes and hedges until she got into the center of an orange grove, which concealed a broad plain in its bosom; in the middle again of this, lofty cedars, interwoven with low myrtle shrubs, shaded a marble bath, where Morgana delighted to refresh herself in the heat of the day.

Genelas had spied through the myrtle hedge, and seen the princess in the bath, surrounded by her shadowy attendants—a heavenly sight even for the eye of a maiden, who was herself not deficient in charms! But the Princess was not alone; upon the green bank, where her suite reclined in picturesque groups, lay the arms of a knight, who was sharing with her the coolness of the limpid waters. The eyes of the modest little Welsh maiden were instantly turned away in terror upon seeing Morgana's bathing companion. She, who grieved so much about a kiss too boldly returned, and who deemed the maiden veil that covered her lovely face to be so indispensable—it may be guessed what she thought of the boldness of one of her sex in admitting a man into the very sanctuary of her evening toilette, into the bath itself. She hid her face in her dress, flew back quicker than she had come, and in the greatest confusion entered the hall where Guinevere with her court were waiting for her. The Queen had learned beforehand from her spies that Guiomar had a private interview with Morgana, knew the Princess's improvidence, which had not made the place of meeting inaccessible to the Queen's envoy, and had purposely chosen simple Genelas for that office, to crush the offender so much the more heavily by the innocent way in which the maiden would tell the story.

As we have seen, the project did not altogether succeed. Genelas was too much ashamed at this impudence in one of her own sex, and felt too much repugnance at owning she had witnessed it, to speak with frankness now. She was as much confused as if she had been the offender; her words, her tears petitioned them so earnestly to leave the veil upon Morgana's mysteries, that those who know not how real innocence behaves—and there were few such innocents at Arthur's court—must have been quite mistaken in her.

Genelas was compelled to show the company the way to Morgana's bath, or rather they knew it already, for they might conclude pretty well where it was from the broken speeches of the abashed maiden.

Morgana was so blinded that she had not taken the least measures for her security. She had imagined the court was absent on a hunting-party, settled long before, had forgotten to place any shadowy terrors or spiritual guards at the entrance of the orange grove, and held herself safe under the simple protection of a few locks; great, therefore, was her surprise, when all of a sudden a thousand witnesses appeared at the edge of the marble bath, some speechless with horror, and others with malignant delight, and gazed on her and her companion of the bath, without knowing how to express their feelings.

King Arthur lifted up his eyes and hands to heaven; the knights exerted all their powers of sight to lose nothing of the surprising spectacle; the ladies beat their breasts with averted eyes; and the Queen alone had enough presence of mind to break the silence.

"Really, Princess," she exclaimed, in a tone such as only triumphant malice can form from lips distorted into bitter scorn, "really, Princess, we surprise you here in a singular condition. Genelas, who brought us hither, said nothing of the state in which we were to find you, or we should have spared our eyes this spectacle."

Vexation, wrath, and shame fettered the tongue of the surprised Morgana. Sir Guiomar at first hid his face in his hands, till a sort of instinct, which makes every hero grasp after his arms upon an insult, drove him to the edge of the bath to fetch his sword. In the meantime, Morgana's eyes were so far from being fixed to the earth by any modest confusion that they flashed fire on the surrounders. Revenge was seething in her heart, and doubtless, if she had possessed the power, she would have punished the gazers in the same way that Cynthia once punished the presumptuous huntsman; indeed, she did fill both hands with water, which she scattered about her in a thousand glittering drops; the whole effect, however, of this maneuver was that the bath scene of the new Diana, together with her Endymion and her nymphs,[4] disappeared from the eyes of the spectators in a thin mist, and even the surrounding grove with the whole of the magic country was enveloped in a bluish fog that by degrees passed off, and let the curious company see where they really stood—namely, on a wide plain of yellow sand, scorched up by the burning sun, with a few dusty bushes that spread out their thin withered foliage. In fact, it was precisely the same desert spot that Morgana had originally found here, and by her magic wand converted into gardens.

It may be imagined with what confusion the assembly looked about them, and with what discomfiture they made their way back again under the heat of the midday sun. But at the same time, Morgana had not been able to effect with her wand that which she had probably intended—causing all to forget these events, or at least, to

4. "Cynthia" and "Diana" are alternate names for the goddess of the moon, the hunt, and chastity in classical mythology. Naubert is conflating stories about two different pairs of mortal heroes and moon goddesses. "The presumptuous huntsman" is Actaeon, who came upon Diana / Cynthia bathing with her companion nymphs. she punished him for gazing on her nakedness by changing him into a stag, which was promptly devoured by his own hounds. Endymion, on the other hand, was another hunter who was sleeping on a mountainside when Selene, another moon goddess, saw him and fell in love with him.

doubt their reality. All present knew perfectly well that they had been awake and not asleep, and all, to the infinite delight of the vindictive Queen, protested that while they looked upon Morgana as the greatest of magicians, they at the same time deemed her the most frivolous and shameless creature upon the face of God's earth. King Arthur betrayed his thoughts only by a troubled silence and angry looks; and it was well that the Princess had taken herself off with all her entourage, or else banishment or death would have been the inevitable punishment of her offence. In fact, she had left nothing of hers behind. In the spots formerly occupied by her extensive palaces, nothing was now to be seen but empty spaces, and even the presents which she had made to the King and Queen in gentler hours had vanished from their jewel chests.

Guinevere's project had thus succeeded; she had revenged herself upon her enemy, and had removed her from the court, perhaps forever, but still she was not quite satisfied: it seemed to her that her revenge and triumph might have been yet more complete; many little circumstances might have been omitted from the whole adventure, and as she was accustomed, in the manner of great ladies, to make others suffer for her discontent, and had just then no other object on which to pour out the cup of her wrath, the storm burst upon poor little Genelas; she was that very evening called before the great council of the ladies, tried, and condemned. A thousand sins occurred, which on this occasion were all brought forward to her account; but the most important charge, or at least that which possessed a little semblance of truth, was that she had a secret understanding with the enchantress, and probably participated in her excesses. From the very beginning she had so reluctantly mingled in the plot against the Princess, had at last, when others had imperceptibly involved her in it, behaved so simplemindedly, had so earnestly sought to hide the offender's shameful trespasses, sparing neither prayers nor tears to keep the rest of the court from the way which she had first taken, that her judges deemed it could not be otherwise than that she was a creature of Morgana, an enemy of the Queen, and consequently as wicked and as vicious as those whose part she had so solemnly and simpleheartedly taken.

We, however, know the motives of the little Welsh girl; at least we can swear that sympathy with Morgana's excesses was far from having any place in her innocent heart, though they could not, and would not, see this at Arthur's court. The sentence pronounced upon her case in the Queen's private chamber soon communicated itself to every heart, however much interested in her favor before; she was with general consent banished from court, and abandoned to poverty and misery. Poor creature! To complete her wretchedness, it was only wanting that she should know the fortune which had that day awaited her, and which had by this fatal event alone been thwarted.

Sir Carados, whose heart cleaved to the beautiful maiden, had already spoken of his passion to King Arthur, and intended this evening to make a formal application to the Queen; but now his beloved appeared in so hateful a light!—What his own eyes could not find was supplied by the opinion of others; no one was there to defend the accused, and thus it happened, that, if not his love, yet all his designs in her favor vanished, and he saw her banishment, not without secret tears, but without any effort to defend or save her. "I loved beauty without virtue," he said to himself mournfully; "I loved a deceptive hallucination that I must now forget. But there can be little virtue in women since Genelas is sinful." So saying, he girded on his sword, mounted his horse, and set out to kill the feelings of grief and love in the tumult of warlike adventures.

In the meantime, Genelas left the court of King Arthur as poor as she had entered it, or rather much poorer; then she had possessed a total freedom from care, ignorance of human necessities, and all the evils arising out of them, together with an abundance of joyful hopes; but, alas! these inestimable goods are only the property of childhood, which we must entirely leave behind on entering the age of manhood or womanhood.

Robbed of every means of honest subsistence, driven out into the wide world, alone and friendless, the poor wanderer could not be without care, and could hardly possess any great stock of hopes for the future. She wandered many a day and many a night, living sparingly on that which she had saved up in happier times, and which was hardly worth naming. It is true, indeed, that King Arthur had sent after her a traveling gift, but her enemies had taken care to intercept it. Genelas was too beautiful to have many women friends; it was no secret that she had pleased many eyes, and above all, the sparkling black eyes of brave Carados—reason enough for most ladies, even for Queen Guinevere, to hate her mortally, and to rejoice that this feeling could just now be so admirably concealed under the mask of the love of virtue.

It was late one evening that the pilgrim, on reaching a village, felt an excess of weariness which made her apprehend the end of all her travels. She had wandered for many days with scanty nourishment, little rest, exposed to the sun's heat and the chilling rains; what wonder then that at last her strength failed, and she sank down almost senseless before a cottage which stood alone by the roadside, about twenty paces from the village?

* * *

[Genelas is sheltered by an old woman named Rose, who gives her spinning to do, and recounts her own tale of family jealousy and loss; she is saved from destitution by a mysterious pilgrim who blesses her spinning after she treats him kindly. One day the pilgrim returns, and gives Genelas a supply of yarn.]

The spindles were quickly filled with a web which might shame the threads of Arachne[5] in fineness and the rainbow in brilliance of color. The mysterious donor came regularly once a week in Rose's absence to fetch what was spun and never forgot to say, "Spin, maiden, the stuff for your cloak of honor; spin, maiden, spin the threads of your fortune!" But when he took away the last of the spinning, and brought no fresh materials with him, terror and sadness fell upon the poor Welsh maiden, and she exclaimed to Rose: "Ah, Mother, some change of fortune is at hand with me, since I lack the wool to spin; and what change can it be that will not snatch me from your arms, and how can I be happy without you?" Rose endeavored to comfort her, but tears stood in her own eyes at the thought of being separated from the child of her heart.

At length that which she had feared from the pilgrim's prophecy really happened. A message came from the King, summoning Genelas to court, and she was obliged to obey. "Ah!" she exclaimed, folding her kind mother in her arms for the last time, "must I then exchange your society for the motley crowds of folly?—give up my dear spinning-wheel for the business of idleness and luxury, and the peaceful silence of this hut for the persecutions that await me at court?"

Such were the lamentations of Genelas, and she would have found still more reason for lament had she known the real cause of her recall to court.

Great ladies have ever in the execution of their secret affairs made use of very subordinate agents, who, in recompense, possess much influence with them and can speak many a word to the advantage or disadvantage of their friends or enemies. Such was the relationship, as we have already mentioned, between Lady Guinevere and

---

5. In Greek myth, a mortal weaver so accomplished she dared to compete with Athena, goddess of weaving and other arts.

Magdalene; the latter, therefore, who grudged Rose any pleasure, even the company of sweet Genelas, needed nothing else to remove her than to give the Queen a hint of Morgana's visits, and these she had learnt with her usual curiosity by listening at the window to the conversation of the two spinners.

Guinevere could not bear the idea of an alliance between Morgana and the young Welsh maiden; she hated both and had an indefinite fear of mischief to herself if they should make common cause. To prevent this, an order from the cabinet was hastily issued, and Genelas was obliged to submit to the journey which gave her so much pain. As she followed the royal envoy, Rose stood at the door and wept; Magdalene, too, stood before her cottage and bade farewell to the traveler, but the tone of the farewell betrayed the heart which uttered it.

Genelas arrived at court and did not even enjoy the favor of being presented to the Queen, but was immediately set about menial offices, which were hardly suited to a servant of the wardrobe. For her part she could not conceive why they had torn her from her beloved solitude, when they seemed so little to need or value her. She surely would have seen that her presence was required only for the sake of watching her more closely, if her innocence could have acknowledged its own value; but she had soon occasion to imagine another cause for her not being allowed to remain any longer in the quiet of obscurity. The hero, Carados, had come back again to court after many victories to receive his reward from the hands of King Arthur, and it was strongly suggested that, in lieu of all other recompense, he would demand the hand of one of the Queen's maids of honor.

"Ah!" sighed Genelas, "that is the reason of my being called hither. All these women hate me, as is evident from their haughty, scornful glances whenever they pass by me; they know that Carados loved me before the loss of my good name made me unworthy of him, and now they want to triumph over me, to make me the witness of a good fortune which, in truth, belongs only to her whose virtue no one can question."

Whitsuntide[6] was approaching, when the King was always wont to hold open court, and this time it was to be kept with more than usual splendor, as, owing to Arthur's indisposition, the preceding Christmas festivities had been canceled: for you must not imagine that the court of the old monarch was like the courts of our days, when every morning brings with it a fresh scene of pleasure. No, it was three, or, at most, four times a year, on high holy days, that the monarchs of the olden days unveiled the splendor of their courts; the rest of the year they led a happy private life amidst their family and their household in the obscurity of their castles. At these times of quiet, if war did not call upon them, the men occupied themselves with state affairs and the chase, while the ladies, even such as Lady Guinevere, found themselves obliged to have recourse to the needle and the spinning wheel, if they were not to die of boredom.

It may be imagined with what eagerness the lovers of pleasure, after so long an abstinence, looked toward such a festival, where all was industriously collected that could gratify the senses. Great and early bustle was made with the preparations for the important day, that they might amuse their minds agreeably in the tedious interval and unite the retelling of past adventures, which never failed on such occasions, with the hope of those that were to be.

* * *

6. The week of Pentecost, beginning the seventh Sunday after Easter.

King Arthur had appointed this day for the celebration of the peacock-festival, of which, my dear readers—knowing your experience in the manners of other times—I need not say anything, except that the first course at dinner was opened with a dish in which was a peacock floating in an aromatic sauce. This dish had to be prepared and served up by the lady of the house, even if she were a queen, as in the present case. The regal bird which was now to decorate the table stood forth in all the splendors of his tail, a golden crown circled his head, and from his beak blue flames incessantly fell into a silver dish, a display invented by the complaisant enchantress Morgana to give a still more splendid appearance to the dish, which was to be served up by the Queen, for at this time both parties conducted themselves as sisters.

The King, the Princes, and the knights were already assembled in the lofty banquet hall, and every moment expected to see the Queen enter with the dish in her hands, followed by her ladies, and preceded by the minstrels and harpers; but a delay took place from a little quarrel for precedence amongst the actresses in the ceremony. In the meantime King Arthur had retired to a window with his favorite, Sir Gawain, when, lo! a handsome page came trotting up the street on a snow-white palfrey, dressed in sky-blue velvet, and carrying before him on his horse a purple-colored portmanteau. At the great castle gate he dismounted nimbly from his horse, tied him to the railings, took his portmanteau under his arm, and ascended the stairs into the royal banquet hall. Upon entering he uncovered his head, bent his knee before the King, and said, "I am sent to you, sire, by a lady of the highest rank in another land, who through me begs a favor at your hands."

"It is granted to her," replied Arthur, bending his head with a gracious smile. The page thanked him, arose, and placed his portmanteau on a side table, that he might undo it and take out its contents.

O ye men! boast not that nature has given more curiosity to the weaker sex than to yourselves! Never did a company of ladies press forward with more eagerness to peek at a novelty produced from the portmanteau of a stranger than did these heroes of the British king.

"Gently! gently, good sirs!" cried the page; "allow me air to breathe, and room to show my curiosities."

At this expostulation all drew back a little, and from every mouth came an exclamation of wonder, for a sight met their eyes, beautiful beyond what any lover of finery could imagine. This was a cloak as large and broad as the coronation robe of an emperor, adorned with all the colors of the rainbow, transparent as a jewel, and of a web so fine and delicate, that it was only with the help of the green spectacles of some old gentlemen that the sharp eyes of the younger ones could discover the threads.

"This garment," continued the page, as he kept back the intruders from incautiously touching the wonderful web, "this garment was spun by maiden hands, of materials more precious than silk, and woven in an elfin land, and so prepared by the most profound magic that it can only fit one person in this court, and for her it is intended. The favor, sire, which my noble mistress begs of you, is, that she may be permitted to present this garment to that woman amongst your ladies who has never committed any infidelity to her husband or her lover, and who, besides, surpasses all her contemporaries in virtue and inward excellence."

"And who is the happy one," cried all with one mouth, "who is to receive this wonderful garment of honor?"

"That will show itself," replied the stranger; "for, by virtue of the royal promise, every lady must try on the cloak, that we may see what virtue and fidelity dwell in the hearts of British women."

"That will be a glorious exhibition!" cried Sir Gawain, rubbing his hands, and laughing, "permit me, sire, to fetch the ladies, for I can scarcely wait for the things we are like to see."

Without waiting for an answer, Gawain ran to the ladies, who had just commenced the procession of the peacock, with the court minstrels playing and singing lustily before them. With difficulty he suppressed his laughter as he said, "Ladies, I entreat you to quicken your steps; presents have come from a foreign land, which the King destines for her who shall be recognized for the fairest amongst you."

At these misleading words the cheeks of the Queen began to glow more warmly, her heart beat in the victory, which she thought undoubted, and her hands trembled so much that she was scarcely able to hold the heavy peacock-dish. The others too felt their share of unquiet sensations; only Morgana was somewhat pale, and stepped a few paces aside, as if she meant to leave the procession, but she suddenly bethought herself and followed the rest, who, without time or order, quite contrary to the custom of the peacock-festival, hastened into the hall and found the King and his nobles employed in admiring the wonderful cloak. During this the King, from certain misgivings, had endeavored to persuade the page from the public trial of the cloak, or at least to exclude the Queen from so dangerous a test, but all was in vain; the page insisted upon the royal word and proved beyond contradiction that this too was contained in the allowance of his request.

"My friends," said the King, as the ladies rushed in, "here is a priceless cloak, which I deem a gift for her who is fully entitled to it."

"Oh, I see already," said Queen Guinevere, giving her dish into the hands of a chamberlain, "I see that it will fit me as if made for me, and I will try it on first. But, tell me—I understand this is a trial of beauty; is it true that she, whom this gown fits, is the fairest?"

"Oh, yes!—the fairest!—undoubtedly the fairest in the world!" cried the King and his knights with one voice.

Guinevere, who did not perceive the double meaning in this speech, hastened to throw on the cloak and gain the prize, which, as she imagined, belonged to her before all others; but what were the feelings of the bystanders, when instead of flowing about her in proper ample folds, and fitting closely about the waist only, the mantle suddenly shrunk up to so small a size that it could scarcely pass for a three-cornered neck-kerchief, stretching itself out on one side to a narrow point, while on the other it lost itself amidst the headdress! The worst part of all this was, that from the wriggling of the mantle the rest of the dress fell into disorder, and revealed more of her person than was agreeable to the decorum of the age.

"Well!" said Guinevere, who alone seemed to be blind to this spectacle, "well, what is your opinion? Shall I win the prize?"

"For Heaven's sake, Madam, throw it off," exclaimed the King, blushing up to his ears and hiding her naked figure with his own robe. "for Heaven's sake, throw off the abominable thing that was not made for you; remove yourself as quickly as possible, and do not show yourself again for some time to come; for there is more in this matter than you imagine."

"Remove myself!" cried the Queen, half ashamed, half angry, for she was now partly sensible of her situation, "remove myself! Certainly not, till I see whether these ladies are more fortunate than I have been."

Upon this Sir Iwain, the King's son, took the cloak from her with stifled laughter and presented it to fair Iselda, the bride of the brave Hector, saying, "Fair Lady, who keep your lovers pining in your chains for twenty years, perhaps this costly garment was intended for you." The fair one instantly put it on, proud of seeing it flow down so decorously to her ankles; but behind her arose a loud laughter, and as the spectators did not feel it requisite to use so much forbearance with her as they had done with the Queen, she soon found out in what a singular way she appeared to them.

With looks of profound contempt the faithful Hector took the treacherous garment from his strict mistress and brought it to the proud Rosalia and the pious Isabella, whom he almost compelled by force to put it on. "It is but just," he said, "that your husbands, who are so ready to laugh at others, should see their own darlings put to the proof."

Great was the triumph of honest Hector, when he saw that these ladies were caught with their virtue down as had been his own cruel Iselda, who had seated herself on a distant couch in shame, and did not dare to lift up her eyes.

"Ah, woe! Ah, woe!" cried the Seneschal, upon seeing that the Lady Agnes and the wild Britomarte met with precisely the same fate as their companions had done. "Fidelity of British ladies, what has become of you?"

"Fidelity!" exclaimed the Queen, "What do you mean by that? Is this a trial of beauty or of virtue?"

"Of virtue, gracious lady," replied the Seneschal, laughing immoderately, "of virtue; and one might almost congratulate you for being at least the best amongst your ladies, for, compared to what we have now seen, what happened to you was nothing."

"Insolent jester!" exclaimed the Queen, "you deserve to be severely punished. But it is not enough that you laugh at the fate of these poor ladies; we will see how it is with the fidelity of your own wife."

At the Queen's command the fat Lady Seneschal was compelled, notwithstanding all her protests, to try on the treacherous cloak. Luckily for her, she had the pious Countess of Brittany, Lady Ellinor, for a companion, or else her shame would have been intolerable; for the garment fitted her so ill and presented such strange sights to the spectators that they averted their eyes.

"Take comfort, ladies," said the Seneschal, "you are not the only ones liable to this misfortune, nor am I the only one amongst the deceived husbands. However, that there may be some order amongst the tried and untried ladies, you, who have already tried the virtue of the cloak, will be pleased to seat yourselves by the side of the distressed Iselda, who is lamenting her mishap in the corner yonder."

The countess and the Lady Seneschal followed, their heads drooping, to the bench on which Rosalia, Isabella, Agnes, and Britomarte had already arranged themselves of their own accord, all with downcast eyes and none venturing to address a single syllable to their neighbors.

Now that the real nature of the trial of the cloak was thoroughly known amongst the ladies, there was not one who did not wish herself a hundred miles away from King Arthur's court. All were sweating with fear and sought a thousand excuses for not putting on the abominable garment; even the compassionate King, when he saw their distress, turned to the bearer of the unlucky present and said, "My friend, it seems to me that you had better remove yourself with your cloak, for it is made clumsily, and will certainly not fit any of these ladies, married or unmarried."

"Great King," cried the page, "where is your word?—No; you have pledged yourself once for all, and I will not stir from the spot, till, amongst the ladies of your court, I have found her for whom this prize of fidelity and virtue is destined."

* * *

[After every lady in court is humiliated, the Queen sends for Genelas, wishing to see her shamed as well. We learn that Genelas has seen Sir Carados going to church with his younger sister, and believes she has a rival for his love.]

Genelas was found lying upon her bed, still indisposed, but she was used to obeying and followed the Queen's messenger without questions and without opposition. A few paces from the royal apartment Sir Carados was waiting for her; from the Queen's words he had learnt her presence, and hastened to meet her with trembling, that he might warn her of the impending misfortune.

"Lady," he said, "I come to lead you back to your chamber, or wherever else you may think proper; my heart still speaks for you, notwithstanding the scenes with Morgana, and I should unwillingly see you taking a part in the things which are now going on in the royal hall."

The terrified Genelas drew her hand away from his and asked what he meant. He explained as well as he was able, but still she did not comprehend him and left him with an angry look, occasioned by jealousy of his companion on the day of the church procession. Carados followed sadly, while she entered the hall with all the ease of conscious innocence, and with a modest curtsy asked what they wanted of her?

"Nothing, child," said the Queen with a malicious laugh, "but that you should try on this cloak. It shall be yours if it fit you."

Genelas stared mightily at this liberality of the Queen's, for the cloak waved toward her in the bearer's hands in all its splendor, and with each moment discovered a fresh brilliance in the wonderful web. What maiden is there, whose heart would not beat faster at the sight of a new garment? Genelas blushed with delight at this regal present and exclaimed, "For me? This costly garment for me? Oh, how have I deserved such kindness? I, who imagined myself obliterated from the memory of my Queen?"

Genelas fell upon her knees, and in the most captivating manner kissed the hands of the malicious Guinevere, who only bade her rise and set to work immediately. The delighted maiden tripped joyfully to the page, to take from his hands the miraculous gift, still ignorant of its real nature, but Sir Carados was close behind her and whispered in her ear, "Suffer anything rather than put on this cloak." Genelas could not at all comprehend this strange importunity of the knight; moreover, since the first day of the festival she had entertained a peculiar aversion to him, which made her inclined to put the worst construction upon all he said or did. She looked upon him as the disturber of her happiness, made as if she heard nothing of his admonition, and boldly flung the magic garment over her shoulders. Carados turned away his face, the knights drew nearer, the ladies on the couch began a malicious whispering, and the Queen collected all the evil of her heart in a single look to beat to the earth the chastised girl in the state in which she soon hoped to see her. But what were the Queen's feelings, what were the feelings of all who envied the young maiden, when the cloak quietly arranged itself about the slim figure of Genelas, without leaving a single tuck, and when from the mouths of the collected knighthood resounded a loud exclamation of "She is the maiden! She is the maiden of rare virtue and fidelity, for whom the wonderful garment was made!"

Genelas stood there in all her splendor, without being able to comprehend why so slight a matter as the putting on of a cloak should be accompanied by such loud acclamations. Her inquiring looks wandered around from one to the other, but the clamor continued, and it was not for some time that Sir Carados—who could scarcely speak from transport at the unexpected outcome of this ticklish affair—found an opportunity of explaining in few words, that by this very putting on of the cloak, which to her seemed so trifling, she had accomplished a feat which concerned the happiness of her life.

Ashamed, confused, confounded at the praise which poured in upon her from all sides, the charming girl stood in the midst of a circle that grew thicker and thicker around her. Her cheeks glowed, her eyes were sunk to earth, her right hand lay in the hand of the delighted Carados, who murmured a thousand words of joy, which she only half heard and in her confusion still less understood, while her left played with the folds of the billowing garment.

"Pray, put an end to this farce," cried Guinevere, who could scarce contain herself for envy. "Why do you intoxicate the poor fool with your admiration, before you know whether she more than half deserves it? Let us examine her first on all sides, before you trumpet forth her praises."

With these words she turned the trembling maiden round before the assembly twice or thrice to spy out any defects, but, lo! the cloak floated about the girl in such graceful folds on all sides that the male spectators unanimously exclaimed, "She is without reproach!" Genelas, however, did not think so; she suddenly recollected an adventure, which, she imagined, rendered her unworthy of the general approbation, and when with these repentant thoughts she cast down her eyes upon her bosom, and found it more exposed than the decorous manners of that period allowed, she was covered with deeper blushes and her eyes swam in tears.

"Treacherous cloak!" she cried, and with her hands covered her bosom, which was as beautiful as the heart that beat within it, "Treacherous cloak! Fold yourself more closely about me; I will willingly confess the fault I once committed."

"There, you see!" cried Guinevere; "she is like the rest of us. Confess, you godless creature, confess your sin this moment and put off the garment, which does not belong to you."

"Gently," cried the page; "gently, fair Lady: one must be blind not to see the difference between you and this innocent soul; we have not yet forgotten certain things. The mantle is incontestably her right, and if she choose to render herself yet more worthy of it by the confession of a peccadillo, it is for no one to prevent her."

"Ah!" said Genelas, "I will confess—willingly confess, so that this shame may be taken from me. I once had a lover—I loved him more perhaps than I ought to do, and thus it happened, when he kissed me in the dusk, that I—that I was so bold as—as to return his kiss."

"And the fortunate man," asked Carados, "the fortunate man, who led you into this mighty fault, was—"

A glance, cast at the speaker from the soft dove's eyes of the fair one, replied to this question.

"Oh, heavenly girl!" cried Sir Carados, "it was I then!—I!—Mine was thy heart, mine the first kiss of thy love, mine the fidelity which distinguishes thee from thousands of thy race!"

No sooner had Genelas made her confession than the cloak fitted decorously about her snowy bosom and left her at liberty to give up to her lover the right hand, which he was endeavoring to possess himself of, although she did not yet well know what to think of him, for the church procession was still fresh in her mind.

But the Queen, to whom this scene was for many reasons intolerable, gave orders to the attendants that they should sound the dinner gong, complaining that the peacock paté was getting cold over the farce. All accordingly placed themselves at table, the knights unanimously protesting that Genelas should yield precedence to no one but the Queen and should sit between the King and Sir Carados. It was, however, by no means Guinevere's intention that Genelas should be introduced to the royal table; she objected that the Welsh maiden held no place at court entitling her to such an honor. But to these objections no answer was made, and the matter remained as it had been settled.

During the whole dinner-time the knights did not cease to lift up the praises of fidelity, while the ladies repasted in sad silence, not one of them venturing to raise up her eyes, and indeed it was as if they had not been present, for no one spoke to them; all attended to Genelas only, who sat by the side of her lover, splendid as a queen and modest as a nun. The only person that sought to give a turn to the conversation was the page, who had been invited to sit at the dinner-table. He brought forward all manner of jests; they were, however, of such a nature that it was easy to see he was laughing at King Arthur's court. Thus toward the end of the meal he drew a boar's head from the middle of the table to his own place, and swore a lofty oath that no knight who had an unfaithful wife or mistress would be able to cut a morsel from it. Herewith he got up to present it in his own person to the knights and nobles, but all recollected the spectacle with the cloak and very gravely begged to be excused. Some, who were too hard pressed by the knavish boy, flung their knives under the table, or protested that they had no knives, while others had, as they said, made a vow never to carve for themselves at dinner. But Sir Carados gracefully cut up the boar's head, presenting a piece to each of the company, and the first and daintiest piece to Genelas.

The knights, however, fell more readily into the snare when the page requested a golden horn, and, having filled it with wine, presented it to the King, with the assurance that only he could empty the cup without spilling a drop who had never been faithless to his beloved. It had been hitherto believed that the fidelity of men was not of so delicate a nature as the fidelity of women, and the knights and princes therefore drank boldly, in the hope that a few trifling gallantries would not be reckoned against them. But, oh heavens! what a sight was there! King Arthur, indeed, spilled the least, but amongst the rest were many who could not bring a drop of the precious wine to their mouths, but missed the way thither in the most ridiculous manner imaginable and soaked themselves and their mistresses.

The ladies now began to lift up their heads a little and to gaze at the knights more boldly. Some even ventured a slight titter and a few words of mockery, when the page commanded silence, for the turn had now come to Sir Carados, who confidently took up the brimming goblet and drained it to the health of the truest and fairest maiden in the world, without spilling a drop.

"Lady! Lady!" said the page to Genelas, "Happy is the man who calls you wife; but happy also is the wife of such a man."

Genelas was silent, not altogether believing in the veracity of the horn, for she still dwelt upon the fair companion in the church-procession. But little Edda, who was present, had only once to call Sir Carados brother, and every doubt was removed.

All now got up from the table, and still Genelas could not keep her eyes for a moment from the page, who again solemnly declared her to be the rightful owner of the magic cloak. She endeavored to get a tête-à-tête with him, and succeeded before the party broke up.

"Tell me, pray, who you are," she said, "I am puzzled by your appearance. The whole assembly calls you a young page, yet to me you seem the very reverse. I discover in you the form and features of a venerable old man, who once provided me with work and hope during the time of my poverty."

"Do not ask too much," replied the stranger with a smile. "Know me, or know me not, it is all the same to me, but never forget that the threads of which your garment of honor was woven, were spun by your own hand in the time of your adversity."

Genelas had perhaps gone on with her questions, but the cloak-bearer was sent for to the King, who drew him aside, saying, "Tell me, pray, who is the high and noble lady that sent you to us with your wonderful present?"

Before the page could answer, the Queen drew him to the other side to ask the same question. And now the questioners, male and female, increased so much about him that he found no better way of helping himself than by vanishing altogether.

"It is Morgana who has played us this trick," said the Queen, as her way was lighted to bed.

"It is Morgana!" exclaimed all.

But Genelas was much happier in her guess that the page was no other than the kindhearted German household spirit, the friend and protectress of female virtue, for whose favor she was indebted to honest Rose.

The next day Sir Carados solicited the hand of fair Genelas of Wales and obtained it without any opposition. She brought him nothing but her well-earned cloak and a heart full of loyalty and virtue, a dowry with which in those simple times people were wont to be contented. Soon after he hastened away with her from Arthur's seductive court to his lands in Scotland, where they were accompanied by Genelas's old friend, Rose, who willingly left her cottage and the neighborhood of Magdalene to lead a life of heaven at the side of the child of her heart.

*   *   *

Jacob Grimm   and   Wilhelm Grimm
1785–1863   1786–1859

Important philologists, medievalists, and cultural historians in their time, Jacob and Wilhelm Grimm are best known today for their legacy as folklorists: the *Grimms' Fairy Tales,* originally published as *Nursery and Household Tales (Kinder–und Hausmärchen;* 1812–1815). Their scholarly thoroughness established the science of folklore, but their creative editing defined the modern genre of the fairy tale, from "Once upon a time" to "happily ever after."

Born into a large bourgeois Hessian family, Jacob and Wilhelm lost their comfortable home when their father died in 1796, and they were sent to live with an aunt in Kassel. They attended the University of Marburg to become lawyers like their father, but under the influence of their literature and history professors, Clemens Brentano and Friedrich Karl von Savigny, devoted themselves instead to German medieval studies. By 1808, when their mother died leaving them responsible for four younger siblings, they had already begun collecting traditional stories. They had also begun a twenty-three-year career as private librarians in Kassel, first to the occupying Bonaparte king of Westphalia, and afterward to the restored Elector of Kassel. During this period they published many collections of medieval and modern folktales, including some two hundred stories in the two annotated scholarly tomes of *Nursery and Household Tales.* Wilhelm married Dorothea Wild in 1825, and the unmarried Jacob lived with them. Having received several honorary doctorates, the brothers accepted professorships at the University of Göttingen in the German kingdom of

Hanover, but within a few years were dismissed and exiled for their refusal to accept the new king's repeal of Hanover's liberal constitution. In 1840 Jacob and Wilhelm were elected to the Berlin Academy, which supported them on a stipend thereafter. There, while Wilhelm continued his ceaseless revisions of the *Nursery and Household Tales,* Jacob took the lead in making contributions to historical linguistics (a law of sound change is named after him), the history of German law and customs, and the study of German pagan mythology (upon which composer Richard Wagner drew so heavily). They also launched the first comprehensive German dictionary. Wilhelm died in the middle of the letter "D," but Jacob survived as far as "F."

Many German authors (including Benedikte Naubert) had been collecting and writing fairy tales since the mid-eighteenth century, influenced both by the highly artful French efforts of the previous century (including those of Charles Perrault) and by the German Romantic idealization of "naive poetry" and "folk poetry" as oral, unschooled, vigorously direct expressions of eternal human truths that had somehow preserved the characteristic traditions of pre-Christian European peoples intact. These now had to be recorded before they died out under the pressures of industrialization. Indeed the Grimms found so few "folk poet" informants left that they relied mainly on literary women who were readers and writers of fairy tales, as well as on written sources in libraries. By comparing different versions of a tale, they thought they could derive its "original," most essentially German core, freed from elements they viewed as foreign influences. This editorial process included simplifying language to erase the traces of the urbane French tradition that still influenced other German writers of fairy tales. Thus they arrived at the stock phrases we all memorized as children. Their folktale project, like their massive works on Germanic philology and law, supported the idea that shared language and traditions constituted one German people or nation, even though German speakers shared neither one state nor one church. When literary critics objected that the *Nursery Tales* might not be suitable reading for children, however, the Grimms realized that making them so could sell more books. In later editions they shortened the collection, cut the extramarital sex, and compensated with extra violence to reinforce the moral message—creating the tales we know and love today. "All-Kinds-of-Fur," a particularly brutal and perplexing tale with variants in most European traditions, is told by Perrault as "Donkey-Skin" (p. 31). It has fascinated recent critics, who have interpreted it from anthropological, psychoanalytic, narratological, and feminist viewpoints.

All-Kinds-of-Fur[1]

Once there was a king who had a wife with golden hair, and she was so beautiful that the like of her was not to be found on earth. By chance she fell ill, and when she felt that she was nigh unto death, she called the king and said, "If after my death you wish to remarry, take no one who's not just as beautiful as I and who hasn't golden hair like mine. That you must promise me." When the king had given his word, she closed her eyes and died.

For a long time the king was inconsolable and had no thought of taking a second wife. Finally his councilors said, "There's no other way out, the king must remarry so that we may have a queen." Messengers were sent about far and wide to look for a bride who in beauty might be quite the late queen's equal, but such a one was not to be found in the whole world, and even if she had been found, there was no one with such golden hair. So the messengers returned with nothing accomplished.

Now the king had a daughter who was just as beautiful as her deceased mother and also had the same golden hair. Once when she was grown up, the king looked at

---

1. Translated by Francis P. Magoun Jr. and Alexander H. Krappe.

her and noticed that in every respect she was like his late wife and suddenly fell violently in love with her. Then he said to his councilors, "I wish to marry my daughter, for she is the image of my deceased wife; if I don't marry her, I shan't be able to find a bride who resembles my wife." On hearing this the councilors were aghast and said, "God has forbidden a father to marry his daughter. No good can come from sin, and the realm will be brought to perdition." The daughter was even more frightened when she learned of her father's resolve; she hoped, however, still to dissuade him from his plan. "Before complying with your wish," she said to him, "I must first have three dresses, one as golden as the sun, one as silvery as the moon, and one as glittering as the stars. I further demand a cloak made up of a thousand kinds of pelts and furs, and every animal in your realm must contribute a piece of its skin to it." She thought, however, "It's quite impossible to procure that and thus I shall divert my father from his evil thoughts." But the king persisted in his plan, and the most skillful maidens in his kingdom had to weave the three dresses, one as golden as the sun, one as silvery as the moon, and one as glittering as the stars. His huntsmen had to catch all animals in his realm and remove a piece of their pelts; from that was made a cloak of a thousand kinds of fur. Finally, when everything was ready, the king had the cloak fetched, spread it out before her, and said, "The wedding will be tomorrow."

When the king's daughter saw that there was no longer any hope of changing her father's mind, she decided to run away. In the night when everybody was asleep, she got up and from among her jewels took three things, a gold ring, a tiny gold spinning wheel, and a tiny gold reel. The three dresses of the sun, the moon, and the stars she put into a nutshell, donned the cloak of all kinds of fur, and blackened her hands and face with soot. Then she commended herself to God and went off, walking the whole night until she came to a big forest. Since she was tired, she sat down in a hollow tree and fell asleep.

The sun rose, but she slept on and kept on sleeping when it was already broad daylight. By chance the king to whom the forest belonged was hunting in it, and when his dogs came to the tree, they snuffed, ran around and round it, and barked. "Go see what kind of game has hidden itself there," said the king to the huntsmen. The latter obeyed the order and on their return said, "A queer animal is lying in the hollow tree, the like of which we have never seen before: on its skin are a thousand kinds of fur, and it's lying asleep there." "See if you can take it alive," said the king, "then tie it in the cart and bring it along." When the huntsmen took hold of the girl, she woke up very frightened and cried out to them, "I'm a poor child, forsaken by father and mother. Have pity on me and take me with you." Then they said, "All-Kinds-of-Fur, you're fit for the kitchen. Just come with us; you can sweep up the ashes there." So they put her in the cart and drove home to the royal palace. They assigned her a cubbyhole under the stairs where no light of day penetrated and said, "You can live and sleep there, furry creature." Then she was sent to the kitchen where she carried wood and water, poked the fire, plucked the poultry, sorted the vegetables, swept up the ashes, and did all the dirty work.

For a long time All-Kinds-of-Fur lived there quite wretchedly. Alas, fair king's daughter, what you still have to go through! It once happened, however, that a party was being celebrated in the palace; then she said to the chef, "May I go upstairs for a little while and look on? I'll stand outside the door." "All right, go along," answered the chef, "but you must be back here in half an hour and collect the ashes." She took her oil lamp, went to her cubbyhole, took off the fur cloak, and washed the soot from her hands and face, so that her full beauty came to light again. Then she opened the nut and took out the dress that shone like the sun and, when that was done, went upstairs to the party. Everybody made way for her, for no one knew her and they didn't doubt but that she was a king's daughter. Then the king came to meet her, offered her his hand, and danced with her, thinking to himself, "I've never laid eyes on a girl so beautiful as she." When the dance was over, she curtsied and, as the king was looking around, disappeared, and no one knew where. The sentries stationed outside the palace were summoned and questioned, but no one had seen her.

She had, however, run into her cubbyhole, quickly taken off her dress, blackened her hands and face, put on the fur cloak, and once again was All-Kinds-of-Fur. When she went into the kitchen and was about to start work and sweep up the ashes, the chef said, "Don't bother till tomorrow; instead, cook the king's pudding. I, too, want to look on a little upstairs. But don't you let a single hair fall in; if you do, you'll get nothing more to eat in the future." The chef went off, and All-Kinds-of-Fur cooked the pudding for the king, a bread pudding, as best she could. When it was ready, she fetched her gold ring from the cubbyhole and put it in the bowl in which the pudding was served. When the ball was over, the king had the pudding brought and ate it, and it tasted so good to him that he thought he'd never eaten a better. When he reached the bottom, he saw a gold ring lying there and couldn't imagine how it got there. He had the chef summoned. On hearing the order the chef was frightened and said to All-Kinds-of-Fur, "You surely let a hair drop into the pudding; if so, you'll get a beating." When he entered the king's presence, the latter asked who'd cooked the pudding. "I did," answered the chef. "That's not true," said the king, "for it was a different kind and much better cooked than usual." "I must confess," answered the chef, "that I didn't cook it; the furry creature did." "Go and have her come up," said the king.

When All-Kinds-of-Fur came, the king asked, "Who are you?" "I'm a poor child who no longer has either a father or a mother." "Why are you in my palace?" "I'm good for nothing except to have the boots thrown at my head," she answered. He asked further, "Where did you get the ring that was in the pudding?" "I don't know anything about the ring," she answered. So the king could find out nothing and had to send her away again.

Some time later there was another party. As before, All-Kinds-of-Fur begged the chef for leave to look on. "Yes," he answered, "but be sure to come back in half an hour and cook the king the bread pudding he's so fond of." She ran to her cubbyhole, hurriedly washed herself, took out of the nut the dress which was as silvery as the moon, and put it on. Then, looking like a king's daughter, she went upstairs, and the king came to meet her and was glad to see her again, and since the dance was just beginning, they danced together. When the dance was over, she again disappeared so quickly that the king couldn't see where she'd gone. She jumped into her cubbyhole, turned herself into the furry creature again, and went into the kitchen to cook the bread pudding. When the chef was upstairs, she fetched the gold spinning-wheel and put it in the bowl so that the pudding was served on top of it. It was taken to the king, who ate it and liked it as much as the time before and summoned the chef. The latter again had to admit that it was All-Kinds-of-Fur who'd cooked the pudding. Again All-Kinds-of-Fur was brought before the king, but she answered that she was good only to have the boots thrown at her head and that she knew nothing at all about the tiny gold spinning-wheel.

When for the third time the king arranged a party, it went the same as before. To be sure the chef said, "You're a witch, furry creature, and always put something into the pudding to make it so good that the king likes it better than what I cook," but since she begged so hard, he allowed her to go there for the allotted time. Now she put on a dress which was as glittering as the stars and thus clad went into the hall. Again the king danced with the beautiful maiden and thought she'd never before been so beautiful. While he was dancing and without her noticing it, he put a gold ring on her finger and gave orders that the dance should last quite long. When it was at an end, he wanted to hold her hands tight, but she tore herself away and slipped so quickly among the crowd that she disappeared before his eyes. She ran as fast as she could to her cubbyhole under the stairs, but because she'd stayed out too long, indeed more than half an hour, she hadn't time to take off the beautiful dress but merely threw her fur cloak over it. Neither did she in her haste quite cover herself with soot, but one of her fingers remained white. All-Kinds-of-Fur now hurried into the kitchen, cooked the bread pudding for the king and, when the chef was gone, put the gold reel in it. When the king found the reel at the bottom of the bowl, he summoned All-Kinds-of-Fur. Then noticing her white finger and seeing the ring he had put on her during the dance, he seized her by the hand and held her tight, and when she wanted to tear herself away and run off, her fur cloak opened a little and her starry dress gleamed forth. The king seized the cloak and tore it off. Then her golden hair appeared, and she stood there in full splendor and could no longer conceal herself. When she'd wiped the soot and ashes from her face, she was more beautiful than anybody had ever before seen on earth. "You are my dear bride," said the king, "and we shall never part." Then the wedding was celebrated and they lived happily until their death.

↤ ⊨◈⊨ ↦

Coyote Tales

The indigenous peoples of North America had highly developed traditions of storytelling, ranging from tales of hunting and recent adventure back to mythic tales of creation and early times, such as the Navajo *Story of the Emergence,* which appears on page 683. These tales circulated widely around the continent, differently inflected in the varying natural and social settings in which they were told and retold. As early as the seventeenth century, French missionaries had begun to collect some of these tales, recognizing them as keys to native culture and beliefs. It was in the nineteenth century, though, that students of the new field of folklore began to collect them systematically, and to study and classify them. Among the most common types were "trickster tales"—stories involving a devious, self-seeking, yet powerful and even sacred character, often in animal form. Animals and humans have a close relation in Amerindian cultures, in which a person will often have a spirit double or guardian, usually in animal form. In many native cultures, sorcerers could change themselves into animal form at will, a practice recorded by the Spanish friar Ruiz de Alarcón in seventeenth-century Mexico (see Volume C).

Particularly in the western and southwestern regions of North America, a common form for the trickster figure was (and still is today) that of the coyote, an elusive animal found on the edges of settlements, a scavenger and forager, able to survive in harsh conditions. The three coyote tales included here show several sides of this multifaceted character, who constantly seeks to get his way by trickery and double-dealing. Sometimes he is successful, but often he is foiled by his own deceit or his own appetites, including his insatiable curiosity. "Coyote and Bull" shows Coyote puffed up with pride and heading for a fall—a motif that goes back to Aesop. In "Coyote as Medicine Man," on the other hand, a sexually voracious Coyote gets everything he wants, thanks to his ability to transform himself in uncanny ways. Some of the tales of this sort were so explicit that the nineteenth-century folklorists couldn't bring themselves to render them in English at all, even for the select readership of scholarly journals, and translated them instead into Latin. In many tales, Coyote transgresses the bounds of propriety and even of physical possibility, committing cannibalism or incest, even changing himself into a woman and becoming pregnant. In "The Origin of Eternal Death" he and his chief, Eagle, cross the border between the living and the dead, with tragic consequences for the entire world.

Coyote and Bull[1]

Coyote was going along upstream hungry, as usual. He came upon a big, fat buffalo bull. Coyote said to him, "Friend, I am hungry. Is it so impossible that you change me into a bull just like you, so that I, too, could become fat and sleek?" Bull heeded him not the least. He only wandered away grazing and not a word would he reply to Coyote. Coyote was insistent. He said again and again, "I wish that I, too, were a bull so that I could get fat." Finally Bull got tired of hearing this and said to him, "Coyote! You are forever foolhardy in the things you do; you could never do what I might ask of you. You are becoming a great bother." Coyote replied, "No, friend, I will do exactly what you tell me to do. Here I see you fat and sleek. Here is much grass and you live well, while, you see, I am painfully hungry. I will do just anything you tell me."

Bull then said to him, "Then go over there and lie down." Coyote accordingly went and lay down. "Absolutely do not flee; do not move when I dash at you. You must, absolutely, remain still and I will heave you upward with my horns."—"Yes, friend, why should I flee?" replied Coyote as he lay down. Bull went off to the side and there he incited himself to terrific anger. He tore up the turf; he threw dirt upward; he bellowed and breathed clouds of vapor from his nostrils. He became terribly angry and then he dashed upon Coyote. But Coyote had been glancing at Bull and had seen him become so terrible. He saw Bull come at him and he jumped quickly aside.

"Now that is what I said—that you would run away," Bull said to him. "Let me try again, just once more," Coyote said. "I won't move next time." But Bull went away even though Coyote beseeched him weepingly. Coyote followed, tearfully entreating him, "Once more, just once more; I will not run away again." Bull said to him at last, "You are most bothersome to me. Now I will try you once more and if you move do not beg me anymore, for I will heed you never again. We are trying for the last time." Coyote placed himself on the designated spot again and Bull went aside, as before, to become terribly angry. Now he dashed at Coyote.

This time Coyote steeled himself and Bull threw him high into the air with his horns. Coyote fell and suddenly became a buffalo bull. He walked away and went along grazing. He would see all kinds of things and eat them. Then finally he parted with the other bull, which now wandered off somewhere feeding. Here now another coyote met him and recognized him as the erstwhile Coyote. "Oh, friend, how is it, friend, that you have become like that? I am terribly hungry; I wish that you would make me like that, too." Coyote-Bull only looked at him sullenly, and walked away to feed, unmindful of what the other said. The coyote insisted, "Friend, make a bull of me, too. I fare piteously and you are very fat." Coyote-Bull then spoke to him, "You are very bothersome. You would never do what I asked you."—"Yes, friend. I will follow out absolutely every word you say. Try me."—"You've been a nuisance to me," Coyote-Bull said to him, "but place yourself there and I will dash upon you angrily and toss you into the air with my horns. You are absolutely not to move. If you run away don't tearfully entreat me for another chance."

The coyote now placed himself there while Bull made himself angry. He bellowed and pawed the ground. He imitated in every way those things that he had seen the other bull do. Now Bull dashed upon him, and oh! he picked him up and hurled him upward with his horns. Now coyote fell—*thud!* To the ground he fell—still a coyote. At the very same moment Bull, too, changed back into a coyote. Here they

---

1. Translated by Archie Phinney.

were suddenly standing there, both coyotes. They stormed and they scolded each other, "You! You've caused me to change back into a coyote. There I was a bull living happily and you caused me to change back into a coyote!"—"Ha, you imitator! You thought you could make me into a bull too, as the other one did to you." Now one chased the other up the valley. The coyotes chased each other. There one lost interest and forgot that, "Thus I was acting silly—I thought I'd become a bull." He went along up the valley from there unmindful of all that had happened.

Coyote as Medicine-Man[1]

A certain old man was sitting in the trail with his penis wrapped about him just like a rope. And then Coyote passed by him and went on a little beyond. He saw some women jumping up and down in the water. And then he thought: "I shall borrow from the old man his penis." He went over to him and said to him: "Friend, would you not lend me your penis?" And then the man said to him: "All right, I shall lend it to you." So then Coyote took it and carried it along with him. Then he put it on to his own penis.

Then he shoved it under water right where the women were jumping up and down. One of the women jumped up, the penis got between her legs, and it remained stuck a little ways. And then she became ill.

Then the other women took hold of her and brought her yonder to shore. They saw that something was sticking to her, but they could do nothing with her; they could not cut it out of her with anything. And then they took hold of her and carried her a little farther away from the water. Coyote was far off across the river, and they dragged him into the water. Coyote shouted: "Split a stone; with it you will cut it off." They said: "What did some person tell us? He said, 'Cut it off with a stone knife.'" And then they looked for it and found a stone. They split it, and with the same they cut off the penis from her. It had run up right into her. That Coyote over yonder cut it all off. Then he turned his penis all back to himself.

Immediately Coyote went on again; he arrived somewhere, and laid himself down there. Now this woman was sick; they took her with them and straightway carried her home. They looked for a medicine-man and found the Raven. They said to him: "Now you will treat her"; then he assented. He went to treat her; he had consented to do so. And then he doctored and doctored until he said: "There is nothing in her body, there is no sickness in her body." Thus did speak the Raven.

And then the people said: "Yonder is a certain Coyote, who is a medicine-man." Then they went and said to him: "What do you think, will you treat her? We have come for you." And then he said: "Well, I could not go so far on foot; there must be five women without husbands. No! five women will have to come for me; they will just carry me on their backs." And then they went and said to five women who had no husbands: "Now you will go and bring the old medicine-man." Coyote yonder split some alder-bark and chewed at it. Then the women came to meet him, and he said to them: "I am sick in my breast." Then he spat; he showed them that what he had spit out was red and pretended that it was blood.

"You will just carry me on your backs so that my head is downward, in order that the blood may slowly go down to the ground. If my head is turned upwards, my mouth will perhaps become filled with blood, so that I shall die. It is good that my

---

1. Translated by Louis Simpson.

head be down; I shall not die." One of the women straightway took him on her back; the youngest one carried him first; she carried him with his head turned down. She went along with him. And then straightway he put his hands between her legs. Immediately he stuck his hands into her private parts and fingered them. She thought: "Oh! the old man is bad; the old man did not do good to me." So then she threw him down on the ground. Then he spat blood when she had thrown him down. One of the older sisters spoke, and said to her: "It is not good that you have hurt the old man."

And then one of the women again took him on her back. She went along with him. Straightway again, as before, he treated her; again he put his hands into her private parts. She did not carry him long; she also threw him down. Again one of the sisters said to her: "It is not good that you have thrown him down; you have hurt the old man. Look at him; again blood is flowing out of his mouth, he is coughing." And then she also put him on her back; now she was the third to carry him. To her also he did as before; he fingered her private parts. She did not carry him long, but threw him down also. And then again one of the women said to them: "Oh! you have not treated the old man well. Now he is continually spitting out much blood, the blood is flowing out of his mouth; you have hurt him badly."

And then the fourth woman took him on her back. That woman also went along with him. He treated her also as before, fingering her private parts. She also threw him down. Behold, now they were approaching to where the girl was lying sick in the house. Now another one of the women, the oldest of all,—she was their oldest sister,—said to them: "How you have treated the old medicine-man! Look, blood is flowing out of his mouth; now he is close to dying. Why have you done thus to the old man?" The four women said among themselves: "Thus has the old man done to me myself." One again said in like manner: "He fingered my private parts." They said to one another: "Now she too will find out; she will think that the old man is bad, after all."

Now also the other one, the fifth, took him on her back and went along with him. Her also he treated as before. Now the house was near by, and there she threw him down. And then people were gotten where the woman lay sick who should sing for him, while he was to treat her; they obtained animals of such kind from the land, large deer who could make much noise; they were to sing out loud.

Coyote, the medicine-man, said: "Now lay her down carefully." And then they laid her down; the people who were to sing for him seated themselves. The medicine-man said: "I alone would treat her. Put something around her here to hide her from view, so that I may treat her well." And then they took rushes and put them over her to hide her from view. Now there he sat by her, and said to them: "If I turn my hand up, then you shall sing."

Then he took up the song, and they started in singing. And then he treated her; he spread apart her legs. He stuck his penis into her and copulated with her. She called out: "The old one is copulating with me." He put up his hand and said to them: "Now go ahead, sing hard." And then hard they sang and sang. The two parts of the penis stuck together. Truly, that was the same penis which they had cut off with the stone knife; that Coyote penetrated her halfways, thus he copulated with her. The two parts of the penis recognized each other, they stuck together.

And then he pulled it out of her. Straightway she became well. Her mother asked her: "How are you feeling now? Have you now become well?"—"Now I have become well, but the old one has copulated with me."—"Well, never mind, just keep quiet;

now the old one has done well to you." And then the old man was told: "Now she has become your wife." He said: "I do not want a woman. I am walking about without particular purpose; I desire no woman." Then he went out of the house; he left them.

The Origin of Eternal Death[1]

Coyote had a wife and two children, and so had Eagle. Both families lived together. Eagle's wife and children died, and a few days later Coyote experienced the same misfortune. As the latter wept, his companion said: "Do not mourn: that won't bring your wife back. Make ready your moccasins, and we'll go somewhere." So the two prepared for a long journey, and set out westward.

After four days they were close to the ocean; on one side of a body of water they saw houses. Coyote called across, "Come with a boat!" "Never mind; stop calling," bade Eagle. He produced an elderberry stalk, made a flute, put the end into the water, and whistled. Soon they saw two persons come out of a house, walk to the water's edge, and enter a canoe. Said Eagle, "Do not look at those people when they land." The boat drew near, but a few yards from the shore it stopped, and Eagle told his friend to close his eyes. He then took Coyote by the arm and leaped to the boat. The two persons paddled back, and when they stopped a short distance from the other side Eagle again cautioned Coyote to close his eyes, and then leaped ashore with him.

They went to the village, where there were many houses, but no people were in sight. Everything was still as death. There was a very large underground house, into which they went. In it was found an old woman sitting with her face to the wall, and lying on the floor on the other side of the room was the moon. They sat down near the wall.

"Coyote," whispered Eagle, "watch that woman and see what she does when the sun goes down!" Just before the sun set they heard a voice outside calling: "Get up! Hurry! The sun is going down, and it will soon be night. Hurry, hurry!" Coyote and Eagle still sat in a corner of the chamber watching the old woman. People began to enter, many hundreds of them, men, women, and children. Coyote, as he watched, saw Eagle's wife and two daughters among them, and soon afterward his own family. When the room was filled, Nikshiamchasht, the old woman, cried, "Are all in?" Then she turned about, and from a squatting posture she jumped forward, then again and again, five times in all, until she alighted in a small pit beside the moon. This she raised and swallowed, and at once it was pitch dark. The people wandered about, hither and thither, crowding and jostling, unable to see. About daylight a voice from outside cried, "Nikshiamshasht, all get through!" The old woman then disgorged the moon, and laid it back in its place on the floor; all the people filed out, and the woman, Eagle, and Coyote were once more alone.

"Now, Coyote," said Eagle, "could you do that?" "Yes, I can do that," he said. They went out, and Coyote at Eagle's direction made a box of boards, as large as he could carry, and put into it leaves from every kind of tree and blades from every kind of grass. "Well," said Eagle, "If you're sure you remember just how she did this, let's go in and kill her." So they entered the house and killed her, and buried the body. Her dress they took off and put on Coyote, so that he looked just like her, and he sat down in her place. Eagle then told him to practice what he had seen, by turning around and jumping as the old woman had done. So Coyote tuned about and jumped five times, but the last leap was a little short, yet he managed to slide into the hole. He put the moon into his mouth, but, try as he would, a thin edge still showed, and he covered it

1. Translated by Edward S. Curtis.

with his hands. Then he laid it back in its place and resumed his seat by the wall, waiting for sunset and the voice of the chief outside.

The day passed, the voiced called, and the people entered. Coyote turned about and began to jump. Some thought there was something strange about the manner of jumping, but others said it was really the old woman. When he came to the last jump and slipped into the pit, many cried out that this was not the old woman, but Coyote quickly lifted the moon and put it into his mouth, covering the edge with his hands. When it was completely dark, Eagle placed the box in the doorway. Throughout the long night Coyote retained the moon in his mouth, until he was almost choking, but at last the voice of the chief was heard from the outside, and the dead began to file out. Every one walked into the box, and Eagle quickly threw the cover over and tied it. The sound was like that of a great swarm of flies. "Now, my brother, we are through," said Eagle. Coyote removed the dress and laid it down beside the moon, and Eagle threw the moon into the sky, where it remained. The two entered the canoe with the box, and paddled toward the east.

When they landed, Eagle carried the box. Near the end of the third night Coyote heard somebody talking; there seemed to be many voices. He awakened his companion, and said, "There are many people coming." "Don't worry," said Eagle; "it's all right." The following night Coyote heard the talking again, and, looking about, he discovered that the voices came from the box which Eagle had been carrying. He placed his ear against it, and after a while distinguished the voice of his wife. He smiled, and broke into laughter, but he said nothing to Eagle. At the end of the fifth night and the beginning of their last day of traveling, he said to his friend, "I'll carry the box now; you've carried it a long way." "No," replied Eagle, "I will take it; I am strong." "Let me carry it," insisted the other; "suppose we come to where people live, and they should see the chief carrying the load. How would that look?" Still Eagle retained his hold on the box, but as they went along Coyote kept begging, and about noon, wearying of the subject, Eagle gave him the box. So Coyote had the load, and every time he heard the voice of his wife he would laugh. After a while he contrived to fall behind, and when Eagle was out of sight around a hill he began to open the box, in order to release his wife. But no sooner was the cover lifted than it was thrown back violently, and the dead people rushed out into the air with such force that Coyote was thrown to the ground. They quickly disappeared in the west. Eagle saw the cloud of dead people rising in the air, and came hurrying back. He found one man left there, a cripple who had been unable to rise; he threw him into the air, and the dead man floated away swiftly.

"Look what you've done, with your curiosity and haste!" said Eagle. "If we had brought these dead all the way back, people would not die forever, but only for a season, like these plants, whose leaves we have brought. Hereafter trees and grasses will die only in the winter, but in the spring they'll be green again. So it would have been with the people." "Let's go back and catch them again," proposed Coyote; but Eagle objected: "They won't go to the same place, and we wouldn't know how to find them; they will be where the moon is, up in the sky."

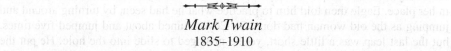

Mark Twain
1835–1910

In 1865 a young journalist got into trouble in San Francisco by writing articles on local political corruption. Deciding he should make himself scarce for a while, Samuel Clemens took a job at a California mining camp called Angel's Camp. Nearby at Jackass Hill, he heard a rambling tale about a jumping frog that failed to jump, and decided to write it up. Under the pen name "Mark Twain"—a riverboat term for dangerously shallow water—he had been writing humorous articles for newspapers, following several years as crew and pilot of Mississippi steamboats, and further time as a journalist and occasional prospector in Nevada. He then moved to San Francisco, where he became friendly with Artemis Ward, a leading humorist of the day, who invited him to contribute some sketches of Western life to a collection. "The Celebrated Jumping Frog of Calaveras County" reached Ward too late for his book, but it was published by the New York *Evening Post*. In 1867 it became the title story for Twain's first book, and his career was launched as America's greatest comic writer.

As in many of his later books, from *The Innocents Abroad* (1869) to *The Adventures of Huckleberry Finn* (1884), in this comic sketch Twain recreates the vivid language of oral storytelling with both a satiric wit and a warm affection. He draws on the tradition of the animal tale, adapted to the realistic setting of the mining camp; the animals in the story don't talk, but they are remarkably human in their attitudes and emotions, while the human actors play out old patterns of boasting and trickery well established in traditions like the Native American trickster tales. Twain's own language slyly mixes colloquial speech with clichés of sentimental fiction and of folkloristic research, in a brilliant performance on the borders between the oral and the written, producing a hilarious confrontation between the sophisticated city-dweller and the irrepressible man of the people.

The Celebrated Jumping Frog of Calaveras County

In compliance with the request of a friend of mine, who wrote me from the East, I called on good-natured, garrulous old Simon Wheeler, and inquired after my friend's friend, Leonidas W. Smiley, as requested to do, and I hereunto append the result. I have a lurking suspicion that *Leonidas W.* Smiley is a myth; that my friend never knew such a personage; and that he only conjectured that if I asked old Wheeler about him, it would remind him of his infamous *Jim* Smiley, and he would go to work and bore me to death with some exasperating reminiscence of him as long and as tedious as it should be useless to me. If that was the design, it succeeded.

I found Simon Wheeler dozing comfortably by the bar-room stove of the dilapidated tavern in the decayed mining camp of Angel's, and I noticed that he was fat and bald-headed, and had an expression of winning gentleness and simplicity upon his tranquil countenance. He roused up, and gave me good day. I told him that a friend of mine had commissioned me to make some inquiries about a cherished companion of his boyhood named *Leonidas W.* Smiley—*Rev. Leonidas W.* Smiley, a young minister of the Gospel, who he had heard was at one time a resident of Angel's Camp. I added that if Mr. Wheeler could tell me anything about this Rev. Leonidas W. Smiley, I would feel under many obligations to him.

Simon Wheeler backed me into a corner and blockaded me there with his chair, and then sat down and reeled off the monotonous narrative which follows this paragraph. He never smiled, he never frowned, he never changed his voice from the gentle-flowing key to which he tuned his initial sentence, he never betrayed the slightest suspicion of enthusiasm; but all through the interminable narrative there ran a vein of impressive earnestness and sincerity, which showed me plainly that, so far from his imagining that there was anything ridiculous or funny about his story, he regarded it as a really important matter, and admired its two heroes as men of transcendent genius in *finesse*. I let him go on in his own way, and never interrupted him once.

"Rev. Leonidas W. H'm, Reverend Le—well, there was a feller here once by the name of *Jim* Smiley, in the winter of '49—or maybe it was the spring of '50—I don't recollect exactly, somehow, though what makes me think it was one or the other is because I remember the big flume warn't finished when he first come to the camp; but anyway, he was the curiousest man about always betting on anything that turned up you ever see, if he could get anybody to bet on the other side; and if he couldn't he'd change sides. Any way that suited the other man would suit *him*—any way just so's he got a bet, *he* was satisfied. But still he was lucky, uncommon lucky; he most always come out winner. He was always ready and laying for a chance; there couldn't be no solit'ry thing mentioned but that feller'd offer to bet on it, and take ary side you please, as I was just telling you. If there was a horse-race, you'd find him flush or you'd find him busted at the end of it; if there was a dog-fight, he'd bet on it; if there was a cat-fight, he'd bet on it; if there was a chicken-fight, he'd bet on it; why, if there was two birds setting on a fence, he would bet you which one would fly first; or if there was a camp-meeting, he would be there reg'lar to bet on Parson Walker, which he judged to be the best exhorter about here, and so he was too, and a good man. If he even see a straddle-bug start to go anywheres, he would bet you how long it would take him to get to—to wherever he was going to, and if you took him up, he would foller that straddle-bug to Mexico but what he would find out where he was bound for and how long he was on the road. Lots of the boys here has seen that Smiley, and can tell you about him. Why, it never made no difference to *him*—he'd bet on *any* thing—the dangdest feller. Parson Walker's wife laid very sick once, for a good while, and it seemed as if they warn't going to save her; but one morning he come in, and Smiley up and asked him how she was, and he said she was considerable better—thank the Lord for his inf'nite mercy—and coming on so smart that with the blessing of Prov'-dence she'd get well, yet; and Smiley, before he thought, says, 'Well, I'll resk two-and-a-half she don't anyway.'

"Thish-yer Smiley had a mare—the boys called her the fifteen-minute nag, but that was only in fun, you know, because of course she was faster than that—and he used to win money on that horse, for all she was so slow and always had the asthma, or the distemper, or the consumption, or something of that kind. They used to give her two or three hundred yards' start, and then pass her under way; but always at the fag end of the race she'd get excited and desperate like, and come cavorting and strad-dling up, and scattering her legs around limber, sometimes in the air, and sometimes out to one side among the fences, and kicking up m-o-r-e dust and raising m-o-r-e racket with her coughing and sneezing and blowing her nose—and *always* fetch up at the stand just about a neck ahead, as near as you could cipher it down.

"And he had a little small bull-pup, that to look at him you'd think he warn't worth a cent but to set around and look ornery and lay for a chance to steal something. But as soon as money was up on him he was a different dog; his under-jaw'd begin to stick out like the fo'castle of a steamboat, and his teeth would uncover and shine like the furnaces. And a dog might tackle him and bully-rag him, and bite him, and throw him over his shoulder two or three times, and Andrew Jackson[1]—which was the name of the pup—Andrew Jackson would never let on but what *he* was satisfied, and hadn't expected nothing else—and the bets being doubled and doubled on the other side all the time, till the money was all up; and then all of a sudden he would grab that other dog jest by the j'int of his hind leg and freeze to it—not chaw, you understand, but only just grip and hang on till they throwed up the sponge, if it was a year. Smiley al-

---

1. The populist seventh president of the United States (1767–1845).

ways come out winner on that pup, till he harnessed a dog once that didn't have no hind legs, because they'd been sawed off in a circular saw, and when the thing had gone along far enough, and the money was all up, and he come to make a snatch for his pet holt, he see in a minute how he'd been imposed on, and how the other dog had him in the door, so to speak, and he 'peared surprised, and then he looked sorter discouraged-like, and didn't try no more to win the fight, and so he got shucked out bad. He give Smiley a look, as much as to say his heart was broke, and it was *his* fault, for putting up a dog that hadn't no hind legs for him to take holt of, which was his main dependence in a fight, and then he limped off a piece and laid down and died. It was a good pup, was that Andrew Jackson, and would have made a name for hisself if he'd lived, for the stuff was in him and he had genius—I know it, because he hadn't no opportunities to speak of, and it don't stand to reason that a dog could make such a fight as he could under them circumstances if he hadn't no talent. It always makes me feel sorry when I think of that last fight of his'n, and the way it turned out.

"Well, thish-yer Smiley had rat-tarriers, and chicken cocks, and tomcats and all them kind of things, till you couldn't rest, and you couldn't fetch nothing for him to bet on but he'd match you. He ketched a frog one day, and took him home, and said he cal'lated to educate him; and so he never done nothing for three months but set in his back yard and learn that frog to jump. And you bet you he *did* learn him, too. He'd give him a little punch behind, and the next minute you'd see that frog whirling in the air like a doughnut—see him turn one summerset, or maybe a couple, if he got a good start, and come down flat-footed and all right, like a cat. He got him up so in the matter of ketching flies, and kep' him in practice so constant, that he'd nail a fly every time as fur as he could see him. Smiley said all a frog wanted was education, and he could do 'most anything—and I believe him. Why, I've seen him set Dan'l Webster[2] down here on this floor—Dan'l Webster was the name of the frog—and sing out, 'Flies, Dan'l, flies!' and quicker'n you could wink he'd spring straight up and snake a fly off'n the counter there, and flop down on the floor ag'in as solid as a gob of mud, and fall to scratching the side of his head with his hind foot as indifferent as if he hadn't no idea he'd been doin' any more'n any frog might do. You never see a frog so modest and straightfor'ard as he was, for all he was so gifted. And when it come to fair and square jumping on a dead level, he could get over more ground at one straddle than any animal of his breed you ever see. Jumping on a dead level was his strong suit, you understand; and when it come to that, Smiley would ante up money on him as long as he had a red.[3] Smiley was monstrous proud of his frog, and well he might be, for fellers that had traveled and been everywheres all said he laid over any frog that ever *they* see.

"Well, Smiley kep' the beast in a little lattice box, and he used to fetch him downtown sometimes and lay for a bet. One day a feller—a stranger in the camp, he was—come acrost him with his box, and says:

"'What might it be that you've got in the box?'

"And Smiley says, sorter indifferent-like, 'It might be a parrot, or it might be a canary, maybe, but it ain't—it's only just a frog.'

"And the feller took it, and looked at it careful, and turned it round this way and that, and says, 'H'm—so 'tis. Well, what's *he* good for?'

"'Well,' Smiley says, easy and careless, 'he's good enough for *one* thing, I should judge—he can outjump any frog in Calaveras County.'

---

2. Lawyer, senator, and Secretary of State (1782–1852),   3. A cent.
famous as an orator.

"The feller took the box again, and took another long, particular look, and give it back to Smiley, and says, very deliberate, 'Well,' he says, 'I don't see no p'ints about that frog that's any better'n any other frog.'

"'Maybe you don't,' Smiley says. 'Maybe you understand frogs and maybe you don't understand 'em; maybe you've had experience, and maybe you ain't only a am-ature, as it were. Anyways, I've got *my* opinion, and I'll resk forty dollars that he can outjump any frog in Calaveras County.'

"And the feller studied a minute, and then says, kinder sad-like, 'Well, I'm only a stranger here, and I ain't got no frog; but if I had a frog, I'd bet you.'

"And then Smiley says, 'That's all right—that's all right—if you'll hold my box a minute, I'll go and get you a frog.' And so the feller took the box, and put up his forty dollars along with Smiley's, and set down to wait.

"So he set there a good while thinking and thinking to himself, and then he got the frog out and prized his mouth open and took a teaspoon and filled him full of quail-shot—filled him pretty near up to his chin—and set him on the floor. Smiley he went to the swamp and slopped around in the mud for a long time, and finally he ketched a frog, and fetched him in, and give him to this feller, and says:

"'Now, if you're ready, set him alongside of Dan'l, with his fore paws just even with Dan'l's, and I'll give the word.' Then he says, 'One—two—three—*git!*' and him and the feller touched up the frogs from behind, and the new frog hopped off lively, but Dan'l give a heave, and hysted up his shoulders—so—like a Frenchman, but it warn't no use—he couldn't budge; he was planted as solid as a church, and he could-n't no more stir than if he was anchored out. Smiley was a good deal surprised, and he was disgusted too, but he didn't have no idea what the matter was, of course.

"The feller took the money and started away; and when he was going out at the door, he sorter jerked his thumb over his shoulder—so—at Dan'l, and says again, very deliberate, 'Well,' he says, '*I* don't see no p'ints about that frog that's any bet-ter'n any other frog.'

"Smiley he stood scratching his head and looking down at Dan'l a long time, and at last he says, 'I do wonder what in the nation that frog throw'd off for—I wonder if there ain't something the matter with him—he 'pears to look mighty baggy, somehow.' And he ketched Dan'l by the nap of the neck, and hefted him, and says, 'Why blame my cats if he don't weigh five pound!' and turned him upside down and he belched out a double handful of shot. And then he see how it was, and he was the maddest man—he set the frog down and took out after that feller, but he never ketched him. And—"

[Here Simon Wheeler heard his name called from the front yard, and got up to see what was wanted.] And turning to me as he moved away, he said: "Just set where you are, stranger, and rest easy—I ain't going to be gone a second."

But, by your leave, I did not think that a continuation of the history of the enter-prising vagabond *Jim* Smiley would be likely to afford me much information con-cerning the Rev. *Leonidas W.* Smiley, and so I started away.

At the door I met the sociable Wheeler returning, and he buttonholed me and recommenced:

"Well, thish-yer Smiley had a yaller one-eyed cow that didn't have no tail, only just a short stump like a bannanner, and—"

However, lacking both time and inclination, I did not wait to hear about the af-flicted cow, but took my leave.

🔆 END OF CROSSCURRENTS: THE FOLK AND THEIR TALES 🔆

William Wordsworth
1770–1850

William Wordsworth's father was steward to the largest landowner in the Lake District, in England's remote northwest. It was wild country, and Lord Lonsdale suited it; Wordsworth's parents both died before he was fourteen, and the rapacious Lord withheld his inheritance for almost two decades. Wordsworth was happier in his early school than at university in Cambridge, and he spent his twenties restlessly, wandering about England and France, suspected of radical political activities possibly extending even to spying for the French, and writing his earliest poetry. He had a daughter in France; he may have intended to marry the mother, Annette Vallon, but international hostilities kept them apart. A bequest allowed him to settle modestly in the countryside with his talented sister Dorothy. In 1797 he met the younger, more precocious Coleridge, and in 1798 they published *Lyrical Ballads,* a joint collection of poems that enjoyed moderate and growing success, becoming the foundation of Wordsworth's reputation as the greatest English poet of the nineteenth century. "The very image of Wordsworth, as I prefigured it to my own planet-struck eye, crushed my faculties as before Elijah or Saint Paul," Thomas De Quincey growled in 1839 in a bitter essay devoted to the poet, while in 1879 the great Victorian critic Matthew Arnold, in the introduction to a volume of Wordsworth's verse, called him "undoubtedly the most considerable [poet] in our language from the Elizabethan age to the present time."

Wordsworth's subsequent life was moderately full of incident, domestically content, upstanding, enhanced by his promotion of public causes, yet in no sense remarkable. After a cold winter with Dorothy in Germany, where Coleridge was studying the language and the new German philosophers, he settled with her in the Lake District. His poetical output henceforth was steady and various: songs and ballads, long narrative poems, formal odes and elevated philosophical meditations, and over 500 sonnets, often on political and religious topics including the injustices of slavery and of the death penalty. He slowly advanced from his early poverty to considerable wealth and retreated from revolutionary politics into staunch conservatism; in 1802 he bid farewell to Annette and married a childhood friend; in 1813 the growing family moved to a grand house in the Lakes; in 1843 he was finally named Poet Laureate. Though full of learning, he demonstrates, like Shakespeare, that a great poet need not be a great man. He was physically unattractive, spoke in an uncouth North Country accent, was never gregarious, and grew increasingly vain and condescending. "I do not conceive," writes De Quincey, "that Wordsworth could have been an amiable boy." William Hazlitt, a political antagonist, opens an appreciation in a volume entitled *The Spirit of the Age,* with rapier-edged praise. "Mr. Wordsworth's genius is a pure emanation of the Spirit of the Age. Had he lived in any other period of the world, he would never have been heard of."

The ordinariness of Wordsworth's life and the lack of personal charisma are an important part of the story. He is the great poet of the commonplace and of the natural. "Wordsworth's poetry," wrote Arnold, is "as inevitable as Nature herself. It might seem that Nature not only gave him the matter for his poem, but wrote his poem for him. He has no style." Condemning the artificial language of eighteenth-century poetry, Wordsworth aspired to write as "a man speaking to men" (Preface to *Lyrical Ballads*). His best-selling book was a prose *Guide to the Lakes,* where he protests against development desecrating the landscape. Fittingly, for an apostle of local values and cultures, his fame is limited to the English-speaking world. Within that world, no one did more to create a reverence for plants and flowers, for children and simple souls, for universal and unadorned humanity, even as he scorned those who lacked what one of his best-known lyrics calls "natural piety."

My heart leaps up when I behold
   A rainbow in the sky:
So was it when my life began;
So is it now I am a Man;
So be it when I shall grow old,
   Or let me die!
The Child is father of the Man;
And I could wish my days to be
Bound each to each by natural piety.

Before Wordsworth in England and Goethe in Germany it had never occurred to anyone to make a cult of simplicity. Poetry was supposed to be learned, "to instruct and to delight," as the Latin poet Horace had written. Wordsworth doesn't so much reject such traditional values as completely transform them. The rainbow poem does contain instructive hints at the end, but opens in unfettered delight. In moral life, leaping yields to binding. But in emotion, the ecstasy takes precedence. Pivoting on the "now" of an immediate present, the poet recognizes both what he preserves in memory and what he risks losing in reality. In linking past to future, he suggests how the child's naive excitement and the adult's reflective sensibility depend on one another; if the child remains buried in the man, so the man was already nascent in the child. And the divine rainbow serves as the emblem of the unity of all life that can be recognized if we shun the false sophistication of learned culture. "A Man" (the individual Wordsworth) rhymes naively and perfectly with "the Man" (humanity in general).

Often, Wordsworth's simplicity is harder won and more fragile. "To the Cuckoo" represents many poems addressed to or written about birds and flowers, yearning for their careless abandon or their self-sufficiency. "Tintern Abbey," one of Wordsworth's greatest achievements, looks to a sublimer natural scene, records the loss and recovery of childhood feelings with greater complexity and in more stages than the rainbow poem, and pits the impoverished inhabitants of its Welsh setting against the dehumanizing "din" of cities. Even more troubled are "Nutting," with its hints of a rape of the natural scene, and the Westminster Bridge sonnet, where the majestic calm hides intimations of death ("And all that mighty heart is lying still") in a poem associated with Wordsworth's farewell journey to Annette Vallon. "Mark the Concent'red Hazels," representative of Wordsworth's later period, returns to a bower like that in "Nutting," but with lowered sight lines and reduced intensity. It exposes the paradox of a bourgeois humility at risk of turning into patriotic complacency. Poems like this one can be as indispensable to understanding the crosscurrents of natural piety as are Goethe's critique of modernization at the end of *Faust* or Thoreau's cultivation of wildness.

Wordsworth's great ambition was to write an extended philosophical poem in three parts. He completed only the first part, *The Excursion,* his longest poem, published to a lukewarm reception in 1815. As an introduction he projected an autobiographical poem, begun between in 1798 and 1799 as a fragment of 978 lines and expanded and reworked throughout his life. Apart from brief excerpts, the poem was withheld during his lifetime and published only in 1850 under the posthumous title *The Prelude.* Describing childhood memories and traumas, adolescent travels and trials, and the political fervor of his early adulthood, *The Prelude* contains much of Wordsworth's most eloquent and famous poetry. The passages included here represent several of Wordsworth's most important roles—the revolutionary modernizer of cultural traditions, the prophet of the natural world, the innovative explorer of conscious and unconscious passions, and the partisan of justice for the oppressed. Epic themes are scattered throughout *The Prelude,* transformed and psychologized until they remain barely recognizable: the prophetic dream in Book 5, the wandering journey to a new world in Book 6, the heavenly journey of Book 14. The philosophical passage from Book 11 reorients readers from ancient myth to the natural world and human reason, while the two great mountain expeditions of Books 6 and 14 correct hubris and reward submission to higher ideals of imagination and vision: notice how Wordsworth looks down as he climbs Mount Snowdon, "With forehead bent / Earthward" (14.28–29). The entire *Prelude* is full of such moments of mystery that translate the hidden motions of the spirit into bodily impulses, "as if in opposition set up / Against an enemy, I panted up / With eager pace" (14.29–31). Among the most fantastic and complex of these moments is the dream of the Arab in Book 5, where hallucinatory figures from Wordsworth's schooling blend with cultural and national fears and with private anxieties about abandonment and obliteration. Finally, the historical resonances of these fears are unfolded in the books on the French Revolution, where Wordsworth recounts his youthful enthusiasms for a government of freedom and reason and the ensuing depression at the inevitable disappointments.

No other writer so richly expresses the struggles of a newly industrialized and highly stratified urban culture to retain its anchor in unforced relations among humans and in contact with natural and local settings. Perhaps the poet's mixture of simplicity and arrogance was necessary to capture these contending impulses to their fullest. At the end of one of his grandest short poems, "Ode: Intimations of Immortality from Recollections of Early Childhood," Wordsworth puts lines that memorably combine his capacious philanthropy, his indulgent sympathy for the humble creatures of the human and natural worlds, and his intricate psychological insight into sadness and joy, taking his own feelings as the model for the universe:

> Thanks to the human heart by which we live,
> Thanks to its tenderness, its joys, and fears,
> To me the meanest flower that blows can give
> Thoughts that do often lie too deep for tears.

Lines Composed a Few Miles above Tintern Abbey
On Revisiting the Banks of the Wye During a Tour, July 13, 1798

Five years have past; five summers, with the length
Of five long winters! and again I hear
These waters, rolling from their mountain-springs
With a soft inland murmur.—Once again
5   Do I behold these steep and lofty cliffs,
That on a wild secluded scene impress
Thoughts of more deep seclusion; and connect
The landscape with the quiet of the sky.
The day is come when I again repose
10   Here, under this dark sycamore, and view
These plots of cottage-ground, these orchard-tufts,
Which at this season, with their unripe fruits,
Are clad in one green hue, and lose themselves
'Mid groves and copses. Once again I see
15   These hedge-rows, hardly hedge-rows, little lines
Of sportive wood run wild: these pastoral farms,
Green to the very door; and wreaths of smoke
Sent up, in silence, from among the trees!
With some uncertain notice, as might seem
20   Of vagrant dwellers in the houseless woods,
Or of some Hermit's cave, where by his fire
The Hermit sits alone.

These beauteous forms,
Through a long absence, have not been to me
As is a landscape to a blind man's eye:
25   But oft, in lonely rooms, and 'mid the din
Of towns and cities, I have owed to them
In hours of weariness, sensations sweet,
Felt in the blood, and felt along the heart;
And passing even into my purer mind,
30   With tranquil restoration:—feelings too
Of unremembered pleasure: such, perhaps,
As have no slight or trivial influence
On that best portion of a good man's life,
His little, nameless, unremembered, acts
35   Of kindness and of love. Nor less, I trust,
To them I may have owed another gift,
Of aspect more sublime; that blessed mood
In which the burthen of the mystery,
In which the heavy and the weary weight
40   Of all this unintelligible world,
Is lightened:—that serene and blessed mood,
In which the affections gently lead us on,—
Until, the breath of this corporeal frame
And even the motion of our human blood
45   Almost suspended, we are laid asleep
In body, and become a living soul:
While with an eye made quiet by the power
Of harmony, and the deep power of joy,
We see into the life of things.

        If this
50   Be but a vain belief, yet, oh! how oft—
In darkness and amid the many shapes
Of joyless daylight; when the fretful stir
Unprofitable, and the fever of the world,
Have hung upon the beatings of my heart—
55   How oft, in spirit, have I turned to thee,
O sylvan Wye! thou wanderer thro' the woods,
How often has my spirit turned to thee!

    And now, with gleams of half-extinguished thought,
With many recognitions dim and faint,
60   And somewhat of a sad perplexity,
The picture of the mind revives again:
While here I stand, not only with the sense
Of present pleasure, but with pleasing thoughts
That in this moment there is life and food
65   For future years. And so I dare to hope,
Though changed, no doubt, from what I was when first
I came among these hills; when like a roe

I bounded o'er the mountains, by the sides
Of the deep rivers, and the lonely streams,
70 Wherever nature led: more like a man
Flying from something that he dreads than one
Who sought the thing he loved. For nature then
(The coarser pleasures of my boyish days,
And their glad animal movements all gone by)
75 To me was all in all.—I cannot paint
What then I was. The sounding cataract
Haunted me like a passion: the tall rock,
The mountain, and the deep and gloomy wood,
Their colours and their forms, were then to me
80 An appetite; a feeling and a love,
That had no need of a remoter charm,
By thought supplied, nor any interest
Unborrowed from the eye.—That time is past,
And all its aching joys are now no more,
85 And all its dizzy raptures. Not for this
Faint° I, nor mourn nor murmur; other gifts   *lose heart*
Have followed; for such loss, I would believe,
Abundant recompense. For I have learned
To look on nature, not as in the hour
90 Of thoughtless youth; but hearing oftentimes
The still, sad music of humanity,
Nor harsh nor grating, though of ample power
To chasten and subdue. And I have felt
A presence that disturbs me with the joy
95 Of elevated thoughts; a sense sublime
Of something far more deeply interfused,
Whose dwelling is the light of setting suns,
And the round ocean and the living air,
And the blue sky, and in the mind of man:
100 A motion and a spirit, that impels
All thinking things, all objects of all thought,
And rolls through all things. Therefore am I still
A lover of the meadows and the woods,
And mountains; and of all that we behold
105 From thus green earth; of all the mighty world
Of eye, and ear,—both what they half create,[1]
And what perceive; well pleased to recognise
In nature and the language of the sense
The anchor of my purest thoughts, the nurse,
110 The guide, the guardian of my heart, and soul
Of all my moral being.

---

1. In a note Wordsworth signals that this phrase is borrowed from the popular long meditative poem *Night Thoughts* (1742–1746) by Edward Young: The senses "half create the wondrous world they see" (6.427).

                     Nor perchance,
If I were not thus taught, should I the more
Suffer my genial° spirits to decay: *creative*
For thou art with me here upon the banks

115   Of this fair river; thou my dearest Friend,
My dear, dear Friend; and in thy voice I catch
The language of my former heart, and read
My former pleasures in the shooting lights
Of thy wild eyes. Oh! yet a little while

120   May I behold in thee what I was once,
My dear, dear Sister! and this prayer I make,
Knowing that Nature never did betray
The heart that loved her; 'tis her privilege,
Through all the years of this our life, to lead

125   From joy to joy: for she can so inform
The mind that is within us, so impress
With quietness and beauty, and so feed
With lofty thoughts, that neither evil tongues,
Rash judgments, nor the sneers of selfish men,

130   Nor greetings where no kindness is, nor all
The dreary intercourse of daily life,
Shall e'er prevail against us, or disturb
Our cheerful faith, that all which we behold
Is full of blessings. Therefore let the moon

135   Shine on thee in thy solitary walk;
And let the misty mountain-winds be free
To blow against thee: and, in after years,
When these wild ecstasies shall be matured
Into a sober pleasure; when thy mind

140   Shall be a mansion for all lovely forms,
Thy memory be as a dwelling-place
For all sweet sounds and harmonies; oh! then,
If solitude, or fear, or pain, or grief,
Should be thy portion,° with what healing thoughts   *dowry*

145   Of tender joy wilt thou remember me,
And these my exhortations! Nor, perchance—
If I should be where I no more can hear
Thy voice, nor catch from thy wild eyes these gleams
Of past existence—wilt thou then forget

150   That on the banks of this delightful stream
We stood together; and that I, so long
A worshipper of Nature, hither came
Unwearied in that service: rather say
With warmer love—oh! with far deeper zeal

155   Of holier love. Nor wilt thou then forget,
That after many wanderings, many years
Of absence, these steep woods and lofty cliffs,
And this green pastoral landscape, were to me
More dear, both for themselves and for thy sake!

Nutting

It seems a day
(I speak of one from many singled out)
One of those heavenly days that cannot die;
When, in the eagerness of boyish hope,
5   I left our cottage-threshold, sallying forth
With a huge wallet o'er my shoulders slung,
A nutting-crook in hand; and turned my steps
Tow'rd some far-distant wood, a Figure quaint,
Tricked out in proud disguise of cast-off weeds°   *clothing*
10   Which for that service had been husbanded,
By exhortation of my frugal Dame—
Motley accoutrement, of power to smile
At thorns, and brakes, and brambles,—and, in truth,
More ragged than need was! O'er pathless rocks,
15   Through beds of matted fern, and tangled thickets,
Forcing my way, I came to one dear nook
Unvisited, where not a broken bough
Drooped with its withered leaves, ungracious sign
Of devastation; but the hazels rose
20   Tall and erect, with tempting clusters hung,
A virgin scene!—A little while I stood,
Breathing with such suppression of the heart
As joy delights in; and, with wise restraint
Voluptuous, fearless of a rival, eyed
25   The banquet;—or beneath the trees I sate°   *sat*
Among the flowers, and with the flowers I played;
A temper known to those who, after long
And weary expectation, have been blest
With sudden happiness beyond all hope.
30   Perhaps it was a bower beneath whose leaves
The violets of five seasons re-appear
And fade, unseen by any human eye;
Where fairy water-breaks do murmur on
For ever; and I saw the sparkling foam,
35   And—with my cheek on one of those green stones
That, fleeced with moss, under the shady trees,
Lay round me, scattered like a flock of sheep—
I heard the murmur and the murmuring sound,
In that sweet mood when pleasure loves to pay
40   Tribute to ease; and, of its joy secure,
The heart luxuriates with indifferent things,
Wasting its kindliness on stocks° and stones,   *tree stumps*
And on the vacant air. Then up I rose,
And dragged to earth both branch and bough, with crash
45   And merciless ravage: and the shady nook
Of hazels, and the green and mossy bower,
Deformed and sullied, patiently gave up
Their quiet being: and, unless I now

Confound my present feelings with the past;
50 Ere from the mutilated bower I turned
Exulting, rich beyond the wealth of kings,
I felt a sense of pain when I beheld
The silent trees, and saw the intruding sky.—
Then, dearest Maiden, move along these shades
55 In gentleness of heart; with gentle hand
Touch—for there is a spirit in the woods.

from LYRICAL BALLADS (1800, 1802)
from Preface

The first Volume of these Poems has already been submitted to general perusal. It was published, as an experiment, which, I hoped, might be of some use to ascertain, how far, by fitting to metrical arrangement a selection of the real language of men in a state of vivid sensation, that sort of pleasure and that quantity of pleasure may be imparted, which a Poet may rationally endeavor to impart. * * *

They who have been accustomed to the gaudiness and inane phraseology of many modern writers, if they persist in reading this book to its conclusion, will, no doubt, frequently have to struggle with feelings of strangeness and awkwardness: they will look round for poetry, and will be induced to inquire by what species of courtesy these attempts can be permitted to assume that title. * * * I hope therefore the Reader will not censure me, if I attempt to state what I have proposed to myself to perform.

[THE PRINCIPAL OBJECT OF THE POEMS. HUMBLE AND RUSTIC LIFE]

The principal object, then, which I proposed to myself in these Poems was to choose incidents and situations from common life, and to relate or describe them, throughout, as far as was possible, in a selection of language really used by men, and, at the same time, to throw over them a certain colouring of imagination, whereby ordinary things should be presented to the mind in an unusual way; and further, and, above all, to make these incidents and situations interesting by tracing in them, truly though not ostentatiously, the primary laws of our nature: chiefly as far as regards the manner in which we associate ideas in a state of excitement. Low and rustic life was generally chosen, because in that condition, the essential passions of the heart find a better soil in which they can attain their maturity, are less under restraint, and speak a plainer and more emphatic language; because in that condition of life our elementary feelings co-exist in a state of greater simplicity, and, consequently, may be more accurately contemplated, and more forcibly communicated; because the manners of rural life germinate from those elementary feelings; and from the necessary character of rural occupations, are more easily comprehended; and are more durable; and, lastly, because in that condition the passions of men are incorporated with the beautiful and permanent forms of nature. The language, too, of these men is adopted (purified indeed from what appear to be its real defects, from all lasting and rational causes of dislike or disgust) because such men hourly communicate with the best objects from which the best part of language is originally derived; and because, from their rank in society and the sameness and narrow circle of their intercourse, being less under the influence of social vanity they convey their feelings and notions in simple and unelaborated expressions. Accordingly, such a language, arising out of repeated experience and regular feelings, is a more permanent, and a far more philosophical language, than that which is frequently substituted for it by Poets, who think that they are conferring honour upon themselves and their art, in proportion as they separate themselves from the sympathies of men, and indulge in arbitrary and capricious habits of expression, in order to furnish food for fickle tastes, and fickle appetites of their own creation.[1]

["THE SPONTANEOUS OVERFLOW OF POWERFUL FEELINGS"]

[A]ll good poetry is the spontaneous overflow of powerful feelings: but though this be true, Poems to which any value can be attached, were never produced on any variety of subjects but by a man who, being possessed of more than usual organic sensibility, had also thought long and deeply. For our continued influxes of feeling are modified and directed by our thoughts, which are indeed the representatives of all our past feelings; and, as by contemplating the relation of these general representatives to each other we discover what is really important to men, so, by the repetition and continuance of this act, our feelings will be connected with important subjects, till at length, if we be originally possessed of much sensibility, such habits of mind will be produced, that, by obeying blindly and mechanically the impulses of those habits, we shall describe objects, and utter sentiments, of such a nature and in such connection with each other, that the understanding of the being to whom we address ourselves, if he be in a healthful state of association, must necessarily be in some degree enlightened, and his affections ameliorated.

I have said that each of these poems has a purpose. * * * I should mention one other circumstance which distinguishes these Poems from the popular Poetry of the day; it is this, that the feeling therein developed gives importance to the action and situation, and not the action and situation to the feeling. * * * I will not suffer a sense of false modesty to prevent me from asserting, that I point my Reader's attention to this mark of distinction, far less for the sake of these particular Poems than from the general importance of the subject. The subject is indeed important! For the human mind is capable of being excited without the application of gross and violent stimulants; and he must have a very faint perception of its beauty and dignity who does not know this, and who does not further know, that one being is elevated above another, in proportion as he possesses this capability. It has therefore appeared to me, that to endeavour to produce or enlarge this capability is one of the best services in which, at any period, a Writer can be engaged; but this service, excellent at all times, is especially so at the present day. For a multitude of causes, unknown to former times, are now acting with a combined force to blunt the discriminating powers of the mind, and unfitting it for all voluntary exertion to reduce it to a state of almost savage torpor. The most effective of these causes are the great national events which are daily taking place, and the increasing accumulation of men in cities, where the uniformity of their occupations produces a craving for extraordinary incident, which the rapid communication of intelligence hourly gratifies.[2] To this tendency of life and manners the literature and theatrical exhibitions of the country have conformed themselves. The invaluable works of our elder writers, I had almost said the works of Shakespear and Milton, are driven into neglect by frantic novels, sickly and stupid German Tragedies, and

---

1. It is worth while here to observe that the affecting parts of Chaucer are almost always expressed in language pure and universally intelligible even to this day [Wordsworth's note].

2. That is, the rapid increase in daily newspaper production at this time. The "events" include the war with France, the Irish rebellion, and the sedition trials at home.

deluges of idle and extravagant stories in verse.[3]—When I think upon this degrading thirst after outrageous stimulation, I am almost ashamed to have spoken of the feeble effort with which I have endeavoured to counteract it; and, reflecting upon the magnitude of the general evil, I should be oppressed with no dishonorable melancholy, had I not a deep impression of certain inherent and indestructible qualities of the human mind, and likewise of certain powers in the great and permanent objects that act upon it, which are equally inherent and indestructible; and did I not further add to this impression a belief, that the time is approaching when the evil will be systematically opposed, by men of greater powers, and with far more distinguished success.

[THE LANGUAGE OF POETRY]

Having dwelt thus long on the subjects and aim of these Poems, I shall request the Reader's permission to apprize him of a few circumstances relating to their *style,* in order, among other reasons, that I may not be censured for not having performed what I never attempted. The Reader will find that personifications of abstract ideas rarely occur in these volumes; and, I hope, are utterly rejected as an ordinary device to elevate the style, and raise it above prose. I have proposed to myself to imitate, and, as far as is possible, to adopt the very language of men; and assuredly such personifications do not make any natural or regular part of that language. They are, indeed, a figure of speech occasionally prompted by passion, and I have made use of them as such; but I have endeavoured utterly to reject them as a mechanical device of style, or as a family language which Writers in metre seem to lay claim to by prescription. I have wished to keep my Reader in the company of flesh and blood, persuaded that by so doing I shall interest him. I am, however, well aware that others who pursue a different track may interest him likewise; I do not interfere with their claim, I only wish to prefer a different claim of my own. There will also be found in these volumes little of what is usually called poetic diction; I have taken as much pains to avoid it as others ordinarily take to produce it; this I have done for the reason already alleged, to bring my language near to the language of men, and further, because the pleasure which I have proposed to myself to impart is of a kind very different from that which is supposed by many persons to be the proper object of poetry. I do not know how, without being culpably particular, I can give my Reader a more exact notion of the style in which I wished these poems to be written, than by informing him that I have at all times endeavoured to look steadily at my subject, consequently, I hope that there is in these Poems little falsehood of description, and that my ideas are expressed in language fitted to their respective importance. Something I must have gained by this practice, as it is friendly to one property of all good poetry, namely good sense; but it has necessarily cut me off from a large portion of phrases and figures of speech which from father to son have long been regarded as the common inheritance of Poets. * * *

To illustrate the subject in a general manner, I will here adduce a short composition of Gray,[4] who was at the head of those who, by their reasonings, have attempted to widen the space of separation betwixt Prose and Metrical composition, and was more than any other man curiously elaborate in the structure of his own poetic diction.

---

3. For example, sentimental melodramas and the popular Gothic novels of Ann Radcliffe and "Monk" Lewis.
4. Thomas Gray (1716–1771) is best known for "Elegy Written in a Country Church-Yard" (1751). The poem Wordsworth quotes (adding italics) is "Sonnet on the Death of Richard West" (1775).

In vain to me the smiling mornings shine,
And reddening Phœbus° lifts his golden fire: *sun god*
The birds in vain their amorous descant° join,   *song*
Or cheerful fields resume their green attire:
These ears, alas! for other notes repine;°   *languish*
A different object do these eyes require;
My lonely anguish melts no heart but mine;
And in my breast the imperfect joys expire;
Yet morning smiles the busy race to cheer,
And new-born pleasure brings to happier men;
The fields to all their wonted tribute bear;
To warm their little loves the birds complain.
I fruitless mourn to him that cannot hear,
And weep the more because I weep in vain.

It will easily be perceived, that the only part of this Sonnet which is of any value is the lines printed in Italics: it is equally obvious, that, except in the rhyme, and in the use of the single word "fruitless" for fruitlessly, which is so far a defect, the language of these lines does in no respect differ from that of prose.

By the foregoing quotation I have shown that the language of Prose may yet be well adapted to Poetry; and I have previously asserted that a large portion of the language of every good poem can in no respect differ from that of good Prose. I will go further. I do not doubt that it may be safely affirmed, that there neither is, nor can be, any essential difference between the language of prose and metrical composition.

[WHAT IS A POET?]

What is a Poet? To whom does he address himself? And what language is to be expected from him? He is a man speaking to men: a man, it is true, endued with more lively sensibility, more enthusiasm and tenderness, who has a greater knowledge of human nature, and a more comprehensive soul, than are supposed to be common among mankind; a man pleased with his own passions and volitions, and who rejoices more than other men in the spirit of life that is in him; delighting to contemplate similar volitions and passions as manifested in the goings-on of the Universe, and habitually impelled to create them where he does not find them. To these qualities he has added a disposition to be affected more than other men by absent things as if they were present; an ability of conjuring up in himself passions, which are indeed far from being the same as those produced by real events, yet (especially in those parts of the general sympathy which are pleasing and delightful) do more nearly resemble the passions produced by real events, than anything which, from the motions of their own minds merely, other men are accustomed to feel in themselves; whence, and from practice, he has acquired a greater readiness and power in expressing what he thinks and feels, and especially those thoughts and feelings which, by his own choice, or from the structure of his own mind, arise in him without immediate external excitement.

But, whatever portion of this faculty we may suppose even the greatest Poet to possess, there cannot be a doubt but that the language which it will suggest to him, must, in liveliness and truth, fall far short of that which is uttered by men in real life, under the actual pressure of those passions, certain shadows of which the Poet thus produces, or feels to be produced, in himself. However exalted a notion we would wish to cherish of the character of a Poet, it is obvious, that, while he describes and imitates passions, his situation is altogether slavish and mechanical, compared with the freedom and power of real and substantial action and suffering. So that it will be the wish of the Poet to bring his feelings near to those of the persons whose feelings he describes, nay, for short spaces of time perhaps, to let himself slip into an entire delusion, and even confound and identify his own feelings with theirs; modifying only the language which is thus suggested to him, by a consideration that he describes for a particular purpose, that of giving pleasure. Here, then, he will apply the principle on which I have so much insisted, namely, that of selection; on this he will depend for removing what would otherwise be painful or disgusting in the passion; he will feel that there is no necessity to trick out or to elevate nature: and, the more industriously he applies this principle, the deeper will be his faith that no words, which his fancy or imagination can suggest, will be to be compared with those which are the emanations of reality and truth.

[“EMOTION RECOLLECTED IN TRANQUILLITY”]

I have said that Poetry is the spontaneous overflow of powerful feelings: it takes its origin from emotion recollected in tranquillity: the emotion is contemplated till by a species of reaction the tranquillity gradually disappears, and an emotion, kindred to that which was before the subject of contemplation, is gradually produced, and does itself actually exist in the mind. In this mood successful composition generally begins.

Composed upon Westminster Bridge, Sept. 3, 1802[1]

Earth has not anything to show more fair:
Dull would he be of soul who could pass by
A sight so touching in its majesty:
This City now doth, like a garment, wear
5   The beauty of the morning; silent, bare,
Ships, towers, domes, theatres, and temples lie
Open unto the fields, and to the sky;
All bright and glittering in the smokeless air.
Never did sun more beautifully steep
10   In his first splendour, valley, rock, or hill;
Ne'er saw I, never felt, a calm so deep!
The river glideth at his own sweet will:
Dear God! the very houses seem asleep;
And all that mighty heart is lying still!

My heart leaps up

My heart leaps up when I behold
    A Rainbow in the sky:
So was it when my life began;
So is it now I am a Man;
5   So be it when I shall grow old,
    Or let me die!

1. Composed on the roof of a coach, on my way to France [Wordsworth's note, 1843].

The Child is Father of the Man;
And I could wish my days to be
Bound each to each by natural piety.

Ode:
Intimations of Immortality from Recollections of Early Childhood

The Child is Father of the Man;
And I could wish my days to be
Bound each to each by natural piety.

1

There was a time when meadow, grove, and stream,
The earth, and every common sight,
  To me did seem
  Apparelled in celestial light,
5 The glory and the freshness of a dream.
It is not now as it hath been of yore;—
  Turn wheresoe'er I may,
  By night or day,
The things which I have seen I now can see no more.

2

10 The Rainbow comes and goes,
  And lovely is the Rose,
  The Moon doth with delight
Look round her when the heavens are bare,
  Waters on a starry night
15 Are beautiful and fair;
  The sunshine is a glorious birth;
  But yet I know, where'er I go,
That there hath past away a glory from the earth.

3

Now, while the birds thus sing a joyous song,
20 And while the young lambs bound
  As to the tabor's° sound,   *small drum*
To me alone there came a thought of grief:
A timely utterance gave that thought relief,
  And I again am strong:
25 The cataracts blow their trumpets from the steep;
No more shall grief of mine the season wrong;
I hear the Echoes through the mountains throng,
The Winds come to me from the fields of sleep,
  And all the earth is gay;
30   Land and sea
  Give themselves up to jollity,
  And with the heart of May
Doth every Beast keep holiday;—
  Thou Child of Joy,
35 Shout round me, let me hear thy shouts, thou happy Shepherd-boy!

4

Ye blessèd Creatures, I have heard the call
   Ye to each other make; I see
The heavens laugh with you in your jubilee;
   My heart is at your festival,
40   My head hath its coronal,°   *flower wreath*
The fulness of your bliss, I feel—I feel it all.
   Oh evil day! if I were sullen
   While Earth herself is adorning,
     This sweet May-morning,
45   And the Children are culling
     On every side,
In a thousand valleys far and wide,
Fresh flowers; while the sun shines warm,
And the Babe leaps up on his Mother's arm:—
50   I hear, I hear, with joy I hear!
—But there's a Tree, of many, one,
A single Field which I have looked upon,
Both of them speak of something that is gone:
   The Pansy[1] at my feet
55   Doth the same tale repeat:
Whither is fled the visionary gleam?
Where is it now, the glory and the dream?

5

Our birth is but a sleep and a forgetting:
The Soul that rises with us, our life's Star,°   *the sun*
60   Hath had elsewhere its setting,
     And cometh from afar:
   Not in entire forgetfulness,
   And not in utter nakedness,
But trailing clouds of glory do we come
65   From God, who is our home:
Heaven lies about us in our infancy!
Shades of the prison-house begin to close
   Upon the growing Boy,
But He beholds the light, and whence it flows,
70   He sees it in his joy;
The Youth, who daily farther from the east
   Must travel, still is Nature's Priest,
   And by the vision splendid
   Is on his way attended;
75 At length the Man perceives it die away,
And fade into the light of common day.

6

Earth fills her lap with pleasures of her own;
Yearnings she hath in her own natural kind,

1. From the French *pensée,* "thought," this flower is its
emblem.

And, even with something of a Mother's mind,
  And no unworthy aim,
  The homely° Nurse doth all she can   *simple*
To make her Foster-child, her Inmate° Man,   *resident*
  Forget the glories he hath known,
And that imperial palace whence he came.

7

Behold the Child among his new-born blisses,
A six years' Darling of a pigmy size!
See, where 'mid work of his own hand he lies,
Fretted° by sallies of his mother's kisses,   *worn*
With light upon him from his father's eyes!
See, at his feet, some little plan or chart,
Some fragment from his dream of human life,
Shaped by himself with newly-learnèd art;
  A wedding or a festival,
  A mourning or a funeral;
   And this hath now his heart,
  And unto this he frames his song:
   Then will he fit his tongue
To dialogues of business, love, or strife;
  But it will not be long
  Ere this be thrown aside,
  And with new joy and pride
The little Actor cons another part;
Filling from time to time his "humorous stage"[2]
With all the Persons, down to palsied Age,
That Life brings with her in her equipage;
  As if his whole vocation
  Were endless imitation.

8

Thou, whose exterior semblance doth belie
  Thy Soul's immensity;
Thou best Philosopher, who yet dost keep
Thy heritage, thou Eye among the blind,
That, deaf and silent, read'st the eternal deep,
Haunted for ever by the eternal mind,—
  Mighty Prophet! Seer blest!
  On whom those truths do rest,
Which we are toiling all our lives to find,
In darkness lost, the darkness of the grave;
Thou, over whom thy Immortality
Broods like the Day, a Master o'er a Slave,
A Presence which is not to be put by;
Thou little Child, yet glorious in the might
Of heaven-born freedom on thy being's height,

---

2. A phrase from the dedicatory sonnet for Samuel Daniel's *Musophilus* (1599), referring to the different character types of Renaissance drama, defined by their "humors" (natural temperaments).

Why with such earnest pains dost thou provoke
The years to bring the inevitable yoke,
125 Thus blindly with thy blessedness at strife?
Full soon thy Soul shall have her earthly freight,
And custom lie upon thee with a weight,
Heavy as frost, and deep almost as life!

9

O joy! that in our embers
130 Is something that doth live,
That nature yet remembers
What was so fugitive!
The thought of our past years in me doth breed
Perpetual benediction: not indeed
135 For that which is most worthy to be blest;
Delight and liberty, the simple creed
Of Childhood, whether busy or at rest,
With new-fledged hope still fluttering in his breast:—
Not for these I raise
140 The song of thanks and praise;
But for those obstinate questionings
Of sense and outward things,
Fallings from us, vanishings;
Blank misgivings of a Creature
145 Moving about in worlds not realised,°   *seeming unreal*
High instincts before which our mortal Nature
Did tremble like a guilty Thing surprised:
But for those first affections,
Those shadowy recollections,
150 Which, be they what they may,
Are yet the fountain light of all our day,
Are yet a master light of all our seeing;
Uphold us, cherish, and have power to make
Our noisy years seem moments in the being
155 Of the eternal Silence: truths that wake,
To perish never;
Which neither listlessness, nor mad endeavour,
Nor Man nor Boy,
Nor all that is at enmity with joy,
160 Can utterly abolish or destroy!
Hence in a season of calm weather
Though inland far we be,
Our Souls have sight of that immortal sea
Which brought us hither,
165 Can in a moment travel thither,
And see the Children sport upon the shore,
And hear the mighty waters rolling evermore.

10

Then sing, ye Birds, sing, sing a joyous song!
And let the young Lambs bound

170   As to the tabor's sound!
    We in thought will join your throng,
          Ye that pipe and ye that play,
          Ye that through your hearts to-day
          Feel the gladness of the May!
175 What though the radiance which was once so bright
    Be now for ever taken from my sight,
        Though nothing can bring back the hour
    Of splendour in the grass, of glory in the flower;
          We will grieve not, rather find
180   Strength in what remains behind;
          In the primal sympathy
          Which having been must ever be;
          In the soothing thoughts that spring
          Out of human suffering;
185   In the faith that looks through death,
    In years that bring the philosophic mind.

                        11

    And O, ye Fountains, Meadows, Hills, and Groves,
    Forebode not any severing of our loves!
    Yet in my heart of hearts I feel your might;
190 I only have relinquished one delight
    To live beneath your more habitual sway.
    I love the Brooks which down their channels fret,
    Even more than when I tripped lightly as they;
    The innocent brightness of a new-born Day
195   Is lovely yet;
    The Clouds that gather round the setting sun
    Do take a sober colouring from an eye
    That hath kept watch o'er man's mortality;
    Another race hath been, and other palms° are won.   *prizes*
200 Thanks to the human heart by which we live,
    Thanks to its tenderness, its joys, and fears,
    To me the meanest° flower that blows can give   *humblest*
    Thoughts that do often lie too deep for tears.

To the Cuckoo

    O blithe New-comer! I have heard,
    I hear thee and rejoice.
    O Cuckoo! shall I call thee Bird,
    Or but a wandering Voice?

5   While I am lying on the grass
    Thy twofold shout I hear,
    From hill to hill it seems to pass
    At once far off, and near.

    Though babbling only to the Vale,
10   Of sunshine and of flowers,

Thou bringest unto me a tale
Of visionary hours.

Thrice welcome, darling of the Spring!
Even yet thou art to me
15   No bird, but an invisible thing,
A voice, a mystery;

The same whom in my schoolboy days
I listened to; that Cry
Which made me look a thousand ways
20   In bush, and tree, and sky.

To seek thee did I often rove
Through woods and on the green;
And thou wert still a hope, a love;
Still longed for, never seen.

25   And I can listen to thee yet;
Can lie upon the plain
And listen, till I do beget
That golden time again.

O blessèd Bird! the earth we pace
30   Again appears to be
An unsubstantial, faery place;
That is fit home for Thee!

Mark the concentred hazels that enclose

Mark the concentred hazels that enclose
Yon old grey Stone, protected from the ray
Of noontide suns:—and even the beams that play
And glance, while wantonly the rough wind blows,
5   Are seldom free to touch the moss that grows
Upon that roof, amid embowering gloom,
The very image framing of a Tomb,
In which some ancient Chieftain finds repose
Among the lonely mountains.—Live, ye trees!
10   And thou, grey Stone, the pensive likeness keep
Of a dark chamber where the Mighty sleep:
For more than Fancy to the influence bends
When solitary Nature condescends
To mimic Time's forlorn humanities.

from THE PRELUDE
from Book Fifth. Books

[THE DREAM OF THE ARAB]

50   One day, when from my lips a like complaint
Had fallen in presence of a studious friend,

He with a smile made answer, that in truth
'Twas going far to seek disquietude;
But on the front of his reproof confessed
55 That he himself had oftentimes given way
To kindred hauntings. Whereupon I told,
That once in the stillness of a summer's noon,
While I was seated in a rocky cave
By the sea-side, perusing, so it chanced,
60 The famous history of the errant knight°   *Don Quixote*
Recorded by Cervantes, these same thoughts
Beset me, and to height unusual rose,
While listlessly I sate, and, having closed
The book, had turned my eyes toward the wide sea.
65 On poetry and geometric truth,
And their high privilege of lasting life,
From all internal injury exempt,
I mused, upon these chiefly: and at length,
My senses yielding to the sultry air,
70 Sleep seized me, and I passed into a dream.
I saw before me stretched a boundless plain
Of sandy wilderness, all black and void,
And as I looked around, distress and fear
Came creeping over me, when at my side,
75 Close at my side, an uncouth shape appeared
Upon a dromedary, mounted high.
He seemed an Arab of the Bedouin tribes:°   *desert nomads*
A lance he bore, and underneath one arm
A stone, and in the opposite hand, a shell
80 Of a surpassing brightness. At the sight
Much I rejoiced, not doubting but a guide
Was present, one who with unerring skill
Would through the desert lead me; and while yet
I looked and looked, self-questioned what this freight
85 Which the new-comer carried through the waste
Could mean, the Arab told me that the stone
(To give it in the language of the dream)
Was "Euclid's Elements;"[1] and "This," said he,
"Is something of more worth"; and at the word
90 Stretched forth the shell, so beautiful in shape,
In colour so resplendent, with command
That I should hold it to my ear. I did so,
And heard that instant in an unknown tongue,
Which yet I understood, articulate sounds,
95 A loud prophetic blast of harmony;
An Ode, in passion uttered, which foretold

---

1. Wordsworth had learned mathematics out of the 3rd century B.C.E. Greek treatise on geometry. Much Greek philosophical and scientific culture was first transmitted to medieval Europe via translations from Arabic.

Destruction to the children of the earth
By deluge, now at hand. No sooner ceased
The song, than the Arab with calm look declared
100   That all would come to pass of which the voice
Had given forewarning, and that he himself
Was going then to bury those two books:
The one that held acquaintance with the stars,
And wedded soul to soul in purest bond
105   Of reason, undisturbed by space or time;
The other that was a god, yea many gods,
Had voices more than all the winds, with power
To exhilarate the spirit, and to soothe,
Through every clime, the heart of human kind.
110   While this was uttering, strange as it may seem,
I wondered not, although I plainly saw
The one to be a stone, the other a shell;
Nor doubted once but that they both were books,
Having a perfect faith in all that passed.
115   Far stronger, now, grew the desire I felt
To cleave unto this man; but when I prayed
To share his enterprise, he hurried on
Reckless of me: I followed, not unseen,
For oftentimes he cast a backward look,
120   Grasping his twofold treasure.—Lance in rest,
He rode, I keeping pace with him; and now
He, to my fancy, had become the knight
Whose tale Cervantes tells; yet not the knight,
But was an Arab of the desert too;
125   Of these was neither, and was both at once.
His countenance, meanwhile, grew more disturbed;
And, looking backwards when he looked, mine eyes
Saw, over half the wilderness diffused,
A bed of glittering light: I asked the cause:
130   "It is," said he, "the waters of the deep
Gathering upon us"; quickening then the pace
Of the unwieldly creature he bestrode,
He left me: I called after him aloud;
He heeded not; but, with his twofold charge
135   Still in his grasp, before me, full in view,
Went hurrying o'er the illimitable waste,
With the fleet waters of a drowning world
In chase of him; whereat I waked in terror,
And saw the sea before me, and the book,
140   In which I had been reading, at my side.

from Book Sixth. Cambridge and the Alps[1]

[CROSSING THE ALPS]

517   Well might a stranger look with bounding heart
        Down on a green recess, the first I saw
        Of those deep haunts, an aboriginal vale,
520   Quiet and lorded over and possessed
        By naked huts, wood-built, and sown like tents
        Or Indian cabins over the fresh lawns
        And by the river side.
                   That very day,
525   From a bare ridge we also first beheld
        Unveiled the summit of Mont Blanc,[2] and grieved
        To have a soulless image on the eye
        That had usurped upon a living thought
        That never more could be. The wondrous Vale
530   Of Chamouny stretched far below, and soon
        With its dumb cataracts and streams of ice,
        A motionless array of mighty waves,
        Five rivers broad and vast, made rich amends,
        And reconciled us to realities;
535   There small birds warble from the leafy trees,
        The eagle soars high in the element,
        There doth the reaper bind the yellow sheaf,
        The maiden spread the haycock in the sun,
        While Winter like a well-tamed lion walks,
540   Descending from the mountain to make sport
        Among the cottages by beds of flowers.

        Whate'er in this wide circuit we beheld,
        Or heard, was fitted to our unripe state
        Of intellect and heart. With such a book
545   Before our eyes, we could not choose but read
        Lessons of genuine brotherhood, the plain
        And universal reason of mankind,
        The truths of young and old. Nor, side by side
        Pacing, two social pilgrims, or alone
550   Each with his humour, could we fail to abound
        In dreams and fictions, pensively composed:
        Dejection taken up for pleasure's sake,
        And gilded sympathies, the willow wreath,°   *a symbol of sorrow*
        And sober posies° of funereal flowers,   *bouquets*
555   Gathered among those solitudes sublime

---

1. Book 6 describes a journey Wordsworth took with a college friend in 1790 through revolutionary France into Switzerland. The atmosphere shortly after the fall of the Bastille on 14 July 1789, is called "golden hours" earlier in the book.

2. At 15,771 feet, Mt. Blanc, the highest peak in the Alps, dwarfs the British mountains that Wordsworth loved to hike. It was celebrated by British travelers and poets of the Romantic decades. Chamonix is the lush valley underneath the north face of the mountain.

From formal gardens of the lady Sorrow,
Did sweeten many a meditative hour.

    Yet still in me with those soft luxuries
Mixed something of stern mood, an under-thirst
560   Of vigour seldom utterly allayed.
And from that source how different a sadness
Would issue, let one incident make known.
When from the Vallais we had turned, and clomb°   *climbed*
Along the Simplon's[3] steep and rugged road,
565   Following a band of muleteers, we reached
A halting-place, where all together took
Their noon-tide meal. Hastily rose our guide,
Leaving us at the board; awhile we lingered,
Then paced the beaten downward way that led
570   Right to a rough stream's edge, and there broke off;
The only track now visible was one
That from the torrent's further brink held forth
Conspicuous invitation to ascend
A lofty mountain. After brief delay
580   Crossing the unbridged stream, that road we took,
And clomb with eagerness, till anxious fears
Intruded, for we failed to overtake
Our comrades gone before. By fortunate chance,
While every moment added doubt to doubt,
585   A peasant met us, from whose mouth we learned
That to the spot which had perplexed us first
We must descend, and there should find the road,
Which in the stony channel of the stream
Lay a few steps, and then along its banks;
590   And, that our future course, all plain to sight,
Was downwards, with the current of that stream.
Loth to believe what we so grieved to hear,
For still we had hopes that pointed to the clouds,
We questioned him again, and yet again;
595   But every word that from the peasant's lips
Came in reply, translated by our feelings,
Ended in this,—*that we had crossed the Alps.*

    Imagination—here the Power so called
Through sad incompetence of human speech,
600   That awful Power rose from the mind's abyss
Like an unfathered vapour that enwraps,
At once, some lonely traveller. I was lost;
Halted without an effort to break through;
But to my conscious soul I now[4] can say—
605   "I recognise thy glory": in such strength

3. A pass leading from the Swiss canton of Valais into
Italy. The first proper road through the Simplon Pass was
built under Napoleon at the start of the 19th century.
4. I.e., at the time of writing, in 1804.

Of usurpation, when the light of sense
Goes out, but with a flash that has revealed
The invisible world, doth greatness make abode,
There harbours; whether we be young or old,
610 Our destiny, our being's heart and home,
Is with infinitude, and only there;
With hope it is, hope that can never die,
Effort, and expectation, and desire,
And something evermore about to be.
615 Under such banners militant, the soul
Seeks for no trophies, struggles for no spoils
That may attest her prowess, blest in thoughts
That are their own perfection and reward,
Strong in herself and in beatitude
620 That hides her, like the mighty flood of Nile
Poured from his fount of Abyssinian clouds
To fertilise the whole Egyptian plain.[5]

    The melancholy slackening that ensued
Upon those tidings by the peasant given
625 Was soon dislodged. Downwards we hurried fast,
And, with the half-shaped road[6] which we had missed,
Entered a narrow chasm. The brook and road
Were fellow-travellers in this gloomy strait,
And with them did we journey several hours
630 At a slow pace. The immeasurable height
Of woods decaying, never to be decayed,
The stationary blasts of waterfalls,
And in the narrow rent at every turn
Winds thwarting winds, bewildered and forlorn,
635 The torrents shooting from the clear blue sky,
The rocks that muttered close upon our ears,
Black drizzling crags that spake by the way-side
As if a voice were in them, the sick sight
And giddy prospect of the raving stream,
640 The unfettered clouds and region of the Heavens,
Tumult and peace, the darkness and the light—
Were all like workings of one mind, the features
Of the same face, blossoms upon one tree;
Characters° of the great Apocalypse,   *written signs*
645 The types and symbols of Eternity,
Of first, and last, and midst, and without end.[7]

5. The military language in this verse paragraph may evoke Napoleon, who catapulted to power in 1799 following a successful Egyptian campaign and who triumphantly led the French army through a nearby Alpine pass into Italy in 1800.
6. The coinage "half-shaped" evidently means that there was an actual road only part of the way, and otherwise a mere track that was hard to identify. An illustrated description by Patrick Vincent of the route as it currently exists may be found at <www.rc.umd.edu/features/features/simplon>.
7. Wordsworth echoes the biblical description of the Apocalypse in Revelation 1:8: "I am Alpha and Omega, the beginning and the ending, saith the Lord."

from Book Eleventh. France[1]

105 O pleasant exercise of hope and joy!
    For mighty were the auxiliars° which then stood   *allies*
    Upon our side, us who were strong in love!
    Bliss was it in that dawn to be alive,
    But to be young was very Heaven! O times,
110 In which the meagre, stale, forbidding ways
    Of custom, law, and statute, took at once
    The attraction of a country in romance!
    When Reason seemed the most to assert her rights
    When most intent on making of herself
115 A prime enchantress—to assist the work,
    Which then was going forward in her name!
    Not favoured spots alone, but the whole Earth,
    The beauty wore of promise—that which sets
    (As at some moments might not be unfelt
120 Among the bowers of Paradise itself)
    The budding rose above the rose full blown.
    What temper° at the prospect did not wake   *temperament*
    To happiness unthought of? The inert
    Were roused, and lively natures rapt° away!   *enraptured*
125 They who had fed their childhood upon dreams,
    The play-fellows of fancy, who had made
    All powers of swiftness, subtilty, and strength
    Their ministers,—who in lordly wise had stirred
    Among the grandest objects of the sense,
130 And dealt with whatsoever they found there
    As if they had within some lurking right
    To wield it;—they, too, who of gentle mood
    Had watched all gentle motions, and to these
    Had fitted their own thoughts, schemers more mild,
135 And in the region of their peaceful selves;—
    Now was it that *both* found, the meek and lofty
    Did both find helpers to their hearts' desire,
    And stuff at hand, plastic° as they could wish,—   *malleable*
    Were called upon to exercise their skill,
140 Not in Utopia,—subterranean fields,—
    Or some secreted island, Heaven knows where!
    But in the very world, which is the world
    Of all of us,—the place where, in the end,
    We find our happiness, or not at all!

145   Why should I not confess that Earth was then
    To me, what an inheritance, new-fallen,

---

1. Wordsworth was in Paris from late October until mid-December 1792, at a critical point, just after the first guillotinings on August 10 ("License," line 163) and the declaration of a Republic on September 21 ("Liberty") but before the execution of the King on 21 January 1793. It remains unknown whether he ever worked as "an active partisan" (line 153) alongside the British and American radicals then in Paris. The remainder of Book 11 describes his disillusionment with the growing tyranny of the revolutionaries.

Seems, when the first time visited, to one
Who thither comes to find in it his home?
He walks about and looks upon the spot
150   With cordial transport, moulds it and remoulds,
And is half pleased with things that are amiss,
'Twill be such joy to see them disappear.

    An active partisan, I thus convoked
From every object pleasant circumstance
155   To suit my ends; I moved among mankind
With genial feelings still predominant;
When erring, erring on the better part,
And in the kinder spirit; placable,
Indulgent, as not uninformed that men
160   See as they have been taught—Antiquity
Gives right to error; and aware, no less,
That throwing off oppression must be work
As well of License as of Liberty;
And above all—for this was more than all—
165   Not caring if the wind did now and then
Blow keen upon an eminence that gave
Prospect so large into futurity;
In brief, a child of Nature, as at first,
Diffusing only those affections wider
170   That from the cradle had grown up with me,
And losing, in no other way than light
Is lost in light, the weak in the more strong.

from Book Fourteenth. Conclusion

[ASCENT OF SNOWDON][1]

11   It was a close, warm, breezeless summer night,
Wan, dull, and glaring,° with a dripping fog   *wet (dialect)*
Low-hung and thick that covered all the sky;
But, undiscouraged, we began to climb
15   The mountain-side. The mist soon girt us round,
And, after ordinary travellers' talk
With our conductor, pensively we sank
Each into commerce with his private thoughts:
Thus did we breast the ascent, and by myself
20   Was nothing either seen or heard that checked
Those musings or diverted, save that once
The shepherd's lurcher,° who, among the crags,   *hunting dog*
Had to his joy unearthed a hedgehog, teased
His coiled-up prey with barkings turbulent.

---

1. The ascent of Mt. Snowdon in Wales—at 3,560 feet the highest peak in Britain—took place in the summer of 1791.

25   This small adventure, for even such it seemed
      In that wild place and at the dead of night,
      Being over and forgotten, on we wound
      In silence as before. With forehead bent
      Earthward, as if in opposition set
30   Against an enemy, I panted up
      With eager pace, and no less eager thoughts.
      Thus might we wear a midnight hour away,
      Ascending at loose distance each from each,
      And I, as chanced, the foremost of the band;
35   When at my feet the ground appeared to brighten,
      And with a step or two seemed brighter still;
      Nor was time given to ask or learn the cause,
      For instantly a light upon the turf
      Fell like a flash, and lo! as I looked up,
40   The Moon hung naked in a firmament
      Of azure without cloud, and at my feet
      Rested a silent sea of hoary mist.
      A hundred hills their dusky backs upheaved
      All over this still ocean; and beyond,
45   Far, far beyond, the solid vapours stretched,
      In headlands, tongues, and promontory shapes,°   *mock shapes in the clouds*
      Into the main° Atlantic, that appeared   *ocean*
      To dwindle, and give up his majesty,
      Usurped upon far as the sight could reach.
50   Not so the ethereal vault; encroachment none
      Was there, nor loss; only the inferior stars
      Had disappeared, or shed a fainter light
      In the clear presence of the full-orbed Moon,
      Who, from her sovereign elevation, gazed
55   Upon the billowy ocean, as it lay
      All meek and silent, save that through a rift—
      Not distant from the shore whereon we stood,
      A fixed, abysmal, gloomy, breathing-place—
      Mounted the roar of waters, torrents, streams
60   Innumerable, roaring with one voice!
      Heard over earth and sea, and, in that hour,
      For so it seemed, felt by the starry heavens.

         When into air had partially dissolved
      That vision, given to spirits of the night
65   And three chance human wanderers, in calm thought
      Reflected, it appeared to me the type
      Of a majestic intellect, its acts
      And its possessions, what it has and craves,
      What in itself it is, and would become.
70   There I beheld the emblem of a mind
      That feeds upon infinity, that broods
      Over the dark abyss, intent to hear
      Its voices issuing forth to silent light

In one continuous stream; a mind sustained
75   By recognitions of transcendent power,
In sense conducting to ideal form,
In soul of more than mortal privilege.
One function, above all, of such a mind
Had Nature shadowed there, by putting forth,
80   'Mid circumstances awful and sublime,
That mutual domination which she loves
To exert upon the face of outward things,
So moulded, joined, abstracted, so endowed
With interchangeable supremacy,
85   That men, least sensitive, see, hear, perceive,
And cannot choose but feel. The power, which all
Acknowledge when thus moved, which Nature thus
To bodily sense exhibits, is the express
Resemblance of that glorious faculty
90   That higher minds bear with them as their own.
This is the very spirit in which they deal
With the whole compass of the universe:
They from their native selves can send abroad
Kindred mutations; for themselves create
95   A like existence; and, whene'er it dawns
Created for them, catch it, or are caught
By its inevitable mastery,
Like angels stopped upon the wing by sound
Of harmony from Heaven's remotest spheres.
100 Them the enduring and the transient both
Serve to exalt; they build up greatest things
From least suggestions; ever on the watch,
Willing to work and to be wrought upon,
They need not extraordinary calls
105 To rouse them; in a world of life they live,
By sensible impressions not enthralled,
But by their quickening impulse made more prompt
To hold fit converse with the spiritual world,
And with the generations of mankind
110 Spread over time, past, present, and to come,
Age after age, till Time shall be no more.
Such minds are truly from the Deity,
For they are Powers; and hence the highest bliss
That flesh can know is theirs—the consciousness
115 Of Whom they are, habitually infused
Through every image and through every thought,
And all affections° by communion raised   *emotions*
From earth to heaven, from human to divine;
Hence endless occupation for the Soul,
120 Whether discursive or intuitive;[2]

2. By reasoning or by direct insight.

Hence cheerfulness for acts of daily life,
Emotions which best foresight need not fear,
Most worthy then of trust when most intense.
Hence, amid ills that vex and wrongs that crush

125 Our hearts—if here the words of Holy Writ
May with fit reverence be applied—that peace
Which passeth understanding,[3] that repose
In moral judgments which from this pure source
Must come, or will by man be sought in vain.

3. Philippians 4:7: "the peace of God, which passeth all understanding."

══╪ PERSPECTIVES ╪══
Romantic Nature

"Love of Nature Leading to Love of Mankind." The title of Book 8 of Wordsworth's epic poem *The Prelude* could serve as a label for much of the enterprise of Romanticism. Birds and flowers, rivers and mountains form the subjects of many of the most famous poems of the era, of key stretches of the novels, vast amounts of travel writing, the most characteristic painting in England and Germany, and important philosophical and scientific works. Of course, poets and artists have always admired nature and depicted the scenery in their writings and paintings. But nature was newly central to the Romantic sensibility, and in ways that continue to form our ecological sensibility today.

Chaucer's medieval *Canterbury Tales* opens with a beautiful spring scene. The point, however, is to set the pilgrims on their journey; nature bears a moral and religious impress: "So pricketh hem nature in hir courages. / Than longen folk to goon on pilgrimages." Dante similarly notes the landscape as he starts underway, in the second canto of the *Inferno*. But here the pilgrim is set apart from nature: "The day was now departing; the dark air released the living beings of the earth from work and weariness; and I myself alone . . ." There is nature, and there is the heart of man, and nature (or the goddess Natura) sends man on his way, or holds him back from his heavenly destination. Nature is setting or mediator, but never end in itself. Only late in the sixteenth century, and then very gradually, did painters even began to depict landscape scenes without humans or divinities in them.

The history of gardening is instructive and important. In the seventeenth century the French set the fashion, with architecturally inspired gardens of neat squares and fountains and rigidly pruned trees. In the eighteenth century the so-called English garden came into style, with informal vistas, lawns, and brooks. Still, and in a succession of different modes, gardens remained tamed and carefully manicured. In his "Epistle to Burlington" (1731) Alexander Pope, a famous gardener in his own right, blamed one kind—"Grove nods at grove, each alley has a brother, / And half the platform just reflects the other"—and praised a more informal and more productive scene, "Whose ample lawns are not ashamed to feed / The milky heifer and deserving steed." But it would never have occurred to Pope to write poems celebrating a field mouse, as did Robert Burns, or a cuckoo or weed as did Wordsworth. Pope may have preferred a more natural garden, but it was still a garden. In contrast, the park in Coleridge's "Kubla Khan" is watered by brooks as meandering as the raw countryside of England.

Perhaps the most famous lines in all of eighteenth-century poetry are found in Thomas Gray's "Elegy Written in a Country Churchyard" (1751):

> Full many a gem of purest ray serene,
> The dark unfathomed caves of ocean bear:
> Full many a flower is born to blush unseen,
> And waste its sweetness on the desert air.

Poems of sensibility like this one drew attention to the hidden, unnoticed beauties of nature. Still, even Gray and his contemporaries wanted to extract the gems for human use, to bring flowers where they wouldn't be wasted. The natural scene remains an allegory: the flower and gem represent the country dwellers who lack the proper education and opportunities to develop their gifts. Things have changed by the time Wordsworth praises a mysterious girl he called Lucy in 1798, in his song "She dwelt among th' untrodden ways." Now the comparisons go the other way; it's not that the isolated beauties of nature are like people but that she is like them:

> A Violet by a mossy stone,
> Half hidden from the Eye!

—Fair, as a star when only one
 Is shining in the sky!

Most surprising to us about older attitudes toward nature is perhaps the fear of mountains. In his *Sacred Theory of the Earth* (first published in Latin in 1681) Bishop Thomas Burnet notoriously called them "wild, vast and indigested Heaps of Stone and Earth," and the "Ruins of a broken World." There are obvious reasons. Nights were dark, roads were bad, there were no snowplows, carriages were unheated, there was always the risk in unpoliced border regions of encountering savage animals or even more savage people. Many residues of this old terror survive—for instance, in the haunted Sleepy Hollow portrayed by Washington Irving, or in the mysterious forest of Ludwig Tieck's "Blond Eckbert," and in Kubla Khan's ice caves. But the Romantics were learning not just to delight in nature's unadorned beauties but equally to revere the grandest and even the most forbidding regions. Rousseau, Swiss by birth, retreated into natural isolation in times of stress. Wordsworth crossed the Alps and climbed Mount Snowdon (the highest peak in the British Isles), and he and Coleridge loved to hike the most isolated and remote reaches of the Lake District, in the far northwest of England. For Emerson, nature displays the power of divinity, and Thoreau caps the turn to nature in all her majestic savagery with the spring vision that climaxes *Walden* and with his famous cry, "We need the tonic of wildness."

Three characteristics of nature might be identified as elements of the Romantic vision. First, Romantic nature is particular. While it may still retain the aura that earlier surrounded nature as either a Paradise or a fallen realm, it is watched and understood first in its own right. Rousseau was never happier than when cataloguing the plants of his retreat on the Island of Saint-Pierre, Goethe amassed an enormous and meticulously inventoried rock collection, Droste-Hülshoff and Thoreau were scrupulous and knowledgeable observers of the characteristics and habits of the plants and animals around them. This was the age of natural history, when scientists and laypeople refined the catalogue of species originally drawn up by Linnaeus (Carl von Linné, 1707–1778), when paleontologists studied fossils and geologists first began speculating about the ages of the earth, and when some daring writers on astronomy, beginning with the young Immanuel Kant, even started imagining histories of the universe. The Romantics localized nature in both place and time.

Second, Romantic nature isn't just composed of living beings but is itself a living thing. In "Tintern Abbey" Wordsworth says, "We see into the life of things," while Goethe has Faust describe the ecstasy of the waterfall at the end of "A Beautiful Landscape," the first scene of *Faust, Part 2,* and Thoreau writes, "I love to see that Nature is so rife with life that myriads can be afforded to be sacrificed and suffered to prey on one another." In each of these cases, the writer celebrates a life force larger than any individual. Notice how old the scene often looks to Romantic writers. Keats's nightingale has sung for millennia, and his autumn seems to live beyond its limits when the "soft-dying day" becomes the home for "gathering swallows"; Droste-Hülshoff's "In the Grass" is a moment that "hastens" and yet "lingers," as she drowses while nature lives on. *Vitalism* is the formal name for the belief in a life that is larger than life and an age that is older yet more continuous than any recorded time. The Romantics were vitalists to their very core, with an instinctive belief that nature is holier and more valuable than any mere sign or evidence of divinity.

Third, Romantic nature is grand. Even its tiniest elements are of infinite value, and its most imposing monuments are less threatening than inspiring. The period's name for this grandeur is sublimity. In its oldest English usage, the term "sublime" meant uplifting, and that sense remained the underpinning for all later meanings. Earlier writers and painters certainly also admired nature's grandeurs but typically found them intimidating; the Romantics found them elevating. Nature was no longer a realm of occult powers to be mastered by magicians like Shakespeare's Prospero or the legendary Renaissance wonder-worker Dr. Faustus, but rather a domain of wondrous, living order to be penetrated by the human intellect and experienced by

Caspar David Friedrich, *Wanderer Above Sea of Fog,* 1818.

the human body. Each of the three main divisions of Dante's *Divine Comedy* ends with the word "stars" in witness of the pilgrim's humility before God. When Kant contemplates the stars, he allies them with his own exaltation of spirit. Emerson's nature-ecstasy is the culmination of the Romantic cult of the particular, living grandeur of nature that has become so much a part of our modern sense of the nature's incomparable value in all its forms, in itself and for our cultural and spiritual lives. "Standing on the bare ground—my head bathed by the blithe air and uplifted into infinite space—all mean egotism vanishes. I become a transparent eyeball; I am nothing; I see all; the currents of the Universal being circulate through me; I am part or parcel of God."

Jean-Jacques Rousseau
1712–1778

Musician, novelist, and educational and political theorist, Jean-Jacques Rousseau was among the greatest thinkers of his age and surely the most unsettling. He was a slashing polemicist with a message of peace and brotherhood, and he was the apostle of a society founded upon the common agreement of its members (the "social contract") whose writings helped inspire the Revolution that tore apart the fabric of the old regime. Proud of his bourgeois, Swiss Protestant origins and ambivalent to the point of paranoia about his status in Parisian society, he resented countless imaginary slights, quarreled with all his friends and supporters, and—despite an uncanny understanding of child psychology that emerges in his still influential writings on pedagogy—he secretly gave his five children up for adoption. His last writings, and arguably the most influential of all, retell his life and meditate on the nature of experience and the experience of nature. Turbulent sexual and social adventures fill the *Confessions,* while the *Reveries of a Solitary Wanderer* chronicle a devotion to the natural environment unparalleled in its day for its intensity. Like Thoreau after him, Rousseau spent hours, days, and weeks observing and collecting the plants in a restricted, protected setting. While Thoreau's theme is life, Rousseau's is time and eternity. He virtually invented the daydream reverie that became a nineteenth-century staple. The hard-won self-satisfaction of "feeling the pleasure of my existence without taking the trouble to think" became an ideal for Wordsworth and for a whole cult of simplicity; the prayer, "I should wish for this instant to last forever," became the great wager of Goethe's Faust. The ecstatic imaginative richness compensating for the (mostly) imaginary persecutions of society was Rousseau's final bequest, in these posthumous works with their unprecedented explorations of the emotional life of a human being.

PRONUNCIATIONS:
Rousseau: Roo-SOH
Thérèse Levasseur: Tay-REZ Le-vas-SIR
Môtiers: Moh-ti-AY

from Reveries of the Solitary Walker[1]
Fifth Walk

Of all the places where I have lived (and I have lived in some charming ones) none has made me so truly happy or left me such tender regrets as the Island of Saint-Pierre in the middle of the Lake of Bienne.[2] This little island, which the people of Neuchâtel call the "Île de la Motte," is scarcely known even in Switzerland. To my knowledge it has never yet been mentioned by any traveler. Yet it is very agreeable and wonderfully well situated for the happiness of those who like to live within narrow bounds— and even if I may be the only person ever to have had such a life thrust on him by destiny, I cannot believe that I am the only one to possess so natural a taste, though I have never yet encountered it in anyone else.

The shores of the Lake of Bienne are wilder and more romantic than those of Lake Geneva,[3] since the rocks and woods come closer to the water, but they are no

---

1. Translated by Peter France.
2. On September 6, 1765, Rousseau and his mistress Thérèse Levasseur were attacked at his residence in the town of Môtiers by a crowd throwing stones. His first refuge, from September 12 until October 25, was a small

island nearby where he had spent a long week the previous July. Saint-Pierre means Saint Peter; "pierre" is also the French word for stone.
3. Where Rousseau was born.

less pleasing. There may be fewer ploughed fields and vineyards, fewer towns and houses, but there is more natural greenery and there are more meadows and secluded spots shaded by woodlands, more frequent and dramatic changes of scenery. Since these happy shores are free of broad roads suitable for carriages, the region is little visited by travelers, but it is fascinating for those solitary dreamers who love to drink deeply of the beauty of nature and to meditate in a silence which is unbroken but for the cry of eagles, the occasional song of birds and the roar of streams cascading down from the mountains. In the middle of this beautiful, nearly circular expanse of water lie two small islands, one of them inhabited, cultivated and some half a league in circumference, the other one smaller, uninhabited, untilled, and bound one day to be eaten away by the constant removal of earth from it to make good the damage inflicted by waves and storms upon its neighbor. Thus it is that the substance of the poor always goes to enrich the wealthy.

There is only one house in the whole island, but it is a large, pleasant and commodious one, belonging like the island to the Hospital of Bern, and inhabited by a Steward together with his family and servants. He keeps a well-stocked farmyard, with fish-ponds and runs for game-birds. Small as it is, the island is so varied in soil and situation that it contains places suitable for crops of every kind. It includes fields, vineyards, woods, orchards, and rich pastures shaded by coppices and surrounded by shrubs of every variety, all of which are kept watered by the shores of the lake; on one shore an elevated terrace planted with two rows of trees runs the length of the island, and in the middle of this terrace there is a pretty summer-house where the people who live round the lake meet and dance on Sundays during the wine harvest.

It was on this island that I took refuge after the stoning at Môtiers. I found the place so delightful and so conducive to the life that suited me, that resolving to end my days there, I was concerned only lest I might not be allowed to carry out this plan, conflicting as it did with the scheme to carry me off to England,[4] the first signs of which I was already beginning to detect. Troubled by forebodings, I could have desired that this place of refuge be made my lifelong prison, that I be shut up here for the rest of my days, deprived of any chance or hope of escaping and forbidden all communication with the mainland, so that not knowing what went on in the world, I should forget its existence and be forgotten by those who lived in it.

I was barely allowed to spend two months on this island, but I could have spent two years, two centuries and all eternity there without a moment's boredom, even though all the company I had, apart from Thérèse, was that of the Steward, his wife and his household—all certainly very good people, and nothing more, but this was exactly what I needed. I look upon these two months as the happiest time of my life, so happy that I would have been content to live all my life in this way, without a moment's desire for any other state.

What then was this happiness, and wherein lay this great contentment? The men of this age would never guess the answer from a description of the life I led there. Precious *far niente*[5] was my first and greatest pleasure, and I set out to taste it in all its sweetness, and everything I did during my stay there was in fact no more than the delectable and necessary pastime of a man who has dedicated himself to idleness.

4. Rousseau had been cordially invited to England by the wealthy dilettante Horace Walpole. In January 1766 he left Paris to stay with the philosopher David Hume. Rousseau stormed out in March and proceeded to publish accusations against his hosts.
5. Idleness.

The hope that they would ask nothing better than to let me stay in the isolated place in which I had imprisoned myself, which I could not leave unaided and unobserved, and where I could have no communication or correspondence with the outside world except with the help of the people surrounding me, this hope encouraged me to hope likewise that I might end my days more peacefully than I had lived till then, and thinking that I would have all the time in the world to settle in, I began by making no attempt at all to install myself. Arriving there unexpectedly, alone and empty-handed, I sent in turn for my companion, my books and my few belongings, which I had the pleasure of leaving just as they were, unpacking not a single box or trunk and living in the house where I intended to end my days, as if it had been an inn which I was to leave the following day. Everything went along so well as it was that to try to order things better would have been to spoil them. One of my greatest joys was above all to leave my books safely shut up and to have no escritoire.[6] When I was forced to take up my pen to answer the wretched letters I received, I reluctantly borrowed the Steward's escritoire and made haste to return it in the vain hope that I might never need to borrow it again. Instead of all these gloomy old papers and books, I filled my room with flowers and grasses, for I was then in the first flush of enthusiasm for botany, a taste soon to become a passion, which I owed to Doctor d'Ivernois.[7] Not wanting to spend the time on serious work, I needed some agreeable pastime which would give me no more trouble than an idler likes to give himself. I set out to compose a *Flora Petrinsularis*[8] and to describe every single plant on the island in enough detail to keep me busy for the rest of my days. They say a German once wrote a book about a lemon-skin; I could have written one about every grass in the meadows, every moss in the woods, every lichen covering the rocks—and I did not want to leave even one blade of grass or atom of vegetation without a full and detailed description. In accordance with this noble plan, every morning after breakfast, which we all took together, I would set out with a magnifying glass in my hand and my *Systema Naturae*[9] under my arm to study one particular section of the island, which I had divided for this purpose into small squares, intending to visit them all one after another in every season. Nothing could be more extraordinary than the raptures and ecstasies I felt at every discovery I made about the structure and organization of plants and the operation of the sexual parts in the process of reproduction, which was at this time completely new to me. Before progressing to rarer plants, I was delighted to observe in the common species the distinctions between families of which I had previously been completely unaware. The forking of the self-heal's two long stamens, the springiness of those of the nettle and wall pellitory,[1] the way the seed bursts out from the fruit of the box and balsam, all these innumerable little tricks of fertilization which I was observing for the first time filled me with joy, and I went about asking people if they had seen the horns of the self-heal just as La Fontaine[2] asked if they had read Habakkuk. After two or three hours I would come back with a rich harvest, enough to occupy me at home all the afternoon if it should rain. The rest of the morning I spent going with the Stew-

---

6. Writing desk.
7. Jean-Antoine d'Ivernois (1703–1765), a physician and botanist who had studied the plants of the region.
8. A botanical guide to the flora of the Island of Saint-Pierre.
9. The great work of the Swedish naturalist Carolus Linnaeus (1707–1778), first published in 1735, which established the modern system of Latin names of plants and animals.

1. Self-heal, nettle, and wall pellitory are medicinal plants.
2. Jean de La Fontaine, the author of the famous fables (see p. 24), is actually said to have admired the apocryphal book Baruch, rather than the Old Testament book Habakkuk.

ard, his wife and Thérèse to see the laborers working at the harvest, and usually to lend them a hand; often people coming to see me from Bern found me perched up in a big tree with a bag round my waist, which I would fill with fruit and then lower to the ground on the end of a rope. My morning exercise and its attendant good humor made it very pleasant to take a rest at dinner-time, but when the meal went on too long and fine weather called me, I could not wait till the others had finished, and leaving them at table I would make my escape and install myself all alone in a boat, which I would row out into the middle of the lake when it was calm; and there, stretching out full-length in the boat and turning my eyes skyward, I let myself float and drift wherever the water took me, often for several hours on end, plunged in a host of vague yet delightful reveries, which though they had no distinct or permanent subject, were still in my eyes infinitely to be preferred to all that I had found most sweet in the so-called pleasures of life. Often reminded by the declining sun that it was time to return home, I found myself so far from the island that I was forced to row with all my might in order to arrive before nightfall. At other times, rather than strike out into the middle of the lake, I preferred to stay close to the green shores of the island, where the clear water and cool shade often tempted me to bathe. But one of my most frequent expeditions was to go from the larger island to the smaller one, disembarking and spending the afternoon there, either walking in its narrow confines among the sallows,[3] alders, persicarias and shrubs of all kinds, or else establishing myself on the summit of a shady hillock covered with turf, wild thyme and flowers, including even red and white clover which had probably been sown there at some time in the past, a perfect home for rabbits, which could multiply there in peace, without harming anything or having anything to fear. I put the idea to the Steward, who sent for rabbits from Neuchâtel, both bucks and does, and we proceeded in great ceremony, his wife, one of his sisters, Thérèse and I, to install them on the little island, where they were beginning to breed before my departure and where they will doubtless have flourished if they have been able to withstand the rigors of winter. The founding of this little colony was a great day. The pilot of the Argonauts[4] was not prouder than I was, when I led the company and the rabbits triumphantly from the large island to the small one; and I was gratified to see that the Steward's wife, who was extremely afraid of water and could not step into a boat without feeling unwell, embarked confidently under my command and showed no sign of fear during the crossing.

When the lake was not calm enough for boating, I would spend the afternoon roaming about the island, stopping to sit now in the most charming and isolated corners where I could dream undisturbed, and now on the terraces and little hills, where I could let my eyes wander over the beautiful and entrancing spectacle of the lake and its shores, crowned on one side by the near-by mountains and on the other extending in rich and fertile plains where the view was limited only by a more distant range of blue mountains.

As evening approached, I came down from the heights of the island, and I liked then to go and sit on the shingle[5] in some secluded spot by the edge of the lake; there the noise of the waves and the movement of the water, taking hold of my senses and driving all other agitation from my soul, would plunge it into a delicious reverie in which night often stole upon me unawares. The ebb and flow of the water, its continuous yet undulating noise, kept lapping against my ears and my eyes, taking the place

3. Willows; persicaria is an aquatic plant.
4. The expedition led by Jason to retrieve the Golden

Fleece.
5. Pebbly bank.

of all the inward movements which my reverie had calmed within me, and it was enough to make me pleasurably aware of my existence, without troubling myself with thought. From time to time some brief and insubstantial reflection arose concerning the instability of the things of this world, whose image I saw in the surface of the water, but soon these fragile impressions gave way before the unchanging and ceaseless movement which lulled me and without any active effort on my part occupied me so completely that even when time and the habitual signal called me home I could hardly bring myself to go.

After supper, when the evening was fine, we all went out once again to walk on the terrace and breathe the coolness of the lake air. We would sit down to rest in the summer-house, and laugh and talk, and sing some old song which was fully the equal of all our modern frills and fancies, and then we would go off to bed satisfied with our day and only wishing for the next day to be the same.

Such, apart from unforeseen and troublesome visits, was the way I spent my time on this island during the weeks I lived there. I should like to know what there was in it that was attractive enough to give me such deep, tender and lasting regrets that even fifteen years later I am incapable of thinking of this beloved place without being overcome by pangs of longing.

I have noticed in the changing fortunes of a long life that the periods of the sweetest joys and keenest pleasures are not those whose memory is most moving and attractive to me. These brief moments of madness and passion, however powerfully they may affect us, can because of this very power only be infrequent points along the line of our life. They are too rare and too short-lived to constitute a durable state, and the happiness for which my soul longs is not made up of fleeting moments, but of a single and lasting state, which has no very strong impact in itself, but which by its continuance becomes so captivating that we eventually come to regard it as the height of happiness.

Everything is in constant flux on this earth.[6] Nothing keeps the same unchanging shape, and our affections, being attached to things outside us, necessarily change and pass away as they do. Always out ahead of us or lagging behind, they recall a past which is gone or anticipate a future which may never come into being; there is nothing solid there for the heart to attach itself to. Thus our earthly joys are almost without exception the creatures of a moment; I doubt whether any of us knows the meaning of lasting happiness. Even in our keenest pleasures there is scarcely a single moment of which the heart could truthfully say: "Would that this moment could last for ever!"[7] And how can we give the name of happiness to a fleeting state which leaves our hearts still empty and anxious, either regretting something that is past or desiring something that is yet to come?

But if there is a state where the soul can find a resting-place secure enough to establish itself and concentrate its entire being there, with no need to remember the past or reach into the future, where time is nothing to it, where the present runs on indefinitely but this duration goes unnoticed, with no sign of the passing of time, and no other feeling of deprivation or enjoyment, pleasure or pain, desire or fear than the

---

6. Rousseau shares this sentiment with Montaigne, notably seen in the opening of "Of Repentance" (*Essays* 3.2): "The world is but a perennial movement."
7. This phrase is echoed by the wager between Faust and

Mephisto in Goethe's play: "If ever to the moment I shall say: / Beautiful moment, do not pass away! / . . . / The clock may stop, the clock-hands fall, / And time come to an end for me!" (lines 1699–1706).

simple feeling of existence,[8] a feeling that fills our soul entirely, as long as this state lasts, we can call ourselves happy, not with a poor, incomplete and relative happiness such as we find in the pleasures of life, but with a sufficient, complete and perfect happiness which leaves no emptiness to be filled in the soul. Such is the state which I often experienced on the Island of Saint-Pierre in my solitary reveries, whether I lay in a boat and drifted where the water carried me, or sat by the shores of the stormy lake, or elsewhere, on the banks of a lovely river or a stream murmuring over the stones.

What is the source of our happiness in such a state? Nothing external to us, nothing apart from ourselves and our own existence; as long as this state lasts we are self-sufficient like God. The feeling of existence unmixed with any other emotion is in itself a precious feeling of peace and contentment which would be enough to make this mode of being loved and cherished by anyone who could guard against all the earthly and sensual influences that are constantly distracting us from it in this life and troubling the joy it could give us. But most men being continually stirred by passion know little of this condition, and having only enjoyed it fleetingly and incompletely they retain no more than a dim and confused notion of it and are unaware of its true charm. Nor would it be desirable in our present state of affairs that the avid desire for these sweet ecstasies should give people a distaste for the active life which their constantly recurring needs impose upon them. But an unfortunate man who has been excluded from human society, and can do nothing more in this world to serve or benefit himself or others, may be allowed to seek in this state a compensation for human joys, a compensation which neither fortune nor mankind can take away from him.

It is true that such compensations cannot be experienced by every soul or in every situation. The heart must be at peace and its calm untroubled by any passion. The person in question must be suitably disposed and the surrounding objects conducive to his happiness. There must be neither a total calm nor too much movement, but a steady and moderate motion, with no jolts or breaks. Without any movement life is mere lethargy. If the movement is irregular or too violent it arouses us from our dreams; recalling us to an awareness of the surrounding objects, it destroys the charm of reverie and tears us from our inner self, bowing us once again beneath the yoke of fortune and mankind and reviving in us the sense of our misfortunes. Complete silence induces melancholy; it is an image of death. In such cases the assistance of a happy imagination is needed, and it comes naturally to those whom Heaven has blessed with it. The movement which does not come from outside us arises within us at such times. Our tranquillity is less complete, it is true, but it is also more agreeable when pleasant and insubstantial ideas barely touch the surface of the soul, so to speak, and do not stir its depths. One needs only enough of such ideas to allow one to be conscious of one's existence while forgetting all one's troubles. This type of reverie can be enjoyed anywhere where one is undisturbed, and I have often thought that in the Bastille, and even in a dungeon with not a single object to rest my eyes on, I could still have dreamed pleasantly.

But it must be admitted that this happened much more easily and agreeably in a fertile and lonely island, naturally circumscribed and cut off from the rest of the world, where I saw nothing but images of delight, where there was nothing to recall painful memories, where the company of the few people who lived there was attractive and

---

8. Cf. Wordsworth, *Prelude* 2.399–402: "I was then / Contented, when with bliss ineffable / I felt the sentiment of Being spread / O'er all that moves and all that seemeth still."

pleasing without being interesting enough to absorb all my attention, and where I could devote the whole day without care or hindrance to the pastimes of my choice or to the most blissful indolence. It was without doubt a fine opportunity for a dreamer who is capable of enjoying the most delightful fantasies even in the most unpleasant settings, and who could here feed on them at leisure, enriching them with all the objects which his senses actually perceived. Emerging from a long and happy reverie, seeing myself surrounded by greenery, flowers and birds, and letting my eyes wander over the picturesque far-off shores which enclosed a vast stretch of clear and crystalline water, I fused my imaginings with these charming sights, and finding myself in the end gradually brought back to myself and my surroundings, I could not draw a line between fiction and reality; so much did everything conspire equally to make me love the contemplative and solitary life I led in that beautiful place. Would that it could come again! Would that I could go and end my days on that beloved island, never leaving it nor seeing again any inhabitants of the mainland who might recall the memory of the calamities of every kind which it has been their pleasure to heap upon me for so many years! They would soon be forgotten for ever; of course they might not similarly forget me, but what could that matter to me, so long as they were kept from troubling my quiet retreat? Set free from all the earthly passions that are born of the tumult of social life, my soul would often soar out of this atmosphere and would converse before its time with the celestial spirits whose number it hopes soon to swell. I know that mankind will never let me return to this happy sanctuary, where they did not allow me to remain. But at least they cannot prevent me from being transported there every day on the wings of imagination and tasting for several hours the same pleasures as if I were still living there. Were I there, my sweetest occupation would be to dream to my heart's content. Is it not the same thing to dream that I am there? Better still, I can add to my abstract and monotonous reveries charming images that give them life. During my moments of ecstasy the sources of these images often escaped my senses; but now, the deeper the reverie, the more vividly they are present to me. I am often more truly in their midst and they give me still greater pleasure than when I was surrounded by them. My misfortune is that as my imagination loses its fire this happens less easily and does not last so long. Alas, it is when we are beginning to leave this mortal body that it most offends us!

Immanuel Kant
1724–1804

Immanuel Kant lived and died quietly in Königsberg, an intellectual and commercial center then in the cold northeast reaches of Prussia and today the Russian city of Kaliningrad. Beginning in his mid-fifties, he published a series of abstract philosophical treatises that transformed conceptions of human existence. Fully aware of the extraordinary nature of his achievement, he himself spoke of a "Copernican revolution in philosophy" in the preface to his *Critique of Pure Reason*. At the start lay the insight that all knowledge is shaped by perception, and consequently all truths of human experience by the forms of consciousness. One consequence, especially in Kant's more emotive followers, was to exalt the mind immeasurably; another was to lay pitiless responsibility for all our actions on rational thought. Kant's rigorous moralism, an extreme form of the biblical Golden Rule, was equally seductive for radical revolutionaries in France (whom he supported) and for conservative apostles of duty like Goethe in Germany and Thomas Carlyle and George Eliot in Victorian England. Nature becomes an eternal model, commanding compliance with its elevated truths and reminding us of the universal values shining through the night of passions and desires that so intrigued Kant's younger contemporaries.

from Critique of Practical Reason[1]

Two things fill the mind with ever new and increasing admiration and awe, the oftener and the more steadily we reflect on them: *the starry heavens above and the moral law within.* I have not to search for them and conjecture them as though they were veiled in darkness or were in the transcendent region beyond my horizon; I see them before me and connect them directly with the consciousness of my existence.[2] The former begins from the place I occupy in the external world of sense, and enlarges my connection therein to an unbounded extent with worlds upon worlds and systems of systems, and moreover into limitless times of their periodic motion, its beginning and continuance. The second begins from my invisible self, my personality, and exhibits me in a world which has true infinity, but which is traceable only by the understanding, and with which I discern that I am not in a merely contingent but in a universal and necessary connection, as I am also thereby with all those visible worlds. The former view of a countless multitude of worlds annihilates, as it were, my importance as an *animal creature,* which after it has been for a short time provided with vital power, one knows not how, must again give back the matter of which it was formed to the planet it inhabits (a mere speck in the universe). The second, on the contrary, infinitely elevates my worth as an *intelligence* by my personality, in which the moral law reveals to me a life independent on animality and even on the whole sensible world—at least so far as may be inferred from the destination assigned to my existence by this law, a destination not restricted to conditions and limits of this life, but reaching into the infinite.

But though admiration and respect may excite to inquiry, they cannot supply the want of it. What, then, is to be done in order to enter on this in a useful manner and one adapted to the loftiness of the subject? Examples may serve in this as a warning, and also for imitation. The contemplation of the world began from the noblest spectacle that the human senses present to us, and that our understanding can bear to follow in their vast reach; and it ended—in astrology. Morality began with the noblest attribute of human nature, the development and cultivation of which give a prospect of infinite utility; and ended—in fanaticism or superstition. So it is with all crude attempts where the principal part of the business depends on the use of reason, a use which does not come of itself, like the use of the feet, by frequent exercise, especially when attributes are in question which cannot be directly exhibited in common experience. But after the maxim had come into vogue, though late, to examine carefully beforehand all the steps that reason purposes to take, and not to let it proceed otherwise than in the track of a previously well-considered method, then the study of the structure of the universe took quite a different direction, and thereby attained an incomparably happier result. The fall of a stone, the motion of a sling, resolved into their elements and the forces that are manifested in them, and treated mathematically, produced at last that clear and henceforward unchangeable insight into the system of the world, which as observation is continued may hope always to extend itself, but need never fear to be compelled to retreat.

---

1. Translated by T. K. Abbott.

2. Kant borrows this phrase from Rousseau's *Fifth Reverie,* published six years earlier.

→ ≍◈≍ ←

William Blake
1757–1827

"When the Sun rises do you not see a round Disk of fire somewhat like a Guinea? O no no, I see an Innumerable company of the Heavenly host crying 'Holy Holy Holy is the Lord God Almighty.' I question not my Corporeal or Vegetative Eye any more than I would Question a Window concerning a Sight. I look through it & not with it." So William Blake, the visionary engraver and poet, commented on his painting of the Last Judgment. A favorite phrase in his mystical epic poems is "He became what he beheld." Sights mesmerized and transported Blake. A uniquely skilled craftsman and a radical thinker never content with religious, political, or sexual orthodoxies, he found the natural world inspiring (as in "The Ecchoing Green," from his "Songs of Innocence") and terrifying (as in "The Tyger," from the "Songs of Experience"). The Tiger's "fearful symmetry" evokes the art of the engraver who arduously incises a steel plate to make a reverse image of the eventual picture; it evokes the exhilarating but frightening correspondence of a powerless man with the vital flux of the universe; and it evokes the almost Kantian sublimity of a supposed constellation that might guide him through the dark night of his labors—or might threaten him under a social regime that he considered unfeeling and repressive. Blake shared with his tamer contemporaries a devotion to the natural world, but he rejected naturalism in favor of his eccentric kind of religious exaltation.

The Ecchoing Green

The Sun does arise,
And make happy the skies.
The merry bells ring
To welcome the Spring.
5   The sky-lark and thrush,
The birds of the bush,
Sing louder around,
To the bells chearful sound
While our sports shall be seen
10   On the Ecchoing Green.

Old John with white hair
Does laugh away care,
Sitting under the oak,
Among the old folk,
15   They laugh at our play,
And soon they all say,
Such such were the joys
When we all girls & boys,
In our youth-time were seen,
20   On the Ecchoing Green.

Till the little ones weary
No more can be merry
The sun does descend,
And our sports have an end:

25 Round the laps of their mothers
   Many sisters and brothers,
   Like birds in their nest,
   Are ready for rest;
   And sport no more seen,
30 On the darkening Green.

The Tyger

Tyger Tyger, burning bright,
In the forests of the night;
What immortal hand or eye,
Could frame thy fearful symmetry?

5 In what distant deeps or skies,
Burnt the fire of thine eyes?
On what wings dare he aspire?[1]
What the hand, dare sieze the fire?

And what shoulder, & what art,
10 Could twist the sinews of thy heart?
And when thy heart began to beat,
What dread hand? & what dread feet?

What the hammer? what the chain,
In what furnace was thy brain?
15 What the anvil? what dread grasp,
Dare its deadly terrors clasp!

When the stars threw down their spears
And water'd heaven with their tears:[2]
Did he smile his work to see?
20 Did he who made the Lamb make thee?[3]

Tyger Tyger burning bright,
In the forests of the night:
What immortal hand or eye,
Dare frame thy fearful symmetry?

John Keats
1795–1821

The short and chubby son of a successful stable-keeper who died before his son was ten, John
Keats spent his life aspiring for recognition from the same classes that the well-born Percy

1. An allusion to Icarus, who, with his father Dedalus,
fashioned wings of feathers and wax to escape from
prison. Icarus became enchanted with flight and, ignoring
his father's cautions, soared too close to the sun; the wax
melted and he fell to his death in the sea.
2. In the war in Heaven, in Book 6 of Milton's *Paradise*

Lost, Satan, rebelling against God's authority, is defeated
by the Son and driven down to Hell. Blake's verb leaves it
undecidable whether the stars "threw down their spears"
in desperate surrender or in defiance.
3. An allusion to Jesus, "The Lamb of God" (John 1:29
and 1:36).

Shelley (a close friend) and Lord Byron rebelled against. Hence Keats goes in for self-display while shunning self-assertion. "A poet . . . has no identity," he writes in one of his eloquent letters, and another praises "*Negative Capability,* that is when man is capable of being in uncertainties, Mysteries, doubts, without an irritable reaching after fact & reason." Via ardent self-suppression he sought the eternal validation of artistic perfection, opening his dream epic *Endymion* with the famous line, "A thing of beauty is a joy forever." His poetry expresses radical humanitarianism that bemoans "where men grow pale and spectre-thin and die," without sacrificing formal rigor and stylistic polish. In his odes he mimics ancient ritual formulas: he addresses the nightingale and autumn like divinities to be approached with the greatest hesitation; he tells their histories, imagines their advent as if a god has descended to earth, prays to them, and absorbs their lessons. While the speaker remains static—contemplating the urn, caught in half-slumber while listening to the nightingale—his negative capability embroiders the encounters with richly imagined scenes, hints of romantic adventure, mythical situations, biblical legend, Virgilian pastoral, Miltonic paradise. No other poet so densely sums up both the pagan and the Christian cultural heritage in such intricately ornamented small poems. Jointly obsessed with mortality and with eternity, Keats seems destined to have endured the tragic death he suffered from tuberculosis at the age of twenty-five.

Ode to a Nightingale[1]

1

My heart aches, and a drowsy numbness pains
    My sense, as though of hemlock I had drunk,
Or emptied some dull opiate to the drains
    One minute past, and Lethe-wards had sunk:[2]
5   'Tis not through envy of thy happy lot,
      But being too happy in thine happiness,—
        That thou, light-winged Dryad° of the trees,   *wood-nymph*
          In some melodious plot
    Of beechen green, and shadows numberless,
10   Singest of summer in full-throated ease.

2

O, for a draught of vintage!° that hath been   *wine*
    Cool'd a long age in the deep-delved° earth,   *dug*
Tasting of Flora° and the country green,   *goddess of flowers*
    Dance, and Provençal[3] song, and sunburnt mirth!
15   O for a beaker full of the warm South,
      Full of the true, the blushful Hippocrene,[4]
        With beaded bubbles winking at the brim,
          And purple-stained mouth;
    That I might drink, and leave the world unseen,[5]
20   And with thee fade away into the forest dim:

3

Fade far away, dissolve, and quite forget

---

1. In Greek legend Philomela had been raped by her brother-in-law Tereus, who cut out her tongue to ensure her silence. After she revealed the crime by weaving the story into a robe, the gods changed her into a nightingale.
2. Hemlock (extracted from a flowering plant unrelated to the North American tree) is a sedative; in large doses, such as Socrates', it is fatal; an opiate is any sense-duller, particularly opium, widely used as a painkiller; Lethe is the mythic river of the underworld whose waters produce forgetfulness of previous life.
3. Provence is a region in southern France famed for troubadours.
4. The fountain of the muses on Mount Helicon.
5. "Unseen" can modify both "I" and "world."

What thou among the leaves hast never known,
   The weariness, the fever, and the fret
Here, where men sit and hear each other groan;
25   Where palsy shakes a few, sad, last gray hairs,
      Where youth grows pale, and spectre-thin, and dies;
        Where but to think is to be full of sorrow
          And leaden-eyed despairs,
     Where Beauty cannot keep her lustrous eyes,
30   Or new Love pine at them beyond to-morrow.

4

Away! away! for I will fly to thee,
   Not charioted by Bacchus and his pards,[6]
But on the viewless wings of Poesy,
   Though the dull brain perplexes and retards:
35   Already with thee! tender is the night,

      And haply° the Queen-Moon is on her throne,   *happily, perhaps*
        Cluster'd around by all her starry Fays;°   *fairies*
          But here there is no light,
     Save what from heaven is with the breezes blown
40   Through verdurous glooms and winding mossy ways.

5

I cannot see what flowers are at my feet,
   Nor what soft incense hangs upon the boughs,
But, in embalmed darkness, guess each sweet
   Wherewith the seasonable month endows
45   The grass, the thicket, and the fruit-tree wild;
      White hawthorn, and the pastoral eglantine;
        Fast fading violets cover'd up in leaves;
          And mid-May's eldest child,
     The coming musk-rose, full of dewy wine,
50   The murmurous haunt of flies on summer eves.

6

Darkling° I listen; and, for many a time   *in the dark*
   I have been half in love with easeful Death,
Call'd him soft names in many a mused rhyme,
   To take into the air my quiet breath;
55   Now more than ever seems it rich to die,
      To cease upon the midnight with no pain,
        While thou art pouring forth thy soul abroad
          In such an ecstasy!
     Still wouldst thou sing, and I have ears in vain—
60   To thy high requiem° become a sod.   *funeral mass*

7

Thou wast not born for death, immortal Bird!
   No hungry generations tread thee down;
The voice I hear this passing night was heard

---

6. Bacchus, god of wine and revelry, whose chariot is drawn by leopards.

In ancient days by emperor and clown:°   *rustic, peasant*

65   Perhaps the self-same song that found a path

      Through the sad heart of Ruth, when, sick for home,

        She stood in tears amid the alien corn;[7]

          The same that oft-times hath

      Charm'd magic casements, opening on the foam

70   Of perilous seas, in faery lands forlorn.

              8

Forlorn! the very word is like a bell

      To toll me back from thee to my sole self!

Adieu! the fancy cannot cheat so well

      As she is fam'd to do, deceiving elf.

75   Adieu! adieu! thy plaintive anthem fades

      Past the near meadows, over the still stream,

        Up the hill-side; and now 'tis buried deep

          In the next valley-glades:

      Was it a vision, or a waking dream?

80   Fled is that music:—Do I wake or sleep?

To Autumn[1]

        1

Season of mists and mellow fruitfulness,

      Close bosom-friend of the maturing sun;

Conspiring with him how to load and bless

      With fruit the vines that round the thatch-eaves[2] run;

5   To bend with apples the moss'd cottage-trees,

      And fill all fruit with ripeness to the core;

        To swell the gourd, and plump the hazel shells

With a sweet kernel; to set budding more,

      And still more, later flowers for the bees,

10   Until they think warm days will never cease,

        For Summer has o'er-brimm'd their clammy cells.

        2

Who hath not seen thee oft amid thy store?

      Sometimes whoever seeks abroad may find

Thee sitting careless on a granary floor,

15   Thy hair soft-lifted by the winnowing wind;

Or on a half-reap'd furrow sound asleep,

      Drows'd with the fume of poppies while thy hook°   *scythe*

        Spares the next swath and all its twined flowers:

And sometimes like a gleaner thou dost keep

20   Steady thy laden head across a brook;

---

7. See Ruth 1–2: compelled by famine to leave her home, Ruth eked out a living as a gleaner in faraway fields.
1. Composed 19–21 September 1819 in Winchester, a tranquil town in southern England, from which Keats wrote to a friend: "How beautiful the season is now— How fine the air. A temperate sharpness about it. . . . I never lik'd stubble fields so much as now—Aye better than the chilly green of the spring. Somehow a stubble plain looks warm—in the same way that some pictures look warm—this struck me so much in my sunday's walk that I composed upon it."
2. The eaves of thatched cottage roofs.

> Or by a cyder-press, with patient look,
>   Thou watchest the last oozings hours by hours.
>
>   3
>
> Where are the songs of Spring? Ay, where are they?
>   Think not of them, thou hast thy music too,—
> 25 While barred clouds bloom the soft-dying day,
>   And touch the stubble-plains with rosy hue;
> Then in a wailful choir the small gnats mourn
>   Among the river sallows,[3] borne aloft
>   Or sinking as the light wind lives or dies;
> 30 And full-grown lambs loud bleat from hilly bourn;°   *boundary, region*
>   Hedge-crickets sing; and now with treble soft°   *faint high pitch*
>   The red-breast whistles from a garden-croft;°   *enclosure*
>   And gathering swallows twitter in the skies.

Annette von Droste-Hülshoff
1797–1848

German artists tended to feel marginal in the first half of the nineteenth century, and none more so than Annette von Droste-Hülshoff. The unmarried daughter of declining nobility, she cared for her widowed mother and other ailing family members, though she herself was often in ill health. Her mother selected appropriate contacts for her lively daughter and only grudgingly allowed her first collection of poems to appear in 1838. As a female Catholic kept cloistered by her aristocratic relatives, Droste suffered more than the usual ambivalence in relationships with intellectuals of her generation, mostly Protestant bourgeois. Nevertheless, her poems commanded immediate respect and lasting fame. A larger collected edition appeared in 1844; Robert Schumann asked her for an opera libretto in the following year. She has remained the most honored woman poet of the century from Continental Europe. Unusually well educated in both music and natural history, Droste combines precise realistic detail with a compelling need to overcome the boundaries of individuality. Her speakers suffer from the limitation of their senses and point of view; they long to move from the margins to the centers of being that had become so inaccessible for late Romantics.

PRONUNCIATION:
   Annette von Droste-Hülshoff: ahn-NET-tuh fon DRO-stuh HILZ-hoff

The Heath-Man[1]

> "Go children, shun the quarry's depths,
> The sun is setting, weaker hums
> The bee's flight now, befogged in sleep,
> An ashen cloth floats on the deep,
> 5 The heath-man comes."
>
> Along the bank the boys play on,
> They pluck at grass stems, skip a stone,
> They paddle at the water's edge,

---

3. Willows (an emblem of death).   1. Translated by Jane K. Brown.

Catch dragon flies above the bog
10   And watch with joy the water spinner
Long-legged flee into the sedge.

"You children, don't lie in the grass!—
Look, where just now the bee flew past,
How steaming mist engulfs the bells.
15   The hare peers shyly from the bush,
The heath-man swells!"

The reed scarce lifts its heavy head
Above the fog, the beetle sneaks
Into its hole, and on the stalk
20   The torpid moth yet higher creeps,
To flee before the humid smoke
That rises underneath its wings.

"You children, stay here close to home!
Don't go beyond the quarry's edge;
25   See how grey the thornbush grows,
The song thrush groans upon its nest,
The heath-man brews!"—

You see the herdsman's pipe now glowing,
Ahead of him his herd is flowing,
30   As Proteus² homeward drives his flock
Of seals across the greying waves.
The swallows twitter round the eaves,
And melancholy crows the cock.

"You children, stay close by the house!
35   See how the damp flat band of mist
About the garden gate-latch twines;
A false light floats now in the depths,
The heath-man climbs!"—

Now just the pine trees' highest tips
40   Protrude green summits from the mist,
Like junipers above the snow;
A gentle bubbling swells the moor,
A feeble whine, a sighing hiss
From out the hollow surges forth.

45   "You children, come, come quickly in!
The Jack-o'-lantern lights his lamp,
The toad puffs up, snake in the fen;
It's eerie now to be abroad,
The heath-man walks!"—

50   The topmost needle sinks, the spruce
Dissolves in smoke, the fog-sprites come,

2. A subject or son of Poseidon, god of the sea.

Upwelling slowly from the moor,
Then glide away on giant limbs;
A mad light flickers in the sedge,
55   The toads strike up at water's edge.

And now a feeble glowing seems
To penetrate the giant's limbs;
It boils up, it tints the waves,
The north, the north bursts into flame—
60   Arrows burning, fire-spears fly,
Horizon all a lava stream!

"God save us! how it flares and booms,
And sulphur burns atop the dunes!
You children, fold your hands and pray,
65   That brings us plague and troubled times—
The heath-man's ablaze!"

In the Grass

Sweet repose, sweet reeling in grass,
Enveloped in fragrance of green,
Deep stream, deep deep drunken stream,
When the cloud dissolves in the blue,
5   When on my tired, swimming head
Sweetly laughter flutters down,
Dear voice murmurs, and trickles
Down like linden blooms onto a grave.

When in the breast the dead ones then,
10   Every corpse stretches and stirs,
Quietly, quietly draws its breath,
Moves its tight-drawn lashes,
Dead love, dead joy, dead time,
All the treasures, immured in the dust
15   Touch one another, timidly sounding,
As tiny bells wave in the breeze.

Hours, more fleeting are you than the kiss
Of a beam on the sorrowing lake,
Than the song of the passing bird,
20   That drops like dew from the heights,
Than the glittering beetle's flash,
As it hastes through the sun's path,
Than the ardent clasp of a hand
As it lingers a final time.

25   Yet, o heaven, this alone
Ever for me: for the song
Of each bird free in the sky
Please, a soul, to fly with him,

But for each scanty beam
30   This my iridescent hem,
For each warm hand my clasp,
And for every joy my dream.

+⌗⬩⌗+

Giacomo Leopardi
1798–1837

In his elegy *In Memoriam* (1850), Tennyson wrote of "Nature, red in tooth and claw." Charles Darwin studied the struggle for existence and the survival of the fittest. "Spring" welcomed Thoreau with a dead horse emerging from beneath the ice. But none of these individuals—nor even his predecessor Byron—matched Giacomo Leopardi for powerful gloom. Cursed with a penetrating intellect and sensibility, a loveless upbringing, miserable health, and poverty, Leopardi had all the makings of what he became, one of the century's greatest pessimists. He is said to have been capable of good cheer, though when he desired like many other Romantics to share the joy of the birds (as his mordant philosophical dialogue says), it was partly because "they are equally adapted to tolerating extremes of cold and of heat." Better a bird than an Icelander, at all events. If his nature is grim, however, it is also sublime, and he expresses a respect for natural forces as compellingly as anyone in his century. It is a sign of his importance that "The ages that are dead" of "The Infinite" form a link between Dante's *Inferno* and Eliot's *Waste Land*.

PRONUNCIATION:
Giacomo Leopardi: JAH-co-mo lay-o-PAR-dee

The Infinite[1]

This lonely hill was always dear to me,
And this hedgerow, that hides so large a part
Of the far sky-line from my view. Sitting and gazing,
I fashion in my mind what lie beyond—
5   Unearthly silences, and endless space,
And very deepest quiet; then for a while
The heart is not afraid. And when I hear
The wind come blustering among the trees
I set that voice against this infinite silence:
10   And then I call to mind Eternity,
The ages that are dead, and the living present
And all the noise of it. And thus it is
In that immensity my thought is drowned:
And sweet to me the foundering in that sea.

Dialogue Between Nature and an Icelander

An Icelander, who had traveled over a great part of the world and had lived in many different lands, was wandering in the heart of Africa. As he was crossing the Equator, in a place no man had ever visited before, something befell him that resembled what

---

1. Translated by Iris Origo & John Heath-Stubbs.

happened to Vasco da Gama as he was sailing round the Cape of Good Hope, when he saw that very Cape, the keeper of the Southern Seas, coming toward him in the form of a giant, to dissuade him from entering those unknown waters. The Icelander saw in the distance a very large bust, which at first he believed to be of stone, like the colossal figures he had seen many years before on Easter Island.[1] But as he came closer, he discovered that it was a great figure of a woman, sitting erect on the ground, with her back and elbow resting against a mountain. It was no statue but a living woman, with a countenance both beautiful and terrible, and very black eyes and hair. She gazed at him intently, in silence, for some time, and at last she said:

NATURE: Who are you? and what do you seek in these lands where your race is unknown?

ICELANDER: I am a poor Icelander, who is attempting to run away from Nature; and having fled from her for almost all my life, in a hundred different regions of the earth, I am now attempting to escape from her here.

NATURE: So does the squirrel fly from the rattlesnake, until it falls into the snake's jaws of its own accord. I am she from whom you are trying to escape.

ICELANDER: Nature?

NATURE: None other.

ICELANDER: This grieves me to the heart; I am certain that no greater misfortune than this could overtake me.

NATURE: You might have considered that I was likely to dwell in these parts, where you must know that my power is more felt than elsewhere. But what was it that made you run away from me?

ICELANDER: You must know that in my early youth a very short experience of life sufficed to persuade me of its vanity and of the folly of men, who are constantly at war with each other for the sake of pleasures, which bring no delight, and possessions, which give no profit, and who endure and inflict upon each other innumerable anxieties and evils, which both distress and injure them. And the further they are from happiness, the more they seek it. For these reasons, having renounced all other desires, I decided to live an obscure and peaceful life, without causing any trouble to anyone, or attempting in any way to better my condition, or contending with other men for any earthly good. And having given up all hope of pleasure, as a thing denied to our race, I had no other aim than the avoidance of suffering. I do not mean that I intended to abstain from every occupation or from physical toil; for you well know that fatigue is as unlike discomfort, as tranquillity is unlike idleness. But hardly had I begun to put this resolve into practice than I at once discovered by experience how vain it is, if one lives among one's fellows, to believe it possible that by causing no suffering to others, one can avoid being injured oneself; or that even if one always gives way to other men, and is content with the least of everything, even that small respite or amount will not be denied to one. But I easily freed myself from the nuisance of other people by leaving their company and taking refuge in solitude—a thing that can easily be obtained on my native island.

Having taken this step, and leading a life that lacked even a mirage of pleasure, I yet found that I could not avoid suffering; for the length of the winter, with its intense cold, and the extreme heat of the summer, which are characteristic of that region, were constantly tormenting me. And the fire, close to which I was

---

1. An island in the South Pacific famous for its many huge stone carvings.

obliged to spend most of my time, parched my flesh, while its smoke hurt my eyes, so that I could not preserve myself from continual discomfort either indoors or out. Nor could I preserve the tranquillity toward which all my wishes were directed, since fearful storms, both from land and sea, the rumblings and threatenings of Mount Hecla, and the dread of fires—very common in wooden houses like ours— never ceased to trouble me. Such discomforts as these, in a monotonous life that had no other desire or hope and hardly any other preoccupation than to achieve tranquillity, acquire a considerable importance, and seem much more weighty than they would be if the greater part of one's mind were occupied with the cares of civilized life or the troubles caused by other men.

Having thus observed that the more I withdrew and almost shrank within myself, so that my existence should neither cause trouble nor injury to anything in the world, the less could I prevent other things from disquieting and troubling me, I decided to try a change of country and of climate, and see if there was any part of the world where, if I gave no offense, I would not be offended, and where, if I could not find enjoyment, I would avoid suffering. And I also reached this decision owing to an idea that perhaps you had allotted to the human race only a single climate and certain regions of the earth (as you have done for all other kinds of animals and plants) and that beyond this region men could not prosper or even live, save with a difficulty and wretchedness that should not be imputed to you, but only to themselves, for having disregarded and gone beyond the boundaries that your laws have laid down for human habitation.

I searched through almost the whole world and became acquainted with almost every country, always keeping to my resolve of not causing any injury, or as little as possible, to any other creature, and only seeking a peaceful life. But I have been scorched with heat in the tropics, benumbed with cold at the poles, afflicted in temperate climates by the changeableness of the weather, and shaken everywhere by the violence of the elements. I have seen many places in which no day passes without a storm, which is the same as to say that every day you assault and attack the men who live there and who have never done you any harm. In other places the habitual serenity of the sky is balanced by the frequency of earthquakes and the number and violence of volcanoes or subterranean commotions; while winds and furious hurricanes prevail in regions free from other forms of violence. Sometimes I have felt the roof giving way over my head beneath a great weight of snow. Sometimes, owing to an excess of rain, I have been obliged to run away at full speed from streams pursuing me, as if I had done them some injury. Many wild beasts, to whom I had not given the least provocation, have tried to devour me, many snakes to poison me; and in several places flying insects came close to stripping my very bones. I will not enumerate the daily perils by which a man is threatened every day; so that an ancient philosopher could find no better prescription against fear, than the observation that everything should equally be feared. Disease, too, has not spared me, even though I always have been and still am, not only temperate but continent with regard to physical pleasures.

I often greatly wonder that you should have instilled into us such a strong and insatiable craving for pleasure, without which our life, being deprived of its most natural desire, is an imperfect thing; and that, on the other hand, you should have ordained that the enjoyment of such pleasures should be the most harmful of all things human to our physical health and strength, the most calamitous in its general effects, and the most pernicious to the length of life itself. But even though I have almost always and completely abstained from every pleasure, I have not been able to avoid many and various diseases, some of which have threatened my life, and others the loss of a limb, or have offered the prospect of perpetually living a life even more wretched than before; and all of them have oppressed me, body and soul, with a thousand hardships and sufferings. Certainly, though each one of us discovers, in times of illness, new and unfamiliar evils and an even greater unhappiness than usual (as if human life were not already sufficiently wretched), you have not granted to us, in compensation, periods of great and exceptional good health, which might afford us some delights, extraordinary both in their nature and intensity. In regions that mostly lie beneath the snow, I have nearly been blinded, as often happens to the Laplanders in their own country. Sun and air—elements that are vital and necessary to our life and therefore cannot be shunned—constantly injure us, the one by its heat and even its light, the other by its dampness or cold; so that a man can never be exposed to the one or the other without some major or minor inconvenience.

In short, I do not recollect having spent a single day of my life without some form of suffering, while I cannot even count those which have gone by without a trace of enjoyment. Therefore I perceive that suffering is as unavoidable and necessary for us as the lack of pleasure, and that a peaceful life, of any kind, is as impossible as an unquiet one without wretchedness. And thus I have reached the conclusion that you are the avowed enemy of mankind and of all other animals and even of your own works, for now you ensnare us, now threaten us, now attack us, now sting us, now smite us, now tear us to pieces, and always both insult and persecute us. By habit and by destiny you are the destroyer of your own family, your children, your own flesh and blood. Therefore I have ceased to hope, having realized that while men may cease to persecute those who fly or hide from them owing to a real wish for escape or obscurity, you, for no reason whatever, will never cease to pursue us until we are completely laid low. And I already see the approach of the sad and bitter years of old age: a true and evident evil, or rather, an accumulation of all the most burdensome evils and troubles—and these, too, are not accidental, but are planned and ordered by you to be the fate of all living creatures. All this each one of us foresees from the time of his childhood, and begins to prepare himself for from his twenty-fifth year, as he observes the gradual process, through no fault of his own, of decay and loss; so that barely one third of the life of man is given up to an early flowering, a few moments only to maturity and perfection, and all the rest to decline and the evils that it brings.

NATURE: But did you think that the world was made for your sake? You must have known that in my works, my laws, and my operations, with a very few exceptions, I have always been ruled, as I am now, by considerations that have little to do with the happiness or unhappiness of mankind. When I injure you in any way or by any means, I very seldom am aware of it, as I also usually do not know when I am giving you some delight or benefit. And I do not do certain things or perform certain actions, as you believe, for either your pleasure or your profit. And finally, if I should happen to destroy all of mankind, I would do so unawares.

ICELANDER: Let us suppose that a man invited me of his own accord and very pressingly to his country house, and that I, to please him, accepted. And suppose I were given a crumbling and ruined cell to dwell in, where I was in perpetual danger of being crushed, and which was damp, stinking, and open to wind and rain. Imagine that he took no trouble to entertain me or to make me comfortable, but scarcely furnished me with enough food to keep me alive, and that in addition he permitted his sons and household to insult, mock, threaten, and beat me. If I complained to him of this ill-treatment, and he were to answer: "Did I build this house for you? Do I keep my children and household for your service? I have other things to think about than your amusements and your comfort." To this I would reply: "My friend, just as you did not build your house for my use, so it was in your power not to invite me to dwell there. But since it was you who wished me to come, was it not your part to arrange, in so far as you could, for me to live there without suffering and danger?" So I say now. I well know that you have not created the world for the service of men. I am more inclined to believe that you created and ordered it for the express purpose of treating them ill. But now I ask you: Did I request you to bring me into the world? Or did I intrude into it violently, against your will? If you yourself put me there with your own hands, by your own desire, and without my knowledge, and in such a manner that I could neither refuse nor resist, is it not your duty, if not to keep me happy and contented within this kingdom of yours, at least to forbid that I should be tormented and molested, and to see that my dwelling there should do me no harm? And I say this not only for myself but on behalf of the whole human race and all other animals and living creatures.

NATURE: You plainly show that you have not realized that the life of the universe is a perpetual circle of production and destruction, each of which is linked to the other in such a way that each constantly serves the other. And this cycle is necessary to conserve the existence of the world, for if either of these elements should fail, the world would swiftly be dissolved. Thus, if anything within the world were free from suffering, the world itself would be harmed.

ICELANDER: All philosophers, I am told, reason like this. But since that which is destroyed suffers, and that which destroys derives no pleasure and is in turn destroyed itself, tell me what no philosopher can: for whose pleasure or use is this most unhappy life of the universe preserved, at the expense of the suffering and death of all the things composing it?

While they were engaged in these discussions and others of the same kind, it is said that two lions appeared. They were so thin and so worn out by hunger that they hardly had the strength to devour the Icelander; but they did; and, having recovered a little, kept themselves alive for another day.

But there are some people who deny this tale and say instead that a very violent wind, which rose up while the Icelander was speaking, cast him to the ground and piled above him a splendid mausoleum of sand, beneath which he was completely dried up and turned into a fine mummy. He was then discovered by some travelers and placed in the museum of a European city, I know not which.

—◄◆►—

Ralph Waldo Emerson
1803–1882

"A man is a bundle of relations, a knot of roots, whose flower and fruitage is the world. His faculties refer to natures out of him and predict the world he is to inhabit, as the fins of the fish foreshow that water exists, or the wings of an eagle in the egg presupposed air." "A foolish consistency is a hobgoblin of little minds." No writer of the century—not even Thoreau or Nietzsche—coined such resonant phrases as did Ralph Waldo Emerson. A survivor from a large, sickly family, drawing on a peaceable constitution, an iron will, and a powerful voice, he made himself into his country's greatest spokesperson for personal integrity and imaginative vision. Emerson began his career working himself emotionally and economically free from a vocation in the Unitarian Church, transformed himself from a successful if free-spirited preacher into a thrilling public speaker, and eventually (though not early on) became one of the most insistent and admired proponents of abolition. He didn't write books, but he did publish his lectures. He called the best-known ones "essays," reviving a term coined for the personal ruminations of Michel de Montaigne and the moral exhortations of Francis Bacon. But Emerson's essays (and also the early, independent pamphlet entitled "Nature") are not so much confessional documents as what Coleridge called lay sermons. He rejected aspects of organized religion, but really only to replace it with a religion of nature and of the human spirit.

   Est deus in nobis, "There is a god in us," is an ancient pagan saying, one of the many moments of Virgil's *Eclogues* that has haunted the European imagination for millennia. Emerson, equally immersed in the Bible and the Greek and Roman classics, updates it into the world of science and modern government. He is capable of alluding deftly to the most abstruse philosophical doctrines—such as Hume's and Kant's attacks on the reality of the external world or of "things in themselves"—and of turning them into soaring affirmations of the vitality of lived experience: "Whether nature enjoy a substantial existence without, or is only in the apocalypse of the mind, it is alike useful and alike venerable to me." "Useful" is the most striking word here, evoking what the second section of "Nature" calls "Commodity," the conspiracy ("breathing together") of all things toward the common good. His so-called Transcendentalism is the ringing voice of optimism we need when we've read too much of the old-worldly Leopardi, even as Leopardi's world-weary humility corrects for the utopian buoyancy emerging from a small town in the New World.

from Nature

CHAPTER I

To go into solitude, a man needs to retire as much from his chamber as from society. I am not solitary whilst I read and write, though nobody is with me. But if a man would be alone, let him look at the stars. The rays that come from those heavenly worlds, will separate between him and vulgar things. One might think the atmosphere was made transparent with this design, to give man, in the heavenly bodies, the perpetual presence of the sublime. Seen in the streets of cities, how great they are! If the stars should appear one night in a thousand years, how would men believe and adore; and preserve for many generations the remembrance of the city of God which had been shown! But every night come out these preachers of beauty, and light the universe with their admonishing smile.

   The stars awaken a certain reverence, because though always present, they are always inaccessible; but all natural objects make a kindred impression, when the mind is open to their influence. Nature never wears a mean appearance. Neither does the wisest man extort all her secret, and lose his curiosity by finding out all her perfection. Nature never became a toy to a wise spirit. The flowers, the animals, the mountains, reflected all the wisdom of his best hour, as much as they had delighted the simplicity of his childhood.

   When we speak of nature in this manner, we have a distinct but most poetical sense in the mind. We mean the integrity of impression made by manifold natural objects. It is this which distinguishes the stick of timber of the wood-cutter, from the tree of the poet. The charming landscape which I saw this morning, is indubitably made up of some twenty or thirty farms. Miller owns this field, Locke that, and Manning the woodland beyond. But none of them owns the landscape. There is a property in the horizon which no man has but he whose eye can integrate all the parts, that is, the poet. This is the best part of these men's farms, yet to this their land-deeds give them no title.

To speak truly, few adult persons can see nature. Most persons do not see the sun. At least they have a very superficial seeing. The sun illuminates only the eye of the man, but shines into the eye and the heart of the child. The lover of nature is he whose inward and outward senses are still truly adjusted to each other; who has retained the spirit of infancy even into the era of manhood. His intercourse with heaven and earth, becomes part of his daily food. In the presence of nature, a wild delight runs through the man, in spite of real sorrows. Nature says,—he is my creature, and maugre[1] all his impertinent griefs, he shall be glad with me. Not the sun or the summer alone, but every hour and season yields its tribute of delight; for every hour and change corresponds to and authorizes a different state of the mind, from breathless noon to grimmest midnight. Nature is a setting that fits equally well a comic or a mourning piece. In good health, the air is a cordial of incredible virtue. Crossing a bare common, in snow puddles, at twilight, under a clouded sky, without having in my thoughts any occurrence of special good fortune, I have enjoyed a perfect exhilaration. Almost I fear to think how glad I am. In the woods too, a man casts off his years, as the snake his slough, and at what period soever of life, is always a child. In the woods, is perpetual youth. Within these plantations of God, a decorum and sanctity reign, a perennial festival is dressed, and the guest sees not how he should tire of them in a thousand years. In the woods, we return to reason and faith. There I feel that nothing can befal me in life,—no disgrace, no calamity, (leaving me my eyes,) which nature cannot repair. Standing on the bare ground,—my head bathed by the blithe air, and uplifted into infinite space,—all mean egotism vanishes. I become a transparent eye-ball. I am nothing. I see all. The currents of the Universal Being circulate through me; I am part or particle of God. The name of the nearest friend sounds then foreign and accidental. To be brothers, to be acquaintances,—master or servant, is then a trifle and a disturbance. I am the lover of uncontained and immortal beauty. In the wilderness, I find something more dear and connate than in streets or villages. In the tranquil landscape, and especially in the distant line of the horizon, man beholds somewhat as beautiful as his own nature.

The greatest delight which the fields and woods minister, is the suggestion of an occult relation between man and the vegetable. I am not alone and unacknowledged. They nod to me and I to them. The waving of the boughs in the storm, is new to me and old. It takes me by surprise, and yet is not unknown. Its effect is like that of a higher thought or a better emotion coming over me, when I deemed I was thinking justly or doing right.

Yet it is certain that the power to produce this delight, does not reside in nature, but in man, or in a harmony of both. It is necessary to use these pleasures with great temperance. For, nature is not always tricked[2] in holiday attire, but the same scene which yesterday breathed perfume and glittered as for the frolic of the nymphs, is overspread with melancholy today. Nature always wears the colors of the spirit. To a man laboring under calamity, the heat of his own fire hath sadness in it. Then, there is a kind of contempt of the landscape felt by him who has just lost by death a dear friend. The sky is less grand as it shuts down over less worth in the population.

---

1. Despite.   2. Decked out.

from Self-Reliance

A foolish consistency is the hobgoblin of little minds, adored by little statesmen and philosophers and divines. With consistency a great soul has simply nothing to do. He may as well concern himself with his shadow on the wall. Speak what you think now in hard words and to-morrow speak what to-morrow thinks in hard words again, though it contradict every thing you said to-day.—"Ah, so you shall be sure to be misunderstood."—Is it so bad then to be misunderstood? Pythagoras was misunderstood, and Socrates, and Jesus, and Luther, and Copernicus, and Galileo, and Newton, and every pure and wise spirit that ever took flesh. To be great is to be misunderstood.

I suppose no man can violate his nature. All the sallies of his will are rounded in by the law of his being, as the inequalities of Andes and Himmaleh[1] are insignificant in the curve of the sphere. Nor does it matter how you gauge and try him. A character is like an acrostic[2] or Alexandrian stanza; read it forward, backward, or across, it still spells the same thing. In this pleasing contrite wood-life[3] which God allows me, let me record day by day my honest thought without prospect or retrospect, and, I cannot doubt, it will be found symmetrical, though I mean it not and see it not. My book should smell of pines and resound with the hum of insects. The swallow over my window should interweave that thread or straw he carries in his bill into my web also. We pass for what we are. Character teaches above our wills. Men imagine that they communicate their virtue or vice only by overt actions, and do not see that virtue or vice emit a breath every moment.

There will be an agreement in whatever variety of actions, so they be each honest and natural in their hour. For of one will, the actions will be harmonious, however unlike they seem. These varieties are lost sight of at a little distance, at a little height of thought. One tendency unites them all. The voyage of the best ship is a zigzag line of a hundred tacks. See the line from a sufficient distance, and it straightens itself to the average tendency. Your genuine action will explain itself and will explain your other genuine actions. Your conformity explains nothing. Act singly, and what you have already done singly will justify you now. Greatness appeals to the future. If I can be firm enough to-day to do right and scorn eyes, I must have done so much right before as to defend me now. Be it how it will, do right now. Always scorn appearances and you always may. The force of character is cumulative. All the foregone days of virtue work their health into this. What makes the majesty of the heroes of the senate and the field, which so fills the imagination? The consciousness of a train of great days and victories behind. They shed a united light on the advancing actor. He is attended as by a visible escort of angels. That is it which throws thunder into Chatham's[4] voice, and dignity into Washington's port,[5] and America into Adams's eye. Honor is venerable to us because it is no ephemera.[6] It is always ancient virtue. We worship it to-day because it is not of to-day. We love it and pay it homage because it is not a trap for our love and homage, but is self-dependent, self-derived, and therefore of an old immaculate pedigree, even if shown in a young person.

---

1. Himalayas.
2. A poem in which the first letters of the lines spell a word or phrase. Alexandrian stanza refers to the so-called "shape poems" written in Greek in ancient Alexandria (and imitated by Renaissance poets); by using lines of various length, the poets and scribes gave these poems the recognizable outline of a familiar object such as (the best-known example) an altar.
3. Retreat, hermitage.
4. William Pitt, Earl of Chatham (1708–1788), a famous orator and wartime leader.
5. Bearing, deportment.
6. Momentary phenomenon.

I hope in these days we have heard the last of conformity and consistency. Let the words be gazetted[7] and ridiculous henceforward. Instead of the gong for dinner, let us hear a whistle from the Spartan fife.[8] Let us never bow and apologize more. A great man is coming to eat at my house. I do not wish to please him; I wish that he should wish to please me. I will stand here for humanity, and though I would make it kind, I would make it true. Let us affront and reprimand the smooth mediocrity and squalid contentment of the times, and hurl in the face of custom and trade and office, the fact which is the upshot of all history, that there is a great responsible Thinker and Actor working wherever a man works; that a true man belongs to no other time or place, but is the centre of things. Where he is, there is nature. He measures you and all men and all events. Ordinarily every body in society reminds us of somewhat else, or of some other person. Character, reality, reminds you of nothing else; it takes place of the whole creation. The man must be so much that he must make all circumstances indifferent. Every true man is a cause, a country, and an age; requires infinite spaces and numbers and time fully to accomplish his design; and posterity seem to follow his steps as a train of clients. A man Cæsar is born, and for ages after we have a Roman Empire. Christ is born, and millions of minds so grow and cleave to his genius that he is confounded with virtue[9] and the possible of man. An institution is the lengthened shadow of one man; as, Monachism, of the Hermit Antony; the Reformation, of Luther; Quakerism, of Fox; Methodism, of Wesley; Abolition, of Clarkson.[1] Scipio,[2] Milton called "the height of Rome"; and all history resolves itself very easily into the biography of a few stout and earnest persons.

Let a man then know his worth, and keep things under his feet. Let him not peep or steal, or skulk up and down with the air of a charity-boy, a bastard, or an interloper in the world which exists for him. But the man in the street, finding no worth in himself which corresponds to the force which built a tower or sculptured a marble god, feels poor when he looks on these. To him a palace, a statue, or a costly book have an alien and forbidding air, much like a gay equipage, and seem to say like that, "Who are you, Sir?" Yet they all are his, suitors for his notice, petitioners to his faculties that they will come out and take possession. The picture waits for my verdict; it is not to command me, but I am to settle its claims to praise. That popular fable of the sot who was picked up dead-drunk in the street, carried to the duke's house, washed and dressed and laid in the duke's bed, and, on his waking, treated with all obsequious ceremony like the duke, and assured that he had been insane,[3] owes its popularity to the fact that it symbolizes so well the state of man, who is in the world a sort of sot, but now and then wakes up, exercises his reason and finds himself a true prince.

Our reading is mendicant and sycophantic.[4] In history our imagination plays us false. Kingdom and lordship, power and estate, are a gaudier vocabulary than private John and Edward in a small house and common day's work; but the things of life are the same to both; the sum total of both is the same. Why all this deference to Alfred and Scanderbeg and Gustavus?[5] Suppose they were virtuous; did they wear out

---

7. Exposed by publication in the newspaper.
8. Ancient Sparta based its military superiority on severe discipline and frugality.
9. Confused with virtue itself, as if every human possibility were contained within him.
1. St. Anthony (251?–350), the father of monastic discipline; George Fox (1624–1691), John Wesley (1703–1791), founders of the Quaker and Methodist sects; Thomas

Clarkson (1760–1846), British antislavery campaigner.
2. Roman general (236–183 B.C.E.) who defeated the Africans under Hannibal, praised in *Paradise Lost* 9.510.
3. The "popular fable" is enacted in the opening scenes of Shakespeare's *Taming of the Shrew*.
4. Begging and servile.
5. Scanderbeg (c. 1404–1468), Albanian national hero; Gustavus Adolphus (1594–1632), Swedish king and hero.

virtue? As great a stake depends on your private act to-day as followed their public and renowned steps. When private men shall act with original views, the lustre will be transferred from the actions of kings to those of gentlemen.

The world has been instructed by its kings, who have so magnetized the eyes of nations. It has been taught by this colossal symbol the mutual reverence that is due from man to man. The joyful loyalty with which men have everywhere suffered the king, the noble, or the great proprietor to walk among them by a law of his own, make his own scale of men and things and reverse theirs, pay for benefits not with money but with honor, and represent the law in his person, was the hieroglyphic[6] by which they obscurely signified their consciousness of their own right and comeliness, the right of every man.

The magnetism which all original action exerts is explained when we inquire the reason of self-trust. Who is the Trustee? What is the aboriginal Self, on which a universal reliance may be grounded? What is the nature and power of that science-baffling star, without parallax,[7] without calculable elements, which shoots a ray of beauty even into trivial and impure actions, if the least mark of independence appear? The inquiry leads us to that source, at once the essence of genius, of virtue, and of life, which we call Spontaneity or Instinct. We denote this primary wisdom as Intuition, whilst all later teachings are tuitions. In that deep force, the last fact behind which analysis cannot go, all things find their common origin. For the sense of being which in calm hours rises, we know not how, in the soul, is not diverse from things, from space, from light, from time, from man, but one with them and proceeds obviously from the same source whence their life and being also proceed. We first share the life by which things exist and afterwards see them as appearances in nature and forget that we have shared their cause. Here is the fountain of action and of thought. Here are the lungs of that inspiration which giveth man wisdom and which cannot be denied without impiety and atheism. We lie in the lap of immense intelligence, which makes us receivers of its truth and organs of its activity. When we discern justice, when we discern truth, we do nothing of ourselves, but allow a passage to its beams. If we ask whence this comes, if we seek to pry into the soul that causes, all philosophy is at fault. Its presence or its absence is all we can affirm. Every man discriminates between the voluntary acts of his mind and his involuntary perceptions, and knows that to his involuntary perceptions a perfect faith is due. He may err in the expression of them, but he knows that these things are so, like day and night, not to be disputed. My wilful actions and acquisitions are but roving; the idlest reverie, the faintest native emotion, command my curiosity and respect. Thoughtless people contradict as readily the statement of perceptions as of opinions, or rather much more readily; for they do not distinguish between perception and notion. They fancy that I choose to see this or that thing. But perception is not whimsical, but fatal.[8] If I see a trait, my children will see it after me, and in course of time all mankind—although it may chance that no one has seen it before me. For my perception of it is as much a fact as the sun.

The relations of the soul to the divine spirit are so pure that it is profane to seek to interpose helps. It must be that when God speaketh he should communicate, not one thing, but all things; should fill the world with his voice; should scatter forth light, nature, time, souls, from the centre of the present thought; and new date and new create the whole. Whenever a mind is simple and receives a divine wisdom, old things pass

6. Symbol.   8. Fated, compelled, determined.
7. Measurable position.

away—means, teachers, texts, temples fall; it lives now, and absorbs past and future into the present hour. All things are made sacred by relation to it—one as much as another. All things are dissolved to their centre by their cause, and in the universal miracle petty and particular miracles disappear. If therefore a man claims to know and speak of God and carries you backward to the phraseology of some old mouldered nation in another country, in another world, believe him not. Is the acorn better than the oak which is its fulness and completion? Is the parent better than the child into whom he has cast his ripened being? Whence then this worship of the past? The centuries are conspirators against the sanity and authority of the soul. Time and space are but physiological colors which the eye makes, but the soul is light: where it is, is day; where it was, is night; and history is an impertinence and an injury if it be any thing more than a cheerful apologue[9] or parable of my being and becoming.

Man is timid and apologetic; he is no longer upright; he dares not say "I think," "I am," but quotes some saint or sage. He is ashamed before the blade of grass or the blowing[1] rose. These roses under my window make no reference to former roses or to better ones; they are for what they are; they exist with God to-day. There is no time to them. There is simply the rose; it is perfect in every moment of its existence. Before a leaf-bud has burst, its whole life acts; in the full-blown flower there is no more; in the leafless root there is no less. Its nature is satisfied and it satisfies nature in all moments alike. But man postpones or remembers; he does not live in the present, but with reverted eye laments the past, or, heedless of the riches that surround him, stands on tiptoe to foresee the future. He cannot be happy and strong until he too lives with nature in the present, above time.

This should be plain enough. Yet see what strong intellects dare not yet hear God himself unless he speak the phraseology of I know not what David, or Jeremiah, or Paul. We shall not always set so great a price on a few texts, on a few lives. We are like children who repeat by rote the sentences of grandames and tutors, and, as they grow older, of the men of talents and character they chance to see—painfully recollecting the exact words they spoke; afterwards, when they come into the point of view which those had who uttered these sayings, they understand them and are willing to let the words go; for at any time they can use words as good when occasion comes. If we live truly, we shall see truly. It is as easy for the strong man to be strong, as it is for the weak to be weak. When we have new perception, we shall gladly disburden the memory of its hoarded treasures as old rubbish. When a man lives with God, his voice shall be as sweet as the murmur of the brook and the rustle of the corn.

And now at last the highest truth on this subject remains unsaid; probably cannot be said; for all that we say is the far-off remembering of the intuition. That thought by what I can now nearest approach to say it, is this. When good is near you, when you have life in yourself, it is not by any known or accustomed way; you shall not discern the footprints of any other; you shall not see the face of man; you shall not hear any name; the way, the thought, the good, shall be wholly strange and new. It shall exclude example and experience. You take the way from man, not to man. All persons that ever existed are its forgotten ministers. Fear and hope are alike beneath it. There is somewhat low even in hope. In the hour of vision there is nothing that can be called gratitude, nor properly joy. The soul raised over passion beholds identity and eternal causation, perceives the self-existence of Truth and Right, and calms itself with

9. Fable.   1. Blooming.

knowing that all things go well. Vast spaces of nature, the Atlantic Ocean, the South Sea; long intervals of time, years, centuries, are of no account. This which I think and feel underlay every former state of life and circumstances, as it does underlie my present, and what is called life and what is called death.

Life only avails, not the having lived. Power ceases in the instant of repose; it resides in the moment of transition from a past to a new state, in the shooting of the gulf, in the darting to an aim. This one fact the world hates; that the soul *becomes;* for that forever degrades the past, turns all riches to poverty, all reputation to a shame, confounds the saint with the rogue, shoves Jesus and Judas equally aside. Why then do we prate of self-reliance? Inasmuch as the soul is present there will be power not confident but agent.[2] To talk of reliance is a poor external way of speaking. Speak rather of that which relies because it works and is. Who has more obedience than I masters me, though he should not raise his finger. Round him I must revolve by the gravitation of spirits. We fancy it rhetoric when we speak of eminent virtue. We do not yet see that virtue is Height, and that a man or a company of men, plastic[3] and permeable to principles, by the law of nature must overpower and ride all cities, nations, kings, rich men, poets, who are not.

This is the ultimate fact which we so quickly reach on this, as on every topic, the resolution of all into the ever-blessed ONE. Self-existence is the attribute of the Supreme Cause, and it constitutes the measure of good by the degree in which it enters into all lower forms. All things real are so by so much virtue as they contain. Commerce, husbandry, hunting, whaling, war, eloquence, personal weight, are somewhat, and engage my respect as examples of its presence and impure action. I see the same law working in nature for conservation and growth. Power is, in nature, the essential measure of right. Nature suffers nothing to remain in her kingdoms which cannot help itself. The genesis and maturation of a planet, its poise and orbit, the bended tree recovering itself from the strong wind, the vital resources of every animal and vegetable, are demonstrations of the self-sufficing and therefore self-relying soul.

Thus all concentrates: let us not rove; let us sit at home with the cause. Let us stun and astonish the intruding rabble of men and books and institutions by a simple declaration of the divine fact. Bid the invaders take the shoes from off their feet, for God is here within. Let our simplicity judge them, and our docility to our own law demonstrate the poverty of nature and fortune beside our native riches.

Henry David Thoreau
1817–1862

"The fact will one day flower out into a truth." Much is packed into this aphorism from Thoreau's voluminous and meticulous journals. A Harvard graduate of good family and modest means, partly supported by his close friend Ralph Waldo Emerson, he went to live for two years in a cabin on Walden Pond, just outside Concord, Massachusetts, collecting facts, looking for nature and, through nature, toward Truth. Thoreau doesn't represent a back-to-nature movement, any more than Wordsworth does, and perhaps less than Rousseau, his most obvious model. One chapter of his great book *Walden* is called "Reading," another is "Higher Laws,"

---

2. Active.   3. Pliant.

and even as the book increasingly concentrates on animals and plants, it is in the service of exalted hopes for humanity. "We need the tonic of wildness," he says near the end of "Spring," in the curiously matter-of-fact tone that makes him the soberest and most reflective of visionaries; that is, we need a cure but also a bracing wake-up. Thoreau's most famous books (mostly, apart from *Walden*, published posthumously) concern his wanderings, as does his famous essay "Walking," which speaks for American destiny: "We go eastward to realize history and study the workings of art and literature, retracing the steps of the race; we go westward as into the future, with a spirit of enterprise and adventure." The spirit of enterprise led him to a ringing defense of individual conscience in "Civil Disobedience," as well as to the millennial hopes that he shares—though in a distinctive voice—with Wordsworth on Mount Snowdon, as with many other hopeful spirits: "There is more day to dawn. The sun is but a morning star."

from *Walden*

from Spring

Our village life would stagnate if it were not for the unexplored forests and meadows which surround it. We need the tonic of wildness,—to wade sometimes in marshes where the bittern and the meadow-hen lurk, and hear the booming of the snipe; to smell the whispering sedge where only some wilder and more solitary fowl builds her nest, and the mink crawls with its belly close to the ground. At the same time that we are earnest to explore and learn all things, we require that all things be mysterious and unexplorable, that land and sea be infinitely wild, unsurveyed and unfathomed by us because unfathomable. We can never have enough of Nature. We must be refreshed by the sight of inexhaustible vigor, vast and Titanic features, the sea-coast with its wrecks, the wilderness with its living and its decaying trees, the thunder cloud, and the rain which lasts three weeks and produces freshets.[1] We need to witness our own limits transgressed, and some life pasturing freely where we never wander. We are cheered when we observe the vulture feeding on the carrion which disgusts and disheartens us and deriving health and strength from the repast. There was a dead horse in the hollow by the path to my house, which compelled me sometimes to go out of my way, especially in the night when the air was heavy, but the assurance it gave me of the strong appetite and inviolable health of Nature was my compensation for this. I love to see that Nature is so rife with life that myriads can be afforded to be sacrificed and suffered to prey on one another; that tender organizations can be so serenely squashed out of existence like pulp,—tadpoles which herons gobble up, and tortoises and toads run over in the road; and that sometimes it has rained flesh and blood! With the liability to accident, we must see how little account is to be made of it. The impression made on a wise man is that of universal innocence. Poison is not poisonous after all, nor are any wounds fatal. Compassion is a very untenable ground. It must be expeditious. Its pleadings will not bear to be stereotyped.

Early in May, the oaks, hickories, maples, and other trees, just putting out amidst the pine woods around the pond, imparted a brightness like sunshine to the landscape, especially in cloudy days, as if the sun were breaking through mists and shining faintly on the hill-sides here and there. On the third or fourth of May I saw a loon in the pond, and during the first week of the month I heard the whippoorwill, the brown-thrasher, the veery, the wood-pewee, the che-wink, and other birds. I had heard the

1. Rushing streams.

wood-thrush long before. The phoebe had already come once more and looked in at my door and window, to see if my house was cavern-like enough for her, sustaining herself on humming wings with clinched talons, as if she were held by the air, while she surveyed the premises. The sulphur-like pollen of the pitch-pine soon covered the pond and the stones and rotten wood along the shore, so that you could have collected a barrel-ful. This is the "sulphur showers" we hear of. Even in Calidas'[2] drama of Sacontala, we read of "rills dyed yellow with the golden dust of the lotus." And so the seasons went rolling on into summer, as one rambles in high and higher grass.

Thus was my first year's life in the woods completed; and the second year was similar to it. I finally left Walden September 6th, 1847.

from Conclusion

To the sick the doctors wisely recommend a change of air and scenery. Thank Heaven, here is not all the world. The buck-eye does not grow in New England, and the mocking-bird is rarely heard here. The wild goose is more of a cosmopolite than we; he breaks his fast in Canada, takes a luncheon in the Ohio, and plumes himself for the night in a southern bayou. Even the bison, to some extent, keeps pace with the seasons, cropping the pastures of the Colorado only till a greener and sweeter grass awaits him by the Yellowstone. Yet we think that if rail fences are pulled down, and stone-walls piled up on our farms, bounds are henceforth set to our lives and our fates decided. If you are chosen town-clerk, forsooth, you cannot go to Tierra del Fuego[1] this summer: but you may go to the land of infernal fire nevertheless. The universe is wider than our views of it.

Yet we should oftener look over the tafferel[2] of our craft, like curious passengers, and not make the voyage like stupid sailors picking oakum. The other side of the globe is but the home of our correspondent. Our voyaging is only great-circle sailing, and the doctors prescribe for diseases of the skin merely. One hastens to Southern Africa to chase the giraffe; but surely that is not the game he would be after. How long, pray, would a man hunt giraffes if he could? Snipes and woodcocks also may afford rare sport; but I trust it would be nobler game to shoot one's self.—

> Direct your eye right inward, and you'll find
> A thousand regions in your mind
> Yet undiscovered. Travel them, and be
> Expert in home-cosmography.[3]

What does Africa,—what does the West stand for? Is not our own interior white[4] on the chart? black though it may prove, like the coast, when discovered. Is it the source of the Nile, or the Niger, or the Mississippi, or a North-West Passage around this continent, that we would find? Are these the problems which most concern mankind? Is Franklin the only man who is lost, that his wife should be so earnest to find him? Does Mr. Grinnell know where he himself is?[5] Be rather the Mungo Park, the Lewis and Clarke and Frobisher,[6] of your own streams and oceans; explore your

---

2. Thoreau knew the ancient Indian drama Sakuntala in a version published by Sir William Jones in 1789.
1. "The land of fire," the southern tip of South America.
2. Taffrail, the rail at the stern of a ship.
3. From "To My Honoured Friend Sir Ed. P. Knight," by William Habington (1605–1664), a minor Catholic poet.
4. An unexplored blank space on a map.
5. Sir John Franklin (1786–1847), a British explorer lost

trying to find the Northwest Passage (open water through the Arctic) and sought by Henry Grinnell (1799–1874), among others.
6. Mungo Park (1771–1806), a Scotsman who explored the Niger basin in Africa. William Clark (1770–1838) and Meriwether Lewis (1774–1809) explored the Columbia River. Sir Martin Frobisher (1535–1594), an Englishman, sought the Northwest Passage.

own higher latitudes,—with shiploads of preserved meats to support you, if they be necessary; and pile the empty cans sky-high for a sign. Were preserved meats invented to preserve meat merely? Nay, be a Columbus to whole new continents and worlds within you, opening new channels, not of trade, but of thought. Every man is the lord of a realm beside which the earthly empire of the Czar is but a petty state, a hummock left by the ice. Yet some can be patriotic who have no *self*-respect, and sacrifice the greater to the less. They love the soil which makes their graves, but have no sympathy with the spirit which may still animate their clay. Patriotism is a maggot in their heads. What was the meaning of that South-Sea Exploring Expedition,[7] with all its parade and expense, but an indirect recognition of the fact, that there are continents and seas in the moral world, to which every man is an isthmus or an inlet, yet unexplored by him, but that it is easier to sail many thousand miles through cold and storm and cannibals, in a government ship, with five hundred men and boys to assist one, than it is to explore the private sea, the Atlantic and Pacific Ocean of one's being alone.

> "Erret, et extremos alter scrutetur Iberos.
> Plus habet hic vitae, plus habet ille viae."

> Let them wander and scrutinize the outlandish Australians.
> I have more of God, they more of the road.[8]

It is not worth the while to go round the world to count the cats in Zanzibar. Yet do this even till you can do better, and you may perhaps find some "Symmes' Hole"[9] by which to get at the inside at last. England and France, Spain and Portugal, Gold Coast and Slave Coast, all front on this private sea; but no bark from them has ventured out of sight of land, though it is without doubt the direct way to India. If you would learn to speak all tongues and conform to the customs of all nations, if you would travel farther than all travelers, be naturalized in all climes, and cause the Sphinx to dash her head against a stone, even obey the precept of the old philosopher, and Explore thyself.[1] Herein are demanded the eye and the nerve. Only the defeated and deserters go to the wars, cowards that run away and enlist. Start now on that farthest western way, which does not pause at the Mississippi or the Pacific, nor conduct toward a worn-out China or Japan, but leads on direct, a tangent to this sphere, summer and winter, day and night, sun down, moon down, and at last earth down too.

It is said that Mirabeau[2] took to highway robbery "to ascertain what degree of resolution was necessary in order to place one's self in formal opposition to the most sacred laws of society." He declared that "a soldier who fights in the ranks does not require half so much courage as a foot-pad"—"that honor and religion have never stood in the way of a well-considered and firm resolve." This was manly, as the world goes; and yet it was idle, if not desperate. A saner man would have found himself often enough "in formal opposition" to what are deemed "the most sacred laws of society," through obedience to yet more sacred laws, and so have tested his resolution

---

7. A U.S. Navy expedition conducted between 1829 and 1842.

8. An epigram by the 4th century Latin poet Claudian. Note that in place of the Roman reference to the passage past Spain ("Iberos," the Iberians) into the open ocean Thoreau puts Australia, which an American of his day might have considered similarly exotic.

9. Captain John Symmes declared in 1818 that the earth was hollow and open at both poles.

1. When Oedipus answered the riddle of the Sphinx, she killed herself by dashing her head against a rock. Thoreau then varies the proverbial maxim "Know thyself," chiseled into the Temple of Apollo and echoed by many Greek philosophers.

2. Honoré Gabriel Riqueti, Comte de Mirabeau (1749–1791), a moderate leader in the French Revolution.

without going out of his way. It is not for a man to put himself in such an attitude to society, but to maintain himself in whatever attitude he find himself through obedience to the laws of his being, which will never be one of opposition to a just government, if he should chance to meet with such.

I left the woods for as good a reason as I went there. Perhaps it seemed to me that I had several more lives to live, and could not spare any more time for that one. It is remarkable how easily and insensibly we fall into a particular route, and make a beaten track for ourselves. I had not lived there a week before my feet wore a path from my door to the pond-side; and though it is five or six years since I trod it, it is still quite distinct. It is true, I fear that others may have fallen into it, and so helped to keep it open. The surface of the earth is soft and impressible by the feet of men; and so with the paths which the mind travels. How worn and dusty, then, must be the highways of the world, how deep the ruts of tradition and conformity! I did not wish to take a cabin passage, but rather to go before the mast and on the deck of the world, for there I could best see the moonlight amid the mountains. I do not wish to go below now.

I learned this, at least, by my experiment; that if one advances confidently in the direction of his dreams, and endeavors to live the life which he has imagined, he will meet with a success unexpected in common hours. He will put some things behind, will pass an invisible boundary; new, universal, and more liberal laws will begin to establish themselves around and within him; or the old laws be expanded, and interpreted in his favor in a more liberal sense, and he will live with the license of a higher order of beings. In proportion as he simplifies his life, the laws of the universe will appear less complex, and solitude will not be solitude, nor poverty poverty, nor weakness weakness. If you have built castles in the air, your work need not be lost; that is where they should be. Now put the foundations under them.

It is a ridiculous demand which England and America make, that you shall speak so that they can understand you. Neither men nor toadstools grow so. As if that were important, and there were not enough to understand you without them. As if Nature could support but one order of understandings, could not sustain birds as well as quadrupeds, flying as well as creeping things, and *hush* and *who,* which Bright[3] can understand, were the best English. As if there were safety in stupidity alone. I fear chiefly lest my expression may not be *extra-vagant* enough, may not wander far enough beyond the narrow limits of my daily experience, so as to be adequate to the truth of which I have been convinced. *Extra vagance!* it depends on how you are yarded. The migrating buffalo, which seeks new pastures in another latitude, is not extravagant like the cow which kicks over the pail, leaps the cow-yard fence, and runs after her calf, in milking time. I desire to speak somewhere *without* bounds; like a man in a waking moment, to men in their waking moments; for I am convinced that I cannot exaggerate enough even to lay the foundation of a true expression. Who that has heard a strain of music feared then lest he should speak extravagantly any more forever? In view of the future or possible, we should live quite laxly and undefined in front, our outlines dim and misty on that side; as our shadows reveal an insensible perspiration toward the sun. The volatile truth of our words should continually betray the inadequacy of the residual statement. Their truth is instantly *translated;* its literal monument alone remains. The words which express our faith and piety are not definite; yet they are significant and fragrant like frankincense to superior natures.

---

3. Conventional name for an ox. "Hush" and "who" are cattlemen's lingo for go and stop.

Why level downward to our dullest perception always, and praise that as common sense? The commonest sense is the sense of men asleep, which they express by snoring. Sometimes we are inclined to class those who are one-and-a-half witted with the half-witted, because we appreciate only a third part of their wit. Some would find fault with the morning-red, if they ever got up early enough. "They pretend," as I hear, "that the verses of Kabir[4] have four different senses; illusion, spirit, intellect, and the exoteric doctrine of the Vedas;" but in this part of the world it is considered a ground for complaint if a man's writings admit of more than one interpretation. While England endeavors to cure the potato-rot, will not any endeavor to cure the brain-rot, which prevails so much more widely and fatally?

I do not suppose that I have attained to obscurity, but I should be proud if no more fatal fault were found with my pages on this score than was found with the Walden ice. Southern customers objected to its blue color, which is the evidence of its purity, as if it were muddy, and preferred the Cambridge ice, which is white, but tastes of weeds. The purity men love is like the mists which envelop the earth, and not like the azure ether beyond.

Some are dinning in our ears that we Americans, and moderns generally, are intellectual dwarfs compared with the ancients, or even the Elizabethan men. But what is that to the purpose? A living dog is better than a dead lion.[5] Shall a man go and hang himself because he belongs to the race of pygmies, and not be the biggest pygmy that he can? Let every one mind his own business, and endeavor to be what he was made.

Why should we be in such desperate haste to succeed, and in such desperate enterprises? If a man does not keep pace with his companions, perhaps it is because he hears a different drummer. Let him step to the music which he hears, however measured or far away. It is not important that he should mature as soon as an apple-tree or an oak. Shall he turn spring into summer? If the condition of things which we were made for is not yet, what were any reality which we can substitute? We will not be shipwrecked on a vain reality. Shall we with pains erect a heaven of blue glass over ourselves, though when it is done we shall be sure to gaze still at the true ethereal heaven far above, as if the former were not?

* * *

There is an incessant influx of novelty into the world, and yet we tolerate incredible dulness. I need only suggest what kind of sermons are still listened to in the most enlightened countries. There are such words and joy and sorrow, but they are only the burden of a psalm, sung with a nasal twang, while we believe in the ordinary and mean. We think that we can change our clothes only. It is said that the British Empire is very large and respectable, and that the United States are a first-rate power. We do not believe that a tide rises and falls behind every man which can float the British Empire like a chip, if he should ever harbor it in his mind. Who knows what sort of seventeen-year locust will next come out of the ground? The government of the world I live in was not framed, like that of Britain, in after-dinner conversations over the wine.

The life in us is like the water in the river. It may rise this year higher than man has ever known it, and flood the parched uplands; even this may be the eventful year, which will drown out all our muskrats. It was not always dry land where we dwell. I see far inland the banks which the stream anciently washed, before science began to

---

4. A 15th-century mystic, known to Thoreau from a French history of Hindu literature. The Vedas are the old- est Hindu scriptures.

5. Ecclesiastes 9:4.

record its freshets.[6] Every one has heard the story which has gone the rounds of New England, of a strong and beautiful bug which came out of the dry leaf of an old table of apple-tree wood, which had stood in a farmer's kitchen for sixty years, first in Connecticut, and afterwards in Massachusetts,—from an egg deposited in the living tree many years earlier still, as appeared by counting the annual layers beyond it; which was heard gnawing out for several weeks, hatched perchance by the heat of an urn. Who does not feel his faith in a resurrection and immortality strengthened by hearing of this? Who knows what beautiful and winged life, whose egg has been buried for ages under many concentric layers of woodenness in the dead dry life of society, deposited at first in the alburnum[7] of the green and living tree, which has been gradually converted into the semblance of its well-seasoned tomb,—heard perchance gnawing out now for years by the astonished family of man, as they sat round the festive board,—may unexpectedly come forth from amidst society's most trivial and hand-selled[8] furniture, to enjoy its perfect summer life at last!

I do not say that John or Jonathan[9] will realize all this; but such is the character of that morrow which mere lapse of time can never make to dawn. The light which puts out our eyes is darkness to us. Only that day dawns to which we are awake. There is more day to dawn. The sun is but a morning star.

━✦━ END OF PERSPECTIVES: ROMANTIC NATURE ━✦━

━✦━

Johann Wolfgang Goethe
1749–1832

Johann Wolfgang Goethe was an amazing figure by anyone's standards. Not only did he write *Faust,* the epic drama of the scholar's pact with the devil that has come to embody the West and its fatal love affair with knowledge and technology, but he wrote seven other major plays and innumerable smaller ones. He wrote the most popular novel of the eighteenth century (*The Sorrows of Young Werther*), one of the most influential novels of the nineteenth century (*Wilhelm Meister's Apprenticeship*), and a profoundly modern novel of adultery (*Elective Affinities*) that has been widely influential in the twentieth century. He wrote more than a thousand pages of odes, ballads, songs, sonnets, bawdy love elegies, didactic poems, satires, short epics, and other verse. The standard edition of his works and letters runs to 144 volumes.

Goethe was born in 1749 but didn't settle down to literature as his real vocation until he was fifty years old, and he continued to pursue many other interests until his death in 1832. He drew, painted, sculpted, and collected art; he directed the Weimar court theater and personally trained the actors; he published contributions in geology, botany, comparative anatomy, chemistry, meteorology, and especially optics; he was a government official in the small duchy of Saxe-Weimar-Eisenach in central Germany, responsible at different times for mines, roads, finances, the university and all libraries and museums. And from age twenty-five until his death he was Germany's most famous personality and most visited cultural attraction. In his day the French Revolution brought an end to the old feudal order of Europe and ushered in the earliest version of the modern mass society in which we live today: as the greatest European writer of his age he is the cultural figure who embodies for us most clearly the beginning of the modern world.

---

6. Rushing streams.
7. Soft wood, close to the bark.
8. Shoddy.

9. John (Bull), a stock name for an Englishman; Jonathan, an American.

Goethe was educated at home by his wealthy father, who intended his son to be a lawyer and eventually an influential member of the government in the free city of Frankfurt am Main, where Goethe's maternal grandfather had been the mayor. The son had other ideas. He did finally earn a law degree, but spent most of his time at the universities of Leipzig and Strasbourg studying drawing and medicine, as well as socializing and writing poetry. Under the influence of his friend Johann Gottfried Herder (1744–1803), who coined the term "folk song," Goethe scoured the countryside collecting songs—and pursuing his love life. From the combination of his superb schooling and the language of the people, he forged a poetry previously unheard in European culture, in which an individual voice spoke its most personal feelings without constraint in simple song or even in the apparent spontaneity of free verse. Already a quarter of a century before Wordsworth his poetry seemed to express human experience directly, and for the next two hundred years his example convinced scholars and general readers that true poetry was autobiographical.

In 1775 Goethe took advantage of his status as Germany's most famous writer (he was twenty-six!) to leave Frankfurt and settle in Weimar, long an artistic and cultural center, where the young Duke soon invited him to join the government. He threw himself into governing and practical activity and, gradually, science. In 1782 he was ennobled, adding "von" to his name. By 1786, tired of governing and of his platonic relationship with the difficult (and married) lady-in-waiting Charlotte von Stein, he fled to Italy, where for eighteen months he studied the art, the geology, and the people. He returned from Italy a changed man: he resigned his political responsibilities (but kept his salary), and he also entered into a common-law marriage with Christiane Vulpius, a young woman from the lower middle class. Goethe lived in Weimar for the remainder of his life. Milestones were the 1792 military campaign against France in which he accompanied the Duke and which he chronicled movingly; a profound friendship established in 1794 with the great dramatist Friedrich Schiller (1759–1804); the German defeat of 1806 by Napoleon at Jena, the neighboring city in the Duchy, followed immediately by formalizing his relationship with Christiane. He began a vast autobiography, *Poetry and Truth* (published in installments beginning in 1810), and devoted himself to his longest book, the thousand-page *Treatise on Optics* (1810). Christiane died in 1816. The major books published in his last years were the *West-Easterly Divan* (1819), a volume of verse written in the manner of the great fourteenth-century Persian poet Hafiz, and an experimental antinovel (*Wilhelm Meister's Journeyman Years,* 1832). The second part of *Faust,* last retouched only weeks before his death, was reserved for posthumous publication.

Assessments of Goethe as a person vary. To some he has seemed aloof, "Olympian," conservative in an era of change; to others he has appeared broadly tolerant, concerned for the welfare of citizens, supportive of countless rival and younger artists even if he did not share their tastes, a nation-builder who was at the same time a committed internationalist. The fifth act of *Faust II* displays his compassionate insight into the ravages of industrialization; earlier, anti-Napoleonic works were powerful pleas for peace in a time of war-mongering. He was an advocate for authentic cultural artifacts worldwide, inventing the term "world literature" and taking an active interest in poetic production from beyond Europe, as can be seen in the poems in imitation of Chinese and Persian verse included in our selection. Religious readers used to consider him immoral, while some recent biographers have suspected frigidity. He has been blamed for condescension toward Christiane and praised for insisting that she be accepted among his friends; he married her late and mourned her death less than that of his close friend Friedrich Schiller, but then few ministers of state married their lower-class mistresses at all. All seem to agree on his commitment to the famous last lines of *Faust,* "Eternal Womanhood / Draws us on high."

FAUST   What remains beyond question is the power of Goethe's literary achievement, which is embodied above all in *Faust,* the epic drama to which he kept returning from age twenty-three until his death. Georg Faust was a wandering charlatan who lived from about 1480 to 1540. An anonymous chapbook—a cheap pamphlet for popular consumption—appeared in 1587 recounting his pact with the devil, adventures, and eventual death and damnation. In England the playwright Christopher Marlowe wrote his famous version, *The Tragical History of Dr. Faustus,* about 1590, though Goethe probably didn't read it until 1818, decades after he took up the theme. In Germany the Faust legend lived on in numerous versions of the chapbook and in street theater and puppet plays, the form in which Goethe first became acquainted with the story. Along with other contemporaries, he imagined it as the vehicle for a grand work, though unlike them he treated it as a European legend more than as a strictly Germanic one. He began work on it in 1773. Scenes amounting to about half of the eventual first part were published in 1790 as *Faust: A Fragment.* The entire first part appeared in print in 1808, though it was staged only in 1829. Around the turn of the century he began work on the second part, which he worked on at intervals for the rest of his life, putting the final touches to the manuscript just weeks before he died in 1832. It was published shortly after his death. The first and only complete theatrical performance, a two-day, twenty-two-hour spectacle, ran successively in three cities (Hannover, Berlin, and Vienna) between 1999 and 2001.

Faust is incredibly varied, yet consistent in its intense human sympathies. Goethe didn't hesitate to juxtapose the individual tragedy of Margareta, the heroine of Part I, with the ribald humor of the apes of Witch's Kitchen. He strove to integrate both normal and eccentric people into social and natural totalities. His devil is humane, his god tolerant. From Shakespeare he learned to portray the interactions of all different social classes on stage. Whereas Marlowe had presented Faust's story as high tragedy in his play *Dr. Faustus,* Goethe transforms the scholar's pact with the devil into a sporting bet, endorsed by the Lord in person. Marlowe's Faustus sells his soul for twenty-four years of service leading to wealth and power, but Goethe's Faust will receive from the devil access to all of human experience—its joys and woes—and only when he ceases to desire more experience will he die. And far from embodying a grim vision of degradation, the devil Mephistopheles is urbane and witty as well as immoral, and is often referred to by the almost friendly nickname "Mephisto." In this radically secular revision of the traditional myth, human experience is all.

Unique to Goethe's sense for the human is the way he always foregrounds ordinary people against larger contexts of nature, culture, and history. Nature is not only the object of veneration, as for Rousseau, or the eternal ground of human existence, as for Wordsworth, but the essential creative force that makes all things exist in time. It embraces the entry of all things into life, their departure from it, and all their developmental transformations in between. Thus does Faust's opening monologue express his greatest desire:

> I ought rather to ask,
> To grant me a vision of Nature's forces
> That bind the world, all its seeds and sources
> And innermost life.

Nature encompasses all being from the inanimate, the geological and elemental up the entire chain of being. All manifestations of nature are connected by a web of analogies that can be described with the same basic spiral of development: the forces that Goethe names polarity and enhancement govern phenomena as diverse as the polarization of light, the development of plants, and the weaving of damask linen. All around us, nature is nevertheless ineffable, not fully accessible to human understanding. In the human sphere its force is often represented by love. Animal spirits, sexual attraction, the desire for knowledge, the mystique of childhood, and above all the eternal feminine—these are all forms of the teeming life of nature. Nature's creative power, in turn, finds a conscious equivalent in culture; as a result art becomes an object worthy of the same attention as nature. Through art, as through nature, Goethe's characters, and by implication his readers, learn to know their essential humanity, their place in nature and in the cosmos. The philosopher Immanuel Kant (whose works Goethe studied carefully) argued that the world in which we live is the world constructed through our faculties of perception; just so, Faust discovers that he must learn about nature through representations of it, mostly plays-within-plays, that he himself constructs, and that are preceded by the elaborately stagy Prelude on the Stage and the Prologue in Heaven that follows.

Since nature is constantly changing, it can be comprehended only as a historical phenomenon. *Poetry and Truth* is the first autobiography to explain the development of the author's identity through generous analysis of the history—political, social, cultural—of his times. Nature itself has a history of change; Goethe's concern with the history of the earth and with what came to be called evolution was widely recognized, by Darwin among many others. History not only enters the details of plot but pervades Goethe's style at every point. His works are so varied precisely because they explore so many different historical modes. In *Faust* Goethe evokes and often parodies a vast range of styles: the Bible, Greek tragedy and comedy, medieval troubadour lyric, Dante, Shakespeare, sixteenth-century German comedy, folk song, Renaissance masque, Spanish Golden Age drama, French neoclassicism, the sentimentalism of eighteenth-century Germany and England all the way up to Lord Byron, for whose death in 1824 he set a eulogy at the end of the third act of Part II. That every age and society is a distinct culture with its own value was one of the great insights of the late eighteenth century. Goethe's friend Herder was one of the great early proponents of this "historicism" that refused to judge different societies by a uniform yardstick, while Goethe gave it its most memorable poetic incarnation.

Goethe's concerns thus extend from the depths of the human psyche to the limits of the universe, from the most profound kind of interiority to the most patient and attentive external observation. All objects of knowledge for Goethe are at once external and internal, objective and subjective. Like all the Romantics, Goethe grappled unceasingly with the division between self and world opened up by Kant's metaphysics, and he reflects the dominant philosophy constantly in the opposed pairs that people *Faust*. A work that stretches (as the Prelude says) "from heaven, through the world, right down to hell," that ranges from the mythic origins of classical antiquity to modern industrial society, that mixes popular and ritual forms with the latest in theatrical fashion and technical advances, is the prototype of what has come to be known, not surprisingly, as cosmic drama.

PRONUNCIATIONS:
  Altmayer: ALT-mai-er
  Baucis: BOW-tsis
  Brander: BRAHN-der
  Faust: fowst
  Goethe: GER-te
  Gretchen: GRAYT-shen
  Lieschen: LEEZ-shen
  Lynceus: LINK-oys
  Mephistopheles: me-fis-TO-fe-leez
  Mignon: MIN-yohn
  Philemon: phi-LAY-mohn
  Siebel: ZEE-bel
  Wagner: VAG-ner

Faust[1]

PART I

Dedication[2]

Uncertain shapes, visitors from the past
At whom I darkly gazed so long ago,
My heart's mad fleeting visions—now at last
Shall I embrace you, must I let you go?
5   Again you haunt me: come then, hold me fast!
Out of the mist and murk you rise, who so
Besiege me, and with magic breath restore,
Stirring my soul, lost youth to me once more.

You bring back memories of happier days
10   And many a well-loved ghost again I greet;
As when some old half-faded legend plays
About our ears, lamenting strains repeat
My journey through life's labyrinthine maze,
Old griefs revive, old friends, old loves I meet,
15   Those dear companions, by their fate's unkind
Decree cut short, who left me here behind.

They cannot hear my present music, those
Few souls who listened to my early song:
They are far from me now who were so close,
20   And their first answering echo has so long
Been silent. Now my voice is heard, who knows
By whom? I shudder as the nameless throng
Applauds it. Are they living still, those friends
Whom once it moved, scattered to the world's ends?

25   And I am seized by long unwonted yearning
For that still, solemn spirit-realm which then
Was mine: these hovering lisping tones returning
Sigh as from some Aeolian harp,[3] as when
I sang them first: I tremble, and my burning
30   Tears flow, my stern heart melts to love again.
All that I now possess seems far away
And vanished worlds are real to me today.

PRELUDE ON THE STAGE

[*The Director. The Poet. The Clown*[4]]

DIRECTOR: Well, here we are on German soil,

---

1. Translated by David Luke.
2. Written in 1797, when Goethe was contemplating finishing Part 1 of *Faust,* about eight years after the most recently composed sections. Early portions had been written in the 1770s, with other scenes at intervals through the 1780s. He subsequently continued working on the first

part, finally completing it in 1806.
3. A wind harp, frequently associated with poetic inspiration.
4. Actor. Frequently played by the same actor as Mephistopheles. Similarly, Faust and the Lord often play the Poet and the Director, respectively.

My friends. Tell me, you two have stood
35   By me in bad times and in good:
How shall we prosper now? My toil,
Indeed my pleasure, is to please the mob;
And they're a tolerant public, I'll admit.
The posts and boards are up, and it's our job
40   To give them all a merry time of it.
They're in their seats, relaxed, eyes opened wide,
Waiting already to be mystified.
I know how to content popular taste;
But I've a problem here, it must be said:
45   Their customary fare's not of the best—
And yet they are appallingly well-read.
How shall we give them something fresh and new,
That's entertaining and instructive too?
I like to see them all throng through the gate
50   Into our wooden paradise, to watch
Them push and shove and labor up that straight
And narrow way, like babes about to hatch!
Our box-office, while it's still broad daylight,
Is under siege; before it's even four
55   They want their tickets. Tooth and nail they fight,
Like some half-famished crowd outside a baker's door.
Only the poet's magic so holds sway
Over them all: make it, my friend, today!
POET: Do not remind me of that motley throng,
60   Spare me the sight of them! Our spirits fail
And flounder in that stream, we are swept along,
Against the unruly flood what can prevail?
Give me the quietness where I belong,
The poet's place, the stillness never stale,
65   The love and friendship! Only there our art
Thrives on the blessed nurture of the heart.
Deep in the soul an impulse there can flow,
An early song still lisping and unclear;
Well-formed or ill, its momentary show
70   Too soon from Time's wild crest will disappear.
Often unseen and darkly it must grow,
Reaching its ripeness after many a year.
What glisters is the moment's, born to be
Soon lost; true gold lives for posterity.
CLOWN: Must we bring in posterity? Suppose
Posterity were all I thought about,
Who'd keep the present public's boredom out?
They must be entertained, it's what one owes
To them. And with a lad like me
80   Performing, they're enjoying what they see!
Communicate and please! You'll not retire
Then into semi-solitude,

Resentful of the public's fickle mood;
The wider circle's easier to inspire.
85   So do what's needed, be a model poet!
Let Fancy's choirs all sing, and interweave
Reason, sense, feeling, passion—but, by your leave,
Let a good vein of folly still run through it!
DIRECTOR: And let's have enough action, above all!
90   They come to look, they want a spectacle.
Let many things unfold before their eyes,
Let the crowd stare and be amazed, for then
You'll win their hearts, and that's to win the prize;
You'll join the ranks of famous men.
95   Mass alone charms the masses; each man finds
Something to suit him, something to take home.
Give much, and you'll have given to many minds;
They'll all leave here contented to have come.
And let your piece be all in pieces too!
100   You'll not go wrong if you compose a stew:
It's quick to make and easy to present.
Why offer them a whole? They'll just fragment
It anyway, the public always do.
POET: I note you don't despise such a *métier*,[5]
105   And have no sense of how it ill beseems
True art. If I were to do things your way,
I'd join the bungling amateurs, it seems.
DIRECTOR: Such a reproach offends me not a whit.
My aim is our success: I must adopt
110   The proper method of achieving it.
What tool's best, when there's soft wood to be chopped?
Consider who you're writing for! They come,
Some of them, from sheer boredom; some
Arrive here fully sated after feeding;
115   Others again have just been reading
The newspapers, God help us all.
They come with absent thoughts, as if to a masked ball;
Mere curiosity brings them. As for the display
Of ladies and their finery, why, they
120   Eke out the show, and ask me for no pay!
Why do you dream your lofty dreams of art?
Why do full houses flatter you as well?
Take a look at our patrons: you can tell
Half of them have no taste, and half no heart.
125   One will be looking forward to a game
Of cards after the play, another to a night
In some girl's arms. Poor foolish poet, why invite
Your Muse to toil for this? Make it your aim

5. Job, trade.

Merely to give them more—give them excess!
130 It's such a hard job to amuse them
That your best plan is to confuse them:
Do that, and you'll be certain of success—
Now what's the matter? Pain, or ecstasy?
POET: Leave me, and find some other willing slave!
135 Must the poet forgo what Nature gave
Him as his birthright, forfeit wantonly
For you that noble gift? How else does he
Move all men's hearts, what power but his invents
The conquest of the elements?
140 Song bursts forth from him, a harmonious whole
Engulfs the world and draws it back into his soul.
Nature spins out her thread, endlessly long,
At random on her careless spindle wound;[6]
All individual lives in chaos throng
145 Together, mixed like harsh discordant sound.
Who divides up this dull monotonous drift
Into a living rhythm? Who can lift
Particular things into a general sense
Of some great music's sacred congruence?
150 When passions rage, who makes the tempest sing,
The sunset glow when solemn thought prevails?
Who scatters all the blossoms of the spring
On his beloved's path? Who makes a crown
Of mere green leaves the symbol of renown
155 For high distinction? What is this that fills
Olympus, joins the gods in unity?—
The power of Man, revealed in Poetry!
CLOWN: Use them then, these delightful powers,
And do your poet's work, rather as when
160 One falls in love to pass the amorous hours.
One meets by chance, one lingers, one is smitten,
And one's involvement gradually increases;
Happiness grows, but soon enough it ceases;
Joy ends in tears. And somehow then
165 It all becomes a novel, ready written.
Let's give them that, let's make that kind of show!
Use real life and its rich variety!
They're living it, but unreflectingly;
They'll notice this or that they didn't know.
170 Colorful changing scenes and little sense,
Much error, mixed with just a grain of truth—
That's the best drink for such an audience;
They'll be refreshed and edified. That way
It will attract the flower of our youth:

---

6. In contrast to the classical Fates, who measured out people's destiny on their spindles.

175	They'll hear your words, and think them revelation,
	And every tender soul suck from your play
	A sustenance of melancholy sensation.
	Each will find something in it to excite him
	For what he'll see's already there inside him.
180	They're young yet, ready still to laugh or cry;
	Fancy still pleases, rhetoric lifts them high.
	The old and hardened are a thankless brood,
	But growing minds can still show gratitude.
POET:	Ah, give me back those years when I
185	Myself was still developing,
	When songs poured forth unceasingly
	And thick and fast as from a spring!
	Then still my world was misty-veiled,
	Then promised wonders were in bud;
190	I picked the myriad flowers that filled
	Those valleys in such plenitude.
	My poverty was rich profusion;
	I longed for truth and loved illusion.
	Give unchecked passion back to me,
195	Those deep delights I suffered then,
	Love's power, and hatred's energy—
	Give back my youth to me again!
CLOWN:	My friend, youth's what one needs, of course, when one
	Is in the thick of battle with the foe,
200	Or when sweet girls are hanging on
	One's neck and simply won't let go,
	Or when the finish of a race
	Beckons far off to victory,
	Or when one's danced at furious pace
205	Then spends the night in revelry:
	But boldly, gracefully to play
	Upon the lyre, choose one's own goal
	And reach it by some charming way
	On random motions of the soul—
210	Such is the older poet's task; and we
	Respect you none the less. The proverb's wrong, you see:
	Age is no second childhood—age makes plain,
	Children we were, true children we remain.
DIRECTOR:	Come, that's enough of words! What I
215	Want now is deeds. While you, my friends,
	Exchange these well-turned compliments,
	The time for useful work slips by.
	Why all this talk of the right mood?
	It won't just come by dithering.
220	Command your Muses, and they'll sing
	To order, if you're any good!
	You know what we expect of you:
	We're thirsty for a potent brew.

Prepare it now! What's not begun
225   Today will still be left undone
Tomorrow. Never miss a day,
But boldly and with resolution
Seize Chance's forelock and waylay
The possible before it slips away;
230   A started task compels completion.

On German stages, as you know no doubt,
Producers like to try things out;
So make sure now we have machines
And plenty of spectacular scenes!
235   Use the sunshine and moonshine lights,
Use starlight—we have stars galore,
Water and fire and rocky heights,
And birds and animals by the score!
Thus on these narrow boards[7] you'll seem
240   To explore the entire creation's scheme—
And with swift steps, yet wise and slow
From heaven, through the world, right down to hell you'll go!

PROLOGUE IN HEAVEN

[*The Lord. The Heavenly Hosts, then Mephistopheles. The three Archangels advance.*]

RAPHAEL: The sun proclaims its old devotion
In rival song with brother spheres,
245   And still completes in thunderous motion
The circuits of its destined years.
Angelic powers, uncomprehending.
Are strengthened as they gaze their fill;
Thy works, unfathomed and unending,
250   Retain the first day's splendor still.

GABRIEL: The glorious earth, with mind-appalling
Swiftness, upon itself rotates,
And with the deep night's dreadful falling
Its primal radiance alternates.
255   High cliffs stand deep in ocean weather,
Wide foaming waves flood out and in,
And cliffs and seas rush on together
Caught in the globe's unceasing spin.

MICHAEL: And turn by turn the tempests raging
260   From sea to land, from land to sea,
Build up, in passion unassuaging,[8]
Their chain of furious energy.
The thunder strikes, its flash is faster,
It spreads destruction on its way—

---

7. The stage.   8. Uncalmable.

265 But we, thy messengers,[9] O master,
   Revere thy gently circling day.
THE THREE IN CHORUS: And each of us, uncomprehending,
   Is strengthened as we gaze our fill;
   For all thy works, sublime, unending,
270 Retain their first day's splendor still.
MEPHISTOPHELES: Your Grace, since you have called on us again
   To see how things are going, and since you
   Have been quite pleased to meet me now and then,
   I thought I'd come and join your retinue.
275 Forgive me, but grand words are not my trick;
   I cut a sorry figure here, I know,
   But you would laugh at my high rhetoric
   If you'd not left off laughing long ago.
   The solar system I must leave unsung,
280 And to mankind's woes lend my humbler tongue.
   The little earth-god still persists in his old ways,
   Ridiculous as ever, as in his first days.
   He'd have improved if you'd not given
   Him a mere glimmer of the light of heaven;
285 He calls it Reason, and it only has increased
   His power to be beastlier than a beast.
   He is—if I may say so, sir—
   A little like the long-legged grasshopper,
   Which hops and flies, and sings its silly songs
290 And flies, and drops straight back to grass where it belongs.
   Indeed, if only he would stick to grass!
   He pokes his nose in all the filth he finds, alas.
THE LORD: And that is all you have to say?
   Must you complain each time you come my way?
295 Is nothing right on your terrestrial scene?
MEPHISTOPHELES: No, sir! The earth's as bad as it has always been.
   I really feel quite sorry for mankind;
   Tormenting them myself's no fun, I find.
THE LORD: Do you know Faust?
MEPHISTOPHELES: The doctor? Do you mean—
THE LORD: My servant.
MEPHISTOPHELES: Ah, he serves you well, indeed!
   He scorns earth's fare and drinks celestial mead.
   Poor fool, his ferment drives him far!
   He half knows his own madness, I'll be bound.
   He'd pillage heaven for its brightest star,
305 And earth for every last delight that's to be found;
   Not all that's near nor all that's far
   Can satisfy a heart so restless and profound.
THE LORD: He serves me, but still serves me in confusion;

---

9. "Angel" comes from the Greek word for "messenger."

I will soon lead him into clarity.
310   A gardener knows, one day this young green tree
Will blossom and bear fruit in rich profusion.

MEPHISTOPHELES: If I may be his guide, you'll lose him yet;
I'll subtly lead him my way, if you'll let
Me do so; shall we have a bet?

THE LORD: He lives on earth, and while he is alive
You have my leave for the attempt;
Man errs, till he has ceased to strive.

MEPHISTOPHELES: I thank your Grace; for dead men never tempt
Me greatly, I confess. In this connection
320   I like to see a full and fresh complexion;
A corpse is an unwelcome visitor.
The cat-and-mouse game is what I prefer.

THE LORD: Well, go and try what you can do!
Entice that spirit from its primal source,
325   And lead him, if he's not too hard for you
To grasp, on your own downward course—
And then, when you have failed, with shame confess:
A good man, in his dark, bewildered stress,
Well knows the path from which he should not stray.

MEPHISTOPHELES: No doubt; it's a short journey anyway.
I'll win my wager without much delay.
And when I do, then, if I may,
I'll come back here and boast of my success.
I'll make him greedy for the dust, the way
335   The serpent was, my famous ancestress![1]

THE LORD: Indeed, you may feel free to come and call.
You are a type I never learnt to hate;
Among the spirits who negate,
The ironic scold offends me least of all.
340   Man is too apt to sink into mere satisfaction,
A total standstill is his constant wish:
Therefore your company, busily devilish,
Serves well to stimulate him into action.
But you, the authentic sons of God, enfold
345   With praise the abundant beauty of the world;
Love, as you do, the eternal Process, which
Is ever living and forever rich;
Its vanishing phenomena will last,
By your angelic thoughts made firm and fast.

[*The heavens close, the Archangels disperse.*]

MEPHISTOPHELES: I like to see him sometimes, and take care
Not to fall out with him. It's civil

---

1. In Genesis 3:14 God punishes the serpent for tempting Eve by condemning him to crawl forever on his belly: "and dust you shall eat, all the days of your life."

Of the old fellow, such a *grand seigneur,*°   *noble lord*
To have these man-to-man talks with the Devil!

The First Part of the Tragedy

NIGHT

[A high-vaulted, narrow Gothic room.]

FAUST *[sitting restlessly at his desk]*:
Well, that's Philosophy I've read,
355   And Law and Medicine, and I fear
Theology too, from A to Z;
Hard studies all, that have cost me dear.
And so I sit, poor silly man,
No wiser now than when I began.
360   They call me Professor and Doctor, forsooth.
For misleading many an innocent youth
These last ten years now, I suppose,
Pulling them to and fro by the nose;
And I see all our search for knowledge is vain,
365   And this burns my heart with bitter pain.
I've more sense, to be sure, than the learned fools,
The masters and pastors, the scribes from the schools;
No scruples to plague me, no irksome doubt,
No hell-fire or devil to worry about—
370   Yet I take no pleasure in anything now;
For I know I know nothing, I wonder how
I can still keep up the pretense of teaching
Or bettering mankind with my empty preaching.
Can I even boast any worldly success?
375   What fame or riches do I possess?
No dog would put up with such an existence!
And so I am seeking magic's assistance,
Calling on spirits and their might
To show me many a secret sight,
380   To relieve me of the wretched task
Of telling things I ought rather to ask,
To grant me a vision of Nature's forces
That bind the world, all its seeds and sources
And innermost life—all this I shall see,
385   And stop peddling in words that mean nothing to me.
Oh sad full moon, my friend, why must
You see me suffer? Look your last!
Here at this desk so many a night
I've watched and waited for your light
390   To visit me again and shine
Over this paper world of mine.
Oh, take me to the hilltops, there
To wander in the sweet moonlit air,
By mountain caves, through fields to roam,

395   Hovering with spirits in your gloam,
       Cleansed of book-learning's fog and stew
       And healed by bathing in your dew!

       God, how these walls still cramp my soul,
       This cursèd, stifling prison-hole
400   Where even heaven's dear light must pass
       Dimly through panes of painted glass!
       Hemmed in by books to left and right
       Which worms have gnawed, which dust-layers choke,
       And round them all, to ceiling-height,
405   This paper stained by candle-smoke,
       These glasses, boxes, instruments,
       All stuffed and cluttered anyhow,
       Ancestral junk—look at it now,
       Your world, this world your brain invents!

410   And can you still ask why your heart
       Is pent and pining in your breast,
       Why you obscurely ache and smart,
       Robbed of all energy and zest?
       For here you sit, surrounded not
415   By living Nature, not as when
       God made us, but by reek and rot
       And mouldering bones of beasts and men.

       Come, flee into the open land!
       And this great book of magic lore,
420   By Nostradamus'[2] very hand,
       Shall be my guide, I'll need no more;
       By it I'll see the stars in course,
       And as great Nature rules my mind
       Discover the inner psychic force,
425   The spirit speaking to its kind!
       This arid speculation's vain,
       The sacred diagrams are clear:
       Spirits, you hover close—be plain
       And answer me, if you can hear!

       [*He throws open the book and sees the Sign of the Macrocosm.*[3]]

430   Ha! as I look, what sudden ecstasy
       Floods all my senses, how I feel it flowing
       Through every vein, through every nerve in me,
       Life's sacred joy and youth's renewal glowing!
       Did not some god write these mysterious
435   Signs, by whose might my soul is filled
       With peace again, my poor heart healed,
       And by whose secret impetus

---

2. Author of a 16th-century collection of prophecies.   3. A mystical diagram in a book of alchemy, showing the solar system.

The powers of Nature all about me are revealed?
Am I a god? Light fills my mind;
440 In these pure lines and forms appear
All Nature's workings, to my inner sense made clear.
That sage's words at last I understand:
"The spirit-world is open wide,
Only your heart has closed and died;
445 Come, earth-disciple, boldly lave
Your bosom in the dawn's red wave!"

[*He gazes at the sign.*]

How it all lives and moves and weaves
Into a whole! Each part gives and receives,
Angelic powers ascend and redescend
450 And each to each their golden vessels lend;
Fragrant with blessing, as on wings
From heaven through the earth and through all things
Their movement thrusts, and all in harmony it sings!
How great a spectacle! But that, I fear,
455 Is all it is. Oh, endless Nature, where
Shall I embrace you? Where, you breasts that flow
With life's whole life? All earth and heaven hangs
On you, who slake the thirsty pangs
Of every heart—and must I languish vainly so?

[*He turns impatiently to another page of the book and sees the Sign of the Earth Spirit.*[4]]

460 How differently this sign affects me! You,
Spirit of Earth, are closer to me,
Fresh strength already pulses through me,
I glow already from wine so new!
Now, to go out into the world and bear
465 The earth's whole pain and joy, all this I dare;
To fight with tempests anywhere,
And in the grinding shipwreck stand and not despair!
Clouds gather over me—
The full moon hides its face—
470 My lamp burns low!
Mist rises—red fire flashes round
My head, and from the vaulted roof
A chill breathes down and strikes
A shudder into me!
475 Spirit I long to summon, now I feel
You hovering round me, oh reveal
Yourself! Ha, this pain tears my heart!
A new sensation
Stirs all my senses into perturbation!

4. The Earth Spirit is Goethe's invention.

480   I am committed: you shall come, you must
  Appear to me, though you may strike me into dust!

[*He seizes the book and secretly pronounces the spirit's sign. A red flame flashes, the spirit appears in the flame.*]

THE SPIRIT: Who is calling me?
FAUST [*turning away*]: Ah, you are too terrible!
THE SPIRIT: You have drawn me to you with mighty power,
  Sucked at my sphere for many an hour,
  And now—
FAUST: Alas, this sight's unbearable!
THE SPIRIT: You groan and sigh to have me appear,
  To hear my voice, to behold my face:
  Your soul's great plea compels me to this place
  And I have come! What pitiable fear
490 Seizes you, Faust the superman! Where is the call
  Of your creative heart, that carried all
  The world and gave it birth, that shook with ecstasy,
  Swelling, upsurging to the heights where we,
  The spirits, live? Where are you, you whose song
495 I heard besieging me so loud and strong?
  Can this be you? Now that my breath blows round you,
  In the depths of terror I have found you,
  Shrinking and writhing like a worm!
FAUST: Am I to quail before you, shape of flame?
  It is I, Faust! you and I are the same!
THE SPIRIT: In life like a flood, in deeds like a storm
  I surge to and fro,
  Up and down I flow!
  Birth and the grave
505 An eternal wave,
  Turning, returning,
  A life ever burning:
  At Time's whirring loom I work and play
  God's living garment I weave and display.
FAUST: Oh busy spirit! from end to end
  Of the world you roam: how close you are to me!
THE SPIRIT: You match the spirit you can comprehend:
  I am not he. [*It vanishes.*]
FAUST [*collapsing*]: Not you!
515 Who is he then?
  I, made in God's image
  And not even like you!

[*There is a knock at the door.*]

  Oh, devil take him, it's that dry-as-dust
  Toady, my famulus![5] Why must

---

5. Assistant.

520   He interrupt me and destroy
       This supreme hour of visionary joy?

    [*Enter Wagner in a nightgown and nightcap, carrying a lamp. Faust turns to him impatiently.*]

WAGNER: Excuse me, sir! I heard your declamation:
       You were reading a Greek tragedy, no doubt?
       That art is one of powerful persuasion
525   These days; I'd like to learn what it's about.
       I've often heard it said an actor might
       Give lessons to a parson.

FAUST: You are right,
       If the parson himself's an actor too;
       As sometimes is the case.

WAGNER: Oh dear, what can one do,
530   Sitting day after day among one's books!
       The world's so distant, and one never looks
       Even through a spyglass at it; so how can
       One learn to bring about the betterment of man?

FAUST: Give up pursuing eloquence, unless
535   You can speak as you feel! One's very heart
       Must pour it out, with primal power address
       One's hearers and compel them with an art
       Deeper than words. Clip and compile, and brew
       From the leavings of others your ragoût
540   Of rhetoric, pump from your embers
       A few poor sparks that nobody remembers!
       Children will gape and fools admire,
       If that's the audience to which you aspire.
       But what can blend all hearts into a whole?
545   Only the language of the soul.

WAGNER: But one must know how to deliver a tirade.[6]
       I fear my training still is uncompleted.

FAUST: Why don't you learn to ply an honest trade?
       Why be a fool with tinkling bells?
550   Stick to right thinking and sound sense, it tells
       Its own tale, little artifice is needed;
       If you have something serious to say,
       Drop the pursuit of words! This play
       Of dazzling oratory, this paper decoration
555   You fiddle with and offer to the world—
       Why, the dry leaves in autumn, whirled
       About by foggy winds, carry more inspiration!

WAGNER: Alas, our life is short,
       And art is long, they say!
560   My scholarly pursuits, how sore they weigh
       Upon my heart and mind! One ought
       To learn the means of mounting to the sources,

6. A speech in a play.

Yet even this task almost passes my resources;
For we poor devils, by the time we've got
565   Less than halfway, we die, as like as not.
FAUST: A manuscript—is that the sacred spring
That stills one's thirst for evermore?
Refreshment! It's your own soul that must pour
It through you, if it's to be anything.
WAGNER: Excuse me, but it's very pleasant
Studying epochs other than the present,
Entering their spirit, reading what they say,
And seeing how much wiser we have grown today.
FAUST: Oh yes indeed, a wisdom most sublime!—
575   My friend, the spirit of an earlier time,
To us it is a seven-sealed mystery;
And what you learned gentlemen would call
Its spirit, is its image, that is all,
Reflected in your own mind's history.
580   And what a sight it often is! Enough
To run a mile from at first glance. A vast
Old rubbish-dump, an attic of the past,
At best a royal tragedy—bombastic stuff
Full of old saws, most edifying for us,
585   The strutting speeches of a puppet-chorus!
WAGNER: But the great world! The heart and mind of man!
We all seek what enlightenment we can.
FAUST: Ah yes, we say "enlightenment," forsooth!
Which of us dares to call things by their names?
590   Those few who had some knowledge of the truth,
Whose full heart's rashness drove them to disclose
Their passion and their vision to the mob, all those
Died nailed to crosses or consigned to flames.
You must excuse me, friend, the night's half through.
595   We shall speak further on the next occasion.
WAGNER: I'd stay awake all night, and gladly too,
Enjoying such a learned conversation.
Tomorrow morning, being Easter Day,
I'll ask you some more questions, if I may.
600   I've studied now for years with zeal and zest;
Already I know much I must know all the rest. [Exit.]
FAUST: Why does he not despair? A mind so void
And blinkered, so benighted and earthbound!
Greedy for gold, he scratches in the ground,
605   And when he finds some worms he's overjoyed.

Why, when those spirit-voices filled the air
About me, must the speech of such a man
Intrude? And yet for once I can
Thank you, poor mortal wretch: for when despair
610   Was close to me and madness had assailed
My mind, when like a dwarf I seemed to shrink

Before that giant vision, and I quailed,
Dwindling to nothingness—you snatched me from the brink.

615 I, God's own image! Ah, how close it shone,
The mirror of eternal verity!
I fed upon its light and clarity
Within myself, all mortal limits gone,
And with presumption too extreme
Of free, superangelic strength, divine
620 Creative life, thought even now to stream
Through Nature's veins—what sudden shame was mine!
A voice of thunder dashed me from that dream.

Not close to you, not like you; this I dare
No longer claim to be. I had the power
625 To summon you, but could not hold you there.
I felt in that ecstatic hour
So small, and yet so great: and then
You hurled me back so cruelly
Into the changeful common state of men.
630 What must I do now? who shall counsel me?
What urge claims my obedience?
Alas, not only pain, even activity
Itself can stop our life's advance.

The spirit's noblest moments, rare and high,
635 Are choked by matter's alien obtrusion,
And rich with this world's goods, we cry
Scorn on those better things as mere illusion.
Life-giving intuitions of great worth
Are stifled in the muddle of the earth.

640 Imagination, once a flight sublime
That soared in hope beyond the swirl of time,
Now, as each joy is drowned beyond redress,
Sinks down inside us into pettiness:
Care makes its nest in the heart's deepest hole
645 And secretly torments the soul;
Its restless rocking motion mars our mind's content.
Its masks are ever-changing, it appears
As house and home, as wife and child, it will invent
Wounds, poisons, fires and floods—from all
650 These blows we flinch before they ever fall,
And for imagined losses shed continual tears.

I am not like a god! Too deeply now I feel
This truth. I am a worm stuck in the dust,
Burrowing and feeding, where at last I must
655 Be crushed and buried by some rambler's heel.

Is this not dust, filling a hundred shelves
On these high walls that hem me in?
These thousand useless toys that thrust themselves

At me in this moth-mumbled rubbish-bin?
660 How shall I find fulfillment in this jail,
Reading the thousand-times-reprinted tale
Of man's perpetual strife and stress
And rare occasional happiness?—
You hollow skull, what does your grinning say?
665 That brain, in the confusion of its youth,
Like mine, once sought the ethereal dawn of truth
But in the heavy dusk went piteously astray.
And you old instruments, how you too mock,
What scorn your wheels, cogs, pulleys pour on me!
670 I reached the gate, you were to be the key:
Your bit's a well-curled beard, but it won't fit the lock.
We snatch in vain at Nature's veil,
She is mysterious in broad daylight,
No screws or levers can compel her to reveal
675 The secrets she has hidden from our sight.
Useless mechanical contrivances, retained
Because my father used them, old smoke-stained
Parchments that have lain here, untouched by toil,
Since my dull lamp first burnt its midnight oil!
680 I should have squandered all my poor inheritance,
Not sat here sweating while it weighed me down.
What we are born with, we must make our own
Or it remains a mere appurtenance
And is not ours: a load of unused things,
685 Not the live moment's need, raised on the moment's wings.

But what is this? My eyes, magnetically drawn,
Are fixed on that one spot, where I can see
That little flask: why does sweet light break over me,
As when in a dark wood the gentle moonbeams dawn?

690 Unique alembic![7] Reverently I lift
You down and greet you. Now, most subtle gift
Compounded of the wit and art of man,
Distillment of all drowsy syrups, kind
Quintessence of all deadly and refined
695 Elixirs, come, and serve your master as you can!
I see you, and am healed as with a balm,
I seize you, and my striving soul grows calm;
And borne upon my spirit's ebbing tide,
Little by little drifting out to sea,
700 I tread on its bright mirror—far and wide
As new dawn breaks, new shores are beckoning me!

A fiery chariot[8] on light wings descends

---

7. Distilling apparatus.
8. The sunrise is here described using an image that is both biblical and classical (Apollo, god of light and rea- son, drives the sun across the sky) and biblical (a fiery chariot takes the prophet Elijah up to heaven, 2 Kings 2:11).

And hovers by me! I will set forth here
On a new journey to the heaven's ends,
705   To pure activity in a new sphere!
O sublime life, o godlike joy! And how
Do I, the ertswhile worm, deserve it now?
I will be resolute, and turn away
For ever from the earth's sweet day.
710   Dread doors, though all men sneak and shuffle past
You, I'll confront you, tear you open wide!
Here it is time for me to prove at last
That by his noble deeds a man is deified;
Time not to shrink from the dark cavern where
715   Our fancy damns itself to its own tortured fate;
Time to approach the narrow gate
Ringed by the eternal flames of hell's despair;
Time to step gladly over this great brink,
And if it is the void, into the void to sink!

720   Old goblet of pure crystal, come, now let
Me take you from your shelf and sheath. Long years
Have passed since last I thought of you; and yet
At bygone feasts you were the cup that cheers
The solemn guests, the gleaming beaker
725   Raised to the toast by many a speaker!
Your rich engraved pictorial decorations,
The drinker's task, his rhyming explanations
Before in one long draught he drained you down—
These I recall, from revels long ago;
730   I passed you round, I praised your art to show
My wit. Now I shall not do so.
I have a potion here whose work's soon done;
Its dizzying liquid fills you, dark and brown.
I made and mixed it well, as I know how.
735   And so, with all my heart, I raise it now:
With this last festive drink I greet the rising sun!

[*He sets the cup to his lips. There is a peal of bells and a sound of choral singing.*]

CHORUS OF ANGELS: Christ is ris'n from the dead!
Hail to all mortal men,
From sin's insidious bane,
740   From their inherited
Bondage set free again!
FAUST: What lilting tones are these, what notes profound
Cry to me: Do not drink! Have they such power?
And do these bells with their dull booming sound
745   Announce the Easter festival's first hour?
Is this already the angelic song
Of solace, heard above the grave that night so long

Ago, when the new covenant was sealed and bound?
CHORUS OF WOMEN: Spices we brought and myrrh,
750   We who befriended him,
Faithfully laid him here,
Lovingly tended him;
Clean linen, swaddling-bands,
We wound with our own hands.
755   Who can have come today
Taking our Lord away?
CHORUS OF ANGELS: Christ is raised, Christ is blest!
He bore mankind's ordeal,
Loving their joys to feel,
760   Suffering the stripes that heal:
He passed the test!
FAUST: You gentle, puissant choirs of heaven, why
Do you come seeking me? The dust is stronger!
Go, chant elsewhere to tenderer souls! For I
765   Can hear the message, but believe no longer.
Wonders are dear to faith, by it they live and die.
I cannot venture to those far-off spheres,
Their sweet evangel[9] is not for my ears.
And yet—these strains, so long familiar, still
770   They call me back to life. There was a time
Of quiet, solemn sabbaths when heaven's kiss would fill
Me with its love's descent, when a bell's chime
Was deep mysterious music, and to pray
Was fervent ecstasy. I could not understand
775   The sweet desire that drove me far away
Out through the woods, over the meadowland:
There I would weep a thousand tears and feel
A whole world come to birth, my own yet real.
Those hymns would herald youthful games we played
780   To celebrate the spring. As I recall
That childhood, I am moved, my hand is stayed,
I cannot take this last and gravest step of all.
Oh sing, dear heaven-voices, as before!
Now my tears flow, I love the earth once more!
CHORUS OF DISCIPLES: Now from his burial
Christ has gone up on high,
Living, no more to die,
Glorious, imperial;
He in creative zest
790   Into the heavens has grown.
On the earth-mother's breast
We still must weep alone;
Yet though we here endure
Exile and anguish,

---

9. Gospel, good news.

795   Master, it is in your
       Joy that we languish!
CHORUS OF ANGELS: Christ is raised from the tomb,
       Snatched from corruption's womb!
       Rise and be joyful, all
800   You whom earth's bonds enthrall!
       Brothers, o blessed few,
       Sharers of love's food, who
       Praise him in deeds you do,
       Pilgrims whose words renew
805   Man's hope of glory: you
       Know that your Lord is near,
       See, he is here!

from OUTSIDE THE TOWN WALL[1]

AN OLD PEASANT: Why, Doctor, now that's very kind
       To join us for your Easter walk,
       Being such a learned gentleman,
       And not look down on us poor folk!
985   Now, here's a jug of finest ale;
       You are the man we've filled it for,
       And in your honor this we wish,
       That it may quench your thirst, and more:
       There's many a drop in this cup I raise—
990   May their number be added to your days!
FAUST: I thank you all; this drink refreshes,
       And I return your kind good wishes.

[*The people gather round.*]

THE OLD PEASANT: Yes, sir, indeed! we all are glad
       To see you on this day of cheer,
995   For long ago, when times were bad,
       You wished us well for many a year.
       There's many of us might now be dead
       Who've lived on to a healthy age
       Because your father stopped the spread
1000   Of plague, and cooled the fever's rage.
       You were young then, you went about
       Visiting every hospital:
       So many corpses they brought out,
       But you came out alive and well;
1005   Though many a hard time you had too.
       You helped us, and the Lord helped you.
ALL: Long life to our good doctor! May
       He help us yet for many a day.
FAUST: Give thanks to Him who gave these skills
1010   And helps mankind in all its ills.

1. Faust and Wagner walk out among the peasants celebrating the spring and Easter.

[*He walks on with Wagner.*]

WAGNER: Ah, what a sense of your own greatness must
You have as all these people honor you!
Happy the man whose gifts bring him such true
Advantage, as is only just!
1015   They all ask questions, fathers point you out
To sons, they all rush up to see
You pass, the fiddling stops, they stand about
To stare instead of dancing, and the sky
Is full of cheers and caps thrown high;
1020   They very nearly drop on bended knee
As if the Sacred Host were being carried by!

FAUST: A few steps further, to that rock up there;
Now let us rest here from our walk. This place is one
Where I would often sit and meditate alone,
1025   Keeping strict fast, in anguished prayer.
Here, full of hope, firm in belief,
I sought to alter heaven's will;
I groaned, I wrung my hands in grief—
The pestilence continued still.
1030   Now I feel mocked by this mob's adulation.
If only you could read my mind and know
How little we did, so long ago,
I and my father, to deserve such commendation!
My father was a man respected, yet obscure,
1035   Who labored honestly with never a pause,
Though by his own eccentric methods to be sure,
Studying Nature's sacred cyclic laws.
With the initiated few
He practiced in the Black Laboratory,[2]
1040   Mixing, by this or that strange recipe,
Elements in an ill-assorted brew.
Thus in tepid immersion he would wed
The Lily to the Lion bold and red;
Then with intenser heat he forced this bridal pair
1045   From one glass chamber to the other—by and by
The Young Queen was engendered there,
The rainbow-hued precipitate: this, then,
Was our specific. Still the sick would die,
But no one asked why none got well again.
1050   So in these valleys and these villages,
With those hell-syrups as our remedies,
We, worse than any plague, raged far and wide.
I myself poisoned thousands, I saw how

---

2. Faust here describes chemical operations in the language of alchemy. In his laboratory Faust's father produced his failed "specific" (medication: the precipitate called the Young Queen by marrying (combining) the Red Lion (mercuric oxide) with the Lily (hydrochloric acid).

| | They all wasted away and perished—now |
| 1055 | Men praise that cynical mass-homicide. |

WAGNER: Sir, do not let that trouble you!
To practice a transmitted skill
With a good conscience and good will
Is all an honest man need do.

1060 If one respects one's father in one's youth,
One will have learnt from him with pleasure;
If as a man one then adds to our store of truth,
One's own son will do this in even greater measure.

FAUST: Happy are they who still hope this is so,

1065 While ignorance surrounds us like an ocean!
The very thing one needs one does not know,
And what one knows is needless information.
But let us put these gloomy thoughts away
And let the precious present hour confound them!

1070 Look how they gleam in the last light of day,
Those little huts with green all round them!
Evening has come, our sun is westering now—
But it speeds on to bring new life elsewhere.
Oh if some wings would raise me, if somehow

1075 I could follow its circuit through the air!
For then as I strove onwards I should see
A silent sunset world for ever under me,
The hills aglow, the valleys lost in dreams,
The silver brooks poured into golden streams;

1080 No mountain-range would stop me, not with all
Its rugged chasms; at divine speed I fly,
The sea already greets my wondering eye
With its warm gulfs where now the sun's rays fall.
Now the god seems at last to sink and set,

1085 But a new impulse drives me yet:
I hasten on to drink his endless light,
The day ahead, behind my back the night,
The sky above me and the waves below . . .
A pleasing dream; but the sun vanishes

1090 And it is over. Wings, alas, may grow
Upon our soul, but still our body is
Earthbound. And yet, by inborn instinct given
To each of us, our hearts rise up and soar
For ever onwards, when we hear the lark outpour

1095 Its warbling song, lost in the blue of heaven,
Or when we see the wing-spread eagle hover
Above wild cliffs which pine-trees cover,
Or across marsh and lakeland watch the crane
Fly homeward to its native haunts again.

WAGNER: I too have known fanciful states of mind,
But to such moods as yours I never was inclined.
One soon grows tired of forests and of fields;

I never envied any bird its wings.
But the pursuit of intellectual things
1105   From book to book, from page to page—what joys that yields!
How fine and snug the winter nights become,
What sweet life courses through one's veins!
Is an old parchment not a whole compendium
Of paradise itself, rewarding all our pains?

FAUST: Only one of our needs is known to you;
You must not learn the other, oh beware!
In me there are two souls, alas, and their
Division tears my life in two.
One loves the world, it clutches her, it binds
1115   Itself to her, clinging with furious lust:
The other longs to soar beyond the dust
Into the realm of high ancestral minds.
Are there no spirits moving in the air,
Ruling the region between earth and sky?
1120   Come down then to me from your golden mists on high,
And to new, many-colored life, oh take me there!
Give me a magic cloak to carry me
Away to some far place, some land untold,
And I'd not part with it for silk or gold
11025   Or a king's crown, so precious it would be!

WAGNER: Oh do not call the dreaded host that swarms
And streams abroad throughout the atmosphere![3]
They bring men danger in a thousand forms,
From the earth's ends they come to plague us here.
1130   Out of the north the sharp-toothed demons fly,
Attacking us with arrow-pointed tongues:
On the east wind they ride to drain us dry
And slake their hunger on our lungs;
The southern desert sends them to beat down
1135   Upon our heads with fiery beams;
The west will bring refreshment, as it seems,
Till in their flooding rains we and the fields must drown.
Their spiteful ears are open to obey
Our summons, for they love to harm and cheat;
1140   They pose as heaven's angels, and though all they say
Is false, their lisping voice is sweet.
But come, the air grows chill, the world is gray
With dusk and mist already; come away!
When evening falls, indoors is best.—
1145   Why do you stand and stare with such surprise?
What twilight thing has seized your interest?

FAUST: There—in the corn and stubble, do you see
That black dog?

WAGNER: Why, of course; of what account is he?

---

3. True to his pedantic nature, Wagner misunderstands Faust's mystical nature spirits as mere weather demons.

FAUST: What do you take him for? Come, use your eyes!
WAGNER: A poodle, acting as a dog will do
                When it has lost its master, I suppose.
FAUST: He's getting closer; round and round he goes
                In a narrowing spiral; no, there's no mistake!
                And as he comes—look, can't you see it too?—
1155   A streak of fire follows in his wake!
WAGNER: An ordinary black poodle is all I
                Can see; no doubt some trick of light deceives your eye.
FAUST: It is some magic he is weaving, so
                Subtly about our feet, some future knot!
WAGNER: He's nervous, jumping round us, since we're not
                His master, but two men he doesn't know.
FAUST: The circle shrinks; now he is on our ground.
WAGNER: You see! he's not a phantom, just a hound.
                He's doubtful still, he growls, he lies down flat,
1165   He wags his tail. All dogs do that.
FAUST: Come to us! Come to heel! Come here!
WAGNER: He's just a foolish poodle-beast, I fear.
                Stand still, and he will dance attendance on you;
                Speak to him, and he'll put his forepaws on you;
1170   Drop something, and he'll find it, that's his trick—
                He'll jump into the water for your stick.
FAUST: No doubt you're right; no spirit after all,
                But merely a conditioned animal.
WAGNER: A well-trained dog is one who can
1175   Find favor even with a learned man.
                Our students taught him to behave this way;
                He far excels his teachers, I must say.

    [*They pass through the gate into the town.*]

                    F A U S T ' S   S T U D Y   (1)

FAUST [*entering with the poodle*]:
                Now I have left the fields and hills
                Where now the night's dark veil is spread;
1180   Night wakes our better part, and fills
                Our prescient soul with holy dread.
                The active turmoil leaves my mind,
                All wilder passions sleep and cease;
                Now I am moved to love mankind,
1185   To love God too, and am at peace.
                Stop running about, you poodle-clown!
                Why are you snuffling there by the door?
                Go behind the stove! Keep still, lie down!
                You have my best cushion, I can't do more.
1190   On that path down the hill you jumped and ran
                For our delectation, and that was fun;
                I will entertain you now if I can,

As a welcome guest, but a silent one.
Back in our little narrow cell
1195 We sit, the lamp glows soft and bright,
And in our heart and mind as well
Self-knowledge sheds its kindly light.
Reason once more begins to speak,
And hope once more is blossoming;
1200 We long to find life's source, to seek
Life's fountainhead, to taste life's spring.
Poodle, stop growling! It does not agree
With my high tone, and my soul's sacred joys
Are interrupted by your animal noise.
1205 We know what scorn and mockery
Uncomprehending man will pour
On anything he has not heard before—
The good, the beautiful, the true;
Must dogs start muttering at it too?

1210 But now, that deep contentment in my breast,
Alas, wells up no more, in spite of all my best
Endeavors. Oh, how soon the stream runs dry,
And in what parching thirst again we lie!
How often this has happened to me!
1215 And yet, there is a remedy:
We learn to seek a higher inspiration,
A supernatural revelation—
And where does this shine in its fullest glory.
If not in that old Gospel story?
1220 Here is the Greek text; I am moved to read
Its sacred words, I feel the need
Now to translate them true and clear
Into the German tongue I hold so dear.

[*He opens a volume and prepares to write.*]

"In the beginning was the Word":[4] why, now
1225 I'm stuck already! I must change that; how?
Is then "the word" so great and high a thing?
There is some other rendering,
Which with the spirit's guidance I must find.
We read: "In the beginning was the Mind."
1230 Before you write this first phrase, think again;
Good sense eludes the overhasty pen.
Does "mind" set worlds on their creative course?
It means: "In the beginning was the Force."
So it should be—but as I write this too,
1235 Some instinct warns me that it will not do.

4. The opening line of John's Gospel.

The spirit speaks! I see how it must read,
And boldly write: "In the beginning was the Deed!"

If we are to share this room in peace,
Poodle, this noise has got to cease,
1240 This howling and barking has got to end!
My invitation did not extend
To so cacophonous a friend.
In my study I won't put up with it.
One of us two will have to quit.
1245 I am sorry that we must part so;
The door stands open, you may go.
But what is this I see?
Can it be happening naturally?
Is it real? Is it a dream or not?
1250 How long and broad my poodle has got!
He heaves himself upright:
This is no dog, if I trust my sight!
What hobgoblin have I brought home somehow?
He looks like a hippopotamus now,
1255 With fearsome jaws and fiery eyes.
Aha! you'll get a surprise!
With this hybrid half-brood of hell
King Solomon's Key[5] works very well.

SPIRITS [*outside in the passage*]:
He's caught! There's one caught in there!
1260 Don't follow him, don't go in!
Like a fox in a gin
An old hell-lynx is trapped; beware!
But now wait and see!
Hover round, hover
1265 Up and down, he'll recover,
He'll set himself free;
We'll lend a hand to him,
We'll not abandon him;
He's been polite to us,
1270 Always done right by us!

FAUST: First, to defeat this beast,
I need the Spell of the Four,[6] at least.
Salamander, burn!
Water-nymph, twist and turn!
1275 Sylph of the air, dissolve!
Goblin, dig and delve!
When the elements are known,
Each in its own

---

5. A magic book popular from the 16th to the 18th century.

6. The four elements: fire (salamander), water (nymph), air (sylph), and earth (goblin or incubus).

Rembrandt van Rijn, *The Scholar in His Study,* c. 1652, often known as *Faust in His Study,* was used as the frontispiece to *Faust: A Fragment* (1790), Goethe's first publication of scenes from Part 1.

Qualities and powers,
1280   The mastery is ours
Over all and each,
By this knowledge and speech.
Salamander, in flame
Vanish as you came!
1285   Murmur and mingle,
Nymph of the sea-dingle![7]
Blaze like a meteor,
Sylph-creature!
Serve in the house for us,
1290   Incubus, incubus!
Come out of him, show yourself thus or thus!
None of those four
Has passed through my door.
The beast just lies there grinning at me.
1295   I've not yet hurt him, evidently.

7. Dell or hollow.

Wait! I can sing
A more powerful spell!
Are you from hell,
You fugitive thing?

1300 Then behold this Sign
Which they fear and know,
The black hosts below!
Now he swells up with bristling spine.
Vile reprobate!

1305 Do you read this name?
He who is nameless,
Uncreated, timeless,
In all worlds the same,
Pierced in impious hate?

1310 Behind the stove he shrinks from my spells;
Like an elephant he swells.
The whole room is filled by this devil-dog.
He wants to dissolve into a fog.
Do not rise to the ceiling, I forbid you!

1315 Lie down at your master's feet, I bid you!
You will see that I utter no idle warning;
With sacred fire I shall set you burning!
Do not dare the might
Of the Thrice-Effulgent Light!8

1320 Do not dare the might
Of my strongest magic of all!

MEPHISTOPHELES [*stepping out from behind the stove as the mist disperses, dressed as a medieval wandering student*]:
Why all this fuss? How can I serve you, sir?

FAUST: So that was the quintessence of the cur!
A student-tramp! How very comical.

MEPHISTOPHELES: Sir, I salute your learning and your wit!
1325   You made me sweat, I must admit.

FAUST: What is your name?

MEPHISTOPHELES: The question is absurd,
Surely, in one who seeks to know
The inmost essence, not the outward show,
1330   And has such deep contempt for the mere word.

FAUST: Ah, with such gentlemen as you
The name often conveys the essence too,
Clearly enough; we say Lord of the Flies,9
Destroyer, Liar—each most fittingly applies.
1335   Well then, who are you?

MEPHISTOPHELES: Part of that Power which would
Do evil constantly, and constantly does good.

FAUST: This riddle has, no doubt, some explanation.

---

8. The sign of the Trinity.

9. Translates Beelzebub, a biblical name for the devil.

MEPHISTOPHELES: I am the spirit of perpetual negation;
        And rightly so, for all things that exist
1340   Deserve to perish, and would not be missed—
        Much better it would be if nothing were
        Brought into being. Thus, what you men call
        Destruction, sin, evil in short, is all
        My sphere, the element I most prefer.
FAUST: You seem complete and whole, yet say you are a part?
MEPHISTOPHELES: I speak the modest truth, I use no art.
        Let foolish little human souls
        Delude themselves that they are wholes.
        I am part of that part which once, when all began,
1350   Was all there was; part of the Darkness before man
        Whence light was born, proud light, which now makes futile war
        To wrest from Night, its mother, what before
        Was hers, her ancient place and space. For light depends
        On the corporeal worlds—matter that sends
1355   Visible light out, stops light in its stride
        And by reflected light is beautified.
        So, light will not last long, I fear;
        Matter shall be destroyed, and light shall disappear.
FAUST: Well! now I know your high vocation:
1360   Failing that grand annihilation
        You try it on a smaller scale.
MEPHISTOPHELES: And frankly, I must own, here too I fail.
        The Something, this coarse world, this mess,
        Stands in the way of Nothingness,
1365   And despite all I've undertaken,
        This solid lump cannot be shaken—
        Storms, earthquakes, fire and flood assail the land
        And sea, yet firmly as before they stand!
        And as for that damned stuff, the brood of beasts and men,
1370   That too is indestructible, I've found;
        I've buried millions—they're no sooner underground
        Than new fresh blood will circulate again.
        So it goes on; it drives me mad. The earth,
        The air, the water, all give birth:
1370   It germinates a thousandfold,
        In dry or wet, in hot or cold!
        Fire is still mine, that element alone—
        Without it, I could call no place my own.
FAUST: And so the ever-stirring, wholesome energy
1380   Of life is your arch-enemy;
        So in cold rage you raise in vain
        Your clenched satanic fist. Why, you
        Strange son of chaos! think again,
        And look for something else to do!
MEPHISTOPHELES: On such a point there's much to say;
        We'll talk again another day.

This time I'll take my leave—if, by your leave, I may.

FAUST: Why not? We are acquainted now,
          And you are welcome to come back
1390   And visit me some time, somehow.
          Here is the window, there's the door;
          I even have a chimney-stack.

MEPHISTOPHELES: I must confess that on the floor,
          Across your threshold, you have put
1395   A certain obstacle—a witch's foot—

FAUST: You mean, that pentagram[1] I drew
          Hinders a gentleman from hell?
          Then how did you get in? Well, well!
          How did I fool a sprite like you?

MEPHISTOPHELES: It's not well drawn; look closely, sir!
          One of the outside angles—there,
          You see? the lines do not quite meet.

FAUST: How curious! how very neat!
          And so you are my prisoner.
1405   A lucky chance, I do declare!

MEPHISTOPHELES: The poodle skipped in without noticing,
          But now it's quite another thing:
          The Devil can't skip out again.

FAUST: Why don't you use the window, then?

MEPHISTOPHELES: Devils and spirits have a law, as you may know:
          They must use the same route to come and go.
          We enter as we please; leaving, we have no choice.

FAUST: So even hell has laws? Good; in that case
          One might conclude a pact with you
1415   Gentlemen, and a guaranteed one too?

MEPHISTOPHELES: Whatever is promised, you shall have your due,
          There'll be no quibbling, no tergiversation.
          But that all needs mature consideration;
          We shall discuss it by and by.
1420   Meanwhile I must most earnestly
          Repeat my plea to be released.

FAUST: Come, stay a little while at least,
          To edify me with your conversation.

MEPHISTOPHELES: Excuse me now: I soon will reappear
1425   And tell you anything you wish to hear.

FAUST: I did not pursue you, you know;
          You put your own head in the noose.
          Don't catch the Devil and let go,
          They say—it's harder when he's on the loose.

MEPHISTOPHELES: Very well, if you wish, I will remain
          And help you while the time away;
          But I insist you let me entertain
          You with my arts in a befitting way.

---

1. A five-pointed star.

FAUST: Certainly, you are welcome to do so;
1435   But you must make it an amusing show.
MEPHISTOPHELES: My friend, you shall in this one night,
          In this one hour, know greater sensuous delight
          Than in a whole monotonous year!
          Delicate spirits now will bring
1440   You visions, and will charm your ear
          With song; theirs is no empty conjuring.
          Your palate also shall be sated,
          Your nostrils sweetly stimulated,
          Your sense of touch exhilarated.
1445   We are all ready, all are in
          Our places—come, at once, begin!

SPIRITS:
          Vanish, you darkling
          Vaults there above us!
          Now let the sweeter
1450   Blue of the ether
          Gaze in and love us!
          Are not the darkling
          Clouds disappearing?
          Starlight is sparkling,
1455   Suns of a gentler
          Brightness appearing.
          Children of light dance
          Past in their radiance,
          Swaying, inclining,
1460   Hovering, shining:
          Passionate yearning
          Follows them burning.
          And their long vesture
          Streams out and flutters,
1465   Streams out and covers
          Arbor and pasture,
          Where lovers ponder
          As they surrender
          Each to each other.
1470   Arbor and bower,
          Full fruit and flower!
          Vines shed their burden
          Into the winepress
          Rich with their ripeness;
1475   Wines foam unending
          In streams descending,
          Through precious gleaming
          Stones they are streaming,
          Leaving behind them
1480   Heights that confined them,
          Pleasantly winding

Round the surrounding
Hills and their verdure,
To lakes expanding.
1485 Birds drink their pleasure,
Soaring to sunlight,
Flying to far bright
Islands that shimmer,
Trembling, enticing,
1490 Where the waves glimmer,
Where echo answers
Songs of rejoicing
Shouted in chorus,
Where we see dancers
1495 Leaping before us
Out over green fields;
Over the green hills
Some of them climbing,
Some of them over
1500 Lake-waters swimming,
Some of them hover;
All seeking life, each
Seeking a distant star
Where love and beauty are
1505 Far beyond speech.
MEPHISTOPHELES: He sleeps! Well done, my airy cherubim!
How soon your lullaby enchanted him!
This concert puts me in your debt.
Faust, you are not the man to hold the Devil yet!
1510 Go on deluding him with sweet dream-shapes,
Plunge him into a sea where he escapes
Reality. As for this threshold, I know how
To split the spell: I need a rat's tooth now.
No need to conjure in this place for long!
1515 I hear them scuttling, soon they'll hear my song.

The master of all rats and mice,
All flies and frogs and bugs and lice,
Commands you to poke forth your snout
And gnaw this floor to let me out!
1520 I'll smear it for you with some drops
Of oil. Aha! see, out he hops!
Now set to work. The point where I was stuck
Is at the front here. What a piece of luck!
One little bite more and it's done.—²
1525 Now, Faust, until we meet again, dream on!
FAUST [*waking*]: Have I been twice deluded in one day?
The spirit-orgy vanishes: it seems
I merely saw the Devil in my dreams,

2. At Mephisto's command the rat gnaws a large enough hole in the pentagram for him to wiggle past.

And had a dog that ran away!

from FAUST'S STUDY (2)

FAUST: A knock? Come in!—Who is this bothering me
          Again?

MEPHISTOPHELES: I'm back!

FAUST: Come in!

MEPHISTOPHELES: You must say it three
          Times over.

FAUST: Well, come in!

MEPHISTOPHELES [*entering*]:   Well done!
          I think we're going to get on
          Together, you and I. To cheer
1535   You up, I've come dressed as a cavalier:
          In scarlet, with gold trimmings, cloak
          Of good stiff silk, and in my hat
          The usual cock's feather; take
          A fine long pointed rapier,
1540   And one's complete. So, my dear sir,
          Be ruled by me and do just that:
          Wear clothes like mine, strike out, be free,
          And learn what the good life can be.

FAUST: The earth's a prison—one can't get away
1545   From it, whatever clothes one wears.
          I'm still too young to lack desires,
          Not young enough now for mere play.
          What satisfaction can life hold?
          Do without, do without! That old
1550   Command pursues us down the years
          Endlessly echoing in our ears—
          The same old hoarse repeated song
          Heard hour by hour our whole life long!
          With each new dawn I wake aghast,
1555   My eyes with bitter tears are filled
          To think that when this day has passed
          I'll not have had one single wish fulfilled,
          That even my presentiments of joy
          Will die of nagging scruples, and life's mess
1560   Of trivial impediments destroy
          My active soul's creativeness.
          When the night falls, I seek my bed
          With anxious fears, with many a sigh,
          But find no peace: with sights of dread
1565   Wild dreams torment me as I lie.
          And though a god lives in my heart,
          Though all my powers waken at his word,
          Though he can move my every inmost part—
          Yet nothing in the outer world is stirred.

1570   Thus by existence tortured and oppressed
        I crave for death, I long for rest.
MEPHISTOPHELES: And yet death never is a wholly welcome guest.
FAUST: Happy the man whom glorious death has crowned
        With bloodstained victor's laurels, happy he
1575   Whose sudden sweet surcease is found
        In some girl's arms, after wild revelry!
        And I, who saw that mighty Spirit's power,
        Why did I not expire with joy in that same hour!
MEPHISTOPHELES: And yet, in that same night, someone who mixed a brown
1580   Elixir did not drink it down.
FAUST: You seem to like eavesdropping.
MEPHISTOPHELES: I am not
        Omniscient, but I know a lot.
FAUST: In that great turmoil and distress
        Sweet well-known echoing notes deceived
1585   My ear, old childhood joys relieved
        My homesick heart—this I confess.
        But now I curse all flattering spells
        That tempt our souls with consolation,
        All that beguilingly compels
1590   Us to endure earth's tribulation!
        A curse first on the high pretences
        Of our own intellectual pride!
        A curse on our deluded senses
        That keep life's surface beautified!
1595   A curse upon our dreams of fame,
        Of honor and a lasting name!
        A curse upon vain property,
        On wife and child and husbandry!
        A curse on Mammon,[3] when his gold
1600   Lures us to rash heroic deeds,
        Or when his easeful arms enfold
        Us softly, pampering all our needs!
        I curse the nectar of the grape,
        I curse love's sweet transcendent call,
1605   My curse on faith! My curse on hope!
        My curse on patience above all!
CHORUS OF INVISIBLE SPIRITS: Alas, alas,
        You have destroyed
        The beautiful world!
1610   At a blow of your clenched fist
        It falls, struck down
        By a demigod, it disappears.[4]

3. The god of evil wealth.
4. Not a literal destruction (such as the baboon imagines
at line 2406), but a metaphorical destruction of beauty

through Faust's curse. The name Faust derives from the
Latin for "blessed" (*faustus*); Goethe here puns on
"Faust," the German word for fist.

            Into the void
            We carry its fragments, with our tears
1615   We mourn
            The beauty that is lost.
            Mightiest
            Of the sons of earth,
            Let it be built anew
1620   More splendidly, let it come to birth
            Again, within you:
            Begin new
            Ways of living,
            With your mind clear,
1625   New light receiving,
            New music to hear.
MEPHISTOPHELES: My little sprites
            Are performing their rites:
            Full of wise exhortations
1630   And invitations
            To worlds unknown
            Of living and doing.
            Why sit here alone,
            They say, stifling and stewing?
1635   Stop playing with your misery,
            That gnaws your vitals like some carrion-bird!
            Even the worst human society
            Where you feel human, is to be preferred!
            I don't of course propose that we
1640   Should merely mingle with the common herd;
            I'm not exactly a grandee,
            But if you'd fancy getting through
            Your life in partnership with me,
            I shall with pleasure, without more ado,
1645   Wholly devote myself to you.
            You shall have my company,
            And if you are satisfied,
            I shall be your servant, always at your side!
FAUST: And what is your reward for this to be?
MEPHISTOPHELES: Long years will pass till we need think of that.
FAUST: No, no! The Devil has his tit-for-tat;
            He is an egoist, he'll not work for free,
            Merely to benefit humanity.
            State your conditions, make them plain and clear!
1655   Servants like you can cost one dear.
MEPHISTOPHELES: In this world I will bind myself to cater
            For all your whims, to serve and wait on you;
            When we meet in the next world, some time later,
            Wages in the same kind will then fall due.

FAUST: The next world? Well, that's no great matter;
            Here is a world for you to shatter—
            Smash this one first, then let the next be born!
            Out of this earth all my contentment springs,
            This sun shines on my sufferings;
1665   First wean me from all earthly things—
            What happens then's not my concern.
            That's something I've no wish to hear:
            Whether there's hatred still or love
            In that remote supernal sphere,
1670   And who's below and who's above.
MEPHISTOPHELES: Why, in that case, be bold and dare!
            Bind yourself to me, begin life anew:
            You soon will see what I can do.
            No man has ever known a spectacle so rare.
FAUST: Poor devil! What can you offer to me?
            A mind like yours, how can it comprehend
            A human spirit's high activity?
            But have you food that leaves one still unsatisfied,
            Quicksilver-gold that breaks up in
1680   One's very hands? Can you provide
            A game that I can never win,
            Procure a girl whose roving eye
            Invites the next man even as I lie
            In her embrace? A meteoric fame
1685   That fades as quickly as it came?
            Show me the fruit that rots before it's plucked
            And trees that change their foliage every day!
MEPHISTOPHELES: I shall perform as you instruct;
            All these delights I can purvey.
1690   But there are times in life, my friend,
            When one enjoys mere quiet satisfaction.
FAUST: If ever I lie down in sloth and base inaction,
            Then let that moment be my end!
            If by your false cajolery
1695   You lull me into self-sufficiency,
            If any pleasure you can give
            Deludes me, let me cease to live!
            I offer you this wager!
MEPHISTOPHELES: Done!
FAUST: And done again!
            If ever to the moment I shall say:
1700   Beautiful moment, do not pass away!
            Then you may forge your chains to bind me,
            Then I will put my life behind me,
            Then let them hear my death-knell toll,
            Then from your labors you'll be free,

1705   The clock may stop, the clock-hands fall,
        And time come to an end for me!
MEPHISTOPHELES: We shall remember this; think well what you are doing.
FAUST: That is your right. This bet, which I may lose,
          Is no bravado. I must be pursuing
1710   My purpose: once I stand still, I shall be
          A slave—yours or no matter whose.
MEPHISTOPHELES: At the doctoral feast I shall display
          My willing servitude to you this very day.
          One small request—I am sure you'll understand;
1715   It's just in case—I'd like a line or two in your own hand.
FAUST: Poor pedant! Must it be in writing too?
          Is a man's plighted word a thing unknown to you?
          My spoken word must rule my life's whole course
          For ever: is this not enough?
1720   The world streams on with headlong force,
          And a promise arrests me. What strange stuff
          Of dreams composes us! A pledge that binds
          Is a thing rooted in our minds,
          And we accept this. Happy is the man
1725   Of pure and constant heart, who can
          Regret no choice, no loss! But parchments signed and sealed
          Are ghosts that haunt and daunt us; the word dies
          Upon the very pen we wield,
          And wax and leather tyrannize
1730   Our lives. Well, devil, which is it to be:
          Bronze, marble, parchment, paper? Answer me:
          What pen, what tool, what chisel shall I use?
          The medium is yours to choose!
MEPHISTOPHELES: Come, come, sir, this excited flood
1735   Of rhetoric's quite out of place.
          The merest scrap of paper meets the case.
          And—for your signature, a drop of blood.
FAUST: If that is all you want, I'll willingly go through
          With such a farce to humor you.
MEPHISTOPHELES: Blood is a juice with curious properties.
FAUST: But you need have no fear that I will break
          This bond. To strive with all my energies—
          Just that is what I undertake.
          I have been too puffed up with pride:
1745   I see now I belong beside
          Merely the likes of you. With scorn
          That mighty Spirit spurned me, Nature's door
          Is closed, the thread of thought is torn,
          Books sicken me, I'll learn no more.
1750   Now let us slake hot passions in
          The depths of sweet and sensual sin!
          Make me your magics—I'll not care to know
          What lies behind their outward show.

Let us plunge into the rush of things,
1755   Of time and all its happenings!
And then let pleasure and distress,
Disappointment and success,
Succeed each other as they will;
Man cannot act if he is standing still.

MEPHISTOPHELES: Nothing shall limit you; if you wish, sir,
To sample every possible delight,
To snatch your pleasures in full flight,
Then let it be as you prefer.
Enjoy them boldly, grasp at what you want!

FAUST: I tell you, the mere pleasure's not the point!
To dizzying, painful joy I dedicate
Myself, to refreshing frustration, loving hate!
I've purged the lust for knowledge from my soul;
Now the full range of suffering it shall face,
1770   And in my inner self I will embrace
The experience allotted to the whole
Race of mankind; my mind shall grasp the heights
And depths, my heart know all their sorrows and delights.
Thus I'll expand myself, and their self I shall be,
1775   And perish in the end, like all humanity.

MEPHISTOPHELES: Oh, take my word for it, I who have chewed
For centuries on this stale food—
From birth to death a man may do his best,
But this old leavened lump he'll not digest!
1780   We do assure you, such totality
Is only for a god; perpetual light
Is God's alone, me and my kind
He has banished to darkness, and you'll find
You men must live with day and night.

FAUST: Yet I swear I'll achieve it!

MEPHISTOPHELES: Bravely said!
But there's a problem, I'm afraid;
For time is short, and art is long.[5]
Might I suggest you take along
With you some well-known poet? He will teach
1790   You many things: his thoughts will reach
Out far and wide, all sorts of virtues crown
Your noble head at his behest:
The courage of the lion,
The stag's velocity,
1795   The Italian's fiery zest,
The north's tenacity!
He'll find out for you how to mingle guile
With magnanimity, and while
You're still a young warm-blooded man,

5. The Christian devil Mephistopheles here quotes a classical adage.

1800   How to fall in love by a prearranged plan.
The result, I'm sure, would be well worth meeting;
"Mr. Microcosm!" shall be my respectful greeting.
FAUST: What am I then, if it's impossible
To win that crown of our humanity,
1805   To be what all my senses ache to be?
MEPHISTOPHELES: You are just what you are. Do what you will;
Wear wigs, full-bottomed, each with a million locks,
Stand up yards high on stilts or actor's socks—
You're what you are, you'll be the same man still.
FAUST: How uselessly I've laboured to collect
The treasures of the human intellect,
And now I sit and wonder what I've done.
I feel no new strength surging in my soul
I'm not a hairsbreadth taller, I'm not one
1815   Step nearer to the infinite goal.
MEPHISTOPHELES: My dear good sir, I fear your view
Of things is all too common in our day.
Revise it; and let's see what we can do
Before life's pleasures fleet away.
1820   Confound it, man, one's hands and feet of course
Belong to one, so do one's head and arse!
But all the things that give me pleasure,
Are they not mine too, for good measure?
Suppose I keep six stallions, don't you see
1825   The strength of each of them's a part of me?
What a fine fellow I have grown,
Trotting with twenty-four feet of my own!
So come, drop all this cogitation, stir
Yourself, explore the world with me. I say
1830   A philosophic ponderer
Is like a poor beast led astray
By some malignant sprite, to graze on desert ground
When fine green grass is growing all around!
FAUST: How do we start?
MEPHISTOPHELES: First we get out of here!
1835   What sort of prison-hole is this? What mere
Shadow of life you live, when all you do
Just bores your pupils and bores you!
Let your fat colleagues take the strain!
Stop threshing empty straw! Why, even when
1840   There's really something you could teach the poor lads, then
It's something you're forbidden to explain.
Ah, I hear one of them outside your door!
FAUST: I can't see any students now.
MEPHISTOPHELES: He's waited a long time, poor chap,
1845   We'll have to comfort him somehow.
Come, let me have your gown and cap.
What a disguise! I'll look my best in it.

[He dresses up as Faust.]

    Now leave all this to me and to my native wit.
    I'll only need a quarter of an hour.
1850   Meanwhile, make ready for our great Grand Tour!

[Exit Faust.]

MEPHISTOPHELES *[in Faust's long gown]*:
    Scorn reason, despise learning, man's supreme
    Powers and faculties; let your vain dream
    Of magic arts be fortified with sweet
    Flatteries by the Spirit of Deceit,
1855   And you're mine, signature or none!—
    Fate has endowed him with the blind
    Impatience of an ever-striving mind;
    In headlong haste it drives him on,
    He skips the earth and leaves its joys behind.
1860   I'll drag him through life's wastes, through every kind
    Of meaningless banality;
    He'll struggle like a bird stuck fast, I'll bind
    Him hand and foot; in his voracity
    He'll cry in vain for food and drink, he'll find
1865   Them dangling out of reach—ah, yes!
    Even without this devil's bond that he has signed
    He's doomed to perish nonetheless!

* * *[6]

A WITCH'S KITCHEN

[A low hearth with a large cauldron hanging over the fire. In the steam that rises from it various apparitions are seen. A female baboon is sitting by the cauldron skimming it, taking care not to let it run over. The male baboon with their young sits nearby warming himself. The walls and ceiling are decorated with strange witch-parapher-nalia. Faust and Mephistopheles enter.]

FAUST: I'm sick of all this crazy magic stuff!
    Is this your vaunted therapy,
    This mess of raving mad absurdity?
2340   Advice from an old witch! Am I to slough
    Off thirty years, become as good as new,
    By swallowing her stinking brew?
    God help me now, if that's the best
    Hope you can offer! Has man's mind
2345   Devised no other method, can we find
    No nobler balm in Nature's treasure-chest?
MEPHISTOPHELES: You're talking sense again now, my dear sir!

---

6. In the omitted scenes Mephistopheles, impersonating Faust, makes fun of a newly arrived student, then sets out with Faust on their adventures. They begin with the raucous low life of a Leipzig tavern, where Mephisto scares the drunken patrons with fire, then deludes them with visions of happiness while he escapes with Faust, bringing him to visit a witch.

There is another means to your rejuvenation,
But it's a very different operation;
I doubt if it's what you'd prefer.

FAUST: I wish to know it.

MEPHISTOPHELES: Very well;
You'll need no fee, no doctor and no spell.
Go out onto the land at once, begin
To dig and delve, be primitive

2355   In body and mind, be bound within
Some altogether narrower sphere;
Eat food that's plain and simple, live
Like cattle with the cattle, humbly reap
The fields you have manured with your own dung;

2360   Believe me, that will make you young
And keep you young until your eightieth year!

FAUST: I'm not used to all that; it's no good now
Trying to learn the simple life. A spade
Is something I could never use.

MEPHISTOPHELES: Then I'm afraid

2365   The witch will have to show us how.

FAUST: Why do we need this hag? Can't you
Prepare the necessary brew?

MEPHISTOPHELES: The Devil's busy, sir! Why, I could build
A thousand bridges by the time that stuff's distilled!

2370   I have the secret art, indeed,
But not the patience I should need.
Quiet laborious years must run their course;
Time alone can ferment that subtle force.
And there's a deal of ceremony

2375   To go with it—too weird for me.
The Devil taught the witch her tricks,
But she makes potions he can't mix.

[*Seeing the animals.*]

Why, look! what charming kith and kin!
This is her manservant, that's her maid.

[*To the animals.*]

2380   It seems your mistress is not in?

THE ANIMALS: Dining out!
Up the chimney-spout!
She's been delayed!

MEPHISTOPHELES: How long do her trips last, if I may be told?

THE ANIMALS: Till we leave the fire, till our paws get cold.

MEPHISTOPHELES [*to Faust*]: Delightful creatures, don't you agree?

FAUST: I think they're dreary disgusting brutes.

MEPHISTOPHELES: Not at all; their conversation suits
Me very well, as you can see.

[*To the animals.*]

2390   So, what are you stirring there in that pot,
         You damnable apes? What mess have you got?
THE ANIMALS: It's charity soup, very light to digest.
MEPHISTOPHELES: I'm sure your public will be impressed.
THE MALE BABOON [*bounding up to Mephistopheles and coaxing him*]:
         O please, throw the dice!
2395   To be rich is so nice,
         It's so nice to be winning!
         Being poor isn't funny,
         And if I had money
         My head would stop spinning!
MEPHISTOPHELES: This monkey thinks a lucky thing to do
         Would be to play the lottery too!

     [*Meanwhile the young baboons have been playing with a large globe, which they roll forward.*]

THE MALE BABOON: The world is this ball:
         See it rise and fall
         And roll round and round!
2405   It's glass, it will break,
         It's an empty fake—
         Hear the hollow sound!
         See it glow here and shine,
         See it glitter so fine!
2410   "I'm alive!" it sings.
         O my son, beware of it,
         Keep clear of it:
         You must die, like all things!
         It's made of clay;
2415   Clay gets broken, they say.
MEPHISTOPHELES: What's the use of that sieve?
THE MALE BABOON [*lifting it down*]: If you were a thief
         I could tell straight away![7]

     [*He scampers across to the female and makes her look through it.*]

         Look through the sieve!
2420   You can name the thief,
         And you mustn't say.
MEPHISTOPHELES [*approaching the fire*]: And what's this pot?
THE BABOONS: Poor ignorant sot!

         Doesn't know why the pot,
2425   Why the cauldron's there!

MEPHISTOPHELES: You insolent beast!
THE MALE BABOON: Take this whisk, at least,
         And sit down in the chair!

7. A folk belief.

[*He makes Mephistopheles sit down.*]

FAUST [*who in the meantime has been standing in front of a mirror, alternately*
          moving towards it and backing away from it]:
          Oh, heavenly image! What is this I see
2430   Appearing to me in this magic glass?
          Love, carry me to where she dwells, alas,
          Oh, lend the swiftest of your wings to me!
          If I so much as move from this one spot,
          If I dare to approach her, then she seems
2435   To fade, I see her as in misty dreams!
          The loveliest image of a woman! Is this not
          Impossible, can woman be so fair?
          I see in that sweet body lying there
          The quintessence of paradise! How can one
2440   Believe such things exist beneath the sun?
MEPHISTOPHELES: Well, if a god has worked hard for six days
          And on the seventh gives himself high praise,
          You'd think it would be reasonably well done!—
          Look your fill at her now. I'll find
2445   A little darling for you of that kind;
          Then you can try your luck. If you succeed
          In winning her, you'll be a happy man indeed!

[*Faust keeps gazing into the mirror. Mephistopheles, lolling in the chair and
playing with the whisk, goes on talking.*]

          Well, here I sit, a king enthroned in state;
          My sceptre's in my hand, my crown I still await.
THE ANIMALS [*who have been scampering about with each other in a bizarre fashion
          and now bring a crown for Mephistopheles, offering it to him with loud
          screeches*]:
          Oh sir, be so good
          As to mend this old crown
          With sweat and with blood!

[*They handle the crown clumsily and break it into two pieces, which they then
scamper about with.*]

          Now it's done! It falls down!—
          We can talk, see and hear,
2455   We can rhyme loud and clear!
FAUST [*gazing at the mirror*]:
          Oh God! have I gone mad? I'm quite distraught!
MEPHISTOPHELES [*indicating the animals*]:
          I think I'm going a bit crazy too.
THE ANIMALS: And when our rhymes fit
          We're in luck: that's the thought,
2460   That's the meaning of it!
FAUST [*as above*]: My heart's on fire, what shall I do?
          Quick, let's leave now, let's get away!

MEPHISTOPHELES [*remaining seated, as above*]:
>Well, one must certainly admit
>These apes are honest poets, in their way!

[*The cauldron, which the female baboon has been neglecting, begins to boil over, and a great tongue of flame blazes up into the chimney. The witch comes down through the flame, screaming hideously.*]

THE WITCH: Ow! ow! ow! ow!
>You damned brute, you damned filthy sow!
>Not minding the pot! You've burnt me now,
>You filthy brute!

[*Seeing Faust and Mephistopheles.*]

>What's this here? Who
2470 >The hell are you?
>Who let you in?
>What does this mean?
>May hell's hot pains
>Burn in your bones!

[*She plunges the skimming-ladle into the cauldron and splashes flames at Faust, Mephistopheles, and the animals. The animals whine.*]

MEPHISTOPHELES [*reversing the whisk in his hand and striking out with the handle at the glasses and pots*]:
>Split! Split in two!
>That's spilt your stew!
>That's spoilt your cooking!
>I'm only joking,
>Hell-hag! You croon,
2480 >I beat the tune!

[*The witch recoils in rage and terror.*]

>Do you know me now? Skinny, cadaverous bitch,
>Do you know your lord and master? Why don't I
>Smash you to pieces, tell me why,
>You and your ape-familiars? Must I teach
2485 >You some respect for my red doublet? What
>Is this cock's feather, eh? My face,
>Have I been hiding it? You learn your place,
>Old hag! Am I to name myself or not?
THE WITCH: Oh master, pardon my rude greeting!
2490 >But where's your cloven hoof, your horse's leg?
>And your two ravens? Sir, I beg
>To be excused!
MEPHISTOPHELES: Well, well, and so
>You are for once; it's true, I know,
>Some time has passed since our last meeting.
2495 >Besides, civilization, which now licks

Us all so smooth, has taught even the Devil tricks;
The northern fiend's becoming a lost cause—
Where are his horns these days, his tail, his claws?
As for my foot, which I can't do without,
2500   People would think me odd to go about
With that; and so, like some young gentlemen,
I've worn false calves since God knows when.
THE WITCH [*capering about*]: I'm crazy with excitement now I see
Our young Lord Satan's back again!
MEPHISTOPHELES: Woman, don't use that name to me!
THE WITCH: Why, sir, what harm's it ever done?
MEPHISTOPHELES: The name has been a myth too long.
Not that man's any better off—the Evil One
They're rid of, evil is still going strong.
2510   Please call me "Baron," that will do.
I'm just a gentleman, like others of my kind.
My blood's entirely noble, you will find;
My coat of arms may be inspected too.

[*He makes an indecent gesture.*]

THE WITCH [*shrieking with laughter*]: Ha! ha! You haven't changed a bit!
2515   Still the same bad lad, by the looks of it!
MEPHISTOPHELES [*to Faust*]: Mark well, my dear sir! This is how
One deals with witches.
THE WITCH: Tell me now,
Gentlemen, what might be your pleasure?
MEPHISTOPHELES: A good glass of the you-know-what;
2520   But please, the oldest vintage you have got—
Years give it strength in double measure.
THE WITCH: Certainly! I've a bottle on this shelf,
I sometimes take a swig from it myself;
By now it's even quite stopped stinking.
2525   A glass for you can well be spared.
[*Aside.*] But as you know, it's not for casual drinking—
This man will die of it unless he's been prepared.
MEPHISTOPHELES: No, it will do him good—he's a good friend
Of ours, and I can safely recommend
2530   Your kitchen to him. Draw your circle, say
Your spells, pour him a cup without delay!

[*The witch, with strange gestures, draws a circle and places magic objects in it; as she does so the glasses and pots begin to ring and hum and make music. Finally she fetches a massive tome and puts the baboons in the circle, where they are made to act as a reading-desk for her and hold the torch. She beckons Faust to approach her.*]

FAUST [*to Mephistopheles*]: Look, what use is all this to me?
These crazy antics, all that stupid stuff,
The woman's vulgar trickery—
2535   I know and hate them well enough!
MEPHISTOPHELES: Rubbish, man! Can't you see a joke?

Don't be pedantic! You must understand,
As a doctor she's got to hoke and poke
If her medicine's to take effect as planned.

[*He makes Faust step into the circle.*]

THE WITCH [*beginning to declaim from the book with great emphasis*]:

Now hear and see!
From one make ten,
Take two, and then
At once take three,
And you are rich!
2545   Four doesn't score.
But, says the witch,
From five and six
Make seven and eight;
That puts it straight.
2550   And nine is one,
And ten is none.
The witch's twice-times-table's done.
FAUST: She's obviously raving mad.
MEPHISTOPHELES: Oh, she has still much more to say!
2555   I know it well, the whole book reads that way.
It's cost me more time than I had.
A complete paradox, you see,
Fills fools and wise men with a sense of mystery.
My friend, the art's both new and old:
2560   Let error, not the truth be told—
Make one of three and three of one;
That's how it always has been done.
Thus to their heart's content they dogmatize,
Plague take the silly chattering crew!
2565   Men hear mere words, yet commonly surmise
Words must have intellectual content too.
THE WITCH [*continuing*]:
The lofty might
Of wisdom's light,
Hid from the vulgar throng:
2570   It costs no thought,
It's freely taught,
We know it all along!
FAUST: What rubbish is the crone repeating?
My head's half split by this entire
2575   Performance; it's like some massed choir
Of fifty thousand idiots bleating.
MEPHISTOPHELES: Enough, enough, excellent sibyl! Bring
Your cocktail, pour it, fill the cup
Right to the brim, quick, fill it up!
2580   This drink won't harm my friend, he knows a thing
Or two already; many a strong potation

He's swallowed during his initiation!

[*The witch, with great ceremony, pours the potion into a cup; as Faust raises it to his lips it flames up a little.*]

Come, down with it! Don't dither so!
Soon it will warm the cockles of your heart.

2585   You're practically the Devil's bedfellow,
      And fire still makes you flinch and start!

[*The witch opens the circle. Faust steps out of it.*]

Let's go! You must keep moving now.
THE WITCH: I hope my potion whets your appetite!
MEPHISTOPHELES [*to the Witch*]: And if I can do you a good turn somehow,
2590   Just tell me on Walpurgis Night.[8]
THE WITCH: Here is a song, sir, you might like to sing;
      You'll find it has a special virtue in it.
MEPHISTOPHELES [*to Faust*]: Do as I say, come, let's be off this minute;
      You must let yourself sweat, this thing
2595   Must soak right through your guts. Then you shall learn
      How to appreciate your noble leisure,
      And soon, to your consummate pleasure,
      Cupid[9] will stir in you, you'll feel him dance and burn.
FAUST: Let me look once more in the glass before we go—
      That woman's lovely shape entrances me.
MEPHISTOPHELES: No, no!
      Before you in the flesh you soon will see
      The very paragon of femininity.

[*Aside.*] With that elixir coursing through him,
Soon any woman will be Helen[1] to him.

* * *[2]

EVENING

[*A small well-kept room.*]

MARGARETA [*plaiting and binding up her hair*]:
      I'd like to find out, I must say,
      Who that gentleman was today.
2680   A handsome man, I do admit,
      And a nobleman by the looks of it.
      I could tell by something in his eyes.
      And he wouldn't have had the cheek otherwise.

[*Exit. Mephistopheles and Faust enter.*]

---

8. The night of April 30, when witches were supposed to engage in Satanic rituals on the Brocken, the highest peak of the Harz Mountains.
9. God of love.
1. Helen of Troy, famous for her fatal beauty.

2. Faust, transformed into a dashing youth, meets Margareta, a lower-class girl, and demands that Mephisto seduce her for him. (Later she is also called by her nickname Gretchen.)

MEPHISTOPHELES: Come in, keep quiet! Come, don't delay!

FAUST [*after a pause*]:   Leave me alone, please go away.

MEPHISTOPHELES [*taking a look round the room*]:

      Very neat and tidy, I must say. [*Exit.*]

FAUST [*gazing up and about him*]:

      Welcome, sweet twilight, shining dim all through

      This sanctuary! Now let love's sweet pain

      That lives on hope's refreshing dew

2690   Seize and consume my heart again!

      How this whole place breathes deep content

      And order and tranquillity!

      What riches in this poverty,

      What happiness in this imprisonment!

[*He sinks into the leather armchair by the bed.*]

2695   Oh let me rest here: long ago, among

      Their joys and sorrows, others sat on you,

      Embraced and welcomed! Ah, how often too

      Round this, their grandsire's throne, the children clung!

      My love herself, at Christmas time, a young

2700   Rosy-cheeked child, glad at some gift, knelt here

      Perhaps, and kissed his wrinkled hand so dear!

      What order, what completeness I am made

      To sense in these surroundings! It is yours,

      Dear girl, your native spirit that ensures

2705   Maternal daily care, the table neatly laid,

      The crisp white sand strewn on the floors!

      Oh godlike hand, by whose dear skill and love

      This little hut matches the heavens above!

      And here!

[*He draws aside a curtain from the bed.*]

         What fierce joy seizes me! I could

2710   Stand gazing here for ever. Nature, you

      Worked this sweet wonder, here the inborn angel grew

      Through gentle dreams to womanhood.

      Here the child lay, her tender heart

      Full of warm life, here the pure love

2715   Of God's creative forces wove

      His likeness by their sacred art!

      And I! What purpose brings me? What

      Profound emotion stirs me! What did I

      Come here to do? Why do I sigh?

2720   Poor wretch! Am I now Faust or not?

      Is there some magic hovering round me here?

      I was resolved, my lust brooked no delay—

      And now in dreams of love I wilt and melt away!

Are we mere playthings of the atmosphere?

2725 If she came in this instant, ah, my sweet,
How she would punish me! How small
The great Don Juan would feel, how he would fall
In tears of languor at her feet!

MEPHISTOPHELES [*entering*]: Quick, she's down there, she'll be here any minute.

FAUST: Take me away! I'll never come again!

MEPHISTOPHELES: Here's quite a heavy box with nice things in it;
I got it—somewhere else. Now then,
Into her cupboard with it, quick, before we're seen.
I tell you, when she finds that stuff

2735 She'll go out of her mind; I've put enough
Jewelry in there to seduce a queen.
A child's a child, of course, and play's just play.

FAUST: I don't know if I should—

MEPHISTOPHELES: Now what's the fuss about?
You'd like to keep it for yourself, no doubt?

2740 Let me advise you then, Sir Lecher-Lust,
Stop wasting the fine time of day,
And spare me further tasks! I trust
You're not a miser too? I scratch my pate
And bite my nails and calculate—

[*He puts the jewel-case in the cupboard and locks it up again.*]

2745 Quick, we must go!—
How I'm to please your sweetheart for you
And make her want you and adore you;
And now you hesitate
As if this were your lecture-room

2750 Where in gray professorial gloom
Physics and metaphysics wait!
We must go! [*They leave.*]

MARGARETA [*coming in with a lamp*]:
It's so hot and sultry in here somehow,

[*She opens the window.*]

And yet it's quite cool outside just now.

2755 I've got a feeling something's wrong—
I hope my mother won't be long.
It's a sort of scare coming over me—
What a silly baby I must be!

[*She begins singing as she undresses.*]

There once was a king of Thule.[3]

2760 Of the far north land of old:
His dying lady he loved so truly

---

3. Ultima Thule was the ancient name for the far north.

She gave him a cup of gold.

There was no thing so dear to the king,
And every time he wept
2765   As he drained that cup at each banqueting,
So truly his faith he kept.

And at last, they say, on his dying day
His kingdom was willed and told,
And his son and heir got all his share—
2770   But the king kept the cup of gold.

They feasted long with wine and song,
And there with his knights sat he,
In the ancestral hall, in his castle tall
On the cliffs high over the sea.

2775   The old man still drank as his life's flame sank,
Then above the waves he stood,
And the sacred cup he raised it up,
Threw it down to the raging flood.

He watched it fall to the distant shore
2780   And sink in the waters deep;
And never a drop that king drank more,
For he'd closed his eyes to sleep.

[She opens the cupboard to put her clothes in, and sees the jewel case.]

However did this pretty box get here?
I left the cupboard locked; how very queer!
2785   Whatever can be in it? Perhaps my mother lent
Some money on it, and it's meant
As a security. Oh dear!
It's got a ribbon with a little key—
I think I'll open it, just to see!
2790   What's this? Oh God in heaven, just look!
I've never seen such things before!
These jewels would be what a princess wore
At the highest feast in the feast-day book!
I wonder how that necklace would suit me?
2795   Whose can these wonderful things be?

[She puts on some of the jewelry and looks at herself in the glass.]

If even the earrings were only mine!
My, what a difference it makes!
We young girls have to learn, it takes
More than just beauty; that's all very fine,
2800   But everyone just says "she's pretty,"
And they seem to say it out of pity.
Gold's all they care
About, gold's wanted everywhere;
For us poor folk there's none to spare.

[Faust walking up and down deep in thought. Enter Mephistopheles.]

MEPHISTOPHELES: By the pangs of despised love! By the fires of hell!
    I wish I knew something worse, to curse it as well!
FAUST: Whatever's the matter? You do look odd
    What a sour face for a fine day!
MEPHISTOPHELES: May the devil take me, I would say,
2810   If I weren't the Devil myself, by God.
FAUST: Are you right in the head? Excuse me if I smile;
    These rages aren't your usual style.
MEPHISTOPHELES: Just think: those jewels for Gretchen that I got,
    A priest has been and swiped the lot!—
2815   Her mother took one look, and hey!
    She had the horrors straight away.
    That woman's got a good nose all right,
    Snuffling her prayer-book day and night,
    With any commodity she can tell
2820   Profane from sacred by the smell:
    And as for those jewels, she knew soon enough
    There was something unholy about that stuff.
    "My child," she exclaimed, ill-gotten wealth
    Poisons one's spiritual health.
2825   To God's blessed Mother it must be given,
    And she will reward us with manna from heaven!
    How Meg's face fell, poor little minx!
    It's a gift-horse after all, she thinks,
    And whoever so kindly brought it—how can
2830   There be anything godless about such a man?
    Ma sends for the priest, and he, by glory!
    Has no sooner heard their little story
    And studied the spoils with great delight,
    Than he says: "Dear ladies, you are quite right!
2835   Who resists the tempter shall gain a crown.
    The Church can digest all manner of meat,
    It's never been known to over-eat
    Although it has gulped whole empires down;
    Holy Church's stomach alone can take
2840   Ill-gotten goods without stomach-ache!"
FAUST: It's common; many a king and Jew
    Has a well-filled belly of that kind too.
MEPHISTOPHELES: So he sweeps every ring and chain and brooch,
    As if they were peanuts, into his pouch:
2845   Takes it no less for granted, indeed,
    Than if it were all just chickenfeed—
    Promises them celestial reward
    And leaves them thanking the blessed Lord.
FAUST: And Gretchen?
MEPHISTOPHELES: Sitting there all of a dither,

2850   Doesn't know what to do or why or whether.
         Can't get the jewels out of her mind—
         Or the gentleman who had been so kind.
FAUST: I can't bear my darling to be sad.
         Get another lot for her! The ones she had
2855   Weren't all that remarkable anyway.
MEPHISTOPHELES: Oh indeed, for my lord it's mere child's play!
FAUST: Do as I tell you!—And one thing more:
         Get to know that friend of hers next door!
         Do something, devil, stir your feet!
2860   And get some more jewels for my sweet!
MEPHISTOPHELES: With pleasure, sir, whatever you say.

     [*Exit Faust.*]

         He's just like all the lovesick fools I know;
         To please their darlings they would blow
         The sun and moon and stars out at one go. [*Exit.*]

                THE NEIGHBOR'S HOUSE

MARTHA [*alone*]: My husband, may God pardon him!
         He didn't treat me right. For shame!
         Just went off into the world one day.
         Left me a grass widow, as they say.
         Yet I've never done him any wrong;
2870   I loved him truly all along. [*She weeps.*]
         He may even be dead. Oh, my poor heart bleeds!
         —A death certificate's what one needs.

     [*Enter Margareta*]

MARGARETA: Martha!
MARTHA: Gretchen dear! What a face!
MARGARETA: Martha, I feel quite faint! There's been
2875   This second box—I found it in
         My cupboard there—an ebony case
         Of the grandest jewels you ever saw;
         Much richer than the one before!
MARTHA: Now this time you mustn't tell your mother,
2880   Or the priest'll get it, just like the other.
MARGARETA: Oh, look at this! Just look at this!
MARTHA [*trying out some of the jewels on her*]:
         Aren't you a lucky little miss!
MARGARETA: But I can't wear them in the street, or go
         To church and be seen in them, you know.[4]
MARTHA: Just come whenever you can to me,
         And put on your jewels secretly—
         Walk about in front of the looking-glass here,

---

4. Clothing and ornamentation were regulated by law, according to the social rank of the wearer.

And we'll enjoy them together, my dear.
Then when there's a feast-day or some occasion,
2890   Let people see one little thing, then another,
A necklace at first, a pearl earring; your mother
May not notice, or we'll make up some explanation.
MARGARETA: But all this jewelry—who can have brought it?
I think there's something funny about it.

[*There is a knock at the door.*]

2895   Oh God, perhaps that's my mother!
MARTHA [*looking through the peep-hole*]:   No!
It's some gentleman I don't know—
Come in!

[*Enter Mephistopheles*]

MEPHISTOPHELES: If I may make so bold!
Forgive me, ladies; I'm looking for
Frau Martha Schwertlein,[5] who lives here, I'm told.

[*He steps back respectfully on seeing Margareta*]

MARTHA: That's me; how can I oblige you, sir?
MEPHISTOPHELES [*aside to her*]: Now that I know you, that will do;
You have a fine lady visiting you.
Excuse my taking the liberty;
I'll call again later when you're free.
MARTHA [*aloud*]: Do you hear that, child! What a rigmarole!
He takes you for a lady, bless your soul!
MARGARETA: Oh sir, you're much too kind to me;
I'm a poor young woman—this jewelry
I'm trying on, it isn't mine.
MEPHISTOPHELES: Why, it's not just the jewels that are fine;
You have a manner, a look in your eyes.
Then I may stay? What a pleasant surprise.
MARTHA: Now, I'm sure your business is interesting—
MEPHISTOPHELES: I hope you'll pardon the news I bring;
2915   I'm sorry to grieve you at our first meeting.
Your husband is dead, and sends his greeting.
MARTHA: What, dead? My true love! Alas the day!
My husband's dead! I shall pass away!
MARGARETA: Oh, don't despair, Frau Martha dear!
MEPHISTOPHELES: Well, it's a sad tale you shall hear.
MARGARETA: I hope I shall never love; I know
It would kill me with grief to lose someone so.
MEPHISTOPHELES: Joy and grief need each other, they can't be parted.
MARTHA: Good sir, pray tell me how he died.

---

5. "Schwertlein" means "little sword," an off-color joke.

MEPHISTOPHELES: In Padua, by St. Anthony's[6] side,
　　　　There they interred your late departed,
　　　　In a spot well suited, by God's grace,
　　　　To be his last cool resting-place.
MARTHA: And have you brought nothing else for me?
MEPHISTOPHELES: Ah, yes: he requests you solemnly
　　　　To have three hundred masses sung for his repose.
　　　　For the rest, my hands are empty, I fear.
MARTHA: What! No old medal, not a souvenir
　　　　Or trinket any poor apprentice will lay by,
2935　　Stuffed in his satchel, and would rather die
　　　　In penury than sell or lose?
MEPHISTOPHELES: I much regret it, ma'am; but truthfully,
　　　　Your husband wasn't one to waste his property.
　　　　And he rued his faults, but his luck he cursed—
2940　　The second more bitterly than the first.
MARGARETA: Oh, why have people such ill luck! I'm sad for them.
　　　　I promise to pray for him with many a requiem.
MEPHISTOPHELES: What a charming child you are! I'd say
　　　　You deserve to be married straight away.
MARGARETA: Oh, I'm still too young, that wouldn't be right.
MEPHISTOPHELES: If a husband won't do, then a lover might.
　　　　Why not? It's life's greatest blessing and pleasure
　　　　To lie in the arms of so sweet a treasure.
MARGARETA: That's not the custom in this country, sir.
MEPHISTOPHELES: Custom or not, it does occur.
MARTHA: Tell me the rest!
MEPHISTOPHELES:　　　　　　I stood by his deathbed;
　　　　It was pretty filthy, it must be said.
　　　　But he died as a Christian, on half-rotten straw.
　　　　His sins were absolved, though he felt he had many more.
2955　　"I hate myself," he cried, "for what I've done;
　　　　Away from my trade, away from my wife to run.
　　　　I'm tormented by that memory.
　　　　If only she could forgive me in this life!—"
MARTHA [weeping]: Oh, he's long been forgiven by his loving wife!
MEPHISTOPHELES: "—But God knows, she was more to blame than me."
MARTHA: Why, that's a lie! What, lie at the point of death!
MEPHISTOPHELES: He was delirious at his last breath,
　　　　If I am any judge of such events.
　　　　"I had my time cut out," he said,
2965　　"Providing her with children, then with bread—
　　　　Which meant bread in the very widest sense.
　　　　And then I got no peace to eat my share."
MARTHA: Had he forgotten all my faithful loving care,
　　　　Slaving for him all day and night?

---

6. St. Anthony of Padua, the patron saint of brides and wives.

MEPHISTOPHELES: Why no, he had remembered that all right.
       He told me: "When we sailed away from Malta,
       For my wife and brats I said a fervent prayer,
       And by heaven's will, our luck began to alter:
       We took a Turkish ship and boarded her—
2975   The mighty Sultan's treasure-ship! We fought
       Them bravely and deserved our prize.
       And as for me, this bold adventure brought
       Me in a dividend of some size."
MARTHA: What's that? Where is it? Has he buried it?
MEPHISTOPHELES: Who knows now where the four winds carried it!
       He fell in with a lovely lady-friend
       In Naples, visiting the place for fun;
       And fun he got—the kindnesses she'd done,
       They left their mark on him till his life's end.[7]
MARTHA: The scoundrel! Stealing his own children's bread!
       Not even want and poverty
       Could stop his vices and debauchery!
MEPHISTOPHELES: Well, there you are, you see; so now he's dead.
       If I were in your place, you know,
2990   I'd mourn him for a decent twelvemonth, then,
       Having looked round a little, choose another beau.
MARTHA: Oh dear, after my first, it will be hard
       To find a second man like him again!
       He was a jolly fellow—everyone enjoyed him;
2995   He just was far too fond of wandering abroad,
       And foreign women, foreign wine,
       And it was that damned gambling that destroyed him.
MEPHISTOPHELES: Well, I daresay it was a fine
       Arrangement, if for his part he
3000   Allowed you equal liberty.
       On such terms, I would hardly hesitate
       Myself to be your second mate.
MARTHA: Oh, sir, you like to have your little joke with me!
MEPHISTOPHELES [aside]: While there's still time I'd best get out of here;
3005   She'd hold the Devil to his word, that's clear.

   [To Gretchen.]

       And you, my child, are you still fancy-free?
MARGARETA: I don't quite understand.
MEPHISTOPHELES [aside]:   Now there's sweet innocence!
       [Aloud.] Ladies, good day to you!
MARGARETA: Good day!
MARTHA: Sir, one more thing:
       I'd like to have some proper evidence—

---

7. Syphilis was known as "the Naples disease."

3010   The details of my husband's death and burying.
           I've always liked things orderly and neat;
           I want to read it in the weekly notice-sheet.
MEPHISTOPHELES: Indeed, ma'am; when two witnesses agree,
           The truth's revealed infallibly.
3015   I have a companion; he and I
           Can go before the judge to testify.
           I'll bring him here.
MARTHA: Oh by all means do!
MEPHISTOPHELES: And this young miss will be here too?—
           He's a fine lad; seen the world all right;
3020   Very nice to ladies, very polite.
MARGARETA: I shall blush with shame to meet him, I fear.
MEPHISTOPHELES: You need blush before no king, my dear.
MARTHA: I've a garden at the back; so, gentlemen.
           Please come this evening, we'll expect you then.

                         A STREET

FAUST: Well, what news now? Is it going ahead?
MEPHISTOPHELES: Ah, bravo! So you're well alight!
           Gretchen will soon be in your bed.
           We're to meet her at her neighbour's house tonight.
           That Martha's a proper witch, good Lord,
3030   I couldn't have picked you a better bawd.
FAUST: Good.
MEPHISTOPHELES: But she asks a service of us too.
FAUST: That's fair enough; what do we have to do?
MEPHISTOPHELES: We swear a deposition, warranting
           That her late husband's bones now are
3035   Buried in hallowed ground in Padua.
FAUST: Brilliant; so first we have to travel there.
MEPHISTOPHELES: *Sancta simplicitas!*[8] Why should we care?
           Just testify; no need to make the visit.
FAUST: If that's your scheme, then I'll do no such thing.
MEPHISTOPHELES: Oh, holy Willie! That's your scruple, is it?
           So this is the first time in your career
           That you'll have borne false witness? Have you not
           Laid down authoritative definitions
           Of God and of the world, of all that's there and here,
3045   Man's mind and heart, his motives and conditions,
           With brazen confidence, with all the pride you've got?
           But pause to think—confess, as you draw breath:
           Of all those matters you knew not a jot
           More than of Martha Schwertlein's husband's death!

8. Holy simplicity!

FAUST: You are, and always were, a sophist[9] and a liar.

MEPHISTOPHELES: And your standards of truth, I know, are so much higher.
          In all good faith, tomorrow, we shall find
          You turning little Gretchen's mind
          With vows of love, and nonsense of that kind.

FAUST: It will come from my heart.

MEPHISTOPHELES: A splendid vow!
          Eternal love, faithfulness to the end,
          Unique all-powerful passion—yes, my friend,
          That will come from the heart too, will it now?

FAUST: Yes! Let me be! It shall!—This deep commotion
3060   And turmoil in me, I would speak
          Its name, find words for this emotion—
          Through the whole world my soul and senses seek
          The loftiest words for it: this flame
          That burns me, it must have a name!
3065   And so I say: eternal, endless, endless—why,
          You devil, do you call all that a lie?

MEPHISTOPHELES: I am right nonetheless.

FAUST: Listen to me—
          And understand, before I burst a lung:
          Insist on being right, and merely have a tongue,
3070   And right you'll be.
          But now let's go, I'm sick of all this chatter.
          And you are right; I've no choice in the matter.

                    A GARDEN

[Margareta walking up and down with Faust, Martha with Mephistopheles.]

MARGARETA: I'm quite ashamed, I feel you're being so kind
          And condescending, just to spare
3075   My feelings, sir! A traveler
          Must be polite, and take what he can find.
          I know quite well that my poor conversation
          Can't entertain a man of education.

FAUST: One look, one word from you—that entertains
3080   Me more than any this wise world contains.

          [He kisses her hand.]

MARGARETA: Sir, you put yourself out! How can you kiss my hand?
          It's so nasty and rough; I have to do
          Such a lot of housework with it. If you knew
          How fussy Mother is, you'd understand!

          [They pass on.]

MARTHA: So, sir, you're always traveling, I believe?

---

9. False reasoner.

MEPHISTOPHELES: Alas, constraints of duty and vocation!
        Sometimes a place is very hard to leave—
        But it's just not one's destination.
MARTHA: I dare say, when one's young and strong,
3090   It's good to roam the world and to be free;
        But there are bad times coming before long,
        And creeping to one's grave alone—oh, you'd be wrong
        To be a bachelor then, sir, believe me!
MEPHISTOPHELES: I view with horror that approaching fate.
MARTHA: Then think again, while it's not yet too late!

    [They pass on.]

MARGARETA: Yes, out of sight out of mind it will be!
        And though you talk politely—after all,
        You've many friends, and I'm sure they are all
        More intellectual than me.
FAUST: My sweet, believe me, what's called intellect
        Is often shallowness and vanity.
MARGARETA: How so?
FAUST: Oh, why can simple innocence not know
        Itself, or humble lowliness respect
        Its own great value, feel the awe that's due
3105   To generous Nature's dearest, greatest boon—
MARGARETA: You'll sometimes think of me, and then forget me soon;
        But I'll have time enough to think of you.
FAUST: So you're alone a lot?
MARGARETA: Oh yes, you see, our household's not
3110   Big, but one has to see to it;
        And we've no maid. I cook and sweep and knit
        And sew, all day I'm on my feet.
        And my mother insists everything's got
        To be so neat!
3115   Not that she's really poor in any way,
        In fact, we're better off than most folk, I should say.
        We got some money when my father died,
        A little house and garden just outside
        The town. But mine's a quiet life now, that's true.
3120   My brother's a soldier, he's not here.
        My little sister, she died too.
        I had such trouble with her, the poor little dear,
        And yet I'd gladly have it all again to do,
        I loved her so.
FAUST: A darling, just like you.
MARGARETA: I brought her up: she got so fond of me.
        She was born after Father's death, you see,
        And Mother was so desperately ill then
        We thought she never would be well again,
        And she got better slowly, very gradually.
3130   She couldn't possibly, you know,

Give the baby her breast; and so
I had to feed her, all alone,
With milk and water; she became my own,
And in my arms and on my breast
3135   She smiled and wriggled and grew and grew.
FAUST: That must have been great happiness for you.
MARGARETA: But very hard as well, although I did my best.
At night she had her little cradle by
My bed; she'd hardly need to move, and I
3140   Was wide awake.
Then I would have to feed her, or else take
Her into bed with me, or if she went
On crying, I'd get up and jog her to and fro.
And then, the washing started at cock-crow;
3145   Then I would shop and cook. That's how I spent
The whole of every blessed day.
So you see, sir, it's not all play!
But you eat well, and you sleep well that way.

[*They pass on.*]

MARTHA: We women do have an unlucky fate!
3150   A confirmed bachelor's hard to educate.
MEPHISTOPHELES: I'm sure it takes a lady of your kind,
Madam, to make one change one's mind.
MARTHA: But tell me truly now, sir: have you never
Lost your hard heart to any woman ever?
MEPHISTOPHELES: One's own fireside, we are so often told,
And a good wife, are worth silver and gold.[1]
MARTHA: I'm asking: have you never felt the inclination—?
MEPHISTOPHELES: I've always been treated with great consideration.
MARTHA: I meant: have things not been serious at any time?
MEPHISTOPHELES: Trifling with ladies is a very serious crime.
MARTHA: Oh, you don't understand!
MEPHISTOPHELES: That grieves me, I confess!
But I do understand—your great obligingness.

[*They pass on.*]

FAUST: You knew me again, sweetheart, immediately,
Here in the garden? Is it really true?
MARGARETA: You saw me cast my eyes down, didn't you.
FAUST: And you've forgiven the liberty
I took outside the church, the insulting way
I spoke to you the other day?
MARGARETA: It was a shock—you see, it never had
3170   Happened before. No one ever says bad
Things of me, and I thought: did I somehow
Seem lacking in modesty to him just now?

---

1. Mephisto's proverbial wisdom partly derives from the Bible: "Who can find a virtuous woman? For her price is far above rubies" (Proverbs 31:10).

He suddenly just thinks, quite without shame:
"I'll pick this girl up;" maybe I'm to blame?
3175   I must confess that something in my heart,
I don't know what, began quite soon to take your part;
In fact I got quite cross with myself, too,
For not being quite cross enough with you.
FAUST: Oh my sweet!
MARGARETA: Wait!

[She picks a daisy and begins pulling off the petals one by one.]

FAUST: What's this for? A bouquet?
MARGARETA: No!
FAUST: What?
MARGARETA: You'll laugh at me; it's just a game we play.

[She murmurs as she picks off the petals.]

FAUST: What's this you're murmuring?
MARGARETA [*half aloud*]:   He loves me—loves me not
FAUST: You dear beloved little thing!
MARGARETA [*continuing*]:   Loves me—not—loves me—not—

[Pulling off the last petal and exclaiming with joy.]

He loves me!
FAUST: Yes, my love! The flower speaks,
3185   And let it be your oracle! He loves you:
Do you know what that means? He loves you!

[He clasps both her hands in his.]

MARGARETA: I'm trembling all over!
FAUST: Don't be afraid! Oh, let my eyes,
My hands on your hands tell you what
3190   No words can say:
To give oneself entirely and to feel
Ecstasy that must last for ever!
For ever!—For its end would be despair.
No, never-ending! Never-ending!

[Margareta presses his hands, frees herself and runs away. He stands lost in thought for a moment, then follows her. Martha enters with Mephistopheles]

MARTHA: It's getting dark.
MEPHISTOPHELES: Yes, and we must be gone.
MARTHA: I would gladly invite you to stay on,
But this place has sharp eyes, and sharp tongues too.
It's as if they all had nothing else to do,
Day in, day out,
3200   But try to sniff their neighbors' business out.
It's wicked! But one can't escape their talk.
And our young pair?
MEPHISTOPHELES: Gone fluttering up that garden walk;
Wild wayward butterflies!

MARTHA: He seems to have found
     His true love.
MEPHISTOPHELES: So has she. That's how the world goes round!

A SUMMERHOUSE

[*Margareta runs in, hides behind the door, puts a fingertip to her lips and peeps through a crack.*]

MARGARETA: He's coming!
FAUST [*entering*]:   Little rogue! I've caught you now,
     You tease! [*He kisses her.*]
MARGARETA [*throwing her arms round him and returning his kiss*]:
     Darling, I love you so. I can't say how!

[*Mephistopheles knocks at the door.*]

FAUST [*stamping his foot*]: Who's there?
MEPHISTOPHELES: A friend!
FAUST: A beast!
MEPHISTOPHELES: It's time to leave, I fear.
MARTHA [*entering*]: Yes, sir, it's getting late.
FAUST: May I not escort you, then?
MARGARETA: My mother would—Goodbye!
FAUST: Then I must go, my dear?
     Goodbye!
MARTHA: Adieu!
MARGARETA: Till we soon meet again!

[*Faust and Mephistopheles leave.*]

     Oh goodness gracious, what a lot
     Of clever thoughts in his head he's got!
     I'm so ashamed, I just agree
     With all he says, poor silly me.
3215   I'm just a child and don't know a thing,
     How can he find me so interesting?

from A FOREST CAVERN

FAUST [*alone*]: Oh sublime Spirit![2] You have given me,
     Given me all I asked for. From the fire
     You turned your face to me, and not in vain.
3220   You gave me Nature's splendor for my kingdom,
     And strength to grasp it with my heart. No mere
     Cold curious inspection was the privilege
     You granted me, but to gaze deep, as into
     The heart of a dear friend. Before my eyes,
3225   Opened by you, all living creatures move
     In sequence: in the quiet woods, the air,
     The water, now I recognize my brothers.

2. The Earth Spirit (lines 460–513).

And when the storm-struck forest roars and jars,
When giant pines crash down, whose crushing fall
3230   Tears neighboring branches, neighboring tree-trunks with them,
And drones like hollow thunder through the hills:
Then in this cavern's refuge, where you lead me,
You show me to myself, and my own heart's
Profound mysterious wonders are disclosed.

3235   And when the pure moon lifts its soothing light
As I look skywards, then from rocky cliffs
And dewy thickets the ensilvered shapes
Of a lost world, hovering there before me,
Assuage the austere joy of my contemplation.

3240   Oh now I feel this truth, that for mankind
No boon is perfect. To such happiness,
Which brings me ever nearer to the gods,
You added a companion, who already
Is indispensable to me, although
3245   With one cold mocking breath he can degrade me
In my own eyes, and turn your gifts to nothing.
He stirs my heart into a burning fire
Of passion for that lovely woman's image.
Thus from my lust I stumble to fulfilment,
3250   And in fulfilment for more lust I languish.

* * * [3]

GRETCHEN'S ROOM

[Gretchen at her spinning-wheel, alone.]

GRETCHEN: My heart's so heavy,
3375   My heart's so sore,
How can ever my heart
Be at peace any more?

How dead the whole world is,
How dark the day,
3380   How bitter my life is
Now he's away!

My poor head's troubled,
Oh what shall I do?
My poor mind's broken
3385   And torn in two.

My heart's so heavy,
My heart's so sore,
How can ever my heart
Be at peace any more?

3390   When I look from my window
It's him I must see;

---

3. In the omitted lines Faust complains to Mephisto that he is torn by pity for Gretchen.

I walk out wondering
Where can he be?

Oh his step so proud
3395   And his head so high
And the smile on his lips
And the spell of his eye,

And his voice, like a stream
Of magic it is,
3400   And his hand pressing mine
And his kiss, his kiss!

My heart's so heavy,
My heart's so sore,
How can ever my heart
3405   Be at peace any more?

My body's on fire
With wanting him so;
Oh when shall I hold him
And never let go

3410   And kiss him at last
As I long to do,
And swoon on his kisses
And die there too!

MARTHA'S GARDEN

[*Margareta. Faust.*]

MARGARETA Promise me, Heinrich.
FAUST: Whatever I can!
MARGARETA: Then tell me what you think about religion.
         I know you are a dear good man,
         But it means little to you, I imagine.
FAUST: My darling, let's not talk of that. You know
         I'd give my life for you, I love you so:
3420   I wouldn't want to take anyone's faith away.
MARGARETA: One must believe! That's not right what you say!
FAUST: Ah, must one?
MARGARETA: Oh, if only I could show you!
         You don't respect the holy Sacraments, do you?
FAUST: I do.
MARGARETA: But you don't want them! You don't go
3425   To Mass or to confession, that I know.
         Do you believe in God?
FAUST: My dear, how can
         Anyone dare to say: I believe in Him?
         Ask a priest how, ask a learned man,
         And all their answers merely seem
3430   To mock the questioner.

MARGARETA: Then you don't believe?
FAUST: My sweet beloved child, don't misconceive
         My meaning! Who dare say God's name?
         Who dares to claim
         That he believes in God?
3435   And whose heart is so dead
         That he has ever boldly said:
         No, I do not believe?
         Embracing all things,
         Holding all things in being,
3440   Does He not hold and keep
         You, me, even Himself?
         Is not the heavens' great vault up there on high,
         And here below, does not the earth stand fast?
         Do everlasting stars, gleaming with love,
3445   Not rise above us through the sky?
         Are we not here and gazing eye to eye?
         Does all this not besiege
         Your mind and heart,
         And weave in unseen visibility
3450   All round you its eternal mystery?
         Oh, fill your heart right up with all of this,
         And when you're brimming over with the bliss
         Of such a feeling, call it what you like!
         Call it joy, or your heart, or love, or God!
3455   I have no name for it. The feeling's all there is:
         The name's mere noise and smoke—what does it do
         But cloud the heavenly radiance?
MARGARETA: Well, I suppose all that makes sense;
         I think the priest says something like that too—
3460   Just in the wording there's a difference.
FAUST: It is what all men say,
         All human hearts under the blessed day
         Speak the same message, each
         In its own speech:
3465   May I not speak in mine?
MARGARETA: It sounds all very well, all very fine
         But there's still something wrong about it,
         For you're not a Christian, I truly doubt it!
FAUST: Sweetheart!
MARGARETA: It's always worried me
3470   To see you keep such company.
FAUST: What do you mean?
MARGARETA: That man you have with you—
         I hate him, upon my soul I do!
         It pierces me to the heart like a knife.
         I've seen nothing so dreadful in all my life
3475   As that man's face and its ugly sneer.
FAUST: My poor child, why, there's nothing to fear!

MARGARETA: It's just that his presence offends me so!
　　　　　I don't usually dislike people, you know!
　　　　　And I'd gaze at you just as long as I can,
3480　　　But it makes my blood freeze to see that man—
　　　　　And I think he's a scoundrel, anyway.
　　　　　If I wrong him, God pardon what I say!
FAUST: Well, you know, some people just are rather odd.
MARGARETA: I wouldn't live with a man like that!
　　　　　As soon as he steps through the door, you can tell
　　　　　You're being looked so mockingly at
　　　　　And half fiercely as well;
　　　　　And he cares for nothing, not man nor God.
　　　　　It's as if he'd a mark on his brow that said
3490　　　That he never has loved, that his heart is dead.
　　　　　Each time you put your arms round me
　　　　　I'm yours so completely, so warm, so free!
　　　　　But I close up inside at the sight of him.
FAUST: Dear fancy, sweet foreboding whim!
MARGARETA: It upsets me so much, each time I see
　　　　　Him coming, that I even doubt
　　　　　If I still love you, when he's about.
　　　　　Besides, when he's there, I never could pray,
　　　　　And that's what's eating my heart away.
3500　　　Dear Heinrich, tell me you feel the same way!
FAUST: You've just taken against him, and that's all.
MARGARETA: I must go home now.
FAUST: 　　　　　　　　　　Oh, tell me whether
　　　　　We can have some peaceful hour together,
　　　　　Lie breast to breast and mingle soul with soul!
MARGARETA: Oh, if only I slept alone it would be all right,
　　　　　I'd leave you my door unbolted tonight.
　　　　　But my mother sleeps lightly, and if she
　　　　　Were to wake up and catch us, oh goodness me,
　　　　　I'd drop down dead on the very spot!
FAUST: My darling, there need be no such surprise.
　　　　　Look, take this little flask I've got:
　　　　　You must put just three drops in her drink
　　　　　And into a sweet, sound sleep she'll sink.
MARGARETA: What would I not do for your sake!
3515　　　But she'll be all right again, she'll wake?
FAUST: Would I suggest it otherwise?
MARGARETA: I look at you, dear Heinrich, and somehow
　　　　　My will is yours, it's not my own will now.
　　　　　Already I've done so many things for you,
3520　　　There's—almost nothing left to do.

　　　[Exit. Enter Mephistopheles]

MEPHISTOPHELES: Pert monkey! Has she gone?
FAUST: 　　　　　　　　　　　　　　Still eavesdropping and spying?

MEPHISTOPHELES: I listened to it all most carefully.
    The learned Doctor was catechized![4]
    I hope he will find it edifying.
3525 Girls always check up, if they're well-advised,
    On one's simple old-world piety;
    Their theory is, if he swallows all
    That stuff, he'll be at our beck and call.
FAUST: To your vile mind, of course, it's merely quaint
3530 That that dear loving soul, filled with her faith,
    The only road to heaven that she knows,
    Should so torment herself, poor saint,
    Thinking her lover's damned to everlasting death!
MEPHISTOPHELES: You supersensual sensual wooer,
3535 A pretty maid has led you by the nose.
FAUST: You misborn monster, spawn of fire and shit!
MEPHISTOPHELES: And physiognomy,[5] how well she's mastered it!
    When I'm around she feels—just what, she's not quite sure;
    My face, forsooth! conceals some runic spell;
3540 She guesses I'm a genius certainly,
    Perhaps indeed the Devil as well.
    So, it's to be tonight—?
FAUST: What's that to you?
MEPHISTOPHELES: I take a certain pleasure in it too!

AT THE WELL

[Gretchen and Lieschen with water jugs.]

LIESCHEN: You've heard about Barbara, haven't you?
GRETCHEN: No; I hardly see anyone.
LIESCHEN: Well, it's true!
    She's done it at last; Sybil told me today.
    Made a fool of herself. That's always the way
    With those airs and graces.
GRETCHEN: But what?
LIESCHEN: It stinks!
    There's two to feed now when she eats and drinks!
GRETCHEN: Oh! . . .
LIESCHEN: And serve her right at last, I say.
    Throwing herself at the lad for so long!
    Always on his arm, always walking along,
    Off to the villages, off to the dance;
3555 Oh, she had an eye to the main chance!
    Such a beauty, of course, she must lead the way!
    He courts her with pastries and wine every day;
    She's even so shameless, the little minx,
    That she can accept presents from him, she thinks!

---

4. Quizzed concerning his faith.   5. The "science" of discerning character from the face.

3560   Cuddling and petting hour by hour—
        Well, now she's lost her little flower!
GRETCHEN: Poor thing!
LIESCHEN: Don't tell me you're sorry for her!
        Why, all the rest of us, there we were,
        Spinning, our mothers not letting us out
3565   In the evenings, while she's sitting about
        In dark doorways with her fancy man,
        Lingering in alleys as long as they can!
        Well, now she'll have her church penance to do,
        And sit in her smock on the sinner's pew!
GRETCHEN: But surely he'll marry her now!
LIESCHEN: Not he!
        A smart boy like that, there are fish in the sea
        In plenty for him; he's not such a fool!
        Anyway, he's left.
GRETCHEN: That's wrong of him!
LIESCHEN: Well,
        If she gets him, she'll get the rest of it too.
3575   The boys'll snatch the flowers from her head,
        And we'll throw her none, just chopped straw instead![6] [Exit.]

GRETCHEN [as she walks home]: What angry things I used to say
        When some poor girl had gone astray!
        I used to rack my brains to find
3580   Words to condemn sins of that kind;
        Blacker than black they seemed to be,
        And were still not black enough for me,
        And I crossed myself and made such a to-do—
        Now that sin of others is my sin too!
3585   Oh God! but all that made me do it
        Was good, such dear love drove me to it!

B Y   A   S H R I N E   I N S I D E   T H E   T O W N   W A L L

[An icon of the Mater Dolorosa stands in the above with vases of flowers in front
of it. Gretchen puts fresh flowers into the vases, then prays.]

GRETCHEN:
        O Virgin Mother, thou
        Who art full of sorrows, bow
        Thy face in mercy to my anguish now!

3590   O Lady standing by
        Thy Son to watch Him die,
        Thy heart is pierced to hear His bitter cry.

        Seeking the Father there
        Thy sighs rise through the air

6. Traditional behavior when an unwed mother married.

3595   From his death-agony, from thy despair.

    Who else can know
    The pain that so
    Burns in my bones like fire from hell?
    How my wretched heart is bleeding,
3600   What it's dreading, what it's needing,
    Lady, only you can tell!

    Wherever I go, wherever,
    It never stops, just never;
    Oh how it hurts and aches!
3605   When I'm alone, I'm crying,
    I cry as if I'm dying,
    I cry as my heart breaks.

    The flower-pots by my window
    I watered with tears like dew
3610   When in the early morning
    I picked these flowers for you.

    The early sun was gleaming,
    I sat up in my bed
    My eyes already streaming
3615   As the new dawn turned red.
    Help! Save me from shame and death!—O thou
    Who art full of sorrows, thou
    Most holy Virgin, bow
    Thy face in mercy to my anguish now!

NIGHT. THE STREET OUTSIDE GRETCHEN'S DOOR

VALENTINE [*a soldier, Gretchen's brother*]:
    I used to drink with the other chaps;
    That's when one likes to boast. Perhaps
    They'd start to sing their girl-friends' praises—
    All lovely girls, like a ring of roses;
    And round and round the full toasts went.
3625   I'd sit there calm and confident,
    With my elbows on the table-top;
    Sit there and stroke my beard meanwhile,
    Wait for their blethering to stop,
    Then fill my glass and with a smile
3630   I'd say: All honor where honor's due!
    But in this whole land is there one girl who
    Can compare with Meg, my sister so sweet,
    One worthy to fasten the shoes to her feet?
    Then clink! The toasts went round again,
3635   And some of the fellows exclaimed: he's right!
    She's the pride of her sex, she's the heart's delight!
    And the boasters and praisers sat silent then.

And now—what now?—Shall I tear my hair,
Shall I run up the walls?—I could despair.
3640   Every one of those blackguards now is free
To sneer and wrinkle his nose at me;
I must sweat, like a debtor who can't pay,
At each chance remark that drops my way!
Oh, yes! I could knock out their brains! But why?
3645   I still couldn't tell them they're telling a lie!

Who's there? Who's sneaking to her door?
There are two of them, if I know the score.
If it's him, I'll take him while I can—
He'll not leave here a living man!

[Enter Faust and Mephistopheles.]

FAUST: Look, through the window of the sacristy
The sanctuary lamp gleams up and glows,
Yet to each side, how dim, how weak it shows,
As darkness clusters round it! So in me
Night falls and thickens in my heart.

MEPHISTOPHELES: Well, I could act a tom-cat's part,
Slinking the streets to find a way
Up to the rooftops where I'll play!
I feel a healthy appetite
For some thieving, some lechery tonight.
3660   Walpurgis, Night of the Wild Witching,[7]
Is coming soon; already I'm twitching
With expectation. Just you wait!
One doesn't sleep through that fine date.

FAUST: Is that your buried gold that's rising now,[8]
3665   Back there? It blooms, it shines at us somehow!

MEPHISTOPHELES: Quite so; you soon will have the pleasure
Of lifting out the pot of treasure.
I took a squint into it too;
Fine silver coins I've raised for you.

FAUST: Was there no jewelry you could find?
My mistress loves those golden toys.

MEPHISTOPHELES: I did see something of the kind;
A necklace. Pearls that are her eyes.[9]

FAUST: That's good; it makes me sad to go
3675   Without a gift to her, you know.

MEPHISTOPHELES: Come now, you should get used to ladies;
Sometimes one enjoys their favors gratis.
But look! The stars are in the sky,
And being a gifted artist, I

---

7. See note to line 2590.
8. In lines 2675–77 (omitted from our selection) Mephisto has implied that he will locate buried treasure to seduce Gretchen. There was a folk belief that buried treasure would shine at night.

9. This allusion to a famous song in Shakespeare's *Tempest* does not originate with Goethe but was added by the translator, in the spirit of the many other Shakespeare allusions in *Faust*.

3680   Will now sing her a moral song,
        To confuse her sense of right and wrong.

[*He sings, accompanying himself on a zither.*]

        Who stands before
        Her sweetheart's door
        Once more, once more,
3685   With early morning starting?
        Poor Kate, beware!
        You'll enter there
        A maid so fair—
        No maid you'll be departing!

3690   Men must have fun,
        But when it's done
        They'll up and run—
        They're thieves, why should they linger?
        Poor darlings all,
3695   Beware your fall:
        Do nothing at all
        Till you've got the ring on your finger!

VALENTINE: Who are you serenading here?
        Damned ratcatcher![1] The devil take
3700   Your zither first; God's blood! I'll make
        Him take the singer next, d'you hear?

MEPHISTOPHELES: The instrument's a write-off, I'm afraid.

VALENTINE: Now draw, and there'll be corpses made!

MEPHISTOPHELES: Doctor, don't back away! Now, quick!
3705   Keep close to me, move as I do.
        Come on, out with your tickle-stick!
        Now lunge! I'll parry him for you.

VALENTINE: Well, parry this one!

MEPHISTOPHELES: Certainly!

VALENTINE: And that!

MEPHISTOPHELES: Why not?

VALENTINE: The devil it must be!
3710   What fencing's this? I think my hand's gone lame.

MEPHISTOPHELES [*to Faust*]: Strike now!

VALENTINE [*falling*]:   Oh God!

MEPHISTOPHELES: Now the poor lout is tame!
        But now let's go! We must get out of here;
        They'll start a hue and cry, and all that chatter.
        The police I can deal with, but I fear
3715   The High Assize is quite another matter.[2]

[*Exit with Faust.*]

---

1. A triple allusion: (1) to Mephisto's self-description as a "tomcat" a few lines earlier, though Valentine cannot actually hear the conversation between Mephisto and Faust; (2) to the Pied Piper of Hamelin, subject of a ballad by Goethe; (3) to a line in Shakespeare's *Midsummer Night's* *Dream* (3.1.75) leading up to a deadly duel: "Tybalt, you ratcatcher, will you walk?"

2. The high court pronounced sentence in God's name, causing problems for Mephisto.

MARTHA [*at her window*]: Come out! Come out!

GRETCHEN [*at her window*]:   Please, fetch a light!

MARTHA: They're cursing and shouting! There's a fight!

THE CROWD [*gathering*]: There's someone dead, there's one!

MARTHA [*coming out of her house*]: Where did the murderers run?

GRETCHEN [*coming out of her house*]: Who's lying here?

THE CROWD: Your mother's son.

GRETCHEN: Oh God in heaven! What have they done!

VALENTINE: I'm dying; it's a thing soon said,

> And even sooner the thing's real.
>
> You women-folk, why weep and wail?

3725   Just hear me speak before I'm dead.

[*They all gather round him.*]

> Meg, listen: you're still a poor young chit,
>
> You've not yet got the hang of it,
>
> You're bungling things, d'you see?
>
> Just let me tell you in confidence:

3730   Since you're a whore now, have some sense

> And do it properly!

GRETCHEN: My brother! God! What do you mean?

VALENTINE: Leave God out of this little scene!

> What's done is done, I'm sorry to say,

3735   And things must go their usual way.

> You started in secret with one man;
>
> Soon others will come where he began,
>
> And when a dozen have joined the queue
>
> The whole town will be having you!

3740   Let me tell you about disgrace:

> It enters the world as a secret shame,
>
> Born in the dark without a name,
>
> With the hood of night about its face.
>
> It's something that you'll long to kill.

3745   But as it grows, it makes its way

> Even into the light of day;
>
> It's bigger, but it's ugly still!
>
> The filthier its face has grown,
>
> The more it must be seen and shown.

3750   There'll come a time, and this I know,

> All decent folk will abhor you so,
>
> You slut! That like a plague-infected
>
> Corpse you'll be shunned, you'll be rejected,
>
> They'll look at you and your heart will quail,

3755   Their eyes will all tell the same tale!

> You'll have no gold chains or jewelry then,
>
> Never stand in church by the altar again,

Never have any pretty lace to wear
At the dance, for you'll not be dancing there!
3760   Into some dark corner may you creep
Among beggars and cripples to hide and weep;
And let God forgive you as he may—
But on earth be cursed till your dying day!
MARTHA: Commend your soul to God's mercy too!
3765   Will you die with blasphemy on you?
VALENTINE: Vile hag, vile bawd! If I could take
You by the skinny throat and shake
The life out of you, that alone,
For all my sins it would atone.
GRETCHEN: Oh, brother—how can I bear it—how—
VALENTINE: I tell you, tears won't mend things now.
When you and your honor came to part,
That's when you stabbed me to the heart.
I'll meet my Maker presently—
3775   As the soldier I'm still proud to be.

[*He dies.*]

A C A T H E D R A L

[*A Mass for the Dead. Organ and choral singing. Gretchen in a large congregation. An Evil Spirit behind Gretchen.*]

THE EVIL SPIRIT: How different things were for you, Gretchen,
When you were still all innocence,
Approaching that altar,
Lisping prayers from your little
3780   Worn prayer-book;
Your heart had nothing in it
But God and child's play!
Gretchen!
What are you thinking?
3785   What misdeed burdens
Your heart now? Are you praying
For your mother's soul, who by your doing
Overslept into long, long purgatorial pains?
Whose blood stains your doorstep?
3790   —And under your heart is there not
Something stirring, welling up already,
A foreboding presence,
Feared by you and by itself?
GRETCHEN: Oh God! Oh God!
3795   If I could get rid of these thoughts
That move across me and through me,
Against my will!
THE CHOIR: *Dies irae, dies illa*

Solvet saeclum in favilla.[3]

[*Organ.*]

THE EVIL SPIRIT: God's wrath seizes you!
        The Last Trumpet scatters its sound!
        The graves shudder open!
        And your heart
        That was at rest in its ashes
3805   Is resurrected in fear,
        Fanned again to the flames
        Of its torment!

GRETCHEN: Let me get away from here!
        It's as if the organ
3810   Were choking me
        And the singing melting
        The heart deep down in me!

THE CHOIR: *Judex ergo cum sedebit,*
        Quidquid latet adparebit,
3815   *Nil inultum remanebit.*[4]

GRETCHEN: I can't breathe!
        The great pillars
        Are stifling me,
        The vaulted roof
3820   Crushes me!—Give me air!

THE EVIL SPIRIT: Hide yourself! Sin and shame
        Cannot be hidden,
        Air? Light?
        Woe on you!

THE CHOIR: *Quid sum miser tunc dicturus?*
        Quem patronum rogaturus,
        Cum vix justus sit securus?[5]

THE EVIL SPIRIT: Souls in bliss
        Have turned their faces from you.
3830   They shrink from touching you,
        For they are pure!
        Woe!

THE CHOIR:
        Quid sum miser tunc dicturus?

GRETCHEN: Neighbor! Your smelling-salts!

[*She faints.*]

* * *[6]

---

3. A Latin hymn, part of the Requiem Mass for the dead: "Day of wrath, that day / Shall dissolve the world into cinders."

4. "Thus when the judge sits, / everything hidden will be manifest / and nothing will remain unavenged."

5. "What am I, miserable, then to say? / What patron shall I call on? / When scarcely the just man is secure?"

6. Mephisto next leads Faust to the orgy at the Walpurgis Night (see note to line 2590). Faust is caught up in the wild dancing until distracted by a vision of Gretchen.

from WALPURGIS NIGHT

FAUST: Then I saw—
MEPHISTOPHELES: What?
FAUST: Mephisto, look! Right over there:
          A young girl stands, so pale, so fair,
4185   All by herself! How slowly she moves now,
          As if her feet were fastened somehow!
          And as I look, it seems to me
          It's poor dear Gretchen that I see!
MEPHISTOPHELES: Let it alone! That is no wholesome vision,
4190   But a dead thing, a magic apparition;
          I warn you to avoid it. Come,
          And keep your distance, or its stare will seize
          Your living blood, almost to stone you'll freeze.
          You have heard of the Gorgon,[7] I presume.
FAUST: It's true, it's true! Those eyes are open wide,
          Closed by no loving hand! I know
          Gretchen's sweet body which I have enjoyed,
          Her breast that lay by mine not long ago!
MEPHISTOPHELES: Gullible fool! That's the enchanter's art:
4200   She takes the shape of every man's sweetheart!
FAUST: Alas, what anguish, what delight!
          I cannot tear my eyes from this one sight!
          How strange it is: her lovely neck's arrayed
          With one encircling scarlet thread,
4205   No wider than the edge of a knife-blade!
MEPHISTOPHELES: Yes, yes, I see it too. She can transport her head
          Under her arm if you prefer;
          Perseus, as you know, beheaded her.
          You are obsessed by these illusions still.
4210   Come, let's just climb this little hill.
          It's like Vienna's new suburban park;[8]
          What fun! And if they've not deluded me,
          It's actually a theater. What a lark!
          What's going on?
MR AT-YOUR-SERVICE:[9] The show starts again presently!
4215   It's a new piece, the last of seven.
          That's how our plays are always given.
          A dilettante wrote all these;
          The cast are dilettantes too.
          My dilettante-duty, if you please,
          Is now to raise the curtain; so, good sirs,
4220   Excuse me!
MEPHISTOPHELES: Well met here, the pack of you!

7. A female monster in Greek mythology, with snakes instead of hair; any mortal who looked at her would be
turned to stone. She was beheaded by the Greek hero
Perseus.
8. The Prater, a large public park then at the edge of Vienna,

opened in 1766.
9. The impresario of the "Walpurgis Night's Dream," a
farcical interlude satirizing contemporary Weimar society
that follows Faust's vision of Gretchen.

The Blocksberg's[1] the right place for amateurs.

* * *

A GLOOMY DAY. OPEN COUNTRY.

[Faust and Mephistopheles.]

FAUST: In misery! In despair! Pitiably wandering about the country for so long, and now a prisoner! Locked up in prison as a criminal and suffering such torment, the sweet hapless creature! So this is what it has come to! This!—Vile treacherous demon, and you told me nothing!—Yes, stand there, stand there and roll your devilish eyes in fury! Stand and affront me by your unendurable presence! A prisoner! In utter ruin, delivered over to evil spirits and the judgment of cold heartless mankind! And meanwhile you lull me with vulgar diversions, hide her growing plight from me and leave her helpless to her fate!

MEPHISTOPHELES: She is not the first.

FAUST: You dog! You repulsive monster! Oh infinite Spirit, change him back, change this reptile back into the form of a dog, the shape he used so often when it amused him to trot along ahead of me at night, suddenly rolling at the feet of innocent wayfarers and leaping on their backs as they fell! Change him back into his favorite shape, let him crawl before me in the sand on his belly, let me trample this reprobate under my feet!—Not the first!—Oh grief, grief that no human soul can grasp, to think that more than one creature has sunk to such depths of wretchedness, that the sins of all the others were not expiated even by the first, as it writhed in its death-agony before the eyes of the eternally merciful God! I am stricken to my life's very marrow by the misery of this one girl—and you calmly sneer at the fate of thousands!

MEPHISTOPHELES: Well, here we are again at the end of our wit's tether, the point where your poor human brains always snap! Why do you make common cause with us, if you can't stand the pace? Why try to fly if you've no head for heights? Did we force ourselves on you, or you on us?

FAUST: Stop baring your greedy fangs at me, it makes me sick!—Oh you great splendid Spirit, who deigned to appear to me, who know my heart and my soul, why did you chain me to this vile companion, who gorges his appetite on ruin and drinks refreshment from destruction?

MEPHISTOPHELES: Have you done talking?

FAUST: Save her! Or woe betide you! May the most hideous curse lie upon you for thousands of years!

MEPHISTOPHELES: I cannot loose the Avenger's bonds or open his bolts!—Save her!— Who was it who ruined her? I, or you?

[Faust glares about him in speechless rage.]

Are you snatching for the thunder? A good thing it was not given to you wretched mortals, to blast your adversary when he makes an innocent reply! That's the way of tyrants, venting their spleen when they're in an embarrassing pass.

FAUST: Take me to her! I'll have her set free!

---

1. The mountain upon whose summit (the Brocken) the Walpurgis Night takes place. Goethe himself climbed it three times, but Faust and Mephisto get sidetracked on the way to the revelries by the vision of Gretchen and by the ensuing satiric interlude omitted here as in most stage performances).

MEPHISTOPHELES: And what of the risk you'll run? I tell you, on that town there lies blood-guilt by your hand. Over the grave of the man you killed there hover avenging spirits, waiting for the murderer to return.

FAUST: Must I hear that from you too? May the murder and death of a world come upon you, you monster! Take me to her, I tell you, and free her!

MEPHISTOPHELES: I will take you, and I will tell you what I can do. Have I all the power in heaven and earth? I will bemuse the jailer's senses, you can take his keys and bring her out with your own human hand! I'll keep watch, the magic horses will be ready, and I'll carry you both to safety. That I can do.

FAUST: Let's go at once!

Night. In Open Country.

[Faust and Mephistopheles storming past on black horses.]

FAUST: What's that moving around on the gallows-mound?

MEPHISTOPHELES: I don't know what they're doing and stewing.

FAUST: Up and down they hover, they stoop, they swoop.

MEPHISTOPHELES: A guild of witches!

FAUST: They're scattering something, it's a ritual deed.

MEPHISTOPHELES: Ride on! Ride on!

A Prison

FAUST [*with a bundle of keys and a lamp, by a small iron door*]:
    That shudder comes again—how long a time
    Since last I felt this grief for all man's woe!
    She lies behind this cold, damp wall, I know;
    And her loving heart's illusion was her crime.
    Do I pause as I enter this place?
4410   Am I afraid to see her face?
    Quick! She must die if I keep hesitating so.

[He grasps the lock. Margareta's voice sings from inside.]

MARGARETA: Who killed me dead?
    My mother, the whore!
    Who ate my flesh?
4415   My father, for sure!
    Little sister gathered
    The bones he scattered;
    In a cool, cool place they lie.
    And then I became a birdie so fine,
4420   And away I fly—away I fly.

FAUST [*unlocking the door*]:
    She doesn't know her lover's listening at the door,
    Hearing the clank of chains, straw rustling on the floor.

[He enters the cell.]

MARGARETA [*hiding her face on her straw mattress*]:
    Oh! Oh! They're coming! Bitter death!

FAUST [*softly*]: Quiet! Quiet! I've come to set you free.

MARGARETA [*crawling towards his feet*]: If you are human, then have pity on me!

FAUST: You'll waken the jailers, speak under your breath!

[*He takes up her chains to unlock them.*]

MARGARETA [*on her knees*]: Oh, hangman, who gave you this power
            Over me? Who said
            You could fetch me at this midnight hour?
4430   Have pity! Tomorrow morning I'll be dead,
            Isn't that soon enough for you?

[*She stands up.*]

            I'm still so young, still so young too!
            And already I must die!
            I was pretty too, and that's the reason why.
4435   My lover was with me, now he's far away.
            They tore my garland off, and threw the flowers away.
            Why are you clutching at me like this?
            Oh spare me! What have I done amiss?
            Let me live! Must I beg you, must I implore
4440   You in vain? I've never even seen you before!

FAUST: How can I bear this any more!

MARGARETA: I'm in your power now, I'm ready to go.
            Just let me feed my baby first.
            I was cuddling it all last night, you know.
4445   They took it from me; that was just
            To hurt me. I killed it, is what they say.
            Now things will never be the same.
            They're wicked people: they sing songs against me!
            There's an old tale that ends that way—
4450   Who told them it meant me?

FAUST [*throwing himself at her feet*]:
            It's your lover, I'm here at your feet, I came
            To free you from this dreadful place!

MARGARETA [*kneeling down beside him*]:
            Oh, let's kneel, and call on the saints for grace!
            Look, under that stair,
4455   Under the door,
            Hell's boiling there!
            You can hear the voice
            Of his angry roar!

FAUST [*aloud*]: Gretchen! Gretchen!

MARGARETA [*hearing her name*]: That was my lover's voice!

[*She jumps to her feet. Her chains fall off.*]

            Where is he? I heard him call to me.
            No one shall stop me, I am free!
            To his arms I'll fly,
4465   On his breast I'll lie!

He stood and called "Gretchen"! I recognized him!
Through the wailing and gnashing of Hell so grim,
Through the Devil's rage, through his scorn and sneer,
I knew it was his voice, so loving and dear!

FAUST: I am here!

MARGARETA: It is you! Oh, tell me once again!
[*Embracing him.*] It's him! It's him! Where's all my suffering, then?
Where are my chains, my prison and my fear?
It's you! You've come to rescue me from here
And I am saved!—

4475   I think it's here again, that street
Where I first saw you; and by and by
We're waiting again, Martha and I,
In that lovely garden where we used to meet.

FAUST [*trying to leave with her*]: Come! Come with me!

MARGARETA: Oh stay!

4480   I love being anywhere when you're not away!

[*Caressing him.*]

FAUST: No, don't delay!
Or we shall have to pay
Most bitterly for this!

MARGARETA: What, you've forgotten so soon how to kiss?

4485   We're together again, my sweetest friend,
And our kissing's come to an end?
In your arms, why do I tremble so?
A whole heaven used to close in on me,
You spoke and you looked so lovingly;

4490   I was stifled with kisses, you'd never let go.
Oh kiss me now!
Or I'll show you how!

[*She embraces him.*]

Oh! Your lips are dumb,
They've nothing to say!

4495   Why has your love gone cold?
Who can have come
Between us to take it away?

[*She turns away from him.*]

FAUST: Come! Follow me! Darling, you must be bold!
I'll hug you later on ten-thousandfold,

4500   Just follow me now! It's all I ask of you!

MARGARETA [*turning to him*]: But is it you, can it be really true?

FAUST: It's me! Come!

MARGARETA: You undid my chains, they fell apart,
And you will take me back to your heart.
How is it you don't find me a vile thing?

4505   Do you really know, my dear, who you are rescuing?

FAUST:	Come! Come! The deep night's giving way to dawn!
MARGARETA:	My mother's dead; I poisoned her, you see.
	I drowned my child when it was born.
	Hadn't it been God's gift to you and me?

4510 To you as well—It is you! Can I trust
This not to be a dream?
Your hand! Your dear hand!—Ugh, but it's wet! You must
Wipe off the blood! To me there seem
To be bloodstains on it. Oh my God,

4515 What did you do!
Put away your sword,
I beg of you!

FAUST: Forget what happened, let it be!
You are killing me.

MARGARETA: Oh no, you must survive!
I'll tell you about the graves now, I'll describe
Them to you. You must arrange all this,
Tomorrow as ever is.
You must choose the places. Mother must have the best,

4525 And my brother right next to her with his,
And me a little further off—
But not too far! Just far enough.
And my little baby at my right breast.
There'll be no one else to lie with me!—

4530 When I clung to your side so tenderly,
Oh, that was so blessed, a joy so sweet!
But I can't seem to do it now as I could;
When I come, I seem to be dragging my feet,
And you seem to be pushing me back somehow.

4535 Yet it's still you, you're still gentle and good!

FAUST: If you feel that it's me, come with me now!

MARGARETA: Out there?

FAUST: Into freedom!

MARGARETA: If my grave's out there,
If death is waiting, come with me! No,

4540 From here to my everlasting tomb
And not one step further I'll go!—
You're leaving? Oh Heinrich, if only I could come!

FAUST: You can! Just want to! I've opened the door!

MARGARETA: I can't leave; for me there's no hope any more.

4545 What's the use of escaping? They'll be watching for me.
It's so wretched to have to beg one's way
Through life, and with a bad conscience too,
And to wander abroad; and if I do,
In the end they'll catch me anyway!

FAUST: I'll stay with you always!

MARGARETA: Quick, oh, quick!
Save your poor baby!
Just follow the path

Up the stream, uphill,
4555   Over the bridge,
The wood's just beyond;
In there, on the left, by the fence—
He's in the pond!
Oh, catch hold of him!
4560   He's struggling still,
He's trying to swim!
Save him! Save him!

FAUST: Oh, stop, stop! Think what it is you say!
Just one step, and we're on our way.

MARGARETA: Oh, quick, let's get to the other side
Of the hill! My mother sits on a stone
Up there—oh it's cold, I'm so terrified!—
My mother's sitting up there on a stone,
She's wagging her head, she's all alone,
4570   Not beckoning, not nodding her poor heavy head;
She slept so long that she'll never wake.
She slept so that we could be happy in bed!
Oh, those were good times, and no mistake.

FAUST: If persuasion's no use, if that's how it must be,
4575   I'll have to carry you off with me.

MARGARETA: Don't touch me! Put me down! No, no!
I'll not be compelled! Don't clutch me so!
I was always willing, as well you know.

FAUST: The day's dawning! Oh sweetheart! Sweetheart!

MARGARETA: The day! Yes, it's day! The last day dawning!
I thought it would be my wedding morning.
Now you've been with Gretchen, don't tell anyone.
Oh, my garland's spoilt!
What's done is done!
4585   We'll meet later on;
But I shan't be dancing.
I can't hear them, but the crowd's advancing.
There are so many there,
The streets and the square
4590   Are all full; the bell tolls; they break the white rod.[2]
Oh how they bind me and seize me, oh God!
Now I'm on the execution-chair,
And at every neck in this whole great throng
The blade strikes when that sword is swung.
4595   The world lies silent as the grave.

FAUST: Oh why was I born, at such a cost!

MEPHISTOPHELES [appearing outside the door]:
Come! One more moment and you're lost!
What's all this dallying, parleying and dithering!
My night-steeds are quivering,
4600   The sun's nearly risen.

2. Sign of final condemnation.

MARGARETA: What's that? It came out of the floor of my prison!
        It's him! It's him! Send him away!
        He can't come! This place is sacred today!
        He wants me!
FAUST: You're to live!
MARGARETA: Oh my God, I await
        Your righteous judgment!
MEPHISTOPHELES [*to Faust*]:
4605   Come! Come! Or I'll leave
        You both to your fate!
MARGARETA: Oh Father, save me, do not reject me,
        I am yours! Oh holy angels, receive
        Me under your wings, surround me, protect me!—
4610   Heinrich! You frighten me.
MEPHISTOPHELES: She is condemned!
A VOICE [*from above*]:   She is redeemed!
MEPHISTOPHELES [*to Faust*]:   Come to me!

    [*He vanishes with Faust.*]

[*Margareta's*] VOICE [*from the cell, dying away*]: Heinrich! Heinrich!

Faust, Part II

ACT 1

A BEAUTIFUL LANDSCAPE

[*Faust, lying among grass and flowers, exhausted and restless, trying to sleep. Dusk. Spirits, graceful little shapes, hovering and circling round.*]

ARIEL[3] [*his song accompanied by Aeolian harps*]:

        When the blossoms hovering
        Rain on meadows green and new,
4615   All earth's children feel the spring,
        Bright with universal dew.
        Come then, little elfin spirits,
        All alike to help and bless;
        Ours to heed no sins or merits
4620   But to pity man's distress.
        You, round this mortal's head circling in air,
        Heal now his heart, in noble elfin fashion:
        Soothe its fierce conflict and the bitter passion
        Of self-reproach's burning darts, make clean
4625   His soul of all the horrors it has seen.
        Four are night's vigils:[4] now with fair
        Contentment fill each one immediately.
        First lay his head where it is soft and cool,

3. The spirit of the air in Shakespeare's *Tempest*. The wind harps that accompany him are associated with poetic inspiration.

4. The three-hour segments into which the night watch was divided.

4630

> Then bathe him in the dew of Lethe:[5] see,
> His clenched limbs will relax, he will be free,
> As he gains strength and feels the day before him.
> Obey the highest elfin rule,
> And to the sacred light restore him!

CHORUS [*singly and in two or more voices, by turns and together*]:

4635

> When a fragrance has descended
> All about the green-girt plain,
> Richer air with mist-clouds blended,
> Evening dusk comes down again;
> Lulls to infant-sweet reposing,
> Rocks the heart with whispering sighs,

4640

> And this wanderer feels it closing
> On his daylight-weary eyes.

> Now to night the world surrenders,
> Sacred love joins star to star;
> Little sparkles, greater splendors,

4645

> Glitter near and gleam from far,
> Glitter in the lake reflecting,
> Gleam against the clear night sky;
> Deepest seals of rest protecting
> Glows the full moon strong and high.

4650

> Soon the hours have slipped away,
> Pain and happiness are past;
> Trust the light of the new day,
> Feel your sickness will not last!
> Green the valleys, hillsides swelling,

4655

> Bushing thick to restful shade,
> And the fields, their wealth foretelling,
> Rippling ripe and silver-swayed!

> Have you wishes without number?
> Watch the promise of the dawn!

4660

> Lightly you are wrapped in slumber:
> Shed this husk and be reborn!
> Venture boldly; hesitation
> Is for lesser men—when deeds
> Are a noble mind's creation,

4665

> All his enterprise succeeds.

[*A tremendous roaring sound heralds the approach of the sun.*]

ARIEL: Hear the tempest of the Hours![6]

> For to spirit-ears like ours
> Day makes music at its birth.
> Hear it! Gates of rock are sundering

---

5. The classical river of forgetfulness between the land of the living and the land of the dead.

6. Greek goddesses of the seasons, often associated with the sun-god.

4670   And the sun-god's wheels are thundering:
   See, with noise light shakes the earth!
   Hear it blare, its trumpets calling,
   Dazzling eyes and ears appalling,
   Speechless sound unheard for dread!

4675   Quickly, into flowers deep,
   Into rocks and foliage creep,
   Hide where elves in silence sleep:
   Ear it strikes is stricken dead.

FAUST: How strong and pure the pulse of life is beating!
4680   Dear earth, this night has left you still unshaken,
   And at my feet you breathe refreshed; my greeting
   To you, ethereal dawn! New joys awaken
   All round me at your bidding: beckoning distance,
   New-stirring strength, new resolution taken

4685   To strive on still towards supreme existence.—
   A gloaming-shine reveals the reborn world,
   The forest sings with myriad-voiced insistence,
   Through vale and dale the morning mists have curled,
   But heaven's radiance pierces them, descending,
4690   And branch and bough appear, revived, unfurled
   From the vaporous chasm, their slumber ending,
   Now deep-down colors grow distinct, as flower
   And leaf gleam moistly, tremulous pearls suspending.
   Oh paradise again, oh encircling power!

4695   Let me look up!—Each giant summit-height
   Proclaims already this most solemn hour:
   They are the first to taste the eternal light,
   As we shall, when its downward course is ended.
   Now the green-slanting meadow-slopes are bright
4700   Again, each detail new and clear and splendid,
   And day spreads stepwise with the dark's downsinking:
   See, the sun rises!—But my eyes offended
   Turn away dazzled, from this great sight shrinking.

   And thus, when with our heart's whole hope for guide
4705   Towards our goal we have struggled on unthinking,
   And find fulfilment's portals open wide—
   From those unfathomed depths a sudden mass
   Of fire bursts forth, we stand amazed: we tried
   To set the torch of life alight—alas,
4710   A sea of flame engulfs us, ah what flame
   Of love or hate, burning, consuming us
   With pain and joy, which strangely seem the same!
   We look back earthwards, hiding from this blaze
   Behind a youthful veil of awestruck shame.

4715   So be it! I will turn from the sun's rays.
   At that rock-riving torrent, with increasing
   Ecstasy at that waterfall I gaze:

From cliff to cliff it pours down never-ceasing,
It foams and streams a thousand thousandfold,
4720   Spray upon spray high in the air releasing.
But from this tumult, marvelous to behold,
The rainbow blooms, changing yet ever still;
Now vanishing and now drawn clear and bold.
How cool the moisture of its scattering spill!
4725   I watch a mirror here of man's whole story,
And plain it speaks, ponder it as you will:
Our life's a spectrum-sheen of borrowed glory.

* * *[7]

A DARK GALLERY

[*Faust. Mephistopheles.*]

MEPHISTOPHELES: These gloomy passages! Why do you drag me here?
        Was all that high society
6175   Not fun enough? There's plenty of good cheer
        Still to enjoy, and much fine trickery!
FAUST: No need to speak of it; in the old days
        You played that game a hundred tedious ways.
        Now stop your slithering to and fro
6180   And tell me what I need to know.
        They're pestering me now for action:
        The Steward, the Chamberlain want satisfaction.
        The Emperor demands to see
        Helen and Paris, here, immediately;
6185   The ideal man and woman, to appear
        Before his eyes, in figures plain and clear.
        So get to work! I mustn't break my word.
MEPHISTOPHELES: You promised that? How frivolous, how absurd!
FAUST: Let me inform you that your pranks
6190   Have consequences, my good friend.
        We made him rich and earned his thanks,
        And now he must be entertained.
MEPHISTOPHELES: You think this task's a simple one;
        But it's a steeper stair to climb,
6195   A stranger region than you've ever known,
        Which by your new commitments you now dare
        To tread, conjuring Helen out of time
        Like phantom paper-money from the air.
        Easy, you think?—Witches I can supply,
6200   Ghost-goblins, changelings, curious succubi;
        But Satan-sweethearts, though quite charming in their way,
        Can't pass for Homer's heroines even today.

---

7. In omitted scenes Mephisto, posing as jester at a decadent Renaissance court, leads Faust in an elaborate masque. Fire breaks out and Faust saves the Emperor by extinguishing it. Mephisto has printed paper money to "magically" revive the failing economy. During the festivities, the Emperor has commanded Mephisto and Faust to show him the Greek beauty Helen, over whom the Trojan War was fought after the Trojan prince Paris abducted her. Since Helen is a classical figure beyond the reach of the Christian devil, Mephisto enlists Faust's aid.

FAUST: So, here we go again, your old lament!
           With you there's never any guarantee;
6205   Nothing gets done without an extra fee,
           Everything is a problem you invent.
           She'll come at once, as I know very well!
           Two mumbled words from you will summon her.
MEPHISTOPHELES: Pagans are not my period, sir;
6210   They're lodged in their own special hell.
           But there's a way.
FAUST: Divulge it instantly!
MEPHISTOPHELES: I do not like to; this is high mystery.
           Enthroned in solitude are goddesses—
           No place, no space around them, time still less;
6215   I mention them with some uneasiness.
           They are *the Mothers*.[8]
FAUST [*startled*]:   Mothers!
MEPHISTOPHELES: You dread the name?
FAUST: The Mothers! But how strange "the mothers" sounds!
MEPHISTOPHELES: Indeed; we hesitate ourselves to speak
           Of these great goddesses, and your mortal minds
6220   Have never known them. Go to the depths to seek
           Their dwelling! If we need them, you're to blame.
FAUST: Which is the way?
MEPHISTOPHELES: No way! A path untrodden
           Which none may tread; a way to the forbidden,
           The unmoved, the inexorable. Make preparation!
6225   There'll be no locks to unlock, no bolts to slide:
           On solitudes you will drift far and wide.
           Do you know solitude and desolation?
FAUST: If these are your wise saws, you might as well
           Not speak. They've a witch-kitchen smell;
6230   This is all stuff from long ago.
           The world was with me, was it not? And there
           I learnt and taught nothing but empty air.
           If ever I talked sense, told what I know,
           They'd shout me down still louder; finally,
6235   Embracing desert solitude to flee
           From the vile tricks society played on me,
           Rather than have no company at all
           I invoked the Devil, as you will recall.
MEPHISTOPHELES: Yet even if you'd swum the ocean through
6240   And known its boundlessness, even then
           You would see waves roll by and roll again;
           Even at the dreadful drowning-point, there too
           You would see something. In the still sea-green
           There would be darting dolphins to be seen;

---

8. Goethe apparently drew the name "the Mothers" from vague Classical sources, but there is no precedent for Mephisto's fantastic and comic use of the name.

6245   There'd be the clouds, sun, moon and starry sky—
        But in the eternal void you'll say goodbye
        To sight, not hear the step that steps so far,
        Not rest a foot on where you are.
FAUST: You talk like any ancient mystagogue[9]
6250   Addressing neophytes with words to fog
        Their simple minds; but here *per contra*.[1] I
        Am sent into your void to magnify
        My art and strength there; I am to cat's-paw
        Your chestnuts from the fire. Come then! let's claw
6255   The meaning out of this. I hope to see
        Your Nothing turn to Everything for me.
MEPHISTOPHELES: My compliments, sir, as you take your leave;
        You know the Devil well, I do believe.
        Now take this key.
FAUST: That little thing!
MEPHISTOPHELES: First seize
6260   It firmly, and respect it, if you please.
FAUST: It grows in my hand! It shines, it's all a-glitter!
MEPHISTOPHELES: Perhaps you now appreciate it better.
        Follow it downwards, for this key can read
        The hidden map: to the Mothers it will lead.
FAUST [*shuddering*]: The Mothers! Every time it strikes such fear
        Into my heart, this word I dare not hear.
MEPHISTOPHELES: Are you so limited, that a new word
        Disturbs you, merely one you've not yet heard?
        Let nothing trouble you in sound or sense:
6270   By now you should be used to strange events.
FAUST: Yet must I turn to stone? Not so I'll thrive!
        Our sense of awe's what keeps us most alive.
        The world chokes human feeling more and more,
        But deep dread still can move us to the core.
MEPHISTOPHELES: Descend then! I could say ascend; there's no
        Distinction. Flee from all that has been born
        To the unbound realm of empty shapes; return
        To savor what has vanished long ago.
        Like drifting coils of cloud they will approach you:
6280   Brandish the key, for then they cannot touch you.
FAUST [*with enthusiasm*]: I seize it, and at once my spirits rise,
        I feel new strength for this great enterprise.
MEPHISTOPHELES: A glowing tripod will alert your fall
        That it has reached the deepest depth of all.
6285   And by that tripod's light you'll see the Mothers;
        Some sitting, as the case may be, and others
        Who stand or walk. Formation, transformation,
        The eternal Mind's eternal delectation.
        You'll pass unseen: the whole world of creatures swarms

---

9. Leader of a mystic cult.   1. On the contrary.

6290   As images round them; they see empty forms
         And nothing else. But you will be in great
         Peril still, and you must be bold: go straight
         To the tripod, touch it with the key.

[*Faust strikes a decisive commanding attitude with the key.*]

MEPHISTOPHELES [*watching him*]:   Just so!
         Then, slave-like, it will follow where you go;
6295   Good fortune's wings will raise you, never fear!
         Before they miss it, you'll be back up here.
         And once you've got that brazier, then you may
         Summon the famous pair into the day.
         No one has ever dared before to do
6300   This deed, and it will be achieved by you.
         The incense-cloud, with magic to compel it,
         Will assume any godlike shape you tell it.
FAUST: Well then, what now?
MEPHISTOPHELES: Strive downwards; stamp, and you
         Will sink; you'll rise again by stamping too.

[*Faust stamps and disappears into the earth.*]

6305   I hope he's well protected by that key.
         Will he get back, I wonder? We shall see.

* * *[2]

ACT 2

A LABORATORY

[*In medieval style, with elaborate clumsy apparatus for fantastic purposes.*]

WAGNER [*at his furnace*]: That dreadful bell's reverberation
6820   Comes shuddering through the sooty walls.
         Too long my doubtful expectation
         Has waited for what now befalls.
         From blackness to illumination
         The deep alembic[3] now has passed,
6825   And like a living coal at last
         A fine carbuncular[4] fire is glowing,
         Into the dark its brilliance throwing:
         An incandescent white shines through!
         Let me succeed, just this once more!—
6830   Oh God, who's rattling at my door?
MEPHISTOPHELES [*entering*]: A well-meant greeting, sir, to you!
WAGNER [*anxiously*]: Greetings, by this hour's ruling star!
         [*sotto voce*[5]]: But hold your words and breath: I am not far
         From a great work's goal, now to be displayed.

---

2. Faust projects an image of Helen on a screen. He falls
in love with her, as do the men at court. Chaos and an explosion ensue. Mephisto brings Faust back to his old laboratory, where Wagner is now making an artificial man.

3. Distilling apparatus.
4. Fiery red.
5. Under his breath.

MEPHISTOPHELES [*sotto voce*]:   What great work's that?
WAGNER [*in a whisper*]:   A man is being made.
MEPHISTOPHELES: A man? So you have locked an amorous pair
      Up in your chimney-stack somehow?
WAGNER: Why, God forbid! That method's out of fashion now:
      Procreation's sheer nonsense, we declare!
6840   That tender point where life used to begin,
      That gentle power springing from within,
      Taking and giving, programmed to portray
      Itself, to assimilate what came its way
      From near or far—all that's now null and void;
6845   By animals, no doubt, it's still enjoyed,
      But man henceforth, being so highly gifted,
      Must have an origin much more uplifted.

    [*Turning to the furnace.*]

      See how it gleams!—Now we may hope to see
      Results. The ingredients—our manifold
6850   *Materia anthropica,*[6] they are called—
      We mix in a retort most patiently,
      With all due care, and so by perlutation[7]
      And proper double-distillation,
      They quietly reach their consummation.

    [*Turning to the furnace again.*]

6855   It works! The moving mass is clarified,
      And our conviction fortified:
      These mysteries we thought only great Nature knew,
      Our expertise now dares attempt them too!
      Her way with living matter was to organize it,
6860   And we have learnt to crystallize it.
MEPHISTOPHELES: When we live long, we learn a thing
      Or two; nothing surprises any more.
      I have, in my long years of wandering,
      Seen crystallized humanity before.
WAGNER [*who has been staring intently at the retort*]:
      It flashes, swells and rises! One
      More moment and it will be done.
      Great plans seem mad at first, but one day we
      Shall laugh at what is bred haphazardly;
      And one day, too, some great brain will create
6870   A brain designed to think and cerebrate!

    [*Gazing at the retort in delight.*]

      The glass is struck into harmonious sound.
      Ah, now it cannot fail! It clouds and clears:
      And moving daintily around

---

6. Human matter.   7. Cementing together.

A well-formed tiny little man appears.
6875   What more do I, what more does the world need?
The secret is at last made known.
Now hear this music: it has grown
To a voice, and into speech, indeed!

THE HOMUNCULUS[8] [*in the retort, to Wagner*]:
Well, dad! It worked, you see! And how are you?
6880   Come now, embrace me tenderly—but do
Be careful, please, my glass must not be cracked.
That is the way things are, in fact:
For natural growth the world's too small a place,
But art must be enclosed in its own space.

[*To Mephistopheles.*]

6885   So you are here as well, my mocking cousin?
I am much obliged; the moment was well chosen.
Our good luck brings this timely call by you.
Since I exist, I must find things to do:
I'd like to set to work this very day,
6890   And you know how to set me on my way.

WAGNER: Just one word, please! It's so embarrassing,
The way I'm questioned on this sort of thing.
For instance: no one yet can understand
How soul and body seem to have been planned
6895   To fit so perfectly and cling so tight,
Yet each torments the other day and night.
Furthermore—

MEPHISTOPHELES: Stop, stop! One should ask him rather
Why man and woman can't endure each other.
My friend, you'll never get such matters straight.
6900   There's work to do here: our small guest can't wait.

THE HOMUNCULUS: What's to be done?

MEPHISTOPHELES [*pointing to a side-door*]: A case for you to cure.

WAGNER [*still gazing into the retort*]:
You are a little darling, to be sure!

[*The side-door opens, Faust is seen lying on the couch.*]

THE HOMUNCULUS [*astonished*]: Remarkable!—

[*The retort slips out of Wagner's hands, hovers over Faust and illuminates him.*]

Delightful place![9]—Clear streams
In a dense grove, and women making ready
6905   To bathe; enchanting! Better still already!
But one shines brighter than them all, she seems
Descended from great heroes, gods perhaps.
She sets her foot in the translucent pool;
Life's noble flame in her sweet body dips

---

8. Little man.
9. Homunculus now describes Faust's dream of Leda,

Queen of Sparta, who gave birth to Helen of Troy after
Zeus, in the shape of a swan, made love to her.

6910   Into the yielding crystal and grows cool.—
        But now, what flurry of quick wings, what whirring
        Is this, in the smooth surface splashing, stirring?
        The girls flee in alarm: the queen, calm-eyed,
        Remains alone, but her heart fills with pride
6915   And womanly contentment as she sees
        The prince of swans come nestling to her knees,
        Docile yet bold. He seems to like it there.—
        And round them all at once has risen a veil
        Of mist, thick-woven to conceal
6920   The loves of this most charming pair.
MEPHISTOPHELES: What a strange tale! Your fantasies at least
        Are out of all proportion to your size.
        I can see nothing—
THE HOMUNCULUS: Why should you! Your eyes
        Are northern, steeped in medieval mist;
6925   In that mad world of monks and armor-plated
        Knights, naturally your vision's obfuscated.
        Dark ages are your proper habitat.

        [*Looking round.*]

        Black mouldering stones, arches in Gothic style
        And absurd curlicues—how drab, how vile!
6930   If he wakes up here, like as not
        He'll drop dead on the very spot.
        Nude women, swans and woodland streams
        I saw in his prophetic dreams.
        In this dank hole he'd have no future;
6935   Neither would I, despite my unfastidious nature.
        Away with him!
MEPHISTOPHELES: I welcome this solution.
THE HOMUNCULUS: Order a warrior to fight,
        Or a young girl to dance all night,
        And things soon reach their right conclusion.
6940   And let me see—tonight is Classical
        Walpurgis Night,[1] as I recall.
        A lucky chance, I do declare!
        He'll be in his own element there.
MEPHISTOPHELES: I know of no such date.
THE HOMUNCULUS: Indeed!
6945   You'll not have heard of it, you and your breed.
        Romantic ghosts are all they know in hell;
        A proper ghost is classical as well.
MEPHISTOPHELES: But where do we go, where do we start exploring?
        My ancient history colleagues are so boring.
THE HOMUNCULUS: Satan, the north-west is your stamping-ground!

---

1. A scene of Goethe's invention (omitted from our selections) as an analogue to the Walpurgis Night of Part 1 (see note to line 3833). It takes place on the Thessalian Fields, on the bank of the Peneus River, a noted resort of witches and also the location where Caesar defeated Pompey in the battle of Pharsalus in 48 B.C.E.

But for this trip, south-eastward we are bound,
To the great plain where the Peneus flows;
Tree-lined, bush-lined its moist meandering goes.
Out to the mountain glens the lowlands rise,
6955   And up there, old and new, Pharsalus lies.

MEPHISTOPHELES: Ugh! why do you remind me of those gory
Wars between slaves and tyrants? That old story,
How stale it is! Their battle is begun
All over again as soon as it is done;
6960   They never guess they merely are the dupes
Of Asmodeus,[2] who really rules the troops.
They call it fighting for their liberty;
Slaves against slaves in fact, it seems to me.

THE HOMUNCULUS: Just let them squabble; men will never mend.
6965   Each one asserts himself as best he can
From boyhood on, and so becomes a man.
The question here is how to cure our friend.
If you've a remedy, then try it now;
If not, leave it to me to find out how.

MEPHISTOPHELES: My Blocksberg[3] magic might be what he'd need
But pagan rules forbid me to proceed.
The Greeks were never much good anyway!
But you are charmed by their free sensuous play,[4]
They lure mankind to many a sinful blessing;
6975   The sins we sell are gloomy and depressing.
And so, what now?

THE HOMUNCULUS: But you do like some sport,
I think; Thessalian witches are the sort
Of thing that might appeal to you.

MEPHISTOPHELES [lustfully]: Thessalian witches! If I've heard aright,
6980   They're persons well worth meeting, that is true;
Not for concubinage night after night,
I hardly think that that would do.
But for a visit, for a try—

THE HOMUNCULUS: We need
Your cloak! And wrap it round our gentleman!
6985   This cloth will bear you, as you know it can,
And carry both of you with speed;
I'll light the way ahead.

WAGNER [anxiously]:   And I?

THE HOMUNCULUS: Why, you
Must stay at home: you have great things to do.
Study old manuscripts, learn from their lore
6990   How to collect life's elements together
And carefully compose them each to other;

2. A Jewish spirit of marital discord.
3. A reference to the Walpurgis Night in Part 1; see the notes to lines 2590 and 4222.
4. Mephisto here makes fun of Goethe's ideal of the Greek spirit, which combined erotic sensuousness with the perfected freedom ("play") of the body as perceived by the senses.

Consider *what*, consider *how* still more.
I meanwhile, traveling the world about,
Shall light on some essential point, no doubt.
6995 Then our great work will have achieved its end;
Such striving merits such reward, my friend!
Gold, honor, fame, health and longevity;
Service to science, virtue too—maybe!
Farewell!

WAGNER [*sadly*]:
Farewell! This parting's pain
7000 And grief; I fear we'll never meet again.

MEPHISTOPHELES: So, off to Greece then!—Judging
by your arts,
Cousin, you are a mannikin of parts.
[*Ad spectatores.*°]   *to the spectators*
Just fancy that! One does depend
On one's own creatures, in the end.

*** [5]

A C T 3

from I N N E R C O U R T Y A R D O F A C A S T L E

[*After a long procession of pages and squires has descended, Faust appears at
the top of the stairway dressed as a medieval knight. He comes down slowly and with
dignity.*]

CHORUS LEADER [*gazing at him*]: Unless the gods have done here as they sometimes do,
Conferring on him only fleetingly a wondrous form,
A lofty dignity, a presence to enchant
9185 But only for a while: then shall this prince succeed
In all he undertakes, whether in wars with men
Or in the lesser war with the fairest of our sex.
For truly he is to be preferred to many whom I
Have seen, though greatly I admired them none the less.
9190 With slow and solemn, with restrained respectful pace
This lord draws near; now turn your eyes to him, oh queen!

FUAST [*approaching, with a man in chains at his side*]:
Not here the solemn greeting that was due
The ceremonious welcome: instead I bring
To you that servant, closely bound in chains,
9195 Who robbed me of my duty, failing his.
Kneel here, to make confession of your guilt
To this most noble lady! This, great queen,
Is the possessor of rare far-seeing eyes

---

5. The lengthy and raucous Classical Walpurgis Night,
occupying most of Act 2, culminates in three forms of
love: Mephisto finds his obscene Classical counterparts;
Homunculus is "born" by breaking out of his glass vessel, crashes into the sea, and dies; and Faust witnesses an
ecstatic celebration of the four elements celebrating the
birth of Galatea, the successor to Venus as goddess of

beauty. Preceding our excerpt Act 3 opens in the style of
a Greek tragedy, with Helen and a chorus suffering in
time of war. In the passage included here, Faust acts on
the side of the northern tribes that overthrew the Roman
Empire (see lines 9281–88), and rescues the ancient
Greek beauty into the modern world.

Whom I appointed to the high look-out tower,
9200   Thence to observe whatever showed itself
In heaven's surrounding space and the wide earth:
He was to watch whatever stirred within
The circle of the hills, or in the valley,
Or near the castle, be it flocks and herds
9205   Or an invading army; we protect
The former, stand against the latter. But
Today, what dereliction! You arrive,
And he does not announce you. No reception
Honoured so high a guest. This miscreant's life
9210   Is forfeit, and his guilty blood already
Should have been spilt, but that it is for you
Alone to punish or pardon, as you please.

HELEN: You grant high dignity, in making me
Both judge and ruler, even though it were
9215   Only to tempt me, as I may surmise.
But I do my first duty as a judge
By hearing the accused. You, therefore, speak!

LYNCEUS THE WATCHMAN[6]:
Let me kneel and let me gaze,
Let me die or let me live:
9220   To this lady, whom the gods give,
I devote my mortal days.

I have watched a mystery:
As I waited for the dawn,
Eastward peering, suddenly
9225   In the south the sun was born.

And my eyes were drawn aside—
Not a peak nor valley there,
Sky nor earth they now descried:
Only her, uniquely fair.

9230   Like the lynx on topmost bough
With keen vision I am blessed;
But to wake I laboured now
As by some dark dream oppressed.

Where was I? What could restore me?
9235   Towers, ramparts, where were they?
Such a goddess stood before me
As the mists were swept away!

Eyes and heart towards her turning,
I had drunk her gentle light,
9240   And her beauty, dazzling, burning,
Burned and dazzled my poor sight.

6. Lynceus, whose name evokes the sharp-eyed lynx, was one of the ancient Greek sailors who searched for the Golden
Fleece. Here his name seems to be transferred to a medieval watchman serving the invading forces. Yet he has an eye for
classical beauty, and as he survives into the much later era of Act 5, he may be a timeless survivor from antiquity.

I forgot the watchman's duty
And my watch-horn's promised call.
Doom me now to death; yet beauty
9245   Tames the anger in us all.

HELEN: I must not punish a misfortune I myself
Have brought about. Alas, how pitiless
Has been my fate, doomed everywhere to drive
Men's hearts to madness, that they neither spared
9250   Themselves nor reverenced any other thing!
They ravished and seduced and fought and snatched
Me hither and thither: heroes, demigods,
Gods, demons, led me wandering to and fro.
My single form confused the world, still more
9255   My double;[7] now I am threefold, fourfold ruin.
Take away this good man and set him free;
Let no shame strike one whom a god has crazed.

FAUST: A double sight, oh queen, amazes me:
Your surely-speeding arrow, and its victim.
9260   I see the bow that winged it on its way,
And him who felt the wound. Arrows apace
Assail me now, I sense their feathering flight
At me from all sides, here within the castle.
What has become of me? My truest followers
9265   You turn to rebels all at once, my walls
You weaken. Will my army now obey
Me, or this conquering unconquered lady?
What choice now, but to give myself and all
My supposed wealth to you in vassalage?
9270   Let me then at your feet, freely and truly,
Confess you mistress, who had but to appear
And take at once your place upon the throne.

LYNCEUS [with a treasure-chest, followed by men bringing others]:
Queen, we return from near and far
To beg one glance, rich as we are!
9275   What man is there that looks at you
And is not prince and beggar too?

What am I now? What have I been?
What must I will or do, oh queen?
My piercing sight, what can it see?
9280   Your bright throne casts it back at me.

Out of the east we came, and so
The west was conquered and laid low;
A weighty army, wide and strong,
From head to tail none knew how long.

9285   The first would fall, the next would stand,
A third was ready spear in hand;

---

7. There was a legend that Zeus sent a phantom Helen of Troy while keeping the real Helen safe in Egypt.

Each reinforced a hundredfold,°   *uncounted*
And a slain thousand fell untold.

So we rushed on like storm and flame,
9290   Conquering and ruling as we came;
One day I gave the orders, then
The plunder fell to other men.

We looked around with greedy eyes:
The loveliest woman was one man's prize,
9295   Others took horses by the score
Or prancing bulls, as spoils of war.

But I would peer with my sharp sight
At all things rare and recondite:
I sought what no one else possessed,
9300   Cared not a straw for all the rest.

I hunted treasure's every trace,
Clear vision led me to the place,
No pocket hid its wealth from me,
Locked chests were glass, my eyes the key.

9305   Mine it became, a hoard of gold
And precious stones. The emerald
Now of all gems is worthiest
To glow so green upon your breast;

And let a pearl from deepest sea
9310   Now by your cheek hang tremblingly—
So red it blooms, no rubies dare
To add their pale adornment there.

Oh queen, so great a gathering
Of riches to your throne I bring;
9315   Much blood was shed in warlike fray,
Its harvest at your feet I lay.
These coffers all are full, and yet
More iron coffers I can get;
If I may be your slave, all these
9320   Shall fill your vaulted treasuries.

For scarcely were you here enthroned
Than all bowed down to you and owned
Their minds, their wealth, their power in thrall
To you, the loveliest form of all.

9325   All this was mine, I held it fast,
I let it go, to you it passed.
I thought it worthy: now I see
This lofty treasure's nullity.

All's vanished now I called my own,
9330   Withered it lies like grass that's mown.
Lady, with one glad look restore

Its value to it all once more!

FAUST: Remove at once this burden boldly won;
Uncensured it shall be, yet unrewarded.

9335   All that my castle's deep interior hides
Is hers already: a specific gift
Is otiose. Go, and lay out the treasures
In proper order. Raise on high the lofty
Image of unseen splendor! Let the vaulted

9340   Roofs glitter like skies freshly starred; plant here
Strange paradises of unliving life.
Where she will walk, let many carpets rich
With flowers unroll before her: let her feet
Fall upon softest ground, and brightest radiance,

9345   Dazzling to all but gods, confront her eyes.

LYNCEUS: Little, my lord, is this you ask,
Your command's a trifling task;
For this beauty all extol
Rules us all, goods, life and soul.

9350   All the army now is tame,
Every sword is blunt and lame;
And this form beyond compare
Dulls the sun and chills the air.
All's made empty, poor and base

9355   By the riches of her face. [Exit.]

HELEN [to Faust]: I wish to speak with you, but I would have you
Seated here at my side! This empty place
Calls for the master, and makes mine secure.

FAUST: First, as I kneel, accept my faithful homage,

9360   Most noble princess! Let me kiss the hand
That lifts me to your side; confirm me now
As the co-regent of your realm which knows
No boundaries, and let me be for you
Admirer, servant, guardian, all in one!

HELEN: Manifold wonders I have seen and heard,
And in amazement I have much to ask.
But tell me why the speech of that good man
Had something strange about it, strange and friendly:
Each sound seems to accommodate the next,

9370   And when one word has settled in the ear
Another follows to caress the first.[8]

FAUST: It is the way our peoples speak; I know
That if this pleases you, our music too
Will charm your hearing, ravish your inmost heart.

9375   But it is best we practice it at once,
Talking by turns, for that calls forth the skill.

---

8. Rhyme was unknown to classical Greek and Roman verse. Originally Helen and the chorus speak in the unrhymed, 12-syllable lines that were standard in Greek tragedy. At his entry (where this selection begins) Faust has introduced the 10-syllable blank verse associated with Renaissance plays such as Marlowe's *Dr. Faustus*. Lynceus then speaks in rhymed verse, which Helen has never heard before, and which strikes her (in a common Romantic-period image) as a loving embrace of words. Learning to rhyme brings her out of the ancient world.

HELEN: Then say, how shall I learn such lovely speech?
FAUST: It is not hard: say what your heart will teach.
          And when one's heart is full, one turns to see
          Who'll share the rapture—
HELEN: Share it now with me!
FAUST: No past recalled, nor future time to guess;
          Only the present—
HELEN: is our happiness.
FAUST: It is treasure and gain, possession and
          A pledge: but what must seal the pledge?
HELEN: My hand.
CHORUS: Who would find fault with our queen for
          Granting this castle's lord
          Some signs of her favor?
          For we must confess that we all are now
          Captives, as we have been before
9390   So often already since the shameful
          Fall of Troy, and our grievous
          Journey, labyrinthine, fear-haunted.

          Women accustomed to men's love
          May not be choosers, but
9395   Their knowledge is expert.
          For whether to golden-haired shepherd boys
          Or to swarthy bristling fauns,⁹
          As the case may be or the occasion:
          Equal rights will be granted,
9400   Making them free of° their soft limbs.   *possessors of*

          Nearer they sit, closer already,
          Leaning against each other;
          Shoulder to shoulder, knee to knee,
          Hand in hand they are cradled
9405   On the soft cushions
          Of the magnificent throne.
          Our rulers do not forebear to make
          Their secret pleasures
          Proudly and exuberantly
9410   Public before the gaze of their people.
HELEN: I feel so far away, and yet so near;
          How willingly I say: Look, I am here!
FUAST: Breathless I seem, words tremble and lose power;
          This is a dream, in no place, at no hour.
HELEN: I am as one long past, and yet so new;
          To you bound fast, to an unknown stranger true.
FAUST: Why puzzle, why insist? Our unique role

---

9. Not fawns (young deer) but rural semi-divinities, human above and goat below.

Bids us exist; one moment means the whole.

* * *[1]

from ACT 5

OPEN COUNTRY

A WANDERER: There they are, so dark and strong,
   Those old lindens, as before;
11045 I have wandered for so long,
   Now I find them here once more!
   And the hut that sheltered me,
   Tempest-tossed as I was then,
   On the sand-dunes here I see:
11050 This is the same place again!
   And my hosts? That fine old couple
   Rescued me with ready will:
   They were pious gentle people—
   Can I hope to find them still?
11055 They were old at our first meeting.
   Shall I knock or call?—My greeting
   To you, if the gods still bless
   You with your life of kindliness!
BAUCIS [*a very old little woman*]:[2]
   Stranger dear, speak softly please,
11060 Softly! My old husband, he's
   Resting still. He needs the length
   Of his nights, for short days' strength.
THE WANDERER: Dear old woman, is it true,
   Can I still be thanking you
11065 For my young life you and he
   Long ago saved from the sea?
   Baucis! You, who when death coldly
   Kissed me, warmed my freezing blood?

[*The husband enters.*]

   You, Philemon, who so boldly
11070 Snatched my treasure from the flood?
   Yours the hospitable fire,
   Yours the bell with silver tone,
   You, my rescuers from dire
   Peril, you my help alone!

---

1. In the conclusion to Act 3, Faust and Helen have a son, Euphorion (modeled on Lord Byron), who dies attempting to fly and is followed into the underworld by Helen. Act 4 returns to Germany for battles between rival emperors. Faust, helped by Mephisto's magic, aids one of the emperors to win and is awarded a fiefdom in the Netherlands, where he glories in helping mankind by building dikes to create new farmland.

2. The aged couple Baucis and Philemon are the subjects of a tale in Ovid's Latin mythological epic *Metamorphoses*. They offered hospitality to Zeus and Hermes, who were refused shelter by all others while traveling in disguise. The gods flooded the lands, except for the hut belonging to the old couple, which became a temple; Philemon was transformed into an oak and Baucis into a linden.

11075   Now, to ease my heart's emotion,
         I must look upon this shore;
         I must kneel and pray once more,
         Gazing on the boundless ocean.

[*He steps forward across the sand-dune.*]

PHILEMON [*to Baucis*]: Quickly now, let's lay the table
11080   Here among the flowers and trees.
         Let him go; he'll stare, unable
         To believe the change he sees.

[*Standing by The Wanderer.*]

         Look! Your enemies of old,
         The fierce foaming waves, have been
11085   Turned into a park; behold
         Now this paradisal scene!
         I was not young enough to lend
         My helping hands to this endeavor;
         Soon my strength was at an end;
11090   The sea was further off than ever.
         Those wise lords, they sent bold slaves:
         Dams and dikes built in a day
         Stole the birthright of the waves
         And usurped the ocean's sway.
11095   Now green fields and gardens lie,
         Woods and villages have grown
         Up all round. But come, the sun
         Will be setting by and by,
         Let us eat. Those distant white
11100   Sails seek haven for the night;
         Now like nesting birds they know
         Here's a port where they can go.
         Thus it is; you must look far
         Now to find the sea's blue shore,
11105   For dense between, on wide new land,
         New human habitations stand.

[*The three sit at table in the little garden.*]

BAUCIS: You are silent? And no food
         Has refreshed you, stranger dear?
PHILEMON: Tell him about the wonders; you'd
11110   Like to talk, he'd like to hear.
BAUCIS: Yes, the wonders. I'm still worried
         By strange doings we have seen.
         Things unnaturally hurried;
         Things not as they should have been.
PHILEMON: Can the Emperor sin? He named him°
         Feudal lord of all the coast;
         Even a herald, marching past

Faust

With his trumpet-call, proclaimed him.
It began here near the dune,
11120   That first foothold on the flood;
There were tents and huts. But soon
In green fields a palace stood.
BAUCIS: Slaves toiled vainly: blow by blow,
Pick and shovel made no way.
11125   Then we saw the night-flames glow—
And a dam stood there next day.
They used human sacrifice:
Fire ran down, like rivers burning.
All night long we heard the cries—
11130   A canal was built by morning.
He is godless, for he sorely
Wants our hut, our clump of trees.
As a neighbor he's too lordly;
We must serve him, if you please!
PHILEMON: Yet a fine new house he's found
For us on the polder-ground.
BAUCIS: I'd not trust that soil for long.
Stay up here where you belong!
PHILEMON: Come, let's watch the sun's last ray,
11140   When our chapel bell we've tolled.
Let us kneel there, let us pray,
Trusting our God, as of old.

A PALACE

[*A large ornamental park, with a long straight canal. Faust in extreme old age, walking about pensively. Lynceus the watchman speaks through a megaphone.*]

LYNCEUS: The sun sinks, the last ships appear,
Gaily they pass the harbor bar,
11145   Soon a tall vessel will be here
In the canal; how merry are
Those fluttering pennants! Each one plays
From a proud standing mast; the crew
Are sharing the good fortune too
11150   That greets you in your latter days.

[*The chapel bell sounds from the sand dune.*]

FAUST [*starting up angrily*]:
Damned bell! A treacherous wound that flies
As from a sniper's shot behind me!
Out there my endless kingdom lies,
But this vexation at my back,
11155   These teasing envious sounds remind me
My great estate's not pure! That line
Of linden-trees, that little shack,

That crumbling chapel, are not mine.
On that green place I may not tread

11160   Another's shadow falls like dread;
It irks my feet, my eyes, my ear—
How can I get away from here!

LYNCEUS THE WATCHMAN [*as above*]:
Now, in the evening breeze, all hail
To this fine ship with swelling sail!

11165   How swift it glides, its load how high—
Sacks, boxes, piled against the sky!

[*A splendid boat appears, richly loaded with a variety of products from distant lands. Enter Mephistopheles and The Three Mighty Men.*³]

CHORUS: Welcome ashore!
We're back again!
Long live the master,

11170   Say his men!

[*They land; the cargo is brought ashore.*]

MEPHISTOPHELES: We have done well and had good sport;
We hope my lord will be content.
We'd only two ships when we went,
With twenty now we're back in port.

11175   Our cargo richly testifies
To our great deeds that won this prize.
The ocean sets one's notions free:
Who's plagued by scruple out at sea?
To catch a fish, to catch a ship,

11180   The only way is grab and grip;
And once three ships have come one's way,
A fourth is easy grappling-prey.
Then guess what chance a fifth will stand!
For might is right, by sea or land.

11185   Not *how* but *how much*—that's what's counted!
What seaman does not take for granted
The undivided trinity
Of war and trade and piracy?

THE THREE MIGHTY MEN: No thanks to meet us,

11190   No word to greet us!
Our master thinks
Our cargo stinks.
His face expresses
Great displeasure;

11195   He does not like
This princely treasure.

MEPHISTOPHELES: There's no more for you
On the house.
You took your cut,

3. Mephisto's assistants.

11200   So what's the grouse?
THE THREE: That's mere penny
       For our pains:
       We ask fair shares
       Of all the gains!
MEPHISTOPHELES: Go up there first
       And set out all
       The valuables
       Hall by hall.
       He'll see the richest
11210   Show on earth;
       Then he'll work out
       Just what it's worth,
       Decide he can
       Afford a treat,
11215   And order a feast-day
       For the fleet.
       Tomorrow the pretty birds° we'll see;   *prostitutes*
       They're my responsibility.

[The cargo is removed.]

MEPHISTOPHELES [*to Faust*]: Why these dark looks, this frowning brow?
11220   Sublime good fortune greets you now:
       By your high wisdom, the sea-shore
       And sea are reconciled once more;
       Now from the land in easy motion
       The ships glide swiftly to the ocean;
11225   And thus, here in this royal place,
       The whole world lies in your embrace!
       Your kingdom started on this spot;
       The first shed stood here, did it not?
       Here the first shallow trench was tried
11230   Where now the plashing oars are plied.
       Your lofty plan, our industry,
       Have made you lord of land and sea.
       From here—
FAUST: *Here!* That damned word again,
       The theme and burden of my pain!
11235   You are no fool: I must tell you
       It cuts my very heart in two,
       I'll not bear it another day!
       Yet as I say it, even I
       Feel shame. The old couple must give way!
11240   I chose that linden clump as my
       Retreat: those few trees not my own
       Spoil the whole world that is my throne.
       From branch to branch I planned to build
       Great platforms, to look far afield,
11245   From panoramic points to gaze

At all I've done; as one surveys
From an all-mastering elevation
A masterpiece of man's creation.
I'd see it all as I have planned:
11250   Man's gain of habitable land.

This is the sharpest torment: what
A rich man feels he has not got!
That linden-scent, that chapel-chime
Haunt me like some grim funeral-time.
11255   My will, my sovereign command
Is broken on that mound of sand!
How shall I cure my mental hell
That rages at that little bell!

MEPHISTOPHELES: Indeed, such matter for distress
11260   Must turn your life to bitterness.
These cursèd tinkling sounds we hear
Must stink in every noble ear.
Ding-donging, tintinnabulating,
Clear evening skies obnubilating:°   *clouding over*
1165   Every event of life it blights.
From that first bath to our last rites—
As if life were some dream-like thing
That fades away from dong to ding!

FAUST: Their stubbornness, their opposition
11270   Ruins my finest acquisition;
And in fierce agony I must
Grow weary now of being just.

MEPHISTOPHELES: Why scruple then at this late hour?
Are you not—a colonial power?

FAUST: Well, do it! Clear them from my path!—
A fine new cottage, as you know,
I've built, where the old folk can go.

MEPHISTOPHELES: We'll lift them up and whisk them to it;
A moment's work, they'll scarcely know it.
11280   They'll suffer it with a good grace
And settle down in their new place.

[*At his shrill whistle, The Three Mighty Men appear.*]

Come, we have orders from my lord;
Tomorrow there'll be a feast on board.

THE THREE: We've had a poor reception here;
11285   A feast's an excellent idea. [*Exeunt.*]

MEPHISTOPHELES [*ad spectatores*]:°   *aside*
The same old story! No doubt you
Have heard of Naboth's vineyard too. (*I Kgs.* 21)[3]

---

3. King Ahab, helped by Queen Jezebel in a murderous seizure of Naboth's vineyard, was denounced by the prophet Elijah. The biblical reference appears in Goethe's text: the devil here does not merely quote scripture, but even annotates his citation.

DEEP NIGHT

LYNCEUS THE WATCHMAN [*on the castle tower, singing*]:

    A watchman by calling,
    Far-sighted by birth,
11290 From this tower, my dwelling,
    I gaze at the earth:

    At the earth near and far,
    At the world far and near,
    At the moon and the stars,
11295 At the woods and the deer.

    A beauty eternal
    In all things I see,
    And the world and myself
    Are both pleasing to me.

11300 Oh blest are these eyes,
    All they've seen and can tell:
    Let it be as it may—
    They have loved it so well!

[*A pause.*]

    But I keep my watch so high,
11305 Alas, not only for delight!
    What dread terror of the night
    Spreads its threat across the sky?[4]
    Fiery sparks are scattering, spraying
    Through the twin-dark linden-trees:
11310 Higher still the flames are playing,
    Fanned to heat by their own breeze!
    Now the hut's ablaze all through,
    That was moist and mossy green;
    Too late now for rescue—who
11315 Can bring help to such a scene?
    Smoke will choke the good old couple,
    At their hearth so carefully
    Kept and tended, poor old people,
    What a dreadful tragedy!
11320 Flames lick up, black mossy beams
    Now are turned to burning red:
    How grim this wild inferno seems!
    Can they escape it? Have they fled?
    Tongues of fearful lightning rise
11325 Through those leaves and branches tall;
    Dried-up boughs burn flickerwise;
    Charred and breaking, soon they fall.
    Cursèd eyes, why must I see?
    Take your gift away from me!—

---

4. The watchman's speech, reporting disaster, is a common device in Classical tragedy.

11330   By their downward-crashing weight
          Now the little chapel's crushed;
          Snaking pointed flames have rushed
          Up to crown the tree-tops' fate.
          Hollow trunks in fiery showing
11335   To their very roots are glowing.

   [*A long pause; singing.*]

          Something lovely to behold
          Has vanished like an old tale told.

FAUST [*on the balcony, looking towards the sand-dunes*]:
          From overhead, what song of woe?
          Its words and music came too slow.
11340   My watchman wails: and inwardly
          The impatient deed now vexes me.
          What if the linden-trees are gone,
          Their trunks half-charred, a direful sight—
          I'll quickly build a watch-tower on
11345   That place, and scan the infinite!
          I see the new house over there,
          That soon will shelter that old pair;
          They'll praise my generous patronage
          And pass a peaceable old age.

MEPHISTOPHELES and THE THREE [*from below*]:
          We're back, sir, with due promptitude;
          Regrettably, they misconstrued
          Our meaning, and some force was needed.
          We knocked and banged, but were not heeded.
          We rattled on, and banged some more,
11355   Till there it lay, the rotten door.
          We threatened them and made a din:
          They would not budge, or ask us in,
          And as is common in such cases
          They just sat on with stolid faces.
11360   On your behalf, our zeal not lacking,
          We grabbed them then and sent them packing.
          They didn't linger long—the pair
          Dropped dead of terror then and there.
          A stranger, lurking with them, drew
11365   His sword and was soon dealt with too.
          The fight was brief and violent;
          Some coals were scattered, and up went
          Some straw; the merry blazing fire
          Is now a triple funeral pyre.

FAUST: And this you claim to have done for me?
          I said exchange, not robbery!
          Deaf savages! I curse this deed;

Now share my curse, your folly's meed!
THE OTHERS, IN CHORUS: The moral's plain, hear it who can:
11375   Never resist the powerful man.
          Don't put up a bold fight, or you
          Risk house and home, and your life too. [*Exeunt.*]
FAUST [*on the balcony*]: The stars have hid their gleam and glow,
          The fire sinks and glimmers low;
11380   A breeze still fans its embers free
          And blows the reek across to me.
          A rash command, too soon obeyed!—
          What comes now, like a hovering shade?

MIDNIGHT

[*Enter Four Gray Women.*]

THE FIRST: My name is Want.
THE SECOND: My name is Debt.
THE THIRD: My name is Care.
THE FOURTH: My name is Need.
THREE OF THEM: The door will not open, we'll never get in.
          This is a rich man's house, there's no way in.
WANT: I am a shadow there.
DEBT: I am as nothing there.
NEED: They pay no heed to me, for they need nothing there.
CARE: You are locked out, sisters, you cannot stay.
          But through his keyhole Care finds a way.

[*Care vanishes.*]

WANT: Come then, my gray sisters, for you must be gone.
DEBT: I'll follow you closely, sister, lead on!
NEED: Need follows you, sister, as close as a breath.
ALL THREE: The dark clouds are drifting, the stars disappearing:
          From far off, from far off, another is nearing!
          Our brother is coming; he comes—brother Death.

[*Exeunt.*]

FAUST [*in the palace*]: I saw four come, I only saw three go.
          What their speech meant I do not know.
11400   They talked of *debt,* and then another word
          That almost rhymed—could it be *death* I heard?
          A dark and hollow sound, a ghostly sigh.
          I have not broken through to freedom yet.
          I must clear magic from my path, forget
11405   All magic conjurations—for then I
          Would be confronting Nature all alone:
          Man's life worth while, man standing on his own!

So it was once, before I probed the gloom
And dared to curse myself, with words of doom
11410   That cursed the world. The air is swarming now
With ghosts we would avoid if we knew how.
How logical and clear the daylight seems
Till the night weaves us in its web of dreams!
As we return from dewy fields, dusk falls
11415   And birds of mischief croak their ominous calls.
All round us lurks this superstition's snare;
Some haunting, half-seen thing cries out Beware!
We shrink back in alarm, and are alone.
Doors creak, and no one enters.

[*In sudden alarm.*]

                                             Is someone
11420   There at the door?
CARE: You ask, need I reply?
FAUST: And who are you?
CARE: I am here, here am I.
FAUST: Go away!
CARE: I am here where I should be.
FAUST [*at first angry, then calmer, to himself*]:
I must take care to use no sorcery.
CARE: Though no human ear can hear me,
11425   Yet the echoing heart must fear me;
In an ever-changed disguise
All men's lives I tyrannize.
On the roads and on the sea
Anxiously they ride with me;
11430   Never looked for, always there,
Cursed and flattered. I am Care:
Have I never crossed your path?
FAUST: I merely raced across the earth,
Seized by the hair each passing joy,
11435   Discarded all that did not satisfy;
What slipped my grasp, I let it go again.
I have merely desired, achieved, and then
Desired some other thing. Thus I have stormed
Through life; at first with pride and violence,
11440   But now less rashly, with more sober sense.
I've seen enough of this terrestrial sphere.
There is no view to the Beyond from here:
A fool will seek it, peer with mortal eyes
And dream of human life above the skies!
11445   Let him stand fast in this world, and look round
With courage: here so much is to be found!
Why must he wander into timelessness?

What his mind grasps, he may possess.
Thus let him travel all his earthly day:
11450 Though spirits haunt him, let him walk his way,
Let both his pain and joy be in his forward stride—
Each moment leave him still unsatisfied!

CARE: When a man is in my keeping,
All his world is dead or sleeping;
11455 Everlasting dusk descending,
Sun not moving, dark not ending.
Though each outward sense be whole,
Night has nested in his soul;
Riches stand around him staling,
11460 Unpossessed and unavailing;
Gladness, sadness are mere whim,
Plenty cannot nourish him,
He delays both joy and pain
Till the day has passed again,
11465 And on time-to-come intent
Comes to no accomplishment.

FAUST: Stop! You'll not put that blight on me!
I will not listen to such stuff.
Leave me! Your wretched litany
11470 Can drive wise men to madness soon enough.

CARE: Shall he come or shall he go?
He can't choose, he does not know.
In the middle of the road,
See, he staggers, tremble-toed!
11475 Wanders deeper in the maze,
Sees the whole world crookedways,
Burdening himself and others;
Still he breathes, yet chokes and smothers—
Not quite choked, yet life-bereft,
11480 Stubborn, though with hope still left.
Such a ceaseless downward course,
Bitter may not, must by force,
Now released, now re-pursued,
Restless sleep and tasteless food,
11485 Binds him in a static state,
Makes him hell's initiate.

FAUST: Horrible phantoms! Thus you still conspire
Again against mankind and yet again;
Even indifferent days you turn into a dire
11490 Chaotic nexus of entangling pain.
Demons, I know, are hard to exorcize,
The spirit-bond is loath to separate:
But though the creeping power of Care be great,
This power I will never recognize!

CARE: Suffer it then; for as I go

I leave a curse where I have passed.
Men live their lives in blindness: so
Shall even Faust be blinded at the last!

[*She breathes on him. Exit.*]

FAUST [*blinded*]: Night seems to close upon me deeper still,
11500   But in my inmost soul a bright light shines.
I hasten to complete my great designs:
My words alone can work my mastering will.
Rise from your sleep, my servants, every man!
Give visible success to my bold plan!
11505   Set to work now with shovel and with spade:
I have marked it all out, let it be made!
With a well-ordered project and with hard
Toil we shall win supreme reward;
Until the edifice of this achievement stands,
11510   One mind shall move a thousand hands.

THE GREAT FORECOURT OF THE PALACE

[*Torches. Mephistopheles as overseer leading a gang of Lemurs.*[5]]

MEPHISTOPHELES: Come now, my lemur-goblins, patched-Up semi-skeletons,
With mouldering sinews still attached
To move your rattling bones!
LEMURS [*in chorus*]: We came at once, sir, when you called;
Is there—we did half hear of it—
A plot of land here to be sold,
And shall we get our share of it?
Here are the chains, here are the posts
11520   To measure out the site.
Why did you summon us poor ghosts?
We can't remember quite.
MEPHISTOPHELES: There's no need for these mysteries;
Just use yourselves as measuring-rods!
11525   The tallest of you can lie down lengthwise,
The rest stand round and cut away the sods.
A rectangle of earth dug deep,
A good old-fashioned place to sleep!
From palace to this narrow house descending—
11530   That always was the stupid story's ending.
LEMURS [*digging with mocking gestures*]:

In youth when I did love, did love
Methought 'twas very sweet,
And night and day to music gay
I danced with nimble feet.

---

5. Not the monkeys called lemurs, but Classical spirits of the evil dead.

11535 But Age with his crutch and cunning clutch
Has come to trip me now.
By a grave I stumbled, and in I tumbled;
They'd left it open somehow.

FAUST [*comes out of the palace, groping at the doorpost*]:
The clash of spades: how it delights my heart!
11540 These are my many workmen; here they toil,
The alienated earth to reconcile,
To keep the ocean and the land apart,
To rule the unruly waves once more.

MEPHISTOPHELES [*aside*]: And yet it's us you're working for
11545 With all your foolish dams and dikes;
Neptune,° the water-devil, likes   *sea god*
To think of the great feast there'll be
When they collapse. Do what you will, my friend,
You all are doomed! They are in league with me,
11550 The elements, and shall destroy you in the end.

FAUST: Overseer!

MEPHISTOPHELES: Sir!

FAUST: I need more workers; bring
Them to me by the hundred! Use persuasion,
Cajole or bully them, try everything,
Inducements, money, force! This excavation
11555 Must go ahead; the ditch I've now begun—
I must know daily how much has been done.

MEPHISTOPHELES [*sotto voce*]:°
                                                        under his breath
The digging has gone well today;
No ditch or dike, but dust to dust,[6] they say.

FAUST: A swamp surrounds the mountains' base;
11560 It poisons all I have achieved till now.
I'll drain it too; that rotten place
Shall be my last great project. I see how
To give those millions a new living-space:
They'll not be safe, but active, free at least.
11565 I see green fields, so fertile: man and beast
At once shall settle that new pleasant earth,
Bastioned by great embankments that will rise
About them, by bold labor brought to birth.
Here there shall be an inland paradise:
11570 Outside, the sea, as high as it can reach,
May rage and gnaw; and yet a common will,
Should it intrude, will act to close the breach.
Yes! to this vision I am wedded still,
And this as wisdom's final word I teach:
11575 Only that man earns freedom, merits life,
Who must reconquer both in constant daily strife.

---

6. Once again the devil quotes Christian material, this time the prayer for the dead.

In such a place, by danger still surrounded,
Youth, manhood, age, their brave new world have founded.
I long to see that multitude, and stand
11580   With a free people on free land!
Then to the moment I might say:
Beautiful moment, do not pass away!
Till many ages shall have passed
This record of my earthly life shall last.
11585   And in anticipation of such bliss
What moment could give me greater joy than this?

[*Faust sinks back, the Lemures seize him and lay him on the ground.*]

MEPHISTOPHELES: Poor fool! Unpleasured and unsatisfied,
          Still whoring after changeful fantasies,
          This last, poor, empty moment he would seize,
11590   Content with nothing else beside.
          How he resisted me! But in the end
          Time wins; so here you lie, my senile friend.
          The clock has stopped—

CHORUS: Has stopped! Like midnight it is stilled.
          The clock-hands fall.

MEPHISTOPHELES: They fall. All is fulfilled.[7]

CHORUS: All's over now.

MEPHISTOPHELES: Over! A stupid word! Why "over"? What can be
          "Over" is just not there; it's all the same to me!
          Why bother to go on creating?
          Making, then endlessly annihilating!
11600   "Over and past!" What's that supposed to mean?
          It's no more than if it had never been,
          Yet it goes bumbling round as if it were.
          The Eternal Void is what I'd much prefer.

BURIAL RITES

A LEMUR [*solo*]: Why is the house so poorly made,
11605   And hempen the shrouding-sheet?

LEMURS [*in chorus*]: 'Twas built with pickaxe and with spade,
          And for such a guest 'tis meet.

A LEMUR [*solo*]: Who furnished it so ill, who took
          The table and chairs away?

LEMURS [*in chorus*]: Not yours to own, 'twas all on loan,
          The creditors came today.

MEPHISTOPHELES: The body's down, the spirit I'll soon fix,
          I'll show him his own blood-scribed document—
          Yet souls come hard these days, their friends invent
11615   Loopholes, and try to play the Devil tricks.
          Our older methods gave offense,

---

7. Mephisto echoes the last words of Jesus on the Cross (John 19:30).

Our new ones don't commend us greatly;
I used to do it all myself, but lately
I've had to send for adjutants.

11620   Things are no longer what they were!
Traditional custom, the old rules inspire
No confidence now; there's nothing one can trust.
In former times a man would breathe his last,
Out popped the soul as quick as any mouse,
11625   And snap! my waiting claws would close on it.
But nowadays it hesitates to quit
The gloomy corpse, its dark disgusting house;
Till in the end the elements at strife
Drive out the wretched scrap of life.
11630   I rack my brains about it night and day:
When, how, and *where*'s the question—who can say?
Old Death has lost his old decisive style;
Even the *whether*'s doubtful a long while.[8]
Often I've watched stiff limbs with lustful eyes—
11635   Sham-dead again! They twitch and squirm and rise.

[*He makes fantastic summoning gestures, like a flank-man drilling troops.*]

Come on then, at the double now, my friends,
Straight-horns and crooked-horns! Good solid fiends
Of the old school. And bring the jaws of hell,[9]
Please, gentlemen, along with you as well!
11640   Hell has a multiplicity of jaws, it's true,
And swallows up by rank and by degree;
Although in future those rules too
Will be relaxed, presumably.

[*The frightful jaws of hell open up on the left.*]

The fangs gape; through the arching orifice
11645   Hell's maw spews up a fiery ocean,
And in the seething murk of the abyss
I see the Infernal City's ceaseless conflagration.
The red surf surges to the teeth: "At last,"
Think damned souls, swimming up, "here's rescue!" But the vast
11650   Hyena-crunch reclaims them; with dismay
They must pursue their incandescent way.
Amusing those odd corners look as well;
What horrors a small area can contain!
It's supposed to scare sinners; they remain,
11655   However, total skeptics about hell.

[*To the fat devils with short straight horns.*]

Now, you pot-bellied red-faced rascals, you!

8. Premature burial was a topic for lively discussion in late 18th-century Germany.

9. A common setting in medieval drama, anticipated at the end of Prelude in the Theater, line 242.

How fat you are! Hot brimstone in your guts,
No doubt; you stiff-necked lumps, you no-necked clots!
Watch here for a sudden phosphorescent glow:
11660   It's called the soul, "Psyche"[1]—pull off its wings!
Without them, souls are nasty worm-like things.
I'll stamp it with my seal; off with it then
Into the fire-storm!
                              You, the gentlemen
Resembling bladders, guard his lower parts!
11665   Don't let our prey squeeze out there—we don't know
Exactly, but it might live where he farts;
Perhaps its whimsy takes it to do so—
Or in the navel maybe; that's a place
It likes. Watch that, or you'll be in disgrace!

[*To the thin devils with long crooked horns.*]

11670   You, flanking giants, you tall gangling fools,
Snatch at the air—keep practicing, and keep
Your arms straight! Spread your claws, they're good sharp tools;
Don't let our fluttering bird give you the slip!
It must be tired of its old lodging now;
11675   And genius, too—that must soar up somehow.

[*A flash of glory from above right.*]

THE HEAVENLY HOST: Follow, bright envoys,
          Companions of heaven,
          Unhurriedly soaring:
          Let sin be forgiven,
11680   Earth-creatures restoring,
          All natures partaking;
          Let each feel the trace
          As you pause at the place
          Of your hovering grace!

MEPHISTOPHELES: Now what cacophony is this, what jangling
          Noise from above, unwelcome as that light?
          A boyish-girlish callow twing-a-twangling,
          Fit for some pious nun or acolyte!
          In vain we hatched that supersubtle plot
11690   To lay the human population waste;
          Our most outrageous trick, just fancy what?
          Exactly suits their dim religious taste.
          The hypocrites, the riff-raff! Here they are!
          That's how they've cheated us of many a prize;
11695   They fight with our own weapons in this war—
          They're devils too, but in disguise.

---

1. "Psyche" is the Greek for both soul and butterfly.

You there! Hold firm, on your eternal shame!
Stand round the grave, and guard it like hell's flame!
CHORUS OF ANGELS [*scattering roses*]:
Roses resplendent,
11700   Roses balm-redolent,
Floating and hovering,
Stem-wing and petal-wing,
Rosebuds reopening,
Blossom recovering,
11705   Secretly succouring:
Hasten to him and bring
Crimson and green of spring,
Make him a paradise
Here where he lies!
MEPHISTOPHELES [*to the demons*]:
11710   What's all this flinching, twitching? Did they teach
You that in hell? Stand fast, and let them throw
Bouquets about! To battle-stations, each
Ugly man-jack of you! They think they'll snow
Hot fiends up under flower-power! Blow,
11715   And they'll all wither, they'll all fade and bleach!
Snuff them out, snuffle-snouts!—Enough, enough!
The whole flight's blighted with your stinking puff!
Just take it easy! Shut your mouths and noses!
Damn you, you're blowing far too hard!
11720   Can't you learn moderation? Look, those roses,
They're not just withering, they're all black and charred—
They're burning! Here they come, the poisoned flames.
Stand and resist, in the three devils' names!—
They're losing heart, they might as well retire.
11725   My devils smell a new, insinuating fire!
ANGELS [*in chorus*]: Flowers of blessedness,
Flames with your dancing light,
Spreaders of happiness,
Powers of love that bless,
11730   Givers of heart's delight:
True words that shine and last,
Brightness in ether lost,
For the eternal host
World without night!
MEPHISTOPHELES: Damn you, my satan-wimps! Now, by my wrath,
They're standing on their heads; oh, shame on you!
The louts are turning cartwheels—the whole crew
Goes plunging arsewise back into perdition.
May you enjoy your well-deserved hot bath!
11740   But I'll not budge from my position.

[*Striking out at the roses as they float down.*]

Begone, will-o'-the-wisps! You're bright lights, yes,
But once I catch you, you're a sticky mess.
Ugh! Get away from me, you fluttering pack!—
They cling like pitch and sulphur to my back.

ANGELS [*in chorus*]: What has no part in you
You have no need of it,
What frets the heart in you
Do not take heed of it.
If the defenses fail
11750   Our strength must then prevail.
Love: for by love alone
Heaven is won.

MEPHISTOPHELES: My head's on fire, my heart and guts as well:
This is worse than the flames of hell!
11755   Some superdiabolic element
Is piercing me. Is this the pain that's meant,
Why unrequited lovers wail Alas!
And crane their necks to see their mistress pass?

Even I! What twists my head towards them somehow?
11760   I was their mortal enemy till now:
Even the sight of them was more than I could bear.
Am I possessed, then, by some alien force?
I like the look of these nice boys—of course
I do! What's this? Why can't I curse and swear?
11765   I'd like to know who's going to be
The fool in future, if they make a fool of me!
Young ruffians, how I hate them all! Yet I confess
They're damned attractive none the less!—
My dears, would I be wrong to guess you are
11770   By any chance cousins of Lucifer?
You're pretty! I must give you all a kiss!
I think you'll suit me at a time like this.
I feel so comfy and so natural,
As if I'd seen you many times before;
11775   So curiously cat-randy, and the more
I contemplate you, the more beautiful
You get. Come closer, please! Just one sweet glance!

THE ANGELS: We are coming; why do you shrink as we advance?
As we draw near, stand your ground if you can!

[*The Angels circle round, filling the entire stage.*]

MEPHISTOPHELES [*pushed forward to the proscenium*]:
11780   You give us a bad name as sprites of hell,
And yet the witchcraft's yours: your goblin-spell
Seduces woman and seduces man!
Damn this for an adventure! Can this be
The element of love, can it be real?
11785   I burn all over, I can scarcely feel

My burnt hump where those flowers got at me.
You dither about so, my dears: come down!
Those lovely limbs should move more worldly-wise.
It's true it suits you well, that serious frown;
11790   But to see you smile would be a sweet surprise!
Just once, please! It would give me such delight!
Just smile the little smile that lovers use—
A modulation of the mouth, that's right!
You tall boy there, now you I'd not refuse;
11795   But why this unbecoming priestly air?
Give me a lustful look instead, ah yes!
And please, be all a little nakeder!
Those flowing robes are decent to excess.
They turn—the rear view is too tantalizing!
11800   Delicious monkeys! ah, how appetizing!
CHORUS OF ANGELS: Turn, burning flames of love,
Turn into clarity!
So to the self-condemned
Truth shall bring liberty;
11805   Freed from the evil spell
They shall win through as well
Into the blessed throng
Where all belong.
MEPHISTOPHELES [*pulling himself together*]:
What's wrong with me? I'm out in boils all over,
11810   Like Job![2] A self-repugnant spectacle;
And yet a triumph, when one sees the whole
Depths of oneself, and trusts them to recover.
My noble devil-parts are saved alive!
Those love-charms, as mere eczema they thrive;
11815   The whole damned bonfire's now a burnt-out case,
And once again I curse the whole angelic race!
CHORUS OF ANGELS: Blaze, holy fire! These
Whom you surround here
Sweet life have found here
11820   For all to share.
With single voice now
Cry and rejoice now!
The spirit breathes
In a purified air.

[*They soar upwards, carrying Faust's immortal part.*]

MEPHISTOPHELES [*looking round*]:
11825   But what is this? They've gone! Where can they be?
You halflings, I've been caught off duty!
You've hovered off to heaven with my booty!

---

2. The man tormented by Satan to test his faith with God. His story is told in the biblical Book of Job.

That's why they snuffled round this grave; I see!
I've lost my greatest, my most precious prize.
11830 That lofty soul who pledged himself to me—
Filched cunningly before my very eyes!
Now who shall I complain to? Who
Will give me justice, give me back what's mine?
Poor fool, at your age you've been tricked. A fine
11835 Mess you are in, and well deserve it too!
I've misbehaved, there's no one else to blame,
I'm in disgrace. The whole investment lost;
All that good work for nothing! Common lust,
Absurd infatuation puts to shame
11840 The hard-boiled Devil. And if even my
Wisdom's no match for such tomfoolery—
Then to this strange love-madness I extend
My compliments, since it could catch me in the end!

* * *

from MOUNTAIN GORGES[3]

DOCTOR MARIANUS [*prostrated in adoration*]:
Gaze aloft—the saving eyes
See you all, such tender
Penitents; look up and render
Thanks, to blest renewal rise!
12100 May each nobler spirit never
Fail to serve thee; Virgin, Mother,
Queen, oh keep us in thy favor,
Goddess, kind for ever!

CHORUS MYSTICUS:
All that must disappear
12105 Is but a parable;
What lay beyond us, here
All is made visible;
Here deeds have understood
Words they were darkened by;
12110 Eternal Womanhood
Draws us on high.

To the Moon[1]

Bush and vale you fill again
With a misty glow,
Softly you at last unchain
My entire soul.

---

3. In the final scene Faust's redemption is celebrated by the soul of Gretchen, the Holy Virgin, and Catholic holy figures. Included here is the famous hymn to the feminine that closes the play.
1. This and the following poems are translated by Jane K. Brown.

5   O'er my valley floor you send
Your tender, soothing gaze,
Like the eye of gentle friend
Over all my days.

Every echo moves my heart
10   Of glad or troubled mood,
Wandering 'twixt joy and smart
In my solitude.

Flow then, flow then, dearest stream!
Ne'er shall I be gay,
15   Play and kiss dissolved in dream,
And loyalty away.

O that which I once possessed,
Precious ever yet!
That in torment without rest
20   We can ne'er forget!

Murmur, stream, and flow along,
Without rest or ease,
Murmur, whisper to my song
Fluid melodies,

25   When you on a winter night
Loose your raging floods,
Or amid spring's splendor bright,
You nurture youthful buds.

Happy he who from the rest
30   Turns and does not hate,
Holds a friend unto his breast
So to contemplate

What from human ken apart
Or else not in sight,
35   Through the mazes of the heart
Wanders in the night.

Erlking[1]

Who rides so late through night wind wild?
It is the father with his child.
He has the boy safe in his arm,
He holds him tight, he keeps him warm.—

5   My son, why hide your face in fear?—
Don't you see, father, the Erlking here?
The alder king, with train and crown?—
My son, it's mist come from the ground.—

---

1. From the Danish for "king of the elves." In German "Erle" means an alder tree or bush, typical riverside vegetation.

10   "You lovely child, come go with me!
      Such pretty games I'll play with thee;
      The shore is lined with blooms untold;
      My mother dresses in cloth of gold."

      My father, my father, and can you not hear
      What Erlking whispers into my ear?—
15   Be quiet, ah stay quiet, my child!
      In the dead leaves the wind rustles mild.—

      "Now won't you go, dear boy, with me?
      My daughters shall wait on you prettily;
      They'll lead the night-dance mid shadows deep
20   And rock and dance and sing you to sleep."

      My father, my father, and can you not see
      Erlking's daughters beyond the dark tree?
      My son, my son, I'm certain, I say,
      It's only old willows gleaming so grey.—

25   "I love you, your face enchants my sight,
      And if you're not willing, then I shall use might."
      My father, my father, he's grasping my arm!
      The alder king has done me harm.

      The father shudders, he speeds o'er the field,
30   He holds in his arms the groaning child,
      Arrives at home with pain and dread;
      In his arms the child was dead.

Mignon[1]

      Know you the land where flowering lemon grows,
      In leafy dark the golden orange glows,
      A gentle wind breathes from the azure sky,
      The myrtle stands so still, the laurel high,
5   You surely know?
                'Tis there! 'tis there
      With you, o my beloved, I would go.

      Know you the house? Its roof on columns tall,
      Its shimmering rooms, its heart a shining hall,
      And marble statues stand and gaze at me:
10   What have they done, poor little child, to thee?
      You surely know?
                'Tis there! 'tis there
      With you, o my protector, I would go.

---

1. From Goethe's novel *Wilhelm Meister's Apprenticeship*. Mignon is a mysterious child with shadowy memories of her Italian birthplace.

Know you the heights with bridges made of cloud?
The mule-train seeks its way in misty shroud,
15 In caverns dwell the dragons' ancient brood,
The cliff falls sheer, and over it the flood;
You surely know?
         'Tis there! 'tis there
That our way leads, o father, let us go!

Dusk Descended from on High[1]

Dusk descended from on high,
Now all nearness is afar;
Yet first lifted in the sky
Nobly lit the evening star!
5 All dislimns° to shape unknown,   *loses form*
Stealthily the mists arise;
Blacker still the darkness grown
Rests within the lake's deep skies.

Now I sense in eastern regions
10 Moonlight's shining ardent gleam,
Slender willow's hair-fine legions
Dance upon the nearby stream.
Through the play of moving shadows
Quivers Luna's° magic glow,   *the moon*
15 Through the eye then coolness tiptoes
Soothing to the heart below.

Blissful Yearning[1]

Tell it no one, but to sages,
Since the crowd at once will blame it:
To the life I vow my praises
That desires to die enflamèd.

5 In the cool of lovers' evenings,
Procreated, procreating,
You fall prey to foreign feeling,
While the candle's calmly shining.

You remain embraced no longer
10 In the darkness-deepened shading,
And new yearning ever stronger
Sweeps you on to higher mating.

Distance could not slow your passage,

1. The eighth of 14 short poems, aiming to recreate the brevity and nature symbolism of the brief fragments of Eastern poetry available to Goethe. The cycle goes under the cumbersome title "Chinese-German Diaries and Annals."

1. From Goethe's last volume of poetry, *West-Eastern Divan*, written in homage to the poet Hafiz (d.1389), whom Goethe read in German translation. "Divan" is the Persian name for a collection of poems.

Wingèd and enthralled you came,
15   And at last, athirst for brightness,
Moth, you are consumed in flame.

And until you have the rest,
Namely: Die and grow!
You are but a darkling guest
20   On the earth below.

━━◄╳►━━

George Gordon, Lord Byron
1788–1824

"I have just learned that my cousin Lord Byron is dead at Missolinghi. The great heart has ceased to beat. He was great, and a heart, no piddling ovary for feelings. Yes, this man was great, in pain he discovered new worlds, like a Prometheus he defied human miseries and the even more miserable gods of humanity, and the fame of his name penetrated to the icebergs of Thule and the burning deserts of the East." So wrote Europe's second most popular poet (and sometime Byron translator) Heinrich Heine about the titanic Englishman, and for once the superlatives are not hyperbole. Byron was not literally Heine's cousin, of course, but Byronic feelings had become so pervasive that all readers felt his pulse.

Byron's universality was social, sexual, political, economic, and emotional. The offspring of two degenerate noble families, he spent his childhood in poverty in Scotland after his father, Captain John "Mad Jack" Byron, died (possibly by suicide) in France. In 1798 he unexpectedly inherited a title and a fortune from a great uncle, William "the Wicked Lord" Byron. With attractive looks when not overweight and athletic prowess despite congenital lameness, the poet attracted uncounted female and some male lovers, both young and old. While studying at Harrow and Cambridge, he mixed study with financial as well as emotional extravagances. He soon began writing both sentimental and savagely satirical poetry, traveled between 1809 and 1811 (with Napoleonic France inaccessible) to the Mediterranean countries, as far as the Turkish possessions of Albania and Greece. Upon his return he briefly served in the House of Lords, and he fell in love with a half-sister whom he hadn't met before adolescence. He married unhappily in 1815, partly for money, partly to escape scandal; his wife left him the next year, shortly after the birth of a daughter. Within a few months he was driven out of England for good by rumors—very possibly true—that he had fathered his sister's daughter. In Switzerland he consorted with Percy Shelley, who had left his wife and child for the sixteen-year-old Mary Wollstonecraft Godwin (soon to be Mary Shelley, the author of *Frankenstein*), and with Mary's stepsister, Claire Clairmont, by whom Byron had another daughter. He spent the following years in Italy, loving many but primarily involved with a married seventeen-year-old noblewoman. Having experienced both deprivation and abundance in his childhood, and being perpetually both an iconoclast and a joiner, Byron followed his idealist enthusiasm back to Greece, where he participated heroically in the ultimately victorious campaign for Greek independence, only to die tragically of battlefield fever.

Byron's whirlwind existence was accompanied by equally prolific writing. He became famous in 1812 with the publication of the first two cantos of *Childe Harold's Pilgrimage* (continuations appeared in 1816 and 1818), a grand poem of exalted passion, natural sublimity, and disillusion in the stately, nine-line stanza of Spenser, as illustrated by a famous stanza from the fourth canto that combines political ardor with Byron's trademark existential nihilism:

> Roll on, thou deep and dark blue Ocean—roll!
> Ten thousand fleets sweep over thee in vain;
> Man marks the earth with ruin—his control
> Stops with the shore; upon the watery plain
> The wrecks are all thy deed, nor doth remain
> A shadow of man's ravage, save his own,
> When for a moment, like a drop of rain,
> He sinks into thy depths with bubbling groan,
> Without a grave, unknell'd, uncoffin'd, and unknown.

Byron's reputation was further enhanced by a series of verse tales of adventure mostly set in the eastern Mediterranean and beyond, as well as by somber, sometimes sexually or religiously daring poetic tragedies.

Byron's genius was too variable, however, to be captured by a single mood. As the narrator of *Don Juan* says, "I hate inconstancy . . . And yet . . ." What suited him best of all (though it was more difficult to translate and played a lesser role in his Continental fame) was the comic mode with which he had begun and to which he returned in his final years, and which Pushkin brilliantly imitated in *Eugene Onegin* (p. 296). For some successful experiments in 1818 as well as his masterpiece *Don Juan* he adopted the quicksilver eight-line stanza of the Italian Renaissance. With its rapid-fire *abababcc* rhyme scheme, often employing elaborate trick rhymes, the stanza lent itself to displays of virtuosic high spirits, as in its dedicatory attack on the older, now conservative poets of the so-called Lake School: Wordsworth, Coleridge, and their erstwhile friend Robert Southey.

> Bob Southey! You're a poet—Poet-laureate,
>   And representative of all the race,
> Although 'tis true that you turn'd out a Tory at
>   Last,—yours has lately been a common case;
> And now, my Epic Renegade! what are ye at?
>   With all the Lakers, in and out of place?
> A nest of tuneful persons, to my eye
> Like "four and twenty Blackbirds in a pye."

With his naughtiness transfigured into this kind of bad-boy humor, Byron makes room for purified versions of his other selves. His Don Juan (comically pronounced to rhyme with "true one") is no longer the swashbuckling daredevil of the tradition represented by the da Ponte–Mozart opera (see Volume D), but rather a beautiful *homme fatal*. He resembles Byron in his unhappy parentage and in the strong swimming that saves him from a terrible shipwreck, though unlike his creator Juan is slender and unhobbled. Women flock to him unsought, and he experiences love, nature, enslavement, travels through the Mediterranean, to Russia, and eventually even to England, all with a kind of dreamlike wonder that gives a unique delicacy to the enormous poem, left unfinished at Byron's death.

Byronic passion and moodiness are aristocratic poses in which multitudes may share. He exposes emotion with unmatched finesse, and then he exposes the very artifices with which actors strike their poses. "A long, long kiss of youth, and love, / And beauty" captures adolescent yearnings in simple diction. And when he then calls the kiss a "heart-quake," the invented word perfectly captures both the violence and the self-centeredness of first loves. As the next canto says, "In her first passion woman loves her lover, / In all the others all she loves is love." Yet if this sounds condescending toward women, it is important to remember that the narrative voice is itself a pose. The canto has begun with the bravado of "Hail, Muse! *et cetera*," and so Byron exposes both the power and the fragility of love together with the power and fragility of anyone who claims to understand love. Human insight is founded directly on human instability: that is the message that grew directly out of Byron's biography and the turmoil of the age as he experienced it, and nowhere is the message communicated with anything like the refinement of Byron's masterpiece.

PRONUNCIATION:
   Don Juan: dawn JOO-uhn

from DON JUAN

from Canto 2

Return we to Don Juan. He begun
1330   To hear new words, and to repeat them; but
Some feelings, universal as the sun,
   Were such as could not in his breast be shut
More than within the bosom of a nun:
   He was in love,—as you would be, no doubt,
1335   With a young benefactress—so was she,
Just in the way we very often see.

168

And every day by daybreak—rather early
   For Juan, who was somewhat fond of rest—
She came into the cave, but it was merely
1340   To see her bird reposing in his nest;
And she would softly stir his locks so curly,
   Without disturbing her yet slumbering guest,
Breathing all gently o'er his cheek and mouth,
As o'er a bed of roses the sweet south.°   *the south wind*

169

1345   And every morn his colour freshlier came,
   And every day help'd on his convalescence;
'Twas well, because health in the human frame
   Is pleasant, besides being true love's essence,
For health and idleness to passion's flame
1350   Are oil and gunpowder; and some good lessons
Are also learnt from Ceres and from Bacchus,[2]
Without whom Venus will not long attack us.

* * *

172

Both were so young, and one so innocent,
1370   That bathing pass'd for nothing: Juan seem'd
To her, as 'twere, the kind of being sent,
   Of whom these two years she had nightly dream'd,
A something to be loved, a creature meant
   To be her happiness, and whom she deem'd

---

1. The 16-year-old Juan has been caught in an incriminating situation with a married older woman and sent away from his native Seville. Caught in a shipwreck, he awakens on an island, tended by a young maiden named Haidée.
2. Ceres, goddess of grain; Bacchus, wine god

1375 To render happy; all who joy would win
  Must share it,—Happiness was born a twin.

173

  It was such pleasure to behold him, such
   Enlargement of existence to partake
  Nature with him, to thrill beneath his touch,
1380 To watch him slumbering, and to see him wake:
  To live with him for ever were too much;
   But then the thought of parting made her quake:
  He was her own, her ocean-treasure, cast
  Like a rich wreck—her first love, and her last.

174

1385 And thus a moon roll'd on, and fair Haidée
   Paid daily visits to her boy, and took
  Such plentiful precautions, that still he
   Remain'd unknown within his craggy nook;
  At last her father's prows put out to sea,
1390 For certain merchantmen upon the look,
  Not as of yore to carry off an Io,[3]
  But three Ragusan vessels bound for Scio.[4]

175

  Then came her freedom, for she had no mother,
   So that, her father being at sea, she was
1395 Free as a married woman, or such other
   Female, as where she likes may freely pass,
  Without even the incumbrance of a brother,
   The freest she that ever gazed on glass:
  I speak of Christian lands in this comparison,
1400 Where wives, at least, are seldom kept in garrison.

176

  Now she prolong'd her visits and her talk
   (For they must talk), and he had learnt to say
  So much as to propose to take a walk,—
   For little had he wander'd since the day
1405 On which, like a young flower snapp'd from the stalk,
   Drooping and dewy on the beach he lay,—
  And thus they walk'd out in the afternoon,
  And saw the sun set opposite the moon.

177

  It was a wild and breaker-beaten coast,
1410 With cliffs above, and a broad sandy shore,
  Guarded by shoals and rocks as by an host,°   *army*
   With here and there a creek, whose aspect wore
  A better welcome to the tempest-tost;

---

3. The Greek historian Herodotus opens his history of the Persian Wars with the story of a Greek princess named Io; the Persians accused the Phoenicians of carrying her off to Egypt, while the Phoenicians claimed she fled in shame after becoming pregnant by the ship's captain.

4. Ragusa was a city-state with a large merchant fleet on the Adriatic coast across from Italy; Scio is the island of Chios, off the Turkish coast.

And rarely ceased the haughty billow's roar,
1415   Save on the dead long summer days, which make
The outstretch'd ocean glitter like a lake.

178
And the small ripple spilt upon the beach
    Scarcely o'erpass'd the cream of your champagne,
When o'er the brim the sparkling bumpers reach,
1420   That spring-dew of the spirit! the heart's rain!
Few things surpass old wine; and they may preach
    Who please,—the more because they preach in vain,—
Let us have wine and woman, mirth and laughter,
Sermons and soda water the day after.

179
1425   Man, being reasonable, must get drunk;
    The best of life is but intoxication:
Glory, the grape, love, gold, in these are sunk
    The hopes of all men, and of every nation;
Without their sap, how branchless were the trunk
1430   Of life's strange tree, so fruitful on occasion:
But to return,—Get very drunk; and when
You wake with head-ache, you shall see what then.

180
Ring for your valet—bid him quickly bring
    Some hock° and soda-water, then you'll know   *white wine*
1435   A pleasure worthy Xerxes[5] the great king;
    For not the blest sherbet, sublimed[6] with snow,
Nor the first sparkle of the desert-spring,
    Nor Burgundy° in all its sunset glow,   *red wine*
After long travel, ennui, love, or slaughter,
1440   Vie with that draught of hock and soda-water.

181
The coast—I think it was the coast that I
    Was just describing—Yes, it *was* the coast—
Lay at this period quiet as the sky,
    The sands untumbled, the blue waves untost,
1445   And all was stillness, save the sea-bird's cry,
    And dolphin's leap, and little billow crost
By some low rock or shelve, that made it fret
Against the boundary it scarcely wet.

182
And forth they wandered, her sire being gone,
1450   As I have said, upon an expedition;
And mother, brother, guardian, she had none,
    Save Zoe, who, although with due precision
She waited on her lady with the sun,
    Thought daily service was her only mission,

---

5. The pleasure-loving king who led the Persians to war against the Greeks in the 5th century.

6. Distilled or refined with heat. Byron eccentrically uses the word to suggest perfect ("sublime") cooling.

1455   Bringing warm water, wreathing her long tresses,
        And asking now and then for cast-off dresses.

183

    It was the cooling hour, just when the rounded
        Red sun sinks down behind the azure hill,
    Which then seems as if the whole earth it bounded,
1460   Circling all nature, hush'd, and dim, and still,
    With the far mountain-crescent half surrounded
        On one side, and the deep sea calm and chill
    Upon the other, and the rosy sky,
    With one star sparkling through it like an eye.

184

1465   And thus they wander'd forth, and hand in hand,
        Over the shining pebbles and the shells,
    Glided along the smooth and harden'd sand,
        And in the worn and wild receptacles
    Work'd by the storms, yet work'd as it were plann'd,
1470   In hollow halls, with sparry° roofs and cells,   *crystal-containing*
    They turn'd to rest; and, each clasp'd by an arm,
    Yielded to the deep twilight's purple charm.

185

    They look'd up to the sky, whose floating glow
        Spread like a rosy ocean, vast and bright;
1475   They gazed upon the glittering sea below,
        Whence the broad moon rose circling into sight;
    They heard the waves splash, and the wind so low,
        And saw each other's dark eyes darting light
    Into each other—and, beholding this,
1480   Their lips drew near, and clung into a kiss;

186

    A long, long kiss, a kiss of youth, and love,
        And beauty, all concentrating like rays
    Into one focus, kindled from above;
        Such kisses as belong to early days,
1485   Where heart, and soul, and sense, in concert° move,   *concord*
        And the blood's lava, and the pulse a blaze,
    Each kiss a heart-quake,—for a kiss's strength,
    I think, it must be reckon'd by its length.

187

    By length I mean duration; theirs endured
1490   Heaven knows how long—no doubt they never reckon'd;
    And if they had, they could not have secured
        The sum of their sensations to a second:
    They had not spoken; but they felt allured,
        As if their souls and lips each other beckon'd,
1495   Which, being join'd, like swarming bees they clung—
    Their hearts the flowers from whence the honey sprung.

188

    They were alone, but not alone as they

Who shut in chambers think it loneliness;
The silent ocean, and the starlight bay,
1500   The twilight glow, which momently grew less,
The voiceless sands, and dropping caves, that lay
Around them, made them to each other press,
As if there were no life beneath the sky
Save theirs, and that their life could never die.

189

1505   They fear'd no eyes nor ears on that lone beach,
They felt no terrors from the night;[7] they were
All in all to each other; though their speech
Was broken words, they *thought* a language there,—
And all the burning tongues the passions teach
1510   Found in one sigh the best interpreter
Of nature's oracle—first love,—that all
Which Eve has left her daughters since her fall.

190

Haidée spoke not of scruples, ask'd no vows,
Nor offer'd any; she had never heard
1515   Of plight and promises to be a spouse,
Or perils by a loving maid incurr'd;
She was all which pure ignorance allows,
And flew to her young mate like a young bird,
And never having dreamt of falsehood, she
1520   Had not one word to say of constancy.

191

She loved, and was beloved—she adored,
And she was worshipp'd; after nature's fashion,
Their intense souls, into each other pour'd,
If souls could die, had perish'd in that passion,—
1525   But by degrees their senses were restored,
Again to be o'ercome, again to dash on;
And, beating 'gainst *his* bosom, Haidée's heart
Felt as if never more to beat apart.

192

Alas! they were so young, so beautiful,
1530   So lonely, loving, helpless, and the hour
Was that in which the heart is always full,
And, having o'er itself no further power,
Prompts deeds eternity cannot annul,
But pays off moments in an endless shower
1535   Of hell-fire—all prepared for people giving
Pleasure or pain to one another living.

193

Alas! for Juan and Haidée! they were
So loving and so lovely—till then never,
Excepting our first parents, such a pair

---

7. Cf. Psalm 91:5: "Thou shalt not be afraid for the terror by night."

1540 Had run the risk of being damn'd for ever;
  And Haidée, being devout as well as fair,
   Had, doubtless, heard about the Stygian river,[8]
  And hell and purgatory—but forgot
  Just in the very crisis she should not.

       194

1545 They look upon each other, and their eyes
   Gleam in the moonlight; and her white arm clasps
  Round Juan's head, and his around her lies
   Half buried in the tresses which it grasps;
  She sits upon his knee, and drinks his sighs,
1550 He hers, until they end in broken gasps;
  And thus they form a group that's quite antique,
  Half naked, loving, natural, and Greek.

       195

  And when those deep and burning moments pass'd,
   And Juan sunk to sleep within her arms,
1555 She slept not, but all tenderly, though fast,
   Sustain'd his head upon her bosom's charms;
  And now and then her eye to heaven is cast,
   And then on the pale cheek her breast now warms,
  Pillow'd on her o'erflowing heart, which pants
1560 With all it granted, and with all it grants.

       196

  An infant when it gazes on a light,
   A child the moment when it drains the breast,
  A devotee when soars the Host° in sight,   *communion wafer*
   An Arab with a stranger for a guest,
1565 A sailor when the prize has struck[9] in fight,
   A miser filling his most hoarded chest,
  Feel rapture; but not such true joy are reaping
  As they who watch o'er what they love while sleeping.

       197

  For there it lies so tranquil, so beloved,
1570 All that it hath of life with us is living;
  So gentle, stirless, helpless, and unmoved,
   And all unconscious of the joy 'tis giving;
  All it hath felt, inflicted, pass'd, and proved,
   Hush'd into depths beyond the watcher's diving;
1575 There lies the thing we love with all its errors
  And all its charms, like death without its terrors.

       198

  The lady watch'd her lover—and that hour
   Of Love's, and Night's, and Ocean's solitude,
  O'erflow'd her soul with their united power;
1580 Amidst the barren sand and rocks so rude

8. The Styx is the river of forgetfulness surrounding the realm of the dead in Greek mythology.

9. Surrendered, the "prize" is the ship taken for booty.

She and her wave-worn love had made their bower,
   Where nought upon their passion could intrude,
And all the stars that crowded the blue space
Saw nothing happier than her glowing face.

          199

1585   Alas! the love of women! it is known
     To be a lovely and a fearful thing;
For all of theirs upon that die is thrown,
     And if 'tis lost, life hath no more to bring
To them but mockeries of the past alone,
1590   And their revenge is as the tiger's spring,
Deadly, and quick, and crushing; yet, as real
Torture is theirs, what they inflict they feel.

          200

They are right; for man, to man so oft unjust,
     Is always so to women; one sole bond
1595   Awaits them, treachery is all their trust;
     Taught to conceal, their bursting hearts despond
Over their idol, till some wealthier lust
     Buys them in marriage—and what rests beyond?
A thankless husband, next a faithless lover,
1600   Then dressing, nursing, praying, and all's over.

          201

Some take a lover, some take drams° or prayers,   *drinks*
     Some mind their household, others dissipation,
Some run away, and but exchange their cares,
     Losing the advantage of a virtuous station;
1605   Few changes e'er can better their affairs,
     Theirs being an unnatural situation,
From the dull palace to the dirty hovel:
Some play the devil, and then write a novel.[1]

          202

Haidée was Nature's bride, and knew not this:
1610   Haidée was Passion's child, born where the sun
Showers triple light, and scorches even the kiss
     Of his gazelle-eyed daughters; she was one
Made but to love, to feel that she was his
     Who was her chosen: what was said or done
1615   Elsewhere was nothing. She had nought to fear,
Hope, care, nor love beyond,—her heart beat *here*.

          203

And oh! that quickening of the heart, that beat!
     How much it costs us! yet each rising throb
Is in its cause as its effect so sweet,
1620   That Wisdom, ever on the watch to rob
Joy of its alchemy, and to repeat
     Fine truths; even Conscience, too, has a tough job

---

1. Byron alludes to a discarded mistress, Lady Caroline Lamb, who had written a novel about their relationship.

To make us understand each good old maxim,
So good—I wonder Castlereagh[2] don't tax 'em.

204

1625 And now 'twas done—on the lone shore were plighted
Their hearts; the stars, their nuptial torches, shed
Beauty upon the beautiful they lighted:
Ocean their witness, and the cave their bed,
By their own feelings hallow'd and united,
1630 Their priest was Solitude, and they were wed:
And they were happy, for to their young eyes
Each was an angel, and earth paradise.

205

Oh, Love! of whom great Caesar was the suitor,[3]
Titus the master, Antony the slave,
1635 Horace, Catullus, scholars, Ovid tutor,
Sappho[4] the sage blue-stocking, in whose grave
All those may leap who rather would be neuter—
(Leucadia's rock still overlooks the wave)—
Oh, Love! thou art the very god of evil,
1640 For, after all, we cannot call thee devil.

206

Thou mak'st the chaste connubial state precarious,
And jestest with the brows of mightiest men:
Caesar and Pompey, Mahomet, Belisarius,[5]
Have much employ'd the muse of history's pen:
1645 Their lives and fortunes were extremely various,
Such worthies Time will never see again;
Yet to these four in three things the same luck holds,
They all were heroes, conquerors, and cuckolds.

207

Thou mak'st philosophers; there's Epicurus
1650 And Aristippus, a material crew![6]
Who to immoral courses would allure us
By theories quite practicable too;
If only from the devil they would insure us,
How pleasant were the maxim (not quite new),
1655 "Eat, drink, and love; what can the rest avail us?"
So said the royal sage Sardanapalus.[7]

208

But Juan! had he quite forgotten Julia?
And should he have forgotten her so soon?
I can't but say it seems to me most truly a

---

2. Robert Stewart, Viscount Castlereagh, foreign secretary 1812–1822.
3. Julius Caesar was Cleopatra's suitor, Mark Antony her slave. Titus (Roman emperor, 79–81 C.E.) dismissed his unpopular mistress when he ascended the throne. Horace, Catullus, and Ovid were great love poets.
4. The lyric poet Sappho was known both for living in an all-female community and for jumping to her death off

the Leucadian rock because of unrequited love for a youth named Phaon. "Blue-stocking" is a mildly condescending term for a woman with literary interests.
5. Famous men of antiquity who had unfaithful wives.
6. Ancient philosophers popularly thought to advocate sensual indulgence.
7. A legendary, dissolute Assyrian.

1660 Perplexing question; but, no doubt, the moon
    Does these things for us, and whenever newly a
      Strong palpitation rises, 'tis her boon,
    Else how the devil is it that fresh features
    Have such a charm for us poor human creatures?

              209

1665 I hate inconstancy—I loathe, detest,
      Abhor, condemn, abjure the mortal made
    Of such quicksilver clay that in his breast
      No permanent foundations can be laid;
    Love, constant love, has been my constant guest,
1670   And yet last night, being at a masquerade,
    I saw the prettiest creature, fresh from Milan,
    Which gave me some sensations like a villain.

              210

    But soon Philosophy came to my aid,
      And whisper'd, "Think of every sacred tie!"
1675 "I will, my dear Philosophy!" I said,
      "But then her teeth, and then, oh, Heaven! her eye!
    I'll just inquire if she be wife or maid,
      Or neither—out of curiosity."
    "Stop!" cried Philosophy, with air so Grecian
1680 (Though she was masqued then as a fair Venetian).

            211

    "Stop!" so I stopp'd.—But to return: that which
      Men call inconstancy is nothing more
    Than admiration due where nature's rich
      Profusion with young beauty covers o'er
1685 Some favour'd object; and as in the niche
      A lovely statue we almost adore,
    This sort of adoration of the real
    Is but a heightening of the "beau ideal."

            212

    'Tis the perception of the beautiful,
1690   A fine extension of the faculties,
    Platonic, universal, wonderful,
      Drawn from the stars, and filter'd through the skies,
    Without which life would be extremely dull;
      In short, it is the use of our own eyes,
1695 With one or two small senses added, just
    To hint that flesh is form'd of fiery dust.

            213

    Yet 'tis a painful feeling, and unwilling,
      For surely if we always could perceive
    In the same object graces quite as killing
1700   As when she rose upon us like an Eve,
    'Twould save us many a heart-ache, many a shilling
      (For we must get them any how, or grieve)
    Whereas, if one sole lady pleased for ever,

How pleasant for the heart, as well as liver!

214

1705 The heart is like the sky, a part of heaven,
　　　But changes night and day too, like the sky;
　　Now o'er it clouds and thunder must be driven,
　　　And darkness and destruction as on high:
　　But when it hath been scorch'd, and pierced, and riven,
1710　　Its storms expire in water-drops; the eye
　　Pours forth at last the heart's-blood turn'd to tears,
　　Which make the English climate of our years.

215

　　The liver is the lazaret of bile,[8]
　　　But very rarely executes its function,
1715 For the first passion stays there such a while,
　　　That all the rest creep in and form a junction,
　　Like knots of vipers on a dunghill's soil,
　　　Rage, fear, hate, jealousy, revenge, compunction,
　　So that all mischiefs spring up from this entrail,
1720 Like earthquakes from the hidden fire call'd "central."

216

　　In the mean time, without proceeding more
　　　In this anatomy, I've finish'd now
　　Two hundred and odd stanzas as before,
　　　That being about the number I'll allow
1725 Each canto of the twelve, or twenty-four;
　　　And, laying down my pen, I make my bow,
　　Leaving Don Juan and Haidée to plead
　　For them and theirs with all who deign to read.

from Canto 3

1

Hail, Muse! *et cetera.*—We left Juan sleeping,
　　Pillow'd upon a fair and happy breast,
And watch'd by eyes that never yet knew weeping,
　　And lov'd by a young heart, too deeply blest
5 To feel the poison through her spirit creeping,
　　Or know who rested there,[1] a foe to rest
Had soil'd the current of her sinless years,
And turn'd her pure heart's purest blood to tears.

2

Oh, Love! what is it in this world of ours
10　　Which makes it fatal° to be loved? Ah why　　　　　*destined*
With cypress branches° hast thou wreathed thy bowers,　　*sign of sorrow*
　　And made thy best interpreter a sigh?
As those who dote on odors pluck the flowers,
　　And place them on their breast—but place to die—

---

8. The liver is the abode ("lazaret," a hospice) of passion,　1. Know that the person who rested there . . .
including anger ("bile").

15   Thus the frail beings we would fondly cherish
      Are laid within our bosoms but to perish.

                          3
      In her first passion woman loves her lover,
          In all the others all she loves is love,
      Which grows a habit she can ne'er get over,
20   And fits her loosely—like an easy glove,
      As you may find, whene'er you like to prove° her: *test*
          One man alone at first her heart can move;
      She then prefers him in the plural number,
      Not finding that the additions much encumber.

                          4
25   I know not if the fault be men's or theirs;
          But one thing's pretty sure; a woman planted—
      (Unless at once she plunge for life in prayers)—
          After a decent time must be gallanted;°   *courted*
      Although, no doubt, her first of love affairs
30   Is that to which her heart is wholly granted;
      Yet there are some, they say, who have had *none*,
      But those who have ne'er end with only *one*.

                          5
      'Tis melancholy, and a fearful sign
          Of human frailty, folly, also crime,
35   That love and marriage rarely can combine,
          Although they both are born in the same clime;
      Marriage from love, like vinegar from wine—
          A sad, sour, sober beverage—by time
      Is sharpen'd from its high celestial flavour
40   Down to a very homely° household savour.   *domestic*

                          6
      There's something of antipathy, as 't were,
          Between their present and their future state;
      A kind of flattery that's hardly fair
          Is used until the truth arrives too late—
45   Yet what can people do, except despair?
          The same things change their names at such a rate;
      For instance—passion in a lover's glorious,
      But in a husband is pronounced uxorious.[2]

                          7
      Men grow ashamed of being[3] so very fond,
50   They sometimes also get a little tired
      (But that, of course, is rare), and then despond:
          The same things cannot always be admired,
      Yet 'tis "so nominated in the bond,"[4]
          That both are tied till one shall have expired.
55   Sad thought! to lose the spouse that was adorning

---

2. Overindulgent to one's wife.   4. Quoted from Shakespeare, *Merchant of Venice* 4.1.258.
3. One syllable.

Our days, and put one's servants into mourning.

8

There's doubtless something in domestic doings,
    Which forms, in fact, true love's antithesis:
Romances paint at full length people's wooings,
60   But only give a bust[5] of marriages;
For no one cares for matrimonial cooings,
    There's nothing wrong in a connubial kiss:
Think you, if Laura had been Petrarch's wife,[6]
He would have written sonnets all his life?

9

65 All tragedies are finish'd by a death,
    All comedies are ended by a marriage;
The future states of both are left to faith,
    For authors fear description might disparage
The worlds to come of both, or fall beneath,
70   And then both worlds would punish their miscarriage;
So leaving each their priest and prayer-book ready,
They say no more of Death or of the Lady.

from Canto 4

26

Juan and Haidée gazed upon each other
    With swimming looks of speechless tenderness,
Which mix'd all feelings—friend, child, lover, brother,
    All that the best can mingle and express
205 When two pure hearts are pour'd in one another,
    And love too much, and yet can not love less;
But almost sanctify the sweet excess
By the immortal wish and power to bless.

27

Mix'd in each other's arms, and heart in heart,
210   Why did they not then die?—they had° lived too long   *would have*
Should an hour come to bid them breathe apart;
    Years could but bring them cruel things or wrong,
The world was not for them, nor the world's art
    For beings passionate as Sappho's song;[1]
215 Love was born *with* them, *in* them, so intense,
It was their very spirit—not a sense.

28

They should have lived together deep in woods,
    Unseen as sings the nightingale; they were
Unfit to mix in these thick solitudes
220   Call'd social, haunts of Hate, and Vice, and Care:

5. A partial, upper-body portrait.
6. Francesco Petrarca (1304–1374) was the first great love poet of modern Europe. His poems celebrate a woman named Laura, whom he had seen briefly.
1. The famous Greek poet of bittersweet love.

How lonely every freeborn creature broods!
   The sweetest song-birds nestle in a pair;
The eagle soars alone; the gull and crow
Flock o'er their carrion, just like men below.

29

225 Now pillow'd cheek to cheek, in loving sleep,
   Haidée and Juan their siesta took,
A gentle slumber, but it was not deep,
   For ever and anon a something shook
Juan, and shuddering o'er his frame would creep;
230   And Haidée's sweet lips murmur'd like a brook
A wordless music, and her face so fair
Stirr'd with her dream as rose-leaves with the air;

30

Or as the stirring of a deep clear stream
   Within an Alpine hollow, when the wind
235 Walks o'er it, was she shaken by the dream,
   The mystical usurper of the mind—
O'erpowering us to be whate'er may seem
   Good to the soul which we no more can bind;
Strange state of being! (for 't is still to be)
240 Senseless to feel, and with seal'd eyes to see.

31

She dream'd of being alone on the sea-shore,
   Chain'd to a rock; she knew not how, but stir
She could not from the spot, and the loud roar
   Grew, and each wave rose roughly, threatening her;
245 And o'er her upper lip they seem'd to pour,
   Until she sobb'd for breath, and soon they were
Foaming o'er her lone head, so fierce and high—
Each broke to drown her, yet she could not die.

32

Anon—she was released, and then she stray'd
250   O'er the sharp shingles° with her bleeding feet,   *seashore pebbles*
And stumbled almost every step she made;
   And something roll'd before her in a sheet,
Which she must still pursue howe'er afraid;
   'Twas white and indistinct, nor stopp'd to meet
255 Her glance nor grasp, for still she gazed and grasp'd,
And ran, but it escaped her as she clasp'd.

33

The dream changed; in a cave she stood, its walls
   Were hung with marble icicles; the work
Of ages on its water-fretted halls,
260   Where waves might wash, and seals might breed and lurk;
Her hair was dripping, and the very balls
   Of her black eyes seemed turn'd to tears, and murk
The sharp rocks look'd below each drop they caught,
Which froze to marble as it fell, she thought.

34

265   And wet, and cold, and lifeless at her feet,
       Pale as the foam that froth'd on his dead brow,
   Which she essay'd in vain to clear, (how sweet
       Were once her cares, how idle seem'd they now!)
   Lay Juan, nor could aught renew the beat
270   Of his quench'd heart: and the sea dirges low
   Rang in her sad ears like a mermaid's song,
   And that brief dream appear'd a life too long.

35

   And gazing on the dead, she thought his face
       Faded, or alter'd into something new—
275   Like to her father's features, till each trace
       More like and like to Lambro's[2] aspect grew—
   With all his keen worn look and Grecian grace;
       And starting, she awoke, and what to view?
   On! Powers of Heaven! what dark eye meets she there?
280   'Tis—'tis her father's—fix'd upon the pair!

36

   Then shrieking, she arose, and shrieking fell,
       With joy and sorrow, hope and fear, to see
   Him whom she deem'd a habitant where dwell
       The ocean-buried, risen[3] from death, to be
285   Perchance the death of one she loved too well:
       Dear as her father had been to Haidée,
   It was a moment of that awful kind—
   I have seen such—but must not call to mind.

37

   Up Juan sprang to Haidée's bitter shriek,
290   And caught her falling, and from off the wall
   Snatch'd down his sabre, in hot haste to wreak
       Vengeance on him who was the cause of all:
   Then Lambro, who till now forbore to speak,
       Smiled scornfully, and said, "Within my call,
295   A thousand scimitars await the word;
   Put up, young man, put up your silly sword."

38

   And Haidée clung around him; "Juan, 'tis—
       'Tis Lambro—'tis my father! Kneel with me—
   He will forgive us—yes—it must be—yes.
300   Oh! dearest father, in this agony
   Of pleasure and of pain—even while I kiss
       Thy garment's hem with transport, can it be
   That doubt should mingle with my filial joy?
   Deal with me as thou wilt, but spare this boy."

2. Haidée's father.   3. One syllable.

39

305   High and inscrutable the old man stood,
          Calm in his voice, and calm within his eye—
      Not always signs with him of calmest mood:
          He look'd upon her, but gave no reply;
      Then turn'd to Juan, in whose cheek the blood
310   Oft came and went, as there resolved to die;
      In arms, at least, he stood, in act to spring
      On the first foe whom Lambro's call might bring.

40

      "Young man, your sword"; so Lambro once more said:
          Juan replied, "Not while this arm is free."
315   The old man's cheek grew pale, but not with dread,
          And drawing from his belt a pistol, he
      Replied, "Your blood be then on your own head."
          Then look'd close at the flint, as if to see
      'Twas fresh—for he had lately used the lock—
320   And next proceeded quietly to cock.

41

      It has a strange quick jar upon the ear,
          That cocking of a pistol, when you know
      A moment more will bring the sight to bear
          Upon your person, twelve yards off, or so;
325   A gentlemanly distance, not too near,
          If you have got a former friend for foe;
      But after being fired at once or twice,
      The ear becomes more Irish,° and less nice.°   *hotheaded / finicky*

42

      Lambro presented, and one instant more
330   Had stopp'd this Canto, and Don Juan's breath,
      When Haidée threw herself her boy before;
          Stern as her sire: "On me," she cried, "let death
      Descend—the fault is mine; this fatal shore
          He found—but sought not. I have pledged my faith;
335   I love him—I will die with him: I knew
      Your nature's firmness—know your daughter's too."

43

      A minute past, and she had been all tears,
          And tenderness, and infancy: but now
      She stood as one who champion'd human fears—
340   Pale, statue-like, and stern, she woo'd the blow;
      And tall beyond her sex, and their compeers,
          She drew up to her height, as if to show
      A fairer mark; and with a fix'd eye scann'd
      Her father's face—but never stopp'd his hand.

44

345   He gazed on her, and she on him; 'twas strange
          How like they look'd! the expression was the same;
      Serenely savage, with a little change

In the large dark eye's mutual-darted flame;
For she too was as one who could avenge,
350   If cause should be—a lioness, though tame.
Her father's blood before her father's face
Boil'd up, and proved her truly of his race.

45

I said they were alike, their features and
      Their stature differing but in sex and years;
355   Even to the delicacy of their hand
      There was resemblance, such as true blood wears;
And now to see them, thus divided, stand
      In fix'd ferocity, when joyous tears
And sweet sensations, should have welcomed both,
360   Shows what the passions are in their full growth.

46

The father paused a moment, then withdrew
      His weapon, and replaced it; but stood still,
And looking on her, as to look her through,
      "Not *I*," he said, "have sought this stranger's ill;
365   Not *I* have made this desolation: few
      Would bear such outrage, and forbear to kill;
But I must do my duty—how thou hast
Done thine, the present vouches for the past.

47

"Let him disarm; or, by my father's head,
370   His own shall roll before you like a ball!"
He raised his whistle, as the word he said,
      And blew; another answer'd to the call,
And rushing in disorderly, though led,
      And arm'd from boot to turban, one and all,
375   Some twenty of his train came, rank on rank;
He gave the word, "Arrest or slay the Frank."°   *European*

48

Then, with a sudden movement, he withdrew
      His daughter; while compress'd within his clasp,
'Twixt her and Juan interposed the crew;
380   In vain she struggled in her father's grasp—
His arms were like a serpent's coil: then flew
      Upon their prey, as darts an angry asp,
The file of pirates; save the foremost, who
Had fallen, with his right shoulder half cut through.

49

385   The second had his cheek laid open; but
      The third, a wary, cool old sworder, took
The blows upon his cutlass, and then put
      His own well in; so well, ere you could look,
His man was floor'd, and helpless at his foot,
390   With the blood running like a little brook
From two smart sabre gashes, deep and red—

One on the arm, the other on the head.

50

And then they bound him where he fell, and bore
    Juan from the apartment: with a sign
395 Old Lambro bade them take him to the shore,
    Where lay some ships which were to sail at nine.
They laid him in a boat, and plied the oar
    Until they reach'd some galliots,° placed in line;   *fast boats*
On board of one of these, and under hatches,
400 They stow'd him, with strict orders to the watches.

51

The world is full of strange vicissitudes,
    And here was one exceedingly unpleasant:
A gentleman so rich in the world's goods,
    Handsome and young, enjoying all the present,
405 Just at the very time when he least broods
    On such a thing is suddenly to sea sent,
Wounded and chain'd, so that he cannot move,
And all because a lady fell in love.

⊷ ⊷ ≡◆≡ ⊶ ⊶

Ghalib
1797–1869

One of the greatest poets of modern times in two different languages, Persian and Urdu, Ghalib
was a religious skeptic whose verses are filled with echoes of the Qur'an. A court poet with little reverence for power, Ghalib was a writer of passionate love poetry and an ironic observer of
his own passion. He was born in Agra, in Muslim northern India, as Mirza Asadullah Beg
Khan, a descendant of Turkish aristocrats who had come to India seeking to improve their fortunes. His father was killed in battle when he was four years old; his mother and her children
then moved in with a wealthy brother, who soon died as well. The children received the education of aristocrats, but they had little wealth of their own. At age thirteen, Ghalib was married
into a noble family in Delhi, then the capital of the Mughal Empire. He wrote much of his most
famous Urdu poetry over the next several years, shifting to Persian at around age twenty.
Though the young poet took the lofty pen name of Ghalib ("Victorious"), he was financially
dependent on inconsistent patrons, and his own love of wine and gambling left him often in
debt. In a capital of lavish homes, Ghalib never owned a home himself, and even possessed few
books, often borrowing from friends and storing his own poems in their libraries.

Ghalib's patrons didn't really know what to make of him, in part because of his unortho-
dox personal habits and his skeptical, tolerant religious beliefs, and in part for the mysterious
beauty of his poems. By the age of eleven he had begun composing poetry in both Persian and
Urdu (the common speech of much of north India, derived from Hindi and written in the Arabic
alphabet). By his late teens he was already writing many of his most striking and original poems, particularly in the verse form of the *ghazal* or "conversation with the beloved." Such poems could be addressed either to an earthly beloved or to God; in Ghalib's verse, it is often difficult to say which is the case, or whether the poem is addressed to both at once. (In the

translations below, the translators use the term "the Great One" to keep these possibilities open.) The *ghazal* is a highly structured poetic form, with strict rules of rhyme and repetition of a key phrase in each of its couplets. In lesser hands, the rhymes can drive the meaning, and the imagery may remain simple or even hackneyed, but Ghalib fashioned his couplets into individual gems, linked together in ways that can be hard to sort out but that cumulatively create powerful images of desire and loss. Ghalib was well aware that his poems weren't generally easy to grasp on a first hearing, and he wrote a *ghazal*—pointedly brief and direct—about this very problem:

> I agree, O heart, that my ghazals are not easy to take in.
> When they hear my work, experienced poets
>
> Tell me I should write something easier to understand.
> I have to write what's difficult, otherwise it is difficult to write.

Like Byron, his contemporary, Ghalib was an aristocratic rebel, a self-styled outsider who sought and enjoyed the admiration of the more conventional readers who read him despite their discomfort with his free-living and free-thinking ways. Like Byron as well, Ghalib made himself a leading figure within his own poems. *Ghazals* had traditionally ended with a coda mentioning the poet's name, often in relatively impersonal fashion, but Ghalib's poems build up a powerful persona of a witty, sophisticated, melancholy commentator on his own life and on life in general. Ghalib is typically indirect in his social and political references, but his verses reflect his ambivalent skepticism toward secular power and religious orthodoxy. Seen in the context of his times, his poems become a personal mirror (a recurrent image in his lyrics) of the declining decades of the Mughal Empire, at a time when British involvement in India was rapidly increasing.

Ghalib was deeply critical of the harshness of British rule, yet he also admired the city planning and prosperity they had introduced in Calcutta. He didn't support the 1857 revolt (or as the British called it, the "Mutiny") against colonial rule, and was shocked at the extent of British reprisals, in which many of his friends were hanged or exiled. An added personal loss was the destruction of the homes and libraries of two friends where many of his poems were housed. Hundreds survived, though, scattered about on paper and in people's memories; one poem was said to have been preserved when a beggar, seeking alms, came to his door and recited it.

Though he wrote for the Mughal emperor and other aristocrats, Ghalib was never a model court poet, and he didn't conceal his lack of admiration for the emperor's own poetry. For the middle decades of his life he enjoyed less royal favor than the emperor's less talented poetry teacher, Zauq; finally, upon Zauq's death in 1847, the emperor rather reluctantly appointed Ghalib his court poet. Ghalib wrote Persian poems in praise of the king, while once again turning to writing *ghazals* in Urdu, until his death in 1869 at the age of seventy-two. Since then, Ghalib has been regarded as the greatest writer of Urdu *ghazals* of any era.

In a classic *ghazal,* both lines of the poem's opening couplet must end with the same word or phrase, which then serves as a refrain at the end of each succeeding couplet. A rhyming word or phrase must appear just before this refrain, and the same rhyme must be carried through the entire poem. The *ghazal* has no set length and no fixed meter, but all the lines in a given *ghazal* have to be of the same length. The translations below strive to convey the condensed, revelatory beauty of Ghalib's verse rather than the formal patterning of rhymes, but this patterning can be experienced directly in the Resonance section that follow Ghalib's verses.

These poems were written in English by the contemporary Kashmiri-American poet Agha Shahid Ali, and they brilliantly transmute Ghalib's favored form, often responding to Ghalib's work either explicitly or indirectly. "Of Snow," for example, published posthumously after

Ali's early death in 2001, brings Ghalib's classic themes of wine, poetry, lost love, and religious doubt into the world of jet travel and modernist poetry. Like Ghalib's poems, Ali's *ghazals* are deeply personal, even contemplative, and full of charm and sly wit, seen especially in the turns of phrase producing each new version of the poem's rhyme, and in the personal couplet that concludes the poem and gives a final twist to its themes. Unlike Ghalib, Ali often gives his verse an openly social and political force, describing his own personal dislocation across continents and cultures. In his 1997 collection *The Country Without a Post Office,* he wrote about the ongoing strife in his homeland of Kashmir—still bitterly disputed between India and Pakistan. In other poems he meditates on the struggles of displaced peoples elsewhere, evoking a wide range of exiles, from Jews and Palestinians, to medieval mystics, to Oscar Wilde. Like Ghalib, Shahid Ali was finally at home only in his own verses.

I'm neither the loosening of song[1]

I'm neither the loosening of song nor the close-drawn tent of music;
I'm the sound, simply, of my own breaking.[2]

You were meant to sit in the shade of your rippling hair;
I was made to look further, into a blacker tangle.

5   All my self-possession is self-delusion;
what violent effort, to maintain this nonchalance!

Now that you've come, let me touch you in greeting
as the forehead of the beggar touches the ground.

No wonder you came looking for me, you
10   who care for the grieving, and I the sound of grief.

Come now: I want you: my only peace[1]

Come now: I want you: my only peace.
I've passed the age of fencing and teasing.

This life: a night of drinking and poetry.
Paradise: a long hangover.

5   Tears sting my eyes; I'm leaving
lest the other guests see my weakness.

I is another, the rose no rose this year;
without a meaning to perceive, what is perception?

Ghalib: no hangover will cure a man like you
10   knowing as you do the aftertaste of all sweetness.

When I look out, I see no hope for change[1]

When I look out, I see no hope for change.
I don't see how anything in my life can end well.

---

1. Translated by Adrienne Rich.
2. The term used, *shikast,* means defeat or breaking; it is also used for a note out of tune.

1. Translated by Adrienne Rich.
1. Translated by Robert Bly and Sunil Dutta, as are the rest of the Ghalib poems.

Their funeral date is already decided, but still
People complain that they can't sleep.

5   When young, my love-disasters made me burst out laughing.
Now even funny things seem sober to me.

I know the answer—that's what keeps me quiet.
Beyond that it's clear I know how to speak.

Why shouldn't I scream? I can stop. Perhaps
10   The Great One notices Ghalib only when he stops screaming.

This is the spiritual state I am in:
About myself, there isn't any news.

I do die; the longing for death is so strong it's killing me.
Such a death comes, but the other death doesn't come.

15   What face will you wear when you visit the Kaaba?[2]
Ghalib, you are shameless even to think of that.

If King Jamshid's diamond cup breaks that's it

If King Jamshid's diamond cup breaks, that's it.[1]
But my clay cup I can easily replace, so it's better.

The delight of giving is deeper when the gift hasn't been demanded.
I like the God-seeker who doesn't make a profession of begging.

5   When I see God, color comes into my cheeks.
God thinks—this is a bad mistake—that I'm in good shape.

When a drop falls in the river, it becomes the river.
When a deed is done well, it becomes the future.

I know that Heaven doesn't exist, but the idea
10   Is one of Ghalib's favorite fantasies.

One can sigh, but a lifetime is needed to finish it

One can sigh, but a lifetime is needed to finish it.
We'll die before we see the tangles in your hair loosened.

There are dangers in waves, in all those crocodiles with their jaws open.
The drop of water goes through many difficulties before it becomes a pearl.

5   Love requires waiting, but desire doesn't want to wait.
The heart has no patience; it would rather bleed to death.

I know you will respond when you understand the state of my soul,
But I'll probably become earth before all that is clear to you.

2. Sacred shrine in Mecca, which every Muslim hopes to visit at least once.

1. The legendary Persian king Jamshid could see the future inside his jeweled cup.

When the sun arrives the dew on the petal passes through existence.
10   I am also me until your kind eye catches sight of me.

How long is our life? How long does an eyelash flutter?
The warmth of a poetry gathering is like a single spark.[1]

Oh Ghalib, the sorrows of existence, what can cure them but death?
There are so many colors in the candle flame, and then the day comes.

When the Great One gestures to me

When the Great One gestures to me, the message does not become clear.
When love words are spoken, I get six or seven meanings.

I must tell you, God, this woman doesn't grasp my meaning.
Give her a second heart, please, if you don't give me a second tongue.

5   Her eyebrows do make a bow, but the rest is unclear.
What are her eyes? An arrow or something else?

You come into town, and I still grieve. Of course I can go
To the market and buy another heart and another life.

I'm good at smashing rocks with my head, but it looks as if
10   Someone on this street has been strewing boulders.

My soul is full and it would be good to drain the blood.
The problem is limits; I have only two eyes.

Even though my head flies off, I love to hear her voice
As she remarks to the executioner: "You're doing well."

15   People get a real sense of what the sun is like
When I let the light reflect off one of my scars.

I could have had some peace, had I not fallen in love with you.
If I hadn't died, I could have done a lot more crying and sighing.

A river keeps rising when its bed is not available.
20   When my nature becomes dammed, it just keeps moving.

We know there is more than one good poet in the world,
But the experts say that Ghalib's little jests are great.

For tomorrow's sake, don't skimp with me on wine today

For tomorrow's sake, don't skimp with me on wine today.
A stingy portion implies a suspicion of heaven's abundance.

The horse of life is galloping; we'll never know the stopping place.
Our hands are not touching the reins, nor our feet the stirrups.

---

1. Poets and their friends would gather for long evenings of poetry and feasting.

5   I keep a certain distance from the reality of things.
     It's the same distance between me and utter confusion.

     The scene, the one looking, and the ability to see are all the same.
     If that is so, why am I confused about what is in front of me?

     The greatness of a river depends on its magnificent face.
10   If we break it into bubbles and drops and waves, we are lost.

     She is not free from her ways to increase her beauty.
     The mirror she sees is on the inside of her veil.

     What we think is obvious is so far beyond our comprehension.
     We are still dreaming even when we dream we are awake.

15   From the smell of my friend's friend I get the smell of my friend.
     Listen, Ghalib, you are busy worshiping God's friend.

I am confused: should I cry over my heart, or slap my chest?

     I am confused: should I cry over my heart, or slap my chest?
     If I could afford it, I'd have a man paid to cry.

     My jealousy is so strong that I refuse to name the street where you live.
     In view of that, "How do I get there?" doesn't make much sense.

5   I was forced to walk to his house a thousand times.
     I wish I'd never known about that path you like so much.

     It's clear to her that my fate is nothing and nobody.
     If I had known that, I would not have thrown away my house.

     Fools typically mistake simple desire for a form of worship.
10   Do I desire a hard woman or do I worship a stone?[1]

     I walk for a short distance with each fast-moving stream.
     But that's because I don't know who the guide is.

     I was so carefree I forgot the roads to my friend's house.
     Now how can I discover who I am?

15   I judge the whole world on the basis of my imagination.
     I think that every person loves a true work of art.

She has a habit of torture, but doesn't mean to end the love

     She has a habit of torture, but doesn't mean to end the love.
     Such oppression is only teasing; we don't imagine it as a test.

     Which of my mouths shall I use to thank her for this delight?
     I know she inquires about me even though no word is exchanged.

---

1. Perhaps alluding to the Black Stone enshrined at Mecca, which Muslim pilgrims kiss to obtain forgiveness of sin; it is said to have been given to Adam on his expulsion from Paradise.

5   The one who tortures likes us, and we like the torturers.
    So if she's not kind, we have to say she's not unkind.

    If you don't give me a kiss, at least curse at me.
    That means you have a tongue if you don't have a mouth.

    If your heart is still in one piece, cut your chest with a dagger.
10 If eyelashes are not soaked with blood, put a knife in your heart.

    The heart is an embarrassment to the chest if it's not on fire.
    Releasing a breath brings shame if it's not a fountain of flame.

    Well, it's not a loss for me if my madness has destroyed our house.
    Giving up a large house for a wilderness is a good bargain.

15 You ask me what is written on my forehead? It shows marks
    From being rubbed on the stone floor before some god.

    Gabriel[1] sends praise to me for my poems;
    That happens even though Gabriel speaks a different language.

    For the price of one kiss she sets my whole life—
20 Because she knows Ghalib is only about half alive.

For my weak heart this living in the sorrow house

For my weak heart this living in the sorrow house is more than enough.
The shortage of rose-colored wine is also more than enough.

I'm embarrassed, otherwise I'd tell the wine-server
That even the leftovers in the cup are, for me, enough.

5   No arrow comes flying in; I am safe from hunters.
    The comfort level I experience in this cage is more than enough.

    I don't see why the so-called elite people are so proud
    When the ropes of custom that tie them down are clear enough.

    It's hard for me to distinguish sacrifice from hypocrisy,
10 When the greed for reward in pious actions is obvious enough.

    Leave me alone at the Zam Zam Well; I won't circle the Kaaba.[1]
    The wine stains on my robe are already numerous enough.

    If we can't resolve this, it will be a great injustice.
    She is not unwilling and my desire is more than strong enough.

15 The blood of my heart has not completely exited through my eyes.
    O death, let me stay a while, the work we have to do is abundant enough.

---

1. Archangel who brought divine revelations to Muhammad, "guidance and glad tidings for those who believe" (*Qur'an* 2:97).

1. The poet will remain at an oasis short of the pilgrim's destination of the Kaaba, the sacred shrine at Mecca.

It's difficult to find a person who has no opinion about Ghalib.
He is a good poet, but the dark rumors about him are more than enough.

Religious people are always praising the Garden of Paradise

Religious people are always praising the Garden of Paradise.
To us ecstatics it's a bouquet left on the bedstand of forgetfulness.

Her eyelashes are so sharp it's hard to describe the pain.
Each drop of eye blood is like a necklace made of coral.

5   If this world gave me free time, I could show you fireworks.
My heart has many scars; each scar signifies a tree all on fire.

You know what the reflected sunlight does to dewdrops.
Your beauty has the same effect on the house of mirrors.

In my beginning there was already the essence of my end.
10   Lightning doesn't care about the crop, it wants the farmer.

In my silence there are thousands of blood-soaked desires.
I am like a candle that has gone out on the grave of a poor man.

I think you must be making love today with that man I hate.
Otherwise why would you smile so mischievously in my dream?

15   Ghalib, I think we have caught sight of the road to death now.
Death is a string that binds together the scattered beads of the universe.

Only a few faces show up as roses

Only a few faces show up as roses; where are the rest?
This dust must be concealing so many poets and saints.

The Seven Pleiades hid behind a veil all day.[1]
At night they changed their minds, and became naked.

5   During the night of separation red tears flow from my eyes.
I will imagine my eyes as two burning candles.

We'll seek revenge in heaven from these hard-hearted beauties.
Of course that presupposes that their destination is heaven.

That man on whose arm your hair is spread out
10   Owns three things: sleep, a quiet mind, and night.

When I visited the Garden, it was as if I started a school.
Even the birds gave poetry readings after hearing me cry.

O God, why do these glances of hers keep invading my heart?
What luck do I have? When I look, I see her lids.

---

1. The translators use the Pleiades as an equivalent to a cluster of three stars called "Daughters of the Bier" in Urdu.

15   All the good words I could remember I gave to the doorman.
How can I change her painful jibes now into blessings?

Whenever a man's hand closes around a cup of wine,
That energy-enhancer, he believes the lines in his palm are life's rivers.

20   I believe in one God only, and my religion is breaking rules:
When all sects go to pieces, they'll become part of the true religion.

When a human being becomes used to sorrow, then sorrow disappears;
Obstacle after obstacle fell on me, and the road was easy.

If Ghalib keeps pouring out the salt of his tears,
Dear people, I say the whole world will become a ruin.

I agree that I'm in a cage, and I'm crying

I agree that I'm in a cage, and I'm crying.
But my crying doesn't affect the happy birds in the garden.

The wound I have in my chest did not bring one tear from you.
But that wound made even the eye of the needle weep.

5   When people began to talk about chains for my ankles,
The gold under the ground began to twist, pushing the iron away.

The essence of faith is loyalty and devotion.
It's all right to bury in the Kaaba the Brahman who died worshiping in the
    temple.[1]

My destiny was always to have my head cut off.
10   Whenever I see a sword, my neck bends by habit.

I can sleep well at night because I was robbed during the day.
I have to thank the robber for providing such a relaxed sleep.

Why should we bother about diamonds if we can write poems?
We have our own chests to dig in; why bother traveling to the mines?

Each time I open my mouth, the Great One says

Each time I open my mouth, the Great One says: "You—you, who are
  you?"
Help me, how would you describe the style of such a conversation?

A spark is lacking in awe. Lightning lacks playfulness.
Neither has the Great One's adroit fierceness.

5   My jealousy arises because my rival gets to speak to you;
Otherwise it's okay if he ruins my reputation.

Blood makes my whole shirt stick to my body.
The good thing is I don't have to repair my collar.

---

1. A Brahman is a member of the Hindu priestly caste, who would never ordinarily be admitted to the precincts of the Muslim shrine at Mecca.

10   With the whole body cindered, the heart was clearly burnt.
Digging into the ashes, what's the point of that?

Blood flowing along through the veins doesn't impress us.
If blood doesn't drop from the eyes, it's not real blood.

My main attraction to Heaven has always been its wine—
That musky, fuschia-colored wine we've been promised.

15   If it's drinking time, I need large containers.
Let's put away these mingy cups and flagons.

My gift of speech is gone but even if I still had it
What reason would I have to put desire into words?

Since he's a friend of the Emperor, he oozes arrogance.[1]
20   How else can Ghalib gain any respect?

My heart is becoming restless again

My heart is becoming restless again;
And my fingernails start looking for my chest.

My fingernails are clawing down toward my heart again.
It must be the right time for planting red tulips.

5   The eyes that are filled with desire have a goal—
The curtained hoodah[1] where the elegant rider sits.

The eye's habit is to buy and sell disreputable goods.
The heart is an enthusiastic purchaser of humiliation.

I'm still giving out the same hundred colorful complaints.
10   Tears are falling now, but a hundred times more.

Because my heart wants so much to look at my lover's beautiful feet,
It has become a scene of great unrest like the paintings of the Last Day.

Beauty is passing by once more and showing her style
So we know that someone will shortly die in the public square.

15   We die over and over for the same unfaithful person.
Our life has fallen back into the old familiar ways.

The whole world is sinking into darkness and corruption
Because she has just thrown back her beautiful hair.

Once more the mashed pieces of the heart send in their petitions
20   Asking why the pain in this world is so repetitive.

The amount of ecstasy has to make some sense, Ghalib.
There must be something hiding behind the curtain.

---

1. Said to be an allusion to the favored court poet Zauq.   1. A canopied seat for nobility riding on an elephant.

~~~

RESONANCE

Agha Shahid Ali[1]
Ghazal

Pale hands I loved beside the Shalimar

—Laurence Hope[2]

Where are you now? Who lies beneath your spell tonight
before you agonize him in farewell tonight?

Pale hands that once loved me beside the Shalimar:
Whom else from rapture's road will you expel tonight?

5   Those "Fabrics of Cashmere—" "to make Me beautiful—"
"Trinket"—to gem—"Me to adorn—How—tell"—tonight?

I beg for haven: Prisons, let open your gates—
A refugee from Belief seeks a cell tonight.

Executioners near the woman at the window.
10   Damn you, Elijah, I'll bless Jezebel tonight.[3]

Lord, cried out the idols, *Don't let us be broken;
Only we can convert the infidel tonight.*[4]

Has God's vintage loneliness turned to vinegar?
He's poured rust into the Sacred Well tonight.

15   In the heart's veined temple all statues have been smashed.
No priest in saffron's left to toll its knell tonight.[5]

He's freed some fire from ice, in pity for Heaven;
he's left open—for God—the doors of Hell tonight.

And I, Shahid, only am escaped to tell thee—
20   God sobs in my arms. Call me Ishmael tonight.[6]

Of Snow

Husband of Water, where is your Concubine of Snow?
Has she laced your flooded desert with a wine of snow?

---

1. Born in New Delhi in 1949, Agha Shahid Ali was raised a Muslim in the northern Indian region of Kashmir, site of prolonged, ongoing conflicts between Hindu nationalists and Muslim separatists. After completing college in India, he emigrated to the United States, where he earned a Ph.D. and an M.F.A. in the 1980s. Before his death in 2001 he directed several creative writing programs and published seven volumes of poetry. Ali wrote many *ghazals* in English, using the classical form to reflect on contemporary romantic, social, and political conflicts.
2. Pen name of Adela Nicolson (1865–1904), whose *Indian Love Lyrics* freely adapted Indian poets, in melodramatic style: "To have—to hold—and—in time—let

go!" Her poem "Kashmiri Song" begins, "Pale hands I loved beside the Shalimar, / Where are you now? Who lies beneath your spell?"
3. In 1 Kings 21, the prophet Elijah announces God's condemnation of Queen Jezebel, who serves the god Ba'al and has slain God's prophets.
4. Muhammad purified the shrine of Mecca by destroying the idols that had been set there in pre-Islamic times.
5. Hindu priests wear saffron-colored robes.
6. "Call me Ishmael" is the opening sentence of Melville's *Moby-Dick,* whose narrator alone survived the wrecking of his ship. In the Bible and the Qur'an, Ishmael is the traditional forefather of the Arabs.

What a desert we met in—the foliage was lush!—
a cactus was dipped into every moonshine of snow.

5   One song is so solitaire in our ring of mountains,
its echo climbs to cut itself at each line of snow.

The sky beyond its means is always beside itself
till (by the plane) each peak rises, a shrine of snow.

Snowmen, inexplicably, have gathered in the Sahara
10 to melt and melt and melt for a Palestine of snow.

Kali[1] turned to ice one winter, her veins transparent—
on her lips blood froze. A ruby wine of snow!

If Lorca were alive he would again come to New York,[2]
bringing back to my life that one Valentine of snow.

15 Do you need to make angels, really, who then vanish
or are angels all you can undermine of snow?

I who believe in prayer but could never in God
place roses at your grave with nothing to divine of snow.

When he drinks in winter, Shahid kisses his enemies.
20 For Peace, then, let bars open at the first sign of snow.

❧

━━━✦━━━

Alexander Sergeyevich Pushkin
1799–1837

Some poets lead the lives of insurance executives. A few, indeed, have been. Not Alexander Sergeyevich Pushkin, who was as romantic as any of his heroes. He was descended from nobility on both sides, but on his mother's side the noble ancestor, his Abyssinian great-grandfather, bequeathed to the poet a dark complexion and became the subject of Pushkin's first major prose work, "The Moor of Alexander the Great." Pushkin made his brilliant poetic debut in his teens and was rewarded with a government post in Moscow, where he spent some years sowing wild oats. But an "Ode to Liberty" aroused the tsar's wrath, and he found himself exiled to the untamed south of the country, where he relished the Caucasian scenery and dabbled in its conspiratorial politics. Irate at an assignment to inspect locust damage, he got himself dismissed and sent to a family estate in the provincial town of Pskov, where he was kept under secret watch. He managed to extricate himself from a failed rebellion, the so-called Decembrist uprising of 1825, then captivated the new tsar Nicholas, who made him a kind of mascot, pampered and guarded. He married in 1831, received a modest salaried position in Saint Petersburg, and

---

1. Hindu goddess of destruction.
2. Federico García Lorca, Spanish surrealist poet; see

Volume F for a selection from his 1929 cycle *Poet in New York.*

contrived with difficulty to support four children born within six years. The fire was by no means out, however. It flared up in 1837 when Pushkin backed into a duel with a Dutch baron, married to his wife's sister and accused of flirting with his wife. The Dutchman was slightly wounded; the poet died.

Russia wanted a national poet, and Pushkin filled the bill to perfection. In the previous century Catherine the Great, who ruled from 1762–1796, had worked to westernize and modernize the country, importing leading French and German intellectuals. The upper classes were culturally French. But the failed Napoleonic invasion of 1812 led the once liberal tsar Alexander I to retreat into reaction, leaving the country at Nicholas's accession with much ferment and little direction. There were plenty of writers in Western European modes, but none to capture the popular imagination until Pushkin came along. He wrote with equal success lyric poems, Byronic narratives with native themes, plays, and prose narratives, the longest of which, "The Captain's Daughter," is a historical fiction in Scott's panoramic manner concerning a Cossack rebel against Catherine the Great. He became the founding figure of Russian national literature, as well as the inspiration for the Russian musical school; operas based on his works were composed by Glinka (*Russlan and Ludmilla,* 1842), Mussorgsky (*Boris Godunov,* 1870, rev. 1872), Tchaikovsky (*Eugene Onegin,* 1877; *Queen of Spades,* 1890), Rimsky-Korsakov (*Mozart and Salieri,* 1897), Stravinsky (*Mavra,* 1922), and others.

Russia sought to be not just a national kingdom but a great empire. To the east it considered itself divinely ordained to bring civilization to the fierce tribes of Central Asia and the Oriental despotism extending in all directions from Turkey. Meanwhile, in the west it wanted to compete with Europe on its own terms, through the window to the west, the city of Saint Petersburg, founded on the Baltic coast in the eighteenth century by Peter the Great. The delicate balancing act was to assert cultural independence without denying participation; typically, even the city's name is German in form. ("Burg," which means "town," would be "grad" in Russian; in 1917 the city was briefly renamed Petrograd, before entering into its Communist identity as Leningrad.) With his French education and his facility in English and Italian, his deep Russian pedigree, and his "Oriental" ancestry, Pushkin was the perfect figure to represent imperial aspirations. He was fiercely liberal at times, yet ultimately compliant. He wrote in polished Western forms such as the couplets of "The Bronze Horseman." His lyrics show a responsiveness to a nature sensibility resembling Wordsworth's; his story "The Queen of Spades" plays into the fashion for the fantastic tale. At the same time, his Russian themes elevate his native country to all the beauty, sublimity, and dignity of the long-established realms of Europe. All these elements can be found in perfection in his last and most eloquent verse tale, "The Bronze Horseman."

PRONUNCIATIONS:
   Pushkin: PUSH-kin
   Onegin: ahn-YAY-gin
   Nevá: nye-VAH

I Visited Again[1]

. . . I visited again
That corner of the earth where once I spent,
In placid exile, two unheeded years.
A decade's gone since then—and in my life
5   There have been many changes—in myself,

---

1. Translated by Avram Yarmolinsky. Suspected of atheism, Pushkin spent two years (1824–1826) in closely supervised internal exile at his mother's estate of Mikhailovskoe. This poem reflects a return visit in September 1835.

Who from the general law am not exempt,
There have been changes, too—but here once more
The past envelops me, and suddenly
It seems that only yesterday I roamed
10   These groves.

Here stands the exile's cottage, where
I lived with my poor nurse. The good old woman
Has passed away[2]—no longer do I hear
Through the thin wall her heavy tread as she
Goes on her busy rounds.

Here is the hill
15   Upon whose wooded crest I often sat
Unstirring, staring down upon the lake—
Recalling, as I looked, with melancholy,
Another shore, and other waves I knew . . .
Among the golden meadows, the green fields,
20   It stretches its blue breadth, the same still lake:
A fisherman across its lonely waters
Is rowing now, and dragging in his wake
A wretched net. Upon the sloping shores
Are scattered hamlets—and beyond them there
25   A mill squats crookedly—it scarcely stirs
Its wings in this soft wind . . .

Upon the edge
Of the ancestral acres, on the spot
Where the rough road, trenched by the heavy rains,
Begins its upward climb, three pine-trees rise—
30   One stands apart, and two are close together,
And I remember how, of moonlight nights,
When I rode past, their rustling greeted me
Like a familiar voice. I took that road,
I saw the pines before me once again.
35   They are the same, and on the ear the same
Familiar whisper breaks from shaken boughs,
But at the base, beside their aged roots
(Where I remembered only barrenness),
Has sprung a fair young grove, and I observe
40   A verdant family; the bushes crowd
Like children in their shadow. And apart,
Alone as ever, their glum comrade stands,
Like an old bachelor, about whose feet
There stretches only bareness as before.
45   I hail you, race of youthful newcomers!
I shall not witness your maturity,
When you shall have outgrown my ancient friends,

2. In May 1835.

And with your shoulders hide their very heads
From passers-by. But let my grandson hear
50   Your wordless greeting when, as he returns,
Content, light-hearted, from a talk with friends,
He too rides past you in the dark of night,
And thinks, perhaps, of me.

The Bronze Horseman[1]
A Petersburg Tale

INTRODUCTION[2]

Upon the brink of the wild stream
He[3] stood, and dreamt a mighty dream.
He gazed far off. Near him the spreading
river poured by; with flood abeam,
5   alone, a flimsy skiff was treading.
Scattered along those shores of bog
and moss were huts of blackened log,
the wretched fisher's squalid dwelling;
forests, impervious in the fog
10   to hidden suns, all round were telling
their whispered tale.
　　　　　　　And so thought He:
"From here, proud Sweden will get warning;
just here is where a city'll be
founded to stop our foes from scorning;
15   here Nature destines us to throw
out over Europe a window;
to stand steadfast beside the waters;
across waves unknown to the West,
all flags will come, to be our guest—
20   and we shall feast in spacious quarters."

A century went by—a young
city, of Northern lands the glory
and pride, from marsh and overhung
forest arose, story on story:
25   where, earlier, Finland's fisher sank—
of Nature's brood the most downhearted—
alone on the low-lying bank,
his ropy net in the uncharted
current, today, on brinks that hum
30   with life and movement, there have come
enormous mansions that are justling

1. Translated by Charles Johnston.
2. "The Bronze Horseman" tells a story founded on a real flood in November 1824. The grand modern city of Saint Petersburg was built on swampland on the Baltic Sea, looking out toward Finland and the then powerful kingdom of Sweden.
3. Peter the Great, who founded Saint Petersburg in 1703.

with graceful towers; and vessels here
from earth's extremities will steer
until the rich quayside is bustling.
35   Nevá[4] now sports a granite face;
bridges are strung across her waters;
in darkly verdant garden-quarters
her isles have vanished without trace;
old Moscow's paled before this other
40   metropolis; it's just the same
as when a widowed Empress-Mother
bows to a young Tsaritsa's° claim.   *Princess's*

I love you, Peter's own creation;
I love your stern, your stately air,
45   Nevá's majestical pulsation,
the granite that her quaysides wear,
your railings with their iron shimmer,
your pensive nights in the half-gloom,
translucent twilight, moonless glimmer,
50   when, sitting lampless in my room,
I write and read; when, faintly shining,
the streets in their immense outlining
are empty, given up to dreams;
when Admiralty's needle gleams;
55   when not admitting shades infernal
into the golden sky, one glow
succeeds another, and nocturnal
tenure has one half-hour to go;
I love your brutal winter, freezing
60   the air to so much windless space;
by broad Nevá the sledges breezing;
brighter than roses each girl's face;
the ball, its brilliance, din, and malice;
bachelor banquets and the due
65   hiss of the overflowing chalice,
and punch's radiance burning blue.
I love it when some warlike duty
livens the Field of Mars, and horse
and foot impose on that concourse
70   their monolithic brand of beauty;
above the smooth-swaying vanguard
victorious, tattered flags are streaming,
on brazen helmets light is gleaming,
helmets that war has pierced and scarred.
75   I love the martial detonation,
the citadel in smoke and roar,

---

4. The river along which the city is built.

when the North's Empress to the nation
has given a son for empire, or
when there's some new triumph in war
80   victorious Russia's celebrating;
or when Nevá breaks the blue ice,
sweeps it to seaward, slice on slice,
and smells that days of spring are waiting.

Metropolis of Peter, stand,
85   steadfast as Russia, stand in splendor!
Even the elements by your hand
have been subdued and made surrender;
let Finland's waves forget the band
of hate and bondage down the ages,
90   nor trouble with their fruitless rages
Peter the Great's eternal sleep!

A fearful time there was: I keep
its memory fresh in retrospection . . .
My friends, let me turn up for you
95   the dossiers of recollection.
Grievous the tale will be, it's true . . .

PART ONE

On Petrograd,° the darkened city,   *Saint Petersburg*
November, chill and without pity,
blasted; against its noble brink
Nevá was splashing noisy billows;
5   its restless mood would make one think
of sufferers tossing on their pillows.
The hour was late and dark; the rain
angrily lashed the window-pane,
the wind blew, pitifully shrieking.
10   From house of friends, about this time,
young Evgeny came home . . .
                My rhyme
selects this name to use in speaking
of our young hero. It's a sound
I like; my pen has long been bound
15   in some way with it; further naming
is not required, though lustre flaming
in years gone by might have lit on
his forebears, and perhaps their story
under Karamzin's[5] pen had shone,
20   resounding to the nation's glory;
but now by all, both high and low,

5. Nikolai Mikhailovich Karamzin (1766–1826), prose writer.

it's quite forgotten. Our hero
lives in Kolomna,[6] has employment
in some bureau, tastes no enjoyment
25   of wealth or fashion's world, and no
regret for tales of long ago.

So Evgeny came home and, shaking
his greatcoat, got undressed for bed—
but lay long hours awake, his head
30   with various thoughts disturbed and aching.
What did he think about? The fact
that he was penniless; that packed
mountains of work must be surmounted
to earn him freedom, fame, and ease;
35   that wit and money might be counted
to him from God; and that one sees
fellows on permanent vacation,
dull-witted, idle, in whose station
life runs as smooth as in a dream;
40   that he'd served two years altogether . . .
And he thought also that the weather
had got no gentler; that the stream
was rising, ever higher lifting;
that soon the bridges might be shifting;
45   that maybe from Parasha° he   *his beloved*
would be cut off, two days or three.

These were his dreams. And a great sadness
came over him that night; he wished
the raindrops with less raging madness
50   would lash the glass, that the wind swished
less drearily . . .

             At last his failing
eyes closed in sleep. But look, the gloom
of that foul-weather night is paling,
and a weak daylight fills the room . . .
55   A dreadful day it was!

                All night
Nevá against the gales to seaward
had battled, but been blown to leeward
by their ungovernable might . . .
That morning, on the quayside, fountains
60   of spray held an admiring crowd,
that pressed to watch the watery mountains,
the foaming waves that roared so loud.
But now, blocked by the headwinds blowing
in from the Gulf, Nevá turned back,

6. A part of Saint Petersburg.

65   in sullen, thunderous fury flowing,
and flooded all the islands; black,
still blacker grew the day; still swelling,
Nevá exploded, raging, yelling,
in kettle-like outbursts of steam—
70   until, mad as a beast, the stream
pounced on the city. From its path
everyone fled, and all around
was sudden desert . . . At a bound
cellars were under inundation,
75   canals leapt rails, forgot their station—
and Triton-Petropol[7] surfaced
with waters lapping round his waist.

Siege and assault! The waves, malicious,
like thieves, burst in through windows; vicious
80   rowboats, careering, smash the panes;
stalls are engulfed; piteous remains,
débris of cabins, roofing, boarding,
wares that a thrifty trade's been hoarding,
poor household goods, dashed all astray,
85   bridges the storm has snatched away,
and scooped-up coffins, helter-skelter
swim down the streets!
             All sense alike
God's wrath, and wait for doom to strike.
Everything's ruined: bread and shelter!
and where to find them?
90   That deathlike,
that frightful year, Tsar Alexander[8]
still ruled in glory. He came out
on the balcony, in grief, in doubt,
and said: "A Tsar is no commander
95   against God's elements." Deep in thought
he gazed with sorrow and confusion,
gazed at the wreck the floods had wrought.
The city squares gave the illusion
of lakes kept brimming to profusion
100   by torrent-streets. The palace stood
sad as an island in the ocean.
And then the Tsar spoke out, for good
or evil set in farflung motion
his generals on their dangerous way
105   along those streets of boisterous waters
to save the people in their quarters,
drowning, unhinged by terror's sway.

7. Triton is a Greek sea god who rides the waves on sea
horses. Petropol is a Greek form of the name Petersburg.

8. Alexander I (1777–1825).

And then in Peter's square, where lately
a corner-mansion rose, and stately
110 from its high porch, on either side,
caught as in life, with paws suspended,
two lions,[9] sentry-like, attended—
perched up on one, as if to ride,
arms folded, motionless, astride,
115 hatless, and pale with apprehension,
Evgeny sat. His fear's intention
not for himself, he never knew
just how the greedy waters grew,
how at his boots the waves were sucking,
120 how in his face the raindrops flew;
or how the stormwind, howling, bucking,
had snatched his hat away. His view
was fixed in darkest desperation,
immobile, on a single spot.
125 Mountainous, from the perturbation
down in the depths, the waves had got
on their high horses, raging, pouncing;
the gale blew up, and, with it, bouncing
wreckage . . . Oh, God, oh God! for there—
130 close to the seashore—almost where
the Gulf ran in, right on the billow—
a fence, untouched by paint, a willow,
a flimsy cottage; *there* were they,
a widow and his dream, her daughter,
135 Parasha . . . or perhaps he may
have dreamt it all? Fickle as water,
our life is as dreamlike as smoke—
at our expense, fate's private joke.
As if by sorcery enchanted,
140 high on the marble fixed and planted,
he can't dismount! And all about
is only water. Looking out,
with back turned to him, on the retching
waves of Nevá in their wild course
145 from his fast summit, arm outstretching,
the Giant rides on his bronze horse.[1]

PART TWO

But by now, tired of helter-skelter
ruin and sheer rampaging, back
Nevá was flowing, in its track

9. Statues at the entrance to the War Ministry.   1. Monument to Peter the Great.

admiring its own hideous welter;
5   its booty, as it made for shelter,
it slung away. With his grim crew
so any robber chief will do;
bursting his way into a village,
he'll hack and thrust and snatch and pillage;
10   rape, havoc, terror, howl and wail!
Then, loaded down with loot, and weary—
fear of pursuers makes them leery—
the robbers take the homeward trail
and as they flee they scatter plunder.

15   So, while the water fell asunder,
the road came up. And fainting, pale,
in hope and yearning, fear and wonder,
Evgeny hurries at full steam
down to the scarcely falling stream.
20   And yet, still proud, and still exulting,
the waves, still furious and insulting,
boiled as if over flames alight;
they still were lathered, foaming, seething
and deeply the Nevá was breathing
25   just like a horse flown from a fight.
Evgeny looks: a skiff is waiting—
Godsent—he rushes, invocating
the ferryman, who without a care
for just a few copecks quite gladly
30   agrees to take him, though still madly
the floods are boiling everywhere.
The boatman fought the agonizing
billows like an experienced hand;
the cockboat with its enterprising
35   crew was quite ready for capsizing
at any moment—but dry land
at last it gained.
                            Evgeny, tearful,
rushes along the well-known ways
towards the well-known scene. His gaze
40   finds nothing it can grasp: too fearful
the sight! before him all is drowned,
or swept away, or tossed around;
cottages are askew, some crumbled
to sheer destruction, others tumbled
45   off by the waves; and all about,
as on a field of martial rout,
bodies lie weltered. Blankly staring,
Evgeny, uncomprehending, flies,
faint from a torment past all bearing,
50   runs to where fate will meet his eyes,

fate whose unknown adjudication
still waits as under seal of wax.
And now he's near his destination
and here's the Gulf, here . . . in his tracks
55   Evgeny halts . . . the house . . . where ever?
he goes back, he returns. He'd never. . .
he looks . . . he walks . . . he looks again:
here's where their cottage stood; and then
here was the willow. Gates were standing
60   just here—swept off, for sure. But where's
the cottage gone? Not understanding,
he walked round, full of boding cares,
he talked to himself loud and gruffly,
and then he struck his forehead roughly
65   and laughed and laughed.
                              In deepest night
the city trembled at its plight;
long time that day's events were keeping
the citizenry all unsleeping
as they rehearsed them.
                              Daylight's ray
70   fell out of tired, pale clouds to play
over a scene of calm—at dawning
yesterday's hell had left no trace.
The purple radiance of the morning
had covered up the dire event.
75   All in its previous order went.
Upon highways no longer flowing,
people as everyday were going
in cold indifference, and the clerk
left where he'd sheltered in the dark
80   and went to work. The daring bosses
of commerce, unperturbed, explore
Nevá's inroads upon their store,
and plan to take their heavy losses
out on their neighbor. From backyards
85   boats are removed.
                              That bard of bards,
Count Khvostov,[2] great poetic master,
begins to sing Nevá's disaster
in unforgettable ballades.

But spare, I pray you, spare some pity
90   for my poor, poor Evgeny, who
by the sad happenings in the city
had wits unhinged. Still the halloo

2. Count D. I. Khvostov (1757–1835), a minor poet.

of tempest and Nevá was shrieking
into his ear; pierced through and through
95   by frightful thoughts, he roamed unspeaking;
some nightmare held him in its thrall.
A week went by, a month—and all
the time he never once was seeking
his home. That small deserted nook,
100   its lease expired, his landlord took
for a poor poet. His possessions
Evgeny never went to claim.
Soon to the world and its professions
a stranger, all day long he came
105   and went on foot, slept by the water;
scraps thrown from windows of the quarter
his only food; always the same,
his clothes wore out to shreds. Malicious
children would stone him; he received
110   from time to time the coachman's vicious
whiplash, for he no more perceived
which way was which, or what direction
led where; he never seemed to know
where he was going, he was so
115   plunged in tumult of introspection.
And so his life's unhappy span
he eked out—neither beast nor man—
not this, nor that—not really living
nor yet a ghost . . .
                              He slept one night
120   by the Nevá. Summer was giving
its place to autumn. Full of spite,
a bad wind blew. In mournful fight
against the embankment, waves were splashing,
their crests on the smooth steps were smashing
125   for all the world like suppliant poor
at some hard-hearted judge's door.
Evgeny woke. Raindrops were falling
in midnight gloom; the wind was calling
piteously—on it, far off, hark,
130   the cry of sentries in the dark . . .
Evgeny rose, and recollection
brought up past horrors for inspection;
he stood in haste, walked off from there,
then halted, and began to stare
135   in silence, with an insensately
wild look of terror on his face.
He was beside the pillared, stately
front of a mansion. In their place,
caught as in life, with paws suspended,
140   two lions, sentry-like, attended,

and there, above the river's course,
atop his rock, fenced-off, defended
on his dark summit, arm extended,
the Idol rode on his bronze horse.

145   Evgeny shuddered. Thoughts were hatching
in frightful clarity. He knew
that spot, where floods ran raging through—
where waves had massed, voracious, snatching,
a riot-mob, vindictive, grim—
150   the lions, and the square, and him
who, motionless and without pity,
lifted his bronze head in the gloom,
whose will, implacable as doom,
had chosen seashore for his city.
155   Fearful he looked in that half-light!
Upon his forehead, what a might
of thought, what strength of concentration!
what fire, what passion, and what force
are all compact in that proud horse!
160   He gallops—to what destination?
On the cliff-edge, O lord of fate,
was it not you, O giant idol,
who, pulling on your iron bridle,
checked Russia, made her rear up straight?

165   Around the hero's plinth of granite
wretched Evgeny, in a daze,
wandered, and turned a savage gaze
on the autocrat of half the planet.
A steely pressure gripped his chest.
170   His brow on the cold railing pressed,
over his eyes a mist was lowering,
and through his heart there ran a flame;
his blood was seething; so he came
to stand before the overpowering
175   image, with teeth and fists again
clenched as if some dark force possessed him.
"Take care," he whisperingly addressed him,
"you marvel-working builder, when . . ."
He shivered with bitter fury, then
180   took headlong flight. He had the impression
that the grim Tsar, in sudden race
of blazing anger, turned his face
quietly and without expression . . .
and through the empty square he runs,
185   but hears behind him, loud as guns
or thunderclap's reverberation,
ponderous hooves in detonation
along the shuddering roadway—

as, lighted by the pale moon-ray,
190   one arm stretched up, on headlong course,
after him gallops the Bronze Rider,
after him clatters the Bronze Horse.
So all night long, demented strider,
wherever he might turn his head—
195   everywhere gallops the Bronze Rider
pursuing him with thunderous tread.

And from then on, if he was chancing
at any time to cross that square,
a look of wild distress came glancing
200   across his features; he would there
press hand to heart, in tearing hurry,
as if to chase away a worry;
take his worn cap off; never raise
up from the ground his distraught gaze,
205   but sidle off.

           A small isle rises
close to the foreshore. Now and then,
a fisher moors alongside, when
late from his catch, with nets and prizes,
and cooks his poor meal on the sand;
210   or some official comes to land,
out for a Sunday's pleasure-boating,
on the wild islet. Not a blade
of grass is seen. There, gaily floating,
the floods had washed up as they played
215   a flimsy cottage. Above water
it showed up like a bush, quite black—
last spring they moved it. The small quarter,
empty, was shipped away, all rack
and ruin. Near it, my dim-witted
220   my mad Evgeny there they found . . .
His cold corpse in that self-same ground
to God's good mercy they committed.

from Eugene Onegin[1]
CHAPTER 1

42

Capricious belles of lofty station!
You were the first that he forswore;
For nowadays in our great nation.
The manner grand can only bore.
5   I wouldn't say that ladies never

---

1. Translated by J. E. Falen.

Discuss a Say or Bentham[2]—ever;
But generally, you'll have to grant,
Their talk's absurd, if harmless, cant.
On top of which, they're so unerring,
10   So dignified, so awfully smart,
So pious and so chaste of heart,
So circumspect, so strict in bearing,
So inaccessibly serene,
Their very sight brings on the spleen.

43

You too, young mistresses of leisure,
Who late at night are whisked away
In racing droshkies° bound for pleasure   *carriages*
Along the Petersburg *chaussée*°—   *boulevard*
5   He dropped you too in sudden fashion.
Apostate from the storms of passion,
He locked himself within his den
And, with a yawn, took up his pen
And tried to write. But art's exaction
10   Of steady labor made him ill,
And nothing issued from his quill;
So thus he failed to join the faction
Of writers—whom I won't condemn
Since, after all, I'm one of them.

44

Once more an idler, now he smothers
The emptiness that plagues his soul
By making his the thoughts of others—
A laudable and worthy goal.
5   He crammed his bookshelf overflowing,
Then read and read—frustration growing:
Some raved or lied, and some were dense;
Some lacked all conscience; some, all sense;
Each with a different dogma girded;
10   The old was dated through and through,
While nothing new was in the new;
So books, like women, he deserted,
And over all that dusty crowd
He draped a linen mourning shroud.

45

I too had parted with convention,
With vain pursuit of worldly ends;
And when Eugene drew my attention,
I liked his ways and we made friends.
5   I liked his natural bent for dreaming,
His strangeness that was more than seeming,

---

2. Jean-Baptiste Say (1767-1832), liberal French economist; Jeremy Bentham (1748–1832), radical British economist and social thinker.

The cold sharp mind that he possessed;
I was embittered, he depressed;
With passion's game we both were sated;
10   The fire in both our hearts was pale;
Our lives were weary, flat, and stale;
And for us both, ahead there waited—
While life was still but in its morn—
Blind fortune's malice and men's scorn.

46

He who has lived as thinking being
Within his soul must hold men small;
He who can feel is always fleeing
The ghost of days beyond recall;
5   For him enchantment's deep infection
Is gone; the snake of recollection
And grim repentance gnaws his heart.
All this, of course, can help impart
Great charm to private conversation;
10   And though the language of my friend
At first disturbed me, in the end
I liked his caustic disputation—
His blend of banter and of bile,
His somber wit and biting style.

47

How often in the summer quarter,
When midnight sky is limpid-light
Above the Neva's[3] placid water—
The river gay and sparkling bright,
5   Yet in its mirror not reflecting
Diana's[4] visage—recollecting
The loves and intrigues of the past,
Alive once more and free at last,
We drank in silent contemplation
10   The balmy fragrance of the night!
Like convicts sent in dreaming flight
To forest green and liberation,
So we in fancy then were borne
Back to our springtime's golden morn.

48

Filled with his heart's regrets, and leaning
Against the rampart's granite shelf,
Eugene stood lost in pensive dreaming
(As once some poet drew himself).
5   The night grew still . . . with silence falling,
Only the sound of sentries calling,
Or suddenly from Million Street

---

3. The river on which Saint Petersburg is built.   4. Goddess of the moon.

Some distant droshky's rumbling beat;
Or floating on the drowsy river,
10   A lonely boat would sail along,
While far away some rousing song
Or plaintive horn would make us shiver.
But sweeter still, amid such nights,
Are Tasso's octaves' soaring flights.[5]

49

O Adriatic! Grand Creation!
O Brenta![6] I shall yet rejoice,
When, filled once more with inspiration,
I hear at last your magic voice!
5   It's sacred to Apollo's choir;[7]
Through Albion's[8] great and haughty lyre
It speaks to me in words I know.
On soft Italian nights I'll go
In search of pleasure's sweet profusion;
10   A fair Venetian at my side,
Now chatting, now a silent guide,
I'll float in gondola's seclusion;
And she my willing lips will teach
Both love's and Petrarch's ardent speech.[9]

50

Will freedom come—and cut my tether?
It's time, it's time! I bid her hail;
I roam the shore, await fair weather,
And beckon to each passing sail.
5   O when, my soul, with waves contesting,
And caped in storms, shall I go questing
Upon the crossroads of the sea?
It's time to quit this dreary lee
And land of harsh, forbidding places;
10   And there, where southern waves break high,
Beneath my Africa's warm sky,[1]
To sigh for somber Russia's spaces,
Where first I loved, where first I wept,
And where my buried heart is kept.

51

Eugene and I had both decided
To make the foreign tour we'd planned;
But all too soon our paths divided,
For fate took matters into hand.
5   His father died—quite unexpected,

5. Torquato Tasso (1544–1595), author of the epic poem
Jerusalem Delivered, in eight-line stanzas ("octaves").
6. River in northern Italy, along which many grand villas
were built in the Renaissance; empties into the Adriatic
near Venice.
7. The Muses.

8. England, homeland of Lord Byron, the most famous
poet (lyricist, "lyre"-master) of the age.
9. Francesco Petrarca (1304–1374), the greatest writer of
love sonnets.
1. A reference to Pushkin's African great-grandfather.

And round Eugene there soon collected
The greedy horde demanding pay.
Each to his own, or so they say.
Eugene, detesting litigation
10   And quite contented with his fate,
Released to them the whole estate . . .
With no great sense of deprivation;
Perhaps he also dimly knew
His aged uncle's time was due.

52

And sure enough a note came flying;
The bailiff wrote as if on cue:
Onegin's uncle, sick and dying,
Would like to bid his heir adieu.
5   He gave the message one quick reading,
And then by post Eugene was speeding,
Already bored, to uncle's bed,
While thoughts of money filled his head.
He was prepared—like any craven—
10   To sigh, deceive, and play his part
(With which my novel took its start);
But when he reached his uncle's haven,
A laid-out corpse was what he found,
Prepared as tribute for the ground.

53

He found the manor fairly bustling
With those who'd known the now deceased;
Both friends and foes had come ahustling,
True lovers of a funeral feast.
5   They laid to rest the dear departed;
Then, wined and dined and heavy-hearted,
But pleased to have their duty done,
The priests and guests left one by one.
And here's Onegin—lord and master
10   Of woods and mills and streams and lands;
A country squire, there he stands,
That former wastrel and disaster;
And rather glad he was, it's true,
That he'd found something else to do.

54

For two full days he was enchanted
By lonely fields and burbling brook,
By sylvan shade that lay implanted
Within a cool and leafy nook.
5   But by the third he couldn't stick it:
The grove, the hill, the field, the thicket—
Quite ceased to tempt him any more
And, presently, induced a snore;
And then he saw that country byways—

10   With no great palaces, no streets,
     No cards, no balls, no poets' feats—
     Were just as dull as city highways;
     And spleen, he saw, would dog his life,
     Like shadow or a faithful wife.

55

     But I was born for peaceful roaming,
     For country calm and lack of strife;
     My lyre sings! And in the gloaming
     My fertile fancies spring to life.
5   I give myself to harmless pleasures
     And *far niente*° rules my leisures: *idleness*
     Each morning early I'm awake
     To wander by the lonely lake
     Or seek some other sweet employment:
10   I read a little, often sleep,
     For fleeting fame I do not weep.
     And was it not in past enjoyment
     Of shaded, idle times like this,
     I spent my days of deepest bliss?

56

     The country, love, green fields and flowers,
     Sweet idleness! You have my heart.
     With what delight I praise those hours
     That set Eugene and me apart.
5   For otherwise some mocking reader
     Or, God forbid, some wretched breeder
     Of twisted slanders might combine
     My hero's features here with mine
     And then maintain the shameless fiction
10   That, like proud Byron, I have penned
     A mere self-portrait in the end;
     As if today, through some restriction,
     We're now no longer fit to write
     On any theme but our own plight.

57

     All poets, I need hardly mention,
     Have drawn from love abundant themes;
     I too have gazed in rapt attention
     When cherished beings filled my dreams.
5   My soul preserved their secret features;
     The Muse then made them living creatures:
     Just so in carefree song I paid
     My tribute to the mountain maid,
     And sang the Salghir[2] captives' praises.
10   And now, my friends, I hear once more
     That question you have put before:

2. A river in Crimea, land of the Tatars.

"For whom these sighs your lyre raises?
To whom amid the jealous throng
Do you today devote your song?

58

"Whose gaze, evoking inspiration,
Rewards you with a soft caress?
Whose form, in pensive adoration,
Do you now clothe in sacred dress?"

5 Why no one, friends, as God's my witness,
For I have known too well the witless
And maddened pangs of love's refrain.
Oh, blest is he who joins his pain
To fevered rhyme: for thus he doubles

10 The sacred ecstasy of art;
Like Petrarch then, he calms the heart,
Subduing passion's host of troubles,
And captures worldly fame to boot!—
But I, in love, was dense and mute.

59

The Muse appeared as love was ending
And cleared the darkened mind she found.
Once free, I seek again the blending
Of feeling, thought, and magic sound.

5 I write . . . and want no more embraces;
My straying pen no longer traces,
Beneath a verse left incomplete,
The shapes of ladies' heads and feet.
Extinguished ashes won't rekindle,

10 And though I grieve, I weep no more;
And soon, quite soon, the tempest's core
Within my soul will fade and dwindle:
And *then* I'll write this world a song
That's five and twenty cantos long!

60

I've drawn a plan and know what's needed,
The hero's named, the plotting's done;
And meantime I've just now completed
My present novel's Chapter One.

5 I've looked it over most severely;
It has its contradictions, clearly,
But I've no wish to change a line;
I'll grant the censor's right to shine
And send these fruits of inspiration

10 To feed the critics' hungry pen.
Fly to the Neva's water then,
My spirit's own newborn creation!
And earn me tribute paid to fame:
Distorted readings, noise, and blame!

≈⁺ PERSPECTIVES ⁺≈
The National Poet

"What is a People in the Higher Meaning of the Word, and What is Love of Fatherland?" In the nineteenth century, Johann Gottlieb Fichte's question was suddenly everywhere. There was as yet no German nation-state (as Fichte was writing in 1808, he was surrounded by Napoleon's troops), and existing loyalties to groups larger or smaller than the state (like cities, empires, and religions) could not suffice to bring it into being. Ethnic nations seeking to become political nation-states, like Germany and Italy, tried to imagine themselves into a state of wholeness that didn't yet exist. This involved looking back at the ballads, folktales, customs, and historical experiences that its prospective members shared across space and time. But it was also necessary to invent what wasn't yet there. Hence all through the nineteenth century we find the literary ambition that James Joyce was to ascribe to Stephen Dedalus in *A Portrait of the Artist as a Young Man* as he leaves colonial Ireland for an artistic career: "to forge in the smithy of my soul the uncreated conscience of my race." Johann Wolfgang Goethe in Germany, Giacomo Leopardi in Italy, and Adam Mickiewicz in Poland are poets who rose to meet a moment of national self-definition. There are many others. Sándor Petőfy recited his "National Song" on the steps of Hungary's National Museum in the midst of the 1848 upheaval, inciting a patriotic crowd to rise up and free the country from Hapsburg oppression. José Rizal of the Philippines was still writing poetry for his fatherland while awaiting execution.

Whether or not the poet expressed it himself—the national poet was generally expected to be a man—a national ambition was often forced upon him retroactively by a nation hungry for heroes. The great Vietnamese poet Nguyen Du certainly intended his unfortunate, resilient heroine Kieu to stand metaphorically for his country's long struggles for independence, yet Nguyen Du himself would have been surprised to find his verse novel attaining the status of a national epic over the course of the nineteenth century—a status it retains to this day. And born among Italian speakers on the Ionian island of Zakynthos (in Italian, Zante) and educated in Italian, Dionysius Solomos began writing in Greek only after the outbreak of the Greek War of Independence. He wrote his "Hymn to Liberty" in the midst of the war, and it is said that by 1825, when the poem was already in its third edition, it was read in the original Greek in every European country. Goethe called Solomos "the Byron of the East." Yet Solomos didn't participate in that national struggle, and after its triumph he chose to remain in an area of Greece that was still under British rule. At the end of his life he turned back to writing in Italian. His editors, eager to sustain the ideal image of a national poet, omitted from his works sentiments that were inadequately patriotic. His acknowledged masterpiece, "The Free Besieged," a much-reworked fragment that began as the account of the tragic siege of Missolonghi, has been seen by many readers as pulling away from the political issues of the War of Independence in favor of more universal themes of freedom and nature.

Like Solomos, Adam Mickiewicz too emerged from a multilingual and multiethnic context. Raised in what was then Lithuania, he developed a poetic vision of Polish national identity that was more capacious than might have been expected. Though he believed that a resurrected Poland would become the savior of all nations, he was no Orientalist. He saw the Tatars to the east as a brother people, equally victimized by the expansion of Russian imperial power, and showed reverence both for Islam and for Judaism. His greatness marks a moment before the rise of patriotic anti-Semitism, when Jewish and Catholic Poles could imagine fighting together for a nation to be held in common. His *Konrad Wallenrod* makes an intriguing parallel to the mixed loyalties in American captivity narratives.

Johann Heinrich Wilhelm Tischbein, *Goethe in the Roman Campagna,* 1786.

"America has yet morally and artistically organized nothing," Walt Whitman wrote in *Democratic Vistas* (1871). "She seems singularly unaware that the models of persons, books, manners, &c,. appropriate for former conditions and European lands, are but exiles and exotics here." Answering Emerson's call for a new voice to sing a new country, Whitman thought he would be perfect for the part. And, with his celebration of American energies of change and expansive self-definition, many subsequent poets have agreed that he was. In his own time, however, Whitman was far too marginal to mainstream American values and poetic taste to be acknowledged in his self-appointed role as America's bard. Despite the recognition he received from Emerson and some others, Whitman wasn't canonized as a great poet of the nation until well into the twentieth century. By then, much the same ambition and accomplishment can be noted in poets as otherwise diverse as W. B. Yeats, Rabindranath Tagore, Leopold Senghor, Aimé Césaire, and Amilcar Cabral.

⊷ ≈◊≊ ⊶

Nguyen Du
1765–1820

For nearly two centuries, Nguyen Du has been seen as the greatest national poet in the modern history of Vietnam—a country that has repeatedly had to struggle to have an independent national existence at all. Ruled by China for a thousand years until the tenth century, Vietnam had been largely independent until Nguyen Du's time, but the old order was changing.

A single dynasty, the Le, had ruled Vietnam for 350 years, but then a popular rebellion known as the Tay-son movement began in southern Vietnam in the early 1770s, and by 1789 the monarchy had fallen. Much as in France in the same years, a period of social upheaval followed—including modest redistribution of wealth from rich to poor. These upheavals ended in 1802 with the establishment of a new royal line, the Nguyen house. Not related to this new household, Nguyen Du was a loyalist of the deposed older dynasty, but like many other former Le officials, he reluctantly supported the new dynasty as an improvement over near anarchy. He served the new government in various capacities, including briefly as an ambassador to China.

His primary vocation, though, was as a lyric and narrative poet. Verse novels had become popular in Vietnam, often loosely based on Chinese prose narratives, and in the troubled years of revolution and dynastic struggle, Nguyen Du turned to a sixteenth-century novel called *The Tale of Chin, Yün, and Ch'iao*. Its author, Hsü Wei, had taken part in a campaign in China to suppress a revolt by a populist rebel named Tu Hai. Tu Hai proved too powerful for the Ming emperor to defeat directly, but Tu Hai had a favorite concubine named Wang Ts'ui-ch'iao (Vuong Thuy Kieu in the Chinese-inflected literary Vietnamese of Nguyen Du's day). She persuaded Tu Hai to surrender, whereupon the emperor had him murdered; Kieu then threw herself into a river. In the original version of the novel, she drowned, but Hsü Wei revised the story in a sequel and had her rescued and reunited with her family.

Nguyen Du took up this material and remade it into an extraordinary tale, focusing not on the rebel leader but on Kieu, whom he made into a picaresque heroine, a consummate survivor in a chaotic world. Sudden death and political violence first deprive Kieu of her betrothed and then force her into prostitution, followed by a series of abrupt reversals in fortune. All too trusting of the various shady characters who promise to help her, mourning her lost love yet also quite ready to fall in love again—and again—Kieu rises to every challenge and does what she must, aware that her sufferings play out faults in past lives recorded in the underworld Book of the Damned. Among her many talents, Kieu is presented as a superb poet, and her poetry gets her out of more than one tight situation. As the Resonance by a contemporary Vietnamese poet shows, Kieu came to be seen as a stand-in for Nguyen Du himself, struggling to stay afloat— and to express himself—in a swiftly changing political situation. In this, Kieu can be compared to Byron's Don Juan and Pushkin's Eugene Onegin, poets' alter egos whose romantic misadventures provide the basis for a broad-based, tragicomic survey of European social and political upheavals in these same years.

Both Nguyen Du and his heroine came to symbolize Vietnam as a whole, though depending on the political needs of the moment, Kieu and her creator could be praised as survivors or excoriated as immoral and disloyal. The relevance of their story only increased as Vietnam lost its independence to France, becoming absorbed in the 1880s into colonial French Indochina, at which point the Vietnamese elite had to face the choice of cooperation or ostracism. Recurrent efforts for national liberation gained momentum during and after World War II. Drawn-out conflicts ensued, first with France and then between the Chinese-supported north and the American-supported south in the Vietnam War of 1965–1973. After a further period of civil conflict, an independent, united Vietnam was established by the communist government of Ho Chi Minh—himself a poet and someone who could quote long stretches of *The Tale of Kieu* from memory.

Nguyen Du's masterpiece continues to resonate on many levels. In addition to the direct political implications that can be drawn from the story, it has long served more generally as a model of the adaptation of classical themes to a modern context. Nguyen Du repeatedly refers to the Confucian classics and China's great T'ang dynasty poets, yet the old images and techniques serve decidedly new purposes, as Kieu fashions a path for herself from the dramatic

Kieu's family lived in the capital, Beijing.

beginning of the story to its surprising end, bending to circumstances without betraying her highest values, always refusing to take the expected way out. Nguyen Du gives rich and psychologically nuanced portrayals of Kieu, her family, friends, lovers, and her many scheming enemies, in a swift-paced and often humorous narrative that carries heroine and reader alike through shocking events in a disintegrating world.

PRONUNCIATIONS:

    Nguyen Du: NWEN DOO
    Hsian-Ching: SHAO-JING
    Kieu: K'YOU
    Ky Thuc: KEY TOOK
    Tu Hai: TOO HIGH
    Vuong Quan: VWONG KWAHN
    Van: VAHN

Reading Hsiao-Ching[1]

West Lake flower garden: a desert, now.
Alone, at the window, I read through old pages.
A smudge of rouge, a scent of perfume, but
I still weep.
5   Is there a Fate for books?
Why mourn for a half-burned poem?
There is nothing, there is no one to question,
And yet this misery feels like my own.
Ah, in another three hundred years
10   Will anyone weep, remembering my Fate?

from The Tale of Kieu[1]

   A hundred years—in this life span on earth
talent and destiny are apt to feud.
You must go through a play of ebb and flow
and watch such things as make you sick at heart.
5   Is it so strange that losses balance gains?
Blue Heaven's wont to strike a rose from spite.

   By lamplight turn these scented leaves and read
a tale of love recorded in old books.
Under the Chia-ching reign when Ming held sway,
10 all lived at peace—both capitals stood strong.[2]
   There was a burgher in the clan of Vuong.
a man of modest wealth and middle rank.
He had a last-born son, Vuong Quan—his hope
to carry on a line of learned folk.
15 Two daughters, beauties both, had come before:
Thúy Kieu was oldest, younger was Thuy Van.
Bodies like slim plum branches, snow-pure souls:
each her own self, each perfect in her way.
   In quiet grace Van was beyond compare:
20 her face a moon, her eyebrows two full curves;
her smile a flower, her voice the song of jade;
her hair the sheen of clouds, her skin white snow.
   Yet Kieu possessed a keener, deeper charm,
surpassing Van in talents and in looks.
25 Her eyes were autumn streams, her brows spring hills.
Flowers grudged her glamour, willows her fresh hue.
A glance or two from her, and kingdoms rocked!

---

1. Translated by Nguyen Ngoc Bich and Burton Raffel. A talented woman poet at the turn of the 17th century, Feng Hsiao-Ching was forced to become a concubine to a man whose primary wife isolated her. Hsiao-Ching died of grief, whereupon the vengeful first wife burned her manuscript; only a few poems survived.

1. Translated by Huynh Sanh Thong, from whom the following footnotes are adapted.
2. There were two capitals in Ming Dynasty China: Peking in the north (where Kieu's family lived) and Nanking in the south. The emperor Chia-ch'ing ruled from 1522–1566.

Supreme in looks, she had few peers in gifts.
By Heaven blessed with wit, she knew all skills:
30 she could write verse and paint, could sing and chant.
Of music she had mastered all five tones
and played the lute far better than Ai Chang.[3]
She had composed a song called *Cruel Fate*
to mourn all women in soul-rending strains.
35 A paragon of grace for womanhood,
she neared that time when maidens pinned their hair.[4]
She calmly lived behind drawn shades and drapes,
as wooers swarmed, unheeded, by the wall.

Swift swallows and spring days were shuttling by—
40 of ninety radiant ones three score had fled.
Young grass spread all its green to heaven's rim;
some blossoms marked pear branches with white dots.
Now came the Feast of Light in the third month[5]
with graveyard rites and junkets on the green.
45 As merry pilgrims flocked from near and far,
the sisters and their brother went for a stroll.

Fine men and beauteous women on parade:
a crush of clothes, a rush of wheels and steeds.
Folks clambered burial knolls to strew and burn
50 sham gold or paper coins, and ashes swirled.

Now, as the sun was dipping toward the west,
the youngsters started homeward, hand in hand.
With leisured steps they walked along a brook,
admiring here and there a pretty view.
55 The rivulet, babbling, curled and wound its course
under a bridge that spanned it farther down.
Beside the road a mound of earth loomed up
where withered weeds, half yellow and half green.

Kieu asked: "Now that the Feast of Light is on,
60 why is no incense burning for this grave?"
Vuong Quan told her this tale from first to last:
"She was a famous singer once, Dam Tien.
Renowned for looks and talents in her day,
she lacked not lovers jostling at her door.
65 But fate makes roses fragile—in mid-spring
off broke the flower that breathed forth heaven's scents.
From overseas a stranger came to woo
and win a girl whose name spread far and wide.
But when the lover's boat sailed into port,
70 he found the pin had snapped, the vase had crashed.[6]
A death-still silence filled the void, her room;

---

3. A famous classical lutist. The traditional Chinese scale has five tones.
4. Chinese girls would pin up their hair at age 15 as they reached marriageable age.

5. Spring festival when people visit graves and make offerings to the dead.
6. Chinese metaphors for the death of one's beloved.

all tracks of horse or wheels had blurred to moss.
He wept, full of a grief no words could tell:
'Harsh is the fate that has kept us apart!
75 Since in this life we are not meant to meet,
let me pledge you my troth for our next life.'
He purchased both a coffin and a hearse
and rested her in dust beneath this mound,
among the grass and flowers. For many moons,
80 who's come to tend a grave that no one claims?"
    A well of pity lay within Kieu's heart:
as soon as she had heard her tears burst forth.
"How sorrowful is women's lot!" she cried.
"We all partake of woe, our common fate.
85 Creator, why are you so mean and cruel,
blighting green days and fading rose-fresh cheeks?
Alive, she played the wife to all the world,
alas, to end down there without a man!
Where are they now who shared in her embrace?
90 Where are they now who lusted for her charms?
Since no one else gives her a glance, a thought,
I'll light some incense candles while I'm here.
I'll mark our chance encounter on the road—
perhaps, down by the Yellow Springs,[7] she'll know."
95   She prayed in mumbled tones, then she knelt down
to make a few low bows before the tomb.
Dusk gathered on a patch of wilted weeds—
reed tassels swayed as gently blew the breeze.
She pulled a pin out of her hair and graved
100 four lines of stop-short verse on a tree's bark.
Deeper and deeper sank her soul in trance—
all hushed, she tarried there and would not leave.
The cloud on her fair face grew darker yet:
as sorrow ebbed or flowed, tears dropped or streamed.
105   Van said: "My sister, you should be laughed at,
lavishing tears on one long dead and gone!"
"Since ages out of mind," retorted Kieu,
"harsh fate has cursed all women, sparing none.
As I see her lie there, it hurts to think
110 what will become of me in later days."
    "A fine speech you just made!" protested Quan.
"It jars the ears to hear you speak of her
and mean yourself. Dank air hangs heavy here—
day's failing, and there's still a long way home."
115   Kieu said: "When one who shines in talent dies,
the body passes on, the soul remains.
In her, perhaps, I've found a kindred heart:

7. The underworld.

let's wait and soon enough she may appear."
Before they could respond to what Kieu said,
120   a whirlwind rose from nowhere, raged and raved.
It blustered, strewing buds and shaking trees
and scattering whiffs of perfume in the air.
They strode along the path the whirlwind took
and plainly saw fresh footprints on the moss.
125   They stared at one another, terror-struck.
"You've heard the prayer of my pure faith!" Kieu cried.
"As kindred hearts, we've joined each other here—
transcending life and death, soul sisters meet."
Dam Tien had cared to manifest herself:
130   to what she'd written Kieu now added thanks.
A poet's feelings, rife with anguish, flowed:
she carved an old-style poem on the tree.[8]

To leave or stay—they all were wavering still
when nearby rang the sound of harness bells.
135   They saw a youthful scholar come their way
astride a colt he rode with slackened rein.
He carried poems packing half his bag,
and tagging at his heels were some page boys.
His frisky horse's coat was dyed with snow.
140   His gown blent tints of grass and pale blue sky.
He spied them from afar, at once alit
and walked toward them to pay them his respects.
His figured slippers trod the green—the field
now sparkled like some jade-and-ruby grove.
145   Young Vuong stepped forth and greeted him he knew
while two shy maidens hid behind the flowers.
He came from somewhere not so far away,
Kim Trong, a scion of the noblest stock.
Born into wealth and talent, he'd received
150   his wit from heaven, a scholar's trade from men.
Manner and mien set him above the crowd:
he studied books indoors, lived high abroad.
Since birth he'd always called this region home—
he and young Vuong were classmates at their school.
155   His neighbors' fame had spread and reached his ear:
two beauties locked in their Bronze Sparrow Tower![9]
But, as if hills and streams had barred the way,
he had long sighed and dreamt of them, in vain.
How lucky, in this season of new leaves,
160   to roam about and find his yearned-for flowers!
He caught a fleeting glimpse of both afar:
spring orchid, autumn mum—a gorgeous pair!

---

8. A free-form poem, better suited than the short quatrain to express a flood of feelings.

9. Two sisters over whom rival warlords fought in the third century.

Beautiful girl and talented young man—
what stirred their hearts their eyes still dared not say.
165   They hovered, rapture-bound, 'tween wake and dream:
they could not stay, nor would they soon depart.
The dusk of sunset prompted thoughts of gloom—
he left, and longingly she watched him go.
Below a stream flowed clear, and by the bridge
170   a twilit willow rustled threads of silk.

When Kieu got back behind her flowered drapes,
the sun had set, the curfew gong had rung.
Outside the window, squinting, peeped the moon—
gold spilled on waves, trees shadowed all the yard.
175   East drooped a red camellia, toward the next house:
as dewdrops fell, the spring branch bent and bowed.
Alone, in silence, she beheld the moon,
her heart a raveled coil of hopes and fears:
"Lower than that no person could be brought!
180   It's just a bauble then, the glittering life.
And who is he? Why did we chance to meet?
Does fate intend some tie between us two?"
Her bosom heaved in turmoil—she poured forth
a wondrous lyric fraught with all she felt.
185   The moonlight through the blinds was falling slant.
Leaning against the window, she drowsed off.
Now out of nowhere there appeared a girl
of worldly glamour joined to virgin grace:
face washed with dewdrops, body clad in snow,
190   and hovering feet, two golden lotus blooms.
With joy Kieu hailed the stranger, asking her:
"Did you stray here from that Peach Blossom Spring?"[1]
"We two are sister souls," the other said.
"Have you forgotten? We just met today!
195   My cold abode lies west of here, out there,
above a running brook, below a bridge.
By pity moved, you stooped to notice me
and strew on me poetic pearls and gems.
I showed them to our League Chief[2] and was told
200   your name is marked in the Book of the Damned.
We both reap what we sowed in our past lives:
of the same League, we ride the selfsame boat.
Well, ten new subjects our League Chief just set:
again please work your magic with a brush."
205   Kieu did as asked and wrote—with nymphic grace
her hand dashed off ten lyrics at one stroke.
Dam Tien read them and marveled to herself:

---

1. A hidden earthly paradise described in a famous prose-
poem by the Chinese poet-recluse T'ao Ch'ien.

2. An underworld immortal, head of the League of Sorrow.

"Rich-wrought embroidery from a heart of gold!
Included in the Book of Sorrow Songs,
210   they'll yield the palm to none but win first prize."
    The caller crossed the doorsill, turned to leave,
but Kieu would hold her back and talk some more.
A sudden gust of wind disturbed the blinds,
and Kieu awakened, knowing she had dreamed.
215   She looked, but nowhere could she see the girl,
though hints of perfume lingered here and there.

* * *

    How strange, the race of lovers! Try as you will,
you can't unsnarl their hearts' entangled threads.
245   Since Kim was back inside his book-lined walls,
he could not drive her from his haunted mind.
He drained the cup of gloom: it filled anew—
one day without her seemed three autumns long.
Silk curtains veiled her windows like dense clouds,
250   and toward the rose within he'd dream his way.
The moon kept waning, oil kept burning low:
his face yearned for her face, his heart her heart.
The study-room turned icy, metal-cold—
brushes lay dry, lute strings hung loose on frets.
255   Hsiang bamboo blinds stirred rustling in the wind—
incense roused longing, tea lacked love's sweet taste.
If fate did not mean them to join as mates,
why had the temptress come and teased his eyes?
Forlorn, he missed the scene, he missed the girl:
260   he rushed back where by chance the two had met.
A tract of land with grasses lush and green,
with waters crystal-clear he saw naught else.
The breeze at twilight stirred a mood of grief—
the reeds waved back and forth as if to taunt.

[*The love-smitten Kim rents a house next to Kieu's, and they talk across the wall between their gardens. When Kieu's parents go off to a family gathering, she throws caution to the wind and steals away to Kim's house, where she admires his paintings and he admires her poetry. Reluctantly, Kieu returns home at day's end.*]

    News of her folks she learned when she reached home:
430   her feasting parents would not soon be back.
She dropped silk curtains at the entrance door,
then crossed the garden in dark night, alone.
The moon through branches cast shapes bright or dark—
through curtains glimmered flickers of a lamp.
435   The student at his desk had nodded off,
reclining half awake and half asleep.
The girl's soft footsteps woke him from his drowse:
the moon was setting as she hovered near.

He wondered—was this Wu-hsia the fairy hill,[3]
440   where he was dreaming now a spring night's dream?
        "Along a lonesome, darkened path," she said,
        "for love of you I found my way to you.
        Now we stand face to face—but who can tell
        we shan't wake up and learn it was a dream?"
445   He bowed and welcomed her, then he replaced
        the candle and refilled the incense urn.
        Both wrote a pledge of troth, and with a knife
        they cut in two a lock of her long hair.
        The stark bright moon was gazing from the skies
450   as with one voice both mouths pronounced the oath.
        Their hearts' recesses they explored and probed,
        etching their vow of union in their bones.
        Both sipped a nectar wine from cups of jade—
        silks breathed their scents, the mirror glassed their selves.
455   "The breeze blows cool, the moon shines clear," he said,
        "but in my heart still burns a thirst unquenched.
        The pestle's yet to pound on the Blue Bridge—[4]
        I fear my bold request might give offense."
        She said: "By the red leaf, the crimson thread,
460   we're bound for life—our oath proves mutual faith.
        Of love make not a sport, a dalliance,
        and what would I begrudge you otherwise?"
        He said: "You've won wide fame as lutanist:
        like Chung Tzu-ch'i I've longed to hear you play."[5]
465   "It's no great art, my luting," answered she,
        "but if you so command, I must submit."
        In the back porch there hung his moon-shaped lute:
        he hastened to present it in both hands,
        at eyebrow's height. "My petty skill," she cried,
470   "is causing you more bother than it's worth!"
        By turns she touched the strings, both high and low,
        to tune all four to five tones, then she played.
        An air, *The Battlefield of Han and Ch'u,*
        made one hear bronze and iron clash and clang.
475   The Ssu-ma tune, *A Phoenix Seeks His Mate,*[6]
        sounded so sad, the moan of grief itself.
        Here was Chi K'ang's famed masterpiece, *Kuang-ling*—
        was it a stream that flowed, a cloud that roamed?
        Crossing the Border-gate—here was Chao-chun,
480   half lonesome for her lord, half sick for home.

3. Home of a nymph who visited a Chinese king in a dream and made love to him.
4. In a folktale, a task that needed to be accomplished before a marriage would be allowed.
5. The only person who could fully appreciate the playing of the famed lute player Po Ya; when Chung died, Po cut the strings of his lute and played no more.

6. The ancient writer Ssu-ma Hsiang-ju won the heart of his beloved by playing this tune, leading her to elope with him against her father's wishes. Kieu next plays a tune by a famous recluse, then a song associated with a classical beauty, Wang Chao-chin, forced to marry a Tartar Khan against her wishes.

Clear notes like cries of egrets flying past;
dark tones like torrents tumbling in mid-course.
Andantes languid as a wafting breeze;
allegros rushing like a pouring rain.

485   The lamp now flared, now dimmed—and there he sat
hovering between sheer rapture and deep gloom.
He'd hug his knees or he'd hang down his head—
he'd feel his entrails wrenching, knit his brows.
"Indeed, a master's touch," he said at last,

490   "but it betrays such bitterness within!
Why do you choose to play those plaintive strains
which grieve your heart and sorrow other souls?"
"I'm settled in my nature," she replied.
"Who knows why Heaven makes one sad or gay?

495   But I shall mark your golden words, their truth,
and by degrees my temper may yet mend."

A fragrant rose, she sparkled in full bloom,
bemused his eyes, and kindled his desire.
When waves of lust had seemed to sweep him off,

500   his wooing turned to wanton liberties.
She said: "Treat not our love as just a game—
please stay away from me and let me speak.
What is a mere peach blossom that one should
fence off the garden, thwart the bluebird's quest?

505   But you've named me your bride—to serve her man,
she must place chastity above all else.
They play in mulberry groves along the P'u,[7]
but who would care for wenches of that ilk?
Are we to snatch the moment, pluck the fruit,

510   and in one sole day wreck a lifelong trust?
Let's ponder those love stories old and new—
what well-matched pair could equal Ts'ui and Chang?[8]
Yet passion's storms did topple stone and bronze:
she cloyed her lover humoring all his whims.

515   As wing to wing and limb to limb they lay,
contempt already lurked beside their hearts.
Under the western roof the two burned out
the incense of their vow, and love turned shame.
If I don't cast the shuttle in defense,[9]

520   we'll later blush for it—who'll bear the guilt?
Why force your wish on your shy flower so soon?
While I'm alive, you'll sometime get your due."

The voice of sober reason gained his ear,
and tenfold his regard for her increased.

525   As silver paled along the eaves, they heard

---

7. The mulberry groves were favored for illicit meetings
between lovers.
8. The most famous lovers in Chinese literature, from a
semi-autobiographical story by the T'ang poet Yuan Chen

(779–831).
9. A girl hurled a shuttle at an unwanted suitor, breaking
his teeth.

an urgent call from outside his front gate.
She ran back toward her chamber while young Kim
rushed out and crossed the yard where peaches bloomed.

530   The brushwood gate unbolted, there came in
a houseboy with a missive fresh from home.
It said Kim's uncle while abroad had died,
whose poor remains were now to be brought back.
To far Liao-yang, beyond the hills and streams,[1]
he'd go and lead the cortege, Father bade.

535   What he'd just learned astounded Kim—at once
he hurried to her house and broke the news.
In full detail he told her how a death,
striking his clan, would send him far away:
"We've scarcely seen each other—now we part.

540   We've had no chance to tie the marriage tie.
But it's still there, the moon that we swore by:
not face to face, we shall stay heart to heart.
A day will last three winters far from you:
my tangled knot of grief won't soon unknit.

545   Care for yourself, my gold, my jade, that I,
at the world's ends, may know some peace of mind."
She heard him speak, her feelings in a snarl.
With broken words, she uttered what she thought:
"Why does he hate us so who spins silk threads?

550   Before we've joined in joy we part in grief.
Together we did swear a sacred oath:
my hair shall gray and wither, not my love.
What matter if I must wait months and years?
I'll think of my wayfaring man and grieve.

555   We've pledged to wed our hearts—I'll never leave
and play my lute aboard another's boat.
As long as hills and streams endure, come back,
remembering her who is with you today."
They lingered hand in hand and could not part,

560   but now the sun stood plumb above the roof.
Step by slow step he tore himself away—
at each farewell their tears would fall in streams.
Horse saddled and bags tied in haste, he left:
they split their grief in half and parted ways.

565   Strange landscapes met his mournful eyes—on trees
cuckoos galore, at heaven's edge some geese.
Grieve for him who must bear through wind and rain
a heart more loaded down with love each day.

There she remained, her back against the porch,
570   her feelings snarled like raveled skeins of silk.
Through window bars she gazed at mists beyond—

---

1. A region in Manchuria, several hundred miles away.

a washed-out rose, a willow gaunt and pale.
    Distraught, she tarried walking back and forth
when from the birthday feast her folks returned.
575 Before they could trade news of health and such,
in burst a mob of bailiffs on all sides.
    With cudgels under arm and swords in hand,
those fiends and monsters rushed around, berserk.
They cangued them both,[2] the old man, his young son—
580 one cruel rope trussed two dear beings up.
Then, like bluebottles buzzing through the house,
they smashed workbaskets, shattered looms to bits.
They grabbed all jewels, fineries, personal things,
scooping the household clean to fill greed's bag.
585   From nowhere woe had struck—who'd caused it all?
Who'd somehow set the snare and sprung the trap?
Upon inquiry it was later learned
some knave who sold raw silk had brought a charge.
Fear gripped the household—cries of innocence
590 shook up the earth, injustice dimmed the clouds.
All day they groveled, begged, and prayed—deaf ears
would hear no plea, harsh hands would spare no blow.
A rope hung each from girders, by his heels—
rocks would have broken, let alone mere men.
595 Their faces spoke sheer pain and fright—this wrong
could they appeal to Heaven far away?
Lawmen behaved that day as is their wont,
wreaking dire havoc just for money's sake.

    By what means could she save her flesh and blood?
600 When evil strikes, you bow to circumstance.
As you must weigh and choose between your love
and filial duty, which will turn the scale?
She put aside all vows of love and troth—
a child first pays the debts of birth and care.
605 Resolved on what to do, she said: "Hands off—
I'll sell myself and Father I'll redeem."
    There was an elderly scrivener surnamed Chung,
a bureaucrat who somehow had a heart.
He witnessed how a daughter proved her love
610 and felt some secret pity for her plight.
Planning to pave this way and clear that path,
he reckoned they would need three hundred liang.
He'd have her kinsmen freed for now, bade her
provide the sum within two days or three.
615   Pity the child, so young and so naïve—
misfortune, like a storm, swooped down on her.
To part from Kim meant sorrow, death in life—

2. A cangue is a wooden yoke, fastened around the neck of a criminal as a punishment.

would she still care for life, much less for love?
A raindrop does not brood on its poor fate;
620   a leaf of grass repays three months of spring.
        Matchmakers were advised of her intent—
brisk rumor spread the tidings near and far.

[*Kieu agrees to a hasty marriage to a middle-aged man named Scholar Ma, who
pays off her debt to Chung. Before the wedding, Kieu instructs her younger sister,
Van, to marry her beloved Kim in her place once he finally returns. Kieu then leaves,
in tears, with Ma.*]

        A carriage, flower-decked, arrived outside
780   with flutes and lutes to bid dear kin part ways.
        She grieved to go, they grieved to stay behind:
tears soaked stone steps as parting tugged their hearts.
        Across a twilit sky dragged sullen clouds—
grasses and branches drooped, all drenched with dew.
785   He led her to an inn and left her there
within four walls, a maiden in her spring.
        The girl felt torn between dire dread and shame—
she'd sadly brood, her heart would ache and ache.
        A rose divine lay fallen in vile hands,
790   once kept from sun or rain for someone's sake:
        "If only I had known I'd sink so low,
I should have let my true love pluck my bud.
        Because I fenced it well from the east wind,
I failed him then and make him suffer now.
795   When we're to meet again, what will be left
of my poor body here to give much hope?
        If I indeed was born to float and drift,
how can a woman live with such a fate?"
        Upon the table lay a knife at hand—
800   she grabbed it, hid it wrapped inside her scarf:
        "Yes, if and when the flood should reach my feet,
this knife may later help decide my life."
        The autumn night wore on, hour after hour—
alone, she mused, half wakeful, half asleep.
805   She did not know that Scholar Ma, the rogue,
had always patronized the haunts of lust.
        The rake had hit a run of blackest luck:
in whoredom our whoremaster sought his bread.
        Now, in a brothel, languished one Dame Tu
810   whose wealth of charms was taxed by creeping age.
        Mere hazard, undesigned, can bring things off:
sawdust and bitter melon met and merged.[3]
        They pooled resources, opening a shop

---

3. Proverbial phrase for mutual cheating by two swindlers.

to sell their painted dolls all through the year.

815 Country and town they scoured for "concubines"
whom they would teach the trade of play and love.
With Heaven lies your fortune, good or ill,
and woe will pick you if you're marked for woe.
Pity a small, frail bit of womankind,

820 a flower sold to board a peddler's boat.
She now was caught in all his bag of tricks:
a paltry bridal gift, some slapdash rites.
He crowed within: "The flag has come to hand!
I view rare jade—it stirs my heart of gold!

825 The kingdom's queen of beauty! Heaven's scent!
One smile of hers is worth pure gold—it's true.
When she gets there, to pluck the maiden bud,
princes and gentlefolk will push and shove.
She'll bring at least three hundred liang, about

830 what I have paid—net profit after that.
A morsel dangles at my mouth—what God
serves up I crave, yet money hate to lose.
A heavenly peach within a mortal's grasp:
I'll bend the branch, pick it, and quench my thirst.

835 How many flower-fanciers on earth
can really tell one flower from the next?
Juice from pomegranate skin and cockscomb blood
will heal it up and lend the virgin look.
In dim half-light some yokel will be fooled:

840 she'll fetch that much, and not one penny less.
If my old broad finds out and makes a scene,
I'll take it like a man, down on my knees!
Besides, it's still a long, long way from home:
if I don't touch her, later she'll suspect."

845 Oh, shame! A pure camellia had to let
the bee explore and probe all ins and outs.
A storm of lust broke forth—it would not spare
the flawless jade, respect the pristine scent.
All this spring night was one bad dream—she woke

850 to lie alone beneath the nuptial torch.
Her tears of silent grief poured down like rain—
she hated him, she loathed herself as much:
"What breed is he, a creature foul and vile?
My body's now a blot on womanhood.

855 What hope is left to cherish after this?
A life that's come to this is life no more."
By turns she cursed her fate, she moaned her lot.
She grabbed the knife and thought to kill herself.
She mulled it over: "If I were alone,

860 it wouldn't matter—I've two loved ones, though.
If trouble should develop afterwards,
an inquest might ensue and work their doom.

Perhaps my plight will ease with passing time.
Sooner or later, I'm to die just once."
865   While she kept tossing reasons back and forth,
a rooster shrilly crowed outside the wall.
The watchtower horn soon blared through morning mists,
so Ma gave orders, making haste to leave.
Oh, how it rends the heart, the parting hour,
870   when horse begins to trot and wheels to jolt!

She traveled far, far into the unknown.
Bridges stark white with frost, woods dark with clouds.
Reeds huddling close while blew the cold north wind:
an autumn sky for her and her alone.

[*Taken to a brothel in a distant town, Kieu stabs herself, but survives. She tries to escape but is caught and beaten, then forced to work as a prostitute. She does so for several months, with no hope of release.*]

1275   Now, as a brothel patron, came a man:
Ky Tam of the Thuc clan, a well-read breed.
He'd followed Father leaving Hsi in Ch'ang
to open at Lin-tzu a trading shop.
Kieu's fame as queen of beauty had reached him—
1280   he called and left his card in her boudoir.
Behind the tasseled drapes he faced the flower:
his fancy relished each of all her charms.
The young camellia, shimmering on its stem,
would glow still brighter with each fresh spring shower!
1285   Man and girl, girl and man in fevered clasp:
on a spring night, how can one quell the heart?
Of course, when two kin spirits meet, one tie
soon binds them in a knot none can yank loose.
They'd tryst and cling together night or day.
1290   What had begun as lust soon turned to love.
It chanced that, by a stroke of timely luck,
his father went away to journey home.
And more bewitched than ever, our young man
would often see his darling these spring days.
1295   On wind-swept balconies, in moon-washed yards,
they'd sip rare liquor, improvise linked verse.
With incense burned at dawn, with tea at noon,
they'd play chess games, perform duets on lutes.
One dizzy round of pleasures caught them both—
1300   they knew each other's moods, grew more attached.

[*Kieu has misgivings—young Thuc is married back home—but she agrees to let him ransom her from the brothel, and they begin living together. Kieu urges young Thuc to openly make her his concubine and tell his wife, but he fears his wife's jealousy and keeps putting it off.*]

As lovers joined their lives beneath one roof,
their love grew deeper, deeper than the sea.
Like fire and incense, mutual passion burned—
her jade-and-lotus beauty gleamed and glowed.

1385   For half a year they lived as intimates.
Now, in the courtyard, planes mixed gold with jade.
Along the hedge, frost-hardy mums peeped out.
And lo, the father came a-riding back.

He stormed and thundered in his towering wrath—
1390   filled with concern, he thought to split the pair.
Determined, he passed judgment straightaway:
in her old whorehouse he'd put back the whore.

The father's verdict was clear-cut, forthright—
yet, making bold, the son entreated him:
1395   "I know my many crimes—if thunderbolts
or hatchet blows strike me, I'll die content.
But now my hand has dipped in indigo:[4]
a fool grown wise still can't undo what's done.
Even if I had her for just one day,
1400   who'd hold a lute and then rip off its strings?
If you will not relent and grant me grace,
I'd rather lose my life than play her false."

Those stubborn words aroused the old man's bile,
so at the hall of law he lodged complaint.
1405   Over a peaceful earth the waves now surged—
the prefect sent a warrant for the pair.
They walked behind the sheriff, then at court
they fell upon their knees, still side by side.

They raised their eyes and saw an iron mask—
1410   the prefect, strutting power, spoke harsh words:
"Young wastrel, you have had your foolish fling—
and she, that slut, is nothing but a cheat.
A cast-off rose with all its scent gone stale,
she's put on rouge and powder, duping boors.
1415   To judge the state of things from his complaint,
it's out of joint with either one of you.
I shall uphold the law and try the case.
There are two paths—you're free to opt for which:
either I'll mete out punishment by the book
1420   or to the whorehouse I'll remand the whore."

"Once and for all my mind's made up!" she cried.
"The spider's web shall not catch me again.
Muddy or clear, it's still my life to live.
I shall endure the thunder of the law!"
1425   The judge declared: "The law be carried out!"
A peony in shackles, cuffs, and cangue.

---

4. An indelible dye.

Resigned, she dared not cry her innocence—
tears stained her cheeks and pain knit tight her brows.
Down on a floor of dust and mud, her face
1430   a tarnished glass, her frame a thin plum branch.
    Oh, poor young Thuc! Consider his sad plight:
he watched her from afar, his entrails torn.
"She suffers so because of me!" he moaned.
"Had I but listened, she'd be spared this wrong.
1435   How ever can a shallow mind think deep?
So now I've caused her all this grief and shame."
    The judge had overheard young Thuc's lament—
by pity moved, he asked for more details.
At once the lover sobbed his story out,
1440   recounting all she'd said when he proposed:
"She pondered what might happen, soon or late,
aware that she herself could come to this.
Because I chose to take it all in hand,
I've brought this woe on her—it's my own fault."
1445   The judge felt sorry when he heard those words—
he smoothed his brow and figured some way out.
"If what you've told me is the truth," he said,
"this harlot, after all, knows right from wrong."
"Though just a lowly woman," Thuc went on,
1450   "she's learned to ply the brush and scribble verse."
"But she must be perfection!" laughed the judge.
"Well, write a piece, The Cangue, and strut your art."
The girl complied—she raised the brush and wrote,
then laid the sheet of paper on his desk.
1455   "It tops the height of T'ang!" he cried in praise.[5]
"All gold on earth can't buy her gifts and charms.
The man of parts has met the woman fair:
a finer match could Chou and Ch'en have bred?
Let's put an end to all this fight and feud:
1460   why sow discord and break a love duet?
When people come before a court of law,
inside the rules of justice mercy dwells.
Your son's own mate belongs within your clan:
forget your own displeasure and forgive."
1465   A wedding he decreed—wind-borne, took off
the bridal carriage, torches raced the stars.
A band of piping flutes and throbbing drums
led bride and groom to their connubial niche.
Old Thuc admired her virtues, prized her gifts—
1470   from him no more harsh word or stormy scene.
Lilies and orchids bathed their home in scents
as bitter sorrow turned to sweeter love.

---

5. The T'ang dynasty (618–906) was the peak period of Chinese poetry.

Time flew amidst delights of wine or chess:
peach red had waned, now lotus green would wax.

1475 Behind their curtains, on a silent night,
she felt misgivings, told him what she felt:
"Since this frail girl found her support in you,
geese followed swallows—almost gone, a year.
Yet not a day's brought news from your own home.

1480 With your new bride, you've cooled toward your old mate.
It seems, upon reflection, rather odd:
from talk and gossip who could have saved us?
The mistress of your household—so I've heard—
does what is proper, says what is correct.

1485 Oh, how I dread all such uncommon souls!
It's hard to plumb the ocean's pits and depths.
We've lived together for these full twelve months—
from her we could not have concealed the fact.
If for so long you've got no news of her,

1490 then something must be brewing in that hush.
Now go back home immediately, I beg you:
you'll please her and we'll know what's in her mind.
If you drag out this game of hide-and-seek
and put off telling her, it just won't work."

1495 He heard those words of counsel, said with calm,
and braced himself to think of going home.
Next day he spoke to Father of his plans—
the old man, too, urged him to make the trip.

* * *

Why tell what our wayfaring man went through?
Let's talk about the mistress of his hearth.
Known as Miss Hoan, she wore a great clan name:

1530 her father ruled the Civil Office Board.
On happy winds of chance Thuc had met her,
and they had tied the nuptial knot long since.
Living above reproach, Miss Hoan could wield
the surest hand in catching one at fault.

1535 His garden boasted now a fresh-blown rose—
so she had heard from every mouth but his.
The fire of wrath kept smoldering in her breast
against the knave whose fickle heart had roamed:
"If only he'd confessed, told me the truth,

1540 I might have favored her with my good grace.
I'd be a fool to lose my stately calm
and gain the stigma of a jealous shrew.
But he's thought fit to pull his boyish prank
and hide his open secret—what a farce!

1545 He's fancied distance keeps me unaware.
Let's hide and seek—I too shall play his game.
I entertain no worry on this score:
the ant's inside the cup—where can it crawl?

I'll make them loathe and shun each other's sight.
1550   I'll crush her so she cannot rear her head.
I'll rub the spectacle in his bare face
and make the traitor feel my iron hand."
      She locked her anger deep inside her heart
and let all rumors breeze right past her ears.

[*While Thuc is visiting Miss Hoan, she sends men to Lin-tzu to kidnap Kieu; they make it appear that she has died in a fire. Kieu is taken to Miss Hoan's family's home and forced to work under the new name of Flower the Slave. Thuc returns to Lin-tzu to find her supposedly dead; while he stays there in mourning, Miss Hoan has Kieu brought to work in her own household. Kieu still doesn't know who her employer is.*]

      While months reeled on, with worries close at hand,
1790   could Thuc suspect what happened far away?
Since from Lin-tzu his lovebird had flown off,
an empty chamber kept a lonesome man.
He saw her eyebrow in the crescent moon,
breathed hints of old perfume and ached for her.
1795   Just as the lotus wilts, the mums bloom forth—
time softens grief, and winter turns to spring.
Where could he find her he had once so loved?
He called it fate and duller throbbed his pain.
      Nostalgia woke some yearning in his breast
1800   and, sick for home, he made his long way back.[6]
She met him at the gate, she gushed with joy.
Once they had traded news of health and such,
she had all drapes rolled up; then she bade Kieu
appear and greet the lord on his return.
1805   As Kieu came out, she faltered at each step,
for from a distance she perceived the truth:
"Unless the sun and lights have tricked my eyes,
who else but my own Thuc is sitting there?
So now I must confront the blatant fact:
1810   beyond all doubt, she's caught me in her trap.
Could such a hellish plot be hatched on earth?
Why has mankind so erred and bred a fiend?
As bride and groom we two were duly joined—
she splits us into slave and master now.
1815   The face displays sweet smiles, but deep inside
the heart will scheme to kill without a knife.
We stand as far apart as sky and earth:
alas, what now to say, what now to do?"
      She grew bewildered gazing at his face,
1820   her heart a raveled knot of silken threads.
Too awed to disobey, she bowed her head

---

6. To his wife, Miss Hoan.

and prostrated herself upon the floor.
The husband was dismayed, at his wits' end:
"Woe's me! But isn't she right here, my Kieu?
1825   What cause or reason led her to this plight?
Alas, we're caught—and I know by whose hands!"
        Lest he'd betray himself, he'd breathe no word
but could not stop his tears from spilling out.
His lady fixed him with a glare and asked:
1830   "You just came home—why look so woebegone?"
"I just took off my mourning," answered he.
"I think of my lost mother and still grieve."
She sang his praises: "What a loving son!
Let's drink to your return, drown autumn gloom."
1835   Husband and wife exchanged repeated toasts
while Kieu stood by and from the bottle poured.
The lady would berate her, finding fault,
would make her kneel and offer up each drink.
He'd act like one demented more and more
1840   as tears kept flowing while the liquor ebbed.
Averting eyes, he'd talk and laugh by fits;
then, pleading drunk, he'd try a safe retreat.
"You slave," the lady snapped, "persuade the lord
to drain his cup or I shall have you thrashed."
1845   Grief bruised his vitals, panic struck his soul—
he took the proffered cup and quaffed the gall.
The lady talked and laughed as though half drunk—
to crown the evening, she devised a sport.
She said: "That slave has mastered all the arts—
1850   she'll play the lute, treat you to some good piece."
        All dizzied, in a daze, Kieu bowed and sat
before the thin gauze screen to tune the lute.
Four strings together seemed to cry and moan
in tones that wrenched him who was feasting there.
1855   Both heard the selfsame voice of silk and wood—
she smiled and gloated while he wept within.
When he could check his welling tears no more,
he stooped his head and tried to wipe them off.
Again the mistress shouted at the slave:
1860   "Why play that doleful tune and kill our joy?
Don't you give thought to anything you do?
I'll punish you if you distress the lord."
He waxed more frantic still—to lay the storm,
he'd hurriedly attempt a laugh, a grin.
1865   The waterclock now marked the night's third watch—
the lady eyed their faces, looking pleased.
She gloried in her soul: "This sweet revenge
makes up for grief that festered in my breast."
But shrunk with shame and choked with rage inside,
1870   he nursed a wound that rankled more and more.

To share one pillow they regained their niche—
Kieu huddled by her lamp, awake all night
"So now she has unveiled her own true face.
How weird, that jealous humor in her blood!
1875 To split two lovebirds, she contrived it all—
she'd part and tear us from each other's eyes.
Now we're a gulf, a world apart—she's all,
I'm nothing now; she's always right, I'm wrong.
So gently it holds us, her iron hand!
1880 How can we struggle free and save our love?
Frail woman that I was, I tripped and fell:
shall I be rescued whole from furious waves?"
Alone, she brooded far into the night—
as ebbed the lampion's oil, her tears still flowed.

1885   Kieu served there day and night. Once, face to face,
the mistress asked the servant how she fared.
She chose her words with care, gave this reply:
"I sometimes sorrow for my lot in life."
The lady turned to Thuc, requesting him:
1890 "Please grill the slave, pry loose the facts from her."
          He felt all torn and rent within his heart,
for he could not confess nor bear the scene.
Afraid he'd draw more outrage on her head,
he ventured, in soft tones, to question her.
1895 Head bowed, the girl knelt down upon the floor
and of her past wrote out a brief account.
Submitted to the lady, it was read—
it seemed to touch some chord inside her heart.
Forthwith she handed it to him and said:
1900 "We should admire her gifts, deplore her woes.
Had fortune favored her with wealth and rank,
she could have graced a palace cast in gold.
A woman bobs upon the sea of life:
so blessed with talent, yet so cursed by fate!"
1905   "Indeed, you speak the utter truth," he said.
"Misfortune's never spared a single rose.
The rule has held since ages out of mind:
show mercy, treat her with a gentler hand."
          The lady said: "In her report she begged
1910 to make her home within the Void's great gate.[7]
Well, I'll be pleased to grant her that one wish
and help her break the cycle of her woes.
There in our garden is the Kuan-yin shrine,
with everblooming lotus, tall bo tree,[8]
1915 with many plants and flowers, rocks and pools:

---

7. The door to nirvana, a general name for Buddhism.
8. The lotus and bo tree are central symbols of Buddhist

enlightenment. Kuan-yin is the Buddhist Goddess of
Mercy, Listener to the World's Cries.

let her go there to tend the shrine and pray."
The dawn's first glow was glimmering in the skies—
they bore five offerings, incense, flowers, and such,
led Kieu to Buddha's temple: there she pledged
1920   to live by all three vows and five commands.[9]
For a cassock she doffed the slave's blue smock,
and as a nun she now was called Pure Spring.
She was to light the temple morn and eve,
while Spring and Autumn served as altar maids.
1925   So Kieu took refuge in the garden, near
the Purple Grove, far from the world's red dust.
What could she still expect of human ties?

[*Thuc makes a secret visit to Kieu, and they admit their mutual grief. To their shock, Miss Hoan is nearby and overhears them. Sure that some new revenge is brewing, Kieu flees. She ends up with a supposedly compassionate man, but he hands her over to another brothel, where she once again becomes a sought-after beauty.*]

2165   Cool breeze, clear moon—her nights were going round
when from the far frontier a guest turned up.
A tiger's beard, a swallow's jaw, and brows
as thick as silkworms—he stood broad and tall.
A towering hero, he outfought all foes
2170   with club or fist and knew all arts of war.
Between the earth and heaven he lived free:
he was Tu Hai, a native of Yueh-tung.
Plying his oar, he roved the streams and lakes
with sword and lute upon his shoulders slung.
2175   In town for fun, he heard loud praise of Kieu—
love for a woman bent a hero's will.
He brought his calling card to her boudoir—
thus eyes met eyes and heart encountered heart.
"Two kindred souls have joined," Tu said to Kieu.
2180   "We're not those giddy fools who play at love.
For long I've heard them rave about your charms,
but none's won favor yet in your clear eyes.
How often have you lucked upon a *man*?
Why bother with caged birds or fish in pots?"
2185   She said: "My lord, you're overpraising me.
For who am I to slight this man or that?
Within I crave the touchstone for the gold—
but whom can I turn to and give my heart?
As for all those who come and go through here,
2190   am I allowed to sift real gold from brass?"
"What lovely words you utter!" Tu exclaimed.

---

9. She is taking the vows of a nun and vowing to keep the commandments against killing, stealing, lewdness, lying, and the drinking of alcohol.

"They call to mind the tale of Prince P'ing-yuan.[1]
Come here and take a good, close look at me
to see if I deserve a bit of trust."

2195   "It's large, your heart," she said. "One of these days,
Chin-yang[2] shall see a dragon in the clouds.
If you care for this weed, this lowly flower,
tomorrow may I count on your good grace?"
        Well pleased, he nodded saying with a laugh:

2200   "Through life how many know what moves one's soul?
Those eyes be praised that, keen and worldly-wise,
can see the hero hid in common dust!
Your words prove you discern me from the rest—
we'll sit together when I sit on high."

2205   Two minds at one, two hearts in unison—
unbidden, love will seek those meant for love.
        Now he approached a go-between—through her
he paid some hundred liang for Kieu's release.
They picked a quiet spot, built their love nest:

2210   a sumptuous bed and curtains decked with gods.
The hero chose a phoenix as his mate;
the beauty found a dragon for her mount.

[*Tu Hai embarks on a series of battles, emerging in control of a wide region, then makes Kieu his formal bride. Once they are married, Kieu tells him her full life story, and he summons the people who have dealt with her, to receive her judgment. Kieu pardons the weak Thuc and even his (now contrite) wife Miss Hoan, but has Scholar Ma and the other pimps and bawds executed. Tu Hai then resumes his wars of conquest.*]

        Bamboos split fast; tiles slip, soon fall apart:
2440   his martial might now thundered far and wide.
In his own corner he installed his court
for peace or war and cut the realm in two.
Time after time he stormed across the land
and trampled down five strongholds in the South.

2445   He fought and honed his sword on wind and dust,
scorning those racks for coats, those sacks for rice.
He stalked and swaggered through his border fief,
with no less stature than a prince, a king.
Who dared oppose his flag, dispute his sway?

2450   For five years, by the sea, he reigned sole lord.
        There was an eminent province governor,
Lord Ho Ton Hien, who plied a statesman's craft.
The emperor sent him off with special powers
to quell revolt and rule the borderland.

---

1. Kieu's appeal makes Tu Hai think of the prince P'ing-yüan, who found great loyalty in a low-born subordinate.

2. Location where the founder of the T'ang dynasty ascended the throne.

2455   He knew Tu Hai would prove a gallant foe—
but then, in all his plans, Kieu had a voice.
He camped his troops and feigned to seek a truce,
sending an envoy with rich gifts for Tu.
For Kieu some presents, too: two waiting maids,
2460   a thousand pounds of finest jade and gold.
     When his headquarters got the plea for peace,
Lord Tu himself felt gnawing doubts and thought,
"My own two hands have built this realm—at will,
I've roamed the sea of Ch'u, the streams of Wu.
2465   If I turn up at court, bound hand and foot,
what will become of me, surrendered man?
Why let them swaddle me in robes and skirts?
Why play a duke so as to cringe and crawl?
Had I not better rule my march domain?
2470   For what can they all do against my might?
At pleasure I stir heaven and shake earth—
I come and go, I bow my head to none."
     But trust in people moved Kieu's guileless heart:
sweet words and lavish gifts could make her yield.
2475   "A fern that floats on water," she now thought,
"I've wandered long enough, endured enough.
Let's swear allegiance to the emperor's throne—
we'll travel far up fortune's royal road.
Public and private ends will both be met,
2480   and soon I may arrange to go back home.
A lord's own consort, head erect, I'll walk
and make my parents glow with pride and joy.
Then, both the state above, my home below,
I'll have well served as liege and daughter both.
2485   Is that not better than to float and drift,
a skiff the waves and waters hurl about?"
     When they discussed the wisest course to take,
she sought to win him over to her views:
"The emperor's munificence," she would say,
2490   "has showered on the world like drenching rain.
His virtues and good works have kept the peace,
placing each subject deeply in his debt.
Since you rose up in arms, dead men's white bones
have piled head-high along the Wayward Stream.[3]
2495   Why should you leave an ill repute behind?
For ages who has ever praised Huang Ch'ao?[4]
Why not accept high post and princely purse?
Is there some surer avenue to success?"
     Her words struck home: he listened, giving ground.
2500   He dropped all schemes for war and sued for peace.

---

3. River with a shifting riverbed, scene of bloody battles between the Chinese and the Tartars.

4. A failed scholar, whose unsuccessful rebellion in 884 seriously weakened the T'ang dynasty.

The envoy he received with pomp and rites—
he pledged to lay down arms, disband his troops.
    Trusting the truce they'd sworn below the walls,
Lord Tu let flags hang loose, watch-drums go dead.
2505   He slackened all defense—imperial spies
observed his camp and learned of its true state.
Lord Ho conceived a ruse to snatch this chance:
behind a screen of gifts he'd poise his troops.
The flying flag of friendship led the van,
2510   with gifts in front and weapons hid behind.
    Lord Tu suspected nothing, caught off guard—
in cap and gown, he waited at the gate.
Afield, Lord Ho now gave the secret cue:
flags on all sides unfurled and guns fired off.
2515   The fiercest tiger, taken unawares,
will lick the dust and meet an abject end.
Now doomed, Tu fought his one last fight on earth
to show them all a soldier's dauntless heart.
When his brave soul left him to join the gods,
2520   he still stood on his feet amidst his foes.
His body, firm as rock and hard as bronze,
who in the whole wide world could shake or move?

* * *

2565   The troops proclaimed their victory with a feast.
Strings twanged, flutes piped—all reveled and caroused.
The lord forced Kieu to wait on him—half drunk,
he bade her play the lute she'd daily played.
It moaned like wind and rain—five fingertips
2570   dripped blood upon four strings. When gibbons howl,
cicadas wail, they cannot match such grief.
Ho listened, knitting brows and shedding tears.
He asked: "What are you playing there? It sounds
like all the world's dark sorrows rolled in one."
2575   "My lord, this tune's called *Cruel Fate*," she said.
"I wrote it for the lute when I was young,
in days long gone. But now, of cruel fate
you have a victim under your own eyes."
    Entranced, he heard her; spellbound, he watched her.
2580   O miracle, love disturbed an iron mask!
"We're destined for each other," said the lord.
"Let me restring your lute and make it whole."
"I am a fallen woman," answered she.
"My conscience bears a person's wrongful death.
2585   And what's there left of me, a faded flower?
My heartstrings broke just like Hsiao-lin's lute strings.[5]
Pity a woman—I'll bless my fortune if

---

5. Hsiao Lin was a concubine of an ancient king of Ch'i; forced to wed another man against her will, she wrote a poem comparing her broken heart to the broken strings of her lute.

I see the elms back home before I die."
Flushed with success, Lord Ho had drunk too much—
2590   but he regained his senses as light dawned.
He thought, "I am a noble of the realm,
whom both my betters and the rabble watch.
Does it become a lord to toy with love?
Now, how should I untangle this affair?"
2595   So at the morning levee, he resolved
to carry his expedient out forthwith.
Who dare protest the word a mandarin speaks?
Kieu was compelled to wed a tribal chief.
How wayward you can be, O Marriage God,
2600   at random tying couples with your threads!
The bridal carriage took her to his boat—
curtains came down, the nuptial lamp lit up.

Willow all withered, peach blossom all seared—
her freshness was all gone, not one spark left.
2605   Let waves and sands entomb her self, annul
her parents' love and care, her gifts of mind.
Mere flotsam seaborne toward the world's far bounds,
where could she find a grave and rest her bones?

[*Distraught at having advised Tu Hai to his betrayal, Kieu throws herself into a river to drown. Carried far downstream, she is found by fishermen, who leave her at the hermitage of an old nun, Giac Duyen, who had met her before and had a premonition they would meet again. Kieu now embraces a nun's life with joy. The scene shifts to the home of Kieu's first beloved, Kim, who has followed her wishes and married her sister, Van. Years have passed with no news of Kieu, but then Van—now a prominent government official—is posted to the region of Lin-tzu, where Kieu now is. Van has a dream in which Kieu appears to her. Sure that she must be nearby, they make inquiries, and are told she has drowned. As they set up a memorial stone at the river, Giac Duyen happens by and reveals that Kieu is living with her. Kim, Van, and her aged parents eagerly make their way along the overgrown path to the old nun's hermitage.*]

All knelt and bowed their thanks to old Giac Duyen,
then in a group they followed on her heels.
They cut and cleared their way through reed and rush,
their loving hearts half doubting yet her word.
3005   By twists and turns they edged along the shore,
pushed past that jungle, reached the Buddha's shrine.
In a loud voice, the nun Giac Duyen called Kieu,
and from an inner room she hurried out.
She glanced and saw her folks—they all were here:
3010   Father looked still quite strong, and Mother spry;
both sister Van and brother Quan grown up;
and over there was Kim, her love of yore.
Could she believe this moment, what it seemed?

Was she now dreaming open-eyed, awake?
3015   Tear-pearls dropped one by one and damped her smock—
she felt such joy and grief, such grief and joy.
     She cast herself upon her mother's knees
and, weeping, told of all she had endured.
"Since I set out to wander through strange lands,
3020   a wave-tossed fern, some fifteen years have passed.
I sought to end it in the river's mud—
who could have hoped to see you all on earth?"
     The parents held her hands, admired her face:
that face had not much changed since she left home.
3025   The moon, the flower, lashed by wind and rain
for all that time, had lost some of its glow.
What scale could ever weigh their happiness?
Present and past, so much they talked about!
The two young ones kept asking this or that
3030   while Kim looked on, his sorrow turned to joy.
Before the Buddha's altar all knelt down
and for Kieu's resurrection offered thanks.
     At once they ordered sedans decked with flowers—
old Vuong bade Kieu be carried home with them.
3035   "I'm nothing but a fallen flower," she said.
"I drank of gall and wormwood half my life.
I thought to die on waves beneath the clouds—
how could my heart nurse hopes to see this day?
Yet I've survived and met you all again,
3040   and slaked the thirst that long has parched my soul.
This cloister's now my refuge in the wilds—
to live with grass and trees befits my age.
I'm used to salt and greens in Dhyana fare;[6]
I've grown to love the drab of Dhyana garb.
3045   Within my heart the fire of lust is quenched—
why should I roll again in worldly dust?
What good is that, a purpose half achieved?
To nunhood vowed, I'll stay here till the end.
I owe to her who saved me sea-deep debts—
3050   how can I cut my bonds with her and leave?"
     Old Vuong exclaimed: "Other times, other tides!
Even a saint must bow to circumstance.
You worship gods and Buddhas—who'll discharge
a daughter's duties, keep a lover's vows?
3055   High Heaven saved your life—we'll build a shrine
and have our Reverend come; live there near us."
Heeding her father's word, Kieu had to yield:
she took her leave of cloister and old nun.
     The group returned to Kim's own yamen[7] where,

6. The simple fare of monks and nuns.   7. A government official's residence.

3060   for their reunion, they all held a feast.
After mum wine instilled a mellow mood,
Van rose and begged to air a thought or two;
"It's Heaven's own design that lovers meet,
so Kim and Kieu did meet and swear their troth.

3065   Then, over peaceful earth wild billows swept,
and in my sister's place I wedded him.
Amber and mustard seed, lodestone and pin!
Besides, 'when blood is spilt, the gut turns soft.'[8]
Day after day, we hoped and prayed for Kieu

3070   with so much love and grief these fifteen years.
But now the mirror cracked is whole again:
wise Heaven's put her back where she belongs.
She still loves him and, luckily, still has him—
still shines the same old moon both once swore by.

3075   The tree still bears some three or seven plums,
the peach stays fresh—it's time to tie the knot!"
     Kieu brushed her sister's speech aside and said:
"Why now retell a tale of long ago?
We once did pledge our troth, but since those days,

3080   my life has been exposed to wind and rain.
I'd die of shame discussing what's now past—
let those things flow downstream and out to sea!"
     "A curious way to put it!" Kim cut in.
"Whatever you may feel, your oath remains.

3085   A vow of troth is witnessed by the world,
by earth below and heaven far above.
Though things may change and stars may shift their course,
sworn pledges must be kept in life or death.
Does fate, which brought you back, oppose our love?

3090   We two are one—why split us in two halves?"
     "A home where love and concord reign," Kieu said,
"whose heart won't yearn for it? But I believe
that to her man a bride should bring the scent
of a close bud, the shape of a full moon.

3095   It's priceless, chastity—by nuptial torch,
am I to blush for what I'll offer you?
Misfortune struck me—since that day the flower
fell prey to bees and butterflies, ate shame.
For so long lashed by rain and swept by wind,

3100   a flower's bound to fade, a moon to wane.
My cheeks were once two roses—what's now left?
My life is done—how can it be remade?
How dare I, boldfaced, soil with worldly filth
the homespun costume of a virtuous wife?

3105   You bear a constant love for me, I know—

8. Linked by blood, family members share each other's pain; they had been drawn together as inevitably as an iron pin is drawn to a magnet or a mustard seed to a piece of amber.

but where to hide my shame by bridal light?
From this day on I'll shut my chamber door:
though I will take no vows, I'll live a nun.
If you still care for what we both once felt,
3110   let's turn it into friendship—let's be friends.
Why speak of marriage with its red silk thread?
It pains my heart and further stains my life."
     "How skilled you are in spinning words!" Kim said.
"You have your reasons—others have their own.
3115   Among those duties falling to her lot,
a woman's chastity means many things.
For there are times of ease and times of stress:
in crisis, must one rigid rule apply?
True daughter, you upheld a woman's role:
3120   what dust or dirt could ever sully you?
Heaven grants us this hour: now from our gate
all mists have cleared; on high, clouds roll away.
The faded flower's blooming forth afresh,
the waning moon shines more than at its full.
3125   What is there left to doubt? Why treat me like
another Hsiao, a passerby ignored?"[9]
     He argued, pleaded, begged—she heard him through.
Her parents also settled on his plans.
Outtalked, she could no longer disagree:
3130   she hung her head and yielded, stifling sighs.
     They held a wedding-feast—bright candles lit
all flowers, set aglow the red silk rug.
Before their elders groom and bride bowed low—
all rites observed, they now were man and wife.
3135   In their own room they traded toasts, still shy
of their new bond, yet moved by their old love.
Since he, a lotus sprout, first met with her,
a fresh peach bud, fifteen full years had fled.
To fall in love, to part, to reunite—
3140   both felt mixed grief and joy as rose the moon.
     The hour was late—the curtain dropped its fringe:
under the light gleamed her peach-blossom cheeks.
Two lovers met again—out of the past,
a bee, a flower constant in their love.
3145   "I've made my peace with my own fate," she said.
"What can this cast-off body be good for?
I thought of your devotion to our past—
to please you, I went through those wedding rites.
But how ashamed I felt in my own heart,
3150   lending a brazen front to all that show!

9. After the wife of a commoner named Hsiao was abducted and married to a powerful official, she refused to acknowledge her former husband in the street.

Don't go beyond the outward marks of love—
perhaps, I might then look you in the face.
But if you want to get what they all want,
glean scent from dirt, or pluck a wilting flower,
3155   then we'll flaunt filth, put on a foul display,
and only hate, not love, will then remain.
When you make love and I feel only shame,
then rank betrayal's better than such love.
If you must give your clan a rightful heir,
3160   you have my sister—there's no need for me.
What little chastity I may have saved,
am I to fling it under trampling feet?
More tender feelings pour from both our hearts—
why toy and crumple up a faded flower?"
3165   "An oath bound us together," he replied.
"We split, like fish to sea and bird to sky.
Through your long exile how I grieved for you!
Breaking your troth, you must have suffered so.
We loved each other, risked our lives, braved death—
3170   now we two meet again, still deep in love.
The willow in mid-spring still has green leaves—
I thought you still attached to human love.
But no more dust stains your clear mirror now:
your vow can't but increase my high regard.
3175   If I long searched the sea for my lost pin,
it was true love, not lust, that urged me on.
We're back together now, beneath one roof:
to live in concord, need two share one bed?"
        Kieu pinned her hair and straightened up her gown,
3180   then knelt to touch her head in gratitude:
"If ever my soiled body's cleansed of stains,
I'll thank a gentleman, a noble soul.
The words you spoke came from a kindred heart:
no truer empathy between two souls.
3185   A home, a refuge—what won't you give me?
My honor lives again as of tonight."
        Their hands unclasped, then clasped and clasped again—
now he esteemed her, loved her all the more.
They lit another candle up, refilled
3190   the incense urn, then drank to their new joy.
His old desire for her came flooding back—
he softly asked about her luting skill.
        "Those strings of silk entangled me," she said,
"in sundry woes which haven't ceased till now.
3195   Alas, what's done regrets cannot undo—
but I'll obey your wish just one more time."
        Her elfin fingers danced and swept the strings—
sweet strains made waves with curls of scentwood smoke.
Who sang this hymn to life and peace on earth?

3200   Was it a butterfly or Master Chuang?[1]
        And who poured forth this rhapsody of love?
        The king of Shu or just a cuckoo-bird?[2]
        Clear notes like pearls dropped in a moon-lit bay.
        Warm notes like crystals of new Lan-t'ien jade.
3205   His ears drank in all five tones of the scale—
        all sounds which stirred his heart and thrilled his soul.
        "Whose hand is playing that old tune?" he asked.
        "What sounded once so sad now sounds so gay!
        It's from within that joy or sorrow comes—
3210   have bitter days now set and sweet ones dawned?"
        "This pleasant little pastime," answered she,
        "once earned me grief and woe for many years.
        For you my lute just sang its one last song—
        henceforth, I'll roll its strings and play no more."
3215   The secrets of their hearts were flowing still
        when cocks crowed up the morning in the east.
        Kim spoke, told all about their private pact.
        All marveled at her wish and lauded her—
        a woman of high mind, not some coquette
3220   who'd with her favors skip from man to man.
            Of love and friendship they fulfilled both claims—
        they shared no bed but joys of lute and verse.
        Now they sipped wine, now played a game of chess,
        admiring flowers, waiting for the moon.
3225   Their wishes all came true since fate so willed,
        and of two lovers marriage made two friends.
            As pledged, they built a temple on a hill,
        then sent a trusted man to fetch the nun.
        When he got there, he found doors shut and barred—
3230   he saw a weed-grown rooftop, moss-filled cracks.
        She'd gone to gather simples,° he was told: *herbs*
        the cloud had flown, the crane had fled—but where?
        For old times' sake, Kieu kept the temple lit,
        its incense candles burning night and day.
3235   The twice-blessed home enjoyed both weal and wealth.
        Kim climbed the office ladder year by year.
        Van gave him many heirs: a stooping tree,
        a yardful of sophoras and cassia shrubs.[3]
        In rank or riches who could rival them?
3240   Their garden throve, won glory for all times.

            This we have learned: with Heaven rest all things.
        Heaven appoints each human to a place.
        If doomed to roll in dust, we'll roll in dust;

1. In the Daoist classic *Chuang Tzu,* Chuang dreams he is a butterfly but then wonders whether in fact a butterfly is dreaming it is a man.
2. Wang-ti, King of Shu, carried on an adulterous affair with the wife of his minister, then fled in disgrace and turned into a cuckoo.
3. A "stooping tree" is a first-ranked wife; the ornamental shrubs are her children.

we'll sit on high when destined for high seats.

3245   Does Heaven ever favor anyone,
bestowing both rare talent and good luck?
In talent take no overweening pride,
for talent and disaster form a pair.[4]
Our karma[5] we must carry as our lot—
3250   let's stop decrying Heaven's whims and quirks.
Inside ourselves there lies the root of good:
the heart outweighs all talents on this earth.

    May these crude words, culled one by one and strung,
beguile an hour or two of your long night.

✌

RESONANCE

Che Lan Vien: Thoughts on Nguyen[1]

Born into those foul times of dusk and dust,
you reached and touched no soul mate by your side.
Your sorrow matched the fate of humankind:
Kieu spoke your thoughts and crystallized your life.

5   Kings rose and fell—the poem still abides.
You fought and won your feats on waves of words.
You planted stakes in the Bach-dang of time:[2]
our language and the moon forever shine.

Tam raised her goby fish in a dark well—[3]
10   you nursed and loved the idiom scholars scorned.
But let a reader call: some line of *Kieu*
will from the well rise like a drop of blood.

All storms of life created you—their pearl.
Alas, a pearl is wont to shun the world.
15   You ushered in the age through your strait gate:
the crushing of Ch'ing troops you left outside.

Why borrow foreign scenes? Our land flows not
with one Ch'ien-t'ang but many fateful streams.[4]
Why split yourself? Nguyen Du, To Nhu, Thanh Hien:[5]
20   the tears in Kieu merge all three into one.

---

4. The word for "talent" (*tai*) sounds like "misfortune" (*tai*).
5. Destiny across successive lives.
1. Translated by Huynh Sanh Thong. Che Lan Vien (pen name of Phan Ngoc Hoan, 1920–1989), was a prominent poet of Vietnam's struggle for independence from France. Under colonial rule, which ended in 1954, Che Lan Vien couldn't publish poems of open opposition, and so like Nguyen Du before him, he often wrote of struggles against China in the medieval period. His "Thoughts on Nguyen" shows how Nguyen's heroine Kieu has been seen as a stand-in for the poet himself, as well as for Vietnam as a whole.

2. The tidal Bach-dang River in northern Vietnam was the site of several victories against Chinese invaders in the 9th through 12th centuries. The Vietnamese would plant sharp stakes in the riverbed just below the high-water mark, and lure Chinese war boats onto them.
3. An orphan, Tam raised a goby fish as her only friend; it was then killed by her wicked stepmother, and when Tam came and called for her fish, only a clot of blood rose to the surface.
4. The Ch'ien-t'ang is the river from which Kieu is rescued at the end of the tale.
5. To Nhu and Thanh Hien were pen names of Nguyen Du.

Need we one century more to feel for Nguyen?[6]
Mourning our nightfalls, we soon grieve for his.
We love kings' calls to arms, yet we shall not
forget those frost-white reeds along Kieu's road.

Anna Letitia Barbauld
1743–1825

What was the result, in the early nineteenth century, when a woman claimed to speak for and
about her nation? Women writers were happily conceded domestic topics like childhood and
household. Could they escape the sphere of domesticity and reflect instead on wider themes,
like the present and future role of their nation on the world stage? The experience of Anna Letitia Barbauld is instructive.

Superbly educated in the rich culture of English Dissent—the schools, churches, and magazines of Protestants outside the official Church of England—Barbauld certainly seemed to
have the necessary cultural authority. Her first book of verse, *Poems* (1773), went through five
editions in four years. She coauthored a book of prose pieces with her brother and ran a school
with her husband, a Dissenting clergyman, before going on to publish numerous other volumes
on her own, including editions of major eighteenth-century writers as well as literature for children. Among the original poems for which she is best remembered today, especially notable are
the domestic realism of "Washing-Day" (1797) and the apocalyptic vision of England in decay,
a meditation on the futility of years of aggressive counterrevolutionary warfare against
Napoleon, in "Eighteen Hundred and Eleven" (1812).

The uncompromising anti-imperialism of this poem called down on Barbauld the savagely
misogynistic condemnation of John Wilson Croker, a writer for the conservative *Quarterly Review*. Barbauld was so crushed by this review that she stopped writing forever. This episode il-
lustrates the fragility of the position women had gained in the world of letters. But the episode
is not entirely about gender. Felicia Hemans (1793–1835) may not have been Britain's national
poet, but she produced something like a national poem for the country. Hemans's "Casabi-
anca," better known as "The boy stood on the burning deck," was one of the century's most recited (and most parodied) poems. It makes a neat contrast with Barbauld's "Eighteen Hundred
and Eleven," for it celebrated the patriotic heroism of the British campaign against Napoleon in
Egypt. And the male critic Francis Jeffrey, famous for his disapproval of the English Romantics and their radicalism, was as generous in his praise of Hemans as Croker was ungenerous
toward Barbauld. Today, however, Barbauld can be read as a compelling public voice, a national poet in everything but the name.

The Mouse's Petition to Dr. Priestley[1]

O hear a pensive prisoner's prayer,
   For liberty that sighs;

---

6. Alluding to Nguyen Du's poem "Reading Hsiao-
Ching" (page 307).
1. The title in early editions is "The Mouse's Petition,
Found in the trap where he had been confined all
night," accompanied by a motto from Virgil's *Aeneid*
(6.853): "Parcere subjectis & debellare superbos" [To

spare the conquered, and subdue the proud]. Joseph
Priestley (1733–1804), political radical and eminent
chemist who discovered oxygen, had been testing the
properties of gases on captured household mice. Tradition has it that Barbauld's petition succeeded, and this
mouse was released.

And never let thine heart be shut
　　Against the wretch's cries!

5　For here forlorn and sad I sit,
　　Within the wiry grate;
And tremble at the approaching morn,
　　Which brings impending fate.

If e'er thy breast with freedom glowed,
10　　And spurned a tyrant's chain,
Let not thy strong oppressive force
　　A free-born mouse detain!

O do not stain with guiltless blood
　　Thy hospitable hearth;
15　Nor triumph that thy wiles betrayed
　　A prize so little worth.

The scattered gleanings of a feast
　　My frugal meals supply;
But if thine unrelenting heart
20　　That slender boon deny,—

The cheerful light, the vital air,
　　Are blessings widely given;
Let nature's commoners enjoy
　　The common gifts of heaven.

25　The well-taught philosophic mind
　　To all compassion gives:
Casts round the world an equal eye,
　　And feels for all that lives.

If mind,—as ancient sages taught,—
30　　A never-dying flame,
Still shifts through matter's varying forms,
　　In every form the same;

Beware, lest in the worm you crush
　　A brother's soul you find;
35　And tremble lest thy luckless hand
　　Dislodge a kindred mind.

Or, if this transient gleam of day
　　Be *all* of life we share,
Let pity plead within thy breast
40　　That little *all* to spare.

So may thy hospitable board
　　With wealth and peace be crowned;
And every charm of heartfelt ease
　　Beneath thy roof be found.

45　So when destruction lurks unseen,
　　Which men, like mice, may share,

May some kind angel clear thy path,
   And break the hidden snare.

Washing-Day

". . . And their voice,
Turning again towards childish treble, pipes
And whistles in its sound."[1]

The Muses are turned gossips; they have lost
  The buskined° step, and clear, high-sounding phrase,   *tragic*
Language of gods. Come, then, domestic Muse,
In slipshod measure° loosely prattling on[2]   *loose meters*
5   Of farm or orchard, pleasant curds and cream,
Or drowning flies, or shoe lost in the mire
By little whimpering boy, with rueful face;
Come, Muse, and sing the dreaded Washing-day.
Ye who beneath the yoke of wedlock bend,
10 With bowed soul, full well ye ken the day
Which week, smooth sliding after week, brings on
Too soon;—for to that day nor peace belongs,
Nor comfort; ere the first gray streak of dawn,
The red-armed washers come and chase repose.
15 Nor pleasant smile, nor quaint device of mirth,
E'er visited that day: the very cat,
From the wet kitchen's scared and reeking° hearth,   *smoking*
Visits the parlor,—an unwonted guest.
The silent breakfast-meal is soon despatched;
20 Uninterrupted, save by anxious looks
Cast at the lowering° sky, if sky should lower.   *threatening*
From that last evil, O preserve us, heavens!
For should the skies pour down, adieu to all
Remains of quiet: then expect to hear
25 Of sad disasters,—dirt and gravel stains
Hard to efface, and loaded lines at once
Snapped short,—and linen-horse° by dog thrown down,   *drying rack*
And all the petty miseries of life.
Saints have been calm while stretched upon the rack,
30 And Guatimozin[3] smiled on burning coals;
But never yet did housewife notable°   *efficient*
Greet with a smile a rainy washing-day.
But grant the welkin° fair, require not thou   *the heavens*
Who call'st thyself perchance the master there,
35 Or study swept, or nicely dusted coat,

1. Shakespeare, loosely quoted from *As You Like It* (2.7 161–63), Jaques's speech on the seven ages of man.
2. The Muse of slipshod meters wears shoes that are loose and so slip off and hobble her pace. Barbauld depicts this plight, however, in a line of perfect iambic (foot) measures.
3. Cuauhtemoc, the last Aztec emperor of Mexico, tortured and executed by Cortés in 1525.

Or usual 'tendance,—ask not, indiscreet,
Thy stockings mended, though the yawning rents
Gape wide as Erebus;[4] nor hope to find
Some snug recess impervious: shouldst thou try
40 The 'customed garden-walks, thine eyes shall rue
The budding fragrance of thy tender shrubs,
Myrtle or rose, all crushed beneath the weight
Of coarse checked apron,—with impatient hand
Twitched off when showers impend: or crossing lines
45 Shall mar thy musings, as the wet, cold sheet
Flaps in thy face abrupt. Woe to the friend
Whose evil stars have urged him forth to claim
On such a day the hospitable rites!
Looks, blank at best, and stinted courtesy,
50 Shall he receive. Vainly he feeds his hopes
With dinner of roast chicken, savory pie,
Or tart, or pudding:—pudding he nor tart
That day shall eat; nor, though the husband try,
Mending what can't be helped, to kindle mirth
55 From cheer deficient, shall his consort's brow
Clear up propitious: the unlucky guest
In silence dines, and early slinks away.
I well remember, when a child, the awe
This day struck into me; for then the maids,
60 I scarce knew why, looked cross, and drove me from them:
Nor soft caress could I obtain; nor hope
Usual indulgences; jelly or creams,
Relic of costly suppers, and set by
For me their petted one, or buttered toast,
65 When butter was forbid; or thrilling tale
Of ghost or witch or murder,—so I went
And sheltered me beside the parlor fire:
There my dear grandmother, eldest of forms,
Tended the little ones, and watched from harm,
70 Anxiously fond, though oft her spectacles
With elfin cunning hid, and oft the pins
Drawn from her ravelled stockings, might have soured
One less indulgent.—
At intervals my mother's voice was heard,
75 Urging despatch: briskly the work went on,
All hands employed to wash, to rinse, to wring,
To fold, and starch, and clap, and iron, and plait.
Then would I sit me down, and ponder much
Why washings were. Sometimes through hollow bowl
80 Of pipe amused we blew, and sent aloft
The floating bubbles; little dreaming then

---

4. In Greek myth, the dark passage through which souls enter Hades.

To see, Montgolfier,[5] thy silken ball
Ride buoyant through the clouds,—so near approach
The sports of children and the toils of men.
85 Earth, air, and sky, and ocean hath its bubbles,
And verse is one of them,—this most of all.

Eighteen Hundred and Eleven[1]

Still the loud death-drum, thundering from afar,
O'er the vext nations pours the storm of war:
To the stern call still Britain bends her ear,
Feeds the fierce strife, the alternate hope and fear;
5 Bravely, though vainly, dares to strive with Fate,
And seeks by turns to prop each sinking state.
Colossal power with overwhelming force
Bears down each foot of Freedom in its course;
Prostrate she lies beneath the despot's° sway,   *Napoleon's*
10 While the hushed nations curse him—and obey.

Bounteous in vain, with frantic man at strife,
Glad Nature pours the means—the joys of life;
In vain with orange-blossoms scents the gale,
The hills with olives clothes, with corn the vale;
15 Man calls to Famine, nor invokes in vain,
Disease and Rapine follow in her train;
The tramp of marching hosts disturbs the plough,
The sword, not sickle, reaps the harvest now,
And where the soldier gleans the scant supply,
20 The helpless peasant but retires to die;
No laws his hut from licensed outrage shield,
And war's least horror is the ensanguined field.

Fruitful in vain, the matron counts with pride
The blooming youths that grace her honored side;
25 No son returns to press her widowed hand,
Her fallen blossoms strew a foreign strand.
—Fruitful in vain, she boasts her virgin race,
Whom cultured arts adorn and gentlest grace;
Defrauded of its homage, Beauty mourns
30 And the rose withers on its virgin thorns.
Frequent, some stream obscure, some uncouth name,
By deeds of blood is lifted into fame;
Oft o'er the daily page some soft one bends
To learn the fate of husband, brothers, friends,
35 Or the spread map with anxious eye explores,

5. In 1783, in France, the Montgolfier brothers launched
the first hot-air balloon.
1. This dark satire was published as a quarto pamphlet. Its
somber tone reflects the times: Britain had been at war
with France almost continuously since 1793. At home, the
economy had sunk, and distress was widespread;
Napoleon controlled the Continent and blockaded British
trade; George III had lapsed into madness; conditions
with America were strained and verging on war, which
broke out the following year.

Its dotted boundaries and pencilled shores,
Asks where the spot that wrecked her bliss is found,
And learns its name but to detest the sound.

And think'st thou, Britain, still to sit at ease,
40 An island queen amidst thy subject seas,
While the vext billows, in their distant roar,
But soothe thy slumbers, and but kiss thy shore?
To sport in wars, while danger keeps aloof,
Thy grassy turf unbruised by hostile hoof?
45 So sing thy flatterers;—but, Britain, know,
Thou who hast shared the guilt must share the woe.
Nor distant is the hour; low murmurs spread,
And whispered fears, creating what they dread;
Ruin, as with an earthquake shock, is here,
50 There, the heart-witherings of unuttered fear,
And that sad death, whence most affection bleeds,
Which sickness, only of the soul, precedes.
Thy baseless wealth dissolves in air away,
Like mists that melt before the morning ray:²
55 No more on crowded mart or busy street
Friends, meeting friends, with cheerful hurry greet;
Sad, on the ground thy princely merchants bend
Their altered looks, and evil days portend,
And fold their arms, and watch with anxious breast
60 The tempest blackening in the distant West.°   *the United States*

Yes, thou must droop; thy Midas dream is o'er;
The golden tide of Commerce leaves thy shore,
Leaves thee to prove the alternate ills that haunt
Enfeebling Luxury and ghastly Want;
65 Leaves thee, perhaps, to visit distant lands,
And deal the gifts of Heaven with equal hands.

Yet, O my Country, name beloved, revered,
By every tie that binds the soul endeared,
Whose image to my infant senses came
70 Mixt with Religion's light and Freedom's holy flame!
If prayers may not avert, if 't is thy fate
To rank amongst the names that once were great,
Not like the dim, cold Crescent³ shalt thou fade,
Thy debt to Science and the Muse unpaid;
75 Thine are the laws surrounding states revere,
Thine the full harvest of the mental year,
Thine the bright stars in Glory's sky that shine,
And arts that make it life to live are thine.
If westward streams the light that leaves thy shores,

---

2. An echo of Shakespeare's Prospero, on the vanishing of the illusions he has wrought; *The Tempest* 4.1.150–56.

3. Symbol of the Muslim empire that formerly ruled much of Spain.

80   Still from thy lamp the streaming radiance pours.
        Wide spreads thy race from Ganges° to the pole,   *river in India*
        O'er half the Western world thy accents roll:
        Nations beyond the Apalachian hills[4]
        Thy hand has planted and thy spirit fills:
85   Soon as their gradual progress shall impart
        The finer sense of morals and of art,
        Thy stores of knowledge the new states shall know,
        And think thy thoughts, and with thy fancy glow;
        Thy Lockes, thy Paleys,[5] shall instruct their youth,
90   Thy leading star direct their search for truth;
        Beneath the spreading platane's° tent-like shade,   *Asian plane-tree*
        Or by Missouri's rushing waters laid,
        "Old Father Thames" shall be the poet's theme,
        Of Hagley's woods[6] the enamored virgin dream,
95   And Milton's tones the raptured ear enthrall,
        Mixt with the roaring of Niagara's fall;
        In Thomson's glass the ingenuous youth shall learn
        A fairer face of Nature to discern;
        Nor of the bards that swept the British lyre
100   Shall fade one laurel, or one note expire.
        Then, loved Joanna,[7] to admiring eyes
        Thy storied groups in scenic pomp shall rise;
        Their high-souled strains and Shakespeare's noble rage
        Shall with alternate passion shake the stage.
105   Some youthful Basil from thy moral lay
        With stricter hand his fond desires shall sway;
        Some Ethwald, as the fleeting shadows pass,
        Start at his likeness in the mystic glass;
        The tragic Muse resume her just control,
110   With pity and with terror purge the soul,
        While wide o'er transatlantic realms thy name
        Shall live in light and gather all its fame.
        Where wanders Fancy down the lapse of years,
        Shedding o'er imaged woes untimely tears?
115   Fond, moody power! as hopes—as fears prevail,
        She longs, or dreads, to lift the awful veil,
        On visions of delight now loves to dwell,
        Now hears the shriek of woe or Freedom's knell:
        Perhaps, she says, long ages past away,
120   And set in western wave our closing day,
        Night, Gothic night, again may shade the plains
        Where Power is seated, and where Science reigns;

---

4. The United States had begun to expand westward with the Louisiana Purchase of 1803.
5. John Locke, author of *An Essay Concerning Human Understanding* (1690) and *Two Treatises on Civil Government* (1690); William Paley, author of *The Principles of Moral and Political Philosophy* (1785), *Evidences of*

Christianity (1794), and *Natural Theology* (1802).
6. The estate of Lord Lyttelton, celebrated in *The Seasons* (1726–1730), a poem by James Thomson ("Thomson's glass," i.e., mirror, line 97).
7. Joanna Baillie, whose *Plays on the Passions* include *Count Basil* (1798) and *Ethwald* (1802).

England, the seat of arts, be only known
By the gray ruin and the mouldering stone;
125 That Time may tear the garland from her brow,
And Europe sit in dust, as Asia now.

Yet then the ingenuous youth whom Fancy fires
With pictured glories of illustrious sires,
With duteous zeal their pilgrimage shall take
130 From the Blue Mountains,° or Ontario's lake,   *in Pennsylvania*
With fond, adoring steps to press the sod
By statesmen, sages, poets, heroes, trod;
On Isis'° banks to draw inspiring air,   *river in Oxford*
From Runnymede[8] to send the patriot's prayer;
135 In pensive thought, where Cam's° slow waters wind,   *Cambridge river*
To meet those shades that ruled the realms of mind;
In silent halls to sculptured marbles bow,
And hang fresh wreaths round Newton's awful brow.[9]
Oft shall they seek some peasant's homely shed,
140 Who toils, unconscious of the mighty dead,
To ask where Avon's[1] winding waters stray,
And thence a knot of wild flowers bear away;
Anxious inquire where Clarkson,[2] friend of man,
Or all-accomplished Jones[3] his race began;
145 If of the modest mansion aught remains
Where Heaven and Nature prompted Cowper's[4] strains;
Where Roscoe, to whose patriot breast belong
The Roman virtue and the Tuscan song,
Led Ceres to the black and barren moor
150 Where Ceres never gained a wreath before:[5]
With curious search their pilgrim steps shall rove
By many a ruined tower and proud alcove,
Shall listen for those strains that soothed of yore
Thy rock, stern Skiddaw, and thy fall, Lodore;[6]
155 Feast with Dun Edin's° classic brow their sight,   *Edinburgh's*
And "visit Melross by the pale moonlight."[7]

But who their mingled feelings shall pursue
When London's faded glories rise to view?
The mighty city, which by every road,
160 In floods of people poured itself abroad
Ungirt by walls, irregularly great,

---

8. The meadow on the banks of the Thames where King John signed the Magna Carta in 1215.
9. Sir Isaac Newton (1642–1727), philosopher, physicist, and mathematician, was professor at Cambridge University.
1. The Avon flows through Stratford, home of Shakespeare.
2. Abolitionist Thomas Clarkson.
3. Sir William Jones (1746–1794), distinguished scholar of Indian language and law.
4. The poet William Cowper, here cited as author of

Olney Hymns (1779).
5. William Roscoe (1753–1831) was a noted agricultural improver, a scholar, and opponent of the war. The claim that he led Ceres, the Roman goddess of agriculture, where she had never succeeded before, alludes to his achievement of growing high-quality crops on moorland.
6. Skiddaw, a mountain, and Lodore, the site of a waterfall, are two tourist spots in the Lake District.
7. Sir Walter Scott, *The Lay of the Last Minstrel* (1805), 2.1. The ruined abbey was famously picturesque.

No jealous drawbridge, and no closing gate;
Whose merchants (such the state which commerce brings)
Sent forth their mandates to dependent kings;
165 Streets, where the turbaned Moslem, bearded Jew,
And woolly Afric, met the brown Hindu;
Where through each vein spontaneous plenty flowed,
Where Wealth enjoyed, and Charity bestowed.
Pensive and thoughtful shall the wanderers greet
170 Each splendid square, and still, untrodden street;
Or of some crumbling turret, mined by time,
The broken stairs with perilous step shall climb,
Thence stretch their view the wide horizon round,
By scattered hamlets trace its ancient bound,
175 And, choked no more with fleets, fair Thames survey
Through reeds and sedge pursue his idle way.

With throbbing bosoms shall the wanderers tread
The hallowed mansions of the silent dead.
Shall enter the long aisle and vaulted dome°   St. Paul's Cathedral
180 Where Genius and where Valor find a home;
Awe-struck 'midst chill sepulchral marbles breathe,
Where all above is still, as all beneath;
Bend at each antique shrine, and frequent turn
To clasp with fond delight some sculptured urn,
185 The ponderous mass of Johnson's form to greet,
Or breathe the prayer at Howard's sainted feet.[8]

Perhaps some Briton, in whose musing mind
Those ages live which Time has cast behind,
To every spot shall lead his wondering guests
190 On whose known site the beam of glory rests;
Here Chatham's[9] eloquence in thunder broke,
Here Fox persuaded, or here Garrick[1] spoke;
Shall boast how Nelson,[2] fame and death in view,
To wonted victory led his ardent crew,
195 In England's name enforced, with loftiest tone,
Their duty,—and too well fulfilled his own:
How gallant Moore,[3] as ebbing life dissolved,
But hoped his country had his fame absolved.
Or call up sages whose capacious mind
200 Left in its course a track of light behind;

---

8. Statues of the critic and lexicographer Samuel Johnson (1709–1784) and of the prison reformer John Howard (1726–1790) stand in the nave of St. Paul's.
9. William Pitt, first Earl of Chatham (1708–1778), a famous orator and the dominant political figure of his time.
1. Charles James Fox (1749–1806), leader of the Whig opposition; David Garrick (1717–1779), celebrated Shakespearean actor.
2. "Every reader will recollect the sublime telegraphic

dispatch, 'England expects every man to do his duty'" [Barbauld's note], sent by Admiral Horatio Nelson (1758–1805), to his fleet, just before he was killed in the victory of the Battle of Trafalgar.
3. "I hope England will be satisfied," were the last words of General Moore [Barbauld's note]. Sir John Moore died while commanding the British retreat at the Battle of Coruña (1809).

Point where mute crowds on Davy's[4] lips reposed,
And Nature's coyest secrets were disclosed;
Join with their Franklin, Priestley's injured name,[5]
Whom, then, each continent shall proudly claim.

205 Oft shall the strangers turn their eager feet
The rich remains of ancient art to greet,
The pictured walls with critic eye explore,
And Reynolds be what Raphael was before.[6]
On spoils from every clime their eyes shall gaze,
210 Egyptian granites and the Etruscan vase;
And when 'midst fallen London they survey
The stone where Alexander's ashes lay,[7]
Shall own with humbled pride the lesson just
By Time's slow finger written in the dust.
215 There walks a Spirit o'er the peopled earth,
Secret his progress is, unknown his birth;
Moody and viewless° as the changing wind,   *invisible*
No force arrests his foot, no chains can bind;
Where'er he turns, the human brute awakes,
220 And, roused to better life, his sordid hut forsakes:
He thinks, he reasons, glows with purer fires,
Feels finer wants, and burns with new desires:
Obedient Nature follows where he leads;
The steaming marsh is changed to fruitful meads;
225 The beasts retire from man's asserted reign,
And prove his kingdom was not given in vain.
Then from its bed is drawn the ponderous ore,
Then Commerce pours her gifts on every shore,
Then Babel's towers and terraced gardens rise,
230 And pointed obelisks invade the skies;
The prince commands, in Tyrian purple drest,
And Egypt's virgins weave the linen vest.
Then spans the graceful arch the roaring tide,
And stricter bounds the cultured fields divide.
235 Then kindles Fancy, then expands the heart,
Then blow° the flowers of Genius and of Art;   *bloom*
Saints, heroes, sages, who the land adorn,
Seem rather to descend than to be born;
While History, 'midst the rolls consigned to fame,
240 With pen of adamant inscribes their name.

The Genius now forsakes the favored shore,[8]
And hates, capricious, what he loved before;

4. Sir Humphry Davy (1778–1829), inventor of the miner's safety lamp, gave public lectures on chemistry at the Royal Institution.
5. Benjamin Franklin (1706–1790) and Joseph Priestley corresponded about their work on electricity.
6. Sir Joshua Reynolds (1723–1792), the leading British portrait painter and first president of the Royal Academy;

Raffaelo Sanzio (1483–1520), the great Italian Renaissance artist.
7. A sarcophagus brought for display at the recently opened British Museum in 1802 was thought to be that of Alexander the Great; among the "Egyptian granites" was the Rosetta stone.
8. An echo of Milton's elegy, *Lycidas*, 183.

Then empires fall to dust, then arts decay,
And wasted realms enfeebled despots sway;°   *rule*
245 Even Nature's changed; without his fostering smile
Ophir° no gold, no plenty yields the Nile;   *region famed for gold*
The thirsty sand absorbs the useless rill,
And spotted plagues from putrid fens distil.
In desert solitudes then Tadmor sleeps,
250 Stern Marius then o'er fallen Carthage weeps;⁹
Then with enthusiast love the pilgrim roves
To seek his footsteps in forsaken groves,
Explores the fractured arch, the ruined tower,
Those limbs disjointed of gigantic power;
255 Still at each step he dreads the adder's sting,
The Arab's javelin, or the tiger's spring;
With doubtful caution treads the echoing ground,
And asks where Troy or Babylon is found.

And now the vagrant Power no more detains
260 The vale of Tempe or Ausonian plains;¹
Northward he throws the animating ray,
O'er Celtic nations bursts the mental day;
And, as some playful child the mirror turns,
Now here, now there, the moving lustre burns;
265 Now o'er his changeful fancy more prevail
Batavia's dykes than Arno's purple vale;²
And stinted suns, and rivers bound with frost,
Than Enna's plains or Baia's viny coast;
Venice the Adriatic weds in vain,
270 And Death sits brooding o'er Campania's plain;³
O'er Baltic shores and through Hercynian groves,°   *the Black Forest*
Stirring the soul, the mighty impulse moves;
Art plies his tools, and Commerce spreads her sail,
And wealth is wafted in each shifting gale.
275 The sons of Odin° tread on Persian looms,   *Norsemen*
And Odin's daughters breathe distilled perfumes;
Loud minstrel bards, in Gothic halls, rehearse
The Runic rhyme, and "build the lofty verse."⁴
The Muse, whose liquid notes were wont to swell
280 To the soft breathings of the Æolian shell,
Submits, reluctant, to the harsher tone,
And scarce believes the altered voice her own.

9. Tadmor is the biblical name for Palmyra, an ancient Syrian city. The Roman consul Gaius Marius (157–86 B.C.E.), driven out of power by Sulla, fled to Africa, where he was denied entry; Plutarch records his lament to the governor: "Tell him, then, that thou hast seen Marius a fugitive, seated amid the ruins of Carthage." The Romans had destroyed the city in 146 B.C.E.
1. The vale of Tempe in Greece; Ausonia, Virgil's name for Italy: hence, the realms of classical literature.
2. Batavia is the Netherlands; the river Arno runs through

Florence.
3. Enna is a valley in Sicily; Baia is a Roman resort on the Bay of Naples. In a grand ceremony, each year the city of Venice symbolically wed the Adriatic. Campania is the province around Capua and Naples, a site of infamous malarial swamps.
4. Milton, *Lycidas* (1637): "Who would not sing for Lycidas? he knew / Himself to sing, and build the lofty rhyme" (10–11). Runic: mysteriously lettered.

And now, where Cæsar saw with proud disdain
The wattled hut and skin of azure stain,[5]
285   Corinthian columns rear their graceful forms,
And light verandas brave the wintry storms,
While British tongues the fading fame prolong
Of Tully's eloquence and Maro's song.[6]
Where once Bonduca[7] whirled the scythed car,
290   And the fierce matrons raised the shriek of war,
Light forms beneath transparent muslins float,
And tutored voices swell the artful note.
Light-leaved acacias and the shady plane
And spreading cedar grace the woodland reign;
295   While crystal walls the tenderer plants confine,
The fragrant orange and the nectared pine;
The Syrian grape there hangs her rich festoons,
Nor asks for purer air or brighter noons:
Science and Art urge on the useful toil,
300   New mould a climate and create the soil,
Subdue the rigor of the Northern Bear,
O'er polar climes shed aromatic air,
On yielding Nature urge their new demands,
And ask not gifts, but tribute, at her hands.

305   London exults:—on London Art bestows
Her summer ices and her winter rose;
Gems of the East her mural crown adorn,
And Plenty at her feet pours forth her horn.°   *cornucopia*
While even the exiles her just laws disclaim,
310   People a continent, and build a name:
August she sits, and with extended hands
Holds forth the book of life to distant lands.

But fairest flowers expand but to decay;
The worm is in thy core, thy glories pass away;
315   Arts, arms, and wealth destroy the fruits they bring;
Commerce, like beauty, knows no second spring.
Crime walks thy streets, Fraud earns her unblest bread,
O'er want and woe thy gorgeous robe is spread,
And angel charities in vain oppose:
320   With grandeur's growth the mass of misery grows.
For, see,—to other climes the Genius soars,
He turns from Europe's desolated shores;
And lo! even now, 'midst mountains wrapt in storm,
On Andes' heights[8] he shrouds his awful form;

5. In his *Gallic Wars*, Julius Caesar noted that the ancient
Scots warriors painted themselves blue.
6. Marcus Tullius Cicero (106–43 B.C.E.) won renown by
his denunciations of the traitor Catiline; "Maro" is Publius Virgilius Maro (70–19 B.C.E.), author of the *Aeneid*.
7. Boadicea, properly Boudicca, a Celtic queen who revolted against the Romans, was finally defeated, and took

her own life (C.E. 61).
8. The first of a series of references to the spreading resistance to colonialism in South America: the Andes are
mountains in Peru, Chimborazo is a mountain in Ecuador,
La Plata a city in Argentina, Potosi a city in Bolivia celebrated for its silver.

325   On Chimborazo's summits treads sublime,
        Measuring in lofty thought the march of Time;
        Sudden he calls: "'Tis now the hour!" he cries,
        Spreads his broad hand, and bids the nations rise.
        La Plata hears amidst her torrents' roar;
330   Potosi hears it, as she digs the ore:
        Ardent, the Genius fans the noble strife,
        And pours through feeble souls a higher life,
        Shouts to the mingled tribes from sea to sea,
        And swears—Thy world, Columbus, shall be free.[9]

RESONANCE

John Wilson Croker: from *A Review of "Eighteen Hundred and Eleven"*[1]

Our old acquaintance Mrs. Barbauld turned satirist! The last thing we should have expected, and, now that we have seen her satire, the last thing that we could have desired.

May we (without derogating too much from that reputation of age and gravity of which critics should be so chary) confess that we are yet young enough to have had early obligations to Mrs. Barbauld; and that it really is with no disposition to retaliate on the fair pedagogue of our former life, that on the present occasion, we have called her up to correct her exercise?

But she must excuse us if we think that she has wandered from the course in which she was respectable and useful, and miserably mistaken both her powers and her duty, in exchanging the birchen for the satiric rod, and abandoning the superintendance of the "ovilia" [lambs] of the nursery, to wage war on the "reluctantes dracones" [struggling lawgivers], statesmen, and warriors, whose misdoings have aroused her indignant muse.

We had hoped, indeed, that the empire might have been saved without the intervention of a lady-author: we even flattered ourselves that the interests of Europe and of humanity would in some degree have swayed our public councils, without the descent of (dea ex machina)[2] Mrs. Anna Letitia Barbauld in a quarto, upon the theatre where the great European tragedy is now performing. Not such, however, is her opinion; an irresistible impulse of public duty—a confident sense of commanding talents—have induced her to dash down her shagreen[3] spectacles and her knitting needles, and to sally forth. * * *

The poem, for so out of courtesy we shall call it, is entitled Eighteen Hundred and Eleven, we suppose, because it was written in the year 1811; but this is a mere

9. Christopher Columbus, landing in the Caribbean islands in 1492, claimed Central and South America for Spain.

1. Published in 1812 in the seventh issue of the *Quarterly Review*. Croker established a reputation in his native Ireland as an academic, man of letters, and lawyer. He entered Parliament in 1806 and served steadily until the Reform Bill of 1832, which he opposed. His knowledge of Irish affairs quickly drew Tory favor: he was backed by Arthur Wellesley, later the Duke of Wellington, and in 1810 named secretary to the admiralty, a crucial post in wartime Britain that he held until 1830. Croker was an authority on the French Revolution and an editor of 18th-

century memoirs and letters, but his literary notoriety rests on his contributions to the *Quarterly Review*, for which he wrote from its founding in 1809 until 1845. His reviews include a scathing notice of Keat's *Endymion* (1818), and he was particularly harsh on works by women. His biases provoked equally violent resentments. William Hazlitt, wielding an ethnic slur, called him "a talking potato"; Thomas Babington Macaulay "detested [him] more than cold boiled veal."

2. The "god(dess) from the machine," a device of Greek drama, proverbial for a revelation that produces a sudden ending.

3. An untanned leather.

conjecture, founded rather on our inability to assign any other reason for the name, than in any particular relation which the poem has to the events of the last year. We do not, we confess, very satisfactorily comprehend the meaning of all the verses which this fatidical [prophetic] spinster has drawn from her poetical distaff;[4] but of what we do understand we very confidently assert that there is not a topic in "Eighteen Hundred and Eleven" which is not quite as applicable to 1810 or 1812, and which, in our opinion, might not, with equal taste and judgment, have been curtailed, or dilated, or transposed, or omitted, without any injustice whatever to the title of the poem, and without producing the slightest discrepancy between the frontispiece and the body of the work. * * *

Upon this melancholy night, however, a bright day dawns, and all the little sense with which Mrs. Barbauld set out, now dissolves away in blissful visions of American glory. This Genius of her's which "walks the *peopled* earth," "viewless and secret," suddenly *appears* walking on the summit of Chimberaço, (which never was nor can be *peopled*,) displays his "*viewless*" form on the Andes, and "*secretly*" arouses, by loud exclamations, all the nations of the western continent.

> "Ardent the Genius fans the noble strife,
> And pours through feeble souls a higher life;
> Shouts to the mingled tribes from sea to sea,
> And *swears*—Thy world, Columbus, shall be free."

And with this oath concludes "Eighteen Hundred and Eleven," upon which we have already wasted too much time. One word, however, we must seriously add. Mrs. Barbauld's former works have been of some utility; her "Lessons for Children," her "Hymns in Prose," her "Selections from the Spectator," et id genus omne [works of that kind], though they display not much of either taste or talents, are yet something better than harmless: but we must take the liberty of warning her to desist from satire, which indeed is satire on herself alone; and of entreating, with great earnestness, that she will not, for the sake of this ungrateful generation, put herself to the trouble of writing any more party pamphlets in verse. We also assure her, that we should not by any means impute it to want of taste or patriotism on her part, if, for her country, her fears were less confident, and for America her hopes less ardent; and if she would leave both the victims and the heroes of her political prejudices to the respective judgment which the impartiality of posterity will not fail to pronounce.

Adam Mickiewicz
1798–1855

The man who was to become Poland's greatest poet and foremost cultural icon was born not in Poland—which had recently been partitioned by Russia, Prussia, and Austria—but in what was then the Grand Duchy of Lithuania and is now Belarus. At that time Lithuania was a huge territory reaching almost to the Black Sea and including Balts, Cossacks, Tatars, and the largest

---

4. The slur on Barbauld as a spinster was nasty—she had recently been widowed. A distaff holds wool to be spun.

Jewish population in the world. The Polishness that Adam Mickiewicz tried hard to create and defend, in this region of ever-shifting borders, did not stop him from opening his *Pan Tadeusz* with the words, "Lithuania, my fatherland . . ." Both as a writer and as a national leader, Mickiewicz was forever finding ways to reach out to other cultures and peoples.

As a student at the University of Vilnius, Mickiewicz became involved with the Filomats, or "lovers of learning," a student group interested in sex as well as revolutionary politics (they invented an "Erometer" for measuring passion). Arrested by the tsarist police, Mickiewicz was imprisoned and exiled to Odessa, where he wrote and met other revolutionaries. His lover in Odessa was the mistress of the tsar's chief of police and herself an informer. The play *Konrad Wallenrod,* written soon after his departure, is the story of a double agent whose national loyalties cannot be taken for granted.

On hearing of the 1830 uprising in Warsaw, Mickiewicz traveled to what is now Poland (a portion then occupied by Prussia) for what turned out to be the first and only time. Less than a year later, after guerrilla campaigns against Russian troops, the uprising collapsed and he was obliged to flee. In the last twenty years of his life he wrote little and devoted himself instead to the struggle for Polish independence. He taught classics and Slavic literature in Switzerland and France, championed Emerson, and befriended the American feminist Margaret Fuller during her stay in Paris. In early 1848 he was in Italy, organizing a voluntary Polish army to fight against Austria. After its defeat he returned to Paris and edited a daily, *La Tribune des Peuples,* in which he advocated a program of radical social reforms and international solidarity. When the Crimean War broke out, he rushed to Istanbul to launch a Polish legion, and it was there that he died in 1855. Yet since Poland won its independence, no poet has continued to live more intensely in the feelings of his homeland than Mickiewicz.

Seeing every land as a land of exile and yet seeking everywhere for the secret signs of a national belonging that was denied him, Mickiewicz produced poetic landscapes of extraordinary complexity and ambivalence. In the Crimea, which has seen centuries of conflict between Christian and Muslim civilizations, he exults in a scenery that seems to rise above such conflicts. In the heart of the Lithuanian forest, which he likens to the depths of the sea, he doesn't discover the treasure of national feeling that one might have expected to find there. Speaking of national struggle, he anticipates the possibility that, looking back from "the dim anonymous aftermath," it may all seem to have been in vain.

PRONUNCIATION:

Mickiewicz: mees-KYAY-vitz

Chatir Dah[1]

Trembling the Muslim comes to kiss the foot of your crags,
Mast on Crimea's raft, towering Chatir Dah![2]
Minaret of the World! Mightiest Padishah[3]
Of Mountains! From the plain Fugitive into the Clouds!

5   As great Gabriel once stood over portals of Eden,
You at Heaven's Gate watch, wrapped in your forest cloak,
And, in turban of clouds with lightning flashes bespangled,
On your forehead you wear janissaries[4] of dread.

---

1. Translated by John Saly.
2. A mountain in what is now Ukraine.

3. The Ottoman term for emperor.
4. Elite soldiers in the Ottoman army.

Hot sun may roast our limbs, mountain mists blind our eyes,
10   Locusts may eat our grain, infidels burn our homes,
You, Chatir Dah, would still, unmindful of man's fate,

Rise between earth and sky, Dragoman[5] of Creation;
Far spreads the plain at your feet, home of men and of thunder,
15   But you can only hear what God to nature speaks.

The Ruins of the Castle of Balaklava[1]

These shapeless heaps of rubbish, which were castles,
Once your pride and your defence, O infertile Crimea!
Lie today on the mountains like skulls of giants,
Inhabited by the reptile
5   Or by men more abject than the reptile.

Let us climb the tower, search out traces of armories;
What do I see! an inscription.
Perhaps the name of a hero
Terror of armies, who sleeps in oblivion,
10   Surrounded like an insect with the leaves of the wild vine.

Here Greeks have chiseled Attic ornaments into the walls;
There the Italians gave fetters to the Mongols,
And the pilgrim to Mecca murmured the words of the namaz.[2]

Today the vultures crown the tombs
15   With their black wings,
As on the ramparts of a city exterminated by the plague
A flag of death eternally flies.

Zosia in the Kitchen Garden[1]

Swimming knee-deep, she trawls among the fronds,
In wrinkled waves for vegetable fish.
First the foot finds, and then the hand responds;
She stoops and gathers for a luncheon dish.

5   Her right hand raised as if to pluck the air,
Attentively she dawdles down the rows;
Her eyes look down, her bright and straying hair
Stirs in the straw hat's shadow, as she goes.

The count is watching, like a crane that stands
10   With neck outstretched, outside the feeding flock,
One leg cranked up, a stone in its lean hand
Clawed close, to fall and wake it with the shock.

---

5. Official interpreter in Middle Eastern countries.
1. Translated by Louise Bogan.

2. Part of Muslim prayer.
1. Translated by Donald Davie.

A voice distracts. He turns. She's there no more.
The leaves return to quiet like a flood
15 Cut by a wing. The basket that she bore
Rides the green swell, capsizing where she stood.

The Lithuanian Forest[1]

Who has explored the Lithuanian woods
Into the deepest kernel of the thicket?
Hard by the shore the fisherman scarce knows
The twilit seabed and the tide-rocked groves;
5 Likewise the wary huntsman skirts this forest,
Reading a darkened face but ignorant
Of far-delved secrets hidden in its heart.
For those who ventured deep into the brush,
Tearing their way through tangled undergrowth,
10 Have come upon a rampart piled high
With man-sized logs and riveted by roots
To giant stumps; a moat of dark morass
And thousand streams girdle this obstacle
Behind a screen of rank nettles and thorn;
15 The ground is strewn with wasps' and hornets' nests,
Anthills, and serpents coiled beneath the weed.
But if somehow you overcame this wall,
Death lurks beyond: in pools like dens of wolves
Half overspread with grass and bottomless.
20 These ghoulish wells, covered with bloody rust
Upon their iridescent surfaces,
Belch forth a fume of such malignant stench
That every nearby tree sloughs off her bark
And drops her poisoned leaves: here devils dwell.
25 Humped trunks with filthy fungi beards, these trees
Sit round the water, bald, wormlike and dwarfed,
Witches would huddle so around their kettle
Boiling the mangled body of a man.
Beyond the lakes of death no one has passed,
30 Even the eye is beaten back: dense mist
Steams up forever from the quaking bog
And settles on its dreadful solitude.

Hands That Fought[1]

Hands that fought to defend the people
The people will sever and let fall
And names beloved of the people
The people will somehow not recall

---

1. Translated by John Saly.   1. Translated by Clark Mills.

5
All must dissolve: crisis and merit
Uproar of elemental wrath
And nameless people will inherit
The dim anonymous aftermath

To a Polish Mother[1]
A poem written in 1830

O Polish mother! If in your son's eyes
    There ever gleams the genius's greatness,
If on his childish brow there will arise
    Of the ancient Poles pride and nobleness;

5
If turning his back on his playmates' crowd,
    He runs to the bard who sings of past deeds,
If he listens heedfully, his head bowed,
    When they tell him of his forefathers' feats:

O Polish mother! Your son plays the wrong part!
    Kneel before Our Lady of Sorrows
10
And look at the sword which pierces Her heart:
    The foe will strike your breast with the same blows.

For though the whole world may in peace flower,
    Though powers, peoples, minds, may join in action,
15
Your son is called to a fight without splendor
    And to martyrdom . . . without resurrection.

Soon bid him go to a solitary lair
    To ponder long . . . on rushes rest his head,
Breathe damp and putrid vapors in the air,
20
    And with the venomous serpent share his bed.

There he will learn to conceal his anger,
    Keep his thoughts unfathomed, like a deep lake,
Poison with soft talk, as with putrid vapor,
    Cut a lowly figure like the cold snake.

Song of the Bard[1]

Before Lithuania is struck by pestilence,
Its coming is divined by the seer's eye;
For if in the bards' words we have confidence,
Then oft on deserted graveyards and meadows
5
The maid of murrain[2] appears for all to spy
Dressed in white, on her brow a fiery wreath glows,

1. Translated by Michael J. Mikós.
1. Translated by Michael J. Mikós.

2. Pestilence, disease of cattle.

Taller than trees in Białowieża land,
A bloodstained kerchief she waves in her hand.

    Castle sentries hide under helmets their eyes,
10   And peasants' dogs, their muzzles in the ground,
Dig, sniff death, and howl their terrible cries.
The maid strides, her ominous paces bound
For villages, castles, and wealthy towns;
And every time her bloody kerchief she waves
15   A palace turns into a desert at once,
Wherever she passes, arise fresh graves.

    An ill-boding vision! Yet more disasters
Augurs for Lithuanians from the German side
A shining helmet with ostrich feathers,
20   And a loose mantle, with a black cross outside.

    Wherever such a specter has passed by,
Fall of towns and hamlets counts not a whit:
For the whole country becomes a grave thereby.
Ah, he who can save the Lithuanian nature,
25   Come here, on the nations' grave we shall sit,
We will meditate, sing, and cry together.

    O native tale! The ark of covenant
Between the ancient and more recent years:
To you the armor of their knight people grant,
30   The thread of your thought, and your heart's flowers.

    O ark! You can't be wrecked by any ill winds
Unless you are debased by your own kin;
O native song, you stand guard protecting
The national temple where memories dwell,
35   With the help of an archangel's voice and wings—
At times you hold the sword of the archangel.

    The flame will gnaw at historical pictures,
The armed robbers will ravage the treasures,
The song unscathed, will make the rounds of throngs,
40   And if the wicked people do not know
How to nurse it with hope and feed with sorrow,
It flees to the hills, cleaves to ruined donjons,
And from there tells tales of the ancient gestes.
So does a nightingale, from a house ablaze
45   It flies out, sits on the roof, briefly stays,
When the roof falls down, it flees to the forests,
And with a loud voice, over graves and cinders,
It sings a mourning song to travelers.

    I've heard the songs—a hundred year old peasant,
50   His plowshare turning up bones in its trail,

Would halt and would play on a pipe instrument
A prayer for the dead; or in a rhymed wail
Praised you, great sires—yet with no descendant.
The echoes respond, from afar I listened,
55   Both view and song made me more dejected,
For only I saw him and heard his tale.

    As archangel's trumpet on the day of doom
Will call the dead past to rise from the tomb,
So at the sound of song, bones under my feet
60   Rejoined and grew into enormous forms.
Columns and rooftops arise from defeat,
On deserted lakes splash uncounted oars,
And castles come into view with open gates,
Princes' coronets, warriors' armor plates,
65   The poets sing, the maidens join in dance—
I was roused cruelly from my glorious trance.

    My native mountains and forests are gone.
Thought, on the weary-laden feathers borne,
Falls, it clings to the home fireside steadfast;
70   The lute fell silent in a benumbed hand,
Among rueful wail of people from my land
I do not often hear the voice of the past!
Yet still the sparks of youthful fervor smolder
Deep in my breast, they often kindle fire,
75   Revive my soul and brighten memory's pyre.
Then memory, like a lamp with crystal cover
Adorned with scenes by the painter's brushes,
Although dimmed with dust and countless blemishes,
If you put a candle inside its heart,
80   It will lure the eyes with fresh color once more,
It will spread on the palace walls as before
Bright-colored tapestries, though obscured in part.

    If I could only pour my own desire
Into listeners' breasts and revive the figures
85   Of the dead past; if I knew how to fire
With ringing words at the hearts of my brothers:
Then perhaps for just that single moment,
When they became moved by the native song,
They would feel their hearts beating as of yore,
90   They would feel their souls as before great and strong
And they would live as nobly that instant,
As their forefathers lived their whole lives before.

    But why recall the ages that passed by?
The singer will not condemn his own times,
95   For a great man is alive and nearby,
I'll sing of him; Lithuanians, learn from these rhymes!

Dionysios Solomos
1798–1857

Dionysios Solomos was born on the island of Zakynthos in 1798, the illegitimate son of a noble Venetian father and one of his father's Greek servants. He was not a likely candidate to become Greece's national poet. Unlike most of Greece, Zakynthos wasn't ruled by the Ottomans; a Venetian colony, it was made a British protectorate in 1815 and remained one during Solomos's lifetime. The Venetians among whom he grew up spoke Greek badly, if at all. Solomos was educated in Italy, and his first poems were written in Italian.

Inspired by the outbreak of the Greek national independence struggle in 1821, Solomos turned to his mother's language, which didn't yet exist in modern written form, to compose his "Hymn to Liberty," a poem that made him famous throughout Europe.

Solomos's masterpiece, "The Free Besieged," is an enigmatic fragment based on the siege of Missolonghi, a heroic defeat in the War of Independence. In the course of revision, the poem became a reflection on freedom itself within a framework of natural beauty and harsh necessity.

PRONUNCIATION:
Dionysios Solomos: dee-oh-NEE-zee-ohs so-low-MOHS

The Free Besieged[1]
Draft III

1

Oh you Mother, magnanimous in suffering and glory,
Though all your children may live in a profound secret,
In meditation and in dream, what has graced my eyes
My very eyes to see you in the deserted forest,
5   Which quite suddenly has wreathed your deathless feet
(Look) with Easter Palms, the greenery of Palm Sunday!
My ears missed your holy step, my eyes missed your figure,
Serene you are like the sky enriched by all its beauties,
That show in many places, in others they are hidden;
10   But, Goddess, may I hear at last the sound of your voice
At once to make it a gift to the Hellenic nation?
On Greece's rocks and dried grass glory dwells forever.

[*The Goddess responds by ordering the poet to sing of the siege of Missolonghi.[2]*]

2

Deeds, words, and deep thoughts—motionless I stare—
Myriads of blossoms, colorful, cover the grassy carpet,
15   White, scarlet, and blue, invite bees of golden hue.
Away, one lives among friends, but here, in death's presence.

1. Translated by M. B. Raizas.
2. Capital of a regional government during the Greek War of Independence against the Ottomans. The town was successfully defended against an Ottoman siege between 1822–1823. It was there that the poet Byron died of an illness in 1824. During a second siege, the Greek forces attempted to attack the besiegers and were destroyed with great loss of life.

Often at the break of dawn, and in the midst of day,
When the waters turn dark, and the stars grow in numbers,
Beaches, rocks, and the open sea suddenly leap up and quiver.
20   "Arabic chargers, English guns, Turkish shots, French minds!
A mighty ocean makes war and strikes the tiny cottage;
Alas! In a while uncovered the few bosoms remain;
Thunder, are you deathless, have you never known rest?"
That's what a sailor from abroad says bending over the prow.
25   All round in fear the islands, they all weep and pray,
And the cross-shaped domed temple and the most modest shrine
Amid incense and lighted candles listen to their pain.
Hatred, though, made heard its odious voice also:
"Fisherwoman, take your hook and go cast elsewhere."

30   Often at the break of dawn, and in the midst of day,
When the waters turn dark, and the stars grow in numbers,
Beaches, rocks, and the open sea suddenly leap up and quiver,
An old man, who had stuck his life to the fish-hook
Cast it away, missed his mark, and pacing he cried:
35   "Arabic chargers, English guns, Turkish shots, French minds!
Alas, a mighty ocean strikes hard at the tiny cottage;
In a little while uncovered the few bosoms remain;
Thunder, are you deathless, have you never known rest?
Oh desolation I can see, come, let's weep together."

3

40   The war has not exhausted them, it has become their life.
. . . . cannot prevent
The girls from singing songs, the boys from playing games.

4

Out of clouds ever black, out of the pitch of darkness,
. . . .
45   But sun-like then invisible ether of a world in symbol
The flag pole appears, with the brave warriors underneath it,
And up there, on its highest top, the banner in full glory,
That speaks and murmurs and its Cross waves in the air
In all the space around it, the brave wind of valor,
50   The sky looked on proudly and the whole earth applauded;
And every voice stirring then toward the light echoed;
Most noble blossoms of love scattering all around:
"Unconquered, rich, and beautiful, venerable, too, and holy!"

5

The eyes, by now grown used to the endless desolation,
55   Shone and smiled, and the blackened lips thus spoke:
"My boy, joyful by the door with the din you raise;
Hare, the hunter's after you, but you linger in the plain;
Seagull, you spit snail and clam shells and sea foam."
At this moment, he eases his dragging steps a while,
60   Toward the tiny fort turns his eyes once more,

While to his wounded chest his sword tightly presses,
As his great heart within is beating full of sorrow.

6

TEMPTATION

Eros and April linked hand in hand began to dance with joy,
And Nature found her greatest and her sweetest hour;
65 Out of swelling shadows enfolding dew and scent came
A most exquisite melody, languorous, soft, and faint.
Water clear and sweet, full of charm and magic
Flows and pours itself into a fragrant abyss,
Taking the perfume with it, leaving coolness behind,
70 Showing to the sun all the wealth of its sources.
It runs here and there and sings like a nightingale.
But over the water of the lake, that is still and white
Still wherever you look at it, all-white to the bottom,
With a little, unknown shadow a butterfly plays,
75 That amid fragrance had slept inside a wild lily.
My seer, light-of-shadow, tell us what you saw tonight:
"A night full of miracles, a most enchanted night!
There was no breeze stirring on earth, nor on sky or ocean,
Not even as much as makes a bee brushing a tiny blossom.
80 Around something motionless that glows in the lake
The round face of the moon merges in close embrace,
And a fair maiden comes forth dressed in its silver light."

7

Deserted the eyes that you call, oh golden wind of life.

8

[*Polylas, one of the most important characters in the poem, is an orphan girl whom the other older women had brought up and all loved as their own daughter. One of the most glorious fighters, whom she had loved during the time of happiness, fell in the war, so her heart sinks from hope to misery. She finds consolation, however, observing her beloved persons and the supreme example of the other women. These suffice somehow to explain this passage, in which the enthused girl turns to the Angel, whom she had seen in her dream offering her his wings; she then turns to the women to tell them that she wants the wings indeed, not to fly away, but to keep them folded while awaiting there with them the hour of death. After that, her imagination flies to the past when, while she was ill, she was comforted "by the peaceful and fond breathing" of the other women who were sleeping beside her; and finally to the young man she had seen dancing the day of victory.*]

Angel, why only in dreams to me wings you offer?
85 In the name of your Maker, the desert space needs them.
Look at me here flapping them into the wind of freedom,
Without a kiss, a farewell, a glance, oh queens mine!
I want to have them myself, and folded up to keep them,

Here, where love's fountains flow charming in delight.

90   And I heard you say, "Bird, how sweet is your own voice!"
Like a bird now bosom sing, before the sword shall cut you;
Innocent breathing comforts me in the dense lonely night;
Let us together to the sword, and let me first among you!
The slanting fez, when we dance, adorns buds on the ears,

95   The eyes tell of a great love for the world on high,
The light is beautiful to see shining full of magic!

9

My innards and the ocean never have known calmness.
As many fruit and flowers the arms are that encircle you.

10

From charging horses I run and from the saber's terror.

100   Futile vanity of dream, she is herself dream-like!
The strange world traveler turned then and addressed me,
Divine was her smiling, moist with tears, and said she:
Cut the water at its spring, channel it to the garden,
The paradise of the soul that's grown amid fragrance.

11

[One of the women resorts to thinking of death as her only salvation, with the joy experienced by a little bird.]

105   When it joyfully salutes a shady paradise
With a flutter of wing and a welcome sound,
(the moment when it is tired from a long trip, in the heat of the
    summer sun.)

12

Yonder I see womenfolk, most brave, with children
Round the fire they have lit and with sadness fed it

110   With their few most dear things and their beds of honor,
Motionless, sightless, tearless, untroubled all remain;
And sparkles fly into their hair and their worn clothes;
Quickly, ashes show up—their empty palms must be filled.

13

Swords are raised facing a flood of foes determined

115   To open among them a path leading them all to freedom,
Afar, with brothers free at last; here, death only frees them.

14

[A woman during the sortie.]

Muskets galore and Turkish swords!
The dried reel goes through them.

15

120   Suddenly the black clouds are torn by a sun-like glare,
And small white houses are seen upon the green grass slope.

Ralph Waldo Emerson
1803–1882

"Every thought is also a prison," Ralph Waldo Emerson wrote in "The Poet" (1844); "every heaven is also a prison." Emerson doesn't tell us that America is or can be a heaven on earth; most of "The Poet" isn't about the United States at all, but about what we would now call the Romantic imagination and its heroic and necessary ability to "make it new." In a world suddenly bereft of traditional certitudes, poets become "liberating gods." They are or will be liberators—Emerson doesn't claim that they already exist—because they will be able to find the poetry waiting in the ordinary things and ordinary people of everyday modern life. It is this democratic impulse rather than an aggressive celebration of national tradition or identity that provokes Emerson to say that "America is a poem in our eyes." This was the cue for the entrance onto the American stage of Walt Whitman. For more on Emerson, see the introduction to his essay "Nature" on page 119.

from The Poet

I look in vain for the poet whom I describe. We do not, with sufficient plainness, or sufficient profoundness, address ourselves to life, nor dare we chant our own times and social circumstance. If we filled the day with bravery, we should not shrink from celebrating it. Time and nature yield us many gifts, but not yet the timely man, the new religion, the reconciler, whom all things await. Dante's praise is, that he dared to write his autobiography in colossal cipher, or into universality. We have yet had no genius in America, with tyrannous eye, which knew the value of our incomparable materials, and saw, in the barbarism and materialism of the times, another carnival of the same gods whose picture he so much admires in Homer; then in the middle age; then in Calvinism. Banks and tariffs, the newspaper and caucus, methodism and unitarianism, are flat and dull to dull people, but rest on the same foundations of wonder as the town of Troy, and the temple of Delphos, and are as swiftly passing away. Our logrolling, our stumps and their politics, our fisheries, our Negroes, and Indians, our boats, and our repudiations, the wrath of rogues, and the pusillanimity of honest men, the northern trade, the southern planting, the western clearing, Oregon, and Texas, are yet unsung. Yet America is a poem in our eyes: its ample geography dazzles the imagination, and it will not wait long for metres. If I have not found that excellent combination of gifts in my countrymen which I seek, neither could I aid myself to fix the idea of the poet by reading now and then in Chalmers's collection of five centuries of English poets. These are wits, more than poets, though there have been poets among them. But when we adhere to the ideal of the poet, we have our difficulties even with Milton and Homer. Milton is too literary, and Homer too literal and historical.

Walt Whitman
1819–1892

In the preface to *Leaves of Grass* (1855), the first of six editions of his masterwork, Walt Whitman wrote, "The Americans of all nations at any time upon the earth have probably the fullest poetic nature. The United States themselves are essentially the greatest poem." This was patriotic boasting, but it had the virtue of celebrating a new democratic diversity within the nation. Calling himself "an American," the poet was also claiming to be "one of the roughs"—not just a Wordsworthian man among men, but a poet whose mission was to include those seen as actively dangerous to official versions of the nation, such as the urban crowd of immigrants, prostitutes, and homosexuals.

Largely self-educated, from a family of modest means but strong intellectual interests, Whitman spent his early life as a schoolteacher on rural Long Island and as a printer in Brooklyn. Some have seen his distinctive long lines as expressing a professional printer's view of poetry, based on making the most of available space. He was also a political journalist; he was fired from the Brooklyn *Daily Eagle* in 1847 for his opposition to the extension of slavery into western territories. A Bohemian life in New York suited both his homosexuality and his urge to think of himself as the nation incarnate, large enough to embrace everyone and everything, whether literally or figuratively. "Do I contradict myself?" he famously asked. "Very well then I contradict myself, / I am large, I contain multitudes." Nothing was too prosaic for his lines, rhymeless and suspiciously close to prose, to see, hear, and feel as part of some larger rhythm—a rhythm reminiscent at once of the industrial city and of the King James Bible. The revolutionary freshness and sensuality of Whitman's language, frank about bodily functions and exploding with present participles that force us to experience reality as instant-by-instant process, sometimes leave the impression that Whitman himself is ready to leap off the page and into the reader's arms. Poets around the world have testified to the power of his voice to liberate them from conventions gone stale.

Working for the Bureau of Indian Affairs, Whitman could see Indians as victims but also write in praise of General George Armstrong Custer. After the Civil War he was not ahead of his white contemporaries, and behind many of them, in his attitude toward newly freed blacks, to whom he was hesitant to extend the right to vote. His inclusiveness could be a way of not choosing. By the end of his life, he was a cult figure, but one that expressed the nation's own contradictions.

I Hear America Singing

I hear America singing, the varied carols I hear,
Those of mechanics, each one singing his as it should be blithe and strong,
The carpenter singing his as he measures his plank or beam,
The mason singing his as he makes ready for work, or leaves off work,
5   The boatman singing what belongs to him in his boat, the deck-hand singing
      on the steamboat deck,
The shoemaker singing as he sits on his bench, the hatter singing as he stands,
The wood-cutter's song, the ploughboy's on his way in the morning, or at
      noon intermission or at sundown,
The delicious singing of the mother, or of the young wife at work, or of the
      girl sewing or washing,
Each singing what belongs to him or her and to none else,
10   The day what belongs to the day—at night the party of young fellows, ro-
      bust, friendly,
Singing with open mouths their strong melodious songs.

from Song of Myself

1

I celebrate myself, and sing myself,
And what I assume you shall assume,
For every atom belonging to me as good belongs to you.

I loafe and invite my soul,
5   I lean and loafe at my ease observing a spear of summer grass.

My tongue, every atom of my blood, form'd from this soil, this air,
Born here of parents born here from parents the same, and their parents the
    same,
I, now thirty-seven years old in perfect health begin,
Hoping to cease not till death.

10   Creeds and schools in abeyance,
Retiring back a while suffced at what they are, but never forgotten,
I harbor for good or bad, I permit to speak at every hazard,
Nature without check with original energy.

2

Houses and rooms are full of perfumes, the shelves are crowded with
    perfumes,
I breathe the fragrance myself and know it and like it,
The distillation would intoxicate me also, but I shall not let it.
The atmosphere is not a perfume, it has no taste of the distillation, it is
    odorless,
5   It is for my mouth forever, I am in love with it,
I will go to the bank by the wood and become undisguised and naked,
I am mad for it to be in contact with me.

The smoke of my own breath,
Echoes, ripples, buzz'd whispers, love-root, silk-thread, crotch and vine,
10   My respiration and inspiration, the beating of my heart, the passing of blood
    and air through my lungs,
The sniff of green leaves and dry leaves, and of the shore and dark-color'd
    sea-rocks, and of hay in the barn,
The sound of the belch'd words of my voice loos'd to the eddies of the
    wind,
A few light kisses, a few embraces, a reaching around of arms,
The play of shine and shade on the trees as the supple boughs wag,
15   The delight alone or in the rush of the streets, or along the fields and
    hill-sides,
The feeling of health, the full-noon trill, the song of me rising from bed and
    meeting the sun.

Have you reckon'd a thousand acres much? have you reckon'd the earth
    much?
Have you practis'd so long to learn to read?
Have you felt so proud to get at the meaning of poems?
20   Stop this day and night with me and you shall possess the origin of all
    poems,
You shall possess the good of the earth and sun, (there are millions of suns
    left),
You shall no longer take things at second or third hand, nor look through
    the eyes of the dead, nor feed on the spectres in books,
You shall not look through my eyes either, nor take things from me,

25   You shall listen to all sides and filter them from your self,

* * *

4

Trippers and askers surround me,
People I meet, the effect upon me of my early life or the ward and city I live
    in, or the nation,
The latest dates, discoveries, inventions, societies, authors old and new,
My dinner, dress, associates, looks, compliments, dues,
5   The real or fancied indifference of some man or woman I love,
The sickness of one of my folks or of myself, or ill-doing or loss or lack of
    money, or depressions or exaltations,
Battles, the horrors of fratricidal war, the fever of doubtful news, the fitful
    events;
These come to me days and nights and go from me again,
But they are not the Me myself.

10   Apart from the pulling and hauling stands what I am,
Stands amused, complacent, compassionating, idle, unitary,
Looks down, is erect, or bends an arm on an impalpable certain rest,
Looking with side-curved head curious what will come next,
Both in and out of the game and watching and wondering at it.
15   Backward I see in my own days where I sweated through fog with linguists
    and contenders,
I have no mockings or arguments, I witness and wait.

5

I believe in you my soul, the other I am must not abase itself to you,
And you must not be abased to the other.

Loafe with me on the grass, loose the stop from your throat,
Not words, not music or rhyme I want, not custom or lecture, not even the
    best,
5   Only the lull I like, the hum of your valvèd voice.

I mind how once we lay such a transparent summer morning,
How you settled your head athwart my hips and gently turn'd over upon
    me,
And parted the shirt from my bosom-bone, and plunged your tongue to my
    bare-stript heart,
And reach'd till you felt my beard, and reach'd till you held my feet.

10   Swiftly arose and spread around me the peace and knowledge that pass all
    the argument of the earth,
And I know that the hand of God is the promise of my own,
And I know that the spirit of God is the brother of my own,
And that all the men ever born are also my brothers, and the women my sis-
    ters and lovers,
And that a kelson[1] of the creation is love,
15   And limitless are leaves stiff or drooping in the fields,
And brown ants in the little wells beneath them,

---

1. A line of timber that holds the floor and the keel of a boat together.

And mossy scabs of the worm fence, heap'd stones, elder, mullein[2] and
    poke-weed.

6

A child said *What is the grass?* fetching it to me with full hands,
How could I answer the child? I do not know what it is any more than he.

I guess it must be the flag of my disposition, out of hopeful green stuff
    woven.

Or I guess it is the handkerchief of the Lord,
A scented gift and remembrancer designedly dropt,
Bearing the owner's name someway in the corners, that we may see and re-
    mark, and say *Whose?*
Or I guess the grass is itself a child, the produced babe of the vegetation.

Or I guess it is a uniform hieroglyphic,
And it means, Sprouting alike in broad zones and narrow zones,
Growing among black folks as among white,
Kanuck, Tuckahoe, Congressman, Cuff, I give them the same, I receive
    them the same.

And now it seems to me the beautiful uncut hair of graves.

Tenderly will I use you curling grass,
It may be you transpire from the breasts of young men,
It may be if I had known them I would have loved them,
It may be you are from old people, or from offspring taken soon out of their
    mothers' laps,
And here you are the mothers' laps.

This grass is very dark to be from the white heads of old mothers,
Darker than the colorless beards of old men,
Dark to come from under the faint red roofs of mouths.
O I perceive after all so many uttering tongues,
And I perceive they do not come from the roofs of mouths for nothing.

I wish I could translate the hints about the dead young men and women,
And the hints about old men and mothers, and the offspring taken soon out
    of their laps.

What do you think has become of the young and old men?
And what do you think has become of the women and children?
They are alive and well somewhere,
The smallest sprout shows there is really no death,
And if ever there was it led forward life, and does not wait at the end to ar-
    rest it,
And ceas'd the moment life appear'd.

All goes onward and outward, nothing collapses,
And to die is different from what any one supposed, and luckier.

* * *

2. A common plant.

50

There is that in me—I do not know what it is—but I know it is in me.

Wrench'd and sweaty—calm and cool then my body becomes,
I sleep—I sleep long.

I do not know it—it is without name—it is a word unsaid,
It is not in any dictionary, utterance, symbol.

Something it swings on more than the earth I swing on,
To it the creation is the friend whose embracing awakes me.
Perhaps I might tell more. Outlines! I plead for my brothers and sisters.

Do you see O my brothers and sisters?
It is not chaos or death—it is form, union, plan—it is eternal life—it is
    Happiness.

51

The past and present wilt—I have fill'd them, emptied them,
And proceed to fill my next fold of the future.

Listener up there! what have you to confide to me?
Look in my face while I snuff the sidle of evening,
(Talk honestly, no one else hears you, and I stay only a minute longer.)

Do I contradict myself?
Very well then I contradict myself,
(I am large, I contain multitudes.)

I concentrate toward them that are nigh, I wait on the door-slab.

Who has done his day's work? who will soonest be through with his
    supper?
Who wishes to walk with me?
Will you speak before I am gone? will you prove already too late?

52

The spotted hawk swoops by and accuses me, he complains of my gab and
    my loitering.

I too am not a bit tamed, I too am untranslatable,
I sound my barbaric yawp over the roofs of the world.

The last scud of day holds back for me,
It flings my likeness after the rest and true as any on the shadow'd wilds,
It coaxes me to the vapor and the dusk.

I depart as air, I shake my white locks at the runaway sun,
I effuse my flesh in eddies, and drift it in lacy jags.

I bequeath myself to the dirt to grow from the grass I love,
If you want me again look for me under your boot-soles.

You will hardly know who I am or what I mean,
But I shall be good health to you nevertheless,
And filter and fibre your blood.
Failing to fetch me at first keep encouraged,

15   Missing me one place search another,
       I stop somewhere waiting for you.

Crossing Brooklyn Ferry

1

Flood-tide below me! I see you face to face!
Clouds of the west—sun there half an hour high—I see you also face to face.

Crowds of men and women attired in the usual costumes, how curious you
   are to me!
On the ferry-boats the hundreds and hundreds that cross, returning home,
   are more curious to me than you suppose,
5   And you that shall cross from shore to shore years hence are more to me,
       and more in my meditations, than you might suppose.

2

The impalpable sustenance of me from all things at all hours of the day,
The simple, compact, well-join'd scheme, myself disintegrated, every one
   disintegrated yet part of the scheme,
The similitudes of the past and those of the future,
The glories strung like beads on my smallest sights and hearings, on the
   walk in the street and the passage over the river,
10   The current rushing so swiftly and swimming with me far away,
The others that are to follow me, the ties between me and them,
The certainty of others, the life, love, sight, hearing of others.
Others will enter the gates of the ferry and cross from shore to shore,
Others will watch the run of the flood-tide,
15   Others will see the shipping of Manhattan north and west, and the heights of
       Brooklyn to the south and east,
Others will see the islands large and small;
Fifty years hence, others will see them as they cross, the sun half an hour
   high,
A hundred years hence, or ever so many hundred years hence, others will
   see them,
Will enjoy the sunset, the pouring-in of the flood-tide, the falling-back to
   the sea of the ebb-tide.

3

20   It avails not, time nor place—distance avails not,
I am with you, you men and women of a generation, or ever so many gener-
   ations hence,
Just as you feel when you look on the river and sky, so I felt,
Just as any of you is one of a living crowd, I was one of a crowd,
Just as you are refresh'd by the gladness of the river and the bright flow, I
   was refresh'd,
25   Just as you stand and lean on the rail, yet hurry with the swift current, I
       stood yet was hurried,
Just as you look on the numberless masts of ships and the thick-stemm'd
   pipes of steamboats, I look'd.

I too many and many a time cross'd the river of old,
Watched the Twelfth-month sea-gulls, saw them high in the air floating
    with motionless wings, oscillating their bodies,
Saw how the glistening yellow lit up parts of their bodies and left the rest in
    strong shadow,
30   Saw the slow-wheeling circles and the gradual edging toward the south,
Saw the reflection of the summer sky in the water,
Had my eyes dazzled by the shimmering track of beams,
Look'd at the fine centrifugal spokes of light round the shape of my head in
    the sunlit water,
Look'd on the haze on the hills southward and south-westward,
35   Look'd on the vapor as it flew in fleeces tinged with violet,
Look'd toward the lower bay to notice the vessels arriving,
Saw their approach, saw aboard those that were near me,
Saw the white sails of schooners and sloops, saw the ships at anchor,
The sailors at work in the rigging or out astride the spars,
40   The round masts, the swinging motion of the hulls, the slender serpentine
    pennants,
The large and small steamers in motion, the pilots in their pilot-houses,
The white wake left by the passage, the quick tremulous whirl of the
    wheels,
The flags of all nations, the falling of them at sunset,
The scallop-edged waves in the twilight, the ladled cups, the frolicsome
    crests and glistening,
45   The stretch afar growing dimmer and dimmer, the gray walls of the granite
    storehouses by the docks,
On the river the shadowy group, the big steam-tug closely flank'd on each
    side by the barges, the hay-boat, the belated lighter,
On the neighboring shore the fires from the foundry chimneys burning high
    and glaringly into the night,
Casting their flicker of black contrasted with wild red and yellow light over
    the tops of houses, and down into the clefts of streets.

4

These and all else were to me the same as they are to you,
50   I loved well those cities, loved well the stately and rapid river,
The men and women I saw were all near to me,
Others the same—others who look back on me because I look'd forward to
    them,
(The time will come, though I stop here to-day and to-night.)

5

What is it then between us?
55   What is the count of the scores or hundreds of years between us?

Whatever it is, it avails not—distance avails not, and place avails not,
I too lived, Brooklyn of ample hills was mine,
I too walk'd the streets of Manhattan island, and bathed in the waters
    around it,
I too felt the curious abrupt questionings stir within me.
60   In the day among crowds of people sometimes they came upon me,

In my walks home late at night or as I lay in my bed they came upon me,
I too had been struck from the float forever held in solution,
I too had receiv'd identity by my body,
That I was I knew was of my body, and what I should be I knew I should be
    of my body.

6

65   It is not upon you alone the dark patches fall,
The dark threw its patches down upon me also,
The best I had done seem'd to me blank and suspicious,
My great thoughts as I supposed them, were they not in reality meagre?
Nor is it you alone who know what it is to be evil,
70   I am he who knew what it was to be evil,
I too knitted the old knot of contrariety,
Blabb'd, blush'd, resented, lied, stole, grudg'd,
Had guile, anger, lust, hot wishes I dared not speak,
Was wayward, vain, greedy, shallow, sly, cowardly, malignant,
75   The wolf, the snake, the hog, not wanting in me,
The cheating look, the frivolous word, the adulterous wish, not wanting,
Refusals, hates, postponements, meanness, laziness, none of these
    wanting,
Was one with the rest, the days and haps of the rest,
Was call'd by my nighest name by clear loud voices of young men as they
    saw me approaching or passing,
80   Felt their arms on my neck as I stood, or the negligent leaning of their flesh
    against me as I sat,
Saw many I loved in the street or ferry-boat or public assembly, yet never
    told them a word,
Lived the same life with the rest, the same old laughing, gnawing, sleeping,
Play'd the part that still looks back on the actor or actress,
The same old role, the role that is what we make it, as great as we like,
85   Or as small as we like, or both great and small.

7

Closer yet I approach you,
What thought you have of me now, I had as much of you—I laid in my
    stores in advance,
I consider'd long and seriously of you before you were born.

Who was to know what should come home to me?
90   Who knows, but I am enjoying this?
Who knows, for all the distance, but I am as good as looking at you now,
    for all you cannot see me?

8

Ah, what can ever be more stately and admirable to me than mast-hemm'd
    Manhattan?
River and sunset and scallop-edg'd waves of flood-tide?
The sea-gulls oscillating their bodies, the hay-boat in the twilight, and the
    belated lighter?
95   What gods can exceed these that clasp me by the hand, and with voices I
    love call me promptly and loudly by my nighest name as I approach?

What is more subtle than this which ties me to the woman or man that looks
    in my face?
Which fuses me into you now, and pours my meaning into you?

We understand then do we not?
What I promis'd without mentioning it, have you not accepted?
100   What the study could not teach—what the preaching could not accomplish
    is accomplish'd, is it not?

        9
Flow on, river! flow with the flood-tide, and ebb with the ebb-tide!
Frolic on, crested and scallop-edg'd waves!
Gorgeous clouds of the sunset! drench with your splendor me, or the men
    and women generations after me!
Cross from shore to shore, countless crowds of passengers!
105   Stand up, tall masts of Manhattan! stand up, beautiful hills of Brooklyn!
Throb, baffled and curious brain! throw out questions and answers!
Suspend here and everywhere, eternal float of solution!
Gaze, loving and thirsting eyes, in the house or street or public assembly!
Sound out, voices of young men! loudly and musically call me by my nigh-
    est name!
110   Live, old life! play the part that looks back on the actor or actress!
Play the old role, the role that is great or small according as one makes it!
Consider, you who peruse me, whether I may not in unknown ways be look-
    ing upon you;
Be firm, rail over the river, to support those who lean idly, yet haste with
    the hasting current;
Fly on, sea-birds! fly sideways, or wheel in large circles high in the air;
115   Receive the summer sky, you water, and faithfully hold it till all downcast
    eyes have time to take it from you!
Diverge, fine spokes of light, from the shape of my head, or any one's head,
    in the sunlit water!
Come on, ships from the lower bay! pass up or down, white-sail'd
    schooners, sloops, lighters!
Flaunt away, flags of all nations! be duly lower'd at sunset!
Burn high your fires, foundry chimneys! cast black shadows at night-fall!
    cast red and yellow light over the tops of the houses!
120   Appearances, now or henceforth, indicate what you are,
You necessary film, continue to envelop the soul,
About my body for me, and your body for you, be hung our divinest
    aromas,
Thrive, cities—bring your freight, bring your shows, ample and sufficient
    rivers,
Expand being than which none else is perhaps more spiritual,
125   Keep your places, objects than which none else is more lasting.

You have waited, you always wait, you dumb, beautiful ministers,
We receive you with free sense at last, and are insatiate henceforward,
Not you any more shall be able to foil us, or withhold yourselves from us,
We use you, and do not cast you aside—we plant you permanently within us,
130   We fathom you not—we love you—there is perfection in you also,

You furnish your parts toward eternity,
Great or small, you furnish your parts toward the soul.

As I lay with my head in your lap camerado

As I lay with my head in your lap camerado,
The confession I made I resume, what I said to you and the open air I re-
    sume,
I know I am restless and make others so,
I know my words are weapons full of danger, full of death,
5   For I confront peace, security, and all the settled laws, to unsettle them,
I am more resolute because all have denied me than I could ever have been
    had all accepted me,
I heed not and have never heeded either experience, cautions, majorities,
    nor ridicule,
And the threat of what is call'd hell is little or nothing to me,
And the lure of what is call'd heaven is little or nothing to me;
10   Dear camerado! I confess I have urged you onward with me, and still urge
    you, without the least idea what is our destination,
Or whether we shall be victorious, or utterly quell'd and defeated.

O Captain! My Captain![1]

O Captain! my Captain! our fearful trip is done,
The ship has weather'd every rack, the prize we sought is won,
The port is near, the bells I hear, the people all exulting,
While follow eyes the steady keel, the vessel grim and daring;
5   But O heart! heart! heart!
        O the bleeding drops of red,
           Where on the deck my Captain lies,
             Fallen cold and dead.

O Captain! my Captain! rise up and hear the bells;
10   Rise up—for you the flag is flung—for you the bugle trills,
For you bouquets and ribbon'd wreaths—for you the shores a-crowding,
For you they call, the swaying mass, their eager faces turning;
      Here Captain! dear father!
        The arm beneath your head!
15   It is some dream that on the deck,
          You've fallen cold and dead.

My Captain does not answer, his lips are pale and still,
My father does not feel my arm, he has no pulse nor will,
The ship is anchor'd safe and sound, its voyage closed and done,
20   From fearful trip the victor ship comes in with object won:
      Exult O shores, and ring O bells!
        But I with mournful tread,
          Walk the deck my Captain lies,
            Fallen cold and dead.

---

1. Published in a collection entitled *Memories of President Lincoln*, after Lincoln's assassination in 1865.

Prayer of Columbus

A batter'd, wreck'd old man,
Thrown on this savage shore, far, far from home,
Pent by the sea and dark rebellious brows, twelve dreary months,
Sore, stiff with many toils, sicken'd and nigh to death,
5   I take my way along the island's edge,
Venting a heavy heart.

I am too full of woe!
Haply I may not live another day;
I cannot rest O God, I cannot eat or drink or sleep,
10   Till I put forth myself, my prayer, once more to Thee.
Breathe, bathe myself once more in Thee, commune with Thee,
Report myself once more to Thee,

Thou knowest my years entire, my life,
My long and crowded life of active work, not adoration merely;
15   Thou knowest the prayers and vigils of my youth,
Thou knowest my manhood's solemn and visionary meditations,
Thou knowest how before I commenced I devoted all to come to Thee,
Thou knowest I have in age ratified all those vows and strictly kept them,
Thou knowest I have not once lost nor faith nor ecstasy in Thee,
20   In shackles, prison'd, in disgrace, repining not,
Accepting all from Thee, as duly come from Thee.

All my emprises° have been fill'd with Thee,   *enterprises*
My speculations, plans, begun and carried on in thought of Thee,
Sailing the deep or journeying the land for Thee;
25   Intentions, purports, aspirations mine, leaving results to Thee.

O I am sure they really came from Thee,
The urge, the ardor, the unconquerable will,
The potent, felt, interior command, stronger than words,
A message from the Heavens whispering to me even in sleep,
30   These sped me on.
By me and these the work so far accomplished,
By me earth's elder cloy'd and stifled lands uncloy'd, unloos'd,
By me the hemispheres rounded and tied, the unknown to the known.

The end I know not, it is all in Thee,
35   O small or great I know not—haply what broad fields, what lands,
Haply the brutish measureless human undergrowth I know,
Transplanted there may rise to stature, knowledge worthy Thee,
Haply the swords I know may there indeed be turn'd to reaping-tools,
Haply the lifeless cross I know, Europe's dead cross, may bud and blossom
    there.

40   One effort more, my altar this bleak sand;
That Thou O God my life hast lighted,
With ray of light, steady, ineffable, vouchsafed° of Thee,   *bestowed*
Light rare untellable, lighting the very light,
Beyond all signs, descriptions, languages;

45   For that O God, be it my latest word, here on my knees,
    Old, poor, and paralyzed, I thank Thee.

    My terminus near,
    The clouds already closing in upon me,
    The voyage balk'd, the course disputed, lost,
50   I yield my ships to Thee.
    My hands, my limbs grow nerveless,
    My brain feels rack'd, bewilder'd,
    Let the old timbers part, I will not part,
    I will cling fast to Thee, O God, though the waves buffet me,
55   Thee, Thee at least I know.

    Is it the prophet's thought I speak, or am I raving?
    What do I know of life? what of myself?
    I know not even my own work past or present,
    Dim ever-shifting guesses of it spread before me,
60   Of newer better worlds, their mighty parturition,
    Mocking, perplexing me.

    And these things I see suddenly, what mean they?
    As if some miracle, some hand divine unseal'd my eyes,
    Shadowy vast shapes smile through the air and sky,
65   And on the distant waves sail countless ships,
    And anthems in new tongues I hear saluting me.

END OF PERSPECTIVES: THE NATIONAL POET

⇌ PERSPECTIVES ⇌
On the Colonial Frontier

Much of nineteenth-century history involves the conquest of non-European regions by Europeans. Often conquest was followed—or even precipitated—by a flow of European settlers. Alongside the scramble of the European imperialist nations to carve up most of Africa, much of Asia, and all of the Pacific, colonies were established, expanded, and consolidated throughout North and South America, Australia, and New Zealand. The native inhabitants, whose wishes were not consulted, saw their homelands invaded and their resources seized. They themselves were often expelled or violently eliminated. The colonial frontier where all this happened is among the century's preeminent literary spaces, both real and imagined. But what was this frontier, and what sort of literature did it give rise to?

That literature is largely the record of the victors. It was they who construed the American frontier, in critic Mary Lawlor's words, "as a border zone that harbored mystery and danger, but that ultimately opened onto a plentiful, inviting space where the desires of common citizens, if they were diligent and brave, might be richly fulfilled." This was not the promise or the experience of the natives whom these common citizens encountered there. And yet one-sided as this literature might appear, the combination of danger and desire Lawlor describes makes the frontier something more than a zone of brutalizing stereotypes deployed so as to justify violent subjugation. In James Fenimore Cooper, as in Walter Scott, we find a powerful identification with the wildness and nobility of the "primitives" on the other side of the frontier line and a fear that encroaching modernity will mean a fundamental loss. The Sioux-American doctor Charles Eastman, or Ohiyesa, tells the story of his double education, first Indian and then white, with an irrepressible sense that "civilization" is not the monopoly of the whites. The Hawaiian poems that follow Ohiyesa's narrative show how amused and intrigued the native populations could be by their new neighbors and the innovations like water-sprinklers they brought to their homes away from home.

While America moved west, Russia moved east and south. Russia's advance was uneven and precarious, thanks to the fierce resistance of the native peoples of the Caucasus region, including the Chechens against whom the future novelist Mikhail Lermontov fought. And the same might be said of the attitude that Lermontov brought to his mission. Many Russians already felt themselves split between Western and Slavic identities, and this division within left its imprint on the Russian version of what the cultural critic Edward Said calls Orientalism. It's as if they had to ask: How can we denigrate these Orientals if we are perhaps Orientals ourselves? At least intermittently, Lermontov suspected that he was aiding in the barbaric repression of people who lived in inoffensive harmony with nature and that this harmony might offer him a redemptive antidote to the civilizational malaise he and his hero had caught in the metropolis.

The historian Frederick Jackson Turner, who identified the frontier with the natural and legitimate drive for American independence from Europe, indignantly rejected any parallel between America's westward expansion and European colonization. The eastward march of European Russia makes problems for his case. Nineteenth-century Argentina, which had become independent from Spain in 1816, tells a slightly different story. It also saw the gradual occupation of Indian lands in the interior by waves of incoming Europeans hungry for farms of their own. Yet it was not the Indians themselves who came to represent the wildness of the frontier. Early expectations that the country was rich in silver (which resulted in its misleading names, beginning with Río de la Plata, "Silver River") proved mistaken, and there was thus less demand for Indian slave labor than elsewhere in Latin America. European settlers made up the bulk of the population, and it was the tension between city dwellers turned toward Europe and the farmers of the distant interior that divided the country both politically and culturally. The Argentine

Daylight at Last! The Advance Column of the Emin Pasha Relief Expedition Emerging from the Great Forest. From Henry Morton Stanley, *In Darkest Africa,* 1890. In his best-selling book, the journalist and explorer H. M. Stanley described his near-fatal expedition to rescue Edward Schnitzer, who held office as the Emin Pasha, governor of the British Equitorial Province of Egypt. The governor had been trapped by rebels at a frontier fort on the shore of Lake Albert in east central Africa. Stanley reached the lake after a grueling overland trek from the Congo. Here, walking stick in hand, Stanley surveys the scene with heroic sang-froid as his native troops rejoice at his success in guiding them through the hostile wilderness to their destination.

writer Domingo Sarmiento portrayed a conflict between "we" and "they," where "they" are feudal landlords and uncivilized gauchos, while "we" are rational urbanites. For Sarmiento, unlike Frederick Jackson Turner, all that is worst about his country comes from the frontier.

The early Catholic missions established in Argentina were called "Reducciones" (reductions), to convey the idea that their purpose was to "reduce" the so-called savages to a domesticated and civilized state. In the Philippines, which Spain had conquered three centuries before, the Church again played a central part. The Philippines wasn't a settler colony; like British India, it was run by relatively few Europeans. The moving line where progress and modernity ran up against their supposed opposites was dictated by the Church, which enjoyed enormous political as well as ideological power. In José Rizal's *Noli Me Tangere,* that line runs through the middle of an elegant drawing room.

⁕ ⚔ ⁕

Mikhail Lermontov
1814–1841

Born to a noble Russian family, Mikhail Lermontov began his university studies in Moscow, but after a clash with the university authorities, he left for Saint Petersburg to prepare for a career in the cavalry. Posted with his regiment of the Imperial Guard to a suburb of Saint Petersburg in 1834, he had plenty of time for writing, which had become his real passion. In 1837, however, he witnessed the fatal wounding of Pushkin in a duel (see page 283) and concluded, along with many others, that Russia's greatest poet had been murdered. In a poem called "The Death of a Poet," Lermontov blamed the ruling circles of Russia under Tsar Nicholas I. The regime reacted by exiling him to the distant Caucasus, where there was still fierce resistance to Russian expansion.

From the writer's point of view, this exile was perhaps a blessing in disguise. As a child Lermontov had twice been taken to the Caucasus by his grandmother for treatment at the mineral springs of Pyatigorsk, and the wild mountain scenery and its exotic Asian inhabitants had made a powerful impression on him. It was there that he wrote his first poem, "Cherkesy," about the life of the Caucasian highlanders. Now the Caucasus again served as an inspiration for his poetry, and in 1839, back in Saint Petersburg, Lermontov began his most famous novel, situating it against a Caucasian backdrop. After a taste of the city's social whirl, another duel led to another Caucasian exile in 1840. At the beginning of June, Lermontov's unit participated in battles in Chechnya, and he was commended for his bravery. But his own side proved more dangerous to him. Perhaps as a result of intrigues by the secret police, he was provoked into another duel, this time with a fellow officer, in July 1841 and was killed. He was not quite twenty-seven. He was buried at Pyatigorsk.

"Bela" is the opening story in *A Hero of Our Time,* published serially beginning in 1840, which consists of five separate stories, each an episode in the life of its somewhat Byronic hero, Pechorin. Pechorin (named for a river, like Pushkin's Onegin) was like Onegin a representative of the "superfluous" man, a line of Russian literary characters distinguished by disillusioned cynicism and the waste of superior talents, whether because of the mediocrity of the world around them or because of their own lack of high moral purpose. In his disregard for other people, Pechorin may seem to leave the realm of morals behind altogether. Does his capacity for strong feeling and self-questioning make him a genuine hero, or only such a hero as his "time" will permit, a symptom of what ails Russia itself? From the moment that "Bela" was published, readers wondered how critical and how sympathetic Lermontov was toward Pechorin, and they continue to wonder. In his preface, Lermontov refuses to answer. Knowing that Lermontov, like his hero, was capable of distancing himself from the powers he served, we may also wonder how sympathetic he may have been toward the wild and colorful Caucasian natives whom the Imperial Russian army had come there to subdue.

PRONUNCIATIONS:
Azamat: ah-zah-MAHT
Kazbich: kaz-BEECH
Lermontov: LYAIR-mon-toff
Maxim Maximych: mak-SEEM mak-SEEM-each
Grigori Pechorin: gree-GOH-ree peh-CHOH-reen

Bela[1]

I was travelling along the post road from Tiflis. The only luggage in the carriage was one small portmanteau half-full of travel notes about Georgia. Fortunately for you the greater part of them has been lost since then, though luckily for me the case and the rest of the things in it have survived.

The sun was already slipping behind a snow-capped ridge when I drove into Koishaur Valley. The Ossetian coachman, singing at the top of his voice, urged his horses on relentlessly to reach the summit of Koishaur Mountain before nightfall. What a glorious spot this valley is! All around it tower formidable mountains, reddish crags draped with hanging ivy and crowned with clusters of plane trees, yellow cliffs grooved by torrents, with a gilded fringe of snow high above, while down below the Aragva embraces a nameless stream that noisily bursts forth from a black, gloom-filled gorge, and then stretches in a silvery ribbon into the distance, its surface shimmering like the scaly back of a snake.

On reaching the foot of Koishaur Mountain we stopped outside a *dukhan*[2] where some twenty Georgians and mountaineers made up a noisy assemblage; nearby a camel caravan had halted for the night. I had to hire oxen to haul my carriage to the top of the confounded mountain for it was already autumn and a thin layer of ice covered the ground, and the climb was about two versts in length.

There was nothing for it but to hire six oxen and several Ossetians. One of them hoisted my portmanteau on his shoulder and the others set to helping the oxen along, doing little more than shout, however.

Behind my carriage came another pulled by four oxen with no visible exertion although the vehicle was piled high with baggage. This rather surprised me. In the wake of the carriage walked its owner, puffing at a small silver inlaid Kabardian pipe. He was wearing an officer's coat without epaulettes and a shaggy Cherkess cap. He looked about fifty or so, his swarthy face betrayed a long acquaintanceship with the Caucasian sun, and his prematurely grey moustache belied his firm step and vigorous appearance. I went up to him and bowed; he silently returned my greeting, blowing out an enormous cloud of smoke.

"I take it we are fellow travellers?"

He bowed again, but did not say a word.

"I suppose you are going to Stavropol?"

"Yes, sir, I am . . . with some government baggage."

"Will you please explain to me how it is that four oxen easily manage to pull your heavy carriage while six beasts can barely haul my empty one with the help of all these Ossetians?"

He smiled shrewdly, casting an appraising glance at me.

"I daresay you haven't been long in the Caucasus?"

1. Translated by M. Parker.   2. Caucasian tavern.

"About a year," I replied.

He smiled again.

"Why do you ask?"

"No particular reason, sir. They're terrific rogues, these Asiatics! You don't think their yelling helps much, do you? You can't tell what the devil they're saying. But the oxen understand them all right; hitch up twenty of the beasts if you wish and they won't budge once those fellows begin yelling in their tongue. . . . Terrific cheats, they are. And what can you do to them? They do like to skin the traveller. Spoiled, they are, the scoundrels . . . you'll see they'll make you tip them too. I know them by now, they won't fool me!"

"Have you served long in these parts?"

"Yes, ever since Alexei Petrovich[3] was here," he replied, drawing himself up. "When he arrived at the line I was a sub-lieutenant, and under him was promoted twice for service against the mountaineers."

"And now?"

"Now I am in the third line battalion. And you, may I ask?"

I told him.

This brought the conversation to an end and we walked along side by side in silence. On top of the mountain we ran into snow. The sun set and night followed day without any interval in between as is usual in the South; thanks to the glistening snow, however, we could easily pick out the road which still continued to climb, though less steeply than before. I gave orders to put my portmanteau in the carriage and replace the oxen with horses, and turned to look back at the valley down below for the last time, but a thick mist that rolled in waves from the gorges blanketed it completely and not a single sound reached us from its depths. The Ossetians vociferously besieged me, demanding money for vodka; but the captain shouted at them in such a threatening manner that they dispersed in a moment.

"You see what they are like!" he grumbled. "They don't know enough Russian to ask for a piece of bread, but they've learned to beg for tips: 'Officer, give me money for vodka!' Even the Tatars are better; they're teetotalers at least. . . ."

Another verst[4] remained to the post station. It was quiet all around, so quiet that you could trace the flight of a mosquito by its buzz. A deep gorge yawned black to the left; beyond it and ahead of us the dark-blue mountain peaks wrinkled with gorges and gullies and topped by layers of snow loomed against the pale sky that still retained the last glimmer of twilight. Stars began to twinkle in the dark sky, and strangely enough it seemed that they were far higher here than in our northern sky. On both sides of the road naked black boulders jutted up from the ground, and here and there some shrubs peeped from under the snow; not a single dead leaf rustled, and it was pleasant to hear in the midst of this lifeless somnolence of nature the snorting of the tired post horses and the uneven tinkling of the Russian carriage bells.

"Tomorrow will be a fine day," I observed, but the captain did not reply. Instead he pointed to a tall mountain rising directly ahead of us.

"What's that?" I asked.

"Gud-Gora."

"Yes?"

"See how it smokes?"

---

3. Alexei Petrovich Yermolov, governor-general of Georgia from 1817 to 1827.

4. Russian measure of distance, about two-thirds of a mile.

Indeed, Gud-Gora was smoking; light wisps of mist crept along its sides while a black cloud rested on the summit, so black that it stood out as a blotch even against the dark sky.

We could already make out the post station and the roofs of the huts around it, and welcoming lights were dancing ahead when the gusts of cold raw wind came whistling down the gorge and it began to drizzle. Barely had I thrown a felt cape over my shoulders than the snow came. I looked at the captain with respect now. . . .

"We'll have to stay here overnight," he said, annoyed. "You can't journey through the hills in a blizzard like this. See any avalanches on Krestovaya?" he asked a coachman.

"No, sir," the Ossetian replied. "But there's a lot just waiting to come down."

As there was no room for travellers at the post house, we were given lodgings in a smoky hut. I invited my fellow traveller to join me at tea for I had with me a cast iron teakettle—my sole comfort on my Caucasian travels.

The hut was built against a cliff. Three wet, slippery steps led up to the door. I groped my way in and stumbled upon a cow, for these people have a cowshed for an ante-room. I could not make out where to go; on one side sheep were bleating and on the other a dog growled. Fortunately a glimmer of light showed through the gloom and guided me to another opening that looked like a door. Here a rather interesting scene confronted me: the spacious hut with a roof supported by two smoke-blackened posts was full of people. A fire built on the bare earth crackled in the middle and the smoke, forced back by the wind through the opening in the roof, hung so thick that it took some time before I could distinguish anything around me. Around the fire sat two old women, a swarm of children and a lean Georgian man, all of them dressed in tatters. There was nothing to do but to make ourselves comfortable by the fire and light up our pipes, and soon the teakettle was singing merrily.

"Pitiable creatures!" I observed to the captain, nodding toward our grimy hosts who stared at us silently with something like stupefaction.

"A dull-witted people," he replied. "Believe me, they can't do a thing, nor can they learn anything either. Our Kabardians or Chechens, rogues and vagabonds though they be, are at least good fighters, whereas these take no interest even in arms: you won't find a decent dagger on a single one of them. But what can you expect from Ossetians!"

"Were you long in Chechna?"

"Quite a while—ten years garrisoning a fort with a company, out Kamenny Brod way. Do you know the place?"

"Heard of it."

"Yes, sir, we had enough of the ruffians; now, thank God, things are quieter, but there was a time when you couldn't venture a hundred paces beyond the rampart without some hairy devil stalking you, ready to put a halter around your neck or a bullet through the back of your head the moment he caught you napping. But they were stout fellows anyway."

"You must have had a good many adventures?" I asked, spurred by curiosity.

"Aye, many indeed. . . ."

Thereupon he began to pluck at the left tip of his moustache, his head drooped and he sank into deep thought. I very badly wanted to get some sort of story out of him—a desire that is natural to anyone who travels about recording things. In the meantime the tea came to a boil; I dug out two travellers' tumblers from my portmanteau, poured out tea and placed one before the captain. He took a sip and muttered as if to himself: "Yes, many indeed!" The exclamation raised my hopes, for I knew that Caucasian oldtimers like to talk; they seldom have a chance to do so, for a man may be stationed a full five years with a company somewhere in the backwoods without anyone to greet him with a "Goodday" (that mode of address does not belong to the sergeant's vocabulary). And there is so much to talk about: the wild, strange people all around, the constant dangers, and the remarkable adventures; one cannot help thinking it is a pity that we record so little of it.

"Would you care to add a little rum?" I asked. "I have some white rum from Tiflis, it will warm you up in this cold."

"No, thanks, I don't drink."

"How is that?"

"Well . . . swore off the stuff. Once when I was still a sub-lieutenant we went on a bit of a spree, you know how it happens, and that very night there was an alarm. So we showed up before the ranks on the gay side, and there was the devil to pay when Alexei Petrovich found out. Lord preserve me from seeing a man as furious as he was; we escaped being court-martialled by a hair's breadth. That's the way it is: sometimes you got to spend a whole year without seeing anyone, and if you take to drink you're done for."

On hearing this I nearly lost hope.

"Take even the Cherkess," he went on. "As soon as they drink their fill of *boza* at a wedding or a funeral the fight begins. Once I barely managed to escape alive although I was the guest of a peaceable prince."

"How did it happen?"

"Well," he filled and lit his pipe, took a long draw on it, and began the story, "you see, I was stationed at the time at a fort beyond the Terek with a company—that was nearly five years back. Once in the autumn a convoy came with foodstuffs, and with it an officer, a young man of about twenty-five. He reported to me in full dress uniform and announced that he had been ordered to join me at the fort. He was so slim and pale and his uniform so immaculate that I could tell at once that he was a newcomer to the Caucasus. 'You must have been transferred here from Russia?' I asked him. 'Yes, sir,' he replied. I took his hand and said: 'Glad to have you here, very glad. It'll be a bit dull for you . . . but we'll get along very well, I'm sure. Call me simply Maxim Maximych, if you like, and, another thing, you need not bother wearing full dress uniform. Just come around in your forage cap.' He was shown his quarters and he settled down in the fort."

"What was his name?" I asked Maxim Maximych.

"Grigori Alexandrovich Pechorin. A fine chap he was, I assure you, though a bit queer. For instance, he would spend days on end hunting in rain or cold; everybody else would be chilled and exhausted, but not he. Yet sometimes a mere draught in his room would be enough for him to claim he had caught cold; a banging shutter might make him start and turn pale, yet I myself saw him go at a wild boar singlehanded; sometimes you couldn't get a word out of him for hours on end, but when he occasionally did start telling stories you'd split your sides laughing. . . . Yes, sir, a most curious sort of fellow he was, and, apparently, rich too, judging by the quantity of expensive trinkets he had."

"How long was he with you?" I asked.

"A good year. That was a memorable year for me; he caused me plenty of trouble, God forgive him! But after all, there are people who are predestined to have all sorts of odd things happen to them!"

"Odd things?" I exclaimed eagerly as I poured him some more tea.

"I'll tell you the story. Some six versts from the fort there lived a peaceable prince. His son, a lad of about fifteen, got into the habit of riding over to see us; not a day passed that he didn't come for one reason or another. Grigori Alexandrovich and I really spoiled him. What a scapegrace he was, ready for anything, whether it was to lean down from his saddle to pick up a cap from the ground while galloping by or to try his hand at marksmanship. But there was one bad thing about him: he had a terrible weakness for money. Once for a joke Grigori Alexandrovich promised him a gold piece if he stole the best goat from his father's herd, and what do you think? The very next night he dragged the animal in by the horns. Sometimes, if we just tried teasing him, he would flare up and reach for his dagger. 'Your head's too hot for your own good, Azamat,' I would tell him. 'That's *yaman*[5] for your topknot!'

"Once the old prince himself came over to invite us to a wedding; he was giving away his elder daughter and since we were *kunaks*[6] there was no way of declining, you know, Tatar or not. So we set out. A pack of barking dogs met us in the village. On seeing us the women hid themselves; the faces we did catch a glimpse of were far from pretty. 'I had a much better opinion of Cherkess women,' Grigori Alexandrovich said to me. 'You wait a while,' I replied, smiling. I had something up my sleeve.

"There was quite a crowd assembled in the prince's house. It's the custom among Asiatics, you know, to invite to their weddings everyone they chance to meet. We were welcomed with all due honours and shown to the best room. Before going in, though, I took care to note where they put our horses, just in case something unforeseen happened, you know."

"How do they celebrate weddings?" I asked the captain.

"Oh, in the usual way. First the mullah reads them something from the Koran, then presents are given to the newlyweds and all their relatives. They eat and drink *boza*, until finally the horsemanship display begins, and there is always some kind of filthy, tattered creature riding a mangy lame nag playing the buffoon to amuse the company. Later, when it grows dark, what we would call a ball begins in the best room. Some miserable old man strums away on a three-stringed . . . can't remember what they call it . . . something like our balalaika. The girls and young men line up in two rows facing each other, clap their hands and sing. Then one of the girls and a man step into the centre and begin to chant verses to each other improvising as they go while the rest pick up the refrain. Pechorin and I occupied the place of honour, and as we sat there the host's younger daughter, a girl of sixteen or so, came up to him and sang to him . . . what should I call it . . . a sort of compliment."

"You don't remember what she sang by any chance?"

"Yes, I think it went something like this: 'Our young horsemen are stalwart and their coats are encrusted with silver, but the young Russian officer is more stalwart still and his epaulettes are of gold. He is like a poplar among the others, yet he shall neither grow nor bloom in our orchard.' Pechorin rose, bowed to her, pressing his hand to his forehead and heart, and asked me to reply to her. Knowing their language well I translated his reply.

"When she walked away I whispered to Grigori Alexandrovich: 'Well, what do you think of her?'

5. Tatar for "bad."   6. *Kunak* means "acquaintance" [Lermontov's note].

"'Exquisite,' replied he. 'What is her name?' 'Her name is Bela,' replied I.

"And indeed, she was beautiful: tall, slim, and her eyes as black as a chamois looked right into your soul. Pechorin fell silent and did not take his eyes off her, and she frequently stole a glance at him. But Pechorin was not the only one who admired the pretty princess: from a corner of the room another pair of eyes, fixed and flaming, stared at her. I looked closer and recognized my old acquaintance Kazbich. He was a man you couldn't say was friendly, though there was nothing to show he was hostile towards us. There were a good many suspicions but he was never caught at any trickery. Occasionally he brought rams to us at the fort and sold them cheap, but he never bargained: you had to pay him what he asked; he would never cut a price even if his life depended on it. It was said about him that he would ride out beyond the Kuban with the *Abreks*,[7] and to tell the truth, he did look like a brigand: he was short, wiry and broad-shouldered. And clever he was, as clever as the devil! The *beshmet*[8] he wore was always torn and patched, but his weapons were set in silver. As for his horse, it was famous in all Kabarda, and indeed, you couldn't think of a better horse. The horsemen all around had very good reason to envy him, and time and again they tried to steal the animal, but in vain. I can still see that horse as if it were before me now: as black as pitch, with legs like taut violin strings and eyes no worse than Bela's. He was a strong animal too, could gallop fifty versts at a stretch, and as for training, he would follow his master like a dog and even recognized his voice. Kazbich never bothered to tether the animal. A regular brigand horse!

"That evening Kazbich was more morose than I had ever seen him, and I noticed that he had a coat of mail under his *beshmet*. 'There must be a reason for the armour,' thought I. 'He is evidently scheming something.'

"It was stuffy indoors, so I stepped out into the fresh air. The night was settling on the hills and the mist was beginning to weave in and out among the gorges.

"It occurred to me to look into the shelter where our horses stood and see whether they were being fed, besides which caution is never amiss. After all, I had a fine horse and a good many Kabardians had cast fond glances at him and said: '*Yakshi tkhe, chek yakshi!*'[9]

"I was picking my way along the fence when suddenly I heard voices; one of the speakers I recognized right away: it was that scapegrace Azamat, our host's son. The other spoke more slowly and quietly. 'I wonder what they're up to,' thought I. 'I hope it's not about my horse.' I dropped down behind the fence and cocked my ears, trying not to miss a word. It was impossible to catch everything, for now and then the singing and the hum of voices from the hut drowned out the conversation.

"'That's a fine horse you have,' Azamat was saying 'Were I the master of my house and the owner of a drove of three hundred mares, I'd give half of them for your horse, Kazbich!'

"'So it's Kazbich,' thought I and remembered the coat of mail.

"'You're right,' Kazbich replied after a momentary silence, 'you won't find another like him in all Kabarda. Once, beyond the Terek it was, I rode with the *Abreks* to pick up some Russian horses. We were unlucky though, and had to scatter. Four Cossacks came after me; I could already hear the *gyaurs*[1] shouting behind me, and ahead of me was a thicket. I bent low in the saddle, trusted myself to Allah and for the

---

7. Mountaineers who waged guerrilla war against the Russian conquerors.
8. Quilted jacket.

9. "Good horse, very good."
1. Pejorative Muslim term for unbelievers.

first time in my life insulted the horse by striking him. Like a bird he flew between the branches; the thorns tore my clothes and the dry Karagach twigs lashed my face. The horse leapt over stumps and crashed through the brush chest on. It would have been better for me to slip off him in some glade and take cover in the woods on foot, but I could not bear to part with him so I held on, and the Prophet rewarded me. Some bullets whistled past overhead; I could hear the Cossacks, now dismounted, running along my trail. . . . Suddenly a deep gully opened up in front; my horse hesitated for a moment, and then jumped. But on the other side his hind legs slipped off the sheer edge and he was left holding on by the forelegs. I dropped the reins and slipped into the gully. This saved the horse, who managed to pull himself up. The Cossacks saw all this, but none of them came down into the ravine to look for me; they probably gave me up for dead. Then I heard them going after my horse. My heart bled as I crawled through the thick grass of the gully until I was out of the woods. Now I saw some Cossacks riding out from the thicket into the open and my Karagyoz galloping straight at them. With a shout they made a dash for him. They chased him for a long time. One of them almost got a halter around his neck once or twice; I trembled, turned away and began praying. Looking up a few moments later I saw my Karagyoz flying free as the wind, his tail streaming while the *gyaurs* trailed far behind in the plain on their exhausted horses. I swear by Allah this is the truth! I sat in my gully until far into the night. And what do you think happened, Azamat? Suddenly through the darkness I heard a horse running along the brink of the gully, snorting, neighing and stamping his hoofs; I recognized the voice of my Karagyoz, for it was he, my comrade! Since then we have never parted.'

"You could hear the man patting the smooth neck of the horse and addressing him with all kinds of endearments.

"'Had I a drove of a thousand mares,' said Azamat, 'I would give it to you for your Karagyoz.'

"'*Iok*,[2] I wouldn't take it,' replied Kazbich indifferently.

"'Listen, Kazbich,' Azamat coaxed him. 'You are a good man and a brave horseman; my father fears the Russians and does not let me go into the mountains. Give me your horse and I will do anything you want, I'll steal for you my father's best musket or sabre, whatever you wish—and his sabre is a real *gurda*,[3] lay the blade against your hand and it will cut deep into the flesh; mail like yours won't stop it.'

"Kazbich was silent.

"'When I first saw your horse,' Azamat went on, 'prancing under you, his nostrils dilated and sparks flying under his hoofs, something strange happened in my soul, and I lost interest in everything. I have disdained my father's best horses, ashamed to be seen riding them, and I have been sick at heart. In my misery I have spent days on end sitting on a crag, thinking of nothing but your fleet-footed Karagyoz with his proud stride and sleek back as straight as an arrow, his blazing eyes looking straight into mine as if he wanted to speak to me. I shall die, Kazbich, if you will not sell him to me,' said Azamat in a trembling voice.

"I thought I heard him sob; and I must tell you that Azamat was a most stubborn lad and even when he was younger nothing could ever make him cry.

"In reply to his tears I heard something like a laugh.

---

2. "No."   3. A kind of sword.

"'Listen!' said Azamat his voice firm now. 'You see I am ready to do anything. I could steal my sister for you if you want. How she can dance and sing! And her gold embroidery is something wonderful! The Turkish Padishah[4] himself never had a wife like her. If you want her, wait for me tomorrow night in the gorge where the stream flows; I shall go by with her on the way to the next village—and she'll be yours. Isn't Bela worth your steed?'

"For a long, long time Kazbich was silent. At last instead of replying he began softly singing an old song:[5]

Ours are the fairest of maidens that be:
Eyes like the stars, by their light do I see.
Sweet flits the time when we cosset a maid,
Sweeter's the freedom of any young blade.
Wives by the dozen are purchased with gold,
A mettlesome steed is worth riches untold;
Swift o'er the plains like a whirlwind he flies,
Never betrays you, and never tells lies.

"In vain Azamat pleaded with him; he tried tears, flattery, and cajolery, until finally Kazbich lost patience with him:

"'Get away with you, boy! Are you mad? You could never ride my horse! He'd throw you after the first three paces and you'd smash your head against a rock.'

"'Me?' Azamat screamed in a fury, and his child's dagger rang against the coat of mail. A strong arm flung him back and he fell against the wattle fence so violently that it shook. 'Now the fun will begin,' thought I and dashed into the stable, bridled our horses and led them to the yard at the back. Two minutes later a terrific uproar broke out in the hut. This is what happened: Azamat ran into the hut in a torn *beshmet* shouting that Kazbich had tried to kill him. Everybody rushed out and went for their arms—and the fun was on! There was screaming and shouting and shots were fired, but Kazbich was already on his horse spinning around like a demon in the midst of the crowd and warding off assailants with his sabre. 'Bad business to get mixed up in this,' said I to Grigori Alexandrovich as I caught him by the arm. 'Hadn't we better clear out as fast as we can?'

"'Let's wait a bit and see how it ends.'

"'It's sure to end badly; that's what always happens with these Asiatics, as soon as they have their fill of drink they go slashing each other.' We mounted and rode home."

"What happened to Kazbich?" I asked impatiently.

"What can happen to these people?" replied the captain, finishing his glass of tea. "He got away, of course."

"Not even wounded, was he?" I asked.

"The Lord only knows. They're tough, the rogues! I have seen some of them in engagements; a man may be cut up into ribbons with bayonets and still he continues brandishing his sabre." After a brief silence the captain went on, stamping his foot:

"There is one thing I'll never forgive myself for. When we got back to the fort, some devil prompted me to tell Grigori Alexandrovich what I had overheard behind the fence. He laughed—the fox—though he was already cooking up a scheme."

"What was it? I should like to hear it."

---

4. Ottoman term for emperor.
5. I apologize to my readers for having put Kazbich's

song, which of course was told to me in prose, into verse; but habit is second nature [Lermontov's note].

"I suppose I'll have to tell you. Since I began telling the story, I might as well finish.

"Some four days later Azamat rode up to the fort. As usual, he went in to see Grigori Alexandrovich, who always had some delicacies for him. I was there too. The talk turned to horses, and Pechorin began to praise Kazbich's horse; as spirited and beautiful as a chamois the steed was, and as Pechorin put it, there simply was no other horse like it in all the world.

"The Tatar boy's eyes lit up, but Pechorin pretended not to notice it; I tried to change the subject, but at once he brought it back to Kazbich's horse. This happened each time Azamat came. About three weeks later I noticed that Azamat was growing pale and wasting away as they do from love in novels. What was it all about?

"You see, I got the whole story later. Grigori Alexandrovich egged him on to a point when the lad was simply desperate. Finally he put it point-blank: I can see, Azamat, that you want that horse very badly. Yet you have as little chance of getting it as of seeing the back of your own head. Now tell me what would you give if someone gave it to you?'

"'Anything he asks,' replied Azamat.

"'In that case I'll get the horse for you, but on one condition. . . . Swear you will carry it out?'

"'I swear. . . . And you must swear too!'

"'Good! I swear you'll get the horse, only you have to give me your sister Bela in exchange. Karagyoz shall be her *kalym*[6]! I hope the bargain suits you.'

"Azamat was silent.

"'You don't want to? As you wish. I thought you were a man, but I see you're still a child: you're too young to ride in the saddle.'

"Azamat flared up. 'What about my father?' he asked.

"'Doesn't he ever go anywhere?'

"'That's true, he does. . . .'

"'So you agree?'

"'I agree,' whispered Azamat, pale as death itself. 'When?'

"'The next time Kazbich comes here; he has promised to bring a dozen sheep. The rest is my business. And you take care of your end of the bargain, Azamat!'

"So they arranged the whole business, and I must say it was a bad business indeed. Later I said so to Pechorin, but he only replied that the primitive Cherkess girl ought to be happy to have such a fine husband as himself, for, after all, he would be her husband according to the local custom, and that Kazbich was a brigand who should be punished anyway. Judge for yourself, what could I say against this? But at the time I knew nothing about the conspiracy. So one day Kazbich came asking whether we wanted sheep and honey, and I told him to bring some the day after. 'Azamat,' Grigori Alexandrovich said to the lad, 'tomorrow Karagyoz will be in my hands. If Bela is not here tonight you will not see the horse. . . .'

"'Good!' said Azamat and galloped back to his village. In the evening Grigori Alexandrovich armed himself and rode out of the fort. How they managed everything, I don't know—but at night they both returned and the sentry saw a woman lying across Azamat's saddle with hands and feet tied and head wrapped in a veil."

"And the horse?" I asked the captain.

6. Dowry.

"Just a moment, just a moment. Early the next morning Kazbich came, driving along the dozen sheep he wanted to sell. Tying his horse to a fence, he came to see me and I regaled him with tea, for, scoundrel though he was, he nevertheless was a *kunak* of mine.

"We began to chat about this and that. Suddenly I saw Kazbich start; his face twisted and he dashed for the window, but it unfortunately opened to the backyard. What's happened?' I asked.

"'My horse . . . horse!' he said, shaking all over.

"And true enough, I heard the beat of hoofs. 'Some Cossack must have arrived.'

"'No! *Urus yaman, yaman,*'[7] he cried and dashed out like a wild panther. In two strides he was in the courtyard; at the gates of the fort a sentry barred his way with a musket, but he leaped over the weapon and began running down the road. In the distance a cloud of dust whirled—it was Azamat urging on the spirited Karagyoz. Kazbich drew his gun from its holster and fired as he ran. For a minute he stood motionless until he was certain he had missed; then he screamed, dashed the gun to pieces against the stones, and rolled on the ground crying like a baby. . . . People from the fort gathered around him—but he did not see anyone, and after standing about for a while they all went back. I had the money for the sheep placed next to him, but he did not touch it; he only lay there face down like a corpse. Would you believe it, he lay like that all through the night? Only the next morning he returned to the fort to ask whether anyone could tell him who the thief was. A sentry who had seen Azamat untie the horse and gallop off did not think it necessary to conceal the fact. When Kazbich heard the name his eyes flashed and he set out for the village where Azamat's father lived.

"What did the father do?"

"The whole trouble was that Kazbich did not find him; he had gone off somewhere for six days or so. Had he not done so could Azamat have carried off his sister?

"The father returned to find both daughter and son gone. The lad was a wily one; he knew very well that his head wouldn't be worth anything if he got caught. So he has been missing ever since; most likely he joined some *Abrek* band and perhaps ended his mad career beyond the Terek, or maybe the Kuban. And that's no more than he deserved!

"I must admit that it wasn't easy for me either. As soon as I learned that the Cherkess girl was at Grigori Alexandrovich's, I put on my epaulettes and strapped on my sword and went to see him.

"He was lying on the bed in the first room, one hand under his head and the other holding a pipe that had gone out. The door leading to the next room was locked, and there was no key in the lock; all this I noticed at once. I coughed and stamped my heels on the threshold, but he pretended not to hear.

"'Ensign! Sir!' I said as severely as I could. 'Don't you realize that I've come to see you?'

"'Ah, how do you do, Maxim Maximych. Have a pipe,' he replied without getting up.

"'I beg your pardon! I am no Maxim Maximych: I am a captain to you!'

"'Oh, it's all the same. Would you care to have some tea? If you only knew what a load I've got on my mind!'

"'I know everything,' I replied, walking up to the bed.

7. "Russian bad, bad."

"'That's all the better, then. I am in no mood to go over it again.'

"'Ensign, you have committed an offence for which I too may have to answer. . . .'

"'Well, why not? Have we not always shared everything equally?'

"'This is no time to joke. Will you surrender your sword?'

"'Mitka, the sword!'

"Mitka brought the sword. Having thus done my duty. I sat down on the bed and said: 'Listen here, Grigori Alexandrovich, you'd best admit that it's wrong.'

"'What's wrong?'

"'To have kidnapped Bela. What a scoundrel that Azamat is! Come, now, admit it,' I said to him.

"'Why should I? She happens to please me.'

"What would you have me reply to that? I did not know what to do. Nevertheless after a moment's silence I told him he would have to give the girl back if her father insisted.

"'I don't see why I should!'

"'But what if he finds out that she is here?'

"'How will he?'

"Again I was in a blind alley.

"'Listen, Maxim Maximych,' said Pechorin, rising, 'you're a good soul—if we give the girl to that barbarian he'll either kill her or sell her. What has been done cannot be undone, and it won't do to spoil things by being overzealous. You keep my sword, but leave her with me. . . .'

"'Supposing you let me see her,' said I.

"'She's behind that door; I myself have been trying in vain to see her. She sits there in a corner all huddled up in her shawl and will neither speak nor look at you; she's as timid as a gazelle. I hired the *dukhan* keeper's wife who speaks Tatar to look after her and get her accustomed to the idea that she is mine—for she will never belong to anyone but myself,' he added, striking the table with his fist.

"I reconciled myself to this too. . . . What would you have had me do? There are people who always get their own way."

"What happened in the end?" I asked Maxim Maximych. "Did he actually win her over or did she pine away in captivity longing for her native village?"

"Now why should she have longed for her native village? She could see the very same mountains from the fort as she had seen from the village, and that's all these barbarians want. Moreover, Grigori Alexandrovich gave her some present every day. At first she proudly tossed the gifts aside without a word, whereupon they became the property of the *dukhan* keeper's wife and stimulated her eloquence. Ah, gifts! What wouldn't a woman do for a bit of coloured rag! But I digress. . . . Grigori Alexandrovich strove long and hard to win her; in the meantime he learned to speak Tatar and she began to understand our language. Little by little she learned to look at him, at first askance, but she was always melancholy and I too could not help feeling sad when I heard her from the next room singing her native songs in a low voice. I shall never forget a scene I once witnessed while passing the window: Bela was seated on a bench, her head bowed, and Grigori Alexandrovich stood before her. 'Listen, my peri,'[8] he was saying, 'don't you realize that sooner or later you must be mine—why

---

8. Fair one; in Persian mythology, an angel or fairy.

then do you torment me so? Or perhaps you love some Chechen? If you do, I will let you go home at once.' She shuddered barely perceptibly and shook her head. 'Or,' he went on, 'am I altogether hateful to you?' She sighed. 'Perhaps your faith forbids your loving me?' She grew pale but did not say a word. 'Believe me, there is only one Allah for all people, and if he permits me to love you why should he forbid you to return my love?' She looked him straight in the face as if struck by this new thought; her eyes betrayed suspicion and sought reassurance. And what eyes she had! They shone like two coals.

"'Listen to me, sweet, kind Bela!' Pechorin continued. 'You can see how I love you. I am ready to do anything to cheer you; I want you to be happy, and if you keep on grieving, I shall die. Tell me, you will be more cheerful?' She thought for a moment, her black eyes searching his face, then smiled tenderly and nodded in agreement. He took her hand and began to persuade her to kiss him; but she resisted weakly and repeated over and over again: 'Please, please, no, no.' He became persistent; she trembled and began to sob. 'I am your captive, your slave,' she said, 'and of course you can force me.' And again there were tears.

"Grigori Alexandrovich struck his forehead with his fist and ran into the next room. I went in to him; he was gloomily pacing up and down with arms folded. 'What now, old chap?' I asked him. 'She's not a woman, but a she-devil!' he replied. 'But I give you my word that she will be mine!' I shook my head. 'Do you want to wager?' he said. 'I'll give her a week.' 'Done!' We shook on it and parted.

"The next day he sent a messenger to Kizlyar to make diverse purchases and there was no end to the array of various kinds of Persian cloth that was brought back.

"'What do you think, Maxim Maximych,' he said as he showed me the gifts, 'will an Asiatic beauty be able to resist a battery like this?' 'You don't know Cherkess women,' I replied. 'They're nothing like Georgian or Transcaucasian Tatar women— nothing like them. They have their own rules of conduct; different upbringing, you know.' Grigori Alexandrovich smiled and began whistling a march air.

"It turned out that I was right: the gifts did only half the trick; she became more amiable and confiding—but nothing more. So he decided to play his last card. One morning he ordered his horse saddled, dressed in Cherkess fashion, armed himself, and went in to her. 'Bela,' he said, 'you know how I love you. I decided to carry you off believing that when you came to know me you would love me too. But I made a mistake; so, farewell, I leave you the mistress of everything I have, and if you wish, you can return to your father—you are free, I have wronged you and must be punished. Farewell, I shall ride away, where, I don't know. Perhaps it will not be long before I am cut down by a bullet or a sabre blow; when that happens, remember me and try to forgive me.' He turned away and extended his hand to her in parting. She did not take the hand, nor did she say a word. Standing behind the door I saw her through the crack, and I was sorry for her—such a deathly pallor had spread over her pretty little face. Hearing no reply, Pechorin took several steps towards the door. He was trembling, and do you know, I quite believe he was capable of actually doing what he threatened. The Lord knows that's the kind of man he was. But barely had he touched the door when she sprang up, sobbing, and threw her arms around his neck. Believe me, I also wept standing there behind the door, that is, I didn't exactly weep, but— well, anyway it was silly."

The captain fell silent.

"I might as well confess," he said after a while, tugging at his moustache, "I was annoyed because no woman had ever loved me like that."

"How long did their happiness last?" I asked.

"Well, she admitted that Pechorin had often appeared in her dreams since the day she first saw him and that no other man had ever made such an impression on her. Yes, they were happy!"

"How boring!" I exclaimed involuntarily. Indeed, I was expecting a tragic end and it was a shock to see my hopes collapse so suddenly. "Don't tell me the father did not guess she was with you in the fort?"

"I believe he did suspect. A few days later, however, we heard that the old man had been killed. This is how it happened. . . ."

My interest was again aroused.

"I must tell you that Kazbich got the idea that Azamat had stolen the horse with his father's consent, at least I think so. So he lay in ambush one day some three versts beyond the village when the old man was returning from his futile search for his daughter. The old man had left his liegemen lagging behind and was plunged deep in thought as he rode slowly down the road through the deepening twilight, when Kazbich suddenly sprang cat-like from behind a bush, leapt behind him on the horse, cut him down with a blow of his dagger and seized the reins. Some of the liegemen saw it all from a hill, but though they set out in pursuit they could not overtake Kazbich."

"So he compensated himself for the loss of his horse and took revenge as well," I said in order to draw an opinion out of my companion.

"Of course he was absolutely right according to their lights," said the captain.

I was struck by the ability of the Russian to reconcile himself to the customs of the peoples among whom he happens to live. I do not know whether this mental quality is a virtue or a vice, but it does reveal a remarkable flexibility and that sober common sense which forgives evil wherever it feels it to be necessary, or impossible to eradicate.

Meanwhile we had finished our tea. Outside the horses had been harnessed long since and were now standing shivering in the snow; the paling moon in the western sky was about to immerse itself in the black clouds that trailed like tattered bits of a rent curtain from the mountain peaks in the distance. We stepped out into the open. Contrary to the prediction of my companion, the weather had cleared and promised a calm morning. The garlands of stars, intertwined in a fantastic pattern in the far heavens, went out one after another as the pale glimmer of the East spread out over the dark lilac sky, gradually casting its glow on the steep mountainsides blanketed by virginal snow. To right and left yawned gloomy, mysterious abysses, and the mist, coiling and twisting like a snake, crawled into them along the cracks and crevices of the cliffs as if in apprehension of coming day.

There was a great peace in the heavens and on earth as there is in the hearts of men at morning prayers. Only now and then the cold east wind came in gusts ruffling the hoary manes of the horses. We set out, the five lean nags hauling our carriages with difficulty along the tortuous road up Gud-Gora. We walked behind, setting stones under the wheels when the horses could pull no longer; it seemed as if the road must lead straight to heaven, for it rose higher and higher as far as the eye could see and finally was lost in the cloud that had been reposing on the mountain summit since the day before like a vulture awaiting its prey. The snow crunched underfoot; the air grew so rare that it was painful to breathe; I continually felt the blood rushing to my head, yet a feeling of elation coursed through my being and somehow it felt good to be so much above the world—a childish feeling, I admit, but as we drift farther away from the conventions of society and draw closer to nature we willy-nilly become children again: the soul is unburdened of whatever it has acquired and it becomes what it once was and what it will surely be again. Anyone who has had occasion as I have to roam in the deserted mountains, feasting his eyes upon their fantastic shapes and eagerly inhaling the invigorating air of the gorges, will understand my urge to describe, to portray, to paint these magic canvases. At last we reached the summit of Gud-Gora, and paused to look around us: a grey cloud rested on the mountain top and its cold breath held the threat of an imminent blizzard; but the east was so clear and golden that we, that is, the captain and I, utterly failed to notice it. . . . Yes, the captain too: for simple hearts feel the beauty and majesty of nature a hundred times more keenly than do we, rapturous tellers of stories spoken or written.

"You are no doubt accustomed to these magnificent scenes," I said to him.

"Yes, sir, you can get accustomed even to the whining of bullets, I mean, accustomed to concealing the involuntary quickening of your pulse."

"On the contrary, I have been told that to some old soldiers it is sweet music."

"Yes, it is sweet too, if you please; but only because it makes the heart beat faster. Look," he added, pointing to the east, "what heavenly country!"

Indeed it was a panorama I can hardly hope to see again: below us lay the Koishaur Valley, the Aragva and another river tracing their course across it like two silver threads; a bluish mist crept over it, seeking refuge in the nearest nooks from the warm rays of the morning; to the right and to the left the mountain ridges, one higher than the other, crisscrossed and stretched out into the distance covered with snow and brush. Mountains as far as the eye could see, but no two crags alike—and all this snow burned with a rosy glitter so gay and so vivid that one would fain have stayed there for ever. The sun barely showed from behind a dark-blue mountain which only the experienced eye could distinguish from a storm cloud, but above it stretched a crimson belt to which my comrade now drew my attention. "I told you," he exclaimed, "there's bad weather ahead; we'll have to hurry or it may catch us on Krestovaya. Look lively, there!" he shouted to the coachmen.

Chains were passed through the wheels for brakes to prevent them from skidding. Leading the horses by their bridles we began the descent. To the right of us was a cliff, and to the left an abyss so deep that an Ossetian village at the bottom looked like a swallow's nest; I shuddered at the thought that a dozen times a year some courier rides through the night along this road too narrow for two carts to pass, without alighting from his jolting carriage. One of our drivers was a Russian peasant from Yaroslavl, the other an Ossetian. The Ossetian took the leading horse by the bridle after unhitching the first pair in good time and taking every other possible precaution, but our heedless Russian did not even bother to get down from the box. When I suggested that he might have shown some concern if only for my portmanteau, which I had no desire to go down into the abyss to recover, he replied: "Don't worry, sir! With God's help we'll get there just as well as they. This is not the first time we've done it." And he was right; true, we might not have got through safely, yet we did. And if all men gave the matter more thought they would realize that life is not worth worrying over too much. . . .

Perhaps you wish to hear the story of Bela to the end? Firstly, however, I am not writing a novel but simply travel notes, and hence I cannot make the captain resume his story sooner than he actually did. So you will have to wait, or, if you wish to do so, skip a few pages; only I do not advise you to, for the crossing of Mount Krestovaya (or le Mont St. Christophe as the learned Gamba calls it) is worthy of your interest. And so we descended from Gud-Gora to Cherlova-Dolina. That is a romantic name for you. Perhaps you already visualize the den of the Evil Spirit among the inaccessible crags—but if you do, you are mistaken: Chertova-Dolina derives its name from the world "*cherta*" and not "*chort,*" for the boundary of Georgia once passed here.[9] The valley was buried under snowdrifts which gave the scene a rather strong resemblance to Saratov, Tambov and other *pleasant* spots in our mother country.

"There's Krestovaya," said the captain as we came down to Cherlova-Dolina, pointing to a hill shrouded by snow. On the summit the black outline of a stone cross was visible, and past it ran a barely discernible road which was used only when the road along the moutainside was snowbound. Our drivers said that there were no snowslides yet and in order to spare the horses they took us the roundabout way. Around a turn in the road we came upon five Ossetians who offered us their services, and seizing hold of the wheels and shouting, they began to help our carriage along. The road was dangerous indeed. To our right masses of snow hung overhead ready, it seemed, to crash down into the gorge with the first blast of wind. Some sections of the narrow road were covered with snow, which here and there gave way underfoot; others had been turned to ice under the action of the sun's rays and night frosts, so that we made headway with difficulty. The horses kept on slipping, and to the left of us yawned a deep fissure with a turbulent stream at the bottom that now slipped out of sight under a crust of ice, now plunged in frothy fury amidst black boulders. It took us all of two hours to skirt Mount Kreslovaya—two hours to negotiate two versts. In the meantime the clouds came lower and it began to hail and snow. The wind bursting into the gorges howled and whistled like Solovey the Brigand,[1] and soon the stone cross was blotted out by the mist which was coming in waves from the East, each wave thicker than the other. Incidentally, there is a queer but generally accepted legend about this cross which claims it was raised by Emperor Peter I when he travelled through the Caucasus. Yet, in the first place, Peter was only in Daghestan, and, secondly, an inscription in big letters on the cross announced it had been put up on the orders of General Yermolov, in 1824, to be exact. Despite the inscription, the legend had taken such firm root that one is at a loss to know what to believe, all the more so since we are not accustomed to put our faith in inscriptions.

We had another five versts to descend along the ice-coated rocky ledges and through soft snow before reaching the station at Kobi. The horses were exhausted and we thoroughly chilled, while the blizzard blew harder and harder much like our native, northern snowstorms, except that its wild refrain was sadder and more mournful. "You too, my exile," thought I, "are mourning your wide, boundless steppes where there was space to spread out your icy wings, whilst here you are choked and hemmed in like the eagle who beats against the bars of his iron cage."

"Looks bad!" the captain was saying. "Nothing but mist and snow. Watch out or we'll find ourselves dropping into a crevice or getting stuck in some wretched hole, and the Baidara down there will probably be running too high to cross. That's Asia for you! The rivers are as unreliable as the people."

The drivers shouted and cursed as they whipped the snorting, balking horses which refused to take another step in spite of the persuasion of the whip. "Your Honour," one of the drivers finally said, "we can't reach Kobi today. Had we not better turn

---

9. A play of words in the original Russian. *Cherta* means "line" and *chort* is "devil."

1. Legendary Russian bandit, so strong that he could fell a person just by whistling.

to the left while there is still time? Over on that slope there are some huts, I believe. Travellers always halt there in bad weather." Then he added, pointing to an Ossetian: "They say they will guide us there if you give them some money for vodka."

"I know it, brother, I know without you telling me!" said the captain. "These rogues! They'll do anything for a tip."

"All the same you have to admit that we'd be worse off without them," said I.

"Maybe, maybe," he muttered, "but I know these guides! They can tell by instinct when to take advantage of you; as if you couldn't find your way without them."

So we turned to the left and somehow after a good deal of trouble made our way to the scanty refuge consisting of two huts built of slabs and stones and surrounded by a wall of the same material. The tattered inhabitants gave us a cordial welcome. Later I found out that the government pays and feeds them on condition that they take in wayfarers who are caught by the storm.

"It's all for the best," said I, taking a seat by the fire. "Now you will be able to tell me the rest of the story about Bela; I am sure that wasn't the end of it."

"What makes you so sure?" replied the captain, with a sly smile and a twinkle in his eye.

"Because things don't happen like that. Anything that begins so strangely must end in the same way."

"Well, you guessed right. . . ."

"Glad to hear it."

"It's all very well for you to be glad, but for me it is really sad to recall. She was a fine girl, Bela was! I grew as fond of her in the end as if she were my own daughter, and she loved me too. I ought to tell you that I have no family; I haven't heard about my father or mother for some twelve years now, and it didn't occur to me to get myself a wife earlier—and now, you must admit, it would no longer be seemly. So I was happy to have found someone to pet. She would sing to us or dance the Lezghinka. . . . And how she danced! I've seen our provincial fine ladies and once some twenty years ago I was at the Nobles' Club in Moscow, but none of them could hold a candle to her. Grigori Alexandrovich dressed her up like a doll, petted and fondled her, and she grew so lovely that it was amazing. The tan disappeared from her face and arms and her cheeks grew rosy. . . . How gay she was and how she used to tease me, the little vixen. . . . May God forgive her!"

"What happened when you told her about her father's death?"

"We kept it from her for a long time, until she became accustomed to her new position. And when she was told, she cried for a couple of days and then forgot about it.

"For about four months everything went splendidly. Grigori Alexandrovich, I must have already told you, had a passion for hunting. Some irresistible force used to draw him to the forest to stalk wild boar or goats, and now he had scarcely ventured beyond the ramparts. Then I noticed he was growing pensive again; he would pace up and down the room with his arms folded behind his back One day without saying a word to anyone he took his gun and went out, and was lost for the whole morning that happened once, twice, and then more and more frequently. Things are going badly, I thought, something must have come between them!

"One morning when I dropped in to see them I found Bela sitting on the bed wearing a black silk *beshmet*, so pale and sad that I was really alarmed.

"'Where's Pechorin?' I asked.

"'Hunting.'

"'When did he leave? Today?'

"She did not reply, it seemed difficult for her to speak.

"'No, yesterday,' she finally said with a deep sigh.

"'I hope nothing has happened to him.'

"'All day yesterday I thought and thought,' she said her eyes full of tears, 'and imagined all kinds of terrible things. First I thought a wild boar had injured him then that the Chechen had carried him off to the mountains. . . . And now it already seems to me that he doesn't love me.'

"'Truly, my dear, you couldn't have imagined anything worse!'

"She burst into tears, and then proudly raised her head dried her tears, and continued:

"'If he doesn't love me, what prevents him from sending me home? I am not forcing myself on him. And if this goes on I shall leave myself; I, am not his slave, I am a prince's daughter!'

"I began reasoning with her. 'Listen, Bela, he can't sit here all the time as if tied to your apron strings. He's a young man and likes to hunt. He'll go and he'll come back, and if you are going to mope he'll only get tired of you the sooner.'

"'You are right,' she replied. 'I shall be gay.' Laughing, the seized her tambourine and began to sing and dance. for me. But very soon she threw herself on the bed again and hid her face in her hands.

"What was I to do with her? You see, I had never had dealings with women. I racked my brains for some way to comfort her but could not think of anything. For a time we both were silent. A most unpleasant situation. I assure you!

"At length I said: 'Would you like to go for a walk with me on the rampart? The weather's fine.' It was September, and the day was really wonderful, sunny but not too hot, the mountains as clearly visible as if laid out on a platter. We went out, and in silence walked up and down the breastwork. After a while she sat down on the turf and I sat next to her. It's really funny to recall how I fussed over her like a nursemaid.

"Our fort was situated on an elevation, and the view from the parapet was excellent: on one side was a wide open space intersected by gullies and ending in a forest that stretched all the way to the top of the mountain ridge, and here and there on this expanse you could see the smoke of villages and droves of grazing horses; on the other side flowed a small rivulet bordered by dense brush that covered the flinty hills merging with the main chain of the Caucasus. We were sitting in a corner of a bastion whence we had a perfect view of either side. As I scanned the landscape, a man riding a grey horse emerged from the woods and came closer and closer, until he finally stopped on the far side of the rivulet some hundred sagenes or so from where we were and began spinning around on his horse like mad. What the devil was that?

"'You've younger eyes than I, Bela, see if you can make out that horseman,' said I. 'I wonder whom he is honouring with a visit.'

"She looked and cried out: 'It's Kazbich!'

"'Ah, the brigand! Has he come to mock at us? Now I could see it was Kazbich: the same swarthy features, and as tattered and dirty as ever. 'That's my father's horse,' Bela said, seizing my arm; she trembled like a leaf and her eyes flashed. 'Aha, my little one,' thought I, 'brigand blood tells in you too.'

"'Come here,' I called to a sentry, 'take aim and knock that fellow off for me and you'll get a ruble in silver.' 'Yes, Your Honour, only he doesn't stay still. . . .' 'Tell him to,' said I laughing. 'Hey, there!' shouted the sentry waving his arm, 'wait a minute, will you, stop spinning like a top!' Kazbich actually paused to listen, probably thinking we wanted to parley, the insolent beggar! My grenadier took aim . . .

bang! . . . and missed, for as soon as the powder flashed in the pan, Kazbich gave a jab to the horse making it leap aside. He stood up in his stirrups, shouted something in his own language, shook his whip in the air—and in a flash was gone.

"'You ought to be ashamed of yourself!' I said to the sentry.

"'Your Honour! He's gone off to die,' he replied. 'Such a cussed lot they are you can't kill them with one shot.'

"A quarter of an hour later Pechorin returned from the chase. Bela ran to meet him and threw her arms around his neck, and not a single complaint, not a single reproach for his long absence did I hear. . . . Even I had lost patience with him. 'Sir,' said I, 'Kazbich was on the other side of the river just now and we fired at him; you could easily have run into him too. These mountaineers are vengeful people, and do you think he does not know you helped Azamat? I'll wager he saw Bela here. And I happen to know that a year ago he was very much attracted by her—told me so himself in fact. Had he had any hope of raising a substantial *kalym* he surely would have courted her. . . .' Pechorin was grave now. 'Yes,' he said, 'we have to be more careful . . . Bela, after today you must not go out on the rampart any more.'

"That evening I had a long talk with him; it grieved me that he had changed toward the poor girl, for besides being out hunting half the time, he began to treat her coldly, rarely showing her any affection. She began to waste away visibly, her face grew drawn, and her big eyes lost their lustre. Whenever I asked her. 'Why are you sighing, Bela? Are you sad?' she would reply 'No.' 'Do you want anything?' 'No!' 'Are you grieving for your kinsfolk?' 'I have no kinsfolk.' For days on end you couldn't get more than 'yes' or 'no' out of her.

"I resolved to have a talk with him about this. 'Listen, Maxim Maximych,' he replied, 'I have an unfortunate character; whether it is my upbringing that made me like that or God who created me so, I do not know. I know only that if I cause unhappiness to others I myself am no less unhappy. I realize this is poor consolation for them—but the fact remains that it is so. In my early youth after leaving the guardianship of my parents, I plunged into all the pleasures money could buy, and naturally these pleasures grew distasteful to me. Then I went into society, but soon enough grew tired of it; I fell in love with beautiful society women and was loved by them, but their love only spurred on my ambition and vanity while my heart remained desolate. . . . I began to read and to study, but wearied of learning too; I saw that neither fame nor happiness depended on it in the slightest, for the happiest people were the ignorant and fame was a matter of luck, to achieve which you only had to be shrewd. And I grew bored. . . . Soon I was transferred to the Caucasus; this was the happiest time of my life. I hoped that boredom would not survive under Chechen bullets—but in vain; in a month I had become so accustomed to their whine and the proximity of death that, to tell the truth, the mosquitoes bothered me more, and life became more boring than ever because I had now lost practically my last hope. When I saw Bela at her home, when I held her on my lap and first kissed her raven locks, I foolishly thought she was an angel sent down to me by a compassionate Providence. . . . Again I erred: the love of a barbarian girl is little better than that of a well-born lady; the ignorance and simplicity of the one are as boring as the coquetry of the other. I still love her, if you wish, I am grateful to her for a few rather blissful moments, I am ready to give my life for her, but I am bored with her. I don't know whether I am a fool or a scoundrel; but the fact is that I am to be pitied as much, if not more than she. My soul has been warped by the world, my mind is restless, my heart insatiable; nothing suffices me: I grow accustomed to sorrow as readily as to joy, and my life becomes emptier from day to day. Only one expedient is left for me, and that is to travel. As soon as possible I shall set out—not for Europe, God forbid—but for America, Arabia, India—and perhaps I shall die somewhere on the road! At least I am sure that with the help of storms and bad roads this last resort will not soon cease to be a consolation. He talked long in this vein and his words seared themselves in my memory for it was the first time I had heard such talk from a man of twenty-five, and, I hope to God, the last. Amazing! You probably were in the capital recently; perhaps you can tell me," the captain went on, addressing me, "whether the young people there are all like that?"

I replied that there are many who say the same, and that most likely some of them are speaking the truth; that, on the whole, disillusionment, having begun like all vogues in the upper strata of society, had descended to the lower which wear it threadbare, and that now those who are really bored the most endeavour to conceal that misfortune as if it were a vice. The captain did not understand these subtleties, and he shook his head and smiled slyly:

"It was the French, I suppose, who made boredom fashionable?"

"No, the English."

"Ah, so that's it!" he replied. "Of course, they've always been inveterate drunkards!"

Involuntarily I recalled one Moscow lady who claimed Byron was nothing more than a drunkard. The captain's remark however, was more excusable, for in order to abstain from drink he naturally tried to reassure himself that all misfortunes in the world are caused by intemperance.

"Kazbich did not come again," he went on with his story. "Still, for some unknown reason, I could not get rid of the idea that his visit had not been purposeless and that he was scheming something evil.

"Once Pechorin persuaded me to go hunting wild boar with him. I tried to resist, for what was a wild boar to me, but finally he did make me go with him. We set out early in the morning, taking five soldiers with us. Until ten o'clock we poked about the reeds and the woods without seeing a single animal. 'What do you say to turning back?' said I. 'What's the use of being stubborn? You can see for yourself the day has turned out to be unlucky.' But Grigori Alexandrovich did not want to return empty-handed in spite of the heat and fatigue. . . . That's how he was; if he set his mind on something he had to get it; his mother must have spoiled him as a child. At last around noon we came upon a cussed boar! . . bang! . . bang! . . but no: the beast slipped into the reeds . . . yes, it was indeed our unlucky day. After a bit of a rest we turned for home.

"We rode side by side, in silence, reins hanging loose, and had almost reached the fort, though we could not yet see it for the brush, when a shot rang out. We looked at each other, and the same suspicion flashed through our minds. Galloping in the direction of the sound, we saw a group of soldiers huddled together on the rampart, pointing to the field where a horseman was careering into the distance at breakneck speed with something white across his saddle, Grigori Alexandrovich yelled not a whit worse than any Chechen, drew his gun from its holster and dashed in pursuit, and I after him.

"Luckily, because of our poor hunting luck, our horses were quite fresh; they strained under the saddle, and with every moment we gained on our quarry. Finally I recognized Kazbich, though I could not make out what he was holding in front of him. I drew abreast of Pechorin and shouted to him: 'It's Kazbich!' He looked at me, nodded and struck his horse with the crop.

"At last we were within gunshot of Kazbich. Whether his horse was exhausted or whether it was worse than ours I do not know, but he was unable to get much speed out of the animal in spite of his efforts to urge it on. I am sure he was thinking of his Karagyoz then. . . .

"I looked up and saw Pechorin aiming. 'Don't shoot!' I yelled. 'Save the charge, we'll catch up with him soon enough.' That's youth for you: always foolhardy at the wrong time. . . . But the shot rang out and the bullet wounded the horse in a hind leg; the animal made another dozen leaps before it stumbled and fell on its knees. Kazbich sprang from the saddle, and now we saw he was holding a woman bound in a veil in his arms. It was Bela . . . poor Bela! He shouted something to us in his own language and raised his dagger over her. . . . There was no time to waste and I fired at random. I must have hit him in the shoulder, for his arm suddenly dropped. When the smoke dispersed there was the wounded horse lying on the ground and Bela next to it, while Kazbich, who had thrown away his gun, was scrambling up a cliff through the underbrush like a cat. I wanted to pick him off but my gun was unloaded now. We slipped out of the saddle and ran toward Bela. The poor girl lay motionless, blood streaming from her wound. The villain! Had he struck her in the heart, it all would have been over in a moment, but to stab her in the back in the foulest way! She was unconscious. We tore the veil into strips and bandaged the wound as tightly as we could. In vain Pechorin kissed her cold lips; nothing could bring her back to consciousness.

"Pechorin mounted his horse and I raised her up from the ground, somehow managing to place her in front of him in the saddle. He put his arm around her and we started back. After several minutes of silence, Grigori Alexandrovich spoke: 'Listen, Maxim Maximych, we'll never get her home alive at this pace.' 'You're right,' I said, and we spurred the horses to full gallop. At the fort gates a crowd was awaiting us. We carried the wounded girl gently into Pechorin's quarters and sent for the surgeon. Although he was drunk, he came at our summons, and after examining the wound said the girl could not live more than a day. But he was wrong. . . ."

"She recovered then?" I asked the captain seizing his arm, glad in spite of myself.

"No," he replied, "The surgeon was wrong only in that she lived another two days."

"But tell me how did Kazbich manage to kidnap her?"

"It was like this: disobeying Pechorin's instructions, she had left the fort and gone to the river. It was very hot, and she had sat down on a rock and dipped her feet into the water. Kazbich crept up, seized and gagged her, dragged her into the bushes, jumped on his horse and galloped off. She managed to scream, however, and the sentries gave the alarm, fired after him but missed, and that's when we arrived on the scene."

"Why did Kazbich want to carry her off?"

"My dear sir! These Cherkess are a nation of thieves. Their fingers itch for anything that lies unguarded; whether they need it or not, they steal—they just can't help themselves! Besides he had long had his eye on Bela."

"And she died?"

"Yes, but she suffered a great deal, and we too were worn out watching her. About ten o'clock at night she regained consciousness; we were sitting at her bedside. As soon as she opened her eyes she asked for Pechorin. 'I am here, beside you, my *janechka*,' (that is, darling in our language) he replied taking her hand. 'I shall die,' she said. We began to reassure her, saying that the surgeon had promised to cure her without fail, but she shook her head and turned to the wall. She did not want to die!

"During the night she grew delirious. Her head was on fire and every now and then she shook with fever. She was now talking incoherently about her father and brother; she wanted to go back to her mountains and home. . . . Then she also talked about Pechorin, calling him all kinds of tender names or reproaching him for not loving his *janechka* any more. . . .

"He listened in silence, his head resting on his hands. But throughout it all I did not notice a single tear on his lashes; whether he was actually incapable of weeping or whether he held himself in check, I do not know. As for myself, I had never witnessed anything more heart-rending.

"By morning the delirium passed. For about an hour she lay motionless pale and so weak that her breathing was barely perceptible. Presently she felt better and began to speak again, but can you guess of what? Such thoughts can occur only to the dying. She regretted that she was not a Christian and that in the world beyond her soul would never meet Grigori Alexandrovich's, that some other woman would be his soulmate in paradise. It occured to me that she might be baptized before death, but when I suggested this she gazed at me in indecision for a long time, unable to say a word. At last she replied that she would die in the faith she had been born. So the whole day passed. How she changed in that day! Her pallid cheeks grew sunken, her eyes seemed to become larger and larger, and her lips were burning. The fever within her was like a red-hot iron pressing upon her breast.

"The second night came, and we sat at her bedside without closing an eyelid. She was in terrible agony, she moaned, but as soon as the pain subsided a little she tried to assure Grigori Alexandrovich that she was feeling better, urged him to get some sleep, and kissed his hand and clung to it with her own. Just before daybreak the agony of death set in, and she tossed on the bed, tearing off the bandage so that the blood flowed again. When the wound was dressed she calmed down for a moment and asked Pechorin to kiss her. He knelt next to the bed, raised her head from the pillow and pressed his lips against hers, which were now growing chill; she entwined her trembling arms tightly around his neck as if by this kiss she wished to give her soul to him. Yes, it was well that she died! What would have happened to her had Grigori Alexandrovich left her? And that was bound to happen sooner or later. . . .

"The first half of the next day she was quiet, silent and submissive in spite of the way our surgeon tortured her with poultices and medicine. 'My good man!' I protested. 'You yourself said she would not live, why then all these medicines of yours?' 'Got to do it, just the same, Maxim Maximych,' he replied, 'so that my conscience should be at peace.' Conscience indeed!

"In the afternoon she was tortured by thirst. We opened the windows, but it was hotter outside than in the room. We placed ice next to her bed, but nothing helped. I knew that this unbearable thirst was a sign that the end was approaching, and I said so to Pechorin. 'Water, water,' she repeated hoarsely, raising herself from the bed.

"He went white as a sheet, seized a glass, filled it with water, and gave it to her. I covered my face with my hands and began to recite a prayer, I can't remember which. Yes, sir, I had been through a great deal in my time, had seen men die in hospitals and on the battlefield, but it had been nothing like this! I must confess that there was something else that made me sad; not once before her death did she remember me, and I think I loved her like a father. Well. . . . May God forgive her! But then who am I that anyone should remember me on his deathbed?

"As soon as she had drunk the water she felt better, and some three minutes later she passed away. We pressed a mirror to her lips, but nothing showed on it. I led Pechorin out of the room, and then we walked on the fort wall, pacing back and forth side by side for a long while without uttering a word, arms crossed behind our backs. It angered me to detect no sign of emotion on his face, for in his place I should have died of grief. Finally, he sat down on the ground in the shade and began to trace some design in the sand with a stick. I began to speak, wishing to console him, more for the sake of good form than anything else, you know, whereupon he looked up and laughed. . . . That laugh sent cold shivers running up and down my spine. . . . I went to order the coffin.

"I confess that it was partly for diversion that I occupied myself with this business. I covered the coffin with a piece of tarlatan I had and ornamented it with some Cherkess silver lace Grigori Alexandrovich had bought for her.

"Early the next morning we buried her beyond the fort, next to the spot on the river bank where she had sat that last time; the small grave has now been surrounded by white acacia and elder bushes. I wanted to put up a cross, but that was a bit awkward, you know, for after all she was not a Christian. . . ."

"What did Pechorin do?" I asked.

"He was ailing for a long time and lost weight, the poor chap. But we never spoke about Bela after that. I saw it would be painful for him, so why should I have mentioned her? Some three months later he was ordered to join the . . . regiment, and he went to Georgia. Since then we have not met. Oh yes, I remember someone telling me recently that he had returned to Russia, though it had not been mentioned in the corps orders. In general it takes a long time before news reaches us here."

Here, probably to dispel his sad memories, he launched upon a long dissertation concerning the disadvantages of hearing year-old tidings.

I neither interrupted him nor listened.

An hour later it was already possible to continue our journey. The blizzard had died down and the sky cleared up, and we set out. On the road, however, I could not help directing the conversation back to Bela and Pechorin.

"Did you ever happen to hear what became of Kazbich?" I asked.

"Kazbich? Really, I don't know. I have heard that the Shapsugi have a Kazbich on their right flank, a bold fellow who wears a red *beshmet*, rides at a trot under our fire and bows with exaggerated politeness whenever a bullet whistles near him, but I doubt whether it's the same man."

Maxim Maximych and I parted at Kobi, for I took the post chaise and he could not keep pace with me because of his heavy baggage. At the time we did not think we would ever meet again, yet we did, and if you wish, I will tell you about it, but that is a story in itself. . . . You must admit, however, that Maxim Maximych is a man you can respect? If you do admit it, I shall be amply rewarded for my story, long though it may be.

Domingo Sarmiento
1811–1888

An educational reformer, author, and politician, Domingo Faustino Sarmiento began his career at the age of sixteen, fighting in the Argentine civil war in 1827 and then escaping to exile in Chile. But it was *The Life of Juan Facundo Quiroga* (published in 1845 in Chile) that made him a household name throughout Argentina and Latin America. The book is a biography of a gaucho proto-dictator who rose to power in the 1820s and 1830s by organizing peasants in the countryside (his slogan was "Religion or death!"). To Sarmiento, he was a prime example of barbarism, sharing much of the blame for the subsequent tyranny of Juan Manuel de Rosas, then ruling Argentina with an iron hand. More ambitious than most biographies, *Facundo*—subtitled *Civilization and Barbarism*—was intended to explain the conditions in Argentina under which personalized tyranny, or *caudillismo*, could flourish. In 1852, Sarmiento helped in the overthrow of Rosas and was able to abandon his exile for what turned out to be a long and distinguished career in Argentine politics, including a stint as President of the Argentine Republic (1868–1874). His American translator and lover, Mary Mann, wife of the educator Horace Mann, once told him, "To me you are not a man, but a nation."

To others Sarmiento has seemed less loyal to his nation than it deserved. Many Latin Americans have seen his concept of civilization as too approving of European ideas and institutions and too uncritical of the United States, to which he served as Argentina's ambassador. Opposing voices like José Martí and Roberto Fernández Retamar have resisted the example and influence of the United States and accused Sarmiento not only of disrespect for everything native to Latin America, but of welcoming the extinction of the Indians as "savages" incapable of "progress." Yet indigenism and anti-indigenism don't exhaust the complications here. Argentina differs from most Latin American countries in a crucial respect. When the Spanish conquerors arrived, they found far fewer indigenous people, and the absence of silver meant that they had less use for Indian slave labor. The role of "barbarian" in Sarmiento is played first and foremost by the gauchos, who are often descendants of European settlers, racially indistinguishable from city dwellers.

The gaucho is at least as central to Argentine identity as the cowboy is to the self-image of the United States. In both cases these frontier figures embody urban ambivalence about the entirely welcome advance of modernity. For Sarmiento himself, modernity couldn't come quickly enough. He felt that the barbarism of the gauchos resulted from the wildness and emptiness of the land itself, and his solution was more European settlers—ideally, northern Europeans, considered more sober and industrious. This argument is a kind of mirror image of Turner's famous "frontier thesis" in the United States: here the frontier represents all that is worst, not all that is best about the nation. Yet *Facundo* was described by the Spanish philosopher Miguel de Unamuno as less a history than a historical novel. And if so, we must be alert for subtle, perhaps unconscious sympathies that blur the lines between civilization and barbarism, the rational urbanite and the brute from the borderlands. As with other examples of the popular genre of *literatura gauchesca* (literature about the gauchos, to be distinguished from *literatura gaucha*, literature written by the gauchos themselves), there are always interesting questions about what such figures represent.

PRONUNCIATIONS:

Juan Facundo Quiroga: wahn fah-COUN-doh key-ROH-gah
Domingo Sarmiento: doe-MEAN-goh sahr-MYEN-toh
Villafañe: vee-ah-FAN-yay

from Life of Juan Facundo Quiroga: Civilization and Barbarism[1]

Chapter 10

CIVIL WAR

What has become of Facundo in the mean time? At Tablada he had lost everything,—arms, officers, men, reputation; everything except rage and valor. Moral, governor of Rioja, taken aback by the news of this unlooked-for disaster, availed himself of a

---

1. Translated by Mary Mann.

slight excuse for leaving the city, and from Sañogasta sent Quiroga a despatch offering him what assistance the province could afford. Before the expedition the friendship between this nominal governor and the all-powerful commander had somewhat cooled. Quiroga thought he had not had the full number of armed men that he considered due him from the result of the census, in addition to the troops already in the province, and which had come from Tucuman, San Juan, Catamarca, etc. And another circumstance strengthened the suspicions with which Quiroga regarded the governor. Sañogasta was the manorial residence of the Dorias Dávilas, the enemies of the commander; and the governor, foreseeing what the suspicions of Facundo would deduce from the date of the despatch, dated it from Uanchin, a place about four leagues distant. But Quiroga knew that Moral was in Sañogasta, and all his doubts were confirmed. Fontanel and Barcena, two of Facundo's odious instruments, were sent out with a party to scour the country for the purpose of impressing as many men as they could find, but the inhabitants took care to escape, so that they were not very successful in their day's hunt, and returned with only eleven persons who were shot upon the spot. Don Inocencio Moral, an uncle of the governor, with his two sons, one only fourteen years of age, were among the victims of that day. There was also among them a Don Mariano Pasos, who had once before incurred the anger of Quiroga. When he was starting on one of his previous expeditions, this man, seeing the disorderly troops, had said to a fellow-merchant, "What men for fighting!" Quiroga, hearing it, had the two criticizers brought before him; one was tied to a post and received two hundred lashes, while the other stood by awaiting his share. The latter, however, was spared when his turn came, and afterwards became the governor of Rioja and a great friend of Quiroga.

Meanwhile, Governor Moral, knowing what he might expect, fled from the province, but he was eventually caught, and received seven hundred lashes for his ingratitude, for it was he who had shared the eighteen thousand dollars extorted from Dorrego.

That Barcena before mentioned was ordered to assassinate the commissioner of the English mining company; and I heard from himself the details of this atrocious murder, which he committed in his own house, desiring his wife and children to stand out of the way of the balls and sword-cuts.

Barcena accompanied Oribe in his expedition to Cordova; and during a ball given in honor of the triumph over Lavalle,[2] threw the bloody heads of three young men into the hall where their families were dancing. This Barcena was the leader of the band of Mazorqueros which went with the army sent to Cordova in persecution of Lavalle, a regularly organized band, each Mazorquero wearing at his side a knife with a blade curved like a small cimeter,[3] which was invented by Rosas himself for the purpose of beheading men dexterously.

What motive could Quiroga have had for these atrocities? He is said to have told Oro at Mendoza that his only object was to inspire terror. And again, during the continual assassinations of wretched peasants, on his way to the headquarters at Atiles, one of the Villafañes said to him in a tone of fear and compassion, "Is it not enough, General?" "Don't be a fool," Quiroga answered; "how else can I establish my power!" This was his one method,—terror with the citizen, that he might fly and leave his fortune; terror with the gaucho, to make him support a cause in which he had no

---

2. General Juan Lavalle, opponent of Rosas' dictatorship, installed as governor of Buenos Aires in 1828 and re-   placed by Rosas the following year.
3. Scimitar, sword.

personal interest. With him terror took the place of administrative power, enthusiasm, tactics, everything. And it cannot be denied that terror, as a means of government, produces much larger results than patriotism or liberty. Russia has made use of it from the time of Ivan, and has conquered the most barbarous nations; the bandits of the forest obey the chief, wielding this power which controls the fiercest natures. It is true that it degrades men, impoverishes them, and takes from them all elasticity of mind, but it extorts more from a state in one day than it would have given in ten years; and what does the rest matter to the Czar of Russia, the bandit chief, or the Argentine commander?

Facundo ordered all the inhabitants of Rioja to emigrate to the Llanos under pain of death, and the order was literally obeyed. It is hard to find a motive for this useless emigration. Quiroga was not apt to fear, yet he might have feared at the moment; for the Unitarios were raising an army in Mendoza to take possession of the government; Tucuman and Salta were on the north; and on the east, Cordova, Tablada, and General Paz; he was, therefore, pretty well surrounded, and a general hunt might very well have brought the Tiger of the Llanos at bay. These terrorists do have their moments of fear: Rosas cried like a child when he heard of the rebellion at Chascomus, and eleven huge trunks were packed with his effects ready to fly an hour before news came of the victory of Alvarez. But woe to the people when such moments have passed! Then follow *September massacres,* and pyramids of human heads arise in the squares!

Notwithstanding the order of Facundo, two persons remained in Rioja—a young girl and a priest. The story of Severa Villafañe is a pitiful romance; a fairy tale in which the loveliest princess is a wandering fugitive, sometimes disguised as a shepherdess, sometimes begging a morsel of bread, or for protection from a frightful giant,—a cruel Bluebeard. Severa had the misfortune to excite the lust of the tyrant, and made superhuman efforts to escape his persecution. It was not only virtue resisting seduction, but the unconquerable repugnance of a delicate woman who detests those coarse types of brute force. A beautiful woman will sometimes barter something of her honor for something of the glory which surrounds a celebrated man; not for the glory which depends on the debasement of others for its brilliancy, but the glory which was the cause of Madame de Maintenon's[4] frailty, or the literary glory to which Madame Roland and other such women are said to have sacrificed their reputations. For whole years Severa resisted. At one time she came near being poisoned by her tiger; at another, Quiroga, in a fit of desperation, tried to poison himself with opium. Once she escaped with difficulty from the hands of some of his creatures, and again she was surprised by Quiroga in her own court-yard, where he seized her by the arm, beat her with his fist until she was covered with blood, then threw her upon the ground and kicked in her skull with the heel of his boot. And was there no one to protect this poor girl, no relatives, no friends! One might well think so; yet she belonged to the first families of Rioja; General Villafañe was her uncle, she had brothers who witnessed the outrages; and there was a curé who shut the doors against her when she sought a refuge in the sanctuary. Finally, Severa fled to Catamarca and went into a convent; two years afterwards, when Facundo was passing through that place, he forced his way into the convent, and ordered the nuns into his presence; at the sight of him one nun uttered a cry and fell senseless upon the floor—it was Severa.

---

4. Secretly married to French King Louis XIV in 1685.

But we must return to the encampment at Atiles, where an army was preparing for the purpose of recovering the reputation lost at Tablada. Two Unitarios of San Juan had fallen into the hands of the tyrant: a young Chilian by the name of Castroy Calvo, and Alexandro Carril. Quiroga asked the latter how much he would give for his life.

"Twenty-five thousand dollars," he answered, trembling.

"And you, sir," asked Quiroga, of the other, "how much will you give?"

"I can only give four thousand," said Castro. "I am only a merchant and have no property."

They sent to San Juan for the money, and behold thirty thousand dollars collected for the war at a very small cost. While waiting for the money, Facundo lodged them under a carob-tree, and employed them in making cartridges, paying them two reals a day for their work.

The governor of San Juan, hearing of the efforts made by the family of Carril to collect this ransom, took advantage of the knowledge. As governor of the city he could not exactly shoot his own citizens, though an independent Federal,[5] and neither did he have the power to extort money from the Unitarios.[6] But he ordered all the political prisoners in the gaols to be sent to the camp at Atiles to join the army. The mothers and wives understood what fate they were to expect, and first one, and then another and another, succeeded in scraping together the sums necessary to keep back their sons and husbands from the den of the Tiger. Thus Quiroga governed in San Juan merely by the terror of his name.

When the brothers Aldao were all powerful in Mendoza, and had not left in Rioja one man, old or young, married or single, who was able to carry arms, Facundo transported his headquarters to San Juan, where there were still many wealthy Unitarios. There he soon ordered six hundred lashes to a citizen noted for his influence, talent, and wealth, and walked himself by the side of the cart which carried his expiring victim through the streets; for Facundo was very careful about this part of his administration; and not at all like Rosas, who, from his private room where he was taking his *maté*, sent Mazorqueros to execute the atrocities afterward charged upon the *federal enthusiasm* of the people. Not thinking this example sufficient, Facundo seized upon an old man, whom he accused—or scarcely troubled himself to accuse—of having served as a guide to some fugitives, and had him shot without permitting him to speak a word; for this heaven-sent defender of the faith cared very little whether his victims confessed or not.

Public opinion being thus prepared, there were no sacrifices the city of San Juan was not ready to make for the defense of the Confederation; contributions were given in without remonstrance, and arms appeared as if by magic. The Aldaos triumphed in the incapacity of the Unitarios to violate the treaty of Pilar, and then Quiroga left for Mendoza. There no additional terror was needed, for the daily executions ordered by the monk Aldao had paralyzed the city; but Facundo thought it necessary to justify the terror carried everywhere by his name. Some young men of San Juan had been made prisoners, and these, at least, belonged to him. He asked one of them how many guns he could furnish by the end of four days; the young man answered that if he might have time to send to Chili for them, he would do all he could. Quiroga repeated, "How many can you furnish now?"

---

5. The party of the dictator Rosas.   6. The main opposition party.

"None," was the answer; and the next moment his body was taken away to be buried, six others soon following. The same question was put orally or in writing to the prisoners from Mendoza, and the answers were more or less satisfactory. Among these was a General Alvarado, who was brought before Facundo.

"Sit down, General," he said. "How soon can you deliver six thousand dollars for your ransom?"

"Sir, I cannot bring it at all; I have no money."

"But you have friends who would not let you be shot," said Quiroga.

"No, sir; I have none. I was only passing through the province when I was induced by the public wish to take charge of the government."

"Where would you like to go?" continued Quiroga, after a moment of silence.

"Wherever you may order, sir."

"What do you think of San Juan?"

"Just as you please, sir."

"How much money do you need?"

"None, I thank you, sir."

Facundo went to a desk and opening a bag of gold, said, "Take what you need, General."

"Thanks, sir, nothing."

An hour later the carriage of General Alvarado was at his door with his baggage in it, and also General Villafañe, who conducted him to San Juan, and on his arrival there, gave him a hundred ounces of gold from General Quiroga, begging him not to refuse it.

This would seem to prove that Quiroga's heart was not entirely dead to noble impressions. Alvarado was an old soldier, a grave and prudent general, who had given him no trouble. He afterward said of him,—"That Alvarado is a good soldier, but he doesn't understand our warfare."

At San Juan they brought before him a Frenchman named Barreau, who had written about him as only a Frenchman can write. Facundo asked him if he was the author of the abusive articles, and was answered in the affirmative.

"Then what do you expect?"

"Death, sir," said the man; but Quiroga threw him a purse, saying, "There, take that, and go somewhere else to be hung."

At Tucuman, Quiroga one day lay stretched on a bench, when an Andalusian came up and asked for the General.

"He is in there," said Quiroga; "what do you want with him?"

"I have come to pay the four hundred dollars' contribution he has charged upon me,—the fellow gets his living easy."

"Do you know the General, friend?"

"No, and I don't want to know him, the rogue!"

"Come in and take a drink," said Quiroga, but at that moment an aide came up, and began: "General—."

"General!" cried the man, opening his eyes, "so you are the General! Ah, General," he continued, falling on his knees, "I am a poor devil,—you wouldn't be the ruin of me,—the money is all ready, General,—come, don't be angry, now!"

Facundo burst into a loud laugh, told the man to make himself easy, and giving him back the contribution, only took two hundred of it as a loan, which he afterwards faithfully repaid. Two years after this, a paralyzed beggar called out to him in the streets of Buenos Ayres,—

"Good-bye, General, I am the Andalusian of Tucuman, and I'm paralyzed." Facundo gave him six dollars.

These things prove the theory, which the modern drama has exhibited with so much brilliancy, namely, that in the darkest characters of history there will always be found a ray of light, however totally it seems sometimes to vanish.

But let us resume the course of public events. After the solemn inauguration of terror in Mendoza, Facundo retired to Retamo, whither the Aldao brothers had carried a contribution of a hundred thousand dollars extorted from the Unitarios. There they gambled day and night, playing for enormous stakes, until Facundo had won the hundred thousand dollars.

A year passed in preparations for the war, and at the end of 1830 a new and formidable army, composed of divisions recruited in Rioja, San Juan, Mendoza, and San Luis, marched against Cordova. General Paz, desirous of avoiding bloodshed, though sure of winning new laurels should an engagement take place, sent Major Pawnero, an officer of prudence, energy, and sagacity, to meet Quiroga with proposals of peace, and even of alliance. It might be thought that Quiroga would be disposed to accept any reasonable opportunity for adjustment; but the intervention of the Buenos Ayres commission, which had no other object than to prevent any adjustment, and his own pride and presumption on finding himself at the head of a more powerful and better disciplined army than the first, made him reject the peace proposals of the more modest General Paz. Facundo had this time arranged something like a plan for the campaign. Communications established in the Sierra de Cordova had excited the pastoral population to rebellion; General Villafañe approached on the north with the division from Catamarca, while Facundo came up from the south. It was not very difficult for General Paz to see through the designs of Quiroga, and to disappoint them. One night the army disappeared from the immediate neighborhood of Cordova, no one knew where; it had been seen by many persons, but in different places at the same time. If there has ever been in America anything like the complicated strategy of Bonaparte's campaigns in Italy, it was when Paz made forty companies cross the Sierra de Cordova and take a position where they would inevitably intercept all fugitives from a regular battle. The Montonera, paralyzed, surrounded on all sides, fell into the net which had been spread for it. It is not necessary to give the particulars of that memorable battle. General Paz, in his despatch, gave the number of his loss as seventy, for appearance sake, but in fact, he had only lost twelve men in a contest with eight thousand men, and twenty pieces of artillery. A simple maneuvre had defeated the valiant Quiroga; and the army which had cost so many tears and horrors of all kinds, only served to show Facundo's bad management, and to give to Paz several thousand useless prisoners.

━━ ✦ ━━

Charles A. Eastman (Ohiyesa)
1858–1939

Soon after his birth in 1858 near the present-day site of Saint Paul, Minnesota, the man we have come to call Charles Alexander Eastman received the Sioux name of Hadakah, meaning "the pitiful last," for his mother died, leaving Eastman and his four siblings in the care of their paternal grandmother. Eastman's mother, Mary Eastman, had been the child of Captain Seth Eastman, an artist stationed at Fort Snelling; her grandfather on her mother's side was Chief Cloud-man of the Mdewakanton Sioux. Eastman's father was Many Lightnings, a Wahpeton Sioux. Many Lightnings was destined to have an unusually dramatic influence over his son's life.

In 1862, the so-called Santee Sioux, who included both groups, revolted against the poverty, starvation, and government fraud that they suffered on the reservation. Father and son were separated during the uprising. Eastman, now under the name of Ohiyesa ("the winner") thanks to his skill at lacrosse, was taken to Canada by his grandmother and uncle, who believed Many Lightnings had been killed by the army. But when Ohiyesa was fifteen, and ready to take revenge against the American soldiers for his father's death, Many Lightnings suddenly reappeared, very much alive and having converted in prison to Christianity. He had come to take his son back to a peaceful life in America—the story told to a white audience in *From the Deep Woods to Civilization* (1916).

What follows is an extraordinary if ambivalent story of successful cultural adaptation. Ohiyesa learns to read and write English, becomes a Christian, takes his anglicized name, graduates from Dartmouth, and is awarded a medical degree by Boston University. But as soon as he tries to put his medical skills to good use on behalf of his people, serving as government physician at the Pine Ridge Agency, he finds himself a witness to the infamous massacre of Wounded Knee, a section of his book that has won it many readers over the decades. Aside from his work as a lecturer and a writer (he authored eleven books), Eastman was employed for many years by the Bureau of Indian Affairs, an organization that Indians had historical reasons to suspect. But Eastman has largely escaped epithets like "apple" (red on the outside, white on the inside) and "Uncle Tomahawk," for he used his hard-won skills in tireless efforts to improve the lot of his fellow Indians.

from The Deep Woods to Civilization

I

THE WAY OPENS

One can never be sure of what a day may bring to pass. At the age of fifteen years, the deepening current of my life swung upon such a pivotal day, and in the twinkling of an eye its whole course was utterly changed; as if a little mountain brook should pause and turn upon itself to gather strength for the long journey toward an unknown ocean.

From childhood I was consciously trained to be a man; that was, after all, the basic thing; but after this I was trained to be a warrior and a hunter, and not to care for money or possessions, but to be in the broadest sense a public servant. After arriving at a reverent sense of the pervading presence of the Spirit and Giver of Life, and a deep consciousness of the brotherhood of man, the first thing for me to accomplish was to adapt myself perfectly to natural things—in other words, to harmonize myself with nature. To this end I was made to build a body both symmetrical and enduring— a house for the soul to live in—a sturdy house, defying the elements. I must have faith and patience; I must learn self-control and be able to maintain silence. I must do with as little as possible and start with nothing most of the time, because a true Indian always shares whatever he may possess.

I felt no hatred for our tribal foes. I looked upon them more as the college athlete regards his rivals from another college. There was no thought of destroying a nation, taking away their country or reducing the people to servitude, for my race rather honored and bestowed gifts upon their enemies at the next peaceful meeting, until they had adopted the usages of the white man's warfare for spoliation and conquest.

There was one unfortunate thing about my early training, however; that is, I was taught never to spare a citizen of the United States, although we were on friendly terms with the Canadian white men. The explanation is simple. My people had been turned out of some of the finest country in the world, now forming the great states of Minnesota and Iowa. The Americans pretended to buy the land at ten cents an acre, but never paid the price; the debt stands unpaid to this day. Because they did not pay, the Sioux protested; finally came the outbreak of 1862 in Minnesota, when many settlers were killed, and forthwith our people, such as were left alive, were driven by the troops into exile.

My father, who was among the fugitives in Canada, had been betrayed by a half-breed across the United States line, near what is now the city of Winnipeg. Some of the party were hanged at Fort Snelling, near St. Paul. We supposed, and, in fact, we were informed that all were hanged. This was why my uncle, in whose family I lived, had taught me never to spare a white man from the United States.

During the summer and winter of 1871, the band of Sioux to which I belonged—a clan of the Wah petons, or "Dwellers among the Leaves"—roamed in the upper Missouri region and along the Yellowstone River. In that year I tasted to the full the joy and plenty of wild existence. I saw buffalo, elk, and antelope in herds numbering thousands. The forests teemed with deer, and in the "Bad Lands" dwelt the Big Horns or Rocky Mountain sheep. At this period, grizzly bears were numerous and were brought into camp quite commonly, like any other game.

We frequently met and camped with the Hudson Bay half-breeds in their summer hunt of the buffalo, and we were on terms of friendship with the Assiniboines and the Crees, but in frequent collision with the Blackfeet, the Gros Ventres, and the Crows. However, there were times of truce when all met in peace for a great midsummer festival and exchange of gifts. The Sioux roamed over an area nearly a thousand miles in extent. In the summer we gathered together in large numbers, but towards fall we would divide into small groups or bands and scatter for the trapping and the winter hunt. Most of us hugged the wooded river bottoms; some depended entirely upon the buffalo for food, while others, and among these my immediate kindred, hunted all kinds of game, and trapped and fished as well.

Thus I was trained thoroughly for an all-round outdoor life and for all natural emergencies. I was a good rider and a good shot with the bow and arrow, alert and alive to everything that came within my ken. I had never known nor ever expected to know any life but this.

In the winter and summer of 1872, we drifted toward the southern part of what is now Manitoba. In this wild, rolling country I rapidly matured, and laid, as I supposed, the foundations of my life career, never dreaming of anything beyond this manful and honest, unhampered existence. My horse and my dog were my closest companions. I regarded them as brothers, and if there was a hereafter, I expected to meet them there. With them I went out daily into the wilderness to seek inspiration and store up strength for coming manhood. My teachers dreamed no more than I of any change in my prospects. I had now taken part in all our tribal activities except that of war, and was nearly old enough to be initiated into the ritual of the war-path. The world was full of natural rivalry; I was eager for the day.

I had attained the age of fifteen years and was about to enter into and realize a man's life, as we Indians understood it, when the change came. One fine September morning as I returned from the daily hunt, there seemed to be an unusual stir and excitement as I approached our camp. My faithful grandmother was on the watch and met me to break the news. "Your father has come—he whom we thought dead at the hands of the white men," she said.

It was a day of miracle in the deep Canadian wilderness, before the Canadian Pacific[1] had been even dreamed of, while the Indian and the buffalo still held sway over the vast plains of Manitoba east of the Rocky Mountains. It was, perhaps, because he was my honored father that I lent my bewildered ear to his eloquent exposition of the so-called civilized life, or the way of the white man. I could not doubt my own father, so mysteriously come back to us, as it were, from the spirit land; yet there was a voice within saying to me, "A false life! a treacherous life!"

In accordance with my training, I asked few questions, although many arose in my mind. I simply tried silently to fit the new ideas like so many blocks into the pattern of my philosophy, while according to my untutored logic some did not seem to have straight sides or square corners to fit in with the cardinal principles of eternal justice. My father had been converted by Protestant missionaries, and he gave me a totally new vision of the white man, as a religious man and a kindly. But when he related how he had set apart every seventh day for religious duties and the worship of God, laying aside every other occupation on that day, I could not forbear exclaiming, "Father! and does he then forget God during the six days and do as he pleases?"

"Our own life, I will admit, is the best in a world of our own, such as we have enjoyed for ages," said my father. "But here is a race which has learned to weigh and measure everything, time and labor and the results of labor, and has learned to accumulate and preserve both wealth and the records of experience for future generations. You yourselves know and use some of the wonderful inventions of the white man, such as guns and gunpowder, knives and hatchets, garments of every description, and there are thousands of other things both beautiful and useful.

"Above all, they have their Great Teacher, whom they call Jesus, and he taught them to pass on their wisdom and knowledge to all other races. It is true that they have subdued and taught many peoples, and our own must eventually bow to this law; the sooner we accept their mode of life and follow their teaching, the better it will be for us all. I have thought much on this matter and such is my conclusion."

There was a mingling of admiration and indignation in my mind as I listened. My father's two brothers were still far from being convinced; but filial duty and affection overweighed all my prejudices. I was bound to go back with him as he desired me to do, and my grandmother and her only daughter accompanied us on the perilous journey.

The line between Canada and the United States was closely watched at this time by hostile Indians, therefore my father thought it best to make a dash for Devil's Lake, in North Dakota, where he could get assistance if necessary. He knew Major Forbes, who was in command of the military post and the agency. Our guide we knew to be an unscrupulous man, who could easily betray us for a kettle of whisky or a pony. One of the first things I observed was my father's reading aloud from a book every morning and evening, followed by a very strange song and a prayer. Although all he said was in Indian, I did not understand it fully. He apparently talked aloud to the "Great Mystery," asking for our safe guidance back to his home in the States. The first reading of this book of which I have any recollection was the twenty-third Psalm, and the first hymn he sang in my presence was to the old tune of Ortonville. It was his Christian faith and devotion which was perhaps the strongest influence toward my change of heart and complete change of my purpose in life.

1. Railroad.

I think it was at our second encampment that we met a large caravan of Canadian half-breeds accompanied by a band of Northern Ojibways. As was usual with the former, they had plenty of whisky. They were friendly enough with us, at least while sober, but the Indians were not. Father showed them his papers as a United States citizen and a letter from Major Forbes, telling of his peaceful mission, but we could not trust our ancestral enemies, the Ojibways, especially when excited with strong drink. My father was calm and diplomatic throughout, but thus privately instructed me:

"My son, conceal yourself in the woods; and if the worst comes you must flee on your swift pony. Before daylight you can pass the deep woods and cross the Assiniboine River." He handed me a letter to Major Forbes. I said, "I will try," and as soon as it was dark, I hid myself, to be in readiness. Meanwhile, my father called the leading half-breeds together and told them again that he was under the protection of his government, also that the Sioux would hold them responsible if anything happened to us. Just then they discovered that another young brave and I were not to be found, which made them think that father had dispatched us to the nearest military post for help. They immediately led away their drunken comrades and made a big talk to their Ojibway friends, so that we remained undisturbed until morning.

Some days later, at the south end of Devil's Lake, I left our camp early to shoot some ducks when the morning flight should begin. Suddenly, when out of sight of the others, my eye caught a slight movement in the rank grass. Instinctively I dropped and flattened myself upon the ground, but soon a quick glance behind me showed plainly the head of a brave hidden behind a bush. I waited, trying to figure out some plan of escape, yet facing the probability that I was already surrounded, until I caught sight of another head almost in front and still another to my left.

In the moments that elapsed after I fully realized my situation, I thought of almost everything that had happened to me up to that day; of a remarkable escape from the Ojibways, of the wild pets I had had, and of my playmates in the Canadian camps whom I should never see again. I also thought with more curiosity than fear of the "Great Mystery" that I was so soon to enter. As these thoughts were passing through my mind, I carelessly moved and showed myself plainly to the enemy.

Suddenly, from behind the nearest bush, came the sound of my own Sioux tongue and the words, "Are you a Sioux?" Possibly my countenance may not have changed much, but certainly I grew weak with surprise and relief. As soon as I answered "Yes!" I was surrounded by a group of warriors of my tribe, who chuckled at the joke that had come so near to costing me my life, for one of them explained that he had been on the point of firing when I exposed myself so plainly that he saw I was not an Ojibway in war paint but probably a Sioux like himself.

After a variety of adventures, we arrived at the canvas city of Jamestown, then the terminal point of the Northern Pacific railroad. I was out watering the ponies when a terrific peal of thunder burst from a spotless blue sky, and indeed seemed to me to be running along the surface of the ground. The terrified ponies instantly stampeded, and I confess I was not far behind them, when a monster with one fiery eye poked his head around a corner of the hill. When we reached camp, my father kindly explained, and I was greatly relieved.

It was a peaceful Indian summer day when we reached Flandreau, in Dakota Territory, the citizen Indian settlement, and found the whole community gathered together to congratulate and welcome us home.

II

MY FIRST SCHOOL DAYS

It was less than a month since I had been a rover and a hunter in the Manitoba wilderness, with no thoughts save those which concern the most free and natural life of an Indian. Now, I found myself standing near a rude log cabin on the edge of a narrow strip of timber, overlooking the fertile basin of the Big Sioux River. As I gazed over the rolling prairie land, all I could see was that it met the sky at the horizon line. It seemed to me vast and vague and endless, as was my conception of the new trail which I had taken and my dream of the far-off goal.

My father's farm of 160 acres, which he had taken up and improved under the United States homestead laws,[2] lay along the north bank of the river. The nearest neighbor lived a mile away, and all had flourishing fields of wheat, Indian corn and potatoes. Some two miles distant, where the Big Sioux doubled upon itself in a swinging loop, rose the mission church and schoolhouse, the only frame building within forty miles.

Our herd of ponies was loose upon the prairie, and it was my first task each morning to bring them into the log corral. On this particular morning I lingered, finding some of them, like myself, who loved their freedom too well and would not come in.

The man who had built the cabin—it was his first house, and therefore he was proud of it—was tall and manly looking. He stood in front of his pioneer home with a resolute face.

He had been accustomed to the buffalo-skin teepee all his life, until he opposed the white man and was defeated and made a prisoner of war at Davenport, Iowa. It was because of his meditations during those four years in a military prison that he had severed himself from his tribe and taken up a homestead. He declared that he would never join in another Indian outbreak, but would work with his hands for the rest of his life.

"I have hunted every day," he said, "for the support of my family. I sometimes chase the deer all day. One must work, and work hard, whether chasing the deer or planting corn. After all, the corn-planting is the surer provision."

These were my father's new views, and in this radical change of life he had persuaded a few other families to join him. They formed a little colony at Flandreau, on the Big Sioux River.

To be sure, his beginnings in civilization had not been attended with all the success that he had hoped for. One year the crops had been devoured by grasshoppers, and another year ruined by drought. But he was still satisfied that there was no alternative for the Indian. He was now anxious to have his boys learn the English language and something about books, for he could see that these were the "bow and arrows" of the white man.

"O-hee-ye-sa!" called my father, and I obeyed the call. "It is time for you to go to school, my son," he said, with his usual air of decision. We had spoken of the matter more than once, yet it seemed hard when it came to the actual undertaking.

I remember quite well how I felt as I stood there with eyes fixed upon the ground.

2. Signed by Abraham Lincoln in 1862, the Homestead Act provided 160 acres of public land free of charge (except for a small filing fee) to anyone 21 years of age or head of a family, a citizen or person who had filed for citizenship, who had lived on the land and cultivated it for at least five years.

"And what am I to do at the school?" I asked finally, with much embarrassment.

"You will be taught the language of the white man, and also how to count your money and tell the prices of your horses and of your furs. The white teacher will first teach you the signs by which you can make out the words on their books. They call them A, B, C, and so forth. Old as I am, I have learned some of them."

The matter having been thus far explained, I was soon on my way to the little mission school, two miles distant over the prairie. There was no clear idea in my mind as to what I had to do, but as I galloped along the road I turned over and over what my father had said, and the more I thought of it the less I was satisfied. Finally I said aloud:

"Why do we need a sign language, when we can both hear and talk?" And unconsciously I pulled on the lariat and the pony came to a stop. I suppose I was half curious and half in dread about this "learning white men's ways." Meanwhile the pony had begun to graze.

While thus absorbed in thought, I was suddenly startled by the yells of two other Indian boys and the noise of their ponies' hoofs. I pulled the pony's head up just as the two strangers also pulled up and stopped their panting ponies at my side. They stared at me for a minute, while I looked at them out of the corners of my eyes.

"Where are you going? Are you going to our school?" volunteered one of the boys at last.

To this I replied timidly: "My father told me to go to a place where the white men's ways are taught, and to learn the sign language."

"That's good—we are going there too! Come on, Red Feather, let's try another race! I think, if we had not stopped, my pony would have outrun yours. Will you race with us?" he continued, addressing me; and we all started our ponies at full speed.

I soon saw that the two strange boys were riding erect and soldier-like. "That must be because they have been taught to be like the white man," I thought. I allowed my pony a free start and leaned forward until the animal drew deep breaths, then I slid back and laid my head against the pony's shoulder, at the same time raising my quirt, and he leaped forward with a will! I yelled as I passed the other boys, and pulled up when I reached the crossing. The others stopped, too, and surveyed pony and rider from head to foot, as if they had never seen us before.

"You have a fast pony. Did you bring him back with you from Canada?" Red Feather asked. "I think you are the son of Many Lightnings, whom he brought home the other day," the boy added.

"Yes, this is my own pony. My uncle in Canada always used him to chase the buffalo, and he has ridden him in many battles." I spoke with considerable pride.

"Well, as there are no more buffalo to chase now, your pony will have to pull the plow like the rest. But if you ride him to school, you can join in the races. On the holy days the young men race horses, too." Red Feather and White Fish spoke both together, while I listened attentively, for everything was strange to me.

"What do you mean by the 'holy days'?" I asked.

"Well, that's another of the white people's customs. Every seventh day they call a 'holy day', and on that day they go to a 'Holy House', where they pray to their Great Mystery. They also say that no one should work on that day."

This definition of Sunday and churchgoing set me to thinking again, for I never knew before that there was any difference in the days.

"But how do you count the days, and how do you know what day to begin with?" I inquired.

"Oh, that's easy! The white men have everything in their books. They know how many days in a year, and they have even divided the day itself into so many equal parts; in fact, they have divided them again and again until they know how many times one can breathe in a day," said White Fish, with the air of a learned man.

"That's impossible," I thought, so I shook my head.

By this time we had reached the second crossing of the river, on whose bank stood the little mission school. Thirty or forty Indian children stood about, curiously watching the newcomer as we came up the steep bank. I realized for the first time that I was an object of curiosity, and it was not a pleasant feeling. On the other hand, I was considerably interested in the strange appearance of these school-children.

They all had on some apology for white man's clothing, but their pantaloons belonged neither to the order *short* nor to the *long*. Their coats, some of them, met only half-way by the help of long strings. Others were lapped over in front, and held on by a string of some sort fastened round the body. Some of their hats were brimless and others without crowns, while most were fantastically painted. The hair of all the boys was cut short, and, in spite of the evidences of great effort to keep it down, it stood erect like porcupine quills. I thought, as I stood on one side and took a careful observation of the motley gathering, that if I had to look like these boys in order to obtain something of the white man's learning, it was time for me to rebel.

The boys played ball and various other games, but I tied my pony to a tree and then walked up to the schoolhouse and stood there as still as if I had been glued to the wall. Presently the teacher came out and rang a bell, and all the children went in, but I waited for some time before entering, and then slid inside and took the seat nearest the door. I felt singularly out of place, and for the twentieth time wished my father had not sent me.

When the teacher spoke to me, I had not the slightest idea what he meant, so I did not trouble myself to make any demonstration, for fear of giving offense. Finally he asked in broken Sioux: "What is your name?" Evidently he had not been among the Indians long, or he would not have asked that question. It takes a tactician and a diplomat to get an Indian to tell his name! The poor man was compelled to give up the attempt and resume his seat on the platform.

He then gave some unintelligible directions, and, to my great surprise, the pupils in turn held their books open and talked the talk of a strange people. Afterward the teacher made some curious signs upon a blackboard on the wall, and seemed to ask the children to read them. To me they did not compare in interest with my bird's-track and fish-fin studies on the sands. I was something like a wild cub caught overnight, and appearing in the corral next morning with the lambs. I had seen nothing thus far to prove to me the good of civilization.

Meanwhile the children grew more familiar, and whispered references were made to the "new boy's" personal appearance. At last he was called "Baby" by one of the big boys; but this was not meant for him to hear, so he did not care to hear. He rose silently and walked out. He did not dare to do or say anything in departing. The boys watched him as he led his pony to the river to drink and then jumped upon his back and started for home at a good pace. They cheered as he started over the hills: "Hoo-oo! hoo-oo! there goes the long-haired boy!"

When I was well out of sight of the school, I pulled in my pony and made him walk slowly home.

"Will going to that place make a man brave and strong?" I asked myself. "I must tell my father that I cannot stay here. I must go back to my uncle in Canada, who taught me to hunt and shoot and to be a brave man. They might as well try to make a buffalo build houses like a beaver as to teach me to be a white man," I thought.

It was growing late when at last I appeared at the cabin. "Why, what is the matter?" quoth my old grandmother, who had taken especial pride in me as a promising young hunter. Really, my face had assumed a look of distress and mental pressure that frightened the superstitious old woman. She held her peace, however, until my father returned.

"Ah," she said then, "I never fully believed in these new manners! The Great Mystery cannot make a mistake. I say it is against our religion to change the customs that have been practiced by our people ages back—so far back that no one can remember it. Many of the school-children have died, you have told me. It is not strange. You have offended Him, because you have made these children change the ways he has given us. I must know more about this matter before I give my consent." Grandmother had opened her mind in unmistakable terms, and the whole family was listening to her in silence.

Then my hard-headed father broke the pause. "Here is one Sioux who will sacrifice everything to win the wisdom of the white man! We have now entered upon this life, and there is no going back. Besides, one would be like a hobbled pony without learning to live like those among whom we must live."

During father's speech my eyes had been fixed upon the burning logs that stood on end in the huge mud chimney in a corner of the cabin. I didn't want to go to that place again; but father's logic was too strong for me, and the next morning I had my long hair cut, and started in to school in earnest.

I obeyed my father's wishes, and went regularly to the little day-school, but as yet my mind was in darkness. What has all this talk of books to do with hunting, or even with planting corn? I thought. The subject occupied my thoughts more and more, doubtless owing to my father's decided position on the matter; while, on the other hand, my grandmother's view of this new life was not encouraging.

I took the situation seriously enough, and I remember I went with it where all my people go when they want light—into the thick woods. I needed counsel, and human counsel did not satisfy me. I had been taught to seek the "Great Mystery" in silence, in the deep forest or on the height of the mountain. There were no mountains here, so I retired into the woods. I knew nothing of the white man's religion; I only followed the teaching of my ancestors.

When I came back, my heart was strong. I desired to follow the new trail to the end. I knew that, like the little brook, it must lead to larger and larger ones until it became a resistless river, and I shivered to think of it. But again I recalled the teachings of my people, and determined to imitate their undaunted bravery and stoic resignation. However, I was far from having realized the long, tedious years of study and confinement before I could begin to achieve what I had planned.

"You must not fear to work with your hands," said my father, "but if you are able to think strongly and well, that will be a quiver full of arrows for you, my son. All of the white man's children must go to school, but those who study best and longest need not work with their hands after that, for they can work with their minds. You may plow the five acres next the river, and see if you can make a straight furrow as well as a straight shot."

I set to work with the heavy breaking-plow and yoke of oxen, but I am sorry to admit that the work was poorly done. "It will be better for you to go away to a higher school," advised my father.

It appears remarkable to me now that my father, thorough Indian as he was, should have had such deep and sound conceptions of a true civilization. But there is the contrast—my father's mother! whose faith in her people's philosophy and training could not be superseded by any other allegiance.

To her such a life as we lead today would be no less than sacrilege. "It is not a true life," she often said. "It is a sham. I cannot bear to see my boy live a made-up life!"

Ah, grandmother! you had forgotten one of the first principles of your own teaching, namely: "When you see a new trail, or a footprint that you do not know, follow it to the point of knowing."

"All I want to say to you," the old grandmother seems to answer, "is this: Do not get lost on this new trail."

"I find," said my father to me, "that the white man has a well-grounded religion, and teaches his children the same virtues that our people taught to theirs. The Great Mystery has shown to the red and white man alike the good and evil, from which to choose. I think the way of the white man is better than ours, because he is able to preserve on paper the things he does not want to forget. He records everything—the sayings of his wise men, the laws enacted by his counselors."

I began to be really interested in this curious scheme of living that my father was gradually unfolding to me out of his limited experience.

"The way of knowledge," he continued, "is like our old way in hunting. You begin with a mere trail—a footprint. If you follow that faithfully, it may lead you to a clearer trail—a track—a road. Later on there will be many tracks, crossing and diverging one from the other. Then you must be careful, for success lies in the choice of the right road. You must be doubly careful, for traps will be laid for you, of which the most dangerous is the spirit-water, that causes a man to forget his self-respect," he added, unwittingly giving to his aged mother material for her argument against civilization.

The general effect upon me of these discussions, which were logical enough on the whole, although almost entirely from the outside, was that I became convinced that my father was right.

My grandmother had to yield at last, and it was settled that I was to go to school at Santee agency, Nebraska, where Dr. Alfred L. Riggs was then fairly started in the work of his great mission school, which has turned out some of the best educated Sioux Indians. It was at that time the Mecca of the Sioux country; even though Sitting Bull and Crazy Horse were still at large, harassing soldiers and emigrants alike, and General Custer had just been placed in military command of the Dakota Territory.

━━ ⚔ ━━

Hawaiian Songs
1860s–1890s

First settled by Polynesians around 400 C.E., the lush volcanic Hawaiian islands in the central Pacific developed a rich oral culture over the centuries, as well as a sturdy independence supported by formidable warriors. The Hawaiians maintained sporadic contact with Tahiti and other Polynesian societies but governed themselves, with powerful chieftains emerging on the major islands. The first European to see Hawaii was the English explorer James Cook, who landed there in 1778 and was killed on a return visit the next year. Contacts with Europeans gradually increased, though Hawaii's isolation, and its skilled warriors, maintained the islands' independence for many years. One unexpected result of European contact was actually to strengthen central Hawaiian government. Using European weapons, a chieftain named Kamehameha succeeded in seizing control over the whole of Hawaii, and for most of the nineteenth century the country was ruled by a native monarchy, until the United States annexed Hawaii in 1898. The islands remained a U.S. territory until the population voted for statehood in 1959.

The nineteenth-century Hawaiian leaders accepted the presence of Christian missionaries, who gradually converted much of the population, but they strove to maintain as much of their culture as possible, including the long-established traditions of dances and of songs, composed by both men and women. Some of the songs below were composed by the Hawaiian royalty themselves. Based on older forms, these poems reflect the Hawaiians' often amused fascination with European ways and European imports, from pianos to water sprinklers. They record as well the Hawaiians' sense of the dramatic opening up of the world, from the comic song of "Bill the Ice Skater," who boasts of skills acquired far away while serving in the merchant marine, to an extraordinary song by King Ka-lā-kaua, recalling his 1881 journey around the world. Such a journey would have been unthinkable for any Hawaiian a century before, and indeed Ka-lā-kaua was the first sitting monarch in history to make a world tour. He visited Japan, China, India, Egypt, and several European capitals, meeting with the Pope in Rome and Queen Victoria in London before going on to Washington to meet with President Chester Arthur. His song expresses his astonishment at the scope of all he has seen, as well as his enduring pride in his own society and the love of his people. The King's year-long journey, indeed, helped to foster the loyalty his poem praises. As a local newspaper noted on his return, "What a contrast for His Majesty between the October of 1880, and the October of 1881. Then distrust, misrepresentation, and much disloyalty in certain quarters; though the heart of the people was true at the time. Now all loyalty and enthusiasm . . . met the royal gaze at every side."

Forest Trees of the Sea[1]

No, it is not too soon.

I have seen in my heart
that sea of forest trees
of tall-masted ships returning
5   to Honolulu's harbor of Māmala,
making every sea-murmur a word—
Māmala's murmur of unresting love.

Love's home is Diamond Head.
Love's shelter is where Pearl Harbor hills reach out to sea.
10   Love's gaze is keen and long.

Perhaps I should write a letter.
Perhaps I should show my love by asking his:
Come back, dear love, bring ease to me,
comfort of mind.

1. Translated by Mary Kawena Pukui and Alfons L. Korn.

15 For you I sing my song
    of forest trees on the unresting sea.

Piano at Evening[1]

O Piano I heard at evening,
where are you?

Your music haunts me far into the night
like the voice of landshells
5 trilling sweetly
near the break of day.

I remember when my dear and I
visited aboard the *Nautilus*[2]
and saw our first looking glass.

10 I remember the upland of Ma'eli'eli
where the mists creeping in and out
threaded their way between the old
houses of thatch.

Again I chant my refrain
15 of long ago and a piano singing
far into the night.

Bill the Ice Skater

Bill's home again.
Now he's an ice skater.
Back from his seafaring,
when Bill opens his mouth
5 the words come a-tumbling—
you never heard such jargon!

"Mi no hao!" says Bill.[1]

Everything jibber-jabber,
jabber-jibber,
10 pell mell!

This is my song about
Bill the ice skater.

The Pearl[1]

I have traveled over many lands and distant seas,
to India afar and China renowned.

---

1. Composed c. 1872 by a young chanter named Pālea after first hearing a piano.
2. A British sailing vessel.
1. "Me know how."

1. Composed by King Ka-l,ā-kaua in 1881. His title alludes to Jesus' comparison of the word of God to "a pearl of great price" (Matthew 3:46).

I have touched the shores of Africa and the boundaries of Europe,
and I have met the great ones of all the lands.

5   As I stood at the side of heads of governments,
next to leaders proud of their rule, their authority over their own,
I realized how small and weak is the power I hold.
For mine is a throne established upon a heap of lava.
They rule where millions obey their commands.
10   Only a few thousands can I count under my care.

Yet one thought came to me of which I may boast,
that of all beauties locked within the embrace of these shores,
one is a jewel more precious than any owned by my fellow monarchs.
I have nothing in my Kingdom to dread.

15   I mingle with my people without fear.
My safety is no concern, I require no bodyguards.
Mine is the boast that a pearl of great price has fallen to me from above.
Mine is the loyalty of my people.

A Feather Chant for Ka-pi'o-lani at Wai-mānalo[1]

Now at Wai-mānalo your heap of feathers and our offering,
gifts fashioned for you by the people of Mololani.

She sits, the beautiful Chiefess, in her place of honor
journeying onward to Moku-lua.

5   Entrancing thoughts fill the mind
when eyes mirror Moku-manu's charm.

Birds circle about the sky, poise
in dipping flight over the waves.

Proudly the royal flag flies acknowledged,
10   greeted by Mālei, guardian goddess of this shore.

Now the sacred kapu[2] of the sea is lifted,
made free by the Chiefess in her journey.

It is she who glides in beauty
over billows of the ever-surging sea.

15   Cold spray pierces, the skin of the Chiefess warms within
from its own ruddy glow.

Now that the telephone makes work such a trifle,
how easy to converse with the best beloved!

O Ka-pi'o-lani, answer to our call!
20   You are the woman we praise, this lei of affection is yours.

---

1. Site of a sugar plantation on the island of Oahu, established by English settlers, who had installed one of the newly invented American telephones rapidly becoming popular on the island. The chant was composed in honor of a visit to the plantation by Queen Ka-pi'o-lani.
2. Precinct.

The Sprinkler[1]

O whirly-water
gentle rain shower on the move
what do you think you're up to
circling, twirling so quietly?

CHORUS

5   You there! You there!
(bass) Yea, yea—coming up!
(hips swinging) As you revolve,
when—oh, when
(bass) will you—will you—
10 will you ever hold still?
Amazing
the way you take over: irresistible.
Come, slow down a little—
so I can drink!

⤏ ⚹ ⤎

José Rizal
1861–1896

Considered the father of Philippine independence as well as the founder of modern Philippine literature, José Rizal squeezed an enormous amount of life into his thirty-five years: two novels, much poetry and journalism, a medical practice, and tireless political activism. Born into a wealthy, racially mixed family, he studied medicine in Manila, then completed his training as an ophthalmologist in Europe while making his début as a writer with essays critical of Spanish rule in his country and in particular the influence of the wealthy Catholic orders. In 1886 he published his darkly comic masterpiece, *Noli Me Tangere* ("Touch me not"). Written in Spanish (then spoken by approximately 3 percent of Filipinos), the book was immediately banned in his homeland. Like so many other figures who would one day be celebrated as national heroes, he was perpetually at odds with the government and spent much of his short life outside his country. After five years living in Spain and Hong Kong, writing and practicing medicine, he returned to the Philippines in 1892 as sentiment built in favor of liberation from Spain. Soon after founding the Liga Filipina, which he insisted was oriented toward reform rather than revolution, he was captured by the authorities and condemned to internal exile far from the capital in Dapitan, where he proceeded to build a school and a hospital. In 1896 he was arrested again while on his way to Cuba and returned to Manila, where he was accused of "promoting rebellion" and executed. His patriotic poem "Mi ultimo adiós" ("My Last Farewell"), was written as he awaited the firing squad and smuggled out of the jail in an alcohol burner. It is still read by students in the Philippines, and his complex heritage continues to be actively debated there.

Noli Me Tangere is the somewhat prophetic story of a deeply charismatic figure very like Rizal himself. Returning to his country after years in Europe, he finds himself on a collision course with the corrupt, semi feudal power of the Spanish priesthood. Yet he is also confused by the question of what is to be done. The title refers to Jesus' words to Mary Magdalene shortly after his resurrection: "Touch me not, for I am not yet ascended to my Father." In the

---

1. Said to have been composed by Queen Lili'u-o-ka-lani around 1891, after she noticed a lawn sprinkler at the home of an American neighbor.

novel's first scene, which demonstrates the attitudes of the Spanish colonial rulers, we hear indirectly of the death of the "very worthy person" who turns out to be the father of the protagonist, now traveling in Europe, and of Father Damaso's shady role in the father's burial.

PRONUNCIATIONS:

Damaso: da-MAH-so
José Rizal: ho-ZAY ree-ZAHL
Laruja: la-ROO-ha

from Noli Me Tangere[1]

1

A GATHERING

Towards the end of October, Don Santiago de los Santos, popularly known as Capitan Tiago, was hosting a dinner which, in spite of its having been announced only that afternoon, against his wont, was already the theme of all conversation in Binondo, in the neighboring districts, and even in Intramuros. Capitan Tiago was reputed to be a most generous man, and it was known that his home, like his country, never closed its door to anything, as long as it was not business, or any new or bold idea.

Like an electric jolt the news circulated around the world of social parasites: the pests or dregs which God in His infinite goodness created and very fondly breeds in Manila. Some went in search of shoe polish for their boots, others for buttons and cravats, but all were preoccupied with the manner in which to greet with familiarity the master of the house, and thus pretend that they were old friends, or to make excuses, if the need arose, for not having been able to come much earlier.

This dinner was being given in a house on Anloague Street, and since we can no longer recall its number, we will try to describe it in such a way as to make it still recognizable—that is, if earthquakes have not ruined it. We do not believe that its owner would have had it pulled down, this task being ordinarily taken care of by God, or Nature, with whom our government also has many projects under contract.

It is a sufficiently large building, of the style prevalent in many parts of the country, situated towards a bend of the Pasig river, called by many the Binondo creek, which plays, as do all rivers in Manila, the multiple roles of bathing place, drainage and sewage, laundering area, fishing ground, means of transport and communication, and even source of potable water, if the Chinese water hauler or peddler finds it convenient. It is noteworthy that this dynamic artery of the district where the traffic is heavy and entangled, a distance of almost one kilometer, relies only on a one-way wooden bridge rickety for a stretch of six months, and impassable the rest of the year, so much so that during the dry season horses take advantage of this permanent status quo to jump from the bridge into the water below, to the great surprise of the distracted mortals inside the coach who are either dozing or contemplating the progress of the times.

The house we allude to is somewhat low and misaligned—perhaps the architect who designed it could not see well, or this could have been the effect of earthquakes and hurricanes—no one can rightly say.

---

1. Translated by Soledad Lacson-Locsi.

A wide stairway with green balustrades and rug-covered steps leads to the house from an entrance hall overlaid with painted glazed tiles, amidst potted green plants and baskets of flowers atop porcelain pedestals of motley colors and fantastic designs.

Since no porters or servants ask for the invitation cards, let us go up. You who read me, friend or foe, if you are attracted to the sounds of the orchestra, to the bright lights, or by the unmistakable tinkling of glass and silverware, and wish to see how parties are in the Pearl of the Orient—I would find it more pleasurable and convenient to spare you the description of the house, but this is just as important. Generally speaking, we mortals are like tortoises: we are valued and classified according to our shells; for this and for other qualities as well, the mortals of the Philippines are the same as tortoises.

Once up we immediately find ourselves in a spacious living room, dubbed a *caida*, I don't know why, which this evening is being utilized as the dining room and at the same time as the orchestra hall.

At the center is a long table, profusely and elegantly decorated, which seems to wink temptingly at the freeloaders with sweet promises; and to threaten the timid youth or the unsophisticated lass with two mortal hours in the company of strangers whose language and conversation tend to have a jargon all their own.

In contrast to these earthly preparations we have before us a motley parade of picture frames aligned on the wall, representing religious themes such as *Purgatory, Hell, The Last Judgment, Death of the Just Man,* and *Death of the Sinner.* In the background, encased in an elegant and splendid Renaissance-style frame by Arevalo, is a curious piece of canvas of wide proportions depicting two old women. The inscription reads: "Our Lady of Peace and Good Voyage, venerated in Antipolo, in the guise of a beggar who visits the pious and well-known Capitana Ines in her sick bed." If the canvas does not reveal much taste or art, it has, however, extreme realism: the sick woman already appears like a cadaver in a stage of decomposition, with yellowish and bluish tints in her features; the glasses, objects and other utensils speak of a long history of illness. They are depicted so minutely and accurately to the last detail that the onlooker is able to catch a glimpse of their contents. Contemplating these paintings which excite the appetite and inspire bucolic thoughts, sets one to thinking that perhaps the cunning owner of the house knew the character of most of those who would be seated at the table, and to partly disguise his thoughts, caused precious Chinese lamps to hang from the platform, also bird cages without their occupants, crystal balls of quicksilver, red, green and blue colors, wilting orchids, desiccated puffer fish called *botetes,* and so forth, hiding completely the view on the other side of the river with ornately carved wooden arches, semi-Chinese and semi-European in style; leaving a view of the big *azotea* or terrace with lots of greenery; *emparrados* or green bowers made with the branches of propped vines and half-lighted by small multi-colored paper lanterns.

Those who are to partake of the meal are gathered in the living room surrounded by colossal mirrors and sparkling chandeliers. Over there on a pine platform is the magnificent grand piano purchased at an exorbitant price, and rendered still more costly this evening since nobody is playing it. In the living room is a giant-sized painting in oil of a handsome man in full dress suit, stiff, erect and very correct down to the gold tasseled cane which he holds in his bejewelled fingers. The picture seems to say: "Hm! Look at how much I have on! See how serious I am!"

The furniture is elegant, but somewhat uncomfortable and unhealthy: the owner of the house is more concerned with the luxury of his household than with any hygienic consideration for the well-being of his guests.

It is as if he were telling them: "Dysentery is such a terrible thing, but you are seated on chairs imported from Europe. It is not every day that one can sit on a chair like this."

The living room is almost full of people: the men separated from the women, as they are in Roman Catholic churches and Jewish synagogues. The ladies, a few young Filipinas and Spaniards, open their mouths to suppress yawns, but cover their faces instantly with their fans, scarcely making a sound. Whatever attempts at conversation are ventured dwindle into monosyllables, like the sounds one hears at night, caused by rats and lizards. Is it, perhaps, the different images of Our Lady hanging from the wall between the mirrors, which makes them silent and assume a religious composure; or are the women here an exception?

The only woman receiving the ladies was Capitan Tiago's old cousin, she of kindly features, who speaks quite bad Spanish. All her manners and urbanity were reduced to offering the Spaniards a tray of cigars and a compound of betel nut, leaves and lime for chewing; and to giving her hand to be kissed by the Filipinas exactly as the friars did. The poor ancient ended in boredom and, taking advantage of the sound of a plate breaking, left the living room in haste, muttering:

"Jesus! You wait, vile despicable creatures . . . !" and never reappeared.

As to the men, they are already making more noise. Some cadets are talking animatedly but in hushed tones in one corner of the living room, looking at everyone now and then, and pointing their fingers at various persons, laughing among themselves more or less quietly. On the other hand, two foreigners attired in white, with hands crossed behind their backs, and without saying a word, are pacing back and forth across the living room like bored passengers on board a ship. All the great excitement and heightened interest emanates from a group of two religious friars, two civilians and a military man around a small table with bottles of wine and English biscuits.

The soldier is a veteran Teniente, tall and with sullen features, looking like a duke of Alba, a straggler in the ranks of the *Guardia Civil;* he talks little, but is brief and harsh. One of the friars, a young Dominican handsome to the point of prettiness, the epitome of pulchritude, and brilliant as his gold-mounted eyeglasses, is possessed of an early maturity. He was the parish priest of Binondo, and had been in previous years a university professor at San Juan de Letran. He was reputed to be a consummate dialectician, so much so that in those times when the Dominicans dared to cross wits in subtleties with the seculars, the very capable commentator, B. de Luna, was never able to embroil nor catch him: the disputations of Padre Sibyla left him like an angler attempting to catch eels with ropes. The Dominican speaks little, but appears to weigh his words.

In contrast, the other friar, a Franciscan, is talking much and gesticulating more. In spite of his hair starting to turn gray, he seems to have conserved well his vigor and robustness. His features are correct, his glance not very reassuring; his wide jaws and his herculean build give him the appearance of a Roman patrician in disguise. Against your will you find yourself reminded of one of the three monks described by Heine in his book *Gods in Exile,* who in the September Equinox somewhere in the Tyrol were cruising a lake in a boat at midnight and deposited each time on the palm of the poor boatman a silver coin as cold as ice, which filled him with fear. However, Padre Damaso is not mysterious like those monks; he is jolly and if the sound of his voice is brusque like that of a man who has never bitten his tongue and who believes everything he utters is sacrosanct and cannot be improved upon, his gay and frank laughter erases this disagreeable impression, even to the extent that one feels bound to forgive him his sockless feet and a pair of hairy legs which would fetch the fortune of a Mendieta in the Quiapo fair.

One of the civilians, a small man with dark whiskers, is notable for his nose, which, judging from its dimensions, should not have been his; the other, a blond youth, has the appearance of a newcomer to the country. The Franciscan was keeping up a lively discussion with this young man:

"You will see," the former was saying, "when you have been in this country for a few months you will become convinced about what I am telling you: it is one thing to govern in Madrid and another to stay in the Philippines."

"But . . ."

"I, for instance," continued Padre Damaso, raising his voice a bit more in order not to allow the other to reply, "I who have been for twenty-three years thriving on bananas and rice in this country, I can speak with authority about it. Don't give me theories or rhetoric. I know the *indio*.[2] You must take into account the fact that when I arrived in this country I was assigned to a town, small, it is true, but highly dedicated to agriculture. I did not understand the Tagalog[3] dialect well then, but the women made their confessions to me, and we understood each other. And they became so fond of me that three years later, when I was being transferred to a bigger town made vacant by the death of the *indio* parish priest, all of them wept to see me go and gave me a sendoff with gifts and music."

"But that only shows . . ."

"Wait! wait! Don't be too quick! My successor stayed for less time than I, and when he left town, had more people saying goodbye, more tears and more music despite the fact that he flogged them more, and had raised parish fees to almost double."

"But you will allow me . . ."

"Even more so, in the town of San Diego where I stayed twenty years, and which I . . . left only a few months ago. (He seems much disgusted.) Twenty years, no one can deny it, are more than sufficient to get to know a town. San Diego had six thousand souls and I knew every inhabitant as if I had given him birth and nourished him. I knew which one was lame; which side of his shoe pinched his foot; which one was making love to which *dalaga;* how many indiscretions this one had and with whom; who was the real father of the boy, etc. All made their confessions to me; they took good care to fulfill their duties. Let Santiago, the master of the house, bear me out. He has many properties in San Diego and it is in San Diego that we became friends. Well, you will see what the *indio* is like: when I left, only some old women and some tertiary sisters saw me off. And I had stayed there for twenty years!"

"But I do not see what this has to do with taking away the monopoly of tobacco," answered the blond man, taking advantage of a pause in the conversation while the friar was sipping a glass of sherry.

Padre Damaso, taken by surprise, almost dropped his wine glass. For a moment he looked at the young man squarely face to face and . . .

"What? How come?" he exclaimed with great surprise. "But is it possible that you do not see that which is clear as daylight? Don't you see, son of God, that this is palpable proof that the reforms of the ministries are irrational?"

This time it was the blond man who was left perplexed; the Teniente knitted his eyebrows further; the diminutive man was shaking his head either in approval of

---

2. Spanish for "Indian." Pejorative term for Philippine natives.

3. A language, not a dialect, spoken by the largest cultural-linguistic group in the Philippines.

Padre Damaso, or in disagreement with him. The Dominican then started to turn his back to them.

"Do you believe so?" the young man finally was able to ask seriously, looking at the friar curiously.

"Do I believe it? As I believe in the Gospel. The *indio* is so indolent!"

"Oh! Forgive me for interrupting," said the young man, lowering his voice and moving his chair slightly closer. "You have uttered a word which evokes all my interest. Is such indolence naturally inherent in the native, or do we, as a foreign traveler has said, justify with this indolence our own, our failings and our colonial system? He was speaking of the other colonies whose inhabitants are of the same race . . ."

"Oh no, just envy. Ask Señor Laruja who also knows the country, ask him if the ignorance and indolence of the *indio* have any equal."

"Actually," replied the small man who had been alluded to, "nowhere in the world can be found another more indolent than the *indio*, nowhere in the world."

"Nor one as vicious and as ungrateful!"

"Nor one so uncouth!"

The blond man began to look uneasily at everybody.

"Gentlemen," he said in a low voice, "I believe we are in the home of an *indio* . . . those young ladies . . ."

"Bah! Don't be so apprehensive! Santiago does not consider himself a native, and besides he is not present and even if he were . . . those are the foolish statements of newcomers. Let a few months pass and you will change opinion after you have frequented many fiestas and their *bailujan*, slept in many beds and eaten plenty of *tinola*."

"What you call *tinola*, is it a fruit of the lotus variety which causes some men to be sort of forgetful?"

"What lotus or what lottery!" answered Padre Damaso laughing.

"You must have bells in your head. *Tinola* is a *gulay* of chicken and squash. How long has it been since you arrived?"

"Four days," answered the youth, somewhat piqued.

"Did you come as an employee?"

"No sir! I came on my own to get to know the country."

"Man, what a rare bird you are," exclaimed Padre Damaso regarding the other with curiosity. "Coming on your own and for nonsensical notions! What a phenomenon! There being so many books . . . just by having two finger-widths of forehead . . . many have written such great books! Just having two finger-widths of forehead . . ."

"Your Reverence, Padre Damaso, you were saying," the Dominican brusquely interrupted, cutting into the conversation, "that you spent 20 years in the town of San Diego and you left it . . . was not your Reverence contented . . . with the town?"

At this question, asked so casually and almost carelessly, Padre Damaso suddenly lost his aplomb and laughter.

"No!" he growled brusquely, and let his full weight fall hard against the back of the chair.

The Dominican went on in an indifferent tone: "It must be painful to leave a town where one has stayed twenty years and which one knows as well as the habit one wears. I, at least, felt deeply when leaving Camiling, and I had been there only a few months . . . but my superiors did that for the good of the community . . . it was also for my own good."

For the first time that evening Padre Damaso seemed much preoccupied. Suddenly he banged his fist against the arm of the chair and, breathing forcefully, exclaimed: "Oh! Is there religion or not, that is, are the parish priests free or not? The country is being lost . . . it is lost!"

And again, he pounded with his fist.

All those in the living room, startled, turned towards the group. The Dominican, much surprised, raised his head to peer at the Franciscan from beneath his glasses. The two foreigners who were strolling stopped for a moment, looked at each other, slightly agape, and continued their walk.

"He is in a bad humor because you did not address him as Your Reverence," murmured the blond youth to Señor Laruja.

"What does Your Reverence mean? What is the matter?" asked both the Dominican and the military man in different tones.

"That is why many calamities come! The government supports the heretics against the ministers of God!" continued the Franciscan, raising his fists vigorously.

"What do you mean?" the sullen Teniente asked, half rising.

"What do I mean?" Padre Damaso repeated, raising his voice and confronting the Teniente. "I say what I want to say! I mean that when the parish priest throws out of the cemetery the corpse of a heretic, nobody, not even the King himself, has the right to interfere, much less impose punishments. That little general . . . a calamity of a little general . . ."

"Padre! His Excellency is Vice-Royal Patron!" shouted the Teniente, getting up.

"Some excellency or Vice-Royal Patron!" answered the Franciscan, also getting up.

"In other times he would have been dragged down the stairs as the religious orders did one time to the impious Governor Bustamante. Those were really days of faith!"

"I am warning you that I will not allow . . . His Excellency represents His Majesty, the King . . ."

"What King! What nobody? For us there is no King but the legitimate . . ."

"Halt!" shouted the Teniente threateningly, as if he were addressing his soldiers. "You take back what you have said, or tomorrow, promptly, I will report to His Excellency!"

"Go ahead—this very moment, go ahead!" replied Padre Damaso with sarcasm, approaching the Teniente with doubled fists. "Do you think that because I wear a habit I lack . . . Go ahead! I will even lend you my carriage!"

The matter was taking a comical turn; fortunately the Dominican intervened.

"Gentlemen," he said in an authoritative tone and with that nasal twang that is so becoming to all friars:

"Do not confuse matters, or look for offenses where there are none. We should distinguish in the words of Padre Damaso two things: the words of the man, and those of the priest. The words of the latter as such, per se, can never offend because they come from the absolute truth. In those of the man a subdistinction has to be made: those which are said *ab irato*[4] and those which are said *ab ore* but not *in corde;* and those which are said *ex corde.* These last are the only ones that can offend; and that is, accordingly: if already *in mente,* pre-existing for a motive, or only coming *per accidens,* in the heat of argument, if there is . . ."

"Well, I—*per accidens* and for myself—know the motives, Padre Sibyla!" interrupted the soldier, seeing himself embroiled in so many distinctions, and fearing that

---

4. These are Latin expressions: *ab irato:* out of rage; *ab ore:* from the mouth; *in corde:* in the heart; *in mente:* in the mind; *per accidens:* by accident.

if these continued he would not come out of it guiltless. "I know the motives, and Your Reverence will make the distinctions. During the absence of Padre Damaso from San Diego, his assistant buried the body of a very worthy person—yes, Sir, a highly worthy person. I had met him many times in his home; he had honored me with his hospitality. That he had never gone to confession, so what? I myself do not confess either; but to claim that he committed suicide is a lie, a calumny! A man like him, having a son in whom he had placed all his affection and hopes; a man who had faith in God; who was cognizant of his duties towards society; a man who was honest and just, does not commit suicide. Thus I speak, and am silent as to other things, with which I bid for Your Reverence's grateful acknowledgement."

And, turning his back on the Franciscan, he proceeded:

"Well, this priest upon his return to the town, after maltreating the poor assistant priest, made him exhume the body, and remove it from the cemetery to bury it—I don't know where. The town of San Diego had the cowardice not to protest; the deceased had no relatives and his only son is in Europe, but His Excellency learned about it, and since he is a man of righteous heart, asked for the punishment; and Padre Damaso was transferred to another town. This is the whole story. Now let Your Reverence make your distinctions."

And having said this he left the group.

"I regret very much having touched a subject so delicate without any previous knowledge," said Padre Sibyla with compunction. "But finally the people got the advantage of the exchange . . ."

"That it has gained. And what about the losses in the transfer . . . and the papers . . . and all that have been misplaced . . ." interrupted Padre Damaso, blurting out, scarcely able to contain his fury.

Gradually the gathering settled down to its former tranquil state.

Some guests had arrived, among them an old hobbled Spaniard, with gentle and harmless features, leaning on the arm of an aged Filipina, heavily curled and made-up, attired in European costume.

The group greeted the couple amiably. Doctor de Espadaña and his wife, the *doctora* Doña Victorina, joined the group we have already met. There were some journalists, store owners or keepers, mutually greeting each other, conversing on one side and another, not knowing what to do.

"But can you tell me, Señor Laruja, how fares the owner of the house?" asked the blond young man. "I have not yet been introduced to him."

"They say he has gone out. I too have not seen him."

"Here there is no need for introductions," Padre Damaso interpolated, "Santiago is a good sort."

"A man who did not invent gunpowder," added Laruja.

"Señor Laruja, you also," exclaimed Doña Victorina with mild reproach, fanning herself. "How can the poor man invent gunpowder which, according to what they say, was invented by the Chinese long ago?"

"The Chinese? Are you mad?" exclaimed Padre Damaso. "Forget it. It was invented by a Franciscan, one of my order, by a Padre I don't recall, a certain Savalls, in the seventh century."

"A Franciscan! Well, this one could have been a missionary in China, this Padre Savalls," replied the lady who did not easily give up on her own views.

"Madam, you must be meaning Schwartz," replied Padre Sibyla without looking at her.

"I don't know. Padre Damaso said Savalls. I can do no less than repeat."

"Well! Savalls or Chevas—what does it matter? One letter does not make him Chinese," replied the Franciscan with ill humor.

"And it was in the fourteenth century and not in the seventh," added the Dominican in a condescending tone, as if to mortify the other's pride.

"Well! a century more or a century less will not make him a Dominican!"

"Man! Don't be upset, Your Reverence!" said Padre Sibyla, smiling. "All the better that he invented it. Thus he has saved his brothers that much labor."

"And Padre Sibyla, you say that it was done in the fourteenth century?" asked Doña Victorina with great interest. "Before or after Christ?"

⇒+ END OF PERSPECTIVES: ON THE COLONIAL FRONTIER +⇐

THE ROMANTIC FANTASTIC

People have always told stories of ghosts and demons, magic and mystery. They are part of the hallowed mysteries of religions, of popular legends and children's bedtime stories. Gods visit humans to tragic and redemptive effect in the drama of many cultures. Goethe's *Faust* was only one of a flow of narratives, tragedies, operas, and even puppet plays about the magician that began in the sixteenth century and continues to the present. In that sense there is nothing new about the fascination with the fantastic in the Romantic period. But earlier ghosts were usually intruders from alien realms (like the terrifying visions of Shakespeare's Hamlet and Macbeth), or else they resided on hidden islands like the fantastic creatures in *The Tempest*. In the decades around 1800 occult forces seemed to enter history, society, and the human mind. It was the age that discovered both electromagnetism and hypnotism (or mesmerism, named for F. A. Mesmer, 1734–1815), and that thought the two forces might be the same. Magic became part of the serious business of life, dreams and madness began to be seen as components of psychic reality rather than signs of divine revelation or sinful alienation.

"A specter is haunting Europe—the specter of the Communist Party," Karl Marx and Friedrich Engels declared, opening *The Communist Manifesto* with a ghost. Their great predecessor, the eighteenthe-century economist Adam Smith, put one at the center of *The Wealth of Nations,* in a passage that has echoed ever since: "every individual . . . intends only his own gain, [but] he is . . . led by an invisible hand to promote an end which was no part of his intention." Poets and novelists made high art out of what earlier might have seemed mere frivolities. During a cold Swiss summer together, the young Mary Wollstonecraft, her lover Percy Shelley, and Lord Byron "occasionally amused ourselves with German stories of ghosts . . . .These tales excited in us a playful desire of imitation," and from that was born *Frankenstein; or, The Modern Prometheus* (first published in 1818), a serious novel of contemporary mythology and science, with powerful insights into human emotions and modern social conditions. Ghost stories were no joke, and no merely theatrical sensation. Almost all Romantic-era writing engages with the mysteries of real life. Wordsworth's "thoughts that do often lie too deep for tears" (Immortality Ode) arise from the unconscious, and Percy Shelley's "Ode to the West Wind" makes meteorology transcendental when it compares autumn leaves to "ghosts from an enchanter fleeing." The invisible hand is never far away. And a great many works make it the center of attention.

Magic can be the topic directly, as in *Faust,* or it can be an aura of mystery within nature, as in Droste-Hülshoff's haunting ballads. However, perhaps most characteristic of all are many works that straddle the border between reality and the unknown. Coleridge's "Kubla Khan" portrays the poetic imagination, driven by opium, opening realms of vast power and sexual seduction; his "Rime of the Ancient Mariner," told at the door to a wedding-feast, concerns crossing "the line" (the equator) into a world of spiritual persecution. In Tieck's "Fair-haired Eckbert" childhood is haunted and haunts the adults who wish to repress their past, while fairy-tale motifs of the wicked witch in the woods and of the bird that lays golden eggs form part of the hazy underground of family romance and infantile sexuality. Balzac's "Sarrasine" turns the spotlight on high society and fine art to reveal sordid and hidden perversions. Edgar Allan Poe is famous for his "Tales of Mystery and Imagination," which encompass the worlds of magic and science and the new world of criminal detection; "The Pit and the Pendulum" offers yet a fourth realm of occult power in the form of political persecution. Everywhere surprising us, and everywhere giving us the slip, the Romantic fantastic lies perpetually in wait at the edges of experiences that we all share.

Samuel Taylor Coleridge
1772–1834

In dividing with Wordsworth the responsibilities for their pathbreaking volume, *Lyrical Ballads* (1798), Samuel Taylor Coleridge took as his province "persons and characters supernatural, or at least romantic; yet so as to transfer from our inward nature a human interest and a semblance of truth sufficient to procure for these shadows of imagination that willing suspension of disbelief for the moment, which constitutes poetic faith." This famous sentence from Coleridge's autobiographical and critical memoir *Biographia Literaria* (1817) condenses much of the brilliance of this most brilliant of Romantic poets and intellectuals. Coleridge was an early and devoted student of German philosophy, with its notion that the truths of the world originate in subjective perceptions ("semblance of truth"); he began as a universalist minister and ended as an influential apostle of conservative Anglicanism ("disbelief," "faith"); he was the age's greatest dramatic critic ("persons and characters"); he was, early and late, a deeply concerned moralist ("human interest"). And his poetic vision was informed by the drug addiction that arose in his mid-twenties from the then commonplace medical use of opium.

"The Rime of the Ancient Mariner" imitates popular ballads in its supernatural narrative, its loose, four-line stanza form, and its snatches of refrain and repetition, but it transcends all its models in length, dramatic intensity, and psychological depth. The story is a patchwork of incidents and images drawn from Coleridge's vast reading in legend and travel literature. Nature is a protagonist, though all perceptions are then filtered through the consciousness of the characters and the multiple narrators. Hence sin and judgment become tangled and subjective issues, with almost cinematic shifts in perspective and evaluation. The framing wedding and the pious hermit who receives the Mariner on land suggest a conventional religious context; the supernatural actions and the background legend of the accursed Wandering Jew evoke primitive superstitions; the nautical setting of exploration alludes to contemporary debates about imperial expansion. Coleridge's daring "Rime of the Ancyent Marinere," as it was originally called, opened the first edition of *Lyrical Ballads*. Subsequently Wordsworth demoted it to next-to-last, just before his own "Tintern Abbey," on account of its difficult story and antique language. In multiple layers of revision, Coleridge modernized the text and added the marginal glosses, which orient the reader through yet another narrative perspective, with a more pronounced Christian coloration than the verse text has. The resulting poem is a mixture of hallucination, psychological study, philosophical meditation, and social and ethical fable, written with an unparalleled mastery of pacing and hectic excitement.

"Kubla Khan" was written in 1797, but published only in 1816. Coleridge first called it an unfinished dream vision; later he wrote that a visitor interrupted the composition. Yet fragments were a popular vehicle in the Romantic period; Wordsworth published bits of *The Prelude* in *Lyrical Ballads,* and Goethe's *Faust: A Fragment* (1790) preceded the completed *Faust: Part I.* In its short compass "Kubla Khan" combines elements as richly as does "The Rime of the Ancient Mariner": with a sexual temptress and a seductive natural scene, folk legend and interest in exotic peoples and settings, political tyranny and popular rebellion, the religion of art and the exultation of the individual consciousness, hints of self-pity and proclamations of prophetic genius, the poem offers a synopsis of Romantic motifs as complete as can be found in any poem of its length.

Kubla Khan[1]
Or, A Vision in a Dream. A Fragment.

The following fragment is here published at the request of a poet of great and deserving celebrity,[2] and, as far as the Author's own opinions are concerned, rather as a psychological curiosity, than on the ground of any supposed *poetic* merits.

In the summer of the year 1797, the Author, then in ill health, had retired to a lonely farm-house between Porlock and Linton, on the Exmoor confines of Somerset and Devonshire. In consequence of a slight indisposition, an anodyne[3] had been prescribed, from the effects of which he fell asleep in his chair at the moment that he was reading the following sentence, or words of the same substance, in "Purchas's Pilgrimage":[4] "Here the Khan Kubla commanded a palace to be built, and a stately garden thereunto. And thus ten miles of fertile ground were inclosed with a wall." The Author continued for about three hours in a profound sleep, at least of the external senses, during which time he has the most vivid confidence, that he could not have composed less than from two to three hundred lines; if that indeed can be called composition in which all the images rose up before him as *things,* with a parallel production of the correspondent expressions, without any sensation or consciousness of effort. On awaking he appeared to himself to have a distinct recollection of the whole, and taking his pen, ink, and paper, instantly and eagerly wrote down the lines that are here preserved. At this moment he was unfortunately called out by a person on business from Porlock, and detained by him above an hour, and on his return to his room, found, to his no small surprise and mortification, that though he still retained some vague and dim recollection of the general purport of the vision, yet, with the exception of some eight or ten scattered lines and images, all the rest had passed away like the images on the surface of a stream into which a stone had been cast, but, alas! without the after restoration of the latter:

> Then all the charm
> Is broken—all that phantom-world so fair
> Vanishes, and a thousand circlets spread,
> And each mis-shape[s] the other. Stay awhile,
> Poor youth! who scarcely dar'st lift up thine eyes—
> The stream will soon renew its smoothness, soon
> The visions will return! And lo, he stays,
> And soon the fragments dim of lovely forms
> Come trembling back, unite, and now once more
> The pool becomes a mirror.[5]

Yet from the still surviving recollections in his mind, the Author has frequently purposed to finish for himself what had been originally, as it were, given to him. Σαμερον αδιον ασω:[6] but the to-morrow is yet to come.

---

1. Kubla Khan was the grandson of Genghis Khan and Emperor of China in the thirteenth century.
2. Byron.
3. A painkiller, probably laudanum.
4. A collection of often fantastical accounts of foreign lands compiled by Samuel Purchas (1613). As a boy, Coleridge was an avid reader of such literature.
5. From Coleridge's *The Picture* (lines 91–100).
6. "I'll sing more sweetly tomorrow." Adapted from Theocritus, *Idyls* 1.145.

Kubla Khan

In Xanadu did Kubla Khan
A stately pleasure-dome decree:
Where Alph,[7] the sacred river, ran
Through caverns measureless to man
5   Down to a sunless sea.
So twice five miles of fertile ground
With walls and towers were girdled round:
And there were gardens bright with sinuous rills,
Where blossomed many an incense-bearing tree;
10 And here were forests ancient as the hills,
Enfolding sunny spots of greenery.

But oh! that deep romantic chasm which slanted
Down the green hill athwart a cedarn cover!
A savage place! as holy and enchanted
15 As e'er beneath a waning moon was haunted
By woman wailing for her demon-lover!
And from this chasm, with ceaseless turmoil seething,
As if this earth in fast thick pants were breathing,
A mighty fountain momently was forced:
20 Amid whose swift half-intermitted burst
Huge fragments vaulted like rebounding hail,
Or chaffy grain beneath the thresher's flail:
And, 'mid these dancing rocks at once and ever
It flung up momently the sacred river.
25 Five miles meandering with a mazy motion
Through wood and dale the sacred river ran,
Then reached the caverns measureless to man,
And sank in tumult to a lifeless ocean:
And 'mid this tumult Kubla heard from far
30 Ancestral voices prophesying war!
    The shadow of the dome of pleasure
    Floated midway on the waves;
    Where was heard the mingled measure
    From the fountain and the caves.
35 It was a miracle of rare device,
A sunny pleasure-dome with caves of ice!

    A damsel with a dulcimer
      In a vision once I saw:
      It was an Abyssinian maid,
40   And on her dulcimer she played,
      Singing of Mount Abora.[8]
      Could I revive within me
      Her symphony and song,
    To such a deep delight 'twould win me,

7. Probably named for Alpheus, a Sicilian river supposed
in legend to flow underground and re-emerge as a famous
fountain.

8. An invented name, possibly varied from Milton,
Paradise Lost 4.280–82: "where Abassin Kings their is-
sue guard, / Mount Amara, though this by some supposed
/ True Paradise under the Ethiop Line."

45   That with music loud and long,
        I would build that dome in air,
        That sunny dome! those caves of ice!
        And all who heard should see them there,
        And all should cry, Beware! Beware!
50   His flashing eyes, his floating hair!
        Weave a circle round him thrice,
        And close your eyes with holy dread,
        For he on honey-dew hath fed,
        And drunk the milk of Paradise.

The Rime of the Ancient Mariner[1]

IN SEVEN PARTS

Part 1

An ancient Mariner meeteth three Gallants bidden to a wedding feast, and detaineth one.

It is an ancient Mariner,
And he stoppeth one of three.
"By thy long gray beard and glittering eye,
Now wherefore stopp'st thou me?

"The Bridegroom's doors are opened wide,   5
And I am next of kin;
The guests are met, the feast is set:
May'st hear the merry din."

He holds him with his skinny hand,
"There was a ship," quoth he.   10
"Hold off! unhand me, grey-beard loon!"
Eftsoons° his hand dropt he.   *immediately*

The Wedding-Guest is spellbound by the eye of the old seafaring man, and constrained to hear his tale.

He holds him with his glittering eye—
The Wedding-Guest stood still,
And listens like a three years' child: 15
The Mariner hath his will.

The Wedding-Guest sat on a stone:
He cannot choose but hear;
And thus spake on that ancient man,
The bright-eyed Mariner.   20

"The ship was cheered, the harbour cleared,
Merrily did we drop
Below the kirk,° below the hill.   *church*
Below the lighthouse top.

1. The poem is prefaced by a Latin epigraph from the English theologian Thomas Burnet's *Archaeologiae Philosophicae* (1692): "I can easily believe that there are more invisible creatures in the universe than visible ones. But who will tell us to what family each belongs, their ranks and relationships, and what their distinguishing characteristics may be? What do they do? Where do they live? The human mind has always circled around these matters without finding satisfaction. But I do not doubt that it is beneficial sometimes to contemplate in the mind, as in a picture, the image of a grander and better world; for if the mind becomes used to the trival things of everyday life, it may limit itself too much and decline completely into worthless thinking. Meanwhile, however, we must be on the lookout for the truth, keeping a sense of proportion so that we can distinguish what is sure from what is uncertain, and day from night."

The Mariner tells how
the ship sailed southward
with a good wind and
fair weather, till it
reached the line.°

The Sun came up upon the left,   25
Out of the sea came he!
And he shone bright, and on the right
Went down into the sea.   *equator*

Higher and higher every day,
Till over the mast at noon—"   30
The Wedding-Guest here beat his breast,
For he heard the loud bassoon.

The Wedding-Guest
heareth the bridal music;
but the Mariner
continueth his tale.

The bride hath paced into the hall,
Red as a rose is she;
Nodding their heads before her goes   35
The merry minstrelsy.

The Wedding-Guest he beat his breast,
Yet he cannot choose but hear;
And thus spake on that ancient man,
The bright-eyed Mariner.   40

The ship driven by a
storm toward the south
pole.

"And now the STORM-BLAST came, and he
Was tyrannous and strong:
He struck with his o'ertaking wings,
And chased us south along.

With sloping masts and dipping prow,   45
As who pursued with yell and blow
Still treads the shadow of his foe,
And forward bends his head,
The ship drove fast, loud roared the blast,
And southward aye we fled.   50

And now there came both mist and snow,
And it grew wondrous cold:
And ice, mast-high, came floating by,
As green as emerald.

The land of ice, and of
fearful sounds where no
living thing was to be
seen.

And through the drifts the snowy clifts°   *cliffs or clefts*
Did send a dismal sheen:
Nor shapes of men nor beast we ken—
The ice was all between.

The ice was here, the ice was there,
The ice was all around: 60
It cracked and growled, and roared and howled,
Like noises in a swound!°   *swoon*

Till a great sea-bird
called the Albatross,
came through the snow-
fog, and was received
with great joy and
hospitality.

At length did cross an Albatross,
Through the fog it came;
As if it had been a Christian soul,   65
We hailed it in God's name.

It ate the food it ne'er had eat,°   *eaten*
And round and round it flew.
The ice did split with a thunder-fit;

The helmsman steered us through!   70

And lo! the Albatross
proveth a bird of good
omen, and followeth the
ship as it return
northward through fog
and floating ice.

And a good south wind sprung up behind;
The Albatross did follow,
And every day, for food or play,
Came to the mariner's hollo!

In mist or cloud, on mast or shroud,°   *supporting rope*
It perched for vespers nine;°   *nine evenings*
Whiles all the night, through fog-smoke white,
Glimmered the white Moon-shine."

The ancient Mariner
inhospitably killeth the
pious bird of good omen.

"God save thee, ancient Mariner!
From the fiends, that plague thee thus!—   80
Why look'st thou so?"—With my cross-bow
I shot the ALBATROSS.

Part 2

The Sun now rose upon the right:
Out of the sea came he,
Still hid in mist, and on the left   85
Went down into the sea.

And the good south wind still blew behind,
But no sweet bird did follow,
Nor any day for food or play
Came to the mariners' hollo!   90

His shipmates cry out
against the ancient
Mariner, for killing the
bird of good luck.

And I had done a hellish thing,
And it would work 'em woe:
For all averred, I had killed the bird
That made the breeze to blow.
Ah wretch! said they, the bird to slay,   95
That made the breeze to blow!

But when the fog cleared
off, they justify the same,
and thus make
themselves accomplices
in the crime.

Nor dim nor red, like God's own head,
The glorious Sun uprist:
Then all averred, I had killed the bird
That brought the fog and mist.   100
'Twas right, said they, such birds to slay,
That bring the fog and mist.

The fair breeze
continues; the ship enters
the Pacific Ocean, and
sails northward, even
until it reaches the Line.

The fair breeze blew, the white foam flew,
The furrow followed free;
We were the first that ever burst   105
Into that silent sea.

The ship hath been
suddenly becalmed.

Down dropt the breeze, the sails dropt down,
'Twas sad as sad could be;
And we did speak only to break
The silence of the sea!   110

Gustave Doré, illustration from an 1875 edition of *The Rime of the Ancient Mariner*.

All in a hot and copper sky,
The bloody Sun, at noon,
Right up above the mast did stand,
No bigger than the Moon.

Day after day, day after day,   115
We stuck, nor breath nor motion;
As idle as a painted ship
Upon a painted ocean.

And the Albatross begins to be avenged.

Water, water, every where,
And all the boards did shrink;   120
Water, water, every where,
Nor any drop to drink.

The very deep did rot: O Christ!
That ever this should be!
Yea, slimy things did crawl with legs   125
Upon the slimy sea.

About, about, in reel and rout
The death-fires° danced at night;   *phosphorescent plankton*
The water, like a witch's oils,
Burnt green, and blue and white.   130

A Spirit had followed them; one of the invisible inhabitants of this planet, neither departed souls nor angels; concerning whom the learned Jew, Josephus, and the Platonic Constantinopolitan, Michael Psellus, may be consulted. They are very numerous, and there is no climate or element without one or more.

And some in dreams assuréd were
Of the Spirit that plagued us so;
Nine fathom deep he had followed us
From the land of mist and snow.

And every tongue, through utter drought,   135
Was withered at the root;
We could not speak, no more than if
We had been choked with soot.

The shipmates, in their sore distress, would fain throw the whole guilt on the ancient Mariner: in sign whereof they hang the dead sea-bird round his neck.

Ah! well a-day! what evil looks
Had I from old and young!   140
Instead of the cross, the Albatross
About my neck was hung.

Part 3

There passed a weary time. Each throat
Was parched, and glazed each eye.
A weary time! a weary time!   145
How glazed each weary eye,
When looking westward, I beheld
A something in the sky.

The ancient Mariner beholdeth a sign in the element afar off.

At first it seemed a little speck,
And then it seemed a mist;
It moved and moved, and took at last   150
A certain shape, I wist.°   *knew*

A speck, a mist, a shape, I wist!
And still it neared and neared:
As if it dodged a water-sprite,   155
It plunged and tacked and veered.

At its nearer approach, it seemeth him to be a ship; and at a dear ransom he freeth his speech from the bonds of thirst.

With throats unslaked, with black lips baked,
We could nor laugh nor wail;
Through utter drought all dumb we stood!
I bit my arm, I sucked the blood,   160
And cried, A sail! a sail!

With throats unslaked, with black lips baked,
Agape they heard me call:

A flash of joy;

Gramercy!° they for joy did grin,   *many thanks*
And all at once their breath drew in,   165
As° they were drinking all.   *as if*

And horror follows. For can it be a ship that comes onward without wind or tide?

See! see! (I cried) she tacks no more!
Hither to work us weal;°   *benefit*
Without a breeze, without a tide,
She steadies with upright keel!   170

The western wave was all a-flame.
The day was well nigh done!
Almost upon the western wave

Rested the broad bright Sun;
When that strange shape drove suddenly   175
Betwixt us and the Sun.

It seemeth him but the
skeleton of a ship.

And straight the Sun was flecked with bars,
(Heaven's Mother send us grace!)
As if through a dungeon-grate he peered
With broad and burning face.   180

And its ribs are seen as
bars on the face of the
setting Sun.

Alas! (thought I, and my heart beat loud)
How fast she nears and nears!
Are those *her* sails that glance in the Sun,
Like restless gossameres?°   *cobwebs*

The Spectre-Woman and
her Death-mate, and no
other on board the
skeleton-ship.

Are those her ribs through which the Sun   185
Did peer, as through a grate?
And is that Woman all her crew?
Is that a DEATH? and are there two?
Is DEATH that woman's mate?

Like vessel, like crew!

Her lips were red, *her* looks were free,   190
Her locks were yellow as gold:

Death and Life-in-Death
have diced for the ship's
crew, and she (the latter)
winneth the ancient
Mariner.

Her skin was as white as leprosy,
The Night-mair LIFE-IN-DEATH was she,
Who thicks man's blood with cold.

The naked hulk alongside came,   195
And the twain were casting dice;
"The game is done! I've won! I've won!"
Quoth she, and whistles thrice.

No twilight within the
courts of the Sun.

The Sun's rim dips; the stars rush out:
At one stride comes the dark;   200
With far-heard whisper, o'er the sea,
Off shot the spectre-bark.

At the rising of the
Moon,

We listened and looked sideways up!
Fear at my heart, as at a cup,
My life-blood seemed to sip!   205
The stars were dim, and thick the night,
The steersman's face by his lamp gleamed white;
From the sails the dew did drip—
Till clomb above the eastern bar
The hornéd Moon, with one bright star   210
Within the nether tip.

One after another,

One after one, by the star-dogged Moon,
Too quick for groan or sigh,
Each turned his face with a ghastly pang,
And cursed me with his eye.   215

His shipmates drop down dead.

Four times fifty living men,
(And I heard nor sigh nor groan)
With heavy thump, a lifeless lump,
They dropped down one by one.

But Life-in-Death begins her work on the ancient Mariner.

The souls did from their bodies fly,—
They fled to bliss or woe!
And every soul, it passed me by,
Like the whizz of my cross-bow!   220

Part 4

The Wedding-Guest feareth that a Spirit is talking to him;

"I fear thee, ancient Mariner!
I fear thy skinny hand!
And thou art long, and lank, and brown,
As is the ribbed sea-sand.   225

I fear thee and thy glittering eye,
And thy skinny hand, so brown."—

But the ancient Mariner assureth him of his bodily life, and proceedeth to relate his horrible penance.

Fear not, fear not, thou Wedding-Guest!   230
This body dropt not down.

Alone, alone, all, all alone,
Alone on a wide wide sea!
And never a saint took pity on
My soul in agony.   235

He despiseth the creatures of the calm,

The many men, so beautiful!
And they all dead did lie:
And a thousand thousand slimy things
Lived on; and so did I.

And envieth that *they* should live, and so many lie dead.

I looked upon the rotting sea,   240
And drew my eyes away;
I looked upon the rotting deck,
And there the dead men lay.

I looked to heaven, and tried to pray;
But or ever° a prayer had gusht,   *even before*
A wicked whisper came, and made
My heart as dry as dust.

I closed my lids, and kept them close,
And the balls like pulses beat;
For the sky and the sea, and the sea and the sky   250
Lay like a load on my weary eye,
And the dead were at my feet.

But the curse liveth for him in the eye of the dead men.

The cold sweat melted from their limbs,
Nor rot nor reek did they:
The look with which they looked on me   255
Had never passed away.

In his loneliness and fixedness he yearneth towards the journeying Moon, and the stars that still sojourn, yet still move onward; and every where the blue sky belongs to them, and is their appointed rest, and their native country and their own natural homes, which they enter unannounced, as lords that are certainly expected and yet there is a silent joy at their arrival.	An orphan's curse would drag to hell A spirit from on high; But oh! more horrible than that Is the curse in a dead man's eye! Seven days, seven nights, I saw that curse, And yet I could not die. The moving Moon went up the sky, And nowhere did abide: Softly she was going up, And a star or two beside—	260 265

	Her beams bemocked the sultry main,° Like April hoar-frost spread; But where the ship's huge shadow lay, The charméd water burnt alway A still and awful red.	*open sea* 270

By the light of the Moon he beholdeth God's creatures of the great calm.	Beyond the shadow of the ship, I watched the water-snakes: They moved in tracks of shining white, And when they reared, the elfish light Fell off in hoary° flakes.	 275 *frost-colored*

	Within the shadow of the ship I watched their rich attire: Blue, glossy green, and velvet black, They coiled and swam; and every track Was a flash of golden fire.	 280

Their beauty and their happiness. He blesseth them in his heart.	O happy living things! no tongue Their beauty might declare: A spring of love gushed from my heart, And I blessed them unaware: Sure my kind saint took pity on me, And I blessed them unaware.	 285

The spell begins to break.	The self-same moment I could pray; And from my neck so free The Albatross fell off, and sank Like lead into the sea.	 290

Part 5

	Oh sleep! it is a gentle thing, Beloved from pole to pole! To Mary Queen the praise be given! She sent the gentle sleep from Heaven, That slid into my soul.	 295

By grace of the holy Mother, the ancient Mariner is refreshed with rain.	The silly² buckets on the deck, That had so long remained,	

2. Either blessed or rustic.

I dreamt that they were filled with dew;
And when I awoke, it rained.   300

My lips were wet, my throat was cold,
My garments all were dank;
Sure I had drunken in my dreams,
And still my body drank.

I moved, and could not feel my limbs: 305
I was so light—almost
I thought that I had died in sleep,
And was a blessèd ghost.

He heareth sounds and seeth strange sights and commotions in the sky and the element.

And soon I heard a roaring wind:
It did not come anear;   310
But with its sound it shook the sails,
That were so thin and sere.°   *worn*

The upper air burst into life!
And a hundred fire-flags° sheen,°   *meteors / gleamed*
To and fro they were hurried about!   315
And to and fro, and in and out,
The wan stars danced between.

And the coming wind did roar more loud,
And the sails did sigh like sedge;°   *rush-like grass*
And the rain poured down from one black cloud;   320
The Moon was at its edge.

The thick black cloud was cleft, and still
The Moon was at its side:
Like waters shot from some high crag,
The lightning fell with never a jag,   325
A river steep and wide.

The bodies of the ship's crew are inspired° and the ship moves on;

The loud wind never reached the ship,
Yet now the ship moved on!
Beneath the lightning and the Moon   *animated*
The dead men gave a groan.   330

They groaned, they stirred, they all uprose,
Nor spake, nor moved their eyes;
It had been strange, even in a dream,
To have seen those dead men rise.

The helmsman steered, the ship moved on;   335
Yet never a breeze up-blew;
The mariners all 'gan work the ropes,
Where they were wont to do;
They raised their limbs like lifeless tools—
We were a ghastly crew.   340

The body of my brother's son
Stood by me, knee to knee:

The body and I pulled at one rope,
But he said naught to me.

"I fear thee, ancient Mariner!"   345
Be calm, thou Wedding-Guest!
'Twas not those souls that fled in pain,
Which to their corses° came again,   *corpses*
But a troop of spirits blest:

For when it dawned—they dropped their arms,   350
And clustered round the mast;
Sweet sounds rose slowly through their mouths,
And from their bodies passed.

Around, around, flew each sweet sound,
Then darted to the Sun;   355
Slowly the sounds came back again,
Now mixed, now one by one.

Sometimes a-dropping from the sky
I heard the sky-lark sing;
Sometimes all little birds that are,   360
How they seemed to fill the sea and air
With their sweet jargoning!°   *warbling*

And now 'twas like all instruments,
Now like a lonely flute;
And now it is an angel's song,   365
That makes the heavens be mute.

It ceased; yet still the sails made on
A pleasant noise till noon,
A noise like of a hidden brook
In the leafy mouth of June,   370
That to the sleeping woods all night
Singeth a quiet tune.

Till noon we quietly sailed on,
Yet never a breeze did breathe:
Slowly and smoothly went the ship,   375
Moved onward from beneath.

Under the keel nine fathom deep,
From the land of mist and snow,
The spirit slid: and it was he
That made the ship to go.   380
The sails at noon left off their tune,
And the ship stood still also.

The Sun, right up above the mast,
Had fixed her to the ocean:
But in a minute she 'gan stir,   385
With a short uneasy motion—

Backwards and forwards half her length
With a short uneasy motion.

Then like a pawing horse let go,
She made a sudden bound: 390
It flung the blood into my head,
And I fell down in a swound.

How long in that same fit I lay,
I have not to declare;
But ere my living life returned,   395
I heard and in my soul discerned
Two voices in the air.

The Polar Spirit's fellow-daemons, the invisible inhabitants of the element, take part in his wrong; and two of them relate, one to the other, that penance long and heavy for the ancient Mariner hath been accorded to the Polar Spirit, who returneth southward.

"Is it he?" quoth one, "Is this the man?
By him who died on cross,
With his cruel bow he laid full low   400
The harmless Albatross.

The spirit who bideth° by himself   *abides*
In the land of mist and snow,
He loved the bird that loved the man
Who shot him with his bow."   405

The other was a softer voice,
As soft as honey-dew.
Quoth he, "The man hath penance done,
And penance more will do."

Part 6

FIRST VOICE.

"But tell me, tell me! speak again,   410
Thy soft response renewing—
What makes that ship drive on so fast?
What is the ocean doing?"

SECOND VOICE.

"Still as a slave before his lord,
The ocean hath no blast;   415
His great bright eye most silently
Up to the Moon is cast—

If he may know which way to go;
For she guides him smooth or grim.
See, brother, see! how graciously   420
She looketh down on him."

FIRST VOICE.

The Mariner hath been cast into a trance; for the angelic power causeth the vessel to drive northward faster than human life could endure.

"But why drives on that ship so fast,
Without or wave or wind?"

SECOND VOICE.

"The air is cut away before,

And closes from behind.   425
Fly, brother, fly! more high, more high!
Or we shall be belated:
For slow and slow that ship will go,
When the Mariner's trance is abated."

I woke, and we were sailing on   430
As in a gentle weather:
'Twas night, calm night, the moon was high;
The dead men stood together.

All stood together on the deck,
For a charnel-dungeon fitter: 435
All fixed on me their stony eyes,
That in the Moon did glitter.

The pang, the curse, with which they died,
Had never passed away:
I could not draw my eyes from theirs,   440
Nor turn them up to pray.

And now this spell was snapt: once more
I viewed the ocean green,
And looked far forth, yet little saw
Of what had else been seen—   445

Like one, that on a lonesome road
Doth walk in fear and dread,
And having once turned round walks on,
And turns no more his head;
Because he knows, a frightful fiend   450
Doth close behind him tread.

But soon there breathed a wind on me,
Nor sound nor motion made:
Its path was not upon the sea,
In ripple or in shade.   455

It raised my hair, it fanned my cheek
Like a meadow-gale of spring—
It mingled strangely with my fears,
Yet it felt like a welcoming.

Swiftly, swiftly flew the ship,   460
Yet she sailed softly too:
Sweetly, sweetly blew the breeze—
On me alone it blew.

Oh! dream of joy! is this indeed
The light-house top I see?   465
Is this the hill? is this the kirk?
Is this mine own countree?

We drifted o'er the harbour-bar,
And I with sobs did pray—
O let me be awake, my God!
Or let me sleep alway.   470

The harbour-bay was clear as glass,
So smoothly it was strewn!
And on the bay the moonlight lay,
And the shadow of the Moon.   475

The rock shone bright, the kirk no less,
That stands above the rock:
The moonlight steeped in silentness
The steady weathercock.

And the bay was white with silent light,   480
Till rising from the same,
Full many shapes, that shadows were,
In crimson colors came.

The angelic spirits leave the dead bodies,

A little distance from the prow
Those crimson shadows were:
I turned my eyes upon the deck—   485
Oh, Christ! what saw I there!

And appear in their own forms of light.

Each corse lay flat, lifeless and flat,
And, by the holy rood!°   *cross*
A man all light, a seraph-man,°   *angel*
On every corse there stood.

This seraph-band, each waved his hand:
It was a heavenly sight!
They stood as signals to the land,
Each one a lovely light;   495

This seraph-band, each waved his hand,
No voice did they impart—
No voice; but oh! the silence sank
Like music on my heart.

But soon I heard the dash of oars,   500
I heard the Pilot's cheer;
My head was turned perforce away
And I saw a boat appear.

The Pilot and the Pilot's boy,
I heard them coming fast: 505
Dear Lord in Heaven! it was a joy
The dead men could not blast.

I saw a third—I heard his voice:
It is the Hermit good!
He singeth loud his godly hymns   510
That he makes in the wood.

He'll shrieve° my soul, he'll wash away   *absolve*
The Albatross's blood.

Part 7

This Hermit good lives in that Wood
Which slopes down to the sea.   515
How loudly his sweet voice he rears!
He loves to talk with marineres
That come from a far countree.

He kneels at morn, and noon, and eve—
He hath a cushion plump: 520
It is the moss that wholly hides
The rotted old oak-stump.

The skiff-boat neared: I heard them talk,
"Why, this is strange, I trow!
Where are those lights so many and fair,   525
That signal made but now?"

"Strange, by my faith!" the Hermit said—
"And they answered not our cheer!
The planks looked warped! and see those sails,
How thin they are and sere!   530
I never saw aught like to them,
Unless perchance it were

Brown skeletons of leaves that lag
My forest-brook along;
When the ivy-tod° is heavy with snow,   *bushy mass of ivy*
And the owlet whoops to the wolf below,
That eats the she-wolf's young."

"Dear Lord! it hath a fiendish look—
(The Pilot made reply)
I am a-feared"—"Push on, push on!"   540
Said the Hermit cheerily.

The boat came closer to the ship,
But I nor spake nor stirred;
The boat came close beneath the ship,
And straight a sound was heard.   545

Under the water it rumbled on,
Still louder and more dread:
It reached the ship, it split the bay;
The ship went down like lead.

Stunned by that loud and dreadful sound,   550
Which sky and ocean smote,
Like one that hath been seven days drowned

My body lay afloat;
But swift as dreams, myself I found
Within the Pilot's boat.   555

Upon the whirl, where sank the ship,
The boat spun round and round;
And all was still, save that the hill
Was telling of the sound.

I moved my lips—the Pilot shrieked   560
And fell down in a fit;
The holy Hermit raised his eyes,
And prayed where he did sit.

I took the oars: the Pilot's boy,
Who now doth crazy go,   565
Laughed loud and long, and all the while
His eyes went to and fro.
"Ha! ha!" quoth he, "full plain I see,
The Devil knows how to row."

And now, all in my own countree,   570
I stood on the firm land!
The Hermit stepped forth from the boat,
And scarcely he could stand.

*The ancient Mariner
earnestly entreateth the
Hermit to shrieve him;
and the penance of life
falls on him.*

"O shrieve me, shrieve me, holy man!"
The Hermit crossed his brow.   575
"Say quick," quoth he, "I bid thee say—
What manner of man art thou?"

Forthwith this frame of mine was wrenched
With a woful agony,
Which forced me to begin my tale;   580
And then it left me free.

*And ever and anon
throughout his future life
an agony constraineth
him to travel from land
to land;*

Since then, at an uncertain hour,
That agony returns:
And till my ghastly tale is told,
This heart within me burns.   585

I pass, like night, from land to land;
I have strange power of speech;
That moment that his face I see,
I know the man that must hear me:
To him my tale I teach.   590

What loud uproar bursts from that door!
The wedding-guests are there:
But in the garden-bower the bride
And bride-maids singing are:
And hark the little vesper-bell,   595
Which biddeth me to prayer!

O Wedding-Guest! this soul hath been
Alone on a wide wide sea:
So lonely 'twas, that God himself
Scarce seeméd there to be.   600

O sweeter than the marriage-feast,
'Tis sweeter far to me,
To walk together to the kirk
With a goodly company!—

To walk together to the kirk,   605
And all together pray,
While each to his great Father bends,
Old men, and babes, and loving friends
And youths and maidens gay!

And to teach, by his own Farewell, farewell! but this I tell   610
example, love and   To thee, thou Wedding-Guest!
reverence to all things He prayeth well, who loveth well
that God made and   Both man and bird and beast.
loveth.

He prayeth best, who loveth best
All things both great and small;   615
For the dear God who loveth us,
He made and loveth all.

The Mariner, whose eye is bright,
Whose beard with age is hoar,
Is gone: and now the Wedding-Guest   620
Turned from the bridegroom's door.

He went like one that hath been stunned,
And is of sense forlorn:
A sadder and a wiser man,
He rose the morrow morn.   625

Ludwig Tieck
1773–1853

In an age of geniuses, the Berlin-born Ludwig Tieck was chiefly a great craftsman. Apart from Goethe, most of the geniuses died young or burned out in Germany as in England. Tieck kept on going. He began with a prolific decade of Romantic novels and folktales; historical fiction about artists; absurdist dramas, including his riotous send-up, *Puss-in-Boots,* and vast pageant dramas in verse, inspired in part by the great Spanish playwrights of the seventeenth century. In his middle age he became an influential literary essayist; in his later years he wrote a number of unremarkable realist tales and novels that were much to the taste of the time and also entertained his contemporaries as a spellbinding public reader. With one exception, his most-read works to this day are his translations—first of *Don Quixote,* then of Elizabethan drama, and finally of Shakespeare. Tieck was the leading member of a team responsible for the still-standard complete translation of Shakespeare, making the English dramatist virtually an honorary founding father of German letters.

And so, Tieck might have remained honored, admired, and occasionally read, perhaps somewhat like one of his great American imitators, Washington Irving. But for one moment, in 1797, genius struck. Nothing in Tieck's life explains the deeply disturbing tale of "Fair-haired Eckbert," nor, despite some later attempts, did he ever again match its shattering power. But this story has deeply marked German culture to the present day and—perhaps because of its accessibility and verbal simplicity—resonates throughout the fantasy literature of Europe.

Sophisticated writers of the period loved to try their hand at writing tales, partly in the manner of the *Märchen,* the German fairy tale popularized worldwide by Jakob and Wilhelm Grimm, and partly under the spell of the *Thousand and One Nights.* In France and England it was the exotic side of that collection that predominated, above all in the numerous Eastern Tales beloved throughout the century. German writers responded especially to the haunted darkness found in many of the tales. Magical tales proliferated in the later decades of the eighteenth century, typically urbanely semiserious in tone and moralizing in outlook. The young Tieck wrote many such entertaining tales.

"Fair-haired Eckbert" begins in a casual tone, with its hero of middle age and middle stature, and its setting, as was common, vaguely medieval in feeling. But Tieck's desire to probe the mode is signaled early on when Eckbert says, "Do not take my narrative for a *Märchen.*" Something grander is at stake, for once, and the story becomes the supernatural mystery of human identity. From a gloomy domestic scene, we graduate to an increasingly sordid tale of childhood abuse and trauma, of lost identity, and uncanny haunting. Finally, at the end, Eckbert's world collapses around him, as the fairy-tale motifs come home to roost in his psyche and reality crashes into madness.

The themes rendered here with such stark vividness are many of the same ones that were to become staples for Sigmund Freud a century later. Dream symbolism was more fully developed in later decades in the dark fantasies of E. T. A. Hoffmann and Edgar Allan Poe, but no one in Tieck's day gives a richer or more economical rendering of infantile sexuality, the melancholic loss of self, and the power of repetition that became equally far-reaching aspects of Freud's system. And not even Freud managed to recapture the nostalgia for lost innocence with such immediacy. If one brief story transcends the rest of Tieck's very impressive career, one word almost carries the story away with it. That word, coined by Tieck, is *Waldeinsamkeit,* forest solitude. With it, Tieck memorably registers the nature yearning that was growing in Germany as throughout Europe and America. As the refrain of the song that returns three times, in ever more demonic forms, *Waldeinsamkeit* is both a primal value and a primitive fear. By popularizing it, Tieck's story became one of the great sources of ecological passion and contest of the last two centuries.

PRONUNCIATIONS:

Ludwig Tieck: LUD-vig TEEK
Walther: VAL-ter
Bertha: BAY-tuh
Strohmian: SHTROH-mee-an
Waldeinsamkeit: VALT-AYN-zam-kayt

Fair-haired Eckbert[1]

In a district of the Harz[2] dwelt a knight, whose common designation in that quarter was Fair-haired Eckbert. He was about forty years of age, scarcely of middle stature,

---

1. Translated by Thomas Carlyle.

2. Mountains in north-central Germany, reputed to house witches.

and short light-colored locks lay close and sleek round his pale and sunken countenance. He led a retired life, had never interfered in the feuds of his neighbors; indeed, beyond the outer wall of his castle he was seldom to be seen. His wife loved solitude as much as he; both seemed heartily attached to one another; only now and then they would lament that heaven had not blessed their marriage with children.

Few came to visit Eckbert, and when guests did happen to be with him, their presence made but little alteration in his customary way of life. Temperance abode in his household, and Frugality herself appeared to be the mistress of the entertainment. On these occasions Eckbert was always cheerful and lively; but when he was alone, you might observe in him a certain mild reserve, a still, retiring melancholy.

His most frequent guest was Philip Walther, a man to whom he had attached himself after finding in him a way of thinking like his own. Walther's residence was in Franconia,[3] but he would often stay for half a year in Eckbert's neighborhood, gathering plants and minerals, and then sorting and arranging them. He lived on a small independency, and was connected with no one. Eckbert frequently attended him in his sequestered walks; year after year a closer friendship grew between them.

There are hours in which a man feels grieved that he should have a secret from his friend, which, till then, he may have kept with niggard anxiety; some irresistible desire lays hold of our heart to open itself wholly, to disclose its inmost recesses to our friend, that he may become our friend still more. It is in such moments that tender souls unveil themselves, and stand face to face; and at times it will happen, that the one recoils affrighted from the countenance of the other.

It was late in autumn, when Eckbert, one cloudy evening, was sitting, with his friend and his wife Bertha, by the parlor fire. The flame cast a red glimmer through the room, and sported on the ceiling; the night looked sullenly in through the windows, and the trees without rustled in wet coldness. Walther complained of the long road he had to travel; and Eckbert proposed to him to stay where he was, to while away half of the night in friendly talk, and then to take a bed in the house till morning. Walther agreed, and the whole was speedily arranged: by and by wine and supper were brought in; fresh wood was laid upon the fire; the talk grew livelier and more confidential.

The cloth being removed, and the servants gone, Eckbert took his friend's hand, and said to him, "Now you must let my wife tell you the history of her youth; it is curious enough, and you should know it."

"With all my heart," said Walther; and the party again drew round the hearth.

It was now midnight; the moon looked fitfully through the breaks of the driving clouds. "You must not reckon me a babbler," began the lady. "My husband says you have so generous a mind, that it is not right in us to hide aught from you. Only do not take my narrative for a fairy tale, however strangely it may sound.

"I was born in a little village; my father was a poor herdsman. Our circumstances were not of the best; often we knew not where to find our daily bread. But what grieved me far more than this, were the quarrels that my father and mother often had about their poverty, and the bitter reproaches they cast on one another. Of myself too, I heard nothing said but ill; they were forever telling me that I was a silly, stupid child, that I could not do the simplest turn of work; and in truth I was extremely inexpert and helpless. I let things fall; I neither learned to sew nor spin; I could be of no use to my parents; only their straits I understood too well. Often I would sit in a cor-

---

3. A region south of the Harz, now the northern portion of the state of Bavaria.

ner, and fill my little heart with dreams of how I would help them, if I should all at once grow rich; how I would overflow them with silver and gold, and feast myself on their amazement. Or sometimes spirits came hovering up, and showed me buried treasures, or gave me little pebbles that changed into precious stones. In short, the strangest fancies occupied me, and when I had to rise and help with anything, my inexpertness was still greater, as my head was giddy with these motley visions.

"My father in particular was always very cross to me; he scolded me for being such a burden to the house; indeed he often used me rather cruelly, and it was very seldom that I got a friendly word from him. In this way I had struggled on to near the end of my eighth year; and now it was seriously fixed that I should begin to do or learn something. My father still maintained that it was nothing but caprice in me, or a lazy wish to pass my days in idleness: accordingly he set upon me with furious threats; and as these made no improvement, he one day gave me a most cruel chastisement, and added that the same should be repeated day after day, since I was nothing but a useless sluggard.

"That whole night I wept abundantly; I felt myself so utterly forsaken, I had such a sympathy with myself that I even longed to die. I dreaded the break of day; I knew not on earth what I was to do or try. I wished from my very heart to be clever, and could not understand how I should be worse than the other children of the place. I was on the borders of despair.

"At the dawn of day I arose, and scarcely knowing what I did, unfastened the door of our little hut. I stepped upon the open field; next minute I was in a wood, where the light of the morning had yet hardly penetrated. I ran along, not looking round; for I felt no fatigue, and I still thought my father would catch me, and in his anger at my flight would beat me worse than ever.

"I had reached the other side of the forest, and the sun was risen a considerable way; I saw something dim lying before me, and a thick fog resting over it. Before long my path began to mount, at one time I was climbing hills, at another winding among rocks; and I now guessed that I must be among the neighboring mountains, a thought that made me shudder in my loneliness. For, living in the plain country, I had never seen a hill; and the very word mountains, when I heard talk of them, had been a sound of terror to my young ear. I had not the heart to go back, my fear itself drove me on; often I looked round affrighted when the breezes rustled over me among the trees, or the stroke of some distant woodman sounded far through the still morning. And when I began to meet with charcoal-men and miners, and heard their foreign way of speech, I nearly fainted for terror.

"I passed through several villages, begging now and then, for I felt hungry and thirsty, and fashioning my answers as I best could when questions were put to me. In this manner I had wandered on some four days, when I came upon a little footpath, which led me farther and farther from the highway. The rocks about me now assumed a different and far stranger form. They were cliffs so piled on one another, that it looked as if the first gust of wind would hurl them all this way and that. I knew not whether to go on or stop. Till now I had slept by night in the woods, for it was the finest season of the year, or in some remote shepherd's hut; but here I saw no human dwelling at all, and could not hope to find one in this wilderness; the crags grew more and more frightful: I had many a time to glide along by the very edge of dreadful abysses. By degrees, my footpath became fainter, and at last all traces of it vanished from beneath me. I was utterly comfortless; I wept and screamed; and my voice came echoing back from the rocky valleys with a sound that terrified me. The night now came on, and I sought out a mossy nook to lie down in. I could not sleep for in the darkness I heard the strangest noises. Sometimes I took them to come from wild beasts, sometimes from wind moaning through the rocks, sometimes from unknown birds. I prayed, and did not sleep till towards morning.

"When the light came upon my face, I awoke. Before me was a steep rock; I climbed up, in the hope of discovering some outlet from the waste, perhaps of seeing houses or men. But when I reached the top, there was nothing still, so far as my eye could reach, but a wilderness of crags and precipices. All was covered with a dim haze; the day was gray and troubled, and no tree, no meadow, not even a bush could I find, only a few shrubs shooting up stunted and solitary in the narrow clefts of the rocks. I cannot utter what a longing I felt but to see one human creature, any living mortal, even though I had been afraid of hurt from him. At the same time I was tortured by a gnawing hunger. I sat down, and made up my mind to die. After a while, however, the desire of living gained the mastery; I roused myself, and wandered forward amid tears and broken sobs all day. In the end, I hardly knew what I was doing. I was tired and spent, I scarcely wished to live, and yet I feared to die.

"Towards night the country seemed to grow a little kindlier; my thoughts, my desires revived, the wish for life awoke in all my veins. I thought I heard the rushing of a mill afar off; I redoubled my steps, and how glad, how light of heart was I, when at last I actually gained the limits of the barren rocks, and saw woods and meadows lying before me, with soft green hills in the distance! I felt as if I had stepped out of hell into a paradise; my loneliness and helplessness no longer frightened me.

"Instead of the hoped-for mill, I came upon a waterfall, which, in truth, considerably dampened my joy. I was lifting a drink from it in the hollow of my hand, when all at once I thought I heard a slight cough some little way from me. Never in my life was I so joyfully surprised as at this moment: I went near, and at the border of the wood saw an old woman sitting on the ground. She was dressed almost wholly in black; a black hood covered her head, and the greater part of her face; in her hand she held a crutch.

"I came up to her, and begged for help; she made me sit by her, and gave me bread, and a little wine. While I ate, she sang in a screeching tone some kind of hymn. When she had done, she told me I might follow her.

"The offer charmed me, strange as the old woman's voice and look appeared. With her crutch she limped away pretty fast, and at every step she twisted her face so oddly, that at first I was like to laugh. The wild rocks retired behind us more and more; we crossed a pleasant meadow, then passed through a considerable stretch of woods. The sun was just going down when we stepped out of the woods, and I never shall forget the aspect and the feeling of that evening. Everything had dissolved into the softest golden red; the trees were standing with their tops in the glow of the sunset; on the fields lay a mild brightness; the woods and the leaves of the trees were standing motionless; the pure sky looked like an open paradise, and the gushing of the brooks, and, from time to time, the rustling of the trees, resounded through the serene stillness, as in pensive joy. My young soul was here first taken with a forethought of the world and its vicissitudes. I forgot myself and my conductress; my spirit and my eyes were wandering among the shining clouds.

"We now mounted an eminence planted with birch-trees; from the top we looked into a green valley, likewise full of birches; and down below, in the middle of them, was a little hut. A glad barking reached us, and immediately a little, nimble dog came springing round the old woman, fawned on her, and wagged its tail; it next came to me, viewed me on all sides, and then turned back with a friendly look to its old mistress.

"On reaching the bottom of the hill, I heard the strangest song, as if coming from the hut, and sung by some bird. It ran thus:

> Alone in wood so gay
> 'Tis good to stay,
> Morrow like today,
> Forever and aye:
> O, I do love to stay
> Alone in wood so gay.

"These few words were continually repeated, and to describe the sound, it was as if you heard forest-horns and shawms[4] sounded together from a far distance.

"My curiosity was wonderfully on the stretch; without waiting for the old woman's permission, I stepped into the hut. It was already dusk. Here all was neatly swept and orderly; some bowls were standing in a cupboard, some strange-looking casks or pots on a table; in a glittering cage, hanging by the window, was a bird, and this in fact proved to be the singer. The old woman coughed and panted: it seemed as if she never would get over her fatigue. She patted the little dog, she talked with the bird, which only answered her with its accustomed song; and as for me, she did not seem to recollect that I was there at all. Looking at her so, many qualms and fears came over me; for her face was in perpetual motion; and, besides, her head shook from old age, so that, for my life, I could not make out what sort of countenance she had.

"Having gathered strength again, she lit a candle, covered a very small table, and brought out supper. She now looked round for me, and bade me take a little cane chair. I was thus sitting close facing her, with the light between us. She folded her bony hands, and prayed aloud, still twisting her countenance, so that I was once more on the point of laughing; but I took strict care that I might not make her angry.

"After supper she again prayed, then showed me a bed in a low narrow closet; she herself slept in the room. I did not remain awake long, for I was half stupefied; but in the night I now and then awoke, and heard the old woman coughing, and between-whiles talking with her dog and her bird, which last seemed dreaming, and replied with only one or two words of its rhyme. This, with the birches rustling before the window, and the song of a distant nightingale, made such a wondrous combination, that I never fairly thought I was awake, but only falling out of one dream into another still stranger.

"The old woman awoke me in the morning, and soon after gave me work. I was put to spin, which I now learned very easily; I had likewise to take charge of the dog and the bird. I soon learned my business in the house and now felt as if it all must be so. I never once remembered that the old woman had so many singularities, that her dwelling was mysterious, and lay apart from all men, and that the bird must be a very strange creature. Its beauty, indeed, always struck me, for its feathers glittered with all possible colors: the fairest deep blue, and the most burning red alternated about his neck and body; and when singing, he blew himself proudly out, so that his feathers looked still finer.

"My old mistress often went abroad, and did not come again till night; on these occasions I went out to meet her with the dog, and she used to call me child and daughter. In the end I grew to like her heartily, as our mind, especially in childhood, will become accustomed and attached to anything. In the evenings she taught me to

---

4. A woodwind instrument, predecessor of the oboe.

read; and this was afterwards a source of boundless satisfaction to me in my solitude, for she had several ancient hand-written books, that contained the strangest stories.

"The recollection of the life I then led is still singular to me: visited by no human creature, secluded in the circle of so small a family; for the dog and the bird made the same impression on me that in other cases long-known friends produce. I am surprised that I have never since been able to recall the dog's name, a very odd one, often as I then pronounced it.

"Four years I had passed in this way (I must now have been nearly twelve), when my old dame began to put more trust in me, and at length told me a secret. The bird, I found, laid every day an egg, in which there was a pearl or a jewel. I had already noticed that she often tended to the cage in private, but I had never troubled myself farther on the subject. She now gave me charge of gathering these eggs in her absence, and carefully storing them up in the strange looking pots. She would leave me food, and sometimes stay away longer, for weeks, for months. My little wheel kept humming round, the dog barked, the bird sang; and withal there was such a stillness in the neighborhood, that I do not recollect of any storm or foul weather all the time I stayed there. No one wandered thither; no wild beast came near our dwelling. I was satisfied, and worked along in peace from day to day. One would perhaps be very happy, could he pass his life so undisturbedly to the end.

"From the little that I read, I formed quite marvelous notions of the world and its people, all taken from myself and my society. When I read of witty persons, I could not figure them but like the little dog; great ladies, I conceived, were like the bird; all old women like my mistress. I had read somewhat of love, too; and often, in fancy, I would tell myself strange stories. I thought up the fairest knight on earth, adorned him with all perfections, without knowing rightly, after all my labor, how he looked; but I could feel a hearty pity for myself when he ceased to love me. I would then, in thought, make long, melting speeches, or perhaps aloud, to try if I could win him back. You smile! These young days are, in truth, far away from us all.

"I now liked better to be left alone, for I was then sole mistress of the house. The dog loved me, and did all I wanted; the bird replied to all my questions with his rhyme; my wheel kept briskly turning, and at bottom I had never any wish for change. When my dame returned from her long wanderings, she would praise my diligence; she said her house, since I belonged to it, was managed far more perfectly. She took a pleasure in my growth and healthy looks. In short, she treated me in all points like her daughter.

"'Thou art a good girl, child,' said she once to me, in her creaking tone; 'if thou continuest so, it will be well with thee: but none ever prospers when he leaves the straight path; punishment will overtake him, though it may be late.' I gave little heed to this remark of hers at the time, for in my temper and movements I was very lively; but by night it occurred to me again, and I could not understand what she meant by it. I considered all the words attentively. I had read of riches, and at last it struck me that her pearls and jewels might perhaps be something precious. Ere long this thought grew clearer to me. But the straight path, and leaving it? What could she mean by this?

"I was now fourteen; it is the misery of man that he arrives at understanding through the loss of innocence. I now saw well enough that it lay with me to take the jewels and the bird in the old woman's absence, and go forth with them and see the world of which I had read. Perhaps, too, it would then be possible that I might meet that fairest of all knights, who forever dwelt in my memory.

"At first this thought was nothing more than any other thought; but when I used to be sitting at my wheel, it still returned to me, against my will. I sometimes followed it so far, that I already saw myself adorned in splendid attire, with princes and knights around me. On awakening from these dreams, I would feel a sadness when I looked up, and found myself still in the little cottage. For the rest, if I went through my duties, the old woman troubled herself little about what I thought or felt.

"One day she went out again, telling me that she should be away on this occasion longer than usual; that I must take strict charge of everything, and not let the time hang heavy on my hands. I had a sort of fear on taking leave of her, for I felt as if I should not see her anymore. I looked long after her, and knew not why I felt so sad; it was almost as if my purpose had already stood before me, without myself being conscious of it.

"Never did I tend the dog and the bird with such diligence as now; they were nearer to my heart than formerly. The old woman had been gone some days, when I rose one morning in the firm mind to leave the cottage, and set out with the bird to see this world they talked so much of. I felt pressed and hampered in my heart: I wished to stay where I was, and yet the thought of that afflicted me. There was a strange contention in my soul, as if between two discordant spirits. One moment my peaceful solitude would seem to me so beautiful; the next the image of a new world, with its many wonders, would again enchant me.

"I knew not what to make of it. The dog leaped up continually about me, the sunshine spread abroad over the fields, the green birch-trees glittered. I always felt as if I had something I must do in haste; so I caught the little dog, tied him up in the room, and took the cage with the bird under my arm. The dog writhed and whined at this unusual treatment; he looked at me with begging eyes, but I feared to have him with me. I also took one pot of jewels, and concealed it by me; the rest I left.

"The bird turned its head very strangely when I crossed the threshold; the dog tugged at his cord to follow me, but he was forced to stay.

"I did not take the road to the wild rocks, but went in the opposite direction. The dog still whined and barked, and it touched me to the heart to hear him; the bird tried once or twice to sing; but as I was carrying him, the shaking put him out.

"The farther I went, the fainter grew the barking, and at last it altogether ceased. I wept, and had almost turned back, but the longing to see something new still hindered me.

"I had got across the hills, and through some forests, when the night came on, and I was forced to turn aside into a village. I was very shy on entering the inn; they showed me to a room and bed, and I slept pretty quietly, except that I dreamed of the old woman, and her threatening me.

"My journey had not much variety; the farther I went, the more was I afflicted by the recollection of my old mistress and the little dog. I considered that in all likelihood the poor thing would die of hunger, and often in the woods I thought my dame would suddenly meet me. Thus amid tears and sobs I went along; when I stopped to rest, and put the cage on the ground, the bird struck up his song, and brought but too keenly to my mind the fair habitation I had left. As human nature is forgetful, I imagined that my former journey, in my childhood, had not been so sad and woeful as the present. I wished to be as I was then.

"I had sold some jewels, and now, after wandering on for several days, I reached a village. At the very entrance I was struck with something strange; I felt terrified and knew not why, but I soon bethought myself, for it was the village where I was born! How amazed was I! How the tears ran down my cheeks for gladness, for a thousand singular remembrances! Many things were changed: new houses had been built, some just raised when I went away were now fallen, apparently destroyed by fires; everything was far smaller and more confined than I had fancied. It rejoiced my very heart that I should see my parents once more after such an absence. I found their little cottage, the well-known threshold; the door-latch was standing as of old, and it seemed to me as if I had shut it only yesternight. My heart beat violently, I hastily lifted that latch, but faces I had never seen before looked up and gazed at me. I asked for the shepherd Martin; they told me that his wife and he were dead three years ago. I drew back quickly, and left the village weeping aloud.

"I had figured out so beautifully how I would surprise them with my riches; by the strangest chance, what I had only dreamed in childhood was become reality, and now it was all in vain, they could not rejoice with me, and that which had been my first hope in life was lost forever.

"In a pleasant town I rented a small house and garden, and took to myself a maid. The world, in truth, proved not so wonderful as I had painted it, but I forgot the old woman and my former way of life rather more, and on the whole I was contented.

"For a long while the bird had ceased to sing; I was therefore not a little frightened, when one night he suddenly began again, and with a different rhyme. He sang:

> Alone in wood so gay,
> Ah, far away!
> But thou wilt say
> Some other day,
> 'Twere best to stay
> Alone in wood so gay.

"Throughout the night I could not close an eye; all things again occurred to my remembrance, and I felt, more than ever, that I had not acted rightly. When I rose, the sight of the bird distressed me greatly; he looked at me continually, and his presence did me ill. There was now no end to his song; he sang it louder and more shrilly than he had been wont. The more I looked at him, the more he pained and frightened me; at last I opened the cage, put in my hand, and grasped his neck. I squeezed my fingers hard together, he looked at me pleadingly, I slackened them; but he was dead. I buried him in the garden.

"After this, there often came a fear over me of my maid; I looked back upon myself, and fancied she might rob me or even murder me. For a long while I had been acquainted with a young knight, whom I altogether liked. I bestowed on him my hand; and with this, Sir Walther, ends my story."

"Ay, you should have seen her then," said Eckbert warmly; "seen her youth, her loveliness, and what a charm her lonely way of life had given her. She seemed to me a miracle and I loved her beyond all measure. I had no fortune; it was through her love these riches came to me. We moved hither, and our marriage has at no time caused us any regret."

"But with our tattling," added Bertha, "it is growing very late; we must go to sleep."

She rose, and proceeded to her chamber; Walther, with a kiss of her hand, wished her good-night, saying, "Many thanks, noble lady; I can well imagine you beside your strange bird, and how you fed poor little *Strohmian*."

Walther likewise went to sleep; Eckbert alone still walked in a restless humor up and down the room. "Are not men fools?" said he at last. "I myself occasioned this recital of my wife's history, and now such confidence appears to me improper! Will he not abuse it? Will he not communicate the secret to others? Will he not, for such is human nature, cast unblessed thoughts on our jewels, and form pretexts and lay plans to get possession of them?"

It now occurred to him that Walther had not taken leave of him so cordially as might have been expected after such a mark of trust: the soul once set upon suspicion finds in every trifle something to confirm it. Eckbert, on the other hand, reproached himself for such ignoble feelings toward his worthy friend; yet still he could not cast them out. All night he plagued himself with such uneasy thoughts, and got very little sleep.

Bertha was unwell next day, and could not come to breakfast. Walther did not seem to trouble himself much about her illness and left her husband also rather coolly. Eckbert could not comprehend such conduct; he went to see his wife, and found her in a feverish state; she said last night's story must have agitated her.

From that day, Walther visited the castle of his friend but seldom, and when he did appear, it was but to say a few trivial words and then depart. Eckbert was exceedingly distressed by this demeanor. To Bertha or Walther he indeed said nothing of it; but to any person his internal disquietude was visible enough.

Bertha's sickness wore an aspect more and more serious; the doctor grew alarmed—the red had vanished from his patient's cheeks, and her eyes were becoming more and more inflamed. One morning she summoned her husband to her bedside; the nurses were ordered to withdraw.

"Dear Eckbert," she began, "I must disclose a secret to you, which has almost taken away my senses, which is ruining my health, unimportant trifle as it may appear. You may remember, often as I talked of my childhood, I could never call to mind the name of the dog that was so long beside me. Now, that night on taking leave, Walther all at once said to me, 'I can well imagine you, and how you fed poor little *Strohmian*.' Is it chance? Did he guess the name; did he know it, and speak it on purpose? If so, how stands this man connected with my destiny? At times I struggle with myself as if I but imagined this mysterious business; but, alas! it is certain, too certain. I felt a shudder that a stranger should help me to recall the memory of my secrets. What do you think, Eckbert?"

Eckbert looked at his sick and agitated wife with deep emotion; he stood silent and thoughtful, then spoke some words of comfort to her, and went out. In a distant chamber, he walked to and fro in indescribable disquiet. Walther, for many years, had been his sole companion; and now this person was the only mortal in the world whose existence pained and oppressed him. It seemed as if he should be gay and light of heart, were that one thing but removed. He took his crossbow, to dissipate these thoughts, and went to hunt.

It was a rough stormy winter day; the snow was lying deep on the hills, and bending down the branches of the trees. He roved about; the sweat was standing on his brow. He found no game, and this embittered his ill humor. All at once he saw an object moving in the distance; it was Walther gathering moss from the trunks of trees. Scarce knowing what he did, he cocked his bow; Walther looked round, and made a threatening gesture, but the bolt was already flying, and he sank transfixed by it.

Eckbert felt relieved and calmed, yet a certain horror drove him home to his castle. It was a good way distant; he had wandered far into the woods. On arriving, he found Bertha dead; before her death, she had spoken much of Walther and the old woman.

For a great while after this occurrence, Eckbert lived in the deepest solitude; he had all along been melancholy, for the strange history of his wife disturbed him, and he had dreaded some unlucky incident or other, but at present he was utterly at variance with himself. The murder of his friend arose incessantly before his mind; he lived in the anguish of continual remorse.

To dissipate his feelings, he occasionally visited the neighboring town, where he mingled in society and its amusements. He longed for a friend to fill the void in his soul; and yet, when he remembered Walther, he would shudder at the thought of meeting with a friend, for he felt convinced that, with any friend, he must be unhappy. He had lived so long with his Bertha in lovely calmness; the friendship of Walther had cheered him through so many years; and now both of them were suddenly swept away. As he thought of these things, there were many moments when his life appeared to him some fabulous tale, rather than the actual history of a living man.

A young knight named Hugo made advances to the silent, melancholy Eckbert and appeared to have a true affection for him. Eckbert felt exceedingly surprised, but he met the knight's friendship with great readiness, because he had so little anticipated it. The two were now frequently together. Hugo showed his friend all possible attentions. One scarcely ever went to ride without the other; in all companies they got together. In a word, they seemed inseparable.

Eckbert was never happy longer than a few transitory moments, for he felt too clearly that Hugo loved him only by mistake, that he knew him not and was unacquainted with his history. He was seized again with the same old longing to unbosom himself wholly, that he might be sure whether Hugo was his friend or not. But again his apprehensions, and the fear of being hated and abhorred, withheld him. There were many hours in which he felt so much impressed with his entire worthlessness that he believed no mortal not a stranger to his history could entertain regard for him. Yet still he was unable to withstand his urge; on a solitary ride, he disclosed his whole history to Hugo, and asked if he could love a murderer. Hugo seemed touched, and tried to comfort him. Eckbert returned to town with a lighter heart.

But it seemed to be his doom that, in the very hour of confidence, he should always find materials for suspicion. Scarcely had they entered the public hall, when, in the glitter of the many lights, Hugo's looks had ceased to satisfy him. He thought he noticed a malicious smile. He remarked that Hugo did not speak to him as usual, that he talked with the rest, and seemed to pay no heed to him. In the party was an old knight, who had always shown himself the enemy of Eckbert, had often asked about his riches and his wife in a peculiar style. With this man Hugo was conversing; they were speaking privately, and casting looks at Eckbert. The suspicions of the latter seemed confirmed; he thought himself betrayed, and a tremendous rage took hold of him. As he continued gazing, suddenly he discerned the countenance of Walther, all his features, all the form so well known to him. He gazed, and looked, and felt convinced that it was none but Walther who was talking to the knight. His horror cannot be described; in a state of frenzy he rushed out of the hall, left the town overnight, and after many wanderings, returned to his castle.

Here, like an unquiet spirit, he hurried to and fro from room to room. No thought would stay with him; out of one frightful idea he fell into another still more frightful, and sleep never visited his eyes. Often he believed that he was mad, that a disturbed imagination was the origin of all this terror; then, again, he recollected Walther's features, and the whole grew more and more a riddle to him. He resolved to take a journey, that he might reduce his thoughts to order; the hope of friendship, the desire of social intercourse, he had now forever given up.

He set out, without prescribing to himself any certain route; indeed, he took small heed of the country he was passing through. Having hastened on some days at the quickest pace of his horse, he, on a sudden, found himself entangled in a labyrinth of rocks, from which he could discover no outlet. At length he met an old peasant, who took him by a path leading past a waterfall: he offered him some coins for his guidance, but the peasant would not have them. "What do you think of that?" said Eckbert to himself. "I could believe that this man, too, was none but Walther." He looked round once more, and it was Walther. Eckbert spurred his horse as fast as it could gallop, over meads and forests, till it sank exhausted to the earth. Regardless of this, he hastened forward on foot.

In a dreamy mood he mounted a hill. He fancied he caught the sound of lively barking at a little distance; the birch-trees whispered in the intervals, and in the strangest notes he heard this song:

> Alone in wood so gay,
> Once more I stay;
> None dare me slay,
> The evil far away:
> Ah, here I stay,
> Alone in wood so gay.

Now it was all over with Eckbert's senses, with his consciousness; it was all a riddle that he could not solve, whether he was dreaming now, or had before dreamed of a woman named Bertha. The marvelous was mingled with the common: the world around him seemed enchanted, and he himself was incapable of thought or recollection.

A crooked, bent old woman crawled coughing up the hill with a crutch. "Art thou bringing me my bird, my pearls, my dog?" cried she to him. "See how injustice punishes itself! No one but I was Walther, was Hugo."

"God of heaven!" said Eckbert, muttering to himself, "in what frightful solitude have I passed my life?"

"And Bertha was thy sister."

Eckbert sank to the ground.

"Why did she leave me deceitfully? All would have been fair and well; her time of trial was already finished. She was the daughter of a knight, who had her nursed in a shepherd's house; the daughter of thy father."

"Why have I always had a forecast of this dreadful thought?" cried Eckbert.

"Because in early youth thy father told thee: he could not keep this daughter by him because she was the child of another woman."

Eckbert lay distracted and dying on the ground. In dull, hollow confusion he heard the old woman speaking, the dog barking, and the bird repeating its song.

⊷—⊱⊰⊶—⊷

Honoré de Balzac
1799–1850

Honoré de Balzac was a force of nature. He was a prodigious eater, "fearsome at the table, like a pig," we are told. He was a prodigious lover of three countesses in succession, and an even more prodigious writer of love letters, which he exchanged at long distance with the Polish Countess Hanska for seventeen years, until she agreed to marry him a few months before his death. The son of a hospital administrator, he was a tempestuous businessman who amassed enormous debts in failed publishing schemes and then devoted his enormous energies to paying them off through his literary sales. A man of infinite goodwill, he was a great friend of many great men and women. As a writer he knew no rival. After a decade producing now forgotten potboilers, he found his stride with the historical novel *The Chouans* (1829) and the gothic novel *The Wild-Ass's Skin* (1831), whose protagonist puts his life into the control of a magic skin that grants his slightest wish but shrinks away with each one until it disappears and he dies. From 1830 onward Balzac is said to have written an average of 2,000 pages a year, a pace exceeding even Walter Scott's and matched, among major figures, perhaps only by Anthony Trollope.

Balzac's greatest fame is perhaps as a chronicler of society. He can be credited with inventing the novel of business, and money is counted, inherited, earned, wagered, and needed in his works to an unprecedented degree. He excelled equally at depicting high society—to which his countesses gave him access—and rural poverty, such as he must have seen in and around his native town of Tours. But he wishes to penetrate as well as to portray; Paris for him is a realm of display but also of deep mysteries—the secrets of business, of crime, of the human heart. He was a fictional dramatist, ever seeking spectacular discoveries, and an early practitioner of detective fiction. Finally, he was also the greatest writer of supernatural fiction in the century of Mary Shelley, E. T. A. Hoffmann, Edgar Allan Poe, and Robert Louis Stevenson. The stories and novels that he grouped under the rubric of "Philosophical Studies" use magic to explore the psychological obsessions that drive and distort human passions.

Balzac described himself as a scientific observer and classifier of humanity. There are over 2,000 named characters in his mature fiction. In another innovation beginning in 1834, he started to reintroduce them in new books (as well as inserting them in his voluminous revisions of earlier work); so, for instance, Nucingen, who is mentioned once in passing in "Sarrasine," appears centrally in the story "The Firm of Nucingen" and in the novel *Old Goriot,* perhaps the first great novelistic representation of old age. Prodigious in his memory as in everything else, Balzac made very few slips in coordinating so many life histories. He began to group his works into categories, calling them scenes of private, provincial, Parisian, political, military, and country life. ("Sarrasine" is one of the "Scenes of Parisian Life.") And then in the 1840s he gave the growing corpus the collective title *The Human Comedy.* The title echoes Dante's *Divine Comedy* in its ambition to depict all facets of society—French society in Balzac's case—and not just to survey but to understand and to judge. It is not the divine afterlife, but the true heart of earthly life that Balzac claimed to master.

Though a great fantasist, Balzac is also the first unequivocal master of realist fiction. He describes settings voluminously, chronicles daily life, governmental regulation, fashion, disease, and many different occupations, and paints the landscape in precise detail. As a social novelist, he leaves out only Dante's ideal realm, the sky, and children, since they aren't yet full members of society. (Goethe and Austen were the great pathbreakers in the fictional representation of children, followed in Balzac's day by Dickens.) He excels at plots of social manipulation, but is also the most Romantic of novelists. Exotic and mysterious characters abound, as do psychological manipulation and even, in some works, magic. Passion is everywhere, equally memorable in powerful tales of sexual love as in the passions of parents for their offspring, of aristocrats for status, authors for fame, misers for gold, and peasants for land. Throughout his fiction, real characters (like Rousseau and his friend Diderot in "Sarrasine") rub elbows with invented personages.

Consequently, readers have long disputed which is the "true" Balzac, the realist or the Romantic. But the early masterwork "Sarrasine" shows what a mistake it is to separate the facets of Balzac's genius. At once a mystery of passion and of money, it opens with a double view, first on the garden, and then on a brilliant aristocratic salon. As if to undermine any simple dualism, the natural setting looks supernatural, while the festival of life harbors death in its midst. The ghostly man's wrinkles are described in realistic detail, the glamorous woman's ravishing beauty in the most Romantically generalized impressions. Throughout the story, identities keep shifting, above all sexual identities. The women are more forceful than the men; the bizarre, aged figure at the center appears feminine, but so does the son of the noble family. For much of the telling, it seems that the title figure will also be the central one, but that too proves deceptive. Most unnatural of all in appearance is the tender love of the daughter Marianina for the decrepit old man, yet the realist reveals her devotion to be at once the most natural and the most corrupt element in the entire ensemble. In this tale of shape-shifting and psychic haunting, the real is the Romantic, body is musical spirit, all that glitters really is gold but of a soul-destroying sort. Yet the comedy in this human tragedy is that no one is at fault; there is vanity galore and some malice but not, in this story, anything that could be characterized as sin.

PRONUNCIATIONS:
Honoré de Balzac: OH-no-RAY duh bal-ZAHC
Sarrasine: sa-ra-ZEEN

Sarrasine[1]

I was deep in one of those daydreams which overtake even the shallowest of men, in the midst of the most tumultuous parties. Midnight had just sounded from the clock of the Elysée-Bourbon.[2] Seated in a window recess and hidden behind the sinuous folds of a silk curtain, I could contemplate at my leisure the garden of the mansion where I was spending the evening. The trees, partially covered with snow, stood out dimly against the grayish background of a cloudy sky, barely whitened by the moon. Seen amid these fantastic surroundings, they vaguely resembled ghosts half out of their shrouds, a gigantic representation of the famous Dance of the Dead.[3] Then, turning in the other direction, I could admire the Dance of the Living! a splendid salon decorated in silver and gold, with glittering chandeliers, sparkling with candles. There, milling about, whirling around, flitting here and there, were the most beautiful women of Paris, the richest, the noblest, dazzling, stately, resplendent with diamonds, flowers in their hair, on their bosoms, on their heads, strewn over dresses or in garlands at their feet. Light, rustling movements, voluptuous steps, made the laces, the silk brocades, the gauzes, float around their delicate forms. Here and there, some overly animated glances darted forth, eclipsing the lights, the fire of the diamonds, and stimulated anew some too-ardent hearts. One might also catch movements of the head meaningful to lovers, and negative gestures for husbands. The sudden outbursts of the gamblers' voices at each unexpected turn of the dice, the clink of gold, mingled with the music and the murmur of conversation, and to complete the giddiness of this mass of people intoxicated by everything seductive the world can hold, a haze of perfume and general inebriation played upon the fevered mind. Thus, on my right, the dark and silent image of death; on my left, the seemly bacchanalias[4] of life: here, cold nature, dull, in mourning; there, human beings enjoying themselves. On the borderline between these two so different scenes, which, a thousand times repeated in various guises, make Paris the world's most amusing and most philosophical[5] city, I was

---

1. Translated by Richard Miller.
2. Palatial building used to host foreign princes and princesses; nowadays, the residence of the French president.
3. A 15th-century painting in a church in Lübeck North

Germany.
4. Greco-Roman revelries in honor of Bacchus, the wine god.
5. Enlightened.

making for myself a moral macédoine,[6] half pleasant, half funereal. With my left foot I beat time, and I felt as though the other were in the grave. My leg was in fact chilled by one of those insidious drafts which freeze half our bodies while the other half feels the humid heat of rooms, an occurrence rather frequent at balls.

"Monsieur de Lanty hasn't owned this house for very long, has he?"

"Oh yes. Maréchal Carigliano sold it to him nearly ten years ago."

"Ah!"

"These people must have a huge fortune."

"They must have."

"What a party! It's shockingly elegant."

"Do you think they're as rich as M. de Nucingen or M. de Gondreville?"

"You mean you don't know?" . . .

I stuck my head out and recognized the two speakers as members of that strange race which, in Paris, deals exclusively with "whys" and "hows," with "Where did they come from?" "What's happening?" "What has she done?" They lowered their voices and walked off to talk in greater comfort on some isolated sofa. Never had a richer vein been offered to seekers after mystery. Nobody knew what country the Lanty family came from, or from what business, what plunder, what piratical activity, or what inheritance derived a fortune estimated at several millions. All the members of the family spoke Italian, French, Spanish, English, and German perfectly enough to create the belief that they must have spent a long time among these various peoples. Were they gypsies? Were they freebooters?

"Even if it's the devil," some young politicians said, "they give a marvelous party."

"Even if the Count de Lanty had robbed a bank, I'd marry his daughter any time!" cried a philosopher.

Who wouldn't have married Marianina, a girl of sixteen whose beauty embodied the fabled imaginings of the Eastern poets! Like the sultan's daughter, in the story of the Magic Lamp,[7] she should have been kept veiled. Her singing put into the shade the partial talents of Malibran, Sontag, and Fodor,[8] in whom one dominant quality has always excluded over-all perfection; whereas Marianina was able to bring to the same level purity of sound, sensibility, rightness of movement and pitch, soul and science, correctness and feeling. This girl was the embodiment of that secret poetry, the common bond among all the arts, which always eludes those who search for it. Sweet and modest, educated and witty, no one could eclipse Marianina, save her mother.

Have you ever encountered one of those women whose striking beauty defies the inroads of age and who seem at thirty-six more desirable than they could have been fifteen years earlier? Their visage is a vibrant soul, it glows; each feature sparkles with intelligence; each pore has a special brilliance, especially in artificial light. Their seductive eyes refuse, attract, speak or remain silent; their walk is innocently knowledgeable; their voices employ the melodious wealth of the most coquettishly soft and tender notes. Based on comparisons, their praises flatter the self-love of the most sentient. A movement of their eyebrows, the least glance, their pursed lips, fill with a kind of terror those whose life and happiness depend upon them. Inexperienced in love and influenced by words, a young girl can be seduced; for this kind of woman,

---

6. A medley (from the French dish featuring a mixture of fruits or vegetables).

7. The story of Aladdin in the *Thousand and One Nights*.

8. Maria Malibran (1808–1836), Henriette Sontag (1806–1854), and Joséphine Mainville-Fodor (1789–1870) were famous opera singers.

however, a man must know, like M. de Jaucourt,[9] not to cry out when he is hiding in a closet and the maid breaks two of his fingers as she shuts the door on them. In loving these powerful sirens, one gambles with one's life. And this, perhaps, is why we love them so passionately. Such was the Countess de Lanty.

Filippo, Marianina's brother, shared with his sister in the Countess's marvelous beauty. To be brief, this young man was a living image of Antinous,[1] even more slender. Yet how well these thin, delicate proportions are suited to young people when an olive complexion, strongly defined eyebrows, and the fire of velvet eyes give promise of future male passion, of brave thoughts! If Filippo resided in every girl's heart as an ideal, he also resided in the memory of every mother as the best catch in France.

The beauty, the fortune, the wit, the charms of these two children, came solely from their mother. The Count de Lanty was small, ugly, and pock-marked; dark as a Spaniard, dull as a banker. However, he was taken to be a deep politician, perhaps because he rarely laughed, and was always quoting Metternich or Wellington.[2]

This mysterious family had all the appeal of one of Lord Byron's poems, whose difficulties each person in the fashionable world interpreted in a different way: an obscure and sublime song in every strophe. The reserve maintained by M. and Mme de Lanty about their origin, their past life, and their relationship with the four corners of the globe had not lasted long as a subject of astonishment in Paris. Nowhere perhaps is Vespasian's axiom[3] better understood. There, even bloodstained or filthy money betrays nothing and stands for everything. So long as high society knows the amount of your fortune, you are classed among those having an equal amount, and no one asks to see your family tree, because everyone knows how much it cost. In a city where social problems are solved like algebraic equations, adventurers have every opportunity in their favor. Even supposing this family were of gypsy origin, it was so wealthy, so attractive, that society had no trouble in forgiving its little secrets. Unfortunately, however, the mystery of the Lantys presented a continuing source of curiosity, rather like that contained in the novels of Ann Radcliffe.[4]

Observers, people who make it a point to know in what shop you buy your candlesticks, or who ask the amount of your rent when they find your apartment attractive, had noticed, now and then, in the midst of the Countess's parties, concerts, balls, and routs,[5] the appearance of a strange personage. It was a man. The first time he had appeared in the mansion was during a concert, when he seemed to have been drawn to the salon by Marianina's enchanting voice.

"All of a sudden, I'm cold," a lady had said who was standing with a friend by the door.

The stranger, who was standing next to the women, went away.

"That's odd! I'm warm now," she said, after the stranger had gone. "And you'll say I'm mad, but I can't help thinking that my neighbor, the man dressed in black who just left, was the cause of my chill."

Before long, the exaggeration native to those in high society gave birth to and accumulated the most amusing ideas, the most outrageous expressions, the most ridiculous anecdotes about this mysterious personage. Although not a vampire, a ghoul, or

9. Arnail-François, Marquis de Jaucourt (1757–1852), a prominent politician under both Napoleon and the Restoration monarchy.
1. Antinous (c. 110–130), a model of youthful beauty and the favorite of the Roman Emperor Hadrian.
2. Klemens Count von Metternich (1773–1859) was an Austrian statesman who helped form the alliance against Napoleon; Arthur Wellesley, Duke of Wellington (1769–1852) was a British statesman and general who defeated Napoleon.
3. "An emperor should die standing," attributed to the Roman emperor Vespasian (9–79 C.E.).
4. English Gothic novelist (1764–1823).
5. Fashionable gatherings, generally evening parties.

an artificial man, a kind of Faust or Robin Goodfellow,[6] people fond of fantasy said he had something of all these anthropomorphic natures about him. Here and there, one came across some Germans who accepted as fact these clever witticisms of Parisian scandal-mongering. The stranger was merely an old man. Many of the young men who were in the habit of settling the future of Europe every morning in a few elegant phrases would have liked to see in this stranger some great criminal, the possessor of vast wealth. Some storytellers recounted the life of this old man and provided really curious details about the atrocities he had committed while in the service of the Maharaja of Mysore. Some bankers, more positive by nature, invented a fable about money. "Bah," they said, shrugging their shoulders in pity, "this poor old man is a *tête génoise!*"[7]

"Sir, without being indiscreet, could you please tell me what you mean by a tête génoise?"

"A man, sir, with an enormous lifetime capital and whose family's income doubtless depends on his good health."

I remember having heard at Mme d'Espard's a hypnotist[8] proving on highly suspect historical data that this old man, preserved under glass, was the famous Balsamo, known as Cagliostro.[9] According to this contemporary alchemist, the Sicilian adventurer had escaped death and passed his time fabricating gold for his grandchildren. Last, the bailiff of Ferrette[1] maintained that he had recognized this odd personage as the Count of Saint-Germain.[2] These stupidities, spoken in witty accents, with the mocking air characteristic of atheistic society in our day, kept alive vague suspicions about the Lanty family. Finally, through a strange combination of circumstances, the members of this family justified everyone's conjectures by behaving somewhat mysteriously toward this old man, whose life was somehow hidden from all investigation.

Whenever this person crossed the threshold of the room he was supposed to inhabit in the Lanty mansion, his appearance always created a great sensation among the family. One might have called it an event of great importance. Filippo, Marianina, Mme de Lanty, and an old servant were the only persons privileged to assist the old man in walking, arising, sitting down. Each of them watched over his slightest movement. It seemed that he was an enchanted being upon whom depended the happiness, the life, or the fortune of them all. Was it affection or fear? Those in society were unable to discover any clue to help them solve this problem. Hidden for whole months in the depths of a secret sanctuary, this family genie would suddenly come forth, unexpectedly, and would appear in the midst of the salons like those fairies of bygone days who descended from flying dragons to interrupt the rites to which they had not been invited. Only the most avid onlookers were then able to perceive the uneasiness of the heads of the house, who could conceal their feelings with unusual skill. Sometimes, however, while dancing a quadrille, Marianina, naïve as she was, would cast a terrified glance at the old man when she spied him among the crowd. Or else Filippo would slip quickly through the throng to his side and would stay near him, tender and attentive, as though contact with others or the slightest breath would destroy this

6. A mischievous fairy in medieval English folklore.
7. A "Genoese head." People from Genoa were proverbially tight-fisted.
8. Hypnotism was a fashionable new discovery by the German physician Franz Anton Mesmer (1734–1815).
9. Giuseppe Balsamo, self-styled Count di Cagliostro (1743–1795), was lionized as a magician in Paris in the 1780s, confined in the Bastille for scandal shortly before the Revolution, then imprisoned in Italy for heresy from 1789 until his death.
1. Probably John-Baptiste de Ferrette, a prominent diplomat who serverd as ambassador to the Grand Duchy of Baden in the Restoration.
2. A mystic and adventurer, seen repeatedly between his recorded death date and 1824.

strange creature. The Countess would make a point of drawing near, without seeming to have any intention of joining them; then, assuming a manner and expression of servitude mixed with tenderness, submission, and power, she would say a few words, to which the old man nearly always deferred, and he would disappear, led off, or, more precisely, carried off, by her. If Mme de Lanty were not present, the Count used a thousand stratagems to reach his side; however, he seemed to have difficulty making himself heard, and treated him like a spoiled child whose mother gives in to his whims in order to avoid a scene. Some bolder persons having thoughtlessly ventured to question the Count de Lanty, this cold, reserved man had appeared never to understand them. And so, after many tries, all futile because of the circumspection of the entire family, everyone stopped trying to fathom such a well-kept secret. Weary of trying, the companionable spies, the idly curious, and the politic all gave up bothering about this mystery.

However, even now perhaps in these glittering salons there were some philosophers who, while eating an ice or a sherbet, or placing their empty punch glass on a side table, were saying to each other: "It wouldn't surprise me to learn that those people are crooks. The old man who hides and only makes his appearance on the first day of spring or winter, or at the solstices, looks to me like a killer . . ."

"Or a confidence man . . ."

"It's almost the same thing. Killing a man's fortune is sometimes worse than killing the man."

"Sir, I have bet twenty louis, I should get back forty."

"But, sir, there are only thirty on the table."

"Ah well, you see how mixed the crowd is, here. It's impossible to play."

"True . . . But it's now nearly six months since we've seen the Spirit. Do you think he's really alive?"

"Hah! at best . . ."

These last words were spoken near me by people I did not know, as they were moving off, and as I was resuming, in an afterthought, my mixed thoughts of white and black, life and death. My vivid imagination as well as my eyes looked back and forth from the party, which had reached the height of its splendor, and the somber scene in the gardens. I do not know how long I meditated on these two faces of the human coin; but all at once I was awakened by the stifled laugh of a young woman. I was stunned by the appearance of the image which arose before me. By one of those tricks of nature, the half-mournful thought turning in my mind had emerged, and it appeared living before me, it had sprung like Minerva[3] from the head of Jove, tall and strong, it was at once a hundred years old and twenty-two years old; it was alive and dead. Escaped from his room like a lunatic from his cell, the little old man had obviously slipped behind a hedge of people who were listening to Marianina's voice, finishing the cavatina from *Tancredi*.[4] He seemed to have come out from underground, impelled by some piece of stage machinery. Motionless and somber, he stood for a moment gazing at the party, the noises of which had perhaps reached his ears. His almost somnambulatory preoccupation was so concentrated on things that he was in the world without seeing it. He had unceremoniously sprung up next to one of the most ravishing women in Paris, a young and elegant dancer, delicately formed, with one of those faces as fresh as that of a child, pink and white, so frail and transparent that a man's glance seems to penetrate it like a ray of sunlight going through ice. They were

3. Roman goddess of war and the arts.   4. Opera by Rossini (1813). Cavatina: a lyrical aria.

both there before me, together, united, and so close that the stranger brushed against her, her gauzy dress, her garlands of flowers, her softly curled hair, her floating sash.

I had brought this young woman to Mme de Lanty's ball. Since this was her first visit to the house, I forgave her her stifled laugh, but I quickly gave her a signal which completely silenced her and filled her with awe for her neighbor. She sat down next to me. The old man did not want to leave this lovely creature, to whom he had attached himself with that silent and seemingly baseless stubbornness to which the extremely old are prone, and which makes them appear childish. In order to sit near her, he had to take a folding chair. His slightest movements were full of that cold heaviness, the stupid indecision, characteristic of the gestures of a paralytic. He sat slowly down on his seat, with circumspection, muttering some unintelligible words. His worn-out voice was like the sound made by a stone falling down a well. The young woman held my hand tightly, as if seeking protection on some precipice, and she shivered when this man at whom she was looking turned upon her two eyes without warmth, glaucous eyes which could only be compared to dull mother-of-pearl.

"I'm afraid," she said, leaning toward my ear.

"You can talk," I answered. "He is very hard of hearing."

"Do you know him?"

"Yes."

Thereupon, she gathered up enough courage to look for a moment at this creature for which the human language had no name, a form without substance, a being without life, or a life without action. She was under the spell of that timorous curiosity which leads women to seek out dangerous emotions, to go see chained tigers, to look at boa constrictors, frightening themselves because they are separated from them only by weak fences. Although the little old man's back was stooped like a laborer's, one could easily tell that he must have had at one time a normal shape. His excessive thinness, the delicacy of his limbs, proved that he had always been slender. He was dressed in black silk trousers which fell about his bony thighs in folds, like an empty sail. An anatomist would have promptly recognized the symptoms of galloping consumption by looking at the skinny legs supporting this strange body. You would have said they were two bones crossed on a tombstone.

A feeling of profound horror for mankind gripped the heart when one saw the marks that decrepitude had left on this fragile machine. The stranger was wearing an old-fashioned gold-embroidered white waistcoat, and his linen was dazzlingly white. A frill of somewhat yellowed lace, rich enough for a queen's envy, fell into ruffles on his breast. On him, however, this lace seemed more like a rag than like an ornament. Centered on it was a fabulous diamond which glittered like the sun. This outmoded luxury, this particular and tasteless jewel, made the strange creature's face even more striking. The setting was worthy of the portrait. This dark face was angular and all sunk in. The chin was sunken, the temples were sunken; the eyes were lost in yellowish sockets. The jawbones stood out because of his indescribable thinness, creating cavities in the center of each cheek. These deformations, more or less illuminated by the candles, produced shadows and strange reflections which succeeded in erasing any human characteristics from his face. And the years had glued the thin, yellow skin of his face so closely to his skull that it was covered all over with a multitude of circular wrinkles, like the ripples on a pond into which a child has thrown a pebble, or star-shaped, like a cracked windowpane, but everywhere deep and close-set as the edges of pages in a closed book. Some old people have presented more hideous portraits; what contributed the most, however, in lending the appearance of an artificial creature to the specter which had risen up before us was the red and white with which he glistened. The eyebrows of his mask took from the light a luster which revealed that they were painted on. Fortunately for the eye depressed by the sight of such ruin, his cadaverous skull was covered by a blond wig whose innumerable curls were evidence of an extraordinary pretension. For the rest, the feminine coquetry of this phantasmagorical personage was rather strongly emphasized by the gold ornaments hanging from his ears, by the rings whose fine stones glittered on his bony fingers, and by a watch chain which shimmered like the brilliants of a choker around a woman's neck. Finally, this sort of Japanese idol had on his bluish lips a fixed and frozen smile, implacable and mocking, like a skull. Silent and motionless as a statue, it exuded the musty odor of old clothes which the heirs of some duchess take out for inventory. Although the old man turned his eyes toward the crowd, it seemed that the movements of those orbs, incapable of sight, were accomplished only by means of some imperceptible artifice; and when the eyes came to rest on something, anyone looking at them would have concluded that they had not moved at all. To see, next to this human wreckage, a young woman whose neck, bosom, and arms were bare and white, whose figure was in the full bloom of its beauty, whose hair rose from her alabaster forehead and inspired love, whose eyes did not receive but gave off light, who was soft, fresh, and whose floating curls and sweet breath seemed too heavy, too hard, too powerful for this shadow, for this man of dust: ah! here were death and life indeed, I thought, in a fantastic arabesque, half hideous chimera,[5] divinely feminine from the waist up.

"Yet there are marriages like that often enough in the world," I said to myself.

"He smells like a graveyard," cried the terrified young woman, pressing against me for protection, and whose uneasy movements told me she was frightened. "What a horrible sight," she went on. "I can't stay here any longer. If I look at him again, I shall believe that death itself has come looking for me. Is he alive?"

She reached out to the phenomenon with that boldness women can summon up out of the strength of their desires; but she broke into a cold sweat, for no sooner had she touched the old man than she heard a cry like a rattle. This sharp voice, if voice it was, issued from a nearly dried-up throat. Then the sound was quickly followed by a little, convulsive, childish cough of a peculiar sonorousness. At this sound, Marianina, Filippo, and Mme de Lanty looked in our direction, and their glances were like bolts of lightning. The young woman wished she were at the bottom of the Seine. She took my arm and led me into a side room. Men, women, everyone made way for us. At the end of the public rooms, we came into a small, semicircular chamber. My companion threw herself onto a divan, trembling with fright, oblivious to her surroundings.

"Madame, you are mad," I said to her.

"But," she replied, after a moment's silence, during which I gazed at her in admiration, "is it my fault? Why does Mme de Lanty allow ghosts to wander about in her house?"

"Come," I replied, "you are being ridiculous, taking a little old man for a ghost."

"Be still," she said, with that forceful and mocking air all women so easily assume when they want to be in the right. "What a pretty room!" she cried, looking around. "Blue satin always makes such wonderful wall hangings. How refreshing it is! Oh! what a beautiful painting!" she went on, getting up and going to stand before a painting in a magnificent frame.

5. Mythological creature, part lion, part goat, part dragon.

We stood for a moment in contemplation of this marvel, which seemed to have been painted by some supernatural brush. The picture was of Adonis[6] lying on a lion's skin. The lamp hanging from the ceiling of the room in an alabaster globe illuminated this canvas with a soft glow which enabled us to make out all the beauties of the painting.

"Does such a perfect creature exist?" she asked me, after having, with a soft smile of contentment, examined the exquisite grace of the contours, the pose, the color, the hair; in short, the entire picture.

"He is too beautiful for a man," she added, after an examination such as she might have made of some rival.

Oh! how jealous I then felt: something in which a poet had vainly tried to make me believe, the jealousy of engravings, of pictures, wherein artists exaggerate human beauty according to the doctrine which leads them to idealize everything.

"It's a portrait," I replied, "the product of the talent of Vien.[7] But that great painter never saw the original and maybe you'd admire it less if you knew that this daub was copied from the statue of a woman."

"But who is it?"

I hesitated.

"I want to know," she added, impetuously.

"I believe," I replied, "that this Adonis is a . . . a relative of Mme de Lanty."

I had the pain of seeing her rapt in the contemplation of this figure. She sat in silence; I sat down next to her and took her hand without her being aware of it! Forgotten for a painting! At this moment, the light footsteps of a woman in a rustling dress broke the silence. Young Marianina came in, and her innocent expression made her even more alluring than did her grace and her lovely dress; she was walking slowly and escorting with maternal care, with filial solicitude, the costumed specter who had made us flee from the music room and whom she was leading, watching with what seemed to be concern as he slowly advanced on his feeble feet. They went together with some difficulty to a door hidden behind a tapestry. There, Marianina knocked softly. At once, as if by magic, a tall, stern man, a kind of family genie, appeared. Before entrusting the old man to the care of his mysterious guardian, the child respectfully kissed the walking corpse, and her chaste caress was not devoid of that graceful cajolery of which some privileged women possess the secret.

"Addio, addio," she said, with the prettiest inflection in her youthful voice.

She added to the final syllable a marvelously well-executed trill, but in a soft voice, as if to give poetic expression to the emotions in her heart. Suddenly struck by some memory, the old man stood on the threshold of this secret hideaway. Then, through the silence, we heard the heavy sigh that came from his chest: he took the most beautiful of the rings which adorned his skeletal fingers, and placed it in Marianina's bosom. The young girl broke into laughter, took the ring, and slipped it onto her finger over her glove; then she walked quickly toward the salon, from which there could be heard the opening measures of a quadrille. She saw us:

"Ah, you were here," she said, blushing.

After having seemed as if about to question us, she ran to her partner with the careless petulance of youth.

---

6. In Greek mythology, a youth of remarkable beauty, the favorite of the goddess Aphrodite.

7. Joseph-Marie Vien (1716–1809): French historical painter, displaced by the Revolution, rehabilitated by Napoleon.

"What did that mean?" my young companion asked me. "Is he her husband? I must be dreaming. Where am I?"

"You," I replied, "you, madame, superior as you are, you who understand so well the most hidden feelings, who know how to inspire in a man's heart the most delicate of feelings without blighting it, without breaking it at the outset, you who pity heartache and who combine the wit of a Parisienne with a passionate soul worthy of Italy or Spain—"

She perceived the bitter irony in my speech; then, without seeming to have heard, she interrupted me: "Oh, you fashion me to your own taste. What tyranny! You don't want me for myself!"

"Ah, I want nothing," I cried, taken aback by her severity. "Is it true, at least, that you enjoy hearing stories of those vivid passions that ravishing Southern women inspire in our hearts?"

"Yes, so?"

"So, I'll call tomorrow around nine and reveal this mystery to you."

"No," she replied, "I want to know now."

"You haven't yet given me the right to obey you when you say: I want to."

"At this moment," she replied with maddening coquetry, "I have the most burning desire to know the secret. Tomorrow, I might not even listen to you . . ."

She smiled and we parted; she just as proud, just as forbidding, and I just as ridiculous as ever. She had the audacity to waltz with a young aide-de-camp; and I was left in turn angry, pouting, admiring, loving, jealous.

"Till tomorrow," she said, around two in the morning, as she left the ball.

"I won't go," I thought to myself. "I'll give you up. You are more capricious, perhaps a thousand times more fanciful . . . than my imagination."

The next evening, we were both seated before a good fire in a small, elegant salon, she on a low sofa, I on cushions almost at her feet, and my eyes below hers. The street was quiet. The lamp shed a soft light. It was one of those evenings pleasing to the soul, one of those never-to-be-forgotten moments, one of those hours spent in peace and desire whose charm, later on, is a matter for constant regret, even when we may be happier. Who can erase the vivid imprint of the first feelings of love?

"Well," she said, "I'm listening."

"I don't dare begin. The story has some dangerous passages for its teller. If I become too moved, you must stop me."

"Tell."

"I will obey."

Ernest-Jean Sarrasine was the only son of a lawyer in the Franche-Comté,[8] I went on, after a pause. His father had amassed six or eight thousand livres of income honestly enough, a professional's fortune which at that time in the provinces, was considered to be colossal. The elder Sarrasine, having but one child and anxious to overlook nothing where his education was concerned, hoped to make a magistrate of him, and to live long enough to see, in his old age, the grandson of Matthieu Sarrasine, farmer of Saint-Dié,[9] seated beneath the lilies and napping through some trial for the greater glory of the law; however, heaven did not hold this pleasure in store for the lawyer.

8. A region in Eastern France, site of peasant uprisings in support of the Revolution.

9. A town in the Lorraine region of northeastern France.

The younger Sarrasine, entrusted to the Jesuits at an early age, evidenced an unusual turbulence. He had the childhood of a man of talent. He would study only what pleased him, frequently rebelled, and sometimes spent hours on end plunged in confused thought, occupied at times in watching his comrades at play, at times dreaming of Homeric heroes. Then, if he made up his mind to amuse himself, he threw himself into games with an extraordinary ardor. When a fight broke out between him and a friend, the battle rarely ended without bloodshed. If he was the weaker of the two, he would bite. Both active and passive by turns, without aptitude and not overly intelligent, his bizarre character made his teachers as wary of him as were his classmates. Instead of learning the elements of Greek, he drew the Reverend Father as he explained a passage in Thucydides[1] to them, sketched the mathematics teacher, the tutors, the Father in charge of discipline, and he scribbled shapeless designs on the walls. Instead of singing the Lord's praises in church, he distracted himself during services by whittling on a pew; or when he had stolen a piece of wood, he carved some holy figure. If he had no wood, paper, or pencil, he reproduced his ideas with bread crumbs. Whether copying the characters in the pictures that decorated the choir, or improvising, he always left behind him some gross sketches whose licentiousness shocked the youngest Fathers; evil tongues maintained that the older Jesuits were amused by them. Finally, if we are to believe school gossip, he was expelled for having, while awaiting his turn at the confessional on Good Friday, shaped a big stick of wood into the form of Christ. The impiety with which this statue was endowed was too blatant not to have merited punishment of the artist. Had he not had the audacity to place this somewhat cynical figure on top of the tabernacle!

Sarrasine sought in Paris a refuge from the effects of a father's curse. Having one of those strong wills that brook no obstacle, he obeyed the commands of his genius and entered Bouchardon's[2] studio. He worked all day, and in the evening went out to beg for his living. Astonished at the young artist's progress and intelligence, Bouchardon soon became aware of his pupil's poverty; he helped him, grew fond of him, and treated him like his own son. Then, when Sarrasine's genius was revealed in one of those works in which future talent struggles with the effervescence of youth, the warmhearted Bouchardon endeavored to restore him to the old lawyer's good graces. Before the authority of the famous sculptor, the parental anger subsided. All Besançon[3] rejoiced at having given birth to a great man of the future. In the first throes of the ecstasy produced by his flattered vanity, the miserly lawyer gave his son the means to cut a good figure in society. For a long time, the lengthy and laborious studies demanded by sculpture tamed Sarrasine's impetuous nature and wild genius. Bouchardon, foreseeing the violence with which the passions would erupt in this young soul, which was perhaps as predisposed to them as Michelangelo's had been, channeled his energy into constant labor. He succeeded in keeping Sarrasine's extraordinary impetuosity within limits by forbidding him to work; by suggesting distractions when he saw him being carried away by the fury of some idea, or by entrusting him with important work when he seemed on the point of abandoning himself to dissipation. However, gentleness was always the most powerful of weapons where this passionate soul was concerned, and the master had no greater control over his student than when he inspired his gratitude through paternal kindness.

---

1. Ancient Greek historian (460?–404? B.C.E.).
2. Edmé Bouchardon (1698–1762), French sculptor.
3. Capital of the Franche–Comté region.

At twenty-two, Sarrasine was necessarily removed from the salutary influence Bouchardon had exercised over his morals and his habits. He reaped the fruits of his genius by winning the sculpture prize established by the Marquis de Marigny,[4] the brother of Mme de Pompadour, who did so much for the arts. Diderot[5] hailed the statue by Bouchardon's pupil as a masterpiece. The King's sculptor, not without great sorrow, saw off to Italy a young man whom he had kept, as a matter of principle, in total ignorance of the facts of life.

For six years, Sarrasine had boarded with Bouchardon. As fanatic in his art as Canova[6] was later to be, he arose at dawn, went to the studio, did not emerge until nightfall, and lived only with his Muse. If he went to the Comédie-Française,[7] he was taken by his master. He felt so out of place at Mme Geoffrin's[8] and in high society, into which Bouchardon tried to introduce him, that he preferred to be alone, and shunned the pleasures of that licentious era. He had no other mistress but sculpture and Clotilde, one of the luminaries of the Opéra. And even this affair did not last. Sarrasine was rather ugly, always badly dressed, and so free in his nature, so irregular in his private life, that the celebrated nymph, fearing some catastrophe, soon relinquished the sculptor to his love of the Arts. Sophie Arnould[9] made one of her witticisms on this subject. She confessed her surprise, I believe, that her friend had managed to triumph over statuary.

Sarrasine left for Italy in 1758. During the journey, his vivid imagination caught fire beneath a brilliant sky and at the sight of the wonderful monuments which are to be found in the birthplace of the Arts. He admired the statues, the frescoes, the paintings, and thus inspired, he came to Rome, filled with desire to carve his name between Michelangelo's and M. Bouchardon's. Accordingly, at the beginning, he divided his time between studio tasks and examining the works of art in which Rome abounds. He had already spent two weeks in the ecstatic state which overwhelms young minds at the sight of the queen of ruins, when he went one evening to the Teatro Argentina, before which a huge crowd was assembled. He inquired as to the causes of this gathering and everyone answered with two names: Zambinella! Jomelli![1] He entered and took a seat in the orchestra, squeezed between two notably fat abbati; however, he was lucky enough to be fairly close to the stage. The curtain rose. For the first time in his life, he heard that music whose delights M. Jean-Jacques Rousseau had so eloquently praised to him at one of Baron d'Holbach's[2] evenings. The young sculptor's senses were, so to speak, lubricated by the accents of Jomelli's sublime harmony. The languorous novelties of these skillfully mingled Italian voices plunged him into a delicious ecstasy. He remained speechless, motionless, not even feeling crowded by the two priests. His soul passed into his ears and eyes. He seemed to hear through every pore. Suddenly a burst of applause which shook the house greeted the prima donna's entrance. She came coquettishly to the front of the stage and greeted the audience with infinite grace. The lights, the general enthusiasm, the

4. Abel François Poisson, Marquis de Marigny (1727–1781): royal architect and art patron; Jeanne-Antoinette Poisson, Marquise de Pompadour (1721–1764): influential mistress of French king Louis XV.
5. Denis Diderot (1713–1784), French philosopher and art critic, and chief editor of the *Encyclopedia.*
6. Antonio Canova (1757–1822), Italian sculptor.
7. National theater of France.
8. Marie-Thérèse Rodet Geoffrin (1699–1777), French

hostess whose salon was a meeting-place of artists and men of letters.
9. Opera singer (1744–1803).
1. Niccolò Jomelli (1714–1774), Italian composer of religious music and operas.
2. Paul-Marie Dietrich, Baron d'Holbach (1723–1789), French philosopher and encyclopedist. The philosopher Rousseau was also a successful composer, the author of an encyclopedia of music, and, by trade, a music copyist.

theatrical illusion, the glamour of a style of dress which in those days was quite attractive, all conspired in favor of this woman. Sarrasine cried out with pleasure.

At that instant he marveled at the ideal beauty he had hitherto sought in life, seeking in one often unworthy model the roundness of a perfect leg; in another, the curve of a breast; in another, white shoulders; finally taking some girl's neck, some woman's hands, and some child's smooth knees, without ever having encountered under the cold Parisian sky the rich, sweet creations of ancient Greece. La Zambinella displayed to him, united, living, and delicate, those exquisite female forms he so ardently desired, of which a sculptor is at once the severest and the most passionate judge. Her mouth was expressive, her eyes loving, her complexion dazzlingly white. And along with these details, which would have enraptured a painter, were all the wonders of those images of Venus revered and rendered by the chisels of the Greeks. The artist never wearied of admiring the inimitable grace with which the arms were attached to the torso, the marvelous roundness of the neck, the harmonious lines drawn by the eyebrows, the nose, and the perfect oval of the face, the purity of its vivid contours and the effect of the thick, curved lashes which lined her heavy and voluptuous eyelids. This was more than a woman, this was a masterpiece! In this unhoped-for creation could be found a love to enrapture any man, and beauties worthy of satisfying a critic. With his eyes, Sarrasine devoured Pygmalion's statue, come down from its pedestal.[3] When La Zambinella sang, the effect was delirium. The artist felt cold; then he felt a heat which suddenly began to prickle in the innermost depth of his being, in what we call the heart, for lack of any other word! He did not applaud, he said nothing, he experienced an impulse of madness, a kind of frenzy which overcomes us only when we are at the age when desire has something frightening and infernal about it. Sarrasine wanted to leap onto the stage and take possession of this woman: his strength, increased a hundredfold by a moral depression impossible to explain, since these phenomena occur in an area hidden from human observation, seemed to manifest itself with painful violence. Looking at him, one would have thought him a cold and senseless man. Fame, knowledge, future, existence, laurels, everything collapsed.

"To be loved by her, or die!" Such was the decree Sarrasine passed upon himself. He was so utterly intoxicated that he no longer saw the theater, the spectators, the actors, or heard the music. Moreover, the distance between himself and La Zambinella had ceased to exist, he possessed her, his eyes were riveted upon her, he took her for his own. An almost diabolical power enabled him to feel the breath of this voice, to smell the scented powder covering her hair, to see the planes of her face, to count the blue veins shadowing her satin skin. Last, this agile voice, fresh and silvery in timbre, supple as a thread shaped by the slightest breath of air, rolling and unrolling, cascading and scattering, this voice attacked his soul so vividly that several times he gave vent to involuntary cries torn from him by convulsive feelings of pleasure which are all too rarely vouchsafed by human passions. He was presently obliged to leave the theater. His trembling legs almost refused to support him. He was limp, weak as a sensitive man who has given way to overwhelming anger. He had experienced such pleasure, or perhaps he had suffered so keenly, that his life had drained away like water from a broken vase. He felt empty inside, a prostration similar to the debilitation that overcomes those convalescing from serious illness.

---

3. In Greek legend, Pygmalion created a statue representing his ideal of womanhood, which then came to life.

Overcome by an inexplicable sadness, he sat down on the steps of a church. There, leaning back against a pillar, he fell into a confused meditation, as in a dream. He had been smitten by passion. Upon returning to his lodgings, he fell into one of those frenzies of activity which disclose to us the presence of new elements in our lives. A prey to this first fever of love derived equally from both pleasure and pain, he tried to appease his impatience and his delirium by drawing La Zambinella from memory. It was a kind of embodied meditation. On one page, La Zambinella appeared in that apparently calm and cool pose favored by Raphael, Giorgione,[4] and every great painter. On another, she was delicately turning her head after having finished a trill, and appeared to be listening to herself. Sarrasine sketched his mistress in every pose: he drew her unveiled, seated, standing, lying down, chaste or amorous, embodying through the delirium of his pencils every capricious notion that can enter our heads when we think intently about a mistress. However, his fevered thoughts went beyond drawing. He saw La Zambinella, spoke to her, beseeched her, he passed a thousand years of life and happiness with her by placing her in every imaginable position; in short, by sampling the future with her. On the following day, he sent his valet to rent a box next to the stage for the entire season. Then, like all young people with lusty souls, he exaggerated to himself the difficulties of his undertaking and first fed his passion with the pleasure of being able to admire his mistress without obstruction. This golden age of love, during which we take pleasure in our own feeling and in which we are happy almost by ourselves, was not destined to last long in Sarrasine's case. Nevertheless, events took him by surprise while he was still under the spell of this vernal hallucination, as naïve as it was voluptuous. In a week he lived a lifetime, spending the mornings kneading the clay by which he would copy La Zambinella, despite the veils, skirts, corsets, and ribbons which concealed her from him. In the evenings, installed in his box early, alone, lying on a sofa like a Turk under the influence of opium, he created for himself a pleasure as rich and varied as he wished it to be. First, he gradually familiarized himself with the overly vivid emotions his mistress's singing afforded him; he then trained his eyes to see her, and finally he could contemplate her without fearing an outburst of the wild frenzy which had seized him on the first day. As his passion became calmer, it grew deeper. For the rest, the unsociable sculptor did not allow his friends to intrude upon his solitude, which was peopled with images, adorned with fantasies of hope, and filled with happiness. His love was so strong, so naïve, that he experienced all the innocent scruples that assail us when we love for the first time. As he began to realize that he would soon have to act, to plot, to inquire where La Zambinella lived, whether she had a mother, uncle, teacher, family, to ponder, in short, on ways to see her, speak to her, these great, ambitious thoughts made his heart swell so painfully that he put them off until later, deriving as much satisfaction from his physical suffering as he did from his intellectual pleasures.

"But," Mme de Rochefide interrupted me, "I still don't see anything about either Marianina or her little old man."

"You are seeing nothing but him!" I cried impatiently, like an author who is being forced to spoil a theatrical effect.

---

4. Raffaello Santi (1483–1520): painter and architect of the Italian High Renaissance; Giorgione (1477–1510): Italian painter.

For several days, I resumed after a pause, Sarrasine had reappeared so faithfully in his box and his eyes had expressed such love that his passion for La Zambinella's voice would have been common knowledge throughout Paris, had this adventure happened there; however, in Italy, madame, everyone goes to the theater for himself, with his own passions, and with a heartfelt interest which precludes spying through opera glasses. Nevertheless, the sculptor's enthusiasm did not escape the attention of the singers for long. One evening, the Frenchman saw that they were laughing at him in the wings. It is hard to know what extreme actions he might not have taken had La Zambinella not come onto the stage. She gave Sarrasine one of those eloquent glances which often reveal much more than women intend them to. This glance was a total revelation. Sarrasine was loved!

"If it's only a caprice," he thought, already accusing his mistress of excessive ardor, "she doesn't know what she is subjecting herself to. I am hoping her caprice will last my whole life."

At that moment, the artist's attention was distracted by three soft knocks on the door of his box. He opened it. An old woman entered with an air of mystery.

"Young man," she said, "if you want to be happy, be prudent. Put on a cape, wear a hat drawn down over your eyes; then, around ten in the evening, be in the Via del Corso in front of the Hotel di Spagna."

"I'll be there," he replied, placing two louis in the duenna's wrinkled hand.

He left his box after having given a signal to La Zambinella, who timidly lowered her heavy eyelids, like a woman pleased to be understood at last. Then he ran home to dress himself as seductively as he could. As he was leaving the theater, a strange man took his arm.

"Be on your guard, Frenchman," he whispered in his ear. "This is a matter of life and death. Cardinal Cicognara[5] is her protector and doesn't trifle."

At that moment, had some demon set the pit of hell between Sarrasine and La Zambinella, he would have crossed it with one leap. Like the horses of the gods described by Homer, the sculptor's love had traversed vast distances in the twinkling of an eye.

"If death itself were waiting for me outside the house, I would go even faster," he replied.

"Poverino!"[6] the stranger cried as he disappeared.

Speaking of danger to a lover is tantamount to selling him pleasures, is it not? Sarrasine's valet had never seen his master take so much care over his toilette. His finest sword, a gift from Bouchardon, the sash Clotilde had given him, his embroidered coat, his silver-brocade waistcoat, his gold snuffbox, his jeweled watches, were all taken from their coffers, and he adorned himself like a girl about to appear before her first love. At the appointed hour, drunk with love and seething with hope, Sarrasine, concealed in his cape, sped to the rendezvous the old woman had given him. The duenna was waiting for him.

"You took a long time," she said. "Come."

She led the Frenchman along several back streets and stopped before a rather handsome mansion. She knocked. The door opened. She led Sarrasine along a labyrinth of stairways, galleries, and rooms which were lit only by the feeble light of the moon, and soon came to a door through whose cracks gleamed bright lights and

---

5. Cardinal Cicognara (1767–1834), Italian statesman and patron of the arts.   6. "Poor little fellow!" (Italian).

from behind which came the joyful sounds of several voices. When at a word from the old woman he was admitted to this mysterious room, Sarrasine was suddenly dazzled at finding himself in a salon as brilliantly lighted as it was sumptuously furnished, in the center of which stood a table laden with venerable bottles and flashing flagons sparkling with ruby facets. He recognized the singers from the theater, along with some charming women, all ready to begin an artists' orgy as soon as he was among them. Sarrasine suppressed a feeling of disappointment and put on a good face. He had expected a dim room, his mistress seated by the fire, some jealous person nearby, death and love, an exchange of confidences in low voices, heart to heart, dangerous kisses and faces so close that La Zambinella's hair would have caressed his forehead throbbing with desire, feverish with happiness.

"*Vive la folie!*"[7] he cried. "*Signori e belle donne,*[8] you will allow me to take my revenge later and to show you my gratitude for the way you have welcomed a poor sculptor."

Having been greeted warmly enough by most of those present, whom he knew by sight, he sought to approach the armchair on which La Zambinella was casually reclining. Ah! how his heart beat when he spied a delicate foot shod in one of those slippers which in those days, may I say, madame, gave women's feet such a coquettish and voluptuous look that I don't know how men were able to resist them. The well-fitting white stockings with green clocks,[9] the short skirts, the slippers with pointed toes, and the high heels of Louis XV's reign may have contributed something to the demoralization of Europe and the clergy.

"Something?" the Marquise replied. "Have you read nothing?"

La Zambinella, I continued, smiling, had impudently crossed her legs and was gently swinging the upper one with a certain attractive indolence which suited her capricious sort of beauty. She had removed her costume and was wearing a bodice that accentuated her narrow waist and set off the satin panniers of her dress, which was embroidered with blue flowers. Her bosom, the treasures of which were concealed, in an excess of coquetry, by a covering of lace, was dazzlingly white. Her hair arranged something like that of Mme du Barry,[1] her face, though it was partially hidden under a full bonnet, appeared only the more delicate, and powder suited her. To see her thus was to adore her. She gave the sculptor a graceful smile. Unhappy at not being able to speak to her without witnesses present, Sarrasine politely sat down next to her and talked about music, praising her extraordinary talent; but his voice trembled with love, with fear and hope.

"What are you afraid of?" asked Vitagliani, the company's most famous singer. "Go ahead; you need fear no rivals here." Having said this, the tenor smiled without another word. This smile was repeated on the lips of all the guests, whose attention contained a hidden malice a lover would not have noticed. Such openness was like a dagger thrust in Sarrasine's heart. Although endowed with a certain strength of character, and although nothing could change his love, it had perhaps not yet occurred to him that La Zambinella was virtually a courtesan,[2] and that he could not have both the pure pleasures that make a young girl's love so delicious and the tempestuous

---

7. Long live madness!
8. Gentlemen and fine ladies.
9. Decorative silk embroidery.

1. Marie-Jeanne Bécu, Comtesse du Barry (1743–1793), last of the mistresses of Louis XV.
2. Prostitute with a courtly or upper-class clientele.

transports by which the hazardous possession of an actress must be purchased. He reflected and resigned himself. Supper was served. Sarrasine and La Zambinella sat down informally side by side. For the first half of the meal, the artists preserved some decorum, and the sculptor was able to chat with the singer. He found her witty, acute, but astonishingly ignorant, and she revealed herself to be weak and superstitious. The delicacy of her organs was reflected in her understanding. When Vitagliani uncorked the first bottle of champagne, Sarrasine read in his companion's eyes a start of terror at the tiny explosion caused by the escaping gas. The love-stricken artist interpreted the involuntary shudder of this feminine constitution as the sign of an excessive sensitivity. The Frenchman was charmed by this weakness. How much is protective in a man's love!

"My strength your shield!" Is this not written at the heart of all declarations of love? Too excited to shower the beautiful Italian with compliments, Sarrasine, like all lovers, was by turns serious, laughing, or reflective. Although he seemed to be listening to the other guests, he did not hear a word they were saying, so absorbed was he in the pleasure of finding himself beside her, touching her hand as he served her. He bathed in a secret joy. Despite the eloquence of a few mutual glances, he was astonished at the reserve La Zambinella maintained toward him. Indeed, she had begun by pressing his foot and teasing him with the flirtatiousness of a woman in love and free to show it; but she suddenly wrapped herself in the modesty of a young girl, after hearing Sarrasine describe a trait which revealed the excessive violence of his character. When the supper became an orgy, the guests broke into song under the influence of the Peralta and the Pedro-Ximenes.[3] There were ravishing duets, songs from Calabria, Spanish seguidillas, Neapolitan canzonettas. Intoxication was in every eye, in the music, in hearts and voices alike. Suddenly an enchanting vivacity welled up, a gay abandon, an Italian warmth of feeling inconceivable to those acquainted only with Parisian gatherings, London routs, or Viennese circles. Jokes and words of love flew like bullets in a battle through laughter, profanities, and invocations to the Holy Virgin or il Bambino.[4] Someone lay down on a sofa and fell asleep. A girl was listening to a declaration of love unaware that she was spilling sherry on the tablecloth. In the midst of this disorder, La Zambinella remained thoughtful, as though terrorstruck. She refused to drink, perhaps she ate a bit too much; however, it is said that greediness in a woman is a charming quality. Admiring his mistress's modesty, Sarrasine thought seriously about the future.

"She probably wants to be married," he thought. He then turned his thoughts to the delights of this marriage. His whole life seemed too short to exhaust the springs of happiness he found in the depths of his soul. Vitagliani, who was sitting next to him, refilled his glass so often that, toward three in the morning, without being totally drunk, Sarrasine could no longer control his delirium. Impetuously, he picked up the woman, escaping into a kind of boudoir next to the salon, toward the door of which he had glanced more than once. The Italian woman was armed with a dagger.

"If you come any closer," she said, "I will be forced to plunge this weapon into your heart. Let me go! You would despise me. I have conceived too much respect for your character to surrender in this fashion. I don't want to betray the feeling you have for me."

3. Spanish dessert wines.

4. The Boy (i.e., the Christ Child).

"Oh no!" cried Sarrasine. "You cannot stifle a passion by stimulating it! Are you already so corrupt that, old in heart, you would act like a young courtesan who whets the emotions by which she plies her trade?"

"But today is Friday," she replied, frightened at the Frenchman's violence.

Sarrasine, who was not devout, broke into laughter. La Zambinella jumped up like a young deer and ran toward the salon. When Sarrasine appeared in her pursuit, he was greeted by an infernal burst of laughter.

He saw La Zambinella lying in a swoon upon a sofa. She was pale and drained by the extraordinary effort she had just made. Although Sarrasine knew little Italian, he heard his mistress saying in a low voice to Vitagliani: "But he will kill me!"

The sculptor was utterly confounded by this strange scene. He regained his senses. At first he stood motionless; then he found his voice, sat down next to his mistress, and assured her of his respect. He was able to divert his passion by addressing the most high-minded phrases to this woman; and in depicting his love, he used all the resources of that magical eloquence, that inspired intermediary which women rarely refuse to believe. When the guests were surprised by the first gleams of morning light, a woman suggested they go to Frascati. Everyone enthusiastically fell in with the idea of spending the day at the Villa Ludovisi. Vitagliani went down to hire some carriages. Sarrasine had the pleasure of leading La Zambinella to a phaeton. Once outside Rome, the gaiety which had been momentarily repressed by each person's battle with sleepiness suddenly revived. Men and women alike seemed used to this strange life, these ceaseless pleasures, this artist's impulsiveness which turns life into a perpetual party at which one laughed unreservedly. The sculptor's companion was the only one who seemed downcast.

"Are you ill?" Sarrasine asked her. "Would you rather go home?"

"I'm not strong enough to stand all these excesses," she replied. "I must be very careful; but with you I feel so well! Had it not been for you, I would never have stayed for supper; a sleepless night and I lose whatever bloom I have."

"You are so delicate," Sarrasine said, looking at the charming creature's pretty face.

"Orgies ruin the voice."

"Now that we're alone," the artist cried, "and you no longer need fear the outbursts of my passion, tell me that you love me."

"Why?" she replied. "What would be the use? I seemed pretty to you. But you are French and your feelings will pass. Ah, you would not love me as I long to be loved."

"How can you say that?"

"Not to satisfy any vulgar passion; purely. I abhor men perhaps even more than I hate women. I need to seek refuge in friendship. For me, the world is a desert. I am an accursed creature, condemned to understand happiness, to feel it, to desire it, and, like many others, forced to see it flee from me continually. Remember, sir, that I will not have deceived you. I forbid you to love me. I can be your devoted friend, for I admire your strength and your character. I need a brother, a protector. Be all that for me, but no more."

"Not love you!" Sarrasine cried. "But my dearest angel, you are my life, my happiness!"

"If I were to say one word, you would repulse me with horror."

"Coquette! Nothing can frighten me. Tell me you will cost me my future, that I will die in two months, that I will be damned merely for having kissed you."

He kissed her, despite La Zambinella's efforts to resist this passionate embrace. "Tell me you are a devil, that you want my money, my name, all my fame! Do you want me to give up being a sculptor? Tell me."

"And if I were not a woman?" La Zambinella asked in a soft silvery voice.

"What a joke!" Sarrasine cried. "Do you think you can deceive an artist's eye? Haven't I spent ten days devouring, scrutinizing, admiring your perfection? Only a woman could have this round, soft arm, these elegant curves. Oh, you want compliments."

She smiled at him sadly, and raising her eyes heavenward, she murmured: "Fatal beauty!"

At that moment her gaze had an indescribable expression of horror, so powerful and vivid that Sarrasine shuddered.

"Frenchman," she went on, "forget this moment of madness forever. I respect you, but as for love, do not ask it of me; that feeling is smothered in my heart. I have no heart!" she cried, weeping. "The stage where you saw me, that applause, that music, that fame I am condemned to, such is my life, I have no other. In a few hours you will not see me in the same way, the woman you love will be dead."

The sculptor made no reply. He was overcome with a dumb rage which oppressed his heart. He could only gaze with enflamed, burning eyes at this extraordinary woman. La Zambinella's weak voice, her manner, her movements and gestures marked with sorrow, melancholy, and discouragement, awakened all the wealth of passion in his soul. Each word was a goad. At that moment they reached Frascati. As the artist offered his mistress his arm to assist her in alighting, he felt her shiver.

"What is wrong? You would kill me," he cried, seeing her grow pale, "if I were even an innocent cause of your slightest unhappiness."

"A snake," she said, pointing to a grass snake which was sliding along a ditch. "I am afraid of those horrid creatures." Sarrasine crushed the snake's head with his heel.

"How can you be so brave?" La Zambinella continued, looking with visible horror at the dead reptile.

"Ah," the artist replied, smiling, "now do you dare deny you are a woman?"

They rejoined their companions and strolled through the woods of the Villa Ludovisi, which in those days belonged to Cardinal Cicognara. That morning fled too quickly for the enamored sculptor, but it was filled with a host of incidents which revealed to him the coquetry, the weakness, and the delicacy of this soft and enervated being. This was woman herself, with her sudden fears, her irrational whims, her instinctive worries, her impetuous boldness, her fussings, and her delicious sensibility. It happened that as they were wandering in the open countryside, the little group of merry singers saw in the distance some heavily armed men whose manner of dress was far from reassuring. Someone said, "They must be highwaymen," and everyone quickened his pace toward the refuge of the Cardinal's grounds. At this critical moment, Sarrasine saw from La Zambinella's pallor that she no longer had the strength to walk; he took her up in his arms and carried her for a while, running. When he came to a nearby arbor, he put her down.

"Explain to me," he said, "how this extreme weakness, which I would find hideous in any other woman, which would displease me and whose slightest indication would be almost enough to choke my love, pleases and charms me in you? Ah, how I love you," he went on. "All your faults, your terrors, your resentments, add an indefinable grace to your soul. I think I would detest a strong woman, a Sappho, a courageous creature, full of energy and passion. Oh, soft, frail creature, how could you be otherwise? That angelic voice, that delicate voice would be an anomaly coming from any body but yours."

"I cannot give you any hope," she said. "Stop speaking to me in this way, because they will make a fool of you. I cannot stop you from coming to the theater; but if you love me or if you are wise, you will come there no more. Listen, monsieur," she said in a low voice.

"Oh, be still," the impassioned artist said. "Obstacles make my love more ardent."

La Zambinella's graceful and modest attitude did not change, but she fell silent as though a terrible thought had revealed some misfortune to her. When it came time to return to Rome, she got into the four-seated coach, ordering the sculptor with imperious cruelty to return to Rome alone in the carriage. During the journey, Sarrasine resolved to kidnap La Zambinella. He spent the entire day making plans, each more outrageous than the other. At nightfall, as he was going out to inquire where his mistress's palazzo was located, he met one of his friends on the threshold.

"My dear fellow," he said, "our ambassador has asked me to invite you to his house tonight. He is giving a magnificent concert, and when I tell you that Zambinella will be there . . ."

"Zambinella," cried Sarrasine, intoxicated by the name, "I'm mad about her!"

"You're like everyone else," his friend replied.

"If you are my friends, you, Vien, Lauterbourg, and Allegrain,[5] will you help me do something after the party?" Sarrasine asked.

"It's not some cardinal to be killed? . . . not . . .?"

"No, no," Sarrasine said, "I'm not asking you to do anything an honest person couldn't do."

In a short time, the sculptor had arranged everything for the success of his undertaking. He was one of the last to arrive at the ambassador's, but he had come in a traveling carriage drawn by powerful horses and driven by one of the most enterprising *vetturini*[6] of Rome. The ambassador's palazzo was crowded; not without some difficulty, the sculptor, who was a stranger to everyone present, made his way to the salon where Zambinella was singing at that very moment.

"Is it out of consideration for the cardinals, bishops, and abbés present," Sarrasine asked, "that *she* is dressed like a man, that she is wearing a snood,[7] kinky hair, and a sword?"

"She? What she?" asked the old nobleman to whom Sarrasine had been speaking. "La Zambinella." "La Zambinella!" the Roman prince replied. "Are you joking? Where are you from? Has there ever been a woman on the Roman stage? And don't you know about the creatures who sing female roles in the Papal States? I am the one, monsieur, who gave Zambinella his voice.[8] I paid for everything that scamp ever had, even his singing teacher. Well, he has so little gratitude for the service I rendered him that he has never consented to set foot in my house. And yet, if he makes a fortune, he will owe it all to me."

Prince Chigi may well have gone on talking for some time; Sarrasine was not listening to him. A horrid truth had crept into his soul. It was as though he had been

5. Philippe Jacqes de Loutherbourg (1740–1812): painter; Christophe-Gabriel Allegrain (1710–1795): sculptor.
6. Coachmen.
7. Hairband.
8. In parts of Italy boys were castrated to keep their voice from changing; the successful ones became highly paid opera singers throughout Europe. They were not typically effeminate like Zambinella. The last major castrato role was in Meyerbeer's *Il Crociato in Egitto*, which premiered in Italy in 1824 and was a hit in Paris in 1825, only a few years before "Sarrasine" was written.

struck by lightning. He stood motionless, his eyes fixed on the false singer. His fiery gaze exerted a sort of magnetic influence on Zambinella, for the *musico* finally turned to look at Sarrasine, and at that moment his heavenly voice faltered. He trembled! An involuntary murmur escaping from the audience he had kept hanging on his lips completed his discomfiture; he sat down and cut short his aria. Cardinal Cicognara, who had glanced out the corner of his eye to see what had attracted his protégé's attention, then saw the Frenchman: he leaned over to one of his ecclesiastical aides-de-camp and appeared to be asking the sculptor's name. Having obtained the answer he sought, he regarded the artist with great attention and gave an order to an abbé, who quickly disappeared.

During this time, Zambinella, having recovered himself, once more began the piece he had so capriciously interrupted; but he sang it badly, and despite all the requests made to him, he refused to sing anything else. This was the first time he displayed that capricious tyranny for which he would later be as celebrated as for his talent and his vast fortune, due, as they said, no less to his voice than to his beauty.

"It is a woman," Sarrasine said, believing himself alone. "There is some hidden intrigue here. Cardinal Cicognara is deceiving the Pope and the whole city of Rome!"

The sculptor thereupon left the salon, gathered his friends together, and posted them out of sight in the courtyard of the palazzo. When Zambinella was confident that Sarrasine had departed, he appeared to regain his composure. Around midnight, having wandered through the rooms like a man seeking some enemy, the *musico* departed. As soon as he crossed the threshold of the palazzo, he was adroitly seized by men who gagged him with a handkerchief and drew him into the carriage Sarrasine had hired. Frozen with horror, Zambinella remained in a corner, not daring to move. He saw before him the terrible face of the artist, who was silent as death.

The journey was brief. Carried in Sarrasine's arms, Zambinella soon found himself in a dark, empty studio. Half dead, the singer remained in a chair, without daring to examine the statue of a woman in which he recognized his own features. He made no attempt to speak, but his teeth chattered. Sarrasine paced up and down the room. Suddenly he stopped in front of Zambinella.

"Tell me the truth," he pleaded in a low, altered voice. "You are a woman? Cardinal Cicognara . . ."

Zambinella fell to his knees, and in reply lowered his head.

"Ah, you are a woman," the artist cried in a delirium, "for even a . . ." He broke off. "No," he continued, "*he* would not be so cowardly."

"Ah, do not kill me," cried Zambinella, bursting into tears. "I only agreed to trick you to please my friends, who wanted to laugh."

"Laugh!" the sculptor replied in an infernal tone. "Laugh! Laugh! You dared play with a man's feelings, you?"

"Oh, have mercy!" Zambinella replied.

"I ought to kill you," Sarrasine cried, drawing his sword with a violent gesture. "However," he went on, in cold disdain, "were I to scour your body with this blade, would I find there one feeling to stifle, one vengeance to satisfy? You are nothing. If you were a man or a woman, I would kill you, but . . ."

Sarrasine made a gesture of disgust which forced him to turn away, whereupon he saw the statue.

"And it's an illusion," he cried. Then, turning to Zambinella: "A woman's heart was a refuge for me, a home. Have you any sisters who resemble you? Then die! But no, you shall live. Isn't leaving you alive condemning you to something worse than death? It is neither my blood nor my existence that I regret, but the future and my heart's fortune. Your feeble hand has destroyed my happiness. What hope can I strip from you for all those you have blighted? You have dragged me down to your level. *To love, to be loved!* are henceforth meaningless words for me, as they are for you. I shall forever think of this imaginary woman when I see a real woman." He indicated the statue with a gesture of despair. "I shall always have the memory of a celestial harpy[9] who thrusts its talons into all my manly feelings, and who will stamp all other women with a seal of imperfection! Monster! You who can give life to nothing. For me, you have wiped women from the earth."

Sarrasine sat down before the terrified singer. Two huge tears welled from his dry eyes, rolled down his manly cheeks, and fell to the ground: two tears of rage, two bitter and burning tears.

"No more love! I am dead to all pleasure, to every human emotion."

So saying, he seized a hammer and hurled it at the statue with such extraordinary force that he missed it. He thought he had destroyed this monument to his folly, and then took up his sword and brandished it to kill the singer. Zambinella uttered piercing screams. At that moment, three men entered and at once the sculptor fell, stabbed by three stiletto thrusts.

"On behalf of Cardinal Cicognara," one of them said.

"It is a good deed worthy of a Christian," replied the Frenchman as he died. These sinister messengers informed Zambinella of the concern of his protector, who was waiting at the door in a closed carriage, to take him away as soon as he had been rescued.

"But," Mme de Rochefide asked me, "what connection is there between this story and the little old man we saw at the Lantys'?"

"Madame, Cardinal Cicognara took possession of Zambinella's statue and had it executed in marble; today it is in the Albani Museum.[1] There, in 1791, the Lanty family found it and asked Vien to copy it. The portrait in which you saw Zambinella at twenty, a second after having seen him at one hundred, later served for Girodet's *Endymion;*[2] you will have recognized its type in the Adonis."

"But this Zambinella—he or she?"

"He, madame, is none other than Marianina's great-uncle. Now you can readily see what interest Mme de Lanty has in hiding the source of a fortune which comes from—"

"Enough!" she said, gesturing to me imperiously. We sat for a moment plunged in the deepest silence.

"Well?" I said to her.

"Ah," she exclaimed, standing up and pacing up and down the room. She looked at me and spoke in an altered voice. "You have given me a disgust for life and for passions that will last a long time. Excepting for monsters, don't all human feelings come down to the same thing, to horrible disappointments? Mothers, our children kill us either by their bad behavior or by their lack of affection. Wives, we are deceived. Mistresses, we are forsaken, abandoned. Does friendship even exist? I would become a nun tomorrow did I not know that I can remain unmoved as a rock amid the storms of life. If the Christian's future is also an illusion, at least it is not destroyed until after death. Leave me."

"Ah," I said, "you know how to punish."

---

9. A savage mythological creature with a woman's head.
1. The Villa Albani in Rome held an important collection of ancient art from 1760 until seized and taken to Paris by Napoleon.

2. Anne-Louis Girodet-Trioson (1767–1824), French painter. Endymion: a beautiful youth in Greek mythology, beloved of Selene, the goddess of the moon.

"Am I wrong?"

"Yes," I replied, with a kind of courage. "In telling this story, which is fairly well known in Italy, I have been able to give you a fine example of the progress made by civilization today. They no longer create these unfortunate creatures."

"Paris is a very hospitable place," she said. "It accepts everything, shameful fortunes and bloodstained fortunes. Crime and infamy can find asylum here; only virtue has no altars here. Yes, pure souls have their home in heaven! No one will have known me. I am proud of that!"

And the Marquise remained pensive.

Edgar Allan Poe
1809–1849

"The death . . . of a beautiful woman is, unquestionably, the most poetical topic in the world." So wrote Edgar Allan poe about his poem "The Raven," in his essay "The Philosophy of Composition" (1846). Life might have suggested otherwise. His actor father vanished while Poe was an infant, and he watched his struggling actress mother succumb to the torments of tuberculosis before his third birthday. He was taken home (but never adopted) by a flint-hearted businessman, John Allan, whose affectionate wife, Frances, died in 1830, also of tuberculosis. Poe attended the University of Virginia and dropped out, entered West Point and contrived to get himself expelled. Thus began a life of drinking and quarreling. Brilliant and driven, Poe gained esteem but never enough money from his poems, stories, and incessant book reviewing. In 1835 he married his thirteen-year-old cousin Virginia Clemm, only to watch her too die of tuberculosis shortly after he published his essay on the philosophy of compositions. Poe himself died in a stupor three years later.

In Poe's experience, then, the death of a beautiful woman was hardly a beautiful death. Rather, Poe was long regarded (in France especially) as the quintessential Romantic writer on account of the unrelieved extremity of emotion and situation in his writings. His works combine the sexually tinged violence against others that we now call sadism with the self-abasement that we call masochism. Poe excelled at bringing to the surface the psychic "blackness of darkness," as "The Pit and the Pendulum" calls it. "The mere consciousness of existence, without thought," as portrayed in this story, replaces the philosopher Jean-Jacques Rousseau's blissful reveries with nightmare, in anticipation of Freud's discovery of the unresolved and amoral drives that surface in dreams. If sado-masochistic fantasy can be poetical, that is because poetry for Poe meant deep-rooted emotion, free from prosaic learning or transient excitement. Poe's attacks on the body and the senses are meant to release sublime energies. Forcibly deprived of its external anchors and drifting in melancholy or in terror, the soul achieves its pure state.

The Pit and the Pendulum[1]

I was sick—sick unto death with that long agony; and when they at length unbound me, and I was permitted to sit, I felt that my senses were leaving me. The sentence—the dread sentence of death—was the last of distinct accentuation which reached my

---

1. The story is prefaced by four lines of Latin poetry that translate as follows: "Here an unholy mob of torturers, with an unquenchable thirst for innocent blood, fed their long frenzy. Our homeland is safe now, the baneful pit destroyed, and what was once a place of savage death is now a scene of life and health." An additional note reads: "Quatrain composed for the gates of a market to be erected upon the site of the Jacobin Club House at Paris." The Jacobins were the most radical group in the French Revolution, responsible for the Terror of 1793. Poe's attribution appears to be groundless.

ears. After that, the sound of the inquisitorial voices seemed merged in one dreamy indeterminate hum. It conveyed to my soul the idea of *revolution*—perhaps from its association in fancy with the burr of a mill-wheel. This only for a brief period; for presently I heard no more. Yet, for a while, I saw; but with how terrible an exaggeration! I saw the lips of the black-robed judges. They appeared to me white—whiter than the sheet upon which I trace these words—and thin even to grotesqueness; thin with the intensity of their expression of firmness—of immoveable resolution—of stern contempt of human torture. I saw that the decrees of what to me was Fate, were still issuing from those lips. I saw them writhe with a deadly locution. I saw them fashion the syllables of my name; and I shuddered because no sound succeeded. I saw, too, for a few moments of delirious horror, the soft and nearly imperceptible waving of the sable draperies which enwrapped the walls of the apartment. And then my vision fell upon the seven tall candles upon the table. At first they wore the aspect of charity, and seemed white slender angels who would save me; but then, all at once, there came a most deadly nausea over my spirit, and I felt every fibre in my frame thrill as if I had touched the wire of a galvanic battery,[2] while the angel forms became meaningless spectres, with heads of flame, and I saw that from them there would be no help. And then there stole into my fancy, like a rich musical note, the thought of what sweet rest there must be in the grave. The thought came gently and stealthily, and it seemed long before it attained full appreciation; but just as my spirit came at length properly to feel and entertain it, the figures of the judges vanished, as if magically, from before me; the tall candles sank into nothingness; their flames went out utterly; the blackness of darkness supervened; all sensations appeared swallowed up in a mad rushing descent as of the soul into Hades. Then silence, and stillness, and night were the universe.

I had swooned; but still will not say that all of consciousness was lost. What of it there remained I will not attempt to define, or even to describe; yet all was not lost. In the deepest slumber—no! In delirium—no! In a swoon—no! In death—no! even in the grave all *is not* lost. Else there is no immortality for man. Arousing from the most profound of slumbers, we break the gossamer web of *some* dream. Yet in a second afterward, (so frail may that web have been) we remember not that we have dreamed. In the return to life from the swoon there are two stages; first, that of the sense of mental or spiritual; secondly, that of the sense of physical, existence. It seems probable that if, upon reaching the second stage, we could recall the impressions of the first, we should find these impressions eloquent in memories of the gulf beyond. And that gulf is—what? How at least shall we distinguish its shadows from those of the tomb? But if the impressions of what I have termed the first stage, are not, at will, recalled, yet, after long interval, do they not come unbidden, while we marvel whence they come? He who has never swooned, is not he who finds strange palaces and wildly familiar faces in coals that glow; is not he who beholds floating in mid-air the sad visions that the many may not view; is not he who ponders over the perfume of some novel flower—is not he whose brain grows bewildered with the meaning of some musical cadence which has never before arrested his attention.

Amid frequent and thoughtful endeavors to remember; amid earnest struggles to regather some token of the state of seeming nothingness into which my soul had lapsed, there have been moments when I have dreamed of success; there have been

2. Luigi Volta invented the chemical battery in 1792, named for his fellow scientist Luigi Galvani. Galvanism was thought to be a means to revive the dead.

brief, very brief periods when I have conjured up remembrances which the lucid reason of a later epoch assures me could have had reference only to that condition of seeming unconsciousness. These shadows of memory tell, indistinctly, of tall figures that lifted and bore me in silence down—down—still down—till a hideous dizziness oppressed me at the mere idea of the interminableness of the descent. They tell also of a vague horror at my heart, on account of that heart's unnatural stillness. Then comes a sense of sudden motionlessness throughout all things; as if those who bore me (a ghastly train!) had outrun, in their descent, the limits of the limitless, and paused from the wearisomeness of their toil. After this I call to mind flatness and dampness; and then all is *madness*—the madness of a memory which busies itself among forbidden things.

Very suddenly there came back to my soul motion and sound—the tumultuous motion of the heart, and, in my ears, the sound of its beating. Then a pause in which all is blank. Then again sound, and motion, and touch—a tingling sensation pervading my frame. Then the mere consciousness of existence,[3] without thought—a condition which lasted long. Then, very suddenly, *thought,* and shuddering terror, and earnest endeavor to comprehend my true state. Then a strong desire to lapse into insensibility. Then a rushing revival of soul and a successful effort to move. And now a full memory of the trial, of the judges, of the sable draperies, of the sentence, of the sickness, of the swoon. Then entire forgetfulness of all that followed; of all that a later day and much earnestness of endeavor have enabled me vaguely to recall.

So far, I had not opened my eyes. I felt that I lay upon my back, unbound. I reached out my hand, and it fell heavily upon something damp and hard. There I suffered it to remain for many minutes, while I strove to imagine where and *what* I could be. I longed, yet dared not to employ my vision. I dreaded the first glance at objects around me. It was not that I feared to look upon things horrible, but that I grew aghast lest there should be *nothing* to see. At length, with a wild desperation at heart, I quickly unclosed my eyes. My worst thoughts, then, were confirmed. The blackness of eternal night encompassed me. I struggled for breath. The intensity of the darkness seemed to oppress and stifle me. The atmosphere was intolerably close. I still lay quietly, and made effort to exercise my reason. I brought to mind the inquisitorial proceedings, and attempted from that point to deduce my real condition. The sentence had passed; and it appeared to me that a very long interval of time had since elapsed. Yet not for a moment did I suppose myself actually dead. Such a supposition, notwithstanding what we read in fiction, is altogether inconsistent with real existence;—but where and in what state was I? The condemned to death, I knew, perished usually at the *autos-da-fé*,[4] and one of these had been held on the very night of the day of my trial. Had I been remanded to my dungeon, to await the next sacrifice, which would not take place for many months? This I at once saw could not be. Victims had been in immediate demand. Moreover, my dungeon, as well as all the condemned cells at Toledo, had stone floors, and light was not altogether excluded.

A fearful idea now suddenly drove the blood in torrents upon my heart, and for a brief period, I once more relapsed into insensibility. Upon recovering, I at once started to my feet, trembling convulsively in every fibre. I thrust my arms wildly above and around me in all directions. I felt nothing; yet dreaded to move a step, lest I should be impeded by the walls of a *tomb*. Perspiration burst from every pore, and

---

3. See Rousseau's "Reverie," page 98.   4. Burning of heretics by the Inquisition.

stood in cold big beads upon my forehead. The agony of suspense grew at length intolerable, and I cautiously moved forward, with my arms extended, and my eyes straining from their sockets, in the hope of catching some faint ray of light. I proceeded for many paces; but still all was blackness and vacancy. I breathed more freely. It seemed evident that mine was not, at least, the most hideous of fates.

And now, as I still continued to step cautiously onward, there came thronging upon my recollection a thousand vague rumors of the horrors of Toledo. Of the dungeons there had been strange things narrated—fables I had always deemed them—but yet strange, and too ghastly to repeat, save in a whisper. Was I left to perish of starvation in this subterranean world of darkness; or what fate, perhaps even more fearful, awaited me? That the result would be death, and a death of more than customary bitterness, I knew too well the character of my judges to doubt. The mode and the hour were all that occupied or distracted me.

My outstretched hands at length encountered some solid obstruction. It was a wall, seemingly of stone masonry—very smooth, slimy, and cold. I followed it up; stepping with all the careful distrust with which certain antique narratives had inspired me. This process, however, afforded me no means of ascertaining the dimensions of my dungeon; as I might make its circuit, and return to the point whence I set out, without being aware of the fact; so perfectly uniform seemed the wall. I therefore sought the knife which had been in my pocket, when led into the inquisitorial chamber; but it was gone; my clothes had been exchanged for a wrapper of coarse serge. I had thought of forcing the blade in some minute crevice of the masonry, so as to identify my point of departure. The difficulty, nevertheless, was but trivial; although, in the disorder of my fancy, it seemed at first insuperable. I tore a part of the hem from the robe and placed the fragment at full length, and at right angles to the wall. In groping my way around the prison, I could not fail to encounter this rag upon completing the circuit. So, at least I thought: but I had not counted upon the extent of the dungeon, or upon my own weakness. The ground was moist and slippery. I staggered onward for some time, when I stumbled and fell. My excessive fatigue induced me to remain prostrate; and sleep soon overtook me as I lay.

Upon awaking, and stretching forth an arm, I found beside me a loaf and a pitcher with water. I was too much exhausted to reflect upon this circumstance, but ate and drank with avidity. Shortly afterward, I resumed my tour around the prison, and with much toil, came at last upon the fragment of the serge. Up to the period when I fell I had counted fifty-two paces, and upon resuming my walk, I had counted forty-eight more;—when I arrived at the rag. There were in all, then, a hundred paces; and, admitting two paces to the yard, I presumed the dungeon to be fifty yards in circuit. I had met, however, with many angles in the wall, and thus I could form no guess at the shape of the vault; for vault I could not help supposing it to be.

I had little object—certainly no hope—in these researches; but a vague curiosity prompted me to continue them. Quitting the wall, I resolved to cross the area of the enclosure. At first I proceeded with extreme caution, for the floor, although seemingly of solid material, was treacherous with slime. At length, however, I took courage, and did not hesitate to step firmly; endeavoring to cross in as direct a line as possible. I had advanced some ten or twelve paces in this manner, when the remnant of the torn hem of my robe became entangled between my legs. I stepped on it, and fell violently on my face.

In the confusion attending my fall, I did not immediately apprehend a somewhat startling circumstance, which yet, in a few seconds afterward, and while I still lay prostrate, arrested my attention. It was this—my chin rested upon the floor of the prison, but my lips and the upper portion of my head, although seemingly at a less elevation than the chin, touched nothing. At the same time my forehead seemed bathed in a clammy vapor, and the peculiar smell of decayed fungus arose to my nostrils. I put forward my arm, and shuddered to find that I had fallen at the very brink of a circular pit, whose extent, of course, I had no means of ascertaining at the moment. Groping about the masonry just below the margin, I succeeded in dislodging a small fragment, and let it fall into the abyss. For many seconds I hearkened to its reverberations as it dashed against the sides of the chasm in its descent; at length there was a sullen plunge into water, succeeded by loud echoes. At the same moment there came a sound resembling the quick opening, and as rapid closing of a door overhead, while a faint gleam of light flashed suddenly through the gloom, and as suddenly faded away.

I saw clearly the doom which had been prepared for me, and congratulated myself upon the timely accident by which I had escaped. Another step before my fall, and the world had seen me no more. And the death just avoided, was of that very character which I had regarded as fabulous and frivolous in the tales respecting the Inquisition. To the victims of its tyranny, there was the choice of death with its direst physical agonies, or death with its most hideous moral horrors. I had been reserved for the latter. By long suffering my nerves had been unstrung, until I trembled at the sound of my own voice, and had become in every respect a fitting subject for the species of torture which awaited me.

Shaking in every limb, I groped my way back to the wall; resolving there to perish rather than risk the terrors of the wells, of which my imagination now pictured many in various positions about the dungeon. In other conditions of mind I might have had courage to end my misery at once by a plunge into one of these abysses; but now I was the veriest of cowards. Neither could I forget what I had read of these pits—that the *sudden* extinction of life formed no part of their most horrible plan.

Agitation of spirit kept me awake for many long hours; but at length I again slumbered. Upon arousing, I found by my side, as before, a loaf and a pitcher of water. A burning thirst consumed me, and I emptied the vessel at a draught. It must have been drugged; for scarcely had I drunk, before I became irresistibly drowsy. A deep sleep fell upon me—a sleep like that of death. How long it lasted of course, I know not; but when, once again, I unclosed my eyes, the objects around me were visible. By a wild sulphurous lustre, the origin of which I could not at first determine, I was enabled to see the extent and aspect of the prison.

In its size I had been greatly mistaken. The whole circuit of its walls did not exceed twenty-five yards. For some minutes this fact occasioned me a world of vain trouble; vain indeed! for what could be of less importance, under the terrible circumstances which environed me, than the mere dimensions of my dungeon? But my soul took a wild interest in trifles, and I busied myself in endeavors to account for the error I had committed in my measurement. The truth at length flashed upon me. In my first attempt at exploration I had counted fifty-two paces, up to the period when I fell; I must then have been within a pace or two of the fragment of serge; in fact, I had nearly performed the circuit of the vault. I then slept, and upon awaking, I must have returned upon my steps—thus supposing the circuit nearly double what it actually was. My confusion of mind prevented me from observing that I began my tour with the wall to the left, and ended it with the wall to the right.

I had been deceived, too, in respect to the shape of the enclosure. In feeling my way I had found many angles, and thus deduced an idea of great irregularity; so potent is the effect of total darkness upon one arousing from lethargy or sleep! The angles were simply those of a few slight depressions, or niches, at odd intervals. The general shape of the prison was square. What I had taken for masonry seemed now to be iron, or some other metal, in huge plates, whose sutures or joints occasioned the depression. The entire surface of this metallic enclosure was rudely daubed in all the hideous and repulsive devices to which the charnel superstition of the monks has given rise. The figures of fiends in aspects of menace, with skeleton forms, and other more really fearful images, overspread and disfigured the walls. I observed that the outlines of these monstrosities were sufficiently distinct, but that the colors seemed faded and blurred, as if from the effects of a damp atmosphere. I now noticed the floor, too, which was of stone. In the centre yawned the circular pit from whose jaws I had escaped; but it was the only one in the dungeon.

All this I saw indistinctly and by much effort: for my personal condition had been greatly changed during slumber. I now lay upon my back, and at full length, on a species of low framework of wood. To this I was securely bound by a long strap resembling a surcingle.[5] It passed in many convolutions about my limbs and body, leaving at liberty only my head, and my left arm to such extent that I could, by dint of much exertion, supply myself with food from an earthen dish which lay by my side on the floor. I saw, to my horror, that the pitcher had been removed. I say to my horror; for I was consumed with intolerable thirst. This thirst it appeared to be the design of my persecutors to stimulate: for the food in the dish was meat pungently seasoned.

Looking upward, I surveyed the ceiling of my prison. It was some thirty or forty feet overhead, and constructed much as the side walls. In one of its panels a very singular figure riveted my whole attention. It was the painted figure of Time as he is commonly represented, save that, in lieu of a scythe, he held what, at a casual glance, I supposed to be the pictured image of a huge pendulum such as we see on antique clocks. There was something, however, in the appearance of this machine which caused me to regard it more attentively. While I gazed directly upward at it (for its position was immediately over my own) I fancied that I saw it in motion. In an instant afterward the fancy was confirmed. Its sweep was brief, and of course slow. I watched it for some minutes, somewhat in fear, but more in wonder. Wearied at length with observing its dull movement, I turned my eyes upon the other objects in the cell.

A slight noise attracted my notice, and, looking to the floor, I saw several enormous rats traversing it. They had issued from the well, which lay just within view to my right. Even then, while I gazed, they came up in troops, hurriedly, with ravenous eyes, allured by the scent of the meat. From this it required much effort and attention to scare them away.

It might have been half an hour, perhaps even an hour, (for I could take but imperfect note of time) before I again cast my eyes upward. What I then saw confounded and amazed me. The sweep of the pendulum had increased in extent by nearly a yard. As a natural consequence, its velocity was also much greater. But what mainly disturbed me was the idea that it had perceptibly *descended.* I now observed—with what horror it is needless to say—that its nether extremity was formed of a crescent of glittering steel, about a foot in length from horn to horn; the horns upward, and the under edge evidently as keen as that of a razor. Like a razor also, it

5. A strap for a horse pack.

seemed massy and heavy, tapering from the edge into a solid and broad structure above. It was appended to a weighty rod of brass, and the whole *hissed* as it swung through the air.

I could no longer doubt the doom prepared for me by monkish ingenuity in torture. My cognizance of the pit had become known to the inquisitorial agents—*the pit* whose horrors had been destined for so bold a recusant as myself—*the pit,* typical of hell, and regarded by rumor as the Ultima Thule[6] of all their punishments. The plunge into this pit I had avoided by the merest of accidents, and I knew that surprise, or entrapment into torment, formed an important portion of all the grotesquerie of these dungeon deaths. Having failed to fall, it was no part of the demon plan to hurl me into the abyss; and thus (there being no alternative) a different and a milder destruction awaited me. Milder! I half smiled in my agony as I thought of such application of such a term.

What boots it to tell of the long, long hours of horror more than mortal, during which I counted the rushing vibrations of the steel! Inch by inch—line by line—with a descent only appreciable at intervals that seemed ages—down and still down it came! Days passed—it might have been that many days passed—ere it swept so closely over me as to fan me with its acrid breath. The odor of the sharp steel forced itself into my nostrils. I prayed—I wearied heaven with my prayer for its more speedy descent. I grew frantically mad, and struggled to force myself upward against the sweep of the fearful scimitar. And then I fell suddenly calm, and lay smiling at the glittering death, as a child at some rare bauble.

There was another interval of utter insensibility; it was brief; for, upon again lapsing into life there had been no perceptible descent in the pendulum. But it might have been long; for I knew there were demons who took note of my swoon, and who could have arrested the vibration at pleasure. Upon my recovery, too, I felt very—oh, inexpressibly sick and weak, as if through long inanition.[7] Even amid the agonies of that period, the human nature craved food. With painful effort I outstretched my left arm as far as my bonds permitted, and took possession of the small remnant which had been spared me by the rats. As I put a portion of it within my lips, there rushed to my mind a half formed thought of joy—of hope. Yet what business had *I* with hope? It was, as I say, a half formed thought—man has many such which are never completed. I felt that it was of joy—of hope; but I felt also that it had perished in its formation. In vain I struggled to perfect—to regain it. Long suffering had nearly annihilated all my ordinary powers of mind. I was an imbecile—an idiot.

The vibration of the pendulum was at right angles to my length. I saw that the crescent was designed to cross the region of the heart. It would fray the serge of my robe—it would return and repeat its operations—again—and again. Notwithstanding its terrifically wide sweep (some thirty feet or more) and the hissing vigor of its descent, sufficient to sunder these very walls of iron, still the fraying of my robe would be all that, for several minutes, it would accomplish. And at this thought I paused. I dared not go farther than this reflection. I dwelt upon it with a pertinacity of attention—as if, in so dwelling, I could arrest *here* the descent of the steel. I forced myself to ponder upon the sound of the crescent as it should pass across the garment—upon the peculiar thrilling sensation which the friction of cloth produces on the nerves. I pondered upon all this frivolity until my teeth were on edge.

---

6. Farthest limit.   7. Starvation.

Down—steadily down it crept. I took a frenzied pleasure in contrasting its downward with its lateral velocity. To the right—to the left—far and wide—with the shriek of a damned spirit; to my heart with the stealthy pace of the tiger! I alternately laughed and howled as the one or the other idea grew predominant.

Down—certainly, relentlessly down! It vibrated within three inches of my bosom! I struggled violently, furiously, to free my left arm. This was free only from the elbow to the hand. I could reach the latter, from the platter beside me, to my mouth, with great effort, but no farther. Could I have broken the fastenings above the elbow, I would have seized and attempted to arrest the pendulum. I might as well have attempted to arrest an avalanche!

Down—still unceasingly—still inevitably down! I gasped and struggled at each vibration. I shrunk convulsively at its every sweep. My eyes followed its outward or upward whirls with the eagerness of the most unmeaning despair; they closed themselves spasmodically at the descent, although death would have been a relief, oh! how unspeakable! Still I quivered in every nerve to think how slight a sinking of the machinery would precipitate that keen, glistening axe upon my bosom. It was *hope* that prompted the nerve to quiver—the frame to shrink. It was *hope*—the hope that triumphs on the rack—that whispers to the death-condemned even in the dungeons of the Inquisition.

I saw that some ten or twelve vibrations would bring the steel in actual contact with my robe, and with this observation there suddenly came over my spirit all the keen, collected calmness of despair. For the first time during many hours—or perhaps days—I *thought*. It now occurred to me that the bandage, or surcingle, which enveloped me, was *unique*. I was tied by no separate cord. The first stroke of the razorlike crescent athwart any portion of the band, would so detach it that it might be unwound from my person by means of my left hand. But how fearful, in that case, the proximity of the steel! The result of the slightest struggle how deadly! Was it likely, moreover, that the minions of the torturer had not foreseen and provided for this possibility! Was it probable that the bandage crossed my bosom in the track of the pendulum? Dreading to find my faint, and, as it seemed, my last hope frustrated, I so far elevated my head as to obtain a distinct view of my breast. The surcingle enveloped my limbs and body close in all directions—*save in the path of the destroying crescent.*

Scarcely had I dropped my head back into its original position, when there flashed upon my mind what I cannot better describe than as the unformed half of that idea of deliverance to which I have previously alluded, and of which a moiety only floated indeterminately through my brain when I raised food to my burning lips. The whole thought was now present—feeble, scarcely sane, scarcely definite,—but still entire. I proceeded at once, with the nervous energy of despair, to attempt its execution.

For many hours the immediate vicinity of the low framework upon which I lay, had been literally swarming with rats. They were wild, bold, ravenous; their red eyes glaring upon me as if they waited but for motionlessness on my part to make me their prey. "To what food," I thought, "have they been accustomed in the well?"

They had devoured, in spite of all my efforts to prevent them, all but a small remnant of the contents of the dish. I had fallen into an habitual see-saw, or wave of the hand about the platter: and, at length, the unconscious uniformity of the movement deprived it of effect. In their voracity the vermin frequently fastened their sharp fangs in my fingers. With the particles of the oily and spicy viand which now remained, I thoroughly rubbed the bandage wherever I could reach it; then, raising my hand from the floor, I lay breathlessly still.

At first the ravenous animals were startled and terrified at the change—at the cessation of movement. They shrank alarmedly back; many sought the well. But this was only for a moment. I had not counted in vain upon their voracity. Observing that I remained without motion, one or two of the boldest leaped upon the frame-work, and smelt at the surcingle. This seemed the signal for a general rush. Forth from the well they hurried in fresh troops. They clung to the wood—they overran it, and leaped in hundreds upon my person. The measured movement of the pendulum disturbed them not at all. Avoiding its strokes they busied themselves with the anointed bandage. They pressed—they swarmed upon me in ever accumulating heaps. They writhed upon my throat; their cold lips sought my own; I was half stifled by their thronging pressure; disgust, for which the world has no name, swelled my bosom, and chilled, with a heavy clamminess, my heart. Yet one minute, and I felt that the struggle would be over. Plainly I perceived the loosening of the bandage. I knew that in more than one place it must be already severed. With a more than human resolution I lay *still*.

Nor had I erred in my calculations—nor had I endured in vain. I at length felt that I was *free*. The surcingle hung in ribands from my body. But the stroke of the pendulum already pressed upon my bosom. It had divided the serge of the robe. It had cut through the linen beneath. Twice again it swung, and a sharp sense of pain shot through every nerve. But the moment of escape had arrived. At a wave of my hand my deliverers hurried tumultuously away. With a steady movement—cautious, sidelong, shrinking, and slow—I slid from the embrace of the bandage and beyond the reach of the scimitar. For the moment, at least, *I was free*.

Free!—and in the grasp of the Inquisition! I had scarcely stepped from my wooden bed of horror upon the stone floor of the prison, when the motion of the hellish machine ceased and I beheld it drawn up, by some invisible force, through the ceiling. This was a lesson which I took desperately to heart. My every motion was undoubtedly watched. Free!—I had but escaped death in one form of agony, to be delivered unto worse than death in some other. With that thought I rolled my eyes nervously around on the barriers of iron that hemmed me in. Something unusual—some change which, at first, I could not appreciate distinctly—it was obvious, had taken place in the apartment. For many minutes of a dreamy and trembling abstraction, I busied myself in vain, unconnected conjecture. During this period, I became aware, for the first time, of the origin of the sulphurous light which illumined the cell. It proceeded from a fissure, about half an inch in width, extending entirely around the prison at the base of the walls, which thus appeared, and were, completely separated from the floor. I endeavored, but of course in vain, to look through the aperture.

As I arose from the attempt, the mystery of the alteration in the chamber broke at once upon my understanding. I have observed that, although the outlines of the figures upon the walls were sufficiently distinct, yet the colours seemed blurred and indefinite. These colours had now assumed, and were momentarily assuming, a startling and most intense brilliancy, that gave to the spectral and fiendish portraitures an aspect that might have thrilled even firmer nerves than my own. Demon eyes, of a wild and ghastly vivacity, glared upon me in a thousand directions, where none had been visible before, and gleamed with the lurid lustre of a fire that I could not force my imagination to regard as unreal.

Unreal!—Even while I breathed there came to my nostrils the breath of the vapour of heated iron! A suffocating odour pervaded the prison! A deeper glow settled each moment in the eyes that glared at my agonies! A richer tint of crimson diffused itself over the pictured horrors of blood. I panted! I gasped for breath! There could be no doubt of the design of my tormentors—oh! most unrelenting! oh! most demoniac of men! I shrank from the glowing metal to the centre of the cell. Amid the thought of the fiery destruction that impended, the idea of the coolness of the well came over my soul like balm. I rushed to its deadly brink. I threw my straining vision below. The glare from the enkindled roof illumined its inmost recesses. Yet, for a wild moment, did my spirit refuse to comprehend the meaning of what I saw. At length it forced—it wrestled its way into my soul—it burned itself in upon my shuddering reason.—Oh! for a voice to speak!—oh! horror!—oh! any horror but this! With a shriek, I rushed from the margin, and buried my face in my hands—weeping bitterly.

The heat rapidly increased, and once again I looked up, shuddering as with a fit of the ague.[8] There had been a second change in the cell—and now the change was obviously in the *form*. As before, it was in vain that I, at first, endeavoured to appreciate or understand what was taking place. But not long was I left in doubt. The Inquisitorial vengeance had been hurried by my two-fold escape, and there was to be no more dallying with the King of Terrors. The room had been square. I saw that two of its iron angles were now acute—two, consequently, obtuse. The fearful difference quickly increased with a low rumbling or moaning sound. In an instant the apartment had shifted its form into that of a lozenge. But the alteration stopped not here—I neither hoped nor desired it to stop. I could have clasped the red walls to my bosom as a garment of eternal peace. "Death," I said, "any death but that of the pit!" Fool! might I have not known that *into the pit* it was the object of the burning iron to urge me? Could I resist its glow? or, if even that, could I withstand its pressure? And now, flatter and flatter grew the lozenge, with a rapidity that left me no time for contemplation. Its centre, and of course, its greatest width, came just over the yawning gulf. I shrank back—but the closing walls pressed me resistlessly onward. At length for my seared and writhing body there was no longer an inch of foothold on the firm floor of the prison. I struggled no more, but the agony of my soul found vent in one loud, long, and final scream of despair. I felt that I tottered upon the brink—I averted my eyes—

There was a discordant hum of human voices! There was a loud blast as of many trumpets! There was a harsh grating as of a thousand thunders! The fiery walls rushed back! An out-stretched arm caught my own as I fell, fainting, into the abyss. It was that of General Lasalle.[9] The French army had entered Toledo. The Inquisition was in the hands of its enemies.

[END OF THE ROMANTIC FANTASTIC]

Gustave Flaubert
1821–1880

Gustave Flaubert was almost twenty-eight when he left France for what was then called "the Orient," a journey that was to last from November 1849 to June 1851. Journeys to the Middle East were in fashion. This was partly because Napoleon's expedition to Egypt (1798–1801) and

---

8. Chills, accompanying a malarial fever.

9. Antoine Charles Louis Lasalle (1775–1809), a hero of Napoleon's Spanish campaign of 1808.

France's strong continuing influence had opened the region to tourism, which increased after France conquered Algeria in 1847. In part, too, people had become full of disgust with the sordid money- and title-grubbing and the social inertia that had followed the epoch of Napoleonic glory. Many of the alienated escaped into exoticism. But in the profundity of his personal alienation, Flaubert had few if any competitors.

Born in 1821 in Rouen, the son of a doctor, Flaubert abandoned the study of law after a brief and not very successful experience. Supported by a private income, he devoted himself with an almost theological intensity to writing. He never married or had an ordinary job, and it was largely writing (including voluminous letters to lovers who were also talented writers) that gave shape to the rest of his life. A perfectionist who worked to discipline his romantic flamboyance, he tried to achieve perfect sentences and perfect detachment. His most famous novel, *Madame Bovary* (1857), scandalized and confused its readers, who couldn't tell whether its author condemned the hungrily misguided aspirations of its adulterous heroine, or secretly identified with them. Prosecuted for "offense to public and religious morality," Flaubert was acquitted but given a severe reprimand and forced to pay the costs of the trial. Subsequent novels added to the sense of public incomprehension, for Flaubert remained absent from his work, refusing to give directions as to how readers were supposed to feel. About *Salammbô* (1862), which fled from the banality of contemporary France into the archaeologically precise strangeness of ancient Carthage, Flaubert famously remarked that few would ever guess how sad he had to be in order to resuscitate this lost kingdom.

Sentimental Education (1869) is set in Paris in the 1840s (the period of Flaubert's own beginnings as a writer) and roughly follows his early passion for an older married woman. But it, too, is distinguished by an apparent disaffection from nearly everything the characters say and do. Franz Kafka, who sets the twentieth-century standard for disaffection, once said that each time he opened Flaubert's book, he felt perfectly at home. *Three Tales* (1877), which includes "A Simple Heart," was a success with the public, but it is simpler only in appearance. Readers have never decided whether Flaubert is or isn't ironic about the servant protagonist of "A Simple Heart," whose life seems empty and who worships a stuffed parrot. Convinced that it was style rather than content that should be decisive, Flaubert once expressed the desire to write a text about "nothing." His extreme horror of cliché and sense of the nothingness lurking behind everyday life are exemplified in two further works, *Bouvard and Pécuchet* and the *Dictionary of Received Ideas,* which were published after his death in 1880.

In 1876, at the funeral of George Sand, a pioneer feminist writer and one of the most famous figures of her generation, Flaubert wept for the loss of his dear friend and long-time correspondent—and for the bad timing that took her away just as he was writing something "exclusively" for her. Sand, who couldn't understand Flaubert's unwillingness to take a moral stand in his fiction, had urged him to write "something down to earth that everybody can enjoy." "A Simple Heart" was his attempt to fulfill her wish. Flaubert insisted that the story was not ironic but intended "to move tender hearts to pity and tears"—just as Sand would have desired. Flaubert would no doubt have appreciated the further irony that we don't know whether or not to trust his own opinion of his story.

PRONUNCIATIONS:
  Aubain: oh-BAHNG
  Félicité: fay-lee-cee-TAY
  Gustave Flaubert: gous-TAHV flow-BARE

A Simple Heart[1]

1

Madame Aubain's servant Félicité was the envy of the ladies of Pont-l'Évêque for half a century.

She received four pounds a year. For that she was cook and general servant, and did the sewing, washing, and ironing; she could bridle a horse, fatten poultry, and churn butter—and she remained faithful to her mistress, unamiable as the latter was.

Mme. Aubain had married a gay bachelor without money who died at the beginning of 1809, leaving her with two small children and a quantity of debts. She then sold all her property except the farms of Toucques and Geffosses, which brought in two hundred pounds a year at most, and left her house in Saint-Melaine for a less expensive one that had belonged to her family and was situated behind the market.

This house had a slate roof and stood between an alley and a lane that went down to the river. There was an unevenness in the levels of the rooms which made you stumble. A narrow hall divided the kitchen from the "parlour" where Mme. Aubain spent her day, sitting in a wicker easy chair by the window. Against the panels, which were painted white, was a row of eight mahogany chairs. On an old piano under the barometer a heap of wooden and cardboard boxes rose like a pyramid. A stuffed armchair stood on either side of the Louis-Quinze chimney-piece, which was in yellow marble with a clock in the middle of it modelled like a temple of Vesta.[2] The whole room was a little musty, as the floor was lower than the garden.

The first floor began with "Madame's" room: very large, with a pale-flowered wallpaper and a portrait of "Monsieur" as a dandy of the period. It led to a smaller room, where there were two children's cots without mattresses. Next came the drawing-room, which was always shut up and full of furniture covered with sheets. Then there was a corridor leading to a study. The shelves of a large bookcase were respectably lined with books and papers, and its three wings surrounded a broad writing-table in darkwood. The two panels at the end of the room were covered with pen-drawings, water-colour landscapes, and engravings by Audran, all relics of better days and vanished splendour. Félicité's room on the top floor got its light from a dormer-window, which looked over the meadows.

She rose at daybreak to be in time for Mass, and worked till evening without stopping. Then, when dinner was over, the plates and dishes in order, and the door shut fast, she thrust the log under the ashes and went to sleep in front of the hearth with her rosary in her hand. Félicité was the stubbornest of all bargainers; and as for cleanness, the polish on her saucepans was the despair of other servants. Thrifty in all things, she ate slowly, gathering off the table in her fingers the crumbs of her loaf—a twelve-pound loaf expressly baked for her, which lasted for three weeks.

At all times of year she wore a print hand-kerchief fastened with a pin behind, a bonnet that covered her hair, grey stockings, a red skirt, and a bibbed apron—such as hospital nurses wear—over her jacket.

Her face was thin and her voice sharp. At twenty-five she looked like forty. From fifty onwards she seemed of no particular age; and with her silence, straight figure, and precise movements she was like a woman made of wood, and going by clockwork.

---

1. Translated by Arthur McDowall.   2. Roman goddess of hearth and home.

2

She had had her love-story like another.

Her father, a mason, had been killed by falling off some scaffolding. Then her mother died, her sisters scattered, and a farmer took her in and employed her, while she was still quite little, to herd the cows at pasture. She shivered in rags and would lie flat on the ground to drink water from the ponds; she was beaten for nothing, and finally turned out for the theft of a shilling which she did not steal. She went to another farm, where she became dairy-maid; and as she was liked by her employers her companions were jealous of her.

One evening in August (she was then eighteen) they took her to the assembly at Colleville. She was dazed and stupefied in an instant by the noise of the fiddlers, the lights in the trees, the gay medley of dresses, the lace, the gold crosses, and the throng of people jigging all together. While she kept shyly apart a young man with a well-to-do air, who was leaning on the shaft of a cart and smoking his pipe, came up to ask her to dance. He treated her to cider, coffee, and cake, and bought her a silk handkerchief; and then, imagining she had guessed his meaning, offered to see her home. At the edge of a field of oats he pushed her roughly down. She was frightened and began to cry out; and he went off.

One evening later she was on the Beaumont road. A big hay-wagon was moving slowly along; she wanted to get in front of it, and as she brushed past the wheels she recognized Theodore. He greeted her quite calmly, saying she must excuse it all because it was "the fault of the drink." She could not think of any answer and wanted to run away.

He began at once to talk about the harvest and the worthies of the commune, for his father had left Colleville for the farm at Les Écots, so that now he and she were neighbours. "Ah!" she said. He added that they thought of settling him in life. Well, he was in no hurry; he was waiting for a wife to his fancy. She dropped her head; and then he asked her if she thought of marrying. She answered with a smile that it was mean to make fun of her.

"But I am not, I swear!"—and he passed his left hand round her waist. She walked in the support of his embrace; their steps grew slower. The wind was soft, the stars glittered, the huge wagon-load of hay swayed in front of them, and dust rose from the dragging steps of the four horses. Then, without a word of command, they turned to the right. He clasped her once more in his arms, and she disappeared into the shadow.

The week after Theodore secured some assignations with her.

They met at the end of farmyards, behind a wall, or under a solitary tree. She was not innocent as young ladies are—she had learned knowledge from the animals—but her reason and the instinct of her honour would not let her fall. Her resistance exasperated Theodore's passion; so much so that to satisfy it—or perhaps quite artlessly—he made her an offer of marriage. She was in doubt whether to trust him, but he swore great oaths of fidelity.

Soon he confessed to something troublesome; the year before his parents had bought him a substitute for the army, but any day he might be taken again, and the idea of serving was a terror to him. Félicité took this cowardice of his as a sign of affection, and it redoubled hers. She stole away at night to see him, and when she reached their meeting-place Theodore racked her with his anxieties and urgings.

At last he declared that he would go himself to the prefecture for information, and would tell her the result on the following Sunday, between eleven and midnight.

When the moment came she sped towards her lover. Instead of him she found one of his friends.

He told her that she would not see Theodore any more. To ensure himself against conscription he had married an old woman, Madame Lehoussais, of Toucques, who was very rich.

There was an uncontrollable burst of grief. She threw herself on the ground, screamed, called to the God of mercy, and moaned by herself in the fields till daylight came. Then she came back to the farm and announced that she was going to leave; and at the end of the month she received her wages, tied all her small belongings with a handkerchief, and went to Pont-l'Évêque.

In front of the inn there she made inquiries of a woman in a widow's cap, who, as it happened, was just looking for a cook. The girl did not know much, but her willingness seemed so great and her demands so small that Mme. Aubain ended by saying: "Very well, then, I will take you."

A quarter of an hour afterwards Félicité was installed in her house.

She lived there at first in a tremble, as it were, at "the style of the house" and the memory of "Monsieur" floating over it all. Paul and Virginie, the first aged seven and the other hardly four, seemed to her beings of a precious substance; she carried them on her back like a horse; it was a sorrow to her that Mme. Aubain would not let her kiss them every minute. And yet she was happy there. Her grief had melted in the pleasantness of things all round.

Every Thursday regular visitors came in for a game of boston,[3] and Félicité got the cards and foot-warmers ready beforehand. They arrived punctually at eight and left before the stroke of eleven.

On Monday mornings the dealer who lodged in the covered passage spread out all his old iron on the ground. Then a hum of voices began to fill the town, mingled with the neighing of horses, bleating of lambs, grunting of pigs, and the sharp rattle of carts along the street. About noon, when the market was at its height, you might see a tall, hook-nosed old countryman with his cap pushed back making his appearance at the door. It was Robelin, the farmer of Geffosses. A little later came Liébard, the farmer from Toucques—short, red, and corpulent—in a grey jacket and gaiters shod with spurs.

Both had poultry or cheese to offer their landlord. Félicité was invariably a match for their cunning, and they went away filled with respect for her.

At vague intervals Mme. Aubain had a visit from the Marquis de Gremanville, one of her uncles, who had ruined himself by debauchery and now lived at Falaise on his last remaining morsel of land. He invariably came at the luncheon hour, with a dreadful poodle whose paws left all the furniture in a mess. In spite of efforts to show his breeding, which he carried to the point of raising his hat every time he mentioned "my late father," habit was too strong for him; he poured himself out glass after glass and fired off improper remarks. Félicité edged him politely out of the house—"You have had enough, Monsieur de Gremanville! Another time!"—and she shut the door on him.

She opened it with pleasure to M. Bourais, who had been a lawyer. His baldness, his white stock, frilled shirt, and roomy brown coat, his way of rounding the arm as he took snuff—his whole person, in fact, created that disturbance of mind which overtakes us at the sight of extraordinary men.

3. A fashionable card game.

As he looked after the property of "Madame" he remained shut up with her for hours in "Monsieur's" study, though all the time he was afraid of compromising himself. He respected the magistracy immensely, and had some pretensions to Latin.

To combine instruction and amusement he gave the children a geography book made up of a series of prints. They represented scenes in different parts of the world: cannibals with feathers on their heads, a monkey carrying off a young lady, Bedouins in the desert, the harpooning of a whale, and so on. Paul explained these engravings to Félicité; and that, in fact, was the whole of her literary education. The children's education was undertaken by Guyot, a poor creature employed at the town hall, who was famous for his beautiful hand and sharpened his penknife on his boots.

When the weather was bright the household set off early for a day at Geffosses Farm.

Its courtyard is on a slope, with the farmhouse in the middle, and the sea looks like a grey streak in the distance.

Félicité brought slices of cold meat out of her basket, and they breakfasted in a room adjoining the dairy. It was the only surviving fragment of a country house which was now no more. The wall-paper hung in tatters, and quivered in the draughts. Mme. Aubain sat with bowed head, overcome by her memories; the children became afraid to speak. "Why don't you play, then?" she would say, and off they went.

Paul climbed into the barn, caught birds, played at ducks and drakes over the pond, or hammered with his stick on the big casks which boomed like drums. Virginie fed the rabbits or dashed off to pick cornflowers, her quick legs showing their embroidered little drawers.

One autumn evening they went home by the fields. The moon was in its first quarter, lighting part of the sky; and mist floated like a scarf over the windings of the Toucques. Cattle, lying out in the middle of the grass, looked quietly at the four people as they passed. In the third meadow some of them got up and made a half-circle in front of the walkers. "There's nothing to be afraid of," said Félicité, as she stroked the nearest on the back with a kind of crooning song; he wheeled round and the others did the same. But when they crossed the next pasture there was a formidable bellow. It was a bull, hidden by the mist. Mme. Aubain was about to run. "No! no! don't go so fast!" They mended their pace, however, and heard a loud breathing behind them which came nearer. His hoofs thudded on the meadow grass like hammers; why, he was galloping now! Félicité turned round, and tore up clods of earth with both hands and threw them in his eyes. He lowered his muzzle, waved his horns, and quivered with fury, bellowing terribly. Mme. Aubain, now at the end of the pasture with her two little ones, was looking wildly for a place to get over the high bank. Félicité was retreating, still with her face to the bull, keeping up a shower of clods which blinded him, and crying all the time, "Be quick! be quick!"

Mme. Aubain went down into the ditch, pushed Virginie first and then Paul, fell several times as she tried to climb the bank, and managed it at last by dint of courage.

The bull had driven Félicité to bay against a rail-fence; his slaver was streaming into her face; another second, and he would have gored her. She had just time to slip between two of the rails, and the big animal stopped short in amazement.

This adventure was talked of at Pont-l'Évêque for many a year. Félicité did not pride herself on it in the least, not having the barest suspicion that she had done anything heroic.

Virginie was the sole object of her thoughts, for the child developed a nervous complaint as a result of her fright, and M. Poupart, the doctor, advised sea-bathing at

Trouville. It was not a frequented place then. Mme. Aubain collected information, consulted Bourais, and made preparations as though for a long journey.

Her luggage started a day in advance, in Liébard's cart. The next day he brought round two horses, one of which had a lady's saddle with a velvet back to it, while a cloak was rolled up to make a kind of seat on the crupper of the other. Mme. Aubain rode on that, behind the farmer. Félicité took charge of Virginie, and Paul mounted M. Lechaptois' donkey, lent on condition that great care was taken of it.

The road was so bad that its five miles took two hours. The horses sank in the mud up to their pasterns, and their haunches jerked abruptly in the effort to get out; or else they stumbled in the ruts, and at other moments had to jump. In some places Liébard's mare came suddenly to a halt. He waited patiently until she went on again, talking about the people who had properties along the road, and adding moral reflections to their history. So it was that as they were in the middle of Toucques, and passed under some windows bowered with nasturtiums, he shrugged his shoulders and said: "There's a Mme. Lehoussais lives there; instead of taking a young man she . . ." Félicité did not hear the rest; the horses were trotting and the donkey galloping. They all turned down a bypath; a gate swung open and two boys appeared; and the party dismounted in front of a manure-heap at the very threshold of the farmhouse door.

When Mme. Liébard saw her mistress she gave lavish signs of joy. She served her a luncheon with a sirloin of beef, tripe, black-pudding, a fricassee of chicken, sparkling cider, a fruit tart, and brandied plums; seasoning it all with compliments to Madame, who seemed in better health; Mademoiselle, who was "splendid" now; and Monsieur Paul, who had "filled out" wonderfully. Nor did she forget their deceased grandparents, whom the Liébards had known, as they had been in the service of the family for several generations. The farm, like them, had the stamp of antiquity. The beams on the ceiling were worm-eaten, the walls blackened with smoke, and the window-panes grey with dust. There was an oak dresser laden with every sort of useful article—jugs, plates, pewter bowls, wolf-traps, and sheep-shears; and a huge syringe made the children laugh. There was not a tree in the three courtyards without mushrooms growing at the bottom of it or a tuft of mistletoe on its boughs. Several of them had been thrown down by the wind. They had taken root again at the middle; and all were bending under their wealth of apples. The thatched roofs, like brown velvet and of varying thickness, withstood the heaviest squalls. The cart-shed, however, was falling into ruin. Mme. Aubain said she would see about it, and ordered the animals to be saddled again.

It was another half-hour before they reached Trouville. The little caravan dismounted to pass Écores—it was an overhanging cliff with boats below it—and three minutes later they were at the end of the quay and entered the courtyard of the Golden Lamb, kept by good Mme. David.

From the first days of their stay Virginie began to feel less weak, thanks to the change of air and the effect of the sea-baths. These, for want of a bathing-dress, she took in her chemise; and her nurse dressed her afterwards in a coastguard's cabin which was used by the bathers.

In the afternoons they took the donkey and went off beyond the Black Rocks, in the direction of Hennequeville. The path climbed at first through ground with dells in it like the green sward of a park, and then reached a plateau where grass fields and arable lay side by side. Hollies rose stiffly out of the briary tangle at the edge of the road; and here and there a great withered tree made zigzags in the blue air with its branches.

They nearly always rested in a meadow, with Deauville on their left, Havre on their right, and the open sea in front. It glittered in the sunshine, smooth as a mirror and so quiet that its murmur was scarcely to be heard; sparrows chirped in hiding and the immense sky arched over it all. Mme. Aubain sat doing her needlework; Virginie plaited rushes by her side; Félicité pulled up lavender, and Paul was bored and anxious to start home.

Other days they crossed the Toucques in a boat and looked for shells. When the tide went out sea-urchins, starfish, and jelly-fish were left exposed; and the children ran in pursuit of the foam-flakes which scudded in the wind. The sleepy waves broke on the sand and unrolled all along the beach; it stretched away out of sight, bounded on the land-side by the dunes which parted it from the Marsh, a wide meadow shaped like an arena. As they came home that way, Trouville, on the hill-slope in the background, grew bigger at every step, and its miscellaneous throng of houses seemed to break into a gay disorder.

On days when it was too hot they did not leave their room. From the dazzling brilliance outside light fell in streaks between the laths of the blinds. There were no sounds in the village; and on the pavement below not a soul. This silence round them deepened the quietness of things. In the distance, where men were caulking, there was a tap of hammers as they plugged the hulls, and a sluggish breeze wafted up the smell of tar.

The chief amusement was the return of the fishing-boats. They began to tack as soon as they had passed the buoys. The sails came down on two of the three masts; and they drew on with the foresail swelling like a balloon, glided through the splash of the waves, and when they had reached the middle of the harbour suddenly dropped anchor. Then the boats drew up against the quay. The sailors threw quivering fish over the side; a row of carts was waiting, and women in cotton bonnets darted out to take the baskets and give their men a kiss.

One of them came up to Félicité one day, and she entered the lodgings a little later in a state of delight. She had found a sister again—and then Nastasie Barette, "wife of Leroux," appeared, holding an infant at her breast and another child with her right hand, while on her left was a little cabin boy with his hands on his hips and a cap over his ear.

After a quarter of an hour Mme. Aubain sent them off; but they were always to be found hanging about the kitchen, or encountered in the course of a walk. The husband never appeared.

Félicité was seized with affection for them. She bought them a blanket, some shirts, and a stove; it was clear that they were making a good thing out of her. Mme. Aubain was annoyed by this weakness of hers, and she did not like the liberties taken by the nephew, who said "thee" and "thou" to Paul. So as Virginie was coughing and the fine weather gone, she returned to Pont-l'Évêque.

There M. Bourais enlightened her on the choice of a boys' school. The one at Caen was reputed to be the best, and Paul was sent to it. He said his good-byes bravely, content enough at going to live in a house where he would have companions.

Mme. Aubain resigned herself to her son's absence as a thing that had to be. Virginie thought about it less and less. Félicité missed the noise he made. But she found an occupation to distract her; from Christmas onward she took the little girl to catechism every day.

3

After making a genuflexion at the door she walked up between the double row of chairs under the lofty nave, opened Mme. Aubain's pew, sat down, and began to look

about her. The choir stalls were filled with the boys on the right and the girls on the
left, and the curé stood by the lectern. On a painted window in the apse the Holy
Ghost looked down upon the Virgin. Another window showed her on her knees before the child Jesus, and a group carved in wood behind the altarshrine represented St.
Michael overthrowing the dragon.

The priest began with a sketch of sacred history. The Garden, the Flood, the
Tower of Babel, cities in flames, dying nations, and overturned idols passed like a
dream before her eyes; and the dizzying vision left her with reverence for the Most
High and fear of his wrath. Then she wept at the story of the Passion. Why had they
crucified Him, when He loved the children, fed the multitudes, healed the blind, and
had willed, in His meekness, to be born among the poor, on the dungheap of a stable?
The sowings, harvests, wine-presses, all the familiar things the Gospel speaks of, were
a part of her life. They had been made holy by God's passing; and she loved the lambs
more tenderly for her love of the Lamb, and the doves because of the Holy Ghost.

She found it hard to imagine Him in person, for He was not merely a bird, but a
flame as well, and a breath at other times. It may be His light, she thought, which flits
at night about the edge of the marshes, His breathing which drives on the clouds, His
voice which gives harmony to the bells; and she would sit rapt in adoration, enjoying
the cool walls and the quiet of the church.

Of doctrines she understood nothing—did not even try to understand. The curé
discoursed, the children repeated their lesson, and finally she went to sleep, waking up
with a start when their wooden shoes clattered on the flagstones as they went away.

It was thus that Félicité, whose religious education had been neglected in her
youth, learned the catechism by dint of hearing it; and from that time she copied all
Virginie's observances, fasting as she did and confessing with her. On Corpus Christi
Day they made a festal altar together.

The first communion loomed distractingly ahead. She fussed over the shoes, the
rosary, the book and gloves; and how she trembled as she helped Virginie's mother to
dress her!

All through the mass she was racked with anxiety. She could not see one side of
the choir because of M. Bourais; but straight in front of her was the flock of maidens,
with white crowns above their hanging veils, making the impression of a field of
snow; and she knew her dear child at a distance by her dainty neck and thoughtful air.
The bell tinkled. The heads bowed, and there was silence. As the organ pealed,
singers and congregation took up the "Agnus Dei"; then the procession of the boys
began, and after them the girls rose. Step by step, with their hands joined in prayer,
they went towards the lighted altar, knelt on the first step, received the sacrament in
turn, and came back in the same order to their places. When Virginie's turn came
Félicité leaned forward to see her; and with the imaginativeness of deep and tender
feeling it seemed to her that she actually was the child; Virginie's face became hers,
she was dressed in her clothes, it was her heart beating in her breast. As the moment
came to open her mouth she closed her eyes and nearly fainted.

She appeared early in the sacristy next morning for Monsieur the curé to give her the
communion. She took it with devotion, but it did not give her the same exquisite delight.

Mme. Aubain wanted to make her daughter into an accomplished person; and as
Guyot could not teach her music or English she decided to place her in the Ursuline
Convent at Honfleur as a boarder. The child made no objection. Félicité sighed and
thought that Madame lacked feeling. Then she reflected that her mistress might be
right; matters of this kind were beyond her.

So one day an old spring-van drew up at the door, and out of it stepped a nun to fetch the young lady. Félicité hoisted the luggage on to the top, admonished the driver, and put six pots of preserves, a dozen pears, and a bunch of violets under the seat.

At the last moment Virginie broke into a fit of sobbing; she threw her arms round her mother, who kissed her on the forehead, saying over and over "Come, be brave! be brave!" The step was raised, and the carriage drove off.

Then Mme. Aubain's strength gave way; and in the evening all her friends—the Lormeau family, Mme. Lechaptois, the Rochefeuille ladies, M. de Houppeville, and Bourais—came in to console her.

To be without her daughter was very painful for her at first. But she heard from Virginie three times a week, wrote to her on the other days, walked in the garden, and so filled up the empty hours.

From sheer habit Félicité went into Virginie's room in the mornings and gazed at the walls. It was boredom to her not to have to comb the child's hair now, lace up her boots, tuck her into bed—and not to see her charming face perpetually and hold her hand when they went out together. In this idle condition she tried making lace. But her fingers were too heavy and broke the threads; she could not attend to anything, she had lost her sleep, and was, in her own words, "destroyed."

To "divert herself" she asked leave to have visits from her nephew Victor.

He arrived on Sundays after mass, rosy-cheeked, bare-chested, with the scent of the country he had walked through still about him. She laid her table promptly and they had lunch, sitting opposite each other. She ate as little as possible herself to save expense, but stuffed him with food so generously that at last he went to sleep. At the first stroke of vespers she woke him up, brushed his trousers, fastened his tie, and went to church, leaning on his arm with maternal pride.

Victor was always instructed by his parents to get something out of her—a packet of moist sugar, it might be, a cake of soap, spirits, or even money at times. He brought his things for her to mend and she took over the task, only too glad to have a reason for making him come back.

In August his father took him off on a coasting voyage. It was holiday time, and she was consoled by the arrival of the children. Paul, however, was getting selfish, and Virginie was too old to be called "thou" any longer; this put a constraint and barrier between them.

Victor went to Morlaix, Dunkirk, and Brighton in succession and made Félicité a present on his return from each voyage. It was a box made of shells the first time, a coffee cup the next, and on the third occasion a large gingerbread man. Victor was growing handsome. He was well made, had a hint of a moustache, good honest eyes, and a small leather hat pushed backwards like a pilot's. He entertained her by telling stories embroidered with nautical terms.

On a Monday, July 14, 1819 (she never forgot the date), he told her that he had signed on for the big voyage and next night but one he would take the Honfleur boat and join his schooner, which was to weigh anchor from Havre before long. Perhaps he would be gone two years.

The prospect of this long absence threw Félicité into deep distress; one more good-bye she must have, and on the Wednesday evening, when Madame's dinner was finished, she put on her clogs and made short work of the twelve miles between Pont-l'Évêque and Honfleur.

When she arrived in front of the Calvary she took the turn to the right instead of the left, got lost in the timber-yards, and retraced her steps; some people to whom she spoke advised her to be quick. She went all round the harbour basin, full of ships, and knocked against hawsers; then the ground fell away, lights flashed across each other, and she thought her wits had left her, for she saw horses up in the sky.

Others were neighing by the quay-side, frightened at the sea. They were lifted by a tackle and deposited in a boat, where passengers jostled each other among cider casks, cheese baskets, and sacks of grain; fowls could be heard clucking, the captain swore; and a cabin-boy stood leaning over the bows, indifferent to it all. Félicité, who had not recognized him, called "Victor!" and he raised his head; all at once, as she was darting forwards, the gangway was drawn back.

The Honfleur packet, women singing as they hauled it, passed out of harbour. Its framework creaked and the heavy waves whipped its bows. The canvas had swung round, no one could be seen on board now; and on the moonsilvered sea the boat made a black speck which paled gradually, dipped, and vanished.

As Félicité passed by the Calvary she had a wish to commend to God what she cherished most, and she stood there praying a long time with her face bathed in tears and her eyes towards the clouds. The town was asleep, coastguards were walking to and fro; and water poured without cessation through the holes in the sluice, with the noise of a torrent. The clocks struck two.

The convent parlour would not be open before day. If Félicité were late Madame would most certainly be annoyed; and in spite of her desire to kiss the other child she turned home. The maids at the inn were waking up as she came in to Pont-l'Évêque.

So the poor slip of a boy was going to toss for months and months at sea! She had not been frightened by his previous voyages. From England or Brittany you came back safe enough; but America, the colonies, the islands—these were lost in a dim region at the other end of the world.

Félicité's thoughts from that moment ran entirely on her nephew. On sunny days she was harassed by the idea of thirst; when there was a storm she was afraid of the lightning on his account. As she listened to the wind growling in the chimney or carrying off the slates she pictured him lashed by that same tempest, at the top of a shattered mast, with his body thrown backwards under a sheet of foam; or else (with a reminiscence of the illustrated geography) he was being eaten by savages, captured in a wood by monkeys, or dying on a desert shore. And never did she mention her anxieties.

Mme. Aubain had anxieties of her own, about her daughter. The good sisters found her an affectionate but delicate child. The slightest emotion unnerved her. She had to give up the piano.

Her mother stipulated for regular letters from the convent. She lost patience one morning when the postman did not come, and walked to and fro in the parlour from her armchair to the window. It was really amazing; not a word for four days!

To console Mme. Aubain by her own example Félicité remarked:

"As for me, Madame, it's six months since I heard . . ."

"From whom, pray?"

"Why . . . from my nephew," the servant answered gently.

"Oh! your nephew!" And Mme. Aubain resumed her walk with a shrug of the shoulders, as much as to say: "I was not thinking of him! And what is more, it's absurd! A scamp of a cabin-boy—what does he matter? . . . whereas my daughter . . . why, just think!"

Félicité, though she had been brought up on harshness, felt indignant with Madame—and then forgot. It seemed the simplest thing in the world to her to lose one's head over the little girl. For her the two children were equally important; a bond in her heart made them one, and their destinies must be the same.

She heard from the chemist that Victor's ship had arrived at Havana. He had read this piece of news in a gazette.

Cigars—they made her imagine Havana as a place where no one does anything but smoke, and there was Victor moving among the negroes in a cloud of tobacco. Could you, she wondered, "in case you needed,' return by land? What was the distance from Pont-l'Évêque? She questioned M. Bourais to find out.

He reached for his atlas and began explaining the longitudes; Félicité's consternation provoked a fine pedantic smile. Finally he marked with his pencil a black, imperceptible point in the indentations of an oval spot, and said as he did so, "Here it is." She bent over the map; the maze of coloured lines wearied her eyes without conveying anything; and on an invitation from Bourais to tell him her difficulty she begged him to show her the house where Victor was living. Bourais threw up his arms, sneezed, and laughed immensely: a simplicity like hers was a positive joy. And Félicité did not understand the reason; how could she when she expected, very likely, to see the actual image of her nephew—so stunted was her mind!

A fortnight afterwards Liébard came into the kitchen at market-time as usual and handed her a letter from her brother-in-law. As neither of them could read she took it to her mistress.

Mme. Aubain, who was counting the stitches in her knitting, put the work down by her side, broke the seal of the letter, started, and said in a low voice, with a look of meaning:

"It is bad news . . . that they have to tell you. Your nephew . . ."

He was dead. The letter said no more.

Félicité fell on to a chair, leaning her head against the wainscot; and she closed her eyelids, which suddenly flushed pink. Then with bent forehead, hands hanging, and fixed eyes, she said at intervals:

"Poor little lad! poor little lad!"

Liébard watched her and heaved sighs. Mme. Aubain trembled a little.

She suggested that Félicité should go to see her sister at Trouville. Félicité answered by a gesture that she had no need.

There was a silence. The worthy Liébard thought it was time for them to withdraw. Then Félicité said:

"They don't care, not they!"

Her head dropped again; and she took up mechanically, from time to time, the long needles on her work-table.

Women passed in the yard with a barrow of dripping linen.

As she saw them through the window-panes she remembered her washing; she had put it to soak the day before, to-day she must wring it out; and she left the room.

Her plank and tub were at the edge of the Toucques. She threw a pile of linen on the bank, rolled up her sleeves, and taking her wooden beater dealt lusty blows whose sound carried to the neighbouring gardens. The meadows were empty, the river stirred in the wind; and down below long grasses wavered, like the hair of corpses floating in the water. She kept her grief down and was very brave until the evening; but once in her room she surrendered to it utterly, lying stretched on the mattress with her face in the pillow and her hands clenched against her temples.

Much later she heard, from the captain himself, the circumstances of Victor's end. They had bled him too much at the hospital for yellow fever. Four doctors held him at once. He had died instantly, and the chief had said: "Bah! there goes another!"

His parents had always been brutal to him. She preferred not to see them again; and they made no advances, either because they forgot her or from the callousness of the wretchedly poor.

Virginie began to grow weaker.

Tightness in her chest, coughing, continual fever, and veinings on her cheek-bones betrayed some deep-seated complaint. M. Poupart had advised a stay in Provence. Mme. Aubain determined on it, and would have brought her daughter home at once but for the climate of Pont-l'Évêque.

She made an arrangement with a job-master, and he drove her to the convent every Tuesday. There is a terrace in the garden, with a view over the Seine. Virginie took walks there over the fallen vine-leaves, on her mother's arm. A shaft of sunlight through the clouds made her blink sometimes, as she gazed at the sails in the distance and the whole horizon from the castle of Tancarville to the lighthouses at Havre. Afterwards they rested in the arbour. Her mother had secured a little cask of excellent Malaga; and Virginie, laughing at the idea of getting tipsy, drank a thimble-full of it, no more.

Her strength came back visibly. The autumn glided gently away. Félicité reassured Mme. Aubain. But one evening, when she had been out on a commission in the neighbourhood, she found M. Poupart's gig at the door. He was in the hall, and Mme. Aubain was tying her bonnet.

"Give me my foot-warmer, purse, gloves! Quicker, come!"

Virginie had inflammation of the lungs; perhaps it was hopeless.

"Not yet!" said the doctor, and they both got into the carriage under whirling flakes of snow. Night was coming on and it was very cold.

Félicité rushed into the church to light a taper. Then she ran after the gig, came up with it in an hour, and jumped lightly in behind. As she hung on by the fringes a thought came into her mind: "The courtyard has not been shut up; supposing burglars got in!" And she jumped down.

At dawn next day she presented herself at the doctor's. He had come in and started for the country again. Then she waited in the inn, thinking that a letter would come by some hand or other. Finally, when it was twilight, she took the Lisieux coach.

The convent was at the end of a steep lane. When she was about half-way up it she heard strange sounds—a death-bell tolling. "It is for someone else," thought Félicité, and she pulled the knocker violently.

After some minutes there was a sound of trailing slippers, the door opened ajar, and a nun appeared.

The good sister, with an air of compunction, said that "she had just passed away." On the instant the bell of St. Leonard's tolled twice as fast.

Félicité went up to the second floor.

From the doorway she saw Virginie stretched on her back, with her hands joined, her mouth open, and head thrown back under a black crucifix that leaned towards her, between curtains that hung stiffly, less pale than was her face. Mme. Aubain, at the foot of the bed which she clasped with her arms, was choking with sobs of agony. The mother superior stood on the right. Three candlesticks on the chest of drawers made spots of red, and the mist came whitely through the windows. Nuns came and took Mme. Aubain away.

For two nights Félicité never left the dead child. She repeated the same prayers, sprinkled holy water over the sheets, came and sat down again, and watched her. At the end of the first vigil she noticed that the face had grown yellow, the lips turned blue, the nose was sharper, and the eyes sunk in. She kissed them several times, and would not have been immensely surprised if Virginie had opened them again; to minds like hers the supernatural is quite simple. She made the girl's toilette, wrapped her in her shroud, lifted her down into her bier, put a garland on her head, and spread out her hair. It was fair, and extraordinarily long for her age. Félicité cut off a big lock and slipped half of it into her bosom, determined that she should never part with it.

The body was brought back to Pont-l'Évêque, as Mme. Aubain intended; she followed the hearse in a closed carriage.

It took another three-quarters of an hour after the mass to reach the cemetery. Paul walked in front, sobbing. M. Bourais was behind, and then came the chief residents, the women shrouded in black mantles, and Félicité. She thought of her nephew; and because she had not been able to pay these honours to him her grief was doubled, as though the one were being buried with the other.

Mme. Aubain's despair was boundless. It was against God that she first rebelled, thinking it unjust of Him to have taken her daughter from her—she had never done evil and her conscience was so clear! Ah, no!—she ought to have taken Virginie off to the south. Other doctors would have saved her. She accused herself now, wanted to join her child, and broke into cries of distress in the middle of her dreams. One dream haunted her above all. Her husband, dressed as a sailor, was returning from a long voyage, and shedding tears he told her that he had been ordered to take Virginie away. Then they consulted how to hide her somewhere.

She came in once from the garden quite upset. A moment ago—and she pointed out the place—the father and daughter had appeared to her, standing side by side, and they did nothing, but they looked at her.

For several months after this she stayed inertly in her room. Félicité lectured her gently; she must live for her son's sake, and for the other, in remembrance of "her."

"Her?" answered Mme. Aubain, as though she were just waking up. "Ah, yes! . . . yes! . . . You do not forget her!" This was an allusion to the cemetery, where she was strictly forbidden to go.

Félicité went there every day.

Precisely at four she skirted the houses, climbed the hill, opened the gate, and came to Virginie's grave. It was a little column of pink marble with a stone underneath and a garden plot enclosed by chains. The beds were hidden under a coverlet of flowers. She watered their leaves, freshened the gravel, and knelt down to break up the earth better. When Mme. Aubain was able to come there she felt a relief and a sort of consolation.

Then years slipped away, one like another, and their only episodes were the great festivals as they recurred—Easter, the Assumption, All Saints' Day. Household occurrences marked dates that were referred to after-wards. In 1825, for instance, two glaziers whitewashed the hall; in 1827 a piece of the roof fell into the courtyard and nearly killed a man. In the summer of 1828 it was Madame's turn to offer the consecrated bread; Bourais, about this time, mysteriously absented himself; and one by one the old acquaintances passed away: Guyot, Liébard, Mme. Lechaptois, Robelin, and Uncle Gremanville, who had been paralysed for a long time.

One night the driver of the mail-coach announced the Revolution of July in Pont-l'Évêque.[4] A new sub-prefect was appointed a few days later—Baron de Larsonnière, who had been consul in America, and brought with him, besides his wife, a sister-in-law and three young ladies, already growing up. They were to be seen about on their lawn, in loose blouses, and they had a negro and a parrot. They paid a call on Mme. Aubain which she did not fail to return. The moment they were seen in the distance Félicité ran to let her mistress know. But only one thing could really move her feelings—the letters from her son.

He was swallowed up in a tavern life and could follow no career. She paid his debts, he made new ones; and the sighs that Mme. Aubain uttered as she sat knitting by the window reached Félicité at her spinning-wheel in the kitchen.

They took walks together along the espaliered wall, always talking of Virginie and wondering if such and such a thing would have pleased her and what, on some occasion, she would have been likely to say.

All her small belongings filled a cupboard in the two-bedded room. Mme. Aubain inspected them as seldom as she could. One summer day she made up her mind to it—and some moths flew out of the wardrobe.

Virginie's dresses were in a row underneath a shelf, on which there were three dolls, some hoops, a set of toy pots and pans, and the basin that she used. They took out her petticoats as well, and the stockings and handkerchiefs, and laid them out on the two beds before folding them up again. The sunshine lit up these poor things, bringing out their stains and the creases made by the body's movements. The air was warm and blue, a blackbird warbled, life seemed bathed in a deep sweetness. They found a little plush hat with thick, chestnut-coloured pile; but it was eaten all over by moth. Félicité begged it for her own. Their eyes met fixedly and filled with tears; at last the mistress opened her arms, the servant threw herself into them, and they embraced each other, satisfying their grief in a kiss that made them equal.

It was the first time in their lives, Mme. Aubain's nature not being expansive. Félicité was as grateful as though she had received a favour, and cherished her mistress from that moment with the devotion of an animal and a religious worship.

The kindness of her heart unfolded.

When she heard the drums of a marching regiment in the street she posted herself at the door with a pitcher of cider and asked the soldiers to drink. She nursed cholera patients and protected the Polish refugees; one of these even declared that he wished to marry her. They quarrelled, however; for when she came back from the Angelus one morning she found that he had got into her kitchen and made himself a vinegar salad which he was quietly eating.

After the Poles came father Colmiche, an old man who was supposed to have committed atrocities in '93.[5] He lived by the side of the river in the ruins of a pigsty. The little boys watched him through the cracks in the wall, and threw pebbles at him which fell on the pallet where he lay constantly shaken by a catarrh;[6] his hair was very long, his eyes inflamed, and there was a tumour on his arm bigger than his head. She got him some linen and tried to clean up his miserable hole; her dream was to establish him in the bakehouse, without letting him annoy Madame. When the tumour

4. The July Revolution overthrew King Charles X, marking the ascendancy of the middle class, who installed a king (Louis-Philippe) more to their liking.

5. During the Reign of Terror at the height of the French Revolution.
6. Racking cough.

burst she dressed it every day; sometimes she brought him cake, and would put him in the sunshine on a truss of straw. The poor old man, slobbering and trembling, thanked her in his worn-out voice, was terrified that he might lose her, and stretched out his hands when he saw her go away. He died; and she had a mass said for the repose of his soul.

That very day a great happiness befell her; just at dinner-time appeared Mme. de Larsonnière's negro, carrying the parrot in its cage, with perch, chain, and padlock. A note from the baroness informed Mme. Aubain that her husband had been raised to a prefecture and they were starting that evening; she begged her to accept the bird as a memento and mark of her regard.

For a long time he had absorbed Félicité's imagination, because he came from America; and that name reminded her of Victor, so much so that she made inquiries of the negro. She had once gone so far as to say "How Madame would enjoy having him!"

The negro repeated the remark to his mistress; and as she could not take the bird away with her she chose this way of getting rid of him.

4

His name was Loulou. His body was green and the tips of his wings rose-pink; his fore-head was blue and his throat golden.

But he had the tiresome habits of biting his perch, tearing out his feathers, sprinkling his dirt about, and spattering the water of his tub. He annoyed Mme. Aubain, and she gave him to Félicité for good.

She endeavoured to train him; soon he could repeat "Nice boy! Your servant, sir! Good morning, Marie!" He was placed by the side of the door, and astonished several people by not answering to the name Jacquot, for all parrots are called Jacquot. People compared him to a turkey and a log of wood, and stabbed Félicité to the heart each time. Strange obstinacy on Loulou's part!—directly you looked at him he refused to speak.

None the less he was eager for society; for on Sundays, while the Rochefeuille ladies, M. de Houppeville, and new familiars—Onfroy the apothecary, Monsieur Varin, and Captain Mathieu—were playing their game of cards, he beat the windows with his wings and threw himself about so frantically that they could not hear each other speak.

Bourais' face, undoubtedly, struck him as extremely droll. Directly he saw it he began to laugh—and laugh with all his might. His peals rang through the courtyard and were repeated by the echo; the neighbours came to their windows and laughed too; while M. Bourais, gliding along under the wall to escape the parrot's eye, and hiding his profile with his hat, got to the river and then entered by the garden gate. There was a lack of tenderness in the looks which he darted at the bird.

Loulou had been slapped by the butcher-boy for making so free as to plunge his head into his basket; and since then he was always trying to nip him through his shirt. Fabu threatened to wring his neck, although he was not cruel, for all his tattooed arms and large whiskers. Far from it; he really rather liked the parrot, and in a jovial humour even wanted to teach him to swear. Félicité, who was alarmed by such proceedings, put the bird in the kitchen. His little chain was taken off and he roamed about the house.

His way of going downstairs was to lean on each step with the curve of his beak, raise the right foot, and then the left; and Félicité was afraid that these gymnastics brought on fits of giddiness. He fell ill and could not talk or eat any longer. There was a growth under his tongue, such as fowls have sometimes. She cured him by tearing the pellicle off with her finger-nails. Mr. Paul was thoughtless enough one day to blow some cigar smoke into his nostrils, and another time when Mme. Lormeau was teasing him with the end of her umbrella he snapped at the ferrule. Finally he got lost.

Félicité had put him on the grass to refresh him, and gone away for a minute, and when she came back—no sign of the parrot! She began by looking for him in the shrubs, by the waterside, and over the roofs, without listening to her mistress's cries of "Take care, do! You are out of your wits!" Then she investigated all the gardens in Pont-l'Évêque, and stopped the passers-by. "You don't ever happen to have seen my parrot, by any chance, do you?" And she gave a description of the parrot to those who did not know him. Suddenly, behind the mills at the foot of the hill she thought she could make out something green that fluttered. But on the top of the hill there was nothing. A hawker assured her that he had come across the parrot just before, at Saint-Melaine, in Mère Simon's shop. She rushed there; they had no idea of what she meant. At last she came home exhausted, with her slippers in shreds and despair in her soul; and as she was sitting in the middle of the garden-seat at Madame's side, telling the whole story of her efforts, a light weight dropped on to her shoulder—it was Loulou! What on earth had he been doing? Taking a walk in the neighbourhood, perhaps!

She had some trouble in recovering from this, or rather never did recover. As the result of a chill she had an attack of quinsy,[7] and soon afterwards an earache. Three years later she was deaf; and she spoke very loud, even in church. Though Félicité's sins might have been published in every corner of the diocese without dishonour to her or scandal to anybody, his Reverence the priest thought it right now to hear her confession in the sacristy only.

Imaginary noises in the head completed her upset. Her mistress often said to her, "Heavens! how stupid you are!" "Yes, Madame," she replied, and looked about for something.

Her little circle of ideas grew still narrower; the peal of church-bells and the lowing of cattle ceased to exist for her. All living beings moved as silently as ghosts. One sound only reached her ears now—the parrot's voice.

Loulou, as though to amuse her, reproduced the click-clack of the turn-spit, the shrill call of a man selling fish, and the noise of the saw in the joiner's house opposite; when the bell rang he imitated Mme. Aubain's "Félicité! the door! the door!"

They carried on conversations, he endlessly reciting the three phrases in his repertory, to which she replied with words that were just as disconnected but uttered what was in her heart. Loulou was almost a son and a lover to her in her isolated state. He climbed up her fingers, nibbled at her lips, and clung to her kerchief; and when she bent her forehead and shook her head gently to and fro, as nurses do, the great wings of her bonnet and the bird's wings quivered together.

When the clouds massed and the thunder rumbled Loulou broke into cries, perhaps remembering the downpours in his native forests. The streaming rain made him absolutely mad; he fluttered wildly about, dashed up to the ceiling, upset everything, and went out through the window to dabble in the garden; but he was back quickly to

7. Tonsillitis.

perch on one of the fire-dogs and hopped about to dry himself, exhibiting his tail and his beak in turn.

One morning in the terrible winter of 1837 she had put him in front of the fire-place because of the cold. She found him dead, in the middle of his cage: head down-wards, with his claws in the wires. He had died from congestion, no doubt. But Félic-ité thought he had been poisoned with parsley, and though there was no proof of any kind her suspicions inclined to Fabu.

She wept so piteously that her mistress said to her, "Well, then, have him stuffed!"

She asked advice from the chemist, who had always been kind to the parrot. He wrote to Havre, and a person called Fellacher undertook the business. But as parcels sometimes got lost in the coach she decided to take the parrot as far as Honfleur herself.

Along the sides of the road were leafless apple-trees, one after the other. Ice covered the ditches. Dogs barked about the farms; and Félicité, with her hands un-der her cloak, her little black sabots and her basket, walked briskly in the middle of the road.

She crossed the forest, passed High Oak, and reached St. Gatien.

A cloud of dust rose behind her, and in it a mail-coach, carried away by the steep hill, rushed down at full gallop like a hurricane. Seeing this woman who would not get out of the way, the driver stood up in front and the positilion shouted too. He could not hold in his four horses, which increased their pace, and the two leaders were grazing her when he threw them to one side with a jerk of the reins. But he was wild with rage, and lifting his arm as he passed at full speed, gave her such a lash from waist to neck with his big whip that she fell on her back.

Her first act, when she recovered consciousness, was to open her basket. Loulou was happily none the worse. She felt a burn in her right cheek, and when she put her hands against it they were red; the blood was flowing.

She sat down on a heap of stones and bound up her face with her handkerchief. Then she ate a crust of bread which she had put in the basket as a precaution, and found a consolation for her wound in gazing at the bird.

When she reached the crest of Ecquemauville she saw the Honfleur lights sparkling in the night sky like a company of stars; beyond, the sea stretched dimly. Then a faintness overtook her and she stopped; her wretched childhood, the disil-lusion of her first love, her nephew's going away, and Virginie's death all came back to her at once like the waves of an oncoming tide, rose to her throat, and choked her.

Afterwards, at the boat, she made a point of speaking to the captain, begging him to take care of the parcel, though she did not tell him what was in it.

Fellacher kept the parrot a long time. He was always promising it for the follow-ing week. After six months he announced that a packing-case had started, and then nothing more was heard of it. It really seemed as though Loulou was never coming back. "Ah, they have stolen him!" she thought.

He arrived at last, and looked superb. There he was, erect upon a branch which screwed into a mahogany socket, with a foot in the air and his head on one side, biting a nut which the bird-stuffer—with a taste for impressiveness—had gilded.

Félicité shut him up in her room. It was a place to which few people were admit-ted, and held so many religious objects and miscellaneous things that it looked like a chapel and bazaar in one.

A big cupboard impeded you as you opened the door. Opposite the window commanding the garden a little round one looked into the court; there was a table by the folding-bed with a water-jug, two combs, and a cube of blue soap in a chipped plate. On the walls hung rosaries, medals, several benign Virgins, and a holy water vessel made out of cocoa-nut; on the chest of drawers, which was covered with a cloth like an altar, was the shell box that Victor had given her, and after that a watering-can, a toy-balloon, exercise-books, the illustrated geography, and a pair of young lady's boots; and, fastened by its ribbons to the nail of the looking-glass, hung the little plush hat! Félicité carried observances of this kind so far as to keep one of Monsieur's frock-coats. All the old rubbish which Mme. Aubain did not want any longer she laid hands on for her room. That was why there were artificial flowers along the edge of the chest of drawers and a portrait of the Comte d'Artois[8] in the little window recess.

With the aid of a bracket Loulou was established over the chimney, which jutted into the room. Every morning when she woke up she saw him there in the dawning light, and recalled old days and the smallest details of insignificant acts in a deep quietness which knew no pain.

Holding, as she did, no communication with anyone, Félicité lived as insensibly as if she were walking in her sleep. The Corpus Christi processions roused her to life again. Then she went round begging mats and candlesticks from the neighbours to decorate the altar they put up in the street.

In church she was always gazing at the Holy Ghost in the window, and observed that there was something of the parrot in him. The likeness was still clearer, she thought, on a crude colour-print representing the baptism of Our Lord. With his purple wings and emerald body he was the very image of Loulou.

She bought him, and hung him up instead of the Comte d'Artois, so that she could see them both together in one glance. They were linked in her thoughts; and the parrot was consecrated by his association with the Holy Ghost, which became more vivid to her eye and more intelligible. The Father could not have chosen to express Himself through a dove, for such creatures cannot speak; it must have been one of Loulou's ancestors, surely. And though Félicité looked at the picture while she said her prayers she swerved a little from time to time towards the parrot.

She wanted to join the Ladies of the Virgin, but Mme. Aubain dissuaded her.

And then a great event loomed up before them—Paul's marriage.

He had been a solicitor's clerk to begin with, and then tried business, the Customs, the Inland Revenue, and made efforts, even, to get into the Rivers and Forests. By an inspiration from heaven he had suddenly, at thirty-six, discovered his real line—the Registrar's Office. And there he showed such marked capacity that an inspector had offered him his daughter's hand and promised him his influence.

So Paul, grown serious, brought the lady to see his mother.

She sniffed at the ways of Pont-l'Évêque, gave herself great airs, and wounded Félicité's feelings. Mme. Aubain was relieved at her departure.

The week after came news of M. Bourais' death in an inn in Lower Brittany. The rumour of suicide was confirmed, and doubts arose as to his honesty. Mme. Aubain studied his accounts, and soon found out the whole tale of his misdoings—embezzled arrears, secret sales of wood, forged receipts, etc. Besides that he had an illegitimate child, and "relations with a person at Dozulé."

---

8. The deposed king Charles X.

These shameful facts distressed her greatly. In March 1853 she was seized with a pain in the chest; her tongue seemed to be covered with film, and leeches did not ease the difficult breathing. On the ninth evening of her illness she died, just at seventy-two.

She passed as being younger, owing to the bands of brown hair which framed her pale, pock-marked face. There were few friends to regret her, for she had a stiffness of manner which kept people at a distance.

But Félicité mourned for her as one seldom mourns for a master. It upset her ideas and seemed contrary to the order of things, impossible and monstrous, that Madame should die before her.

Ten days afterwards, which was the time it took to hurry there from Besançon, the heirs arrived. The daughter-in-law ransacked the drawers, chose some furniture, and sold the rest; and then they went back to their registering.

Madame's armchair, her small round table, her foot-warmer, and the eight chairs were gone! Yellow patches in the middle of the panels showed where the engravings had hung. They had carried off the two little beds and the mattresses, and all Virginie's belongings had disappeared from the cupboard. Félicité went from floor to floor dazed with sorrow.

The next day there was a notice on the door, and the apothecary shouted in her ear that the house was for sale.

She tottered, and was obliged to sit down. What distressed her most of all was to give up her room, so suitable as it was for poor Loulou. She enveloped him with a look of anguish when she was imploring the Holy Ghost, and formed the idolatrous habit of kneeling in front of the parrot to say her prayers. Sometimes the sun shone in at the attic window and caught his glass eye, and a great luminous ray shot out of it and put her in an ecstasy.

She had a pension of fifteen pounds a year which her mistress had left her. The garden gave her a supply of vegetables. As for clothes, she had enough to last her to the end of her days, and she economized in candles by going to bed at dusk.

She hardly ever went out, as she did not like passing the dealer's shop, where some of the old furniture was exposed for sale. Since her fit of giddiness she dragged one leg; and as her strength was failing Mère Simon, whose grocery business had collapsed, came every morning to split the wood and pump water for her.

Her eyes grew feeble. The shutters ceased to be thrown open. Years and years passed, and the house was neither let nor sold.

Félicité never asked for repairs because she was afraid of being sent away. The boards on the roof rotted; her bolster was wet for a whole winter. After Easter she spat blood.

Then Mère Simon called in a doctor. Félicité wanted to know what was the matter with her. But she was too deaf to hear, and the only word which reached her was "pneumonia." It was a word she knew, and she answered softly "Ah! like Madame," thinking it natural that she should follow her mistress.

The time for the festal shrines was coming near. The first one was always at the bottom of the hill, the second in front of the post-office, and the third towards the middle of the street. There was some rivalry in the matter of this one, and the women of the parish ended by choosing Mme. Aubain's courtyard.

The hard breathing and fever increased. Félicité was vexed at doing nothing for the altar. If only she could at least have put something there! Then she thought of the parrot. The neighbours objected that it would not be decent. But the priest gave her permission, which so intensely delighted her that she begged him to accept Loulou, her sole possession, when she died.

From Tuesday to Saturday, the eve of the festival, she coughed more often. By the evening her face had shrivelled, her lips stuck to her gums, and she had vomitings; and at twilight next morning, feeling herself very low, she sent for a priest.

Three kindly women were round her during the extreme unction. Then she announced that she must speak to Fabu. He arrived in his Sunday clothes, by no means at his ease in the funereal atmosphere.

"Forgive me," she said, with an effort to stretch out her arm; "I thought it was you who had killed him."

What did she mean by such stories? She suspected him of murder—a man like him! He waxed indignant, and was on the point of making a row.

"There," said the women, "she is no longer in her senses, you can see it well enough!"

Félicité spoke to shadows of her own from time to time. The women went away, and Mère Simon had breakfast. A little later she took Loulou and brought him close to Félicité with the words:

"Come, now, say good-bye to him!"

Loulou was not a corpse, but the worms devoured him; one of his wings was broken, and the tow was coming out of his stomach. But she was blind now; she kissed him on the forehead and kept him close against her cheek. Mère Simon took him back from her to put him on the altar.

5

Summer scents came up from the meadows; flies buzzed; the sun made the river glitter and heated the slates. Mère Simon came back into the room and fell softly asleep.

She woke at the noise of bells; the people were coming out from vespers. Félicité's delirium subsided. She thought of the procession and saw it as if she had been there.

All the school children, the church-singers, and the firemen walked on the pavement, while in the middle of the road the verger armed with his hallebard and the beadle with a large cross advanced in front. Then came the schoolmaster, with an eye on the boys, and the sister, anxious about her little girls; three of the daintiest, with angelic curls, scattered rosepetals in the air; the deacon controlled the band with outstretched arms; and two censerbearers turned back at every step towards the Holy Sacrament, which was borne by Monsieur the curé, wearing his beautiful chasuble, under a canopy of dark-red velvet held up by four churchwardens. A crowd of people pressed behind, between the white cloths covering the house walls, and they reached the bottom of the hill.

A cold sweat moistened Félicité's temples. Mère Simon sponged her with a piece of linen, saying to herself that one day she would have to go that way.

The hum of the crowd increased, was very loud for an instant, and then went further away.

A fusillade shook the window-panes. It was the postilions saluting the monstrance.[9] Félicité rolled her eyes and said as audibly as she could: "Does he look well?" The parrot was weighing on her mind.

---

9. Golden container displaying the consecrated communion bread.

Her agony began. A death-rattle that grew more and more convulsed made her sides heave. Bubbles of froth came at the corners of her mouth and her whole body trembled.

Soon the booming of the ophicleides,[1] the high voices of the children, and the deep voices of the men were distinguishable. At intervals all was silent, and the tread of feet, deadened by the flowers they walked on, sounded like a flock pattering on grass.

The clergy appeared in the courtyard. Mère Simon clambered on to a chair to reach the attic window, and so looked down straight upon the shrine. Green garlands hung over the altar, which was decked with a flounce of English lace. In the middle was a small frame with relics in it; there were two orange-trees at the corners, and all along stood silver candlesticks and china vases, with sunflowers, lilies, peonies, fox-gloves, and tufts of hortensia. This heap of blazing colour slanted from the level of the altar to the carpet which went on over the pavement; and some rare objects caught the eye. There was a silver-gilt sugar-basin with a crown of violets; pendants of Alençon stone glittered on the moss, and two Chinese screens displayed their landscapes. Loulou was hidden under roses, and showed nothing but his blue forehead, like a plaque of lapis lazuli.

The churchwardens, singers, and children took their places round the three sides of the court. The priest went slowly up the steps, and placed his great, radiant golden sun upon the lace. Everyone knelt down. There was a deep silence; and the censers glided to and fro on the full swing of their chains.

An azure vapour rose up into Félicité's room. Her nostrils met it; she inhaled it sensuously, mystically; and then closed her eyes. Her lips smiled. The beats of her heart lessened one by one, vaguer each time and softer, as a fountain sinks, an echo disappears; and when she sighed her last breath she thought she saw an opening in the heavens, and a gigantic parrot hovering above her head.

from Travels in Egypt[1]
from Flaubert's Travel Notes

Esna. Wednesday, 6 March 1850. Reached Esna about nine in the morning.

... *Bambeh.* While we were breakfasting, an *almeh* came to speak with Joseph. She was thin, with a narrow forehead, her eyes painted with antimony, a veil passed over her head and held by her elbows. She was followed by a pet sheep, whose wool was painted in spots with yellow henna. Around its nose was a black velvet muzzle. It was very wooly, its feet like those of a toy sheep, and it never left its mistress.

We go ashore. The town is like all the others, built of dried mud, smaller than Kena; the bazaars less rich. On the square, Albanian soldiers at a café. The postal authorities "reside" on the square: that is, the effendi comes there to perform his func-

1. Brass wind instruments.
1. Translated by Francis Steegmuller. When Flaubert wrote to Louis Bouilhet from Cairo on January 15th: "We have not yet seen any dancing girls; they are all in exile in Upper Egypt. Good brothels no longer exist in Cairo either," he was referring to an 1834 edict by Mohammed Ali that had prohibited female dancing and prostitution in Cairo and ordered the deportation of all known "courtesans" to three cities—Kena, Esna, and Assuan. The name *almehs* (said to come from the Arabic *awaleim*, "learned women") had originally signified professional women improvisers of songs and poems, but had come to be applied to all female entertainers, and in 1850 meant little more than dancing girls, all of whom were prostitutes as well. Among them Kuchuk Hanem, at Esna, was a star, of whom the travelers had undoubtedly heard in Cairo. Her Turkish name is said to mean either "Pretty Little Princess" or simply "Dancing Woman." [Translator's note.]

tions. School above a mosque, where we go to buy some ink. First visit to the temple, where we stay but a moment. The houses have a kind of square tower, with poles thick with pigeons. In the doorways, a few *almehs,* fewer than at Kena, their dress less brilliant and their aspect less bold.

House of Kuchuk Hanem. Bambeh precedes us, accompanied by her sheep; she pushes open a door and we enter a house with a small courtyard and a stairway opposite the door. On the stairs, opposite us, surrounded by light and standing against the background of blue sky, a woman in pink trousers. Above, she wore only dark violet gauze.

She had just come from the bath, her firm breasts had a fresh smell, something like that of sweetened turpentine; she began by perfuming her hands with rose water.

We went up to the first floor. Turning to the left at the top of the stairs, we entered a square whitewashed room: two divans, two windows, one looking on the mountains, the other on the town.

. . . Kuchuk Hanem is a tall, splendid creature, lighter in coloring than an Arab; she comes from Damascus; her skin, particularly on her body, is slightly coffee-coloured. When she bends, her flesh ripples into bronze ridges. Her eyes are dark and enormous, her eyebrows black, her nostrils open and wide; heavy shoulders, full, apple-shaped breasts. She wore a large tarboosh,[2] ornamented on the top with a convex gold disk, in the middle of which was a small green stone imitating emerald; the blue tassel of her tarboosh was spread out fanwise and fell down over her shoulders; just in front of the lower edge of the tarboosh, fastened to her hair and going from one ear to the other, she had a small spray of white artificial flowers. Her black hair, wavy, unruly, pulled straight back on each side from a center parting beginning at the forehead; small braids joined together at the nape of her neck. She has one upper incisor, right, which is beginning to go bad. For a bracelet she has two bands of gold, twisted together and interlaced, around one wrist. Triple necklace of large hollow gold beads. Earrings: gold disks, slightly convex, circumference decorated with gold granules. On her right arm is tattooed a line of blue writing.

She asks us if we would like a little entertainment, but Max says that first he would like to entertain himself alone with her, and they go downstairs. After he finishes, I go down and follow his example. Ground-floor room, with a divan and a *cafas* [an upturned palm-fibre basket] with a mattress.

Dance. The musicians arrive: a child and an old man, whose left eye is covered with a rag; they both scrape on the *rebabah,* a kind of small round violin with a metal leg that rests on the ground and two horse-hair strings. The neck of the instrument is very long in proportion to the rest. Nothing could be more discordant or disagreeable. The musicians never stop playing for an instant unless you shout at them to do so.

Kuchuk Hanem and Bambeh begin to dance. Kuchuk's dance is brutal. She squeezes her bare breasts together with her jacket. She puts on a girdle fashioned from a brown shawl with gold stripes, with three tassels hanging on ribbons. She rises first on one foot, then on the other—marvellous movement: when one foot is on the ground, the other moves up and across in front of the shin-bone—the whole thing with a light bound. I have seen this dance on old Greek vases.

Bambeh prefers a dance on a straight line; she moves with a lowering and raising of one hip only, a kind of rhythmic limping of great character. Bambeh has henna on

2. Flat-topped brimless hat worn in the Middle East.

her hands. She seems to be a devoted servant to Kuchuk. (She was a chambermaid in Cairo in an Italian household and understands a few words of Italian; her eyes are slightly diseased.) All in all, their dancing—except Kuchuk's step mentioned above—is far less good than that of Hasan el-Belbeissi, the male dancer in Cairo. Joseph's opinion is that all beautiful women dance badly.

Kuchuk took up a *darabukeh.* When she plays it, she assumes a superb pose: the *darabukeh* is on her knees, or rather on her left thigh; the left elbow is lowered, the left wrist raised, and the fingers, as they play, fall quite widely apart on the skin of the *darabukeh;* the right hand strikes flatly, marking the rhythm. She leans her head slightly back, in a stiffened pose, the whole body slightly arched.

Ces dames,[3] and particularly the old musician, imbibe considerable amounts of *raki.* Kuchuk dances with my tarboosh on her head. Then she accompanies us to the end of her quarter, climbing up on our backs and making faces and jokes like any Christian tart.

At the café of *ces dames.* We take a cup of coffee. The place is like all such places—flat roof of sugarcane stalks put together any which way. Kuchuk's amusement at seeing our shaven heads and hearing Max say: *"Allah il allah,"* etc.

Second and more detailed visit to the temple. We wait for the effendi in the café, to give him a letter. Dinner.

We return to Kuchuk's house. The room was lighted by three wicks in glasses full of oil, inserted in tin sconces hanging on the wall. The musicians are in their places. Several glasses of *raki* are quickly drunk; our gift of liquor and the fact that we are wearing swords have their effect.

Arrival of Safiah Zugairah, a small woman with a large nose and eyes that are dark, deep-set, savage, sensual; her necklace of coins clanks like a country cart; she kisses our hands.

The four women seated in a line on the divan singing. The lamps cast quivering, lozenge-shaped shadows on the walls, the light is yellow. Bambeh wore a pink robe with large sleeves (all the costumes are light-colored) and her hair was covered with a black kerchief such as the fellahin wear. They all sang, the *darabukehs* throbbed, and the monotonous rebecs[4] furnished a soft but shrill bass; it was like a rather gay song of mourning.

Coup[5] with Safia Zugairah ('Little Sophie')—I stain the divan. She is very corrupt and writhing, extremely voluptuous. But the best was the second copulation with Kuchuk. Effect of her necklace between my teeth. Her cunt felt like rolls of velvet as she made me come. I felt like a tiger.

Kuchuk dances the Bee. First, so that the door can be closed, the women send away Farghali and another sailor, who up to now have been watching the dances and who, in the background, constituted the grotesque element of the scene. A black veil is tied around the eyes of the child, and a fold of his blue turban is lowered over those of the old man. Kuchuk shed her clothing as she danced. Finally she was naked except for a *fichu*[6] which she held in her hands and behind which she pretended to hide, and at the end she threw down the *fichu.* That was the Bee. She danced it very briefly and said she does not like to dance that dance. Joseph, very excited, kept clapping his hands: *"La, eu, nia, oh! eu, nia, oh!"* Finally, after repeating for us the wonderful step

---

3. These ladies (French).
4. Musical instrument.

5. Act of sexual intercourse (French).
6. Light shawl.

she had danced in the afternoon, she sank down breathless on her divan, her body continuing to move slightly in rhythm. One of the women threw her her enormous white trousers striped with pink, and she pulled them on up to her neck. The two musicians were unblindfolded.

When she was sitting cross-legged on the divan, the magnificent, absolutely sculptural design of her knees.

Another dance: a cup of coffee is placed on the ground; she dances before it, then falls on her knees and continues to move her torso, always clacking the castanets, and describing in the air a gesture with her arms as though she were swimming. That continues, gradually the head is lowered, she reaches the cup, takes the edge of it between her teeth, and then leaps up quickly with a single bound.

She was not too enthusiastic about having us spend the night with her, out of fear of thieves who are apt to come when they know strangers are there. Some guards or pimps (on whom she did not spare the cudgel) slept downstairs in a side room, with Joseph and the negress, an Abyssinian slave who carried on each arm the round scar (like a burn) of a plague-sore. We went to bed; she insisted on keeping the outside. Lamp: the wick rested in an oval cup with a lip; after some violent play, *coup*. She falls asleep with her hand in mine. She snores. The lamp, shining feebly, cast a triangular gleam, the color of pale metal, on her beautiful forehead; the rest of her face was in shadow. Her little dog slept on my silk jacket on the divan. Since she complained of a cough, I put my pelisse over her blanket. I heard Joseph and the guards talking in low voices; I gave myself over to intense reverie, full of reminiscences. Feeling of her stomach against my buttocks. Her mound warmer than her stomach, heated me like a hot iron. Another time I dozed off with my fingers passed through her necklace, as though to hold her should she awake. I thought of Judith and Holofernes sleeping together. At quarter of three, we awake—another *coup,* this time very affectionate. We told each other a great many things by pressure. (As she slept she kept contracting her hands and thighs mechanically, like involuntary shudders.)

I smoke a *sheesheh,* she goes down to talk with Joseph, brings back a bucket of burning charcoal, warms herself, comes back to bed. "*Basta!*"[7]

How flattering it would be to one's pride if at the moment of leaving you were sure that you left a memory behind, that she would think of you more than of the others who have been there, that you would remain in her heart!

In the morning we said goodbye very calmly.

Our two sailors come to carry our things to the *cange,* and after returning to it I do some shooting around Esna. A cotton field under palms and *gassis.* Arabs, donkeys and buffalo going to the fields. The wind was blowing through the slender branches of the *gassis,* whistling as it does in the reeds at home. The sun climbs, the hills are no longer pale pink as they were this morning as I left Kuchuk Hanem's house; the fresh air feels good on my eyes . . . I thought a great deal about that morning (Michaelmas) at the Marquis de Pomereu's, at l'Héron, when I walked all by myself in the park, after the ball: it was during the holidays between my forth and third forms.

I return to the boat and get Joseph . . . We buy meat, a belt.

. . . We meet Bambeh and the fourth woman who played the *darabukeh;* Bambeh saw to our supply of bread; she looked extremely tired.

We left Esna at a quarter before noon. Some Bedouins sold us a gazelle they had killed that morning on the other side of the Nile.

7. Enough (Italian).

Temple of Esna. . . . This temple is 33 m. 70 long and 16 m. 89 wide, the circumference of the columns is 5 m. 37, the total height of the columns is 11 m. 37. There are 24 columns . . . An Arab climbed on to the capital of a column to drop the metric tape. A yellow cow, on the left, poked her head inside . . .

Saturday, 9 March 1850. Assuan. Reached Assuan threading our course between the rocks in midstream; they are dark chocolate-color, with long white streaks of bird-droppings that widen toward the bottom. To the right, bare sand-hills, their summits sharp against the blue sky. The light comes down perpendicular into transparent depths. A negro landscape.

. . . The Governor, on his doorstep, raises both hands to his turban in salute to our *firmans;*[8] beside him, a big fat blond personage wearing several coats—the former governor of Wadi Halfa. A man is brought to him who found some money on the island of Elephantine; he declared it, but he is given the third degree nevertheless, to make sure that he hasn't kept a few coins for himself. Also an army deserter, and a splendidly shaped little Nubian girl whose height they measure with a stick in order to assess the tax that every slave-trader has to pay per head.

In a shop we see an *almeh,* tall, slender, black—or rather, green—frizzy negro hair. Her eyes are dreamy and sad, or, rather, suggestive of negro daydreaming. She rolls her eyes—she is charming in profile. Another, little woman with tousled frizzy hair under her tarboosh—this one is cheerful.

Azizeh. The tall girl is named Azizeh. Her dancing is more expert than Kuchuk's. For dancing she takes off her flowing robe and puts on a cotton dress of European cut. She begins. Her neck slides back and forth on her vertebrae, and more often sideways, as though her head were going to fall off; terrifying effect of decapitation.

She stands on one foot, lifts the other, the knee making a right angle, then brings it down firmly. This is no longer Egypt; it is negro, African, savage—as wild as the other was formal.

* * *

She kissed my hand respectfully and said:

"I am a dancer; my body is suppler than a snake's; if you wish, I can come with my musicians and dance barefoot on the deck of your boat."

"The *cawadja* has seen Kuchuk Hanem at Esna," Joseph answered her.

"Kuchuk Hanem doesn't know how to dance," she replied.

I told Joseph to accept; and towards evening, when the setting sun had tempered the heat and shadows spread over the river bank, the dancer came with her players of the *rebec* and the *darabukeh.*

She was a tall Nubian, born in Korosko, named Azizeh.

She is elegant, and almost awesome, with her black skin, like bronze in its nuances of green and copper; her crinkly hair, full of gold piastres, is barely covered by a yellow kerchief dotted with blue flowers; her markedly slitted eyes seem like silver globes inset with black diamonds, and they are veiled and languid like those of an amorous cat. Her white, even teeth glitter from behind the thin lips of her mouth; a long necklace of sequins hangs down to her belly, which is circled by a girdle of glass beads that I can see through the diaphanous folds of her clothing.

---

8. Ottoman permit or passport.

Her dance is savage, and makes one think involuntarily of the contortions of the negroes of central Africa. Sometimes she uttered a shrill cry, as though to spur the zeal of her musicians. Between her fingers her noisy castanets tinkled and rang unceasingly.

"*Cawadja,* what do you think of Kuchuk Hanem now?" she cried, as she writhed her hips.

She held out her two long arms, black and glistening, shaking them from shoulder to wrist with an imperceptible quivering, moving them apart with soft and quick motions like those of the wings of a hovering eagle. Sometimes she bent completely over backwards, supporting herself on her hands in the position of the dancing Salomé over the left portal of the Rouen cathedral.

All the sailors from the boats moored at Assuan, and the town loungers, and slaves and slave-traders, gathered opposite my *cange* and watched and applauded the strange dancer, who was proud of the admiration she aroused. When she had finished, and I paid her, and she left wishing me *bon voyage* and long prosperity, the crowd around us slowly dispersed; and then I saw a horrible monster climbing on board my boat, dragging himself up the plank that served as gangway for landing.

He crawled towards me, trying to speak, uttering hoarse grunts punctuated by moans that were like appeals for help. Thus he made his way to the divan where I was sitting, seized my hand, which I snatched away from him before he could touch it with his lips, and looked at me with the expression of a hurt dog asking for comfort from his master.

His twisted, ulcerated legs had become so enfeebled as barely to support him; his eyes were infinitely sad, and tears escaped from beneath their reddened, bloated lids; his lips were covered with sores, and with a whitish slobber; his throat was swollen and purple, crusted with blood; his thickened tongue was helpless beneath the shreds of his half-destroyed palate; his voice was but a series of hiccoughs mingled with sobs.

Ah! If, like Candide, I had "inquired into cause and effect, and as to the sufficient reason that had reduced this wretch to such a piteous state," he could have replied, like Pangloss, "Alas—it was love—love, the consolation of the human race, the preserver of the universe, the soul of all sensitive beings—tender love!"

By an irony of fate, this unhappy victim of implacable Venus bore the name of a king, and was called Sultan Ahmed. A *raïs* who was leaving for Cairo agreed to convey him there, and three months later I saw him again, in the hospital of Kasr el-'Aini, rejuvenated, erect, and almost rid of his frightful sores. Egypt is a country created by Aesculapius[9]—all sicknesses are cured there.

---

9. Legendary Greek physician and god of healing.

PERSPECTIVES
Occidentalism—Europe Through Foreign Eyes

As far back as Herodotus in the fifth century B.C.E., travelers had written accounts comparing and contrasting their home culture with the differing practices they had observed abroad. As the major European powers began to establish colonies in distant lands, these accounts took on a new dimension, helping to shape the mutual understandings—and misunderstandings—of civilizations that were becoming more and more interdependent. In the nineteenth century, as the European powers began to gain influence in the broad territories held by the Ottoman Empire, an elaborate pattern developed under the name of "Orientalism"—the study of the East, and especially what Europeans called "the Near East."

That term shows the Orientalists' assumption that Europe was the natural point of reference for surveying the globe: Asia Minor and Mesopotamia were nearer to Paris and London than were China, Japan, and the other countries of the "Far East." Americans, too, adopted these Europe-centered terms, even though in actual fact people would travel west to reach Japan from San Francisco, while England would geographcially be "the near east" to a New Yorker. As the literary and cultural critic Edward Said showed in his influential book *Orientalism* (1978), European accounts of the "mysterious Orient" served to mystify as much as to understand, creating an image of backward civilizations in need of imperial guidance and control.

In the nineteenth century as earlier, though, the discourse wasn't one-sided: travelers from Asia and the Ottoman Empire came in growing numbers to Europe and North America, and wrote home about what they had seen there. Direct accounts by travelers were also seconded by home-based reflections on the advantages and disadvantages of European customs and technologies. Given here are several particularly interesting "Eastern" responses to the "West" from across the course of the century. Collectively these views can be called "occidentalism"—the construction of an image of the west from outside. Like European Orientalism, Middle Eastern and Asian occidentalism was rarely a neutral project aiming at a purely abstract understanding; instead, the writers used their comparisons either to defend their own traditions in the face of European misconceptions, or to press for reform at home. The following selections are no mere summaries of information: the writers seek to bring their comparisons to life by vivid description and the use of telling details. Sometimes, too, the writer becomes a character in the story, a foil for the reader's own understanding. Even when a writer like Chiang Yee seems comically at sea amid the Europeans' strange ways, he is implicitly challenging the reader to look afresh at life at home, as refracted through the image of life abroad.

Najaf Kuli Mirza
Early 19th century

In the summer of 1836, three Persian princes came to England on a life-and-death mission. Following the death in 1834 of the ruler Fath Ali Shah, conflict had broken out among his many sons and grandsons. One son had been proclaimed shah, but then a prince Muhammad, backed by Russia and England, succeeded in taking power and was named shah. Most of his brothers and cousins fell in with the new regime, but a prince named Firman Firman resisted. He was captured and imprisoned in the Persian capital of Tehran, where he soon died under suspicious circumstances. At this point three of his sons had set out on a journey to England, to plead for help. Escaping through Iraq and Syria, where they acquired an interpreter with an excellent knowledge of English, they came to England. During their four-month stay, they

Chiang Yee, *Umbrellas Under Big Ben*, 1937. In this illustration from his book *The Silent Traveller in London* (see p. 535), Chiang Yee turns a classic London scene into a poetic Chinese-style landscape.

charmed various members of the British nobility and enlisted the aid of the Foreign Secretary, Lord Palmerston, who agreed to intercede with Muhammad Shah. The brothers were able to return home, now as their cousin Muhammad's loyal subordinates.

One of the three princes, Najaf Kuli Mirza, was a poet and intellectual ("Mirza" is a title meaning "prince" or "learned man"), and he kept a journal during his voyage. This he wrote up in polished form on his return to Persia, detailing the marvels and the strange customs he had encountered. Though it has no express political purpose, the journal was clearly meant to bolster the tenuous position of the three princess back home, emphasizing their close friendship with Persia's powerful British allies.

The princes' Syrian interpreter, Assad Kayat, realized that the journal might have an audience abroad as well, and he translated it into English under the expansive title *Journal of a Residence in England, and of a Journey from and to Syria, of their Noble Highnesses Reeza Koolee Meerza, Najaf Koolee Meerza, and Taymoor Meerza, of Persia: To Which Are Prefixed Some Particulars Respecting Modern Persia, and the Death of the Late Shah.* As Kayat says in a preface, "It is rarely that the English Public obtain such an opportunity of learning what is said of them by the people of other nations, as in the work now presented. . . . Such a work may teach by comparison the state of civilization to which Britain has attained; the difference between those customs which belong to its own habits and prejudices, and those which are the result of experience, convenience, and propriety." Najaf Kuli Mirza perceptively analyzes British politics, enjoys the flirtatious friendship of unveiled Englishwomen, and observes with wonder and amusement the scenes he encounters, from wax museums to locomotives. A genial, contemplative observer with a poetic cast of mind, Najaf Kuli conveys his views in terms drawn from the Qur'an and the rich traditions of Persian poetry.

from Journal of a Residence in England[1]

[ARRIVAL IN ENGLAND]

About noon we came in sight of the island of England and the seaport of Falmouth. We now adored God the Most High, the most merciful, thanking Him a hundred thousand times for His mercy which has been bestowed upon us. We went upon deck, gazing upon the shore in the same manner as the lover gazes upon his mistress, when waiting to receive her. Thus our eyes looked on the shore with great anxiety till we came to the harbour, and the anchor took its hold upon the bottom of the sea, and the fire was put out. Behold, now we are new born in the world, as if fresh from the womb of our mother. Thanks be given to the Most High, who bestowed upon us as it were a new life in this world.

[LONDON]

Sunday, the 6th, Lord Palmerston, the vizir of foreign affairs (our business being also in his hand), called upon us. He came on the part of government to learn all our plans and views, as he was to inform all the other vizirs of it; he asked us to put everything down in writing: this, I believe, he requested, so that we may always be held responsible by our own written pledge that nothing new should occur. We explained clearly every thing of importance, so that he was satisfied with our reasonable requests; he promised to do every thing in the name of the badishah with Mohammed Shah in our behalf, so that we should be satisfied with our visit to this kingdom, to which we have come from such a great distance. We also proposed some questions to him, to which

---

1. Translated by Assad Kayat.

he gave no answer, but promised to think about them, and let us know the result. We therefore put down all our requests in writing, which were translated by Meerza Ibrahim, a Persian, native of Shiraz, who had been here for the last twelve years. Before Lord Palmerston left us, he took our promise to dine with him on Sunday next.

* * *

Afterwards we visited the great zoological garden, where birds, flowers, and the numerous visitors are indescribable. We saw whatever Wali[2] had already seen, and some which he had not seen, such as the giraffes which had just arrived from Abyssinia. We observed here also a dreadful rhinoceros of an extraordinary size in an iron house. I went near him, and gave him something to eat; but once he got angry, and made a most terrible noise; indeed he was a dreadful beast. Taymoor Meerza took a sketch of him. It is utterly impossible to describe these animals and birds.

Tuesday the 8th, Mohammed Ismael Khan, the ambassador of Oude, called to see us, and he tendered to us his sincere friendship; we also manifested our friendship towards him. We conversed together on several subjects, also on the wonderful arts of this country. We related to him what we saw the day before. He said, "I visited a beautiful place yesterday, a lofty edifice containing a great number of rooms, which contain some beautiful pictures beyond conception: I was perfectly astonished at them." He said, "Will you be pleased to visit it, and let me conduct you there?" Accordingly we ordered the carriage, and with Mohammed Ismael Khan went to see the place which he praised so much.

It is a very lofty edifice of innumerable large rooms, containing from the ground to the roof some most beautiful pictures, such as astonish the mind and affect the heart. But above all, our visit was at a most fortunate hour, when the originals of these pictures were walking about the rooms, so we left gazing at the artificials: and as a matter of course, our heart forced the eye to admire the splendid and beautiful visitors; yet at last we were obliged to return home, quite against the sanction of the heart. In the evening we went to the house of pleasure and music (opera); new plays and representations were performed, with dancing by beauty, such as was before mentioned by Wali. What shall I write? what am I to say? Nothing but that which is mentioned in the Hadith,[3] by the holy lips.[4] "The world is the prison of the Believer, and the paradise of the Infidel." In truth, there is nothing wanting in the paradise, except that grace which the God of the universe has promised to his faithful servants, in the world above; He has given the same to them in the world below, with this difference: theirs is made by hands and is transitory, but ours is eternal and everlasting, and the draught wine of its pleasure is not made from earthly materials. In fine, the Most High, for the sake of fulfilling his word and grace, presented these people with their paradise in this world.[5] I could give no description of these wonderful and delightful representations, &c.

Thursday evening, we were invited to an evening party at a nobleman's, where we observed many expensive articles, and costly furniture. This entertainment might

---

2. Nickname of Najaf Kuli's older brother, Reza.
3. Sayings of the Prophet.
4. Mohammed's lips are what H. R. H. means. I wish that Christian authors in general would show their veneration when speaking of the Lord Jesus Christ [translator's note]. Assad Kayat had been converted to Christianity by the missionaries who taught him English. At several places, he provides footnotes commenting on the Persian princes' Muslim beliefs, either to exhort fellow Chris-

tians to equal piety, or else (as in the next note) to register his discomfort with Najaf Kuli's treatment of Christian beliefs.
5. I would refer the reader to that part of the Journal in which H. R. H. describes his visit to St. Paul's Cathedral. We can easily see that all sights and exhibitions do not produce the same effect on the minds of Asiatics. The question is, which would be most advantageously shown them [translator's note].

have cost 4000 tomâns. All the vizirs of Government and noblemen were present here. There were also some members of the royal family; with all of whom we formed acquaintance and friendship. The people here have a very curious custom, that in their assemblies they do not sit down, neither is there any distinction; there were about 1000 persons, men and women, mixed with each other. Everyone takes the hand of a lady with an angelic face, and begins to converse with her, endeavouring in every respect to please her. They have no jealousy in this; and if a man converses much with his wife at such a time, it would be considered an ignorance from him, or rudeness. When the music commenced, every person, princes, vizirs, nobles, and gentlemen, took a lady by the hand, and went dancing while we were admiring. They who cannot dance are considered neither respectable, nor considered as persons of complete education, particularly so a lady. Many of the ladies asked us to dance with them; now we were puzzled what to say; however, we were obliged to take oath that we did not know how, and that our mother did not care to teach us, and thank God we did never dance. God protect the faithful![6] In truth, it was a splendid assembly.

[A MAGIC LANTERN SHOW]

They invited us up stairs into a large room, half of which was furnished with seats for visitors to sit on, who have to pay some money for entrance. We sat on these seats, and a number of men and women were also seated. The wall opposite to our face was made most elegantly white with paint, so much so, that in the place although dark, yet the face of a man might be seen in this wall; opposite this wall there is another which was just behind us, which had several holes in it, where there are several instruments, which had such a power, a thousand times more than the lustre of the sun. Whenever they touched this apparatus, the array of the loadstone came out of the holes, and gave out such a ray and light that no one dared to look at the wall; but when they moderated the power of the instrument, a man might look at it. The light was so great as to lead anyone to say that all the power of the sun, or the sun itself was in this room.

Afterwards the master brought some water in a glass, which he placed against this light. This drop of water suddenly (praise be to God!) looked as if it were a great sea; in which we observed myriads of animals of different kinds, in forms of leopards, and some as large as elephants, and camels, they were mingled together, and eating each other. All of them had several thousand feet and hands; such a thing had never been thought of, nor would it enter the mind. Indeed, all those that came to see this had no courage to look at these dreadful beasts. The operator was standing by the wall with a stick in his hand, explaining the nature of every one of these animals, and said in the English language, "This is the pure water that you drink every day, without being sensible of the wonderful power of God of the universe displayed in it; and what food he has given you which you do not understand." In the same way the changes of times are hidden, and we do not think of them. One after another he explained, what is their benefit, and what is their injury, that "in this drop of water there are about four millions of different kinds of animals." Thus God the most powerful has concealed from our sight many of the things that are created, existing even in what we swallow daily. After this, he presented on a glass some little insects, such as flies, muskittoes

6. I take the liberty of begging the reader who may feel disposed to argue with the Prince upon the lawfulness of certain representations [such as mixed dancing], to ask himself whether those who profess Christianity are living up to their profession, and are endeavouring to show Mohammedans and other sects that this world is not their paradise [translator's note].

possessing feet, and hands, and hair, of extraordinary form. This magnificence of what we saw in these little insects could never be described; nor would it be believed unless a man in person should go himself and see them. Indeed, we doubted the truth of the spectacle before we rose and were induced to examine the originals. Today we had indeed a very interesting, wonderful exhibition.

[An Evening Party]

In the evening we visited a large garden, beautifully lighted up, and the fireworks that we saw here made us forget all others we had already seen. A garden, a heaven, large, adorned with roses of different colours in every direction, the water was running on the beautiful green, pictures were drawn on every wall. Here and there were young moonly faces selling refreshments. There were burning in this place about two millions of lights, each giving a different colour; the lanterns and lights are so arranged as to make poetry, in such a manner that they have no end. On every side there appeared the moon, and the sun, with the planets, each moving in its orbit;[7] and in every walk there were about 10,000 Frank[8] moons, walking and gazing about, where the roses and their tribes were admiring their beautiful cheeks. Each was taken by the hand, such a company in such a place says to the soul, Behold thy paradise!—pleasure and joy appear; woes and sorrows are banished;—every hand asked for a glass of refreshment to present to the possessors of jasmine hands. Thus we were happy to have in each hand a paradisean companion, and to point out the beauties of the place, in order to draw forth the sweet music of their replies; we left the rose and met a pink! are we awake or in a dream?

[An Underwater Tunnel]

Thursday the 18th, we visited that place which is celebrated over all the world. This was the Thames Tunnel, the construction of which would never enter the human mind. The noble river Thames is navigable for ships of the line; the ships pass over the heads of the people in the following manner: The learned men of England in their wisdom have dug a tunnel under this river. It is constructed in the form of arches, and miraculously lighted with gas, and it is free from all damp. Thus they have most wonderfully succeeded in making a road under the water, like a bridge under the sea, from one side of the river to the other. To this we call the attention of all travellers. In truth, it may be called a glory of this country, and the name is a sufficient reward for the millions of money that have been spent. It is established by the law that any person who passes this tunnel must pay a certain sum, so that in a short time they may receive what they have spent. After this we went to the road of iron, or railroad, which is near the Tunnel. On railroads there are steam-coaches, which go at the incredible rate of forty miles an hour.

[Duels]

The men are very particular in their disputes, which are carried on with great ability. If there should be the widest possible misunderstanding, still they keep up the rules of politeness. If it should rise so high as to produce vindictive feeling, still they carry on their disputes in a genteel style, and bad language (God forbid!) is not used. To be called a liar is the utmost insult: this will lead to a duel; the duel is allowed here.

---

7. A radiant universe of beautiful women.   8. European.

Sometimes this happens in such circumstances as the following: If a man should be at an assembly, and should have something said to him improper or disgraceful, he who feels it to be such would at once leave the room. Then he will relate it to some friend, saying, that he heard so and so, at such a place, in such a party, which he did not like at all. * * *

Then the friends of both endeavour to settle the question between them, but generally, this cannot be effected without fighting the duel. However, when all mediations fail, then the two individuals, accompanied by their respective friends as witnesses, meet at the appointed place, exactly at the fixed hour, which will be published in the newspapers. When the two come to this place with their pistols, then the friends use their utmost influence of mediation; if at last all should be in vain, then they separate from each other a distance of twenty feet, and the signal will be given when both fire. Then it becomes a matter of chance; sometimes both of them are hit and perish, and perhaps no one is hit, or one dies, and the other is saved. Thus the question is finished; this act is permitted by their law which does not condemn it, and it has been a well-known practice among the fools of this nation from the ancient times.

It is quite similar to the old foolish custom of the heathens, who threw both the plaintiff and defendant into the fire, believing that the flame would only burn the criminal and not the innocent. Thus, also, these people believe that the bullet will not hit the innocent, and this old foolish custom is continued among the imprudent class of the Franks; this, however, takes place more in France than other parts. Just at this time we observed in the newspaper that a great man in that country had been killed in this act.

In fine, in former times, the Franks, especially those of England, were like animals and quadrupeds, and had no arts of any description. They dwelt in forests, mountains, and the extreme coasts of the sea, dressed in the skins of animals, eating the natural productions of the earth, and if they had a king, they sometimes killed him; and likewise their kings killed many of the people. These oppressions, outrages, and violations caused always quarrels between the kings and their subjects. Many people, during the height of oppression, had no rest, and were obliged to abandon the country, and go to the New World and other parts. It appears that at different times, according to the wisdom of the Lord the Omnipotent, oppression falls upon the people in different kingdoms, according to the state of their hearts. These horrible outrages which at this time are practised to their extreme in the Asiatic kingdoms,[9] are entirely banished from Europe, where there is no oppression, and cannot be. In all parts and cities of England which we visited, the inhabitants are a very high-minded people, and conduct their affairs with perfect prudence, so much so, that they have no governors, nor do they require civil power. All of them know the law, and what is justice: they obey their laws, which are founded on liberty. Every person enjoys this liberty, and acts according to its laws. Vizirs, princes, even the king himself, has no power to kill a bird. For instance, should the king fire at a bird during the prohibited season, he must stand before the law, and receive the decision thereof; in short, every person is under the law.

---

9. A rare hint at the princes' own troubles. In addition to killing their father after displacing the duly installed shah, Muhammad Shah had disposed of two rivals—his own brothers—by having their eyes put out.

[ENGLISH POLITICS]

The administration consists of two parties. The one is named whig, the other tory.[1] The difference between these two parties is political, that is, every one has a different opinion on policy. Their seats in the Vazaraship, or administration, depend on the House of Commons, that is, if the majority of the House are tories, then the ministers also are tories; and if they be whigs, then the ministers are whigs. They cannot both be in office at the same time. Administration must be of one party alone. It happens sometimes that they are changed, one goes out, and the other comes in. Sometimes the father is a whig, and his son a tory, and two brothers may also be one a tory, and the other a whig. The difference between these two parties is as follows:

The tories in ancient days have always been in office, and thereby they have established to themselves some privileges by which every one is now a possessor of millions of money. As to their policy and their views, they say this:

"Three hundred years ago, we were wild people, and our kingdom then was worse and lower than any other. But through mind, wisdom, and learning, which we have now, we have brought our kingdom to its present height of honour; and as our empire grew larger by our management, why should we now reform and give up our policy which has done all this good?" This being the case, they say they will not give up their views. As to the whigs, they say this:

"We know that it is more prudent to go according to the changes of time and circumstances; moreover, by the old policy, only a few were profited, and as our government is a general one, therefore we must observe that which is best for the whole nation, and that all should be profited, and every person should enjoy the same privileges. It will never do that some should grow rich beyond measure, and others should be left poor. The policy of the whigs is for the advantage of the public in general, and they are most powerful in the House of Commons. Also the present administration is formed of whigs. But there are also a good number of tories in Parliament, who always dispute with the opposite party: in fact, each party uses its utmost power, by proofs and arguments, to establish its own view. Thus they (the two parties) have always great discussions.

There is also in this kingdom another foundation, which is of invaluable importance and exceeding advantage, that is, what they call newspapers. These papers are written by some very clever editors and authors, who are very learned, and poets. They enjoy the confidence of the people. They have large establishments, furnished with every convenience, such as types and presses, and every necessary material. They employ thousands of individuals in these undertakings. Some of them are appointed to go about the different parts of the city, to learn all the news concerning everything that is going on, of life, death, birth, war, quarrels, arrivals, departures, sales, purchases, failures, friendships, disputes, and, in a word, all kinds of information, which they relate daily to the editors. Others go about the king, queen, princes, vizirs, and, in an astonishing manner, they learn what is going on, in detail, and give in an account of it. Likewise some are sent to the different departments of the vizirs, such as the Vizir of Foreign Affairs, who is always visited by foreign ambassadors, political agents, and consuls, and receives news from all parts of the world. Thus the information is collected, and reported in the printing-office. Besides all this, they have agents in every place abroad, to inform them of all foreign news and accidents.

---

1. The Whigs were the major progressive party in the 19th century; the Tories were the conservatives.

[A WAX MUSEUM]

[Najaf Kuli's brothers visit a wax museum on a day he can't go. They decide to play a trick on him, and take him there, pretending they are going to visit the king and queen, whom they are supposed to meet but haven't yet seen.]

About sunset we entered the carriage for the royal palace, on a visit to the Queen. We arrived at the door of the house, supposing this to be the palace. I desired Fraser Sâheb[2] to enter first, and to announce our arrival, and to obtain permission for us to enter. Fraser Sâheb went in, and came out saying that the king has honoured this place with his presence, and that all the royal family are present, as well as the viziers and nobles of state, all in full uniform, in the presence of his Majesty, who is holding a levee.[3] I then entered the place, and found it a splendid hall. The king was sitting on the imperial throne, with the crown on his head, and clad in a splendid royal robe of jewels. In the same manner, the Queen was seated, in her most magnificent robe of precious stones. All the members of the royal family were in their full uniform, making a circle round the King. Dukes, princes, viziers, and nobles, all standing before him. The royal hall was beautifully lighted up, with magnificent chandeliers. When I beheld all this splendour, I said within myself, "I ought to approach the King just as I should my sovereign, the Badishah of Persia, and offer him the same dutiful obedience." Thus I approached nearer to the King, bowing down my head, after our custom, and my brothers stood behind me. The King, much to my surprise, did not appear to acknowledge my presence.

I then asked Fraser Sâheb why the King was uncivil. He said, "I do not know. Perhaps," said he, "the reason is, that it was not the King, but the Queen, who invited you, so that the King has nothing to say to you; let us go to the Queen." I was exceedingly vexed and ashamed of what took place, bowed my head to the ground, and followed Fraser Sâheb to the Queen. Here I observed a throne of marble, inlaid with precious stones and valuable jewels. On this splendid and magnificent throne was seated a young lady, with a face like the moon, dressed in royal robes, worth more than the revenues of Europe. A precious crown was on her head, and she was surrounded by a company of ladies with angelic faces, whose splendour was like the sun at mid-day, all seated upon chairs of gold. I drew near, offering the due respects; all were silent, and nobody replied to my salutation. This was quite the reverse of what I met with at other parties. I began to be quite vexed with Fraser Sâheb, and said to him, "Fraser Sâheb! this gives me to understand that the Queen did not invite me to come, and that she did not wish to see me. It is all through your fault and intermeddling that I have to bear this shame."

One of the ministers, dressed most magnificently, without a hat on his head, was standing before the Queen. I went near this minister, and desired Fraser Sâheb to tell him this, that although the Queen did not invite us, yet we were already in her palace, and it would be only politeness in her to treat us as her guests. Fraser Sâheb interpreted to him what I said, but I observed that this man did not give any answer, neither uttered a word. Praise be to God! what a curious circumstance! I then took his hand, saying, "Why do not you give an answer to my question?" When I shook his hand, he fell down. I then observed that he was dead, and I was astonished to find that all of

---

them also were dead persons. Now my brothers and Fraser Sâheb laughed loudly, and said, "These people are not dead, but all of them are artificial figures of white wax." Verily, no one would ever have thought that they were manufactured by men.

This establishment belongs to a rich nobleman, who inherited it from his father; and it brings him daily an income of a hundred tomâns. Many people from all parts of the world come to visit this wonderful place. In short, I was not satisfied till I examined all of them; and I was perfectly astonished to find that there was not the least difference between the imitation and the imitated. So wonderful are the arts of the Franks.

[FOND FAREWELLS]

In the evening we went to the entertainment of Mrs. R——. Here we met the beautiful circle of the family, our hosts. With fine arms of jasmine colour, hair of ambergris odour, eyes of the gazelle, and conversations sweet as sugar-candy. These lovely houries[4] sat around us with their splendid musical instruments, and with sweet and lovely voices revived the heart. Indeed, here we felt the unpleasant feelings of bidding them good-bye. Oh, how unsupportable is the word—farewell! how is it possible that the body can live without the soul? What a melancholy mixture of night! at first full of joy and pleasure, afterwards full of grief and sorrow at leaving this dear assembly. Alas! for the changes of time! woe! at being far from love!

* * *

Saturday, the 23rd of Jamad the first, or September the 3rd, early in the morning, Fraser Sâheb called upon us, saying that everything requested from Government on our behalf was settled, and that nothing was now wanting; that he was ordered by Government to accompany us as mihmandar[5] to Constantinople, and there to arrange everything respecting our further journey comfortably; and also that he was ready to offer us any possible service in his power for our pleasure, and that carriages, &c., for starting were quite prepared. On this day, about noon, we bade our friends, who came to see us, good-bye, and left London. We were nearly four months in London, spending every other day in a garden, and every second in an exhibition; not a day or a night passed without our receiving some invitation, and it was impossible for us to accept all that were proposed, so that such places as we were more anxiously invited to, and to which we desired to go, were fixed a month previous to our being able to accomplish the engagement. In fine, we cannot even describe an item[6] of the friendship and hospitality which we received from the people of this kingdom, from the king to the poorest, from the highest to the lowest, from both old and young.

During the short time of our stay here, we formed such acquaintance and friendship amongst them, that it caused all of us very insupportable pain to leave each other. Verily we can never forget these friends. All the time of our stay at Mivart's, which is the best hotel, we were the King's guests; indeed the kindness and friendship that he ordered towards us has imposed upon us an obligation for ever. If a man wishes to travel and examine this kingdom, and desires to know much about it; in short, if he should be a philosopher, and should every day and hour visit new arts and exhibitions, &c., were he to remain here a hundred years, he would be unable to see the tenth part. But I have done according to the saying, "If it cannot all be comprehended, it must not all be neglected." In this short time I have written what I have seen and can recollect; it will be taken into consideration that I do not understand their language. May the end be happy!

4. Heavenly women.
5. Guide.

6. A fraction.

Mustafa Sami Effendi
c. 1790–1855

The world's most powerful empire in the fifteenth and sixteenth centuries, the Ottoman Empire had extended from its base in Turkey to control the entire eastern half of the Mediterranean and lands beyond. By the early nineteenth century, though, this extended empire was unraveling. Corruption and division in the capital of Constantinople were hampering the central government's ability to collect taxes and to control its far-flung holdings. Restive local rulers in Egypt, Greece, and Serbia were becoming increasingly independent, Russia had retaken the Crimean peninsula and the northern coast of the Black Sea, and the technologically advanced navies of France and Britain controlled the Mediterranean. A bitter debate raged in Turkey: would the government do best to hold fast to the old ways that had originally built the empire, or should they adopt modern European technologies and methods?

A first attempt at modernization came under Sultan Selim III, who took the throne in 1789. Selim focused on creating an army equipped with modern weapons and trained by European advisers—an army that would be directly loyal to him. In 1807 the older military corps, often loyal to regional rulers, backed a revolt by conservatives, who imprisoned Selim and massacred most of his reformers. A new sultan, Mahmud II, took power in 1808 with conservative support, but he too soon saw that the old policies weren't sufficing to contain the growing internal and external threats to the empire's power and its very existence. By the early 1830s he had succeeded in disbanding the old army and replacing it with a European-style force, and a series of new measures was begun: a national postal system, technical schools to train engineers, and medical schools for doctors.

Such innovations were often modeled on European institutions, but Mahmud was mindful of the reaction that had destroyed Selim's reforms. If they were to succeed, it would be crucial for the new measures to be seen at home as compatible with traditional practice, if possible even as the logical extension of traditional ways. The sultan sent emissaries on fact-finding missions to Europe, and on their return their task was not only to report on useful innovations but also to present them in ways that would be acceptable to conservatives who were deeply suspicious of any capitulation to Christian Europeans. One such report was written in 1838 by an official named Mustafa Sami Effendi; his *Essay on Europe* pointedly details a range of European practices that he feels would be beneficial at home. The chapter included here focuses especially on medical care and on education—aspects that would be stressed in major reforms inaugurated the next year by Sultan Mahmud's successor, Abdul-Mecid I.

As impressed as he is by what he sees in Europe, Mustafa Sami Effendi never suggests that Europe's technical and social advances are the product of some natural Western superiority, as the European Orientalists of the time usually believed. On the contrary, he emphasizes that the Europeans' successes have grown from their own openness to foreign influences—particularly the benefits of medieval Islamic science and philosophy. He thus skillfully brings his report full circle, grounding the latest European innovations in the most traditional Muslim values and achievements.

On the General Conditions of Europe[1]

All countries in Europe are of the Christian religion. The people of five of those countries, that is the people of Great Britain, Prussia, Holland, Sweden and Denmark, are Protestants. Russia is of Orthodox Christian faith and the remaining France, Austria,

---

1. Translated by Laurent Magon.

Spain and other well-known states and governments are of the Catholic faith. But a lot of Catholics live in Protestant countries and likewise there are a lot of Protestants in Catholic countries. However, since nobody is being pressured in matters of religion and faith, anybody who has the suitable skills can be employed in a state duty regardless of his religion, even if he is a Jew.

Men and women, all the people of Europe, are able to read and write. This is particularly true in France where even a simple porter or a shepherd is able to write or read his own letter at least. In short, the Europeans have stretched the frontiers of knowledge and skills and rendered education and tuition easier. There are separate schools and teachers for blind and mute children in most places. These children develop their skills and knowledge during eight or ten years with the help of books and signs which have been specially designed for them. Thanks to these skills and knowledge, they are able to live independently and in prosperity just like healthy people. There are several savants among the deaf, mute and blind people who have written books about philosophy and mathematics. There are even nine- or ten-year-old boys and girls who have a very deep knowledge of geometry and geography as well as of other branches of science.

It is truly admirable that Europeans have spent a lot of time and money for disabled children and that that they have worked so hard in order to spread science throughout their lands, so that people could be saved from ignorance and protected from the degradation of begging. Taking into consideration how they educate disabled boys and girls, one can easily imagine what the knowledge and capacities of healthy people are.

Europeans have grown famous for their organisational skills and their industrial advances in manners of economic and military power as well as in issues related to the prosperity of towns. Indeed everything is organised like the machinery of a clock. For instance, it is above all necessary to protect the health of the human body. In order to achieve this, it is necessary on the one hand to know one's state of health and on the other to know whether the things eaten or drunk are warm or cold and then to act accordingly. Europeans know whether the nature of things is useful or harmful as a result of their skills and their education and thus they can wisely use their bodies. Through experimentation, they are discovering several solutions and cures like the vaccination for smallpox and the quarantine against the plague.

As a result of the abundance of skilled doctors, men and women are treated in well-organised hospitals that exist in every city, town and sometimes even in villages. There are separate hospitals for people from different social classes, for those with contagious diseases, for the old, for the soldiers and for the retired. Patients are easily cured and are healed in a short period of time since there are doctors on duty and pharmacies with every kind of drugs in every hospital. I can testify that I was amazed by the size and the soundness of the buildings of some of the hospitals as well as by the actual neatness of the clothing of the patients, by the cleanliness of the beds and of the rooms and by the carefully prepared food that tasted so good.

Moreover I was stunned when I witnessed that the women who work in the hospitals and take care of the patients do not do it because they are poor. Most of them are the daughters of respected and rich families. With a desire for self-sacrifice, they offer the wealth they inherited from their ancestors or the money their parents consented to give them to the hospitals. Moreover it is with joy that throughout their life they dedicate their own bodies to the service of injured and ill patients.

Patients affected by mental diseases recover just like the rich or poor patients who heal in a relatively little time because of the above-mentioned reasons and facilities, thanks to the perfection and professionalism of the doctors and the good organisation of lunatic asylums in Europe. Asylums are only built in regions where the air is light and clean. They have well-decorated and well-kept gardens with water-jets and fountains. The rooms too are well ordered. They all have stoves for winter days and chandeliers and oil-lamps which can be lit during the night. Every ten patients have a separate nurse who checks their dressings, clothes, food and drinks with appropriate attention. There are doctors on duty who examine and check each patient twice a day.

The patients are treated according to the nature of their illness. For instance, certain women became mad because of the pain engendered by the loss of a child and were brought to the hospital. They are treated by showing them representations of children made in wax. Those who are possessed with the fancy of accumulating possessions, gold and money are quietened by giving them things made of tin and lead that look like coins. The doctors try to heal everyone by going right to the source of the illness. This is why very few do not heal. Moreover the patients are not enchained and are free to walk and wander around the hospital and the above mentioned gardens. But it should be said that, whenever they are disobedient, they are made to wear a heavy shirt made of resistant cloth. Then, they are unable to harm anyone since their hands have been tied behind their back. If this is not enough they are imprisoned in a room without windows that has a glass roof. The room is full of hay. Thus they are unable to harm anybody and if the person were able to tear up his shirt, he would be saved from staying on bare wood or stone since, unlike the bed and the shirt, he could not tear up the hay.

Having made great progress in medicine, the Europeans have reached the conclusion that the remedy for those suffering of mental diseases was to look after them in a pleasing manner. Hence one realises the utter foolishness of the saying current in our lands—*the madman becomes sensible when he is beaten.*

The above given information makes it clear that the Europeans have found easy ways to protect their health and to heal their illnesses with the help of science. Let us now discuss the effects and advantages that science provides in everyday life.

Literacy allows people to calculate their earnings and their business expenditures. Hence they can act accordingly and avoid debts and bankruptcy. Moreover they are protected from disputes and allegations of lies because they write title deeds and contracts when doing business.

Their works and arts progressed with the power of experimentation in chemistry and mathematics. For instance, they are able to produce pure and brilliant mirrors and chinaware using simple earth. More than fifteen hundred books are published every year in several places, but especially in the city of Paris, on various developments and new crafts which they have heard about.

New editions can easily be printed because of the multitude of printing offices. In Europe, books are available on every science, method and system. It is known that several books in European languages can even be found on matters that are considered insignificant, such as the pasturing of sheep and the destruction of mice and other vermin. Their approach has offered them new opportunities and made their countries prosperous. Moreover it is obvious that they have provided advantages to people in other countries too. This is why the sweets and compotes made with the sugar from the talented and expert European importers taste so good and that their velvets and broadcloths suit our costumes and stature so well during festivities.

Let us now talk about the fact that science and education are sources of ease and comfort in everyday life: It is possible to go without hesitation and without asking anybody to any house or shop because numbers are written over the doors of every house and the names are written on the top of every shop. Someone who would like to travel from one province to another can go to whatever city, town or village without having to ask for help from anybody. All the traveller needs to do is to read which road to follow on columns planted in the countryside and on mountains. Thus even a stranger from India could easily find his way.

Moreover there are special books and maps that tell the travellers how long the journey will last and describe the conditions of the regions they will pass through as well as indicate the fare of the ticket for the journey. It would take a few volumes just to describe to what extent science and ingenuity have eased journeys in Europe.

With the knowledge of geometry and dynamics they have managed to flatten the main routes progressively and to transform them into plains, even though there were depressions and mountains that reached to the sky. Now three carts can drive side by side on those roads. There are special officers who are responsible for the main roads. They take care of the maintenance of the roads and of the upkeep of the trees that grow on the right and left of the roads.

There is not a mountain or a valley without a village because all the conditions for the growth in number of human beings are well in place. Travellers can settle, according to their means, in houses called hotels in the city, town or village of their choice. These hotels provide peace of mind and comfort that is not even available in one's own home. Food is served with silver cutlery and dishes. The traveller can rest and sleep under satin-embroidered quilts in rooms that have been furnished with valuable carpets, velvet armchairs and sofas and been decorated with chandeliers and mirrors. The most remarkable aspect of the food served in the above mentioned *khans* and in the apartments of the noble and notables of Europe is that it is medically easy to digest. Moreover the dinner tables are decorated with fresh fruit and flowers, whatever the season including winter, and with various sweets and objects which look like golden chandeliers. But despite this, it should be said that their food cannot be chewed or swallowed by somebody who is not used to it.

But let us return to our discussion: It is not only the travellers who benefit from the maintenance and the levelling of the main roads. For instance, the roads ease the transport of soldiers, provisions, artillery and ammunition during wartime. Moreover, they are also of great use in order to convey with speed to the neighbouring countries the writings and the letters of the state or of the people. There are post offices in every city, town and village. When you want to send even a simple note to another country, or from one district to another in the same city, you hand it over to the post office. It is impossible for the letter not to reach its destination or for it to fall into the hands of strangers. Moreover this service is so well organised that if a letter is posted at twelve o'clock from Paris to London, one can be informed of the exact time of its arrival in London two days later in the morning. There are places of signals which they call telegraph all over the country. They are used in order to communicate faster, when an urgent problem concerning the affairs of the state arises. You may receive news in an hour from a place a hundred hours away with the telegraph.

The degree to which skills and knowledge are needed in every action and work must be clear by now. Moreover it has been understood that the high degree of organisation attained by the Europeans has only been rendered possible by the spread of science and virtue.

Let us now discuss the reasons for their love of science: After pondering the issue, the Europeans have declared that ignorance was the greatest source of shame. The state and the people have decided to pay attention to and work on the crux of the matter. They have built independent schools even for the blind and the deaf and they have founded several educational institutions for each independent branch of science. They pay great attention to educate systematically every girl and boy for at least ten years.

Moreover, progress in one particular science leads to progress in other sciences too. For instance in our country poetry has been an agent for the development of prose. Among the Europeans the development of the mathematical science led to progress in algebra. As a result they have built steam engines thanks to which things that were produced in one year can now be produced in one day. Likewise, the development of chemistry has led to the invention of the science of lithography, thanks to which two thousand books can now be printed in the same amount of time that one book can be written by hand. In this way the literacy of the people has been eased according to individual needs.

The Europeans have suppressed or limited the use of several unnecessary words and expressions by linking their languages to a system. The state has given certificates to the representatives of every guild and anyone writing a book or developing a new skill or ability is being rewarded and honored in a suitable fashion.

Hence their eagerness and ardor grows from day to day. Since no individuals are denied their rights, their work and labour are not lost.

The sciences, to which the Europeans are said to show, day and night, much attention and care, have not originated from their faith or creed. Mathematics and philosophy as well as other branches of sciences and other skills such as logic, astronomy, medicine, geometry, mechanics, arithmetic, chemistry, history, poetry and prose were discovered by ancient Muslim Arabs. The Europeans brought them to their own lands and continued to develop them. Beside the above mentioned branches of science, there are other branches such as geography, physics and the remaining sciences that had already been studied by European scholars to a certain degree.

As everybody knows and as far as I can understand, the state of perfection reached in European provinces and the production of every kind of rare and precious goods is not due to the moderation of the weather or the fertility of the earth. The weather is not enjoyable and the soil is not fertile in any European country but Italy. All their achievements were engendered by the power of science and knowledge.

If science and perfection, which were invented by Muslims and hence are our true heritage, could be spread among the people in the Islamic lands just like in past times, then, since the Islamic lands are the most outstanding places on earth and more particularly since our soils are fertile because God, out of respect to the prophet Muhammad, whose community we are proud to be members of, has decreed that our lands and climate should be abundant and prosperous and moreover since our people are intelligent and wise from birth, all the industry and the organisation, which the Europeans founded using a lot of time and work, could be spread among our people in very little time. This situation would be advantageous in every aspect because we would not need any goods or provisions produced in foreign lands anymore. The money usually spent for those imports would remain in our country. Hence our country and people would become prosperous. Our organisation, our sciences, our perfectionism and our fame would be greater than that of the Europeans. Moreover, our people would learn the true value of patriotism and citizenship because they would be educated. Lodgings and hospitals would be built for the handicapped, for the poor, for the old and the orphans who beg in the markets and bazaars, since this latter degradation injures the sense of honour of everyone. *Madrasas* and convents would be built for the religious teachers and the dervishes.[2] The number of prosperous people would increase in our community because economic power is a consequence of scientific power. They could take care of charitable works such as the restoration of mosques, bridges and fountains that are in ruins. Thus we would most certainly guarantee our future prosperity.

[handwritten marginalia: economic power, consequence, scientific power!]

❈

Hattori Bushō
1842–1908

For centuries, Japan was largely closed to Western products and cultural influence. By the mid-nineteenth century, though, the United States and the European powers were deeply involved in China and were pressuring Japan to open its markets as well. Though Japan was nominally ruled by an emperor, real power had long been controlled by military dictators, the shoguns, and Japan was divided into a patchwork of holdings of feudal barons (daimyo). As the influence of the Western powers grew throughout Asia, many Japanese, including some of the barons, came to feel that their country would be swallowed up also unless Japan could be unified and could develop an industrial economy. After a series of battles, the shogunate was overthrown in 1867, and the old feudal baronies were replaced with a system intended to blend the best of old and new: a strengthened emperor, presiding over a constitutional government.

The young emperor Mutsuhito assumed a new throne name, Meiji ("enlightened rule") and inaugurated the period known as the Meiji era (from 1868 through Meiji's death in 1912). This period saw extraordinary changes, in which the government reclaimed large land holdings from the country's 300 daimyo and radically reformed government, education, and commerce. Within a generation, Japan had moved from an inward-looking, agricultural economy with a thousand-year-old political system to a dynamically expanding industrial economy, holding its own in Asia against the colonial European powers while also adapting many Western concepts and institutions.

These rapid changes were greeted with mixed feelings by many, even as change was widely felt to be unavoidable. Hattori Bushō's bestselling *Tōkyō Shin-hanjō-ki* ("A New Account of the Flourishing City of Tokyo," 1874) gave a skeptical account of the city's changing shape. The chapter included here, "The Western Peep Show," expresses a scornful fascination for the new Western technologies being introduced. Even as Hattori mocks the peep show as tawdry and unsatisfying, he registers the dramatic opening out of a formerly closed society to a tantalizing, unsettling global perspective.

The Western Peep Show[1]

No less than the soaring eagle, the dung fly beats its wings; the naked savage parades himself with the airs of the elegantly clad. Hence it comes about that the peep show has won such popularity and, together with the photograph, proudly flaunts its banners today. It all began when someone opened a place in Asakusa.[2] Within a few months there were peep-show establishments in a number of localities, particularly in the section formerly dominated by mansions of the daimyo. The peep show must have

---

2. Madrases are religious schools; dervishes are men living a religious life of poverty and chastity.
1. Translated by Donald Keene.

2. Neighborhood in central Tokyo being developed as a commercial center.

been an invention of those who eat without tilling the fields and who wear clothes which are not of their own weaving. As yet no respected businessmen seem to be promoting this entertainment.

The viewing parlors are for the most part small painted shacks, the fronts of which have been given a hasty coat of whitewash. The rear, however, is neglected, suggesting nothing so much as a slattern who powders her face but leaves her back dirty. Some of these parlors are several stories tall, and the wooden boards with which they are built are painted to resemble stone, exactly like the entrance to some quack doctor's residence. Inside the building, at intervals several feet apart, are arranged a number of machines, and one goes from one machine to another peeping at its display. The front of the machine has eyes like a giant snake, each of which neatly fits the two human eyes. The viewer peeps at the world as through the eye of a needle, and the cost is a mere one sen. Some machines contain pictures of the scenery of countries all over the world; others are of completely imaginary subjects:

The steel bridge of London is longer than a rainbow; the palace of Paris is taller than the clouds. An enraged Russian general pulls out a soldier's whiskers; a recumbent Italian lady kisses her dog. They have bought an American conflagration to sell us; they have wrapped up a German war to open here. Warships push through the waves in droves; merchant ships enter port in a forest of masts. A steam engine climbs a mountain; a balloon flies in the sky. Seated one may contemplate the Cape of Good Hope; lying down one may gaze at the Mediterranean. The lion which devours the human being invariably kills from the trunk; the black men who paddle boats remain stuck for all eternity to the bottom.[3] You look at a picture of a museum and despise the pawnshop next door; you peep at a great hospital and lament the headaches of others. As the spectator approaches the last peep show he becomes increasingly aware how cheap the admission price has been. In the last show, the Goddess of Beauty lies naked in bed. Her skin is pure white, except for a small black mole under her navel. It is unfortunate that she has one leg lifted, and we cannot admire what lies within. In another scene we regret that only half the body is exposed and we cannot see the behind; in still another we lament that though face to face we cannot kiss the lips. This marvel among marvels, novelty among novelties, is quite capable of startling the eyes of rustics and untutored individuals.

The above are only a few examples of what one can see. Although the peep show is popular entertainment, when compared to other familiar types it is not without its educational benefits. Unlike the "tigers" of Asakusa, which are actually dyed cats, or the "dragons" of Yorozuyo Bridge, which are snakes with painted scales—displays whose falseness becomes apparent in a couple of days, when the paint wears off—the peep shows offer the latest curiosities of the world and the customs of every nation. It is like touring the world at a glance, and should broaden men's knowledge while delighting their eyes. It may be true, as some say, that we cannot be sure whether these pictures are true or false without going to the countries they represent, but they are by no means in the same category with a cat painted like a tiger. But, of course, they are no more than second-hand articles from some old ragpicker's shop.

---

3. Mocking the static, stereotypical nature of the peep show's images.

Okakura Kakuzo
1862–1913

Over the course of a life that bracketed the Meiji era, Okakura Kakuzo became one of the most eloquent voices for the revitalization of traditional Japanese culture amid the changing forces of modernity. Born in the port city of Yokohama, Okakura learned English as a child at a Christian mission school while also studying classical Chinese at a nearby Buddhist temple. Throughout his life, he would seek creative ways to link East and West, classical civilization and modernity. Okakura studied at the newly established Tokyo Imperial University with Ernest Fenollosa, an American art historian who was championing the preservation of traditional Japanese arts and crafts. Okakura then joined Japan's education ministry, and he and Fenollosa traveled to the United States to study methods of arts education. Back in Tokyo, while still in his twenties Okakura became director of the new Tokyo Art School and served as a curator at the Imperial Museum. He resigned his posts, though, following an affair with the wife of a prominent government official, and in 1901 he traveled to India, where he lived with the family of the great Bengali writer Rabindranath Tagore.

In India he began writing in English, seeking to promote intercultural understanding, and in 1904 he moved to the United States, where he served as curator of Japanese art at the Museum of Fine Arts in Boston until his death. His most influential book was *The Book of Tea* (1906), whose opening essay is given here; the pioneering American architect Frank Lloyd Wright later credited Okakura's book as an inspiration for his own "architecture of within." In "The Cup of Humanity" Okakura steers a middle way between the Meiji love of all things new and Western and the conservative hewing to old ways. In the process, he rings changes on the nineteenth-century discourses of "east" and "west." Folded inside his charming evocation of an ancient Japanese custom is a strong critique of Western superficiality, haste, and jingoism, as he simultaneously presents a view of the West and counters Western views of the Orient. For Okakura, the Japanese tea ceremony provides a necessary counterweight to the stresses of modern civilization. At the same time, his book is a plea for cross-cultural understanding, and he portrays tea as a perfect meeting-ground: the most civilized of Oriental customs has become ubiquitous in the West.

The Cup of Humanity

Tea began as a medicine and grew into a beverage. In China, in the eighth century, it entered the realm of poetry as one of the polite amusements. The fifteenth century saw Japan ennoble it into a religion of aestheticism—Teaism.[1] Teaism is a cult founded on the adoration of the beautiful among the sordid facts of everyday existence. It inculcates purity and harmony, the mystery of mutual charity, the romanticism of the social order. It is essentially a worship of the Imperfect, as it is a tender attempt to accomplish something possible in this impossible thing we know as life.

The Philosophy of Tea is not mere aestheticism in the ordinary acceptance of the term, for it expresses conjointly with ethics and religion our whole point of view about man and nature. It is hygiene, for it enforces cleanliness; it is economics, for it shows comfort in simplicity rather than in the complex and costly; it is moral geometry, inasmuch as it defines our sense of proportion to the universe. It represents the true spirit of Eastern democracy by making all its votaries aristocrats in taste.

---

1. Okakura has invented this word, playfully echoing "Taoism," the Buddhist philosophy stressing personal freedom and simplicity.

The long isolation of Japan from the rest of the world, so conducive to introspection, has been highly favourable to the development of Teaism. Our home and habits, costume and cuisine, porcelain, lacquer, painting—our very literature—all have been subject to its influence. No student of Japanese culture could ever ignore its presence. It has permeated the elegance of noble boudoirs, and entered the abode of the humble. Our peasants have learned to arrange flowers, our meanest labourer to offer his salutation to the rocks and waters. In our common parlance we speak of the man "with no tea" in him, when he is insusceptible to the serio-comic interests of the personal drama. Again we stigmatise the untamed aesthete who, regardless of the mundane tragedy, runs riot in the springtide of emancipated emotions, as one "with too much tea" in him.

The outsider may indeed wonder at this seeming much ado about nothing. What a tempest in a tea-cup! he will say. But when we consider how small after all the cup of human enjoyment is, how soon overflowed with tears, how easily drained to the dregs in our quenchless thirst for infinity, we shall not blame ourselves for making so much of the tea-cup. Mankind has done worse. In the worship of Bacchus, we have sacrificed too freely; and we have even transfigured the gory image of Mars.[2] Why not consecrate ourselves to the queen of the Camelias,[3] and revel in the warm stream of sympathy that flows from her altar? In the liquid amber within the ivory-porcelain, the initiated may touch the sweet reticence of Confucius, the piquancy of Laotse, and the ethereal aroma of Sakyamuni himself.[4]

Those who cannot feel the littleness of great things in themselves are apt to overlook the greatness of little things in others. The average Westerner, in his sleek complacency, will see in the tea ceremony but another instance of the thousand and one oddities which constitute the quaintness and childishness of the East to him. He was wont to regard Japan as barbarous while she indulged in the gentle arts of peace: he calls her civilised since she began to commit wholesale slaughter on Manchurian battlefields.[5] Much comment has been given lately to the Code of the Samurai, —the Art of Death which makes our soldiers exult in self-sacrifice; but scarcely any attention has been drawn to Teaism, which represents so much of our Art of Life. Fain would we remain barbarians, if our claim to civilisation were to be based on the gruesome glory of war. Fain would we await the time when due respect shall be paid to our art and ideals.

When will the West understand, or try to understand, the East? We Asiatics are often appalled by the curious web of facts and fancies which has been woven concerning us. We are pictured as living on the perfume of the lotus, if not on mice and cockroaches. It is either impotent fanaticism or else abject voluptuousness. Indian spirituality has been derided as ignorance, Chinese sobriety as stupidity, Japanese patriotism as the result of fatalism. It has been said that we are less sensible to pain and wounds on account of the callousness of our nervous organisation!

Why not amuse yourselves at our expense? Asia returns the compliment. There would be further food for merriment if you were to know all that we have imagined and written about you. All the glamour of the perspective is there, all the unconscious homage of wonder, all the silent resentment of the new and undefined. You have been

2. Bacchus: Greek god of wine; Mars: Roman god of war.
3. Camelias are shrubs of the tea family.
4. Confucius, Laotse, and Sakyamuni were the founders of Confucianism, Taoism, and Buddhism.

5. Westerners had been surprised and impressed when Japan defeated Russia in the Russo-Japanese War (1904–1905) over control of northern China (Manchuria).

loaded with virtues too refined to be envied, and accused of crimes too picturesque to be condemned. Our writers in the past—the wise men who knew—informed us that you had bushy tails somewhere hidden in your garments, and often dined off a fricassee of newborn babes! Nay, we had something worse against you: we used to think you the most impracticable people on the earth, for you were said to preach what you never practiced.

Such misconceptions are fast vanishing amongst us. Commerce has forced the European tongues on many an Eastern port. Asiatic youths are flocking to Western colleges for the equipment of modern education. Our insight does not penetrate your culture deeply, but at least we are willing to learn. Some of my compatriots have adopted too much of your customs and too much of your etiquette, in the delusion that the acquisition of stiff collars and tall silk hats comprised the attainment of your civilisation. Pathetic and deplorable as such affectations are, they evince our willingness to approach the West on our knees. Unfortunately the Western attitude is unfavourable to the understanding of the East. The Christian missionary goes to impart, but not to receive. Your information is based on the meagre translations of our immense literature, if not on the unreliable anecdotes of passing travellers. It is rarely that the chivalrous pen of a Lafcadio Hearn or that of the author of "The Web of Indian Life" enlivens the Oriental darkness with the torch of our own sentiments.[6]

Perhaps I betray my own ignorance of the Tea Cult by being so outspoken. Its very spirit of politeness exacts that you say what you are expected to say, and no more. But I am not to be a polite Teaist. So much harm has been done already by the mutual misunderstanding of the New World and the Old, that one need not apologise for contributing his tithe to the furtherance of a better understanding. The beginning of the twentieth century would have been spared the spectacle of sanguinary warfare if Russia had condescended to know Japan better. What dire consequences to humanity lie in the contemptuous ignoring of Eastern problems! European imperialism, which does not disdain to raise the absurd cry of the Yellow Peril, fails to realise that Asia may also awaken to the cruel sense of the White Disaster. You may laugh at us for having "too much tea," but may we not suspect that you of the West have "no tea" in your constitution?

Let us stop the continents from hurling epigrams at each other, and be sadder if not wiser by the mutual gain of half a hemisphere. We have developed along different lines, but there is no reason why one should not supplement the other. You have gained expansion at the cost of restlessness; we have created a harmony which is weak against aggression. Will you believe it?—the East is better off in some respects than the West!

Strangely enough humanity has so far met in the tea-cup. It is the only Asiatic ceremonial which commands universal esteem. The white man has scoffed at our religion and our morals, but has accepted the brown beverage without hesitation. The afternoon tea is now an important function in Western society. In the delicate clatter of trays and saucers, in the soft rustle of feminine hospitality, in the common catechism about cream and sugar, we know that the Worship of Tea is established beyond question. The philosophic resignation of the guest to the fate awaiting him in the dubious decoction proclaims that in this single instance the Oriental spirit reigns supreme.

6. The American writer Lafcadio Hearn moved to Japan in 1890 and became a citizen; his books included *Japan: An Attempt at Interpretation* (1904). Margaret Noble had recently published *The Web of Indian Life*.

The earliest record of tea in European writing is said to be found in the statement of an Arabian traveller, that after the year 879 the main sources of revenue in Canton were the duties on salt and tea. Marco Polo records the deposition of a Chinese minister of finance in 1285 for his arbitrary augmentation of the tea-taxes. It was at the period of the great discoveries that the European people began to know more about the extreme Orient. At the end of the sixteenth century the Hollanders brought the news that a pleasant drink was made in the East from the leaves of a bush. The travellers Giovanni Batista Ramusio (1559), L. Almeida (1576), Maffeno (1588), Tareira (1610), also mentioned tea. In the last-named year ships of the Dutch East India Company brought the first tea into Europe. It was known in France in 1636, and reached Russia in 1638. England welcomed it in 1650 and spoke of it as "That excellent and by all physicians approved China drink, called by the Chineans Tcha, and by other nations Tay, alias Tee."

Like all good things of the world, the propaganda of Tea met with opposition. Heretics like Henry Saville (1678) denounced drinking it as a filthy custom. Jonas Hanway (Essay on Tea, 1756) said that men seemed to lose their stature and comeliness, women their beauty through the use of tea. Its cost at the start (about fifteen or sixteen shillings a pound) forbade popular consumption, and made it "regalia for high treatments and entertainments, presents being made thereof to princes and grandees." Yet in spite of such drawbacks tea-drinking spread with marvellous rapidity. The coffee-houses of London in the early half of the eighteenth century became, in fact, tea-houses, the resort of wits like Addison and Steele, who beguiled themselves over their "dish of tea." The beverage soon became a necessity of life—a taxable matter. We are reminded in this connection what an important part it plays in modern history. Colonial America resigned herself to oppression until human endurance gave way before the heavy duties laid on Tea. American independence dates from the throwing of tea-chests into Boston harbour.

There is a subtle charm in the taste of tea which makes it irresistible and capable of idealisation. Western humourists were not slow to mingle the fragrance of their thought with its aroma. It has not the arrogance of wine, the self-consciousness of coffee, nor the simpering innocence of cocoa. Already in 1711, says the Spectator: "I would therefore in a particular manner recommend these my speculations to all well-regulated families that set apart an hour every morning for tea, bread and butter; and would earnestly advise them for their good to order this paper to be punctually served up and to be looked upon as a part of the tea-equipage." Samuel Johnson draws his own portrait as "a hardened and shameless tea drinker, who for twenty years diluted his meals with only the infusion of the fascinating plant; who with tea amused the evening, with tea solaced the midnight, and with tea welcomed the morning."

Charles Lamb, a professed devotee, sounded the true note of Teaism when he wrote that the greatest pleasure he knew was to do a good action by stealth, and to have it found out by accident. For Teaism is the art of concealing beauty that you may discover it, of suggesting what you dare not reveal. It is the noble secret of laughing at yourself, calmly yet thoroughly, and is thus humour itself,—the smile of philosophy. All genuine humourists may in this sense be called tea-philosophers,—Thackeray, for instance, and of course, Shakespeare. The poets of the Decadence (when was not the world in decadence?), in their protests against materialism, have, to a certain extent, also opened the way to Teaism. Perhaps nowadays it is in our demure contemplation of the Imperfect that the West and the East can meet in mutual consolation.

The Taoists relate that at the great beginning of the No-Beginning, Spirit and Matter met in mortal combat. At last the Yellow Emperor, the Sun of Heaven, triumphed over Shuhyung, the demon of darkness and earth. The Titan, in his death agony, struck his head against the solar vault and shivered the blue dome of jade into fragments. The stars lost their nests, the moon wandered aimlessly among the wild chasms of the night. In despair the Yellow Emperor sought far and wide for the repairer of the Heavens. He had not to search in vain. Out of the Eastern sea rose a queen, the divine Niuka, horn-crowned and dragon-tailed, resplendent in her armor of fire. She welded the five-coloured rainbow in her magic cauldron and rebuilt the Chinese sky. But it is told that Niuka forgot to fill two tiny crevices in the blue firmament. Thus began the dualism of love—two souls rolling through space and never at rest until they join together to complete the universe. Everyone has to build anew his sky of hope and peace.

The heaven of modern humanity is indeed shattered in the Cyclopean struggle for wealth and power. The world is groping in the shadow of egotism and vulgarity. Knowledge is bought through a bad conscience, benevolence practiced for the sake of utility. The East and the West, like two dragons tossed in a sea of ferment, in vain strive to regain the jewel of life. We need a Niuka again to repair the grand devastation; we await the great Avatar.[7] Meanwhile, let us have a sip of tea. The afternoon glow is brightening the bamboos, the fountains are bubbling with delight, the soughing of the pines is heard in our kettle. Let us dream of evanescence, and linger in the beautiful foolishness of things.

RESONANCE

Chiang Yee: from *The Silent Traveller in London*[1]

[INTRODUCTION]

Anyone who chanced to read my book on the English Lakeland, would never imagine me writing anything about London, as I claimed there to find that living under London fogs had its unpleasant side. I wrote the truth. But nevertheless a reasonable person finds some kind of beauty everywhere. When I stay in London I grow at times very tired of it and at others very fond of it. I have seen many beautiful things in London and certainly made a great many curious reflections on all I saw since I came here five years ago. As I am an Oriental (actually one of those strange Chinese people who "belong to an age gone by" as a London critic said of me) I am bound to look at many things from a different angle. But is it really so different? I very much doubt it myself,

---

7. Incarnation of a god.
1. A painter and calligrapher, Chiang Yee (1903–1977) came to England for a visit in 1933. With political upheavals increasing in China, he didn't succeed in returning for forty years. Though he had only minimal skills in English when he arrived, he studied intensively and rapidly developed a fluent, charming style, first employed in a book on Chinese art and then in *The Silent Traveller: A Chinese Artist in Lakeland* (1937), in which he sketched Wordsworth's Lake Country in Chinese style. *The Silent Traveller in London* (1938) then became a surprise best-seller. A subtle melancholy underlies his warm,

self-deprecating account; claiming to know nothing of politics, he had in fact resigned from the Chinese civil service after a dispute with a powerful warlord. He discusses his fascination with watching British children without mentioning that his own wife and children had been caught up in the Japanese invasion of Manchuria and couldn't get out of China. Like Okakura, Chiang directed his work at a Western audience, using his foreign perspective to help his readers see their own land afresh and at the same time gain a deeper understanding of Chinese culture.

but my readers shall judge for themselves. I have never agreed with people who hold that the various nationalities differ greatly from each other. They may be different superficially, but they eat, drink, sleep, dress, and shelter themselves from wind and rain in the same way. In particular their outlook on life need not vary fundamentally. Individual thought is always individual, and similarity of tastes will always link people without regard for any geographical boundary. You would expect your butcher to think of a frisky young lamb as good to eat, not to look at! A Chinese butcher will think the same as he does!

It always gives me pleasure to jot down my impressions of anything I have seen, and this book on London has been in my mind for quite a long time, but I still feel ashamed to give it form so soon. I quite agree with my friends who tell me that the first impression is always the most fresh and lively. But then one is apt to find later that the first impression was false. Before I came to London, I often heard stories of it from people who had travelled there, or read of it in papers and books; but those accounts were much too general and could bring no clear picture before my mind. I suppose people who hear and read about China must suffer in the same way. Many travellers who have gone to China for only a few months come back and write books about it, including everything from literature and philosophy to domestic and social life, and economic conditions. And some have written without having been there at all. I can only admire their temerity and their skill in generalising on great questions. I expect I suffer together with many others in the world, whose characters have been mis-generalised in some way. I was thought to be a Communist by an English friend because, he declared, all young Chinese were Communists; and another criticised me as a die-hard or one belonging to an age gone by. I was only casually acquainted with them. I can imagine there must be a good number of people who will still wonder why I have no pig-tail on my head, or who think I must be the same sort of person as Mr. Wu or Charlie Chan![2]

A modest person with little ability, who dares not make generalisations on big topics, I would like first of all to advise my readers not to expect from me anything approaching an historical or academic study of London. There are heaps of books written by well-known historians, scholars, and artists, both English and foreign, which deal with all the great features of this city. They are the classics of London; but mine is a book of another sort. As I am diffident of fixing my eyes on big things, I generally glance down on the small ones. There are a great many tiny events which it has given me great joy to look at, to watch, and to think about. And as they are so tiny, other people may have neglected them. This little book can perhaps be called a collection of odds and ends of observations, that may amuse a few people at bedtime, or in idle moments after tea or dinner.

* * *

I suppose most people who know anything about Chinese food have heard the expression "Chop Suey." Since I came to London, I have frequently invited my English friends to a Chinese meal. They generally choose "Chop Suey" from the menu—as soon as they get it, they ask me what it is made of. I simply answer—"made of all things." All Chinese cooks and waiters know their English visitors like this dish. In Chinese it is called "Tsa Tsui," which in the Cantonese pronunciation sounds like "Chop Suey." "Tsa" means "mixed up" and "Tsui" "fragments"; the whole expression means "a mixture of everything." There are some nice pieces of meat and a fine

---

2. Chinese detective, hero of popular novels by Earl Bigger and the Hollywood movies based on them. Mr. Wu is the villain of MGM's 1927 movie *Mr. Wu;* though educated in the West, he stabs his daughter rather than allow her to marry a Westerner.

assortment of vegetables in the dish, but it is made up of bits of all sorts that are left over in the kitchen and has a strange composite flavour. After this explanation, perhaps I can call this book a "Chop Suey of London"; there is nothing of great value in it, but it may be appetising to some.

I am lucky enough to have lived in London during five important years in which big events have happened one after the other, such as the Silver Jubilee, the death of King George V, the Hoare Crisis, the Abdication, the Coronation, the Bus Strike, the Eden Crisis, etc. Such events only happen once in a lifetime. How lucky for an Oriental like me to have seen all these together in a short time! I myself have seen three kings *in the distance* and would, on that account, have been thought a most reverend person if I had lived in the old days of China. Republican China is not much interested in such things.[3]

I shall certainly not try to deal with politics, because I cannot understand them at all. During these five years it has seemed to me everyone in London can talk politics and can interpret them so well that I feel I must be a most stupid man. I appear to shock people when I answer them that I know nothing about politics. An old postman whom I have known for four years had a chat with me one evening when I was posting my letter at the pillar-box near my house. It was just after the invasion of Austria. He asked me what I thought of it and was puzzled when I answered that I had no ideas on the subject. Then I said, "What do you think of the happenings in Abyssinia, Spain, and China?"[4] He answered me very positively that he had plenty of ideas about them, but these three presented quite different problems. Many a person would think like him, and would argue with me vigorously if I declared they were one and the same. Everyone wants peace, so they say, but actually nearly everyone is at war or preparing for it. You can find the word "peace" a good number of times in the newspapers every day, but you will find the same number of "war" there too. Abyssinians were to be civilised. Austrians were under the tyrannical control of Schuschnigg's regime. Lawless Chinese are to be put in order. I can only open my eyes wide in continual amazement at all these events!

* * *

All the friends I have met here have been extremely kind to me. Whenever we meet, they generally ask me whether I have had good news from home. But the news that we get is seldom good. Really, no news is good news for us! Apart from our internal troubles, we have a friendly neighbour[5] who always insists on making friends with us whether we wish it or not. During these five years, any news that appeared in the papers always had something to do with this quarrel. It is interesting for the world to know that a young lady intends to marry an old man by making quarrels before they can really fall in love with each other. Perhaps there has never been a case like this in the history of the world! I can say nothing about this question for my part and do not want to say anything because I am "The Silent Traveller." Besides I have many other and different thoughts in my head. I have wandered about London very silently and really seen a good many things through my silence.

[ABOUT CHILDREN]

After I arrived in London, a friend of mine put me up in a house near Regent's Park Road. As I knew nothing about London then, and as my friend was busy most of the

3. Chiang uses "Republican" in its French sense of "revolutionary." By 1938 Mao Zedong's Communist Party was becoming dominant in the struggle to drive the Japanese invaders out of China.
4. Totalitarian regimes were taking over in each area: Mussolini had invaded Ethiopia (Abyssinia), the Fascist-supported General Franco was waging civil war against the constitutional government of Spain, and China was disputed between Japan and Mao's Communists.
5. Japan.

day, I sometimes just sat in my room and looked out through the window to watch the people passing. Once a little girl of about four or five came to the house opposite. She had a small stick in her hand with which she knocked at the door, for she was too short to reach up to the knocker. Then she stood there for about a quarter or half an hour and seemed to have unlimited patience in waiting for the door to open. She played gracefully with her stick and looked up and down the road. As long as she stood on the doorstep, I could not take my eyes off her. She was very pretty with her little rosy face and her bright green frock. I could not describe how much I was attracted by her and she gave me one of my very first impressions about London. "Does this child come from a very well-educated family or is she simply an unusual type?" I kept posing myself with all sorts of queries about her and eventually my friend told me that I should not wonder about such a common sight too much, otherwise I would never have any time for anything else in London. But I have a real passion for children, I have always been interested in studying their actions and manners—the results of training, upbringing, and national discipline. At this point I cannot help thinking of the influence of mothers especially, and of education! There must always be a difference between English and Chinese because we are brought up in such different traditions and environment. Even our houses are built in a very different style—except in Shanghai, Tientsin, and some other big cities—and our entrance gates are generally kept open all day long and so there is no need to knock for entrance. Brothers, sisters, and cousins, always live together under one roof, so we do not need to look for other companions. I hope my readers will not be surprised if I tell them I was not allowed to go outside the great entrance gate until I was over ten years old! The explanation is quite simple; our house is built on one level and occupies a very big space including several courtyards and a good garden. There are quantities of rooms in which to run about and vast space for walking. And in our estate we even had a small school building inside the garden, as my family is very big and I am the sixteenth child in my generation. Inside the big gate we could enjoy all sorts of fun.

This little girl reminds me of several things I have noticed about the English family. She is certainly one who has had a good upbringing, but is probably an only child, or one of two children. I often wonder whether such terms as "brother," "sister," "uncle," and "aunt" will be in existence in England after a few more generations if English families continue to decrease. Once I read in a paper that "people are more anxious than they have ever been to give their children the best possible chances in life, and they are inclined to be afraid of the increased responsibility that a large family must bring." This is a reasonable fear. However, most English children of the present generation still enjoy very much shouting out "uncle" or "auntie," as I hear in parks whenever I meet them.

I always find interest in watching children's actions and manners, and try to think of what I should have done at the same age. It is curious for me to realise that I shall never do these things again. I always like to see small children feeding birds in London parks. They have a natural love for birds, but they have the sort of possessive love which makes them like to get hold of them or touch them. Yet they make diffident gestures as if they dared not do so. In my observation, when children take out a piece of bread or food, they like to give it themselves to the birds. But as soon as the birds come near their hands, they suddenly throw the food away and give them a fright. Afterwards they smile or laugh as if they asked forgiveness. Oh, this smile touches the very bottom of my heart! Would I do the same? That I cannot tell. But I have seen many people in various situations trying to smile in hypocrisy, which also touches my heart with agony!

* * *

We Chinese here usually have some difficulties in finding a place to live in, because some might not like to take foreigners and some do not want to have children. So Chinese with families have particular embarrassment. At first I did not understand this at all. Once I went to visit a friend in company with a married couple and a child in a pram. As soon as we reached the house, the landlord refused to let the child in as he said that "No children" was in his agreement. We were all surprised because we never heard of such a thing in all our experience at home. I was even more surprised than the others, because I have the belief that everybody must remember his own childhood and must think of that time affectionately. Apparently this is not true. I looked hard for the reason for this unnatural action, until I was suddenly enlightened by reading a cartoon of three children in *Punch*,[6] which runs:

> Pat (play-acting): Have you lodgings to let?
> Barbara: Excuse me, have you any parents?
> Pat: Yes.
> Barbara: I'm 'fraid we never take in children with parents.

This gives me the idea that this sort of prohibition must be rather common in London. But why object to children? Oh, where is their sense of "give and take"?

Shyness and something like a sense of fear seem to me to be born in young children's minds whenever they meet a new thing or person. London's children may be better in this respect than those of any other neighbourhood, because they are used to more variety. But I also think there is some difference in individuals too. I know most Chinese children would not dare to answer questions from foreigners even though they tried to speak the Chinese language; and some of them will gaze at foreigners with great curiosity and smile in watching their actions. I had the same experience being a foreigner here. But the manner of London children talking to their parents or elders gives me a surprise when I compare them with what I would have done in my own younger days. For instance, I sometimes hear a boy of seven or eight shouting out: "Daddy, I don't think you are right." It is quite a reasonable expression which nobody will make any fuss about. But the first time I heard this I wondered to myself how a boy could address his father like that, because we are generally taught not to criticise our elders and especially not our parents. As we are virtually controlled by the Confucian idea,[7] our elders enjoy the privilege of being respected by the young, and it is said they have more experience and therefore more wisdom. According to our ethic of "filial piety," our children are trained not to argue with their parents and upset their feelings, for this would be considered as "not filial." If a young person is insubordinate, he has not an easy position in society. So our children have won the habit of naturally accepting what they are told by their parents. After all, no parent would deliberately lead his children on the wrong road. Of course, it is a disputable point, but such has been the idea we have inherited for centuries. I do not think we should never be allowed at all to say anything contradictory to our parents or elders. When we are grown up, we may address them as follows: "Yes, father, but I think it will be better if we do it by another method." As a rule there are many obstinate parents in China, perhaps even more than in England!

I have heard older children in London discussing their parents and using such expressions as "We are very good friends," or "She or he is very friendly to me." There are many kinds of friendship of course. But I am often puzzled at this word being

---

6. Leading British humor magazine.
7. Confucian philosophy stressed the authority of parents over children as the basis for social stability and good government.

used between children and parents. Although the Oxford dictionary has defined it clearly as: "One joined to another in intimacy and mutual benevolence apart from sexual or family love," yet it seems to me to be used differently nowadays. Parents and children are naturally bound to be together for some time at least, and they have an instinctive love for each other with no time limit. Children may not like their parents when they are told to do this and that, but no normal parents would develop hatred of their *own* children. Even in China, some of our best scholars have strictly criticised the ethics of "filial piety" because they said children were not originally born for the sake of their parents. Yet we all think that children have been very well cared for by the parents after their birth, so they ought to be good (I mean here more than a friendship) to them in return. The word "friend" between parents and children is a bond which I am inclined to think might be broken after a time. To me personally, the link between parents and children is unbreakable, also that between brothers and sisters. There is always something more than friendship in these links. So far we have not come to live under the strain of the entirely mechanically arranged life towards which modern civilisation is tending. Later on, my conception on this point will have to undergo a change! I think we shall then simply become original animals again, and as soon as the child grows up, he or she will run away.

[A STUDY OF NAMES]

To me English names are interesting but puzzling. At first I was struck by the habit of calling different persons by the same Christian name. Passing along a busy street in London, I often hear people being called John or Charlie. In the parks, every second boy seems to answer to Tom or George. At parties, I soon noticed that many ladies were called Jean or Marjorie or Flora. I wondered how they distinguished themselves from each other, if three Johns and four Marjories happened to be together. Once I took part in a friendly conversation and heard a gentleman saying to a friend of mine: "Bill, don't you think this is all right?" "Yes, I think so, Bill," was the answer. I could not help asking my friend why they should address each other like that. He answered: "His name is Bill and mine is too." Then I said: "Don't you feel that you are addressing yourself?" "No, I've never thought of that," he replied. I am still mystified!

A Chinese girl came over here to study in a convent school. I suppose her Chinese name was difficult for the nuns to pronounce, so she was given the English name, "Margaret." But she told me that there were already three students called Margaret and so she was always wondering what was going to happen when this name was called. She found it very difficult at first, and then got to know the difference in the way the nuns called each of them. From her description it seemed a subtle distinction. However, she went on to say that she always looked up when this name was called and then looked at the nun's eyes. She was clever! I have frequently been told by my English friends that they know by instinct. They think my question is unnecessary, so I am still in a puzzle.

Once I read a letter from a lady in the newspaper, in which she said:

> I have recently named my baby daughter Mary Ann. I was aware that this name is out of fashion, and that it was regarded in the near past as somehow humorous; but I was unprepared to find it so unacceptable today as it appears to many of my friends, who advise me to use an abbreviation. Other despised names have turned to favour. Why not Mary Ann?

Presently another correspondent replied in the same paper and said:

> But there are other agencies at work besides fashion. Many names, like Oscar and Jabez, drop out from unpleasant association. A good many disappeared through being used as

subjects of ridicule in music-hall songs; and the War got a bad name for such terms as "Cuthbert" and "Clarence." One never knows what accident may happen to a name to render it unpopular.

From these two passages, I am surprised and interested to learn that a name can be a despised or a favourite one. And an accident may also happen to it to render it unpopular. After all, it seems to me that we in China are certainly wiser on this point, for we choose our own names. It may happen occasionally that two people have the same name because we all pick out a name with a good meaning, but this is only one chance in a million.

I always imagine that English people must be delighted if on reading a novel their name appears in it in such a good context as: "Andrew, you are so wonderful to have done it!" said by a beautiful girl; or, "Stella is the most charming girl I have ever seen," murmured by a handsome young man. But on the other hand, if a man named Henry saw a heading in the evening paper: "Henry—charged with manslaughter," would he read about it?

I have another explanation to offer why English people like to be called by the same names. I suppose they consider that all men are brothers, so they like to address each other by the most popular names they know. Sometimes I have been addressed by some drunkard as "Jack" or "John" when I looked in at some public bar! Besides, kings, queens, princes, and princesses all have the same sort of names as the people, and this is a further sign of the English democratic nature.

I think that in China the choice of our names has undergone a sort of purification from early times. A Chinese book says:

> There are five different ways of choosing names; but we cannot choose one from the name of a country, from an official title, from the names of mountains and rivers, from the terms of secret diseases, from the names of animals and from the names of money.

But in the second century BC even names from these categories were used occasionally. If we go far back, there were persons called by their birthdays and by the number of persons in the generation, and also a lot of people took their names from their occupation. They had very peculiar names too, such as "Black-Kidney," "Black-Arm," "Sheep's Back," "Fox-Hair," and so forth. After a time these were abolished and names for men became most frequently associated with Confucian virtues and those for girls with flowers. But we only have one hundred family names, though we can have as many first names as people care to select. It is funny for me to see that English people can choose only from a limited number of first names, but they can have as many different family names as they like. I am not in a position to discuss their origin or how they changed, but I must say I had a very amusing time going through the London telephone directory from the first name to the last for three whole days! I know people like to hear and know of other people doing stupid things, though they do not like to do them themselves! I found there many English family names which were beyond my imagination. For instance, a very charming girl with beautiful lips may belong to a family called "Campbell," which generally means "disproportionate mouth." A handsome young man belongs to the family of "Cameron," which means "twisted nose." A thief may be called Mr. Noble; a sick man walking very slowly is called Mr. Rush; a dwarf may have the family name "Longfellow"; a member of Parliament is Mr. Butler. Oh, there are too many for me to think of! I can imagine that no lady likes to be born into a family called "Old" or even "Older." Surely no one can help being miserable if he is always called Mr. Poor or Mr. Farthing. It would be interesting to know what the host or hostess would think if one of his or her guests was called "Greedy." I wonder how people address those who have such family names as "Younghusband," "Darling," "Love," "Dear," and so forth when they become intimate friends? A Mr. or Miss Loveless may have many lovers and a Monk is perhaps not a monk! I do not think I should have the courage to speak to a Miss Dare, Miss Male, Mrs. Manly, Lady Marshall, or Madam Strong. Suppose there is a heading in the newspaper: "Miss Middlemiss Missing," I shall be puzzled whether to interpret middlemiss as a middle-sized or middle-aged person if Missing is a family name. You may argue with me that any proper name always has a capital letter at the beginning, but I am afraid that some of my fellow-countrymen who are just beginning to learn English will complain that a sentence such as "English's car runs over" has a grammatical mistake in it, if they do not know that "English" stands for a person's family name. They will never understand the meaning of sentences like "England reaches England" or "London is in London." We generally play games with each other's names, and I suppose it is the same in England, and probably the games will be even more amusing. We very seldom play with family names, because they provide little variety, but in English it will be the other way round. I have tried to work out a short story using only English family names helped by a few prepositions and conjunctions. And I have composed it in the Chinese manner without change in the verb for the third person, without articles, and very seldom using a pronoun. It runs:

> *Coward Man* and *Dark Child*, not *Goodchild, Call Fisherman* and *Buy Fish. Fisherman Handover Herring* to *Child* and *Coward Man Fry Herring* from *Gray* to *Brown. Wise Fox Take Herring* for *Child Making Full Joy* with *Coward Man. Coward Man Walk Down* with *Knife* and *Child Call Loud* that *Man Want* to *Man-Slaughter Child. Whatmore?*

All words in italics are the family names. Once I came across a Cumberland farmer whose name was Lamb. He and a friend of mine were good friends, so they addressed each other by the family name only. As we three sat together, they began talking absorbedly about lamb. My friend said: "Lamb, how is the lamb?" and went on to mention the word frequently in their talk. I must confess that I did not follow the conversation very well!

The harm of blood marriage was known in our early history. Hence persons of the same surname or family name were not allowed to intermarry since the twelfth century BC. Even though our surnames are limited to one hundred, we have never had the case of a couple both having the same family name. A young man from the North will never think of making love to a girl who has the same surname as his, even if she lives in the South. It is interesting to know that English people can marry someone with the same family name, though they have such a vast number of names. For instance, in a paper it says:

> It is announced to-day that Miss Joan Macneill Campbell, elder daughter of Sir George and Lady Campbell, of Pyrford, Surrey, and Calcutta, has been married in Calcutta to Mr. Kenneth Macrae Campbell, younger son of Mr. and Mrs. J. Campbell, of Harrow.

The journalist seemed to be interested, as he added the heading: "Married—kept same name." I do not know whether there is really any harm in this kind of intermarriage, but we Chinese seem to think that same names descend from the same ancestor. I do not think we shall ever change this idea, even in the present march of time! The Chinese is the most conservative race in the world!

There is another difference between English and Chinese names. According to English ways, the Christian name stands first and then comes the family name, but with us it is just the reverse. Since I have been here, I have frequently been called Mr. Yee, but actually I am Mr. Chiang. Some people have been very cautious and addressed me as Mr. Chiang Yee!

Many London street names are also extremely interesting. I would like to quote here some from the "New London Street Dictionary" in *Punch:*

Air Street—Doctors send their patients to this locality for change.
Coldbath Square—Very bracing.
Distaff Lane—Full of spinsters.
Fashion Street—Magnificent sight in the height of the season.
First Street—Of immense antiquity.
Friday Street—Great jealousy felt by all the other days of the week.
Great Smith Street—Which of the Smiths is this?
Idol Lane—Where are the missionaries?
Love Lane—What sort of love? The "love of the turtle?"
Paradise Street and Peerless Street—Difficult to choose between the two.
World's End Passage—Finis.

These certainly grow in interest from the interpreter's definition of them! Though many street names in London are those of Christian saints as well as of kings, princes, and well-known families, yet I do not know why there are several roads called "London Road," as if they were in some other foreign city. I like to think there are places called "Snow Fields" and "Half Moon Street," because I can so rarely see snow or moon in London. Once I went to Rotten Row, but nothing was rotten there; another time I was in Patience Road and could see only people dashing impatiently to and fro. There are two more places in London that have stuck in my memory. They are Meeting House Lane and Makepeace Avenue. I wonder why those people who enjoy meeting and peace conferences do not come over here!

[CONCLUSION]

In the foregoing chapters I have described what I have seen and thought in London during these past five years. I should like to write a great deal more on such things as ghosts, colours, cats, and dogs, all of which have interested me too, but I must not keep my readers longer or they will be exhausted. So I am going to make a long pause, until perhaps after several more years in London I shall be able to draw further conclusions on what I have observed and thought. The more I look at London scenes the more friendly a feeling I have towards them. And the more I learn of the different phases of London life, the surer and deeper is my belief in humanity, love, and beauty. Why should people be separated by terms of race or nation?

London is now my second home. Since my college days I have never stayed anywhere in my own country for more than three years. I like travelling and hope to go on travelling all my life, but London will be my headquarters while I travel in Europe. Besides, these five years, during which London has shown me so much hospitality and entertained me in so many ways, will always be a good memory. I like to think that this book, which is like my claw-marks left on London slush by accident, as I said in the snow chapter, may perhaps not be so ephemeral as most claw-marks and may be seen by many people.

How strange is life, and how wonderful a human being can be! Had I not been born in this age of progression and destruction, fighting side by side, I should probably not have been able to see through life to the very bottom of human nature and hold my faith in its essential goodness. I cannot think that hatred really exists in mankind, in spite of all the evidence which tries to pervert my way of thinking. Between individual and individual there is no such thing. Why should not all we human beings open our eyes wider and try to see the other side? I owe to London's friendship, kindness, and faithfulness a particular debt, which I hope I shall find a way to repay.

By now my readers possibly doubt the truth of my name—the Silent Traveller. Surely I have not appeared to be silent at all. Without further explanation and without trying to compare myself with our great philosopher, Lao Tzu, who wrote *Tao-Te-Ching*, the well-known doctrine of Chinese Taoism, I should like to end by quoting about him the following poem, which was written by Po Chu-I of T'ang dynasty:

> Those who speak know nothing;
> Those who know are silent.
> These words, as I am told,
> Were spoken by Lao-Tzu.
> If we are to believe that Lao-Tzu
> Was himself one who knew,
> How comes it that he wrote a book
> Of five thousand words?

⟳

⇒＋ END OF PERSPECTIVES: OCCIDENTALISM—EUROPE THROUGH FOREIGN EYES ＋⇐

＋⇒✦⇐＋

Elizabeth Barrett Browning
1806–1861

The immense popularity of Elizabeth Barrett Browning in the Victorian era is a bit of a miracle, for in a time famous for its demure conventionality she was celebrated both for her passionate love poems and for her espousal of radical political causes, including feminism, the liberation of Italy from the Austro-Hungarian Empire, and the emancipation of American slaves. In the United States, she was a major inspiration for Emily Dickinson and for the political activist Susan B. Anthony, among many others. In the midst of an extremely precocious childhood—she had written a four-book epic, *The Battle of Marathon,* by the age of twelve—she was struck by illness at fifteen and for many years lived as a semi-invalid. Though dependent on morphine and unable or unwilling to leave her house, she published extensively—a translation of Aeschylus's *Prometheus Bound,* a philosophical poem entitled *An Essay on Mind,* and then the works that made and sealed her reputation: *The Seraphim and Other Poems* (1838) and *Poems* (1844).

In 1845, at the age of forty, she began a correspondence with Robert Browning, a younger and less famous poet. The two married and eloped to Italy in 1846. There Barrett Browning recovered her health, wrote her best work, and gave birth to a son. The couple's correspondence, published posthumously, is considered one of her finest works, as is the collection of love poems written to Browning as their relationship developed and published with the misleading title *Sonnets from the Portuguese* (1850). Her greatest achievement however is considered to be the verse novel *Aurora Leigh* (1856), a sort of female version of Wordsworth's *The Prelude* and the first major poem in English in which the heroine, like the author, is a woman writer.

from Aurora Leigh[1]
from *Book 1*

[SELF-PORTRAIT]

Of writing many books there is no end;
And I who have written much in prose and verse
For others' uses, will write now for mine,—
Will write my story for my better self,
5   As when you paint your portrait for a friend,
Who keeps it in a drawer and looks at it
Long after he has ceased to love you, just
To hold together what he was and is.
I, writing thus, am still what men call young;
10   I have not so far left the coasts of life
To travel inward, that I cannot hear
That murmur of the outer Infinite
Which unweaned babies smile at in their sleep
When wondered at for smiling; not so far,
15   But still I catch my mother at her post
Beside the nursery door, with finger up,
"Hush, hush—here's too much noise!" while her sweet eyes
Leap forward, taking part against her word
In the child's riot. Still I sit and feel
20   My father's slow hand, when she had left us both,
Stroke out my childish curls across his knee,
And hear Assunta's daily jest (she knew
He liked it better than a better jest)
Inquire how many golden scudi[2] went
25   To make such ringlets. O my father's hand,
Stroke heavily, heavily the poor hair down,
Draw, press the child's head closer to thy knee!
I'm still too young, too young, to sit alone.
I write. My mother was a Florentine,
30   Whose rare blue eyes were shut from seeing me
When scarcely I was four years old, my life
A poor spark snatched up from a failing lamp
Which went out therefore. She was weak and frail;
She could not bear the joy of giving life,
35   The mother's rapture slew her. If her kiss
Had left a longer weight upon my lips
It might have steadied the uneasy breath,
And reconciled and fraternised my soul
With the new order. As it was, indeed,

---

1. Barrett Browning called *Aurora Leigh*, a poem in nine books, a "verse novel." It portrays the struggles of a young poet to find her artistic voice and pursue her voca-tion despite the obstacles confronting a woman writer.
2. Italian coins; Assunta was Aurora's nurse.

40   I felt a mother-want about the world,
     And still went seeking, like a bleating lamb
     Left out at night in shutting up the fold,—
     As restless as a nest-deserted bird
     Grown chill through something being away, though what
45   It knows not. I, Aurora Leigh, was born
     To make my father sadder, and myself
     Not overjoyous, truly. Women know
     The way to rear up children (to be just),
     They know a simple, merry, tender knack
50   Of tying sashes, fitting baby-shoes,
     And stringing pretty words that make no sense,
     And kissing full sense into empty words,
     Which things are corals to cut life upon,
     Although such trifles: children learn by such,
55   Love's holy earnest in a pretty play
     And get not over-early solemnised,
     But seeing, as in a rose-bush, Love's Divine
     Which burns and hurts not,—not a single bloom,—
     Become aware and unafraid of Love.
60   Such good do mothers. Fathers love as well
     —Mine did, I know,—but still with heavier brains,
     And wills more consciously responsible,
     And not as wisely, since less foolishly;
     So mothers have God's license to be missed.

65   My father was an austere Englishman,
     Who, after a dry lifetime spent at home
     In college-learning, law, and parish talk,
     Was flooded with a passion unaware,
     His whole provisioned and complacent past
70   Drowned out from him that moment. As he stood
     In Florence, where he had come to spend a month
     And note the secret of Da Vinci's drains,[3]
     He musing somewhat absently perhaps
     Some English question . . . whether men should pay
75   The unpopular but necessary tax
     With left or right hand—in the alien sun
     In that great square of the Santissima[4]
     There drifted past him (scarcely marked enough
     To move his comfortable island scorn)
80   A train of priestly banners, cross and psalm,
     The white-veiled rose-crowned maidens holding up
     Tall tapers, weighty for such wrists, aslant
     To the blue luminous tremor of the air,

---

3. Leonardo da Vinci (1452–1519) was an architect and engineer, as well as an artist; he designed the aqueduct that supplied Milan's water.

4. The Florentine church of the Santissima Annunziata, or Holy Annunciation.

And letting drop the white wax as they went
85 To eat the bishop's wafer[5] at the church;
From which long trail of chanting priests and girls,
A face flashed like a cymbal on his face
And shook with silent clangour brain and heart,
Transfiguring him to music. Thus, even thus,
90 He too received his sacramental gift
With eucharistic meanings; for he loved.

[HER MOTHER'S PORTRAIT]

And as I grew
In years, I mixed, confused, unconsciously,
Whatever I last read or heard or dreamed,
Abhorrent, admirable, beautiful,
150 Pathetical, or ghastly, or grotesque,
With still that face . . . which did not therefore change,
But kept the mystic level of all forms,
Hates, fears, and admirations, was by turns
Ghost, fiend, and angel, fairy, witch, and sprite,
155 A dauntless Muse who eyes a dreadful Fate,
A loving Psyche who loses sight of Love,[6]
A still Medusa[7] with mild milky brows
All curdled and all clothed upon with snakes
Whose slime falls fast as sweat will; or anon
160 Our Lady of the Passion, stabbed with swords
Where the Babe sucked; or Lamia[8] in her first
Moonlighted pallor, ere she shrunk and blinked
And shuddering wriggled down to the unclean;
Or my own mother, leaving her last smile
165 In her last kiss upon the baby-mouth
My father pushed down on the bed for that,—
Or my dead mother, without smile or kiss,
Buried at Florence. All which images,
Concentred on the picture, glassed themselves
170 Before my meditative childhood, as
The incoherencies of change and death
Are represented fully, mixed and merged,
In the smooth fair mystery of perpetual Life.

[AURORA'S EDUCATION]

Then, land!—then, England! oh, the frosty cliffs[9]
Looked cold upon me. Could I find a home

---

5. To take Holy Communion.
6. Psyche was beloved of Cupid (or Eros), whom she had never seen because he always came to her after dark; one night she lit her lamp to look at him as he slept, whereupon he left her.

7. A gorgon, a female monster with serpents for hair, the sight of whom turned people to stone.
8. A monster with the head and upper body of a maiden, and lower body of a serpent.
9. The white chalk cliffs of Dover.

Among those mean red houses through the fog?
And when I heard my father's language first
From alien lips which had no kiss for mine
I wept aloud, then laughed, then wept, then wept,
And some one near me said the child was mad
Through much sea-sickness. The train swept us on:
Was this my father's England? the great isle?
The ground seemed cut up from the fellowship
Of verdure, field from field,[1] as man from man;
The skies themselves looked low and positive,
As almost you could touch them with a hand,
And dared to do it they were so far off
From God's celestial crystals;[2] all things blurred
And dull and vague. Did Shakespeare and his mates
Absorb the light here?—not a hill or stone
With heart to strike a radiant colour up
Or active outline on the indifferent air.

I think I see my father's sister stand
Upon the hall-step of her country-house
To give me welcome. She stood straight and calm,
Her somewhat narrow forehead braided tight
As if for taming accidental thoughts
From possible pulses;[3] brown hair pricked with gray
By frigid use of life (she was not old,
Although my father's elder by a year),
A nose drawn sharply, yet in delicate lines;
A close mild mouth, a little soured about
The ends, through speaking unrequited loves
Or peradventure niggardly half-truths;
Eyes of no colour,—once they might have smiled,
But never, never have forgot themselves
In smiling; cheeks, in which was yet a rose
Of perished summers, like a rose in a book,
Kept more for ruth° than pleasure,—if past bloom,   *remorse*
Past fading also.

        She had lived, we'll say,
A harmless life, she called a virtuous life,
A quiet life, which was not life at all
(But that, she had not lived enough to know),
Between the vicar and the country squires,
The lord-lieutenant looking down sometimes
From the empyrean to assure their souls
Against chance vulgarisms, and, in the abyss,
The apothecary, looked on once a year
To prove their soundness of humility.

255
260
265
270
275
280
285
290
295

---

1. English fields are divided by hedgerows.
2. The stars, or perhaps the crystalline sphere the ancients
believed lay beyond them.
3. Pulsations of strong emotion.

The poor-club exercised her Christian gifts
Of knitting stockings, stitching petticoats,
Because we are of one flesh, after all,
300   And need one flannel° (with a proper sense   *petticoat*
Of difference in the quality)—and still
The book-club, guarded from your modern trick
Of shaking dangerous questions from the crease,[4]
Preserved her intellectual. She had lived
305   A sort of cage-bird life, born in a cage,
Accounting that to leap from perch to perch
Was act and joy enough for any bird.
Dear heaven, how silly are the things that live
In thickets, and eat berries!

I, alas,
310   A wild bird scarcely fledged, was brought to her cage,
And she was there to meet me. Very kind.
Bring the clean water, give out the fresh seed.

* * *

So it was.
385   I broke the copious curls upon my head
In braids, because she liked smooth-ordered hair.
I left off saying my sweet Tuscan words
Which still at any stirring of the heart
Came up to float across the English phrase
390   As lilies (*Bene* or *Che che*[5]), because
She liked my father's child to speak his tongue.
I learnt the collects and the catechism,
The creeds, from Athanasius back to Nice,
The Articles,[6] the Tracts *against* the times[7]
395   (By no means Buonaventure's "Prick of Love"[8]),
And various popular synopses of
Inhuman doctrines never taught by John,[9]
Because she liked instructed piety.
I learnt my complement of classic French
400   (Kept pure of Balzac and neologism[1])
And German also, since she liked a range
Of liberal education,—tongues, not books.
I learnt a little algebra, a little
Of the mathematics,—brushed with extreme flounce
405   The circle of the sciences, because
She misliked women who are frivolous.

---

4. Books were sold with their pages uncut; one had to cut the folds, or creases, to open the pages and read the book.
5. "Good" and "no, indeed" (Italian).
6. The Thirty-nine Articles are the principles of Anglican faith; collects are Anglican prayers.
7. An ironic reference to the High Church movement's *Tracts for the Times,* written by Newman, Keble, and Pusey; thus, the aunt is Low Church.

8. Saint Buonaventure (1221–1274) wrote of ecstatic, mystical Christian experiences; he believed in the power of love over the power of reason.
9. The author of the gospel.
1. Honoré de Balzac (1799–1850), French realist novelist who described things considered unpleasant or immoral, hence unsuitable reading for young ladies. A neologism is a newly coined word.

    I learnt the royal genealogies
    Of Oviedo, the internal laws
    Of the Burmese empire,—by how many feet
410   Mount Chimborazo outsoars Teneriffe.
    What navigable river joins itself
    To Lara, and what census of the year five
    Was taken at Klagenfurt,—because she liked
    A general insight into useful facts.
415   I learnt much music,—such as would have been
    As quite impossible in Johnson's day[2]
    As still it might be wished—fine sleights of hand
    And unimagined fingering, shuffling off
    The hearer's soul through hurricanes of notes
420   To a noisy Tophet;° and I drew . . . costumes   *Hell*
    From French engravings, nereids neatly draped
    (With smirks of simmering godship): I washed in°   *water-colored*
    Landscapes from nature (rather say, washed out).
    I danced the polka and Cellarius,
425   Spun glass, stuffed birds, and modelled flowers in wax,
    Because she liked accomplishments in girls.
    I read a score of books on womanhood
    To prove, if women do not think at all,
    They may teach thinking (to a maiden aunt
430   Or else the author),—books that boldly assert
    Their right of comprehending husband's talk
    When not too deep, and even of answering
    With pretty "may it please you," or "so it is,"—
    Their rapid insight and fine aptitude,
435   Particular worth and general missionariness,
    As long as they keep quiet by the fire
    And never say "no" when the world says "ay,"
    For that is fatal,—their angelic reach
    Of virtue, chiefly used to sit and darn,
440   And fatten household sinners,—their, in brief,
    Potential faculty in everything
    Of abdicating power in it: she owned
    She liked a woman to be womanly,
    And English women, she thanked God and sighed
445   (Some people always sigh in thanking God)
    Were models to the universe. And last
    I learnt cross-stitch, because she did not like
    To see me wear the night with empty hands
    A-doing nothing. So, my shepherdess
450   Was something after all (the pastoral saints
    Be praised for't), leaning lovelorn with pink eyes
    To match her shoes, when I mistook the silks;

2. When informed that a piece of music being played by a young lady was extremely difficult, Samuel Johnson responded, "Would that it had been impossible."

Her head uncrushed by that round weight of hat
So strangely similar to the tortoise-shell
455   Which slew the tragic poet.[3]
                                By the way,
The works of women are symbolical.
We sew, sew, prick our fingers, dull our sight,
Producing what? A pair of slippers, sir,
To put on when you're weary—or a stool
460   To stumble over and vex you . . ."curse that stool!"
Or else at best, a cushion, where you lean
And sleep, and dream of something we are not
But would be for your sake. Alas, alas!
This hurts most, this—that, after all, we are paid
465   The worth of our work, perhaps.

                                In looking down
Those years of education (to return)
I wonder if Brinvilliers suffered more
In the water-torture[4] . . . flood succeeding flood
To drench the incapable throat and split the veins . . .
470   Than I did. Certain of your feebler souls
Go out in such a process; many pine
To a sick, inodorous light; my own endured:
I had relations in the Unseen, and drew
The elemental nutriment and heat
475   From nature, as earth feels the sun at nights,
Or as a babe sucks surely in the dark.
I kept the life thrust on me, on the outside
Of the inner life with all its ample room
For heart and lungs, for will and intellect,
480   Inviolable by conventions. God,
I thank thee for that grace of thine!

                    [DISCOVERY OF POETRY]

815   The cygnet finds the water, but the man
Is born in ignorance of his element
And feels out blind at first, disorganised
By sin i' the blood,—his spirit-insight dulled
And crossed by his sensations. Presently
820   He feels it quicken in the dark sometimes,
When, mark, be reverent, be obedient,
For such dumb motions of imperfect life
Are oracles of vital Deity
Attesting the Hereafter. Let who says

---

3. The Greek playwright Aeschylus was supposed to have been killed when an eagle, mistaking his bald head for a stone, dropped a tortoise on it to break the shell.

4. In 1676 Marie Marguerite, Marquise de Brinvilliers, was tortured by having water forced down her throat, then executed.

825 "The soul's a clean white paper," rather say,
A palimpsest,[5] a prophet's holograph
Defiled, erased and covered by a monk's,—
The apocalypse, by a Longus![6] poring on
Which obscene text, we may discern perhaps
830 Some fair, fine trace of what was written once,
Some upstroke of an alpha and omega
Expressing the old scripture.
                              Books, books, books!
I had found the secret of a garret-room
Piled high with cases in my father's name,
835 Piled high, packed large,—where, creeping in and out
Among the giant fossils of my past,
Like some small nimble mouse between the ribs
Of a mastodon, I nibbled here and there
At this or that box, pulling through the gap,
840 In heats of terror, haste, victorious joy,
The first book first. And how I felt it beat
Under my pillow, in the morning's dark,
An hour before the sun would let me read!
My books! At last because the time was ripe,
845 I chanced upon the poets.

                    As the earth
Plunges in fury, when the internal fires
Have reached and pricked her heart, and, throwing flat
The marts and temples, the triumphal gates
And towers of observation, clears herself
850 To elemental freedom—thus, my soul,
At poetry's divine first finger-touch,
Let go conventions and sprang up surprised,
Convicted of the great eternities
Before two worlds.

                    What's this, Aurora Leigh,
855 You write so of the poets, and not laugh?
Those virtuous liars, dreamers after dark,
Exaggerators of the sun and moon,
And soothsayers in a tea-cup?

                    I write so
Of the only truth-tellers now left to God,
860 The only speakers of essential truth,
Opposed to relative, comparative,
And temporal truths; the only holders by
His sun-skirts, through conventional gray glooms;

---

5. Parchment where the original writing has been scraped off so it can be reused.
6. I.e., imagine that the words of the apocalyse have been erased and written over by Longus, a Greek writer of romances.

865 The only teachers who instruct mankind
From just a shadow on a charnel-wall[7]
To find man's veritable stature out
Erect, sublime,—the measure of a man,
And that's the measure of an angel, says
870 The apostle. Ay, and while your common men
Lay telegraphs, gauge railroads, reign, reap, dine,
And dust the flaunty carpets of the world
For kings to walk on, or our president,
The poet suddenly will catch them up
875 With his voice like a thunder,—"This is soul,
This is life, this word is being said in heaven,
Here's God down on us! what are you about?"
How all those workers start amid their work,
Look round, look up, and feel, a moment's space,
880 That carpet-dusting, though a pretty trade,
Is not the imperative labour after all.

from **Book 2**
[WOMAN AND ARTIST]

Times followed one another. Came a morn
I stood upon the brink of twenty years,
And looked before and after, as I stood
Woman and artist,—either incomplete,
5 Both credulous of completion. There I held
The whole creation in my little cup,
And smiled with thirsty lips before I drank
"Good health to you and me, sweet neighbor mine,
And all these peoples."

I was glad, that day;
10 The June was in me, with its multitudes
Of nightingales all singing in the dark,
And rosebuds reddening where the calyx[1] split.
I felt so young, so strong, so sure of God!
So glad, I could not choose be very wise!
15 And, old at twenty, was inclined to pull
My childhood backward in a childish jest
To see the face of't once more, and farewell!
In which fantastic mood I bounded forth
At early morning,—would not wait so long
20 As even to snatch my bonnet by the strings,
But, brushing a green trail across the lawn
With my gown in the dew, took will and away
Among the acacias of the shrubberies,

7. Wall of a building where bodies or bones are deposited.   1. The green outer leaves which protect a flowerbud.

To fly my fancies in the open air
And keep my birthday, till my aunt awoke
To stop good dreams. Meanwhile I murmured on
As honeyed bees keep humming to themselves,
"The worthiest poets have remained uncrowned
Till death has bleached their foreheads to the bone;
And so with me it must be unless I prove
Unworthy of the grand adversity,
And certainly I would not fail so much.
What, therefore, if I crown myself to-day
In sport, not pride, to learn the feel of it,
Before my brows be numbed as Dante's own
To all the tender pricking of such leaves?
Such leaves! what leaves?"
                              I pulled the branches down
To choose from.
              "Not the bay!² I choose no bay
(The fates deny us if we are overbold),
Nor myrtle—which means chiefly love; and love
Is something awful which one dares not touch
So early o' mornings. This verbena strains
The point of passionate fragrance; and hard by,
This guelder-rose, at far too slight a beck
Of the wind, will toss about her flower-apples.
Ah—there's my choice,—that ivy on the wall,
That headlong ivy! not a leaf will grow
But thinking of a wreath. Large leaves, smooth leaves,
Serrated like my vines, and half as green.
I like such ivy, bold to leap a height
'Twas strong to climb; as good to grow on graves
As twist about a thyrsus;³ pretty too
(And that's not ill) when twisted round a comb."
Thus speaking to myself, half singing it,
Because some thoughts are fashioned like a bell
To ring with once being touched, I drew a wreath
Drenched, blinding me with dew, across my brow,
And fastening it behind so, turning faced
. . . My public!—cousin Romney—with a mouth
Twice graver than his eyes.
                              I stood there fixed,—
My arms up, like the caryatid,⁴ sole
Of some abolished temple, helplessly
Persistent in a gesture which derides
A former purpose. Yet my blush was flame,

25

30

35

40

45

50

55

60

---

2. Laurel; Apollo, the god of poetry, wore a wreath of laurel leaves.
3. Ivy-covered staff carried by the Greek god Dionysus.

4. Female figure with upraised arms, used as a supporting architectural column.

65   As if from flax, not stone.

                                      "Aurora Leigh,
The earliest of Auroras!"[5]

                                        Hand stretched out
I clasped, as shipwrecked men will clasp a hand,
Indifferent to the sort of palm. The tide
Had caught me at my pastime, writing down
70   My foolish name too near upon the sea
Which drowned me with a blush as foolish. "You,
My cousin!"

                          The smile died out in his eyes
And dropped upon his lips, a cold dead weight,
For just a moment, "Here's a book I found!
75   No name writ on it—poems, by the form;
Some Greek upon the margin,—lady's Greek
Without the accents. Read it? Not a word.
I saw at once the thing had witchcraft in't,
Whereof the reading calls up dangerous spirits:
80   I rather bring it to the witch."

                                "My book.
You found it" . . .

                              "In the hollow by the stream
That beech leans down into—of which you said
The Oread in it has a Naiad's heart
And pines for waters."[6]

                            "Thank you."

                                   "Thanks to *you*
85   My cousin! that I have seen you not too much
Witch, scholar, poet, dreamer, and the rest,
To be a woman also."

                            With a glance
The smile rose in his eyes again and touched
The ivy on my forehead, light as air.
90   I answered gravely "Poets needs must be
Or men or women—more's the pity."

                                 "Ah,
But men, and still less women, happily,
Scarce need be poets. Keep to the green wreath,
Since even dreaming of the stone and bronze
95   Brings headaches, pretty cousin, and defiles
The clean white morning dresses."

---

5. Aurora, the goddess of the dawn.

6. An Oread is a tree nymph; a Naiad is a water nymph.

                                   "So you judge!
Because I love the beautiful I must
Love pleasure chiefly, and be overcharged
For ease and whiteness! well, you know the world,
100   And only miss your cousin, 'tis not much.
But learn this; I would rather take my part
With God's Dead, who afford to walk in white
Yet spread His glory, than keep quiet here
And gather up my feet from even a step
105   For fear to soil my gown in so much dust.
I choose to walk at all risks.—Here, if heads
That hold a rhythmic thought, much ache perforce,
For my part I choose headaches,—and to-day's
My birthday."

                        "Dear Aurora, choose instead
110   To cure them. You have balsams."

                                   "I perceive.
The headache is too noble for my sex.
You think the heartache would sound decenter,
Since that's the woman's special, proper ache,
And altogether tolerable, except
115   To a woman."

                        [NO FEMALE CHRIST]

                        "There it is!—
180   You play beside a death-bed like a child,
Yet measure to yourself a prophet's place
To teach the living. None of all these things
Can women understand. You generalise
Oh, nothing,—not even grief! Your quick-breathed hearts,
185   So sympathetic to the personal pang,
Close on each separate knife-stroke, yielding up
A whole life at each wound, incapable
Of deepening, widening a large lap of life
To hold the world-full woe. The human race
190   To you means, such a child, or such a man,
You saw one morning waiting in the cold,
Beside that gate, perhaps. You gather up
A few such cases, and when strong sometimes
Will write of factories and of slaves, as if
195   Your father were a negro, and your son
A spinner in the mills. All's yours and you,
All, coloured with your blood, or otherwise
Just nothing to you. Why, I call you hard
To general suffering. Here's the world half-blind
200   With intellectual light, half-brutalised
With civilisation, having caught the plague

In silks from Tarsus,[7] shrieking east and west
Along a thousand railroads, mad with pain
And sin too! . . . does one woman of you all
205   (You who weep easily) grow pale to see
This tiger shake his cage?—does one of you
Stand still from dancing, stop from stringing pearls,
And pine and die because of the great sum
Of universal anguish?—Show me a tear
210   Wet as Cordelia's,[8] in eyes bright as yours,
Because the world is mad. You cannot count,
That you should weep for this account, not you!
You weep for what you know. A red-haired child
Sick in a fever, if you touch him once,
215   Though but so little as with a finger-tip,
Will set you weeping; but a million sick . . .
You could as soon weep for the rule of three
Or compound fractions. Therefore, this same world,
Uncomprehended by you, must remain
220   Uninfluenced by you.—Women as you are,
Mere women, personal and passionate,
You give us doating mothers, and perfect wives,
Sublime Madonnas, and enduring saints!
We get no Christ from you,—and verily
225   We shall not get a poet, in my mind."

[AURORA'S REJECTION OF ROMNEY]

There he glowed on me
With all his face and eyes. "No other help?"
345   Said he—"no more than so?"[9]

                  "What help?" I asked.
"You'd scorn my help,—as Nature's self, you say,
Has scorned to put her music in my mouth
Because a woman's. Do you now turn round
And ask for what a woman cannot give?"

350   "For what she only can, I turn and ask,"
He answered, catching up my hands in his,
And dropping on me from his high-eaved brow
The full weight of his soul,—"I ask for love,
And that, she can; for life in fellowship
355   Through bitter duties—that, I know she can;

---

7. I.e., with civilized luxuries come evils, just as the trading ships bringing silks from Tarsus—a wealthy center of trade in the ancient Middle East—might also have brought rats that spread the plague.
8. Cordelia weeps when she is reunited with her father (*King Lear*, 4.7.71); her feelings are entirely personal. Romney mentions Cordelia to bolster his argument that women cannot play any role in world affairs because they are incapable of taking a broad view of human suffering.
9. Romney wants to alleviate the misery of the poor through social reform. Aurora has offered her approval of his plans, but he asks if she can offer him another kind of help—i.e., to be his wife or "helpmate" (line 402 below).

For wifehood—will she?"

           "Now," I said, "may God
Be witness 'twixt us two!" and with the word,
Meseemed I floated into a sudden light
Above his stature,—"am I proved too weak

360   To stand alone, yet strong enough to bear
Such leaners on my shoulder? poor to think,
Yet rich enough to sympathise with thought?
Incompetent to sing, as blackbirds can,
Yet competent to love, like HIM?"

                     I paused;

365   Perhaps I darkened, as the lighthouse will
That turns upon the sea. "It's always so.
Anything does for a wife."

                 "Aurora, dear,
And dearly honoured,"—he pressed in at once
With eager utterance,—"you translate me ill.

370   I do not contradict my thought of you
Which is most reverent, with another thought
Found less so. If your sex is weak for art
(And I, who said so, did but honour you
By using truth in courtship), it is strong

375   For life and duty. Place your fecund heart
In mine, and let us blossom for the world
That wants love's colour in the grey of time.
My talk, meanwhile, is arid to you, ay,
Since all my talk can only set you where

380   You look down coldly on the arena-heaps
Of headless bodies, shapeless, indistinct!
The Judgment-Angel scarce would find his way
Through such a heap of generalised distress
To the individual man with lips and eyes,

385   Much less Aurora. Ah, my sweet, come down,
And hand in hand we'll go where yours shall touch
These victims, one by one! till, one by one,
The formless, nameless trunk of every man
Shall seem to wear a head with hair you know,

390   And every woman catch your mother's face
To melt you into passion."

                  "I am a girl,"
I answered slowly; "you do well to name
My mother's face. Though far too early, alas,
God's hand did interpose 'twixt it and me,

395   I know so much of love as used to shine
In that face and another. Just so much;
No more indeed at all. I have not seen
So much love since, I pray you pardon me,

As answers even to make a marriage with
400   In this cold land of England. What you love
Is not a woman, Romney, but a cause:
You want a helpmate, not a mistress, sir,
A wife to help your ends,—in her no end.
Your cause is noble, your ends excellent,
405   But I, being most unworthy of these and that,
Do otherwise conceive of love. Farewell."

"Farewell, Aurora? you reject me thus?"
He said.

         "Sir, you were married long ago.
You have a wife already whom you love,
410   Your social theory. Bless you both, I say.
For my part, I am scarcely meek enough
To be the handmaid of a lawful spouse.
Do I look a Hagar,[1] think you?"

                         "So you jest."

"Nay, so, I speak in earnest," I replied.
415   "You treat of marriage too much like, at least,
A chief apostle: you would bear with you
A wife . . . a sister . . . shall we speak it out?
A sister of charity."

                    "Then, must it be
Indeed farewell? And was I so far wrong
420   In hope and in illusion, when I took
The woman to be nobler than the man,
Yourself the noblest woman, in the use
And comprehension of what love is,—love,
That generates the likeness of itself
425   Through all heroic duties? so far wrong,
In saying bluntly, venturing truth on love,
'Come, human creature, love and work with me,'—
Instead of 'Lady, thou art wondrous fair,
And, where the Graces walk before, the Muse
430   Will follow at the lightning of their eyes,
And where the Muse walks, lovers need to creep:
Turn round and love me, or I die of love.'"

With quiet indignation I broke in.
"You misconceive the question like a man,
435   Who sees a woman as the complement
Of his sex merely. You forget too much
That every creature, female as the male,
Stands single in responsible act and thought

---

1. In Genesis 16, Hagar was the handmaiden of Abraham's lawful wife, Sarah; Hagar bore Abraham a son, Ishmael, when it appeared that Sarah was barren.

As also in birth and death. Whoever says
440   To a loyal woman, 'Love and work with me,'
Will get fair answers if the work and love,
Being good themselves, are good for her—the best
She was born for. Women of a softer mood,
Surprised by men when scarcely awake to life,
445   Will sometimes only hear the first word, love,
And catch up with it any kind of work,
Indifferent, so that dear love go with it.
I do not blame such women, though, for love,
They pick much oakum;[2] earth's fanatics make
450   Too frequently heaven's saints. But *me* your work
Is not the best for,—nor your love the best,
Nor able to commend the kind of work
For love's sake merely. Ah, you force me, sir,
To be overbold in speaking of myself:
455   I too have my vocation,—work to do,
The heavens and earth have set me since I changed
My father's face for theirs, and, though your world
Were twice as wretched as you represent,
Most serious work, most necessary work
460   As any of the economists'. Reform,
Make trade a Christian possibility,
And individual right no general wrong;
Wipe out earth's furrows of the Thine and Mine,
And leave one green for men to play at bowls,[3]
465   With innings for them all! . . . What then, indeed,
If mortals are not greater by the head
Than any of their prosperities? what then,
Unless the artist keep up open roads
Betwixt the seen and unseen,—bursting through
470   The best of your conventions with his best,
The speakable, imaginable best
God bids him speak, to prove what lies beyond
Both speech and imagination? A starved man
Exceeds a fat beast: we'll not barter, sir,
475   The beautiful for barley.—And, even so,
I hold you will not compass your poor ends
Of barley-feeding and material ease,
Without a poet's individualism
To work your universal. It takes a soul,
480   To move a body: it takes a high-souled man,
To move the masses, even to a cleaner stye:
It takes the ideal, to blow a hair's-breadth off
The dust of the actual.—Ah, your Fouriers[4] failed,

---

2. Prisoners and paupers in workhouses were forced to pick oakum (untwist strands of old rope); it was tedious and menial labor.

3. Lawn bowling.
4. François Marie Charles Fourier (1772–1837), a French social theorist who advocated communal property.

Because not poets enough to understand
485 That life develops from within.—For me,
Perhaps I am not worthy, as you say,
Of work like this: perhaps a woman's soul
Aspires, and not creates: yet we aspire,
And yet I'll try out your perhapses, sir,
490 And if I fail . . . why, burn me up my straw[5]
Like other false works—I'll not ask for grace;
Your scorn is better, cousin Romney. I
Who love my art, would never wish it lower
To suit my stature. I may love my art.
495 You'll grant that even a woman may love art,
Seeing that to waste true love on anything
Is womanly, past question."

                    I retain
The very last word which I said that day,
As you the creaking of the door, years past,
500 Which let upon you such disabling news
You ever after have been graver. He,
His eyes, the motions in his silent mouth,
Were fiery points on which my words were caught,
Transfixed for ever in my memory
505 For his sake, not their own. And yet I know
I did not love him . . . nor he me . . . that's sure . . .
And what I said is unrepented of,
As truth is always. Yet . . . a princely man!—
If hard to me, heroic for himself!
510 He bears down on me through the slanting years,
The stronger for the distance. If he had loved,
Ay, loved me, with that retributive face, . . .
I might have been a common woman now
And happier, less known and less left alone,
515 Perhaps a better woman after all,
With chubby children hanging on my neck
To keep me low and wise. Ah me, the vines
That bear such fruit are proud to stoop with it.
The palm stands upright in a realm of sand.
520 And I, who spoke the truth then, stand upright,
Still worthy of having spoken out the truth,
By being content I spoke it though it set
Him there, me here.—O woman's vile remorse,
To hanker after a mere name, a show,
525 A supposition, a potential love!
Does every man who names love in our lives
Become a power for that?

---

5. I.e., destroy my poetry.

from **Book 3**
[THE WOMAN WRITER IN LONDON]

Why what a pettish, petty thing I grow,—
A mere mere woman, a mere flaccid nerve,
A kerchief left out all night in the rain,
Turned soft so,—overtasked and overstrained
40   And overlived in this close London life!
And yet I should be stronger.

Never burn
Your letters, poor Aurora! for they stare
With red seals from the table, saying each,
"Here's something that you know not." Out, alas,
45   'Tis scarcely that the world's more good and wise
Or even straighter and more consequent
Since yesterday at this time—yet, again,
If but one angel spoke from Ararat[1]
I should be very sorry not to hear:
50   So open all the letters! let me read.
Blanche Ord, the writer in the "Lady's Fan,"
Requests my judgment on . . . that, afterwards.
Kate Ward desires the model of my cloak,
And signs "Elisha to you."[2] Pringle Sharpe
55   Presents his work on "Social Conduct," craves
A little money for his pressing debts . . .
From me, who scarce have money for my needs;
Art's fiery chariot which we journey in
Being apt to singe our singing-robes to holes,
60   Although you ask me for my cloak, Kate Ward!
Here's Rudgely knows it,—editor and scribe;
He's "forced to marry where his heart is not,
Because the purse lacks where he lost his heart."
Ah,——lost it because no one picked it up;
65   That's really loss,—(and passable impudence).
My critic Hammond flatters prettily,
And wants another volume like the last.
My critic Belfair wants another book
Entirely different, which will sell (and live?),
70   A striking book, yet not a startling book,
The public blames originalities
(You must not pump spring-water unawares
Upon a gracious public full of nerves):
Good things, not subtle, new yet orthodox,
75   As easy reading as the dog-eared page

1. The mountain where Noah's ark rested after the Flood and where God spoke to Noah (Genesis 8).
2. When the prophet Elijah was carried to heaven in a chariot of fire, his cloak fell to earth and was taken up by his successor Elisha (2 Kings 2.1–15); Kate Ward means that she wants to copy Aurora's cloak.

That's fingered by said public fifty years,
Since first taught spelling by its grandmother,
And yet a revelation in some sort:
That's hard, my critic Belfair. So—what next?
80 My critic Stokes objects to abstract thoughts;
"Call a man John, a woman Joan," says he,
"And do not prate so of *humanities*":
Whereat I call my critic simply, Stokes.
My critic Jobson recommends more mirth
85 Because a cheerful genius suits the times,
And all true poets laugh unquenchably
Like Shakespeare and the gods. That's very hard.
The gods may laugh, and Shakespeare; Dante smiled
With such a needy heart on two pale lips,
90 We cry "Weep rather, Dante." Poems are
Men, if true poems: and who dares exclaim
At any man's door, "Here, 'tis understood
The thunder fell last week and killed a wife
And scared a sickly husband—what of that?
95 Get up, be merry, shout and clap your hands,
Because a cheerful genius suits the times—"?
None says so to the man, and why indeed
Should any to the poem? A ninth seal;[3]
The apocalypse is drawing to a close.
100 Ha,—this from Vincent Carrington,—"Dear friend,
I want good counsel. Will you lend me wings
To raise me to the subject, in a sketch
I'll bring to-morrow—may I? at eleven?
A poet's only born to turn to use:
105 So save you! for the world . . . and Carrington."
"(Writ after.) Have you heard of Romney Leigh,
Beyond what's said of him in newspapers,
His phalansteries[4] there, his speeches here,
His pamphlets, pleas, and statements, everywhere?
110 He dropped *me* long ago, but no one drops
A golden apple—though indeed one day
You hinted that, but jested. Well, at least
You know Lord Howe who sees him . . . whom he sees
And *you* see and I hate to see,—for Howe
115 Stands high upon the brink of theories,
Observes the swimmers and cries 'Very fine,'
But keeps dry linen equally,—unlike
That gallant breaster, Romney. Strange it is,
Such sudden madness seizing a young man

---

3. In Revelation 5.1 there is a book closed with seven
seals, the opening of which will herald the Apocalypse.
The reference to a ninth seal satirically suggests something more extreme than the Apocalypse itself.
4. The communes advocated by the socialist Fourier.

120 To make earth over again,—while I'm content
  To make the pictures. Let me bring the sketch.
  A tiptoe Danae,[5] overbold and hot,
  Both arms a-flame to meet her wishing Jove
  Halfway, and burn him faster down; the face
125 And breasts upturned and straining, the loose locks
  All glowing with the anticipated gold.
  Or here's another on the self-same theme.[6]
  She lies here—flat upon her prison-floor,
  The long hair swathed about her to the heel
130 Like wet seaweed. You dimly see her through
  The glittering haze of that prodigious rain,
  Half blotted out of nature by a love
  As heavy as fate. I'll bring you either sketch.
  I think, myself, the second indicates
  More passion."

135   Surely. Self is put away,
  And calm with abdication. She is Jove,
  And no more Danae—greater thus. Perhaps
  The painter symbolises unaware
  Two states of the recipient artist-soul,
140 One, forward, personal, wanting reverence,
  Because aspiring only. We'll be calm,
  And know that, when indeed our Joves come down,
  We all turn stiller than we have ever been.

        * * *

  Serene and unafraid of solitude,
170 I worked the short days out,—and watched the sun
  On lurid morns or monstrous afternoons
  (Like some Druidic idol's fiery brass
  With fixed unflickering outline of dead heat,
  From which the blood of wretches pent inside
175 Seems oozing forth to incarnadine the air[7])
  Push out through fog with his dilated disk,
  And startle the slant roofs and chimney-pots
  With splashes of fierce colour. Or I saw
  Fog only, the great tawny weltering fog,
180 Involve the passive city, strangle it
  Alive, and draw it off into the void,
  Spires, bridges, streets, and squares, as if a sponge
  Had wiped out London,—or as noon and night
  Had clapped together and utterly struck out
185 The intermediate time, undoing themselves
  In the act. Your city poets see such things

---

5. Carrington has sketched Danae, the beloved of Zeus, whom Zeus visited in a shower of gold.
6. I.e., the second picture is also of Danae and the golden shower ("prodigious rain") that is Zeus.
7. It was believed that ancient Celtic druids performed human sacrifices.

Not despicable. Mountains of the south,
When drunk and mad with elemental wines
They rend the seamless mist and stand up bare,
190   Make fewer singers, haply. No one sings,
Descending Sinai: on Parnassus mount[8]
You take a mule to climb and not a muse
Except in fable and figure: forests chant
Their anthems to themselves, and leave you dumb.
195   But sit in London at the day's decline,
And view the city perish in the mist
Like Pharaoh's armaments in the deep Red Sea,[9]
The chariots, horsemen, footmen, all the host,
Sucked down and choked to silence—then, surprised
200   By a sudden sense of vision and of tune,
You feel as conquerors though you did not fight,
And you and Israel's other singing girls,
Ay, Miriam[1] with them, sing the song you choose.

from Book 5
[Epic Art and Modern Life]

The critics say that epics have died out
140   With Agamemnon and the goat-nursed gods;[1]
I'll not believe it. I could never deem,
As Payne Knight[2] did (the mythic mountaineer
Who travelled higher than he was born to live,
And showed sometimes the goitre in his throat[3]
145   Discoursing of an image seen through fog),
That Homer's heroes measured twelve feet high.
They were but men:—his Helen's hair turned grey
Like any plain Miss Smith's who wears a front;[4]
And Hector's infant whimpered at a plume[5]
150   As yours last Friday at a turkey-cock.
All actual heroes are essential men,
And all men possible heroes: every age,
Heroic in proportions, double-faced,
Looks backward and before, expects a morn
155   And claims an epos.°   *epic poem*

8. Sinai is the mountain where God gave the Commandments to Moses; Parnassus is the mountain where the Muses, the Greek goddesses of the arts and of knowledge, dwelled. The idea is that neither biblical nor classical sources can provide poetic inspiration for the modern poet; only the city can do so.
9. In Exodus 14.21–30, God parts the Red Sea so the Israelites can escape from Egypt but drowns Pharaoh's pursuing armies.
1. Miriam, the sister of Moses and Aaron, led the women of Israel in singing to celebrate the drowning of the Egyptian army (Exodus 15.19–21).

1. Agamemnon led the Greeks in the Trojan War, as chronicled in Homer's epic, the *Iliad;* Zeus was nursed by a goat.
2. Richard Payne Knight (1750–1824), a classical scholar who speculated about Homer and the Elgin marbles.
3. A swelling of the throat (caused by lack of iodine in the water at high altitudes), symbolizing the foolishness of Payne Knight's utterances.
4. Hairpiece worn over the forehead; artificial bangs.
5. When the Trojan warrior Hector tried to embrace his infant son before going into battle, the baby was terrified of his father's plumed helmet.

Ay, but every age

Appears to souls who live in't (ask Carlyle[6])
Most unheroic. Ours, for instance, ours:
The thinkers scout it, and the poets abound
Who scorn to touch it with a finger-tip:

160 A pewter age,[7]—mixed metal, silver-washed;
An age of scum, spooned off the richer past,
An age of patches for old gaberdines,°   *overcoats*
An age of mere transition,[8] meaning nought
Except that what succeeds must shame it quite

165 If God please. That's wrong thinking, to my mind,
And wrong thoughts make poor poems.

Every age,

Through being beheld too close, is ill-discerned
By those who have not lived past it. We'll suppose
Mount Athos carved, as Alexander schemed,

170 To some colossal statue of a man.[9]
The peasants, gathering brushwood in his ear,
Had guessed as little as the browsing goats
Of form or feature of humanity
Up there,—in fact, had travelled five miles off

175 Or ere the giant image broke on them,
Full human profile, nose and chin distinct,
Mouth, muttering rhythms of silence up the sky
And fed at evening with the blood of suns;
Grand torso,—hand, that flung perpetually

180 The largesse of a silver river down
To all the country pastures. 'Tis even thus
With times we live in,—evermore too great
To be apprehended near.

But poets should

Exert a double vision; should have eyes

185 To see near things as comprehensively
As if afar they took their point of sight,
And distant things as intimately deep
As if they touched them. Let us strive for this.
I do distrust the poet who discerns

190 No character or glory in his times,
And trundles back his soul five hundred years,
Past moat and drawbridge, into a castle-court,
To sing—oh, not of lizard or of toad
Alive i' the ditch there,—'twere excusable,

---

6. In *On Heroes and Hero Worship* (1841) Thomas Carlyle urges a renewal of the idea of the heroic.
7. Inferior to the Golden, the Silver, or even the Bronze Age; Hesiod proposed that history is a constant process of decline.
8. In *The Spirit of the Age* (1831) John Stuart Mill says

the present era is "an age of transition."
9. Alexander the Great thought of having Mount Athos carved in the form of a gigantic statue of a conqueror, with a basin in one hand to collect water for the pastures below.

195   But of some black chief, half knight, half sheep-lifter,
      Some beauteous dame, half chattel and half queen,
      As dead as must be, for the greater part,
      The poems made on their chivalric bones;
      And that's no wonder: death inherits death.

200   Nay, if there's room for poets in this world
      A little overgrown (I think there is),
      Their sole work is to represent the age,
      Their age, not Charlemagne's,[1]—this live, throbbing age,
      That brawls, cheats, maddens, calculates, aspires,
205   And spends more passion, more heroic heat,
      Betwixt the mirrors of its drawing-rooms,
      Than Roland with his knights at Roncesvalles.[2]
      To flinch from modern varnish, coat or flounce,
      Cry out for togas and the picturesque,
210   Is fatal,—foolish too. King Arthur's self
      Was commonplace to Lady Guenever;
      And Camelot to minstrels seemed as flat
      As Fleet Street to our poets.[3]

                        Never flinch,
      But still, unscrupulously epic, catch
215   Upon the burning lava of a song
      The full-veined, heaving, double-breasted Age:
      That, when the next shall come, the men of that
      May touch the impress with reverent hand, and say
      "Behold,—behold the paps we all have sucked!
220   This bosom seems to beat still, or at least
      It sets ours beating: this is living art,
      Which thus presents and thus records true life."

+—❦❧—+

Charles Baudelaire
1821–1867

Charles Baudelaire was the consummate modern city-dweller, a bohemian slummer who devoted himself to sex, drugs, alcohol, art, and poetry. His background was typical for an upper-
middle-class child in nineteenth-century France: the young second wife adored by her son, the
father an ancient civil servant (and poet and painter) dead before his son was ten, the detested
and disciplinarian stepfather who sent the boy away to various schools from which he was

---

1. Charlemagne was king of the Franks (768–814) and
emperor of the West, laying the foundation for the Holy
Roman Empire.
2. Legendary hero whose defeat at Roncesvalles (in the
Spanish Pyrenees) was disastrous for Charlemagne's
forces; his exploits are the subject of a medieval epic

poem, *Le Chanson de Roland.*
3. I.e., to his wife Guenevere, even the glorious King
Arthur was ordinary, and his kingdom was no more a subject for the poets of his own time than Fleet Street—location of London publishers and newspaper offices—is for
the poets of the 19th century.

quickly expelled for bad behavior, the inheritance squandered on a dandy's finery and on every debauchery the city could offer, the enforced South Seas voyage to straighten him out, and the return to Paris more determined than ever to live to the fullest the life of the penniless artist. Baudelaire fell tumultuously in love with the mulatta actress Jeanne Duval, among others; he drank to excess while experimenting with hashish and other intoxicants; he accumulated enormous debts, and contracted syphilis in the bargain while exploring the low life of Paris. He also wrote, constantly.

In the mid-1840s, Baudelaire began publishing reviews of the annual *Salons* (art exhibitions), and composing the poems that he would eventually collect in *Les Fleurs du Mal* (*The Flowers of Evil*). He was involved briefly in radical politics, manning the barricades during the Revolution of 1848, where his primary contribution was to exhort the Republicans to shoot down his stepfather, the General Aupick. He achieved his first literary celebrity with a series of translations of the American writer Edgar Allan Poe (page 478). When the first edition of *Les Fleurs du Mal* was finally published in 1857, it was immediately prosecuted for obscenity, the author was fined, and six of the poems were ordered to be excised from further editions. Over the last ten years of his life, as his health deteriorated, Baudelaire revised *Les Fleurs du Mal,* continued publishing criticism, including influential manifesto of modernism, *The Painter of Modern Life,* and began work on a series of prose poems, *Paris Spleen,* which were published posthumously. By the last years of his life, syphilis had rendered him mute and partially paralyzed; he died an invalid at age forty-six, his mother by his side.

The subject matter of Baudelaire's poetry has retained much of its capacity to shock: the necrophilia of "A Martyr," the rotting corpse of "Carrion," the sheer cruelty of "Ragpicker's Wine." But the key to its power is the decorous language and melodic rhythms with which the poems describe the depravity of modern life. In "Carrion," for example, the poet begins with the familiar theme of a lover remembering a walk in a park alongside his beloved, before bringing his reader face-to-face with a different sort of nature:

> Remember, my soul, the thing we saw
> that lovely summer day?
> On a pile of stones where the path turned off,
> that hideous carrion.

Baudelaire favored regular and often intricate rhyme schemes, short and highly structured verse forms such as the sonnet, and the classically French twelve-syllable line called the alexandrine. In the quatrain quoted above, the narrative alexandrines (1 and 3) alternate with the singsong counterpoint of the brief eight-syllable lines (2 and 4):

> Rappelez-vous l'objet que nous vîmes, mon âme,
> Ce beau matin d'été si doux:
> Au détour d'un sentier une charogne infame
> Sur un lit semé de cailloux.

Just as modern life hid unpleasant surprises behind pleasing exteriors, just as the industrial city brought stark contrasts of experience into close proximity, so the *Fleurs du Mal* wrapped cruel and cynical insights inside perfect poetic artifacts of great beauty.

Although the desire to shock the middle class was a fundamental tenet of Baudelaire's bohemianism, his poetry extended that rebellious impulse into a profound expression of despair. Baudelaire is one of the great love poets of the French language, and yet his poetry is more about the impossibility of love in Paris than about its wonders and delights. The poet appears rooted to Paris, but can conceive of love only outside of its bounds, in an exotic place he will never actually see but where he can hope to escape in his imagination: "All is order there, and elegance, / pleasure, peace, and opulence" ("Invitation to the Voyage"). By contrast, love in reality takes place in the fallen world of Paris, sullied by money and spoiled by boredom, a world where "Man is tired of writing, Woman of love" ("Twilight: Daybreak"). The only joy offered by love in the city lies in a momentary glance or a dream of what might have been, as in the sonnet, "In Passing." Once tasted, passion turns to boredom, and novelty gives way to spleen, the bile of someone who yearns for genuine experience but is convinced he will never find it.

Among the citydwellers who inhabit the world of these poems there is scarcely a glimpse of the figures of elegance, wealth, and beauty for which mid-nineteenth-century Paris was renowned; instead, the poet turns his caustic eye to society's exiles, throwing into the face of his bourgeois readers what they would have seen around them every day but never actually registered: the ragpicking beggars, the prostitutes, the drunkards, and the rundown slums. Whatever his society defined as evil or excluded as diseased, Baudelaire placed in his poetry as a figure of warped beauty. Not for the bohemian the easy pleasures of the summer day and the innocent sweetheart of the traditional lyric; the only response to the cruelty of modern life was a crueler beauty and a fiercely ironic gaze on the world.

For his prose poems, Baudelaire wrote in the preface to *Paris Spleen,* he dreamed of creating a "poetic prose" able not only "to adapt itself to the lyrical impulses of the soul" but also "to translate in a song the *Glazier's* strident cry." In these pieces, as in the late essay "The Painter of Modern Life," Baudelaire eschewed the shocking elegance of the *Fleurs du Mal* for a wholeheartedly modern approach. Here, too, we find the twin themes of escape and spleen, but voiced as parables or as short, paradoxical anecdotes. Baudelaire exposed what he saw as the hypocrisy of the standard charitable response to the horrors of the city. If truth and sincerity were no longer to be trusted, then artifice and deceit were preferable; at least they were perversely honest about what they were doing.

Baudelaire brought lyric poetry into the modern world; he invented the persona of the *poète maudit,* the cursed artist who transforms despair into a tool for stripping away the hypocrisies of existence, and who trades in the niceties of society for the grit of the slums. And he perfected another hallmark of modern culture—irony—for he never forgot the fundamentally ridiculous fact that his audience, the "hypocrite reader" of the opening poem of the *Fleurs du Mal,* was not the downtrodden marginals and perverse bohemians of whom he wrote, but the respectable bourgeoisie whom he wanted so desperately to shock. The mythic persona and ironic gaze of Baudelaire's writing resonates through modern poetry from Symbolist admirers such as Rimbaud and Mallarmé to modernist poets such as Pound and Eliot through the American Beat poets of the 1950s all the way to such martyrs to rock music as Jim Morrison, Janis Joplin, and Kurt Cobain.

from THE FLOWERS OF EVIL[1]

To the Reader

Stupidity, delusion, selfishness and lust
torment our bodies and possess our minds,
and we sustain our affable remorse
the way a beggar nourishes his lice.

5   Our sins are stubborn, our contrition lame;
we want our scruples to be worth our while—
how cheerfully we crawl back to the mire:
a few cheap tears will wash our stains away!

Satan Trismegistus[2] subtly rocks
10   our ravished spirits on his wicked bed

1. Translated by Richard Howard.
2. Meaning "triply great," Trismegistus was usually ap- plied to Hermes Trismegistus, legendary author of the Hermetic writings of Egypt and inventor of alchemy.

until the precious metal of our will
is leached out° by this cunning alchemist:³   *filtered out*

the Devil's hand directs our every move—
the things we loathed become the things we love;
15   day by day we drop through stinking shades
quite undeterred on our descent to Hell.

Like a poor profligate who sucks and bites
the withered breast of some well-seasoned trull,°   *prostitute*
we snatch in passing at clandestine joys
20   and squeeze the oldest orange harder yet.

Wriggling in our brains like a million worms,
a demon demos° holds its revels there,   *populace*
and when we breathe, the Lethe⁴ in our lungs
trickles sighing on its secret course.

25   If rape and arson, poison and the knife
have not yet stitched their ludicrous designs
onto the banal buckram° of our fates,   *coarse linen*
it is because our souls lack enterprise!

But here among the scorpions and the hounds,
30   the jackals, apes and vultures, snakes and wolves,
monsters that howl and growl and squeal and crawl
in all the squalid zoo of vices, one

is even uglier and fouler than the rest,
although the least flamboyant of the lot;
35   this beast would gladly undermine the earth
and swallow all creation in a yawn;

I speak of Boredom⁵ which with ready tears
dreams of hangings as it puffs its pipe.
Reader, you know this squeamish monster well,
40   —hypocrite reader,—my alias,—my twin!

The Albatross¹

Often, to pass the time on board, the crew
will catch an albatross, one of those big birds
which nonchalantly chaperone a ship
across the bitter fathoms of the sea.

5   Tied to the deck, this sovereign of space,
as if embarrassed by its clumsiness,

---

3. Alchemy manipulates base metals with corrosive acids
and water preparations to yield precious metals such as
gold and silver.
4. The river of forgetting in the classical underworld.
5. Here as elsewhere in *The Flowers of Evil*, Baudelaire
personifies states of mind and other abstractions as active

forces or characters.
1. Large seabirds with a wingspan reaching over ten feet,
albatrosses spend nearly their entire lives at sea. In
sailors' lore, to cause the death of an albatross was considered extremely bad luck.

pitiably lets its great white wings
drag at its sides like a pair of unshipped oars.

10   How weak and awkward, even comical
this traveller but lately so adroit—
one deckhand sticks a pipestem in its beak,
another mocks the cripple that once flew!

The Poet is like this monarch of the clouds
riding the storm above the marksman's range;
15   exiled on the ground, hooted and jeered,
he cannot walk because of his great wings.

Correspondences

The pillars of Nature's temple are alive
and sometimes yield perplexing messages;
forests of symbols between us and the shrine
remark our passage with accustomed eyes.

5   Like long-held echoes, blending somewhere else
into one deep and shadowy unison
as limitless as darkness and as day,
the sounds, the scents, the colors correspond.[1]

There are odors succulent as young flesh,
10   sweet as flutes, and green as any grass,
while others—rich, corrupt and masterful—

possess the power of such infinite things
as incense, amber, benjamin[2] and musk,
to praise the senses' raptures and the mind's.

The Head of Hair

Ecstatic fleece that ripples to your nape
and reeks of negligence in every curl!
To people my dim cubicle tonight
with memories shrouded in that head of hair,
5   I'd have it flutter like a handkerchief!

For torpid Asia, torrid Africa
—the wilderness I thought a world away—
survive at the heart of this dark continent . . .
As other souls set sail to music, mine,
10   O my love! embarks on your redolent hair.

Take me, tousled current, to where men
as mighty as the trees they live among

1. The theory of a universal analogy between sounds, scents, and colors was frequently voiced in mid-19th-century literary circles; among its proponents were the German writer of fantastic stories, E. T. A. Hoffmann, the French novelist Honoré de Balzac, the eccentric poet Alphonse Esquiros, and Alphonse-Louis Constant, who published occult works under the pseudonym Eliphas Levi.

2. Gum benjamin, the resin of the benzoin tree of Southeast Asia, is used as an aromatic in perfumes.

submit like them to the sun's long tyranny;
ebony sea, you bear a brilliant dream
15   of sails and pennants, mariners and masts,

a harbor where my soul can slake its thirst
for color, sound and smell—where ships that glide
among the seas of golden silk throw wide
their yardarms to embrace a glorious sky
20   palpitating in eternal heat.

Drunk, and in love with drunkenness, I'll dive
into this ocean where the other lurks,
and solaced by these waves, my restlessness
will find a fruitful lethargy at last,
25   rocking forever at aromatic ease.

Blue hair, vault of shadows, be for me
the canopy of overarching sky;
here at the downy roots of every strand
I stupefy myself on the mingled scent
30   of musk and tar and coconut oil for hours . . .

For hours? Forever! Into that splendid mane
let me braid rubies, ropes of pearls to bind
you indissolubly to my desire—
you the oasis where I dream, the gourd
35   from which I gulp the wine of memory.

Carrion

Remember, my soul, the thing we saw
    that lovely summer day?
On a pile of stones where the path turned off,
    the hideous carrion—

5   legs in the air, like a whore—displayed,
    indifferent to the last,
a belly slick with lethal sweat
    and swollen with foul gas.

The sun lit up that rottenness
10   as though to roast it through,
restoring to Nature a hundredfold
    what she had here made one.

And heaven watched the splendid corpse
    like a flower open wide—
15   you nearly fainted dead away
    at the perfume it gave off.

Flies kept humming over the guts
    from which a gleaming clot
of maggots poured to finish off

20   what scraps of flesh remained.

The tide of trembling vermin sank,
    then bubbled up afresh
as if the carcass, drawing breath,
    by *their* lives lived again

25   and made a curious music there—
    like running water, or wind,
or the rattle of chaff the winnower
    loosens in his fan.[1]

Shapeless—nothing was left but a dream
30   the artist had sketched in,
forgotten, and only later on
    finished from memory.

Behind the rocks an anxious bitch
    eyed us reproachfully,
35   waiting for the chance to resume
    her interrupted feast.

—Yet you will come to this offence,
    this horrible decay,
you, the light of my life, the sun
40   and moon and stars of my love!

Yes, you will come to this, my queen,
    after the sacraments,°   *funeral rites*
when you rot underground among
    the bones already there.

45   But as their kisses eat you up,
    my Beauty, tell the worms
I've kept the sacred essence, saved
    the form of my rotted loves!

Invitation to the Voyage

Imagine the magic
    of living together
there, with all the time in the world
    for loving each other,
5   for loving and dying
where even the landscape resembles you:
    the suns dissolved
    in overcast skies
have the same mysterious charm for me
10   as your wayward eyes
    through crystal tears,

---

1. A winnower uses a special fan to toss corn or wheat into the air to separate the lighter husks, the chaff, from the edible grain.

my sister, my child!

All is order there, and elegance,
    pleasure, peace, and opulence.

15   Furniture gleaming
        with the patina
of time itself in the room we would share;
        the rarest flowers
        mingling aromas
20 with amber's uncertain redolence;
        encrusted ceilings
        echoed in mirrors
and Eastern splendor on the walls—
        here all would whisper
25   to the soul in secret
            her sweet mother tongue.

All is order there, and elegance,
    pleasure, peace, and opulence.

        On these still canals
30   the freighters doze
fitfully: their mood is for roving,
        and only to flatter
        a lover's fancy
have they put in from the ends of the earth.
35   By late afternoon
        the canals catch fire
as sunset glorifies the town;
        the world turns to gold
        as it falls asleep
40   in a fervent light.

All is order there, and elegance,
    pleasure, peace, and opulence.

Spleen[1] (II)

Souvenirs?
More than if I had lived a thousand years!

No chest of drawers crammed with documents,
love-letters, wedding-invitations, wills,
5   a lock of someone's hair rolled up in a deed,
hides so many secrets as my brain.
This branching catacombs, this pyramid
contains more corpses than the potter's field:[2]

---

1. In medieval medicine, the spleen was associated with the black bile said to cause melancholy. Baudelaire adapted the English word to express the feeling of bitterness and boredom ("ennui") he considered to be characteristic of modern life.

2. In French *fosse commune*, a burial ground for the poor and for strangers.

I am a graveyard that the moon abhors,
10   where long worms like regrets come out to feed
most ravenously on my dearest dead.
I am an old boudoir where a rack of gowns,
perfumed by withered roses, rots to dust;
where only faint pastels and pale Bouchers[3]
15   inhale the scent of long-unstoppered flasks.

Nothing is slower than the limping days
when under the heavy weather of the years
Boredom, the fruit of glum indifference,
gains the dimension of eternity . . .
20   Hereafter, mortal clay, you are no more
than a rock encircled by a nameless dread,
an ancient sphinx omitted from the map,
forgotten by the world, and whose fierce moods
sing only to the rays of setting suns.

The Swan

to Victor Hugo[1]

1

Andromache, I think of you! That stream,
the sometime witness to your widowhood's
enormous majesty of mourning—that
mimic Simoïs salted by your tears[2]

5   suddenly inundates my memory
as I cross the new Place du Carrousel.[3]
Old Paris is gone (no human heart
changes half so fast as a city's face)[4]

and only in my mind's eye can I see
10   The junk laid out to glitter in the booths
among the weeds and splintered capitals,°   *columns*
blocks of marble blackened by the mud;

there used to be a poultry-market here,
and one cold morning—with the sky swept clean,
15   the ground, too, swept by garbage-men who raised

---

3. The French painter François Boucher (1703–1770) was famous for his delicate colors, easy style, and frivolous subjects, and especially for his female nudes.
1. Celebrated French Romantic poet, novelist and dramatist (1802–1885). Baudelaire sent a manuscript copy of the poem to Hugo, who was in political exile at the time on the Channel Islands.
2. The wife of Hector of Troy, Andromache was claimed as prize of war by Achilles' son Pyrrhus. Abandoned by him, she eventually came to settle in Epirus, where Aeneas visits her in Book 3 of Virgil's *Aeneid*. She and her new husband, Hector's brother Helenus, have built a miniature Troy, complete with a replica of its river, Simois, at the shores of which she weeps over the empty grave of her dead husband.
3. The bohemian artists' quarter where Baudelaire and others of his circle had lived had been demolished in 1849 in order to connect the Louvre with the Tuileries Palace. The Place du Carrousel was established in its place.
4. The loss of *vieux Paris*, the narrow winding streets and old buildings dating back to the medieval city, to the demolitions of 19th-century speculation and improvements, was a refrain through most of the century, especially the second half.

clouds of soot in the icy air—I saw

a swan that had broken out of its cage,
webbed feet clumsy on the cobblestones,
white feathers dragging in the uneven ruts,
20   and obstinately pecking at the drains,

drenching its enormous wings in the filth
as if in its own lovely lake, crying
'Where is the thunder, when will it rain?'
I see it still, inevitable myth,

25   like Daedalus dead-set against the sky—[5]
the sky quite blue and blank and unconcerned—
that straining neck and that voracious beak,
as if the swan were castigating God!

2

Paris changes . . . But in sadness like mine
30   nothing stirs—new buildings, old
neighborhoods turn to allegory,
and memories weigh more than stone.

One image, near the Louvre, will not dissolve:
I think of that great swan in its torment,
35   silly, like all exiles, and sublime,
endlessly longing . . . And again I think

of you, Andromache, dragged off
to be the booty of Achilles' son,
Hector's widow now the wife of Helenus,
40   crouching blindly over an empty grave!

I think of some black woman, starving
and consumptive in the muddy streets,
peering through a wall of fog for those
missing palms of splendid Africa;

45   I think of orphans withering like flowers;
of those who lose what never can be found
again—never! swallowing their tears
and nursing at the she-wolf Sorrow's dugs;

and in the forest of my mind's exile
50   a merciless memory winds its horn:
I hear it and I think of prisoners,
of the shipwrecked, the beaten—and so many more!

In Passing

The traffic roared around me, deafening!
Tall, slender, in mourning—noble grief—

---

5. According to legend, the Greek inventor Daedalus had escaped with his son Icarus from imprisonment in Crete with the help of artificial wings stuck with wax.

a woman passed, and with a jewelled hand
gathered up her black embroidered hem;

5   stately yet lithe, as if a statue walked . . .
And trembling like a fool, I drank from eyes
as ashen as the clouds before a gale
the grace that beckons and the joy that kills.

Lightning . . . then darkness! Lovely fugitive
10   whose glance has brought me back to life! But where
is life—not this side of eternity?

Elsewhere! Too far, too late, or never at all!
Of me you know nothing, I nothing of you—you
whom I might have loved and who knew that too!

Twilight: Evening

It comes as an accomplice, stealthily,
the lovely hour that is the felon's friend;
the sky, like curtains round a bed, draws close,
and man prepares to become a beast of prey.

5   Longed for by those whose aching arms confess:
we earned our daily bread, at last it comes,
evening and the anodyne° it brings   *relief*
to workmen free to sleep and dream of sleep,
to stubborn scholars puzzling over texts,
10   to minds consumed by one tormenting pain . . .
Meantime, foul demons in the atmosphere
dutifully waken—they have work to do—
rattling shutters as they take the sky.
Under the gaslamps shaken by that wind
15   whoredom invades and everywhere at once
debouches° on invisible thoroughfares,   *pours out*
as if the enemy had launched a raid;
it fidgets like a worm in the city's filth,
filching its portion of Man's daily bread.

20   Listen! Now you can hear the kitchens hiss,
the stages yelp, the music drown it all!
The dens that specialize in gambling fill
with trollops and their vague confederates,
and thieves untroubled by a second thought
25   will soon be hard at work (they also serve)
softly forcing doors and secret drawers
to dress their sluts and live a few days more.

This is the hour to compose yourself, my soul;
ignore the noise they make; avert your eyes.
30   Now comes the time when invalids grow worse
and darkness takes them by the throat; they end
their fate in the usual way, and all their sighs

turn hospitals into a cave of the winds.
More than one will not come back for broth
35   warmed at the fireside by devoted hands.

Most of them, in fact, have never known
a hearth to come to, and have never lived.

Twilight: Daybreak

The morning wind rattles the windowpanes
and over the barracks reveille rings out.

Dreams come now, bad dreams, and teen-age boys
burrow into their pillows. Now the lamp
5   that glowed at midnight seems, like a bloodshot eye,
to throb and throw a red stain on the room;
balked by the stubborn body's weight, the soul
mimics the lamplight's struggles with the dawn.
Like a face in tears—the tears effaced by wind—
10   the air is tremulous with escaping things,
and Man is tired of writing, Woman of love.

Here and there, chimneys begin to smoke.
Whores, mouths gaping, eyelids gray as ash,
sleep on their feet, leaning against the walls,
15   and beggar-women, hunched over sagging breasts,
blow on burning sticks, then on their hands.
Now, the hungry feel the cold the worst,
and women in labor suffer the sharpest pains;
now, like a sob cut short by a clot of blood,
20   a rooster crows somewhere; a sea of mist
swirls around the buildings; in the Hôtel-Dieu[1]
the dying breathe their last, while the debauched,
spent by their exertions, sleep alone.

Shivering dawn, in a wisp of pink and green,
25   totters slowly across the empty Seine,
and dingy Paris—old drudge rubbing its eyes—
picks up its tools to begin another day.

Ragpickers' Wine[1]

Look—there! in the streetlamp's dingy glow
—wind rattling the glass, lashing the flame—
out of the muddy labyrinth of streets
teeming with unruly, sordid types,

1. A municipal hospital; the one in Paris dates back to the very early Middle Ages, and was demolished in the late 19th century. It stood on the south side of the Ile de la Cité, catercornered from the Notre Dame Cathedral.
1. Ragpickers, or *chiffonniers*, lived off what they scav-
enged at night from the rags and the garbage of the city. The *chiffonnier* was an important figure for many writers of the many marginal occupations of the nocturnal city, both positive and negative, including poetry.

5   a ragpicker stumbles past, wagging his head
and bumping into walls with a poet's grace,
pouring out his heartfelt schemes to one
and all, including spies of the police.[2]

10   He swears to wonders, lays down noble laws,
reforms the wicked, raises up their prey,
and under the lowering canopy of heaven
intoxicates himself on his own boasts.

More such creatures—who knows where they live?—
wracked by drudgery, ruined by the years,
15   staggering under enormous sacks of junk
—the vomit of surfeited Paris—now appear,

whole armies of them, reeking of sour wine,
comrades in arms, whitened by their wars,
whiskers dropping like surrendered flags . . .
20   Before them wave the banners and the palms—

as if by magic, arches of triumph rise
and in the chaos of exploding flares,
bugle-calls and battle-cries and drums,
they march in glory past a cheering mob!

25   So it is, through frivolous mankind,
that wine like a bright Pactolus pours its gold;[3]
with human tongues it glorifies its deeds
and rules by what it gives, as true kings do.

To drown the spleen and pacify the sloth
30   of these old wrecks who die without a word,
God, taking pity, created Sleep; to which
Man added Wine, the sun's anointed son!

A Martyr
Drawing by an Unknown Master[1]

Among decanters, ivories and gems,
    sumptuous divans[2]
with gold-brocaded silks and fragrant gowns
    trailing languid folds,

2. *Mouchards*, or police and government spies, were om-
nipresent under the July Monarchy of Louis-Philippe
(1830–1848) and the Second Empire of Napoleon III
(1852–1870). *Chiffonniers* were frequently identified
with radical politics.
3. According to Greek myth, King Midas was released
from the enchantment that caused whatever he touched to
become gold by bathing in the river Pactolus, filling it
with gold.
1. Rather than referring to a particular work of art, the

subtitle emphasizes the visual focus of the poem. The
style is of the exotic Romanticism of artists such as Eu-
gène Delacroix, about whose works Baudelaire wrote regularly as an art critic.
2. A decanter is a glass bottle with a stopper in its top;
wine is stored in it after it has been decanted, or poured
off slowly to eliminate sediment. A divan is a low couch
or bed without back or ends; the word comes from the
Persian, and the divan was associated with the Orient.

5   where lilies sorrowing in crystal urns
          exhale their final sigh
       and where, as if the room were under glass,
          the air is pestilent,

       a headless corpse emits a stream of blood
10   the sopping pillows shed
       onto thirsty sheets which drink it up
          as greedily as sand.

       Pale as the visions which our captive eyes
          discover in the dark,
15   the head, enveloped in its sombre mane,
          emeralds still in its ears,

       watches from a stool, a thing apart,
          and from the eyes rolled back
       to whiteness blank as daybreak emanates
20   an alabaster stare.[3]

       The carcass sprawling naked on the bed
          displays without a qualm
       the splendid cynosure[4] which prodigal
          Nature bestowed—betrayed;

25   pink with gold clocks, one stocking clings—
          a souvenir, it seems;
       the garter, gleaming like a secret eye,
          darts a jewelled glance.

       Doubled by a full-length portrait drawn
30   in the same provocative pose,
       the strange demeanor of this solitude
          reveals love's darker side—

       profligate practices and guilty joys,
          embraces bound to please
35   the swarm of naughty angels frolicking
          in the curtains overhead;

       yet judging from the narrow elegance
          of her shoulders sloping down
       past the serpentine curve of her waist
40   to the almost bony hips,

       she still is young!—What torment in her soul,
          what tedium that stung
       her senses gave this body to the throng
          of wandering, lost desires?[5]

---

3. Alabaster is a translucent form of gypsum, usually white, used for carving. The adjective is used as a poetic term to describe something white and smooth, such as skin, or, here, in a more symbolic way, the gaze of a dead eye.

4. A brilliant or beautiful focus of attraction or of admiration.

5. Opinion at the time had it that the real-life model was a singer, Rosine Stoltz, of whom Baudelaire was enamored, and whose profile evidently matched this description.

45   In spite of so much love, did the vengeful man
           she could not, living, sate
       assuage on her inert and docile flesh
           the measure of his lust?

       And did he, gripping her blood-stiffened hair
50   lift up that dripping head
       and press on her cold teeth one final kiss?
           The sullied corpse is still.

       —Far from a scornful world of jeering crowds
           and peering magistrates,
55   sleep in peace, lovely enigma, sleep
           in your mysterious tomb:

       your bridegroom roves, and your immortal form
           keeps vigil when he sleeps;
       like you, no doubt, he will be constant too,
60   and faithful unto death.

from The Painter of Modern Life[1]
from 3. An Artist, Man of the World, Man of Crowds, and Child

The crowd is his domain, just as the air is the bird's, and water that of the fish. His passion and his profession is to merge with the crowd. For the perfect idler, for the passionate observer it becomes an immense source of enjoyment to establish his dwelling in the throng, in the ebb and flow, the bustle, the fleeting and the infinite. To be away from home and yet to feel at home anywhere; to see the world, to be at the very centre of the world, and yet to be unseen of the world, such are some of the minor pleasures of those independent, intense and impartial spirits, who do not lend themselves easily to linguistic definitions. The observer is a prince enjoying his incognito wherever he goes.[2] The lover of life makes the whole world into his family, just as the lover of the fair sex creates his from all the lovely women he has found, from those that could be found, and those who are impossible to find, just as the picture-lover lives in an enchanted world of dreams painted on canvas. Thus the lover of universal life moves into the crowd as though into an enormous reservoir of electricity. He, the lover of life, may also be compared to a mirror as vast as this crowd; to a kaleidoscope endowed with consciousness, which with every one of its movements presents a pattern of life, in all its multiplicity, and the flowing grace of all the elements that go to compose life. It is an ego athirst for the non-ego, and reflecting it at every moment in energies more vivid than life itself, always inconstant and fleeting. "Any man," M. G. once said, in one of those talks he rendered memorable by the intensity of his gaze, and by his eloquence of

---

1. Translated by P. E. Charvet. Although probably written earlier, the article first appeared in 1863. The subject is the Parisian drawings of the Dutch-born artist Constantin Guy (1805–1892), referred to in the text as M. G. ("Mr. G").
2. The metaphor probably refers to Haroun al-Rashid, 8th-century ruler of Baghdad and character in *The Thou-* sand and One Nights, who made a habit of wandering his city at night in disguise. The popularity of *The Thousand and One Nights,* translated into French during the previous century, was an influential factor in the exoticism of French romanticism and symbolism, and in the imagination of the urban idler and wanderer.

gesture, "any man who is not weighed down with a sorrow so searching as to touch all his faculties, and who is bored in the midst of the crowd, is a fool! A fool! and I despise him!"

When, as he wakes up, M. G. opens his eyes and sees the sun beating vibrantly at his window-panes, he says to himself with remorse and regret: "What an imperative command! What a fanfare of light! Light everywhere for several hours past! Light I have lost in sleep! and endless numbers of things bathed in light that I could have seen and have failed to!" And off he goes! And he watches the flow of life move by, majestic and dazzling. He admires the eternal beauty and the astonishing harmony of life in the capital cities, a harmony so providentially maintained in the tumult of human liberty. He gazes at the landscape of the great city, landscapes of stone, now swathed in the mist, now struck in full face by the sun. He enjoys handsome equipages, proud horses, the spit and polish of the grooms, the skilful handling by the page boys, the smooth rhythmical gait of the women, the beauty of the children, full of the joy of life and proud as peacocks of their pretty clothes; in short, life universal. If in a shift of fashion, the cut of a dress has been slightly modified, if clusters of ribbons and curls have been dethroned by rosettes, if bonnets have widened and chignons have come down a little on the nape of the neck, if waist-lines have been raised and skirts become fuller, you may be sure that from a long way off his eagle's eye will have detected it.[3] A regiment marches by, maybe on its way to the ends of the earth, filling the air of the boulevard with its martial airs, as light and lively as hope; and sure enough M. G. has already seen, inspected and analysed the weapons and the bearing of this whole body of troops. Harness, highlights, bands, determined mien, heavy and grim mustachios, all these details flood chaotically into him; and within a few minutes the poem that comes with it all is virtually composed. And then his soul will vibrate with the soul of the regiment, marching as though it were one living creature, proud image of joy and discipline!

But evening comes. The witching hour, the uncertain light, when the sky draws its curtains and the city lights go on. The gaslight stands out on the purple background of the setting sun.[4] Honest men or crooked customers, wise or irresponsible, all are saying to themselves: "The day is done at last!" Good men and bad turn their thoughts to pleasure, and each hurries to his favourite haunt to drink the cup of oblivion. M. G. will be the last to leave any place where the departing glories of daylight linger, where poetry echoes, life pulsates, music sounds; any place where a human passion offers a subject to his eye, where natural man and conventional man reveal themselves in strange beauty, where the rays of the dying sun play on the fleeting pleasure of the "depraved animal!"[5] "Well, there, to be sure, is a day well filled," murmurs to himself a type of reader well-known to all of us; "each one of us has surely enough genius to fill it in the same way." No! few men have the gift of seeing; fewer still have the power to express themselves. And now, whilst others are sleeping, this man is leaning over his table, his steady gaze on a sheet of paper, exactly the same gaze as he directed just now at the things about him, brandishing his pencil, his pen, his brush,

---

3. A rosette is a rose-shaped ornament made of ribbon. A chignon is a coil of (often false) hair piled on the back of a woman's neck. Both were the height of fashion in Paris around 1860.
4. Brighter than the lamps of previous centuries but far dimmer than the electric lights of the 20th century, gas lighting gave night in the 19th-century its characteristic

glow, often described as twilight. It also made nocturnal strolling a leisure activity rather than a proposition fraught with the peril of dark, deserted streets.
5. Baudelaire ironically cites Jean-Jacques Rousseau's assertion in the *Discourse on Inequality* (1755) that natural man, tempted and corrupted by society, becomes a "depraved animal."

splashing water from the glass up to the ceiling, wiping his pen on his shirt, hurried, vigorous, active, as though he was afraid the images might escape him, quarrelsome though alone, and driving himself relentlessly on. And things seen are born again on the paper, natural and more than natural, beautiful and better than beautiful, strange and endowed with an enthusiastic life, like the soul of their creator. The weird pageant has been distilled from nature. All the materials, stored higgledy-piggledy by memory, are classified, ordered, harmonized, and undergo that deliberate idealization, which is the product of a childlike perceptiveness, in other words a perceptiveness that is acute and magical by its very ingenuousness.

4. Modernity

And so, walking or quickening his pace, he goes his way, for ever in search. In search of what? We may rest assured that this man, such as I have described him, this solitary mortal endowed with an active imagination, always roaming the great desert of men, has a nobler aim than that of the pure idler, a more general aim, other than the fleeting pleasure of circumstance. He is looking for that indefinable something we may be allowed to call "modernity," for want of a better term to express the idea in question. The aim for him is to extract from fashion the poetry that resides in its historical envelope, to distil the eternal from the transitory. * * * Modernity is the transient, the fleeting, the contingent; it is one half of art, the other being the eternal and the immovable.

11. In Praise of Make-Up

I know a song so valueless and futile that I scarcely dare quote from it in a work with some claims to being serious; but it expresses very aptly, in vaudeville style, the aesthetic notions of people not given to thinking. "Nature embellishes beauty." It may be presumed that the "poet," had he been able to write his own language properly, would have said: "Simplicity embellishes beauty," which is tantamount to this truth of a wholly unexpected kind: "Nothing embellishes what is."

Most wrong ideas about beauty derive from the false notion the eighteenth century had about ethics.[6] In those days, Nature was taken as a basis, source and prototype of all possible forms of good and beauty. The rejection of original sin is in no small measure responsible for the general blindness of those days.[7] If, however, we are prepared merely to consult the facts that stare us in the face, the experience of all ages, and the *Gazette des Tribunaux*,[8] we can see at once that natures teaches nothing or nearly nothing; in other words, it compels man to sleep, drink, eat and to protect himself as best he can against the inclemencies of the weather. It is nature too that drives man to kill his fellow-man, to eat him, to imprison and torture him; for as soon as we move from the order of necessities and needs to that of luxury and pleasures, we see that nature can do nothing but counsel crime. It is this so-called infallible nature that has produced parricide and cannibalism, and a thousand other abominations,

6. Here again, Baudelaire is thinking primarily about Rousseau, and the various ideas associated with his definition of the "natural man."
7. Whereas the Catholic doctrine of original sin holds that men and women are born in a state of sin as a result of the fall of Adam and Eve, Rousseau's philosophy argued that children are born pure and corrupted by society. Baudelaire will argue that Rousseau's idea is an utter distortion of human nature, while Christianity gives a metaphorical but accurate description of the actual state of affairs.
8. A daily newspaper devoted to the proceedings of the law courts.

which modesty and nice feeling alike prevent our mentioning. It is philosophy (I am referring to the right kind), it is religion that enjoins upon us to succour our poor and enfeebled parents. Nature (which is nothing but the inner voice of self-interest) tells us to knock them on the head. Review, analyse everything that is natural, all the actions and desires of absolutely natural man: you will find nothing that is not horrible. Everything that is beautiful and noble is the product of reason and calculation. Crime, which the human animal took a fancy to in his mother's womb, is by origin natural. Virtue, on the other hand, is *artificial,* supernatural, since in every age and nation gods and prophets have been necessary to teach it to bestialized humanity, and since man by himself would have been powerless to discover it. Evil is done without effort, *naturally,* it is the working of fate; good is always the product of an art. All I have said about nature, as a bad counsellor in matters of ethics, and about reason, as the true power of redemption and reform, can be transferred to the order of beauty. Thus I am led to regard adornment as one of the signs of the primitive nobility of the human soul. The races that our confused and perverted civilization so glibly calls savage, with a quite laughable pride and fatuity, appreciate, just as children do, the high spiritual quality of dress. The savage and the infant show their distaste for the real by their naïve delight in bright feathers of different colours, in shimmering fabrics, in the superlative majesty of artificial shapes, thus unconsciously proving the immateriality of their souls. Woe to him who, like Louis XV (who far from being the product of a true civilization was that of a recurrence of barbarism), drives depravity to the point of appreciating nothing but nature unadorned.[9]

Fashion must therefore be thought of as a symptom of the taste for the ideal that floats on the surface in the human brain, above all the coarse, earthy and disgusting things that life according to nature accumulates, as a sublime distortion of nature, or rather as a permanent and constantly renewed effort to reform nature. For this reason, it has been judiciously observed (though without discovering the cause) that all fashions are charming, or rather relatively charming, each one being a new striving, more or less well conceived, after beauty, an approximate statement of an ideal, the desire for which constantly teases the unsatisfied human mind. But, if we want to enjoy fashions thoroughly, we must not look upon them as dead things; we might as well admire a lot of old clothes hung up, limp and inert, like the skin of St Bartholomew, in the cupboard of a second-hand-clothes dealer.[1] They must be pictured as full of the life and vitality of the beautiful women that wore them. Only in that way can we give them meaning and value. If therefore the aphorism "All fashions are charming" offends you as being too absolute, say—and then you can be sure of making no mistake—all were legitimately charming in their day.

Woman is well within her rights, we may even say she carries out a kind of duty, in devoting herself to the task of fostering a magic and supernatural aura about her appearance; she must create a sense of surprise, she must fascinate; idol that she is, she must adorn herself, to be adored. It follows, she must borrow, from all the arts, the means of rising above nature, in order the better to conquer the hearts and impress the minds of men. It matters very little that the ruse and the artifice be known of all, if

---

9. It is recorded that when Madame Dubarry wanted to avoid receiving the King, she was careful to put on rouge. That was enough; it meant she was closing her door. In beautifying herself she used to put to flight the royal disciple of nature [Baudelaire's note]. Louis XV was King of France from 1715 to 1774; he was remembered primarily for his many mistresses, including, late in his life, the unpopular Comtesse Dubarry (1743–1793).

1. One of the 12 apostles of Jesus, Bartholomew was said to have been martyred by flaying (stripping off the skin) while a missionary in Armenia.

their success is certain, and the effect always irresistible. These are the kind of reflections that lead the philosopher-artist to justify readily all the means employed by women, over the centuries, to consolidate and, so to speak, divinize their fragile beauty. Any enumeration would have to include countless details; but, to limit ourselves to what in our day is commonly called make-up, who can fail to see that the use of rice powder, so fatuously anathematized by innocent philosophers, has as its purpose and result to hide all the blemishes that nature has so outrageously scattered over the complexion, and to create an abstract unity of texture and colour in the skin, which unity, like the one produced by tights, immediately approximates the human being to a statue, in other words to a divine or superior being? As for black pencil for eye effects, and rouge for heightening the colour of the upper part of the cheek, although their use comes from the same principle, the need to surpass nature, the result is destined to satisfy a quite opposite need. Red and black represent life, a supernatural, excessive life; black rings round the eyes give them a deeper and stranger look, a more decisive appearance of a window open on the infinite; the rouge which heightens the glow of cheek-bones confers still greater brightness on the pupils, and gives to a lovely woman's face the mysterious passion of a priestess.

Thus, if I have been properly understood, painting the face is not to be used with the vulgar, unavowable intention of imitating the fair face of nature, or competing with youth. It has, moreover, been observed that artifice does not embellish ugliness, and can only serve beauty. Who would dare assign to art the sterile function of imitating nature?[2] Make-up has no need of concealment, no need to avoid discovery; on the contrary, it can go in for display, if not with affectation, at least with a sort of ingenuousness.

I will readily allow people whose ponderous gravity prevents their looking for beauty in its very minutest manifestations to laugh at my reflections, and to condemn their childish solemnity; the austere judgements of such folk worry me not at all; I am content to appeal to the true artists, and to women who have received at birth a spark of that sacred fire they would feign use to light up their whole being.

from PARIS SPLEEN[1]

To Each His Chimera[2]

Under a huge gray sky, on a huge dusty plain, without paths, without grass, without a thistle, without a nettle, I came upon several men walking along bent over.

Each of them was carrying an enormous Chimera on his back, as heavy as a sack of flour or coal, or the rig of a Roman footsoldier.

Yet the monstrous beast was not an inert weight. On the contrary, she enwrapped and subjugated the man with flexible and powerful muscles; with her two huge claws she hooked onto the breast of her mount; and her fabled head topped the man's forehead, like one of those ghastly helmets which ancient warriors hoped would increase their enemy's terror.

---

2. Baudelaire refers to the classical definition by Aristotle that made *mimesis*, or the imitation of reality, to be the goal of art, and its 19th-century descendant, realism, a dominant literary movement, especially in the novel.
1. Translated by Edward K. Kaplan.

2. In Greek myth, the Chimera was a female monster combining parts of a lion, goat, and dragon. A chimera came to refer to any fantastic idea or figment of the imagination. In this poem, Baudelaire characteristically literalizes the metaphorical meaning.

I questioned one of these men, and I asked him where they were going like that. He answered that he knew nothing about it, not he, nor the others; but that obviously they were going somewhere, since they were driven by an irresistible need to walk.

A curious thing to note: none of these travelers seemed bothered by the ferocious beast hanging around his neck and attached to his back. They seemed to consider it as part of themselves. All their weary and serious faces expressed no sign of despair. Under the sky's splenetic[3] dome, their feet immersed in the dust of a terrain as ravaged as the sky, they made their way with the resigned expression of those who are condemned to hope forever.

And the procession passed by me and descended into the horizon's atmosphere, at that place where the planet's rounded surface hides from the curiosity of the human gaze.

And for a few moments I persistently tried to understand this mystery. But soon insurmountable Indifference swooped down upon me, and I was more heavily oppressed than they were themselves by their overwhelming Chimeras.

Crowds[4]

Not everyone is capable of taking a bath of multitude: enjoying crowds is an art. And only he who can go on a binge of vitality, at the expense of the human species, is he into whom in his cradle a fairy breathed a craving for disguises and masks, hatred of home, and a passion for traveling.

Multitude, solitude: equal and interchangeable terms for the active and fertile poet. He who does not know how to populate his solitude, does not know either how to be alone in a busy crowd.

The poet enjoys the incomparable privilege of being able, at will, to be himself and an other. Like those wandering souls seeking a body, he enters, when he wants, into everyone's character. For him alone, everything is empty. And if certain places seem to exclude him, it is because he considers them not worth the bother of being visited.

The solitary and thoughtful stroller draws a unique intoxication from this universal communion. He who easily espouses crowds knows feverish delights, of which the selfish will be eternally deprived, locked up like a chest, and the lazy, confined like a mollusk. He adopts as his every profession, every joy and every misery circumstances place before him.

What people call love is awfully small, awfully restricted, and awfully weak, compared with that ineffable orgy, that holy prostitution of the soul which gives itself totally, poetry and charity, to the unexpected which appears, to the unknown which passes by.

It is sometimes right to teach the world's happy ones, if only to humiliate their stupid pride for an instant, that there are forms of happiness superior to theirs, more vast and more refined. Founders of colonies, shepherds of peoples, missionary priests exiled to the ends of the earth, probably know something of these mysterious intoxications. And, in the bosom of the vast family created by their genius, they must sometimes laugh at those who pity their fortunes so troubled and their lives so chaste.

---

3. Full of spleen.
4. Compare to the similar sentiments about the stroller

in the urban crowd in "The Painter of Modern Life" (page 581).

Invitation to the Voyage[5]

There exists a magnificent land, a land of Cockaigne, as they say, which I dream of visiting with a familiar confidante.[6] Remarkable land, drowned in the mists of our North, and which we might call the Orient of the West, the China of Europe, so freely does a hearty and capricious fancy flourish there, adorning it so patiently and stubbornly with her learned and delicate vegetation.

A true land of Cockaigne, where everything is beautiful, rich, calm, decent; where excess takes pleasure in mirroring itself in uniformity; where life breathes luxuriant and mellow; where disorder, commotion, and the unexpected are excluded; where happiness is wedded to silence; where even cooking is poetic, both luxuriant and arousing; where everything resembles you, my dear angel.

Do you feel that feverish ailment seizing us in our stark affliction, that longing for unheard-of realms, that anguish of curiosity? A land exists resembling you, where everything is beautiful, rich, calm, and decent; where fancy has built and furnished a western China, where life breathes mellow, where happiness is wedded to silence. There is where we must live, where we must go to die!

Yes, we must go there to breathe, to dream, and to prolong the hours with an infinity of sensations. A musician has written "Invitation to the Waltz."[7] Who then will compose "Invitation to the Voyage," to be presented to the beloved woman, to the favored sister?

Yes, it would be fine to live in that atmosphere—far away, where the slower hours contain more thoughts, where clocks strike happiness with a deeper and more meaningful solemnity.

On glossy panels, or on gilded and darkly rich leathers, blissful pictures live discreetly, quiet and profound, like the souls of the artists who created them. The setting suns, so richly tinting the dining room or the salon, sift through beautiful fabrics or through tall crafted windows divided into many leaded panes. The furniture is huge, curious, weird, armed with locks and hiding places like refined souls. The mirrors, the metals, the fabrics, the silver, and the porcelain play a silent and secretive symphony for the eyes. And a remarkable aroma escapes from everything, from every corner, from the splits in drawers and the creases of fabrics, a *return-here* from Sumatra,[8] which seems to be the apartment's soul.

A true land of Cockaigne, I insist, where everything is rich, tidy, and glossy, like a clean conscience, like a magnificent array of kitchen utensils, like splendid silverware, like colorful jewelry! The world's treasures pour in there, as into the house of a hard-working man who deserves the whole world's best. Remarkable land, superior to others, as Art is to Nature, where dream refashions Nature, where it is corrected, embellished, recast.

May they search, continue to search, may they ceaselessly extend the limits of their happiness, those alchemists of horticulture! May they offer prizes of sixty and of

---

5. Compare to the verse version in *The Flowers of Evil* (page 569). Several of the prose poems reworked titles and themes from the earlier collection.
6. In the legends of medieval Europe, the land of Cockaigne was a place of milk and honey, of luxury and ease where the rivers ran with wine, the trees bore sweets, and cooked meats and fowls offered themselves for the taking.

7. An immensely popular piece composed in 1819 by Carl Maria von Weber (1786–1826).
8. The second-largest island of Indonesia, Sumatra during the 19th century was part of the Dutch East Indies. Its rainforests were an important source of exotic hardwoods as well as of oils and essences for perfumes.

one hundred thousand florins for someone to solve their ambitious problems! As for me, I have found my *black tulip* and my *blue dahlia!*[9]

Incomparable flower, retrieved tulip, allegorical dahlia, isn't it there, to that beautiful land, so quiet and so dreamy, that we must go to live and flourish? Would you not be framed by your analogy there, and could you not mirror yourself, as the mystics say, in your own *correspondence?*[1]

Dreams! always dreams! And the more ambitious and delicate the soul, the more dreams remove it from the possible. Each of us carries within a dose of natural opium, ceaselessly secreted and renewed; and, from birth to death, how many hours can we count filled with concrete delight, with well-executed and resolute action? Will we ever live, will we ever enter that picture painted by my mind, that painting which resembles you?

These treasures, this furniture, this excess, this uniformity, these scents, these miraculous flowers, they are you. Still you again, these wide rivers and calm canals. The enormous ships they sweep along, loaded full with riches, and from which the crew's monotonous songs ascend, these are my thoughts sleeping or flowing on your breast. You lead them gently toward the sea which is the Infinite, all the while reflecting the sky's depths in the transparency of your lovely soul. —And when they reach the native port, wearied by the waves and glutted on the produce of the East, they are still my enriched thoughts returning from the Infinite toward you.

Get High

You must always be high. Everything depends on it: it is the only question. So as not to feel the horrible burden of Time wrecking your back and bending you to the ground, you must get high without respite.

But on what? On wine, on poetry, or on virtue, whatever you like. But get high.

And if sometimes you wake up, on palace steps, on the green grass of a ditch, in your room's gloomy solitude, your intoxication already waning or gone, ask the wind, the waves, the stars, the birds, clocks, ask everything that flees, everything that moans, everything that moves, everything that sings, everything that speaks, ask what time it is. And the wind, the waves, the stars, the birds, clocks, will answer, "It is time to get high! So as not to be the martyred slaves of Time, get high; get high constantly! On wine, on poetry, or on virtue, as you wish."

Any Where Out of the World[2]

This life is a hospital in which every patient is haunted by the desire to change beds. This one wants to suffer in front of the stove, and that one believes he will recover next to the window.

It seems that I would always be content where I am not, and I constantly discuss that question of relocation with my soul.

---

9. Black tulips and blue dahlias were highly sought-after, mythically rare varieties. Alexandre Dumas had published an historical novel about the tulip craze in 17th-century Holland entitled *The Black Tulip* (1850); the songwriter Pierre Dupont had included a waltz called *The Blue Dahlia* in a collection prefaced by Baudelaire (1852–1854).

1. The theory of a universal analogy between sounds, scents and colors was frequently voiced in mid-19th-century literary circles; see the poem "Correspondences" (page 571).

2. The title is in English in the original collection.

"Tell me, my soul, poor benumbed soul, what would you think about residing in Lisbon?[3] It must be warm there, and there you would perk up like a lizard. That city is next to the water; they say it is built of marble, and its populace hates vegetation so much that they rip out all the trees. Now there's a landscape to your liking; a landscape made of light and mineral, and of liquid to reflect them!"

My soul does not answer.

"Since you love calm so much, added to the view of movement, do you want to come reside in Holland, that beatifying land? Perhaps that region whose image you have often admired in museums would divert you. What would you say to Rotterdam, you who love forests of masts, and ships moored at the doorsteps of houses?"[4]

My soul remains mute.

"Batavia would appeal to you more? Besides there we would find the spirit of Europe married to tropical beauty."[5]

Not a word.—Might my soul be dead?

"So have you reached that degree of stupor where you can take pleasure only in your affliction? If it is thus, let's flee toward the countries which are the analogies of Death.—I've just what we need, poor soul! We'll pack our trunks for Tornio.[6] Let's go farther still, to the very edge of the Baltic Sea; still farther away from life, if that is possible; let's settle at the pole. There the sun just obliquely grazes the earth's surface, and the slow alternation of light and night abolishes variety and increases monotony, that one-half of nothingness. There, we can take long baths of darkness, while, to amuse us, the aurora borealis now and then hurls out its pink showers, like reflections of fireworks from Hell!"[7]

At last, my soul explodes, and wisely she shouts at me, "Anywhere! Anywhere! provided it is out of this world!"

Let's Beat Up the Poor!

For two weeks I had shut myself up in my room, and I had surrounded myself with the books fashionable at that time (sixteen or seventeen years ago); I speak of books dealing with the art of making nations happy, wise, and rich, in twenty-four hours. I had thus digested—swallowed, I mean—all the ramblings of all those managers of public happiness—of those who advise all the poor to become slaves, and those who persuade them that they are all dethroned kings.[8]—It will not be considered surprising that I was then in a state of mind bordering on vertigo or idiocy.

Yet I thought that I sensed, shut deep within my intellect, the dim seed of an idea better than all the old wives' formulas I had recently perused in the encyclopedia. But it was only the idea of an idea, something infinitely hazy.

---

3. The capital of Portugal, the port of Lisbon was long the westernmost point of the known world. Called the White City for the characteristic color of its houses and the blinding sunlight of its climate, it had an exotic reputation. Napoleon's forces had held the region briefly during 1807 and 1808.

4. The great Dutch port of Rotterdam had been occupied by the French between 1795 and 1815. The "images" referred to would be 17th-century seascapes, landscapes, still lifes from the height of Dutch trading power and wealth, which hung in the Louvre in Paris.

5. Djakarta, the capital city of Indonesia, was known until 1949 as Batavia. Controlled by the Dutch from 1619, it was rebuilt as a city in the Dutch style.

6. At the border between Sweden and Finland.

7. Baudelaire runs through the exemplary features of the far north: the endless dark of the winter months, the white nights of summer, and the northern lights, or aurora borealis, the spectacular atmospheric displays that light up and color the northern sky.

8. Baudelaire refers back to the revolutionary ideologies of 1848, the insurrection in which he had participated, and in particular to the socialist-anarchist writings of Pierre-Joseph Proudhon (1809–1865), whose ideas he had once admired but which he had come to regard as naïve. In addition, the satire is aimed at contemporary, especially socialist, versions of the tradition of Christian charity toward the poor.

Then I went out quite thirsty. For a passionate craving for shoddy books begets a proportional need for the open air and refreshments.

As I was about to enter a tavern, a beggar held out his hat, with one of those unforgettable looks that would topple thrones, if mind could move matter, and if a hypnotist's eyes could ripen grapes.[9]

At the same time, I heard a voice whispering in my ear, a voice I knew well; the voice of a good Angel, or of a good Demon, who accompanies me everywhere. Since Socrates had his good Demon, why shouldn't I have my good Angel, why shouldn't I have the honor, like Socrates, of acquiring my certificate of insanity, signed by the insightful Lélut and the sagacious Baillarger?[1]

The difference between the Demon of Socrates and mine is that Socrates' one appears to him only to forbid, warn, suggest, persuade. That poor Socrates had only a prohibitive demon; mine is a great approver, mine is a Demon of action, or Demon of combat.

This is what its voice whispered to me: "He alone is equal to another, if he proves it, and he alone is worthy of freedom, if he can conquer it."

Immediately, I pounced on my beggar. With a single punch, I shut one eye, which became, in a second, as big as a ball. I broke one of my nails smashing two of his teeth, and since I didn't feel strong enough to beat up the old man quickly, having been born fragile and not well trained in boxing, with one hand I grabbed him by the collar of his outfit, and I gripped his throat with the other, and I began vigorously to bounce his head against a wall. I should admit that beforehand I had examined the surroundings with a glance, and I had ascertained that in that deserted suburb, for a long enough time, I was beyond the reach of any policeman.

Having next, with a kick directed to his back, forceful enough to break his shoulder blades, floored that weakened sexagenarian, I grabbed a big tree branch lying on the ground, and I beat him with the obstinate energy of cooks trying to tenderize a beefsteak.

Suddenly,—Oh miracle! Oh delight of the philosopher who verifies the excellence of his theory!—I saw that antique carcass turn over, straighten up with a force I would never have suspected in a machine so peculiarly unhinged. And, with a look of hatred that seemed to me *a good omen,* the decrepit bandit flung himself on me, blackened both my eyes, broke four of my teeth, and, with the same tree branch beat me to a pulp.—By my forceful medication, I had thus restored his pride and his life.

Then, I made a mighty number of signs to make him understand that I considered the debate settled, and getting up with the self-satisfaction of a Stoic sophist,[2] I told him, "Sir, *you are my equal!* Please do me the honor of sharing my purse. And remember, if you are a true philanthropist, you must apply to all your colleagues, when they seek alms, the theory I had the *pain* to test upon your back."

He indeed swore that he had understood my theory, and that he would comply with my advice.

---

9. It was a widely held assumption about hypnotism that it could cause plants to grow and fruit to ripen.

1. The 5th-century B.C.E. Athenian philosopher Socrates maintained that a voice, or *daimon,* spoke to him, forbidding him to do certain actions. The 19th-century psychiatrists Jules-Gabriel François Baillarger (1809–1890) and Louis-Francisque de Lélut (1804–1877) had both used this *daimon* to argue that Socrates was clinically insane.

2. Sophism and Stoicism were two schools of ancient Athenian philosophy, which shared a belief that truth could only be perceived in an immediate fashion. They are probably invoked here as epitomes of the figure of the philosopher confronted with the world around him.

RESONANCES

Jules and Edmond Goncourt: from *The Journal*[1]

19 May 1857

Baudelaire, coming out of a tart's rooms, meets Sainte-Beuve on the stairs.[2] Baudelaire: "Ah! I know where you're going!" Sainte-Beuve: "And I know where you've been. But look, I'd rather go and have a chat with you." They go to a café. Sainte-Beuve: "You know, what disgusts me about the philosophers, Cousin and the rest, what makes me positively loathe them, is that they talk of nothing but God and the immortality of the soul.[3] They know perfectly well that the immortality of the soul doesn't exist any more than God does. It's disgusting!" There follows a tirade on atheism in comparison with which the most blasphemous eighteenth-century pamphlet would read like the Gospel according to St. John, with Sainte-Beuve—the same Sainte-Beuve who described Cardinal de Bernis as a sort of Father of the Church[4]—getting angry and excited and attacking God so fiercely as to bring every game of dominoes in the café to a stop.

October 1857

The Café Riche seems to be on the way to becoming the head-quarters of those men of letters who wear gloves.[5] It is strange how places make the people who frequent them. Beneath that white and gold, on that red plush, none of the guttersnipes of literature would dare to venture. Murger, with whom we had dinner, made his profession of faith to us. He is rejecting Bohemia and passing over bag and baggage to the side of the gentlemen of letters: a new Mirabeau.[6]

It is at the far end of the Café Riche, in the room overlooking the Rue Le Peletier, that between eleven o'clock and half-past twelve at night, after the theatre or their work, you will find Saint-Victor, Uchard, About with his ape-like mask fixed in a bogus smile, Aubryet nervously drawing on the tables or insulting all and sundry from the waiters to M. Scribe, Albéric Second, Fiorentino, Villemot, the publisher Lévy, Beauvoir, the last of the Regency drunks, etc.[7]

At the entrance, in the room separated from ours by two pillars, you can see here and there a few ears pricked up and drinking in the talk of our circle. They belong either to dandies frittering away the last of their little fortunes, or to young men from the Stock Exchange, Rothschild's clerks, who have brought along some high-grade tarts

1. Translated by Robert Baldick. Inseparable and insufferable, avant-garde, eccentric, and never married, the Goncourt brothers, Edmond (1822–1896) and Jules (1830–1870), dedicated their lives to what they called "the absolute truth" in a series of realist novels and in their celebrated *Journals,* a detailed record of Parisian life. The passages give a vivid and opinionated sketch of Baudelaire and his social and artistic milieu at the time of the *Fleurs du mal.*
2. Charles-Augustin Sainte-Beuve (1804–1869) was the preeminent literary historian and critic of his generation, author of a weekly column of literary portraits, and an acquaintance of the Goncourt brothers.
3. Victor Cousin (1792–1867), a Christian philosopher.
4. Cardinal de Bernis (1717–1794) was a statesman and libertine who was instrumental in the papal suppression of the order of the Jesuits and later attempted to reconcile the

papacy with the church reforms undertaken by the revolutionary government of France.
5. On the Boulevard des Italiens, the new center of Paris life, the Café Riche was the place to see and be seen not only for elegant writers, intellectuals, and dandies, but for the fashionable elite of the city during the Second Empire.
6. The painter's son, Henri Murger (1822–1861), was author of *Scenes of Bohemian Life,* 1847–1849. By 1857, he had become extremely successful. The Goncourts compare him facetiously to the Count Mirabeau (1749–1791), the statesman and orator who attempted to reconcile the Revolution with the Monarchy.
7. The list includes the names of eminent men of letters, journalists, artists, and publishers. The bookseller Michel Lévy had published Baudelaire's translations of Edgar Allan Poe. Roger de Beauvoir was a famous dandy and rival of Baudelaire.

from the Cirque or Mabille to offer their little appetites the satisfaction of some fruit or a cup of tea and to point out from a distance the leading players in our company.[8]

Baudelaire had supper at the next table to ours. He was without a cravat, his shirt open at the neck and his head shaved, just as if he were going to be guillotined. A single affectation: his little hands washed and cared for, the nails kept scrupulously clean. The face of a maniac, a voice that cuts like a knife, and a precise elocution that tries to copy Saint-Just and succeeds.[9] He denies, with some obstinacy and a certain harsh anger, that he has offended morality with his verse.[1]

Stéphane Mallarmé: The Tomb of Charles Baudelaire[1]

The buried shrine discloses through the tomblike
Mouth of a sewer slobbering mud and rubies
The abomination of some god Anubis
With all its muzzle ablaze like a wild bark[2]

5   Or let the new gas twist the crooked wick[3]
Wiping we know the places where the scab is
Wanly it lights up an immortal pubis
Whose flight sleeps out by streetlamps in the dark[4]

What foliage parched in each duskless town
10   Offered in prayer can bless like her sit down
Against the marble in vain of Baudelaire

With her veil girded absent with a thrill
She his Shade a protective plague in air
That we though we should perish must breathe still.

Arthur Rimbaud: Vowels[1]

A black, E white, I red, U green, O blue: vowels,[2]
One day I will tell your latent birth:
A, black hairy corset of shining flies
Which buzz around cruel stench,

---

8. The powerful house of Rothschild dominated international banking during the 19th century and was synonymous with the financial world of Paris.

9. Son of an army officer like Baudelaire, Louis Saint-Just (1767–1794) was a key Jacobin during the Revolution and instrumental in the Terror that followed. Celebrated for his good looks, charm, and eloquent public speaking, he was also infamous for the ruthlessness that earned him the nickname, "Angel of Death."

1. Three months earlier, as a consequence of the trial of *The Flowers of Evil* for obscenity, Baudelaire had been fined for offending morality and had six poems in the collection suppressed.

1. Translated by Keith Bosley. Strongly influenced by Baudelaire, Stéphane Mallarmé (1842–1898) became a leading practitioner and theorist of the poetic movement known as symbolism. His sonnet "The Tomb of Charles Baudelaire" (1893) transmutes Baudelaire's lucid imagery of a nighttime Paris of sewers and whores into a mysterious nightmare that unfolds in a single, densely packed sentence.

2. Anubis is the ancient Egyptian god of death, with the head of a jackal.

3. Mallarmé contrasts the modern gaslight with the traditional lantern wick.

4. The pubis refers to the bone forming a wall of the pelvis, and more generally to the female genitalia; here it serves as a metaphor for the prostitute.

1. Translated by Wallace Fowlie. Even more than Baudelaire's, Rimbaud's life (1854–1891) was the stuff of legend. He wrote all of his poetry in the space of a few years before he was twenty; he became the protégé and lover of the older poet Verlaine; they ran off to London and Brussels, where Verlaine shot him; he gave up writing, became an arms dealer in Africa, and died at the age of thirty-seven without ever having written another word of poetry. The famous sonnet "Vowels" demonstrates what he called his "alchemy of the verb"; the short prose poems, or "Illuminations," as Rimbaud called them, show how he took Baudelaire's painting of modern life into the realm of symbolism.

2. Like Baudelaire's "Correspondences" (page 571), Rimbaud's sonnet develops the concept of a universal analogy between colors, sounds, and scents. Here, however, the analogy is based in language—the five vowels—rather than Baudelaire's Nature.

5   Gulfs of darkness; E, whiteness of vapors and tents,
    Lances of proud glaciers, white kings, quivering of flowers;
    I, purples, spit blood, laughter of beautiful lips
    In anger or penitent drunkenness;

    U, cycles, divine vibrations of green seas,
10   Peace of pastures scattered with animals, peace of the wrinkles
    Which alchemy prints on heavy studious brows;

    O, supreme Clarion full of strange stridor,
    Silences crossed by worlds and angels:
    —O, the Omega, violet beam from His Eyes![3]

Arthur Rimbaud: City

I am an ephemeral and not-too-discontented citizen of a metropolis obviously modern because every known taste has been avoided in the furnishings and in the outsides of the houses as well as in the layout of the city. Here you would not discover the least sign of any monument of superstition. In short, morals and speech are reduced to their simplest expression. These millions of people who have no need of knowing one another conduct their education, their trade, and their old age with such similarity that the duration of their lives must be several times shorter than, according to some insane statistics, is the case with the people on the continent. From my window, I see new ghosts rolling through thick, everlasting coal smoke—our shadow in the woods, our summer night!—new Eumenides[1] in front of my cottage which is my country and my heart since everything here resembles it—Death without tears, our active daughter and servant, a desperate Love, and a pretty Crime crying in the mud of the street.[2]

Arthur Rimbaud: Departure

 Seen enough. The vision met itself in every kind of air.
  Had enough. Noises of cities in the evening, in the sunlight, and forever.
  Known enough. The haltings of life. Oh! Noises and Visions!
  Departure into new affection and sound.

Leo Tolstoy
1828–1910

Count Leo Tolstoy was born and raised at Yasnaya Polyana, his family's estate located near Moscow. After an early and unsuccessful attempt to reform the estate, he volunteered for the army. He served first with Russian forces seeking to conquer what were called "mountain

---

3. Omega (or "o") is the last letter of the Greek alphabet, alpha (or "a") the first; in Christian mysticism, they stand for the all-encompassing God.
1. The Eumenides, or Furies, were female powers of the underworld in Greek and Roman myth who punished

blood-crimes and broken taboos.
2. Like Baudelaire before him, Rimbaud personifies abstract forces and emotions (Death, Love, Crime) as if they were the deities of the modern city, here London.

tribesmen" in the Caucasus, and then in the Crimean War (1853–1856), in which Russian expansion southward into Orthodox areas of the Ottoman Empire was defeated at great cost by combined Turkish and British armies. Already a published author before beginning his military career, Tolstoy achieved solid success by making use of his military experience to tell realistic, unglamorous tales of the war. He left the army in 1856, traveled around Europe, and before reaching the age of thirty had retired to his estate, whose revenues made it possible for him to spend the rest of his life writing. It was there that he wrote his masterpieces *War and Peace* (1865–1869) and *Anna Karenina* (1875–1877). After a personal crisis (described in *Confession* [1879]) he formulated a personal philosophy involving nonviolence, the renunciation of wealth, and the value of physical labor. This philosophy was an inspiration to such world figures as Mahatma Gandhi. In *What Is Art?* (1897) Tolstoy renounced much of his earlier fiction on moral grounds. But some of his last works are among his greatest, including "The Death of Ivan Ilyich" (1886) and "The Kreutzer Sonata" (1890). In "Hadji Murad" (1896–1904), he returned to the subject of Russia's war of conquest in the Caucasus, but chose a Caucasian protagonist. By the end of Tolstoy's long life, Yasnaya Polyana had become a place of pilgrimage. After a violent quarrel with his wife, Sofia, he left the estate in October 1910, fell ill, and died at a nearby town.

Tolstoy's great counterpart, Dostoevsky, once described Russian literature as "a literature of landowners." He was announcing his desire to write fiction about Russia's urban poor. But the remark also helps explain why, like classical Greece, nineteenth-century Russia sometimes seems to set an unmatchable standard for literary greatness. Russian landowners turned to literature with such passionate seriousness because they could see that their way of life was doomed. The most prophetic, like Tolstoy, could even see that they deserved no better. Their power, based on their ownership of serfs and supporting in turn the increasingly antiquated bureaucratic empire headed by the Czar, appeared to almost everyone as a sign of Russia's backwardness by comparison with Europe. Unless there was some fundamental change, Russia seemed condemned to ongoing feebleness and disrespect, and more humiliations like the Crimean War. Yet what kind of change should there be? Slavophiles, supporters of native Russian traditions, fell back with nationalist fervor on the certainties of the Russian Orthodox tradition or romanticized views of the Russian peasant. But even devout Westernizers joined with them in being critical of the West's version of industrial modernity. There were more questions than answers. Russian writers could see, as their more complacent European contemporaries often did not, that their society had ceased to function, that revolution of some sort was on the horizon, that everything was up in the air. Blocked at the level of political action by the Czarist autocracy, the energy of criticizing the status quo and imagining alternatives went into literature, which took as its ambitious task the largest and most tantalizing mysteries of human existence.

Though Tolstoy's celebration of peasantlike simplicity and hard work shares something with Slavophile primitivism, "After the Ball" shows that Tolstoy's disaffection is both deeper and more complex. When the privileged life of upper-class refinement is suddenly disturbed by an eruption of violence, the rich young protagonist is powerfully moved, but he is moved by an injustice so alien to his way of thinking that he can find no words for it. He has no way of expressing himself except by a quiet refusal—a refusal that can be compared to that of Melville's protagonist in "Bartleby the Scrivener" (page 712).

PRONUNCIATIONS:
Ivan Vasilyevich: ee-VAHN vah-sill-YAY-veetch
Tolstoy: toll-STOY
Varenka: vah-REN-ka

After the Ball[1]

"So you contend a man cannot judge independently of what is good and what is bad, that it is all a matter of environment—that man is a creature of environment. But I contend it is all a matter of chance. And here is what I can say about myself. . . ."

This is what our respected friend Ivan Vasilyevich said at the conclusion of a discussion we had been having about the necessity of changing the environment, the conditions in which men live, before there could be any talk about the improvement of the individual. As a matter of fact, no one had said it was impossible to judge independently of the good and the bad, but Ivan Vasilyevich had a habit of answering thoughts of his own stimulated by a discussion, and recounting experiences from his own life suggested by these thoughts. Often he became so absorbed in the story that he forgot his reason for telling it, especially since he always spoke with great fervor and sincerity. That is precisely what happened in the present case.

"At least I can make this claim with regard to myself. My own life has been molded in that way and no other—not by environment, but by something quite different."

"By what?" we asked.

"That is a long story. If you are to understand, I must tell it all to you."

"Then do."

Ivan Vasilyevich considered a moment and shook his head.

"Yes," he said, "my whole life was changed by a single night, or rather, a morning."

"Why? What happened?"

"It happened that I was deeply in love. I had often been in love before, but never so deeply. It took place a long time ago—her daughters are married women by this time. Her name was B., Varenka B. She was still strikingly beautiful at fifty, but in her youth, when she was eighteen, she was a dream: tall, slender, graceful, and majestic—yes, majestic. She always held herself as erect as if she were unable to bend, with her head tipped slightly backward; this, combined with her beauty and height, even though she was so thin as to be almost bony, gave her a queenly air that would have been intimidating if it had not been for her gay, winning smile, her mouth, her glorious shining eyes, and her whole captivating, youthful being."

"Ivan Vasilyevich certainly does lay it on thick!"

"However thick I were to lay it on, I could not make you understand what she was really like. But that is beside the point. The events I shall recount took place in the forties.

"I was then a student at a provincial university. I don't know whether it was a good or a bad thing, but in those days there were none of your study circles, none of your theorizing, at our university; we were just young and lived in the way of young folk—studying and having a good time. I was a very gay and energetic youth, and rich in the bargain. I owned a spirited carriage horse and used to take the girls out for drives (skating had not yet become the fad); I went on drinking parties with my fellow students (in those days we drank nothing but champagne; if we were out of money, we drank nothing, for we never drank vodka as they do now); but most of all I enjoyed parties and balls. I was a good dancer and not exactly ugly."

"Come, don't be modest," put in one of the listeners. "We've all seen your daguerreotype. You were a very handsome youth."

1. Translated by M. Wettlin.

"Perhaps I was, but that isn't what I wanted to tell you. When my love was at its height I attended a ball given on the last day of Shrovetide by the Marshal of Nobility, a good-natured old man, wealthy, and fond of entertaining. His wife, as amiable as he was, stood beside him to receive us. She was wearing a velvet gown and a diamond tiara in her hair, and her aging neck and shoulders, plump and white, were exposed, as in the portraits of Empress Yelizaveta Petrovna. The ball was magnificent. The ballroom was charming, there were famous serf singers and musicians belonging to a certain landowner who was a lover of music, the food was abundant, the champagne flowed in rivers. Much as I loved champagne, I did not drink—I was drunk with love. But I danced till I dropped. I danced quadrilles, and waltzes, and polonaises, and it goes without saying that I danced as many of them as I could with Varenka. She was wearing a white dress with a pink sash, white kid gloves that did not quite reach her thin, pointed elbows, and white satin slippers. A wretched engineer named Anisimov cheated me out of a mazurka with her. I have never forgiven him for that. He invited her the moment she entered the ballroom, while I had been delayed by calling at the hairdresser's for my gloves. And so instead of dancing the mazurka with her, I danced it with a German girl I had once had a crush on. But I am afraid I was very neglectful of her that evening; I did not talk to her or look at her, for I had eyes for no one but a tall, slender girl in a white dress with a pink sash, with radiant, flushed, dimpled cheeks and soft, gentle eyes. I was not the only one; everyone looked at her and admired her, even the women, though she outshone them all. It was impossible not to admire her.

"Formally I was not her partner for the mazurka, but as a matter of fact I did dance it with her—at least most of it. Without the least embarrassment she danced straight to me down the length of the whole room, and when I leapt up to meet her without waiting for the invitation, she smiled to thank me for guessing what she wanted. When we had been led up to her and she had not guessed my nature, she had given a little shrug of her thin shoulders as she held out her hand to another, turning upon me a little smile of regret and consolation.

"When the figures of the mazurka changed into a waltz, I waltzed with her for a long time, and she smiled breathlessly and murmured *'encore.'* And I waltzed on and on with her, quite unaware of my own body, as if it were made of air."

"Unaware of it? I'm sure you must have been very much aware of it as you put your arm about her waist—aware of not only *your* body, but of hers as well," said one of the guests.

Ivan Vasilyevich suddenly turned crimson and almost shouted:

"That may apply to you, modern youth—all you think of is the body. In our day things were different. The more deeply I loved a girl, the more incorporeal she seemed to me. Today you are aware of legs, ankles, and other things; you disrobe the ladies with whom you are in love, but for me, as Alphonse Karr has said—and a very good writer he was—the object of my love was always clad in bronze raiment. Far from exposing, we tried to hide nakedness, as did the good son of Noah. But you cannot understand this."

"Pay no attention to him. Go on with your story," said another of the listeners.

"Well, I danced mostly with her and did not notice the passage of time. The musicians were so exhausted—you know how it always is at the end of a ball—that they kept playing the mazurka; mamas and papas were rising from the card tables in the drawing room in anticipation of supper; footmen were rushing about. It was going on for three o'clock. We had to take advantage of the few minutes left us. I invited her once more, and for the hundredth time we passed down the length of the room.

"'Will I be your partner for the quadrille after supper?' I asked her as I took her back to her place.

"'Oh, yes, if they do not take me home,' she said with a smile.

"'I won't let them,' I said.

"'Give me my fan,' she said.

"'I am sorry to give it back to you,' I said as I handed her her little white fan.

"'Here, then, to keep you from being sorry,' she said, plucking a feather out of the fan and giving it to me.

"I took the feather, unable to express my rapture and gratitude except with a glance. I was not only gay and content—I was happy, I was blissful, I was benevolent, I was no longer myself, but some creature not of this earth, who knew no evil and could do nothing but good.

"I tucked the feather in my glove and stood riveted to the spot, unable to move away from her.

"'Look, they are asking Papa to dance,' she said, indicating a tall, stately man who was her father, a colonel, in silver epaulettes, standing in the doorway with the hostess and some other women.

"'Varenka, come here,' called the hostess in the diamond tiara.

"Varenka made for the door and I followed her.

"'Do talk your father into dancing with you, *ma chère*.[2] Please do, Pyotr Vladislavich,' said the hostess to the colonel.

"Varenka's father was a tall, handsome, stately, and well-preserved old man. He had a ruddy face with a white mustache curled *à la* Nicholas I, white side whiskers that met his mustache, hair combed forward over his temples, and the same smile as his daughter's lighting up his eyes and lips. He was very well built, with a broad chest swelling out in military style and with a modest display of decorations on it, with strong shoulders and long, fine legs. He was an officer of the old type with a military bearing of the Nicholas school.

"As we came up to the door the colonel was protesting that he had forgotten how to dance, but nevertheless he smiled, reached for his sword, drew it out of its scabbard, handed it to a young man eager to offer his services, and, drawing a suede glove on to his right hand ('Everything according to rule,' he said with a smile), he took his daughter's hand and struck a pose in a quarter turn, waiting for the proper measure to begin.

"As soon as the mazurka phrase was introduced he stamped one foot energetically and swung out with the other, and then his tall heavy figure sailed round the ball-room. He kept striking one foot against the other, now slowly and gracefully, now quickly and energetically. The willowy form of Varenka floated beside him. Imperceptibly and always just in time, she kept lengthening or shortening the step of the little white satin feet to fit his.

"All the guests stood watching the couple's every movement. The feeling I experienced was less admiration than a sort of deep ecstasy. I was especially touched by the sight of the colonel's boots. They were good calfskin boots, but they were heelless and had blunt toes instead of fashionable pointed ones. Obviously they had been made by the battalion cobbler. 'He wears ordinary boots instead of fashionable ones so that he can dress his beloved daughter and take her into society,' I thought to myself, and that is why I was particularly touched by his blunt-toed boots. Anyone could see he had once danced beautifully, but now he was heavy and his legs were not flexible enough

2. My dear (French).

to make all the quick and pretty turns he attempted. But he went twice round the room very well, and everybody applauded when he quickly spread out his feet, then snapped them together again and fell, albeit rather heavily, on one knee. And she smiled as she freed her caught skirt and floated gracefully round him. When he had struggled back to his feet, he touchingly put his hands over his daughter's ears and kissed her on the forehead, then led her over to me, who he thought had been her dancing partner. I told him I was not.

"'It doesn't matter; you dance with her,' he said, smiling warmly as he slipped his sword back into the scabbard.

"Just as the first drop poured out of a bottle brings a whole stream in its wake, so my love for Varenka released all the love in my soul. I embraced the whole world with love. I loved the hostess with her diamond tiara, and her husband, and her guests, and her footmen, and even the wretched Anisimov, who was clearly angry with me. As for her father with his blunt-toed boots and a smile so much like hers—I felt a rapturous affection for him.

"The mazurka came to an end and our hosts invited us to the supper table. But Colonel B. declined, saying that he must be up early in the morning. I was afraid he would take Varenka with him, but she remained behind with her mother.

"After supper I danced the promised quadrille with her. And while it had seemed that my happiness could not be greater, it went on growing and growing. We said nothing of love; I did not ask her, nor even myself, whether she loved me. It was sufficient that I loved her. The only thing I feared was that something might spoil my happiness.

"When I got home, undressed myself and thought of going to bed, I realized that sleep was out of the question. I held in my hand the feather from her fan and one of her gloves, which she had given to me when I put her and her mother into their carriage. As I gazed at these keepsakes I saw her again at the moment when, choosing one of two partners, she had guessed my nature and said in a sweet voice, 'Too proud? Is that it?' then joyfully held out her hand to me; or when, sipping champagne at the supper table, she had gazed at me over her glass with loving eyes. But I saw her best as she danced with her father, floating gracefully beside him, looking at all the admiring spectators with joy and pride for his sake as well as her own. And involuntarily the two of them became merged in my mind and enveloped in one deep and tender feeling.

"At that time my late brother and I lived alone. My brother had no use for society and never went to balls. He was getting ready to take his examinations for a master's degree and was leading the most exemplary of lives. He was asleep. I felt sorry for him as I looked at his head buried in the pillow, half covered by the blanket—sorry because he did not know and did not share the happiness which was mine. Petrusha, our serf valet, met me with a candle and would have helped me undress, but I dismissed him. I was touched by the sight of the man's sleepy face and disheveled hair. Trying to make no noise. I tiptoed to my own room and sat down on the bed. I was too happy, I could not sleep. I found it hot in the room, and so without taking off my uniform I went quietly out into the hall, put on my greatcoat, opened the entrance door, and went out.

"It had been almost five o'clock when I left the ball; about two hours had passed since, so that it was already light when I went out. It was typical Shrovetide weather—misty, with wet snow melting on the roads and water dripping from all the roofs. At that time the B.'s lived on the outskirts of town, at the edge of an open field with a girls' school at one end and a space used for promenading at the other. I went down our quiet little bystreet and came out upon the main street, where I met passersby and carters with timber loaded on sledges whose runners cut through the snow to the very pavement. And everything—the horses bobbing their heads rhythmically under their lacquered yokes, and the carters with bast matting on their shoulders plodding in their enormous boots through the slush beside their sledges, and the houses on either side of the street standing tall in the mist—everything seemed particularly dear and significant.

"When I reached the field where their house stood I saw something big and black at the promenade end of it, and I heard the sounds of a fife and drum. My heart had been singing all this time, and occasionally the strains of the mazurka had come to my mind. But this was different music, harsh and sinister.

"'What could it be?' I wondered, and made my way in the direction of the sounds, down the slippery wagon road that cut across the field. When I had gone about a hundred paces I began to distinguish in the mist a crowd of people. They were evidently soldiers. 'Drilling,' I thought, and continued on my way in the company of a blacksmith in an oil-stained apron and jacket who was carrying a large bundle. A double row of soldiers in black coats were standing facing each other motionless, their guns at their sides. Behind them stood a fifer and a drummerboy who kept playing that shrill tune over and over.

"'What are they doing?' I asked the blacksmith who was standing next to me.

"'Driving a Tatar down the line for having tried to run away,' replied the blacksmith brusquely, glaring at the far end of the double row.

"I looked in the same direction and saw something horrible coming toward me between the rows. It was a man bare to the waist and tied to a horizontal gun held at either end by a soldier. Beside him walked a tall officer in a greatcoat and forage cap whose figure seemed familiar to me. The prisoner, his whole body twitching, his feet squashing through the melting snow, advanced through the blows raining down on him from either side, now cringing back, at which the soldiers holding the gun would pull him forward, now lunging forward, at which the soldiers would jerk him back to keep him from falling. And next to him, walking firmly, never lagging behind, came the tall officer. It was her father, with his ruddy face and white mustache and side whiskers.

"At every blow the prisoner turned his pain-distorted face to the side from which the blow had come, as if in surprise, and kept repeating something over and over through bared white teeth. I could not make out the words until he came closer to me. He was sobbing rather than speaking them. 'Have mercy, brothers; have mercy, brothers.' But the brothers had no mercy, and when the procession was directly opposite me I saw one of the soldiers step resolutely forward and bring his lash down so hard on the Tatar's back that it whistled through the air. The Tatar fell forward, but the soldiers jerked him up, and then another blow fell from the opposite side, and again from this, and again from that. . . . The colonel marched beside him, now glancing down at his feet, now up at the prisoner, drawing in deep breaths of air, blowing out his cheeks, slowly letting the air out between pursed lips. When the procession passed the spot where I was standing I got a glimpse of the prisoner's back through the row of soldiers. It was something indescribable: striped, wet, crimson, outlandish. I could not believe it was part of a human body.

"'God in heaven!' murmured the blacksmith standing next to me.

"The procession moved on. The blows kept falling from both sides on the cringing, floundering creature, the drum kept beating, the fife shrilling, and the tall, stately colonel walking firmly beside the prisoner. Suddenly the colonel stopped and went quickly over to one of the soldiers.

"'Missed? I'll show you!' I heard him say in a wrathful voice. 'Here, take this! And this!' And I saw his strong hand in its suede glove strike the small weak soldier in the face because the man's lash had not come down hard enough on the crimson back of the Tatar.

"'Bring fresh whips!' shouted the colonel. As he spoke he turned round and caught sight of me. Pretending not to recognize me, he gave a vicious, threatening scowl and turned quickly away. I felt so ashamed that I did not know where to turn my eyes, as if I had been caught doing something disgraceful. With hanging head I hurried home. All the way I kept hearing the rolling of the drum, the shrilling of the fife, the words, 'Have mercy, brothers,' and the wrathful, self-confident voice of the colonel shouting, 'Here, take this! And this!' And the aching of my heart was so intense as to be almost physical, making me feel nauseated, so that I had to stop several times. I felt I must throw up all the horror that this sight had filled me with. I do not remember how I reached home and got into bed, but the moment I began to doze off I saw and heard everything all over again. I jumped up.

"'There must be something he knows that I do not know,' I said to myself, thinking of the colonel. 'If I knew what he knows, I would understand, and what I saw would not cause me such anguish.' But rack my brains as I might, I could not understand what it was the colonel knew, and I could not fall asleep until evening, and then only after having gone to see a friend and drinking myself into forgetfulness.

"Do you suppose I concluded that what I had seen was bad? Nothing of the sort. 'If what I saw was done with such assurance and was accepted by everyone as being necessary, it means they know something I do not know,' was the conclusion I came to, and I tried to find out what it was. But I never did. And not having found out, I could not enter military service, as it had been my intention to do, and not only military service, but any service at all, and so I turned out to be the good-for-nothing, that you see."

"We know very well what a 'good-for-nothing' you turned out to be," said one of the guests. "It would be more to the point to say how many people would have turned out to be good-for-nothing had it not been for you."

"Now that's a foolish thing to say," said Ivan Vasilyevich with real vexation.

"Well, and what about your love?" we asked.

"My love? From that day on my love languished. Whenever we went out walking and she smiled that pensive smile of hers, I could not help recalling the colonel out in the field, and this made me feel uncomfortable and unhappy, and I gradually stopped going to see her. My love petered out.

"So that is what sometimes happens, and it is incidents like this that change and give direction to a man's whole life. And you talk about environment," he said.

━━━◦❈◦━━━

Fyodor Dostoevsky
1821–1881

"I am a sick man. . . . I am a spiteful man. I am an unpleasant man." The first words of Fyodor Dostoevsky's *Notes from Underground* (1864) announced a new voice and defined a new epoch. Who had ever dared introduce his story by trying to alienate his readers, listing reasons why we shouldn't listen to him? So as not to be identified with his character, Dostoevsky added a footnote reminding us that this speaker is a fiction. But the note also says that characters like him "not only may, but must exist in our society." In this unnamed hero, or rather antihero (as he calls himself), Dostoevsky was trying to sum up the meaning of the nineteenth century.

Leonid Petrovich Grossman,
Caricature of Dostoevsky.

His own life looks much like an unpleasant preparation for this enterprise. Born in Moscow in 1821, the son of an army doctor, Dostoevsky was destined by his family for the Army Engineering Corps. However, he soon revolted against the study of engineering and threw himself instead into literature and politics. Both interests led him to European writers like Goethe, Hugo, and Balzac, who seemed to embody the spirit of modernity that had produced the French Revolution and continued to shake many of society's deeply rooted ethical values and political structures. Convinced that Russia needed this spiritual agitation, Dostoevsky spent much time and energy translating Balzac's novel *Eugénie Grandet*. And in his own fiction, too, he turned to the new urban realities, writing about the underpaid, rootless, resentful inhabitants of cities like Petersburg who had been forgotten by Russia's "literature of landowners." His great predecessor Nikolai Gogol had already discovered the poor government clerk as a comic figure for Russia's backwardness. "We have all emerged," Dostoevsky wrote, "from under Gogol's *Overcoat.*" But Dostoevsky took this figure more seriously. Wandering the streets of Petersburg at night, especially in the less prosperous sections, he was seeking to integrate clerks and prostitutes, the insulted and the injured, into literature's conversation about the fate of the nation, a conversation that had been restricted to the fashionable salons. Though he used his income from his family to pursue a bohemian life of alternating prodigality and indebtedness, studiously avoiding the middle-class model of hardworking frugality, Dostoevsky was astonishingly productive. In the five years after giving up his army career in 1844, he published ten novels and short stories. He was a celebrity from the age of twenty-four, when his first novel, *Poor Folk* (1845), was hailed by the most important critics of the age.

The next stage in his life is also the most famous. Having joined a left-wing student group centered around a rich young man named Petrashevsky, Dostoevsky was arrested along with the rest of the group in 1849, imprisoned for eight months, and sentenced to death. The eight men were led out in front of a firing squad, then told at the last minute that their lives would be spared. The sentence was commuted to prison in Siberia, where he served four years. There has naturally been much speculation about the impact this near-death experience must have had. Dostoevsky had been troubled by childhood bouts of epilepsy; in Siberia his epilepsy worsened. Politically, he gave up his hopes of progressive reform. Released from prison in 1854, he married in 1857 and finally returned to Petersburg in 1859, where despite continuing government suspicion and interference, he resumed a successful career as novelist and journalist.

He was forty years old, and had been a famous writer for a decade and a half, when the emancipation of the serfs in 1861 marked the beginning of the end of the old landowners' order (two years before Lincoln's Emancipation Proclamation abolished slavery in the United States). Dostoevsky—whose father had been murdered by serfs—wasn't enthusiastic about this democratic transformation. Like other members of the Westernized elite, he watched uneasily the social processes in the materialist West that brought, along with political democracy, a disintegration of age-old moral certainties and a huge, desperate mass of urban poor. Should Russia follow this example? Many thought not, turning against their own Westernized education and even against the self-consciousness it had stimulated in them. Dostoevsky's political ideas became reactionary even by the standards of the day. He wrote odes to members of the Czar's family and expressed a somewhat paranoid fear that socialists and Roman Catholics were conspiring together to destroy the Russian Orthodox Church. For him, Orthodoxy was a desperately needed cultural heritage that set the Russian nation apart from the increasingly godless West, but he saw nothing un-christian in calling on patriotic Russians to invade Turkey and win back Constantinople from the Muslim Turks.

His most directly political novel, *The Possessed* (1867), made use of his early radical experiences in order to satirize progressives, especially wealthy ones like Petrashevsky, with merciless brilliance. Journeys abroad, in part to flee his creditors, provided compelling evidence against the arrogance and spiritual emptiness of the West. These travels also encouraged his compulsive penchant for gambling, which gave self-destructive expression to his belief in free will and contingency, his revolt against the European creed of scientific determinism. But if anti-Western and Slavophile ideas are present in the masterpieces Dostoevsky wrote in the following years, like *The Idiot, Crime and Punishment*, and *The Brothers Karamazov*, they are by no means the single key to the meaning of those novels. Many readers have felt that though he vigorously opposed the subversive modernity of the West, fearing its effect on established values, he knew deep down that established values were weak and indefensible and that humanity would eventually have to face the enormous challenge of what Nietzsche called the revaluation of all values. As he wrote in *The Brothers Karamazov*, Dostoevsky was afraid people would conclude that if there is no God, everything is permitted. Yet to someone like the philosopher Jean-Paul Sartre, it is precisely that existential truth that Dostoevsky forces us to recognize.

The enduring power of *Notes from Underground* comes in part from its ability to hold this question open. The text seems to have been intended as a critique of progressive Westernized intellectuals like Nicolai Chernyshevsky, whose extremely influential novel of ideas *What Is to Be Done?* had argued that society can be improved by following the principle of rational self-interest. Unsurprisingly, it was the aristocratic landowners who preached self-sacrifice rather than self-interest, and Underground Man's contempt for self-interest and "model flats" makes him sound at times like a spokesman for their party. To Dostoevsky's protagonist, it is better to be irrational and free than rational and thus ruled by a calculating materialism. But by putting his ideas in the mouth of such an unreliable narrator, Dostoevsky doesn't permit us simply to agree. He gives us no firm footing anywhere. Like Nietzsche, he asks unpleasantly searching

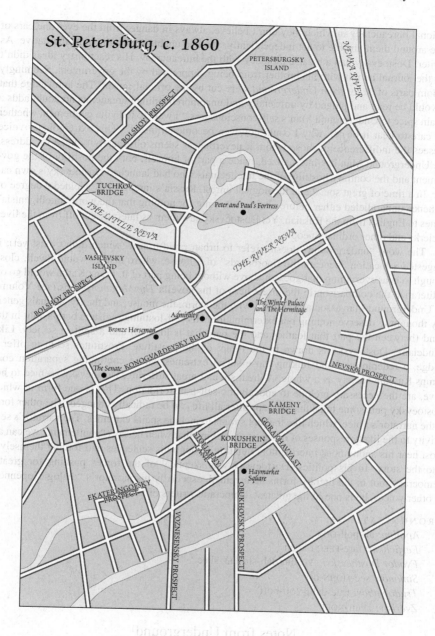

St. Petersburg, c. 1860

questions about values that seem self-evident. Modern humanity prides itself on its self-consciousness. But what after all is the value of self-consciousness? Does it really lead, as it claims, to change for the better? Wouldn't it be better *not* to be Hamlet, to be able simply to act, even in revenge, rather than asking endless philosophical questions about everything? Is the nineteenth century making a tragic mistake when it seizes on Hamlet as an exemplary figure, celebrating consciousness over action?

Clerks, like the former employee of the Civil Service in the story, are Dostoevsky's characteristic types because they are spiteful: hemmed in by the rules and regulations of an archaic, irrational bureaucracy in which they don't believe, always in danger from the eyes and ears of those around them, unable to act independently, yet also unable to imagine any alternative. As a writer, Dostoevsky had a bizarre intimacy with the bureaucracy. His reactionary ideas didn't stop the journal he ran with his brother from being suppressed by the government. Seemingly random parts of *Notes from Underground* were cut by the official censor. The knowledge that he would be read and judged by unfriendly and uncomprehending bureaucrats no doubt adds a certain spice to Underground Man's self-consciousness. "I want to tell you, gentlemen, whether you care to hear it or not, why I could not even become an insect." This extraordinary voice foresees the indifference of those whom it nevertheless seems obstinately obliged to address. The Underground Man has internalized, made a part of himself, both the hostility of the government and the contrary hostility of the intellectuals who had launched Dostoevsky's own career. In a time of great social and ideological unrest, Russia's intellectuals wielded a degree of influence unparalleled either before or since. It is not for nothing that the word "intelligentsia" comes to English from the Russian. Yet Dostoevsky saw them as fatefully cut off from the lives of clerks and other ordinary people.

The word "underground" doesn't refer to urban rapid transit (which didn't exist yet); it suggested a location "beneath the floorboards" of a house, where insects would dwell, close enough to hear everything that goes on above without being part of it. Franz Kafka would go on to literalize the comparison in the insect hero of his novella *The Metamorphosis* (see Volume F). Underground Man associates himself with the worm, the mouse, and the fly, animals generally thought to deserve nothing but extermination. His self-loathing registers both a split in the mind (between the part that loathes and the part that is loathed) and a split in society. Like Baudelaire, Dostoevsky is drawn to the figure of the prostitute. Prostitutes seem to offer a bridge, a redemptive bond linking those social extremes whose continuing separation condemns Russian society as a whole. A great sin and great suffering, Dostoevsky seemed to believe, are the necessary prelude to apocalyptic self-transformation. This is one form in which Dostoevsky puts some hope that perhaps after all life *can* be radically changed. The other form is the narrator's voice, which like the plot strains to include social extremes. The narrator's sensitivity to the likely responses of others is so striking that when he says "gentlemen," we can almost hear his anonymous interlocutors bursting through his sentences and forcing themselves into the story. In his politics, Dostoevsky was skeptical of the forces pushing for greater democracy, but in the literary forms he invented, especially his narrator's "dialogic" openness to other voices, he is one of the greatest democratic writers of all time.

PRONUNCIATIONS:

Apollon: ah-poll-OHN
Ferfichkin: fare-FEECH-keen
Fyodor Dostoevsky: FYO-dur dah-sta-YEF-skee
Simonov: see-MOHN-off
Trudolyubov: true-dahl-YOU-boff
Zverkov: zvair-KOHF

Notes from Underground[1]
Part One
UNDERGROUND

I

I am a sick man . . . I am a spiteful man. I am an unpleasant man. I think my liver is diseased. However, I don't know beans about my disease, and I am not sure what is bothering me. I don't treat it and never have, though I respect medicine and doctors.

---

1. Translated by Ralph E. Matlaw.

Besides, I am extremely superstitious, let's say sufficiently so to respect medicine. (I am educated enough not to be superstitious, but I am.) No, I refuse to treat it out of spite. You probably will not understand that. Well, but *I* understand it. Of course, I can't explain to you just whom I am annoying in this case by my spite. I am perfectly well aware that I cannot "get even" with the doctors by not consulting them. I know better than anyone that I thereby injure only myself and no one else. But still, if I don't treat it, it is out of spite. My liver is bad, well then—let it get even worse!

I have been living like that for a long time now—twenty years. I am forty now. I used to be in the civil service, but no longer am. I was a spiteful official. I was rude and took pleasure in being so. After all, I did not accept bribes, so I was bound to find a compensation in that, at least. (A bad joke but I will not cross it out, I wrote it thinking it would sound very witty; but now that I see myself that I only wanted to show off in a despicable way, I will purposely not cross it out!) When petitioners would come to my desk for information I would gnash my teeth at them, and feel intense enjoyment when I succeeded in distressing some one. I was almost always successful. For the most part they were all timid people—of course, they were petitioners. But among the fops there was one officer in particular I could not endure. He simply would not be humble, and clanked his sword in a disgusting way. I carried on a war with him for eighteen months over that sword. At last I got the better of him. He left off clanking it. However, that happened when I was still young. But do you know, gentlemen, what the real point of my spite was? Why, the whole trick, the real vileness of it lay in the fact that continually, even in moments of the worst spleen, I was inwardly conscious with shame that I was not only not spiteful but not even an embittered man, that I was simply frightening sparrows at random and amusing myself by it. I might foam at the mouth, but bring me some kind of toy, give me a cup of tea with sugar, and I would be appeased. My heart might even be touched, though probably I would gnash my teeth at myself after ward and lie awake at night with shame for months after. That is the way I am.

I was lying when I said just now that I was a spiteful official. I was lying out of spite. I was simply indulging myself with the petitioners and with the officer, but I could never really become spiteful. Every moment I was conscious in myself of many, very many elements completely opposite to that. I felt them positively teeming in me, these opposite elements. I knew that they had been teeming in me all my life, begging to be let out, but I would not let them, would not let them, purposely would not let them out. They tormented me till I was ashamed; they drove me to convulsions, and finally, they bored me, how they bored me! Well, are you not imagining, gentlemen, that I am repenting for something now, that I am asking your forgiveness for something? I am sure you are imagining that. However, I assure you it does not matter to me if you are.

Not only could I not become spiteful, I could not even become anything: neither spiteful nor kind, neither a rascal nor an honest man, neither a hero nor an insect. Now, I am living out my life in my corner, taunting myself with the spiteful and useless consolation that an intelligent man cannot seriously become anything and that only a fool can become something. Yes, an intelligent man in the nineteenth century must and morally ought to be pre-eminently a characterless creature; a man of character, an active man, is pre-eminently a limited creature. That is the conviction of my forty years. I am forty years old now, and forty years, after all, is a whole lifetime; after all, that is extreme old age. To live longer than forty years is bad manners; it is vulgar, immoral. Who does live beyond forty? Answer that, sincerely and honestly. I will tell you who do: fools and worthless people do. I tell all old men that to their face, all those respectable old men, all those silver-haired and reverend old men! I tell the whole world that to its face. I have a right to say so, for I'll go on living to sixty myself. I'll live till seventy! Till eighty! Wait, let me catch my breath.

No doubt you think, gentlemen, that I want to amuse you. You are mistaken in that, too. I am not at all such a merry person as you imagine, or as you may imagine; however, if irritated by all this babble (and I can feel that you are irritated) you decide to ask me just who I am—then my answer is, I am a certain low-ranked civil servant. I was in the service in order to have something to eat (but only for that reason), and when last year a distant relation left me six thousand roubles in his will I immediately retired from the service and settled down in my corner. I used to live in this corner before, but now I have settled down in it. My room is a wretched, horrid one on the outskirts of town. My servant is an old country-woman, spiteful out of stupidity, and, moreover, she always smells bad. I am told that the Petersburg climate is bad for me, and that with my paltry means it is very expensive to live in Petersburg. I know all that better than all these sage and experienced counsellors and monitors. But I am going to stay in Petersburg. I will not leave Petersburg! I will not leave because . . . Bah, after all it does not matter in the least whether I leave or stay.

But incidentally, what can a decent man speak about with the greatest pleasure?

Answer: About himself.

Well, then, I will talk about myself.

II

Now I want to tell you, gentlemen, whether you care to hear it or not, why I could not even become an insect. I tell you solemnly that I wanted to become an insect many times. But I was not even worthy of that. I swear to you, gentlemen, that to be hyperconscious is a disease, a real positive disease. Ordinary human consciousness would be too much for man's everyday needs, that is, half or a quarter of the amount which falls to the lot of a cultivated man of our unfortunate nineteenth century, especially one who has the particular misfortune to inhabit Petersburg, the most abstract and intentional city in the whole world.[2] (There are intentional and unintentional cities.) It would have been quite enough, for instance, to have the consciousness by which all so-called straightforward persons and men of action live. I'll bet you think I am writing all this to show off, to be witty at the expense of men of action; and what is more, that out of ill-bred showing-off, I am clanking a sword, like my officer. But, gentlemen, whoever can pride himself on his diseases and even show off with them?

However, what am I talking about? Everyone does that. They do pride themselves on their diseases, and I, perhaps, more than any one. There is no doubt about it: my objection was absurd. Yet just the same, I am firmly convinced not only that a great deal of consciousness, but that any consciousness is a disease. I insist on it. Let us drop that, too, for a minute. Tell me this: why did it happen that at the very, yes, at the very moment when I was most capable of recognizing every refinement of "all the sublime and beautiful," as we used to say at one time, I would, as though purposely, not only feel but do such hideous things, such that—well, in short, such as everyone

---

2. One of the youngest European cities, Petersburg was established at the beginning of the 18th century by the decree of Tsar Peter the Great, who wanted a "window on the west." Peter's ambition was to turn a marshy wasteland into a harmonious and perfectly ordered Enlightenment capital.

probably does but which, as though purposely, occurred to me at the very time when I was most conscious that they ought not to be done. The more conscious I was of goodness, and of all that "sublime and beautiful," the more deeply I sank into my mire and the more capable I became of sinking into it completely. But the main thing was that all this did not seem to occur in me accidentally, but as though it had to be so. As though it were my most normal condition, and not in the least disease or depravity, so that finally I even lost the desire to struggle against this depravity. It ended by my almost believing (perhaps actually believing) that probably this was really my normal condition. But at first, in the beginning, that is, what agonies I suffered in that struggle! I did not believe that others went through the same things, and therefore I hid this fact about myself as a secret all my life. I was ashamed (perhaps I am even ashamed now). I reached the point of feeling a sort of secret abnormal, despicable enjoyment in returning home to my corner on some disgusting Petersburg night, and being acutely conscious that that day I had again done something loathsome, that what was done could never be undone, and secretly, inwardly gnaw, gnaw at myself for it, nagging and consuming myself till at last the bitterness turned into a sort of shameful accursed sweetness, and finally into real positive enjoyment! Yes, into enjoyment, into enjoyment! I insist upon that. And that is why I have started to speak, because I keep wanting to know for a fact whether other people feel such an enjoyment. Let me explain: the enjoyment here consisted precisely in the hyperconsciousness of one's own degradation; it was from feeling oneself that one had reached the last barrier, that it was nasty, but that it could not be otherwise; that you no longer had an escape; that you could never become a different person; that even if there remained enough time and faith for you to change into something else you probably would not want to change; or if you did want to, even then you would do nothing; because perhaps in reality there was nothing for you to change into. And the worst of it, and the root of it all, was that it all proceeded according to the normal and fundamental laws of hyperconsciousness, and with the inertia that was the direct result of those laws, and that consequently one could not only not change but one could do absolutely nothing. Thus it would follow, as the result of hyperconsciousness, that one is not to blame for being a scoundrel, as though that were any consolation to the scoundrel once he himself has come to realize that he actually is a scoundrel. But enough. Bah, I have talked a lot of nonsense, but what have I explained? Can this enjoyment be explained? But I will explain it! I will get to the bottom of it! That is why I have taken up my pen.

To take an instance, I am terribly vain. I am as suspicious and touchy as a hunchback or a dwarf. But to tell the truth, there have been moments when if someone had happened to slap my face I would, perhaps, have even been glad of that. I say, very seriously, that I would probably have been able to discover a peculiar sort of enjoyment even in that—the enjoyment, of course, of despair; but in despair occur the most intense enjoyments, especially when one is very acutely conscious of one's hopeless position. As for the slap in the face—why then the consciousness of being beaten to a pulp would positively overwhelm one. The worst of it is, no matter how I tried, it still turned out that I was always the most to blame in everything, and what is most humiliating of all, to blame for no fault of my own but, so to say, through the laws of nature. In the first place, to blame because I am cleverer than any of the people surrounding me. (I have always considered myself cleverer than any of the people surrounding me, and sometimes, would you believe it, I have even been ashamed of that. At any rate, all my life, I have, as it were, looked away and I could never look people straight in the eye.) To blame, finally, because even if I were magnanimous, I would only have suffered more from the consciousness of all its uselessness. After all, I would probably never have been able to do anything with my magnanimity—neither to forgive, for my assailant may have slapped me because of the laws of nature, and one cannot forgive the laws of nature; nor to forget, for even if it were the laws of nature, it is insulting all the same. Finally, even if I had wanted to be anything but magnanimous, had desired on the contrary to revenge myself on the man who insulted me, I could not have revenged myself on anyone nor anything because I would certainly never have made up my mind to do anything, even if I had been able to. Why would I not have made up my mind? I want to say a few words about that in particular.

III

After all, people who know how to revenge themselves and to take care of themselves in general, how do they do it? After all, when they are possessed, let us suppose, by the feeling of revenge, then for the time there is nothing else but that feeling left in their whole being. Such a man simply rushes straight toward his object like an infuriated bull with its horns down, and nothing but a wall will stop him. (By the way: facing the wall, such people—that is, the straightforward persons and men of action—are genuinely nonplussed. For them a wall is not an evasion, as for example for us people who think and consequently do nothing; it is not an excuse for turning aside, an excuse for which our kind is always very glad, though we scarcely believe in it ourselves, usually. No, they are nonplussed in all sincerity. The wall has for them something tranquilizing, morally soothing, final—maybe even something mysterious . . . but of the wall later.) Well, such a direct person I regard as the real normal man, as his tender mother nature wished to see him when she graciously brought him into being on the earth. I envy such a man till I am green in the face. He is stupid. I am not disputing that, but perhaps the normal man should be stupid, how do you know? Perhaps it is very beautiful, in fact. And I am all the more convinced of that suspicion, if one can call it so, by the fact that if, for instance, you take the antithesis of the normal man, that is, the hyperconscious man, who has come, of course, not out of the lap of nature but out of a retort (this is almost mysticism, gentlemen, but I suspect this, too), this retort-made man is sometimes so nonplussed in the presence of his antithesis that with his hyperconsciousness he genuinely thinks of himself a mouse and not a man. It may be a hyperconscious mouse, yet it is a mouse, while the other is a man, are therefore, etc. And the worst is, he himself, his very ownself, looks upon himself as a mouse. No one asks him to do so. And that is an important point. Now let us look at this mouse in action. Let us suppose, for instance, that it feels insulted, too (and it almost always does feel insulted), and wants to revenge itself too. There may even be a greater accumulation of spite in it than in *l'homme de la nature et de la vérité*.[3] The base, nasty desire to repay with spite whoever has offended it, rankles perhaps even more nastily in it than in *l'homme de la nature et de la vérité*, because *l'homme de la nature et de la vérité*, through his innate stupidity looks upon his revenge as justice pure and simple; while in consequence of his hyperconsciousness the mouse does not believe in the justice of it. To come at last to the deed itself, to the very act of revenge. Apart from the one fundamental nastiness the unfortunate mouse succeeds in creating around it so many other nastinesses in the form of doubts and questions, adds to the

---

3. A man of nature and of truth (French), ideal of Enlightenment philosophers like Jean-Jacques Rousseau.

one question so many unsettled questions, that there inevitably works up around it a sort of fatal brew, a stinking mess, made up of its doubts, agitations and lastly of the contempt spat upon it by the straightforward men of action who stand solemnly about it as judges and arbitrators, laughing at it till their healthy sides ache. Of course the only thing left for it is to dismiss all that with a wave of its paw, and, with a smile of assumed contempt in which it does not even believe itself, creep ignominiously into its mouse-hole. There, in its nasty, stinking, underground home our insulted, crushed and ridiculed mouse promptly becomes absorbed in cold, malignant and, above all, everlasting spite. For forty years together it will remember its injury down to the smallest, most shameful detail, and every time will add, of itself, details still more shameful, spitefully teasing and irritating itself with its own imagination. It will be ashamed of its own fancies, but yet it will recall everything, it will go over it again and again, it will invent lies against itself pretending that worse things might have happened, and will forgive anything. Maybe it will begin to revenge itself, too, but, as it were, piecemeal, in trivial ways, from behind the stove, incognito, without believing either in its own right to vengeance, or in the success of its revenge, knowing beforehand that from all its efforts at revenge it will suffer a hundred times more than he on whom it revenges itself, while he, probably will not even feel it. On its deathbed it will recall it all over again, with interest accumulated over all the years. But it is just in that cold, abominable half-despair, half-belief, in that conscious burying oneself alive for grief in the underworld for forty years, in that hyperconsciousness and yet to some extent doubtful hopelessness of one's position, in that hell of unsatisfied desires turned inward, in that lever of oscillations, of resolutions taken for ever and regretted again a minute later—that the savor of that strange enjoyment of which I have spoken lies. It is so subtle, sometimes so difficult to analyze consciously, that somewhat limited people, or simply people with strong nerves, will not understand anything at all in it. "Possibly," you will add on your own account with a grin, "people who have never received a slap in the face will not understand it either," and in that way you will politely hint to me that I, too, perhaps, have been slapped in the face in my life, and so I speak as an expert. I'll bet that you are thinking that. But set your minds at rest, gentlemen, I have not received a slap in the face, though it doesn't matter to me at all what you may think about it. Possibly, I even myself regret that I have given so few slaps in the face during my life. But enough, not another word on the subject of such extreme interest to you.

I will continue calmly about people with strong nerves who do not understand a certain refinement of enjoyment. Though in certain circumstances these gentlemen bellow their loudest like bulls, though this, let us suppose, does them the greatest honor, yet, as I have already said, confronted with the impossible they at once resign themselves. Does the impossible mean the stone wall? What stone wall? Why, of course, the laws of nature, the conclusions of natural science, of mathematics. As soon as they prove to you, for instance, that you are descended from a monkey, then it is no use scowling, accept it as a fact. When they prove to you that in reality one drop of your own fat must be dearer to you than a hundred thousand of your fellow creatures, and that this conclusion is the final solution of all so-called virtues and duties and all such ravings and prejudices, then you might as well accept it, you can't do anything about it, because two times two is a law of mathematics. Just try refuting it.

"But really," they will shout at you, "there is no use protesting; it is a case of two times two makes four. Nature does not ask your permission, your wishes, and whether you like or dislike her laws does not concern her. You are bound to accept her as she is, and consequently also all her conclusions. A wall, you see, is a wall—etc., etc." Good God! but what do I care about the laws of nature and arithmetic, when, for some reason, I dislike those laws and the fact that two times two makes four? Of course I cannot break through a wall by battering my head against it if I really do not have the strength to break through it, but I am not going to resign myself to it simply because it is a stone wall and I am not strong enough.

As though such a stone wall really were a consolation, and really did contain some word of conciliation, if only because it is as true as two times two makes four. Oh, absurdity of absurdities! How much better it is to understand it all, to be conscious of it all, all the impossibilities and the stone walls, not to resign yourself to a single one of those impossibilities and stone walls if it disgusts you to resign yourself; to reach, through the most inevitable, logical combinations, the most revolting conclusions on the everlasting theme that you are yourself somehow to blame even for the stone wall, though again it is as clear as day you are not to blame in the least, and therefore grinding your teeth in silent impotence sensuously to sink into inertia, brooding on the fact that it turns out that there is even no one for you to feel vindictive against, that you have not, and perhaps never will have, an object for your spite, that it is a sleight-of-hand, a bit of juggling, a card-sharper's trick, that it is simply a mess, no knowing what and no knowing who, but in spite of all these uncertainties, and jugglings, still there is an ache in you, and the more you do not know, the worse the ache.

IV

"Ha, ha, ha! Next you will find enjoyment in a toothache," you cry with a laugh.

"Well? So what? There is enjoyment even in a toothache," I answer. I had a toothache for a whole month and I know there is. In that case, of course, people are not spiteful in silence, they moan; but these are not sincere moans, they are malicious moans, and the maliciousness is the whole point. The sufferer's enjoyment finds expression in those moans; if he did not feel enjoyment in them he would not moan. It is a good example, gentlemen, and I will develop it. The moans express in the first place all the aimlessness of your pain, which is so humiliating to your consciousness; the whole legal system of Nature on which you spit disdainfully, of course, but from which you suffer all the same while she does not. They express the consciousness that you have no enemy, but that you do have a pain; the consciousness that in spite of all the dentists in the world you are in complete slavery to your teeth; that if someone wishes it, your teeth will leave off aching, and if he does not, they will go on aching another three months; and that finally if you still disagree and still protest, all that is left you for your own gratification is to thrash yourself or beat your wall with your fist as hard as you can, and absolutely nothing more. Well then, these mortal insults, these jeers on the part of someone unknown, end at last in an enjoyment which sometimes reaches the highest degree of sensuality. I beg you, gentlemen, to listen sometimes to the moans of an educated man of the nineteenth century who is suffering from a toothache, particularly on the second or third day of the attack, when he has already begun to moan not as he moaned on the first day, that is, not simply because he has a toothache, not just as any coarse peasant might moan, but as a man affected by progress and European civilization, a man who is "divorced from the soil and the nation of principles," as they call it these days. His moans become nasty, disgustingly spiteful, and go on for whole days and nights. And, after all, he himself knows that he does not benefit at all from his moans; he knows better than any one that he is only lacerating and irritating himself and others in vain; he knows that even the audience for whom he is exerting himself and his whole family now listen to him with loathing, do not believe him for the second, and that deep down they understand that he could moan differently, more simply, without trills and flourishes, and that he is only indulging himself like that out of spite, out of malice. Well, sensuality exists precisely in all these consciousnesses and infamies. "It seems I am troubling you, I am lacerating your hearts, I am keeping everyone in the house awake. Well, stay awake then, you, too, feel every minute that I have a toothache, I am no longer the hero to you now that I tried to appear before, but simply a nasty person, a scoundrel. Well, let it be that way, then! I am very glad that you see through me. Is it nasty for you to hear my foul moans? Well, let it be nasty. Here I will let you have an even nastier flourish in a minute. . . ." You still do not understand, gentlemen? No, it seems our development and our consciousness must go further to understand all the intricacies of this sensuality. You laugh? I am delighted. My jokes, gentlemen, are of course in bad taste, uneven, involved, lacking self-confidence. But of course that is because I do not respect myself. Can a man with consciousness respect himself at all?

V

Come, can a man who even attempts to find enjoyment in the very feeling of self-degradation really have any respect for himself at all? I am not saying this now from any insipid kind of remorse. And, indeed, I could never endure to say, "Forgive me, Daddy, I won't do it again," not because I was incapable of saying it, but, on the contrary, perhaps just because I was too capable of it, and in what a way, too! As though on purpose I used to get into trouble on occasions when I was not to blame in the faintest way. That was the nastiest part of it. At the same time I was genuinely touched and repentant, I used to shed tears and, of course, tricked even myself, though it was not acting in the least and there was a sick feeling in my heart at the time. For that one could not even blame the laws of nature, though the laws of nature have offended me continually all my life more than anything. It is loathsome to remember it all, but it was loathsome even then. Of course, in a minute or so I would realize with spite that it was all a lie, a lie, an affected, revolting lie, that is, all this repentance, all these emotions, these vows to reform. And if you ask why I worried and tortured myself that way, the answer is because it was very dull to twiddle one's thumbs, and so one began cutting capers. That is really it. Observe yourselves more carefully, gentlemen, then you will understand that that's right! I invented adventures for myself and made up a life, so as to live at least in some way. How many times it has happened to me—well, for instance, to take offence at nothing, simply on purpose; and one knows oneself, of course, that one is offended at nothing, that one is pretending, but yet one brings oneself, at last, to the point of really being offended. All my life I have had an impulse to play such pranks, so that in the end, I could not control it in myself. Another time, twice, in fact, I tried to force myself to fall in love. I even suffered, gentlemen, I assure you. In the depth of my heart I did not believe in my suffering, there was a stir of mockery, but yet I did suffer, and in the real, regular way I was jealous, I was beside myself, and it was all out of boredom, gentlemen, all out of boredom; inertia overcame me. After all, the direct, legitimate, immediate fruit of consciousness is inertia, that is, conscious thumb twiddling. I have referred to it already, I repeat, I repeat it emphatically: all straightforward persons and men of action are active just because they are stupid and limited. How can that be explained? This way: as a result of their limitation they take immediate and secondary causes for primary ones, and in that way persuade themselves more quickly and easily than other people do that they have found an infallible basis for their activity, and their minds are at ease and that, you know, is the most important thing. To begin to act, you know, you must first have your mind completely at ease and without a trace of doubt left in it. Well, how am I, for example, to set my mind at rest? Where are the primary causes on which I am to build? Where are my bases? Where am I to get them from? I exercise myself in the process of thinking, and consequently with me every primary cause at once draws after itself another still more primary, and so on to infinity. That is precisely the essence of every sort of consciousness and thinking. It must be a case of the laws of nature again. In what does it finally result? Why, just the same. Remember I spoke just now of vengeance. (I am sure you did not grasp that.) I said that a man revenges himself because he finds justice in it. Therefore he has found a primary cause, found a basis, to wit, justice. And so he is completely set at rest, and consequently he carries out his revenge calmly and successfully, as he is convinced that he is doing a just and honest thing. But, after all, I see no justice in it, I find no sort of virtue in it either, and consequently if I attempt to revenge myself, it would only be out of spite. Spite, of course, might overcome everything, all my doubts, and could consequently serve quite successfully in a place of a primary cause, precisely because it is not a cause. But what can be done if I do not even have spite (after all, I began with that just now)? Again, in consequence of those accursed laws of consciousness, my spite is subject to chemical disintegration. You look into it, the object flies off into air, your reasons evaporate, the criminal is not to be found, the insult becomes fate rather than an insult, something like the toothache, for which no one is to blame, and consequently there is only the same outlet left again—that is, to beat the wall as hard as you can. So you give it up as hopeless because you have not found a fundamental cause. And try letting yourself be carried away by your feelings, blindly, without reflection, without a primary cause, repelling consciousness at least for a time; hate or love, if only not to sit and twiddle your thumbs. The day after tomorrow, at the latest, you will begin despising yourself for having knowingly deceived yourself. The result—a soap-bubble and inertia. Oh, gentlemen, after all, perhaps I consider myself an intelligent man only because all my life I have been able neither to begin nor to finish anything. Granted, granted I am a babbler, a harmless annoying babbler, like all of us. But what is to be done if the direct and sole vocation of every intelligent man is babble, that is, the intentional pouring of water through a sieve?

VI

Oh, if I had done nothing simply out of laziness! Heavens, how I would have respected myself then. I would have respected myself because I would at least have been capable of being lazy; there would at least have been in me one positive quality, as it were, in which I could have believed myself. Question: Who is he? Answer: A loafer. After all, it would have been pleasant to hear that about oneself! It would mean that I was positively defined, it would mean that there was something to be said about me. "Loafer"—why, after all, it is a calling and an appointment, it is a career, gentlemen. Do not joke, it is so. I would then, by rights, be a member of the best club, and would occupy myself only in continually respecting myself. I knew a gentleman who prided himself all his life on being a connoisseur of Lafitte.[4] He considered this as his positive virtue, and never doubted himself. He died, not simply with a tranquil but with a triumphant conscience, and he was completely right. I should have chosen a career for myself then too: I would have been a loafer and a glutton, not a simple one, but, for instance, one in sympathy with everything good and beautiful. How do you like that? I have long had visions of it. That "sublime and beautiful" weighs heavily on my mind at forty. But that is when I am forty, while then—oh, then it would have been different! I would have found myself an appropriate occupation, namely, to drink to the health of everything sublime and beautiful. I would have seized every opportunity to drop a tear into my glass and then to drain it to all that is sublime and beautiful. I would then have turned everything into the sublime and the beautiful; I would have sought out the sublime and the beautiful in the nastiest, most unquestionable trash. I would have become as tearful as a wet sponge. An artist, for instance, paints Ge's picture. At once I drink to the health of the artist who painted Ge's picture, because I love all that is "sublime and beautiful." An author writes "Whatever You Like"; at once I drink to the health of "Whatever You Like" because I love all that is "sublime and beautiful." I would demand respect for doing so, I would persecute anyone who would not show me respect. I would live at ease, I would die triumphantly—why, after all, it is charming, perfectly charming! And what a belly I would have grown, what a triple chin I would have established, what a red nose I would have produced for myself, so that every passer-by would have said, looking at me: "Here is an asset! Here is something really positive!" And, after all, say what you like, it is very pleasant to hear such remarks about oneself in this negative age, gentlemen.

VII

But these are all golden dreams. Oh, tell me, who first declared, who first proclaimed, that man only does nasty things because he does not know his own real interests; and that if he were enlightened, if his eyes were opened to his real normal interests, man would at once cease to do nasty things, would at once become good and noble because, being enlightened and understanding his real advantage, he would see his own advantage in the good and nothing else, and we all know that not a single man can knowingly act to his own disadvantage. Consequently, so to say, he would begin doing good through necessity. Oh, the babe! Oh, the pure, innocent child! Why, in the first place, when in all these thousands of years has there ever been a time when man has acted only for his own advantage? What is to be done with the millions of facts that bear witness that men, *knowingly,* that is, fully understanding their real advantages, have left them in the background and have rushed headlong on another path, to risk, to chance, compelled to this course by nobody and by nothing, but, as it were, precisely because they did not want the beaten track, and stubbornly, wilfully, went off on another difficult, absurd way seeking it almost in the darkness. After all, it means that this stubbornness and willfulness were more pleasant to them than any advantage. Advantage! What is advantage? And will you take it upon yourself to define

4. A fine wine.

with perfect accuracy in exactly what the advantage of man consists of? And what if it so happens that a man's advantage *sometimes* not only may, but even must, consist exactly in his desiring under certain conditions what is harmful to himself and not what is advantageous. And if so, if there can be such a condition then the whole principle becomes worthless. What do you think—are there such cases? You laugh; laugh away, gentlemen, so long as you answer me: have man's advantages been calculated with perfect certainty? Are there not some which not only have been included but cannot possibly be included under any classification? After all, you, gentlemen, so far as I know, have taken your whole register of human advantages from the average of statistical figures and scientific-economic formulas. After all, your advantages are prosperity, wealth, freedom, peace—and so on, and so on. So that a man who, for instance, would openly and knowingly oppose that whole list would, to your thinking, and indeed to mine too, of course, be an obscurantist or an absolute madman, would he not? But, after all, here is something amazing: why does it happen that all these statisticians, sages and lovers of humanity, when they calculate human advantages invariably leave one out? They don't even take it into their calculation in the form in which it should be taken, and the whole reckoning depends upon that. There would be no great harm to take it, this advantage, and to add it to the list. But the trouble is, that this strange advantage does not fall under any classification and does not figure in any list. For instance, I have a friend. Bah, gentlemen! But after all he is your friend, too; and indeed there is no one, no one to whom he is not a friend! When he prepares for any undertaking this gentleman immediately explains to you, pompously and clearly, exactly how he must act in accordance with the laws of reason and truth. What is more, he will talk to you with excitement and passion of the real normal interests of man; with irony he will reproach the short-sighted fools who do not understand their own advantage, for the true significance of virtue; and, within a quarter of an hour, without any sudden outside provocation, but precisely through that something internal which is stronger than all his advantages, he will go off on quite a different tack— that is, act directly opposite to what he has just been saying himself, in opposition to the laws of reason, in opposition to his own advantage—in fact, in opposition to everything. I warn you that my friend is a compound personality, and therefore it is somehow difficult to blame him as an individual. The fact is, gentlemen, it seems that something that is dearer to almost every man than his greatest advantages must really exist, or (not to be illogical) there is one most advantageous advantage (the very one omitted of which we spoke just now) which is more important and more advantageous than all other advantages, for which, if necessary, a man is ready to act in opposition to all laws, that is, in opposition to reason, honor, peace, prosperity—in short, in opposition to all those wonderful and useful things if only he can attain that fundamental, most advantageous advantage which is dearer to him than all.

"Well, but it is still advantage just the same," you will retort. But excuse me, I'll make the point clear, and it is not a case of a play on words, but what really matters is that this advantage is remarkable from the very fact that it breaks down all our classifications, and continually shatters all the systems evolved by lovers of mankind for the happiness of mankind. In short, it interferes with everything. But before I mention this advantage to you, I want to compromise myself personally, and therefore I boldly declare that all these fine systems—all these theories for explaining to mankind its real normal interests, so that inevitably striving to obtain these interests, it may at once become good and noble—are, in my opinion, so far, mere logical exercises! Yes, logical exercises. After all, to maintain even this theory of the regeneration of mankind by means of its own advantage, is, after all, to my mind almost the same thing as—as to claim, for instance, with Buckle, that through civilization mankind becomes softer, and consequently less blood-thirsty, and less fitted for warfare.[5] Logically it does not seem to follow from his arguments. But man is so fond of systems and abstract deductions that he is ready to distort the truth intentionally, he is ready to deny what he can see and hear just to justify his logic. I take this example because it is the most glaring instance of it. Only look about you: blood is being spilled in streams, and in the merriest way, as though it were champagne. Take the whole of the nineteenth century in which Buckle lived. Take Napoleon—both the Great and the present one.[6] Take North America—the eternal union. Take farcical Schleswig-Holstein.[7] And what is it that civilization softens in us? Civilization only produces a greater variety of sensations in man—and absolutely nothing more. And through the development of this variety, man may even come to find enjoyment in bloodshed. After all, it has already happened to him. Have you noticed that the subtlest slaughterers have almost always been the most civilized gentlemen, to whom the various Attilas and Stenka Razins[8] could never hold a candle, and if they are not so conspicuous as the Attilas and Stenka Razins it is precisely because they are so often met with, are so ordinary and have become so familiar to us. In any case if civilization has not made man more bloodthirsty, it has at least made him more abominably, more loathsomely bloodthirsty than before. Formerly he saw justice in bloodshed and with his conscience at peace exterminated whomever he thought he should. And now while we consider bloodshed an abomination, we nevertheless engage in this abomination and even more than ever before. Which is worse? Decide that for yourselves. It is said that Cleopatra (pardon the example from Roman history) was found of sticking gold pins into her slave-girls' breasts and derived enjoyment from their screams and writhing. You will say that that occurred in comparatively barbarous times; that these are barbarous times too, because (also comparatively speaking) pins are stuck in even now; that even though man has now learned to see more clearly occasionally than in barbarous times, he is still far from having *accustomed* himself to act as reason and science would dictate. But all the same you are fully convinced that he will inevitably accustom himself to it when he gets completely rid of certain old bad habits, and when common sense and science have completely re-educated human nature and turned it in a normal direction. You are confident that man will then refrain from erring *intentionally,* and will, so to say, willy-nilly, not want to set his will against his normal interests. More than that: then, you say, science itself will teach man (though to my mind that is a luxury) that he does not really have either caprice or will of his own and that he has never had it, and that he himself is something like a piano key or an organ stop, and that, moreover, laws of nature exist in this world, so that everything he does is not done by his will at all, but is done by itself, according to the laws of nature. Consequently we have only to discover these laws of nature, and man will no longer be responsible for his actions and life will become exceedingly easy for

5. Thomas Buckle (1821–1862) argued in his *History of Civilization in England* that modern society was becoming more and more rational and less dependent on violence to solve disputes.

6. The reference is to Napoleon Bonaparte and his nephew, Louis-Napoleon or Napoleon III, who ruled France as president and then emperor from 1850 to 1870.

7. An area disputed between Denmark and Prussia in the 19th century and eventually seized by Prussia; after World War II it was divided between Denmark and Germany.

8. Leader of a major Cossack and peasant rebellion, 1670–1671.

him. All human actions will then, of course, be tabulated according to these laws, mathematically, like tables of logarithms up to 108,000, and entered in a table; or, better still, there would be published certain edifying works like the present encyclopedic lexicons, in which everything will be so clearly calculated and designated that there will be no more incidents or adventures in the world.

Then—it is still you speaking—new economic relations will be established, all ready-made and computed with mathematical exactitude, so that every possible question will vanish in a twinkling, simply because every possible answer to it will be provided. Then the crystal palace will be built. Then—well, in short, those will be halcyon days. Of course there is no guaranteeing (this is my comment now) that it will not be, for instance, terribly boring then (for what will one have to do when everything is calculated according to the table?) but on the other hand everything will be extraordinarily rational. Of course boredom may lead you to anything. After all, boredom even sets one to sticking gold pins into people, but all that would not matter. What is bad (this is my comment again) is that for all I know people will be thankful for the gold pins then. After all, man is stupid, phenomenally stupid. Or rather he is not stupid at all, but he is so ungrateful that you could not find another like him in all creation. After all, it would not surprise me in the least, if, for instance, suddenly for no reason at all, general rationalism in the midst of the future, a gentleman with an ignoble, or rather with a reactionary and ironical, countenance were to arise and, putting his arms akimbo, say to us all: "What do you think, gentlemen, hadn't we better kick over all that rationalism at one blow, scatter it to the winds, just to send these logarithms to the devil, and to let us live once more according to our own foolish will!" That again would not matter; but what is annoying is that after all he would be sure to find followers—such is the nature of man. And all that for the most foolish reason, which, one would think, was hardly worth mentioning: that is, that man everywhere and always, whoever he may be, has preferred to act as he wished and not in the least as his reason and advantage dictated. Why, one may choose what is contrary to one's own interests, and sometimes one *positively ought* (that is my idea). One's own free unfettered choice, one's own fancy, however wild it may be, one's own fancy worked up at times to frenzy—why that is that very "most advantageous advantage" which we have overlooked, which comes under no classification and through which all systems and theories are continually being sent to the devil. And how do these sages know that man must necessarily need a rationally advantageous choice? What man needs is simply *independent* choice, whatever that independence may cost and wherever it may lead. Well, choice, after all, the devil only knows . . .

VIII

"Ha! ha! ha! But after all, if you like, in reality, there is no such thing as choice," you will interrupt with a laugh. "Science has even now succeeded in analyzing man to such an extent that we know already that choice and what is called freedom of will are nothing other than—"

Wait, gentlemen, I meant to begin with that myself. I admit that I was even frightened. I was just going to shout that after all the devil only knows what choice depends on, and that perhaps that was a very good thing, but I remembered the teaching of science—and pulled myself up. And here you have begun to speak. After all, really, well, if some day they truly discover a formula for all our desires and caprices—that is, an explanation of what they depend upon, by what laws they arise, just how they develop, what they are aiming at in one case or another and so on, and so on, that is, a real mathematical formula—then, after all, man would most likely at once stop to feel desire, indeed, he will be certain to. For who would want to choose by rule? Besides, he will at once be transformed from a human being into an organ stop or something of the sort; for what is a man without desire, without free will and without choice, if not a stop in an organ? What do you think? Let us consider the probability—can such a thing happen or not?

"H'm!" you decide. "Our choice is usually mistaken through a mistaken notion of our advantage. We sometimes choose absolute nonsense because in our stupidity we see in that nonsense the easiest means for attaining an advantage assumed before-hand. But when all that is explained and worked out on paper (which is perfectly possible, for it is contemptible and senseless to assume in advance that man will never understand some laws of nature), then, of course, so-called desires will not exist. After all, if desire should at any time come to terms completely with reason, we shall then, of course, reason and not desire, simply because, after all, it will be impossible to retain reason and *desire* something senseless, and in that way knowingly act against reason and desire to injure ourselves. And as all choice and reasoning can really be calculated, because some day they will discover the laws of our so-called free will—so joking aside, there may one day probably be something like a table of desires so that we really shall choose in accordance with it. After all, if, for instance, some day they calculate and prove to me that I stuck my tongue out at someone because I could not help sticking my tongue out at him and that I had to do it in that particular way, what sort of *freedom* is left me, especially if I am a learned man and have taken my degree somewhere? After all, then I would be able to calculate my whole life for thirty years in advance. In short, if that comes about, then, after all, we could do nothing about it. We would have to accept it just the same. And, in fact, we ought to repeat to ourselves incessantly that at such and such a time and under such and such circumstances. Nature does not ask our leave; that we must accept her as she is and not as we imagine her to be, and if we really aspire to tables and indices and well, even—well, let us say to the chemical retort, then it cannot be helped. We must accept the retort, too, or else it will be accepted without our consent."

Yes, but here I come to a stop! Gentlemen, you must excuse me for philosophizing; it's the result of forty years underground! Allow me to indulge my fancy for a minute. You see, gentlemen, reason, gentlemen, is an excellent thing, there is no disputing that, but reason is only reason and can only satisfy man's rational faculty, while will is a manifestation of all life, that is, of all human life including reason as well as all impulses. And although our life, in this manifestation of it, is often worthless, yet it is life nevertheless and not simply extracting square roots. After all, here I, for instance, quite naturally want to live, in order to satisfy all my faculties for life, and not simply my rational faculty, that is, not simply one-twentieth of all my faculties for life. What does reason know? Reason only knows what it has succeeded in learning (some things it will perhaps never learn; while this is nevertheless no comfort, why not say so frankly?) and human nature acts as a whole, with everything that is in it, consciously or unconsciously, and, even if it goes wrong, it lives. I suspect, gentlemen, that you are looking at me with compassion; you repeat to me that an enlightened and developed man, such, in short, as the future man will be, cannot knowingly desire anything disadvantageous to himself, that this can be proved mathematically. I thoroughly agree, it really can—by mathematics. But I repeat for the hundredth time, there is one case, one only, when man may purposely consciously, desire what is injurious to himself, which is stupid, very stupid—simply in order *to have the right* to desire for himself even what is very stupid and not to be bound by an obligation to desire only what is rational. After all, this very stupid thing, after all, this caprice of ours, may really be more advantageous for us, gentlemen than anything else on earth, especially in some cases. And in particular it may be more advantageous than any advantages even when it does us obvious harm, and contradicts the soundest conclusions of our reason about our advantage—because in any case it preserves for us what is most precious and most important—that is, our personality, our individuality. Some, you see, maintain that this really is the most precious thing for man; desire can, of course, if it desires, be in agreement with reason; particularly if it does not abuse this practice but does so in moderation, it is both useful and sometimes even praiseworthy. But very often, and even most often, desire completely and stubbornly opposes reason, and . . . and . . . and do you know that that, too, is useful and sometimes even praiseworthy? Gentlemen, let us suppose that man is not stupid. (Indeed, after all, one cannot say that about him anyway, if only for the one consideration that, if man is stupid, then, after all, who is wise?) But if he is not stupid, he is just the same monstrously ungrateful! Phenomenally ungrateful. I even believe that the best definition of man is—a creature that walks on two legs and is ungrateful. But that is not all, that is not his worst defect; his worst defect is his perpetual immorality, perpetual—from the days of the Flood to the Schleswig-Holstein period of human destiny. Immorality, and consequently lack of good sense; for it has long been accepted that lack of good sense is due to no other cause than immorality. Try it, and cast a look upon the history of mankind. Well, what will you see? Is it a grand spectacle? All right, grand, if you like. The Colossus of Rhodes,[9] for instance, that is worth something. Mr. Anaevsky may well testify that some say it is the work of human hands, while others maintain that it was created by Nature herself. Is it variegated? Very well, it may be variegated too. If one only took the dress uniforms, military and civilian, of all peoples in all ages—that alone is worth something, and if you take the undress uniforms you will never get to the end of it; no historian could keep up with it. Is it monotonous? Very well. It may be monotonous, too; they fight and fight; they are fighting now, they fought first and they fought last—you will admit that it is almost too monotonous. In short, one may say anything about the history of the world—anything that might enter the most disordered imagination. The only thing one cannot say is that it is rational. The very word sticks in one's throat. And, indeed, this is even the kind of thing that continually happens. After all, there are continually turning up in life moral and rational people, sages, and lovers of humanity, who make it their goal for life to live as morally and rationally as possible, to be, so to speak, a light to their neighbors, simply in order to show them that it is really possible to live morally and rationally in this world. And so what? We all know that those very people sooner or later toward the end of their lives have been false to themselves, playing some trick, often a most indecent one. Now I ask you: What can one expect from man since he is a creature endowed with such strange qualities? Shower upon him every earthly blessing, drown him in bliss so that nothing but bubbles would dance on the surface of his bliss, as on a sea; give him such economic prosperity that he would have nothing else to do but sleep, eat cakes and busy himself with ensuring the con-

9. One of the wonders of the ancient world.

tinuation of world history and even then man, out of sheer ingratitude, sheer libel, would play you some loathsome trick. He would even risk his cakes and would deliberately desire the most fatal rubbish, the most uneconomical absurdity, simply to introduce into all this positive rationality his fatal fantastic element. It is just his fantastic dreams, his vulgar folly, that he will desire to retain, simply in order to prove to himself (as though that were so necessary) that men still are men and not piano keys, which even if played by the laws of nature themselves threaten to be controlled so completely that soon one will be able to desire nothing but by the calendar. And, after all, that is not all: even if man really were nothing but a piano key, even if this were proved to him by natural science and mathematics, even then he would not become reasonable, but would purposely do something perverse out of sheer ingratitude, simply to have his own way. And if he does not find any means he will devise destruction and chaos, will devise sufferings of all sorts, and will thereby have his own way. He will launch a curse upon the world, and, as only man can curse (it is his privilege, the primary distinction between him and other animals) then, after all, perhaps only by his curse will he attain his object, that is, really convince himself that he is a man and not a piano key! If you say that all this, too, can be calculated and tabulated, chaos and darkness and curses, so that the mere possibility of calculating it all beforehand would stop it all, and reason would reassert itself—then man would purposely go mad in order to be rid of reason and have his own way! I believe in that, I vouch for it, because, after all, the whole work of man seems really to consist in nothing but proving to himself continually that he is a man and not an organ stop. It may be at the cost of his skin! But he has proved it; he may become a caveman, but he will have proved it. And after that can one help sinning, rejoicing that it has not yet come, and that desire still depends on the devil knows what!

You will shout at me (that is, if you will still favor me with your shout) that, after all, no one is depriving me of my will, that all they are concerned with is that my will should somehow of itself, of its own free will, coincide with my own normal interests, with the laws of nature and arithmetic.

Bah, gentlemen, what sort of free will is left when we come to tables and arithmetic, when it will all be a case of two times two makes four? Two times two makes four even without my will. As if free will meant that!

IX

Gentlemen, I am joking, of course, and I know myself that I'm joking badly, but after all you know, one can't take everything as a joke. I am, perhaps, joking with a heavy heart. Gentlemen, I am tormented by questions; answer them for me. Now you, for instance, want to cure men or their old habits and reform their will in accordance with science and common sense. But how do you know, not only that it is possible, but also that it is *desirable,* to reform man in that way? And what leads you to the conclusion that it is so *necessary* to reform man's desires? In short, how do you know that such a reformation will really be advantageous to man? And to go to the heart of the matter, why are you *so sure* of your conviction that not to act against his real normal advantages guaranteed by the conclusions of reason and arithmetic is always advantageous for man and must be a law for all mankind? After all, up to now it is only your supposition. Let us assume it to be a law of logic, but perhaps not a law of humanity at all. You gentlemen perhaps think that I am mad? Allow me to defend myself. I agree that man is pre-eminently a creative animal, predestined to strive consciously toward a goal, and to engage in engineering; that is, eternally and incessantly, to build new roads, *wherever they may lead.* But the reason why he sometimes wants to swerve aside may be precisely that he is *forced* to make that road, and perhaps, too, because however stupid the straightforward practical man may be in general, the thought nevertheless will sometimes occur to him that the road, it would seem, almost always does lead *somewhere,* and that the destination it leads to is less important than the process of making it, and that the chief thing is to save the well-behaved child from despising engineering, and so giving way to the fatal idleness, which, as we all know, is the mother of all vices. Man likes to create and build roads, that is beyond dispute. But why does he also have such a passionate love for destruction and chaos? Now tell me that! But on that point I want to say a few special words myself. May it not be that he loves chaos and destruction (after all, he sometimes unquestionably likes it very much, that is surely so) because he is instinctively afraid of attaining his goal and completing the edifice he is constructing? How do you know, perhaps he only likes that edifice from a distance, and not at all at close range, perhaps he only likes to build it and does not want to live in it, but will leave it, when completed, *aux animaux domestiques*[1]—such as the ants, the sheep, and so on, and so on. Now the ants have quite a different taste. They have an amazing edifice of that type, that endures forever—the anthill.

With the anthill, the respectable race of ants began and with the anthill they will probably end, which does the greatest credit to their perseverance and staidness. But man is a frivolous and incongruous creature, and perhaps, like a chessplayer, loves only the process of the game, not the end of it. And who knows (one cannot swear to it), perhaps the only goal on earth to which mankind is striving lies in this incessant process of attaining, or in other words, in life itself, and not particularly in the goal which of course must always be two times two makes four, that is a formula, and after all, two times two makes four is no longer life, gentlemen, but is the beginning of death. Anyway, man has always been somehow afraid of this two times two makes four, and I am afraid of it even now. Granted that man does nothing but seek that two times two makes four, that he sails the oceans, sacrifices his life in the quest, but to succeed, really to find it—he is somehow afraid, I assure you. He feels that as soon as he has found it there will be nothing for him to look for. When workmen have finished their work they at least receive their pay, they go to the tavern, then they wind up at the police station—and there is an occupation for a week. But where can man go? Anyway, one can observe a certain awkwardness about him every time he attains such goals. He likes the process of attaining, but does not quite like to have attained, and that, of course, is terribly funny. In short, man is a comical creature; there seems to be a kind of pun in it all. But two times two makes four is, after all, something insufferable. Two times two makes four seems to me simply a piece of insolence. Two times two makes four is a fop standing with arms akimbo barring your path and spitting. I admit that two times two makes four is an excellent thing, but if we are going to praise everything, two times two makes five is sometimes also a very charming little thing.

And why are you so firmly, so triumphantly convinced that only the normal and the positive—in short, only prosperity—is to the advantage of man? Is not reason mistaken about advantage? After all, perhaps man likes something besides prosperity? Perhaps he likes suffering just as much? Perhaps suffering is just as great an advan-

---

1. Domestic animals (French).

tage to him as prosperity? Man is sometimes fearfully, passionately in love with suffering and that is a fact. There is no need to appeal to universal history to prove that; only ask yourself, if only you are a man and have lived at all. As far as my own personal opinion is concerned, to care only for prosperity seems to me somehow even illbred. Whether it's good or bad, it is sometimes very pleasant to smash things, too. After all, I do not really insist on suffering or on prosperity either. I insist on my caprice, and its being guaranteed to me when necessary. Suffering would be out of place in vaudevilles, for instance; I know that. In the crystal palace it is even unthinkable; suffering means doubt, means negation, and what would be the good of a crystal palace if there could be any doubt about it? And yet I am sure man will never renounce real suffering, that is, destruction and chaos. Why, after all, suffering is the sole origin of consciousness. Though I stated at the beginning that consciousness, in my opinion, is the greatest misfortune for man, yet I know man loves it and would not give it up for any satisfaction. Consciousness, for instance, is infinitely superior to two times two makes four. Once you have two times two makes four, there is nothing left to do or to understand. There will be nothing left but to bottle up your five senses and plunge into contemplation. While if you stick to consciousness, even though you attain the same result, you can at least flog yourself at times, and that will, at any rate, liven you up. It may be reactionary, but corporal punishment is still better than nothing.

X

You believe in a crystal edifice that can never be destroyed; that is, an edifice at which one would neither be able to stick out one's tongue nor thumb one's nose on the sly. And perhaps I am afraid of this edifice just because it is of crystal and can never be destroyed and that one could not even put one's tongue out at it even on the sly.

You see, if it were not a palace but a chicken coop and rain started, I might creep into the chicken coop to avoid getting wet, and yet I would not call the chicken coop a palace out of gratitude to it for sheltering me from the rain. You laugh, you even say that in such circumstances a chicken coop is as good as a mansion. Yes, I answer, if one had to live simply to avoid getting wet.

But what is to be done if I have taken it into my head that this is not the only object in life, and that if one must live one may as well live in a mansion. That is my choice, my desire. You will only eradicate it when you have changed my desire. Well, do change it, tempt me with something else, give me another ideal. But in the meantime, I will not take a chicken coop for a palace. Let the crystal edifice even be an idle dream, say it is inconsistent with the laws of nature and that I have invented it only through my own stupidity, through some old-fashioned irrational habits of my generation. But what do I care if it is inconsistent? Does it matter at all, since it exists in my desires, or rather exists as long as my desires exist? Perhaps you are laughing again? Laugh away; I will put up with all your laughter rather than pretend that I am satisfied when I am hungry. I know, anyway, that I will not be appeased with a compromise, with an endlessly recurring zero, simply because it is consistent with the laws of nature and *really* exists. I will not accept as the crown of my desires a block of buildings with apartments for the poor on a lease of a thousand years and, to take care of any contingency, a dentist's shingle hanging out. Destroy my desires, eradicate my ideals, show me something better, and I will follow you. You may say, perhaps, that it is not worth your getting involved in it; but in that case, after all, I can give you the same answer. We are discussing things seriously; but if you won't deign to give me your attention, then, after all, I won't speak to you, I do have my underground.

But while I am still alive and have desires I would rather my hand were withered than to let it bring one brick to such a building! Don't remind me that I have just rejected the crystal edifice for the sole reason that one cannot put out one's tongue at it. I did not say it at all because I am so fond of putting my tongue out. Perhaps the only thing I resented was that of all your edifices up to now, there has not been a single one at which one could not put out one's tongue. On the contrary, I would let my tongue be cut off out of sheer gratitude if things could be so arranged that I myself would lose all desire to put it out. What do I care that things cannot be so arranged, and that one must be satisfied with model apartments? Why then am I made with such desires? Can I have been made simply in order to come to the conclusion that the whole way I am made is a swindle? Can this be my whole purpose? I do not believe it.

But do you know what? I am convinced that we underground folk ought to be kept in tow. Though we may be able to sit underground forty years without speaking, when we do come out into the light of day and break out we talk and talk and talk.

XI

The long and the short of it is, gentlemen, that it is better to do nothing! Better conscious inertial! And so hurrah for underground!

Though I have said that I envy the normal man to the point of exasperation, yet I would not care to be in his place as he is now (though I will not stop envying him. No, no; anyway the underground life is more advantageous!) There, at any rate, one can— Bah! But after all, even now I am lying! I am lying because I know myself as surely as two times two makes four, that it is not at all underground that is better, but something different, quite different, for which I long but which I cannot find! Damn underground!

I will tell you another thing that would be better, and that is, if I myself believed even an iota of what I have just written. I swear to you, gentlemen, that I do not really believe one thing, not even one word, of what I have just written. That is, I believe it, perhaps, but at the same time, I feel and suspect that I am lying myself blue in the face.

"Then why have you written all this?" you will say to me.

"I ought to put you underground for forty years without anything to do and then come to you to find out what stage you have reached! How can a man be left alone with nothing to do for forty years?"

"Isn't that shameful, isn't that humiliating?" you will say, perhaps, shaking your heads contemptuously. "You long for life and try to settle the problems of life by a logical tangle. And how tiresome, how insolent your outbursts are, and at the same time, how scared you are. You talk nonsense and are pleased with it; you say impudent things and are constantly afraid of them and apologizing for them. You declare that you are afraid of nothing and at the same time try to ingratiate yourself with us. You declare that you are gnashing your teeth and at the same time you try to be witty so as to amuse us. You know that your witticisms are not witty, but you are evidently well satisfied with their literary value. You may perhaps really have suffered, but you have no respect whatsoever for your own suffering. You may be truthful in what you have said but you have no modesty; out of the pettiest vanity you bring your truth to public exposure, to the market place, to ignominy. You doubtlessly mean to say something, but hide your real meaning for fear, because you lack the resolution to say it, and only have a cowardly impudence. You boast of consciousness, but you are unsure of your ground, for though your mind works, yet your heart is corrupted by depravity, and you cannot have a full, genuine consciousness without a pure heart. And how tiresome you are, how you thrust yourself on people and grimace! Lies, lies, lies!"

Of course I myself have made up just now all the things you say. That, too, is from underground. For forty years I have been listening to your words there through a crack under the floor. I have invented them myself. After all there was nothing else I could invent. It is no wonder that I have learned them by heart and that it has taken a literary form.

But can you really be so credulous as to think that I will print all this and give it to you to read too? And another problem; why do I really call you "gentlemen," Why do I address you as though you really were my readers? Such declarations as I intend to make are never printed nor given to other people to read. Anyway, I am not strong-minded enough for that, and I don't see why I should be. But you see a fancy has oc-curred to me and I want to fulfill it at all costs. Let me explain.

Every man has some reminiscences which he would not tell to everyone, but only to his friends. He has others which he would not reveal even to his friends, but only to him-self, and that in secret. But finally there are still others which a man is even afraid to tell himself, and every decent man has a considerable number of such things stored away. That is, one can even say that the more decent he is, the greater the number of such things in his mind. Anyway, I have only lately decided to remember some of my early adventures. Till now I have always avoided them, even with a certain uneasiness. Now, however, when I am not only recalling them, but have actually decided to write them down, I want to try the experiment whether one can be perfectly frank, even with one-self, and not take fright at the whole truth. I will observe, parenthetically, that Heine maintains that a true autobiography is almost an impossibility, and that man is bound to lie about himself. He considers that Rousseau certainly told lies about himself in his con-fessions, and even intentionally lied, out of vanity. I am convinced that Heine is right; I understand very well that sometimes one may, just out of sheer vanity, attribute regular crimes to oneself, and indeed I can very well conceive that kind of vanity. But Heine judged people who made their confessions to the public. I, however, am writing for my-self, and wish to declare once and for all that if I write as though I were addressing read-ers, that is simply because it is easier for me to write in that way. It is merely a question of form, only an empty form—I shall never have readers. I have made this plain already.

I don't wish to be hampered by any restrictions in compiling my notes. I shall not attempt any system or method. I will jot things down as I remember them.

But here, perhaps, someone will take me at my word and ask me: if you really don't count on readers, why do you make such compacts with yourself—and on paper too—that is, that you won't attempt any system or method, that you will jot things down as you remember them, etc., etc.? Why do you keep explaining? Why do you keep apologizing?

Well, there it is, I answer.

Incidentally, there is a whole psychological system in this. Or, perhaps, I am sim-ply a coward. And perhaps also, that I purposely imagine an audience before me in or-der to conduct myself in a more dignified manner while I am jotting things down. There are perhaps thousands of reasons.

And here is still something else. What precisely is my object in writing? If it is not for the public, then after all, why should I not simply recall these incidents in my own mind without putting them down on paper?

Quite so; but yet it is somehow more dignified on paper. There is something more impressive in it; I will be able to criticize myself better and improve my style. Besides, perhaps I will really get relief from writing. Today, for instance, I am partic-ularly oppressed by a certain memory from the distant past. It came back to my mind vividly a few days ago, and since then, has remained with me like an annoying tune that one cannot get rid of. And yet I must get rid of it. I have hundreds of such memories, but at times some single one stands out from the hundreds and oppresses me. For some reason I believe that if I write it down I will get rid of it. Why not try?

Besides, I am bored, and I never do anything. Writing will really be a sort of work. They say work makes man kindhearted and honest. Well, here is a chance for me, anyway.

It is snowing today. A wet, yellow, dingy snow. It fell yesterday too and a few days ago. I rather think that I remembered that incident which I cannot shake off now, apropos of the wet snow. And so let it be a story apropos of the wet snow.

Part Two
APROPOS OF THE WET SNOW

> When from the gloom of corruption
> I delivered your fallen soul
> With the ardent speech of conviction;
> And, full of profound torment,
> Wringing your hands, you cursed
> The vice that ensnared you;
> When, with memories punishing
> Forgetful conscience
> You told me the tale
> Of all that happened before me,
> And suddenly, covering your face,
> Full of shame and horror,
> You tearfully resolved,
> Outraged, shocked. . . .
> *Etc., etc., etc.*
>
> *From the poetry of N. A. Nekrasov.[2]*

I

At that time I was only twenty-four. My life was even then gloomy, disorganized, and solitary to the point of savagery. I made friends with no one and even avoided talking, and hid myself in my corner more and more. At work in the office I even tried never to look at anyone, and I was very well aware that my colleagues looked upon me, not only as a crank, but looked upon me—so I always thought—seemed to look upon me with a sort of loathing. I sometimes wondered why no one except me thought that he was looked upon with loathing. One of our clerks had a repulsive, pock-marked face, which even looked villainous. I believe I would not have dared to look at anyone with such an unsightly face. Another had a uniform so worn that there was an unpleasant smell near him. Yet not one of these gentlemen was disconcerted either by his clothes or his face or in some moral sense. Neither of them imagined that he was looked at with loathing, and even if he had imagined it, it would not have mattered to him, so long as his superiors did not look at him in that way. It is perfectly clear to me now that, owing to my unbounded vanity and, probably, to the high standard I set for my-

2. A poet and journalist (1827–1878) known for his compassionate attention to the sufferings of the peasantry.

self, I very often looked at myself with furious discontent, which verged on loathing, and so I inwardly attributed the same view to everyone. For instance, I hated my face; I thought it disgusting, and even suspected that there was something base in its expression and therefore every time I turned up at the office I painfully tried to behave as independently as possible so that I might not be suspected of being base, and to give my face as noble an expression as possible. "Let my face even be ugly," I thought, "but let it be noble, expressive, and, above all, *extremely* intelligent." But I was absolutely and painfully certain that my face could never express those perfections; but what was worst of all, I thought it positively stupid-looking. And I would have been quite satisfied if I could have looked intelligent. In fact, I would even have put up with looking base if, at the same time, my face could have been thought terribly intelligent.

Of course, I hated all my fellow-clerks, one and all, and I despised them all, yet at the same time I was, as it were, afraid of them. It happened at times that I even thought more highly of them than of myself. It somehow happened quite suddenly then that I alternated between despising them and thinking them superior to myself. A cultivated and decent man cannot be vain without setting an inordinately high standard for himself, and without despising himself at certain moments to the point of hatred. But whether I despised them or thought them superior I dropped my eyes almost every time I met anyone. I even made experiments whether I could face So-and-So's looking at me, and I was always the first to drop my eyes. This tormented me to the point of frenzy. I was also morbidly afraid of being ridiculous, and so I slavishly worshipped the conventional in everything external. I loved to fall into the common rut, and had a whole-hearted terror of any kind of eccentricity in myself. But how could I live up to it? I was morbidly cultivated as a cultivated man of our age should be. They were all dull, and as like one another as so many sheep. Perhaps I was the only one in the office who constantly thought that I was a coward and a slave, and I thought it precisely because I was cultivated. But I did not only think it, in actuality it was really so. I was a coward and a slave. I say this without the slightest embarrassment. Every decent man in our age must be a coward and a slave. That is his normal condition. I am profoundly convinced of that. He is made that way and is constructed for that very purpose. And not only at the present time owing to some casual circumstances, but always, at all times, a decent man must be a coward and a slave. That is the law of nature for all decent people on the earth. If any one of them happens to be brave about something, he need not be comforted or carried away by that; he will funk out just the same before something else. That is how it invariably and inevitably ends. Only asses and mules are brave, and even they are so only until they come up against the wall. It is not even worth while to pay attention to them. Because they don't mean anything at all.

Still another circumstance tormented me in those days: that no one resembled me and that I resembled no one else. "I am alone and they are *every one*," I thought—and pondered.

From that it can be seen that I was still an absolute child.

The very opposite sometimes happened. After all, how vile it sometimes seemed to have to go to the office; things reached such a point that I often came home ill. But all at once, for no rhyme or reason, there would come a phase of skepticism and indifference (everything happened to me in phases), and I would myself laugh at my intolerance and fastidiousness. I would reproach myself with being *romantic*. Sometimes I was unwilling to speak to anyone, while at other times I would not only talk, but even think of forming a friendship with them. All my fastidiousness would suddenly vanish for no rhyme or reason. Who knows, perhaps I never had really had it, and it had simply been affected, and gotten out of books. I have still not decided that question even now. Once I quite made friends with them, visited their homes, played preference, drank vodka, talked of promotions . . . But here let me make a digression.

We Russians, speaking generally, have never had those foolish transcendental German, and still more, French, romantics on whom nothing produces any effect; if there were an earthquake, if all France perished at the barricades, they would still be the same, they would not even change for decency's sake, but would still go on singing their transcendental songs, so to speak, to the hour of their death, because they are fools. We, in Russia, have no fools; that is well known. That is what distinguishes us from foreign lands. Consequently those transcendental natures do not exist among us in their pure form. We only think they do because our "positivistic" journalists and critics of that time, always on the hunt for Kostanzhoglos and Uncle Peter Ivaniches and foolishly accepting them as our ideal,[3] slandered our romantics taking them for the same transcendental sort that exists in Germany or France. On the contrary, the characteristics of our romantics are absolutely and directly opposed to the transcendental European type, and not a single European standard can be applied to them. (Allow me to make use of this word "romantic"—an old fashioned and much-respected word which has done good service and is familiar to all.) The characteristics of our romantics are to understand everything, *to see everything and often to see it incomparably more clearly than our most positivistic minds see it;* to refuse to accept anyone or anything, but at the same time not to despise anything; to give way, to yield, from policy; never to lose sight of a useful practical goal (such as rent-free government quarters, pensions, decorations), to keep their eye on that object through all the enthusiasms and volumes of lyrical poems, and at the same time to preserve "the sublime and the beautiful" inviolate within them to the hour of their death, and also, incidentally, to preserve themselves wrapped in cotton, like some precious jewel if only for the benefit of "the sublime and the beautiful." Our romantic is a man of great breadth and the greatest rogue of all our rogues, I assure you. I can even assure you from experience. Of course all that occurs if he is intelligent. But what am I saying! The romantic is always intelligent, and I only meant to observe that although we have had foolish romantics they don't count, and they were only so because in the flower of their youth they degenerated completely into Germans, and to preserve their precious jewel more comfortably, settled somewhere out there—by preference in Weimar or the Black Forest. I, for instance, genuinely despised my official work and did not openly abuse it simply through necessity because I was in it myself and got a salary for it. And, as a result, take note, I did not openly abuse it. Our romantic would rather go out of his mind (which incidentally happened very rarely) than abuse it, unless he had some other career in view; and he is never kicked out, unless, of course, he is taken to the lunatic asylum as "the King of Spain" and then only if he went very mad. But after all, it is only the thin, fair people who go out of their minds in Russia. Innumerable romantics later in life rise to considerable rank in the service. Their versatility is remarkable! And what a faculty they have for the most contradictory sensations! I was comforted by those thoughts even in those days, and I am so still. That is why there are so many "broad natures" among us who never lose their ideal even in

---

3. Good-hearted, efficient administrators in novels by Dostoevsky's older contemporaries Nikolai Gogol and Ivan Goncharov.

the depths of degradation; and though they never lift a finger for their ideal, though they are arrant thieves and robbers, yet they tearfully cherish their first ideal and are extraordinarily honest at heart. Yes, only among us can the most arrant rogue be absolutely and even loftily honest at heart without in the least ceasing to be a rogue. I repeat, our romantics, after all, frequently become such accomplished rascals (I use the term "rascals" affectionately), suddenly display such a sense of reality and practical knowledge, that their bewildered superiors and the public can only gape in amazement at them.

Their many-sidedness is really astounding, and goodness knows what it may turn itself into under future circumstances, and what lies in store for us later on. They are good stuff! I do not say this out of any foolish or boastful patriotism. But I feel sure that you are again imagining that I am joking. Or perhaps it's just the contrary, and you are convinced that I really think so. Anyway, gentlemen, I shall welcome both views as an honor and a special favor. And do forgive my digression.

I did not, of course, maintain a friendship with my comrades and soon was at loggerheads with them, and in my youthful inexperience I even gave up bowing to them, as though I had cut off all relations. That, however, only happened to me once. As a rule, I was always alone.

In the first place, at home, I spent most of my time reading. I tried to stifle all that was continually seething within me by means of external sensations. And the only source of external sensation possible for me was reading. Reading was a great help, of course, it excited, delighted and tormented me. But at times it bored me terribly. One longed for movement just the same, and I plunged all at once into dark, subterranean, loathsome—not vice but petty vice. My petty passions were acute, smarting, from my continual sickly irritability. I had hysterical fits, with tears and convulsions. I had no resource except reading—that is, there was then nothing in my surroundings which I could respect and which attracted me. I was overwhelmed with depression, too; I had an hysterical craving for contradictions and for contrast, and so I took to vice. I have not said all this to justify myself, after all—but no, I am lying. I did want to justify myself. I make that little observation for my own benefit, gentlemen. I don't want to lie. I vowed to myself I would not.

I indulged my vice in solitude at night, furtively, timidly, filthily, with a feeling of shame which never deserted me, even at the most loathsome moments, and which at such moments drove me to curses. Even then I already had the underground in my soul. I was terribly afraid of being seen, of being met, of being recognized. I visited various completely obscure places.

One night as I was passing a tavern, I saw through a lighted window some gentlemen fighting with billiard cues, and saw one of them thrown out of the window. At another time I would have felt very much disgusted, but then I was suddenly in such a mood that I actually envied the gentleman thrown out of the window, and I envied him so much that I even went into the tavern and into the billiard-room. "Perhaps," I thought, "I'll have a fight, too, and they'll throw me out of the window."

I was not drunk, but what is one to do—after all, depression will drive a man to such a pitch of hysteria. But nothing happened. It seemed that I was not even equal to being thrown out of the window and I went away without having fought.

An officer put me in my place from the very first moment.

I was standing by the billiard-table and in my ignorance blocking up the way, and he wanted to pass; he took me by the shoulders and without a word—without a warning or an explanation—moved me from where I was standing to another spot and passed by as though he had not noticed me. I could even have forgiven blows, but I absolutely could not forgive his having moved me and so completely failing to notice me.

Devil knows what I would then have given for a real regular quarrel—a more decent, a more *literary* one, so to speak. I had been treated like a fly. This officer was over six feet, while I am short and thin. But the quarrel was in my hands. I had only to protest and I certainly would have been thrown out of the window. But I changed my mind and preferred to beat a resentful retreat.

I went out of the tavern straight home, confused and troubled, and the next night I continued with my petty vices, still more furtively, abjectly and miserably than before, as it were, with tears in my eyes—but still I did continue them. Don't imagine, though, that I funked out on the officer through cowardice. I have never been a coward at heart, though I have always been a coward in action. Don't be in a hurry to laugh. There is an explanation for it. I have an explanation for everything, you may be sure.

Oh, if only that officer had been one of the sort who would consent to fight a duel! But no, he was one of those gentlemen (alas, long extinct!) who preferred fighting with cues, or, like Gogol's Lieutenant Pirogov,[4] appealing to the police. They did not fight duels and would have thought a duel with a civilian like me an utterly unseemly procedure in any case—and they looked upon the duel altogether as something impossible, something free-thinking and French, but they were quite ready to insult people, especially when they were over six feet.

I did not funk out through cowardice here but through unbounded vanity. I was not afraid of his six feet, not of getting a sound thrashing and being thrown out of the window; I would probably have had sufficient physical courage; but I lacked sufficient moral courage. What I was afraid of was that everyone present, from the insolent marker down to the lowest little stinking pimply clerk hanging around in a greasy collar, would jeer at me and fail to understand when I began to protest and to address them in literary language. For even now we cannot, after all, speak of the point of honor—not of honor, but of the point of honor (*point d'honneur*)—except in literary language. You cannot allude to the "point of honor" in ordinary language. I was fully convinced (the sense of reality, in spite of all romanticism!) that they would all simply split their sides with laughter and that the officer would not simply, that is, not uninsultingly, beat me, but would certainly prod me in the back with his knee, kick me round the billiard-table that way and only then perhaps have pity and throw me out of the window. Of course, this trivial incident could not have ended like that with me. I often met that officer afterward in the street and observed him very carefully. I am not quite sure whether he recognized me. I imagine not; I judge from certain signs. But I—I stared at him with spite and hatred and so it went on—for several years! My resentment even grew deeper with the years. At first I began making stealthy inquiries about this officer. It was difficult for me to do so, for I knew no one. But one day I heard someone call him by his name in the street when I was following him at a distance, just as though I were tied to him—and so I learned his surname. Another time I followed him to his flat, and for a few pennies learned from the porter where he lived, on which floor, whether he lived alone or with others, and so on—in fact, everything one could learn from a porter. One morning, though I had never tried to write anything before, it suddenly occurred to me to describe this officer in the form

---

4. A cowardly officer in Gogol's story "Nevsky Prospect," who doesn't stand up for his own honor.

of an exposé, in a satire, in a tale. I wrote the tale with relish. I did expose him. I slandered him; at first I so altered his name that it could easily be recognized but on second thought I changed it, and sent the story to the *Annals of the Fatherland*. But at that time such exposés were not yet the fashion and my story was not printed. That was a great vexation to me. Sometimes I was positively choked with resentment. At last I decided to challenge my enemy to a duel. I composed a splendid, charming letter to him, imploring him to apologize to me, and hinting rather plainly at a duel in case of refusal. The letter was so composed that if the officer had had the least understanding of the "sublime and the beautiful" he would certainly have rushed to me to fling himself on my neck and to offer me his friendship. And how fine that would have been! How we would have gotten along! How we would have gotten along! "He could have shielded me with his higher rank, while I could have improved his mind with my culture, and, well—my ideas, and all sorts of things might have happened." Just think, this was two years after his insult to me, and my challenge was the most ridiculous anachronism, in spite of all the ingenuity of my letter in disguising and explaining away the anachronism. But, thank God (to this day I thank the Almighty with tears in my eyes), I did not send the letter to him. Cold shivers run down my back when I think of what might have happened if I had sent it. And all at once I revenged myself in the simplest way, by a stroke of genius! A brilliant thought suddenly dawned upon me. Sometimes on holidays I used to stroll along the sunny side of the Nevsky between three and four in the afternoon. That is, I did not stroll so much as experience innumerable torments, humiliations and resentments; but no doubt that was just what I wanted. I used to wriggle like an eel among the passers-by in the most unbecoming fashion, continually moving aside to make way for generals, for officers of the Guards and the Hussars, or for ladies. In those minutes I used to feel a convulsive twinge at my heart, and hot all the way down my back at the mere thought of the wretchedness of my dress, of the wretchedness and vulgarity of my little wriggling figure. This was a regular martyrdom, a continual, intolerable humiliation at the thought, which passed into an incessant and direct sensation, that I was a fly in the eyes of this whole world, a nasty, disgusting fly—more intelligent, more cultured, more noble than any of them, of course, but a fly that was continually making way for everyone, insulted and humiliated by everyone. Why I inflicted this torment upon myself, why I went to the Nevsky, I don't know. I felt simply *drawn* there at every possible opportunity.

Already then I began to experience a rush of the enjoyment of which I spoke in the first chapter. After my affair with the officer I felt even more drawn there than before: it was on the Nevsky that I met him most frequently, it was *there* that I could admire him. He, too, went there chiefly on holidays. He, too, made way for generals and persons of high rank, and he, too, shifted among them like an eel; but people like me, or even neater than I, he simply walked over; he made straight for them as though there was nothing but empty space before him, and never, under any circumstances, moved aside. I gloated over my resentment watching him and—resentfully made way for him every time. It tormented me that even in the street I could not be on an even footing with him. "Why must you invariably be the first to move aside?" I kept asking myself in hysterical rage, waking up sometimes at three o'clock in the morning. "Why precisely you and not he? After all, there's no regulation about it; after all, there's no written law about it. Let the making way be equal as it usually is when refined people meet; he moves halfway and you move halfway; you pass with mutual respect." But that never happened, and I always made way, while he did not even notice I moved aside for him. And lo and behold the most astounding idea dawned upon me! "What," I thought, "if I meet him and—don't move aside? What if I don't move

aside on purpose, even if I were to bump into him? How would that be?" This audacious idea little by little took such a hold on me that it gave me no peace. I dreamt of
it continually, terribly, and I purposely went to the Nevsky more frequently in order to
picture more vividly how I would do it when I did do it. I was delighted. This plan
seemed to me more and more practical and possible. "Of course I will not really bump
him," I thought, already more good-natured in my joy. "I will simply not turn aside,
will bump against him, not very violently, but just shouldering each other—just as
much as decency permits. I will bump him just as much as he bumps me." At last I
made up my mind completely. But my preparations took a great deal of time. To begin with, when I carried out my plan I would have to look rather more decent, and I
had to think of my clothes. "In any case, if, for instance, there were any sort of public
scandal (and the public there is of the most *superflu:*[5] the Countess walks there;
Prince D. walks there; the whole literary world is there), I would have to be well
dressed; that inspires respect and of itself puts us in some way on equal footing in the
eyes of high society." With that in mind I asked for my salary in advance, and bought
at Churkin's a pair of black gloves and a decent hat. Black gloves seemed to me both
more dignified and *bon ton* than the lemon-colored ones which I had contemplated at
first. "The color is too gaudy, it looks as though one were trying to be conspicuous,"
and I did not take the lemon-colored ones. I had gotten ready a good shirt, with the
bone studs, long beforehand; but my overcoat very much delayed me. The coat in itself was a very good one, it kept me warm; but it was wadded and it had a raccoon
collar which was the height of vulgarity. I had to change the collar at any sacrifice,
and to have a beaver one like an officer's. For this purpose I began visiting the
Gostiny Dvor and after several attempts I lit on a piece of cheap German beaver.
Though these German beavers very soon wear out and look shabby, at first, when
new, they look exceedingly well, and after all, I only needed it for one occasion. I
asked the price; even so, it was too expensive. After thinking it over thoroughly I decided to sell my raccoon collar. The rest of the money—a considerable sum for me, I
decided to borrow from Anton Antonich Syetochkin, my superior, an unassuming
person, but grave and dependable. He never lent money to anyone, but I had, on entering the service, been specially recommended to him by an important personage
who had got me my job. I was terribly worried. To borrow from Anton Antonich
seemed to me monstrous and shameful. I did not sleep for two or three nights, and indeed I did not sleep well in general at that time, I was in a fever; I had a vague sinking
at my heart or suddenly it would start to throb, throb, throb! Anton Antonich was at
first surprised, then he frowned, then he reflected, and did after all lend me the
money, receiving from me a written authorization to take from my salary a fortnight
later the sum that he had lent me. In this way everything was at last ready. The handsome beaver was established in place of the mean-looking raccoon, and I began by
degrees to get to work. It would never have done to act offhand, at random; the plan
had to be carried out skillfully, by degrees. But I must confess that after many efforts
I almost even began to despair; we could not run into each other and that is all there
was to it. I made every preparation, I was quite determined—it seemed as though we
would run into one another directly—and before I knew what I was doing I had
stepped aside for him again and he had passed without noticing me. I even prayed as I
approached him that God would grant me determination. One time I had made up my

5. Useless, redundant (French).

mind thoroughly, but it ended in my stumbling and falling at his feet because at the very last instant when I was only some six inches from him my courage failed me. He very calmly stepped over me, while I flew to one side like a ball. That night I was ill again, feverish and delirious. And suddenly it ended most happily. The night before I had made up my mind not to carry out my fatal plan and to abandon it all, and with that goal in mind I went to the Nevsky for the last time, just to see how I would abandon it all. Suddenly, three paces from my enemy, I unexpectedly made up my mind— I closed my eyes, and we ran full tilt, shoulder to shoulder, into each other! I did not budge an inch and passed him on a perfectly equal footing! He did not even look round and pretended not to notice it; but he was only pretending, I am convinced of that. I am convinced of that to this day! Of course, I got the worst of it—he was stronger, but that was not the point. The point was that I had attained my goal, I had kept up my dignity. I had not yielded a step, and had put myself publicly on an equal social footing with him. I returned home feeling that I was perfectly avenged for everything. I was delighted. I was triumphant and sang Italian arias. Of course, I will not describe to you what happened to me three days later; if you have read my first chapter "Underground," you can guess for yourself. The officer was afterward transferred; I have not seen him now for fourteen years. What is the dear fellow doing now? Whom is he walking over?

II

But the period of my dissipation would end and I always felt terribly sick afterward. It was followed by remorse—I tried to drive it away; I felt too sick. By degrees, however, I grew used to that, too. I grew used to everything, that is, I did not really grow used to it, but rather I voluntarily resigned myself to enduring it. But I had a means of escape that reconciled everything—that was to find refuge in "the sublime and the beautiful," in dreams. Of course I was a terrible dreamer. I would dream for three months on end, tucked away in my corner, and you may believe me that at those moments I had no resemblance to the gentleman who, in his chicken-hearted anxiety, put a German beaver collar on his greatcoat. I suddenly became a hero. I would not have received my six-foot lieutenant even if he had called on me. I could not even picture him before me then. What were my dreams and how I could satisfy myself with them, it is hard to say now, but at the time I did satisfy myself with them, to some extent. Dreams were particularly sweet and vivid after a little vice; they came with remorse and with tears, with curses and transports. There were moments of such positive intoxication, of such happiness, that there was not the faintest trace of irony within me, on my honor. I had faith, hope, love. That is just it. I believed blindly at such times that by some miracle, through some external circumstance, all this would suddenly open out, expand; that suddenly a vista of suitable activity—beneficial, good, and above all, *ready-made* (what sort of activity I had no idea, but the great thing was that it should be all ready for me)—would rise up before me, and I should come out into the light of day, almost riding a white horse and crowned with laurel. I could not conceive of a secondary role for myself, and for that reason I quite contentedly played the lowest one in reality. Either to be a hero or to grovel in the mud—there was nothing between. That was my ruin, for when I was in the mud I comforted myself with the thought that at other times I was a hero, and I took refuge in this hero for the mud: for an ordinary man, say, it is shameful to defile himself, but a hero is too noble to be utterly defiled, and so he might defile himself. It is worth noting that these attacks of "the sublime and the beautiful" visited me even during the period of vice and just at the times when I had sunk to the very bottom. They came in separate spurts, as though reminding me of themselves, but did not banish the vice by their appearance. On the contrary, they seemed to add a zest to it by contrast, and were only sufficiently present to serve as an appetizing sauce. That sauce was made up of contradictions and sufferings, of agonizing inward analysis, and all these torments and pin-pricks lent my vice a certain piquancy, even a significance—in short, completely fulfilled the function of a good sauce. There was even a certain depth of meaning in it. And I could hardly have restrained myself to the simple, vulgar, direct clerk-like vice and have endured all the filthiness of it. What could have attracted me about it then and have driven me at night into the street? No, I had a noble loophole for everything.

And what love, oh Lord, what love I felt at times in those dreams of mine! In those "flights into the sublime and the beautiful"; though it was fantastic love, though it was never applied to anything human in reality, yet there was so much of this love that afterward one did not even feel the impulse to apply it in reality; that would have been a superfluous luxury. Everything, however, always passed satisfactorily by a lazy and fascinating transition into the sphere of art; that is, into the beautiful forms of life, ready made, violently stolen from the poets and novelists and adapted to all sorts of needs and uses. I, for instance, was triumphant over everyone; everyone, of course, lay in the dust and was forced to recognize my superiority spontaneously, and I forgave them all. I, a famous poet, and a courtier, fell in love; I inherited countless millions and immediately devoted them to humanity, and at the same time I confessed before all the people my shameful deeds, which, of course, were not merely shameful, but contained an enormous amount of "the sublime and the beautiful," something in the Manfred[6] style. Everyone would weep and kiss me (what idiots they would be if they did not), while I would go barefoot and hungry preaching new ideas and fighting a victorious Austerlitz against the reactionaries. Then a march would sound, an amnesty would be declared, the Pope would agree to retire from Rome to Brazil; then there would be a ball for the whole of Italy at the Villa Borghese on the shores of Lake Como, Lake Como being for that purpose transferred to the neighborhood of Rome; then would come a scene in the bushes, etc., etc.—as though you did not know all about it! You will say that it is vulgar and base to drag all this into public after all the tears and raptures I have myself admitted. But why is it base? Can you imagine that I am ashamed of it all, and that is was stupider than anything in your life, gentlemen? And I can assure you that some of these fancies were by no means badly composed. Not everything took place on the shores of Lake Como. And yet you are right—it really is vulgar and base. And what is most base of all is that I have now started to justify myself to you. And even more base than that is my making this remark now. But that's enough, or, after all, there will be no end to it; each step will be more base than the last.

I could never stand more than three months of dreaming at a time without feeling an irresistible desire to plunge into society. To plunge into society meant to visit my superior, Anton Antonich Syetochkin. He was the only permanent acquaintance I have had in my life, and I even wonder at the fact myself now. But I even went to see him only when that phase came over me, and when my dreams had reached such a point of bliss that it became essential to embrace my fellows and all mankind immediately. And for that purpose I needed at least one human being at hand who actually

---

6. Brooding, romantic title character in a verse tragedy by Byron.

existed. I had to call on Anton Antonich, however, on Tuesday—his at-home day; so I always had to adjust my passionate desire to embrace humanity so that it might fall on a Tuesday. This Anton Antonich lived on the fourth floor in a house in Five Corners, in four low-pitched rooms of a particularly frugal and sallow appearance, one smaller than the next. He had two daughters and their aunt, who used to pour out the tea. Of the daughters one was thirteen and another fourteen, they both had snub noses, and I was terribly embarrassed by them because they were always whispering and giggling together. The master of the house usually sat in his study on a leather couch in front of the table, with some gray-headed gentleman, usually a colleague from our office or even some other department. I never saw more than two or three visitors there, and those always the same. They talked about the excise duty, about business in the senate, about salaries, about promotions, about His Excellency, and the best means of pleasing him, and so on, and so on. I had the patience to sit like a fool beside these people for four hours at a stretch, listening to them without knowing what to say to them or venturing to say a word. I became stupefied; several times I felt myself perspiring. I was overcome by a sort of paralysis; but that was pleasant and useful for me. On returning home I deferred for a time my desire to embrace all mankind.

I had, however, one other acquaintence of a sort, Simonov, who was an old schoolfellow. Indeed I had a number of schoolfellows in Petersburg, but I did not associate with them and had even given up nodding to them in the street. Perhaps I even transferred into the department I was in simply to avoid their company and to cut off at one stroke all connection with my hateful childhood. Curses on that school and all those terrible years of penal servitude! In short, I parted from my schoolfellows as soon as I got out into the world. There were two or three left to whom I nodded in the street. One of them was Simonov, who had been in no way distinguished at school, was of a quiet and even disposition; but I discovered in him a certain independence of character and even honesty. I don't even suppose that he was particularly limited. I had at one time spent some rather soulful moments with him, but these had not lasted long and had somehow been suddenly clouded over. He was evidently uncomfortable at these reminiscences, and was, it seemed, always afraid that I might take up the same tone again. I suspected that he had an aversion for me, but I still went on going to see him, not being completely certain of it.

And so on one occasion, on a Thursday, unable to endure my solitude and knowing that it was Thursday Anton Antonich's door would be closed, I thought of Simonov. Climbing up four floors to his place, I was thinking that I made the man uncomfortable and that it was a mistake to go to see him. But as it always happened that such reflections impelled me even more strongly, as though purposely, to put myself into a false position, I went in. It was almost a year since I had last seen Simonov.

III

I found two more of my old schoolfellows with him. They seemed to be discussing an important matter. All of them scarcely took any notice of my entrance, which was strange, for I had not seen them for years. Evidently they looked upon me as something on the level of a common fly. I had not been treated like that even at school, although everybody hated me there. I knew, of course, that they must despise me now for my lack of success in the service, and for having let myself sink so low, going about badly dressed and so on which seemed to them a sign of my inaptitude and insignificance. But nevertheless I had not expected such contempt. Simonov even seemed surprised at my turning up. Even in the old days he had always seemed surprised at my coming. All this disconcerted me; I sat down, feeling rather miserable, and began listening to what they were saying.

They were engaged in an earnest and even heated discussion about a farewell dinner these gentlemen wanted to arrange together the very next day for their friend Zverkov, an officer in the army, who was going away to a distant province. Monsieur Zverkov had been all the time at school with me too. I had begun to hate him particularly in the upper classes. In the lower classes he had simply been a pretty, playful boy whom everybody liked. I had hated him, however, even in the lower classes, just because he was a pretty and playful boy. He was always consistently poor in his work, and got worse and worse as he went on; nevertheless he was successfully graduated as influence was exerted on his behalf. During his last year at school he inherited an estate of two hundred serfs, and as almost all of us were poor he even started to boast before us. He was vulgar to the worst degree, but nevertheless he was a good-natured fellow, even when he boasted. In spite of superficial, fantastic and rhetorical notions of honor and dignity, all but a very few of us positively grovelled before Zverkov, and the more so the more he boasted. And they did not grovel for any advantage, but simply because he had been favored by the gifts of nature. Moreover, we came somehow to accept the idea that Zverkov was a specialist in regard to tact and good manners. That particularly infuriated me. I hated the sharp, self-confident tone of his voice, his admiration for his own witticisms, which were terribly stupid, though he was bold in his expressions; I hated his handsome but stupid face (for which I would, however, have gladly exchanged my *intelligent* one), and the free-and-easy military manners in fashion in the 'forties. I hated the way in which he used to talk of his future conquests of women (he did not venture to begin with women until he had officer's epaulettes and was looking forward to them with impatience), and boasted of the duels he would constantly be fighting. I remember how I, invariably so taciturn, suddenly attacked Zverkov, when one day he talked at a leisure moment with his schoolfellows of the affairs he would have in the future and growing as sportive as a puppy in the sun, he all at once declared that he would not leave a single village girl on his estate unnoticed, that that was his *droit de seigneur*,[7] and that if the peasants dared to protest he would have them all flogged and double their taxes, the bearded rascals. Our servile rabble applauded, but I attacked him, not at all out of compassion for the girls and their fathers, but simply because they were applauding such a beetle. I got the better of him on that occasion, but though Zverkov was stupid he was lively and impudent, and so laughed it off, and even in such a way that my victory was not really complete: the laugh was on his side. He got the better of me on several occasions afterward, but without malice, somehow just in jest, casually, in fun. I remained maliciously and contemptuously silent. When we left school he made advances to me; I did not rebuff them much, for I was flattered, but we soon parted naturally. Afterward I heard of his barrack-room success as a lieutenant, and of the *fast life* he was leading. Then there came other rumors—of his *successes* in the service. By then he no longer greeted me in the street, and I suspected that he was afraid of compromising himself by greeting a person as insignificant as I. I also saw him once in the theatre, in the third tier of boxes. By then he was a staff officer. He was twisting and twirling about, ingratiating himself with the daughters of an ancient general. In three years his looks had gotten

---

7. A feudal lord's right to have sex with women on his estate on their wedding night.

considerably worse, though he was still rather handsome and smart. He had somehow swelled, started to put on weight. One could see that by the time he was thirty he would be completely fat. So it was, finally, to this Zverkov that my schoolfellows were going to give a dinner on his departure. They had kept up with him for those three years, though privately they did not consider themselves on an equal footing with him, I am convinced of that.

Of Simonov's two visitors, one was Ferfichkin, a Russianized German—a little fellow with the face of a monkey, a blockhead who was always deriding everyone, a very bitter enemy of mine from our days in the lower classes—a vulgar, impudent, boastful fellow, who affected a most sensitive feeling of personal honor, though, of course, he was a wretched little coward at heart. He was one of those admirers of Zverkov who made up to the latter out of calculation, and often borrowed money from him. Simonov's other visitor, Trudolyubov, was a person in no way remarkable—a military lad, tall with a cold face, quite honest. But he worshipped success of every sort, and was only capable of thinking of promotion. He was some distant relation of Zverkov and this, foolish as it seems, gave him a certain importance among us. He never thought me of any consequence whatever; while his behavior to me was not quite courteous, it was tolerable.

"Well then, with seven roubles each," said Trudolyubov, "twenty-one *roups* from the three of us, we can dine well. Zverkov, of course, won't pay."

"Of course not, since we are inviting him," Simonov decided.

"Can you imagine," Ferfichkin interrupted hotly and conceitedly, like some insolent flunky boasting of his master the general's decorations, "can you imagine that Zverkov will let us pay alone? He will accept from delicacy, but he will order *a half case* on his own."

"Why do we need half a case for the four of us?" observed Trudolyubov, taking notice only of the half case.

"So the three of us, with Zverkov for the fourth, twenty-one roubles, at the Hôtel de Paris at five o'clock tomorrow," Simonov, who had been asked to make the arrangements, concluded finally.

"How about twenty-one roubles?" I asked in some agitation, even offended, apparently; "if you count me it will be twenty-eight, not twenty-one roubles."

It seemed to me that to invite myself so suddenly and unexpectedly would be positively graceful, and that they would all be conquered at once and would look at me with respect.

"Do you want to join, too?" Simonov observed, with displeasure, and seemed to avoid looking at me. He knew me inside out.

It infuriated me that he knew me inside out.

"Why not? After all, I am an old schoolfellow of his too, I believe, and I must admit I feel offended that you have left me out," I said, boiling over again.

"And where were we to find you?" Ferfichkin put in roughly.

"You were never on good terms with Zverkov," Trudolyubov added, frowning. But I had already clutched at the idea and would not let go.

"I do not think that anyone has a right to judge that," I retorted in a shaking voice, as though God only knows what had happened. "Perhaps that is just my reason for wishing it now, that I have not always been on good terms with him."

"Oh, there's no making you out—with these refinements," Trudolyubov jeered.

"We'll put your name down," Simonov decided, addressing me. "Tomorrow at five o'clock at the Hotel de Paris."

"What about the money?" Ferfichkin began in an undertone, indicating me to Simonov, but he broke off, for even Simonov was embarrassed.

"That will do," said Trudolyubov, getting up. "If he wants to come so much, let him."

"But after all it's a private thing, between us friends," Ferfichkin said crossly, as he too picked up his hat. "It's not an official meeting. Perhaps we do not want you at all—"

They went away. Ferfichkin did not salute me in any way as he went out. Trudolyubov barely nodded. Simonov, with whom I remained alone, was in some state of vexed perplexity, and looked at me strangely. He did not sit down and did not ask me to.

"H'm—yes—tomorrow, then. Will you pay your share now? I just ask so as to know," he muttered in embarrassment.

I blazed up in anger but as I did so I remembered that I had owed Simonov fifteen roubles for ages—which I had, indeed, never forgotten, though I had not paid it.

"You will understand, Simonov, that I could have had no idea when I came here—I am very much vexed that I have forgotten—"

"All right, all right, it doesn't matter. You can pay tomorrow after the dinner. After all, I simply wanted to know—Please don't—"

He broke off and began pacing the room still more vexed. As he walked he began to thump with his heels and stomped even louder.

"Am I keeping you?" I asked, after two minutes of silence.

"Oh, no!" he said, starting, "that is—to be truthful—yes. I have to go and see someone—not far from here," he added in a sort of apologetic voice, somewhat ashamed.

"My goodness, but why didn't you say so?" I cried, seizing my cap with, incidentally, an astonishingly free-and-easy air, which was the last thing I would have expected of myself.

"After all, it's close by—not two paces away," Simonov repeated, accompanying me to the front door with a fussy air which did not suit him at all. "So five o'clock, punctually, tomorrow," he called down the stairs after me. He was very glad to get rid of me. I was in a fury.

"What possessed me, what possessed me to force myself upon them?" I gnashed my teeth, as I strode along the street. "For a scoundrel, a pig like that Zverkov! Of course, I had better not go; of course, I can just snap my fingers at them. I am not bound in any way. I'll send Simonov a note by tomorrow's post—"

But what made me furious was that I knew for certain that I would go, that I would purposely go; and the more tactless, the more ill-mannered my going would be, the more certainly I would go.

And there was even a positive obstacle to my going: I had no money. All I had altogether, was nine roubles. But I had to give seven of that to my servant, Apollon, for his monthly wages. That was all I paid him—he had to keep himself.

Not to pay him was impossible, considering his character. But I will talk about that fellow, about that plague of mine, another time.

However, I knew I would go after all and would not pay him his wages.

That night I had the most hideous dreams. No wonder; the whole evening I had been oppressed by memories of my days of penal servitude at school, and I could not shake them off. I was sent to the school by distant relations, upon whom I was dependent and of whom I have heard nothing since—they sent me there, a lonely, silent boy, already crushed by their reproaches, already troubled by doubt, and looking savagely at everything around him. My schoolfellows met me with spiteful and merciless jibes because I was not like any of them. But I could not endure their taunts; I could not give in to them as cheaply as they gave in to one another. I hated them from the first, and shut myself away from everyone in timid, wounded and disproportionate pride. Their coarseness revolted me. They laughed, cynically at my face, at my clumsy figure; and yet what stupid faces they themselves had. In our school the boys' faces somehow degenerated and grew stupider particularly. How many fine-looking boys came to us? In a few years they became repulsive looking. Even at sixteen I wondered at them morosely; even then I was struck by the pettiness of their thoughts, the stupidity of their pursuits, their games, their conversations. They had no understanding of such essential things, they took no interest in such striking, impressive subjects, that I could not help considering them inferior to myself. It was not wounded vanity that drove me to it, and for God's sake do not thrust upon me your hackneyed remarks, repeated to nausea, that "I was only a dreamer, while they even then understood real life." They understood nothing, they had no idea of real life, and I swear that that was what made me most indignant with them. On the contrary, the most obvious, striking reality they accepted with fantastic stupidity and even then had already begun to respect only success. Everything that was just, but oppressed and looked down upon, they laughed at cruelly and shamefully. They took rank for intelligence; even at sixteen they were already talking about a snug berth. Of course a great deal of it was due to their stupidity, to the bad examples that constantly surrounded them in their childhood and boyhood. They were monstrously depraved. Of course much of that, too, was superficial and much was only affected cynicism; of course there were glimpses of youth and freshness in them even beneath their depravity; but even that freshness was not attractive in them, and showed itself in a certain rakishness. I hated them terribly, though perhaps I was worse than any of them. They repaid me in kind, and did not conceal their aversion for me. But by then I did not want them to like me; on the contrary, I continually longed for them to humiliate me. To escape from their derision I purposely began to make all the progress I could with my studies and forced my way to the very top. This impressed them. Moreover, they all began to grasp slowly that I was already reading books none of them could read, and understood things (not forming part of our school curriculum) of which they had not even heard. They took a savage and sarcastic view of it, but were morally impressed, especially as the teachers began to notice me on those grounds. The mockery ceased but the hostility remained, and cold and strained relations were formed between us. In the end I could not stand it myself; with years a craving for society, for friends, developed in me. I attempted to get on friendly terms with some of my schoolfellows; but somehow or other my intimacy with them was always strained and soon ended of itself. Once, indeed, I did have a friend. But I was already a tyrant at heart; I wanted to exercise unlimited power over him; I tried to instil into him a contempt for his surroundings; I required of him a disdainful and complete break with those surroundings. I frightened him with my passionate affection; I reduced him to tears, to convulsions. He was a simple and devoted soul; but when he submitted to me completely I began to hate him immediately and rejected him—as though all I needed him for was to win a victory over him, to subjugate him and nothing else. But I could not subjugate all of them; my friend was not at all like them either, he was, in fact, a rare exception. The first thing I did on leaving school was to give up the special job for which I had been destined so as to break all ties, to curse my past and scatter it to the winds—And goodness knows why, after all that, I should drag myself to that Simonov!

Early next morning I roused myself and jumped out of bed with excitement, as though it were all about to happen at once. But I believed that some radical change in my life was coming, and would inevitably come that day. Owing to its rarity, perhaps, any external event, however trivial, always made me feel as though some radical change in my life would occur immediately. I went to the office as usual, however, but slipped away home two hours early to get ready. The important thing, I thought, is not to be the first to arrive, or they will think I was overjoyed at coming. But there were thousands of such important points to consider, and they all agitated me to the point of impotence. I polished my boots a second time with my own hands; nothing in the world would have induced Apollon to clean them twice a day, as he considered that it was more than his duties required of him. I stole the brushes to clean them from the passage, so that he would not detect it and then start to despise me. Then I minutely examined my clothes, and found that everything looked old, worn and threadbare. I had let myself get too slovenly. My uniform, perhaps, was in good shape, but I could hardly go out to dinner in my uniform. And the worst thing was that on the knee of my trousers was a big yellow stain. I had a foreboding that that stain would in itself deprive me of nine-tenths of my personal dignity. I knew, too, that it was stopping very low to think so. "But this is no time for thinking: now the real thing is beginning," I thought, and my heart sank. I knew, too, perfectly well even then, that I was monstrously exaggerating the facts. But how could I help it? I could not control myself and I was already shaking with fever. With despair I pictured to myself how coldly and disdainfully that "scoundrel" Zverkov would greet me; with what dull-witted, absolutely profound contempt the blockhead Trudolyubov would look at me; with what nasty insolence the beetle Ferfichkin would snigger at me in order to curry favor with Zverkov; how completely Simonov would take it all in, and how he would despise me for the abjectness of my vanity and faint-heartedness, and worst of all how paltry, *unliterary,* commonplace it would all be. Of course the best thing would be not to go at all. But that was the most impossible of all: once I feel impelled to do anything, I am completely drawn into it, head first. I would have jeered at myself ever afterward: "So you funked it, you funked the *real thing,* you funked it!" On the contrary, I passionately longed to show all that "rabble" that I was not at all such a coward as I pictured myself. What is more, even in the acutest paroxysm of this cowardly fever, I dreamed of getting the upper hand, of overcoming them, carrying them away, making them like me—if only for my "elevation of thought and unmistakable wit." They would abandon Zverkov, he would sit on one side, silent and ashamed, while I would crush Zverkov. Then, perhaps, I would be reconciled to him and toast our camaraderie; but what was most spiteful and insulting for me was that I knew even then, knew completely and for certain, that I needed nothing of all this really, that I did not really want to crush, to subdue, to attract them, and that I would be the first not to care a straw, really, for the result, even if I did achieve it. Oh, how I prayed to God for the day to pass quickly! In inexpressible anguish I went to the window, opened a pane and looked out into the turbid darkness of the thickly falling wet snow.

At last my wretched little wall clock hissed out five. I seized my hat trying not to look at Apollon, who had been all day expecting his month's wages, but in his pride was unwilling to be the first to speak about it. I slipped past him and out the door, and jumping into a high-class sledge, on which I spent my last half-rouble, I drove up in grand style to the Hôtel de Paris.

IV

I had already known the day before that I would be the first to arrive. But it was no longer a question of precedence.

Not only were they not there, but I even had difficulty finding our room. The table had still not been completely set. What did it mean? After a good many questions I finally ascertained from the waiters that the dinner had been ordered not for five, but for six o'clock. This was confirmed at the buffet too. I even felt ashamed to go on questioning them. It was still only twenty-five minutes past five. If they changed the dinner hour they ought in any case to have let me know—that is what the post is for, and not to have subjected me to "shame" both in my own eyes and—well, before the waiters. I sat down: the servant began to set the table; I felt even more insulted when he was present. Toward six o'clock they brought in candles, though there were lamps burning in the room. It had not occurred to the waiter, however, to bring them in at once when I arrived. In the next room, two gloomy, angry-looking persons were eating their dinners in silence at two different tables. There was a great deal of noise, even shouting, in a room farther away; one could hear the laughter of a crowd of people, and nasty little shrieks in French; there were ladies at the dinner. In short, it was sickening. I rarely passed a more unpleasant time, so much so that when they did arrive all together punctually at six I was for the first moment overjoyed to see them, as though they were my deliverers, and almost forgot it was incumbent upon me to look insulted.

Zverkov walked in at the head of them; evidently he was the leading spirit. He and all of them were laughing; but, seeing me, Zverkov drew himself up, walked up to me unhurriedly with a slight, rather jaunty bend from the waist, and shook hands with me in a friendly but not over-friendly fashion, with a sort of circumspect courtesy almost like a general's as though in giving me his hand he were warding off something. I had imagined, on the contrary, that as soon as he came in he would immediately break into his former thin, shrieking laugh and fall to making his insipid jokes and witticisms. I had been preparing for them ever since the previous day, but I had never expected such condescension, such high-official courtesy. So, then, he felt himself immeasurably superior to me in every respect! If he had only meant to insult me by that high-official tone, it would still not have mattered, I thought—I could pay him back for it one way or another. But what if, in reality, without the least desire to be offensive, that sheep's-head had seriously acquired the notion that he was immeasurably superior to me and could only look at me in a patronizing way? The very supposition made me gasp.

"I was surprised to hear of your desire to join us," he began, lisping and drawling, which was something new. "You and I seem to have seen nothing of one another. You fight shy of us. You shouldn't. We are not such terrible people as you think. Well, anyway, I am glad to renew our acquaintance."

And he turned carelessly to put down his hat on the window sill.

"Have you been waiting long?" Trudolyubov inquired.

"I arrived punctually at five o'clock as I was informed yesterday," I answered aloud, with an irritability that promised an imminent explosion.

"Didn't you let him know that we had changed the hour?" said Trudolyubov to Simonov.

"No, I didn't. I forgot," the latter replied, with no sign of regret, and without even apologizing to me he went off to order the *hors d'oeuvres*.

"So you've been here a whole hour? Oh, you poor fellow!" Zverkov cried ironically, for according to his notions this was bound to be extremely funny. That scoundrel Ferfichkin followed with his nasty little snigger like a puppy yapping. My position struck him, too, as extremely ludicrous and embarrassing.

"It isn't funny at all!" I cried to Ferfichkin, more and more irritated. "It wasn't my fault, but other people's. They neglected to let me know. It was—it was—it was simply absurd."

"It's not only absurd, but something else as well," muttered Trudolyubov, naïvely taking my part. "You are too complacent about it. It was simply rudeness—unintentional, of course. And how could Simonov—h'm!"

"If a trick like that had been played on me," observed Ferfichkin, "I would—"

"But you should have ordered yourself something," Zverkov interrupted, "or simply asked for dinner without waiting for us."

"You will allow that I might have done that without your permission," I rapped out. "If I waited, it was—"

"Let us sit down, gentlemen," cried Simonov, coming in. "Everything is ready; I can answer for the champagne; it is capitally chilled.—After all, I did not know your address. Where was I to look for you?" He suddenly turned to me, but again he seemed to avoid looking at me. Evidently he had something against me. He must have made up his mind after what happened yesterday.

Everybody sat down: I did the same. It was a round table. Trudolyubov was on my left, Simonov on my right. Zverkov was sitting opposite, Ferfichkin next to him, between him and Trudolyubov.

"Te-e-ell me, are you—in a government agency?" Zverkov went on, attending to me. Seeing that I was embarrassed, he seriously thought that he ought to be friendly to me, and, so to speak, cheer me up. "Does he want me to throw a bottle at his head or something?" I thought, in a fury. In my unaccustomed surroundings I was unnaturally quick to be irritated.

"In the N—office," I answered jerkily, with my eyes on my plate.

"And—ha-ave you a go-od berth? Te-e-ll me, what ma-a-de you leave your former job?"

"What ma-a-de me was that I wanted to leave my original job," I drawled twice as much as he, hardly able to control myself. Ferfichkin snorted. Simonov looked at me ironically. Trudolyubov stopped eating and began looking at me with curiosity.

Zverkov was jarred but he pretended not to notice it.

"A-a-and the remuneration?"

"What remuneration?"

"I mean, your sa-a-lary?"

"Why are you cross-examining me?"

However, I told him at once what my salary was. I blushed terribly.

"It is not very handsome," Zverkov observed majestically.

"Yes, you can't afford to dine in restaurants on that," Ferfichkin added insolently.

"I think it's very low," Trudolyubov observed gravely.

"And how thin you have grown! How you have changed!" added Zverkov, with a shade of venom in his voice, scanning me and my attire with a sort of insolent compassion.

"Oh, spare his blushes," cried Ferfichkin, sniggering.

"My dear sir, permit me to tell you I am not blushing," I broke out at last; "do you hear? I am dining here, at this restaurant, at my own expense, at mine, not at other people's—note that, Monsieur Ferfichkin."

"Wha-at do you mean? Isn't everyone here dining at his own expense? You seem to be—" Ferfichkin let fly at me, turning as red as a lobster, and looking me in the face with fury.

"Tha-at's what I mean," I answered, feeling I had gone too far, "and I imagine it would be better to talk of something more intelligent."

"You intend to show off your intelligence, I suppose?"

"Don't disturb yourself, that would be quite out of place here."

"What are you clacking away like that for, my good sir, eh? Have you gone out of your wits in your *dumb*partment?"

"Enough, gentlemen, enough!" Zverkov cried, authoritatively.

"How stupid it is," muttered Simonov.

"It really is stupid. We have met here, a company of friends, for a farewell dinner to a good comrade and you are settling old scores," said Trudolyubov, rudely addressing himself to me alone. "Yesterday you invited yourself to join us, so don't disturb the general harmony."

"Enough, enough!" cried Zverkov. "Stop it, gentlemen, it's out of place. Better let me tell you how I nearly got married the day before yesterday . . ."

And then followed a burlesque narrative of how this gentleman had almost been married two days before. There was not a word about marriage, however, but the story was adorned with generals, colonels and high courtiers while Zverkov practically took the lead among them. It was greeted with approving laughter; Ferfichkin even squealed.

No one paid any attention to me, and I sat crushed and humiliated.

"Good heavens, these are not the people for me!" I thought. "And what a fool I have made of myself before them! I let Ferfichkin go too far, though. The brutes imagine that it is an honor for me to sit down with them. They don't understand that I do them an honor. I to them and not they to me! I've grown thinner! My clothes! Oh, damn my trousers! Zverkov long ago noticed the yellow stain on the knee . . . But what's the use! I must get up at once, this very minute, take my hat and simply go without a word—out of contempt! And tomorrow I can send a challenge. The scoundrels! After all, I don't care about the seven roubles. They may think . . . Damn it! I don't care about the seven roubles. I'll go this minute!"

Of course I remained.

I drank sherry and Lafitte by the glassful in my distress. Being unaccustomed to it, I quickly became intoxicated and my annoyance increased with the intoxication. I longed all at once to insult them all in a most flagrant manner and then go away. To seize the moment and show what I could do, so that they would say, "Though he is absurd, he's clever," and—and—in short, damn them all!

I scanned them all insolently with my dulled eyes. But they seemed to have forgotten me altogether. *They* were noisy, vociferous, cheerful. Zverkov kept talking. I began to listen. Zverkov was talking about some sumptuous lady whom he had at last led on to declaring her love (of course, he was lying like a horse), and how he had been helped in this affair by an intimate friend of his, a Prince Kolya, an officer in the Hussars, who had three thousand serfs.

"And yet, this Kolya, who has three thousand serfs, has not put in an appearance here tonight at all to see you off," I cut in suddenly. For a minute everyone was silent.

"You are drunk already." Trudolyubov deigned to notice me at last, glancing contemptuously in my direction. Zverkov, without a word, examined me as though I were a little beetle. I dropped my eyes. Simonov made haste to fill up the glasses with champagne.

Trudolyubov raised his glass, as did everyone else but me.

"Your health and good luck on the journey!" he cried to Zverkov. "To old times, gentlemen, to our future, hurrah!"

They all tossed off their glasses, and crowded round Zverkov to kiss him. I did not move; my full glass stood untouched before me.

"Why, aren't you going to drink it?" roared Trudolyubov, losing patience and turning menacingly to me.

"I want to make a toast separately, on my own account . . . and then I'll drink it, Mr. Trudolyubov."

"Disgusting crank!" muttered Simonov.

I drew myself up in my chair and feverishly seized my glass, prepared for something extraordinary, though I did not know myself precisely what I was going to say.

"*Silence!*" cried Ferfichkin, in French. "Now for a display of wit!"

Zverkov waited very gravely, knowing what was coming.

"Lieutenant Zverkov," I began, "let me tell you that I hate phrases, phrasemongers and corseted waists—that's the first point, and there is a second one to follow it."

There was a general stir.

"The second point is: I hate dirty stories and people who tell dirty stories. Especially people who tell dirty stories!

"The third point: I love truth, sincerity and honesty," I went on almost mechanically, for I was beginning to shiver with horror and had no idea how I came to be talking like this. "I love thought, Monsieur Zverkov; I love true comradeship, on an equal footing and not—h'm—I love—but, however, why not? I will drink to your health, too, Monsieur Zverkov. Seduce the Circassian girls, shoot the enemies of the fatherland and—and—to your health, Monsieur Zverkov!"

Zverkov got up from his seat, bowed to me and said:

"I am very much obliged to you."

He was frightfully offended and even turned pale.

"Damn the fellow!" roared Trudolyubov, bringing his fist down on the table.

"Well, he ought to be punched in the nose for that," squealed Ferfichkin.

"We ought to turn him out," muttered Simonov.

"Not a word, gentlemen, not a movement!" cried Zverkov solemnly, checking the general indignation. "I thank you all, but I can show him for myself how much value I attach to his words."

"Mr. Ferfichkin, you will give me satisfaction tomorrow at the latest for your words just now!" I said aloud, turning with dignity to Ferfichkin.

"A duel, you mean? Certainly," he answered. But probably I was so ridiculous as I challenged him and it was so out of keeping with my appearance that everyone, including Ferfichkin, roared with laughter.

"Yes, let him alone, of course! After all, he is completely drunk," Trudolyubov said with disgust.

"I will never forgive myself for letting him join us," Simonov muttered again.

"Now is the time to throw a bottle at their heads," I thought to myself. I picked up the bottle . . . and poured myself a full glass.

"No, I had better sit on to the end," I went on thinking; "you would be pleased, my friends, if I left. Nothing will induce me to go. I'll go on sitting here, and drinking to the end, on purpose, as a sign that I don't attach the slightest importance to you. I will go on sitting and drinking, because this is a public-house and I paid my entrance money. I'll sit here and drink, for I look upon you as so many pawns, as inanimate pawns. I'll sit here and drink—and sing if I want to, yes, sing, for I have the right to—to sing—h'm!"

But I did not sing. I simply tried not to look at any of them. I assumed most unconcerned attitudes and waited with impatience for them to speak *first,* of their own accord. But alas, they did not speak! And oh, how I wished, how I wished at that moment to be reconciled to them! It struck eight, at last nine. They moved from the table to the sofa. Zverkov stretched himself on a couch and put one foot on a round table. The wine was brought there. He did, as a matter of fact, order three bottles on his own account. He didn't, of course, invite me to join them. They all sat round him on the sofa. They listened to him, almost with reverence. It was evident that they were fond of him. "For what? For what?" I wondered. From time to time they were moved to drunken enthusiasm and kissed each other. They talked of the Caucasus, of the nature of true passion, of advantageous jobs in the service, of the income of a Hussar called Podkharzhevsky, whom none of them knew personally and rejoiced that he had a large income; of the extraordinary grace and beauty of a Princess D., whom none of them had ever seen; then it came to Shakespeare's being immortal.

I smiled contemptuously and walked up and down the other side of the room, opposite the sofa, along the wall, from the table to the stove and back again. I tried my very utmost to show them that I could do without them, and yet I purposely stomped with my boots, thumping with my heels. But it was all in vain. They paid no attention at all. I had the patience to walk up and down in front of them that way from eight o'clock till eleven, in one and the same place, from the table to the stove and from the stove back again to the table. "I walk up and down to please myself and no one can prevent me." The waiter who came into the room several times stopped to look at me. I was somewhat giddy from turning round so often; at moments it seemed to me that I was in delirium. During those three hours I was three times soaked with sweat, and then dry again. At times, with an intense, acute pang, I was stabbed to the heart by the thought that ten years, twenty years, forty years would pass, and that even in forty years I would remember with loathing and humiliation those filthiest, most ludicrous, and most terrible moments of my life. No one could have gone out of his way to degrade himself more shamelessly and voluntarily, and I fully realized it, fully, and yet I went on pacing up and down from the table to the stove. "Oh, if you only knew what thoughts and feelings I am capable of, how cultured I am!" I thought at moments, mentally addressing the sofa on which my enemies were sitting. But my enemies behaved as though I did not exist in the room. Once—only once—they turned toward me, just when Zverkov was talking about Shakespeare, and I suddenly gave a contemptuous laugh. I snorted in such an effected and nasty way that they all at once broke off their conversation, and silently and gravely for two minutes watched me walking up and down from the table to the stove, *paying no attention whatsoever to them.* But nothing came of it; they said nothing, and two minutes later they ceased to notice me again. It struck eleven.

"Gentlemen," cried Zverkov, getting up from the sofa, "let us all go there *now!*"

"Of course, of course," the others said.

I turned sharply to Zverkov. I was so exhausted, so broken, that I would have cut my throat to put an end to it. I was in a fever; my hair, soaked with perspiration, stuck to my forehead and temples.

"Zverkov, I beg your pardon," I said abruptly and resolutely. "Ferfichkin, yours too, and everyone's, everyone's; I have insulted you all!"

"Aha! A duel is not in your line, old man," Ferfichkin hissed venomously.

It sent a deep pang to my heart.

"No, it's not the duel I am afraid of, Ferfichkin! I am ready to fight you tomorrow, after we are reconciled. I insist upon it, in fact, and you cannot refuse. I want to show you that I am not afraid of a duel. You will fire first and I will fire into the air."

"He is comforting himself," remarked Simonov.

"He's simply raving," declared Trudolyubov.

"But let us pass. Why are you barring our way? Well, what do you want?" Zverkov answered disdainfully. They were all flushed; their eyes were bright; they had been drinking heavily.

"I asked for your friendship, Zverkov; I insulted you, but—"

"Insulted? You-u insulted me-e-e! Permit me to tell you, sir, that you never, under any circumstances, could possibly insult *me*."

"And that's enough of you. Out of the way!" concluded Trudolyubov. "Let's go."

"Olympia is mine, gentlemen, that's agreed!" cried Zverkov.

"We won't dispute your right, we won't dispute your right," the others answered, laughing.

I stood as though spat upon. The party went noisily out of the room. Trudolyubov struck up some stupid song. Simonov remained behind for a moment to tip the waiters. I suddenly went up to him.

"Simonov! give me six roubles!" I said, decisively and desperately.

He looked at me in extreme amazement, with dulled eyes. He, too, was drunk.

"You don't mean you are even coming with us *there?*"

"Yes."

"I've no money," he snapped out, and with a scornful laugh he went out of the room.

I clutched at his overcoat. It was a nightmare.

"Simonov! I saw you had money, why do you refuse me? Am I a scoundrel? Beware of refusing me; if you knew, if you knew why I am asking! Everything depends upon it! My whole future, my whole plans!"

Simonov pulled out the money and almost flung it at me.

"Take it, if you have no sense of shame!" he pronounced pitilessly, and ran to overtake them.

I was left alone for a moment. Disorder, the remains of dinner, a broken wine-glass on the floor, spilt wine, cigarette butts, intoxication and delirium in my brain, an agonizing misery in my heart and finally the waiter, who had seen and heard all and was looking inquisitively into my face.

"I am going *there!*" I shouted. "Either they will all fall down on their knees to beg for my friendship—or I will give Zverkov a slap in the face!"

V

"So this is it, so this is it at last, a clash with reality," I muttered as I ran headlong downstairs. "This, it seems, is very different from the Pope's leaving Rome and going to Brazil; this, it seems, is very different from the ball on the shores of Lake Como!"

"You are a scoundrel," flashed through my mind, "if you laugh at this now."

"No matter!" I cried, answering myself. "Now everything is lost!"

There was no trace of them left, but that made no difference—I knew where they had gone.

At the steps was standing a solitary night sledge-driver in a rough peasant coat, powdered over with the wet, and, as it were, warm snow that was still falling thickly. It was sultry and warm. The little shaggy piebald horse was also powdered with snow and was coughing, I remember that very well. I made a rush for the roughly made sledge; but as soon as I raised my foot to get into it, the recollection of how Simonov had just given me six roubles seemed to double me up and I tumbled into the sledge like a sack.

"No, I must do a great deal to make up for all that," I cried. "But I will make up for it or perish on the spot this very night. Start!"

We set off. There was an absolute whirl in my head.

"They won't go down on their knees to beg for my friendship. That is a mirage, a cheap mirage, revolting, romantic and fantastical—that is another ball at Lake Como. And so I have to slap Zverkov's face! It is my duty to. And so it is settled; I am flying to give him a slap in the face. Hurry up!"

The cabby tugged at the reins.

"As soon as I go in I'll give it to him. Ought I to say a few words by way of preface before giving him the slap? No, I'll simply go in and give it to him. They will all be sitting in the drawing-room, and he with Olympia on the sofa. That damned Olympia! She laughed at my looks on one occasion and refused me. I'll pull Olympia's hair, pull Zverkov's ears! No, better one ear, and pull him by it round the room. Maybe they will all begin beating me and will kick me out. That is even very likely. No matter! Anyway, I will slap him first; the initiative will be mine; and according to the code of honor that is everything: he will be branded and no blows can wipe off the slap, nothing but a duel can. He will be forced to fight. And let them beat me then. Let them, the ungrateful wretches! Trudolyubov will beat me hardest, he is so strong; Ferfichkin is sure to catch hold from the side and tug at my hair. But no matter, no matter! That's what I am going for. The blockheads will be forced at last to see the tragedy of it all! When they drag me to the door I shall call out to them that in reality they are not worth my little finger." "Get on, driver, get on!" I cried to the driver. He started and flicked his whip, I shouted so savagely.

"We shall fight at daybreak, that's a settled thing. I am through with the Department. Ferfichkin called the Department 'Dumbpartment' before. But where can I get pistols? Nonsense! I'll call my salary in advance and buy them. And powder, and bullets? That's the second's business. And how can it all be done by daybreak? And where am I to get a second? I have no friends. Nonsense!" I cried, lashing myself more and more into a fury. "Nonsense! the first person I meet in the street is bound to be my second, just as he would be bound to pull a drowning man out of water. The strangest things may happen. Even if I were to ask the Director himself to be my second tomorrow, even he would be bound to consent, if only from a feeling of chivalry, and to keep the secret! Anton Antonich—"

The fact is that at that very minute the disgusting absurdity of my plans and the other side of the question were clearer and more vivid to my imagination than they could be to anyone on earth, but—

"Get on, driver, get on, you rascal, get on!"

"Ugh, sir!" said the son of toil.

Cold shivers suddenly ran down me.

"Wouldn't it be better . . . wouldn't it be better . . . to go straight home now? Oh, my God! Why, why did I invite myself to this dinner yesterday? But no, it's impossible. And my three hours' walk from the table to the stove? No, they, they and no one else must pay for my walking up and down! They must wipe out this dishonor! Drive on!"

"And what if they hand me over to the police? They won't dare! They'll be afraid of the scandal. And what if Zverkov is so contemptuous that he refuses to fight a duel? That is even sure to happen, but in that case I'll show them—I will turn up at the posting station when he is setting off tomorrow—I'll catch him by the leg, I'll pull off his coat when he gets into the carriage. I'll get my teeth into his hand, I'll bite him.

See to what lengths you can drive a desperate man! He may hit me on the head and they may pummel me from behind. I will shout to the whole crowd of spectators: 'Look at this young puppy who is driving off to captivate the Circassian girls after letting me spit in his face!'

"Of course, after that everything will be over! The Department will have vanished off the face of the earth. I will be arrested. I will be tried, I will be dismissed from the service, thrown in prison, sent to Siberia, deported. Never mind! In fifteen years when they let me out of prison I will trudge off to him, a begger in rags, I shall find him in some provincial city. He will be married and happy. He will have a grown-up daughter . . . I will say to him: 'Look, monster, at my hollow cheeks and my rags! I've lost everything—my career, my happiness, art, science, *the woman I loved,* and all through you. Here are pistols. I have come to discharge my pistol and—and I . . . forgive you.' Then I will fire into the air and he will hear nothing more of me."

I was actually on the point of tears, though I knew perfectly well at that very moment that all this was out of Pushkin's Silvio and Lermontov's *Masquerade.*[8] And all at once I felt terribly ashamed, so ashamed that I stopped the sledge, stepped out of it and stood still in the snow in the middle of the street. The driver sighed and gazed at me in astonishment.

What was I to do? I could not go on there—that was clearly absurd, and I could not leave things as they were, because that would seem as though—"Heavens, how could I leave things! And after such insults!" "No!" I cried, throwing myself into the sledge again. "It is ordained! It is fate! Drive on, drive on to that place!"

And in my impatience I punched the sledge-driver on the back of the neck.

"What are you up to? What are you hitting me for?" the poor man shouted, but he whipped up his nag so that it began to kick out.

The wet snow was falling in big flakes; I unbuttoned myself. I did not care about it. I forgot everything else, for I had finally decided on the slap, and felt with horror that after all it was going to happen *now, at once,* that it would happen immediately and that *no force could stop it.* The deserted street lamps gleamed sullenly in the snowy darkness like torches at a funeral. The snow drifted under my greatcoat, under my coat, under my necktie, and melted there. I did not cover myself up—after all, all was already lost, anyway. At last we arrived. I jumped out, almost fainting, ran up the steps and began knocking and kicking at the door. My legs, particularly at the knee, felt terribly weak. The door was opened quickly as though they knew I was coming. As a matter of fact, Simonov had warned them that perhaps another would arrive, and this was a place in which one had to give notice and to observe certain precautions. It was one of the "millinery establishments" which were abolished by the police a long time ago. By day it really was a shop; but at night, if one had an introduction, one might visit it for other purposes.

I walked rapidly through the dark shop into the familiar drawing-room, where there was only one candle burning, and stopped in amazement; there was no one there.

"Where are they?" I asked somebody.

But by now, of course, they had separated.

Before me stood a person with a stupid smile, the "madam" herself, who had seen me before. A minute later a door opened and another person came in.

8. An 1835 play by Mikhail Lermontov about love, duty, and honor. Silvio is the vengeful hero of a story by Alexander Pushkin, "The Shot" (1830).

Paying no attention to anything, I strode about the room, and, I believe, I talked to myself. I felt as though I had been saved from death and was conscious of it, joyfully, all over: after all, I would have given that slap. I would certainly, certainly have given it! But now they were not here and—everything had vanished and changed! I looked round. I could not realize my condition yet. I looked mechanically at the girl who had come in and had a glimpse of a fresh, young, rather pale face, with straight, dark eyebrows, and with a grave, as it were, amazed glance, eyes that attracted me at once. I would have hated her if she had been smiling. I began looking at her more intently and, as it were, with effort. I had not fully collected my thoughts. There was something simple and good-natured in her face, but something strangely serious. I am sure that this stood in her way here, and that not one of those fools had noticed her. She could not, however, have been called a beauty, though she was tall, strong-looking, and well built. She was very simply dressed. Something loathsome stirred within me. I went straight up to her—

I happened to look at myself in the mirror. My harassed face struck me as extremely revolting, pale, spiteful, nasty, with disheveled hair. "No matter, I am glad of it," I thought; "I am glad that I shall seem revolting to her; I like that."

VI

. . . Somewhere behind a screen a clock began wheezing, as though under some great pressure, as though someone were strangling it. After an unnaturally prolonged wheezing there followed a shrill, nasty and, as it were, unexpectedly rapid chime—as though someone were suddenly jumping forward. It struck two. I woke up, though I had not really been asleep but only lay semi-conscious.

It was almost completely dark in the narrow, cramped, low-pitched room, cluttered up with an enormous wardrobe and piles of cardboard boxes and all sorts of frippery and litter. The candle stump that had been burning on the table was going out and it gave a faint flicker from time to time. In a few minutes it would be completely dark.

I was not long in coming to myself; everything came back to my mind at once, without an effort, as though it had been in ambush to pounce upon me again. And, indeed, even while I was unconscious, a point continually seemed to remain in my memory that could not ever be forgotten, and around it my dreams moved drearily. But strange to say, everything that had happened to me during that day seemed to me now, on waking, to be in the far, far-away distant past, as though I had long, long ago lived all that down.

My head was heavy. Something seemed to be hovering over me, provoking me, rousing me and making me restless. Misery and gall seemed to surge up in me again and to seek an outlet. Suddenly I saw beside me two wide-open eyes scrutinizing me curiously and persistently. The look in those eyes was coldly detached, sullen, utterly detached, as it were; it weighed heavily on me.

A grim idea came into my brain and passed all over my body, like some nasty sensation, such as one feels when one goes into a damp and mouldy cellar. It was somehow unnatural that those two eyes only now thought of beginning to examine me. I recalled, too, that during those two hours I had not said a single word to this creature, and had, in fact, considered it entirely unnecessary; it had even for some reason gratified me before. Now I suddenly realized vividly how absurd, revolting as a spider, was the idea of vice which, without love, grossly and shamelessly begins directly with that in which true love finds its consummation. For a long time we gazed at each other like that, but she did not drop her eyes before mine and did not change her expression, so that at last, somehow, I felt uncomfortable.

"What is your name?" I asked abruptly, to put an end to it quickly.

"Liza," she answered almost in a whisper, but somehow without any friendliness; she turned her eyes away.

I was silent.

"What weather today—the snow—it's abominable!" I said, almost to myself, putting my arm under my head despondently, and gazing at the ceiling.

She made no answer. This was all outrageous.

"Are you a local girl?" I asked a minute later, almost angrily, turning my head slightly toward her.

"No."

"Where do you come from?"

"From Riga," she answered reluctantly.

"Are you a German?"

"No, Russian."

"Have you been here long?"

"Where?"

"In this house?"

"A fortnight."

She spoke more and more jerkily. The candle went out: I could no longer distinguish her face.

"Have you a father and mother?"

"Yes—no—I have."

"Where are they?"

"There—in Riga."

"What are they?"

"Oh, nothing."

"Nothing? Why, what do they do?"

"Tradespeople."

"Have you always lived with them?"

"Yes."

"How old are you?"

"Twenty."

"Why did you leave them?"

"Oh, for no reason."

That answer meant "Let me alone; I feel wretched." We were silent.

God knows why I did not go away. I felt myself more and more wretched and dreary. The images of the previous day started to flit through my mind in confusion independently of my will. I suddenly recalled something I had seen that morning when, full of anxious thoughts, I was hurrying to the office.

"I saw them carrying a coffin out yesterday and they nearly dropped it," I suddenly said aloud with no desire at all to start a conversation, but just so, almost by accident.

"A coffin?"

"Yes, in the Haymarket; they were bringing it up out of a cellar."

"From a cellar?"

"Not from a cellar, but from a basement. Oh, you know—down below—from a house of ill-fame. It was filthy all round—eggshells, litter—a stench. It was loathsome."

Silence.

"A nasty day to be buried," I began, simply to avoid being silent.

"Nasty, in what way?"

"The snow, the wet." (I yawned.)

"It doesn't matter," she said suddenly, after a brief silence.

"No, it's abominable." (I yawned again.) "The gravediggers must have sworn at getting drenched by the snow. And there must have been water in the grave."

"Why would there be water in the grave?" she asked, with a sort of curiosity, but speaking even more harshly and abruptly than before. I suddenly began to feel provoked.

"Why, there must have been water at the bottom a foot deep. You can't dig a dry grave in Volkovo Cemetery."

"Why?"

"Why? Why, the place is waterlogged. It's a regular marsh. So they bury them in water. I've seen it myself—many times."

(I had never seen it at all, and I had never even been in Volkovo, but had only heard stories of it.)

"Do you mean to say it doesn't matter to you whether you die?"

"But why should I die?" she answered, as though defending herself.

"Why, some day you will die, and you will die just the same as that dead woman. She was—a girl like you. She died of consumption."

"The wench would have died in a hospital, too . . . (She knows all about it already; she said "wench," not "girl.")

"She was in debt to her madam," I retorted, more and more provoked by the discussion; "and went on earning money for her almost up to the very end, though she was in consumption. Some coachmen standing by were talking about her to some soldiers and telling them so. No doubt her former acquaintances. They were laughing. They were going to meet in a pot-house to drink to her memory." (I lied a great deal here.)

Silence followed, profound silence. She did not even stir.

"And is it better to die in a hospital?"

"Isn't it just the same? Besides, why should I die?" she added irritably.

"If not now, a little later."

"Why a little later?"

"Why, indeed? Now you are young, pretty, fresh, you fetch a high price. But after another year of this life you will be very different—you will fade."

"In a year?"

"Anyway, in a year you will be worth less," I continued malignantly. "You will go from here to something lower, another house; a year later—to a third, lower and lower, and in seven years you will come to a basement in the Haymarket. And that's if you are lucky. But it would be much worse if you got some disease, consumption, say— and caught a chill, or something or other. It's not easy to get over an illness in your way of life. If you catch anything you may not get rid of it. And so you would die."

"Oh, well, then I will die," she answered, quite vindictively, and she made a quick movement.

"But after all, it's a pity."

"For whom?"

"Pity for life."

Silence.

"Were you engaged? Eh?"

"What's that to you?"

"Oh, I am not cross-examining you. It's nothing to me. Why are you so cross? Of course you may have had your own troubles. What is it to me? I simply felt sorry."

"For whom?"

"Sorry for you."

"No need," she whispered hardly audibly, and again made a faint movement. That incensed me at once. What! I was so gentle with her, and she—

"Why, what do you think? Are you on the right path, ah?"

"I don't think anything."

"That's what's wrong, that you don't think. Wake up while there is still time. And there is still time. You are still young, good-looking; you might love, be married, be happy—"

"Not all married women are happy," she snapped out in the rude, fast way she had spoken before.

"Not all, of course, but anyway it is much better than the life here. Infinitely better. Besides, with love one can live even without happiness. Even in sorrow life is sweet; life is sweet, however one lives. But here you have nothing except foulness. Phew!"

I turned away with disgust; I was no longer reasoning coldly. I began to feel myself what I was saying and warmed to the subject. I was already longing to expound the cherished *little ideas* I had brooded over in my corner. Something suddenly flared up in me. An object had "appeared" before me.

"Never mind my being here. I am not an example for you. I am, perhaps, even worse than you are. I was drunk when I came here, though," I hastened, however, to say in self-defense. "Besides, a man is no example for a woman. It's a different thing. I may degrade and defile myself, but I am not anyone's slave. I come and go, and there's an end to it. I shake it off, and I am a different man. But you are a slave from the start. Yes, a slave! You give up everything, your whole freedom. If you want to break your chains afterward, you won't be able to; you will be caught more and more in the snares. It is an accursed bondage. I know it. I won't mention anything else, maybe you won't understand it, but tell me: after all, surely you are in debt to your madam already? There, you see," I added, though she made no answer, but only listened in silence, entirely absorbed, "that's bondage for you! You will never buy your freedom. They will see to that. It's like selling your soul to the devil—

"And besides—perhaps I, too, am just as unfortunate, how do you know—and wallow in the mud on purpose, also out of misery? After all, men take to drink out of grief; well, maybe I am here out of grief. Come, tell me, what good is there here? Here you and I—were intimate—just now and did not say one word to one another all the time, and it was only afterward you began staring at me like a wild creature, and I at you. Is that loving? Is that how human beings are intimate? It's hideous, that's what it is!"

"Yes!" she assented sharply and hurriedly.

I was even amazed by the eagerness of this "yes." So the same thought may have been straying through her mind when she was staring at me just before. So she, too, was capable of certain thoughts? "Damn it all, this was curious, this was *kinship?*" I thought, almost rubbing my hands. And indeed how can one fail to manage a young soul like that?

The sport in it attracted me most.

She turned her head nearer to me, and it seemed to me in the darkness that she propped herself on her arm. Perhaps she was scrutinizing me. How I regretted that I could not see her eyes. I heard her deep breathing.

"Why did you come here?" I asked her, with a note of authority already in my voice.

"Oh, I don't know."

"But after all how nice it would be to be living in your own father's house! It's warm and free; you have a nest of your own."

"But what if it's worse than this?"

"I must take the right tone," flashed through my mind. "I may not get far with sentimentality."

But it was only a momentary thought. I swear she really did interest me. Besides, I was exhausted and moody. And after all, cunning so easily goes hand in hand with feeling.

"Who denies it?" I hastened to answer. "Anything may happen. I am, after all, convinced that someone has wronged you and is guiltier toward you than you toward them. After all, I know nothing of your story, but it's not likely a girl like you has come here of her own inclination—"

"What kind of girl am I?" she whispered, hardly audible, but I heard it.

Damn it all, I was flattering her. That was abominable. But perhaps it was a good thing—She was silent.

"See, Liza, I will tell you about myself. If I had had a home from childhood, I shouldn't be what I am now. I often think about that. After all, no matter how bad it may be at home, at least they are your father and mother, and not enemies, strangers. Once a year, at least, they'll show their love for you. Anyway, you know you are at home. I grew up without a home; and perhaps that's why I've turned so—unfeeling."

I waited again.

"Perhaps she doesn't understand," I thought, "and, indeed, it is absurd, this moralizing."

"If I were a father and had a daughter, I believe I should love my daughter more than my sons, really," I began indirectly, as though talking of something else, in order to distract her attention. I confess I blushed.

"Why so?" she asked.

Ah! so she was listening!

"I don't know, Liza. I knew a father who was a stern, strict man, but he used to go down on his knees to his daughter, used to kiss her hands and feet, he couldn't make enough of her, really. When she danced at parties he used to stand for five hours at a stretch without taking his eyes off her. He was mad about her; I understand that! She would fall asleep tired at night, and he would get up to kiss her in her sleep and make the sign of the cross over her. He would go about in a dirty old coat, he was stingy to everyone else, but would spend his last penny for her, giving her expensive presents, and it was a delight to him when she was pleased with what he gave her. Fathers always love their daughters more than mothers do. Some girls live happily at home! And I believe I would never let my daughter marry."

"What next?" she said with a faint smile.

"I would be jealous, I really would. To think that she should kiss anyone else! That she should love a stranger more than her father! It's painful to imagine it. Of course, that's all nonsense, of course every father would be reasonable at last. But I believe before I would let her marry, I would worry myself to death; I would find fault with all her suitors. But I would end by letting her marry whom she herself loved. After all, the one whom the daughter loves always seems the worst to the father. That is always so. So many families get into trouble with that."

"Some are glad to sell their daughters, rather than to marry them honorably."

Ah! So that was it!

"Such a thing, Liza, happens in those accursed families in which there is neither love nor God," I retorted warmly, "and where there is no love, there is no sense either. There are such families, it's true, but I am not speaking of them. You must have seen wickedness in your own family, if you talk like that. You must have been genuinely unlucky. H'm!—that sort of thing mostly comes about through poverty."

"And is it any better among the rich? Even among the poor, honest people live happily."

"H'm—yes. Perhaps. Another thing, Liza, man only likes to count his troubles, but he does not count his joys. If he counted them up as he ought, he would see that every lot has enough happiness provided for it. And what if all goes well with the family, if the blessing of God is upon it, if the husband is a good one, loves you, cherishes you, never leaves you! There is happiness in such a family! Sometimes there is happiness even in the midst of sorrow; and indeed sorrow is everywhere. If you marry *you will find out for yourself*. But think of the first years of married life with one you love: what happiness, what happiness there sometimes is in it! And indeed it's the ordinary thing. In those early days even quarrels with one's husband end happily. Some women get up more quarrels with their husbands the more they love them. Indeed, I knew a woman like that: she seemed to say that because she loved him deeply, she would torment him out of love so that he'd feel it. Did you know that you may torment a man on purpose out of love? Women are particularly given to that, thinking to themselves, 'I will love him so much afterward, I will make so much of him, that it's no sin to torment him a little now.' And everyone in the house rejoices in the sight of you, and you are happy and gay and peaceful and honorable. Then there are some women who are jealous. If the husband goes off someplace—I knew one such woman, she couldn't restrain herself, but would jump up at night and would run off on the sly to find out where he was, whether he was with some other woman. That's already bad. And the woman knows herself it's wrong, and her heart fails her and she suffers, but, after all, she loves—it's all through love. And how sweet it is to make up after quarrels, to admit she was wrong, or to forgive him! And they are both so happy, all at once they become so happy, as though they had met anew, been married over again; as though their love had begun anew. And no one, no one should know what passes between husband and wife if they love one another. And no matter how their quarrels ended they ought not to call in even their own mothers to judge between them and tell tales of one another. They are their own judges. Love is a holy mystery and ought to be hidden from all other eyes, no matter what happens. That makes it holier and better. They respect one another more, and much is built on respect. And if once there has been love, if they have been married for love, why should love pass away? Surely one can keep it! It is rare that one cannot keep it. And if the husband is kind and straightforward, why should not love last? The first phase of married love will pass, it is true, but then there will come a love that is better still. Then there will be the union of souls, they will have everything in common, there will be no secrets between them. And once they have children, the most difficult times will seem to them happy, so long as there is love and courage. Even toil will be a joy, you may deny yourself bread for your children and even that will be a joy. After all, they will love you for it afterward; so you are laying by for your future. As the children grow up you feel that you are an example, a support for them; that even after you die your children will always cherish your thoughts and feelings, because they have received them from you, they will take on your semblance and likeness. So you see it is a great duty. How can it fail to draw the father and mother closer? People say it's a trial to have children. Who says that? It is heavenly joy! Are you fond of little children, Liza? I am awfully fond of them. You know—a little rosy baby boy at your bosom, and what husband's heart is not touched, seeing his wife nursing his child! A plump little rosy baby, sprawling and snuggling, chubby little hands and feet, clean tiny little nails, so tiny that it makes one laugh to look at them; eyes that look as if they understand everything. And while it sucks it clutches at your bosom with its little hand, plays. When its father comes up, the child tears itself away from the bosom, flings itself back, looks at its father, laughs, as though it were God knows how funny, and falls to sucking again. Or it will bite its mother's breast when it is cutting its little teeth while it looks sideways at her with its little eyes as though to say, 'Look, I am biting!' Is not all that a joy when they are all three together, husband, wife and child? One can forgive a great deal for the sake of such moments. Yes, Liza, one must first learn to live oneself before one blames others!"

"It's by pictures, pictures like that one must get at you," I thought to myself, though I did not speak with real feeling, and all at once I flushed crimson. "What if she were suddenly to burst out laughing, what would I do then?" That idea drove me to fury. Toward the end of my speech I really was excited, and now my vanity was somehow wounded. The silence continued. I almost wanted to nudge her.

"Why are you . . ." she began, and stopped. But I understood: there was a quiver of something different in her voice, not abrupt, harsh and unyielding as before, but something soft and shamefaced, so shamefaced that I suddenly felt ashamed and guilty.

"What?" I asked with tender curiosity.

"Why, you . . ."

"What?"

"Why you—speak exactly like a book," she said, and something sarcastic was heard in her voice.

That remark sent a pang to my heart. It was not what I was expecting.

I did not understand that she was hiding her feelings by sarcasm and that this is usually the last refuge of modest and chaste-souled people when the privacy of their soul is coarsely and intrusively invaded, and that their pride makes them refuse to surrender till the last moment and shrink from expressing their feelings to you. I ought to have guessed the truth for the timidity with which she had a number of times attempted her sarcasm, only bringing herself to utter it at last with an effort. But I did not guess, and a spiteful feeling took possession of me.

"Wait a bit!" I thought.

VII

"Oh, hush, Liza! How can you talk about my speaking like a book when it makes even me, an outsider, feel sick? Though I don't look at it as an outsider, for, indeed, all that has touched me to the heart. Is it possible, is it possible that you do not feel sick at being here yourself? Evidently habit does wonders! God knows what habit can do with anyone. Can you really and seriously think that you will never grow old, that you will always be good-looking, and that they will keep you here forever and ever? I say nothing of the filth here. Though let me tell you this about it; about your present life, I mean; even though you are young now, attractive, nice, with soul and feeling, yet you know, as soon as I came to myself just now, I felt at once sick at being here with you! After all, one can only come here when one is drunk. But if you were anywhere else, living as decent people live, I would perhaps be more than attracted by you, I would fall in love with you, would be glad of a look from you, let alone a word. I would hang about your door, would go down on my knees to you, we would become engaged and I would even consider it an honor to do so. I would not dare to have an impure thought about you. But here, after all, I know that I have only to whistle and you have to come with me whether you like it or not. I don't consult your wishes, but you mine. The lowest laborer hires himself as a workman but he doesn't make a slave of himself altogether; besides, he knows that he will be free again. But when will you be free? Only think what you are giving up here! What is it you are making a slave of? It is your soul, together with your body; you are selling your soul which you have no right to dispose of! You give your love to be outraged by every drunkard! Love! But after all, that's everything, but after all, it's a jewel, it's a maiden's treasure, love—why, after all a man would be ready to give his soul, to face death to gain that love. But how much is your love worth now? You can be bought, all of you, body and soul, and there is no need to strive for love when you can have everything without love. And after all, there is no greater insult for a girl than that, do you understand? To be sure, I have heard that they comfort you, poor fools, they let you have lovers of your own here. But after all, that's simply a farce, that's simply a sham, it's just laughing at you, and you are taken in by it! Why, do you suppose he really loves you, that lover of yours? I don't believe it. How can he love you when he knows that you may be called away from him any minute? He would be a vile fellow if he did! Would he have a grain of respect for you? What have you in common with him? He laughs at you and robs you— that is all his love amounts to! You are lucky if he does not beat you. Very likely he does beat you, too. Ask him, if you have one, whether he will marry you. He will laugh in your face, if he doesn't spit in it or give you a blow—yet he may not be worth a plugged nickel himself. And for what have you ruined your life, if you come to think of it? For the coffee they give you to drink and the plentiful meals? But after all, why do they feed you? An honest girl couldn't swallow the food, she would know why she was being fed. You are in debt here, and, of course, you will always be in debt, and you will go on in debt to the end, till the visitors here begin to scorn you. And that will soon happen, don't rely upon your youth—all that flies by, like an express train here, after all. You will be kicked out. And not simply kicked out; long before that they will begin to nag you, scold you, abuse you, as though you had not sacrificed your health for her, had not ruined your youth and your soul for her benefit, but as though you had ruined her, ravaged her, robbed her. And don't expect anyone to take your part; the others, your companions, will attack you, too, to win her favor, for all are in slavery here, and have lost all conscience and pity long ago. They have become utterly vile, and nothing on earth is viler, more loathsome and more insulting than their abuse. And you are laying down everything here, everything unconditionally, youth and health and beauty and hope, and at twenty-two you will look like a woman of thirty-five, and you will be lucky if you are not diseased, pray to God for that! No doubt you are thinking now after all that you have a lark and no work to do! Yet there is no harder or more dreadful work in the world or ever has been. One would think that the heart alone would be worn out with tears. And you won't dare to say a word, not half a word, when they drive you away from here: you will go away as though you were to blame. You will change to another house, then to a third, then somewhere else, till you come down at last to the Haymarket. There you will be beaten at every turn; that is a courtesy there, the visitors there don't know how to be friendly without beating you. You don't believe that it is so hateful there? Go and look for yourself some time, you can see with your own eyes. Once, one New Year's Day, I saw a woman at a door. Her own kind had turned her out as a joke, to give her a taste of the frost because she had been howling too much, and they shut the door behind her. At nine o'clock in the morning she was already completely drunk, dishevelled, half-naked, covered with bruises, her face was powdered, but she had a black eye, blood was trickling from her nose and her teeth; some cabman had just beaten her. She was sitting on the stone steps, a salt fish of some sort was in her hand; she was howling, wailing something about her 'fate' and beating with the fish on the steps, and cabmen and drunken soldiers were crowding in the doorway taunting her. You don't believe that you will ever be like that? I would not like to believe it, either, but how do you know, maybe ten years, eight years ago that very woman with that salt fish came here fresh as a little cherub, innocent, pure, knowing no evil, blushing at every word. Perhaps she was like you, proud, ready to take offence, not like the others; perhaps she looked like a queen, and knew what happiness was in store for the man who would love her and whom she would love. Do you see how it ended? And what if at that very minute when she was beating on the filthy steps with that fish, drunken and dishevelled—what if at that very minute she recalled the pure early days in her father's house, when she used to go to school and the neighbor's son watched for her on the way, declaring that he would love her as long as he lived, that he would devote his life to her, and when they vowed to love one another for ever and be married as soon as they were grown up! No, Liza, it would be a joy for you, a joy if you were to die soon of consumption in some corner, in some cellar like that woman just now. In the hospital, do you say? You will be lucky if they take you, but what if you are still of use to the madam here? Consumption is a queer disease, it is not like fever. The patient goes on hoping till the last minute and says he is all right. He deludes himself. And that's just advantageous for your madam. Don't doubt it, that's how it is; you have sold your soul, and what is more you owe money, so you don't even dare to say a word. But when you are dying, everyone will abandon you, everyone will turn away from you, for then there will be nothing to get from you. What's more, they will reproach you for taking up space, for taking so long to die. You won't even be able to beg for a drink of water without getting abuse. 'Aren't you going to die, you foul wench; you won't let us sleep with your moaning, you make the gentlemen sick.' That's true. I have heard such things said myself. When you are really dying they will push you into the filthiest corner in the cellar; in the damp and darkness; what will your thoughts be, lying there alone? When you die, strange hands will lay you out, with grumbling and impatience; no one will bless you, no one will sigh for you, they will only want to get rid of you as soon as possible; they will buy a coffin, take you to the grave as they did that poor woman today, and celebrate your memory at the tavern. There is slush, filth, wet snow in the grave—no need to put themselves out for you: 'Let her down, Vanyukha; it's just like her "fate" after all, here she goes in, head first, the wench. Shorten the cord, you rascal.' 'It's all right as it is.' 'All right, is it? Why, she's on her side! Wasn't she a human being, too? Well, never mind, cover her up.' And they won't care to waste much time quarreling over you. They will scatter the wet blue clay as quickly as they can and go off to the tavern—and there your memory on earth will end; other women have children who visit their graves, fathers, husbands. While for you there will be neither tear, nor sigh, nor remembrance; no one, no one in the whole wide world will ever come to you; your name will vanish from the face of the earth as though you had never existed, had never been born at all! Nothing but filth and mud, no matter how much you knock on your coffin lid at night, when the dead arise, however you cry: 'Let me out, kind people, to live in the light of day! My life was no life at all; my life has been thrown away like a dirty rag; it was drunk away in the tavern at the Haymarket; let me out, kind people, to live in the world again!'"

And I worked myself up to such a pitch that I began to have a lump in my throat myself and—and suddenly I stopped, sat up in dismay, and bending over apprehensively, began to listen with a beating heart. I had reason to be worried.

I felt for some time that I was turning her soul upside down and breaking her heart, and the more I was convinced of it, the more I wanted to gain my end as quickly and as effectively as possible. The sport, the sport attracted me; yet it was not merely the sport.

I knew I was speaking stiffly, artificially, even bookishly, in short I did not know how to speak except "just like a book." But that did not bother me: after all I knew, I felt, that I would be understood and that this very bookishness would perhaps even be a help. But now, having achieved my effect, I was suddenly panic-stricken. No, I had never, never before witnessed such despair! She was lying face down, pressing her face deep into the pillow and clutching it in both hands. Her heart was being torn. Her youthful body was shuddering all over as though in convulsions. Suppressed sobs rent her bosom and suddenly burst out in weeping and wailing, then she pressed even deeper into the pillow: she did not want anyone here, not a single living soul, to know of her anguish and her tears. She bit the pillow, bit her hand till it bled (I saw that afterward), or, thrusting her fingers into her dishevelled hair, seemed rigid with the effort to restrain herself, holding her breath and clenching her teeth. I began to say something to her, to beg her to calm herself, but felt that I did not dare; and suddenly, all in a sort of chill, almost in terror, began fumbling in the dark, trying hurriedly to get dressed to go. It was dark: try as I would, I could not finish dressing quickly. Suddenly I felt a box of matches and a candlestick with a whole new candle in it. As soon as the room was lighted up, Liza sprang up, sat up in bed, and with a contorted face, with a half-insane smile, looked at me almost senselessly. I sat down beside her and took her hands; she came to herself, made a movement toward me, would have clasped me, but did not dare, and slowly bowed her head before me.

"Liza, my dear, I was wrong to—Forgive me," I began but she squeezed my hand in her fingers so tightly that I felt I was saying the wrong thing and stopped.

"This is my address, Liza, come to me."

"I will come," she whispered resolutely, her head still bowed.

"But now I am going, good-by—till we meet again."

I got up; she, too, stood up and suddenly flushed all over, shuddered, snatched up a shawl that was lying on a chair and muffled herself in it to her chin. As she did this she gave another sickly smile, blushed and looked at me strangely. I felt wretched; I was in haste to get away—to disappear.

"Wait a minute," she said suddenly, in the passage just at the doorway, stopping me with her hand on my overcoat. She put down the candle hastily and ran off; evidently she had thought of something or wanted to show me something. As she ran away she flushed, her eyes shone, and a smile appeared on her lips—what was the meaning of it? Against my will I waited; she came back a minute later with an expression that seemed to ask forgiveness for something. In fact, it was not the same face, nor the same look it had been before: sullen, mistrustful and obstinate. Her look was now imploring, soft, and at the same time trustful, caressing, timid. Children look that way at people they are very fond of, of whom they are asking a favor. Her eyes were a light hazel, they were lovely eyes, full of life, capable of expressing love as well as sullen hatred.

Making no explanation, as though I, as a sort of higher being, must understand everything without explanations, she held out a piece of paper to me. Her whole face was positively beaming at that instant with naïve, almost childish, triumph. I unfolded it. It was a letter to her from a medical student or someone of that sort—a very high-flown and flowery, but extremely respectful, declaration of love. I don't recall the words now, but I remember well enough that through the high-flown phrases there was apparent a genuine feeling, which cannot be feigned. When I had finished reading it I met her glowing, questioning, and childishly impatient eyes fixed upon me. She fastened her eyes upon my face and waited impatiently for what I would say. In a few words, hurriedly, but with a sort of joy and pride, she explained to me that she had been to a dance somewhere, in a private house, at some "very, very nice people's house, a *family* who *still know nothing,* absolutely nothing," for she had only come here so lately and it had all happened—and she hadn't made up her mind to stay and was certainly going away as soon as she had paid her debt—"and at that party there had been that student who had danced with her the whole evening, had talked to her, and it turned out that he had known her in the old days at Riga when he was a child, they had played together, but a very long time ago—and he knew her parents, but *about this* he knew nothing, nothing, nothing whatever, and had no suspicion! And the day after the dance (three days ago) he had sent her that letter through the friend with whom she had gone to the party—and—well, that was all."

She dropped her shining eyes with a sort of bashfulness as she finished.

The poor girl was keeping that student's letter as a treasure and had run to fetch it, her only treasure, because she did not want me to go away without knowing that she, too, was honestly and genuinely loved; that she, too, was addressed respectfully. No doubt that letter was destined to lie in her box and lead to nothing. But it doesn't matter, I am certain that she would guard it as a treasure all her life, as her pride and justification, and now at such a minute she had thought of that letter and brought it with naïve pride to raise herself in my eyes that I might see, that I, too, might think well of her. I said nothing, pressed her hand and went out. I so longed to get away. I walked home all the way in spite of the fact that the wet snow was still falling in large flakes. I was exhausted, shattered, in bewilderment. But behind the bewilderment the truth was already gleaming. The loathsome truth!

VIII

It was some time, however, before I consented to recognize that truth. Waking up in the morning after some hours of heavy, leaden sleep, and immediately realizing all that had happened on the previous day, I was positively amazed at my last night's *sentimentality* with Liza, at all those "horrors and pity of yesterday." After all, to have such an attack of womanish hysteria, pah! I concluded. "And why did I force my address upon her? What if she comes? Let her come, though; it is all right—" But *obviously* that was not now the chief and the most important matter: I had to make haste and at all costs save my reputation in the eyes of Zverkov and Simonov as quickly as possible; that was the chief business. And I was so taken up that morning that I actually forgot all about Liza.

First of all I had to repay at once what I had borrowed the day before from Simonov. I resolved on a desperate course: to borrow fifteen roubles from Anton Antonich. As luck would have it he was in the best of humors that morning, and gave it to me at once, as soon as I asked. I was so delighted at this that, as I signed the I O U with a swaggering air, I told him *casually* that the night before "I had been making merry with some friends at the Hôtel de Paris; we were giving a farewell party to a comrade, in fact, I might say a friend of my childhood, and you know—a desperate rake, spoilt—of course, he belongs to a good family, and has considerable means, a

brilliant career; he is witty, charming, carries on affairs with certain ladies, you understand; we drank an extra 'half-a-case' and—" And after all it went off all right; all this
was said very lightly, unconstrainedly and complacently.

On reaching home I promptly wrote to Simonov.

To this hour I am lost in admiration when I recall the truly gentlemanly, good-humored, candid tone of my letter. With tact and good taste, and, above all, entirely
without superfluous words, I blamed myself for all that had happened. I defended myself, "if only I may still be allowed to defend myself," by alleging that being utterly
unaccustomed to wine, I had been intoxicated by the first glass which (I claimed) I
had drunk before they arrived, while I was waiting for them at the Hotel de Paris between five and six o'clock. I particularly begged Simonov's pardon; I asked him also
to convey my explanations to all the others, especially to Zverkov whom "I remember
as though in a dream" I seem to have insulted. I added that I would have called upon
all of them myself, but that my head ached, and that besides, I was rather ashamed. I
was especially pleased with that "certain lightness," almost carelessness (strictly
within the bounds of politeness, however), which was suddenly reflected in my style,
and better than any possible arguments, gave them at once to understand that I took
rather an independent view of "all that unpleasantness last night"; that I was by no
means so utterly crushed as you, gentlemen, probably imagine; but on the contrary
that I looked at it as a gentleman serenely respecting himself should. "On a young
hero's past no censure is cast!"

"There is, after all, even an aristocratic playfulness about it!" I thought admir-
ingly, as I read over the letter. "And it's all because I am a cultured and educated
man! Others in my place would not have known how to extricate themselves, but here
I have gotten out of it and am as gay as ever again, and all because I am a cultured and
educated man of our day." And, indeed, perhaps, everything really was due to the
wine yesterday. H'm!—well, no, it was not the wine. I drank nothing at all between
five and six while I was waiting for them. I had lied to Simonov; lied shamelessly;
and even now I wasn't ashamed—

Hang it all, though! The important thing was that I was rid of it.

I put six roubles in the letter, sealed it up, and asked Apollon to take it to Simonov. When he learned that there was money in the letter, Apollon became more respectful and agreed to take it. Toward evening I went out for a walk. My head was
still aching and giddy, after yesterday. But as evening came on and the twilight grew
thicker, my impressions changed and grew more and more confused and, after them,
my thoughts. Something was not dead within me, in the depths of my heart and conscience it would not die, and it expressed itself as a burning anguish. For the most part
I jostled my way through the most crowded business streets, along Meshchansky
Street, along Sadovy Street and in the Yusupov Garden. I always particularly liked to
stroll along these streets at dusk just when they become more crowded with people of
all sorts, merchants and artisans going home from their day's work, with faces looking malicious out of anxiety. What I liked was just that cheap bustle, that bare, humdrum prosaic quality. On this occasion all that bustling in the streets irritated me more
than ever. I could not make out what was wrong with me, I could not find the clue.
Something was rising up, rising up continually in my soul, painfully, and refusing to
be appeased. I returned home completely upset; it was just as though some crime
were lying on my conscience.

The thought that Liza was coming worried me continually. It seemed queer to me
that of all yesterday's memories, the memory of her tormented me as it were, particu-

larly, quite separately, as it were. I had succeeded in forgetting everything else by evening time. I dismissed it all and was still perfectly satisfied with my letter to Simonov. But on this point I was not satisfied at all. It was as though I were worried only by Liza. "What if she comes," I thought incessantly. "Well, so what, it's all right, let her come! H'm! it's horrid that she should see how I live for instance. Yesterday I seemed such a—hero to her, while now, H'm! It's horrid, though, that I have let myself sink so low, the room looks like a beggar's. And I brought myself to go out to dinner in such a suit! And my oilcloth sofa with the stuffing sticking out. And my robe, which will not cover me! What tatters. And she will see all this and she will see Apollon. That beast is certain to insult her. He will fasten upon her in order to be rude to me. And I, of course, will be panic-stricken as usual. I will begin to bow and scrape before her and to pull my robe around me, I will begin to smile, to lie. Oh, how foul! And it isn't the foulness of it that matters most! There is something more important, more loathsome, viler! Yes, viler! And to put on that dishonest lying mask again!"

When I reached that thought I flared up all at once.

"Why dishonest? How dishonest? I was speaking sincerely last night. I remember there was real feeling in me, too. What I wanted was to awake noble feelings in her. Her crying was a good thing, it will have a good effect."

Yet I could not feel at ease.

All that evening, even when I had come back home, even after nine o'clock, when I calculated that Liza could not possibly come, she still haunted me, and what was worse, she always came back to my mind in the same position. One moment out of all that had happened last night presented itself before me vividly: the moment when I struck a match and saw her pale, distorted face, with its tortured look. And what a pitiful, what an unnatural, what a distorted smile she had at that moment! But I did not know then that even fifteen years later I would still always picture Liza to myself with that pitiful, distorted, inappropriate smile which was on her face at that minute.

Next day I was ready again to look upon it all as nonsense, due to over-excited nerves, and, above all, as *exaggerated*. I always recognized that as a weak point of mine, and was sometimes very much afraid of it. "I exaggerate everything, that is where I go wrong," I repeated to myself every hour. But, nevertheless, Liza will very likely come still, nevertheless, was the refrain with which all my reflections ended then. I was so uneasy that I sometimes flew into a fury. "She'll come, she is certain to come!" I cried, running about the room, "if not today, she will come tomorrow; she'll seek me out! The damnable romanticism of these *pure hearts!* Oh, the vileness—oh, the silliness—oh, the stupidity of these 'wretched sentimental souls'! Why, how could one fail to understand? How could one possibly fail to understand?"

But at this point I stopped short, and even in great confusion.

"And how few, how few words," I thought, in passing, "were needed; how little of the idyllic (and affectedly, bookishly, artificially idyllic too) had sufficed to turn a whole human life at once according to my will. That's innocence for you! That's virgin soil for you!"

At times the thought occurred to me to go to her, "to tell her all" and beg her not to come to me. But this thought stirred such wrath in me that I believed I would have crushed that "damned" Liza if she had happened to be near me at the time. I would have insulted her, have spat at her, have turned her out, have struck her!

One day passed, however, a second and a third; she did not come and I began to grow calmer, I felt particularly bold and cheerful after nine o'clock, I even began sometimes to dream, and rather sweetly: I, for instance, became the salvation of Liza, simply through her coming to me and my talking to her. I develop her, educate her. Finally, I notice that she loves me, loves me passionately. I pretend not to understand (I don't know, however, why I pretend, just for effect, perhaps). At last all confusion, beautiful, trembling and sobbing, she flings herself at my feet and tells me that I am her savior, and that she loves me better than anything in the world. I am amazed, but—"Liza," I say, "can you really believe that I have noticed your love? I saw it all, I divined it, but I did not dare to approach you first, because I had an influence over you and was afraid that you would force yourself, out of gratitude, to respond to my love, would try to rouse in your heart a feeling which was perhaps absent, and I did not wish that because it would be—tyranny. It would be indelicate (in short, I launch off at that point into European, inexplicably lofty subtleties, à la George Sand),[9] but now, now you are mine, you are my creation, you are pure, you are beautiful, you are my beautiful wife.

> And into my house come bold and free,
> Its rightful mistress there to be.[1]

Then we begin to live together happily, go abroad, etc., etc. In short, in the end it seemed vulgar to me myself, and I began to put out my tongue at myself.

Besides, they won't let her out, "the hussy!" I thought. After all, they don't let them go out very readily, especially in the evening (for some reason I fancied she would have to come in the evening, and precisely at seven o'clock). Though she did say she was not altogether a slave there yet, and had certain rights; so, h'm! Damn it all, she will come, she is sure to come!

It was a good thing, in fact, that Apollon distracted my attention at that time by his rudeness. He drove me beyond all patience! He was the bane of my life, the curse laid upon me by Providence. We had been squabbling continually for years, and I hated him. My God, how I hated him! I believe I had never hated anyone in my life as I hated him, especially at some moments. He was an elderly, dignified man, who worked part of his time as a tailor. But for some unknown reason, he despised me beyond all measure, and looked down upon me insufferably. Though indeed, he looked down upon everyone. Simply to glance at that flaxen, smoothly brushed head, at the tuft of hair he combed up on his forehead and oiled with sunflower oil, at that dignified mouth, always pursed, made one feel one was confronting a man who never doubted himself. He was an insufferable pedant, the greatest pedant I had met on earth, and with that had a vanity only befitting Alexander the Great. He was in love with every button on his coat, every nail on his fingers—absolutely in love with them, and he looked it! In his behavior to me he was an absolute tyrant, spoke very little to me, and if he chanced to glance at me he gave me a firm, majestically self-confident and invariably ironical look that sometimes drove me to fury. He did his work with the air of doing me the greatest favor. Though he did scarcely anything for me, and did not, indeed, consider himself obliged to do anything, there could be no doubt that he looked upon me as the greatest fool on earth, and that the reason he did not "get rid of me" was simply that he could get wages from me every month. He consented "to do nothing" for me for seven roubles a month. Many sins should be forgiven me for what I suffered from him. My hatred reached such a point that sometimes his very walk almost threw me into convulsions. What I loathed particularly was his lisp. His

---

9. George Sand (1804–1876), French woman writer concerned with the liberation of women.

1. These are the concluding lines of the poem by Nekrasov that opens this section (p. 624).

tongue must have been a little too long or something of that sort, for he continually lisped, and seemed to be very proud of it, imagining that it greatly added to his dignity. He spoke in a slow, measured tone, with his hands behind his back and his eyes fixed on the ground. He maddened me particularly when he read the Psalms aloud to himself behind his partition. I waged many a battle over that reading! But he was awfully fond of reading aloud in the evenings, in a slow, even, chanting voice, as though over the dead. It is interesting that he has ended up that way. He hires himself out to read the Psalms over the dead, and at the same time he kills rats and makes shoe polish. But at that time I could not get rid of him, it was as though he were chemically combined with my existence. Besides, nothing would have induced him to consent to leave me. I could not live in a furnished room: my apartment was my privacy, my shell, my cave, in which I concealed myself from all mankind, and Apollon seemed to me, God only knows why, an integral part of that apartment, and for seven whole years I could not get rid of him.

For example, to be two or three days late with his wages was impossible. He would have made such a fuss, I would not have known where to hide my head. But I was so exasperated with everyone during that period, that I made up my mind for some reason and with some object to *punish* Apollon and not to pay him for a fortnight the wages I owed him. I had intended to do this for a long time, for the last two years, simply in order to teach him not to give himself airs with me, and to show him that if I liked I could withhold his wages. I decided to say nothing to him about it, and even to be silent purposely in order to conquer his pride and force him to be the first to speak of his wages. Then I would take the seven roubles out of a drawer, show him I have the money and have put it aside purposely, but that I don't want, I don't want, I simply don't want to pay him his wages, I don't want to just because that is *what I want,* because "I am master and it is for me to decide," because he has been disrespectful, because he is a ruffian; but if he were to ask respectfully I might be softened and give it to him, otherwise he might wait another fortnight, another three weeks, a whole month . . .

But no matter how angry I was, he always got the better of me. I could not even hold out for four days. He began as he always did begin such cases, for there had been such cases already, there had been attempts (and it may be observed I knew all this beforehand, I knew his nasty tactics by heart), to wit: he would begin by fixing upon me an exceedingly severe stare, keeping it up for several minutes at a time, particularly on meeting me or seeing me out of the house. If I held out and pretended not to notice these stares, he would, still in silence, proceed to further tortures. All at once, for no reason at all, he would softly and smoothly walk into my room when I was pacing up and down, or reading, stand at the door, one hand behind his back and one foot forward, and fix upon me a stare more than severe, utterly contemptuous. If I suddenly asked him what he wanted, he would not answer, but continue to stare at me persistently for some seconds longer, then, with a peculiar compression of his lips and a very significant air, deliberately turn round and deliberately go back to his room. Two hours later he would come out again and again present himself before me in the same way. It has happened that in my fury I did not even ask him what he wanted, but simply raised my head sharply and imperiously and began staring back at him. So we stared at one another for two minutes; at last he turned with deliberation and dignity and went back again for two hours.

If I were still not brought to reason by all this, but persisted in my revolt, he would suddenly begin sighing while he looked at me, long, deep sighs as though measuring by them the depths of my moral degradation, and, of course, it ended at last by his triumphing completely: I raged and shouted, but was still forced to do what he wanted.

This time the usual maneuvers of "severe staring" had scarcely begun when I lost my temper and flew at him in a fury. I was irritated beyond endurance even without him.

"Wait," I shouted in a frenzy, as he was slowly and silently turning with one hand behind his back, to go to his room. "Wait! Come back, come back, I tell you!" and I must have bawled so unnaturally, that he turned round and even looked at me with a certain amazement. However, he persisted in saying nothing, and that infuriated me.

"How dare you come and look at me like that without being sent for? Answer!" After looking at me calmly for half a minute, he began turning round again.

"Wait!" I roared, running up to him. "Don't stir! There. Answer, now: what did you come in to look at?"

"If you have any order to give me at the moment, it is my duty to carry it out," he answered, after another silent pause, with a slow, measured lisp, raising his eyebrows and calmly twisting his head from one side to another, all this with exasperating composure.

"That's not it, that is not what I am asking you about, you torturer!" I shouted, shaking with anger. "I'll tell you myself, you torturer, why you came here: you see, I don't give you your wages, you are so proud you don't want to bow down and ask for it, and so you have come to punish me with your stupid stares, to torture me, and you have no sus-pic-ion, you torturer, how stupid it is—stupid, stupid, stupid, stupid!"

He would have turned round again without a word, but I seized him.

"Listen," I shouted to him. "Here's the money, do you see, here it is" (I took it out of the table drawer) "here's the whole seven roubles but you are not going to have it, you . . . are . . . not . . . going . . . to . . . have it until you come respectfully with bowed head to beg my pardon. Do you hear?"

"That cannot be," he answered, with the most unnatural self-confidence.

"It will be so," I said. "I give you my word of honor, it will be!"

"And there's nothing for me to beg your pardon for," he went on, as though he had not noticed my exclamations at all. "Why, besides, you called me a 'torturer,' for which I can summon you at the police station at any time for insulting behavior."

"Go, summon me," I roared, "go at once, this very minute, this very second! You are a torturer all the same! A torturer! A torturer!" But he merely looked at me, then turned, and regardless of my loud calls to him, he walked to his room with an even step and without looking round.

"If it had not been for Liza nothing of this would have happened," I decided inwardly. Then, after waiting a minute, I myself went behind the screen with a dignified and solemn air, though my heart was beating slowly and violently.

"Apollon," I said quietly and emphatically, though I was breathless, "go at once without a minute's delay and fetch the police officer."

He had meanwhile settled himself at his table, put on his spectacles and taken up something to tailor. But, hearing my order, he burst into a guffaw.

"At once, go this minute! Go on, or else you can't imagine what will happen."

"You are certainly not in your right mind," he observed, without even raising his head, lisping as deliberately as ever and threading his needle. "Whoever heard of a man sending for the police against himself? And as for being frightened—you are upsetting yourself about nothing, for nothing will come of it."

"Go!" I shrieked, grabbing him by the shoulder. I felt that in another minute I would hit him.

But I did not notice that suddenly the door from the passage softly and slowly opened at that instant and a figure came in, stopped short, and began staring at us in amazement. I glanced, nearly died with shame, and rushed back to my room. There, clutching at my hair with both hands, I leaned my head against the wall and stood motionless in that position.

Two minutes later I heard Apollon's deliberate footsteps.

"There is *some woman* asking for you," he said, looking at me with peculiar severity. Then he stood aside and let in—Liza. He would not go away, but stared at us sarcastically.

"Go away, go away," I commanded in desperation. At that moment my clock began whirring and wheezing and struck seven.

IX

> And into my house come bold and free,
> Its rightful mistress there to be.
>
> *From the same poetic work*

I stood before her crushed, crestfallen, revoltingly embarrassed, and I believe I smiled as I did my utmost to wrap myself in the skirts of my ragged wadded robe— just exactly as I had imagined the scene not long before in a fit of depression. After standing over us for a couple of minutes Apollon went away, but that did not make me more comfortable. What made it worse was that suddenly, she, too, became embarrassed, more so, in fact, than I would have expected. At the sight of me, of course.

"Sit down," I said mechanically, moving a chair up to the table, and I sat down on the sofa. She obediently sat down at once and gazed at me open-eyed, evidently expecting something from me at once. This naïveté of expectation drove me to fury, but I restrained myself.

She ought to have tried not to notice, as though everything had been as usual, while instead she . . . and I dimly felt that I would make her pay dearly for *all this*.

"You have found me in a strange position, Liza," I began, stammering and knowing that this was the wrong way to begin.

"No, no, don't imagine anything," I cried, seeing that she had suddenly flushed. "I am not ashamed of my poverty. On the contrary, I look on my poverty with pride. I am poor but honorable. One can be poor and honorable," I muttered. "However— would you like tea?"

"No—" she was beginning.

"Wait a minute."

I leapt up and ran to Apollon. I had to get out of the room somehow.

"Apollon," I whispered in feverish haste, flinging down before him the seven roubles which had remained all the time in my clenched fist, "here are your wages. You see I give them to you; but for that you must come to my rescue: bring me tea and a dozen rusks from the restaurant. If you won't go, you'll make a man miserable! You don't know what this woman is. This is—everything! You may be imagining something, but you don't know what a woman she is!"

Apollon, who had already sat down to his work and put on his spectacles again, at first glanced askance at the money without speaking or putting down his needle; then, without paying the slightest attention to me, or making any answer, he went on busying himself with his needle, which he had not yet threaded. I waited before him for several minutes with my arms crossed *à la Napoleon*. My temples were moist with sweat. I was pale, I felt it. But, thank God, he must have been moved to pity, looking at me. Having threaded his needle, he deliberately got up from his seat, deliberately moved back his chair, deliberately took off his spectacles, deliberately counted the money, and finally asking me over his shoulder: "Shall I get a whole pot?" deliberately walked out of the room. As I was going back to Liza, the thought occurred to me on the way: shouldn't I run away just as I was in my robe, no matter where, and let come what may?

I sat down again. She looked at me uneasily. For some minutes we were silent.

"I will kill him," I shouted suddenly, striking the table with my fist so that the ink spurted out of the inkstand.

"What are you saying!" she cried, starting.

"I will kill him! kill him!" I shrieked, suddenly striking the table in absolute frenzy, and at the same time fully understanding how stupid it was to be in such a frenzy.

"You don't know, Liza, what that torturer is to me. He is my torturer. He has gone now to fetch some rusks; he—"

And suddenly I burst into tears. It was an hysterical attack. How ashamed I felt in the midst of my sobs; but still I could not restrain them.

She was frightened. "What is the matter? What is wrong?" she shrieked, fussing around me.

"Water, give me water, over there!" I muttered in a faint voice, though I was inwardly conscious that I could easily have done without water and without muttering in a faint voice. But I was what is called *putting it on*, to save appearances, though the attack was a genuine one.

She gave me water, looking at me in bewilderment. At that moment Apollon brought in the tea. It suddenly seemed to me that this commonplace and prosaic tea was terribly undignified and paltry after all that had happened, and I blushed. Liza even looked at Apollon with alarm. He went out without a glance at us.

"Liza, do you despise me?" I asked, looking at her fixedly, trembling with impatience to know what she was thinking.

She was embarrassed and did not know what to answer.

"Drink your tea," I said to her angrily. I was angry with myself, but, of course, it was she who would have to pay for it. A horrible spite against her suddenly surged up in my heart; I believe I could have killed her. To revenge myself on her I swore inwardly not to say a word to her all the time. "She is the cause of it all," I thought.

Our silence lasted for five minutes. The tea stood on the table; we did not touch it. I had got to the point of purposely refraining from beginning to drink in order to embarrass her further; it was awkward for her to begin alone. Several times she glanced at me with mournful perplexity. I was obstinately silent. I was, of course, myself the chief sufferer, because I was fully conscious of the disgusting meanness of my spiteful stupidity, and yet at the same time I absolutely could not restrain myself.

"I want to—get away—from there altogether," she began, to break the silence in some way, but, poor girl, that was just what she ought not to have spoken about at such a moment, stupid enough even without that to a man so stupid as I was. My heart positively ached with pity for her tactless and unnecessary straightforwardness. But something hideous at once stifled all compassion in me; it even provoked me to greater venom. Let the whole world go to pot. Another five minutes passed.

"Perhaps I am in your way?" she began timidly, hardly audibly, and was getting up.

But as soon as I saw this first impulse of wounded dignity I positively trembled with spite, and at once burst out.

"Why did you come to me, tell me that, please?" I began, gasping for breath and regardless of all logical connection in my words. I longed to have it all out at once, at one burst: I did not even trouble how to begin.

"Why did you come? Answer, answer," I cried, hardly knowing what I was doing. "I'll tell you, my good girl, why you came. You came because I talked *fine sentiments* to you then. So now you are soft as butter and longing for fine sentiments again. So you may as well know, know that I was laughing at you then. And I am laughing at you now. Why are you shuddering? Yes, I was laughing at you! I had been insulted just before, at dinner, by the fellows who came that evening before me. I came to you, meaning to thrash one of them, an officer; but I didn't succeed. I didn't find him; I had to avenge the insult on someone to get my own back again; you turned up, I vented my spleen on you and laughed at you. I had been humiliated, so I wanted to humiliate; I had been treated like a rag, so I wanted to show my power. That's what it was, and you imagined I had come there on purpose to save you, didn't you? Did you imagine that? Did you imagine that?"

I knew that she would perhaps get muddled and not grasp all the details, but I knew, too, that she would grasp the gist of it very well. And so, indeed, she did. She turned white as a handkerchief, tried to say something, and distorted her mouth painfully but she sank on a chair as though she had been felled by an ax. And all the time afterward she listened to me with her lips parted and her eyes wide open, shuddering with awful terror. The cynicism, the cynicism of my words overwhelmed her—

"Save you!" I went on, jumping up from my chair and running up and down the room before her. "Save you from what? But perhaps I am worse than you myself. Why didn't you throw it in my teeth when I was giving you that sermon: 'But you, what did you come here for yourself? Was it to read us a sermon?' Power, power was what I wanted then, sport was what I wanted, I wanted to wring out your tears, your humiliation, your hysteria—that was what I wanted then! After all, I couldn't keep it up then, because I am a wretch, I was frightened, and the devil knows why, gave you my address in my folly. Afterward, before I got home, I was cursing and swearing at you because of that address. I hated you already because of the lies I had told you. Because I only like to play with words, to dream in my mind, but, do you know, what I really want is that you would all go to hell, that is what I want. I want peace; yes, I'd sell the whole world for a farthing right now, so long as I was left in peace. Is the world to go to pot, or am I to go without my tea? I say let the world go to pot as long as I get my tea every time. Did you know that, or not? Well, anyway, I know that I am a blackguard, a scoundrel, an egotist, a sluggard. Here I have been shuddering for the last three days at the thought of your coming. And do you know what has worried me particularly for these three days? That I posed as such a hero to you then, and now you would see me in a wretched torn robe, a beggar, an abomination. I told you just now that I was not ashamed of my poverty; you may as well know that I am ashamed of it; I am more ashamed of it than of anything, more afraid of it than of being found out if I were a thief, because I am as vain as though I had been skinned and the very air blowing on me hurt. Surely by now even you must have realized that I will never forgive you for having found me in this wretched robe, just as I was flying at Apollon like a spiteful sheep-dog at his lackey, and the lackey was jeering at him! And I shall never forgive you for the tears I could not help shedding before you just now, like some silly woman put to shame! And for what I am confessing to you now, I shall never forgive *you,* either! Yes—you must answer for it all because you turned up like this, because I am a blackguard, because I am the nastiest, stupidest, pettiest, absurdest and most envious of all worms on earth, none of whom is a bit better than I am, but who, the devil only knows why, are never embarrassed; while I will always be insulted by every louse, that is my doom! And what is it to me that you don't understand a word of this! And what do I care, what do I care about you, and whether you go to ruin there or not? Do you understand how I will hate you now after saying this, for having been here and listening? After all, a man speaks out like this once in a lifetime and then it is in hysterics! What more do you want? Why, after all, do you still stand there in front of me? Why do you torment me? Why don't you go?"

But at this point a strange thing happened.

I was so accustomed to think and imagine everything from books, and to picture everything in the world to myself just as I had made it up in my dreams beforehand, that I could not even take in this strange circumstance all at once. What happened was this: Liza, wounded and crushed by me, understood a great deal more than I imagined. She understood from all this what a woman understands first of all, if she feels genuine love, that is, that I was myself unhappy.

The frightened and wounded expression on her face was followed first by a look of sorrowful perplexity. When I began to call myself a scoundrel and a blackguard and my tears flowed (that tirade was accompanied throughout by tears) her whole face worked convulsively. She was on the point of getting up and stopping me; when I finished she took no notice of my shouting: "Why are you here, why don't you go away?" but realized only that it must have been very bitter to me to say all this. Besides, she was so crushed, poor girl; she considered herself infinitely beneath me; how could she feel anger or resentment? Suddenly she leapt up from her chair with an irresistible impulse and held out her hands, yearning toward me, though still timid and not daring to stir. At this point there was an upheaval in my heart too. Then she suddenly rushed to me, threw her arms round me and burst into tears. I, too, could not restrain myself, and sobbed as I never had before.

"They won't let me—I can't be—good!" I managed to say, then I went to the sofa, fell on it, face downward, and sobbed on it for a quarter of an hour in genuine hysterics. She knelt near me, put her arms round me and stayed motionless in that position.

But the trouble was that the hysterics could not go on for ever. And (after all, I am writing the loathsome truth) lying face downward on the sofa with my face thrust into my nasty leather pillow, I began by degrees to be aware of a far-away, involuntary but irresistible feeling that after all it would be awkward for me to raise my head now and look Liza straight in the face. Why was I ashamed? I don't know, but I was ashamed. In my overwrought brain the thought also occurred that our parts were after all completely reversed now, that she was now the heroine, while I was just a crushed and humiliated creature as she had been before me that night—four days before . . . And all this came into my mind during the minutes I was lying face down on the sofa!

My God! surely I was not envious of her then?

I don't know, to this day I cannot decide, and at the time, of course, I was still less able to understand what I was feeling than now. I cannot get on without domineering and tyrannizing over someone, after all, but—but, after all, there is no explaining anything by reasoning and consequently it is useless to reason.

I conquered myself, however, and raised my head—I had to do so sooner or later—and I am convinced to this day that it was just because I was ashamed to look at her that another feeling was suddenly kindled and flamed up in my heart—a feeling of mastery and possession. My eyes gleamed with passion, and I gripped her hands tightly. How I hated her and how I was drawn to her at that minute! The one feeling intensified the other. It was almost like an act of vengeance! At first there was a look of amazement, even of terror, on her face, but only for one instant. She warmly and rapturously embraced me.

X

A quarter of an hour later I was rushing up and down the room in frenzied impatience, from minute to minute I went up to the screen and peeped through the crack at Liza. She was sitting on the floor with her head leaning against the bed, and must have been crying. But she did not go away, and that irritated me. This time she understood it all. I had insulted her once and for all, but—there's no need to describe it. She realized that my outburst of passion had been simply revenge, a new humiliation for her and that to my earlier, almost generalized hatred was added now a *personal, envious* hatred—though I do not maintain positively that she understood all this distinctly; but she certainly did fully understand that I was a despicable man, and what was worse, incapable of loving her.

I know I shall be told that this is incredible; that it is incredible to be as spiteful and stupid as I was; it may be added it was strange that I would not love her, or at any rate, appreciate her love. Why is it strange? In the first place, by then I was incapable of love, for, I repeat, with me loving meant tyrannizing and showing my moral superiority. I have never in my life ever been able to imagine any other sort of love, and have nowadays come to the point of sometimes thinking that love really consists in the right—freely given by the beloved object—to be tyrannized over. Even in my underground dreams I did not imagine love in any form except as a struggle. I always began it with hatred and ended it with moral subjugation, and afterward I could never imagine what to do with the subjugated object. And what is there incredible in that, since I had so succeeded in corrupting myself morally, since I was so out of touch with "real life," that I had just thought of reproaching her and putting her to shame for having come to me to hear "fine sentiments," and I did not even guess that she had come not at all to hear fine sentiments, but to love me, because to a woman true resurrection, true salvation from any sort of ruin, and true moral regeneration is contained in love and can only show itself in that form. I no longer hated her so much, however, when I was running about the room and peeping through the crack in the screen. I was only insufferably oppressed by her being here. I wanted her to disappear. I wanted "peace," I wanted to be left alone in my underground world. "Real life" oppressed me with its novelty so much that I could hardly breathe.

But several minutes passed and she still remained without stirring, as though she were unconscious. I had the shamelessness to tap softly at the screen as though to remind her. She started, sprang up, and flew to seek her shawl, her hat, her coat, just as though she were making her escape from me. Two minutes later she came from behind the screen and looked with heavy eyes at me. I gave a spiteful grin, which was forced, however, to *keep up appearances,* and I turned away from her look.

"Good-by," she said, going toward the door.

I ran up to her, seized her hand, opened it, thrust something in it—and closed it again. Then I turned immediately and hurriedly rushed to the other corner of the room, to avoid seeing, anyway—

I meant to lie a moment ago—to write that I did this accidentally, not knowing what I was doing, through foolishness, through losing my head. But I don't want to lie, and so I will say straight out that I opened her hand and put the money in it—from spite. It came into my head to do so while I was running up and down the room and she was sitting behind the screen. But I can say this for certain: though I did that cruel thing purposely, it was not an impulse from the heart, but came from my evil brain. This cruelty was so affected, so purposely made up, so completely a product of the brain, of *books,* that I could not even keep it up for a minute—first I rushed to the corner to avoid seeing her, and then in shame and despair rushed after Liza. I opened the door in the passage and began listening.

"Liza! Liza!" I cried on the stairs, but in a low voice, not boldly.

There was no answer, but it seemed to me I heard her footsteps, lower down on the stairs.

"Liza!" I cried, more loudly.

No answer. But at that minute I heard the stiff outer glass door open heavily with a creak and slam violently. The roar echoed up the stairs.

She had gone. I went back to my room in hesitation. I felt horribly oppressed.

I stood still at the table beside the chair on which she had sat and looked aimlessly before me. A minute passed. Suddenly I started; straight before me on the table I saw—in short, I saw a crumpled blue five-rouble note, the one I had thrust into her hand a minute before. It was the same note; it could be no other, there was no other in the apartment. So she had managed to fling it from her hand on the table at the moment when I had rushed into the farther corner.

So what? I might have expected that she would do that. Might I have expected it? No, I was such an egotist, I was so lacking in respect for people in actuality, that I could not even imagine she would do so. I could not endure it. A moment later I flew like a madman to get dressed, flinging on what I could at random and ran headlong after her. She could not have got two hundred paces away when I ran out into the street.

It was a still night and the snow was coming down in masses and falling almost perpendicularly, blanketing the pavement and the empty street. There was no one in the street, no sound was to be heard. The street lamps gave a disconsolate and useless glimmer. I ran two hundred paces to the intersection and stopped short. Where had she gone? And why was I running after her?

Why? To fall down before her, to sob with remorse, to kiss her feet, to beg her forgiveness! I longed for that. My whole heart was being rent to pieces, and never, never will I recall that minute with indifference. But—what for? I thought. Would I not begin to hate her, perhaps, even tomorrow, just because I had kissed her feet today? Would I give her happiness? Had I not again recognized that day, for the hundredth time, what I was worth? Would I not torment her?

I stood in the snow, gazing into the troubled darkness and pondered this.

"And will it not be better? *Will it not be better?*" I fantasied afterward at home, stifling the living pang of my heart with fantastic dreams. "Will it not be better that she carry the outrage with her forever? Outrage—why, after all, that is purification: it is the most stinging and painful consciousness! Tomorrow I would have defiled her soul and have exhausted her heart, while now the feeling of humiliation will never die in her, and however loathsome the filth awaiting her, that outrage will elevate and purify her—by hatred—h'm!—perhaps by forgiveness also. But will all that make things easier for her, though? . . ."

And, indeed, I will at this point ask an idle question on my own account: which is better—cheap happiness or exalted sufferings? Well, which is better?

So I dreamed as I sat at home that evening, almost dead with the pain in my soul. Never yet had I endured such suffering and remorse, but could there possibly have been the faintest doubt when I ran out from my lodging that I would turn back halfway? I never met Liza again and I have heard nothing about her. I will add, too, that for a long time afterward I remained pleased with the *phrase* about the utility of outrage and hatred, in spite of the fact that I almost fell ill from misery.

Even now, many years later, I somehow remember all this as very bad. I have many bad memories now, but—hadn't I better end my "Notes" here? I believe I made a mistake in beginning to write this *story;* so it's hardly literature so much as corrective punishment. After all, to tell long stories, for example, showing how I have ruined my life by morally rotting in my corner, through lack of fitting environment, through divorce from reality, and vainglorious spite in my underground world, would certainly not be interesting; a novel needs a hero, and all the traits of an anti-hero are *expressly* gathered together here, and what matters most, it all produces an unpleasant impression, for we are all divorced from life, we are all cripples, every one of us, more or less. We are so far divorced from it that we immediately feel a sort of loathing for actual "real life," and so cannot even stand to be reminded of it. After all, we have reached the point of almost looking at actual "real life" as an effort, almost as hard work, and we are all privately agreed that it is better in books. And why do we sometimes fret, why are we perverse and ask for something else? We don't know why ourselves. It would be worse for us if our capricious requests were granted. Come, try, come give anyone of us, for instance, a little more independence, untie our hands, widen the spheres of our activity, relax the controls and we—yes, I assure you—we would immediately beg to be under control again. I know that you will very likely be angry with me for that, and will begin to shout and stamp your feet. "Speak for yourself," you will say, "and for your miseries in your underground holes, but don't dare to say 'all of us.'" Excuse me, gentlemen, after all I do not mean to justify myself with that "all of us." As for what concerns me in particular I have only, after all, in my life carried to an extreme what you have not dared to carry halfway, and what's more, you have taken your cowardice for good sense, and have found comfort in deceiving yourselves. So that perhaps, after all, there is more "life" in me than in you. Look into it more carefully! After all, we don't even know where living exists now, what it is, and what it is called! Leave us alone without books and we will be lost and in a confusion at once—we will not know what to join, what to cling to, what to love and what to hate, what to respect and what to despise. We are even oppressed by being men—men with real *individual* body and blood. We are ashamed of it, we think it a disgrace and try to contrive to be some sort of impossible generalized man. We are still-born, and for many years we have not been begotten by living fathers, and that suits us better and better. We are developing a taste for it. Soon we shall somehow contrive to be born from an idea. But enough; I don't want to write more from "underground" . . .

The "notes" of this paradoxalist do not end here, however. He could not resist and continued them. But it also seems to me that we may stop here.

≪≫

RESONANCES

Friedrich Nietzsche: from *Daybreak*[1]

In this book you will discover a "subterranean man" at work, one who tunnels and mines and undermines. You will see him—presupposing you have eyes capable of seeing this work in the depths—going forward slowly, cautiously, gently inexorable, without betraying very much of the distress which any protracted deprivation of light and air must entail; you might even call him contented, working there in the dark. Does it not seem as though some faith were leading him on, some consolation offering him compensation? As though he perhaps desires this prolonged obscurity, desires to be incomprehensible, concealed, enigmatic, because he knows what he will thereby also acquire: his own morning, his own redemption, his own *daybreak?* . . . He will return, that is certain: do not ask him what he is looking for down there, he will tell you himself of his own accord; this seeming Trophonius[2] and subterranean, as soon as he has 'become a man' again. Being silent is something one completely unlearns if, like him, one has been for so long a solitary mole————

And indeed, my patient friends, I shall now tell you what I was after down there—here in this late preface which could easily have become a funeral oration: for I have returned and, believe it or not, returned safe and sound. Do not think for a moment that I intend to invite you to the same hazardous enterprise! Or even only to the same solitude! For he who proceeds on his own path in this fashion encounters no one: that is inherent in "proceeding on one's own path." No one comes along to help him: all the perils, accidents, malice and bad weather which assail him he has to tackle by himself. For his path is *his alone*—as is, of course, the bitterness and occasional ill-humour he feels at this "his alone": among which is included, for instance, the knowledge that even his friends are unable to divine where he is or whither he is going, that they will sometimes ask themselves: "what? is he going at all? does he still have—a path?"—At that time I undertook something not everyone may undertake: I descended into the depths, I tunnelled into the foundations, I commenced an investigation and digging out of an ancient *faith,* one upon which we philosophers have for a couple of millennia been accustomed to build as if upon the firmest of all foundations—and have continued to do so even though every building hitherto erected on them has fallen down: I commenced to undermine our *faith in morality.* But you do not understand me?

* * *

Do not forget!—The higher we soar, the smaller we seem to those who cannot fly.

---

1. Translated by R. J. Hollingdale. Whereas Dostoevsky wrote highly philosophical novels, the radically skeptical German philosopher Friedrich Nietzsche (1844–1900) wrote philosophy with a novelist's eye and a poet's ear. He shared Dostoevsky's sense of estrangement from the optimistic rationalism of the bourgeois society around him, though unlike Dostoevsky he was deeply opposed to the "slave morality" of Christianity, as he described it. After a brief early career as a professor of philology, he lived in seclusion in Switzerland, Italy, and the south of France, writing searching analyses of morality, rationality, and language, including *Beyond Good and Evil* and *The Genealogy of Morals.* He pays direct tribute to Dostoevsky in the preface to his 1881 collection *Daybreak,* a shifting blend of aphorisms and philosophical mediations by a philosopher turned underground man.

2. In Greek myth, an oracle consulted by descending into a chasm.

We aeronauts of the spirit!—All those brave birds which fly out into the distance, into the farthest distance—it is certain! somewhere or other they will be unable to go on and will perch on a mast or a bare cliff-face—and they will even be thankful for this miserable accommodation! But who could venture to infer from that, that there was *not* an immense open space before them, that they had flown as far as one *could* fly! All our great teachers and predecessors have at last come to a stop and it is not with the noblest or most graceful of gestures that weariness comes to a stop: it will be the same with you and me! But what does that matter to you and me! *Other birds will fly farther!* This insight and faith of ours vies with them in flying up and away; it rises above our heads and above our impotence into the heights and from there surveys the distance and sees before it the flocks of birds which, far stronger than we, still strive whither we have striven, and where everything is still sea, sea, sea![3]—And whither then would we go? Would we *cross* the sea? Whither does this mighty longing draw us, this longing that is worth more to us than any pleasure? Why just in this direction, thither where all the suns of humanity have hitherto *gone down?* Will it perhaps be said of us one day that we too, *steering westward, hoped to reach an India*—but that it was our fate to be wrecked against infinity? Or, my brothers. Or?—

Ishikawa Takuboku: from *The Romaji Diary*[1]

7th April 1909

This morning a violent west wind was roaring through the sky. The windows on the third floor were all rattling, and a dustlike sand from the street below came blowing in the cracks. But in spite of the wind the scattered clouds were motionless.

A springlike sunshine was warming the windowpanes. It was the sort of day when you might be sweating if it weren't for the wind. The old man from the lending library came in, wiping his nose with the palm of his hand. "Terrible wind," said he. "Still, the cherry blossoms all over Tokyo will be opening today. Wind or no wind, it's fine weather."

"Spring has come at last," I said, but of course he couldn't understand my feelings. "Eh! Eh!" answered the old man, "Spring, you know, is a loss as far as we're concerned. Lending books is finished for the season. All my customers would rather go out for a walk than read a book, and I can't say I blame them. The few people who do read books naturally take their time over it."

There is a five-yen bill in my wallet, the remains of what I borrowed yesterday of next month's pay from the company. All morning long I couldn't think about anything else. It must be the way people who normally have money feel when they are

---

3. "Still sea," *noch Meer* in German, plays on the striving to have *noch mehr*—still more.
1. Translated by Donald Keene. Born in 1885 on the island of Hokkaido, in the far north of Japan, Ishikawa Takuboku had set his sights on becoming a poet and novelist. Married and with a young daughter, he left them at home when he came to Tokyo hoping to establish himself. He rented a room and found a low-paying job as a newspaper proofreader, unable to afford to bring his family to join him. In the spring of 1909, consumed with self-doubt, he kept a secret diary from April to June, writing it in Japanese but using "romaji"—the Roman alphabet—so that his family wouldn't be able to read it. The diary records his sharp, ironic observations of life in late Meiji Tokyo, his ambitions, and his despair for the future. A real-life "underground man," Ishikawa was in fact reading widely in Russian literature at the time he wrote this diary. In 1910 he published a volume of experimental poetry, *A Handful of Sand,* and brought his family to Tokyo. All three contracted tuberculosis; Takuboku died of it in 1912.

suddenly deprived of it. Both situations are funny, but though they're funny in quite the same way, there's a big difference in the happiness or grief involved!

Having nothing else to do, I tried to make a table of Romaji. From time to time the memory of my mother and my wife in Hokkaido leapt out of the middle of the table and took possession of me. "Spring has come. It's April! Spring! Spring! The blossoms are opening! It's already a year since I came to Tokyo . . . ! And still I haven't been able to make any arrangements to send for my family." That's the problem that keeps tormenting me, I don't know how many times a day.

Why did I decide to keep this diary in Romaji? Why? I love my wife, and it's precisely because I love her that I don't want her to read this diary. No, that's a lie! It's true that I love her, and it's true that I don't want her to read this, but the two facts are not necessarily related.

Am I a weakling then? No, my trouble comes entirely from the mistaken institution of marriage. Marriage! What an idiotic institution! What's to be done about it?

Today the members of the tennis team from Kyoto University, who are staying in the next room, are having their last day of play. They went off in high spirits.

After eating lunch I went by streetcar as usual to the office, where I corrected proofs with the old men in a corner of the editorial room. About five o'clock in the evening the proofs for the first edition were finished and I went back home: this is my daily stint to earn a living.

On the way back I walked along a street in Hongō, intending to do a little shopping. The cherry trees of the university campus had half-opened their blossoms in just one day.

The world is now completely given over to the spring.

The sound of the footsteps of the people going back and forth crowding the streets somehow exhilarated me. I couldn't help wondering where they had so suddenly appeared from, those beautiful people in beautiful clothes who were streaming by. It's spring, I thought. Then I thought of my wife and little Kyōko.

I had promised myself that I would send for them by April and I haven't—no, I can't.

Oh, my writing is my enemy, and my philosophy nothing but empty logic that I myself ridicule. I seem to desire so many things, but don't they boil down to one small one? Money!

When I got back after ten tonight there was a tremendous racket in the next room. One of the tennis players, having returned drunk from a dinner given in their honor, had smashed the light and was breaking up the frames of the sliding doors.

I met one of the students at the entrance to his room. He was a classmate of mine in high school and is now studying engineering in Kyoto. We carried on a childish conversation until about one in the morning. In the meantime the uproar in the next room had subsided. The spring night deepened, the night of a day which had opened the blossoms all over the city.

In the midst of a city quiet in sleep, I lay awake alone, and, counting the breaths of the calm spring night, I felt how dull and meaningless my life in this little room has been. What must I look like sleeping here all alone in this tiny room, overcome by an indescribable fatigue? The final discovery of human beings must be that the human being itself is not of the slightest importance.

I have lived a long time—over two hundred days—in this little room, filled with heavy uneasiness, and with the shallow hope that I may find something to interest me. How long will it last . . . ? No!

I read in bed the *Collected Stories of Turgenev*.[2]

* * *

9th, Friday

The cherry blossoms are almost in full bloom: it is a warm, calm, perfectly springlike day; the sky in the distance is veiled in mist.

On the tram going back this evening I saw a child who looked just as Kyōko did when I parted from her last spring. She was making a squeak with a toy flute, and as she did so she looked at me bashfully, hiding her laughing face. She was so adorable I felt like taking her in my arms.

The face of the child's mother looked the way I imagine my mother's did when she was young. The nose, the cheeks, the eyes—the whole face was like hers. It wasn't a very refined face!

It is a spring evening sweet as milk. In the distance a frog is croaking. The first frog of the year!

10th, Saturday

Last night I read until past three, and I got up today after ten. A wind from the south is blowing in the clear sky.

The fact that recent short stories have come to be no more than a kind of new form of sketches from life—no—the fact that we have stopped wanting to read them—in other words, the fact that we are dissatisfied with them—shows that the authority of Naturalistic philosophy as a view of life is gradually dying out.

How times change! It cannot be denied that Naturalism[3] was the philosophy we sought out with the greatest eagerness. But before we knew it we had discovered the logical contradictions in it. Then when we had surmounted these contradictions and moved forward, the sword we held in our hands was no longer the sword of Naturalism. I for one am no longer able to content myself with an attitude of detachment. The attitude of the writer toward humanity cannot be one of detachment. He must be a critic. Or a planner for mankind.

The positive Naturalism I have reached is a new idealism. For a long time we despised the word "ideal." As a matter of fact, the kind of ideals we were then holding were, as we discovered, no more than pitiful illusions—no more than a *life illusion*. But we are alive and we must live. The ideal of destroying everything and then building anew with our own hands is no longer just a pitiful illusion. Even if the ideal itself is just a *life illusion,* we cannot live without it. If this deep internal need must also be discarded, there is nothing left for me to do but to die.

What I wrote this morning is a lie. At least in so far as I am concerned it is not a first principle. I do not consider that any human achievement, regardless of the field, is of consequence. I used to think that literature was more admirable and valuable than other things, but that was before I knew what "admirable" meant. Is it possible that anything done by a human being can be admirable? The human being itself is neither admirable nor valuable.

---

2. Ivan Turgenev (1818–1883), Russian writer of tragic, realistic tales, often focusing on the quandaries of Russian intellectuals in a stagnant society.
3. Aesthetic movement championed by Emile Zola and other 19th-century French novelists, who sought to depict social life with scientific detachment, often showing how individual choices and happiness are constrained by social forces.

What I desire is peace of mind. I realized it this evening for the first time. Yes, it is exactly that, beyond any doubt.

I wonder what real assurance—the feeling that there is nothing to worry about—must be like. It has been such a long time since I experienced it—not since I became conscious of what was going on in the world—that I have forgotten.

Of late the most tranquil moments in my life have been the ones spent going back and forth to work on the streetcar. When I am at home doing nothing, I feel as if I should be doing something. But what? That's the problem. Read? Write? But there seems to be nothing to read or write. No, reading and writing are only a part of that "something." Is there anything else I can do besides read and write? That I don't know. But I feel, anyway, as though I should do something. Even when I am thinking of quite carefree things, I feel as if I am always being pursued by that "something." And as a result I can't seem to put my hand to anything.

At the office I wish the time would pass more quickly. It's not that there's anything I especially dislike about the work, or that the surroundings are disagreeable: when I return home early I am pursued by that feeling that I must do "something." I don't know what it is I should be doing, but I'm haunted by that compulsion.

* * *

Of late I have been tempted from time to time by the desire to go where there is no one else. A place with no one else—or at least where no voices are heard, where nothing can be heard which has the remotest connection with me, a place where there is no fear of anyone coming and looking at me—oh, I would like to go there all by myself for a week, ten days, no, even for a day, even for half a day.

I should like to rest my body as I please in a place where no matter what expression I have on my face, no matter what appearance I make, there is no fear of being noticed.

Sometimes, trying to forget this thought, I go to places where there are many people, like the motion pictures. And sometimes, on the other hand, I go when I feel a yearning for people—for young women. But I can't find any satisfaction there either. While I am watching the film, especially if it is the most stupid, childish kind, I do manage to return to the heart of a child, and I can forget everything; but as soon as the film is over and the lights flash on, and I see the countless swarming people, the desire to seek some gayer, more amusing place rises all the stronger within my breast. Sometimes I can smell right in front of my nose the fragrance of hair, or I can feel a warm hand in mine. But at such times my mind is calculating the contents of my pocketbook—or, rather, thinking of how to borrow some money! When I hold a warm hand or breathe the strong perfume of hair, I have the feeling not merely of holding a hand, but of taking in my arms a soft, warm, white body. And how lonely I feel when I return home without having done so! It is not just the loneliness that comes from having been unable to obtain sexual satisfaction: it is the deep terrible despair at not being able to get everything I want.

When I have had a little money I have without hesitation gone, filled with the voice of lust, to those narrow dirty streets.

Since last autumn I have gone thirteen or fourteen times, and I have bought about ten prostitutes. Mitsu, Masa, Kiyo, Mine, Tsuyu, Hana, Aki. . . . I have forgotten the names of some of them. What I sought was a warm, soft, white body: a pleasure in which my body and mind would melt. But those women, the old ones and the ones of fifteen who were still children, had all slept with hundreds or thousands of men.

There is no luster to their faces, their skin is cold and rough, they are so used to men that they feel no excitement. All it amounts to is that for a little while they hire out their private parts to men, and receive a pittance in exchange. Without even bothering to undo their sashes, they say "All right," and lie down just as they are, without the slightest embarrassment.

It doesn't make the least difference to them whether or not there is anyone on the other side of the partition who hears them. All it amounts to is that an excretory process has been effected with thousands of men. They have no desire to heal themselves with a pleasure in which the body and mind melt.

The nervous desire to seek strong excitement did not leave me even when I was receiving the excitement. I have spent the night three or four times.

It is no longer possible for me to go off somewhere all by myself, and yet I can obtain no satisfaction from people. I can't stand the agony of human life itself, but I can't do anything about it. Everything is in shackles, and there is heavy responsibility. What should I do? Hamlet said, *To be or not to be?* But in the present world the question of death has become more complicated than in Hamlet's time. Oh, Ilya![4] Ilya's plan was the greatest plan that any human being could conceive. He tried to escape from life, no, he did escape, and then with all his strength he rushed from life—from this life of ours—into a limitless path of darkness. He dashed out his brains against a stone wall.

Ilya was a bachelor. I always think: how lucky Ilya was to have been a bachelor! There's the difference between the unhappy Ilya and myself.

I am worn out now. And I am seeking peace of mind. What sort of thing is "peace of mind?" Where is it? I can't return to the blank mind I had long ago before I knew pain, not if a hundred years were to elapse. Where is peace of mind?

I want to be sick. For a long time this desire has been lurking in my head. Sick! This word that other people hate sounds as sweet to me as the name of the mountain where I was born. A free life, released from all responsibilities!

Sickness is the only way we have to obtain peace of mind.

* * *

11th, Sunday

Today I had to go to a poetry gathering at Yosano's house.[5] Naturally, there was no likelihood of anything amusing taking place. Hiraide was telling what a big success last night's "Devotees of Pan"[6] had been. Yoshii, who came in late, was saying, "Last night when I got drunk and pissed from Eitai Bridge, a policeman bawled me out." Everybody seems to have been drunk and had a wild time.

As usual we wrote poems on given themes. It must have been about nine o'clock when the selection of poems was completed. Recently I haven't felt like writing serious *uta,*[7] and as usual turned out some mock verses. Here are a couple:

> When I wear shoes
> That make a squeak
> I feel unpleasant, as if
> I tread upon a frog.

---

4. Suicidal hero of "The Three of Them," a story by the radical, working-class Russian writer Maxim Gorky (1868–1936).
5. Yosano Tekkan (1873–1935), a young experimental poet, as was his wife Akiko, mentioned below.
6. A literary club whose members sought to blend European and Japanese traditions.
7. Formal poems.

Your eyes must have
The mechanism of
A fountain pen—
You are always shedding tears.

The man
Whose hands tremble and voice breaks
At sight of a woman
No longer exists.

Akiko suggested that we sit up all night composing poetry. I made some silly excuse and left.

Another precious day wasted. Suddenly a feeling of regret surged up within me. If I was going to look at the cherry blossoms, why didn't I go by myself and look at them as I wanted? A poetry gathering! Of all the stupid things!

* * *

13th, Tuesday

Early this morning I opened my eyes, momentarily wakened by the noise of the maid opening the shutters. Hearing nothing else, I dozed off again, the unconscious sleep of spring. It is a cloudy calm day. All over the city the blossoms are gradually beginning to fall.

A sad letter came from my mother.

Dear Mr. Ishikawa,

I was so happy with the letter you sent to Mr. Miyazaki. I have been waiting every day since, hoping word would come from you, and now it is April already. I am taking care of Kyōko and feeding her, which I have never done before. She is getting bigger every day, and is almost too much for me. Can't you send for her? I beg the favor of a reply. On the sixth and seventh there was a terrible rainstorm. The rain leaked in and we had nowhere to stay. Kyōko was so upset she couldn't sleep. She caught a cold on the second of April and is still not better. Setsuko[8] leaves for work every morning at eight o'clock and doesn't return until five or six. It's so hard for me when she is not here. There's no more household money left. Even one yen will be appreciated. I beg you kindly to send something soon. When do you think we will be able to go to Tokyo? Please let me know. If we don't get an answer from you, it's all over with us. We are all coming, so please make preparations.

Katsu

My mother's letter, in shaky characters, full of spelling mistakes! I don't suppose very many people besides myself could read it. They say Mother was the best student at school when she was a girl. But in forty years of married life with my father, she probably never once wrote a letter. The first one I received from her was two summers ago. I had left Mother alone in Shibutami. She couldn't stand that dreadful town any longer, and she had written out of loneliness, searching in her memory for the completely forgotten characters. Today was the fifth letter I have received since coming to Tokyo. There are fewer mistakes, and the characters are better formed. How sad—my mother's letter!

---

8. Takuboku's wife.

14th, Wednesday

I decided to take off today and tomorrow, and started a story. I'm calling it "The Wooden Horse."

Inspiration in writing seems to be something like sexual desire. The man from the lending library came today and offered me some "unusual" books. Somehow I wanted to read them, and I borrowed two. One is called *The Misty Night in the Blossoms,* the other *The Secrets of Love.* I wasted three hours copying out in Romaji *The Misty Night.*

At night Nakajima came here, together with a minor poet named Uchiyama. Uchiyama's nose has the most extraordinary shape! It looks as if a deformed sweet potato had been stuck in the middle of his face, with a few parings and flattenings here and there. An endless flow of chatter comes from him: he's like one of those unshaven beggars one sees clowning in the streets. On top of everything else, he is practically a midget. I have never seen anyone quite so pathetic-looking. A truly pitiful, farcical innocent—excessively so, perhaps: I felt a strange impulse to smash him in the face. Every serious utterance he makes sounds funny, and when he says something humorous with a sniff of his grotesque nose, he looks as if he is crying.

It started to rain a little before ten. Nakajima professes to be a Socialist, but his is a very aristocratic socialism—he left in a rickshaw. Uchiyama—the poet is a real Socialist—went home under a borrowed umbrella. He really looked a poet.

I wrote three pages of "The Wooden Horse." I longed for Setsuko—not because of the lonely patter of the rain, but because I had been reading *The Misty Night in the Blossoms.*

15th, Thursday

No! Does my need for Setsuko arise simply out of sexual desire? No! No!

My love for her has cooled. That is a fact, a not surprising fact—regrettable but inescapable.

Love is only a part, not the entirety of human life, a diversion, something like a song. Everyone wants at times to sing, and it is a pleasant thing to do. But man cannot spend his whole life in song, and to sing the same tune all the time, however joyous it may be, is sating.

My love has cooled; I am tired of singing that song—it's not that I dislike it. Setsuko is really a good woman. Is there in all the world another such good, gentle, sensible woman? I cannot imagine a better wife than Setsuko. Sometimes, even while I was actually sleeping with Setsuko, I have hungered for other women. But what has that to do with Setsuko? I was not dissatisfied with her. It is simply that men have complex desires.

I have not changed in my love for Setsuko. She was not the only woman I loved, but the one I loved most. Even now, especially during the last few days, I often think of her.

The present marriage system—the whole social system—is riddled with errors. Why must I be tied down because of parents, a wife, or a child? Why must they be victimized because of me? But that, naturally, is quite apart from the fact that I love my parents, Setsuko, and Kyōko.

16th, Friday

What an idiotic thing! Last night I stayed up until three copying in my notebook that pornographic old novel *The Misty Night in the Blossoms*. Ah, me!

I could not control my craving for that intense pleasure!

When I woke about ten this morning I felt a strange mental fatigue. I read the letter from Miyazaki.

Will they all please die, or must I? It's one or the other! I really thought that as I sat down to write an answer. I assured Miyazaki that I am now able to make a living, and said that all I need is the money to move from these lodgings, to rent a house, and to pay the traveling expenses for my family! When I finished writing, I wished I were dead.

I finally got off the one yen to my mother. Out of dislike for writing, out of fear, I have neglected to send it until today. I enclosed it in the letter to Miyazaki.

Tonight Kindaichi[9] came to my room. He talked about all kinds of things, hoping to stir up some literary inspiration in me. I didn't answer—instead, I indulged in a variety of absurd pranks which eventually drove Kindaichi away. I took up my pen immediately. Half an hour went by. I was obliged to give serious consideration again to my inability to write a novel and to the fact that my future is devoid of hope. I went to Kindaichi's room and performed my whole repertory of silly tricks. I painted a huge face on my chest and made all kinds of grimaces, whistled like a thrush, and, in conclusion, took out my knife and acted out the part of the murderer in a play. Kindaichi fled from the room! I certainly must have been thinking something horrible!

I had switched off the light in his room, and stood in the doorway brandishing my knife.

Later, back in my room, we looked at each other in dismay at what had happened. I thought that suicide could not frighten me.

Then, at night, what did I do? *Misty Night in the Blossoms!*

It is about two o'clock. Somewhere off beyond Koishigawa there is a fire, a single dull red line of smoke climbing perpendicularly into the black sky.

A fire!

17th, Saturday

I did not go to work today because I was sure I would be able to write—no, it was because I wanted to take the day off that I decided to write. I attempted to describe last night's thoughts about suicide. I wrote three pages and couldn't think of another line.

I tried to correct some poems, but just spreading out the paper was enough to make me sick.

I thought of writing a story about a man who is arrested by a policeman for sleeping in a vacant house, but couldn't find the energy to lift my pen.

I said to myself, "I positively will give up my literary career."

"If I give up literature, what shall I do?"

Death! That's the only answer.

Either I must have money or else be released from all responsibilities.

Probably this problem will haunt me until I die—I'll think about it in bed!

* * *

---

9. A linguist and scholar of Japan's Ainu minority population, who was living in the room next to Takuboku's.

21st, Wednesday

The cherry trees are in full leaf. When I opened the window this morning, a smoky color of young leaves met my eyes. Yesterday I saw two people in summer hats. It's summer!

At nine o'clock I went to the public bath in Daimachi. I often used to go there when I first came to Tokyo last year. Nothing has changed, except that the seventeen-year-old girl-attendant, the one who seemed fond of me, is no longer there. I could see through the window the shadows of young leaves in the fresh morning sunlight. I returned to all my feelings of a year ago. Then the memory of the dreadful Tokyo summer came back with painful vividness, that summer I spent in lodgings. I was in terrible financial straits, but happy to be escaping even briefly the responsibility of providing for my family. Yes, I was enjoying the sensation of being a "semi-bachelor." I soon abandoned the woman with whom I was having an affair at the time. She's now a geisha in Asakusa. A great deal has changed. I have made a number of new friends and discarded them.

As I scrubbed my body, healthier than it was then, I lost myself in recollections—a year of terrible struggle! *The dreadful summer is coming again on me—the penniless novelist! The dreadful summer! alas! with great pains and deep sorrows of physical struggle, and, other young with the bottomless rapture of hand, Nihilist!*

As I come out of the gate of the bathhouse, the expressful faced woman who sold me the soap yesterday said to me "Good morning" with something calm and favourable gesture.

The bath and the memories bring me some hot and young lightness. I am young, and, at last, the life is not so dark and so painful. The sun shines, and moon is calm. If I do not send the money, or call up them to Tokyo, they—my mother and wife will take other manner to eat. I am young, and young, and young: and I have the pen, the brain, the eyes, the heart and the mind. That is all. All of all. If the inn-master take me out of this room, I will go everywhere—where are many inns and hotels in this capital. To-day, I have only one piece of change: but what then? Nonsence! There are many, many writers in Tokyo. What is that to me? There is nothing. They are writing with their finger-bones and the brush: but I must write with the ink and the G pen! That is all. Ah, the burning summer and the green-coloured struggle!

OTHER AMERICAS

José Martí's "Our America," written in the 1880s while the great Cuban patriot was in exile in the United States, reminded its readers that, in addition to the citizens of the United States, many other people had an equal right to call themselves "American." These other Americans and the other Americas they came from were to become more prominent in the literature of the twentieth century, thanks in part to efforts both literary and political by figures like Martí. In the Latin American nations that were emerging from the traumas of settler colonialism, and even more so in those nations that had yet to win their independence, many people would need several decades and even several generations in order to put together their old (or newly acquired) European languages with their non-European experience and produce what Europeans would recognize as literature. The same was true within the United States. The Mexicans and Native Americans who were still in the process of becoming "American" by conquest, the Irish and Chinese who were building railroads across the country and thus giving it a new unity, were still treated by the majority population as symptoms or causes of a disagreeable disunity. The remarkable texts presented here were exceptional in their time, the first stirrings of what would become a flood of writing in the next century, when the descendants of all of these groups, along with those of the non–Anglo Saxon immigrants from Eastern and Southern Europe who began arriving in the late nineteenth century, had learned English and become (for better or worse) acculturated.

The ideal of freedom that swept the world after the American and French revolutions did not have an equal impact everywhere. French revolutionaries did not welcome Toussaint L'Ouverture's bold application of their thinking to Haiti, a French colony. In the 1850s, there were Cuban nationalists who wanted Cuba, once liberated from the Spanish yoke, to enter the United States—as a slave state. It was because the universal ideals of equality and freedom were not universally observed that African-American slaves like Harriet Jacobs and Frederick Douglass had to struggle, literally and literarily, to assert their own identity both as human beings and as Americans. Everywhere in the literature of the nineteenth century we find images of enclosure and of an escape from it that is possible but by no means certain. An increasing body of writing was produced by and about different kinds of "other" Americans, including women and working-class men less often given voice before. Dickinson and Melville manage to turn the caged conditions of female domesticity and male office-work into opportunities for cosmic statements about the ways in which people are and aren't free. Gilman and Machado de Assis show us the imprisonment of those who are defined as insane and force us to ask how different this is from what is called normal life, while Rubén Darío looks north to Whitman and Theodore Roosevelt to test his self-definition in both literary and political terms.

Hathali Nez and Washington Matthews
dates unknown   1843–1905

The first "other Americans" the European settlers encountered as they spread across the Americas were the people who were already living there. From early colonial times, an important strand in American writing concerned relations between the "Indians" and the new settlers. Whether seen as noble savages or as bloodthirsty devil-worshipers, the native populations of the Americas were usually thought of as inscrutable, their cultures hidden from outsiders or even nonexistent. It was often claimed that the Indians had no laws, no organized religion, and no art beyond the everyday crafts of basketry and weaving. In the nineteenth century the picture

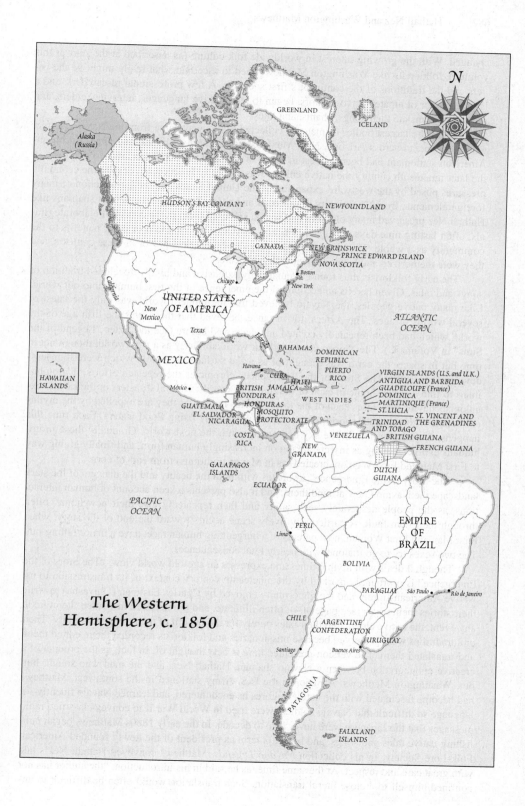

N

GREENLAND

ICELAND

Alaska
(Russia)

HUDSON'S BAY COMPANY

NEWFOUNDLAND

CANADA

NEW BRUNSWICK
PRINCE EDWARD ISLAND
NOVA SCOTIA

California

Chicago •

Boston •
New York •

UNITED STATES
OF AMERICA

*New
Mexico*

ATLANTIC
OCEAN

Texas

Florida

BAHAMAS

DOMINICAN
REPUBLIC

MEXICO

Havana •

CUBA

HAITI

PUERTO
RICO

VIRGIN ISLANDS (U.S. and U.K.)
ANTIGUA AND BARBUDA
GUADELOUPE (France)
DOMINICA
MARTINIQUE (France)
ST. LUCIA

HAWAIIAN
ISLANDS

Mexico •

BRITISH
HONDURAS

JAMAICA

WEST INDIES

ST. VINCENT AND
THE GRENADINES

GUATEMALA
EL SALVADOR
NICARAGUA

HONDURAS

MOSQUITO
PROTECTORATE

TRINIDAD
AND TOBAGO

COSTA
RICA

NEW
GRANADA

VENEZUELA

BRITISH GUIANA
FRENCH GUIANA

DUTCH
GUIANA

GALAPAGOS
ISLANDS

ECUADOR

PACIFIC
OCEAN

PERU

EMPIRE
OF
BRAZIL

Lima •

BOLIVIA

The Western
Hemisphere, c. 1850

PARAGUAY

São Paulo •

• Rio de Janeiro

CHILE

ARGENTINE
CONFEDERATION

URUGUAY

Santiago •

Buenos Aires •

PATAGONIA

FALKLAND
ISLANDS

changed. With the growing interest in worldwide folk culture (as described at the start of this volume), folklorists like Washington Matthews tried to ascertain what really might be the beliefs and the traditions of the continent's first societies. A few professional researchers, and a larger number of amateur investigators, began to learn native languages, interview elders, and record and translate their songs, chants, and tales.

One of the largest bodies of material collected in this way came from the Navajo people, who were spread across Arizona, New Mexico, and southern Colorado and Utah. European-American settlement had been modest in much of this arid, mountainous area, so that even in the later nineteenth century the native culture was still fully functioning, despite the economic pressures posed by the westward expansion of the United States and the introduction of many foreign elements, from Christianity to railroads and rifles. Traditional healers or shamans like Hathali Nez preserved many old tales and songs, and used them in the course of elaborate rituals, often lasting nine days, designed to heal a person or to bring rain or other benefits to the community as a whole. The old stories and songs had a magical power in these contexts, and they were memorized and handed down with great care.

The early folklorists thus found a remarkably extensive and highly developed tradition of songs and tales. Given here is an account of the emergence of the first humans into our world. Like many native peoples, the Navajo believed that the modern world was only the latest of several worlds or ages. The Aztecs, for instance, believed that theirs was the fifth age of the world, which had been repeatedly created and destroyed before (see the Aztec "Legend of the Suns" in Volume C). The Navajo conceived our world similarly as a fifth world, though not in time but in space: the earth was thought of as a flat surface, far below which were four less-developed worlds. "The Story of the Emergence" chronicles the repeated efforts of protohumans to find a secure home in each of the first four worlds. Natural disasters or their own sexual misbehavior forecloses each of the lower worlds in turn, as they are expelled by the mythical beings who rule each world, or are forced upward by rising flood waters. Each time this happens, they find a hole in the sky and emerge into the next world. Gradually these protohumans evolve, starting as insects, taking on increasingly human form, and finally giving way to First Man and First Woman, created (as in Mayan traditions) from ears of corn.

"The Story of the Emergence" resonates with both the beauty and the dangers of the stark landscape the Navajo knew around them, and it also presents a keen account of human interactions, as the people desperately seek safety and then repeatedly lose their new home, often through their own fault. A particularly lively scene occurs toward the end of the story, when First Man and First Woman, now parents of a burgeoning human race, have a major falling-out. The two sexes try to go it alone, with nearly fatal consequences.

Though it deals with mythic times and expresses an age-old world view, "The Story of the Emergence" is profoundly marked by the nineteenth-century context of its transmission to us. Native Americans rarely had the opportunity enjoyed by Charles Eastman (Ohiyesha) to write their stories themselves (see page 404); often illiterate, and uninterested in written literature in any event, the native elders told their tales purely for the benefit of their own community. Their oral traditions were preserved because missionaries and folklorists recorded them, edited them, and translated them. The version presented here is best thought of, in fact, as the product of a creative collaboration between a Navajo shaman, Hathali Nez, and the man who sought him out, Washington Matthews. A major in the U.S. Army stationed in the southwest, Matthews had become fascinated with the native cultures he encountered, and learned Navajo fluently—a language so difficult that Navajo soldiers were used in World War II to convey classified radio messages that the Japanese were never able to decode. In the early 1880s Matthews began publishing native tales and songs, and served a term as president of the newly founded American Folk-Lore Society. In his collection *Navaho Legends*, Matthews conveyed Hathali Nez's tale with great care and respect. At the same time, as he said in his introduction, "the author has not confined himself to a close literal translation. Such translation would often be difficult to understand, and, more often still, be uninteresting reading. . . . Still the writer has taken pains never to exceed the metaphor or descriptive force of the original, and never to add a single thought of his own."

If Matthews never added, he did at times subtract, eliminating repetitions he felt would weary his readers, and toning down the tale's sexual content. The hilarious, obscene argument between First Woman and First Man, for instance, was more than Matthews could bring himself to convey in his text proper, even for his fellow folklorists; he relegated it to an endnote, in small type, buried at the end of his volume. (This passage appears below, in brackets, restored to its proper place in the tale.) Still less acceptable was a detailed account of the aberrant sexual practices that led to the early humans being expelled from the third world; Matthews's note only hints at these events.

Apart from Matthews's direct editorial shaping, it is likely that Hathali Nez's own telling reflects aspects of Navajo contacts with Christian culture. Catholic missionaries had been active in the region for three centuries, and it is probably no coincidence that the story includes some elements that closely resemble the biblical creation account in Genesis, as when the protohumans send out a pair of winged messengers to scout for habitable land after they flee a worldwide Flood. "The Story of the Emergence" as we have it, then, reflects a modern, cross-cultural collaboration even as it conveys an ancient and very distinctive native tradition.

The Story of the Emergence

At Tobilhaskidi (in the middle of the first world), white arose in the east, and they regarded it as day there, they say; blue rose in the south, and still it was day to them, and they moved around; yellow rose in the west and showed that evening had come; then dark arose in the north, and they lay down and slept.

At Tobilhaskidi water flowed out in different directions; one stream flowed to the east, another to the south, and another to the west. There were dwelling-places on the border of the stream that flowed to the east, on that which flowed to the south, and on that which flowed to the west also.

To the east there was a place called Corn, to the south a place called Nahodoola, and to the west a place called Standing Reed. Again, to the east there was a place called One Pot, to the south a place called They Come Often for Water, and to the west a place called House Made of the Red Mountain. Then, again, to the east there was a place called Underground House, to the south a place called Among Aromatic Sumac, and to the west a place called House Made of Red Rock.

Dark ants lived there. Red ants lived there. Dragon flies lived there. Yellow beetles lived there. Hard beetles lived there. Stone-carrier beetles lived there. Black beetles lived there. Coyote-dung beetles lived there. Bats lived there. White-faced beetles lived there. Locusts lived there. White locusts lived there. These twelve people started in life there.

To the east extended an ocean, to the south an ocean, to the west an ocean, and to the north an ocean. In the ocean to the east lay Tieholtsodi; he was chief of the people there. In the ocean to the south lived Thaltlahale (Blue Heron), who was chief of the people there. In the ocean to the west lay Tsal (Frog), who was chief of the people there. In the ocean to the north was Idnidsilkai (White Mountain Thunder), and he was chief of the people there.

The people quarreled among themselves, and this is the way it happened. They committed adultery, one people with another. Many of the women were guilty. They tried to stop it, but they could not. Tieholtsodi, the chief in the east, said: "What shall we do with them? They like not the land they dwell in." In the south Blue Heron spoke to them, and in the west Frog said: "No longer shall you dwell here, I say. I am chief here." To the north White Mountain Lightning said: "Go elsewhere at once. Depart from here!"

When again they sinned and again they quarrelled, Tieholtsodi, in the east, would not speak to them; Blue Heron, in the south, would not speak to them, Frog, in the west, would say nothing; and White Mountain Thunder, in the north, would not speak to them.

Four nights later, the same thing happened. Those who dwelt at the south again committed crime, and again they had contentions. One woman and one man sought to enter in the east to complain to the chief, but they were driven out. In the south they sought to go in where Blue Heron lay, but again they were driven out. In the west, where Frog was the chief, again they tried to enter; but again they were driven out. To the north again they were driven out. The chief said: "None of you shall enter here. Go elsewhere and keep on going." That night at Nahodoola they held a council, but they arrived at no decision. At dawn Tieholtsodi began to talk. "You pay no attention to my words. Everywhere you disobey me; you must go to some other place. Not upon this earth shall you remain." Thus he spoke to them.

Among the women, for four nights they talked about it. At the end of the fourth night, in the morning, as they were rising, something white appeared in the east. It appeared also in the south, the west, and the north. It looked like a chain of mountains, without a break, stretching around them. It was water that surrounded them. Water impassable, water insurmountable, flowed all around. All at once they started.

They went in circles upward till they reached the sky. It was smooth. They looked down; but there the water had risen, and there was nothing else but water there. While they were flying around, a blue head thrust out from the sky and called to them, saying: "In here, to the eastward, there is a hole." They entered the hole and went through it up to the surface of the second world.

The blue one belonged to the Hastsosidiné, or Swallow People. The Swallow People lived there. A great many of their houses, rough and lumpy, lay scattered all around. Each tapered toward the top, and at that part there was a hole for entrance. A great many people approached and gathered around the strangers, but they said nothing.

The first world was red in color; the second world, into which the people had now entered, was blue. They sent out two couriers, a Locust and a White Locust, to the east, to explore the land and see if there were in it any people like themselves. At the end of two days the couriers returned, and said that in one day's travel they had reached the edge of the world—the top of a great cliff that arose from an abyss whose bottom they could not see; but that they found in all their journey no people, no animals of any kind, no trees, no grass, no sage-brush, no mountains, nothing but bare, level ground. The same couriers were then dispatched in turn to the south, to the west, and to the north. They were gone on each journey two days, and when they returned related, as before, that they had reached the edge of the world, and discovered nothing but an uninhabited waste. Here, then, the strangers found themselves in the center of a vast barren plain, where there was neither food nor a kindred people. When the couriers had returned from the north, the Swallows visited the camp of the newly arrived people, and asked them why they had sent out the couriers to the east. "We sent them out," was the reply, "to see what was in the land, and to see if there were any people like ourselves here." "And what did your couriers tell you?" asked the Swallows.

"They told us that they came to the edge of the world, yet found no plant and no living thing in all the land." (The same questions were asked and the same answers given for the other points of the compass.)[1] "They spoke the truth," said the Swallow People. "Had you asked us in the beginning what the land contained, we would have told you and saved you all your trouble. Until you came, no one has ever dwelt in all this land but ourselves." The people then said to the Swallows: "You understand our language and are much like us. You have legs, feet, bodies, heads, and wings, as we have: why cannot your people and our people become friends?" "Let it be as you wish," said the Swallows, and both parties began at once to treat each other as members of one tribe; they mingled one among the other, and addressed one another by the terms of relationship, as, my brother, my sister, my father, my son, and so on.

They all lived together pleasantly and happily for twenty-three days; but on the twenty-fourth night one of the strangers made too free with the wife of the Swallow chief, and next morning, when the latter found out what had happened, he said to the strangers: "We have treated you as friends, and thus you return our kindness. No doubt for such crimes you were driven from the lower world, and now you must leave this. This is our land and we will have you here no longer. Besides, this is a bad land. People are dying here every day, and, even if we spare you, you cannot live here long." The Locusts took the lead on hearing this; they soared upwards; the others followed, and all soared and circled till they reached the sky.

When they reached the sky they found it, like the sky of the first world, smooth and hard with no opening; but while they were circling round under it, they saw a white face peering out at them,—it was the face of Niltsi, the Wind. He called to them and told them if they would fly to the south they would find a hole through which they could pass; so off they flew, as bidden, and soon they discovered a slit in the sky which slanted upwards toward the south; through this slit they flew, and soon entered the third world in the south.

The color of the third world was yellow. Here they found nothing but the Grasshopper People. The latter gathered around the wanderers in great numbers, but said nothing. They lived in holes in the ground along the banks of a great river which flowed through their land to the east. The wanderers sent out the same Locust messengers that they had sent out in the second world to explore the land to the east, to the south, to the west, to the north, to find out what the land contained, and to see if there were any kindred people in it; but the messengers returned from each journey after an absence of two days, saying they had reached the end of the world, and that they had found a barren land with no people in it save the Grasshoppers.

When the couriers returned from their fourth journey, the two great chiefs of the Grasshoppers visited the strangers and asked them why they had sent out the explorers, and the strangers answered that they had sent them out to see what grew in the land, and to find if there were any people like themselves in it. "And what did your couriers find?" said the Grasshopper chiefs. "They found nothing save the bare land and the river, and no people but yourselves." "There is nothing else in the land," said the chiefs. "Long we have lived here, but we have seen no other people but ourselves until you came."

The strangers then spoke to the Grasshoppers, as they had spoken to the Swallows in the second world, and begged that they might join them and become one people with them. The Grasshoppers consented, and the two peoples at once mingled

1. Here Matthews has evidently condensed Nez's account.

among one another and embraced one another, and called one another by the endearing terms of relationship, as if they were all of the same tribe.

As before, all went well for twenty-three days; but on the twenty-fourth one of the strangers served a chief of the Grasshoppers as the chief of the Swallows had been served in the lower world. In the morning, when the wrong was discovered, the chief reviled the strangers and bade them depart. "For such crimes," he said, "I suppose you were chased from the world below: you shall drink no more of our water, you shall breathe no more of our air. Begone!"

Up they all flew again, and circled round and round until they came to the sky above them, and they found it smooth and hard as before. When they had circled round for some time, looking in vain for an entrance, they saw a red head stuck out of the sky, and they heard a voice which told them to fly to the west. It was the head of Red Wind which they saw, and it was his voice that spoke to them. The passage which they found in the west was twisted round like the tendril of a vine; it had thus been made by the wind. They flew up in circles through it and came out in the fourth world. Four of the Grasshoppers came with them; one was white, one blue, one yellow, and one black. We have grasshoppers of these four colors with us to this day.

The surface of the fourth world was mixed black and white. The colors in the sky were the same as in the lower worlds, but they differed in their duration. In the first world, the white, the blue, the yellow, and the black all lasted about an equal length of time every day. In the second world the blue and the black lasted a little longer than the other two colors. In the third world they lasted still longer. In the fourth world there was but little of the white and yellow; the blue and the black lasted most of the time. As yet there was neither sun, moon, nor star.

When they arrived on the surface of the fourth world they saw no living thing; but they observed four great snow-covered peaks sticking up at the horizon,—one at the east, one at the south, one at the west, and one at the north.

They sent two couriers to the east. These returned at the end of two days. They related that they had not been able to reach the eastern mountain, and that, though they had travelled far, they had seen no track or trail or sign of life. Two couriers were then sent to the south. When they returned, at the end of two days, they related that they had reached a low range of mountains this side of the great peak; that they had seen no living creature, but had seen two different kinds of tracks, such as they had never seen before, and they described such as the deer and the turkey make now. Two couriers were next sent to the west. In two days these returned, having failed to reach the great peak in the west, and having seen no living thing and no sign of life. At last two couriers were sent to the north. When these got back to their kindred they said they had found a race of strange men, who cut their hair square in front, who lived in houses in the ground and cultivated fields. These people, who were engaged in gathering their harvest, the couriers said, treated them very kindly and gave them food to eat. It was now evident to the wanderers that the fourth world was larger than any of the worlds below.

The day following the return of the couriers who went to the north, two of the newly discovered race—Kisani (Pueblos) they were called—entered the camp of the exiles and guided the latter to a stream of water. The water was red, and the Kisani told the wanderers they must not walk through the stream, for if they did the water would injure their feet. The Kisani showed them a square raft made of four logs,—a white pine, a blue spruce, and yellow pine, and a black spruce,—on which they might cross; so they went over the stream and visited the homes of the Kisani.

The Kisani gave the wanderers corn and pumpkins to eat, and the latter lived for some time on the food given to them daily by their new friends. They held a council among themselves, in which they resolved to mend their manners for the future and do nothing to make the Kisani angry. The land of the Kisani had neither rain nor snow; the crops were raised by irrigation.

Late in the autumn they heard in the east the distant sound of a great voice calling. They listened and waited, and soon heard the voice nearer and louder. They listened still and heard the voice a third time, nearer and louder than before. Once more they listened, and soon they heard the voice louder still, and clear like the voice of one near at hand. A moment later four mysterious beings appeared to them. These were: Bitsis Lakai, or White Body, a being like the god of this world whom the Navahoes call Hastseyalti; Bitsis Dotliz, or Blue Body, who was like the present Navaho god Tonenili, or Water Sprinkler; Bitsis Litsoi, or Yellow Body; and Bitsis Lizin, or Black Body, who was the same as the present Navaho god of fire, Hastsezini.

These beings, without speaking, made many signs to the people, as if instructing them; but the latter did not understand them. When the gods had gone, the people long discussed the mysterious visit, and tried to make out what the gods meant by the signs they had made. Thus the gods visited four days in succession. On the fourth day, when the other three had departed, Black Body remained behind and spoke to the people in their own language. He said: "You do not seem to understand the signs that these gods make you, so I must tell you what they mean. They want to make more people, but in form like themselves. You have bodies like theirs; but you have the teeth, the feet, and the claws of beasts and insects. The new creatures are to have hands and feet like ours. But you are uncleanly, you smell badly. Have yourselves well cleansed when we return; we will come back in twelve days."

On the morning of the twelfth day the people washed themselves well. The women dried themselves with yellow corn-meal; the men with white corn-meal. Soon after the ablutions were completed they heard the distant call of the approaching gods. It was shouted, as before, four times,—nearer and louder at each repetition,—and, after the fourth call, the gods appeared. Blue Body and Black Body each carried a sacred buckskin. White Body carried two ears of corn, one yellow, one white, each covered at the end completely with grains.[2]

The gods laid one buckskin on the ground with the head to the west; on this they placed the two ears of corn, with their tips to the east, and over the corn they spread the other buckskin with its head to the east; under the white ear they put the feather of a white eagle, under the yellow ear the feather of a yellow eagle. Then they told the people to stand at a distance and allow the wind to enter. The white wind blew from the east, and the yellow wind blew from the west, between the skins. While the wind was blowing, eight of the Mirage People came and walked around the objects on the ground four times, and as they walked the eagle feathers, whose tips protruded from between the buckskins, were seen to move. When the Mirage People had finished their walk the upper buckskin was lifted,—the ears of corn had disappeared; a man and a woman lay there in their stead.

The white ear of corn had been changed into a man, the yellow ear into a woman. It was the wind that gave them life. It is the wind that comes out of our mouths now

2. Yellow corn belongs to the female, white corn to the male. This rule is observed in all Navaho ceremonies. An ear of corn used for sacred purposes must be completely covered with full grains [Matthews's note].

that gives us life. When this ceases to blow we die. In the skin at the tips of our fingers we see the trail of the wind; it shows us where the wind blew when our ancestors were created.

The pair thus created were First Man and First Woman (Atse Hastin and Atse Estsan). The gods directed the people to build an inclosure of brushwood for the pair. When the inclosure was finished, First Man and First Woman entered it, and the gods said to them: "Live together now as husband and wife." At the end of four days hermaphrodite twins were born,[3] and at the end of four days more a boy and a girl were born, who in four days grew to maturity and lived with one another as husband and wife. The primal pair had in all five pairs of twins, the first of which only was barren, being hermaphrodites.

In four days after the last pair of twins was born, the gods came again and took First Man and First Woman away to the eastern mountain where the gods dwelt, and kept them there for four days. When they returned all their children were taken to the eastern mountain and kept there for four days. Soon after they all returned it was observed that they occasionally wore masks, such as Hastseyalti and Hastsehogan wear now, and that when they wore these masks they prayed for all good things,—for abundant rain and abundant crops. It is thought, too, that during their visit to the eastern mountain they learned the awful secrets of witchcraft, for the antihi (witches, wizards) always keep such masks with them and marry those too nearly related to them.

When they returned from the eastern mountain the brothers and sisters separated; and, keeping the fact of their former unlawful marriages secret, the brothers married women of the Mirage People and the sisters married men of the Mirage People. They kept secret, too, all the mysteries they had learned in the eastern mountain. The women thus married bore children every four days, and the children grew to maturity in four days, were married, and in their turn had children every four days. This numerous offspring married among the Kisani, and among those who had come from the lower world, and soon there was a multitude of people in the land.

These descendants of First Man and First Woman made a great farm. They built a dam and dug a wide irrigating ditch. But they feared the Kisani might injure their dam or their crops; so they put one of the hermaphrodites to watch the dam and the other to watch the lower end of the field. The hermaphrodite who watched at the dam invented pottery. He made first a plate, a bowl, and a dipper, which were greatly admired by the people. The hermaphrodite who lived at the lower end of the farm invented the wicker water-bottle. Others made, from thin split boards of cotton-wood, implements which they shoved before them to clear the weeds out of the land. They made also hoes from shoulder-blades of deer and axes of stone. They got their seeds from the Kisani.

Once they killed a little deer, and someone among them thought that perhaps they might make, from the skin of the head, a mask, by means of which they could approach other deer and kill them. They tried to make such a mask but failed; they could not make it fit. They debated over the invention and considered it for four days, but did not succeed. On the morning of the fifth day they heard the gods shouting in the distance. As on a previous occasion, they shouted four times, and after the fourth call they made their appearance. They brought with them heads of deer and of antelope.

3. The Navaho word natli or nutle is here translated as hermaphrodite, because the context shows that reference is made to anomalous creatures. But the word is usually employed to designate that class of men, known perhaps in all wild Indian tribes, who dress as women, and perform the duties usually allotted to women in Indian camps. Such persons are called berdaches (English, bardash) by the French Canadians. . . . The Navahos, in this legend, credit them with the invention of the arts practiced by women [from Matthews's note].

They showed the people how the masks were made and fitted, how the eye-holes were cut, how the motions of the deer were to be imitated, and explained to them all the other mysteries of the deer-hunt. Next day hunters went out and several deer were killed; from these more masks were made, and with these masks more men went out to hunt; after that time the camp had abundance of meat. The people dressed the deer-skins and made garments out of them.

The people from the third world had been in the fourth world eight years when the following incident occurred: One day they saw the sky stooping down and the earth rising up to meet it. For a moment they came in contact, and then there sprang out of the earth, at the point of contact, the Coyote and the Badger. We think now that the Coyote and the Badger are children of the sky. The Coyote rose first, and for this reason we think he is the elder brother of the Badger. At once the Coyote came over to the camp and skulked round among the people, while the Badger went down into the hole that led to the lower world.

First Man told the people the names of the four mountains which rose in the distance. They were named the same as the four mountains that now bound the Navaho land. There was Tsisnadzini in the east, Tsotsil in the south, Dokoslid in the west, and Depentsa in the north, and he told them that a different race of people lived in each mountain.

First Man was the chief of all these people in the fourth world, except the Kisani. He was a great hunter, and his wife, First Woman, was very corpulent. One day he brought home from the hunt a fine fat deer. The woman boiled some of it and they had a hearty meal. When they were done the woman wiped her greasy hands on her dress, [and said: "E'yehe si-tsod" (Thanks, my vagina). "What is that you say?" asked First Man. "E'yehe si-tsod," she repeated. "Why do you speak thus?" he queried; "Was it not I who killed the deer whose flesh you have eaten? Why do you not thank me? Was it *tsod* that killed the deer?" "Yes," she replied; "if it were not for that, you would not have killed the deer. If it were not for that, you lazy men would do nothing. It is that which does all the work." "Then perhaps you women think you can live without the men," he said. "Certainly we can. It is we women who till the fields and gather food; we can live on the produce of our fields, and the seeds and fruits we collect. We have no need of you men." Thus they argued. First Man became more and more angry with each reply that his wife made, until at length, in wrath, he jumped across the fire], remaining by himself in silence for the rest of the night.[4]

Next morning First Man went out early and called aloud to the people: "Come hither, all ye men," he said; "I wish to speak to you, but let all the women stay behind; I do not wish to see them." Soon all the males gathered, and he told them what his wife had said the night before. "They believe," he said, "that they can live without us. Let us see if they can hunt game and till the fields without our help. Let us see what sort of a living they can make by themselves. Let us leave them and persuade the Kisani to come with us. We will cross the stream, and when we are gone over we will keep the raft on the other side." He sent for the hermaphrodites. They came, covered with meal, for they had been grinding corn. "What have you that you have made yourselves?" he asked. "We have each two mealing-stones, and we have cups and bowls and baskets and many other things," they answered. "Then take these all along with

---

4. The bracketed lines appear only in Matthews's endnotes. In the text proper, he simply says that First Woman "made a remark which greatly enraged her husband; they had a quarrel about this, which First Man ended by jumping across the fire."

you," he ordered, "and join us to cross the stream." Then all the men and the hermaphrodites assembled at the river and crossed to the north side on the raft, and they took over with them their stone axes and farm implements and everything they had made. When they had all crossed they sent the raft down to the Kisani for them to cross. The latter came over,—six clans of them,—but they took their women with them. While some of the young men were crossing the stream they cried at parting with their wives; still they went at the bidding of their chief. The men left the women everything the latter had helped to make or raise.

As soon as they had crossed the river some of the men went out hunting, for the young boys needed food, and some set to work to chop down willows and build huts. They had themselves all sheltered in four days.

That winter the women had abundance of food, and they feasted, sang, and had a merry time. They often came down to the bank of the river and called across to the men and taunted and reviled them. Next year the men prepared a few small fields and raised a little corn; but they did not have much corn to eat, and lived a good deal by hunting. The women planted all of the old farm, but they did not work it very well; so in the winter they had a small crop, and they did not sing and make merry as in the previous winter. In the second spring the women planted less, while the men planted more, cleared more land, and increased the size of their farm. Each year the fields and crops of the men increased, while those of the women diminished and they began to suffer for want of food. Some went out and gathered the seeds of wild plants to eat. In the autumn of the third year of separation many women jumped into the river and tried to swim over; but they were carried under the surface of the water and were never seen again. In the fourth year the men had more food than they could eat; corn and pumpkins lay untouched in the fields, while the women were starving.

First Man at length began to think what the effect of his course might be. He saw that if he continued to keep the men and the women apart the race might die out, so he called the men and spoke his thoughts to them. Some said, "Surely our race will perish," and others said, "What good is our abundance to us? We think so much of our poor women starving in our sight that we cannot eat." Then he sent a man to the shore to call across the stream to find if First Woman were still there, and to bid her come down to the bank if she were. She came to the bank, and First Man called to her and asked if she still thought she could live alone. "No," she replied, "we cannot live without our husbands." The men and the women were then told to assemble at the shores of the stream; the raft was sent over and the women were ferried across. They were made to bathe their bodies and dry them with meal. They were put in a corral and kept there until night, when they were let out to join the men in their feasts.

When they were let out of the corral it was found that three were missing. After dark, voices were heard calling from the other side of the river; they were the voices of the missing ones,—a mother and her two daughters. They begged to be ferried over, but the men told them it was too dark, that they must wait until morning. Hearing this, they jumped into the stream and tried to swim over. The mother succeeded in reaching the opposite bank and finding her husband. The daughters were seized by Tieholtsodi, the water monster, and dragged down under the water.

For three nights and three days the people heard nothing about the young women and supposed them lost forever. On the morning of the fourth day the call of the gods was heard,—four times as usual,—and after the fourth call White Body made his appearance, holding up two fingers and pointing to the river. The people supposed that these signs had reference to the lost girls. Some of the men crossed the stream on the raft and looked for the tracks of the lost ones; they traced the tracks to the edge of the water, but no farther. White Body went away, but soon returned, accompanied by Blue Body. White Body carried a large bowl of white shell, and Blue Body a large bowl of blue shell. They asked for a man and a woman to accompany them, and they went down to the river. They put both the bowls on the surface of the water and caused them to spin around. Beneath the spinning bowls the water opened, for it was hollow, and gave entrance to a large house of four rooms. The room in the east was made of the dark waters, the room in the south of the blue waters, the room in the west of the yellow waters, and the room in the north of waters of all colors.

The man and the woman descended and Coyote followed them. They went first into the east room, but there they found nothing; then they went into the south room, but there they found nothing; next they went into the west room, where again they found nothing; at last they went into the north room, and there they beheld the water monster Tieholtsodi, with the two girls he had stolen and two children of his own. The man and the woman demanded the girls, and as he said nothing in reply they took them and walked away. But as they went out Coyote, unperceived by all, took the two children of Tieholtsodi and carried them off under his robe.[5] Coyote always wore his robe folded close around him and always slept with it thus folded, so no one was surprised to see that he still wore his robe in this way when he came up from the waters, and no one suspected that he had stolen the children of Tieholtsodi.

Next day the people were surprised to see deer, turkey, and antelope running past from east to west, and to see animals of six different kinds (two kinds of Hawks, two kinds of Squirrels, the Hummingbird, and the Bat) come into their camp as if for refuge. The game animals ran past in increasing numbers during the three days following. On the morning of the fourth day, when the white light rose, the people observed in the east a strange white gleam along the horizon, and they sent out the Locust couriers to see what caused this unusual appearance. The Locusts returned before sunset, and told the people that a vast flood of waters was fast approaching from the east. On hearing this the people all assembled together, the Kisani with the others, in a great multitude, and they wailed and wept over the approaching catastrophe. They wept and moaned all night and could not sleep.

When the white light arose in the east, next morning, the waters were seen high as mountains encircling the whole horizon, except in the west, and rolling on rapidly. The people packed up all their goods as fast as they could, and ran up on a high hill near by, for temporary safety. Here they held a council. Someone suggested that perhaps the two Squirrels (Hazaitso and Hazaistozi) might help them. "We will try what we can do," said the Squirrels. One planted a piñon seed, the other a juniper seed, and they grew so very fast that the people hoped that they would soon grow so tall that the flood could not reach their tops, and that all might find shelter there. But after the trees grew a little way they began to branch out and grew no higher. Then the frightened people called on the Weasels (Glodsilkai and Glodsilzini). One of these planted a spruce seed and one a pine seed. The trees sprouted at once and grew fast, and again the people began to hope; but soon the trees commenced to branch, and they dwindled to slender points at the top and ceased to grow higher. Now they were in the depths of despair, for the waters were coming nearer every moment, when they saw two men approaching the hill on which they were gathered.

5. Typically tricky behavior by Coyote; see the "Coyote Tales," page 57.

One of the approaching men was old and grayhaired; the other, who was young, walked in advance. They ascended the hill and passed through the crowd, speaking to no one. The young man sat down on the summit, the old man sat down behind him, and the Locust sat down behind the old man,—all facing the east. The elder took out seven bags from under his robe and opened them. Each contained a small quantity of earth. He told the people that in these bags he had earth from the seven sacred mountains. There were in the fourth world seven sacred mountains, named and placed like the sacred mountains of the present Navaho land. "Ah! Perhaps our father can do something for us," said the people. "I cannot, but my son may be able to help you," said the old man. Then they bade the son to help them, and he said he would if they all moved away from where he stood, faced to the west, and looked not around until he called them; for no one should see him at his work. They did as he desired, and in a few moments he called them to come to him. When they came, they saw that he had spread the sacred earth on the ground and planted in it thirty-two reeds, each of which had thirty-two joints. As they gazed they beheld the roots of the reeds striking out into the soil and growing rapidly downward. A moment later all the reeds joined together and became one reed of great size, with a hole in its eastern side. He bade them enter the hollow of the reed through this hole. When they were all safely inside, the opening closed, and none too soon, for scarcely had it closed when they heard the loud noise of the surging waters outside, saying, "*Yin, yin, yin.*"

The waters rose fast, but the reed grew faster, and soon it grew so high that it began to sway, and the people inside were in great fear lest, with their weight, it might break and topple over into the water. White Body, Blue Body, and Black Body were along. Black Body blew a great breath out through a hole in the top of the reed; a heavy dark cloud formed around the reed and kept it steady. But the reed grew higher and higher; again it began to sway, and again the people within were in great fear, whereupon he blew and made another cloud to steady the reed. By sunset it had grown up close to the sky, but it swayed and waved so much that they could not secure it to the sky until Black Body, who was uppermost, took the plume out of his head-band and stuck it out through the top of the cane against the sky, and this is why the reed always carries a plume on its head now.

Seeing no hole in the sky, they sent up the Great Hawk, Ginitso, to see what he could do. He flew up and began to scratch in the sky with his claws, and he scratched and scratched till he was lost to sight. After a while he came back, and said that he scratched to where he could see light, but that he did not get through the sky. Next they sent up a Locust. He was gone a long time, and when he came back he had this story to tell: He had gotten through to the upper world, and came out on a little island in the center of a lake. When he got out he saw approaching him from the east a black Grebe, and from the west a yellow Grebe. One of them said to him: "Who are you and whence come you?" But he made no reply. The other then said: "We own half of this world,—I in the east, my brother in the west. We give you a challenge. If you can do as we do, we shall give you one half of the world; if you cannot, you must die." Each had an arrow made of the black wind. He passed the arrow from side to side through his heart and flung it down to Wonistsidi, the Locust. The latter picked up one of the arrows, ran it from side to side through his heart, as he had seen the Grebes do, and threw it down. The Grebes swam away, one to the east and one to the west, and troubled him no more. When they had gone, two more Grebes appeared, a blue one from the south and a shining one from the north. They spoke to him as the other Grebes had spoken, and gave him the same challenge. Again he passed the arrow through his heart and the Grebes departed, leaving the land to the locust. To this day we see in every locust's sides the holes made by the arrows. But the hole the Locust made in ascending was too small for many of the people, so they sent Badger up to make it larger. When Badger came back his legs were stained black with the mud, and the legs of all badgers have been black ever since. Then First Man and First Woman led the way and all the others followed them, and they climbed up through the hole to the surface of this—the fifth—world.

∽

RESONANCE

Nicholas Black Elk and John G. Neihardt

In August of 1930, the poet John Neihardt (1881–1973) was looking for information on the massacre at Wounded Knee in 1890, the climax of native resistance to Anglo-American control over North America. The branch of the Sioux nation known as the Oglala had been inspired by hopes for a native messiah to mount a late rebellion against the ongoing encroachment of white settlers onto their reservations. The U.S. Army's nighttime massacre of two hundred men, women, and children encamped at Wounded Knee Creek in South Dakota finally crushed their resistance. Raised in Kansas and Nebraska, Neihardt had lived for years next to the Omaha Indian reservation in Nebraska, while making his name as a poet specializing in Western themes; he had been named Poet Laureate of Nebraska in 1923. He was now engaged in composing a five-volume epic poem called *A Cycle of the West,* on the settlement of the western states and their gradual integration into the United States. He was planning for his concluding volume, *The Song of the Messiah,* to focus on the Oglala messianic movement and the final establishment of the contemporary American order.

Not satisfied with the accounts available in print, he traveled to the Pine Ridge Reservation, where the massacre had taken place, hoping to find some informants who could tell him what had happened as they had seen it. There he was introduced to an aged former shaman or "medicine man," Nicholas Black Elk (1863–1950), who was willing to discuss the events at Wounded Knee and the messianic movement that had led up to it. Black Elk took a liking to Neihardt, and offered him much more than expected: he proposed to tell the entire story of his early years as a shaman. At the age of nine Black Elk himself had been given a great vision, in which his heavenly grandfathers had granted him powers of life and death and assigned him the task of uniting his people and restoring their nation. Black Elk had long resigned himself to the fact that he had been unable to carry out this mission, and around 1900 he had become an active Christian and had ceased practicing traditional medicine. Yet on meeting Neihardt he decided it was time to tell his story, to convey his vision before it would die with him.

Neihardt returned for an extended stay in 1931 and heard the whole story, aided by the shorthand skills of his two daughters, with Black Elk's son Ben translating for his father. Neihardt then edited and shaped the oral account into an eloquent portrayal of a vanishing civilization and its religious world vision. *Black Elk Speaks* attracted little attention when the University of Nebraska published it in 1932, but it became a best-seller when it was reissued in 1961, at a time when people were becoming newly interested in native cultures. It has since been widely seen as "a Native American Bible," a unique record of a harmonious worldview of humans living close to a sacred landscape, as well as a moving account of the last native struggle against the eclipse of their culture.

Presented here are Black Elk's childhood vision and the climactic struggle at Wounded Knee, together with the book's opening and closing framing narrative. The "great vision" shows interesting continuities with traditional Native American myths like the Navajo "Story of the Emergence," as Black Elk finds himself flying up into the clouds to receive a panoramic vision of the world as it is, and the new world that he must help his people make. The Wounded Knee episode then brings the story all too vividly back to earth.

Like "The Story of the Emergence," *Black Elk Speaks* is the product of a collaboration between two very different storytellers. Neihardt rephrased and condensed Black Elk's account, producing a highly readable literary text; notably, the poetic opening and closing statements aren't Black Elk's direct words at all but free adaptations of statements made in the body of the book. Neihardt also systematically left out two kinds of material that he saw as detracting from Black Elk's essential message. In the original transcripts (now published under the title *The Sixth Grandfather*), Black Elk presents himself as a warrior as much as a healer, but in Neihardt's version he is preeminently a man of peace. Neihardt's teller is also a deeply unworldly man, wedded to the old ways; rarely does Neihardt hint that Black Elk had become a Christian, baptized as Nicholas—and had long been active as a catechist, teaching Catholic doctrine and evangelizing among his people.

Most importantly, Black Elk had emphasized his people's ongoing hopes for the future, a future that he expected would develop in close interchange with Anglo-American culture. Neihardt deleted such moments from the story, presenting instead a tragic, Romantic image of a lost world, as though Black Elk were the very last of the Last Mohicans. We do learn how close Neihardt has become to Black Elk, who has renamed him "Flaming Rainbow," but nowhere in the book do we learn that Neihardt in turn addressed Black Elk as "Uncle Nick." After all, *Uncle Nick Speaks* would have been a rather different book.

These changes place Neihardt's version squarely within the nineteenth-century folkloristic tradition of his youth—one reason why it appropriately appears in this volume. It has only been more recently that indigenous writers have begun to tell their tales themselves in large numbers and in distinctively different terms, as can be seen in "Perspectives: Indigenous Cultures in the Twentieth Century" in Volume F. Neihardt's romanticization had distorting effects, yet it also had the positive result of gaining Black Elk a large audience once the book was rediscovered. It was Neihardt's poetic and narrative shaping that turned a sometimes rambling oral account into a deeply moving literary work. At the same time, we can now read Neihardt's eloquent account in light of the full transcripts. At several key points in the following selections, footnotes will present material that didn't make it into *Black Elk Speaks,* and at the story's conclusion Neihardt's version is followed by the conclusion as it appears in the transcription, with its direct appeal to a better future through mutual engagement.

from *Black Elk Speaks*

[BLACK ELK BEGINS]

My friend, I am going to tell you the story of my life, as you wish; and if it were only the story of my life I think I would not tell it; for what is one man that he should make much of his winters, even when they bend him like a heavy snow? So many other men have lived and shall live that story, to be grass upon the hills.

It is the story of all life that is holy and is good to tell, and of us two-leggeds sharing in it with the four-leggeds and the wings of the air and all green things; for these are children of one mother and their father is one Spirit.

This, then, is not the tale of a great hunter or of a great warrior, or of a great traveler, although I have made much meat in my time and fought for my people both as boy and man, and have gone far and seen strange lands and men. So also have many others done, and better than I. These things I shall remember by the way, and often they may seem to be the very tale itself, as when I was living them in happiness and sorrow. But now that I can see it all as from a lonely hilltop, I know it was the story of a mighty vision given to a man too weak to use it; of a holy tree that should have flourished in a people's heart with flowers and singing birds, and now is withered; and of a people's dream that died in bloody snow.

But if the vision was true and mighty, as I know, it is true and mighty yet; for such things are of the spirit, and it is in the darkness of their eyes that men get lost.

So I know that it is a good thing I am going to do; and because no good thing can be done by any man alone, I will first make an offering and send a voice to the Spirit of the World, that it may help me to be true. See, I fill this sacred pipe with the bark of the red willow; but before we smoke it, you must see how it is made and what it means. These four ribbons hanging here on the stem are the four quarters of the universe. The black one is for the west where the thunder beings live to send us rain; the white one for the north, whence comes the great white cleansing wind; the red one for the east, whence springs the light and where the morning star lives to give men wisdom; the yellow for the south, whence come the summer and the power to grow.

But these four spirits are only one Spirit after all, and this eagle feather here is for that One, which is like a father, and also it is for the thoughts of men that should rise high as eagles do. Is not the sky a father and the earth a mother, and are not all living things with feet or wings or roots their children? And this hide upon the mouthpiece here, which should be bison hide, is for the earth, from whence we came and at whose breast we suck as babies all our lives, along with all the animals and birds and trees and grasses. And because it means all this, and more than any man can understand, the pipe is holy.

[THE GREAT VISION]

What happened after that until the summer I was nine years old is not a story. There were winters and summers, and they were good; for the Wasichus[1] had made their iron road along the Platte and traveled there. This had cut the bison herd in two, but those that stayed in our country with us were more than could be counted, and we wandered without trouble in our land.

Now and then the voices would come back when I was out alone, like someone calling me, but what they wanted me to do I did not know. This did not happen very often, and when it did not happen, I forgot about it; for I was growing taller and was riding horses now and could shoot prairie chickens and rabbits with my bow. The boys of my people began very young to learn the ways of men, and no one taught us; we just learned by doing what we saw, and we were warriors at a time when boys now are like girls.

It was the summer when I was nine years old, and our people were moving slowly towards the Rocky Mountains. We camped one evening in a valley beside a little creek just before it ran into the Greasy Grass, and there was a man by the name of Man Hip who liked me and asked me to eat with him in his tepee.

While I was eating, a voice came and said: "It is time; now they are calling you." The voice was so loud and clear that I believed it, and I thought I would just go where it wanted me to go. So I got right up and started. As I came out of the tepee, both my thighs began to hurt me, and suddenly it was like waking from a dream, and there wasn't any voice. So I went back into the tepee, but I didn't want to eat. Man Hip looked at me in a strange way and asked me what was wrong. I told him that my legs were hurting me.

---

1. White men; their "iron road" was the Union Pacific Railroad.

The next morning the camp moved again, and I was riding with some boys. We stopped to get a drink from a creek, and when I got off my horse, my legs crumpled under me and I could not walk. So the boys helped me up and put me on my horse; and when we camped again that evening, I was sick. The next day the camp moved on to where the different bands of our people were coming together, and I rode in a pony drag, for I was very sick. Both my legs and both my arms were swollen badly and my face was all puffed up.

When we had camped again, I was lying in our tepee and my mother and father were sitting beside me. I could see out through the opening, and there two men were coming from the clouds, headfirst like arrows slanting down, and I knew they were the same that I had seen before. Each now carried a long spear, and from the points of these a jagged lightning flashed. They came clear down to the ground this time and stood a little way off and looked at me and said: "Hurry! Come! Your Grandfathers are calling you!"

Then they turned and left the ground like arrows slanting upward from the bow. When I got up to follow, my legs did not hurt me any more and I was very light. I went outside the tepee, and yonder where the men with flaming spears were going, a little cloud was coming very fast. It came and stooped and took me and turned back to where it came from, flying fast. And when I looked down I could see my mother and my father yonder, and I felt sorry to be leaving them.

Then there was nothing but the air and the swiftness of the little cloud that bore me and those two men still leading up to where white clouds were piled like mountains on a wide blue plain, and in them thunder beings lived and leaped and flashed.

Now suddenly there was nothing but a world of cloud, and we three were there alone in the middle of a great white plain with snowy hills and mountains staring at us; and it was very still; but there were whispers.

Then the two men spoke together and they said: "Behold him, the being with four legs!"

I looked and saw a bay horse standing there, and he began to speak: "Behold me!" he said, "My life-history you shall see." Then he wheeled about to where the sun goes down, and said: "Behold them! Their history you shall know."

I looked, and there were twelve black horses yonder all abreast with necklaces of bison hoofs, and they were beautiful, but I was frightened, because their manes were lightning and there was thunder in their nostrils.

Then the bay horse wheeled to where the great white giant lives (the north) and said: "Behold!" And yonder there were twelve white horses all abreast. Their manes were flowing like a blizzard wind and from their noses came a roaring, and all about them white geese soared and circled.

Then the bay wheeled round to where the sun shines continually (the east) and bade me look; and there twelve sorrel horses, with necklaces of elk's teeth, stood abreast with eyes that glimmered like the day-break star and manes of morning light.

Then the bay wheeled once again to look upon the place where you are always facing (the south), and yonder stood twelve buckskins all abreast with horns upon their heads and manes that lived and grew like trees and grasses.

And when I had seen all these, the bay horse said: "Your Grandfathers are having a council. These shall take you; so have courage."

Then all the horses went into formation, four abreast—the blacks, the whites, the sorrels, and the buckskins—and stood behind the bay, who turned now to the west and neighed; and yonder suddenly the sky was terrible with a storm of plunging horses in all colors that shook the world with thunder, neighing back.

Now turning to the north the bay horse whinnied, and yonder all the sky roared with a mighty wind of running horses in all colors, neighing back.

And when he whinnied to the east, there too the sky was filled with glowing clouds of manes and tails of horses in all colors singing back. Then to the south he called, and it was crowded with many colored, happy horses, nickering.

Then the bay horse spoke to me again and said: "See how your horses all come dancing!" I looked, and there were horses, horses everywhere—a whole skyful of horses dancing round me.

"Make haste!" the bay horse said; and we walked together side by side, while the blacks, the whites, the sorrels, and the buckskins followed, marching four by four.

I looked about me once again, and suddenly the dancing horses without number changed into animals of every kind and into all the fowls that are, and these fled back to the four quarters of the world from whence the horses came, and vanished.

Then as we walked, there was a heaped up cloud ahead that changed into a tepee, and a rainbow was the open door of it; and through the door I saw six old men sitting in a row. The two men with the spears now stood beside me, one on either hand, and the horses took their places in their quarters, looking inward, four by four. And the oldest of the Grandfathers spoke with a kind voice and said: "Come right in and do not fear." And as he spoke, all the horses of the four quarters neighed to cheer me. So I went in and stood before the six, and they looked older than men can ever be—old like hills, like stars.

The oldest spoke again: "Your Grandfathers all over the world are having a council, and they have called you here to teach you." His voice was very kind, but I shook all over with fear now, for I knew that these were not old men, but the Powers of the World. And the first was the Power of the West; the second, of the North; the third, of the East; the fourth, of the South; the fifth, of the Sky; the sixth, of the Earth. I knew this, and was afraid, until the first Grandfather spoke again: "Behold them yonder where the sun goes down, the thunder beings! You shall see, and have from them my power; and they shall take you to the high and lonely center of the earth that you may see; even to the place where the sun continually shines, they shall take you there to understand."

And as he spoke of understanding, I looked up and saw the rainbow leap with flames of many colors over me.

Now there was a wooden cup in his hand and it was full of water and in the water was the sky.

"Take this," he said. "It is the power to make live, and it is yours." Now he had a bow in his hands. "Take this," he said. "It is the power to destroy, and it is yours."

Then he pointed to himself and said: "Look close at him who is your spirit now, for you are his body and his name is Eagle Wing Stretches."

And saying this, he got up very tall and started running toward where the sun goes down; and suddenly he was a black horse that stopped and turned and looked at me, and the horse was very poor and sick; his ribs stood out.

Then the second Grandfather, he of the North, arose with a herb of power in his hand, and said: "Take this and hurry." I took and held it toward the black horse yonder. He fattened and was happy and came prancing to his place again and was the first Grandfather sitting there.

The second Grandfather, he of the North, spoke again: "Take courage, younger brother," he said; "on earth a nation you shall make live, for yours shall be the power of the white giant's wing, the cleansing wind." Then he got up very tall and started running toward the north; and when he turned toward me, it was a white goose wheeling. I looked about me now, and the horses in the west were thunders and the horses of the north were geese. And the second Grandfather sang two songs that were like this:

> They are appearing, may you behold!
> They are appearing, may you behold!
> The thunder nation is appearing, behold!
>
> They are appearing, may you behold!
> They are appearing, may you behold!
> The white geese nation is appearing, behold!

And now it was the third Grandfather who spoke, he of where the sun shines continually. "Take courage, younger brother," he said, "for across the earth they shall take you!" Then he pointed to where the daybreak star was shining, and beneath the star two men were flying. "From them you shall have power," he said, "from them who have awakened all the beings of the earth with roots and legs and wings." And as he said this, he held in his hand a peace pipe which had a spotted eagle outstretched upon the stem; and this eagle seemed alive, for it was poised there, fluttering, and its eyes were looking at me. "With this pipe," the Grandfather said, "you shall walk upon the earth, and whatever sickens there you shall make well." Then he pointed to a man who was bright red all over, the color of good and of plenty, and as he pointed, the red man lay down and rolled and changed into a bison that got up and galloped toward the sorrel horses of the east, and they too turned to bison, fat and many.

And now the fourth Grandfather spoke, he of the place where you are always facing (the south), whence comes the power to grow. "Younger brother," he said, "with the powers of the four quarters you shall walk, a relative.[2] Behold, the living center of a nation I shall give you, and with it many you shall save." And I saw that he was holding in his hand a bright red stick that was alive, and as I looked it sprouted at the top and sent forth branches, and on the branches many leaves came out and murmured and in the leaves the birds began to sing. And then for just a little while I thought I saw beneath it in the shade the circled villages of people and every living thing with roots or legs or wings, and all were happy. "It shall stand in the center of the nation's circle," said the Grandfather, "a cane to walk with and a people's heart; and by your powers you shall make it blossom."

Then when he had been still a little while to hear the birds sing, he spoke again: "Behold the earth!" So I looked down and saw it lying yonder like a hoop of peoples, and in the center bloomed the holy stick that was a tree, and where it stood there crossed two roads, a red one and a black. "From where the giant lives (the north) to where you always face (the south) the red road goes, the road of good," the Grandfather said, "and on it shall your nation walk. The black road goes from where the thunder beings live (the west) to where the sun continually shines (the east), a fearful road, a road of troubles and of war. On this also you shall walk, and from it you shall have the power to destroy a people's foes. In four ascents you shall walk the earth with power."

2. In the original transcript, Black Elk adds: "At the time I grew up to manhood there was no war and the Indians all became white men and if there had been right feeling among the Indians I would have been the greatest, most powerful medicine man of the ages."

I think he meant that I should see four generations, counting me, and now I am seeing the third.

Then he rose very tall and started running toward the south, and was an elk; and as he stood among the buckskins yonder, they too were elks.

Now the fifth Grandfather spoke, the oldest of them all, the Spirit of the Sky. "My boy," he said, "I have sent for you and you have come. My power you shall see!" He stretched his arms and turned into a spotted eagle hovering. "Behold," he said, "all the wings of the air shall come to you, and they and the winds and the stars shall be like relatives. You shall go across the earth with my power." Then the eagle soared above my head and fluttered there; and suddenly the sky was full of friendly wings all coming toward me.

Now I knew the sixth Grandfather was about to speak, he who was the Spirit of the Earth, and I saw that he was very old, but more as men are old. His hair was long and white, his face was all in wrinkles and his eyes were deep and dim. I stared at him, for it seemed I knew him somehow; and as I stared, he slowly changed, for he was growing backwards into youth, and when he had become a boy, I knew that he was myself with all the years that would be mine at last. When he was old again, he said: "My boy, have courage, for my power shall be yours, and you shall need it, for your nation on the earth will have great troubles. Come."

He rose and tottered out through the rainbow door, and as I followed I was riding on the bay horse who had talked to me at first and led me to that place.

Then the bay horse stopped and faced the black horses of the west, and a voice said: "They have given you the cup of water to make live the greening day, and also the bow and arrow to destroy." The bay neighed, and the twelve black horses came and stood behind me, four abreast.

The bay faced the sorrels of the east, and I saw that they had morning stars upon their foreheads and they were very bright. And the voice said: "They have given you the sacred pipe and the power that is peace, and the good red day." The bay neighed, and the twelve sorrels stood behind me, four abreast.

My horse now faced the buckskins of the south, and a voice said: "They have given you the sacred stick and your nation's hoop, and the yellow day; and in the center of the hoop you shall set the stick and make it grow into a shielding tree, and bloom." The bay neighed, and the twelve buckskins came and stood behind me, four abreast.

Then I knew that there were riders on all the horses there behind me, and a voice said: "Now you shall walk the black road with these; and as you walk, all the nations that have roots or legs or wings shall fear you."

So I started, riding toward the east down the fearful road, and behind me came the horsebacks four abreast—the blacks, the whites, the sorrels, and the buckskins—and far away above the fearful road the daybreak star was rising very dim.

I looked below me where the earth was silent in a sick green light, and saw the hills look up afraid and the grasses on the hills and all the animals; and everywhere about me were the cries of frightened birds and sounds of fleeing wings. I was the chief of all the heavens riding there, and when I looked behind me, all the twelve black horses reared and plunged and thundered and their manes and tails were whirling hail and their nostrils snorted lightning. And when I looked below again, I saw the slant hail falling and the long, sharp rain, and where we passed, the trees bowed low and all the hills were dim.

Now the earth was bright again as we rode. I could see the hills and valleys and the creeks and rivers passing under. We came above a place where three streams made a big one—a source of mighty waters —and something terrible was there. Flames were rising from the waters and in the flames a blue man lived. The dust was floating all about him in the air, the grass was short and withered, the trees were wilting, two-legged and four-legged beings lay there thin and panting, and wings too weak to fly.

Then the black horse riders shouted "Hoka hey!"[3] and charged down upon the blue man, but were driven back. And the white troop shouted, charging, and was beaten; then the red troop and the yellow.

And when each had failed, they all cried together: "Eagle Wing Stretches, hurry!" And all the world was filled with voices of all kinds that cheered me, so I charged. I had the cup of water in one hand and in the other was the bow that turned into a spear as the bay and I swooped down, and the spear's head was sharp lightning. It stabbed the blue man's heart, and as it struck I could hear the thunder rolling and many voices that cried "Un-hee!," meaning I had killed. The flames died. The trees and grasses were not withered any more and murmured happily together, and every living being cried in gladness with whatever voice it had. Then the four troops of horsemen charged down and struck the dead body of the blue man, counting coup; and suddenly it was only a harmless turtle.

You see, I had been riding with the storm clouds, and had come to earth as rain, and it was drouth that I had killed with the power that the Six Grandfathers gave me.[4] So we were riding on the earth now down along the river flowing full from the source of waters, and soon I saw ahead the circled village of a people in the valley. And a Voice said: "Behold a nation; it is yours. Make haste, Eagle Wing Stretches!"

I entered the village, riding, with the four horse troops behind me—the blacks, the whites, the sorrels, and the buckskins; and the place was filled with moaning and with mourning for the dead. The wind was blowing from the south like fever, and when I looked around I saw that in nearly every tepee the women and the children and the men lay dying with the dead.

So I rode around the circle of the village, looking in upon the sick and dead, and I felt like crying as I rode. But when I looked behind me, all the women and the children and the men were getting up and coming forth with happy faces.

And a Voice said: "Behold, they have given you the center of the nation's hoop to make it live."

So I rode to the center of the village, with the horse troops in their quarters round about me, and there the people gathered. And the Voice said: "Give them now the flowering stick that they may flourish, and the sacred pipe that they may know the power that is peace, and the wing of the white giant that they may have endurance and face all winds with courage."

So I took the bright red stick and at the center of the nation's hoop I thrust it in the earth. As it touched the earth it leaped mightily in my hand and was a waga chun,[5] the rustling tree, very tall and full of leafy branches and of all birds singing. And beneath it all the animals were mingling with the people like relatives and making happy cries. The women raised their tremolo of joy, and the men shouted all together: "Here we shall raise our children and be as little chickens under the mother sheo's[6] wing."

3. "Onward!"—a rallying cry in battle.
4. In the transcript, the symbolic interpretation of the slain man as drought doesn't appear here; Neihardt has taken it from a later episode. At this point, the transcript reads: "Everything that had been dead came back to life and

cheered me for killing that enemy. This means that sometime in the future I was going to kill an enemy in some future battle."
5. Cottonwood tree.
6. Prairie hen.

Then I heard the white wind blowing gently through the tree and singing there, and from the east the sacred pipe came flying on its eagle wings, and stopped before me there beneath the tree, spreading deep peace around it.

Then the daybreak star was rising, and a Voice said: "It shall be a relative to them; and who shall see it, shall see much more, for thence comes wisdom; and those who do not see it shall be dark." And all the people raised their faces to the east, and the star's light fell upon them, and all the dogs barked loudly and the horses whinnied.

Then when the many little voices ceased, the great Voice said: "Behold the circle of the nation's hoop, for it is holy, being endless, and thus all powers shall be one power in the people without end. Now they shall break camp and go forth upon the red road, and your Grandfathers shall walk with them."[7] So the people broke camp and took the good road with the white wing on their faces, and the order of their going was like this:

First, the black horse riders with the cup of water; and the white horse riders with the white wing and the sacred herb; and the sorrel riders with the holy pipe; and the buckskins with the flowering stick. And after these the little children and the youths and maidens followed in a band.

Second, came the tribe's four chieftains, and their band was all young men and women.

Third, the nation's four advisers leading men and women neither young nor old.

Fourth, the old men hobbling with their canes and looking to the earth.

Fifth, old women hobbling with their canes and looking to the earth.

Sixth, myself all alone upon the bay with the bow and arrows that the First Grandfather gave me. But I was not the last; for when I looked behind me there were ghosts of people like a trailing fog as far as I could see—grandfathers of grandfathers and grandmothers of grandmothers without number. And over these a great Voice—the Voice that was the South—lived, and I could feel it silent.

And as we went the Voice behind me said: "Behold a good nation walking in a sacred manner in a good land!"

Then I looked up and saw that there were four ascents ahead, and these were generations I should know. Now we were on the first ascent, and all the land was green. And as the long line climbed, all the old men and women raised their hands, palms forward, to the far sky yonder and began to croon a song together, and the sky ahead was filled with clouds of baby faces.

When we came to the end of the first ascent we camped in the sacred circle as before, and in the center stood the holy tree, and still the land about us was all green.

Then we started on the second ascent, marching as before, and still the land was green, but it was getting steeper. And as I looked ahead, the people changed into elks and bison and all four-footed beings and even into fowls, all walking in a sacred manner on the good red road together. And I myself was a spotted eagle soaring over them. But just before we stopped to camp at the end of that ascent, all the marching animals grew restless and afraid that they were not what they had been, and began

---

7. At this point the transcript continues: "In his left hand the spirit held the hoop and in his right hand he held the bow and arrow. He said: 'You shall have this nation and with this bow and arrow on earth your worst enemy you shall conquer.' At the same time he held this wooden cup of water, and he said: 'With this the wildest enemies will be tame.' I could capture anything without being hurt. With that bow and arrow my people should be able to do the same things as I can. They used that on Custer and there wasn't one of them who did not have an arrow in his skin. This worked in the Custer fight very well" (123)—referring to the killing of General Custer and his 200 men at Little Bighorn in 1876.

sending forth voices of trouble, calling to their chiefs. And when they camped at the end of that ascent, I looked down and saw that leaves were falling from the holy tree.

And the Voice said: "Behold your nation, and remember what your Six Grandfathers gave you, for thenceforth your people walk in difficulties."

Then the people broke camp again, and saw the black road before them towards where the sun goes down, and black clouds coming yonder; and they did not want to go but could not stay. And as they walked the third ascent, all the animals and fowls that were the people ran here and there, for each one seemed to have his own little vision that he followed and his own rules; and all over the universe I could hear the winds at war like wild beasts fighting.[8]

And when we reached the summit of the third ascent and camped, the nation's hoop was broken like a ring of smoke that spreads and scatters and the holy tree seemed dying and all its birds were gone. And when I looked ahead I saw that the fourth ascent would be terrible.

Then when the people were getting ready to begin the fourth ascent, the Voice spoke like some one weeping, and it said: "Look there upon your nation." And when I looked down, the people were all changed back to human, and they were thin, their faces sharp, for they were starving. Their ponies were only hide and bones, and the holy tree was gone. And as I looked and wept, I saw that there stood on the north side of the starving camp a sacred man who was painted red all over his body, and he held a spear as he walked into the center of the people, and there he lay down and rolled. And when he got up, it was a fat bison standing there, and where the bison stood a sacred herb sprang up right where the tree had been in the center of the nation's hoop. The herb grew and bore four blossoms on a single stem while I was looking—a blue, a white, a scarlet, and a yellow—and the bright rays of these flashed to the heavens.

I know now what this meant, that the bison were the gift of a good spirit and were our strength, but we should lose them, and from the same good spirit we must find another strength. For the people all seemed better when the herb had grown and bloomed, and the horses raised their tails and neighed and pranced around, and I could see a light breeze going from the north among the people like a ghost; and suddenly the flowering tree was there again at the center of the nation's hoop where the four-rayed herb had blossomed.

I was still the spotted eagle floating, and I could see that I was already in the fourth ascent and the people were camping yonder at the top of the third long rise. It was dark and terrible about me, for all the winds of the world were fighting. It was like rapid gun-fire and like whirling smoke, and like women and children wailing and like horses screaming all over the world.

I could see my people yonder running about, setting the smoke-flap poles and fastening down their tepees against the wind, for the storm cloud was coming on them very fast and black, and there were frightened swallows without number fleeing before the cloud.

Then a song of power came to me and I sang it there in the midst of that terrible place where I was. It went like this:

---

8. "At this point Black Elk remarked: 'I think we are near that place now, and I am afraid something very bad is going to happen all over the world.' He cannot read and knows nothing of world affairs" [Neihardt's note]. The transcript puts Black Elk's concern rather differently: "Black Elk says at this point he has a queer feeling all the time he is telling this, and that he is giving his power away. He feels he will die very soon afterward. His dream has been coming true. . . . He knew something was going to happen in the war [World War I], so he didn't allow his son to go even though he wanted to. In Black Elk's days he has seen the second generation and in the third he thinks something fearful is going to happen."

A good nation I will make live.
This the nation above has said.
They have given me the power to make over.

And when I had sung this, a Voice said: "To the four quarters you shall run for help, and nothing shall be strong before you. Behold him!"[9]

Now I was on my bay horse again, because the horse is of the earth, and it was there my power would be used. And as I obeyed the Voice and looked, there was a horse all skin and bones yonder in the west, a faded brownish black. And a Voice there said: "Take this and make him over; and it was the four-rayed herb that I was holding in my hand. So I rode above the poor horse in a circle, and as I did this I could hear the people yonder calling for spirit power, "A-hey! a-hey! a-hey! a-hey!" Then the poor horse neighed and rolled and got up, and he was a big, shiny, black stallion with dapples all over him and his mane about him like a cloud. He was the chief of all the horses; and when he snorted, it was a flash of lightning and his eyes were like the sunset star. He dashed to the west and neighed, and the west was filled with a dust of hoofs, and horses without number, shiny black, came plunging from the dust. Then he dashed toward the north and neighed, and to the east and to the south, and the dust clouds answered, giving forth their plunging horses without number—whites and sorrels and buckskins, fat, shiny, rejoicing in their fleetness and their strength. It was beautiful, but it was also terrible.

Then they all stopped short, rearing, and were standing in a great hoop about their black chief at the center, and were still. And as they stood, four virgins, more beautiful than women of the earth can be, came through the circle, dressed in scarlet, one from each of the four quarters, and stood about the great black stallion in their places; and one held the wooden cup of water, and one the white wing, and one the pipe, and one the nation's hoop. All the universe was silent, listening; and then the great black stallion raised his voice and sang. The song he sang was this:

> My horses, prancing they are coming.
> My horses, neighing they are coming;
> Prancing, they are coming.
> All over the universe they come.
> They will dance; may you behold them.
> (4 times)
> A horse nation, they will dance. May you behold them.
> (4 times)

His voice was not loud, but it went all over the universe and filled it. There was nothing that did not hear, and it was more beautiful than anything can be. It was so beautiful that nothing anywhere could keep from dancing. The virgins danced, and all the circled horses. The leaves on the trees, the grasses on the hills and in the valleys, the waters in the creeks and in the rivers and the lakes, the four-legged and the two-legged and the wings of the air—all danced together to the music of the stallion's song.

And when I looked down upon my people yonder, the cloud passed over, blessing them with friendly rain, and stood in the east with a flaming rainbow over it.

9. In the transcript, Black Elk goes on to describe the sudden emergence of a flaming dog, whom he kills with an arrow. He interprets this scene as follows: "This meant that when you go to war you should kill your enemy like a dog. . . . If I had gone to war much I would have been able to do much damage, but the enemy couldn't fight back."

Then all the horses went singing back to their places beyond the summit of the fourth ascent, and all things sang along with them as they walked. And a Voice said: "All over the universe they have finished a day of happiness." And looking down I saw that the whole wide circle of the day was beautiful and green, with all fruits growing and all things kind and happy.

Then a Voice said: "Behold this day, for it is yours to make. Now you shall stand upon the center of the earth to see, for there they are taking you."

I was still on my bay horse, and once more I felt the riders of the west, the north, the east, the south, behind me in formation, as before, and we were going east. I looked ahead and saw the mountains there with rocks and forests on them, and from the mountains flashed all colors upward to the heavens. Then I was standing on the highest mountain of them all, and round about beneath me was the whole hoop of the world. And while I stood there I saw more than I can tell and I understood more than I saw; for I was seeing in a sacred manner the shapes of all things in the spirit, and the shape of all shapes as they must live together like one being. And I saw that the sacred hoop of my people was one of many hoops that made one circle, wide as daylight and as starlight, and in the center grew one mighty flowering tree to shelter all the children of one mother and one father. And I saw that it was holy.

Then as I stood there, two men were coming from the east, head first like arrows flying, and between them rose the day-break star. They came and gave a herb to me and said: "With this on earth you shall undertake anything and do it." It was the day-break-star herb, the herb of understanding, and they told me to drop it on the earth. I saw it falling far, and when it struck the earth it rooted and grew and flowered, four blossoms on one stem, a blue, a white, a scarlet, and a yellow; and the rays from these streamed upward to the heavens so that all creatures saw it and in no place was there darkness.[1]

Then the Voice said: "Your Six Grandfathers—now you shall go back to them."

I had not noticed how I was dressed until now, and I saw that I was painted red all over, and my joints were painted black, with white stripes between the joints. My bay had lightning stripes all over him, and his mane was cloud. And when I breathed, my breath was lightning.

Now two men were leading me, head first like arrows slanting upward—the two that brought me from the earth. And as I followed on the bay, they turned into four flocks of geese that flew in circles, one above each quarter, sending forth a sacred voice as they flew: Br-r-r-p, br-r-r-p, br-r-r-p, br-r-r-p!

Then I saw ahead the rainbow flaming above the tepee of the Six Grandfathers, built and roofed with cloud and sewed with thongs of lightning; and underneath it were all the wings of the air and under them the animals and men. All these were rejoicing, and thunder was like happy laughter.

As I rode in through the rainbow door, there were cheering voices from all over the universe, and I saw the Six Grandfathers sitting in a row, with their arms held toward me and their hands, palms out; and behind them in the cloud were faces thronging, without number, of the people yet to be.

"He has triumphed!" cried the six together, making thunder. And as I passed before them there, each gave again the gift that he had given me before—the cup of wa-

---

1. In the transcript, Black Elk is next given an herb of destruction: "It could be used in war and could destroy a nation. . . . I was not old enough when I was supposed to use this herb or else I could have used it and killed many enemies. It was too terrible to use and I was glad that I did not get to use it. This herb is in the Black Hills. Every animal that nears it dies. Around where it grows there are many skeletons always. This medicine belongs only to me—no one else knows what this herb looks like. It looks like a little tree with crinkly leaves, reddish in color."

ter and the bow and arrows, the power to make live and to destroy; the white wing of cleansing and the healing herb; the sacred pipe; the flowering stick. And each one spoke in turn from west to south, explaining what he gave as he had done before, and as each one spoke he melted down into the earth and rose again; and as each did this, I felt nearer to the earth.

Then the oldest of them all said: "Grandson, all over the universe you have seen. Now you shall go back with power to the place from whence you came, and it shall happen yonder that hundreds shall be sacred, hundreds shall be flames! Behold!"

I looked below and saw my people there, and all were well and happy except one, and he was lying like the dead—and that one was myself. Then the oldest Grandfather sang, and his song was like this:

> There is someone lying on earth in a sacred manner.
> There is someone—on earth he lies.
> In a sacred manner I have made him to walk.

Now the tepee, built and roofed with cloud, began to sway back and forth as in a wind, and the flaming rainbow door was growing dimmer. I could hear voices of all kinds crying from outside: "Eagle Wing Stretches is coming forth! Behold him!"

When I went through the door, the face of the day of earth was appearing with the day-break star upon its forehead; and the sun leaped up and looked upon me, and I was going forth alone.

And as I walked alone, I heard the sun singing as it arose, and it sang like this:

> With visible face I am appearing.
> In a sacred manner I appear.
> For the greening earth a pleasantness I make.
> The center of the nation's hoop I have made pleasant.
> With visible face, behold me!
> The four-leggeds and two-leggeds, I have made them to walk;
>
> The wings of the air, I have made them to fly.
> With visible face I appear.
> My day, I have made it holy.

When the singing stopped, I was feeling lost and very lonely. Then a Voice above me said: "Look back!" It was a spotted eagle that was hovering over me and spoke. I looked, and where the flaming rainbow tepee, built and roofed with cloud, had been, I saw only the tall rock mountain at the center of the world.

I was all alone on a broad plain now with my feet upon the earth, alone but for the spotted eagle guarding me. I could see my people's village far ahead, and I walked very fast, for I was homesick now. Then I saw my own tepee, and inside I saw my mother and my father bending over a sick boy that was myself. And as I entered the tepee, some one was saying: "The boy is coming to; you had better give him some water."

Then I was sitting up; and I was sad because my mother and my father didn't seem to know I had been so far away.[2]

---

2. Black Elk goes on to describe various events in his life, particularly the battle against General Custer and the sacred "ghost dances" intended to bring about a revival of the Sioux nation. He also describes a year spent performing in Europe with Buffalo Bill's Wild West Show and another show run by a man named Mexican Joe. Black Elk then ends with the following account of the disaster at Wounded Knee in 1890, when he was 27.

[THE MASSACRE AT WOUNDED KNEE]

We camped on White River, then on White Clay, then on Cheyenne Creek north of Pine Ridge. Most of the Ogalalas were camping near there too.

It was about this time that bad news came to us from the north. We heard that some policemen from Standing Rock had gone to arrest Sitting Bull on Grand River, and that he would not let them take him; so there was a fight, and they killed him.[3]

It was now near the end of the Moon of Popping Trees, and I was twenty-seven years old (December, 1890). We heard that Big Foot was coming down from the Badlands with nearly four hundred people. Some of these were from Sitting Bull's band. They had run away when Sitting Bull was killed, and joined Big Foot on Good River. There were only about a hundred warriors in this band, and all the others were women and children and some old men. They were all starving and freezing, and Big Foot was so sick that they had to bring him along in a pony drag. They had all run away to hide in the Badlands, and they were coming in now because they were starving and freezing. When they crossed Smoky Earth River, they followed up Medicine Root Creek to its head. Soldiers were over there looking for them. The soldiers had everything and were not freezing and starving. Near Porcupine Butte the soldiers came up to the Big Foots, and they surrendered and went along with the soldiers to Wounded Knee Creek where the Brenan store is now.

It was in the evening when we heard that the Big Foots were camped over there with the soldiers, about fifteen miles by the old road from where we were. It was the next morning (December 29, 1890) that something terrible happened.

That evening before it happened, I went in to Pine Ridge and heard these things, and while I was there, soldiers started for where the Big Foots were. These made about five hundred soldiers that were there next morning. When I saw them starting I felt that something terrible was going to happen. That night I could hardly sleep at all. I walked around most of the night.

In the morning I went out after my horses, and while I was out I heard shooting off toward the east, and I knew from the sound that it must be wagon-guns (cannon) going off. The sounds went right through my body, and I felt that something terrible would happen.

When I reached camp with the horses, a man rode up to me and said: "Hey-hey-hey! The people that are coming are fired on! I know it!"

I saddled up my buckskin and put on my sacred shirt. It was one I had made to be worn by no one but myself. It had a spotted eagle outstretched on the back of it, and the daybreak star was on the left shoulder, because when facing south that shoulder is toward the east. Across the breast, from the left shoulder to the right hip, was the flaming rainbow, and there was another rainbow around the neck, like a necklace, with a star at the bottom. At each shoulder, elbow, and wrist was an eagle feather; and over the whole shirt were red streaks of lightning. You will see that this was from my great vision, and you will know how it protected me that day.

I painted my face all red, and in my hair I put one eagle feather for the One Above. It did not take me long to get ready, for I could still hear the shooting over

3. Chief Sitting Bull (c. 1831–1890) led the Dakota Sioux in battles including the killing of Custer and his men. Eventually he was forced to surrender. He was living quietly on his reservation when rumors of renewed war arose; he was dragged from his bed and was killed when he resisted arrest.

there. I started out alone on the old road that ran across the hills to Wounded Knee. I had no gun. I carried only the sacred bow of the west that I had seen in my great vision. I had gone only a little way when a band of young men came galloping after me. The first two who came up were Loves War and Iron Wasichu. I asked what they were going to do, and they said they were just going to see where the shooting was. Then others were coming up, and some older men.

We rode fast, and there were about twenty of us now. The shooting was getting louder. A horseback from over there came galloping very fast toward us, and he said: "Hey-hey-hey! They have murdered him!" Then he whipped his horse and rode away faster toward Pine Ridge.

In a little while we had come to the top of the ridge where, looking to the east, you can see for the first time the monument and the burying ground on the little hill where the church is. That is where the terrible thing started. Just south of the burying ground on the little hill a deep dry gulch runs about east and west, very crooked, and it rises westward to nearly the top of the ridge where we were. It had no name, but the Wasichus sometimes call it Battle Creek now. We stopped on the ridge not far from the head of the dry gulch. Wagon guns were still going off over there on the little hill, and they were going off again where they hit along the gulch. There was much shooting down yonder, and there were many cries, and we could see cavalrymen scattered over the hills ahead of us. Cavalrymen were riding along the gulch and shooting into it, where the women and children were running away and trying to hide in the gullies and the stunted pines.

A little way ahead of us, just below the head of the dry gulch, there were some women and children who were huddled under a clay bank, and some cavalrymen were there pointing guns at them.

We stopped back behind the ridge, and I said to the others: "Take courage. These are our relatives. We will try to get them back." Then we all sang a song which went like this:

> A thunder being nation I am, I have said.
> A thunder being nation I am, I have said.
> You shall live.
> You shall live.
> You shall live.
> You shall live.

Then I rode over the ridge and the others after me, and we were crying: "Take courage! It is time to fight!" The soldiers who were guarding our relatives shot at us and then ran away fast, and some more cavalrymen on the other side of the gulch did too. We got our relatives and sent them across the bridge to the northwest where they would be safe.

I had no gun, and when we were charging, I just held the sacred bow out in front of me with my right hand. The bullets did not hit us at all.

We found a little baby lying all alone near the head of the gulch. I could not pick her up just then, but I got her later and some of my people adopted her. I just wrapped her up tighter in a shawl that was around her and left her there. It was a safe place, and I had other work to do.

The soldiers had run eastward over the hills where there were some more soldiers, and they were off their horses and lying down. I told the others to stay back, and I charged upon them holding the sacred bow out toward them with my right hand.

They all shot at me, and I could hear bullets all around me, but I ran my horse right close to them, and then swung around. Some soldiers across the gulch began shooting at me too, but I got back to the others and was not hurt at all.

By now many other Lakotas, who had heard the shooting, were coming up from Pine Ridge, and we all charged on the soldiers. They ran eastward toward where the trouble began. We followed down along the dry gulch, and what we saw was terrible. Dead and wounded women and children and little babies were scattered all along there where they had been trying to run away. The soldiers had followed along the gulch, as they ran, and murdered them in there. Sometimes they were in heaps because they had huddled together, and some were scattered all along. Sometimes bunches of them had been killed and torn to pieces where the wagon guns hit them. I saw a little baby trying to suck its mother, but she was bloody and dead.

There were two little boys at one place in this gulch. They had guns and they had been killing soldiers all by themselves. We could see the soldiers they had killed. The boys were all alone there and they were not hurt. These were very brave little boys.

When we drove the soldiers back, they dug themselves in, and we were not enough people to drive them out from there. In the evening they marched off up Wounded Knee Creek, and then we saw all that they had done there.

Men and women and children were heaped and scattered all over the flat at the bottom of the little hill where the soldiers had their wagon-guns, and westward up the dry gulch all the way to the high ridge, the dead women and children and babies were scattered.

When I saw this I wished that I had died too, but I was not sorry for the women and children. It was better for them to be happy in the other world, and I wanted to be there too. But before I went there I wanted to have revenge. I thought there might be a day, and we should have revenge.

After the soldiers marched away, I heard from my friend, Dog Chief, how the trouble started, and he was right there by Yellow Bird when it happened. This is the way it was:

In the morning the soldiers began to take all the guns away from the Big Foots, who were camped in the flat below the little hill where the monument and burying ground are now. The people had stacked most of their guns, and even their knives, by the tepee where Big Foot was lying sick. Soldiers were on the little hill and all around, and there were soldiers across the dry gulch to the south and over east along Wounded Knee Creek too. The people were nearly surrounded, and the wagon-guns were pointing at them.

Some had not yet given up their guns, and so the soldiers were searching all the tepees, throwing things around and poking into everything. There was a man called Yellow Bird, and he and another man were standing in front of the tepee where Big Foot was lying sick. They had white sheets around and over them, with eyeholes to look through, and they had guns under these. An officer came to search them. He took the other man's gun, and then started to take Yellow Bird's. But Yellow Bird would not let go. He wrestled with the officer, and while they were wrestling, the gun went off and killed the officer. Wasichus and some others have said he meant to do this, but Dog Chief was standing right there, and he told me it was not so. As soon as the gun went off, Dog Chief told me, an officer shot and killed Big Foot who was lying sick inside the tepee.

Then suddenly nobody knew what was happening, except that the soldiers were all shooting and the wagon-guns began going off right in among the people.

Many were shot down right there. The women and children ran into the gulch and up west, dropping all the time, for the soldiers shot them as they ran. There were only about a hundred warriors and there were nearly five hundred soldiers. The warriors rushed to where they had piled their guns and knives. They fought soldiers with only their hands until they got their guns.

Dog Chief saw Yellow Bird run into a tepee with his gun, and from there he killed soldiers until the tepee caught fire. Then he died full of bullets.

It was a good winter day when all this happened. The sun was shining. But after the soldiers marched away from their dirty work, a heavy snow began to fall. The wind came up in the night. There was a big blizzard, and it grew very cold. The snow drifted deep in the crooked gulch, and it was one long grave of butchered women and children and babies, who had never done any harm and were only trying to run away.

[The End of the Dream]

It was now nearly the middle of the Moon of Frost in the Tepee (January). We heard that soldiers were on Smoky Earth River and were coming to attack us in the O-ona-gazhee. They were near Black Feather's place. So a party of about sixty of us started on the war-path to find them. My mother tried to keep me at home, because, although I could walk and ride a horse, my wound was not all healed yet. But I would not stay; for, after what I had seen at Wounded Knee, I wanted a chance to kill soldiers.

We rode down Grass Creek to Smoky Earth, and crossed, riding down stream. Soon from the top of a little hill we saw wagons and cavalry guarding them. The soldiers were making a corral of their wagons and getting ready to fight. We got off our horses and went behind some hills to a little knoll, where we crept up to look at the camp. Some soldiers were bringing harnessed horses down to a little creek to water, and I said to the others: "If you will stay here and shoot at the soldiers, I will charge over there and get some good horses." They knew of my power, so they did this, and I charged on my buckskin while the others kept shooting. I got seven of the horses; but when I started back with these, all the soldiers saw me and began shooting. They killed two of my horses, but I brought five back safe and was not hit. When I was out of range, I caught up a fine bald-faced bay and turned my buckskin loose. Then I drove the others back to our party.

By now more cavalry were coming up the river, a big bunch of them, and there was some hard fighting for a while, because there were not enough of us. We were fighting and retreating, and all at once I saw Red Willow on foot running. He called to me: "Cousin, my horse is killed!" So I caught up a soldier's horse that was dragging a rope and brought it to Red Willow while the soldiers were shooting fast at me. Just then, for a little while, I was a wanekia[4] myself. In this fight Long Bear and another man, whose name I have forgotten, were badly wounded; but we saved them and carried them along with us. The soldiers did not follow us far into the Badlands, and when it was night we rode back with our wounded to the O-ona-gazhee.

We wanted a much bigger war-party so that we could meet the soldiers and get revenge. But this was hard, because the people were not all of the same mind, and they were hungry and cold. We had a meeting there, and were all ready to go out with more warriors, when Afraid-of-His-Horses came over from Pine Ridge to make peace with Red Cloud, who was with us there. Our party wanted to go out and fight anyway,

---

4. Savior, One Who Makes Live; the term is used both for the Sioux god Wovoka and for Jesus.

but Red Cloud made a speech to us something like this: "Brothers, this is a very hard winter. The women and children are starving and freezing. If this were summer, I would say to keep on fighting to the end. But we cannot do this. We must think of the women and children and that it is very bad for them. So we must make peace, and I will see that nobody is hurt by the soldiers."

The people agreed to this, for it was true. So we broke camp next day and went down from the O-ona-gazhee to Pine Ridge, and many, many Lakotas were already there. Also, there were many, many soldiers. They stood in two lines with their guns held in front of them as we went through to where we camped.

And so it was all over.

I did not know then how much was ended. When I look back now from this high hill of my old age, I can still see the butchered women and children lying heaped and scattered all along the crooked gulch as plain as when I saw them with eyes still young. And I can see that something else died there in the bloody mud, and was buried in the blizzard. A people's dream died there. It was a beautiful dream.

And I, to whom so great a vision was given in my youth,—you see me now a piti-ful old man who has done nothing, for the nation's hoop is broken and scattered. There is no center any longer, and the sacred tree is dead.

[This is the conclusion of Black Elk's account in the published book. In the tran-scripts, a further chapter follows, describing the aftermath of the surrender and re-counting prayers that were sung. At the close of this chapter, Black Elk sums up his experience as follows.]

You have heard what I have said about my people. I had been appointed by my vision to be an intercessor of my people with the spirit powers and concerning that I had decided that sometime in the future I'd bring my people out of the black road into the red road. From my experience and from what I know, and in recalling the past from where I was at that time, I could see that it was next to impossible, but there was nothing like trying. Of course probably the spirit world will help me and I thought I'd just figure on a scheme to have the people be all as one and if I had done this probably we would have been as we were before.

At that time I could see that the hoop was broken and all scattered out and I thought, "I am going to try my best to get my people back into the hoop again." At this time, when I had these things in my mind, I was abroad with strange people. They were not like my people and I couldn't have any clearness of understanding and somehow I had in mind that I was in a strange country and a strange land and that it was not the place nor the habits or religion that the spirits had assigned me, but then I had often wished that someday I might see a day for my people. At that time the wilds were vanishing and it seemed the spirits altogether forgot me and I felt almost like a dead man going around—I was actually dead at this time, that's all. In my vision they had predicted that I was chosen to be intercessor for my people so it was up to me to do my utmost for my people and everything that I did not do for my people, it would be my fault—if my people should perish it seemed that it would be my fault. If I were in poverty my people would also be in poverty, and if I were helpless or died, my peo-ple would die also. But it was up to me to scheme a certain way for myself to prosper for the people. If I prosper, my people would also prosper.

I am just telling you this, Mr. Neihardt. You know how I felt and what I really wanted to do is for us to make that tree bloom. On this tree we shall prosper. Therefore my children and yours are relative-like and therefore we shall go back into the hoop and here we'll cooperate and stand as one. This is why I want to go to Harney Peak, because here I will send the voices to the six grandfathers. And you remember I saw many happy faces behind those six grandfathers and maybe it will be that Mr. Neihardt['s] and my family will be the happy faces. Our families will multiply and prosper after we get this tree to blooming.

❦

•─ ❦ ─•

Herman Melville
1819–1891

Herman Melville's life is one of the best-known stories in nineteenth-century American literature. Born in New York City in 1819, he came from a prosperous and illustrious family; both grandfathers had been officers and heroes in the War of Independence. When he was only twelve, however, his father died bankrupt, and Herman was suddenly obliged to make his way unaided in a world that was harder and scruffier than his childhood had prepared him for. At the age of twenty-one, having already tried out work as a bank clerk (much like the employment he was to make famous in "Bartleby the Scrivener"), an elementary school teacher, and a cabin boy on a transatlantic trading ship, he signed on as an ordinary seaman on a whaling ship bound for the Pacific. In the Marquesas Islands he deserted, making his way to Tahiti. Both experiences confirmed his sense that the Pacific Islanders were being debased by the incursion of American commercial interests. Melville joined in a mutiny, escaped from jail, made his way to Honolulu, then took a berth on another whaling ship as a harpooner. Finally he returned to Boston as an ordinary seaman on a U.S. Navy frigate in 1844. His books based on these South Pacific adventures, *Typee* (1846) and *Omoo* (1847), were enormously successful, and Melville became a literary celebrity while he was still in his twenties.

Newly married and with a growing family, Melville tried his hand at farming in western Massachusetts while working on what is now considered his masterpiece, *Moby-Dick* (1851). Shelves and shelves of critical books have been written about this astonishingly complex sea story, which seems to express the fate of America itself in its captain's allegorical quest for the white whale and the travails and magical multiculturalism of its common sailors. The critic Harry Levin once remarked that Melville criticism is now a larger industry than whaling. It was during this same pre–Civil War period that "Bartleby" was written, along with a magnificent novella about slavery, *Benito Cereno*. In both of these works, a certain malicious trickery is aimed at the reader, one clue that Melville no longer wanted to provide his readership with the relatively lighthearted adventure narratives they had come to expect from him. Readers did not react well to the fiction that followed, and the royalties Melville depended on dried up. He was thirty-six when he completed *The Confidence Man,* which turned out to be the last prose work published in his lifetime. In debt to his publishers, he sought a well-paid government position, but in vain. The farm he had bought with his earnings had to be sold. Discouraged and forgotten as a writer, he earned his living for nineteen years as a customs inspector on the docks of New York. It was only long after his death in 1891 that his reputation began to rise again, this time on the basis of those darker and more difficult works that the audience of the 1850s had rejected. Another masterpiece of insubordination at sea, *Billy Budd,* was published posthumously in 1924.

Now accepted as one of America's greatest writers, Melville invites comparison with such Continental masters as Flaubert and Dostoevsky. Like Flaubert, he alternates between an adventurous exoticism and a stubborn localism suggesting that the most apparently empty and banal sort of stay-at-home existence may open out onto unearthly visions. And like Dostoevsky, who took the white-collar consciousness of the petty bureaucrat as a figure for all modernity, Melville makes the "unreliable" narrative voice into a vessel exploring uncharted seas of existential uncertainty. Bartleby has sometimes been read as a figure for Melville himself, the writer who refused to write what his society demanded of him. But other interpretations are possible of a story so full of sly humor and narrative high jinks, a story that dares us to take vast metaphysical leaps while examining the everyday routine of a Wall Street office.

Bartleby the Scrivener

A Story of Wall Street

I am a rather elderly man. The nature of my avocations for the last thirty years has brought me into more than ordinary contact with what would seem an interesting and somewhat singular set of men, of whom as yet nothing that I know of has ever been written:—I mean the law-copyists or scriveners. I have known very many of them, professionally and privately, and if I pleased, could relate divers histories, at which good-natured gentlemen might smile, and sentimental souls might weep. But I waive the biographies of all other scriveners for a few passages in the life of Bartleby, who was a scrivener the strangest I ever saw or heard of. While of other law-copyists I might write the complete life, of Bartleby nothing of that sort can be done. I believe that no materials exist for a full and satisfactory biography of this man. It is an irreparable loss to literature. Bartleby was one of those beings of whom nothing is ascertainable, except from the original sources, and in his case those are very small. What my own astonished eyes saw of Bartleby, *that* is all I know of him, except, indeed, one vague report which will appear in the sequel.

Ere introducing the scrivener, as he first appeared to me, it is fit I make some mention of myself, my *employés,* my business, my chambers, and general surroundings; because some such description is indispensable to an adequate understanding of the chief character about to be presented.

Imprimis: I am a man who, from his youth upward, has been filled with a profound conviction that the easiest way of life is the best. Hence, though I belong to a profession proverbially energetic and nervous, even to turbulence, at times, yet nothing of that sort have I ever suffered to invade my peace. I am one of those unambitious lawyers who never addresses a jury, or in any way draws down public applause; but in the cool tranquillity of a snug retreat, do a snug business among rich men's bonds and mortgages and title-deeds. All who know me, consider me an eminently *safe* man. The late John Jacob Astor,[1] a personage little given to poetic enthusiasm, had no hesitation in pronouncing my first grand point to be prudence; my next, method. I do not speak it in vanity, but simply record the fact, that I was not unemployed in my profession by the late John Jacob Astor; a name which, I admit, I love to repeat, for it hath a rounded and orbicular sound to it, and rings like unto bullion. I will freely add, that I was not insensible to the late John Jacob Astor's good opinion.

---

1. John Jacob Astor (1763–1848) was the wealthiest man in America at the time of his death, with holdings especially in New York real estate. He was seen by some as a slumlord.

Some time prior to the period at which this little history begins, my avocations had been largely increased. The good old office, now extinct in the State of New York, of a Master in Chancery,[2] had been conferred upon me. It was not a very arduous office, but very pleasantly remunerative. I seldom lose my temper; much more seldom indulge in dangerous indignation at wrongs and outrages; but I must be permitted to be rash here and declare, that I consider the sudden and violent abrogation of the office of Master in Chancery, by the new Constitution, as a—premature act; inasmuch as I had counted upon a life-lease of the profits, whereas I only received those of a few short years. But this is by the way.

My chambers were upstairs at No.— Wall Street. At one end they looked upon the white wall of the interior of a spacious sky-light shaft, penetrating the building from top to bottom. This view might have been considered rather tame than otherwise, deficient in what landscape painters call "life." But if so, the view from the other end of my chambers offered, at least, a contrast, if nothing more. In that direction my windows commanded an unobstructed view of a lofty brick wall, black by age and everlasting shade; which wall required no spy-glass to bring out its lurking beauties, but for the benefit of all near-sighted spectators, was pushed up to within ten feet of my window panes. Owing to the great height of the surrounding buildings, and my chambers being on the second floor, the interval between this wall and mine not a little resembled a huge square cistern.

At the period just preceding the advent of Bartleby, I had two persons as copyists in my employment, and a promising lad as an office-boy. First, Turkey; second, Nippers; third, Ginger Nut. These may seem names, the like of which are not usually found in the Directory. In truth they were nicknames, mutually conferred upon each other by my three clerks, and were deemed expressive of their respective persons or characters. Turkey was a short, pursy Englishman of about my own age, that is, somewhere not far from sixty. In the morning, one might say, his face was of a fine florid hue, but after twelve o'clock, meridian—his dinner hour—it blazed like a grate full of Christmas coals; and continued blazing—but, as it were, with a gradual wane—till 6 o'clock P.M. or thereabouts, after which I saw no more of the proprietor of the face, which, gaining its meridian with the sun, seemed to set with it, to rise, culminate, and decline the following day, with the like regularity and undiminished glory. There are many singular coincidences I have known in the course of my life, not the least among which was the fact, that exactly when Turkey displayed his fullest 'beams from his red and radiant countenance, just then, too, at that critical moment, began the daily period when I considered his business capacities as seriously disturbed for the remainder of the twenty-four hours. Not that he was absolutely idle, or averse to business then; far from it. The difficulty was, he was apt to be altogether too energetic. There was a strange, inflamed, flurried, flighty recklessness of activity about him. He would be incautious in dipping his pen into his inkstand. All his blots upon my documents, were dropped there after twelve o'clock, meridian. Indeed, not only would he be reckless and sadly given to making blots in the afternoon, but some days he went further, and was rather noisy. At such times, too, his face flamed with augmented blazonry, as if cannel coal had been heaped on anthracite. He made an unpleasant racket with his chair; spilled his sand-box; in mending his pens, impatiently split them all to pieces, and threw them on the floor in a sudden passion; stood up and leaned over his

---

2. A court of equity specializing in inheritance of real estate, famous for delay, expense, and injustice.

table, boxing his papers about in a most indecorous manner, very sad to behold in an elderly man like him. Nevertheless, as he was in many ways a most valuable person to me, and all the time before twelve o'clock, meridian, was the quickest, steadiest creature, too, accomplishing a great deal of work in a style not easy to be matched—for these reasons, I was willing to overlook his eccentricities, though indeed, occasionally, I remonstrated with him. I did this very gently, however, because, though the civilest, nay, the blandest and most reverential of men in the morning, yet in the afternoon he was disposed, upon provocation, to be slightly rash with his tongue, in fact, insolent. Now, valuing his morning services as I did, and resolving not to lose them— yet, at the same time, made uncomfortable by his inflamed ways after twelve o'clock; and being a man of peace, unwilling by my admonitions to call forth unseemly retorts from him—I took upon me, one Saturday noon (he was always worse on Saturdays), to hint to him, very kindly, that perhaps now that he was growing old, it might be well to abridge his labours; in short, he need not come to my chambers after twelve o'-clock, but dinner over, had best go home to his lodgings and rest himself till tea-time. But no; he insisted upon his afternoon devotions. His countenance became intolerably fervid, as he oratorically assured me—gesticulating, with a long ruler, at the other side of the room—that if his services in the morning were useful, how indispensable, then, in the afternoon?

"With submission, sir," said Turkey on this occasion, "I consider myself your right-hand man. In the morning I but marshal and deploy my columns; but in the afternoon I put myself at their head, and gallantly charge the foe, thus!"—and he made a violent thrust with the ruler.

"But the blots, Turkey," intimated I.

"True,—but, with submission, sir, behold these hairs! I am getting old. Surely, sir, a blot or two of a warm afternoon is not to be severely urged against grey hairs. Old age—even if it blot the page—is honourable. With submission, sir, we *both* are getting old."

This appeal to my fellow-feeling was hardly to be resisted. At all events, I saw that go he would not. So I made up my mind to let him stay, resolving, nevertheless, to see to it, that during the afternoon he had to do with my less important papers.

Nippers, the second on my list, was a whiskered, sallow, and, upon the whole, rather piratical-looking young man of about five and twenty. I always deemed him the victim of two evil powers—ambition and indigestion. The ambition was evinced by a certain impatience of the duties of a mere copyist—an unwarrantable usurpation of strictly professional affairs, such as the original drawing up of legal documents. The indigestion seemed betokened in an occasional nervous testiness and grinning irritability, causing the teeth to audibly grind together over mistakes committed in copying; unnecessary maledictions, hissed, rather than spoken, in the heat of business; and especially by a continual discontent with the height of the table where he worked. Though of a very ingenious mechanical turn, Nippers could never get this table to suit him. He put chips under it, blocks of various sorts, bits of pasteboard, and at last went so far as to attempt an exquisite adjustment by final pieces of folded blotting-paper. But no invention would answer. If, for the sake of easing his back, he brought the table lid at a sharp angle well up toward his chin, and wrote there like a man using the steep roof of a Dutch house for his desk—then he declared that it stopped the circulation in his arms. If now he lowered the table to his waistbands, and stooped over it in writing, then there was a sore aching in his back. In short, the truth of the matter was, Nippers knew not what he wanted. Or, if he wanted anything, it was to be rid of a scrivener's table altogether. Among the manifestations of his diseased ambition was a fondness he had for receiving visits from certain ambiguous-looking fellows in seedy coats, whom he called his clients. Indeed I was aware that not only was he, at times, considerable of a ward-politician, but he occasionally did a little business at the Justices' courts, and was not unknown on the steps of the Tombs. I have good reason to believe, however, that one individual who called upon him at my chambers, and who, with a grand air, he insisted was his client, was no other than a dun, and the alleged title-deed, a bill. But with all his failings, and the annoyances he caused me, Nippers, like his compatriot Turkey, was a very useful man to me; wrote a neat, swift hand; and, when he chose, was not deficient in a gentlemanly sort of deportment. Added to this, he always dressed in a gentlemanly sort of way; and so, incidentally, reflected credit upon my chambers. Whereas with respect to Turkey, I had much ado to keep him from being a reproach to me. His clothes were apt to look oily and smell of eating-houses. He wore his pantaloons very loose and baggy in summer. His coats were execrable; his hat not to be handled. But while the hat was a thing of indifference to me, inasmuch as his natural civility and deference, as a dependent Englishman, always led him to doff it the moment he entered the room, yet his coat was another matter. Concerning his coats, I reasoned with him; but with no effect. The truth was, I suppose, that a man with so small an income, could not afford to sport such a lustrous face and a lustrous coat at one and the same time. As Nippers once observed, Turkey's money went chiefly for red ink. One winter day I presented Turkey with a highly-respectable looking coat of my own, a padded grey coat, of a most comfortable warmth, and which buttoned straight up from the knee to the neck. I thought Turkey would appreciate the favour, and abate his rashness and obstreperousness of afternoons. But no. I verily believe that buttoning himself up in so downy and blanket-like a coat had a pernicious effect upon him; upon the same principle that too much oats are bad for horses. In fact, precisely as a rash, restive horse is said to feel his oats, so Turkey felt his coat. It made him insolent. He was a man whom prosperity harmed.

Though concerning the self-indulgent habits of Turkey had my own private surmises, yet touching Nippers I was well persuaded that whatever might be his faults in other respects, he was, at least, a temperate young man. But, indeed, nature herself seemed to have been his vintner,[3] and at his birth charged him so thoroughly with an irritable brandy-like disposition, that all subsequent potations were needless. When I consider how, amid the stillness of my chambers, Nippers would sometimes impatiently rise from his seat, and stooping over his table, spread his arms wide apart, seize the whole desk, and move it, and jerk it, with a grim, grinding motion on the floor, as if the table were a perverse voluntary agent, intent on thwarting and vexing him; I plainly perceive that for Nippers, brandy and water were altogether superfluous.

It was fortunate for me that, owing to its peculiar cause—indigestion—the irritability and consequent nervousness of Nippers, were mainly observable in the morning, while in the afternoon he was comparatively mild. So that Turkey's paroxysms only coming on about twelve o'clock, I never had to do with their eccentricities at one time. Their fits relieved each other like guards. When Nipper's was on, Turkey's was off and *vice versa*. This was a good natural arrangement under the circumstances.

Ginger Nut, the third on my list, was a lad some twelve years old. His father was a carman, ambitious of seeing his son on the bench instead of a cart, before he died.

3. Wine maker.

So he sent him to my office as student at law, errand boy, and cleaner and sweeper, at the rate of one dollar a week. He had a little desk to himself, but he did not use it much. Upon inspection, the drawer exhibited a great array of the shells of various sorts of nuts. Indeed, to this quick-witted youth the whole noble science of the law was contained in a nut-shell. Not the least among the employments of Ginger Nut, as well as one which he discharged with the most alacrity, was his duty as cake and apple purveyor for Turkey and Nippers. Copying law papers being proverbially a dry, husky sort of business, my two scriveners were fain to moisten their mouths very often with Spitzenbergs to be had at the numerous stalls nigh the Custom House and Post Office. Also, they sent Ginger Nut very frequently for that peculiar cake—small, flat, round, and very spicy—after which he had been named by them. Of a cold morning, when business was but dull, Turkey would gobble up scores of these cakes, as if they were mere wafers—indeed they sell them at the rate of six or eight for a penny—the scrape of his pen blending with the crunching of the crisp particles in his mouth. Of all the fiery afternoon blunders and flurried rashness of Turkey, was his once moistening a ginger-cake between his lips, and clapping it on to a mortgage for a seal. I came within an ace of dismissing him then. But he mollified me by making an oriental bow and saying—"With submission, sir, it was generous of me to find you in stationery on my own account."

Now my original business—that of a conveyancer and title hunter, and drawer-up of recondite documents of all sorts—was considerably increased by receiving the master's office. There was now great work for scriveners. Not only must I push the clerks already with me, but I must have additional help. In answer to my advertisement, a motionless young man one morning stood upon my office threshold, the door being open, for it was summer. I can see that figure now—pallidly neat, pitiably respectable, incurably forlorn! It was Bartleby.

After a few words touching his qualifications, I engaged him, glad to have among my corps of copyists a man of so singularly sedate an aspect, which I thought might operate beneficially upon the flighty temper of Turkey, and the fiery one of Nippers.

I should have stated before that ground glass folding-doors divided my premises into two parts, one of which was occupied by my scriveners, the other by myself. According to my humour I threw open these doors, or closed them. I resolved to assign Bartleby a corner by the folding-doors, but on my side of them, so as to have this quiet man within easy call, in case any trifling thing was to be done. I placed his desk close up to a small side-window in that part of the room, a window which originally had afforded a lateral view of certain grimy back-yards and bricks, but which, owing to subsequent erections, commanded at present no view at all, though it gave some light. Within three feet of the panes was a wall, and the light came down from far above, between two lofty buildings, as from a very small opening in a dome. Still further to a satisfactory arrangement, I procured a high green folding screen, which might entirely isolate Bartleby from my sight, though not remove him from my voice. And thus, in a manner, privacy and society were conjoined.

At first Bartleby did an extraordinary quantity of writing. As if long famishing for something to copy, he seemed to gorge himself on my documents. There was no pause for digestion. He ran a day and night line, copying by sun-light and by candle-light. I should have been quite delighted with his application, had he been cheerfully industrious. But he wrote on silently, palely, mechanically.

It is, of course, an indispensable part of a scrivener's business to verify the accuracy of his copy, word by word. Where there are two or more scriveners in an office, they assist each other in this examination, one reading from the copy, the other hold-ing the original. It is a very dull, wearisome, and lethargic affair. I can readily imagine that to some sanguine temperaments it would be altogether intolerable. For example, I cannot credit that the mettlesome poet Byron would have contentedly sat down with Bartleby to examine a law document of, say five hundred pages, closely written in a crimpy hand.

Now and then, in the haste of business, it had been my habit to assist in compar-ing some brief document myself, calling Turkey or Nippers for this purpose. One ob-ject I had in placing Bartleby so handy to me behind the screen, was to avail myself of his services on such trivial occasions. It was on the third day, I think, of his being with me, and before any necessity had arisen for having his own writing examined, that, being much hurried to complete a small affair I had in hand, I abruptly called to Bartleby. In my haste and natural expectancy of instant compliance, I sat with my head bent over the original on my desk, and my right hand side-ways, and somewhat nervously extended with the copy, so that immediately upon emerging from his re-treat, Bartleby might snatch it and proceed to business without the least delay.

In this very attitude did I sit when I called to him, rapidly stating what it was I wanted him to do—namely, to examine a small paper with me. Imagine my surprise, nay, my consternation, when without moving from his privacy, Bartleby in a singu-larly mild, firm voice, replied, "I would prefer not to."

I sat awhile in perfect silence, rallying my stunned faculties. Immediately it oc-curred to me that my ears had deceived me, or Bartleby had entirely misunderstood my meaning. I repeated my request in the clearest tone I could assume. But in quite as clear a one came the previous reply, "I would prefer not to."

"Prefer not to," echoed I, rising in high excitement, and crossing the room with a stride. "What do you mean? Are you moon-struck? I want you to help me compare this sheet here—take it," and I thrust it toward him.

"I would prefer not to," said he.

I looked at him steadfastly. His face was leanly composed; his grey eye dimly calm. Not a wrinkle of agitation rippled him. Had there been the least uneasiness, anger, impatience or impertinence in his manner; in other words, had there been any-thing ordinarily human about him; doubtless I should have violently dismissed him from the premises. But as it was, I should have as soon thought of turning my pale plaster-of-paris bust of Cicero out of doors. I stood gazing at him awhile, as he went on with his own writing, and then reseated myself at my desk. This is very strange, thought I. What had one best do? But my business hurried me. I concluded to forget the matter for the present, preserving it for my future leisure. So calling Nippers from the other room, the paper was speedily examined.

A few days after this, Bartleby concluded four lengthy documents, being quadru-plicates of a week's testimony taken before me in my High Court of Chancery. It be-came necessary to examine them. It was an important suit, and great accuracy was im-perative. Having all things arranged, I called Turkey, Nippers and Ginger Nut from the next room, meaning to place the four copies in the hands of my four clerks, while I should read from the original. Accordingly Turkey, Nippers and Ginger Nut had taken their seats in a row, each with his document in hand, when I called to Bartleby to join this interesting group.

"Bartleby! quick, I am waiting."

I heard a slow scrape of his chair legs on the uncarpeted floor, and soon he ap-peared standing at the entrance of his hermitage.

"What is wanted?" said he mildly.

"The copies, the copies," said I hurriedly. "We are going to examine them. There"—and I held toward him the fourth quadruplicate.

"I would prefer not to," he said, and gently disappeared behind the screen.

For a few moments I was turned into a pillar of salt, standing at the head of my seated column of clerks. Recovering myself, I advanced toward the screen, and demanded the reason for such extraordinary conduct.

"*Why* do you refuse?"

"I would prefer not to."

With any other man I should have flown outright into a dreadful passion, scorned all further words, and thrust him ignominiously from my presence. But there was something about Bartleby that not only strangely disarmed me, but in a wonderful manner touched and disconcerted me. I began to reason with him.

"These are your own copies we are about to examine. It is labour saving to you, because one examination will answer for your four papers. It is common usage. Every copyist is bound to help examine his copy. Is it not so? Will you not speak? Answer!"

"I prefer not to," he replied in a flute-like tone. It seemed to me that while I had been addressing him, he carefully revolved every statement that I made; fully comprehended the meaning; could not gainsay the irresistible conclusion; but, at the same time, some paramount consideration prevailed with him to reply as he did.

"You are decided, then, not to comply with my request—a request made according to common usage and common sense?"

He briefly gave me to understand that on that point my judgment was sound. Yes: his decision was irreversible.

It is not seldom the case that when a man is browbeaten in some unprecedented and violently unreasonable way, he begins to stagger in his own plainest faith. He begins, as it were, vaguely to surmise that, wonderful as it may be, all the justice and all the reason are on the other side. Accordingly, if any disinterested persons are present, he turns to them for some reinforcement for his own faltering mind.

"Turkey," said I, "what do you think of this? Am I not right?"

"With submission, sir," said Turkey, with his blandest tone, "I think that you are."

"Nippers," said I, "what do *you* think of it?"

"I think I should kick him out of the office."

(The reader of nice perceptions will here perceive that, it being morning, Turkey's answer is couched in polite and tranquil terms but Nippers's reply in ill-tempered ones. Or, to repeat a previous sentence, Nippers's ugly mood was on duty, and Turkey's off.)

"Ginger Nut," said I, willing to enlist the smallest suffrage in my behalf, "what do *you* think of it?"

"I think, sir, he's a little *luny*," replied Ginger Nut, with a grin.

"You hear what they say," said I, turning towards the screen, "come forth and do your duty."

But he vouchsafed no reply. I pondered a moment in sore perplexity. But once more business hurried me. I determined again to postpone the consideration of this dilemma to my future leisure. With a little trouble we made out to examine the papers without Bartleby, though at every page or two, Turkey deferentially dropped his opinion that this proceeding was quite out of the common; while Nippers, twitching in his chair with a dyspeptic nervousness, ground out between his set teeth occasional hissing maledictions against the stubborn oaf behind the screen. And for his (Nippers's) part, this was the first and the last time he would do another man's business without pay.

Meanwhile Bartleby sat in his hermitage, oblivious to everything but his own peculiar business there.

Some days passed, the scrivener being employed upon another lengthy work. His late remarkable conduct led me to regard his ways narrowly. I observed that he never went to dinner; indeed that he never went any where. As yet I had never of my personal knowledge known him to be outside of my office. He was a perpetual sentry in the corner. At about eleven o'clock though, in the morning, I noticed that Ginger Nut would advance towards the opening in Bartleby's screen, as if silently beckoned thither by a gesture invisible to me where I sat. The boy would then leave the office jingling a few pence, and reappear with a handful of ginger-nuts which he delivered in the hermitage, receiving two of the cakes for his trouble.

He lives, then, on ginger-nuts, thought I; never eats a dinner, properly speaking; he must be a vegetarian then; but no; he never eats even vegetables, he eats nothing but ginger-nuts. My mind then ran on in reveries concerning the probable effects upon the human constitution of living entirely on ginger-nuts. Ginger-nuts are so called because they contain ginger as one of their peculiar constituents, and the final flavouring one. Now what was ginger? A hot, spicy thing. Was Bartleby hot and spicy? Not at all. Ginger, then, had no effect upon Bartleby. Probably he preferred it should have none.

Nothing so aggravates an earnest person as a passive resistance. If the individual so resisted be of a not inhumane temper, and the resisting one perfectly harmless in his passivity; then, in the better moods of the former, he will endeavour charitably to construe to his imagination what proves impossible to be solved by his judgment. Even so, for the most part, I regarded Bartleby and his ways. Poor fellow! thought I, he means no mischief; it is plain he intends no insolence; his aspect sufficiently evinces that his eccentricities are involuntary. He is useful to me. I can get along with him. If I turn him away, the chances are he will fall in with some less indulgent employer, and then he will be rudely treated, and perhaps driven forth miserably to starve. Yes. Here I can cheaply purchase a delicious self-approval. To befriend Bartleby; to humour him in his strange wilfulness, will cost me little or nothing, while I lay up in my soul what will eventually prove a sweet morsel for my conscience. But this mood was not invariable with me. The passiveness of Bartleby sometimes irritated me. I felt strangely goaded on to encounter him in new opposition, to elicit some angry spark from him answerable to my own. But indeed I might as well have essayed to strike fire with my knuckles against a bit of Windsor soap. But one afternoon the evil impulse in me mastered me, and the following little scene ensued:

"Bartleby," said I, "when those papers are all copied, I will compare them with you."

"I would prefer not to."

"How? Surely you do not mean to persist in that mulish vagary?"

No answer.

I threw open the folding-doors near by, and turning upon Turkey and Nippers, exclaimed in an excited manner:

"He says, a second time, he won't examine his papers. What do you think of it, Turkey?"

It was afternoon, be it remembered. Turkey sat glowing like a brass boiler, his bald head steaming, his hands reeling among his blotted papers.

"Think of it?" roared Turkey; "I think I'll just step behind his screen, and black his eyes for him!"

So saying, Turkey rose to his feet and threw his arms into a pugilistic position. He was hurrying away to make good his promise, when I detained him, alarmed at the effect of incautiously rousing Turkey's combativeness after dinner.

"Sit down, Turkey," said I, "and hear what Nippers has to say. What do you think of it, Nippers? Would I not be justified in immediately dismissing Bartleby?"

"Excuse me, that is for you to decide, sir. I think his conduct quite unusual, and indeed unjust, as regards Turkey and myself. But it may only be a passing whim."

"Ah," exclaimed I, "you have strangely changed your mind then—you speak very gently of him now."

"All beer," cried Turkey; "gentleness is effects of beer—Nippers and I dined together to-day. You see how gentle *I* am, sir. Shall I go and black his eyes?"

"You refer to Bartleby, I suppose. No, not to-day, Turkey," I replied; "pray, put up your fists."

I closed the doors, and again advanced towards Bartleby. I felt additional incentives tempting me to my fate. I burned to be rebelled against again. I remembered that Bartleby never left the office.

"Bartleby," said I, "Ginger Nut is away; just step round to the Post Office, won't you? (it was but a three minutes' walk), and see if there is anything for me."

"I would prefer not to."

"You *will* not?"

"I *prefer* not."

I staggered to my desk, and sat there in a deep study. My blind inveteracy returned. Was there any other thing in which I could procure myself to be ignominiously repulsed by this lean, penniless wight?—my hired clerk? What added thing is there, perfectly reasonable, that he will be sure to refuse to do?

"Bartleby!"

No answer.

"Bartleby," in a louder tone.

No answer.

"Bartleby," I roared.

Like a very ghost, agreeably to the laws of magical invocation, at the third summons, he appeared at the entrance of his hermitage.

"Go to the next room, and tell Nippers to come to me."

"I prefer not to," he respectfully and slowly said, and mildly disappeared.

"Very good, Bartleby," said I, in a quiet sort of serenely severe self-possessed tone, intimating the unalterable purpose of some terrible retribution very close at hand. At the moment I half intended something of the kind. But upon the whole, as it was drawing towards my dinner-hour, I thought it best to put on my hat and walk home for the day, suffering much from perplexity and distress of mind.

Shall I acknowledge it? The conclusion of this whole business was, that it soon became a fixed fact of my chambers, that a pale young scrivener, by the name of Bartleby, had a desk there; that he copied for me at the usual rate of four cents a folio (one hundred words); but he was permanently exempt from examining the work done by him, that duty being transferred to Turkey and Nippers, out of compliment doubtless to their superior acuteness; moreover, said Bartleby was never on any account to be despatched on the most trivial errand of any sort; and that even if entreated to take upon him such a matter, it was generally understood that he would prefer not to—in other words, that he would refuse point-blank.

As days passed on, I became considerably reconciled to Bartleby. His steadiness, his freedom from all dissipation, his incessant industry (except when he chose to throw himself into a standing revery behind his screen), his great stillness, his unalterableness of demeanour under all circumstances, made him a valuable acquisition. One prime thing was this,—*he was always there;*—first in the morning, continually through the day, and the last at night. I had a singular confidence in his honesty. I felt my most precious papers perfectly safe in his hands. Sometimes to be sure I could not, for the very soul of me, avoid falling into sudden spasmodic passions with him. For it was exceeding difficult to bear in mind all the time those strange peculiarities, privileges, and unheard of exemptions, forming the tacit stipulations on Bartleby's part under which he remained in my office. Now and then, in the eagerness of despatching pressing business, I would inadvertently summon Bartleby, in a short, rapid tone, to put his finger, say, on the incipient tie of a bit of red tape with which I was about compressing some papers. Of course, from behind the screen the usual answer, "I prefer not to," was sure to come; and then, how could a human creature with the common infirmities of our nature, refrain from bitterly exclaiming upon such perverseness—such unreasonableness. However, every added repulse of this sort which I received only tended to lessen the probability of my repeating the inadvertence.

Here it must be said, that according to the custom of most legal gentlemen occupying chambers in densely-populated law buildings, there were several keys to my door. One was kept by a woman residing in the attic, which person weekly scrubbed and daily swept and dusted my apartments. Another was kept by Turkey for convenience' sake. The third I sometimes carried in my own pocket. The fourth I knew not who had.

Now, one Sunday morning I happened to go to Trinity Church, to hear a celebrated preacher, and finding myself rather early on the ground, I thought I would walk round to my chambers for awhile. Luckily I had my key with me; but upon applying it to the lock, I found it resisted by something inserted from the inside. Quite surprised, I called out; when to my consternation a key was turned from within; and thrusting his lean visage at me, and holding the door ajar, the apparition of Bartleby appeared, in his shirt sleeves, and otherwise in a strangely tattered dishabille, saying quietly that he was sorry, but he was deeply engaged just then, and—preferred not admitting me at present. In a brief word or two, he moreover added, that perhaps I had better walk round the block two or three times, and by that time he would probably have concluded his affairs.

Now, the utterly unsurmised appearance of Bartleby, tenanting my law-chambers of a Sunday morning, with his cadaverously gentlemanly *nonchalance,* yet withal firm and self-possessed, had such a strange effect upon me, that incontinently I slunk away from my own door, and did as desired. But not without sundry twinges of impotent rebellion against the mild effrontery of this unaccountable scrivener. Indeed, it was his wonderful mildness chiefly, which not only disarmed me, but unmanned me, as it were. For I consider that one, for the time, is in a way unmanned when he tranquilly permits his hired clerk to dictate to him, and order him away from his own premises. Furthermore, I was full of uneasiness as to what Bartleby could possibly be doing in my office in his shirt sleeves, and in an otherwise dismantled condition of a Sunday morning. Was anything amiss going on? Nay, that was out of the question. It was not to be thought of for a moment that Bartleby was an immoral person. But what could he be doing there—copying? Nay again, whatever might be his eccentricities, Bartleby was an eminently decorous person. He would be the last man to sit down to his desk in any state approaching to nudity. Besides, it was Sunday; and there was something about Bartleby that forbade the supposition that he would by any secular occupation violate the proprieties of the day.

Nevertheless, my mind was not pacified; and full of a restless curiosity, at last I returned to the door. Without hindrance I inserted my key, opened it, and entered. Bartleby was not to be seen. I looked round anxiously, peeped behind his screen; but it was very plain that he was gone. Upon more closely examining the place, I surmised that for an indefinite period Bartleby must have ate, dressed, and slept in my office, and that too without plate, mirror, or bed. The cushioned seat of a rickety old sofa in one corner bore the faint impress of a lean, reclining form. Rolled away under his desk, I found a blanket; under the empty grate, a blacking box and brush; on a chair, a tin basin, with soap and a ragged towel; in a newspaper a few crumbs of ginger-nuts and a morsel of cheese. Yes, thought I, it is evident enough that Bartleby has been making his home here, keeping bachelor's hall all by himself. Immediately then the thought came sweeping across me, What miserable friendlessness and loneliness are here revealed! His poverty is great; but his solitude, how horrible! Think of it. Of a Sunday, Wall Street is deserted as Petra; and every night of every day it is an emptiness. This building too, which of week-days hums with industry and life, at nightfall echoes with sheer vacancy, and all through Sunday is forlorn. And here Bartleby makes his home; sole spectator of a solitude which he has seen all populous—a sort of innocent and transformed Marius brooding among the ruins of Carthage![4]

For the first time in my life a feeling of overpowering stinging melancholy seized me. Before, I had never experienced aught but a not-unpleasing sadness. The bond of a common humanity now drew me irresistibly to gloom. A fraternal melancholy! For both I and Bartleby were sons of Adam. I remembered the bright silks and sparkling faces I had seen that day, in gala trim, swan-like sailing down the Mississippi of Broadway; and I contrasted them with the pallid copyist, and thought to myself, Ah, happiness courts the light, so we deem the world is gay; but misery hides aloof, so we deem that misery there is none. These sad fancyings—chimeras, doubtless, of a sick and silly brain—led on to other and more special thoughts, concerning the eccentricities of Bartleby. Presentiments of strange discoveries hovered round me. The scrivener's pale form appeared to me laid out, among uncaring strangers, in its shivering winding sheet.

Suddenly I was attracted by Bartleby's closed desk, the key in open sight left in the lock.

I mean no mischief, seek the gratification of no heartless curiosity, thought I; besides, the desk is mine, and its contents, too, so I will make bold to look within. Everything was methodically arranged, the papers smoothly placed. The pigeon holes were deep, and, removing the files of documents, I groped into their recesses. Presently I felt something there, and dragged it out. It was an old bandana handkerchief, heavy and knotted. I opened it, and saw it was a savings' bank. I now recalled all the quiet mysteries which I had noted in the man. I remembered that he never spoke but to answer; that though at intervals he had considerable time to himself, yet I had never seen him reading—no, not even a newspaper; that for long periods he

---

4. Marius (157–86 B.C.E.), Roman general and politician.

would stand looking out, at his pale window behind the screen, upon the dead brick wall; I was quite sure he never visited any refectory or eating-house; while his pale face clearly indicated that he never drank, beer like Turkey, or tea and coffee even, like other men; that he never went anywhere in particular that I could learn; never went out for a walk, unless indeed that was the case at present; that he had declined telling who he was, or whence he came, or whether he had any relatives in the world; that though so thin and pale, he never complained of ill health. And more than all, I remembered a certain unconscious air of pallid—how shall I call it?—of pallid haughtiness, say, or rather an austere reserve about him, which had positively awed me into my tame compliance with his eccentricities, when I had feared to ask him to do the slightest incidental thing for me, even though I might know, from his long-continued motionlessness, that behind his screen he must be standing in one of those dead-wall reveries of his.

Revolving all these things, and coupling them with the recently discovered fact that he made my office his constant abiding place and home, and not forgetful of his morbid moodiness; revolving all these things, a prudential feeling began to steal over me. My first emotions had been those of pure melancholy and sincerest pity; but just in proportion as the forlornness of Bartleby grew and grew to my imagination, did that same melancholy merge into fear, that pity into repulsion. So true it is, and so terrible, too, that up to a certain point the thought or sight of misery enlists our best affections; but, in certain special cases, beyond that point it does not. They err who would assert that invariably this is owing to the inherent selfishness of the human heart. It rather proceeds from a certain hopelessness of remedying excessive and organic ill. To a sensitive being, pity is not seldom pain. And when at last it is perceived that such pity cannot lead to effectual succour, common sense bids the soul be rid of it. What I saw that morning persuaded me that the scrivener was the victim of innate and incurable disorder. I might give alms to his body; but his body did not pain him; it was his soul that suffered, and his soul I could not reach.

I did not accomplish the purpose of going to Trinity Church that morning. Somehow, the things I had seen disqualified me for the time from church-going. I walked homeward, thinking what I would do with Bartleby. Finally, I resolved upon this:—I would put certain calm questions to him the next morning, touching his history, &c., and if he declined to answer them openly and unreservedly (and I suppose he would prefer not), then to give him a twenty dollar bill over and above whatever I might owe him, and tell him, his services were no longer required; but that if in any other way I could assist him, I would be happy to do so, especially if he desired to return to his native place, wherever that might be, I would willingly help to defray the expenses. Moreover, if, after reaching home, he found himself at any time in want of aid, a letter from him would be sure of a reply.

The next morning came.

"Bartleby," said I, gently calling to him behind his screen.

No reply.

"Bartleby," said I, in a still gentler tone, "come here; I am not going to ask you to do anything you would prefer not to do—I simply wish to speak to you."

Upon this he noiselessly slid into view.

"Will you tell me, Bartleby, where you were born?"

"I would prefer not to."

"Will you tell me *anything* about yourself?"

"I would prefer not to."

"But what reasonable objection can you have to speak to me? I feel friendly towards you."

He did not look at me while I spoke, but kept his glance fixed upon my bust of Cicero, which, as I then sat, was directly behind me, some six inches above my head.

"What is your answer, Bartleby?" said I, after waiting a considerable time for a reply, during which his countenance remained immovable, only there was the faintest conceivable tremor of the white attenuated mouth.

"At present I prefer to give no answer," he said, and retired into his hermitage.

It was rather weak in me I confess, but his manner on this occasion nettled me. Not only did there seem to lurk in it a certain calm disdain, but his perverseness seemed ungrateful, considering the undeniable good usage and indulgence he had received from me.

Again I sat ruminating what I should do. Mortified as I was at his behaviour, and resolved as I had been to dismiss him when I entered my office, nevertheless I strangely felt something superstitious knocking at my heart, and forbidding me to carry out my purpose, and denouncing me for a villain if I dared to breathe one bitter word against this forlornest of mankind. At last, familiarly drawing my chair behind his screen, I sat down and said: "Bartleby, never mind then about revealing your history; but let me entreat you, as a friend, to comply as far as may be with the usages of this office. Say now you will help to examine papers to-morrow or next day; in short, say now that in a day or two you will begin to be a little reasonable:—say so, Bartleby."

"At present I would prefer not to be a little reasonable," was his mildly cadaverous reply.

Just then the folding-doors opened, and Nippers approached. He seemed suffering from an unusually bad night's rest, induced by severer indigestion than common. He overheard those final words of Bartleby.

"*Prefer not,* eh?" gritted Nippers—"I'd *prefer* him, if I were you, sir," addressing me—"I'd *prefer* him; I'd give him preferences, the stubborn mule! What is it, sir, pray, that he prefers not to do now?"

Bartleby moved not a limb.

"Mr. Nippers," said I, "I'd prefer that you would withdraw for the present."

Somehow, of late I had got into the way of involuntarily using this word "prefer" upon all sorts of not exactly suitable occasions. And I trembled to think that my contact with the scrivener had already and seriously affected me in a mental way. And what further and deeper aberration might it not yet produce? This apprehension had not been without efficacy in determining me to summary means.

As Nippers, looking very sour and sulky, was departing, Turkey blandly and deferentially approached.

"With submission, sir," said he, "yesterday I was thinking about Bartleby here, and I think that if he would but prefer to take a quart of good ale every day, it would do much towards mending him, and enabling him to assist in examining his papers."

"So you have got the word, too," said I, slightly excited.

"With submission, what word, sir?" asked Turkey, respectfully crowding himself into the contracted space behind the screen, and by so doing, making me jostle the scrivener. "What word, sir?"

"I would prefer to be left alone here," said Bartleby, as if offended at being mobbed in his privacy.

"*That's* the word, Turkey," said I—"*that's* it."

"Oh, *prefer?* oh, yes—queer word. I never use it myself. But, sir, as I was saying, if he would but prefer—"

"Turkey," interrupted I, "you will please withdraw."

"Oh, certainly, sir, if you prefer that I should."

As he opened the folding-door to retire, Nippers at his desk caught a glimpse of me, and asked whether I would prefer to have a certain paper copied on blue paper or white. He did not in the least roguishly accent the word prefer. It was plain that it involuntarily rolled from his tongue. I thought to myself, surely I must get rid of a demented man, who already has in some degree turned the tongues, if not the heads, of myself and clerks. But I thought it prudent not to break the dismission at once.

The next day I noticed that Bartleby did nothing but stand at his window in his dead-wall revery. Upon asking him why he did not write, he said that he had decided upon doing no more writing.

"Why, how now? what next?" exclaimed I, "do no more writing?"

"No more."

"And what is the reason?"

"Do you not see the reason for yourself?" he indifferently replied.

I looked steadfastly at him, and perceived that his eyes looked dull and glazed. Instantly it occurred to me, that his unexampled diligence in copying by his dim window for the first few weeks of his stay with me might have temporarily impaired his vision.

I was touched. I said something in condolence with him. I hinted that, of course, he did wisely in abstaining from writing for a while, and urged him to embrace that opportunity of taking wholesome exercise in the open air. This, however, he did not do. A few days after this, my other clerks being absent, and being in a great hurry to despatch certain letters by the mail, I thought that, having nothing else earthly to do, Bartleby would surely be less inflexible than usual, and carry these letters to the Post Office. But he blankly declined. So, much to my inconvenience, I went myself.

Still added days went by. Whether Bartleby's eyes improved or not, I could not say. To all appearance, I thought they did. But when I asked him if they did, he vouchsafed no answer. At all events, he would do no copying. At last, in reply to my urgings, he informed me that he had permanently given up copying.

"What!" exclaimed I; "suppose your eyes should get entirely well—better than ever before—would you not copy then?"

"I have given up copying," he answered and slid aside.

He remained, as ever, a fixture in my chamber. Nay—if that were possible—he became still more of a fixture than before. What was to be done? He would do nothing in the office: why should he stay there? In plain fact, he had now become a millstone to me, not only useless as a necklace, but afflictive to bear. Yet I was sorry for him. I speak less than truth when I say that, on his own account, he occasioned me uneasiness. If he would but have named a single relative or friend, I would instantly have written, and urged their taking the poor fellow away to some convenient retreat. But he seemed alone, absolutely alone in the universe. A bit of wreckage in the mid-Atlantic. At length, necessities connected with my business tyrannized over all other considerations. Decently as I could, I told Bartleby that in six days' time he must unconditionally leave the office. I warned him to take measures, in the interval, for procuring some other abode. I offered to assist him in this endeavour, if he himself would but take the first step towards a removal. "And when you finally quit me, Bartleby," added I, "I shall see that you go away not entirely unprovided. Six days from this hour, remember."

At the expiration of that period, I peeped behind the screen, and lo! Bartleby was there.

I buttoned up my coat, balanced myself; advanced slowly towards him, touched his shoulder, and said, "The time has come; you must quit this place; I am sorry for you; here is money; but you must go."

"I would prefer not," he replied, with his back still towards me.

"You *must*."

He remained silent.

Now I had an unbounded confidence in this man's common honesty. He had frequently restored to me sixpences and shillings carelessly dropped upon the floor, for I am apt to be very reckless in such shirt-button affairs. The proceeding then which followed will not be deemed extraordinary.

"Bartleby," said I, "I owe you twelve dollars on account; here are thirty-two; the odd twenty are yours.—Will you take it?" and I handed the bills towards him.

But he made no motion.

"I will leave them here then," putting them under a weight on the table. Then taking my hat and cane and going to the door, I tranquilly turned and added—"After you have removed your things from these offices, Bartleby, you will of course lock the door—since every one is now gone for the day but you—and if you please, slip your key underneath the mat, so that I may have it in the morning. I shall not see you again; so good-bye to you. If hereafter in your new place of abode I can be of any service to you, do not fail to advise me by letter. Good-bye, Bartleby, and fare you well.'

But he answered not a word; like the last column of some ruined temple, he remained standing mute and solitary in the middle of the otherwise deserted room.

As I walked home in a pensive mood, my vanity got the better of my pity. I could not but highly plume myself on my masterly management in getting rid of Bartleby. Masterly I call it, and such it must appear to any dispassionate thinker. The beauty of my procedure seemed to consist in its perfect quietness. There was no vulgar bullying, no bravado of any sort, no choleric hectoring, no striding to and fro across the apartment, jerking out vehement commands for Bartleby to bundle himself off with his beggarly traps. Nothing of the kind. Without loudly bidding Bartleby depart—as an inferior genius might have done—I assumed the ground that depart he must; and upon that assumption built all I had to say. The more I thought over my procedure, the more I was charmed with it. Nevertheless, next morning, upon awakening, I had my doubts,—I had some-how slept off the fumes of vanity. One of the coolest and wisest hours a man has, is just after he awakes in the morning. My procedure seemed as sagacious as ever,—but only in theory. How it would prove in practice—there was the rub. It was truly a beautiful thought to have assumed Bartleby's departure; but, after all, that assumption was simply my own, and none of Bartleby's. The great point was, not whether I had assumed that he would quit me, but whether he would prefer so to do. He was more a man of preferences than assumptions.

After breakfast, I walked down town, arguing the probabilities *pro* and *con*. One moment I thought it would prove a miserable failure, and Bartleby would be found all alive at my office as usual; the next moment it seemed certain that I should see his chair empty. And so I kept veering about. At the corner of Broadway and Canal Street, I saw quite an excited group of people standing in earnest conversation.

"I'll take odds he doesn't," said a voice as I passed.

"Doesn't go?—done!" said I, "put up your money."

I was instinctively putting my hand in my pocket to produce my own, when I remembered that this was an election day. The words I had overheard bore no reference to Bartleby, but to the success or non-success of some candidate for the mayoralty. In my intent frame of mind, I had, as it were, imagined that all Broadway shared in my excitement, and were debating the same question with me. I passed on, very thankful that the uproar of the street screened my momentary absent-mindedness.

As I had intended, I was earlier than usual at my office door. I stood listening for a moment. All was still. He must be gone. I tried the knob. The door was locked. Yes, my procedure had worked to a charm; he indeed must be vanished. Yet a certain melancholy mixed with this: I was almost sorry for my brilliant success. I was fumbling under the door mat for the key, which Bartleby was to have left there for me, when accidently my knee knocked against a panel, producing a summoning sound, and in response a voice came to me from within—"Not yet; I am occupied."

It was Bartleby.

I was thunderstruck. For an instant I stood like the man who, pipe in mouth, was killed one cloudless afternoon long ago in Virginia, by summer lightning; at his own warm open window he was killed, and remained leaning out there upon the dreamy afternoon, till some one touched him, and he fell.

"Not gone!" I murmured at last. But again obeying that wondrous ascendency which the inscrutable scrivener had over me—and from which ascendency, for all my chafing, I could not completely escape—I slowly went down stairs and out into the street, and while walking round the block, considered what I should next do in this unheard-of perplexity. Turn the man out by an actual thrusting I could not; to drive him away by calling him hard names would not do; calling in the police was an unpleasant idea; and yet, permit him to enjoy his cadaverous triumph over me,—this too I could not think of. What was to be done? or, if nothing could be done, was there anything further that I could *assume* in the matter? Yes, as before I had prospectively assumed that Bartleby would depart, so now I might retrospectively assume that departed he was. In the legitimate carrying out of this assumption, I might enter my office in a great hurry, and pretending not to see Bartleby at all, walk straight against him as if he were air. Such a proceeding would in a singular degree have the appearance of a home-thrust. It was hardly possible that Bartleby would withstand such an application of the doctrine of assumptions. But, upon second thought, the success of the plan seemed rather dubious. I resolved to argue the matter over with him again.

"Bartleby," said I, entering the office, with a quietly severe expression, "I am seriously displeased. I am pained, Bartleby. I had thought better of you. I had imagined you of such a gentlemanly organization, that in any delicate dilemma slight hint would suffice—in short, an assumption; but it appears I am deceived. Why," I added, unaffectedly starting, "you have not even touched that money yet," pointing to it, just where I had left it the evening previous.

He answered nothing.

"Will you, or will you not, quit me?" I now demanded in a sudden passion, advancing close to him.

"I would prefer *not* to quit you," he replied, gently emphasizing the *not*.

"What earthly right have you to stay here? Do you pay any rent? Do you pay my taxes? Or is this property yours?"

He answered nothing.

"Are you ready to go on and write now? Are your eyes recovered? Could you copy a small paper for me this morning? or help examine a few lines? or step round to the Post Office? In a word, will you do any thing at all, to give a colouring to your refusal to depart the premises?"

He silently retired into his hermitage.

I was now in such a state of nervous resentment that I thought it but prudent to check myself, at present, from further demonstrations. Bartleby, and I were alone. I remembered the tragedy of the unfortunate Adams and the still more unfortunate Colt in the solitary office of the latter; and how poor Colt, being dreadfully incensed by Adams, and imprudently permitting himself to get wildly excited, was at unawares hurried into his fatal act—an act which certainly no man could possibly deplore more than the actor himself. Often it had occurred to me in my ponderings upon the subject, that had that altercation taken place in the public street, or at a private residence, it would not have terminated as it did. It was the circumstance of being alone in a solitary office, upstairs, of a building entirely unhallowed by humanizing domestic associations—an uncarpeted office, doubtless, of a dusty, haggard sort of appearance;—this it must have been, which greatly helped to enhance the irritable desperation of the hapless Colt.

But when this old Adam of resentment rose in me and tempted me concerning Bartleby, I grappled him and threw him. How? Why, simply by recalling the divine injunction: "A new commandment give I unto you, that ye love one another." Yes, this it was that saved me. Aside from higher considerations, charity often operates as a vastly wise and prudent principle—a great safeguard to its possessor. Men have committed murder for jealousy's sake, and anger's sake, and hatred's sake, and selfishness' sake, and spiritual pride's sake; but no man that ever I heard of, ever committed a diabolical murder for sweet charity's sake. Mere self-interest, then, if no better motive can be enlisted, should, especially with high-tempered men, prompt all beings to charity and philanthropy. At any rate, upon the occasion in question, I strove to drown my exasperated feelings toward the scrivener by benevolently construing his conduct. Poor fellow, poor fellow! thought I, he doesn't mean any thing; and besides, he has seen hard times, and ought to be indulged.

I endeavoured also immediately to occupy myself, and at the same time to comfort my despondency. I tried to fancy that in the course of the morning, at such time as might prove agreeable to him, Bartleby, of his own free accord, would emerge from his hermitage, and take up some decided line of march in the direction of the door. But no. Half-past twelve o'clock came; Turkey began to glow in the face, overturn his inkstand, and become generally obstreperous; Nippers abated down into quietude and courtesy; Ginger Nut munched his noon apple; and Bartleby remained standing at his window in one of his profoundest dead-wall reveries. Will it be credited? Ought I to acknowledge it? That afternoon I left the office without saying one further word to him.

Some days now passed, during which at leisure intervals I looked a little into "Edwards on the Will," and "Priestley on Necessity."[5] Under the circumstances, those books induced a salutary feeling. Gradually I slid into the persuasion that these troubles of mine, touching the scrivener, had been all predestinated from eternity, and Bartleby was billeted upon me for some mysterious purpose of an all-wise Providence, which it was not for a mere mortal like me to fathom. Yes, Bartleby, stay there behind your screen, thought I; I shall persecute you no more; you are harmless and

5. Jonathan Edwards (1703–1758), New England Puritan theologian, and Joseph Priestley (1733–1804), English clergyman and scientist and discoverer of oxygen, were both interested in forms of determinism.

noiseless as any of these old chairs; in short, I never feel so private as when I know you are here. At least I see it, I feel it; I penetrate to the predestinated purpose of my life. I am content. Others may have loftier parts to enact; but my mission in this world, Bartleby, is to furnish you with office room for such period as you may see fit to remain.

I believe that this wise and blessed frame of mind would have continued with me had it not been for the unsolicited and uncharitable remarks obtruded upon me by my professional friends who visited the rooms. But thus it often is, that the constant friction of illiberal minds wears out at last the best resolves of the more generous. Though to be sure, when I reflected upon it, it was not strange that people entering my office should be struck by the peculiar aspect of the unaccountable Bartleby, and so be tempted to throw out some sinister observations concerning him. Sometimes an attorney having business with me, and calling at my office, and finding no one but the scrivener there, would undertake to obtain some sort of precise information from him touching my whereabouts; but without heeding his idle talk, Bartleby would remain standing immovable in the middle of the room. So, after contemplating him in that position for a time, the attorney would depart, no wiser than he came.

Also, when a Reference was going on, and the room full of lawyers and witnesses and business was driving fast, some deeply occupied legal gentleman present, seeing Bartleby wholly unemployed, would request him to run round to his (the legal gentleman's) office and fetch some papers for him, Thereupon, Bartleby would tranquilly decline, and yet remain idle as before. Then the lawyer would give a great stare, and turn to me. And what could I say? At last I was made aware that all through the circle of my professional acquaintance, a whisper of wonder was running round, having reference to the strange creature I kept at my office. This worried me very much. And as the idea came upon me of his possibly turning out a long-lived man, and keep occupying my chambers, and denying my authority; and perplexing my visitors; and scandalizing my professional reputation; and casting a general gloom over the premises; keeping soul and body together to the last upon his savings (for doubtless he spent but half a dime a day), and in the end perhaps outlive me, and claim possession of my office by right of his perpetual occupancy: as all these dark anticipations crowded upon me more and more, and my friends continually intruded their relentless remarks upon the apparition in my room, a great change was wrought in me. I resolved to gather all my faculties together, and for ever rid me of this intolerable incubus. Ere revolving any complicated project, however, adapted to this end, I first simply suggested to Bartleby the propriety of his permanent departure. In a calm and serious tone, I commended the idea to his careful and mature consideration. But having taken three days to meditate upon it, he apprised me that his original determination remained the same; in short, that he still preferred to abide with me.

What shall I do? I now said to myself, buttoning up my coat to the last button. What shall I do? what ought I to do? what does conscience say I *should* do with this man, or rather ghost? Rid myself of him, I must; go, he shall. But how? You will not thrust him, the poor, pale, passive mortal,—you will not thrust such a helpless creature out of your door? you will not dishonour yourself by such cruelty? No, I will not, I cannot do that. Rather would I let him live and die here, and then mason up his remains in the wall. What then will you do? For all your coaxing, he will not budge. Bribes he leaves under your own paper-weight on your table; in short, it is quite plain that he prefers to cling to you.

Then something severe, something unusual must be done. What! surely you will not have him collared by a constable, and commit his innocent pallor to the common jail? And upon what ground could you procure such a thing to be done?—a vagrant, is he? What! he a vagrant, a wanderer, who refuses to budge? It is because he will *not* be a vagrant, then, that you seek to count him *as* a vagrant. That is too absurd. No visible means of support: there I have him. Wrong again: for indubitably he *does* support himself, and that is the only unanswerable proof that any man can show of his possessing the means so to do. No more then. Since he will not quit me, I must quit him. I will change my offices; I will move elsewhere; and give him fair notice, that if I find him on my new premises I will then proceed against him as a common trespasser.

Acting accordingly, next day I thus addressed him: "I find these chambers too far from the City Hall; the air is unwholesome. In a word, I propose to remove my offices next week, and shall no longer require your services. I tell you this now, in order that you may seek another place."

He made no reply, and nothing more was said.

On the appointed day I engaged carts and men, proceeded to my chambers, and having but little furniture, everything was removed in a few hours. Throughout all, the scrivener remained standing behind the screen, which I directed to be removed the last thing. It was withdrawn; and being folded up like a huge folio, left him the motionless occupant of a naked room. I stood in the entry watching him a moment, while something from within me upbraided me.

I re-entered, with my hand in my pocket—and—and my heart in my mouth.

"Good-bye, Bartleby; I am going—good-bye, and God some way bless you; and take that," slipping something in his hand. But it dropped upon the floor and then—strange to say—I tore myself from him whom I had so longed to be rid of.

Established in my new quarters, for a day or two I kept the door locked, and started at every footfall in the passages. When I returned to my rooms after any little absence, I would pause at the threshold for an instant, and attentively listen, ere applying my key. But these fears were needless. Bartleby never came nigh me.

I thought all was going well, when a perturbed looking stranger visited me, inquiring whether I was the person who had recently occupied rooms at No.— Wall Street.

Full of forebodings, I replied that I was.

"Then sir," said the stranger, who proved a lawyer, "you are responsible for the man you left there. He refuses to do any copying, he refuses to do anything; and he says he prefers not to; and he refuses to quit the premises."

"I am very sorry, sir," said I, with assumed tranquillity, but an inward tremor, "but, really, the man you allude to is nothing to me—he is no relation or apprentice of mine, that you should hold me responsible for him."

"In mercy's name, who is he?"

"I certainly cannot inform you. I know nothing about him: Formerly I employed him as a copyist; but he has done nothing for me now for some time past."

"I shall settle him then,—good morning, sir."

Several days passed, and I heard nothing more; and though I often felt a charitable prompting to call at the place and see poor Bartleby, yet a certain squeamishness of I know not what withheld me.

All is over with him, by this time, thought I at last, when through another week no further intelligence reached me. But coming to my room the day after, I found several persons waiting at my door in a high state of nervous excitement.

"That's the man—here he comes," cried the foremost one, whom I recognized as the lawyer who had previously called upon me alone.

"You must take him away, sir, at once," cried a portly person among them, advancing upon me, and whom I knew to be the landlord of No.— Wall Street. "These gentlemen, my tenants, cannot stand it any longer; Mr. B————," pointing to the lawyer, "has turned him out of his room," and he now persists in haunting the building generally, sitting upon the banisters of the stairs by day, and sleeping in the entry by night. Everybody here is concerned; clients are leaving the offices; some fears are entertained of a mob; something you must do, and that without delay."

Aghast at this torrent, I fell back before it, and would fain have locked myself in my new quarters. In vain I persisted that Bartleby was nothing to me—no more than to any one else there. In vain:—I was the last person known to have anything to do with him, and they held me to the terrible account. Fearful then of being exposed in the papers (as one person present obscurely threatened) I considered the matter, and at length said, that if the lawyer would give me a confidential interview with the scrivener, in his (the lawyer's) own room, I would that afternoon strive my best to rid them of the nuisance they complained of.

Going up stairs to my old haunt, there was Bartleby silently sitting upon the banister at the landing.

"What are you doing here, Bartleby?" said I.

"Sitting upon the banister," he mildly replied.

I motioned him into the lawyer's room, who then left us.

"Bartleby," said I, "are you aware that you are the cause of great tribulation to me, by persisting in occupying the entry after being dismissed from the office?"

No answer.

"Now one of two things must take place. Either you must do something, or something must be done to you. Now what sort of business would you like to engage in? Would you like to re-engage in copying for some one?"

"No; I would prefer not to make any change."

"Would you like a clerkship in a dry-goods store?"

"There is too much confinement about that. No, I would not like a clerkship; but I am not particular."

"Too much confinement," I cried, "why, you keep yourself confined all the time!"

"I would prefer not to take a clerkship," he rejoined, as if to settle that little item at once.

"How would a bartender's business suit you? There is no trying of the eyesight in that."

"I would not like it at all; though, as I said before, I am not particular."

His unwonted wordiness inspirited me. I returned to the charge.

"Well then, would you like to travel through the country collecting bills for the merchants? That would improve your health."

"No, I would prefer to be doing something else."

"How then would going as a companion to Europe to entertain some young gentleman with your conversation,—how would that suit you?"

"Not at all. It does not strike me that there is anything definite about that. I like to be stationary. But I am not particular."

"Stationary you shall be then," I cried, now losing all patience, and for the first time in all my exasperating connection with him fairly flying into a passion. "If you do not go away from these premises before night, I shall feel bound—indeed I *am* bound—to—to—to quit the premises myself!" I rather absurdly concluded, knowing not with what possible threat to try to frighten his immobility into compliance. Despairing of all further efforts, I was precipitately leaving him, when a final thought occurred to me—one which had not been wholly unindulged before.

"Bartleby," said I, in the kindest tone I could assume under such exciting circumstances, "will you go home with me now—not to my office, but my dwelling—and remain there till we can conclude upon some convenient arrangement for you at our leisure? Come, let us start now, right away."

"No: at present I would prefer not to make any change at all."

I answered nothing; but effectually dodging every one by the suddenness and rapidity of my flight, rushed from the building, ran up Wall Street toward Broadway, and then jumping into the first omnibus, was soon removed from pursuit. As soon as tranquillity returned I distinctly perceived that I had now done all that I possibly could, both in respect to the demands of the landlord and his tenants, and with regard to my own desire and sense of duty, to benefit Bartleby, and shield him from rude persecution. I now strove to be entirely carefree and quiescent; and my conscience justified me in the attempt; though indeed it was not so successful as I could have wished. So fearful was I of being again hunted out by the incensed landlord and his exasperated tenants, that, surrendering my business to Nippers, for a few days I drove about the upper part of the town and through the suburbs, in my rockaway; crossed over to Jersey City and Hoboken, and paid fugitive visits to Manhattanville and Astoria. In fact I almost lived in my rockaway for the time.

When again I entered my office, lo, a note from the landlord lay upon the desk. I opened it with trembling hands. It informed me that the writer had sent to the police, and had Bartleby removed to the Tombs as a vagrant. Moreover, since I knew more about him than any one else, he wished me to appear at that place, and make a suitable statement of the facts. These tidings had a conflicting effect upon me. At first I was indignant; but at last almost approved. The landlord's energetic, summary disposition had led him to adopt a procedure which I do not think I would have decided upon myself; and yet as a last resort, under such peculiar circumstances, it seemed the only plan.

As I afterwards learned, the poor scrivener, when told that he must be conducted to the Tombs, offered not the slightest obstacle, but in his own pale, unmoving way silently acquiesced.

Some of the compassionate and curious bystanders joined the party; and headed by one of the constables, arm-in-arm with Bartleby the silent procession filed its way through all the noise, and heat, and joy of the roaring thoroughfares at noon. The same day I received the note I went to the Tombs, or, to speak more properly, the Halls of Justice. Seeking the right officer, I stated the purpose of my call, and was informed that the individual I described was indeed within. I then assured the functionary that Bartleby was a perfectly honest man, and a greatly to be compassionated (however unaccountable) eccentric. I narrated all I knew, and closed by suggesting the idea of letting him remain in as indulgent confinement as possible till something less harsh might be done—though indeed I hardly knew what. At all events, if nothing else could be decided upon, the alms-house must receive him. I then begged to have an interview.

Being under no disgraceful charge, and quite serene and harmless in all his ways, they had permitted him freely to wander about the prison, and especially in the inclosed grass-platted yards thereof. And so I found him there, standing all alone in the quietest of the yards, his face toward a high wall—while all around, from the narrow slits of the jail windows, I thought I saw peering out upon him the eyes of murderers and thieves.

"Bartleby!"

"I know you," he said, without looking round,—"and I want nothing to say to you."

"It was not I that brought you here, Bartleby," said I, keenly pained at his implied suspicion. "And to you, this should not be so vile a place. Nothing reproachful attaches to you by being here. And see, it is not so sad a place as one might think. Look, there is the sky and here is the grass."

"I know where I am," he replied, but would say nothing more, and so I left him.

As I entered the corridor again a broad, meat-like man in an apron accosted me, and jerking his thumb over his shoulder said—"Is that your friend?"

"Yes."

"Does he want to starve? If he does, let him live on the prison fare, that's all."

"Who are you?" asked I, not knowing what to make of such an unofficially speaking person in such a place.

"I am the grub-man. Such gentlemen as have friends here, hire me to provide them with something good to eat."

"Is this so?" said I, turning to the turnkey.

He said it was. "Well then," said I, slipping some silver into the grub-man's hands (for so they called him), "I want you to give particular attention to my friend there; let him have the best dinner you can get. And you must be as polite to him as possible."

"Introduce me, will you?" said the grub-man, looking at me with an expression which seemed to say he was all impatience for an opportunity to give a specimen of his breeding.

Thinking it would prove of benefit to the scrivener, I acquiesced; and asking the grub-man his name, went up with him to Bartleby.

"Bartleby, this is Mr. Cutlets; you will find him very useful to you."

"Your sarvant, sir, your sarvant," said the grub-man, making a low salutation behind his apron. "Hope you find it pleasant here, sir;—spacious grounds—cool apartments, sir—hope you'll stay with us some time—try to make it agreeable. May Mrs. Cutlets and I have the pleasure of your company to dinner, sir, in Mrs. Cutlets' private room?"

"I prefer not to dine to-day," said Bartleby, turning away. "It would disagree with me; I am unused to dinners." So saying, he slowly moved to the other side of the inclosure and took up a position fronting the dead-wall.

"How's this?" said the grub-man, addressing me with a stare of astonishment. "He's odd, ain't he?"

"I think he is a little deranged," said I, sadly.

"Deranged? deranged is it? Well now, upon my word, I thought that friend of yourn was a gentleman forger; they are always pale and genteel-like, them forgers. I can't help pity 'em—can't help it, sir. Did you know Monroe Edwards?" he added touchingly, and paused. Then, laying his hand pityingly on my shoulder, sighed, "He died of the consumption at Sing-Sing. So you weren't acquainted with Monroe?"

"No, I was never socially acquainted with any forgers. But I cannot stop longer. Look to my friend yonder. You will not lose by it. I will see you again."

Some few days after this, I again obtained admission to the Tombs, and went through the corridors in quest of Bartleby; but without finding him.

"I saw him coming from his cell not long ago," said a turnkey, "maybe he's gone to loiter in the yards."

So I went in that direction.

"Are you looking for the silent man?" said another turnkey passing me. "Yonder he lies—sleeping in the yard there. 'Tis not twenty minutes since I saw him lie down."

The yard was entirely quiet. It was not accessible to the common prisoners. The surrounding walls, of amazing thickness, kept off all sounds behind them. The Egyptian character of the masonry weighed upon me with its gloom. But a soft imprisoned turf grew under foot. The heart of the eternal pyramids, it seemed, wherein by some strange magic, through the clefts grass-seed, dropped by birds, had sprung.

Strangely huddled at the base of the wall—his knees drawn up, and lying on his side, his head touching the cold stones—I saw the wasted Bartleby. But nothing stirred. I paused; then went close up to him; stooped over, and saw that his dim eyes were open; otherwise he seemed profoundly sleeping. Something prompted me to touch him. I felt his hand, when a tingling shiver ran up my arm and down my spine to my feet.

The round face of the grub-man peered upon me now. "His dinner is ready. Won't he dine to-day, either? Or does he live without dining?"

"Lives without dining," said I, and closed the eyes.

"Eh!—He's asleep, ain't he?"

"With kings and counsellors,"[6] murmured I.

There would seem little need for proceeding further in this history. Imagination will readily supply the meagre recital of poor Bartleby's interment. But ere parting with the reader, let me say, that if this little narrative has sufficiently interested him, to awaken curiosity as to who Bartleby was, and what manner of life he led prior to the present narrator's making his acquaintance, I can only reply, that in such curiosity I fully share—but am wholly unable to gratify it. Yet here I hardly know whether I should divulge one little item of rumour, which came to my ear a few months after the scrivener's decease. Upon what basis it rested, I could never ascertain; and hence, how true it is I cannot now tell. But inasmuch as this vague report has not been without a certain strange suggestive interest to me, however sad, it may prove the same with some others; and so I will briefly mention it. The report was this: that Bartleby had been a subordinate clerk in the Dead Letter Office at Washington, from which he had been suddenly removed by a change in the administration. When I think over this rumour I cannot adequately express the emotions which seize me. Dead letters! does it not sound like dead men? Conceive a man by nature and misfortune prone to a pallid hopelessness: can any business seem more fitted to heighten it than that of continually handling these dead letters, and assorting them for the flames? For by the cartload they are annually burned. Sometimes from out the folded paper the pale clerk takes a ring:—the finger it was meant for, perhaps, moulders in the grave; a bank-note sent in swiftest charity:—he whom it would relieve, nor eats nor hungers any more; pardon for those who died despairing; hope for those who died unhoping; good tid-

---

6. Unjustly tormented by Satan, the biblical character Job wishes he'd died at birth, "For then I should have lain down and been quiet . . . with kings and counselors of the earth" (Job 3:13–14).

ings for those who died stifled by unrelieved calamities. On errands of life, these letters speed to death.

Ah Bartleby! Ah humanity!

Frederick Douglass
1818–1895

More than any other individual, Frederick Douglass came to embody the antislavery movement to nineteenth-century Americans. The story of his own escape from slavery was first told to enthusiastic audiences in the North in the early 1840s, while Douglass was working with Northern abolitionists like William Lloyd Garrison. It was then published as the *Narrative of the Life of Frederick Douglass, An American Slave* (1845), and it became a runaway international best-seller.

To his contemporaries, Douglass also exemplified the self-made man, the subject of one of his most popular lectures. When the *Narrative* made Douglass famous at the age of twenty-seven, his accomplishments were already extraordinary. Born in slavery on a farm on the shores of Chesapeake Bay, Douglass was the son of Harriet Bailey and an unknown white man; as a child he was known as Fred Bailey. His mother died when he was seven, and he was sent to Baltimore to work as a servant and errand boy in the home of his master's brother. The seven years he spent in the city taught him the crucial lesson that life could be different. Once back on the farm, he showed his dissatisfaction, and he was hired out for a year to Edward Covey, a local farmer known for his ability to "break" unruly slaves. His successful resistance to being beaten by Covey, a turning point in his life in 1834, is a still larger turning point in his narrative, where it overshadows the escape from slavery itself. As he explains, he was obliged to pass over the details of his escape in silence for fear of retribution against those who had helped him. Later, however, the full story came out. Back in Baltimore again, where he learned the trade of caulking, he escaped north in 1838 with the aid of papers borrowed from a seaman and money from his fiancée, Anna Murray, a free black woman living in Baltimore. The couple settled in New Bedford, Massachusetts, where he hoped to find shipbuilding work, and where Douglass adopted the name by which he is known. He became a lecturer for the Massachusetts Anti-Slavery Society in 1841, and it was the Society that published his *Narrative,* the first and most popular of several autobiographies in which Douglass expanded and updated the story of his life. One motive for writing it down was to assuage the doubts some of his listeners expressed that someone so eloquent and accomplished as Douglass could really have been raised as a slave. He was still technically a slave when he wrote the book, and he feared that the publication of the book might allow him to be tracked down and dragged back to Maryland. This was a reason for the lecture tour to England he immediately undertook. Money gathered from supporters there helped him buy his freedom, and he returned to the United States in 1847.

In Rochester, New York, his home for almost another half century, he launched his own antislavery weekly, *The North Star.* The paper endorsed the movement for the equality of woman (on its front page it declared, "Right is of no sex"), and Douglass himself was the only male to make a substantive contribution to the historic feminist convention at Seneca Falls, New York, in 1848. Nevertheless, the issue of gender remained alive during his lifetime. During Reconstruction, he was attacked by some feminists for putting the need for black men to get the vote in the South ahead of the right to vote for women. And the issue remains alive today. With so many more narratives now in circulation, recent scholarship has asked whether Douglass's escape-from-slavery story has been allowed to take precedence over others, some by women, that couldn't present the slave in the same masculine heroic light of self-reliance and self-making.

Heavily involved as a lobbyist for Lincoln and a recruiter of black men into the Union army, Douglass was rewarded after the war with government appointments: in 1871 Ulysses S. Grant made him assistant secretary to a commission considering the annexation of the Dominican Republic (he recommended annexation); in 1877 Rutherford B. Hayes appointed him U.S. Marshall for the District of Columbia; in 1889 Benjamin Harrison appointed him Minister to Haiti. His wife, Anna, died in 1882; in 1884 he married Helen Pitts, a white woman active in women's rights. By this point there were challenges to his positions as a spokesperson. Some found him too optimistic about the prospects for blacks in the post–Civil War South, others too enthusiastic about self-reliance. About his greatness as a writer, however, there has been no controversy.

Narrative of the Life of Frederick Douglass

An American Slave

CHAPTER 1

I was born in Tuckahoe, near Hillsborough, and about twelve miles from Easton, in Talbot county, Maryland. I have no accurate knowledge of my age, never having seen any authentic record containing it. By far the larger part of the slaves know as little of their ages as horses know of theirs, and it is the wish of most masters within my knowledge to keep their slaves thus ignorant. I do not remember to have ever met a slave who could tell of his birthday. They seldom come nearer to it than planting-time, harvest-time, cherry-time, spring-time, or fall-time. A want of information concerning my own was a source of unhappiness to me even during childhood. The white children could tell their ages. I could not tell why I ought to be deprived of the same privilege. I was not allowed to make any inquiries of my master concerning it. He deemed all such inquiries on the part of a slave improper and impertinent, and evidence of a restless spirit. The nearest estimate I can give makes me now between twenty-seven and twenty-eight years of age. I come to this, from hearing my master say, some time during 1835, I was about seventeen years old.

My mother was named Harriet Bailey. She was the daughter of Isaac and Betsey Bailey, both colored, and quite dark. My mother was of a darker complexion than either my grandmother or grandfather.

My father was a white man. He was admitted to be such by all I ever heard speak of my parentage. The opinion was also whispered that my master was my father; but of the correctness of this opinion, I know nothing; the means of knowing was withheld from me. My mother and I were separated when I was but an infant— before I knew her as my mother. It is a common custom, in the part of Maryland from which I ran away, to part children from their mothers at a very early age. Frequently, before the child has reached its twelfth month, its mother is taken from it, and hired out on some farm a considerable distance off, and the child is placed under the care of an old woman, too old for field labor. For what this separation is done, I do not know, unless it be to hinder the development of the child's affection toward its mother, and to blunt and destroy the natural affection of the mother for the child. This is the inevitable result.

I never saw my mother, to know her as such, more than four or five times in my life; and each of these times was very short in duration, and at night. She was hired by

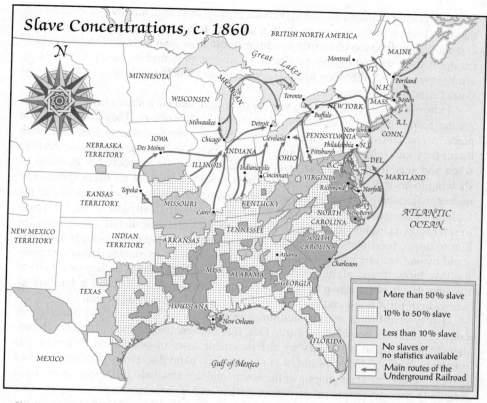

Slave Concentrations, c. 1860

▓	More than 50% slave
░	10% to 50% slave
▒	Less than 10% slave
□	No slaves or no statistics available
←	Main routes of the Underground Railroad

Slave concentrations, by county, in 1860. A network of black and white abolitionists, the Underground Railroad, helped fugitive slaves escape to freedom in the northern states and Canada. Frederick Douglass' journey to freedom carried him from Maryland, where he was born, to New Bedford, Massachusetts.

a Mr. Stewart, who lived about twelve miles from my home. She made her journeys to see me in the night, travelling the whole distance on foot, after the performance of her day's work. She was a field hand, and a whipping is the penalty of not being in the field at sunrise, unless a slave has special permission from his or her master to the contrary—a permission which they seldom get, and one that gives to him that gives it the proud name of being a kind master. I do not recollect of ever seeing my mother by the light of day. She was with me in the night. She would lie down with me, and get me to sleep, but long before I waked she was gone. Very little communication ever took place between us. Death soon ended what little we could have while she lived, and with it her hardships and suffering. She died when I was about seven years old, on one of my master's farms, near Lee's Mill. I was not allowed to be present during her illness, at her death, or burial. She was gone long before I knew any thing about it. Never having enjoyed, to any considerable extent, her soothing presence, her tender and watchful care, I received the tidings of her death with much the same emotions I should have probably felt at the death of a stranger.

Called thus suddenly away, she left me without the slightest intimation of who my father was. The whisper that my master was my father, may or may not be true; and, true or false, it is of but little consequence to my purpose whilst the fact remains, in all its glaring odiousness, that slaveholders have ordained, and by law established, that the children of slave women shall in all cases follow the condition of their mothers; and this is done too obviously to administer to their own lusts, and make a gratification of their wicked desires profitable as well as pleasurable; for by this cunning arrangement, the slaveholder, in cases not a few, sustains to his slaves the double relation of master and father.

I know of such cases; and it is worthy of remark that such slaves invariably suffer greater hardships, and have more to contend with, than others. They are, in the first place, a constant offence to their mistress. She is ever disposed to find fault with them; they can seldom do any thing to please her; she is never better pleased than when she sees them under the lash, especially when she suspects her husband of showing to his mulatto children favors which he withholds from his black slaves. The master is frequently compelled to sell this class of his slaves, out of deference to the feelings of his white wife; and, cruel as the deed may strike any one to be, for a man to sell his own children to human flesh-mongers, it is often the dictate of humanity for him to do so; for, unless he does this, he must not only whip them himself, but must stand by and see one white son tie up his brother, of but few shades darker complexion than himself, and ply the gory lash to his naked back; and if he lisp one word of disapproval, it is set down to his parental partiality, and only makes a bad matter worse, both for himself and the slave whom he would protect and defend.

Every year brings with it multitudes of this class of slaves. It was doubtless in consequence of a knowledge of this fact, that one great statesman of the south predicted the downfall of slavery by the inevitable laws of population. Whether this prophecy is ever fulfilled or not, it is nevertheless plain that a very different-looking class of people are springing up at the south, and are now held in slavery, from those originally brought to this country from Africa; and if their increase will do no other good, it will do away the force of the argument, that God cursed Ham, and therefore American slavery is right. If the lineal descendants of Ham are alone to be scripturally enslaved, it is certain that slavery at the south must soon become unscriptural; for thousands are ushered into the world, annually, who, like myself, owe their existence to white fathers, and those fathers most frequently their own masters.

I have had two masters. My first master's name was Anthony. I do not remember his first name. He was generally called Captain Anthony—a title which, I presume, he acquired by sailing a craft on the Chesapeake Bay. He was not considered a rich slaveholder. He owned two or three farms, and about thirty slaves. His farms and slaves were under the care of an overseer. The overseer's name was Plummer. Mr. Plummer was a miserable drunkard, a profane swearer, and a savage monster. He always went armed with a cowskin and a heavy cudgel. I have known him to cut and slash the women's heads so horribly, that even master would be enraged at his cruelty, and would threaten to whip him if he did not mind himself. Master, however, was not a humane slaveholder. It required extraordinary barbarity on the part of an overseer to affect him. He was a cruel man, hardened by a long life of slaveholding. He would at times seem to take great pleasure in whipping a slave. I have often been awakened at the dawn of day by the most heart-rending shrieks of an own aunt of mine, whom he used to tie up to a joist, and whip upon her naked back till she was literally covered with blood. No words, no tears, no prayers, from his gory victim, seemed to move his iron heart from its bloody purpose. The louder she screamed, the harder he whipped; and where the blood ran fastest, there he whipped longest. He would whip her to make her scream, and whip her to make her hush;

and not until overcome by fatigue, would he cease to swing the blood-clotted cowskin. I remember the first time I ever witnessed this horrible exhibition. I was quite a child, but I well remember it. I never shall forget it whilst I remember any thing. It was the first of a long series of such outrages, of which I was doomed to be a witness and a participant. It struck me with awful force. It was the blood-stained gate, the entrance to the hell of slavery, through which I was about to pass. It was a most terrible spectacle. I wish I could commit to paper the feelings with which I beheld it.

This occurrence took place very soon after I went to live with my old master, and under the following circumstances. Aunt Hester went out one night,—where or for what I do not know,—and happened to be absent when my master desired her presence. He had ordered her not to go out evenings, and warned her that she must never let him catch her in company with a young man, who was paying attention to her, belonging to Colonel Lloyd. The young man's name was Ned Roberts, generally called Lloyd's Ned. Why master was so careful of her, may be safely left to conjecture. She was a woman of noble form, and of graceful proportions, having very few equals, and fewer superiors, in personal appearance, among the colored or white women of our neighborhood.

Aunt Hester had not only disobeyed his orders in going out, but had been found in company with Lloyd's Ned; which circumstance, I found, from what he said while whipping her, was the chief offence. Had he been a man of pure morals himself, he might have been thought interested in protecting the innocence of my aunt; but those who knew him will not suspect him of any such virtue. Before he commenced whipping Aunt Hester, he took her into the kitchen, and stripped her from neck to waist, leaving her neck, shoulders, and back, entirely naked. He then told her to cross her hands, calling her at the same time a d——d b——h. After crossing her hands, he tied them with a strong rope, and led her to a stool under a large hook in the joist, put in for the purpose. He made her get upon the stool, and tied her hands to the hook. She now stood fair for his infernal purpose. Her arms were stretched up at their full length, so that she stood upon the ends of her toes. He then said to her, "Now, you d——d b——h, I'll learn you how to disobey my orders!" and after rolling up his sleeves, he commenced to lay on the heavy cowskin, and soon the warm, red blood (amid heart-rending shrieks from her, and horrid oaths from him) came dripping to the floor. I was so terrified and horror-stricken at the sight, that I hid myself in a closet, and dared not venture out till long after the bloody transaction was over. I expected it would be my turn next. It was all new to me. I had never seen any thing like it before. I had always lived with my grand-mother on the outskirts of the plantation, where she was put to raise the children of the younger women. I had therefore been, until now, out of the way of the bloody scenes that often occurred on the plantation.

CHAPTER 2

My master's family consisted of two sons, Andrew and Richard; one daughter, Lucretia, and her husband, Captain Thomas Auld. They lived in one house, upon the home plantation of Colonel Edward Lloyd. My master was Colonel Lloyd's clerk and superintendent. He was what might be called the overseer of the overseers. I spent two years of childhood on this plantation in my old master's family. It was here that I witnessed the bloody transaction recorded in the first chapter; and as I received my first impressions of slavery on this plantation, I will give some description of it, and of slavery as it there existed. The plantation is about twelve miles north of Easton, in Talbot county, and is situated on the border of Miles River. The principal products raised upon it were tobacco, corn, and wheat. These were raised in great abundance;

so that, with the products of this and the other farms belonging to him, he was able to keep in almost constant employment a large sloop, in carrying them to market at Baltimore. This sloop was named Sally Lloyd, in honor of one of the colonel's daughters. My master's son-in-law, Captain Auld, was master of the vessel; she was otherwise manned by the colonel's own slaves. Their names were Peter, Isaac, Rich, and Jake. These were esteemed very highly by the other slaves, and looked upon as the privileged ones of the plantation; for it was no small affair, in the eyes of the slaves, to be allowed to see Baltimore.

Colonel Lloyd kept from three to four hundred slaves on his home plantation, and owned a large number more on the neighboring farms belonging to him. The names of the farms nearest to the home plantation were Wye Town and New Design. "Wye Town" was under the overseership of a man named Noah Willis. New Design was under the overseership of a Mr. Townsend. The overseers of these, and all the rest of the farms, numbering over twenty, received advice and direction from the managers of the home plantation. This was the great business place. It was the seat of government for the whole twenty farms. All disputes among the overseers were settled here. If a slave was convicted of any high misdemeanor, became unmanageable, or evinced a determination to run away, he was brought immediately here, severely whipped, put on board the sloop, carried to Baltimore, and sold to Austin Woolfolk, or some other slave-trader, as a warning to the slaves remaining.

Here, too, the slaves of all the other farms received their monthly allowance of food, and their yearly clothing. The men and women slaves received, as their monthly allowance of food, eight pounds of pork, or its equivalent in fish, and one bushel of corn meal. Their yearly clothing consisted of two coarse linen shirts, one pair of linen trousers, like the shirts, one jacket, one pair of trousers for winter, made of coarse negro cloth, one pair of stockings, and one pair of shoes; the whole of which could not have cost more than seven dollars. The allowance of the slave children was given to their mothers, or the old women having the care of them. The children unable to work in the field had neither shoes, stockings, jackets, nor trousers, given to them; their clothing consisted of two coarse linen shirts per year. When these failed them, they went naked until the next allowance-day. Children from seven to ten years old, of both sexes, almost naked, might be seen at all seasons of the year.

There were no beds given the slaves, unless one coarse blanket be considered such, and none but the men and women had these. This, however, is not considered a very great privation. They find less difficulty from the want of beds, than from the want of time to sleep; for when their day's work in the field is done, the most of them having their washing, mending, and cooking to do, and having few or none of the ordinary facilities for doing either of these, very many of their sleeping hours are consumed in preparing for the field the coming day; and when this is done, old and young, male and female, married and single, drop down side by side, on one common bed,—the cold, damp floor,—each covering himself or herself with their miserable blankets; and here they sleep till they are summoned to the field by the driver's horn. At the sound of this, all must rise, and be off to the field. There must be no halting; every one must be at his or her post; and woe betides them who hear not this morning summons to the field; for if they are not awakened by the sense of hearing, they are by the sense of feeling: no age nor sex finds any favor. Mr. Severe, the overseer, used to stand by the door of the quarter, armed with a large hickory stick and heavy cowskin, ready to whip any one who was so unfortunate as not to hear, or, from any other cause, was prevented from being ready to start for the field at the sound of the horn.

Mr. Severe was rightly named: he was a cruel man. I have seen him whip a woman, causing the blood to run half an hour at the time; and this, too, in the midst of her crying children, pleading for their mother's release. He seemed to take pleasure in manifesting his fiendish barbarity. Added to his cruelty, he was a profane swearer. It was enough to chill the blood and stiffen the hair of an ordinary man to hear him talk. Scarce a sentence escaped him but that was commenced or concluded by some horrid oath. The field was the place to witness his cruelty and profanity. His presence made it both the field of blood and of blasphemy. From the rising till the going down of the sun, he was cursing, raving, cutting, and slashing among the slaves of the field, in the most frightful manner. His career was short. He died very soon after I went to Colonel Lloyd's; and he died as he lived, uttering, with his dying groans, bitter curses and horrid oaths. His death was regarded by the slaves as the result of a merciful providence.

Mr. Severe's place was filled by a Mr. Hopkins. He was a very different man. He was less cruel, less profane, and made less noise, than Mr. Severe. His course was characterized by no extraordinary demonstrations of cruelty. He whipped, but seemed to take no pleasure in it. He was called by the slaves a good overseer.

The home plantation of Colonel Lloyd wore the appearance of a country village. All the mechanical operations for all the farms were performed here. The shoemaking and mending, the blacksmithing, cartwrighting, coopering, weaving, and grain-grinding, were all performed by the slaves on the home plantation. The whole place wore a business-like aspect very unlike the neighboring farms. The number of houses, too, conspired to give it advantage over the neighboring farms. It was called by the slaves the *Great House Farm*. Few privileges were esteemed higher, by the slaves of the out-farms, than that of being selected to do errands at the Great House Farm. It was associated in their minds with greatness. A representative could not be prouder of his election to a seat in the American Congress, than a slave on one of the out-farms would be of his election to do errands at the Great House Farm. They regarded it as evidence of great confidence reposed in them by their overseers; and it was on this account, as well as a constant desire to be out of the field from under the driver's lash, that they esteemed it a high privilege, one worth careful living for. He was called the smartest and most trusty fellow, who had this honor conferred upon him the most frequently. The competitors for this office sought as diligently to please their overseers, as the office-seekers in the political parties seek to please and deceive the people. The same traits of character might be seen in Colonel Lloyd's slaves, as are seen in the slaves of the political parties.

The slaves selected to go to the Great House Farm, for the monthly allowance for themselves and their fellow-slaves, were peculiarly enthusiastic. While on their way, they would make the dense old woods, for miles around, reverberate with their wild songs, revealing at once the highest joy and the deepest sadness. They would compose and sing as they went along, consulting neither time nor tune. The thought that came up, came out—if not in the word, in the sound;—and as frequently in the one as in the other. They would sometimes sing the most pathetic sentiment in the most rapturous tone, and the most rapturous sentiment in the most pathetic tone. Into all of their songs they would manage to weave something of the Great House Farm. Especially would they do this, when leaving home. They would then sing most exultingly the following words:—

> "I am going away to the Great House Farm!
> 　　O, yea! O, yea! O!"

This they would sing, as a chorus, to words which to many would seem unmeaning jargon, but which, nevertheless, were full of meaning to themselves. I have sometimes thought that the mere hearing of those songs would do more to impress some minds with the horrible character of slavery, than the reading of whole volumes of philosophy on the subject could do.

I did not, when a slave, understand the deep meaning of those rude and apparently incoherent songs. I was myself within the circle; so that I neither saw nor heard as those without might see and hear. They told a tale of woe which was then altogether beyond my feeble comprehension; they were tones loud, long, and deep; they breathed the prayer and complaint of souls boiling over with the bitterest anguish. Every tone was a testimony against slavery, and a prayer to God for deliverance from chains. The hearing of those wild notes always depressed my spirit, and filled me with ineffable sadness. I have frequently found myself in tears while hearing them. The mere recurrence to those songs, even now, afflicts me; and while I am writing these lines, an expression of feeling has already found its way down my cheek. To those songs I trace my first glimmering conception of the dehumanizing character of slavery. I can never get rid of that conception. Those songs still follow me, to deepen my hatred of slavery, and quicken my sympathies for my brethren in bonds. If any one wishes to be impressed with the soul-killing effects of slavery, let him go to Colonel Lloyd's plantation, and, on allowance-day, place himself in the deep pine woods, and there let him, in silence, analyze the sounds that shall pass through the chambers of his soul,—and if he is not thus impressed, it will only be because "there is no flesh in his obdurate heart."

I have often been utterly astonished, since I came to the north, to find persons who could speak of the singing among slaves, as evidence of their contentment and happiness. It is impossible to conceive of a greater mistake. Slaves sing most when they are most unhappy. The songs of the slave represent the sorrows of his heart; and he is relieved by them, only as an aching heart is relieved by its tears. At least, such is my experience. I have often sung to drown my sorrow, but seldom to express my happiness. Crying for joy, and singing for joy, were alike uncommon to me while in the jaws of slavery. The singing of a man cast away upon a desolate island might be as appropriately considered as evidence of contentment and happiness, as the singing of a slave; the songs of the one and of the other are prompted by the same emotion.

CHAPTER 3

Colonel Lloyd kept a large and finely cultivated garden, which afforded almost constant employment for four men, besides the chief gardener, (Mr. M'Durmond.) This garden was probably the greatest attraction of the place. During the summer months, people came from far and near—from Baltimore, Easton, and Annapolis—to see it. It abounded in fruits of almost every description, from the hardy apple of the north to the delicate orange of the south. This garden was not the least source of trouble on the plantation. Its excellent fruit was quite a temptation to the hungry swarms of boys, as well as the older slaves, belonging to the colonel, few of whom had the virtue or the vice to resist it. Scarcely a day passed, during the summer, but that some slave had to take the lash for stealing fruit. The colonel had to resort to all kinds of stratagems to keep his slaves out of the garden. The last and most successful one was that of tarring his fence all around; after which, if a slave was caught with any tar upon his person, it was deemed sufficient proof that he had either been into the garden, or had tried to get in. In either case, he was severely whipped by the chief gardener. This plan worked well; the slaves became as fearful of tar as of the lash. They seemed to realize the impossibility of touching *tar* without being defiled.

The colonel also kept a splendid riding equipage. His stable and carriage-house presented the appearance of some of our large city livery establishments. His horses were of the finest form and noblest blood. His carriage-house contained three splendid coaches, three or four gigs, besides dearborns and barouches of the most fashionable style.

This establishment was under the care of two slaves—old Barney and young Barney—father and son. To attend to this establishment was their sole work. But it was by no means an easy employment; for in nothing was Colonel Lloyd more particular than in the management of his horses. The slightest inattention to these was unpardonable, and was visited upon those, under whose care they were placed, with the severest punishment; no excuse could shield them, if the colonel only suspected any want of attention to his horses—a supposition which he frequently indulged, and one which, of course, made the office of old and young Barney a very trying one. They never knew when they were safe from punishment. They were frequently whipped when least deserving, and escaped whipping when most deserving it. Every thing depended upon the looks of the horses, and the state of Colonel Lloyd's own mind when his horses were brought to him for use. If a horse did not move fast enough, or hold his head high enough, it was owing to some fault of his keepers. It was painful to stand near the stable-door, and hear the various complaints against the keepers when a horse was taken out for use. "This horse has not had proper attention. He has not been sufficiently rubbed and curried, or he has not been properly fed; his food was too wet or too dry; he got it too soon or too late; he was too hot or too cold; he had too much hay, and not enough of grain; or he had too much grain, and not enough of hay; instead of old Barney's attending to the horse, he had very improperly left it to his son." To all these complaints, no matter how unjust, the slave must answer never a word. Colonel Lloyd could not brook any contradiction from a slave. When he spoke, a slave must stand, listen, and tremble; and such was literally the case. I have seen Colonel Lloyd make old Barney, a man between fifty and sixty years of age, uncover his bald head, kneel down upon the cold, damp ground, and receive upon his naked and toil-worn shoulders more than thirty lashes at the time. Colonel Lloyd had three sons—Edward, Murray, and Daniel,—and three sons-in-law, Mr. Winder, Mr. Nicholson, and Mr. Lowndes. All of these lived at the Great House Farm, and enjoyed the luxury of whipping the servants when they pleased, from old Barney down to William Wilkes, the coach-driver. I have seen Winder make one of the house-servants stand off from him a suitable distance to be touched with the end of his whip, and at every stroke raise great ridges upon his back.

To describe the wealth of Colonel Lloyd would be almost equal to describing the riches of Job. He kept from ten to fifteen house-servants. He was said to own a thousand slaves, and I think this estimate quite within the truth. Colonel Lloyd owned so many that he did not know them when he saw them; nor did all the slaves of the outfarms know him. It is reported of him, that, while riding along the road one day, he met a colored man, and addressed him in the usual manner of speaking to colored people on the public highways of the south: "Well, boy, whom do you belong to?" "To Colonel Lloyd," replied the slave. "Well, does the colonel treat you well?" "No, sir," was the ready reply. "What, does he work you too hard?" "Yes, sir." "Well, don't he give you enough to eat?" "Yes, sit, he gives me enough, such as it is."

The colonel, after ascertaining where the slave belonged, rode on; the man also went on about his business, not dreaming that he had been conversing with his master. He thought, said, and heard nothing more of the matter, until two or three weeks afterwards. The poor man was then informed by his overseer that, for having found fault with his master, he was now to be sold to a Georgia trader. He was immediately chained and handcuffed; and thus, without a moment's warning, he was snatched away, and forever sundered, from his family and friends, by a hand more unrelenting than death. This is the penalty of telling the truth, of telling the simple truth, in answer to a series of plain questions.

It is partly in consequence of such facts, that slaves, when inquired of as to their condition and the character of their masters, almost universally say they are contented, and that their masters are kind. The slaveholders have been known to send in spies among their slaves, to ascertain their views and feelings in regard to their condition. The frequency of this has had the effect to establish among the slaves the maxim, that a still tongue makes a wise head. They suppress the truth rather than take the consequences of telling it, and in so doing prove themselves a part of the human family. If they have any thing to say of their masters, it is generally in their masters' favor, especially when speaking to an untried man. I have been frequently asked, when a slave, if I had a kind master, and do not remember ever to have given a negative answer; nor did I, in pursuing this course, consider myself as uttering what was absolutely false; for I always measured the kindness of my master by the standard of kindness set up among slaveholders around us. Moreover, slaves are like other people, and imbibe prejudices quite common to others. They think their own better than that of others. Many, under the influence of this prejudice, think their own masters are better than the masters of other slaves; and this, too, in some cases, when the very reverse is true. Indeed, it is not uncommon for slaves even to fall out and quarrel among themselves about the relative goodness of their masters, each contending for the superior goodness of his own over that of the others. At the very same time, they mutually execrate their masters when viewed separately. It was so on our plantation. When Colonel Lloyd's slaves met the slaves of Jacob Jepson, they seldom parted without a quarrel about their masters; Colonel Lloyd's slaves contending that he was the richest, and Mr. Jepson's slaves that he was the smartest, and most of a man. Colonel Lloyd's slaves would boast his ability to buy and sell Jacob Jepson. Mr. Jepson's slaves would boast his ability to whip Colonel Lloyd. These quarrels would almost always end in a fight between the parties, and those that whipped were supposed to have gained the point at issue. They seemed to think that the greatness of their masters was transferable to themselves. It was considered as being bad enough to be a slave; but to be a poor man's slave was deemed a disgrace indeed!

CHAPTER 4

Mr. Hopkins remained but a short time in the office of overseer. Why his career was so short, I do not know, but suppose he lacked the necessary severity to suit Colonel Lloyd. Mr. Hopkins was succeeded by Mr. Austin Gore, a man possessing, in an eminent degree, all those traits of character indispensable to what is called a first-rate overseer. Mr. Gore had served Colonel Lloyd, in the capacity of overseer, upon one of the out-farms, and had shown himself worthy of the high station of overseer upon the home or Great House Farm.

Mr. Gore was proud, ambitious, and persevering. He was artful, cruel, and obdurate. He was just the man for such a place, and it was just the place for such a man. It afforded scope for the full exercise of all his powers, and he seemed to be perfectly at home in it. He was one of those who could torture the slightest look, word, or gesture, on the part of the slave, into impudence, and would treat it accordingly. There must be no answering back to him; no explanation was allowed a slave, showing himself to have been wrongfully accused. Mr. Gore acted fully up to the maxim laid down by slaveholders,—"It is better that a dozen slaves suffer under the lash, than that the overseer should be convicted, in the presence of the slaves, of having been at fault." No matter how innocent a slave might be—it availed him nothing, when accused by Mr. Gore of any misdemeanor. To be accused was to be convicted, and to be convicted was to be punished; the one always following the other with immutable certainty. To escape punishment was to escape accusation; and few slaves had the fortune to do either, under the overseership of Mr. Gore. He was just proud enough to demand the most debasing homage of the slave, and quite servile enough to crouch, himself, at the feet of the master. He was ambitious enough to be contented with nothing short of the highest rank of overseers, and persevering enough to reach the height of his ambition. He was cruel enough to inflict the severest punishment, artful enough to descend to the lowest trickery, and obdurate enough to be insensible to the voice of a reproving conscience. He was, of all the overseers, the most dreaded by the slaves. His presence was painful; his eye flashed confusion; and seldom was his sharp, shrill voice heard, without producing horror and trembling in their ranks.

Mr. Gore was a grave man, and, though a young man, he indulged in no jokes, said no funny words, seldom smiled. His words were in perfect keeping with his looks, and his looks were in perfect keeping with his words. Overseers will sometimes indulge in a witty word, even with the slaves; not so with Mr. Gore. He spoke but to command, and commanded but to be obeyed; he dealt sparingly with his words, and bountifully with his whip, never using the former where the latter would answer as well. When he whipped, he seemed to do so from a sense of duty, and feared no consequences. He did nothing reluctantly, no matter how disagreeable; always at his post, never inconsistent. He never promised but to fulfil. He was, in a word, a man of the most inflexible firmness and stone-like coolness.

His savage barbarity was equalled only by the consummate coolness with which he committed the grossest and most savage deeds upon the slaves under his charge. Mr. Gore once undertook to whip one of Colonel Lloyd's slaves, by the name of Demby. He had given Demby but few stripes, when, to get rid of the scourging, he ran and plunged himself into a creek, and stood there at the depth of his shoulders, refusing to come out. Mr. Gore told him that he would give him three calls, and that, if he did not come out at the third call, he would shoot him. The first call was given. Demby made no response, but stood his ground. The second and third calls were given with the same result. Mr. Gore then, without consultation or deliberation with any one, not even giving Demby an additional call, raised his musket to his face, taking deadly aim at his standing victim, and in an instant poor Demby was no more. His mangled body sank out of sight, and blood and brains marked the water where he had stood.

A thrill of horror flashed through every soul upon the plantation, excepting Mr. Gore. He alone seemed cool and collected. He was asked by Colonel Lloyd and my old master, why he resorted to this extraordinary expedient. His reply was, (as well as I can remember,) that Demby had become unmanageable. He was setting a dangerous example to the other slaves,—one which, if suffered to pass without some such demonstration on his part, would finally lead to the total subversion of all rule and order upon the plantation. He argued that if one slave refused to be corrected, and escaped with his life, the other slaves would soon copy the example; the result of which would be, the freedom of the slaves, and the enslavement of the whites. Mr. Gore's defence was satisfactory. He was continued in his station as overseer upon the home plantation. His fame as an overseer went abroad. His horrid crime was not even submitted to judicial investigation. It was committed in the presence of slaves, and they of course could neither institute a suit, nor testify against him; and thus the guilty perpetrator of one of the bloodiest and most foul murders goes unwhipped of justice, and uncensured by the community in which he lives. Mr. Gore lived in St. Michael's, Talbot county, Maryland, when I left there; and if he is still alive, he very probably lives there now; and if so, he is now, as he was then, as highly esteemed and as much respected as though his guilty soul had not been stained with his brother's blood.

I speak advisedly when I say this,—that killing a slave, or any colored person, in Talbot county, Maryland, is not treated as a crime, either by the courts or the community. Mr. Thomas Lanman, of St. Michael's, killed two slaves, one of whom he killed with a hatchet, by knocking his brains out. He used to boast of the commission of the awful and bloody deed. I have heard him do so laughingly, saying, among other things, that he was the only benefactor of his country in the company, and that when others would do as much as he had done, we should be relieved of "the d——d niggers."

The wife of Mr. Giles Hick, living but a short distance from where I used to live, murdered my wife's cousin, a young girl between fifteen and sixteen years of age, mangling her person in the most horrible manner, breaking her nose and breastbone with a stick, so that the poor girl expired in a few hours afterward. She was immediately buried, but had not been in her untimely grave but a few hours before she was taken up and examined by the coroner, who decided that she had come to her death by severe beating. The offence for which this girl was thus murdered was this:—She had been set that night to mind Mrs. Hick's baby, and during the night she fell asleep, and the baby cried. She, having lost her rest for several nights previous, did not hear the crying. They were both in the room with Mrs. Hicks. Mrs. Hicks, finding the girl slow to move, jumped from her bed, seized an oak stick of wood by the fireplace, and with it broke the girl's nose and breastbone, and thus ended her life. I will not say that this most horrid murder produced no sensation in the community. It did produce sensation, but not enough to bring the murderess to punishment. There was a warrant issued for her arrest, but it was never served. Thus she escaped not only punishment, but even the pain of being arraigned before a court for her horrid crime.

Whilst I am detailing bloody deeds which took place during my stay on Colonel Lloyd's plantation, I will briefly narrate another, which occurred about the same time as the murder of Demby by Mr. Gore.

Colonel Lloyd's slaves were in the habit of spending a part of their nights and Sundays in fishing for oysters, and in this way made up the deficiency of their scanty allowance. An old man belonging to Colonel Lloyd, while thus engaged, happened to get beyond the limits of Colonel Lloyd's, and on the premises of Mr. Beal Bondly. At this trespass, Mr. Bondly took offence, and with his musket came down to the shore, and blew its deadly contents into the poor old man.

Mr. Bondly came over to see Colonel Lloyd the next day, whether to pay him for his property, or to justify himself in what he had done, I know not. At any rate, this whole fiendish transaction was soon hushed up. There was very little said about it at all, and nothing done. It was a common saying, even among little white boys, that it was worth a half-cent to kill a "nigger," and a half-cent to bury one.

CHAPTER 5

As to my own treatment while I lived on Colonel Lloyd's plantation, it was very similar to that of the other slave children. I was not old enough to work in the field, and there being little else than field work to do, I had a great deal of leisure time. The most I had to do was to drive up the cows at evening, keep the fowls out of the garden, keep the front yard clean, and run of errands for my old master's daughter, Mrs. Lucretia Auld. The most of my leisure time I spent in helping Master Daniel Lloyd in finding his birds, after he had shot them. My connection with Master Daniel was of some advantage to me. He became quite attached to me, and was a sort of protector of me. He would not allow the older boys to impose upon me, and would divide his cakes with me.

I was seldom whipped by my old master, and suffered little from any thing else than hunger and cold. I suffered much from hunger, but much more from cold. In hottest summer and coldest winter, I was kept almost naked—no shoes, no stockings, no jacket, no trousers, nothing on but a coarse tow linen shirt, reaching only to my knees. I had no bed. I must have perished with cold, but that, the coldest nights, I used to steal a bag which was used for carrying corn to the mill. I would crawl into this bag, and there sleep on the cold, damp, clay floor, with my head in and feet out. My feet have been so cracked with the frost, that the pen with which I am writing might be laid in the gashes.

We were not regularly allowanced. Our food was coarse corn meal boiled. This was called *mush*. It was put into a large wooden tray or trough, and set down upon the ground. The children were then called, like so many pigs, and like so many pigs they would come and devour the mush; some with oyster-shells, others with pieces of shingle, some with naked hands, and none with spoons. He that ate fastest got most; he that was strongest secured the best place; and few left the trough satisfied.

I was probably between seven and eight years old when I left Colonel Lloyd's plantation. I left it with joy. I shall never forget the ecstasy with which I received the intelligence that my old master (Anthony) had determined to let me go to Baltimore, to live with Mr. Hugh Auld, brother to my old master's son-in-law, Captain Thomas Auld. I received this information about three days before my departure. They were three of the happiest days I ever enjoyed. I spent the most part of all these three days in the creek, washing off the plantation scurf, and preparing myself for my departure.

The pride of appearance which this would indicate was not my own. I spent the time in washing, not so much because I wished to, but because Mrs. Lucretia had told me I must get all the dead skin off my feet and knees before I could go to Baltimore; for the people in Baltimore were very cleanly, and would laugh at me if I looked dirty. Besides, she was going to give me a pair of trousers, which I should not put on unless I got all the dirt off me. The thought of owning a pair of trousers was great indeed! It was almost a sufficient motive, not only to make me take off what would be called by pig-drovers the mange, but the skin itself. I went at it in good earnest, working for the first time with the hope of reward.

The ties that ordinarily bind children to their homes were all suspended in my case. I found no severe trial in my departure. My home was charmless; it was not home to me; on parting from it, I could not feel that I was leaving any thing which I could have enjoyed by staying. My mother was dead, my grandmother lived far off, so that I seldom saw her. I had two sisters and one brother, that lived in the same house with me; but the early separation of us from our mother had well nigh blotted the fact of our relationship from our memories. I looked for home elsewhere, and was confident of finding none which I should relish less than the one which I was leaving. If, however, I found in my new home hardship, hunger, whipping, and nakedness, I had the consolation that I should not have escaped any one of them by staying. Having already had more than a taste of them in the house of my old master, and having endured them there, I very naturally inferred my ability to endure them elsewhere, and especially at Baltimore; for I had something of the feeling about Baltimore that is expressed in the proverb, that "being hanged in England is preferable to dying a natural death in Ireland." I had the strongest desire to see Baltimore. Cousin Tom, though not fluent in speech, had inspired me with that desire by his eloquent description of the place. I could never point out any thing at the Great House, no matter how beautiful or powerful, but that he had seen something at Baltimore far exceeding, both in beauty and strength, the object which I pointed out to him. Even the Great House itself, with all its pictures, was far inferior to many buildings in Baltimore. So strong was my desire, that I thought a gratification of it would fully compensate for whatever loss of comforts I should sustain by the exchange. I left without a regret, and with the highest hopes of future happiness.

We sailed out of Miles River for Baltimore on a Saturday morning. I remember only the day of the week, for at that time I had no knowledge of the days of the month, nor the months of the year. On setting sail, I walked aft, and gave to Colonel Lloyd's plantation what I hoped would be the last look. I then placed myself in the bows of the sloop, and there spent the remainder of the day in looking ahead, interesting myself in what was in the distance rather than in things near by or behind.

In the afternoon of that day, we reached Annapolis, the capital of the State. We stopped but a few moments, so that I had no time to go on shore. It was the first large town that I had ever seen, and though it would look small compared with some of our New England factory villages, I thought it a wonderful place for its size—more imposing even than the Great House Farm!

We arrived at Baltimore early on Sunday morning, landing at Smith's Wharf, not far from Bowley's Wharf. We had on board the sloop a large flock of sheep; and after aiding in driving them to the slaughter-house of Mr. Curtis on Louden Slater's Hill, I was conducted by Rich, one of the hands belonging on board of the sloop, to my new home in Alliciana Street, near Mr. Gardner's ship-yard, on Fells Point.

Mr. and Mrs. Auld were both at home, and met me at the door with their little son Thomas, to take care of whom I had been given. And here I saw what I had never seen before; it was a white face beaming with the most kindly emotions; it was the face of my new mistress, Sophia Auld. I wish I could describe the rapture that flashed through my soul as I beheld it. It was a new and strange sight to me, brightening up my pathway with the light of happiness. Little Thomas was told, there was his Freddy,—and I was told to take care of little Thomas; and thus I entered upon the duties of my new home with the most cheering prospect ahead.

I look upon my departure from Colonel Lloyd's plantation as one of the most interesting events of my life. It is possible, and even quite probable, that but for the mere circumstance of being removed from that plantation to Baltimore, I should have to-day, instead of being here seated by my own table, in the enjoyment of freedom and the happiness of home, writing this Narrative, been confined in the galling chains of slavery. Going to live at Baltimore laid the foundation, and opened the gateway, to all my subsequent prosperity. I have ever regarded it as the first plain manifestation of that kind providence which has ever since attended me, and marked my life with so many favors. I regarded the selection of myself as being somewhat remarkable. There were a number of slave children that might have been sent from the plantation to Baltimore. There were those younger, those older, and those of the same age. I was chosen from among them all, and was the first, last, and only choice.

I may be deemed superstitious, and even egotistical, in regarding this event as a special interposition of divine Providence in my favor. But I should be false to the earliest sentiments of my soul, if I suppressed the opinion. I prefer to be true to myself, even at the hazard of incurring the ridicule of others, rather than to be false, and incur my own abhorrence. From my earliest recollection, I date the entertainment of a deep conviction that slavery would not always be able to hold me within its foul embrace; and in the darkest hours of my career in slavery, this living word of faith and spirit of hope departed not from me, but remained like ministering angels to cheer me through the gloom. This good spirit was from God, and to him I offer thanksgiving and praise.

CHAPTER 6

My new mistress proved to be all she appeared when I first met her at the door,—a woman of the kindest heart and finest feelings. She had never had a slave under her control previously to myself, and prior to her marriage she had been dependent upon her own industry for a living. She was by trade a weaver; and by constant application to her business, she had been in a good degree preserved from the blighting and dehumanizing effects of slavery. I was utterly astonished at her goodness. I scarcely knew how to behave towards her. She was entirely unlike any other white woman I had ever seen. I could not approach her as I was accustomed to approach other white ladies. My early instruction was all out of place. The crouching servility, usually so acceptable a quality in a slave, did not answer when manifested toward her. Her favor was not gained by it; she seemed to be disturbed by it. She did not deem it impudent or unmannerly for a slave to look her in the face. The meanest slave was put fully at ease in her presence, and none left without feeling better for having seen her. Her face was made of heavenly smiles, and her voice of tranquil music.

But, alas! this kind heart had but a short time to remain such. The fatal poison of irresponsible power was already in her hands, and soon commenced its infernal work. That cheerful eye, under the influence of slavery, soon became red with rage; that voice, made all of sweet accord, changed to one of harsh and horrid discord; and that angelic face gave place to that of a demon.

Very soon after I went to live with Mr. and Mrs. Auld, she very kindly commenced to teach me the A, B, C. After I had learned this, she assisted me in learning to spell words of three or four letters. Just at this point of my progress, Mr. Auld found out what was going on, and at once forbade Mrs. Auld to instruct me further, telling her, among other things, that it was unlawful, as well as unsafe, to teach a slave to read. To use his own words, further, he said, "If you give a nigger an inch, he will take an ell. A nigger should know nothing but to obey his master—to do as he is told to do. Learning would *spoil* the best nigger in the world. Now," said he, "if you teach that nigger (speaking of myself) how to read, there would be no keeping him. It would forever unfit him to be a slave. He would at once become unmanageable, and of no value to his master. As to himself, it could do him no good, but a great deal of harm. It would make him discontented and unhappy." These words sank deep into my heart, stirred up sentiments within that lay slumbering, and called into existence an entirely new train of thought. It was a new and special revelation, explaining dark and mysterious things, with which my youthful understanding had struggled, but struggled in vain. I now understood what had been to me a most perplexing difficulty—to wit, the white man's power to enslave the black man. It was a grand achievement, and I prized it highly. From that moment, I understood the pathway from slavery to freedom. It was just what I wanted, and I got it at a time when I the least expected it. Whilst I was saddened by the thought of losing the aid of my kind mistress, I was gladdened by the invaluable instruction which, by the merest accident, I had gained from my master. Though conscious of the difficulty of learning without a teacher, I set out with high hope, and a fixed purpose, at whatever cost of trouble, to learn how to read. The very decided manner with which he spoke, and strove to impress his wife with the evil consequences of giving me instruction, served to convince me that he was deeply sensible of the truths he was uttering. It gave me the best assurance that I might rely with the utmost confidence on the results which, he said, would flow from teaching me to read. What he most dreaded, that I most desired. What he most loved, that I most hated. That which to him was a great evil, to be carefully shunned, was to me a great good, to be diligently sought; and the argument which he so warmly urged, against my learning to read, only served to inspire me with a desire and determination to learn. In learning to read, I owe almost as much to the bitter opposition of my master, as to the kindly aid of my mistress. I acknowledge the benefit of both.

I had resided but a short time in Baltimore before I observed a marked difference, in the treatment of slaves, from that which I had witnessed in the country. A city slave is almost a freeman, compared with a slave on the plantation. He is much better fed and clothed, and enjoys privileges altogether unknown to the slave on the plantation. There is a vestige of decency, a sense of shame, that does much to curb and check those outbreaks of atrocious cruelty so commonly enacted upon the plantation. He is a desperate slaveholder, who will shock the humanity of his non-slaveholding neighbors with the cries of his lacerated slave. Few are willing to incur the odium attaching to the reputation of being a cruel master; and above all things, they would not be known as not giving a slave enough to eat. Every city slaveholder is anxious to have it known of him, that he feeds his slaves well; and it is due to them to say, that most of them do give their slaves enough to eat. There are, however, some painful exceptions to this rule. Directly opposite to us, on Philpot Street, lived Mr. Thomas Hamilton. He owned two slaves. Their names were Henrietta and Mary. Henrietta was about twenty-two years of age, Mary was about fourteen; and of all the mangled and emaciated creatures I ever looked upon, these two were the most so. His heart must be harder than stone, that could look upon these unmoved. The head, neck, and shoulders of Mary were literally cut to pieces. I have frequently felt her head, and found it nearly covered with festering sores, caused by the lash of her cruel mistress. I do not know that her master ever whipped her, but I have been an eye-witness to the cruelty of Mrs. Hamilton. I used to be in Mr. Hamilton's house nearly every day. Mrs. Hamilton used to sit in a large chair in the middle of the room, with a heavy cowskin always by her side, and scarce an hour passed during the day but was marked by the blood of one of these slaves. The girls seldom passed her without her saying, "Move faster, you *black gip!*" at the same time giving them a blow with the cowskin over the head or shoulders, often drawing the blood. She would then say, "Take that, you *black gip!*"—continuing, "If you don't move faster, I'll move you!" Added to the cruel lashings to which these slaves were subjected, they were kept nearly half-starved. They seldom knew what it was to eat a full meal. I have seen Mary contending with the pigs for the offal thrown into the street. So much was Mary kicked and cut to pieces, that she was oftener called *"pecked"* than by her name.

CHAPTER 7

I lived in Master Hugh's family about seven years. During this time, I succeeded in learning to read and write. In accomplishing this, I was compelled to resort to various stratagems. I had no regular teacher. My mistress, who had kindly commenced to instruct me, had, in compliance with the advice and direction of her husband, not only ceased to instruct, but had set her face against my being instructed by any one else. It is due, however, to my mistress to say of her, that she did not adopt this course of treatment immediately. She at first lacked the depravity indispensable to shutting me up in mental darkness. It was at least necessary for her to have some training in the exercise of irresponsible power, to make her equal to the task of treating me as though I were a brute.

My mistress was, as I have said, a kind and tender-hearted woman; and in the simplicity of her soul she commenced, when I first went to live with her, to treat me as she supposed one human being ought to treat another. In entering upon the duties of a slaveholder, she did not seem to perceive that I sustained to her the relation of a mere chattel, and that for her to treat me as a human being was not only wrong, but dangerously so. Slavery proved as injurious to her as it did to me. When I went there, she was a pious, warm, and tender-hearted woman. There was no sorrow or suffering for which she had not a tear. She had bread for the hungry, clothes for the naked, and comfort for every mourner that came within her reach. Slavery soon proved its ability to divest her of these heavenly qualities. Under its influence, the tender heart became stone, and the lamblike disposition gave way to one of tiger-like fierceness. The first step in her downward course was in her ceasing to instruct me. She now commenced to practise her husband's precepts. She finally became even more violent in her opposition than her husband himself. She was not satisfied with simply doing as well as he had commanded; she seemed anxious to do better. Nothing seemed to make her more angry than to see me with a newspaper. She seemed to think that here lay the danger. I have had her rush at me with a face made all up of fury, and snatch from me a newspaper, in a manner that fully revealed her apprehension. She was an apt woman; and a little experience soon demonstrated, to her satisfaction, that education and slavery were incompatible with each other.

From this time I was most narrowly watched. If I was in a separate room any considerable length of time, I was sure to be suspected of having a book, and was at once called to give an account of myself. All this, however, was too late. The first step had been taken. Mistress, in teaching me the alphabet, had given me the *inch,* and no precaution could prevent me from taking the *ell.*

The plan which I adopted, and the one by which I was most successful, was that of making friends of all the little white boys whom I met in the street. As many of these as I could, I converted into teachers. With their kindly aid, obtained at different times and in different places, I finally succeeded in learning to read. When I was sent of errands, I always took my book with me, and by going one part of my errand quickly, I found time to get a lesson before my return. I used also to carry bread with me, enough of which was always in the house, and to which I was always welcome; for I was much better off in this regard than many of the poor white children in our neighborhood. This bread I used to bestow upon the hungry little urchins, who, in return, would give me that more valuable bread of knowledge. I am strongly tempted to give the names of two or three of those little boys, as a testimonial of the gratitude and affection I bear them; but prudence forbids;—not that it would injure me, but it might embarrass them; for it is almost an unpardonable offence to teach slaves to read in this Christian country. It is enough to say of the dear little fellows, that they lived on Philpot Street, very near Durgin and Bailey's ship-yard. I used to talk this matter of slavery over with them. I would sometimes say to them, I wished I could be as free as they would be when they got to be men. "You will be free as soon as you are twenty-one, *but I am a slave for life!* Have not I as good a right to be free as you have?" These words used to trouble them; they would express for me the liveliest sympathy, and console me with the hope that something would occur by which I might be free.

I was now about twelve years old, and the thought of being *a slave for life* began to bear heavily upon my heart. Just about this time, I got hold of a book entitled "The Columbian Orator." Every opportunity I got, I used to read this book. Among much of other interesting matter, I found in it a dialogue between a master and his slave. The slave was represented as having run away from his master three times. The dialogue represented the conversation which took place between them, when the slave was retaken the third time. In this dialogue, the whole argument in behalf of slavery was brought forward by the master, all of which was disposed of by the slave. The slave was made to say some very smart as well as impressive things in reply to his master—things which had the desired though unexpected effect; for the conversation resulted in the voluntary emancipation of the slave on the part of the master.

In the same book, I met with one of Sheridan's mighty speeches on and in behalf of Catholic emancipation.[1] These were choice documents to me. I read them over and over again with unabated interest. They gave tongue to interesting thoughts of my own soul, which had frequently flashed through my mind, and died away for want of utterance. The moral which I gained from the dialogue was the power of truth over the conscience of even a slaveholder. What I got from Sheridan was a bold denunciation of slavery, and a powerful vindication of human rights. The reading of these documents enabled me to utter my thoughts, and to meet the arguments brought forward to sustain slavery; but while they relieved me of one difficulty, they brought on another even more painful than the one of which I was relieved. The more I read, the more I was led to abhor and detest my enslavers. I could regard them in no other light than a band of successful robbers, who had left their homes, and gone to Africa, and stolen us from our homes, and in a strange land reduced us to slavery. I loathed them as being the meanest as well as the most wicked of men. As I read and contemplated the subject, behold! that very discontentment which Master Hugh had predicted would follow my learning to read had already come, to torment and sting my soul to unutterable anguish. As I writhed under it, I would at times feel that learning to read had been a curse rather than a blessing. It had given me a view of my wretched condition, without the remedy. It opened my eyes to the horrible pit, but to no ladder upon which to get out. In moments of agony, I envied my fellow-slaves for their stupidity. I have often wished myself a beast. I preferred the condition of the meanest reptile to my own. Any thing, no matter what, to get rid of thinking! It was this everlasting thinking of my condition that tormented me. There was no getting rid of it. It was pressed upon me by every object within sight or hearing, animate or inanimate. The

---

1. Richard Brinsley Sheridan (1751–1816), Irish-born playwright and noted political orator, spoke out in the English Parliament in favor of equal rights for Roman Catholics. The Catholic Emancipation Act was finally passed in 1829.

silver trump of freedom had roused my soul to eternal wakefulness. Freedom now appeared, to disappear no more forever. It was heard in every sound, and seen in every thing. It was ever present to torment me with a sense of my wretched condition. I saw nothing without seeing it, I heard nothing without hearing it, and felt nothing without feeling it. It looked from every star, it smiled in every calm, breathed in every wind, and moved in every storm.

I often found myself regretting my own existence, and wishing myself dead; and but for the hope of being free, I have no doubt but that I should have killed myself, or done something for which I should have been killed. While in this state of mind, I was eager to hear any one speak of slavery. I was a ready listener. Every little while, I could hear something about the abolitionists. It was some time before I found what the word meant. It was always used in such connections as to make it an interesting word to me. If a slave ran away and succeeded in getting clear, or if a slave killed his master, set fire to a barn, or did any thing very wrong in the mind of a slaveholder, it was spoken of as the fruit of *abolition*. Hearing the word in this connection very often, I set about learning what it meant. The dictionary afforded me little or no help. I found it was "the act of abolishing," but then I did not know what was to be abolished. Here I was perplexed. I did not dare to ask any one about its meaning, for I was satisfied that it was something they wanted me to know very little about. After a patient waiting, I got one of our city papers, containing an account of the number of petitions from the north, praying for the abolition of slavery in the District of Columbia, and of the slave trade between the States. From this time I understood the words *abolition* and *abolitionist*, and always drew near when that word was spoken, expecting to hear something of importance to myself and fellow-slaves. The light broke in upon me by degrees. I went one day down on the wharf of Mr. Waters; and seeing two Irishmen unloading a scow of stone, I went, unasked, and helped them. When we had finished, one of them came to me and asked me if I were a slave. I told him I was. He asked, "Are ye a slave for life?" I told him that I was. The good Irishman seemed to be deeply affected by the statement. He said to the other that it was a pity so fine a little fellow as myself should be a slave for life. He said it was a shame to hold me. They both advised me to run away to the north; that I should find friends there, and that I should be free. I pretended not to be interested in what they said, and treated them as if I did not understand them; for I feared they might be treacherous. White men have been known to encourage slaves to escape, and then, to get the reward, catch them and return them to their masters. I was afraid that these seemingly good men might use me so; but I nevertheless remembered their advice, and from that time I resolved to run away. I looked forward to a time at which it would be safe for me to escape. I was too young to think of doing so immediately; besides, I wished to learn how to write, as I might have occasion to write my own pass. I consoled myself with the hope that I should one day find a good chance. Meanwhile, I would learn to write.

The idea as to how I might learn to write was suggested to me by being in Durgin and Bailey's ship-yard, and frequently seeing the ship carpenters, after hewing, and getting a piece of timber ready for use, write on the timber the name of that part of the ship for which it was intended. When a piece of timber was intended for the larboard side, it would be marked thus— "L." When a piece was for the starboard side, it would be marked thus— "S." A piece for the larboard side forward, would be marked thus—"L. F." When a piece was for starboard side forward, it would be marked thus—"S. F." For larboard aft, it would be marked thus—"L. A." For starboard aft, it would be marked thus—"S. A." I soon learned the names of these letters, and for what they were intended when placed upon a piece of timber in the ship-yard. I immediately commenced copying them, and in a short time was able to make the four letters named. After that, when I met with any boy who I knew could write, I would tell him I could write as well as he. The next word would be, "I don't believe you. Let me see you try it." I would then make the letters which I had been so fortunate as to learn, and ask him to beat that. In this way I got a good many lessons in writing, which it is quite possible I should never have gotten in any other way. During this time, my copy-book was the board fence, brick wall, and pavement; my pen and ink was a lump of chalk. With these, I learned mainly how to write. I then commenced and continued copying the Italics in Webster's Spelling Book, until I could make them all without looking on the book. By this time, my little Master Thomas had gone to school, and learned how to write, and had written over a number of copybooks. These had been brought home, and shown to some of our near neighbors, and then laid aside. My mistress used to go to class meeting at the Wilk Street meeting-house every Monday afternoon, and leave me to take care of the house. When left thus, I used to spend the time in writing in the spaces left in Master Thomas's copy-book, copying what he had written. I continued to do this until I could write a hand very similar to that of Master Thomas. Thus, after a long, tedious effort for years, I finally succeeded in learning how to write.

CHAPTER 8

In a very short time after I went to live at Baltimore, my old master's youngest son Richard died; and in about three years and six months after his death, my old master, Captain Anthony, died, leaving only his son, Andrew, and daughter, Lucretia, to share his estate. He died while on a visit to see his daughter at Hillsborough. Cut off thus unexpectedly, he left no will as to the disposal of his property. It was therefore necessary to have a valuation of the property, that it might be equally divided between Mrs. Lucretia and Master Andrew. I was immediately sent for, to be valued with the other property. Here again my feelings rose up in detestation of slavery. I had now a new conception of my degraded condition. Prior to this, I had become, if not insensible to my lot, at least partly so. I left Baltimore with a young heart overborne with sadness, and a soul full of apprehension. I took passage with Captain Rowe, in the schooner Wild Cat, and, after a sail of about twenty-four hours, I found myself near the place of my birth. I had now been absent from it almost, if not quite, five years. I, however, remembered the place very well. I was only about five years old when I left it, to go and live with my old master on Colonel Lloyd's plantation; so that I was now between ten and eleven years old.

We were all ranked together at the valuation. Men and women, old and young, married and single, were ranked with horses, sheep, and swine. There were horses and men, cattle and women, pigs and children, all holding the same rank in the scale of being, and were all subjected to the same narrow examination. Silvery-headed age and sprightly youth, maids and matrons, had to undergo the same indelicate inspection. At this moment, I saw more clearly than ever the brutalizing effects of slavery upon both slave and slaveholder.

After the valuation, then came the division. I have no language to express the high excitement and deep anxiety which were felt among us poor slaves during this time. Our fate for life was now to be decided. We had no more voice in that decision than the brutes among whom we were ranked. A single word from the white men was enough—against all our wishes, prayers, and entreaties—to sunder forever the dearest friends, dearest kindred, and strongest ties known to human beings. In addition to the pain of separation, there was the horrid dread of falling into the hands of Master Andrew. He was known to us all as being a most cruel wretch,—a common drunkard, who had, by his reckless mismanagement and profligate dissipation, already wasted a large portion of his father's property. We all felt that we might as well be sold at once to the Georgia traders, as to pass into his hands; for we knew that that would be our inevitable condition,—a condition held by us all in the utmost horror and dread.

I suffered more anxiety than most of my fellow-slaves. I had known what it was to be kindly treated; they had known nothing of the kind. They had seen little or nothing of the world. They were in very deed men and women of sorrow, and acquainted with grief. Their backs had been made familiar with the bloody lash, so that they had become callous; mine was yet tender; for while at Baltimore I got few whippings, and few slaves could boast of a kinder master and mistress than myself; and the thought of passing out of their hands into those of Master Andrew—a man who, but a few days before, to give me a sample of his bloody disposition, took my little brother by the throat, threw him on the ground, and with the heel of his boot stamped upon his head till the blood gushed from his nose and ears—was well calculated to make me anxious as to my fate. After he had committed this savage outrage upon my brother, he turned to me, and said that was the way he meant to serve me one of these days,—meaning, I suppose, when I came into his possession.

Thanks to a kind Providence, I fell to the portion of Mrs. Lucretia, and was sent immediately back to Baltimore, to live again in the family of Master Hugh. Their joy at my return equalled their sorrow at my departure. It was a glad day to me. I had escaped a worse than lion's jaws. I was absent from Baltimore, for the purpose of valuation and division, just about one month, and it seemed to have been six.

Very soon after my return to Baltimore, my mistress, Lucretia, died, leaving her husband and one child, Amanda; and in a very short time after her death, Master Andrew died. Now all the property of my old master, slaves included, was in the hands of strangers,—strangers who had had nothing to do with accumulating it. Not a slave was left free. All remained slaves, from the youngest to the oldest. If any one thing in my experience, more than another, served to deepen my conviction of the infernal character of slavery, and to fill me with unutterable loathing of slaveholders, it was their base ingratitude to my poor old grandmother. She had served my old master faithfully from youth to old age. She had been the source of all his wealth; she had peopled his plantation with slaves; she had become a great grandmother in his service. She had rocked him in infancy, attended him in childhood, served him through life, and at his death wiped from his icy brow the cold death-sweat, and closed his eyes forever. She was nevertheless left a slave—a slave for life—a slave in the hands of strangers; and in their hands she saw her children, her grandchildren, and her great-grandchildren, divided, like so many sheep, without being gratified with the small privilege of a single word, as to their or her own destiny. And, to cap the climax of their base ingratitude and fiendish barbarity, my grandmother, who was now very old, having outlived my old master and all his children, having seen the beginning and end of all of them, and her present owners finding she was of but little value, her frame already racked with the pains of old age, and complete helplessness fast stealing over her once active limbs, they took her to the woods, built her a little hut, put up a little mud-chimney, and then made her welcome to the privilege of supporting herself there in perfect loneliness; thus virtually turning her out to die! If my poor old grandmother now lives, she lives to suffer in utter loneliness; she lives to remember and mourn over the loss of children, the loss of grandchildren, and the loss of great-grandchildren. They are, in the language of the slave's poet, Whittier,—

> Gone, gone, sold and gone
> To the rice swamp dank and lone,
> Where the slave-whip ceaseless swings,
> Where the noisome insect stings,
> Where the fever-demon strews
> Poison with the falling dews,
> Where the sickly sunbeams glare
> Through the hot and misty air:—
> Gone, gone, sold and gone
> To the rice swamp dank and lone,
> From Virginia hills and waters—
> Woe is me, my stolen daughters![2]

The hearth is desolate. The children, the unconscious children, who once sang and danced in her presence, are gone. She gropes her way, in the darkness of age, for a drink of water. Instead of the voices of her children, she hears by day the moans of the dove, and by night the screams of the hideous owl. All is gloom. The grave is at the door. And now, when weighed down by the pains and aches of old age, when the head inclines to the feet, when the beginning and ending of human existence meet, and helpless infancy and painful old age combine together—at this time, this most needful time, the time for the exercise of that tenderness and affection which children only can exercise towards a declining parent—my poor old grandmother, the devoted mother of twelve children, is left all alone, in yonder little hut, before a few dim embers. She stands—she sits—she staggers—she falls—she groans—she dies—and there are none of her children or grandchildren present, to wipe from her wrinkled brow the cold sweat of death, or to place beneath the sod her fallen remains. Will not a righteous God visit for these things?

In about two years after the death of Mrs. Lucretia, Master Thomas married his second wife. Her name was Rowena Hamilton. She was the eldest daughter of Mr. William Hamilton. Master now lived in St. Michael's. Not long after his marriage, a misunderstanding took place between himself and Master Hugh; and as a means of punishing his brother, he took me from him to live with himself at St. Michael's. Here I underwent another most painful separation. It, however, was not so severe as the one I dreaded at the division of property; for, during this interval, a great change had taken place in Master Hugh and his once kind and affectionate wife. The influence of brandy upon him, and of slavery upon her, had effected a disastrous change in the characters of both; so that, as far as they were concerned, I thought I had little to lose by the change. But it was not to them that I was attached. It was to those little Baltimore boys that I felt the strongest attachment. I had received many good lessons from them, and was still receiving them, and the thought of leaving them was painful indeed. I was leaving, too, without the hope of ever being allowed to return. Master Thomas had said he would never let me return again. The barrier betwixt himself and brother he considered impassable.

---

2. John Greenleaf Whittier (1807–1892), "The Farewell: Of a Virginia Slave Mother to Her Daughter Sold into Southern Bondage."

I then had to regret that I did not at least make the attempt to carry out my resolution to run away; for the chances of success are tenfold greater from the city than from the country.

I sailed from Baltimore for St. Michael's in the sloop Amanda, Captain Edward Dodson. On my passage, I paid particular attention to the direction which the steamboats took to go to Philadelphia. I found, instead of going down, on reaching North Point they went up the bay, in a north-easterly direction. I deemed this knowledge of the utmost importance. My determination to run away was again revived. I resolved to wait only so long as the offering of a favorable opportunity. When that came, I was determined to be off.

CHAPTER 9

I have now reached a period of my life when I can give dates. I left Baltimore, and went to live with Master Thomas Auld, at St. Michael's, in March, 1832. It was now more than seven years since I lived with him in the family of my old master, on Colonel Lloyd's plantation. We of course were now almost entire strangers to each other. He was to me a new master, and I to him a new slave. I was ignorant of his temper and disposition; he was equally so of mine. A very short time, however, brought us into full acquaintance with each other. I was made acquainted with his wife not less than with himself. They were well matched, being equally mean and cruel. I was now, for the first time during a space of more than seven years, made to feel the painful gnawings of hunger—a something which I had not experienced before since I left Colonel Lloyd's plantation. It went hard enough with me then, when I could look back to no period at which I had enjoyed a sufficiency. It was tenfold harder after living in Master Hugh's family, where I had always had enough to eat, and of that which was good. I have said Master Thomas was a mean man. He was so. Not to give a slave enough to eat, is regarded as the most aggravated development of meanness even among slaveholders. The rule is, no matter how coarse the food, only let there be enough of it. This is the theory; and in the part of Maryland from which I came, it is the general practice,—though there are many exceptions. Master Thomas gave us enough of neither coarse nor fine food. There were four slaves of us in the kitchen—my sister Eliza, my aunt Priscilla, Henny, and myself; and we were allowed less than a half of a bushel of corn-meal per week, and very little else, either in the shape of meat or vegetables. It was not enough for us to subsist upon. We were therefore reduced to the wretched necessity of living at the expense of our neighbors. This we did by begging and stealing, whichever came handy in the time of need, the one being considered as legitimate as the other. A great many times have we poor creatures been nearly perishing with hunger, when food in abundance lay mouldering in the safe and smoke-house, and our pious mistress was aware of the fact; and yet that mistress and her husband would kneel every morning, and pray that God would bless them in basket and store!

Bad as all slaveholders are, we seldom meet one destitute of every element of character commanding respect. My master was one of this rare sort. I do not know of one single noble act ever performed by him. The leading trait in his character was meanness; and if there were any other element in his nature, it was made subject to this. He was mean; and, like most other mean men, he lacked the ability to conceal his meanness. Captain Auld was not born a slaveholder. He had been a poor man, master only of a Bay craft. He came into possession of all his slaves by marriage; and of all men, adopted slaveholders are the worst. He was cruel, but cowardly. He commanded without firmness. In the enforcement of his rules, he was at times rigid, and at times lax. At times, he spoke to his slaves with the firmness of Napoleon and the fury of a demon; at other times, he might well be mistaken for an inquirer who had lost his way. He did nothing of himself. He might have passed for a lion, but for his ears. In all things noble which he attempted, his own meanness shone most conspicuous. His airs, words, and actions, were the airs, words, and actions of born slaveholders, and, being assumed, were awkward enough. He was not even a good imitator. He possessed all the disposition to deceive, but wanted the power. Having no resources within himself, he was compelled to be the copyist of many, and being such, he was forever the victim of inconsistency; and of consequence he was an object of contempt, and was held as such even by his slaves. The luxury of having slaves of his own to wait upon him was something new and unprepared for. He was a slaveholder without the ability to hold slaves. He found himself incapable of managing his slaves either by force, fear, or fraud. We seldom called him "master;" we generally called him "Captain Auld," and were hardly disposed to title him at all. I doubt not that our conduct had much to do with making him appear awkward, and of consequence fretful. Our want of reverence for him must have perplexed him greatly. He wished to have us call him master, but lacked the firmness necessary to command us to do so. His wife used to insist upon our calling him so, but to no purpose. In August, 1832, my master attended a Methodist camp-meeting held in the Bay-side, Talbot county, and there experienced religion. I indulged a faint hope that his conversion would lead him to emancipate his slaves, and that, if he did not do this, it would, at any rate, make him more kind and humane. I was disappointed in both these respects. It neither made him to be humane to his slaves, nor to emancipate them. If it had any effect on his character, it made him more cruel and hateful in all his ways; for I believe him to have been a much worse man after his conversion than before. Prior to his conversion, he relied upon his own depravity to shield and sustain him in his savage barbarity; but after his conversion, he found religious sanction and support for his slaveholding cruelty. He made the greatest pretensions to piety. His house was the house of prayer. He prayed morning, noon, and night. He very soon distinguished himself among his brethren, and was soon made a class-leader and exhorter. His activity in revivals was great, and he proved himself an instrument in the hands of the church in converting many souls. His house was the preachers' home. They used to take great pleasure in coming there to put up; for while he starved us, he stuffed them. We have had three or four preachers there at a time. The names of those who used to come most frequently while I lived there, were Mr. Storks, Mr. Ewery, Mr. Humphry, and Mr. Hickey. I have also seen Mr. George Cookman at our house. We slaves loved Mr. Cookman. We believed him to be a good man. We thought him instrumental in getting Mr. Samuel Harrison, a very rich slaveholder, to emancipate his slaves; and by some means got the impression that he was laboring to effect the emancipation of all the slaves. When he was at our house, we were sure to be called in to prayers. When the others were there, we were sometimes called in and sometimes not. Mr. Cookman took more notice of us than either of the other ministers. He could not come among us without betraying his sympathy for us, and, stupid as we were, we had the sagacity to see it.

While I lived with my master in St. Michael's, there was a white young man, a Mr. Wilson, who proposed to keep a Sabbath school for the instruction of such slaves as might be disposed to learn to read the New Testament. We met but three times, when Mr. West and Mr. Fairbanks, both class-leaders, with many others, came upon us with sticks and other missiles, drove us off, and forbade us to meet again. Thus ended our little Sabbath school in the pious town of St. Michael's.

I have said my master found religious sanction for his cruelty. As an example, I will state one of many facts going to prove the charge. I have seen him tie up a lame young woman, and whip her with a heavy cowskin upon her naked shoulders, causing the warm red blood to drip; and, in justification of the bloody deed, he would quote this passage of Scripture—"He that knoweth his master's will, and doeth it not, shall be beaten with many stripes."[3]

Master would keep this lacerated young woman tied up in this horrid situation four or five hours at a time. I have known him to tie her up early in the morning, and whip her before breakfast; leave her, go to his store, return at dinner, and whip her again, cutting her in the places already made raw with his cruel lash. The secret of master's cruelty toward "Henny" is found in the fact of her being almost helpless. When quite a child, she fell into the fire, and burned herself horribly. Her hands were so burnt that she never got the use of them. She could do very little but bear heavy burdens. She was to master a bill of expense; and as he was a mean man, she was a constant offence to him. He seemed desirous of getting the poor girl out of existence. He gave her away once to his sister; but, being a poor gift, she was not disposed to keep her. Finally, my benevolent master, to use his own words, "set her adrift to take care of herself." Here was a recently-converted man, holding on upon the mother, and at the same time turning out her helpless child, to starve and die! Master Thomas was one of the many pious slaveholders who hold slaves for the very charitable purpose of taking care of them.

My master and myself had quite a number of differences. He found me unsuitable to his purpose. My city life, he said, had had a very pernicious effect upon me. It had almost ruined me for every good purpose, and fitted me for every thing which was bad. One of my greatest faults was that of letting his horse run away, and go down to his father-in-law's farm, which was about five miles from St. Michael's. I would then have to go after it. My reason for this kind of carelessness, or carefulness, was, that I could always get something to eat when I went there. Master William Hamilton, my master's father-in-law, always gave his slaves enough to eat. I never left there hungry, no matter how great the need of my speedy return. Master Thomas at length said he would stand it no longer. I had lived with him nine months, during which time he had given me a number of severe whippings, all to no good purpose. He resolved to put me out, as he said, to be broken; and, for this purpose, he let me for one year to a man named Edward Covey. Mr. Covey was a poor man, a farm-renter. He rented the place upon which he lived, as also the hands with which he tilled it. Mr. Covey had acquired a very high reputation for breaking young slaves, and this reputation was of immense value to him. It enabled him to get his farm tilled with much less expense to himself than he could have had it done without such a reputation. Some slaveholders thought it not much loss to allow Mr. Covey to have their slaves one year, for the sake of the training to which they were subjected, without any other compensation. He could hire young help with great ease, in consequence of this reputation. Added to the natural good qualities of Mr. Covey, he was a professor of religion—a pious soul—a member and a class-leader in the Methodist church. All of this

3. Quoting Luke 12:47, in which Jesus describes God's punishments at the end of the world, comparing sinners to unfaithful servants.

added weight to his reputation as a "nigger-breaker." I was aware of all the facts, having been made acquainted with them by a young man who had lived there. I nevertheless made the change gladly; for I was sure of getting enough to eat, which is not the smallest consideration to a hungry man.

CHAPTER 10

I left Master Thomas's house, and went to live with Mr. Covey, on the 1st of January, 1833. I was now, for the first time in my life, a field hand. In my new employment, I found myself even more awkward than a country boy appeared to be in a large city. I had been at my new home but one week before Mr. Covey gave me a very severe whipping, cutting my back, causing the blood to run, and raising ridges on my flesh as large as my little finger. The details of this affair are as follows: Mr. Covey sent me, very early in the morning of one of our coldest days in the month of January, to the woods, to get a load of wood. He gave me a team of unbroken oxen. He told me which was the in-hand ox, and which the off-hand one. He then tied the end of a large rope around the horns of the in-hand ox, and gave me the other end of it, and told me, if the oxen started to run, that I must hold on upon the rope. I had never driven oxen before, and of course I was very awkward. I, however, succeeded in getting to the edge of the woods with little difficulty; but I had got a very few rods into the woods, when the oxen took fright, and started full tilt, carrying the cart against trees, and over stumps, in the most frightful manner. I expected every moment that my brains would be dashed out against the trees. After running thus for a considerable distance, they finally upset the cart, dashing it with great force against a tree, and threw themselves into a dense thicket. How I escaped death, I do not know. There I was, entirely alone, in a thick wood, in a place new to me. My cart was upset and shattered, my oxen were entangled among the young trees, and there was none to help me. After a long spell of effort, I succeeded in getting my cart righted, my oxen disentangled, and again yoked to the cart. I now proceeded with my team to the place where I had, the day before, been chopping wood, and loaded my cart pretty heavily, thinking in this way to tame my oxen. I then proceeded on my way home. I had now consumed one half of the day. I got out of the woods safely, and now felt out of danger. I stopped my oxen to open the woods gate; and just as I did so, before I could get hold of my ox-rope, the oxen again started, rushed through the gate, catching it between the wheel and the body of the cart, tearing it to pieces, and coming within a few inches of crushing me against the gate-post. Thus twice, in one short day, I escaped death by the merest chance. On my return, I told Mr. Covey what had happened, and how it happened. He ordered me to return to the woods again immediately. I did so, and he followed on after me. Just as I got into the woods, he came up and told me to stop my cart, and that he would teach me how to trifle away my time, and break gates. He then went to a large gumtree, and with his axe cut three large switches, and, after trimming them up neatly with his pocket-knife, he ordered me to take off my clothes. I made him no answer, but stood with my clothes on. He repeated his order. I still made him no answer, nor did I move to strip myself. Upon this he rushed at me with the fierceness of a tiger, tore off my clothes, and lashed me till he had worn out his switches, cutting me so savagely as to leave the marks visible for a long time after. This whipping was the first of a number just like it, and for similar offences.

I lived with Mr. Covey one year. During the first six months, of that year, scarce a week passed without his whipping me. I was seldom free from a sore back. My awkwardness was almost always his excuse for whipping me. We were worked fully up to the point of endurance. Long before day we were up, our horses fed, and by the first approach of day we were off to the field with our hoes and ploughing teams. Mr. Covey gave us enough to eat, but scarce time to eat it. We were often less than five minutes taking our meals. We were often in the field from the first approach of day till its last lingering ray had left us; and at saving-fodder time, midnight often caught us in the field binding blades.

Covey would be out with us. The way he used to stand it, was this. He would spend the most of his afternoons in bed. He would then come out fresh in the evening, ready to urge us on with his words, example, and frequently with the whip. Mr. Covey was one of the few slaveholders who could and did work with his hands. He was a hard-working man. He knew by himself just what a man or a boy could do. There was no deceiving him. His work went on in his absence almost as well as in his presence; and he had the faculty of making us feel that he was ever present with us. This he did by surprising us. He seldom approached the spot where we were at work openly, if he could do it secretly. He always aimed at taking us by surprise. Such was his cunning, that we used to call him, among ourselves, "the snake." When we were at work in the cornfield, he would sometimes crawl on his hands and knees to avoid detection, and all at once he would rise nearly in our midst, and scream out, "Ha, ha! Come, come! Dash on, dash on!" This being his mode of attack, it was never safe to stop a single minute. His comings were like a thief in the night. He appeared to us as being ever at hand. He was under every tree, behind every stump, in every bush, and at every window, on the plantation. He would sometimes mount his horse, as if bound to St. Michael's, a distance of seven miles, and in half an hour afterwards you would see him coiled up in the corner of the wood-fence, watching every motion of the slaves. He would, for this purpose, leave his horse tied up in the woods. Again, he would sometimes walk up to us, and give us orders as though he was upon the point of starting on a long journey, turn his back upon us, and make as though he was going to the house to get ready; and, before he would get half way thither, he would turn short and crawl into a fence-corner, or behind some tree, and there watch us till the going down of the sun.

Mr. Covey's *forte* consisted in his power to deceive. His life was devoted to planning and perpetrating the grossest deceptions. Every thing he possessed in the shape of learning or religion, he made conform to his disposition to deceive. He seemed to think himself equal to deceiving the Almighty. He would make a short prayer in the morning, and a long prayer at night; and, strange as it may seem, few men would at times appear more devotional than he. The exercises of his family devotions were always commenced with singing; and, as he was a very poor singer himself, the duty of raising the hymn generally came upon me. He would read his hymn, and nod at me to commence. I would at times do so; at others, I would not. My non-compliance would almost always produce much confusion. To show himself independent of me, he would start and stagger through with his hymn in the most discordant manner. In this state of mind, he prayed with more than ordinary spirit. Poor man! such was his disposition, and success at deceiving, I do verily believe that he sometimes deceived himself into the solemn belief, that he was a sincere worshipper of the most high God; and this, too, at a time when he may be said to have been guilty of compelling his woman slave to commit the sin of adultery. The facts in the case are these: Mr. Covey was a poor man; he was just commencing in life; he was only able to buy one slave; and, shocking as is the fact, he bought her, as he said, for *a breeder.* This woman was named Caroline. Mr. Covey bought her from Mr. Thomas Lowe, about six miles from

St. Michael's. She was a large, able-bodied woman, about twenty years old. She had already given birth to one child, which proved her to be just what he wanted. After buying her, he hired a married man of Mr. Samuel Harrison, to live with him one year; and him he used to fasten up with her every night! The result was, that, at the end of the year, the miserable woman gave birth to twins. At this result Mr. Covey seemed to be highly pleased, both with the man and the wretched woman. Such was his joy, and that of his wife, that nothing they could do for Caroline during her confinement was too good, or too hard, to be done. The children were regarded as being quite an addition to his wealth.

If at any one time of my life more than another, I was made to drink the bitterest dregs of slavery, that time was during the first six months of my stay with Mr. Covey. We were worked in all weathers. It was never too hot or too cold; it could never rain, blow, hail, or snow, too hard for us to work in the field. Work, work, work, was scarcely more the order of the day than of the night. The longest days were too short for him, and the shortest nights too long for him. I was somewhat unmanageable when I first went there, but a few months of this discipline tamed me. Mr. Covey succeeded in breaking me. I was broken in body, soul, and spirit. My natural elasticity was crushed, my intellect languished, the disposition to read departed, the cheerful spark that lingered about my eye died; the dark night of slavery closed in upon me; and behold a man transformed into a brute!

Sunday was my only leisure time. I spent this in a sort of beast-like stupor, between sleep and wake, under some large tree. At times I would rise up, a flash of energetic freedom would dart through my soul, accompanied with a faint beam of hope, that flickered for a moment, and then vanished. I sank down again, mourning over my wretched condition. I was sometimes prompted to take my life, and that of Covey, but was prevented by a combination of hope and fear. My sufferings on this plantation seem now like a dream rather than a stern reality.

Our house stood within a few rods of the Chesapeake Bay, whose broad bosom was ever white with sails from every quarter of the habitable globe. Those beautiful vessels, robed in purest white, so delightful to the eye of freemen, were to me so many shrouded ghosts, to terrify and torment me with thoughts of my wretched condition. I have often, in the deep stillness of a summer's Sabbath, stood all alone upon the lofty banks of that noble bay, and traced, with saddened heart and tearful eye, the countless number of sails moving off to the mighty ocean. The sight of these always affected me powerfully. My thoughts would compel utterance; and there, with no audience but the Almighty, I would pour out my soul's complaint, in my rude way, with an apostrophe to the moving multitude of ships:—

"You are loosed from your moorings, and are free; I am fast in my chains, and am a slave! You move merrily before the gentle gale, and I sadly before the bloody whip! You are freedom's swift-winged angels, that fly round the world; I am confined in bands of iron! O that I were free! O, that I were on one of your gallant decks, and under your protecting wing! Alas! betwixt me and you, the turbid waters roll. Go on, go on. O that I could also go! Could I but swim! If I could fly! O, why was I born a man, of whom to make a brute! The glad ship is gone; she hides in the dim distance. I am left in the hottest hell of unending slavery. O God, save me! God, deliver me! Let me be free! Is there any God? Why am I a slave? I will run away. I will not stand it. Get caught, or get clear, I'll try it. I had as well die with ague as the fever. I have only one life to lose. I had as well be killed running as die standing. Only think of it; one hundred miles straight north, and I am free! Try it? Yes! God helping me, I will. It cannot be that I shall live and die a slave. I will take to the water. This very bay shall yet bear me into freedom. The steamboats steered in a north-east course from North Point. I will do the same; and when I get to the head of the bay, I will turn my canoe adrift, and walk straight through Delaware into Pennsylvania. When I get there, I shall not be required to have a pass; I can travel without being disturbed. Let but the first opportunity offer, and, come what will, I am off. Mean-while, I will try to bear up under the yoke. I am not the only slave in the world. Why should I fret? I can bear as much as any of them. Besides, I am but a boy, and all boys are bound to some one. It may be that my misery in slavery will only increase my happiness when I get free. There is a better day coming."

Thus I used to think, and thus I used to speak to myself; goaded almost to madness at one moment, and at the next reconciling myself to my wretched lot.

I have already intimated that my condition was much worse, during the first six months of my stay at Mr. Covey's, than in the last six. The circumstances leading to the change in Mr. Covey's course toward me form an epoch in my humble history. You have seen how a man was made a slave; you shall see how a slave was made a man. On one of the hottest days of the month of August, 1833, Bill Smith, William Hughes, a slave named Eli, and myself, were engaged in fanning wheat. Hughes was clearing the fanned wheat from before the fan, Eli was turning, Smith was feeding, and I was carrying wheat to the fan. The work was simple, requiring strength rather than intellect; yet, to one entirely unused to such work, it came very hard. About three o'clock of that day, I broke down; my strength failed me; I was seized with a violent aching of the head, attended with extreme dizziness; I trembled in every limb. Finding what was coming, I nerved myself up, feeling it would never do to stop work. I stood as long as I could stagger to the hopper with grain. When I could stand no longer, I fell, and felt as if held down by an immense weight. The fan of course stopped; every one had his own work to do; and no one could do the work of the other, and have his own go on at the same time.

Mr. Covey was at the house, about one hundred yards from the treading-yard where we were fanning. On hearing the fan stop, he left immediately, and came to the spot where we were. He hastily inquired what the matter was. Bill answered that I was sick, and there was no one to bring wheat to the fan. I had by this time crawled away under the side of the post and rail-fence by which the yard was enclosed, hoping to find relief by getting out of the sun. He then asked where I was. He was told by one of the hands. He came to the spot, and, after looking at me awhile, asked me what was the matter. I told him as well as I could, for I scarce had strength to speak. He then gave me a savage kick in the side, and told me to get up. I tried to do so, but fell back in the attempt. He gave me another kick, and again told me to rise. I again tried, and succeeded in gaining my feet; but, stooping to get the tub with which I was feeding the fan, I again staggered and fell. While down in this situation, Mr. Covey took up the hickory slat with which Hughes had been striking off the half-bushel measure, and with it gave me a heavy blow upon the head, making a large wound, and the blood ran freely; and with this again told me to get up. I made no effort to comply, having now made up my mind to let him do his worst. In a short time after receiving this blow, my head grew better. Mr. Covey had now left me to my fare. At this moment I resolved, for the first time, to go to my master, enter a complaint, and ask his protection. In order to do this, I must that afternoon walk seven miles; and this, under the circumstances, was truly a severe undertaking. I was exceedingly feeble; made so as much by the kicks and blows which I received, as by the severe fit of sickness to which I had been subjected. I, however, watched my chance, while Covey was looking in an opposite direction, and started for St. Michael's. I succeeded in getting a considerable distance on my way to the woods, when Covey discovered me, and called after me to come back, threatening what he would do if I did not come. I disregarded both his calls and his threats, and made my way to the woods as fast as my feeble state would allow; and thinking I might be overhauled by him if I kept the road, I walked through the woods, keeping far enough from the road to avoid detection, and near enough to prevent losing my way. I had not gone far before my little strength again failed me. I could go no farther. I fell down, and lay for a considerable time. The blood was yet oozing from the wound on my head. For a time I thought I should bleed to death; and think now that I should have done so, but that the blood so matted my hair as to stop the wound. After lying there about three quarters of an hour, I nerved myself up again, and started on my way, through bogs and briers, barefooted and bareheaded, tearing my feet sometimes at nearly every step; and after a journey of about seven miles, occupying some five hours to perform it, I arrived at master's store. I then presented an appearance enough to affect any but a heart of iron. From the crown of my head to my feet, I was covered with blood. My hair was all clotted with dust and blood; my shirt was stiff with blood. My legs and feet were torn in sundry places with briers and thorns, and were also covered with blood. I suppose I looked like a man who had escaped a den of wild beasts, and barely escaped them. In this state I appeared before my master, humbly entreating him to interpose his authority for my protection. I told him all the circumstances as well as I could, and it seemed, as I spoke, at times to affect him. He would then walk the floor, and seek to justify Covey by saying he expected I deserved it. He asked me what I wanted. I told him, to let me get a new home; that as sure as I lived with Mr. Covey again, I should live with but to die with him; that Covey would surely kill me; he was in a fair way for it. Master Thomas ridiculed the idea that there was any danger of Mr. Covey's killing me, and said that he knew Mr. Covey; that he was a good man, and that he could not think of taking me from him; that, should he do so, he would lose the whole year's wages; that I belonged to Mr. Covey for one year, and that I must go back to him, come what might; and that I must not trouble him with any more stories, or that he would himself *get hold of me.* After threatening me thus, he gave me a very large dose of salts, telling me that I might remain in St. Michael's that night, (it being quite late,) but that I must be off back to Mr. Covey's early in the morning; and that if I did not, he would *get hold of me,* which meant that he would whip me. I remained all night, and, according to his orders, I started off to Covey's in the morning, (Saturday morning,) wearied in body and broken in spirit. I got no supper that night, or breakfast that morning. I reached Covey's about nine o'clock; and just as I was getting over the fence that divided Mrs. Kemp's fields from ours, out ran Covey with his cowskin, to give me another whipping. Before he could reach me, I succeeded in getting to the cornfield; and as the corn was very high, it afforded me the means of hiding. He seemed very angry, and searched for me a long time. My behavior was altogether unaccountable. He finally gave up the chase, thinking, I suppose, that I must come home for something to eat; he would give himself no further trouble in looking for me. I spent that day mostly in the woods, having the alternative before me,—to go home and be whipped to death, or stay in the woods and be starved to death. That night, I fell in with Sandy Jenkins, a slave with whom I was somewhat acquainted. Sandy had a free wife, who lived about four miles from Mr. Covey's; and it being Saturday, he was on his way to see her. I told him my circumstances, and he very kindly invited me to go home with him. I went home with him, and talked this whole matter over, and got his advice as to what course it was best for me to pursue. I found Sandy an old adviser. He told me, with great solemnity, I must go back to Covey; but that before I went, I must go with him into another part of the woods, where there was a certain *root,* which, if I would take some of it with me, carrying it *always on my right side,* would render it impossible for Mr. Covey, or any other white man, to whip me. He said he had carried it for years; and since he had done so, he had never received a blow, and never expected to while he carried it. I at first rejected the idea, that the simple carrying of a root in my pocket would have any such effect as he had said, and was not disposed to take it; but Sandy impressed the necessity with much earnestness, telling me it could do no harm, if it did no good. To please him, I at length took the root, and, according to his direction, carried it upon my right side. This was Sunday morning. I immediately started for home; and upon entering the yard gate, out came Mr. Covey on his way to meeting. He spoke to me very kindly, bade me drive the pigs from a lot near by, and passed on towards the church. Now, this singular conduct of Mr. Covey really made me begin to think that there was something in the *root* which Sandy had given me; and had it been on any other day than Sunday, I could have attributed the conduct to no other cause than the influence of that root; and as it was, I was half inclined to think the *root* to be something more than I at first had taken it to be. All went well till Monday morning. On this morning, the virtue of the *root* was fully tested. Long before daylight, I was called to go and rub, curry, and feed, the horses. I obeyed, and was glad to obey. But whilst thus engaged, whilst in the act of throwing down some blades from the loft, Mr. Covey entered the stable with a long rope; and just as I was half out of the loft, he caught hold of my legs, and was about tying me. As soon as I found what he was up to, I gave a sudden spring, and as I did so, he holding to my legs, I was brought sprawling on the stable floor. Mr. Covey seemed now to think he had me, and could do what he pleased; but at this moment—from whence came the spirit I don't know—I resolved to fight; and, suiting my action to the resolution, I seized Covey hard by the throat; and as I did so, I rose. He held on to me, and I to him. My resistance was so entirely unexpected, that Covey seemed taken all aback. He trembled like a leaf. This gave me assurance, and I held him uneasy, causing the blood to run where I touched him with the ends of my fingers. Mr. Covey soon called out to Hughes for help. Hughes came, and, while Covey held me, attempted to tie my right hand. While he was in the act of doing so, I watched my chance, and gave him a heavy kick close under the ribs. This kick fairly sickened Hughes, so that he left me in the hands of Mr. Covey. This kick had the effect of not only weakening Hughes, but Covey also. When he saw Hughes bending over with pain, his courage quailed. He asked me if I meant to persist in my resistance. I told him I did, come what might; that he had used me like a brute for six months, and that I was determined to be used so no longer. With that, he strove to drag me to a stick that was lying just out of the stable door. He meant to knock me down. But just as he was leaning over to get the stick, I seized him with both hands by his collar, and brought him by a sudden snatch to the ground. By this time, Bill came. Covey called upon him for assistance. Bill wanted to know what he could do. Covey said, "Take hold of him, take hold of him!" Bill said his master hired him out to work, and not to help to whip me; so he left Covey and myself to fight our own battle out. We were at it for nearly two hours. Covey at length let me go, puffing and blowing at a great rate, saying that if I had not resisted, he would not have whipped me half so much. The truth was, that he had not whipped me at all. I considered him as getting entirely the worst end of the bargain; for he had drawn no blood from me, but I had from him. The whole six months afterwards, that I spent with Mr. Covey, he never laid the weight of his finger upon me in anger. He would occasionally say, he didn't want to get hold of me again. "No," thought I, "you need not; for you will come off worse than you did before."

This battle with Mr. Covey was the turning-point in my career as a slave. It rekindled the few expiring embers of freedom, and revived within me a sense of my own manhood. It recalled the departed self-confidence, and inspired me again with a determination to be free. The gratification afforded by the triumph was a full compensation for whatever else might follow, even death itself. He only can understand the deep satisfaction which I experienced, who has himself repelled by force the bloody arm of slavery. I felt as I never felt before. It was a glorious resurrection, from the tomb of slavery, to the heaven of freedom. My long-crushed spirit rose, cowardice departed, bold defiance took its place; and I now resolved that, however long I might remain a slave in form, the day had passed forever when I could be a slave in fact. I did not hesitate to let it be known of me, that the white man who expected to succeed in whipping, must also succeed in killing me.

From this time I was never again what might be called fairly whipped, though I remained a slave four years afterwards. I had several fights, but was never whipped.

It was for a long time a matter of surprise to me why Mr. Covey did not immediately have me taken by the constable to the whipping-post, and there regularly whipped for the crime of raising my hand against a white man in defence of myself. And the only explanation I can now think of does not entirely satisfy me; but such as it is, I will give it. Mr. Covey enjoyed the most unbounded reputation for being a first-rate overseer and negro-breaker. It was of considerable importance to him. That reputation was at stake; and had he sent me—a boy about sixteen years old—to the public whipping-post, his reputation would have been lost; so, to save his reputation, he suffered me to go unpunished.

My term of actual service to Mr. Edward Covey ended on Christmas day, 1833. The days between Christmas and New Year's day are allowed as holidays; and, accordingly, we were not required to perform any labor, more than to feed and take care of the stock. This time we regarded as our own, by the grace of our masters; and we therefore used or abused it nearly as we pleased. Those of us who had families at a distance, were generally allowed to spend the whole six days in their society. This time, however, was spent in various ways. The staid, sober, thinking and industrious ones of our number would employ themselves in making corn-brooms, mats, horse-collars, and baskets; and another class of us would spend the time in hunting opossums, hares, and coons. But by far the larger part engaged in such sports and merriments as playing ball, wrestling, running foot-races, fiddling, dancing, and drinking whisky; and this latter mode of spending the time was by far the most agreeable to the feelings of our masters. A slave who would work during the holidays was considered by our masters as scarcely deserving them. He was regarded as one who rejected the favor of his master. It was deemed a disgrace not to get drunk at Christmas; and he was regarded as lazy indeed, who had not provided himself with the necessary means, during the year, to get whisky enough to last him through Christmas.

From what I know of the effect of these holidays upon the slave, I believe them to be among the most effective means in the hands of the slaveholder in keeping down the spirit of insurrection. Were the slaveholders at once to abandon this practice, I have not the slightest doubt it would lead to an immediate insurrection among the slaves. These holidays serve as conductors, or safety-valves, to carry off the rebellious spirit of enslaved humanity. But for these, the slave would be forced up to the wildest desperation; and woe betide the slaveholder, the day he ventures to remove or hinder the operation of those conductors! I warn him that, in such an event, a spirit will go forth in their midst, more to be dreaded than the most appalling earthquake.

The holidays are part and parcel of the gross fraud, wrong, and inhumanity of slavery. They are professedly a custom established by the benevolence of the slaveholders; but I undertake to say, it is the result of selfishness, and one of the grossest frauds committed upon the down-trodden slave. They do not give the slaves this time because they would not like to have their work during its continuance, but because they know it would be unsafe to deprive them of it. This will be seen by the fact, that the slaveholders like to have their slaves spend those days just in such a manner as to make them as glad of their ending as of their beginning. Their object seems to be, to disgust their slaves with freedom, by plunging them into the lowest depths of dissipation. For instance, the slaveholders not only like to see the slave drink of his own accord, but will adopt various plans to make him drunk. One plan is, to make bets on their slaves, as to who can drink the most whisky without getting drunk; and in this way they succeed in getting whole multitudes to drink to excess. Thus, when the slave asks for virtuous freedom, the cunning slave-holder, knowing his ignorance, cheats him with a dose of vicious dissipation, artfully labelled with the name of liberty. The most of us used to drink it down, and the result was just what might be supposed: many of us were led to think that there was little to choose between liberty and slavery. We felt, and very properly too, that we had almost as well be slaves to man as to rum. So, when the holidays ended, we staggered up from the filth of our wallowing, took a long breath, and marched to the field,—feeling, upon the whole, rather glad to go, from what our master had deceived us into a belief was freedom, back to the arms of slavery.

I have said that this mode of treatment is a part of the whole system of fraud and inhumanity of slavery. It is so. The mode here adopted to disgust the slave with freedom, by allowing him to see only the abuse of it, is carried out in other things. For instance, a slave loves molasses; he steals some. His master, in many cases, goes off to town, and buys a large quantity; he returns, takes his whip, and commands the slave to eat the molasses, until the poor fellow is made sick at the very mention of it. The same mode is sometimes adopted to make the slaves refrain from asking for more food than their regular allowance. A slave runs through his allowance, and applies for more. His master is enraged at him; but, not willing to send him off without food, gives him more than is necessary, and compels him to eat it within a given time. Then, if he complains that he cannot eat it, he is said to be satisfied neither full nor fasting, and is whipped for being hard to please! I have an abundance of such illustrations of the same principle, drawn from my own observation, but think the cases I have cited sufficient. The practice is a very common one.

On the first of January, 1834, I left Mr. Covey, and went to live with Mr. William Freeland, who lived about three miles from St. Michael's. I soon found Mr. Freeland a very different man from Mr. Covey. Though not rich, he was what would be called an educated southern gentleman. Mr. Covey, as I have shown, was a well-trained negro-breaker and slave driver. The former (slaveholder though he was) seemed to possess some regard for honor, some reverence for justice, and some respect for humanity. The latter seemed totally insensible to all such sentiments. Mr. Freeland had many of the faults peculiar to slaveholders, such as being very passionate and fretful; but I must do him the justice to say, that he was exceedingly free from those degrading vices to which Mr. Covey was constantly addicted. The one was open and frank and we always knew where to find him. The other was a most artful deceiver, and could be understood only by such as were skilful enough to detect his cunningly-devised frauds. Another advantage I gained in my new master was, he made no pretensions to, or profession of, religion; and this, in my opinion, was truly a great advantage. I assert most unhesitatingly, that the religion of the south is a mere covering for the most horrid crimes,—a justifier of the most appalling barbarity,—a sanctifier of the most hateful frauds,—and a dark shelter under, which the darkest, foulest, grossest, and most infernal deeds of slaveholders find the strongest protection. Were I to be again reduced to the chains of slavery, next to that enslavement, I should regard being the slave of a religious master the greatest calamity that could befall me. For of all slaveholders with whom I have ever met, religious slaveholders are the worst. I have ever found them the meanest and basest, the most cruel and cowardly, of all others. It was my unhappy lot not only to belong to a religious slaveholder, but to live in a community of such religionists. Very near Mr. Freeland lived the Rev. Daniel Weeden, and in the same neighborhood lived the Rev. Rigby Hopkins. These were members and ministers in the Reformed Methodist Church. Mr. Weeden owned, among others, a woman slave, whose name I have forgotten. This woman's back, for weeks, was kept literally raw, made so by the lash of this merciless, *religious* wretch. He used to hire hands. His maxim was, Behave well or behave ill, it is the duty of a master occasionally to whip a slave, to remind him of his master's authority. Such was his theory, and such his practice.

Mr. Hopkins was even worse than Mr. Weeden. His chief boast was his ability to manage slaves. The peculiar feature of his government was that of whipping slaves in advance of deserving it. He always managed to have one or more of his slaves to whip every Monday morning. He did this to alarm their fears, and strike terror into those who escaped. His plan was to whip for the smallest offences, to prevent the commission of large ones. Mr. Hopkins could always find some excuse for whipping a slave. It would astonish one, unaccustomed to a slaveholding life, to see with what wonderful ease a slaveholder can find things, of which to make occasion to whip a slave. A mere look, word, or motion,—a mistake, accident, or want of power,—are all matters for which a slave may be whipped at any time. Does a slave look dissatisfied? It is said, he has the devil in him, and it must be whipped out. Does he speak loudly when spoken to by his master? Then he is getting high-minded, and should be taken down a button-hole lower. Does he forget to pull off his hat at the approach of a white person? Then he is wanting in reverence, and should be whipped for it. Does he ever venture to vindicate his conduct, when censured for it? Then he is guilty of impudence,—one of the greatest crimes of which a slave can be guilty. Does he ever venture to suggest a different mode of doing things from that pointed out by his master? He is indeed presumptuous, and getting above himself; and nothing less than a flogging will do for him. Does he, while ploughing, break a plough,—or, while hoeing, break a hoe? It is owing to his carelessness, and for it a slave must always be whipped. Mr. Hopkins could always find something of this sort to justify the use of the lash, and he seldom failed to embrace such opportunities. There was not a man in the whole county, with whom the slaves who had the getting their own home, would not prefer to live, rather than with this Rev. Mr. Hopkins. And yet there was not a man any where round, who made higher professions of religion, or was more active in revivals,—more attentive to the class, love-feast, prayer and preaching meetings, or more devotional in his family,—that prayed earlier, later, louder, and longer,—than this same reverend slave-driver, Rigby Hopkins.

But to return to Mr. Freeland, and to my experience while in his employment. He, like Mr. Covey, gave us enough to eat; but, unlike Mr. Covey, he also gave us sufficient time to take our meals. He worked us hard, but always between sunrise and sunset. He required a good deal of work to be done, but gave us good tools with which to work. His farm was large, but he employed hands enough to work it, and with ease, compared with many of his neighbors. My treatment, while in his employment, was heavenly, compared with what I experienced at the hands of Mr. Edward Covey.

Mr. Freeland was himself the owner of but two slaves. Their names were Henry Harris and John Harris. The rest of his hands he hired. These consisted of myself, Sandy Jenkins,[4] and Handy Caldwell. Henry and John were quite intelligent, and in a very little while after I went there, I succeeded in creating in them a strong desire to learn how to read. This desire soon sprang up in the others also. They very soon mustered up some old spelling-books, and nothing would do but that I must keep a Sabbath school. I agreed to do so, and accordingly devoted my Sundays to teaching these my loved fellow-slaves how to read. Neither of them knew his letters when I went there. Some of the slaves of the neighboring farms found what was going on, and also availed themselves of this little opportunity to learn to read. It was understood, among all who came, that there must be as little display about it as possible. It was necessary to keep our religious masters at St. Michael's unacquainted with the fact, that, instead of spending the Sabbath in wrestling, boxing, and drinking whisky, we were trying to learn how to read the will of God; for they had much rather see us engaged in those degrading sports, than to see us behaving like intellectual, moral, and accountable beings. My blood boils as I think of the bloody manner in which Messrs. Wright Fairbanks and Garrison West, both class-leaders, in connection with many others, rushed in upon us with sticks and stones, and broke up our virtuous little Sabbath school, at St. Michael's—all calling themselves Christians! humble followers of the Lord Jesus Christ! But I am again digressing.

I held my Sabbath school at the house of a free colored man, whose name I deem it imprudent to mention; for should it be known, it might embarrass him greatly, though the crime of holding the school was committed ten years ago. I had at one time over forty scholars, and those of the right sort, ardently desiring to learn. They were of all ages, though mostly men and women. I look back to those Sundays with an amount of pleasure not to be expressed. They were great days to my soul. The work of instructing my dear fellow-slaves was the sweetest engagement with which I was ever blessed. We loved each other, and to leave them at the close of the Sabbath was a severe cross indeed. When I think that these precious souls are to-day shut up in the prison-house of slavery, my feelings overcome me, and I am almost ready to ask, "Does a righteous God govern the universe? and for what does he hold the thunders in his right hand, if not to smite the oppressor, and deliver the spoiled out of the hand of the spoiler?" These dear souls came not to Sabbath school because it was popular to do so, nor did I teach them because it was reputable to be thus engaged. Every moment they spent in that school, they were liable to be taken up, and given thirty-nine lashes. They came because they wished to learn. Their minds had been starved by their cruel masters. They had been shut up in mental darkness. I taught them, because it was the delight of my soul to be doing something that looked like bettering the condition of my race. I kept up my school nearly the whole year I lived with Mr. Freeland; and, beside my Sabbath school, I devoted three evenings in the week, during the winter, to teaching the slaves at home. And I have the happiness to know, that several

---

4. This is the same man who gave me the roots to prevent my being whipped by Mr. Covey. He was "a clever soul." We used frequently to talk about the fight with Covey, and as often as we did so, he would claim my success as the result of the roots which he gave me. This superstition is very common among the more ignorant slaves. A slave seldom dies but that his death is attributed to trickery [Douglass's note].

of those who came to Sabbath school learned how to read; and that one, at least, is now free through my agency.

The year passed off smoothly. It seemed only about half as long as the year which preceded it. I went through it without receiving a single blow. I will give Mr. Freeland the credit of being the best master I ever had, *till I became my own master.* For the ease with which I passed the year, I was, however, somewhat indebted to the society of my fellow-slaves. They were noble souls; they not only possessed loving hearts, but brave ones. We were linked and interlinked with each other. I loved them with a love stronger than any thing I have experienced since. It is sometimes said that we slaves do not love and confide in each other. In answer to this assertion, I can say, I never loved any or confided in any people more than my fellow-slaves, and especially those with whom I lived at Mr. Freeland's. I believe we would have died for each other. We never undertook to do any thing, of any importance, without a mutual consultation. We never moved separately. We were one; and as much so by our tempers and dispositions, as by the mutual hardships to which we were necessarily subjected by our condition as slaves.

At the close of the year 1834, Mr. Freeland again hired me of my master, for the year 1835. But, by this time, I began to want to live *upon free land* as well as *with Freeland;* and I was no longer content, therefore, to live with him or any other slave-holder. I began, with the commencement of the year, to prepare myself for a final struggle, which should decide my fate one way or the other. My tendency was upward. I was fast approaching manhood, and year after year had passed, and I was still a slave. These thoughts roused me—I must do something. I therefore resolved that 1835 should not pass without witnessing an attempt, on my part, to secure my liberty. But I was not willing to cherish this determination alone. My fellow-slaves were dear to me. I was anxious to have them participate with me in this, my life-giving determination. I therefore, though with great prudence, commenced early to ascertain their views and feelings in regard to their condition, and to imbue their minds with thoughts of freedom. I bent myself to devising ways and means for our escape, and mean-while strove, on all fitting occasions, to impress them with the gross fraud and inhumanity of slavery. I went first to Henry, next to John, then to the others. I found, in them all, warm hearts and noble spirits. They were ready to hear, and ready to act when a feasible plan should be proposed. This was what I wanted. I talked to them of our want of manhood, if we submitted to our enslavement without at least one noble effort to be free. We met often, and consulted frequently, and told our hopes and fears, recounted the difficulties, real and imagined, which we should be called on to meet. At times we were almost disposed to give up, and try to content ourselves with our wretched lot; at others, we were firm and unbending in our determination to go. Whenever we suggested any plan, there was shrinking—the odds were fearful. Our path was beset with the greatest obstacles; and if we succeeded in gaining the end of it, our right to be free was yet questionable—we were yet liable to be returned to bondage. We could see no spot, this side of the ocean, where we could be free. We knew nothing about Canada. Our knowledge of the north did not extend farther than New York; and to go there, and be forever harassed with the frightful liability of being returned to slavery—with the certainty of being treated ten-fold worse than before—the thought was truly a horrible one, and one which it was not easy to overcome. The case sometimes stood thus: At every gate through which we were to pass, we saw a watchman—at every ferry a guard—on every bridge a sentinel—and in every wood a patrol. We were hemmed in upon every side. Here were the difficulties, real or imagined—the good to be sought, and the evil to be shunned. On the one hand, there stood slavery, a stern reality, glaring frightfully upon us,—its robes already crimsoned with the blood of millions, and even now feasting itself greedily upon our own flesh. On the other hand, away back in the dim distance, under the flickering light of the north star, behind some craggy hill or snow-covered mountain, stood a doubtful freedom—half frozen—beckoning us to come and share its hospitality. This in itself was sometimes enough to stagger us; but when we permitted ourselves to survey the road, we were frequently appalled. Upon either side we saw grim death, assuming the most horrid shapes. Now it was starvation, causing us to eat our own flesh;—now we were contending with the waves, and were drowned;—now we were overtaken, and torn to pieces by the fangs of the terrible bloodhound. We were stung by scorpions, chased by wild beasts, bitten by snakes, and finally, after having nearly reached the desired spot,—after swimming rivers, encountering wild beasts, sleeping in the woods, suffering hunger and nakedness,—we were overtaken by our pursuers, and, in our resistance, we were shot dead upon the spot! I say, this picture sometimes appalled us, and made us

> rather bear those ills we had,
> Than fly to others, that we knew not of.[5]

In coming to a fixed determination to run away, we did more than Patrick Henry, when he resolved upon liberty or death. With us it was a doubtful liberty at most, and almost certain death if we failed. For my part, I should prefer death to hopeless bondage.

Sandy, one of our number, gave up the notion, but still encouraged us. Our company then consisted of Henry Harris, John Harris, Henry Bailey, Charles Roberts, and myself. Henry Bailey was my uncle, and belonged to my master. Charles married my aunt: he belonged to my master's father-in-law, Mr. William Hamilton.

The plan we finally concluded upon was, to get a large canoe belonging to Mr. Hamilton, and upon the Saturday night previous to Easter holidays, paddle directly up the Chesapeake Bay. On our arrival at the head of the bay, a distance of seventy or eighty miles from where we lived, it was our purpose to turn our canoe adrift, and follow the guidance of the north star till we got beyond the limits of Maryland. Our reason for taking the water route was, that we were less liable to be suspected as runaways; we hoped to be regarded as fishermen; whereas, if we should take the land route, we should be subjected to interruptions of almost every kind. Any one having a white face, and being so disposed, could stop us, and subject us to examination.

The week before our intended start, I wrote several protections, one for each of us. As well as I can remember, they were in the following words, to wit:—

This is to certify that I, the undersigned, have given the bearer, my servant, full liberty to go to Baltimore, and spend the Easter holidays. Written with mine own hand, &c., 1835.

William Hamilton,

Near St. Michael's, in Talbot county, Maryland.

We were not going to Baltimore; but, in going up the bay, we went toward Baltimore, and these protections were only intended to protect us while on the bay.

As the time drew near for our departure, our anxiety became more and more intense. It was truly a matter of life and death with us. The strength of our determination was about to be fully tested. At this time, I was very active in explaining every difficulty, removing every doubt, dispelling every fear, and inspiring all with the

5. William Shakespeare, *Hamlet*, 3.1.

firmness indispensable to success in our undertaking; assuring them that half was gained the instant we made the move; we had talked long enough; we were now ready to move; if not now, we never should be; and if we did not intend to move now, we had as well fold our arms, sit down, and acknowledge ourselves fit only to be slaves. This, none of us were prepared to acknowledge. Every man stood firm; and at our last meeting, we pledged ourselves afresh, in the most solemn manner, that, at the time appointed, we would certainly start in pursuit of freedom. This was in the middle of the week, at the end of which we were to be off. We went, as usual, to our several fields of labor, but with bosoms highly agitated with thoughts of our truly hazardous undertaking. We tried to conceal our feelings as much as possible; and I think we succeeded very well.

After a painful waiting, the Saturday morning, whose night was to witness our departure, came. I hailed it with joy, bring what of sadness it might. Friday night was a sleepless one for me. I probably felt more anxious than the rest, because I was, by common consent, at the head of the whole affair. The responsibility of success or failure lay heavily upon me. The glory of the one, and the confusion of the other, were alike mine. The first two hours of that morning were such as I never experienced before, and hope never to again. Early in the morning, we went, as usual, to the field. We were spreading manure; and all at once, while thus engaged, I was overwhelmed with an indescribable feeling, in the fulness of which I turned to Sandy, who was near by, and said, "We are betrayed!" "Well," said he, "that thought has this moment struck me." We said no more. I was never more certain of any thing.

The horn was blown as usual, and we went up from the field to the house for breakfast. I went for the form, more than for want of any thing to eat that morning. Just as I got to the house, in looking out at the lane gate, I saw four white men, with two colored men. The white men were on horse-back, and the colored ones were walking behind, as if tied. I watched them a few moments till they got up to our lane gate. Here they halted, and tied the colored men to the gatepost. I was not yet certain as to what the matter was. In a few moments, in rode Mr. Hamilton, with a speed betokening great excitement. He came to the door, and inquired if Master William was in. He was told he was at the barn. Mr. Hamilton, without dismounting, rode up to the barn with extraordinary speed. In a few moments, he and Mr. Freeland returned to the house. By this time, the three constables rode up, and in great haste dismounted, tied their horses, and met Master William and Mr. Hamilton returning from the barn; and after talking awhile, they all walked up to the kitchen door. There was no one in the kitchen but myself and John. Henry and Sandy were up at the barn. Mr. Freeland put his head in at the door, and called me by name, saying, there were some gentlemen at the door who wished to see me. I stepped to the door, and inquired what they wanted. They at once seized me, and, without giving me any satisfaction, tied me—lashing my hands closely together. I insisted upon knowing what the matter was. They at length said, that they had learned I had been in a "scrape," and that I was to be examined before my master; and if their information proved false, I should not be hurt.

In a few moments, they succeeded in tying John. They then turned to Henry, who had by this time returned, and commanded him to cross his hands. "I won't!" said Henry, in a firm tone, indicating his readiness to meet the consequences of his refusal. "Won't you?" said Tom Graham, the constable. "No, I won't!" said Henry, in a still stronger tone. With this, two of the constables pulled out their shining pistols, and swore, by their Creator, that they would make him cross his hands or kill him. Each cocked his pistol, and, with fingers on the trigger, walked up to Henry, saying, at the same time, if he did not cross his hands, they would blow his damned heart out. "Shoot me, shoot me!" said Henry; "you can't kill me but once. Shoot, shoot,—and be damned! *I won't be tied!*" This he said in a tone of loud defiance; and at the same time, with a motion as quick as lightning, he with one single stroke dashed the pistols from the hand of each constable. As he did this, all hands fell upon him, and, after beating him some time, they finally overpowered him, and got him tied.

During the scuffle, I managed, I know not how, to get my pass out, and, without being discovered, put it into the fire. We were all now tied; and just as we were to leave for Easton jail, Betsy Freeland, mother of William Freeland, came to the door with her hands full of biscuits, and divided them between Henry and John. She then delivered herself of a speech, to the following effect:—addressing herself to me, she said, "*You devil! You yellow devil!* it was you that put it into the heads of Henry and John to run away. But for you, you longlegged mulatto devil! Henry nor John would never have thought of such a thing." I made no reply, and was immediately hurried off towards St. Michael's. Just a moment previous to the scuffle with Henry, Mr. Hamilton suggested the propriety of making a search for the protections which he had understood Frederick had written for himself and the rest. But, just at the moment he was about carrying his proposal into effect, his aid was needed in helping to tie Henry; and the excitement attending the scuffle caused them either to forget, or to deem it unsafe, under the circumstances, to search. So we were not yet convicted of the intention to run away.

When we got about half way to St. Michael's, while the constables having us in charge were looking ahead, Henry inquired of me what he should do with his pass. I told him to eat it with his biscuit, and own nothing; and we passed the word around, "*Own nothing;*" and "*Own nothing!*" said we all. Our confidence in each other was unshaken. We were resolved to succeed or fail together, after the calamity had befallen us as much as before. We were now prepared for any thing. We were to be dragged that morning fifteen miles behind horses, and then to be placed in the Easton jail. When we reached St. Michael's, we underwent a sort of examination. We all denied that we ever intended to run away. We did this more to bring out the evidence against us, than from any hope of getting clear of being sold; for, as I have said, we were ready for that. The fact was, we cared but little where we went, so we went together. Our greatest concern was about separation. We dreaded that more than any thing this side of death. We found the evidence against us to be the testimony of one person; our master would not tell who it was; but we came to a unanimous decision among ourselves as to who their informant was. We were sent off to the jail at Easton. When we got there, we were delivered up to the sheriff, Mr. Joseph Graham, and by him placed in jail. Henry, John, and myself, were placed in one room together—Charles, and Henry Bailey, in another. Their object in separating us was to hinder concert.

We had been in jail scarcely twenty minutes, when a swarm of slave traders, and agents for slave traders, flocked into jail to look at us, and to ascertain if we were for sale. Such a set of beings I never saw before! I felt myself surrounded by so many fiends from perdition. A band of pirates never looked more like their father, the devil. They laughed and grinned over us, saying, "Ah, my boys! we have got you, haven't we?" And after taunting us in various ways, they one by one went into an examination of us, with intent to ascertain our value. They would impudently ask us if we would not like to have them for our masters. We would make them no answer, and leave them to find out as best they could. Then they would curse and swear at us, telling us that they could take the devil out of us in a very little while, if we were only in their hands.

While in jail, we found ourselves in much more comfortable quarters than we expected when we went there. We did not get much to eat, nor that which was very good; but we had a good clean room, from the windows of which we could see what was going on in the street, which was very much better than though we had been placed in one of the dark, damp cells. Upon the whole, we got along very well, so far as the jail and its keeper were concerned. Immediately after the holidays were over, contrary to all our expectations, Mr. Hamilton and Mr. Freeland came up to Easton, and took Charles, the two Henrys, and John, out of jail, and carried them home, leaving me alone. I regarded this separation as a final one. It caused me more pain than any thing else in the whole transaction. I was ready for any thing rather than separation. I supposed that they had consulted together, and had decided that, as I was the whole cause of the intention of the others to run away, it was hard to make the innocent suffer with the guilty; and that they had, therefore, concluded to take the others home, and sell me, as a warning to the others that remained. It is due to the noble Henry to say, he seemed almost as reluctant at leaving the prison as at leaving home to come to the prison. But we knew we should, in all probability, be separated, if we were sold; and since he was in their hands, he concluded to go peaceably home.

I was now left to my fate. I was all alone, and within the walls of a stone prison. But a few days before, and I was full of hope. I expected to have been safe in a land of freedom; but now I was covered with gloom, sunk down to the utmost despair. I thought the possibility of freedom was gone. I was kept in this way about one week, at the end of which, Captain Auld, my master, to my surprise and utter astonishment, came up, and took me out, with the intention of sending me, with a gentleman of his acquaintance, into Alabama. But, from some cause or other, he did not send me to Alabama, but concluded to send me back to Baltimore, to live again with his brother Hugh, and to learn a trade.

Thus, after an absence of three years and one month, I was once more permitted to return to my old home at Baltimore. My master sent me away, because there existed against me a very great prejudice in the community, and he feared I might be killed.

In a few weeks after I went to Baltimore, Master Hugh hired me to Mr. William Gardner, an extensive ship-builder, on Fell's Point. I was put there to learn how to calk. It, however, proved a very unfavorable place for the accomplishment of this object. Mr. Gardner was engaged that spring in building two large map-of-war brigs, professedly for the Mexican government. The vessels were to be launched in the July of that year, and in failure thereof, Mr. Gardner was to lose a considerable sum; so that when I entered, all was hurry. There was no time to learn any thing. Every man had to do that which he knew how to do. In entering the ship-yard, my orders from Mr. Gardner were, to do whatever the carpenters commanded me to do. This was placing me at the beck and call of about seventy-five men. I was to regard all these as masters. Their word was to be my law. My situation was a most trying one. At times I needed a dozen pair of hands. I was called a dozen ways in the space of a single minute. Three or four voices would strike my ear at the same moment. It was—"Fred., come help me to cant this timber here."—"Fred., come carry this timber yonder."—"Fred., bring that roller here."—"Fred., go get a fresh can of water."—"Fred., come help saw off the end of this timber."—"Fred., go quick, and get the crowbar."—"Fred., hold on the end of this fall."—"Fred., go to the blacksmith's shop, and get a new punch."—"Hurra, Fred.! run and bring me a cold chisel."—"I say, Fred., bear a hand, and get up a fire as quick as lightning under that steam-box."—"Halloo, nigger!

come, turn this grindstone."—"Come, come! move, move! and *bowse* this timber forward."—"I say, darky, blast your eyes, why don't you heat up some pitch?"—"Halloo! halloo! halloo!" (Three voices at the same time.) "Come here!—Go there!—Hold on where you are! Damn you, if you move, I'll knock your brains out!"

This was my school for eight months; and I might have remained there longer, but for a most horrid fight I had with four of the white apprentices, in which my left eye was nearly knocked out, and I was horribly mangled in other respects. The facts in the case were these: Until a very little while after I went there, white and black ship-carpenters worked side by side, and no one seemed to see any impropriety in it. All hands seemed to be very well satisfied. Many of the black carpenters were freemen. Things seemed to be going on very well. All at once, the white carpenters knocked off, and said they would not work with free colored workmen. Their reason for this, as alleged, was, that if free colored carpenters were encouraged, they would soon take the trade into their own hands, and poor white men would be thrown out of employment. They therefore felt called upon at once to put a stop to it. And, taking advantage of Mr. Gardner's necessities, they broke off, swearing they would work no longer, unless he would discharge his black carpenters. Now, though this did not extend to me in form, it did reach me in fact. My fellow-apprentices very soon began to feel it degrading to them to work with me. They began to put on airs, and talk about the "niggers" taking the country, saying we all ought to be killed; and, being encouraged by the journeymen, they commenced making my condition as hard as they could, by hectoring me around, and sometimes striking me. I, of course, kept the vow I made after the fight with Mr. Covey, and struck back again, regardless of consequences; and while I kept them from combining, I succeeded very well; for I could whip the whole of them, taking them separately. They, however, at length combined, and came upon me, armed with sticks, stones, and heavy handspikes. One came in front with a half brick. There was one at each side of me, and one behind me. While I was attending to those in front, and on either side, the one behind ran up with the handspike, and struck me a heavy blow upon the head. It stunned me. I fell, and with this they all ran upon me, and fell to beating me with their fists. I let them lay on for a while, gathering strength. In an instant, I gave a sudden surge, and rose to my hands and knees. Just as I did that, one of their number gave me, with his heavy boot, a powerful kick in the left eye. My eyeball seemed to have burst. When they saw my eye closed, and badly swollen, they left me. With this I seized the handspike, and for a time pursued them. But here the carpenters interfered, and I thought I might as well give it up. It was impossible to stand my hand against so many. All this took place in sight of not less than fifty white ship-carpenters, and not one interposed a friendly word; but some cried, "Kill the damned nigger! Kill him! kill him! He struck a white person." I found my only chance for life was in flight. I succeeded in getting away without an additional blow, and barely so; for to strike a white man is death by Lynch law,—and that was the law in Mr. Gardner's ship-yard; nor is there much of any other out of Mr. Gardner's ship-yard.

I went directly home, and told the story of my wrongs to Master Hugh; and I am happy to say of him, irreligious as he was, his conduct was heavenly, compared with that of his brother Thomas under similar circumstances. He listened attentively to my narration of the circumstances leading to the savage outrage, and gave many proofs of his strong indignation at it. The heart of my once overkind mistress was again melted into pity. My puffed-out eye and blood-covered face moved her to tears. She took a chair by me, washed the blood from my face, and, with a mother's tenderness, bound up my head, covering the wounded eye with a lean piece of fresh beef. It was almost compensation for my suffering to witness, once more, a manifestation of kindness from this, my once affectionate old mistress. Master Hugh was very much enraged. He gave expression to his feelings by pouring out curses upon the heads of those who did the deed. As soon as I got a little the better of my bruises, he took me with him to Esquire Watson's, on Bond Street, to see what could be done about the matter. Mr. Watson inquired who saw the assault committed. Master Hugh told him it was done in Mr. Gardner's ship-yard, at mid-day, where there were a large company of men at work. "As to that," he said, "the deed was done, and there was no question as to who did it." His answer was, he could do nothing in the case, unless some white man would come forward and testify. He could issue no warrant on my word. If I had been killed in the presence of a thousand colored people, their testimony combined would have been insufficient to have arrested one of the murderers. Master Hugh, for once, was compelled to say this state of things was too bad. Of course, it was impossible to get any white man to volunteer his testimony in my behalf, and against the white young men. Even those who may have sympathized with me were not prepared to do this. It required a degree of courage unknown to them to do so; for just at that time, the slightest manifestation of humanity toward a colored person was denounced as abolitionism, and that name subjected its bearer to frightful liabilities. The watch-words of the bloody-minded in that region, and in those days, were, "Damn the abolitionists!" and "Damn the niggers!" There was nothing done, and probably nothing would have been done if I had been killed. Such was, and such remains, the state of things in the Christian city of Baltimore.

Master Hugh, finding he could get no redress, refused to let me go back again to Mr. Gardner. He kept me himself, and his wife dressed my wound till I was again restored to health. He then took me into the ship-yard of which he was foreman, in the employment of Mr. Walter Price. There I was immediately set to calking, and very soon learned the art of using my mallet and irons. In the course of one year from the time I left Mr. Gardner's, I was able to command the highest wages given to the most experienced calkers. I was now of some importance to my master. I was bringing him from six to seven dollars per week. I sometimes brought him nine dollars per week: my wages were a dollar and a half a day. After learning how to calk, I sought my own employment, made my own contracts, and collected the money which I earned. My pathway became much more smooth than before; my condition was now much more comfortable. When I could get no calking to do, I did nothing. During these leisure times, those old notions about freedom would steal over me again. When in Mr. Gardner's employment, I was kept in such a perpetual whirl of excitement, I could think of nothing, scarcely, but my life; and in thinking of my life, I almost forgot my liberty. I have observed this in my experience of slavery,—that whenever my condition was improved, instead of its increasing my contentment, it only increased my desire to be free, and set me to thinking of plans to gain my freedom. I have found that, to make a contented slave, it is necessary to make a thoughtless one. It is necessary to darken his moral and mental vision, and, as far as possible, to annihilate the power of reason. He must be able to detect no inconsistencies in slavery; he must be made to feel that slavery is right; and he can be brought to that only when he ceases to be a man.

I was now getting, as I have said, one dollar and fifty cents per day. I contracted for it; I earned it; it was paid to me; it was rightfully my own; yet, upon each returning Saturday night, I was compelled to deliver every cent of that money to Master Hugh. And why? Not because he earned it,—not because he had any hand in earning it,—not because I owed it to him,—nor because he possessed the slightest shadow of a right to it; but solely because he had the power to compel me to give it up. The right of the grim-visaged pirate upon the high seas is exactly the same.

CHAPTER 11

I now come to that part of my life during which I planned, and finally succeeded in making, my escape from slavery. But before narrating any of the peculiar circumstances, I deem it proper to make known my intention not to state all the facts connected with the transaction. My reasons for pursuing this course may be understood from the following: First, were I to give a minute statement of all the facts, it is not only possible, but quite probable, that others would thereby be involved in the most embarrassing difficulties. Secondly, such a statement would most undoubtedly induce greater vigilance on the part of slaveholders than has existed heretofore among them; which would, of course, be the means of guarding a door whereby some dear brother bondman might escape his galling chains. I deeply regret the necessity that impels me to suppress any thing of importance connected with my experience in slavery. It would afford me great pleasure indeed, as well as materially add to the interest of my narrative, were I at liberty to gratify a curiosity, which I know exists in the minds of many, by an accurate statement of all the facts pertaining to my most fortunate escape. But I must deprive myself of this pleasure, and the curious of the gratification which such a statement would afford. I would allow myself to suffer under the greatest imputations which evil-minded men might suggest, rather than exculpate myself, and thereby run the hazard of closing the slightest avenue by which a brother slave might clear himself of the chains and fetters of slavery.

I have never approved of the very public manner in which some of our western friends have conducted what they call the *underground railroad,* but which, I think, by their open declarations, has been made most emphatically the *upperground railroad.* I honor those good men and women for their noble daring, and applaud them for willingly subjecting themselves to bloody persecution, by openly avowing their participation in the escape of slaves. I, however, can see very little good resulting from such a course, either to themselves or the slaves escaping; while, upon the other hand, I see and feel assured that those open declarations are a positive evil to the slaves remaining, who are seeking to escape. They do nothing towards enlightening the slave, whilst they do much towards enlightening the master. They stimulate him to greater watchfulness, and enhance his power to capture his slave. We owe something to the slaves south of the line as well as to those north of it; and in aiding the latter on their way to freedom, we should be careful to do nothing which would be likely to hinder the former from escaping from slavery. I would keep the merciless slaveholder profoundly ignorant of the means of flight adopted by the slave. I would leave him to imagine himself surrounded by myriads of invisible tormentors, ever ready to snatch from his infernal grasp his trembling prey. Let him be left to feel his way in the dark; let darkness commensurate with his crime hover over him; and let him feel that at every step he takes, in pursuit of the flying bondman, he is running the frightful risk of having his hot brains dashed out by an invisible agency. Let us render the tyrant no aid; let us not hold the light by which he can trace the footprints of our flying brother. But enough of this. I will now proceed to the statement of those facts, connected with my escape, for which I am alone responsible, and for which no one can be made to suffer but myself.

In the early part of the year 1838, I became quite restless. I could see no reason why I should, at the end of each week, pour the reward of my toil into the purse of my master. When I carried to him my weekly wages, he would, after counting the money, look me in the face with a robber-like fierceness, and ask, "Is this all?" He was satisfied with nothing less than the last cent. He would, however, when I made him six dollars, sometimes give me six cents, to encourage me. It had the opposite effect. I regarded it as a sort of admission of my right to the whole. The fact that he gave me any part of my wages was proof, to my mind, that he believed me entitled to the whole of them. I always felt worse for having received any thing; for I feared that the giving me a few cents would ease his conscience, and make him feel himself to be a pretty honorable sort of robber. My discontent grew upon me. I was ever on the look-out for means of escape; and, finding no direct means, I determined to try to hire my time, with a view of getting money with which to make my escape. In the spring of 1838, when Master Thomas came to Baltimore to purchase his spring goods, I got an opportunity, and applied to him to allow me to hire my time. He unhesitatingly refused my request, and told me this was another stratagem by which to escape. He told me I could go nowhere but that he could get me; and that, in the event of my running away, he should spare no pains in his efforts to catch me. He exhorted me to content myself, and be obedient. He told me, if I would be happy, I must lay out no plans for the future. He said, if I behaved myself properly, he would take care of me. Indeed, he advised me to complete thoughtlessness of the future, and taught me to depend solely upon him for happiness. He seemed to see fully the pressing necessity of setting aside my intellectual nature, in order to contentment in slavery. But in spite of him, and even in spite of myself, I continued to think, and to think about the injustice of my enslavement, and the means of escape.

About two months after this, I applied to Master Hugh for the privilege of hiring my time. He was not acquainted with the fact that I had applied to Master Thomas, and had been refused. He too, at first, seemed disposed to refuse; but, after some reflection, he granted me the privilege, and proposed the following terms: I was to be allowed all my time, make all contracts with those for whom I worked, and find my own employment; and, in return for this liberty, I was to pay him three dollars at the end of each week; find myself in calking tools, and in board and clothing. My board was two dollars and a half per week. This, with the wear and tear of clothing and calking tools, made my regular expenses about six dollars per week. This amount I was compelled to make up, or relinquish the privilege of hiring my time. Rain or shine, work or no work, at the end of each week the money must be forthcoming, or I must give up my privilege. This arrangement, it will be perceived, was decidedly in my master's favor. It relieved him of all need of looking after me. His money was sure. He received all the benefits of slaveholding without its evils; while I endured all the evils of a slave, and suffered all the care and anxiety of a freeman. I found it a hard bargain. But, hard as it was, I thought it better than the old mode of getting along. It was a step towards freedom to be allowed to bear the responsibilities of a freeman, and I was determined to hold on upon it. I bent myself to the work of making money. I was ready to work at night as well as day, and by the most untiring perseverance and industry, I made enough to meet my expenses, and lay up a little money every week. I went on thus from May till August. Master Hugh then refused to allow me to hire my time longer. The ground for his refusal was a failure on my part, one Saturday night, to pay him for my week's time. This failure was occasioned by my attending a camp meeting about ten miles from Baltimore. During the week, I had entered into an engagement with a number of young friends to start from Baltimore to the camp ground early Saturday evening; and being detained by my employer, I was unable to get down to Master Hugh's without disappointing the company. I knew that Master Hugh was in no special need of the money that night. I therefore decided to go to camp meeting, and upon my return pay him the three dollars. I staid at the camp meeting one day longer than I intended when I left. But as soon as I returned, I called upon him to pay him what he considered his due. I found him very angry; he could scarce restrain his wrath. He said he had a great mind to give me a severe whipping. He wished to know how I dared go out of the city without asking his permission. I told him I hired my time, and while I paid him the price which he asked for it, I did not know that I was bound to ask him when and where I should go. This reply troubled him; and, after reflecting a few moments, he turned to me, and said I should hire my time no longer; that the next thing he should know of, I would be running away. Upon the same plea, he told me to bring my tools and clothing home forthwith. I did so; but instead of seeking work, as I had been accustomed to do previously to hiring my time, I spent the whole week without the performance of a single stroke of work. I did this in retaliation. Saturday night, he called upon me as usual for my week's wages. I told him I had no wages; I had done no work that week. Here we were upon the point of coming to blows. He raved, and swore his determination to get hold of me. I did not allow myself a single word; but was resolved, if he laid the weight of his hand upon me, it should be blow for blow. He did not strike me, but told me that he would find me in constant employment in future. I thought the matter over during the next day, Sunday, and finally resolved upon the third day of September, as the day upon which I would make a second attempt to secure my freedom. I now had three weeks during which to prepare for my journey. Early on Monday morning, before Master Hugh had time to make any engagement for me, I went out and got employment of Mr. Butler, at his ship-yard near the drawbridge, upon what is called the City Block, thus making it unnecessary for him to seek employment for me. At the end of the week, I brought him between eight and nine dollars. He seemed very well pleased, and asked me why I did not do the same the week before. He little knew what my plans were. My object in working steadily was to remove any suspicion he might entertain of my intent to run away; and in this I succeeded admirably. I suppose he thought I was never better satisfied with my condition than at the very time during which I was planning my escape. The second week passed, and again I carried him my full wages; and so well pleased was he, that he gave me twenty-five cents, (quite a large sum for a slave-holder to give a slave,) and bade me to make a good use of it. I told him I would.

Things went on without very smoothly indeed, but within there was trouble. It is impossible for me to describe my feelings as the time of my contemplated start drew near. I had a number of warm-hearted friends in Baltimore,—friends that I loved almost as I did my life,—and the thought of being separated from them forever was painful beyond expression. It is my opinion that thousands would escape from slavery, who now remain, but for the strong cords of affection that bind them to their friends. The thought of leaving my friends was decidedly the most painful thought with which I had to contend. The love of them was my tender point, and shook my decision more than all things else. Besides the pain of separation, the dread and apprehension of a failure exceeded what I had experienced at my first attempt. The appalling defeat I then sustained returned to torment me. I felt assured that, if I failed in this attempt, my case would be a hopeless one—it would seal my fate as a slave forever. I could not hope to get off with any thing less than the severest punishment, and being placed beyond the means of escape. It required no very vivid imagination to depict the most frightful scenes through which I should have to pass, in case I failed. The wretchedness of slavery, and the blessedness of freedom, were perpetually before me. It was life and death with me. But I remained firm, and, according to my resolution, on the third day of September, 1838, I left my chains, and succeeded in reaching New York without the slightest interruption of any kind. How I did so,—what means I adopted,—what direction I travelled, and by what mode of conveyance,—I must leave unexplained, for the reasons before mentioned.

I have been frequently asked how I felt when I found myself in a free State. I have never been able to answer the question with any satisfaction to myself. It was a moment of the highest excitement I ever experienced. I suppose I felt as one may imagine the unarmed mariner to feel when he is rescued by a friendly man-of-war from the pursuit of a pirate. In writing to a dear friend, immediately after my arrival at New York, I said I felt like one who had escaped a den of hungry lions. This state of mind, however, very soon subsided; and I was again seized with a feeling of great insecurity and loneliness. I was yet liable to be taken back, and subjected to all the tortures of slavery. This in itself was enough to damp the ardor of my enthusiasm. But the loneliness overcame me. There I was in the midst of thousands, and yet a perfect stranger; without home and without friends, in the midst of thousands of my own brethren—children of a common Father, and yet I dared not to unfold to any one of them my sad condition. I was afraid to speak to any one for fear of speaking to the wrong one, and thereby falling into the hands of money-loving kidnappers, whose business it was to lie in wait for the panting fugitive, as the ferocious beasts of the forest lie in wait for their prey. The motto which I adopted when I started from slavery was this—"Trust no man!" I saw in every white man an enemy, and in almost every colored man cause for distrust. It was a most painful situation; and, to understand it, one must needs experience it, or imagine himself in similar circumstances. Let him be a fugitive slave in a strange land—a land given up to be the hunting-ground for slave holders—whose inhabitants are legalized kidnappers—where he is every moment subjected to the terrible liability of being seized upon by his fellow-men, as the hideous crocodile seizes upon his prey!—I say, let him place himself in my situation—without home or friends—without money or credit—wanting shelter, and no one to give it—wanting bread, and no money to buy it,—and at the same time let him feel that he is pursued by merciless men-hunters, and in total darkness as to what to do, where to go, or where to stay,—perfectly helpless both as to the means of defence and means of escape,—in the midst of plenty, yet suffering the terrible gnawings of hunger,—in the midst of houses, yet having no home,—among fellow-men, yet feeling as if in the midst of wild beasts, whose greediness to swallow up the trembling and half-famished fugitive is only equalled by that with which the monsters of the deep swallow up the helpless fish upon which they subsist,—I say, let him be placed in this most trying situation,—the situation in which I was placed,—then, and not till then, will he fully appreciate the hardships of, and know how to sympathize with, the toil-worn and whip-scarred fugitive slave.

Thank Heaven, I remained but a short time in this distressed situation. I was relieved from it by the humane hand of Mr. David Ruggles, whose vigilance, kindness, and perseverance, I shall never forget. I am glad of an opportunity to express, as far as words can, the love and gratitude I bear him. Mr. Ruggles is now afflicted with blindness, and is himself in need of the same kind offices which he was once so forward in the performance of toward others. I had been in New York but a few days, when Mr.

Ruggles sought me out, and very kindly took me to his boarding-house at the corner of Church and Lespenard Streets. Mr. Ruggles was then very deeply engaged in the memorable *Darg* case, as well as attending to a number of other fugitive slaves, devising ways and means for their successful escape; and, though watched and hemmed in on almost every side, he seemed to be more than a match for his enemies.

Very soon after I went to Mr. Ruggles, he wished to know of me where I wanted to go; as he deemed it unsafe for me to remain in New York. I told him I was a calker, and should like to go where I could get work. I thought of going to Canada; but he decided against it, and in favor of my going to New Bedford, thinking I should be able to get work there at my trade. At this time, Anna,[6] my intended wife, came on; for I wrote to her immediately after my arrival at New York, (not-withstanding my homeless, houseless, and helpless condition,) informing her of my successful flight, and wishing her to come on forthwith. In a few days after her arrival, Mr. Ruggles called in the Rev. J. W. C. Pennington, who, in the presence of Mr. Ruggles, Mrs. Michaels, and two or three others, performed the marriage ceremony, and gave us a certificate, of which the following is an exact copy:—

> This may certify, that I joined together in holy matrimony Frederick Johnson[7] and Anna Murray, as man and wife, in the presence of Mr. David Ruggles and Mrs. Michaels.
>
> James W. C. Pennington.
>
> New York, Sept. 15, 1838.

Upon receiving this certificate, and a five-dollar bill from Mr. Ruggles, I shouldered one part of our baggage, and Anna took up the other, and we set out forthwith to take passage on board of the steamboat John W. Richmond for Newport, on our way to New Bedford. Mr. Ruggles gave me a letter to a Mr. Shaw in Newport, and told me, in case my money did not serve me to New Bedford, to stop in Newport and obtain further assistance; but upon our arrival at Newport, we were so anxious to get to a place of safety, that, notwithstanding we lacked the necessary money to pay our fare, we decided to take seats in the stage, and promise to pay when we got to New Bedford. We were encouraged to do this by two excellent gentlemen, residents of New Bedford, whose names I afterward ascertained to be Joseph Ricketson and William C. Taber. They seemed at once to understand our circumstances, and gave us such assurance of their friendliness as put us fully at ease in their presence. It was good indeed to meet with such friends, at such a time. Upon reaching New Bedford, we were directed to the house of Mr. Nathan Johnson, by whom we were kindly received, and hospitably provided for. Both Mr. and Mrs. Johnson took a deep and lively interest in our welfare. They proved themselves quite worthy of the name of abolitionists. When the stage-drives found us unable to pay our fare, he held on upon our baggage as security for the debt. I had but to mention the fact to Mr. Johnson, and he forthwith advanced the money.

We now began to feel a degree of safety, and to prepare ourselves for the duties and responsibilities of a life of freedom. On the morning after our arrival at New Bedford, while at the breakfast-table, the question arose as to what name I should be called by. The name given me by my mother was "Frederick Augustus Washington Bailey." I, however, had dispensed with the two middle names long before I left

---

6. She was free [Douglass's note].

7. I had changed my name from Frederick *Bailey* to that of *Johnson* [Douglass's note].

Maryland, so that I was generally known by the name of "Frederick Bailey." I started from Baltimore bearing the name of "Stanley." When I got to New York, I again changed my name to "Frederick Johnson," and thought that would be the last change. But when I got to New Bedford, I found it necessary again to change my name. The reason of this necessity was, that there were so many Johnsons in New Bedford, it was already quite difficult to distinguish between them. I gave Mr. Johnson the privilege of choosing me a name, but told him he must not take from me the name of "Frederick." I must hold on to that, to preserve a sense of my identity. Mr. Johnson had just been reading the "Lady of the Lake,"[8] and at once suggested that my name be "Douglass." From that time until now I have been called "Frederick Douglass;" and as I am more widely known by that name than by either of the others, I shall continue to use it as my own.

I was quite disappointed at the general appearance of things in New Bedford. The impression which I had received respecting the character and condition of the people of the north, I found to be singularly erroneous. I had very strangely supposed, while in slavery, that few of the comforts, and scarcely any of the luxuries, of life were enjoyed at the north, compared with what were enjoyed by the slaveholders of the south. I probably came to this conclusion from the fact that northern people owned no slaves. I supposed that they were about upon a level with the non-slaveholding population of the south. I knew *they* were exceedingly poor, and I had been accustomed to regard their poverty as the necessary consequence of their being non-slaveholders. I had somehow imbibed the opinion that, in the absence of slaves, there could be no wealth, and very little refinement. And upon coming to the north, I expected to meet with a rough, hard-handed, and uncultivated population, living in the most Spartan-like simplicity, knowing nothing of the ease, luxury, pomp, and grandeur of southern slaveholders. Such being my conjectures, any one acquainted with the appearance of New Bedford may very readily infer how palpably I must have seen my mistake.

In the afternoon of the day when I reached New Bedford, I visited the wharves, to take a view of the shipping. Here I found myself surrounded with the strongest proofs of wealth. Lying at the wharves, and riding in the stream, I saw many ships of the finest model, in the best order, and of the largest size. Upon the right and left, I was walled in by granite warehouses of the widest dimensions, stowed to their utmost capacity with the necessaries and comforts of life. Added to this, almost every body seemed to be at work, but noiselessly so, compared with what I had been accustomed to in Baltimore. There were no loud songs heard from those engaged in loading and unloading ships. I heard no deep oaths or horrid curses on the laborer. I saw no whipping of men; but all seemed to go smoothly on. Every man appeared to understand his work, and went at it with a sober, yet cheerful earnestness, which betokened the deep interest which he felt in what he was doing, as well as a sense of his own dignity as a man. To me this looked exceedingly strange. From the wharves I strolled around and over the town, gazing with wonder and admiration at the splendid churches, beautiful dwellings, and finely-cultivated gardens; evincing an amount of wealth, comfort, taste, and refinement, such as I had never seen in any part of slaveholding Maryland.

Every thing looked clean, new, and beautiful. I saw few or no dilapidated houses, with poverty-stricken inmates; no halfnaked children and barefooted women, such as I had been accustomed to see in Hillsborough, Easton, St. Michael's, and Baltimore.

8. Walter Scott, "The Lady of the Lake" (1810).

The people looked more able, stronger, healthier, and happier, than those of Maryland. I was for once made glad by a view of extreme wealth, without being saddened by seeing extreme poverty. But the most astonishing as well as the most interesting thing to me was the condition of the colored people, a great many of whom, like myself, had escaped thither as a refuge from the hunters of men. I found many, who had not been seven years out of their chains, living in finer houses, and evidently enjoying more of the comforts of life, than the average of slaveholders in Maryland. I will venture to assert that my friend Mr. Nathan Johnson (of whom I can say with a grateful heart, "I was hungry, and he gave me meat; I was thirsty, and he gave me drink; I was a stranger, and he took me in") lived in a neater house; dined at a better table; took, paid for, and read, more newspapers; better understood the moral, religious, and political character of the nation,—than nine tenths of the slaveholders in Talbot county, Maryland. Yet Mr. Johnson was a working man. His hands were hardened by toil, and not his alone, but those also of Mrs. Johnson. I found the colored people much more spirited than I had supposed they would be. I found among them a determination to protect each other from the blood-thirsty kidnapper, at all hazards. Soon after my arrival, I was told of a circumstance which illustrated their spirit. A colored man and a fugitive slave were on unfriendly terms. The former was heard to threaten the latter with informing his master of his whereabouts. Straightway a meeting was called among the colored people, under the stereotyped notice, "Business of importance!" The betrayer was invited to attend. The people came at the appointed hour, and organized the meeting by appointing a very religious old gentleman as president, who, I believe, made a prayer, after which he addressed the meeting as follows: *"Friends, we have got him here, and I would recommend that you young men just take him outside the door, and kill him!"* With this, a number of them bolted at him; but they were intercepted by some more timid than themselves, and the betrayer escaped their vengeance, and has not been seen in New Bedford since. I believe there have been no more such threats, and should there be hereafter, I doubt not that death would be the consequence.

I found employment, the third day after my arrival, in stowing a sloop with a load of oil. It was new, dirty, and hard work for me; but I went at it with a glad heart and a willing hand. I was now my own master. It was a happy moment, the rapture of which can be understood only by those who have been slaves. It was the first work, the reward of which was to be entirely my own. There was no Master Hugh standing ready, the moment I earned the money, to rob me of it. I worked that day with a pleasure I had never before experienced. I was at work for myself and newly-married wife. It was to me the starting-point of a new existence. When I got through with that job, I went in pursuit of a job of calking; but such was the strength of prejudice against color, among the white calkers, that they refused to work with me, and of course I could get no employment.[9] Finding my trade of no immediate benefit, I threw off my calking habiliments, and prepared myself to do any kind of work I could get to do. Mr. Johnson kindly let me have his wood-horse and saw, and I very soon found myself a plenty of work. There was no work too hard—none too dirty. I was ready to saw wood, shovel coal, carry the hod, sweep the chimney, or roll oil casks,—all of which I did for nearly three years in New Bedford, before I became known to the anti-slavery world.

9. I am told that colored persons can now get employment at caulking in New Bedford—a result of anti-slavery effort [Douglass's note].

In about four months after I went to New Bedford, there came a young man to me, and inquired if I did not wish to take the "Liberator."[1] I told him I did; but, just having made my escape from slavery, I remarked that I was unable to pay for it then. I, however, finally became a subscriber to it. The paper came, and I read it from week to week with such feelings as it would be quite idle for me to attempt to describe. The paper became my meat and my drink. My soul was set all on fire. Its sympathy for my brethren in bonds—its scathing denunciations of slaveholders—its faithful exposures of slavery—and its powerful attacks upon the upholders of the institution—sent a thrill of joy through my soul, such as I had never felt before!

I had not long been a reader of the "Liberator," before I got a pretty correct idea of the principles, measures and spirit of the anti-slavery reform. I took right hold of the cause. I could do but little; but what I could, I did with a joyful heart, and never felt happier than when in an anti-slavery meeting. I seldom had much to say at the meetings, because what I wanted to say was said so much better by others. But, while attending an anti-slavery convention at Nantucket, on the 11th of August, 1841, I felt strongly moved to speak, and was at the same time much urged to do so by Mr. William C. Coffin, a gentleman who had heard me speak in the colored people's meeting at New Bedford. It was a severe cross, and I took it up reluctantly. The truth was, I felt myself a slave, and the idea of speaking to white people weighed me down. I spoke but a few moments, when I felt a degree of freedom, and said what I desired with considerable ease. From that time until now, I have been engaged in pleading the cause of my brethren—with what success, and with what devotion, I leave those acquainted with my labors to decide.

APPENDIX

I find, since reading over the foregoing Narrative, that I have, in several instances, spoken in such a tone and manner, respecting religion, as may possibly lead those unacquainted with my religious views to suppose me an opponent of all religion. To remove the liability of such misapprehension, I deem it proper to append the following brief explanation. What I have said respecting and against religion, I mean strictly to apply to the *slaveholding religion* of this land, and with no possible reference to Christianity proper; for, between the Christianity of this land, and the Christianity of Christ, I recognize the widest possible difference—so wide, that to receive the one as good, pure, and holy, is of necessity to reject the other as bad, corrupt, and wicked. To be the friend of the one, is of necessity to be the enemy of the other. I love the pure, peaceable, and impartial Christianity of Christ: I therefore hate the corrupt, slaveholding, women-whipping, cradle-plundering, partial and hypocritical Christianity of this land. Indeed, I can see no reason, but the most deceitful one, for calling the religion of this land Christianity. I look upon it as the climax of all misnomers, the boldest of all frauds, and the grossest of all libels. Never was there a clearer case of "stealing the livery of the court of heaven to serve the devil in." I am filled with unutterable loathing when I contemplate the religious pomp and show, together with the horrible inconsistencies, which every where surround me. We have men-stealers for ministers, women-whippers for missionaries, and cradle-plunderers for church members. The man who wields the blood-clotted cowskin during the week fills the pulpit on Sunday, and claims to be a minister of the meek and lowly Jesus. The man who robs me of my earnings at the end of each week meets me as a class-leader on Sunday morning, to

---

1. *The Liberator* was an abolitionist newspaper founded in Boston in 1831 by William Lloyd Garrison (1805–1879).

show me the way of life, and the path of salvation. He who sells my sister, for purposes of prostitution, stands forth as the pious advocate of purity. He who proclaims it a religious duty to read the Bible denies me the right of learning to read the name of the God who made me. He who is the religious advocate of marriage robs whole millions of its sacred influence, and leaves them to the ravages of wholesale pollution. The warm defender of the sacredness of the family relation is the same that scatters whole families,—sundering husbands and wives, parents and children, sisters and brothers,—leaving the hut vacant, and the hearth desolate. We see the thief preaching against theft, and the adulterer against adultery. We have men sold to build churches, women sold to support the gospel, and babes sold to purchase Bibles for the *poor heathen! all for the glory of God and the good of souls!* The slave auctioneer's bell and the church-going bell chime in with each other, and the bitter cries of the heart-broken slave are drowned in the religious shouts of his pious master. Revivals of religion and revivals in the slave-trade go hand in hand together. The slave prison and the church stand near each other. The clanking of fetters and the rattling of chains in the prison, and the pious psalm and solemn prayer in the church, may be heard at the same time. The dealers in the bodies and souls of men erect their stand in the presence of the pulpit, and they mutually help each other. The dealer gives his blood-stained gold to support the pulpit, and the pulpit, in return, covers his infernal business with the garb of Christianity. Here we have religion and robbery the allies of each other—devils dressed in angels' robes, and hell presenting the semblance of paradise.

> Just God! and these are they,
> Who minister at thine altar, God of right!
> Men who their hands, with prayer and blessing, lay
> On Israel's ark of light.

> What! preach, and kidnap men?
> Give thanks, and rob thy own afflicted poor?
> Talk of thy glorious liberty, and then
> Bolt hard the captive's door?

> What! servants of thy own
> Merciful Son, who came to seek and save
> The homeless and the outcast, fettering down
> The tasked and plundered slave!

> Pilate and Herod friends!
> Chief priests and rulers, as of old, combine!
> Just God and holy! is that church which lends
> Strength to the spoiler thine?

The Christianity of America is a Christianity, of whose votaries it may be as truly said, as it was of the ancient scribes and Pharisees, "They bind heavy burdens, and grievous to be borne, and lay them on men's shoulders, but they themselves will not move them with one of their fingers. All their works they do for to be seen of men.——They love the uppermost rooms at feasts, and the chief seats in the synagogues, . . . and to be called of men, Rabbi, Rabbi.——But woe unto you, scribes and Pharisees, hypocrites! for ye shut up the kingdom of heaven against men; for ye neither go in yourselves, neither suffer ye them that are entering to go in. Ye devour widows' houses, and for a pretence make long prayers; therefore ye shall receive the greater damnation. Ye compass sea and land to make one proselyte, and when he is made, ye make him twofold more the child of hell than yourselves.——Woe unto you, scribes and Pharisees, hypocrites! for ye pay tithe of mint, and anise, and cumin, and have omitted the weightier matters of the law, judgment, mercy, and faith; these ought ye to have done, and not to leave the other undone. Ye blind guides! which strain at a gnat, and swallow a camel. Woe unto you, scribes and Pharisees, hypocrites! for ye make clean the outside of the cup and of the platter; but within, they are full of extortion and excess.——Woe unto you, scribes and Pharisees, hypocrites! for ye are like unto whited sepulchres, which indeed appear beautiful outward, but are within full of dead men's bones, and of all uncleanness. Even so ye also outwardly appear righteous unto men, but within ye are full of hypocrisy and iniquity."

Dark and terrible as is this picture, I hold it to be strictly true of the overwhelming mass of professed Christians in America. They strain at a gnat, and swallow a camel. Could any thing be more true of our churches? They would be shocked at the proposition of fellowshipping a *sheep*-stealer; and at the same time they hug to their communion a *man*-stealer, and brand me with being an infidel, if I find fault with them for it. They attend with Pharisaical strictness to the outward forms of religion, and at the same time neglect the weightier matters of the law, judgment, mercy, and faith. They are always ready to sacrifice, but seldom to show mercy. They are they who are represented as professing to love God whom they have not seen, whilst they hate their brother whom they have seen. They love the heathen on the other side of the globe. They can pray for him, pay money to have the Bible put into his hand, and missionaries to instruct him; while they despise and totally neglect the heathen at their own doors.

Such is, very briefly, my view of the religion of this land; and to avoid any misunderstanding, growing out of the use of general terms, I mean, by the religion of this land, that which is revealed in the words, deeds, and actions, of those bodies, north and south, calling themselves Christian churches, and yet in union with slaveholders. It is against religion, as presented by these bodies, that I have felt it my duty to testify.

I conclude these remarks by copying the following portrait of the religion of the south, (which is, by communion and fellowship, the religion of the north,) which I soberly affirm is "true to the life," and without caricature or the slightest exaggeration. It is said to have been drawn, several years before the present anti-slavery agitation began, by a northern Methodist preacher, who, while residing at the south, had an opportunity to see slaveholding morals, manners, and piety, with his own eyes. "Shall I not visit for these things? saith the Lord. Shall not my soul be avenged on such a nation as this?"

A Parody
Come, saints and sinners, hear me tell
How pious priests whip Jack and Nell,
And women buy and children sell,
And preach all sinners down to hell,
And sing of heavenly union.

They'll bleat and baa, go *na* like goats,
Gorge down black sheep, and strain at motes,
Array their backs in fine black coats,
Then seize their negroes by their throats,
And choke, for heavenly union.

They'll church you if you sip a dram,
And damn you if you steal a lamb;

Yet rob old Tony, Doll, and Sam,
Of human rights, and bread and ham;
Kidnapper's heavenly union.

They'll loudly talk of Christ's reward,
And bind his image with a cord,
And scold, and swing the lash abhorred,
And sell their brother in the Lord
To handcuffed heavenly union.

They'll read and sing a sacred song,
And make a prayer both loud and long,
And teach the right and do the wrong,
Hailing the brother, sister throng,
With words of heavenly union.

We wonder how such saints can sing,
Or praise the Lord upon the wing,
Who roar, and scold, and whip, and sting,
And to their slaves and mammon cling,
In guilty conscience union.

They'll raise tobacco, corn, and rye,
And drive, and thieve, and cheat, and lie,
And lay up treasures in the sky,
By making switch and cowskin fly,
In hope of heavenly union.

They'll crack old Tony on the skull,
And preach and roar like Bashah bull,
Or braying ass, of mischief full,
Then seize old Jacob by the wool,
And pull for heavenly union.

A roaring, ranting, sleek man-thief,
Who lived on mutton, veal, and beef,
Yet never would afford relief
To needy, sable sons of grief,
Was big with heavenly union.

"Love not the world," the preacher said,
And winked his eye, and shook his head;
He seized on Tom, and Dick, and Ned,
Cut short their meat, and clothes, and bread,
Yet still loved heavenly union.

Another preacher whining spoke
Of One whose heart for sinners broke:
He tied old Nanny to an oak,
And drew the blood at every stroke,
And prayed for heavenly union.

Two others oped their iron jaws,
And waved their children-stealing paws;
There sat their children in gewgaws;

By stinting negroes' backs and maws,
They kept up heavenly union.

All good from Jack another takes,
And entertains their flirts and rakes,
Who dress as sleek as glossy snakes,
And cram their mouths with sweetened cakes;
And this goes down for union.

    Sincerely and earnestly hoping that this little book may do something toward throwing light on the American slave system, and hastening the glad day of deliverance to the millions of my brethren in bonds—faithfully relying upon the power of truth, love, and justice, for success in my humble efforts—and solemnly pledging myself anew to the sacred cause,—I subscribe myself,

FREDERICK DOUGLASS.

Lynn, Mass., April 28, 1845.

Harriet Jacobs
1813–1897

Born a slave in North Carolina, Harriet Jacobs did not put her name on the book by which she is now known, *Incidents in the Life of a Slave Girl* (1861). Though it was her own story she was telling, she called her protagonist by the name of Linda Brent. There were at least two main reasons. In pre–Civil War America fugitive slaves, their families, and those who helped them escape were still in danger. But Jacobs was also doing something extremely risky as a woman. Her story was not only about her successful efforts to avoid being raped by her master, to arrange her children's escape, to hide in a tiny crawl space and then (seven years later) to escape North herself. It was also about her sexual liaison with a white neighbor, which resulted in the birth of her two children. The sexual standards of the day, which she herself often seemed to believe in, were of course harsher for women than for men. Her failure to adhere to these standards threatened her readership in ways most abolitionist narratives did not. By daring to raise the conflicts and complications of her private sexual history to the level of political concern, by suggesting that the sexual standards applied to free women might not hold for women in slavery, Jacobs could be said to have created what her recent editor Jean Fagan Yellin calls "a new kind of female hero." Note the contrast with Frederick Douglass (page 735), whose sexual life plays no part at all in his story.

    Jacobs's efforts to acquire a writer's skills, to get the book written, and then to get it published, much of the time while employed in the North as a nursemaid and while fighting off attempts to recapture her family and return them to slavery, form a story scarcely less heroic than the escape itself. But the story went on. She used the celebrity she had won for herself with her book to bring help to the victims of the Civil War, and later to publicize conditions in the South. *Incidents* was then forgotten until the civil rights and women's movements focused attention once again on her heroic and miraculously articulate voice. It was only in 1981 that the scholar and editor Jean Fagan Yellin was able to establish Jacobs's authorship definitively.

from Incidents in the Life of a Slave Girl, Seven Years Concealed

1

CHILDHOOD

I was born a slave; but I never knew it till six years of happy childhood had passed away. My father was a carpenter, and considered so intelligent and skilful in his trade, that, when buildings out of the common line were to be erected, he was sent for from long distances, to be head workman. On condition of paying his mistress two hundred dollars a year, and supporting himself, he was allowed to work at his trade, and manage his own affairs. His strongest wish was to purchase his children; but, though he several times offered his hard earnings for that purpose, he never succeeded. In complexion my parents were a light shade of brownish yellow, and were termed mulattoes. They lived together in a comfortable home; and, though we were all slaves, I was so fondly shielded that I never dreamed I was a piece of merchandise, trusted to them for safe keeping, and liable to be demanded of them at any moment. I had one brother, William, who was two years younger than myself—a bright, affectionate child. I had also a great treasure in my maternal grandmother, who was a remarkable woman in many respects. She was the daughter of a planter in South Carolina, who, at his death, left her mother and his three children free, with money to go to St. Augustine, where they had relatives. It was during the Revolutionary War; and they were captured on their passage, carried back, and sold to different purchasers. Such was the story my grandmother used to tell me; but I do not remember all the particulars. She was a little girl when she was captured and sold to the keeper of a large hotel. I have often heard her tell how hard she fared during childhood. But as she grew older she evinced so much intelligence, and was so faithful, that her master and mistress could not help seeing it was for their interest to take care of such a valuable piece of property. She became an indispensable personage in the household, officiating in all capacities, from cook and wet nurse, to seamstress. She was much praised for her cooking; and her nice crackers became so famous in the neighborhood that many people were desirous of obtaining them. In consequence of numerous requests of this kind, she asked permission of her mistress to bake crackers at night, after all the household work was done; and she obtained leave to do it, provided she would clothe herself and her children from the profits. Upon these terms, after working hard all day for her mistress, she began her midnight bakings, assisted by her two oldest children. The business proved profitable; and each year she laid by a little, which was saved for a fund to purchase her children. Her master died, and the property was divided among his heirs. The widow had her dower in the hotel, which she continued to keep open. My grandmother remained in her service as a slave; but her children were divided among her master's children. As she had five, Benjamin, the youngest one, was sold, in order that each heir might have an equal portion of dollars and cents. There was so little difference in our ages that he seemed more like my brother than my uncle. He was a bright, handsome lad, nearly white; for he inherited the complexion my grandmother had derived from Anglo-Saxon ancestors. Though only ten years old, seven hundred and twenty dollars were paid for him. His sale was a terrible blow to my grandmother; but she was naturally hopeful, and she went to work with renewed energy, trusting in time to be able to purchase some of her children. She had laid up three hundred dollars, which her mistress one day begged as a loan, promising to pay her soon. The reader probably knows that no promise or writing given to a slave is legally binding; for, according to Southern laws, a slave, *being* property, can *hold* no property. When my grandmother lent her hard earnings to her mistress, she trusted solely to her honor. The honor of a slaveholder to a slave!

To this good grandmother I was indebted for many comforts. My brother Willie and I often received portions of the crackers, cakes, and preserves, she made to sell; and after we ceased to be children we were indebted to her for many more important services.

Such were the unusually fortunate circumstances of my early childhood. When I was six years old, my mother died; and then, for the first time, I learned, by the talk around me, that I was a slave. My mother's mistress was the daughter of my grandmother's mistress. She was the foster sister of my mother; they were both nourished at my grandmother's breast. In fact, my mother had been weaned at three months old, that the babe of the mistress might obtain sufficient food. They played together as children; and, when they became women, my mother was a most faithful servant to her whiter foster sister. On her death-bed her mistress promised that her children should never suffer for any thing; and during her lifetime she kept her word. They all spoke kindly of my dead mother, who had been a slave merely in name, but in nature was noble and womanly. I grieved for her, and my young mind was troubled with the thought who would now take care of me and my little brother. I was told that my home was now to be with her mistress; and I found it a happy one. No toilsome or disagreeable duties were imposed upon me. My mistress was so kind to me that I was always glad to do her bidding, and proud to labor for her as much as my young years would permit. I would sit by her side for hours, sewing diligently, with a heart as free from care as that of any free-born white child. When she thought I was tired, she would send me out to run and jump; and away I bounded, to gather berries or flowers to decorate her room. Those were happy days—too happy to last. The slave child had no thought for the morrow; but there came that blight, which too surely waits on every human being born to be a chattel.

When I was nearly twelve years old, my kind mistress sickened and died. As I saw the cheek grow paler, and the eye more glassy, how earnestly I prayed in my heart that she might live! I loved her; for she had been almost like a mother to me. My prayers were not answered. She died, and they buried her in the little churchyard, where, day after day, my tears fell upon her grave.

I was sent to spend a week with my grandmother. I was now old enough to begin to think of the future; and again and again I asked myself what they would do with me. I felt sure I should never find another mistress so kind as the one who was gone. She had promised my dying mother that her children should never suffer for any thing; and when I remembered that, and recalled her many proofs of attachment to me, I could not help having some hopes that she had left me free. My friends were almost certain it would be so. They thought she would be sure to do it, on account of my mother's love and faithful service. But, alas! we all know that the memory of a faithful slave does not avail much to save her children from the auction block.

After a brief period of suspense, the will of my mistress was read, and we learned that she had bequeathed me to her sister's daughter, a child of five years old. So vanished our hopes. My mistress had taught me the precepts of God's Word: "Thou shalt love thy neighbor as thyself." "Whatsoever ye would that men should do unto you, do ye even so unto them." But I was her slave, and I suppose she did not recognize me as her neighbor. I would give much to blot out from my memory that one great wrong. As a child, I loved my mistress; and, looking back on the happy days I spent with her, I try to think with less bitterness of this act of injustice. While I was with her, she taught me to read and spell; and for this privilege, which so rarely falls to the lot of a slave, I bless her memory.

She possessed but few slaves; and at her death those were all distributed among her relatives. Five of them were my grandmother's children, and had shared the same milk that nourished her mother's children. Notwithstanding my grandmother's long and faithful service to her owners, not one of her children escaped the auction block. These God-breathing machines are no more, in the sight of their masters, than the cotton they plant, or the horses they tend.

2

THE NEW MASTER AND MISTRESS

Dr. Flint, a physician in the neighborhood, had married the sister of my mistress, and I was now the property of their little daughter. It was not without murmuring that I prepared for my new home; and what added to my unhappiness, was the fact that my brother William was purchased by the same family. My father, by his nature, as well as by the habit of transacting business as a skilful mechanic, had more of the feelings of a freeman than is common among slaves. My brother was a spirited boy; and being brought up under such influences, he early detested the name of master and mistress. One day, when his father and his mistress both happened to call him at the same time, he hesitated between the two; being perplexed to know which had the strongest claim upon his obedience. He finally concluded to go to his mistress. When my father reproved him for it, he said, "You both called me, and I didn't know which I ought to go to first."

"You are *my* child," replied our father, "and when I call you, you should come immediately, if you have to pass through fire and water."

Poor Willie! He was now to learn his first lesson of obedience to a master. Grandmother tried to cheer us with hopeful words, and they found an echo in the credulous hearts of youth.

When we entered our new home we encountered cold looks, cold words, and cold treatment. We were glad when the night came. On my narrow bed I moaned and wept, I felt so desolate and alone.

I had been there nearly a year, when a dear little friend of mine was buried. I heard her mother sob, as the clods fell on the coffin of her only child, and I turned away from the grave, feeling thankful that I still had something left to love. I met my grandmother, who said, "Come with me, Linda;" and from her tone I knew that something sad had happened. She led me apart from the people, and then said, "My child, your father is dead." Dead! How could I believe it? He had died so suddenly I had not even heard that he was sick. I went home with my grandmother. My heart rebelled against God, who had taken from me mother, father, mistress, and friend. The good grandmother tried to comfort me. "Who knows the ways of God?" said she. "Perhaps they have been kindly taken from the evil days to come." Years afterwards I often thought of this. She promised to be a mother to her grandchildren, so far as she might be permitted to do so; and strengthened by her love, I returned to my master's. I thought I should be allowed to go to my father's house the next morning; but I was ordered to go for flowers, that my mistress's house might be decorated for an evening party. I spent the day gathering flowers and weaving them into festoons, while the dead body of my father was lying within a mile of me. What cared my owners for that? he was merely a piece of property. Moreover, they thought he had spoiled his children, by teaching them to feel that they were human beings. This was blasphemous doctrine for a slave to teach; presumptuous in him, and dangerous to the masters.

The next day I followed his remains to a humble grave beside that of my dear mother. There were those who knew my father's worth, and respected his memory.

My home now seemed more dreary than ever. The laugh of the little slave-children sounded harsh and cruel. It was selfish to feel so about the joy of others. My brother moved about with a very grave face. I tried to comfort him, by saying, "Take courage, Willie; brighter days will come by and by."

"You don't know any thing about it, Linda," he replied. "We shall have to stay here all our days; we shall never be free."

I argued that we were growing older and stronger, and that perhaps we might, before long, be allowed to hire our own time, and then we could earn money to buy our freedom. William declared this was much easier to say than to do; moreover, he did not intend to *buy* his freedom. We held daily controversies upon this subject.

Little attention was paid to the slaves' meals in Dr. Flint's house. If they could catch a bit of food while it was going, well and good. I gave myself no trouble on that score, for on my various errands I passed my grandmother's house, where there was always something to spare for me. I was frequently threatened with punishment if I stopped there; and my grandmother, to avoid detaining me, often stood at the gate with something for my breakfast or dinner. I was indebted to *her* for all my comforts, spiritual or temporal. It was *her* labor that supplied my scanty wardrobe. I have a vivid recollection of the linsey-woolsey dress given me every winter by Mrs. Flint. How I hated it! It was one of the badges of slavery.

While my grandmother was thus helping to support me from her hard earnings, the three hundred dollars she had lent her mistress were never repaid. When her mistress died, her son-in-law, Dr. Flint, was appointed executor. When grandmother applied to him for payment, he said the estate was insolvent, and the law prohibited payment. It did not, however, prohibit him from retaining the silver candelabra, which had been purchased with that money. I presume they will be handed down in the family, from generation to generation.

My grandmother's mistress had always promised her that, at her death, she should be free; and it was said that in her will she made good the promise. But when the estate was settled, Dr. Flint told the faithful old servant that, under existing circumstances, it was necessary she should be sold.

On the appointed day, the customary advertisement was posted up, proclaiming that there would be a "public sale of negroes, horses, &c." Dr. Flint called to tell my grandmother that he was unwilling to wound her feelings by putting her up at auction, and that he would prefer to dispose of her at private sale. My grandmother saw through his hypocrisy; she understood very well that he was ashamed of the job. She was a very spirited woman, and if he was base enough to sell her, when her mistress intended she should be free, she was determined the public should know it. She had for a long time supplied many families with crackers and preserves; consequently, "Aunt Marthy," as she was called, was generally known, and every body who knew her respected her intelligence and good character. Her long and faithful service in the family was also well known, and the intention of her mistress to leave her free. When the day of sale came, she took her place among the chattels, and at the first call she sprang upon the auction-block. Many voices called out, "Shame! Shame! Who is going to sell *you*, aunt Marthy? Don't stand there! That is no place for *you*." Without saying a word, she quietly awaited her fate. No one bid for her.

At last, a feeble voice said, "Fifty dollars." It came from a maiden lady, seventy years old, the sister of my grandmother's deceased mistress. She had lived forty years under the same roof with my grandmother; she knew how faithfully she had served her owners, and how cruelly she had been defrauded of her rights; and she resolved to protect her. The auctioneer waited for a higher bid; but her wishes were respected; no one bid above her. She could neither read nor write; and when the bill of sale was made out, she signed it with a cross. But what consequence was that, when she had a big heart overflowing with human kindness? She gave the old servant her freedom.

At that time, my grandmother was just fifty years old. Laborious years had passed since then; and now my brother and I were slaves to the man who had defrauded her of her money, and tried to defraud her of her freedom. One of my mother's sisters, called Aunt Nancy, was also a slave in his family. She was a kind, good aunt to me; and supplied the place of both housekeeper and waiting maid to her mistress. She was, in fact, at the beginning and end of every thing.

Mrs. Flint, like many southern women, was totally deficient in energy. She had not strength to superintend her household affairs; but her nerves were so strong, that she could sit in her easy chair and see a woman whipped, till the blood trickled from every stroke of the lash. She was a member of the church; but partaking of the Lord's supper did not seem to put her in a Christian frame of mind. If dinner was not served at the exact time on that particular Sunday, she would station herself in the kitchen, and wait till it was dished, and then spit in all the kettles and pans that had been used for cooking. She did this to prevent the cook and her children from eking out their meagre fare with the remains of the gravy and other scrapings. The slaves could get nothing to eat except what she chose to give them. Provisions were weighed out by the pound and ounce, three times a day. I can assure you she gave them no chance to eat wheat bread from her flour barrel. She knew how many biscuits a quart of flour would make, and exactly what size they ought to be.

Dr. Flint was an epicure. The cook never sent a dinner to his table without fear and trembling; for if there happened to be a dish not to his liking, he would either order her to be whipped, or compel her to eat every mouthful of it in his presence. The poor, hungry creature might not have objected to eating it; but she did object to having her master cram it down her throat till she choked.

They had a pet dog, that was a nuisance in the house. The cook was ordered to make some Indian mush for him. He refused to eat, and when his head was held over it, the froth flowed from his mouth into the basin. He died a few minutes after. When Dr. Flint came in, he said the mush had not been well cooked, and that was the reason the animal would not eat it. He sent for the cook, and compelled her to eat it. He thought that the woman's stomach was stronger than the dog's; but her sufferings afterwards proved that he was mistaken. This poor woman endured many cruelties from her master and mistress; sometimes she was locked up, away from her nursing baby, for a whole day and night.

When I had been in the family a few weeks, one of the plantation slaves was brought to town, by order of his master. It was near night when he arrived, and Dr. Flint ordered him to be taken to the work house, and tied up to the joist, so that his feet would just escape the ground. In that situation he was to wait till the doctor had taken his tea. I shall never forget that night. Never before, in my life, had I heard hundreds of blows fall, in succession, on a human being. His piteous groans, and his "O, pray don't, massa," rang in my ear for months afterwards. There were many conjectures as to the cause of this terrible punishment. Some said master accused him of stealing corn; others said the slave had quarrelled with his wife, in presence of the overseer, and had accused his master of being the father of her child. They were both black, and the child was very fair.

I went into the work house next morning, and saw the cowhide still wet with blood, and the boards all covered with gore. The poor man lived, and continued to quarrel with his wife. A few months afterwards Dr. Flint handed them both over to a slave-trader. The guilty man put their value into his pocket, and had the satisfaction of knowing that they were out of sight and hearing. When the mother was delivered into the trader's hands, she said, "You *promised* to treat me well." To which he replied, "You have let your tongue run too far; damn you!" She had forgotten that it was a crime for a slave to tell who was the father of her child.

From others than the master persecution also comes in such cases. I once saw a young slave girl dying soon after the birth of a child nearly white. In her agony she cried out, "O Lord, come and take me!" Her mistress stood by, and mocked at her like an incarnate fiend. "You suffer, do you?" she exclaimed. "I am glad of it. You deserve it all, and more too."

The girl's mother said, "The baby is dead, thank God; and I hope my poor child will soon be in heaven, too."

"Heaven!" retorted the mistress. "There is no such place for the like of her and her bastard."

The poor mother turned away, sobbing. Her dying daughter called her, feebly, and as she bent over her, I heard her say, "Don't grieve so, mother; God knows all about it; and he will have mercy upon me."

Her sufferings, afterwards, became so intense, that her mistress felt unable to stay; but when she left the room, the scornful smile was still on her lips. Seven children called her mother. The poor black woman had but the one child, whose eyes she saw closing in death, while she thanked God for taking her away from the greater bitterness of life.

5

THE TRIALS OF GIRLHOOD

During the first years of my service in Dr. Flint's family, I was accustomed to share some indulgences with the children of my mistress. Though this seemed to me no more than right, I was grateful for it, and tried to merit the kindness by the faithful discharge of my duties. But I now entered on my fifteenth year—a sad epoch in the life of a slave girl. My master began to whisper foul words in my ear. Young as I was, I could not remain ignorant of their import. I tried to treat them with indifference or contempt. The master's age, my extreme youth, and the fear that his conduct would be reported to my grandmother, made him bear this treatment for many months. He was a crafty man, and resorted to many means to accomplish his purposes. Sometimes he had stormy, terrific ways, that made his victims tremble; sometimes he assumed a gentleness that he thought must surely subdue. Of the two, I preferred his stormy moods, although they left me trembling. He tried his utmost to corrupt the pure principles my grandmother had instilled. He peopled my young mind with unclean images, such as only a vile monster could think of. I turned from him with disgust and hatred. But he was my master. I was compelled to live under the same roof with him—where I saw a man forty years my senior daily violating the most sacred commandments of nature. He told me I was his property; that I must be subject to his will in all things. My soul revolted against the mean tyranny. But where could I turn for protection? No matter whether the slave girl be as black as ebony or as fair as her mistress. In either case, there is no shadow of law to protect her from insult, from violence, or even from death; all these are inflicted by fiends who bear the shape of men. The mistress, who ought to protect the helpless victim, has no other feelings towards her but those of jealousy and rage. The degradation, the wrongs, the vices, that grow out of slavery, are more than I can describe. They are greater than you would willingly believe. Surely, if you credited one half the truths that are told you concerning the helpless millions suffering in this cruel bondage, you at the north would not help to tighten the yoke. You surely would refuse to do for the master, on your own soil, the mean and cruel work which trained bloodhounds and the lowest class of whites do for him at the south.

Every where the years bring to all enough of sin and sorrow; but in slavery the very dawn of life is darkened by these shadows. Even the little child, who is accustomed to wait on her mistress and her children, will learn, before she is twelve years old, why it is that her mistress hates such and such a one among the slaves. Perhaps the child's own mother is among those hated ones. She listens to violent outbreaks of jealous passion, and cannot help understanding what is the cause. She will become prematurely knowing in evil things. Soon she will learn to tremble when she hears her master's footfall. She will be compelled to realize that she is no longer a child. If God has bestowed beauty upon her, it will prove her greatest curse. That which commands admiration in the white woman only hastens the degradation of the female slave. I know that some are too much brutalized by slavery to feel the humiliation of their position; but many slaves feel it most acutely, and shrink from the memory of it. I cannot tell how much I suffered in the presence of these wrongs, nor how I am still pained by the retrospect. My master met me at every turn, reminding me that I belonged to him, and swearing by heaven and earth that he would compel me to submit to him. If I went out for a breath of fresh air, after a day of unwearied toil, his footsteps dogged me. If I knelt by my mother's grave, his dark shadow fell on me even there. The light heart which nature had given me became heavy with sad forebodings. The other slaves in my master's house noticed the change. Many of them pitied me; but none dared to ask the cause. They had no need to inquire. They knew too well the guilty practices under that roof; and they were aware that to speak of them was an offence that never went unpunished.

I longed for some one to confide in. I would have given the world to have laid my head on my grandmother's faithful bosom, and told her all my troubles. But Dr. Flint swore he would kill me, if I was not as silent as the grave. Then, although my grandmother was all in all to me, I feared her as well as loved her. I had been accustomed to look up to her with a respect bordering upon awe. I was very young, and felt shamefaced about telling her such impure things, especially as I knew her to be very strict on such subjects. Moreover, she was a woman of a high spirit. She was usually very quiet in her demeanor; but if her indignation was once roused, it was not very easily quelled. I had been told that she once chased a white gentleman with a loaded pistol, because he insulted one of her daughters. I dreaded the consequences of a violent outbreak; and both pride and fear kept me silent. But though I did not confide in my grandmother, and even evaded her vigilant watchfulness and inquiry, her presence in the neighborhood was some protection to me. Though she had been a slave, Dr. Flint was afraid of her. He dreaded her scorching rebukes. Moreover, she was known and patronized by many people; and he did not wish to have his villany made public. It was lucky for me that I did not live on a distant plantation, but in a town not so large that the inhabitants were ignorant of each other's affairs. Bad as are the laws and customs in a slaveholding community, the doctor, as a professional man, deemed it prudent to keep up some outward show of decency.

O, what days and nights of fear and sorrow that man caused me! Reader, it is not to awaken sympathy for myself that I am telling you truthfully what I suffered in slavery. I do it to kindle a flame of compassion in your hearts for my sisters who are still in bondage, suffering as I once suffered.

I once saw two beautiful children playing together. One was a fair white child; the other was her slave, and also her sister. When I saw them embracing each other, and heard their joyous laughter, I turned sadly away from the lovely sight. I foresaw the inevitable blight that would fall on the little slave's heart. I knew how soon her laughter would be changed to sighs. The fair child grew up to be a still fairer woman. From childhood to womanhood her pathway was blooming with flowers, and overarched by a sunny sky. Scarcely one day of her life had been clouded when the sun rose on her happy bridal morning.

How had those years dealt with her slave sister, the little playmate of her childhood? She, also, was very beautiful; but the flowers and sunshine of love were not for her. She drank the cup of sin, and shame, and misery, whereof her persecuted race are compelled to drink.

In view of these things, why are ye silent, ye free men and women of the north? Why do your tongues falter in maintenance of the right? Would that I had more ability! But my heart is so full, and my pen is so weak! There are noble men and women who plead for us, striving to help those who cannot help themselves. God bless them! God give them strength and courage to go on! God bless those, every where, who are laboring to advance the cause of humanity!

6

THE JEALOUS MISTRESS

I would ten thousand times rather that my children should be the half-starved paupers of Ireland than to be the most pampered among the slaves of America. I would rather drudge out my life on a cotton plantation, till the grave opened to give me rest, than to live with an unprincipled master and a jealous mistress. The felon's home in a penitentiary is preferable. He may repent, and turn from the error of his ways, and so find peace; but it is not so with a favorite slave. She is not allowed to have any pride of character. It is deemed a crime in her to wish to be virtuous.

Mrs. Flint possessed the key to her husband's character before I was born. She might have used this knowledge to counsel and to screen the young and the innocent among her slaves; but for them she had no sympathy. They were the objects of her constant suspicion and malevolence. She watched her husband with unceasing vigilance; but he was well practised in means to evade it. What he could not find opportunity to say in words he manifested in signs. He invented more than were ever thought of in a deaf and dumb asylum. I let them pass, as if I did not understand what he meant; and many were the curses and threats bestowed on me for my stupidity. One day he caught me teaching myself to write. He frowned, as if he was not well pleased; but I suppose he came to the conclusion that such an accomplishment might help to advance his favorite scheme. Before long, notes were often slipped into my hand. I would return them, saying, "I can't read them, sir." "Can't you?" he replied; "then I must read them to you." He always finished the reading by asking, "Do you understand?" Sometimes he would complain of the heat of the tea room, and order his supper to be placed on a small table in the piazza. He would seat himself there with a well-satisfied smile, and tell me to stand by and brush away the flies. He would eat very slowly, pausing between the mouthfuls. These intervals were employed in describing the happiness I was so foolishly throwing away, and in threatening me with the penalty that finally awaited my stubborn disobedience. He boasted much of the forbearance he had exercised towards me, and reminded me that there was a limit to his patience. When I succeeded in avoiding opportunities for him to talk to me at home, I was ordered to come to his office, to do some errand. When there, I was obliged to stand and listen to such language as he saw fit to address to me. Sometimes I so openly expressed my contempt for him that he would become violently enraged, and I wondered why he did not strike me. Circumstanced as he was, he probably thought it was better policy to be forbearing. But the state of things grew worse and worse daily. In desperation I told him that I must and would apply to my grandmother for protection. He threatened me with death, and worse than death, if I made any complaint to her. Strange to say, I did not despair. I was naturally of a buoyant disposition, and always I had a hope of somehow getting out of his clutches. Like many a poor, simple slave before me, I trusted that some threads of joy would yet be woven into my dark destiny.

I had entered my sixteenth year, and every day it became more apparent that my presence was intolerable to Mrs. Flint. Angry words frequently passed between her and her husband. He had never punished me himself, and he would not allow any body else to punish me. In that respect, she was never satisfied; but, in her angry moods, no terms were too vile for her to bestow upon me. Yet I, whom she detested so bitterly, had far more pity for her than he had, whose duty it was to make her life happy. I never wronged her, or wished to wrong her, and one word of kindness from her would have brought me to her feet.

After repeated quarrels between the doctor and his wife, he announced his intention to take his youngest daughter, then four years old, to sleep in his apartment. It was necessary that a servant should sleep in the same room, to be on hand if the child stirred. I was selected for that office, and informed for what purpose that arrangement had been made. By managing to keep within sight of people, as much as possible, during the day time, I had hitherto succeeded in eluding my master, though a razor was often held to my throat to force me to change this line of policy. At night I slept by the side of my great aunt, where I felt safe. He was too prudent to come into her room. She was an old woman, and had been in the family many years. Moreover, as a married man, and a professional man, he deemed it necessary to save appearances in some degree. But he resolved to remove the obstacle in the way of his scheme; and he thought he had planned it so that he should evade suspicion. He was well aware how much I prized my refuge by the side of my old aunt, and he determined to dispossess me of it. The first night the doctor had the little child in his room alone. The next morning, I was ordered to take my station as nurse the following night. A kind Providence interposed in my favor. During the day Mrs. Flint heard of this new arrangement, and a storm followed. I rejoiced to hear it rage.

After a while my mistress sent for me to come to her room. Her first question was, "Did you know you were to sleep in the doctor's room?"

"Yes, ma'am."

"Who told you?"

"My master."

"Will you answer truly all the questions I ask?"

"Yes, ma'am."

"Tell me, then, as you hope to be forgiven, are you innocent of what I have accused you?"

"I am."

She handed me a Bible, and said, "Lay your hand on your heart, kiss this holy book, and swear before God that you tell me the truth."

I took the oath she required, and I did it with a clear conscience.

"You have taken God's holy word to testify your innocence," said she. "If you have deceived me, beware! Now take this stool, sit down, look me directly in the face, and tell me all that has passed between your master and you."

I did as she ordered. As I went on with my account her color changed frequently, she wept, and sometimes groaned. She spoke in tones so sad, that I was touched by her grief. The tears came to my eyes; but I was soon convinced that her emotions arose from anger and wounded pride. She felt that her marriage vows were desecrated, her dignity insulted; but she had no compassion for the poor victim of her husband's perfidy. She pitied herself as a martyr; but she was incapable of feeling for the condition of shame and misery in which her unfortunate, helpless slave was placed.

Yet perhaps she had some touch of feeling for me; for when the conference was ended, she spoke kindly, and promised to protect me. I should have been much comforted by this assurance if I could have had confidence in it; but my experiences in slavery had filled me with distrust. She was not a very refined woman, and had not much control over her passions. I was an object of her jealousy, and, consequently, of her hatred; and I knew I could not expect kindness or confidence from her under the circumstances in which I was placed. I could not blame her. Slaveholders' wives feel as other women would under similar circumstances. The fire of her temper kindled from small sparks, and now the flame became so intense that the doctor was obliged to give up his intended arrangement.

I knew I had ignited the torch, and I expected to suffer for it afterwards; but I felt too thankful to my mistress for the timely aid she rendered me to care much about that. She now took me to sleep in a room adjoining her own. There I was an object of her especial care, though not of her especial comfort, for she spent many a sleepless night to watch over me. Sometimes I woke up, and found her bending over me. At other times she whispered in my ear, as though it was her husband who was speaking to me, and listened to hear what I would answer. If she startled me, on such occasions, she would glide stealthily away; and the next morning she would tell me I had been talking in my sleep, and ask who I was talking to. At last, I began to be fearful for my life. It had been often threatened; and you can imagine, better than I can describe, what an unpleasant sensation it must produce to wake up in the dead of night and find a jealous woman bending over you. Terrible as this experience was, I had fears that it would give place to one more terrible.

My mistress grew weary of her vigils; they did not prove satisfactory. She changed her tactics. She now tried the trick of accusing my master of crime, in my presence, and gave my name as the author of the accusation. To my utter astonishment, he replied, "I don't believe it; but if she did acknowledge it, you tortured her into exposing me." Tortured into exposing him! Truly, Satan had no difficulty in distinguishing the color of his soul! I understood his object in making this false representation. It was to show me that I gained nothing by seeking the protection of my mistress; that the power was still all in his own hands. I pitied Mrs. Flint. She was a second wife, many years the junior of her husband; and the hoary-headed miscreant was enough to try the patience of a wiser and better woman. She was completely foiled, and knew not how to proceed. She would gladly have had me flogged for my supposed false oath; but, as I have already stated, the doctor never allowed any one to whip me. The old sinner was politic. The application of the lash might have led to remarks that would have exposed him in the eyes of his children and grandchildren. How often did I rejoice that I lived in a town where all the inhabitants knew each other! If I had been on a remote plantation, or lost among the multitude of a crowded city, I should not be a living woman at this day.

The secrets of slavery are concealed like those of the Inquisition. My master was, to my knowledge, the father of eleven slaves. But did the mothers dare to tell who was the father of their children? Did the other slaves dare to allude to it, except in whispers among themselves? No, indeed! They knew too well the terrible consequences.

My grandmother could not avoid seeing things which excited her suspicions. She was uneasy about me, and tried various ways to buy me; but the never-changing answer was always repeated: "Linda does not belong to *me*. She is my daughter's property, and I have no legal right to sell her." The conscientious man! He was too scrupulous to *sell* me; but he had no scruples whatever about committing a much greater wrong against the helpless young girl placed under his guardianship, as his daughter's property. Sometimes my persecutor would ask me whether I would like to be sold. I told him I would rather be sold to any body than to lead such a life as I did. On such occasions he would assume the air of a very injured individual, and reproach me for my ingratitude. "Did I not take you into the house, and make you the companion of my own children?" he would say. "Have I ever treated you like a negro? I have never allowed you to be punished, not even to please your mistress. And this is the recompense I get, you ungrateful girl!" I answered that he had reasons of his own for screening me from punishment, and that the course he pursued made my mistress hate me and persecute me. If I wept, he would say, "Poor child! Don't cry! don't cry! I will make peace for you with your mistress. Only let me arrange matters in my own way. Poor, foolish girl! you don't know what is for your own good. I would cherish you. I would make a lady of you. Now go, and think of all I have promised you."

I did think of it.

Reader, I draw no imaginary pictures of southern homes. I am telling you the plain truth. Yet when victims make their escape from this wild beast of Slavery, northerners consent to act the part of bloodhounds, and hunt the poor fugitive back into his den, "full of dead men's bones, and all uncleanness." Nay, more, they are not only willing, but proud, to give their daughters in marriage to slaveholders. The poor girls have romantic notions of a sunny clime, and of the flowering vines that all the year round shade a happy home. To what disappointments are they destined! The young wife soon learns that the husband in whose hands she has placed her happiness pays no regard to his marriage vows. Children of every shade of complexion play with her own fair babies, and too well she knows that they are born unto him of his own household. Jealousy and hatred enter the flowery home, and it is ravaged of its loveliness.

Southern women often marry a man knowing that he is the father of many little slaves. They do not trouble themselves about it. They regard such children as property, as marketable as the pigs on the plantation; and it is seldom that they do not make them aware of this by passing them into the slavetrader's hands as soon as possible, and thus getting them out of their sight. I am glad to say there are some honorable exceptions.

I have myself known two southern wives who exhorted their husbands to free those slaves towards whom they stood in a "parental relation;" and their request was granted. These husbands blushed before the superior nobleness of their wives' natures. Though they had only counselled them to do that which it was their duty to do, it commanded their respect, and rendered their conduct more exemplary. Concealment was at an end, and confidence took the place of distrust.

Though this bad institution deadens the moral sense, even in white women, to a fearful extent, it is not altogether extinct. I have heard southern ladies say of Mr. Such a one, "He not only thinks it no disgrace to be the father of those little niggers, but he is not ashamed to call himself their master. I declare, such things ought not to be tolerated in any decent society!"

10

A PERILOUS PASSAGE IN THE SLAVE GIRL'S LIFE

After my lover went away, Dr. Flint contrived a new plan. He seemed to have an idea that my fear of my mistress was his greatest obstacle. In the blandest tones, he told me that he was going to build a small house for me, in a secluded place, four miles away from the town. I shuddered; but I was constrained to listen, while he talked of his intention to give me a home of my own, and to make a lady of me. Hitherto, I had escaped my dreaded fate, by being in the midst of people. My grandmother had already had high words with my master about me. She had told him pretty plainly what she thought of his character, and there was considerable gossip in the neighborhood about our affairs, to which the open-mouthed jealousy of Mrs. Flint contributed not a little. When my master said he was going to build a house for me, and that he could do it with little trouble and expense, I was in hopes something would happen to frustrate his scheme; but I soon heard that the house was actually begun. I vowed before my Maker that I would never enter it. I had rather toil on the plantation from dawn till dark; I had rather live and die in jail, than drag on, from day to day, through such a living death. I was determined that the master, whom I so hated and loathed, who had blighted the prospects of my youth, and made my life a desert, should not, after my long struggle with him, succeed at last in trampling his victim under his feet. I would do any thing, every thing, for the sake of defeating him. What *could* I do? I thought and thought, till I became desperate, and made a plunge into the abyss.

And now, reader, I come to a period in my unhappy life, which I would gladly forget if I could. The remembrance fills me with sorrow and shame. It pains me to tell you of it; but I have promised to tell you the truth, and I will do it honestly, let it cost me what it may. I will not try to screen myself behind the plea of compulsion from a master; for it was not so. Neither can I plead ignorance or thoughtlessness. For years, my master had done his utmost to pollute my mind with foul images, and to destroy the pure principles inculcated by my grandmother, and the good mistress of my childhood. The influences of slavery had had the same effect on me that they had on other young girls; they had made me prematurely knowing, concerning the evil ways of the world. I knew what I did, and I did it with deliberate calculation.

But, O, ye happy women, whose purity has been sheltered from childhood, who have been free to choose the objects of your affection, whose homes are protected by law, do not judge the poor desolate slave girl too severely! If slavery had been abolished, I, also, could have married the man of my choice; I could have had a home shielded by the laws; and I should have been spared the painful task of confessing what

I am now about to relate; but all my prospects had been blighted by slavery. I wanted to keep myself pure; and, under the most adverse circumstances, I tried hard to preserve my self-respect; but I was struggling alone in the powerful grasp of the demon Slavery; and the monster proved too strong for me. I felt as if I was forsaken by God and man; as if all my efforts must be frustrated; and I became reckless in my despair.

I have told you that Dr. Flint's persecutions and his wife's jealousy had given rise to some gossip in the neighborhood. Among others, it chanced that a white unmarried gentleman had obtained some knowledge of the circumstances in which I was placed. He knew my grandmother, and often spoke to me in the street. He became interested for me, and asked questions about my master, which I answered in part. He expressed a great deal of sympathy, and a wish to aid me. He constantly sought opportunities to see me, and wrote to me frequently. I was a poor slave girl, only fifteen years old.

So much attention from a superior person was, of course, flattering; for human nature is the same in all. I also felt grateful for his sympathy, and encouraged by his kind words. It seemed to me a great thing to have such a friend. By degrees, a more tender feeling crept into my heart. He was an educated and eloquent gentleman; too eloquent, alas, for the poor slave girl who trusted in him. Of course I saw whither all this was tending. I knew the impassable gulf between us; but to be an object of interest to a man who is not married, and who is not her master, is agreeable to the pride and feelings of a slave, if her miserable situation has left her any pride or sentiment. It seems less degrading to give one's self, than to submit to compulsion. There is something akin to freedom in having a lover who has no control over you, except that which he gains by kindness and attachment. A master may treat you as rudely as he pleases, and you dare not speak; moreover, the wrong does not seem so great with an unmarried man, as with one who has a wife to be made unhappy. There may be sophistry in all this; but the condition of a slave confuses all principles of morality, and, in fact, renders the practice of them impossible.

When I found that my master had actually begun to build the lonely cottage, other feelings mixed with those I have described. Revenge, and calculations of interest, were added to flattered vanity and sincere gratitude for kindness. I knew nothing would enrage Dr. Flint so much as to know that I favored another; and it was something to triumph over my tyrant even in that small way. I thought he would revenge himself by selling me, and I was sure my friend, Mr. Sands, would buy me. He was a man of more generosity and feeling than my master, and I thought my freedom could be easily obtained from him. The crisis of my fate now came so near that I was desperate. I shuddered to think of being the mother of children that should be owned by my old tyrant. I knew that as soon as a new fancy took him, his victims were sold far off to get rid of them; especially if they had children. I had seen several women sold, with his babies at the breast. He never allowed his offspring by slaves to remain long in sight of himself and his wife. Of a man who was not my master I could ask to have my children well supported; and in this case, I felt confident I should obtain the boon. I also felt quite sure that they would be made free. With all these thoughts revolving in my mind, and seeing no other way of escaping the doom I so much dreaded, I made a headlong plunge. Pity me, and pardon me, O virtuous reader! You never knew what it is to be a slave; to be entirely unprotected by law or custom; to have the laws reduce you to the condition of a chattel, entirely subject to the will of another. You never exhausted your ingenuity in avoiding the snares, and eluding the power of a hatred tyrant; you never shuddered at the sound of his footsteps, and trembled within hearing of his voice. I know I did wrong. No one can feel it more sensibly than I do. The painful and humiliating memory will haunt me to my dying day. Still, in looking back, calmly, on the events of my life, I feel that the slave woman ought not to be judged by the same standard as others.

The months passed on. I had many unhappy hours. I secretly mourned over the sorrow I was bringing on my grandmother, who had so tried to shield me from harm. I knew that I was the greatest comfort of her old age, and that it was a source of pride to her that I had not degraded myself, like most of the slaves. I wanted to confess to her that I was no longer worthy of her love; but I could not utter the dreaded words.

As for Dr. Flint, I had a feeling of satisfaction and triumph in the thought of telling *him*. From time to time he told me of his intended arrangements, and I was silent. At last, he came and told me the cottage was completed, and ordered me to go to it. I told him I would never enter it. He said, "I have heard enough of such talk as that. You shall go, if you are carried by force; and you shall remain there."

I replied, "I will never go there. In a few months I shall be a mother."

He stood and looked at me in dumb amazement, and left the house without a word. I thought I should be happy in my triumph over him. But now that the truth was out, and my relatives would hear of it, I felt wretched. Humble as were their circumstances, they had pride in my good character. Now, how could I look them in the face? My self-respect was gone! I had resolved that I would be virtuous, though I was a slave. I had said, "Let the storm beat! I will brave it till I die." And now, how humiliated I felt!

I went to my grandmother. My lips moved to make confession, but the words stuck in my throat. I sat down in the shade of a tree at her door and began to sew. I think she saw something unusual was the matter with me. The mother of slaves is very watchful. She knows there is no security for her children. After they have entered their teens she lives in daily expectation of trouble. This leads to many questions. If the girl is of a sensitive nature, timidity keeps her from answering truthfully, and this well-meant course has a tendency to drive her from maternal counsels. Presently, in came my mistress, like a mad woman, and accused me concerning her husband. My grandmother, whose suspicions had been previously awakened, believed what she said. She exclaimed, "O Linda! has it come to this? I had rather see you dead than to see you as you now are. You are a disgrace to your dead mother." She tore from my fingers my mother's wedding ring and her silver thimble. "Go away!" she exclaimed, "and never come to my house, again." Her reproaches fell so hot and heavy, that they left me no chance to answer. Bitter tears, such as the eyes never shed but once, were my only answer. I rose from my seat, but fell back again, sobbing. She did not speak to me; but the tears were running down her furrowed cheeks, and they scorched me like fire. She had always been so kind to me! *So* kind! How I longed to throw myself at her feet, and tell her all the truth! But she had ordered me to go, and never to come there again. After a few minutes, I mustered strength, and started to obey her. With what feelings did I now close that little gate, which I used to open with such an eager hand in my childhood! It closed upon me with a sound I never heard before.

Where could I go? I was afraid to return to my master's. I walked on recklessly, not caring where I went, or what would become of me. When I had gone four or five miles, fatigue compelled me to stop. I sat down on the stump of an old tree. The stars were shining through the boughs above me. How they mocked me, with their bright, calm light! The hours passed by, and as I sat there alone a chilliness and deadly sickness came over me. I sank on the ground. My mind was full of horrid thoughts. I prayed to die; but the prayer was not answered. At last, with great effort I roused myself, and walked some distance further, to the house of a woman who had been a friend of my mother. When I told her why I was there, she spoke soothingly to me; but I could not be comforted. I thought I could bear my shame if I could only be reconciled to my grandmother. I longed to open my heart to her. I thought if she could know the real state of the case, and all I had been bearing for years, she would perhaps judge me less harshly. My friend advised me to send for her. I did so; but days of agonizing suspense passed before she came. Had she utterly forsaken me? No. She came at last. I knelt before her, and told her the things that had poisoned my life; how long I had been persecuted; that I saw no way of escape; and in an hour of extremity I had become desperate. She listened in silence. I told her I would bear any thing and do any thing, if in time I had hopes of obtaining her forgiveness. I begged of her to pity me, for my dead mother's sake. And she did pity me. She did not say, "I forgive you;" but she looked at me lovingly, with her eyes full of tears. She laid her old hand gently on my head, and murmured, "Poor child! Poor child!"

17

THE FLIGHT

Mr. Flint was hard pushed for house servants, and rather than lose me he had restrained his malice. I did my work faithfully, though not, of course, with a willing mind. They were evidently afraid I should leave them. Mr. Flint wished that I should sleep in the great house instead of the servants' quarters. His wife agreed to the proposition, but said I mustn't bring my bed into the house, because it would scatter feathers on her carpet. I knew when I went there that they would never think of such a thing as furnishing a bed of any kind for me and my little one. I therefore carried my own bed, and now I was forbidden to use it. I did as I was ordered. But now that I was certain my children were to be put in their power, in order to give them a stronger hold on me, I resolved to leave them that night. I remembered the grief this step would bring upon my dear old grandmother; and nothing less than the freedom of my children would have induced me to disregard her advice. I went about my evening work with trembling steps. Mr. Flint twice called from his chamber door to inquire why the house was not locked up. I replied that I had not done my work. "You have had time enough to do it," said he. "Take care how you answer me!"

I shut all the windows, locked all the doors, and went up to the third story, to wait till midnight. How long those hours seemed, and how fervently I prayed that God would not forsake me in this hour of utmost need! I was about to risk every thing on the throw of a die; and if I failed, O what would become of me and my poor children? They would be made to suffer for my fault.

At half past twelve I stole softly down stairs. I stopped on the second floor, thinking I heard a noise. I felt my way down into the parlor, and looked out of the window. The night was so intensely dark that I could see nothing. I raised the window very softly and jumped out. Large drops of rain were falling, and the darkness bewildered me. I dropped on my knees, and breathed a short prayer to God for guidance and protection. I groped my way to the road, and rushed towards the town with almost lightning speed. I arrived at my grandmother's house, but dared not see her. She would say, "Linda, you are killing me;" and I knew that would unnerve me. I tapped softly at the window of a room, occupied by a woman, who had lived in the house several years. I knew she was a faithful friend, and could be trusted with my secret. I tapped several times before she heard me. At last she raised the window, and I whispered, "Sally, I have run away. Let me in, quick." She opened the door softly, and said in low tones, "For God's sake, don't. Your grandmother is trying to buy you and de chillern. Mr. Sands was here last week. He tole her he was going away on business, but he wanted her to go ahead about buying you and de chillren, and he would help her all he could. Don't run away, Linda. Your grandmother is all bowed down wid trouble now."

I replied, "Sally, they are going to carry my children to the plantation to-morrow; and they will never sell them to any body so long as they have me in their power. Now, would you advise me to go back?"

"No, chile, no," answered she. "When dey finds you is gone, dey won't want de plague ob de chillern; but where is you going to hide? Dey knows ebery inch ob dis house."

I told her I had a hiding-place, and that was all it was best for her to know. I asked her to go into my room as soon as it was light, and take all my clothes out of my trunk, and pack them in hers; for I knew Mr. Flint and the constable would be there early to search my room. I feared the sight of my children would be too much for my full heart; but I could not go out into the uncertain future without one last look. I bent over the bed where lay my little Benny and baby Ellen. Poor little ones! fatherless and motherless! Memories of their father came over me. He wanted to be kind to them; but they were not all to him, as they were to my womanly heart. I knelt and prayed for the innocent little sleepers. I kissed them lightly, and turned away.

As I was about to open the street door, Sally laid her hand on my shoulder, and said, "Linda, is you gwine all alone? Let me call your uncle."

"No, Sally," I replied, "I want no one to be brought into trouble on my account."

I went forth into the darkness and rain. I ran on till I came to the house of the friend who was to conceal me.

Early the next morning Mr. Flint was at my grandmother's inquiring for me. She told him she had not seen me, and supposed I was at the plantation. He watched her face narrowly, and said, "Don't you know any thing about her running off?" She assured him that she did not. He went on to say, "Last night she ran off without the least provocation. We had treated her very kindly. My wife liked her. She will soon be found and brought back. Are her children with you?" When told that they were, he said, "I am very glad to hear that. If they are here, she cannot be far off. If I find out that any of my niggers have had any thing to do with this damned business, I'll give 'em five hundred lashes." As he started to go to his father's, he turned round and added, persuasively, "Let her be brought back, and she shall have her children to live with her."

The tidings made the old doctor rave and storm at a furious rate. It was a busy day for them. My grandmother's house was searched from top to bottom. As my trunk was empty, they concluded I had taken my clothes with me. Before ten o'clock every vessel northward bound was thoroughly examined, and the law against harboring fugitives was read to all on board. At night a watch was set over the town. Knowing how distressed my grandmother would be, I wanted to send her a message; but it could not be done. Every one who went in or out of her house was closely watched. The doctor said he would take my children, unless she became responsible for them; which of course she willingly did. The next day was spent in searching. Before night, the following advertisement was posted at every corner, and in every public place for miles round:—

$300 REWARD! Ran away from the subscriber, an intelligent, bright, mulatto girl, named Linda, 21 years of age. Five feet four inches high. Dark eyes, and black hair inclined to curl; but it can be made straight. Has a decayed spot on a front tooth. She can read and write, and in all probability will try to get to the Free States. All persons are forbidden, under penalty of the law, to harbor or employ said slave. $150 will be given to whoever takes her in the state, and $300 if taken out of the state and delivered to me, or lodged in jail.

Dr. Flint.

39

THE CONFESSION

For two years my daughter and I supported ourselves comfortably in Boston. At the end of that time, my brother William offered to send Ellen to a boarding school. It required a great effort for me to consent to part with her, for I had few near ties, and it was her presence that made my two little rooms seem home-like. But my judgment prevailed over my selfish feelings. I made preparations for her departure. During the two years we had lived together I had often resolved to tell her something about her father; but I had never been able to muster sufficient courage. I had a shrinking dread of diminishing my child's love. I knew she must have curiosity on the subject, but she had never asked a question. She was always very careful not to say any thing to remind me of my troubles. Now that she was going from me, I thought if I should die before she returned, she might hear my story from some one who did not understand the palliating circumstances; and that if she were entirely ignorant on the subject, her sensitive nature might receive a rude shock.

When we retired for the night, she said, "Mother, it is very hard to leave you alone. I am almost sorry I am going, though I do want to improve myself. But you will write to me often; won't you, mother?"

I did not throw my arms round her. I did not answer her. But in a calm, solemn way, for it cost me great effort, I said, "Listen to me, Ellen; I have something to tell you!" I recounted my early sufferings in slavery, and told her how nearly they had crushed me. I began to tell her how they had driven me into a great sin, when she clasped me in her arms, and exclaimed, "O, don't, mother! Please don't tell me any more."

I said, "But, my child, I want you to know about your father."

"I know all about it, mother," she replied; "I am nothing to my father, and he is nothing to me. All my love is for you. I was with him five months in Washington, and he never cared for me. He never spoke to me as he did to his little Fanny. I knew all the time he was my father, for Fanny's nurse told me so; but she said I must never tell any body, and I never did. I used to wish he would take me in his arms and kiss me, as he did Fanny; or that he would sometimes smile at me, as he did at her. I thought if he was my own father, he ought to love me. I was a little girl then, and didn't know any better. But now I never think any thing about my father. All my love is for you." She hugged me closer as she spoke, and I thanked God that the knowledge I had so much dreaded to impart had not diminished the affection of my child. I had not the slightest idea she knew that portion of my history. If I had, I should have spoken to her long before; for my pent-up feelings had often longed to pour themselves out to some one I could trust. But I loved the dear girl better for the delicacy she had manifested towards her unfortunate mother.

The next morning, she and her uncle started on their journey to the village in New York, where she was to be placed at school. It seemed as if all the sunshine had gone away. My little room was dreadfully lonely. I was thankful when a message came from a lady, accustomed to employ me, requesting me to come and sew in her family for several weeks. On my return, I found a letter from brother William. He thought of opening an anti-slavery reading room in Rochester, and combining with it the sale of some books and stationery; and he wanted me to unite with him. We tried it, but it was not successful. We found warm anti-slavery friends there, but the feeling was not general enough to support such an establishment. I passed nearly a year in the family of Isaac and Amy Post, practical believers in the Christian doctrine of human brotherhood. They measured a man's worth by his character, not by his complexion. The memory of those beloved and honored friends will remain with me to my latest hour.

41

FREE AT LAST

Mrs. Bruce, and every member of her family, were exceedingly kind to me. I was thankful for the blessings of my lot, yet I could not always wear a cheerful countenance. I was doing harm to no one; on the contrary, I was doing all the good I could in my small way; yet I could never go out to breathe God's free air without trepidation at my heart. This seemed hard; and I could not think it was a right state of things in any civilized country.

From time to time I received news from my good old grandmother. She could not write; but she employed others to write for her. The following is an extract from one of her last letters:—

"Dear Daughter: I cannot hope to see you again on earth; but I pray to God to unite us above, where pain will no more rack this feeble body of mine; where sorrow and parting from my children will be no more. God has promised these things if we are faithful unto the end. My age and feeble health deprive me of going to church now; but God is with me here at home. Thank your brother for his kindness. Give much love to him, and tell him to remember the Creator in the days of his youth, and strive to meet me in the Father's kingdom. Love to Ellen and Benjamin. Don't neglect him. Tell him for me, to be a good boy. Strive, my child; to train them for God's children. May he protect and provide for you, is the prayer of your loving old mother."

These letters both cheered and saddened me. I was always glad to have tidings from the kind, faithful old friend of my unhappy youth; but her messages of love made my heart yearn to see her before she died, and I mourned over the fact that it was impossible. Some months after I returned from my flight to New England, I received a letter from her, in which she wrote, "Dr. Flint is dead. He has left a distressed family. Poor old man! I hope he made his peace with God."

I remembered how he had defrauded my grandmother of the hard earnings she had loaned; how he had tried to cheat her out of the freedom her mistress had promised her, and how he had persecuted her children; and I thought to myself that she was a better Christian than I was, if she could entirely forgive him. I cannot say, with truth, that the news of my old master's death softened my feelings towards him. There are wrongs which even the grave does not bury. The man was odious to me while he lived, and his memory is odious now.

His departure from this world did not diminish my danger. He had threatened my grandmother that his heirs should hold me in slavery after he was gone; that I never should be free so long as a child of his survived. As for Mrs. Flint, I had seen her in deeper afflictions than I supposed the loss of her husband would be, for she had buried several children; yet I never saw any signs of softening in her heart. The doctor had died in embarrassed circumstances, and had little to will to his heirs, except such property as he was unable to grasp. I was well aware what I had to expect from the family of Flints; and my fears were confirmed by a letter from the south, warning me to be on my guard, because Mrs. Flint openly declared that her daughter could not afford to lose so valuable a slave as I was.

I kept close watch of the newspapers for arrivals; but one Saturday night, being much occupied, I forgot to examine the Evening Express as usual. I went down into the parlor for it, early in the morning, and found the boy about to kindle a fire with it. I took it from him and examined the list of arrivals. Reader, if you have never been a slave, you cannot imagine the acute sensation of suffering at my heart, when I read the names of Mr. and Mrs. Dodge, at a hotel in Courtland Street. It was a third-rate hotel, and that circumstance convinced me of the truth of what I had heard, that they were short of funds and had need of my value, as *they* valued me; and that was by dollars and cents. I hastened with the paper to Mrs. Bruce. Her heart and hand were always open to every one in distress, and she always warmly sympathized with mine. It was impossible to tell how near the enemy was. He might have passed and repassed the house while we were sleeping. He might at that moment be waiting to pounce upon me if I ventured out of doors. I had never seen the husband of my young mistress, and therefore I could not distinguish him from any other stranger. A carriage was hastily ordered; and, closely veiled, I followed Mrs. Bruce, taking the baby again with me into exile. After various turnings and crossings, and returnings, the carriage stopped at the house of one of Mrs. Bruce's friends, where I was kindly received. Mrs. Bruce returned immediately, to instruct the domestics what to say if any one came to inquire for me.

It was lucky for me that the evening paper was not burned up before I had a chance to examine the list of arrivals. It was not long after Mrs. Bruce's return to her house, before several people came to inquire for me. One inquired for me, another asked for my daughter Ellen, and another said he had a letter from my grandmother, which he was requested to deliver in person.

They were told, "She *has* lived here, but she has left."

"How long ago?"

"I don't know, sir."

"Do you know where she went?"

"I do not, sir." And the door was closed.

This Mr. Dodge, who claimed me as his property, was originally a Yankee pedler in the south; then he became a merchant, and finally a slaveholder. He managed to get introduced into what was called the first society, and married Miss Emily Flint. A quarrel arose between him and her brother, and the brother cowhided him. This led to a family feud, and he proposed to remove to Virginia. Dr. Flint left him no property, and his own means had become circumscribed, while a wife and children depended upon him for support. Under these circumstances, it was very natural that he should make an effort to put me into his pocket.

I had a colored friend, a man from my native place, in whom I had the most implicit confidence. I sent for him, and told him that Mr. and Mrs. Dodge had arrived in New York. I proposed that he should call upon them to make inquiries about his friends at the south, with whom Dr. Flint's family were well acquainted. He thought there was no impropriety in his doing so, and he consented. He went to the hotel, and knocked at the door of Mr. Dodge's room, which was opened by the gentleman himself, who gruffly inquired, "What brought you here? How came you to know I was in the city?"

"Your arrival was published in the evening papers, sir; and I called to ask Mrs. Dodge about my friends at home. I didn't suppose it would give any offence."

"Where's that negro girl, that belongs to my wife?"

"What girl, sir?"

"You know well enough. I mean Linda, that ran away from Dr. Flint's plantation, some years ago. I dare say you've seen her, and know where she is."

"Yes, sir, I've seen her, and know where she is. She is out of your reach, sir."

"Tell me where she is, or bring her to me, and I will give her a chance to buy her freedom."

"I don't think it would be of any use, sir. I have heard her say she would go to the ends of the earth, rather than pay any man or woman for her freedom, because she thinks she has a right to it. Besides, she couldn't do it, if she would, for she has spent her earnings to educate her children."

This made Mr. Dodge very angry, and some high words passed between them. My friend was afraid to come where I was; but in the course of the day I received a note from him. I supposed they had not come from the south, in the winter, for a pleasure excursion; and now the nature of their business was very plain.

Mrs. Bruce came to me and entreated me to leave the city the next morning. She said her house was watched, and it was possible that some clew to me might be obtained. I refused to take her advice. She pleaded with an earnest tenderness, that ought to have moved me; but I was in a bitter, disheartened mood. I was weary of flying from pillar to post. I had been chased during half my life, and it seemed as if the chase was never to end. There I sat, in that great city, guiltless of crime, yet not daring to worship God in any of the churches. I heard the bells ringing for afternoon service, and, with contemptuous sarcasm, I said, "Will the preachers take for their text, 'Proclaim liberty to the captive, and the opening of prison doors to them that are bound'? or will they preach from the text, 'Do unto others as ye would they should do unto you'?" Oppressed Poles and Hungarians could find a safe refuge in that city; John Mitchell was free to proclaim in the City Hall his desire for "a plantation well stocked with slaves;" but there I sat, an oppressed American, not daring to show my face. God forgive the black and bitter thoughts I indulged on that Sabbath day! The Scripture says, "Oppression makes even a wise man mad;" and I was not wise.

I had been told that Mr. Dodge said his wife had never signed away her right to my children, and if he could not get me, he would take them. This it was, more than any thing else, that roused such a tempest in my soul. Benjamin was with his uncle William in California, but my innocent young daughter had come to spend a vacation with me. I thought of what I had suffered in slavery at her age, and my heart was like a tiger's when a hunter tries to seize her young.

Dear Mrs. Bruce! I seem to see the expression of her face, as she turned away discouraged by my obstinate mood. Finding her expostulations unavailing, she sent Ellen to entreat me. When ten o'clock in the evening arrived and Ellen had not returned, this watchful and unwearied friend became anxious. She came to us in a carriage, bringing a well-filled trunk for my journey—trusting that by this time I would listen to reason. I yielded to her, as I ought to have done before.

The next day, baby and I set out in a heavy snow storm, bound for New England again. I received letters from the City of Iniquity, addressed to me under an assumed name. In a few days one came from Mrs. Bruce, informing me that my new master was still searching for me, and that she intended to put an end to this persecution by buying my freedom. I felt grateful for the kindness that prompted this offer, but the idea was not so pleasant to me as might have been expected. The more my mind had become enlightened, the more difficult it was for me to consider myself an article of property; and to pay money to those who had so grievously oppressed me seemed like taking from my sufferings the glory of triumph. I wrote to Mrs. Bruce, thanking her, but saying that being sold from one owner to another seemed too much like slavery; that such a great obligation could not be easily cancelled; and that I preferred to go to my brother in California.

Without my knowledge, Mrs. Bruce employed a gentleman in New York to enter into negotiations with Mr. Dodge. He proposed to pay three hundred dollars down, if Mr. Dodge would sell me, and enter into obligations to relinquish all claim to me or my children forever after. He who called himself my master said he scorned so small an offer for such a valuable servant. The gentleman replied, "You can do as you choose, sir. If you reject this offer you will never get any thing; for the woman has friends who will convey her and her children out of the country."

Mr. Dodge concluded that "half a loaf was better than no bread," and he agreed to the proffered terms. By the next mail I received this brief letter from Mrs. Bruce: "I am rejoiced to tell you that the money for your freedom has been paid to Mr. Dodge. Come home to-morrow. I long to see you and my sweet babe."

My brain reeled as I read these lines. A gentleman near me said, "It's true; I have seen the bill of sale." "The bill of sale!" Those words struck me like a blow. So I was *sold* at last! A human being *sold* in the free city of New York! The bill of sale is on record, and future generations will learn from it that women were articles of traffic in New York, late in the nineteenth century of the Christian religion. It may hereafter prove a useful document to antiquaries, who are seeking to measure the progress of civilization in the United States. I well know the value of that bit of paper; but much as I love freedom, I do not like to look upon it. I am deeply grateful to the generous friend who procured it, but I despise the miscreant who demanded payment for what never rightfully belonged to him or his.

I had objected to having my freedom bought, yet I must confess that when it was done I felt as if a heavy load had been lifted from my weary shoulders. When I rode home in the cars I was no longer afraid to unveil my face and look at people as they passed. I should have been glad to have met Daniel Dodge himself; to have had him seen me and known me, that he might have mourned over the untoward circumstances which compelled him to sell me for three hundred dollars.

When I reached home, the arms of my benefactress were thrown round me, and our tears mingled. As soon as she could speak, she said, "O Linda, I'm *so* glad it's all over! You wrote to me as if you thought you were going to be transferred from one owner to another. But I did not buy you for your services. I should have done just the same, if you had been going to sail for California to-morrow. I should, at least, have the satisfaction of knowing that you left me a free woman."

My heart was exceedingly full. I remembered how my poor father had tried to buy me, when I was a small child, and how he had been disappointed. I hoped his spirit was rejoicing over me now. I remembered how my good old grandmother had laid up her earnings to purchase me in later years, and how often her plans had been frustrated. How that faithful, loving old heart would leap for joy, if she could look on me and my children now that we were free! My relatives had been foiled in all their efforts, but God had raised me up a friend among strangers, who had bestowed on me the precious, long-desired boon. Friend! It is a common word, often lightly used. Like other good and beautiful things, it may be tarnished by careless handling; but when I speak of Mrs. Bruce as my friend, the word is sacred.

My grandmother lived to rejoice in my freedom; but not long after, a letter came with a black seal. She had gone "where the wicked cease from troubling, and the weary are at rest."

Time passed on, and a paper came to me from the south, containing an obituary notice of my uncle Phillip. It was the only case I ever knew of such an honor conferred upon a colored person. It was written by one of his friends, and contained these words: "Now that death has laid him low, they call him a good man and a useful citizen; but what are eulogies to the black man, when the world has faded from his vision? It does not require man's praise to obtain rest in God's kingdom." So they called a colored man a *citizen!* Strange words to be uttered in that region!

Reader, my story ends with freedom; not in the usual way, with marriage. I and my children are now free! We are as free from the power of slaveholders as are the white people of the north; and though that, according to my ideas, is not saying a great deal, it is a vast improvement in *my* condition. The dream of my life is not yet realized. I do not sit with my children in a home of my own. I still long for a hearthstone of my own, however humble. I wish it for my children's sake far more than for my own. But God so orders circumstances as to keep me with my friend Mrs. Bruce. Love, duty, gratitude, also bind me to her side. It is a privilege to serve her who pities my oppressed people, and who has bestowed the inestimable boon of freedom on me and my children.

It has been painful to me, in many ways, to recall the dreary years I passed in bondage. I would gladly forget them if I could. Yet the retrospection is not altogether without solace; for with those gloomy recollections come tender memories of my good old grandmother, like light, fleecy clouds floating over a dark and troubled sea.

Emily Dickinson
1830–1886

As a young child, Emily Dickinson wrote a humor column for a student magazine, and at Mount Holyoke Female Seminary, where she spent a year, she became notorious both for her witty and irreverent compositions and because it was darkly suspected that she had little interest in the fate of her soul or the religious fervor that then prevailed in western Massachusetts. Though she is famous for the secludedness of her life, almost all of it spent in her family's house in Amherst, and for her lack of interest in publishing her poems, only ten of which (out of over 1,100) appeared in print during her lifetime, Dickinson was in fact making history on a world scale, quietly fashioning a revolutionary sensibility of astonishing originality and force.

The comic irreverence is inseparable from her most visionary insights. She writes, with barely subdued sarcasm: "Of God we ask one favor, / That we may be forgiven— / For what, he is presumed to know— / The Crime, from us, is hidden." Refusing to think of pain (one of her frequent subjects) as the result of original sin, she is obliged to face the facts of loss, anxiety, and loneliness without any recourse to the consolation of transcendental ideas, whether religious or secular. Her relation to both the form and the content of New England Protestantism is a complex matter. What is sure is that, imagining Calvinism's Heavenly Father as at once a "Banker" and a "Burglar," a figure of reassuring certitude who is also a thief, breaking and entering in order to steal away the love or self-worth he is supposed to ensure, Dickinson prophesies much of the great women's literature to come, with its analyses of the daughter's ambivalent relation to the patriarchal father. When she talks about how women say the words "my husband," when she looks at the world with the cold, unsentimental eyes of the already dead, she seems to leap with absolute freshness out of her century and into our own.

Given the disparity between Dickinson's bare and simple life and the startlingly new sensibility of her poems, critics have sometimes sought explanation in men, whether the essayist and abolitionist Thomas Wentworth Higginson, with whom she corresponded after sending him some of her poems in 1862, or a mysterious man whom she supposedly loved and who supposedly broke her heart. Higginson's comment after a visit suggests how unready nineteenth-century men were for a woman so distant from conventional femininity: "I never was with anyone who drained my nerve power so much . . . I am glad not to live near her." It seems likely that Dickinson discovered rich emotional resources in those who did live near her, including her family, especially her sister-in-law and next-door neighbor, Susan, and her friends (among whom many of her poems were circulated). She also got a great deal from her voracious reading. Language itself seems to have permitted Dickinson so much travel that transporting her body around in dusty coaches would have been beside the point.

Short and aphoristic, Dickinson's poems use but also extend the simple hymnbook meters of her time and place. They stretch the acceptable criteria of successful rhyming, making room for greater flexibility. Most famously, they often use series of dashes instead of more conventional punctuation, making it uncertain how final a given statement might be. This fracturing of grammar has come to seem less eccentric than modern. It's as if poetry had to catch up to her in order for us to see the true society in which she belongs.

I never lost as much but twice

I never lost as much but twice,
And that was in the sod.
Twice have I stood a beggar
Before the door of God!

5   Angels—twice descending
Reimbursed my store—
Burglar! Banker—Father!
I am poor once more!

Title divine—is mine!

Title divine—is mine!
The Wife—without the Sign!
Acute Degree—conferred on me—
Empress of Calvary!
5   Royal—all but the Crown!
Betrothed—without the swoon
God sends us Women—
When you—hold—Garnet to Garnet—
Gold—to Gold—
10   Born—Bridalled—Shrouded—
In a Day—
Tri Victory
"My Husband"—women say—
Stroking the Melody—
15   Is *this*—the way?

There came a Day at Summer's full

There came a Day at Summer's full,
Entirely for me—
I thought that such were for the Saints,
Where Resurrections—be—

5   The Sun, as common, went abroad,
The flowers, accustomed, blew,
As if no soul the solstice passed
That maketh all things new—

The time was scarce profaned, by speech—
10   The symbol of a word
Was needless, as at Sacrament,
The Wardrobe—of our Lord—

Each was to each The Sealed Church,
Permitted to commune this—time—
15   Lest we too awkward show
At Supper of the Lamb.

The Hours slid fast—as Hours will,
Clutched tight, by greedy hands—
So faces on two Decks, look back,
20   Bound to opposing lands—

And so when all the time had leaked,
Without external sound
Each bound the Other's Crucifix—
We gave no other Bond—

25   Sufficient troth, that we shall rise—
Deposed—at length, the Grave—
To that new Marriage,
Justified—through Calvaries of Love—

It was not Death, for I stood up

It was not Death, for I stood up,
And all the Dead, lie down—
It was not Night, for all the Bells
Put out their Tongues, for Noon.

5   It was not Frost, for on my Flesh
I felt Siroccos[1]—crawl—
Nor Fire—for just my Marble feet
Could keep a Chancel,[2] cool—

And yet, it tasted, like them all,
10   The Figures I have seen

---

1. Oppressively hot Mediterranean wind.   2. The part of a church reserved for those who officiate in the service.

Set orderly, for Burial,
Reminded me, of mine—

As if my life were shaven,
And fitted to a frame,
15 And could not breathe without a key,
And 'twas like Midnight, some—

When everything that ticked—has stopped—
And Space stares all around—
Or Grisly frosts—first Autumn morns,
20 Repeal the Beating Ground—

But, most, like Chaos—Stopless—cool—
Without a Chance, or Spar—
Or even a Report of Land—
To justify—Despair.

After great pain, a formal feeling comes

After great pain, a formal feeling comes—
The Nerves sit ceremonious, like Tombs—
The stiff Heart questions was it He, that bore,
And Yesterday, or Centuries before?

5 The Feet, mechanical, go round—
Of Ground, or Air, or Ought—
A Wooden way
Regardless grown,
A Quartz contentment like a stone—

10 This is the Hour of Lead—
Remembered, if outlived,
As Freezing persons, recollect the Snow—
First—Chill—then Stupor—then the letting go—

I died for Beauty

I died for Beauty—but was scarce
Adjusted in the Tomb
When One who died for Truth, was lain
In an adjoining Room—

5 He questioned softly "Why I failed"?
"For Beauty," I replied—
"And I—for Truth—Themself are One—
We Brethren, are," He said—

And so, as Kinsmen, met a Night—
10 We talked between the Rooms—
Until the Moss had reached our lips—
And covered up—our names—

I dwell in Possibility

I dwell in Possibility—
A fairer House than Prose—
More numerous of Windows—
Superior—for Doors—

5   Of Chambers as the Cedars—
Impregnable of Eye—
And for an Everlasting Roof
The Gambrels[1] of the Sky—

Of Visitors—the fairest—
10   For Occupation—This—
The spreading wide my narrow Hands
To gather Paradise—

I heard a Fly buzz—when I died

I heard a Fly buzz—when I died—
The Stillness in the Room
Was like the Stillness in the Air—
Between the Heaves of Storm—

5   The Eyes around—had wrung them dry—
And Breaths were gathering firm
For that last Onset—when the King
Be witnessed—in the Room—

I willed my Keepsakes—Signed away
10   What portion of me be
Assignable—and then it was
There interposed a Fly—

With Blue—uncertain stumbling Buzz—
Between the light—and me—
15   And then the Windows failed—and then
I could not see to see—

I live with Him—I see His face

I live with Him—I see His face—
I go no more away
For Visitor—or Sundown—
Death's single privacy

5   The Only One—forestalling Mine—
And that—by Right that He
Presents a Claim invisible—
No wedlock—granted Me—

1. Curved or hipped roof.

I live with Him—I hear His Voice—
10   I stand alive—Today—
To witness to the Certainty
Of Immortality—

Taught Me—by Time—the lower Way—
Conviction—Every day—
15   That Life like This—is stopless—
Be Judgment—what it may—

My Life had stood—a Loaded Gun

My Life had stood—a Loaded Gun—
In Corners—till a Day
The Owner passed—identified—
And carried Me away—

5   And now We roam in Sovereign Woods—
And now We hunt the Doe—
And every time I speak for Him—
The Mountains straight reply—

And do I smile, such cordial light
10   Upon the Valley glow—
It is as a Vesuvian face
Had let its pleasure through—

And when at Night—Our good Day done—
I guard My Master's Head—
15   'Tis better than the Eider-Duck's
Deep Pillow—to have shared—

To foe of His—I'm deadly foe—
None stir the second time—
On whom I lay a Yellow Eye—
20   Or an emphatic Thumb—

Though I than He—may longer live
He longer must—than I—
For I have but the power to kill,
Without—the power to die—

Further in Summer than the Birds

Further in Summer than the Birds
Pathetic from the Grass
A minor Nation celebrates
Its unobtrusive Mass.

5   No Ordinance be seen
So gradual the Grace

A pensive Custom it becomes
Enlarging Loneliness.

10 Antiquest felt at Noon
When August burning low
Arise this spectral Canticle[1]
Repose to typify

Remit as yet no Grace
No Furrow on the Glow
15 Yet a Druidic[2] Difference
Enhances Nature now

Tell all the Truth but tell it slant

Tell all the Truth but tell it slant—
Success in Circuit lies
Too bright for our infirm Delight
The Truth's superb surprise
5 As Lightning to the Children eased
With explanation kind
The Truth must dazzle gradually
Or every man be blind—

Joaquim María Machado de Assis
1839–1908

Born in Rio de Janeiro to a Portuguese mother and a Brazilian mulatto father, Machado de Assis was raised in extreme poverty and doesn't seem to have had any education beyond elementary school. His rise to literary greatness is the stuff of Brazilian legend. Between the ages of fifteen and thirty he seems to have worked as typesetter, proofreader, editor, staff writer, and possibly a clerk in a stationery store. In the same years, he also wrote some 6,000 lines of poetry, nineteen plays and opera librettos, twenty-four short stories, and numerous articles and translations. These writings are pervaded by allusions to Portuguese, Greek, Latin, French, and English literature. Self-educated as well as self-made, he had to overcome the disadvantages of epilepsy and stuttering as well as racial prejudice and destitution. By the end of his life, he had become a high-level civil servant while being universally recognized as Brazil's foremost prose writer.

A private man, Machado de Assis did everything in his power to discourage people from explaining his fiction on the basis of his biography. His novels, for which he is best known, are elliptical, ironic, and understated, surprisingly modern in their refusal to give the reader any secure and comfortable perspective on Brazilian society. Along with radical social critique and Swiftian satire, he has a taste for the unreliable narrator. Perhaps the most important advice we get from his fiction is that it can be dangerous not to read attentively. In *Dom Casmurro* (1899),

---

1. Hymn.

2. Having to do with the Druids, priests or magicians among the ancient Celts.

which has been obligatory reading in Brazilian schools for decades, he writes, "Not everything is clear in life or in books." Though he was a big winner himself in the game of life, he knew that society's rules were not fair and that chance played a large role. In *Epitaph of a Small Winner* (1881) he declared that, like Stendhal, he could be content with few readers. But despite his uncompromising high principles and constitutional pessimism, he also knew how to draw with bemused detachment on popular genres like melodrama and farce, and his work has always been extremely well received. His satiric story "The Psychiatrist" can read as a straightforward satire on scientific arrogance and its potential collusion in tyranny—compare with Charlotte Perkins Gilman's "The Yellow Wallaper," which follows. Yet "The Psychiatrist" also pokes fun at the doctor's victims and leaves us with anything but a reassuring vision of "normal" society.

PRONUNCIATIONS:
   Machado de Assis: mah-CHA-doh day ah-CEASE
   Itaguai: EE-tah-GUAI

The Psychiatrist[1]

1. How Itaguai Acquired a Madhouse

The chronicles of Itaguai relate that in remote times a certain physician of noble birth, Simão Bacamarte, lived there and that he was one of the greatest doctors in all Brazil, Portugal, and the Spains.[2] He had studied for many years in both Padua and Coimbra. When, at the age of thirty-four, he announced his decision to return to Brazil and his home town of Itaguai, the King of Portugal tried to dissuade him; he offered Bacamarte his choice between the Presidency of Coimbra University and the office of Chief Expediter of Government Affairs. The doctor politely declined.

"Science," he told His Majesty, "is my only office; Itaguai, my universe."

He took up residence there and dedicated himself to the theory and practice of medicine. He alternated therapy with study and research; he demonstrated theorems with poultices.

In his fortieth year Bacamarte married the widow of a circuit judge. Her name was Dona Evarista da Costa e Mascarenhas, and she was neither beautiful nor charming. One of his uncles, an outspoken man, asked him why he had not selected a more attractive woman. The doctor replied that Dona Evarista enjoyed perfect digestion, excellent eyesight, and normal blood pressure; she had had no serious illnesses and her urinalysis was negative. It was likely she would give him healthy, robust children. If, in addition to her physiological accomplishments, Dona Evarista possessed a face composed of features neither individually pretty nor mutually compatible, he thanked God for it, for he would not be tempted to sacrifice his scientific pursuits to the contemplation of his wife's attractions.

But Dona Evarista failed to satisfy her husband's expectations. She produced no robust children and, for that matter, no puny ones either. The scientific temperament is by nature patient; Bacamarte waited three, four, five years. At the end of this period he began an exhaustive study of sterility. He reread the works of all the authorities (including the Arabian), sent inquiries to the Italian and German universities, and finally recommended a special diet. But Dona Evarista, nourished almost

---

1. Translated by William L. Grossman.

2. The union of the Spanish crowns of Aragon and Castile.

exclusively on succulent Itaguai pork, paid no heed; and to this lack of wifely submissiveness—understandable but regrettable—we owe the total extinction of the Bacamartian dynasty.

The pursuit of science is sometimes itself therapeutic. Dr. Bacamarte cured himself of his disappointment by plunging even deeper into his work. It was at this time that one of the byways of medicine attracted his attention: psychopathology. The entire colony and, for that matter, the kingdom itself could not boast one authority on the subject. It was a field, indeed, in which little responsible work had been done anywhere in the world. Simão Bacamarte saw an opportunity for Lusitanian[3] and, more specifically, Brazilian science to cover itself with "imperishable laurels"—an expression he himself used, but only in a moment of ecstasy and within the confines of his home; to the outside world he was always modest and restrained, as befits a man of learning.

"The health of the soul!" he exclaimed. "The loftiest possible goal for a doctor."

"For a great doctor like yourself, yes." This emendation came from Crispim Soares, the town druggist and one of Bacamarte's most intimate friends.

The chroniclers chide the Itaguai Town Council for its neglect of the mentally ill. Violent madmen were locked up at home; peaceable lunatics were simply left at large; and none, violent or peaceable, received care of any sort. Simão Bacamarte proposed to change all this. He decided to build an asylum and he asked the Council for authority to receive and treat all the mentally ill of Itaguai and the surrounding area. He would be paid by the patient's family or, if the family was very poor, by the Council. The proposal aroused excitement and curiosity throughout the town. There was considerable opposition, for it is always difficult to uproot the established way of doing things, however absurd or evil it may be. The idea of having madmen live together in the same house seemed itself to be a symptom of madness, as many intimated even to the doctor's wife.

"Look, Dona Evarista," said Father Lopes, the local vicar, "see if you can't get your husband to take a little holiday. In Rio de Janeiro, maybe. All this intensive study, a man can take just so much of it and then his mind . . ."

Dona Evarista was terrified. She went to her husband and said that she had a consuming desire to take a trip with him to Rio de Janeiro. There, she said, she would eat whatever he thought necessary for the attainment of a certain objective. But the astute doctor immediately perceived what was on his wife's mind and replied that she need have no fear. He then went to the town hall, where the Council was debating his proposal, which he supported with such eloquence that it was approved without amendment on the first ballot. The Council also adopted a tax designed to pay for the lodging, sustenance, and treatment of the indigent mad. This involved a bit of a problem, for everything in Itaguai was already being taxed. After considerable study the Council authorized the use of two plumes on the horses drawing a funeral coach. Anyone wishing to take advantage of this privilege would pay a tax of a stated amount for each hour from the time of death to the termination of the rites at the grave. The town clerk was asked to determine the probable revenue from the new tax, but he got lost in arithmetical calculations, and one of the Councilmen, who was opposed to the doctor's undertaking, suggested that the clerk be relieved of a useless task.

3. Portuguese.

"The calculations are unnecessary," he said, "because Dr. Bacamarte's project will never be executed. Who ever heard of putting a lot of crazy people together in one house?"

But the worthy Councilman was wrong. Bacamarte built his madhouse on New Street, the finest thoroughfare in Itaguai. The building had a courtyard in the center and two hundred cubicles, each with one window. The doctor, an ardent student of Arabian lore, found a passage in the Koran in which Mohammed declared that the insane were holy, for Allah had deprived them of their judgment in order to keep them from sinning. Bacamarte found the idea at once beautiful and profound, and he had the passage engraved on the façade of the house. But he feared that this might offend the Vicar and, through him, the Bishop. Accordingly, he attributed the quotation to Benedict VIII.

The asylum was called the Green House, for its windows were the first of that color ever seen in Itaguai. The formal opening was celebrated magnificently. People came from the entire region, some even from Rio de Janeiro, to witness the ceremonies, which lasted seven days. Some patients had already been admitted, and their relatives took advantage of this opportunity to observe the paternal care and Christian charity with which they were treated. Dona Evarista, delighted by her husband's glory, covered herself with silks, jewels, and flowers. She was a real queen during those memorable days. Everyone came to visit her two or three times. People not only paid court to her but praised her, for—and this fact does great honor to the society of the time—they thought of Dona Evarista in terms of the lofty spirit and prestige of her husband; they envied her, to be sure, but with the noble and blessed envy of admiration.

2. A Torrent of Madmen

Three days later, talking in an expansive mood with the druggist Crispim Soares, the psychiatrist revealed his inmost thoughts.

"Charity, Soares, definitely enters into my method. It is the seasoning in the recipe, for thus I interpret the words of St. Paul to the Corinthians: 'Though I understand all mysteries and all knowledge . . . and have not charity, I am nothing.' But the main thing in my work at the Green House is to study insanity in depth, to learn its various gradations, to classify the various cases, and finally to discover the cause of the phenomenon and its remedy. This is my heart's desire. I believe that in this way I can render a valuable service to humanity."

"A great service," said Crispim Soares.

"Without this asylum," continued the psychiatrist, "I might conceivably accomplish a little. But it provides far greater scope and opportunity for my studies than I would otherwise have."

"Far greater," agreed the druggist.

And he was right. From all the towns and villages in the vicinity came the violent, the depressed, the monomaniacal—the mentally ill of every type and variety. At the end of four months the Green House was a little community in itself. A gallery with thirty-seven more cubicles had to be added. Father Lopes confessed that he had not imagined there were so many madmen in the world nor that such strange cases of madness existed. One of the patients, a coarse, ignorant young man, gave a speech every day after lunch. It was an academic discourse, with metaphors, antitheses, and apostrophes, ornamented with Greek words and quotations from Cicero, Apuleius, and Tertullian.[4] The Vicar could hardly believe his ears. What, a fellow he had seen only three months ago hanging around street corners!

"Quite so," replied the psychiatrist. "But Your Reverence has observed for himself. This happens every day."

"The only explanation I can think of," said the priest, "is the confusion of languages on the Tower of Babel. They were so completely mixed together that now, probably, when a man loses his reason, he easily slips from one into another."

"That may well be the divine explanation," agreed the psychiatrist after a moment's reflection, "but I'm looking for a purely scientific, human explanation—and I believe there is one."

"Maybe so, but I really can't imagine what it could be."

Several of the patients had been driven mad by love. One of these spent all his time wandering through the building and courtyard in search of his wife, whom he had killed in a fit of jealousy that marked the beginning of his insanity. Another thought he was the morning star. He had repeatedly proposed marriage to a certain young lady, and she had continually put him off. He knew why: she thought him dreadfully dull and was waiting to see if she could catch a more interesting husband. So he became a brilliant star, standing with feet and arms outspread like rays. He would remain in this position for hours, waiting to be supplanted by the rising sun.

There were some noteworthy cases of megalomania. One patient, the son of a cheap tailor, invented a genealogy in which he traced his ancestry back to members of royalty and, through them, ultimately to Jehovah. He would recite the entire list of his male progenitors, with a "begat" to link each father and son. Then he would slap his forehead, snap his fingers, and say it all over again. Another patient had a somewhat similar idea but developed it with more rigorous logic. Beginning with the proposition that he was a child of God, which even the Vicar would not have denied, he reasoned that, as the species of the child is the same as that of the parent, he himself must be a god. This conclusion, derived from two irrefutable premises—one Biblical, the other scientific—placed him far above the lunatics who identified themselves with Caesar, Alexander, or other mere mortals.

More remarkable even than the manias and delusions of the madmen was the patience of the psychiatrist. He began by engaging two administrative assistants—an idea that he accepted from Crispim Soares along with the druggist's two nephews. He gave these young men the task of enforcing the rules and regulations that the Town Council had approved for the asylum. They also kept the records and were in charge of the distribution of food and clothing. Thus, the doctor was free to devote all his time to psychiatry.

"The Green House," he told the Vicar, "now has its temporal government and its spiritual government."

Father Lopes laughed. "What a delightful novelty," he said, "to find a society in which the spiritual dominates."

Relieved of administrative burdens, Dr. Bacamarte began an exhaustive study of each patient: his personal and family history, his habits, his likes and dislikes, his hobbies, his attitudes toward others, and so on. He also spent long hours studying, inventing, and experimenting with psychotherapeutic methods. He slept little and ate little; and while he ate he was still working, for at the dinner table he would read an

4. Three Latin authors; Tertullian was an early Christian theologian.

old text or ponder a difficult problem. Often he sat through an entire dinner without saying a word to Dona Evarista.

3. God Knows What He Is Doing

By the end of two months the psychiatrist's wife was the most wretched of women. She did not reproach her husband but suffered in silence. She declined into a state of deep melancholy, became thin and yellowish, ate little, and sighed continually. One day, at dinner, he asked what was wrong with her. She sadly replied that it was nothing. Then she ventured for the first time to complain a little, saying she considered herself as much a widow now as before she married him.

"Who would ever have thought that a bunch of lunatics . . ."

She did not complete the sentence. Or, rather, she completed it by raising her eyes to the ceiling. Dona Evarista's eyes were her most attractive feature—large, black, and bathed in a vaporous light like the dawn. She had used them in much the same way when trying to get Simão Bacamarte to propose. Now she was brandishing her weapon again, this time for the apparent purpose of cutting science's throat. But the psychiatrist was not perturbed. His eyes remained steady, calm, enduring. No wrinkle disturbed his brow, as serene as the waters of Botafogo Bay. Perhaps a slight smile played on his lips as he said:

"You may go to Rio de Janeiro."

Dona Evarista felt as if the floor had vanished and she were floating on air. She had never been to Rio, which, although hardly a shadow of what it is today, was, by comparison with Itaguai, a great and fascinating metropolis. Ever since childhood she had dreamed of going there. She longed for Rio as a Hebrew in the captivity must have longed for Jerusalem, but with her husband settled so definitively in Itaguai she had lost hope. And now, of a sudden, he was permitting her to realize her dream. Dona Evarista could not hide her elation. Simão Bacamarte took her by the hand and smiled in a manner at once conjugal and philosophical.

"How strange is the therapy of the soul!" he thought. "This lady is wasting away because she thinks I do not love her. I give her Rio de Janeiro and she is well again." And he made a note of the phenomenon.

A sudden misgiving pierced Dona Evarista's heart. She concealed her anxiety, however, and merely told her husband that, if he did not go, neither would she, for of course she could not travel alone.

"Your aunt will go with you," replied the psychiatrist.

It should be noted that this expedient had occurred to Dona Evarista. She had not suggested it, for it would impose great expense on her husband. Besides, it was better for the suggestion to come from him.

"Oh, but the money it will cost!" she sighed.

"It doesn't matter," he replied. "Have you any idea of our income?"

He brought her the books of account. Dona Evarista, although impressed by the quantity of the figures, was not quite sure what they signified, so her husband took her to the chest where the money was kept.

Good heavens! There were mountains of gold, thousands upon thousands of cruzados and doubloons. A fortune! While she was drinking it in with her black eyes, the psychiatrist placed his mouth close to her and whispered mischievously:

"'Who would ever have thought that a bunch of lunatics . . .'"

Dona Evarista understood, smiled, and replied with infinite resignation:

"God knows what he is doing."

Three months later she left for Rio in the company of her aunt, the druggist's wife, one of the druggist's cousins, a priest whom Bacamarte had known in Lisbon and who happened to be in Itaguaí, four maidservants, and five or six male attendants. A small crowd had come to see them off. The farewells were sad for everyone but the psychiatrist, for he was troubled by nothing outside the realm of science. Even Dona Evarista's tears, sincere and abundant as they were, did not affect him. If anything concerned him on that occasion, if he cast a restless and police-like eye over the crowd, it was only because he suspected the presence of one or two candidates for commitment to the Green House.

After the departure the druggist and the psychiatrist mounted their horses and rode homeward. Crispim Soares stared at the road, between the ears of his roan. Simão Bacamarte swept the horizon with his eyes, surveyed the distant mountains, and let his horse find the way home. Perfect symbols of the common man and of the genius! One fixes his gaze upon the present with all its tears and privations; the other looks beyond to the glorious dawns of a future that he himself will shape.

4. A New Theory

As his horse jogged along, a new and daring hypothesis occurred to Simão Bacamarte. It was so daring, indeed, that, if substantiated, it would revolutionize the bases of psychopathology. During the next few days he mulled it over. Then, in his spare time, he began to go from house to house, talking with the townspeople about a thousand and one things and punctuating the conversations with a penetrating look that terrified even the bravest.

One morning, after this had been going on for about three weeks, Crispim Soares received a message that the psychiatrist wished to see him.

"He says it's important," added the messenger.

The druggist turned pale. Something must have happened to his wife! The chroniclers of Itaguaí, it should be noted, dwell upon Crispim's love for his Cesaria and point out that they had never been separated in their thirty years of marriage. Only against this background can one explain the monologue, often overheard by the servants, with which the druggist reviled himself: "You miss your wife, do you? You're going crazy without her? It serves you right! Always truckling to Dr. Bacamarte! Who told you to let Cesaria go traveling? Dr. Bacamarte, that's who. Anything he says, you say amen. So now see what you get for it, you vile, miserable, groveling little lackey! Lickspittle! Flunky!" And he added many other ugly names that a man ought not call his enemies, much less himself. The effect of the message on him, in this state of mind, can be readily imagined. He dropped the drugs he had been mixing and fairly flew to the Green House. Simão Bacamarte greeted him joyfully, but he wore his joy as a wise man should—buttoned up to the neck with circumspection.

"I am very happy," he said.

"Some news of our wives?" asked the druggist in a tremulous voice.

The psychiatrist made a magnificent gesture and replied:

"It is something much more important—a scientific experiment. I say 'experiment,' for I do not yet venture to affirm the correctness of my theory. Indeed, this is the very nature of science, Soares: unending inquiry. But, although only an experiment as yet, it may change the face of the earth. Till now, madness has been thought a small island in an ocean of sanity. I am beginning to suspect that it is not an island at all but a continent."

He fell silent for a while, enjoying the druggist's amazement. Then he explained his theory at length. The number of persons suffering from insanity, he believed, was far greater than commonly supposed; and he developed this idea with an abundance of reasons, texts, and examples. He found many of these examples in Itaguai, but he recognized the fallacy of confining his data to one time and place and he therefore resorted to history. He pointed in particular to certain historical celebrities: Socrates, who thought he had a personal demon; Pascal, who sewed a report of an hallucination into the lining of his coat; Mohammed, Caracalla, Domitian, Caligula, and others. The druggist's surprise at Bacamarte's mingling of the vicious and the merely ridiculous moved the psychiatrist to explain that these apparently inconsistent attributes were really different aspects of the same thing.

"The grotesque, my friend, is simply ferocity in disguise."

"Clever, very clever!" exclaimed Crispim Soares.

As for the basic idea of enlarging the realm of insanity, the druggist found it a little far-fetched; but modesty, his chief virtue, kept him from stating his opinion. Instead, he expressed a noble enthusiasm. He declared the idea sublime and added that it was "something for the noisemaker." This expression requires explanation. Like the other towns, villages, and settlements in the colony at that time, Itaguai had no newspaper. It used two media for the publication of news: hand-written posters nailed to the doors of the town hall and of the main church, and the noisemaker.

This is how the latter medium worked: a man was hired for one or more days to go through the streets rattling a noisemaker. A crowd would gather and the man would announce whatever he had been paid to announce: a cure for malaria, a gift to the Church, some farm land for sale, and the like. He might even be engaged to read a sonnet to the people. The system continually disturbed the peace of the community, but it survived a long time because of its almost miraculous effectiveness. Incredible as it may seem, the noisemaker actually enabled merchants to sell inferior goods at superior prices and third-rate authors to pass as geniuses. Yes, indeed, not all the institutions of the old regime deserve our century's contempt.

"No, I won't announce my theory to the public," replied the psychiatrist. "I'll do something better: I'll act on it."

The druggist agreed that it might be best to begin that way. "There'll be plenty of time for the noisemaker afterwards," he concluded.

But Simão Bacamarte was not listening. He seemed lost in meditation. When he finally spoke, it was with great deliberation.

"Think of humanity," he said, "as a great oyster shell. Our first task, Soares, is to extract the pearl—that is, reason. In other words, we must determine the nature and boundaries of reason. Madness is simply all that lies beyond those limits. But what is reason if not the equilibrium of the mental faculties? An individual, therefore, who lacks this equilibrium in any particular is, to that extent, insane."

Father Lopes, to whom he also confided his theory, replied that he was not quite sure he understood it but that it sounded a little dangerous and, in any case, would involve more work than one doctor could possibly handle.

"Under the present definition of insanity, which has always been accepted," he added, "the fence around the area is perfectly clear and satisfactory. Why not stay within it?"

The vague suggestion of a smile played on the fine and discreet lips of the psychiatrist, a smile in which disdain blended with pity. But he said nothing. Science merely extended its hand to theology—with such assurance that theology was unde-cided whether to believe in itself or in science. Itaguai and the entire world were on the brink of a revolution.

5. THE TERROR

Four days later the population of Itaguai was dismayed to hear that a certain Mr. Costa had been committed to the Green House.

"Impossible!"

"What do you mean, impossible! They took him away this morning."

Costa was one of the most highly esteemed citizens of Itaguai. He had inherited 400,000 cruzados in the good coin of King João V. As his uncle said in the will, the interest on this capital would have been enough to support him "till the end of the world." But as soon as he received the inheritance he began to make loans to people without interest: a thousand cruzados to one, two thousand to another, three hundred to another, eight hundred to another, until, at the end of five years, there was nothing left. If poverty had come to him all at once, the shock to the good people of Itaguai would have been enormous. But it came gradually. He went from opulence to wealth, from wealth to comfort, from comfort to indigence, and from indigence to poverty. People who, five years earlier, had always doffed their hats and bowed deeply to him as soon as they saw him a block away, now clapped him on the shoulder, flicked him on the nose, and made coarse remarks. But Costa remained affable, smiling, sub-limely resigned. He was untroubled even by the fact that the least courteous were the very ones who owed him money; on the contrary, he seemed to greet them with espe-cial pleasure.

Once, when one of these eternal debtors jeered at him and Costa merely smiled, someone said to him: "You're nice to this fellow because you still hope you can get him to pay what he owes you." Costa did not hesitate an instant. He went to the debtor and forgave the debt. "Sure," said the man who had made the unkind remark, "Costa canceled the debt because he knew he couldn't collect it anyway." Costa was no fool; he had anticipated this reaction. Inventive and jealous of his honor, he found a way two hours later to prove the slur unmerited: he took a few coins and loaned them to the same debtor.

"Now I hope . . . ," he thought.

This act of Costa's convinced the credulous and incredulous alike. Thereafter no one doubted the nobility of spirit of that worthy citizen. All the needy, no matter how timid, came in their patched cloaks and knocked on his door. The words of the man who had impugned his motive continued, however, to gnaw like worms at his soul. But this also ended, for three months later the man asked him for one hundred and twenty cruzados, promising to repay it in two days. This was all that remained of the inheritance, but Costa made the loan immediately, without hesitation or interest. It was a means of noble redress for the stain on his honor. In time the debt might have been paid; unfortunately, Costa could not wait, for five months later he was commit-ted to the Green House.

The consternation in Itaguai, when the matter became known, can readily be imagined. No one spoke of anything else. Some said that Costa had gone mad during lunch, others said it had happened early in the morning. They told of the mental at-tacks he had suffered, described by some as violent and frightening, by others as mild and even amusing. Many people hurried to the Green House. There they found poor Costa calm if somewhat surprised, speaking with great lucidity and asking why he had been brought there. Some went and talked with the psychiatrist. Bacamarte approved of their esteem and compassion for the patient, but he explained that science was science and that he could not permit a madman to remain at large. The last person to intercede (for, after what I am about to relate, no one dared go to see the dreadful psychiatrist) was a lady cousin of the patient. The doctor told her that Costa must certainly be insane, for otherwise he would not have thrown away all the money that . . .

"No! Now there you are wrong!" interrupted the good woman energetically. "He was not to blame for what he did."

"No?"

"No, Doctor. I'll tell you exactly what happened. My uncle was not ordinarily a bad man, but when he became angry he was so fierce that he would not even take off his hat to a religious procession. Well, one day, a short time before he died, he discovered that a slave had stolen an ox from him. His face became as red as a pepper; he shook from head to foot; he foamed at the mouth. Then an ugly, shaggy-haired man came up to him and asked for a drink of water. My uncle (may God show him the light!) told the man to go drink in the river—or in hell, for all he cared. The man glared at him, raised his hand threateningly, and uttered this curse: 'Your money will not last more than seven years and a day, as surely as this is the star of David!' And he showed a star of David tattooed on his arm. That was the cause of it all, Doctor—the hex put on the money by that evil man."

Bacamarte's eyes pierced the poor woman like daggers. When she had finished, he extended his hand as courteously as if she had been the wife of the Viceroy and invited her to go and talk with her cousin. The miserable woman believed him. He took her to the Green House and locked her up in the ward for those suffering from delusions or hallucinations.

When this duplicity on the part of the illustrious Bacamarte became known, the townspeople were terrified. No one could believe that, for no reason at all, the psychiatrist would lock up a perfectly sane woman whose only offense had been to intercede on behalf of an unfortunate relative. The case was gossiped about on street corners and in barber shops. Within a short time it developed into a full-scale novel, with amorous overtures by the psychiatrist to Costa's cousin, Costa's indignation, the cousin's scorn, and finally the psychiatrist's vengeance on them both. It was all very obvious. But did not the doctor's austerity and his life of devotion to science give the lie to such a story? Not at all! This was merely a cloak by which he concealed his treachery. And one of the more credulous of the townspeople even whispered that he knew certain other things—he would not say what, for he lacked complete proof—but he knew they were true, he could almost swear to them.

"You who are his intimate friend," they asked the druggist, "can't you tell us what's going on, what happened, what reason . . . ?"

Crispim Soares was delighted. This questioning by his puzzled friends, and by the uneasy and curious in general, amounted to public recognition of his importance. There was no doubt about it, the entire population knew that he, Crispim the druggist, was the psychiatrist's confidant, the great man's collaborator. That is why they all came running to the pharmacy. All this could be read in the druggist's jocund expression and discreet smile—and in his silence, for he made no reply. One, two, perhaps three dry monosyllables at the most, cloaked in a loyal, constant half-smile and full of scientific mysteries which he could reveal to no human being without danger and dishonor.

"There's something very strange going on," thought the townspeople.

But one of them merely shrugged his shoulders and went on his way. He had more important interests. He had just built a magnificent house, with a garden that was a masterpiece of art and taste. His furniture, imported from Hungary and Holland, was visible from the street, for the windows were always open. This man, who had become rich in the manufacture of packsaddles, had always dreamed of owning a sumptuous house, an elaborate garden, and rare furniture. Now he had acquired all these things and, in semi-retirement, was devoting most of his time to the enjoyment of them. His house was undoubtedly the finest in Itaguai, more grandiose than the Green House, nobler than the town hall. There was wailing and gnashing of teeth among Itaguai's social elite whenever they heard it praised or even mentioned—indeed, when they even thought about it. Owned by a mere manufacturer of packsaddles, good God!

"There he is, staring at his own house," the passers-by would say. For it was his custom to station himself every morning in the middle of his garden and gaze lovingly at the house. He would keep this up for a good hour, until called in to lunch.

Although his neighbors always greeted him respectfully enough, they would laugh behind his back. One of them observed that Mateus could make a lot more money manufacturing packsaddles to put on himself—a somewhat unintelligible remark, which nevertheless sent the listeners into ecstasies of laughter.

Every afternoon, when the families went out for their after-dinner walks (people dined early in those days), Mateus would station himself at the center window, elegantly clothed in white against a dark background. He would remain there in a majestic pose for three or four hours, until it was dark. One may reasonably infer an intention on Mateus's part to be admired and envied, although he confessed no such purpose to anyone, not even to Father Lopes. His good friend the druggist nevertheless drew the inference and communicated it to Bacamarte. The psychiatrist suggested that, as the saddler's house was of stone, he might have been suffering from petrophilia, an illness that the doctor had discovered and had been studying for some time. This continual gazing at the house . . .

"No, Doctor," interrupted Crispim Soares vigorously.

"No?"

"Pardon me, but perhaps you don't know . . ." And he told the psychiatrist what the saddler did every afternoon.

Simão Bacamarte's eyes lighted up with scientific voluptuousness. He questioned Crispim at some length, and the answers he received were apparently satisfactory, even pleasant, to him. But there was no suggestion of a sinister intent in the psychiatrist's face or manner—quite the contrary—as he asked the druggist's arm for a little stroll in the afternoon sun. It was the first time he had bestowed this honor on his confidant. Crispim, stunned and trembling, accepted the invitation. Just then, two or three people came to see the doctor. Crispim silently consigned them to all the devils. They were delaying the walk; Bacamarte might even take it into his head to invite one of them in Crispim's stead. What impatience! What anxiety! Finally the visitors left and the two men set out on their walk. The psychiatrist chose the direction of Mateus's house. He strolled by the window five or six times, slowly, stopping now and then and observing the saddler's physical attitude and facial expression. Poor Mateus noticed only that he was an object of the curiosity or admiration of the most important figure in Itaguai. He intensified the nobility of his expression, the stateliness of his pose. . . . Alas! he was merely helping to condemn himself. The next day he was committed.

"The Green House is a private prison," said an unsuccessful doctor.

Never had an opinion caught on and spread so rapidly. "A private prison"—the words were repeated from one end of Itaguai to the other. Fearfully, to be sure, for during the week following the Mateus episode twenty-odd persons, including two or three of the town's prominent citizens, had been committed to the Green House. The psychiatrist said that only the mentally ill were admitted, but few believed him. Then came the popular explanations of the matter: revenge, greed, a punishment from God, a monomania afflicting the doctor himself, a secret plan on the part of Rio de Janeiro to destroy the budding prosperity of Itaguai and ultimately to impoverish this rival municipality, and a thousand other products of the public imagination.

At this time the party of travelers returned from their visit of several weeks to Rio de Janeiro. The psychiatrist, the druggist, Father Lopes, the Councilmen, and several other officials went to greet them. The moment when Dona Evarista laid eyes again on her husband is regarded by the chroniclers of the time as one of the most sublime instants in the moral history of man, because of the contrast between these two extreme (although both commendable) natures. Dona Evarista uttered a cry, stammered a word or two, and threw herself at her husband in a way that suggested at once the fierceness of a wildcat and the gentle affection of a dove. Not so the noble Bacamarte. With diagnostic objectivity, without disturbing for a moment his scientific austerity, he extended his arms to the lady, who fell into them and fainted. The incident was brief; two minutes later Dona Evarista's friends were greeting her and the homeward procession began.

The psychiatrist's wife was Itaguai's great hope. Everyone counted on her to alleviate the scourge. Hence the public acclamation, the crowds in the streets, the pennants, and the flowers in the windows. The eminent Bacamarte, having entrusted her to the arm of Father Lopes, walked contemplatively with measured step. Dona Evarista, on the contrary, turned her head animatedly from side to side, observing with curiosity the unexpectedly warm reception. The priest asked about Rio de Janeiro, which he had not seen since the previous viceroyalty, and Dona Evarista replied that it was the most beautiful sight there could possibly be in the entire world. The Public Gardens, now completed, were a paradise in which she had often strolled—and the Street of Beautiful Nights, the Fountain of Ducks . . . Ah! the Fountain of Ducks. There really were ducks there, made of metal and spouting water through their mouths. A gorgeous thing. The priest said that Rio de Janeiro had been lovely even in his time there and must be much lovelier now. Small wonder, for it was so much larger than Itaguai and was, moreover, the capital. . . . But one could not call Itaguai ugly; it had some beautiful buildings, such as Mateus's mansion, the Green House . . .

"And apropos the Green House," said Father Lopes, gliding skillfully into the subject, "you will find it full of patients."

"Really?"

"Yes, Mateus is there. . . ."

"The saddler?"

"Costa is there too. So is Costa's cousin, and So-and-so, and What's-his-name, and . . ."

"All insane?"

"Apparently," replied the priest.

"But how? Why?"

Father Lopes drew down the corners of his mouth as if to say that he did not know or did not wish to tell what he knew—a vague reply, which could not be repeated to anyone. Dona Evarista found it strange indeed that all those people should have gone mad. It might easily happen to one or another—but to *all* of them? Yet she could hardly doubt the fact. Her husband was a learned man, a scientist; he would not commit anyone to the Green House without clear proof of insanity.

The priest punctuated her observations with an intermittent "undoubtedly . . . undoubtedly . . ."

A few hours later about fifty guests were seated at Simão Bacamarte's table for the home-coming dinner. Dona Evarista was the obligatory subject of toasts, speeches, and verses, all of them highly metaphorical. She was the wife of the new Hippocrates, the muse of science, an angel, the dawn, charity, consolation, life itself. Her eyes were two stars, according to Crispim Soares, and two suns, by a Councilman's less modest figure. The psychiatrist found all this a bit tiresome but showed no signs of impatience. He merely leaned toward his wife and told her that such flights of fancy, although permissible in rhetoric, were unsubstantiated in fact. Dona Evarista tried to accept this opinion; but, even if she discounted three fourths of the flattery, there was enough left to inflate her considerably. One of the orators, for example—Martim Brito, twenty-five, a pretentious fop, much addicted to women—declaimed that the birth of Dona Evarista had come about in this manner: "After God gave the universe to man and to woman, who are the diamond and the pearl of the divine crown" (and the orator dragged this phrase triumphantly from one end of the table to the other), "God decided to outdo God and so he created Dona Evarista."

The psychiatrist's wife lowered her eyes with exemplary modesty. Two other ladies, who thought Martim Brito's expression of adulation excessive and audacious, turned to observe its effect on Dona Evarista's husband. They found his face clouded with misgivings, threats, and possibly blood. The provocation was great indeed, thought the two ladies. They prayed God to prevent any tragic occurrence—or, better yet, to postpone it until the next day. The more charitable of the two admitted (to herself) that Dona Evarista was above suspicion, for she was so very unattractive. And yet not all tastes were alike. Maybe some men . . . This idea caused her to tremble again, although less violently than before; less violently, for the psychiatrist was now smiling at Martim Brito.

When everyone had risen from the table, Bacamarte walked over to him and complimented him on his eulogy of Dona Evarista. He said it was a brilliant improvisation, full of magnificent figures of speech. Had Brito himself originated the thought about Dona Evarista's birth or had he taken it from something he had read? No, it was entirely original; it had come to him as he was speaking and he had considered it suitable for use as a rhetorical climax. As a matter of fact, he always leaned toward the bold and daring rather than the tender or jocose. He favored the epic style. Once, for example, he had composed an ode on the fall of the Marquis of Pombal in which he had said that "the foul dragon of Nihility is crushed in the vengeful claws of the All." And he had invented many other powerful figures of speech. He liked sublime concepts, great and noble images. . . .

"Poor fellow!" thought the psychiatrist. "He's probably suffering from a cerebral lesion. Not a very serious case but worthy of study."

Three days later Dona Evarista learned, to her amazement, that Martim Brito was now living at the Green House. A young man with such beautiful thoughts! The two other ladies attributed his commitment to jealousy on the part of the psychiatrist, for the young man's words had been provocatively bold.

Jealousy? But how, then, can one explain the commitment a short time afterwards of persons of whom the doctor could not possibly have been jealous: innocuous, fun-loving Chico, Fabrício the notary, and many others. The terror grew in intensity. One no longer knew who was sane and who was insane. When their husbands went out in the street, the women of Itaguai lit candles to Our Lady. And some of the men hired bodyguards to go around with them.

Everyone who could possibly get out of town, did so. One of the fugitives, however, was seized just as he was leaving. He was Gil Bernardes, a friendly, polite young man; so polite, indeed, that he never said hello to anyone without doffing his hat and bowing to the ground. In the street he would sometimes run forty yards to shake the hand of a gentleman or lady—or even of a child, such as the Circuit Judge's little boy. He had a special talent for affability. He owed his acceptance by society not only to his personal charm but also to the noble tenacity with which he withstood any number of refusals, rejections, cold shoulders, and the like, without becoming discouraged. And, once he gained entry to a house, he never left it—nor did its occupants wish him to leave, for he was a delightful guest. Despite his popularity and the self-confidence it engendered, Gil Bernardes turned pale when he heard one day that the psychiatrist was watching him. The following morning he started to leave town but was apprehended and taken to the Green House.

"This must not be permitted to continue."

"Down with tyranny!"

"Despot! Outlaw! Goliath!"

At first such things were said softly and indoors. Later they were shouted in the streets. Rebellion was raising its ugly head. The thought of a petition to the government for the arrest and deportation of Simão Bacamarte occurred to many people even before Porfírio, with eloquent gestures of indignation expounded it in his barber shop. Let it be noted—and this is one of the finest pages of a somber history—that as soon as the population of the Green House began to grow so rapidly, Porfírio's profits also increased, for many of his customers now asked to be bled; but private interests, said the barber, have to yield to the public welfare. "The tyrant must be overthrown!" So great was his dedication to the cause that he uttered this cry shortly after he heard of the commitment of a man named Coelho who was bringing a lawsuit against him.

"How can anyone call Coelho crazy?" shouted Porfírio.

And no one answered. Everybody said he was perfectly sane. The legal action against the barber, involving some real estate, grew not out of hatred or spite but out of the obscure wording of a deed. Coelho had an excellent reputation. A few individuals, to be sure, avoided him; as soon as they saw him approaching in the distance they ran around corners, ducked into stores. The fact is, he loved conversation—long conversation, drunk down in large draughts. Consequently he was almost never alone. He preferred those who also liked to talk, but he would compromise, if necessary, for a unilateral conversation with the more taciturn. Whenever Father Lopes, who disliked Coelho, saw him taking his leave of someone, he quoted Dante, with a minor change of his own:

> La bocca sollevò dal fiero pasto
> Quel seccatore . . .[5]

---

5. A revised quotation from Dante's Italian: literally, "He lifted his mouth from his proud meal, that nuisance. . . ."

But the priest's remark did not affect the general esteem in which Coelho was held, for some attributed the remark to mere personal animosity and others thought it was a prayer in Latin.

6. THE REBELLION

About thirty people allied themselves with the barber. They prepared a formal complaint and took it to the Town Council, which rejected it on the ground that scientific research must be tempered neither by hostile legislation nor by the misconceptions and prejudices of the mob.

"My advice to you," said the President of the Council, "is to disband and go back to work."

The group could hardly contain its anger. The barber declared that the people would march to the Green House and destroy it; that Itaguai must no longer be used as a corpse for dissection in the experiments of a medical despot; that several esteemed and even distinguished individuals, not to mention many humble but estimable persons, lay confined in the cubicles of the Green House; that the psychiatrist was clearly motivated by greed, for its compensation varied directly with the number of alleged madmen in his care—

"That's not true," interrupted the President.

"Not true?"

"About two weeks ago we received a communication from the illustrious doctor in which he stated that, in view of the great value, to him as a scientist, of his observations and experiments, he would no longer accept payment from the Council or from the patients' families."

In view of this noble act of self-denial, how could the rebels persist in their attitude? The psychiatrist might, indeed, make mistakes, but obviously he was not motivated by any interest alien to science; and to establish error on his part, something more would be needed than disorderly crowds in the street. So spoke the President, and the entire Council applauded.

The barber meditated for a few moments and then declared that he was invested with a public mandate; he would give Itaguai no peace until the final destruction of the Green House, that "Bastille of human reason"—an expression he had heard a local poet use and which he now repeated with great vigor. Having spoken, he gave his cohorts a signal and led them out.

The Council was faced with an emergency. It must, at all costs, prevent rebellion and bloodshed. To make matters worse, one of the Councilmen who had supported the President was so impressed by the figure of speech, "Bastille of the human reason," that he changed his mind. He advocated adoption of a measure to liquidate the Green House. After the President had expressed his amazement and indignation, the dissenter observed:

"I know nothing about science, but if so many men whom we considered sane are locked up as madmen, how do we know that the real madman is not the psychiatrist himself?"

This Councilman, a highly articulate fellow named Sebastião Freitas, spoke at some length. He presented the case against the Green House with restraint but with firm conviction. His colleagues were dumbfounded. The President begged him at least to help preserve law and order by not expressing his opinions in the street, where they might give body and soul to what was so far merely a whirlwind of uncoordinated atoms. This figure of speech counterbalanced to some extent the one about the

Bastille. Sebastião Freitas promised to take no action for the present but reserved the right to seek the elimination of the Green House by legal means. And he murmured to himself lovingly: "That Bastille of the human reason!"

Nevertheless, the crowd grew. Not thirty but three hundred now followed the barber, whose nickname ought to be mentioned at this point because it gave the rebellion its name: he was called Stewed Corn, and the movement was therefore known as the Revolt of the Stewed Corners. Storming through the streets toward the Green House, they might well have been compared to the mob that stormed the Bastille, with due allowance, of course, for the difference between Paris and Itaguaí.

A young child attached to the household ran in from the street and told Dona Evarista the news. The psychiatrist's wife was trying on a silk dress (one of the thirty-seven she had bought in Rio).

"It's probably just a bunch of drunks," she said as she changed the location of a pin. "Benedita, is the hem all right?"

"Yes, ma'am," replied the slave, who was squatting on the floor, "it looks fine. Just turn a little bit. Like that. It's perfect, ma'am."

"They're not a bunch of drunks, Dona Evarista," said the child in fear. "They're shouting: 'Death to Dr. Bacamarte the tyrant.'"

"Be quiet! Benedita, look over here on the left side. Don't you think the seam is a little crooked? We'll have to rip it and sew it again. Try to make it nice and even this time."

"Death to Dr. Bacamarte! Death to the tyrant!" howled three hundred voices in the street.

The blood left Dona Evarista's face. She stood there like a statue, petrified with terror. The slave ran instinctively to the back door. The child, whom Dona Evarista had refused to believe, enjoyed a moment of unexpressed but profound satisfaction.

"Death to the psychiatrist!" shouted the voices, now closer than before.

Dona Evarista, although an easy prey to emotions of pleasure, was reasonably steadfast in adversity. She did not faint. She ran to the inside room where her husband was studying. At the moment of her precipitate entrance, the doctor was examining a passage in Averroës.[6] His eyes, blind to external reality but highly perceptive in the realm of the inner life, rose from the book to the ceiling and returned to the book. Twice, Dona Evarista called him loudly by name without his paying her the least attention. The third time, he heard and asked what was troubling her.

"Can't you hear the shouting?"

The psychiatrist listened. The shouts were coming closer and closer, threatening, terrifying. He understood. Rising from the armchair, he shut the book and, with firm, calm step, walked over to the bookcase and put the volume back in its place. The insertion of the volume caused the books on either side of it to be slightly out of line. Simão Bacamarte carefully straightened them. Then he asked his wife to go to her room.

"No, no," begged his worthy helpmeet. "I want to die at your side where I belong."

Simão Bacamarte insisted that she go. He assured her that it was not a matter of life and death and told her that, even if it were, it would be her duty to remain alive. The unhappy lady bowed her head, tearful and obedient.

6. Averroës (1126–1198) was a major Islamic philosopher of the Middle Ages, known for his synthesis of Islam with ancient Greek thinkers.

"Down with the Green House!" shouted the Stewed Corners.

The psychiatrist went out on the front balcony and faced the rebel mob, whose three hundred heads were radiant with civism and somber with fury. When they saw him they shouted: "Die! Die!" Simão Bacamarte indicated that he wished to speak, but they only shouted the louder. Then the barber waved his hat as a signal to his followers to be silent and told the psychiatrist that he might speak, provided his words did not abuse the patience of the people.

"I shall say little and, if possible, nothing at all. It depends on what it is that you have come to request."

"We aren't requesting anything," replied the barber, trembling with rage. "We are demanding that the Green House be destroyed or at least that all the prisoners in it be freed."

"I don't understand."

"You understand all right, tyrant. We want you to release the victims of your hatred, your whims, your greed. . . ."

The psychiatrist smiled, but the smile of this great man was not perceptible to the eyes of the multitude: it was a slight contraction of two or three muscles, nothing more.

"Gentlemen," he said, "science is a serious thing and it must be treated seriously. For my professional decisions I account to no one but God and the authorities in my special field. If you wish to suggest changes in the administration of the Green House, I am ready to listen to you; but if you wish me to be untrue to myself, further talk would be futile. I could invite you to appoint a committee to come and study the way I treat the madmen who have been committed to my care, but I shall not, for to do so would be to account to you for my methods and this I shall never do to a group of rebels or, for that matter, to laymen of any description."

So spoke the psychiatrist, and the people were astounded at his words. Obviously they had not expected such imperturbability and such resoluteness. Their amazement was even greater when the psychiatrist bowed gravely to them, turned his back, and walked slowly back into the house. The barber soon regained his self-possession and, waving his hat, urged the mob to demolish the Green House. The voices that took up the cry were few and weak. At this decisive moment the barber felt a surging ambition to rule. If he succeeded in overthrowing the psychiatrist and destroying the Green House, he might well take over the Town Council, dominate the other municipal authorities, and make himself the master of Itaguaí. For some years now he had striven to have his name included in the ballots from which the Councilmen were selected by lot, but his petitions were denied because his position in society was considered incompatible with such a responsibility. It was a case of now or never. Besides, he had carried the street riot to such a point that defeat would mean prison and perhaps banishment or even the scaffold. Unfortunately, the psychiatrist's reply had taken most of the steam out of the Stewed Corners. When the barber perceived this, he felt like shouting: "Wretches! Cowards!" But he contained himself and merely said:

"My friends, let us fight to the end! The salvation of Itaguaí is in your worthy and heroic hands. Let us destroy the foul prison that confines or threatens your children and parents, your mothers and sisters, your relatives and friends, and you yourselves. Do you want to be thrown into a dungeon and starved on bread and water or maybe whipped to death?"

The mob bestirred itself, murmured, shouted, and gathered round the barber. The revolt was emerging from its stupor and threatening to demolish the Green House.

"Come on!" shouted Porfírio, waving his hat.

"Come on!" echoed his followers.

At that moment a corps of dragoons turned the corner and came marching toward the mob.

7. The Unexpected

The mob appeared stupefied by the arrival of the dragoons; the Stewed Corners could hardly believe that the force of the law was being exerted against them. The dragoons halted and their captain ordered the crowd to disperse. Some of the rebels felt inclined to obey, but others rallied around the barber, who boldly replied to the captain:

"We shall not disperse. If you wish, you may take our lives, but nothing else: we will not yield our honor or our rights, for on them depends the salvation of Itaguai."

Nothing could have been more imprudent or more natural than this reply. It reflected the ecstasy inspired by great crises. Perhaps it reflected also an excess of confidence in the captain's forbearance, a confidence soon dispelled by the captain's order to charge. What followed is indescribable. The mob howled its fury. Some managed to escape by climbing into windows or running down the street, but the majority, inspired by the barber's words, snorted with anger and stood their ground. The defeat of the Stewed Corners appeared imminent, when suddenly one third of the dragoons, for reasons not set forth in the chronicles, went over to the side of the rebels. This unexpected reenforcement naturally heartened the Stewed Corners and discouraged the ranks of legality. The loyal soldiers refused to attack their comrades and, one by one, joined them, with the result that in a few minutes the entire aspect of the struggle had changed. The captain, defended by only a handful of his men against a compact mass of rebels and soldiers, gave up and surrendered his sword to the barber.

The triumphant rebels did not lose an instant. They carried the wounded into the nearest houses and headed for the town hall. The people and the troops fraternized. They shouted *vivas* for the King, the Viceroy, Itaguai, and "our great leader, Porfírio." The barber marched at their head, wielding the sword as dexterously as if it had been merely an unusually long razor. Victory hovered like a halo above him, and the dignity of government informed his every movement.

The Councilmen, watching from the windows, thought that the troops had captured the Stewed Corners. The Council formally resolved to send a petition to the Viceroy asking him to give an extra month's pay to the dragoons, "whose high devotion to duty has saved Itaguai from the chaos of rebellion and mob rule." This phrase was proposed by Sebastião Freitas, whose defense of the rebels had so scandalized his colleagues. But the legislators were soon disillusioned. They could now clearly hear the *vivas* for the barber and the shouts of "death to the Councilmen" and "death to the psychiatrist." The President held his head high and said: "Whatever may be our fate, let us never forget that we are the servants of His Majesty and of the people of Itaguai." Sebastião suggested that perhaps they could best serve the Crown and the town by sneaking out the back door and going to the Circuit Judge's office for advice and help, but all the other members of the Council rejected this suggestion.

A few seconds later the barber and some of his lieutenants entered the chamber and told the Town Council that it had been deposed. The Councilmen surrendered and were put in jail. Then the barber's friends urged him to assume the dictatorship of Itaguai in the name of His Majesty. Porfírio accepted this responsibility, although, as he told them, he was fully aware of its weight and of the thorny problems it entailed. He said also that he would be unable to rule without their coöperation, which they promptly promised him. The barber then went to the window and told the people what had happened; they shouted their approval. He chose the title, "Town Protector in the Name of His Majesty and of the People." He immediately issued several important orders, official communications from the new government, a detailed statement to the Viceroy with many protestations of obedience to His Majesty, and finally the following short but forceful proclamation to the people:

> Fellow Itaguaians:
>   A corrupt and irresponsible Town Council was conspiring ígnominiously against His Majesty and against the people. Public opinion had condemned it, and now a handful of citizens, with the help of His Majesty's brave dragoons, have dissolved it. By unanimous consent I am empowered to rule until His Majesty chooses to take formal action in the premises. Itaguaians, I ask only for your trust and for your help in restoring peace and the public funds, recklessly squandered by the Council. You may count on me to make every personal sacrifice for the common good, and you may rest assured that we shall have the full support of the Crown.
>
> Porfírio Caetano das Neves
> Town Protector in the Name of His Majesty and of the People

Everyone remarked that the proclamation said nothing whatever about the Green House, and some considered this ominous. The danger seemed all the greater when, in the midst of the important changes that were taking place, the psychiatrist committed to the Green House some seven or eight new patients, including a relative of the Protector. Everybody erroneously interpreted Bacamarte's action as a challenge to the barber and thought it likely that within twenty-four hours the terrible prison would be destroyed and the psychiatrist would be in chains.

The day ended happily. While the crier with the noisemaker went from corner to corner reading the proclamation, the people walked about the streets and swore they would be willing to die for the Protector. There were very few shouts of opposition to the Green House, for the people were confident that the government would soon liquidate it. Porfírio declared the day an official holiday and, to promote an alliance between the temporal power and the spiritual power, he asked Father Lopes to celebrate the occasion with a Te Deum. The Vicar issued a public refusal.

"May I at least assume," asked the barber with a threatening frown, "that you will not ally yourself with the enemies of the government?"

"How can I ally myself with your enemies," replied Father Lopes (if one can call it a reply), "when you have no enemies? You say in your proclamation that you are ruling by unanimous consent."

The barber could not help smiling. He really had almost no opposition. Apart from the captain of dragoons, the Council, and some of the town bigwigs, everybody acclaimed him; and even the bigwigs did not actually oppose him. Indeed, the people blessed the name of the man who would finally free Itaguai from the Green House and from the terrible Simão Bacamarte.

8. THE DRUGGIST'S DILEMMA

The next day Porfírio and two of his aides-de-camp left the government palace (the new name of the town hall) and set out for the residence of Simão Bacamarte. The barber knew that it would have been more fitting for him to have ordered Bacamarte to come to the palace, but he was afraid the psychiatrist would refuse and so he decided to exercise forbearance in the use of his powers.

Crispim Soares was in bed at the time. The druggist was undergoing continual mental torture these days. His intimacy with Simão Bacamarte called him to the doctor's defense, and Porfírio's victory called him to the barber's side. This victory, together with the intensity of the hatred for Bacamarte, made it unprofitable and perhaps dangerous for Crispim to continue to associate with the doctor. But the druggist's wife, a masculine woman who was very close to Dona Evarista, told him that he owed the psychiatrist an obligation of loyalty. The dilemma appeared insoluble, so Crispim avoided it by the only means he could devise: he said he was sick, and went to bed.

The next day his wife told him that Porfírio and some other men were headed for Simão Bacamarte's house.

"They're going to arrest him," thought the druggist.

One idea led to another. He imagined that their next step would be to arrest him, Crispim Soares, as an accessory. The therapeutic effect of this thought was remarkable. The druggist jumped out of bed and, despite his wife's protests, dressed and went out. The chroniclers all agree that Mrs. Soares found great comfort in the nobility of her husband, who, she assumed, was going to the defense of his friend, and they note with perspicacity the immense power of a thought, even if untrue; for the druggist walked not to the house of the psychiatrist but straight to the government palace. When he got there he expressed disappointment that the barber was out; he had wanted to assure him of his loyalty and support. Indeed, he had intended to do this the day before but had been prevented by illness—an illness that he now evidenced by a forced cough. The high officials to whom he spoke knew of his intimacy with the psychiatrist and therefore appreciated the significance of this declaration of loyalty. They treated the druggist with the greatest respect. They told him that the protector had gone to the Green House on important business but would soon return. They offered him a chair, refreshments, and flattery. They told him that the cause of the illustrious Porfírio was the cause of every true patriot—a proposition with which Crispim Soares heartily agreed and which he proposed to affirm in a vigorous communication to the Viceroy.

9. Two Beautiful Cases

The psychiatrist received the barber immediately. He told him that he had no means of resistance and was therefore prepared to submit to the new government. He asked only that they not force him to be present at the destruction of the Green House.

"The doctor is under a misapprehension," said Porfírio after pause. "We are not vandals. Rightly or wrongly, everybody thinks that most of the people locked up here are perfectly sane. But the government recognizes that the question is purely scientific and that scientific issues cannot be resolved by legislation. Moreover, the Green House is now an established municipal institution. We must therefore find a compromise that will both permit its continued operation and placate the public."

The psychiatrist could not conceal his amazement. He confessed that he had expected not only destruction of the Green House but also his own arrest and banishment. The last thing in the world he would have expected was—

"That is because you don't appreciate the grave responsibility of government," interrupted the barber. "The people, in their blindness, may feel righteous indignation about something that they do not understand; they have a right, then, to ask the government to act along certain lines. The government, however, must remember its duty to promote the public interest, whether or not this interest is in full accord with the demands made by the public itself. The revolution, which yesterday overthrew a corrupt and despicable Town Council, screams for destruction of the Green House. But the government must remain calm and objective. It knows that elimination of the Green House would not eliminate insanity. It knows that the mentally ill must receive treatment. It knows also that it cannot itself provide this treatment and that it even lacks the ability to distinguish the sane from the insane. These are matters for science, not for politics. They are matters requiring the sort of delicate, trained judgment that you, not we, are fitted to exercise. All I ask is that you help me give some degree of satisfaction to the people of Itaguai. If you and the government present a united front and propose a compromise of some sort, the people will accept it. Let me suggest, unless you have something better to propose, that we free those patients who are practically cured and those whose illnesses are relatively mild. In this way we can show how benign and generous we are without seriously handicapping your work."

Simão Bacamarte remained silent for about three minutes and then asked: "How many casualties were there in the fighting yesterday?"

The barber thought the question a little odd, but quickly replied that eleven had been killed and twenty-five wounded.

"Eleven dead, twenty-five wounded," repeated the psychiatrist two or three times.

Then he said that he did not like the barber's suggestion and that he would try to devise a better compromise, which he would communicate to the government within a few days. He asked a number of questions about the events of the day before: the attack by the dragoons, the defense, the change of sides by the dragoons, the Council's resistance, and so on. The barber replied in detail, with emphasis on the discredit into which the Council had fallen. He admitted that the government did not yet have the support of the most important men in the community and added that the psychiatrist might be very helpful in this connection. The government would be pleased, indeed, if it could count among its friends the loftiest spirit in Itaguai and, doubtless, in the entire kingdom. Nothing that the barber said, however, changed the expression on the doctor's austere face. Bacamarte evidenced neither vanity nor modesty; he listened in silence, as impassive as a stone god.

"Eleven dead, twenty-five wounded," repeated the psychiatrist after the visitors had left. "Two beautiful cases. This barber shows unmistakable symptoms of psychopathic duplicity. As for proof of the insanity of the people who acclaim him, what more could one ask than the fact that eleven were killed and twenty-five wounded? Two beautiful cases!"

"Long live our glorious Protector!" shouted thirty-odd people who had been awaiting the barber in front of the house.

The psychiatrist went to the window and heard part of the barber's speech:

" . . . for my main concern, day and night, is to execute faithfully the will of the people. Trust in me and you will not be disappointed. I ask of you only one thing: be peaceful, maintain order. For order, my friends, is the foundation on which government must rest."

"Long live Porfírio!" shouted the people, waving their hats.

"Two beautiful cases," murmured the psychiatrist.

10. The Restoration

Within a week there were fifty additional patients in the Green House, all of them strong supporters of the new government. The people felt outraged. The government was stunned; it did not know how to react. João Pina, another barber, said openly that

Porfírio had "sold his birthright to Simão Bacamarte for a pot of gold"—a phrase that attracted some of the more indignant citizens to Pina's side. Porfírio, seeing his competitor at the head of a potential insurrection, knew that he would be overthrown if he did not immediately change his course. He therefore issued two decrees, one abolishing the Green House and the other banishing the psychiatrist from Itaguai.

João Pina, however, explained clearly and eloquently that these decrees were a hoax, a mere face-saving gesture. Two hours later Porfírio was deposed and João Pina assumed the heavy burden of government. Pina found copies of the proclamation to the people, the explanatory statement to the Viceroy, and other documents issued by his predecessor. He had new originals made and sent them out over his own name and signature. The chronicles note that the wording of the new documents was a little different. For example, where the other barber had spoken of "a corrupt and irresponsible Town Council," João Pina spoke of "a body contaminated by French doctrines wholly contrary to the sacrosanct interests of His Majesty."

The new dictator barely had time to dispatch the documents when a military force sent by the Viceroy entered the town and restored order. At the psychiatrist's request, the troops immediately handed over to him Porfírio and some fifty other persons, and promised to deliver seventeen more of the barber's followers as soon as they had sufficiently recovered from their wounds.

This period in the crisis of Itaguai represents the culmination of Simão Bacamarte's influence. He got whatever he wanted. For example, the Town Council, now reestablished, promptly consented to have Sebastião Freitas committed to the asylum. The psychiatrist had requested this in view of the extraordinary inconsistency of the Councilman's opinions, which Bacamarte considered a clear sign of mental illness. Subsequently the same thing happened to Crispim Soares. When the psychiatrist learned that his close friend and staunch supporter had suddenly gone over to the side of the Stewed Corners, he ordered him to be seized and taken to the Green House. The druggist did not deny his switch of allegiance but explained that he had been motivated by an overwhelming fear of the new government. Simão Bacamarte accepted the explanation as true; he pointed out, however, that fear is a common symptom of mental abnormality.

Perhaps the most striking proof of the psychiatrist's influence was the docility with which the Town Council surrendered to him its own President. This worthy official had declared that the affront to the Council could be washed away only by the blood of the Stewed Corners. Bacamarte learned of this through the Secretary of the Council, who repeated the President's words with immense enthusiasm. The psychiatrist first committed the Secretary to the Green House and then proceeded to the town hall. He told the Council that its President was suffering from hemoferal mania, an illness that he planned to study in depth, with, he hoped, immense benefit to the world. The Council hesitated for a moment and then acquiesced.

From that day on, the population of the asylum increased even more rapidly than before. A person could not utter the most commonplace lie, even a lie that clearly benefited him, without being immediately committed to the Green House. Scandalmongers, dandies, people who spent hours at puzzles, people who habitually inquired into the private lives of others, officials puffed up with authority—the psychiatrist's agents brought them all in. He spared sweethearts but not flirts, for he maintained that the former obeyed a healthful impulse, but that the latter yielded to a morbid desire for conquest. He discriminated against neither the avaricious nor the prodigal: both were committed to the asylum; this led people to say that the psychiatrist's concept of madness included practically everybody.

Some of the chroniclers express doubts about Simão Bacamarte's integrity. They note that, at his instigation, the Town Council authorized all persons who boasted of noble blood to wear a silver ring on the thumb of the left hand. These chroniclers point out that, as a consequence of the ordinance, a jeweler who was a close friend of Bacamarte became rich. Another consequence, however, was the commitment of the ring-wearers to the Green House; and the treatment of these unfortunate people, rather than the enrichment of his friend, may well have been the objective of the illustrious physician. Nobody was sure what conduct on the part of the ring-wearers had betrayed their illness. Some thought it was their tendency to gesticulate a great deal, especially with the left hand, no matter where they were—at home, in the street, even in church. Everybody knows that madmen gesticulate a great deal.

"Where will this man stop?" said the important people of the town. "Ah, if only we had supported the Stewed Corners!"

One day, when preparations were being made for a ball to be held that evening in the town hall, Itaguai was shocked to hear that Simão Bacarmarte had sent his own wife to the asylum. At first everyone thought it was a gag of some sort. But it was the absolute truth. Dona Evarista had been committed at two o'clock in the morning.

"I had long suspected that she was a sick woman," said the psychiatrist in response to a question from Father Lopes. "Her moderation in all other matters was hard to reconcile with her mania for silks, velvets, laces, and jewelry, a mania that began immediately after her return from Rio de Janeiro. It was then that I started to observe her closely. Her conversation was always about these objects. If I talked to her about the royal courts of earlier times, she wanted to know what kind of clothes the women wore. If a lady visited her while I was out, the first thing my wife told me, even before mentioning the purpose of the visit, was how the woman was dressed and which jewels or articles of clothing were pretty and which were ugly. Once (I think Your Reverence will remember this) she said she was going to make a new dress every year for Our Lady of the Mother Church. All these symptoms indicated a serious condition. Tonight, however, the full gravity of her illness became manifest. She had selected the entire outfit she would wear to the ball and had it all fixed and ready. All except one thing: she couldn't decide between a garnet necklace and a sapphire necklace. The day before yesterday she asked me which she should wear. I told her it didn't matter, that they both were very becoming. Yesterday at lunch she repeated the question. After dinner she was silent and pensive. I asked her what was the matter. 'I want to wear my beautiful garnet necklace, but my sapphire one is so lovely.' 'Then wear the sapphire necklace.' 'But then I can't wear the garnet necklace.' In the middle of the night, about half-past one, I awoke. She was not in bed. I got up and went to the dressing-room. There she sat with the two necklaces, in front of the mirror, trying on first one and then the other. An obvious case of dementia. I had her put away immediately."

Father Lopes said nothing. The explanation did not wholly satisfy him. Perceiving this, the psychiatrist told him that the specific illness of Dona Evarista was vestimania; it was by no means incurable.

"I hope to have her well within two weeks and, in any event, I expect to learn a great deal from the study of her case," said the psychiatrist in conclusion.

This personal sacrifice greatly enhanced the public image of the illustrious doctor. Suspicion, distrust, accusations were all negated by the commitment of his own wife whom he loved with all his heart. No one could ever again charge him with motives other than those of science itself. He was beyond doubt a man of integrity and profound objectivity, a combination of Cato and Hippocrates.

11. RELEASE AND JOY

And now let the reader share with the people of Itaguai their amazement on learning one day that the madmen of the Green House had been released.

"All of them?"

"All of them."

"Impossible. Some, maybe. But all?"

"All. He said so himself in a communiqué that he sent today to the Town Council."

The psychiatrist informed the Council, first, that he had checked the statistics and had found that four-fifths of the population of Itaguai was in the Green House; second, that this disproportionately large number of patients had led him to reexamine his fundamental theory of mental illness, a theory that classified as sick all people who were mentally unbalanced; third, that as a consequence of this reexamination in the light of the statistics, he had concluded not only that his theory was unsound but also that the exactly contrary doctrine was true—that is, that normality lay in a lack of equilibrium and that the abnormal, the really sick, were the well balanced, the thoroughly rational; fourth, that in view of the foregoing he would release the persons now confined and would commit to the Green House all persons found to be mentally ill under the new theory; fifth, that he would continue to devote himself to the pursuit of scientific truth and trusted that the Council would continue to give him its support; and sixth, that he would give back the funds he had received for the board and lodging of the patients, less the amounts already expended, which could be verified by examination of his records and accounts.

The amazement of Itaguai was no greater than the joy of the relatives and friends of the former patients. Dinners, dances, Chinese lanterns, music, everything to celebrate the happy occasion. I shall not describe the festivities, for they are merely peripheral to this history; suffice it to say that they were elaborate, long, and memorable.

In the midst of all this rejoicing, nobody noticed the last part of the fourth item in the psychiatrist's communiqué.

12. THE LAST PART OF THE FOURTH ITEM

The lanterns were taken down, the ex-patients resumed their former lives, everything appeared normal. Councilman Freitas and the President returned to their accustomed places, and the Council governed Itaguai without external interference. Porfírio the barber had "experienced everything," as the poet said of Napoleon; indeed, Porfírio had experienced more than Napoleon, for Napoleon was never committed to the Green House. The barber now found the obscure security of his trade preferable to the brilliant calamities of power. He was tried for his crimes and convicted, but the people begged His Majesty to pardon their ex-Protector, and His Majesty did so. The authorities decided not to prosecute João Pina, for he had overthrown an unlawful ruler. The chroniclers maintain that Pina's absolution inspired our adage:

> A judge will never throw the book
> At crook who steals from other crook.

An immoral adage, but immensely useful.

There were no more complaints against the psychiatrist. There was not even resentment for his past acts. Indeed, the former patients were grateful because he had declared them sane; they gave a ball in his honor. The chroniclers relate that Dona Evarista decided at first to leave her husband but changed her mind when she contemplated the emptiness of a life without him. Her devotion to this high-minded man overcame her wounded vanity, and they lived together more happily than ever before.

On the basis of the new psychiatric doctrine set forth in the communiqué, Crispim Soares concluded that his prudence in allying himself with the revolution had been a manifestation of mental health. He was deeply touched by Bacamarte's magnanimity: the psychiatrist had extended his hand to his old friend upon releasing him from the Green House.

"A great man," said the druggist to his wife.

We need not specifically note the release of Costa, Coelho, and the other patients named in this history. Each was now free to resume his previous way of life. Martim Brito, for example, who had been committed because of a speech in excessive praise of Dona Evarista, now made another in honor of the doctor, "whose exalted genius lifted its wings and flew far above the common herd until it rivaled the sun in altitude and in brilliance."

"Thank you," said the psychiatrist. "Obviously I was right to set you free."

Meanwhile, the Town Council passed, without debate, an ordinance to take care of the last part of the fourth item in Bacamarte's communiqué. The ordinance authorized the psychiatrist to commit to the Green House all persons whom he found to be mentally well balanced. But, remembering its painful experience in connection with public reaction to the asylum, the Council added a proviso in which it stated that, since the purpose of the ordinance was to provide an opportunity for the doctor to test his new theory, the authorization would remain in effect for only one year, and the Council reserved the right to close the asylum at any time if the maintenance of public order so required.

Sebastião Freitas proposed an amendment to the effect that under no circumstances were members of the Council to be committed to the Green House. The amendment was adopted almost unanimously. The only dissenting vote was cast by Councilman Galvão. He argued calmly that, in authorizing a scientific experiment on the people of Itaguai, the Council would itself be unscientific if it exempted its members or any other segment of the population from subjection to the experiment. "Our public office," he said, "does not exclude us from the human race." But he was shouted down.

Simão Bacamarte accepted the ordinance with all its restrictions. As for the exemption of the Councilmen, he declared that they were in no danger whatever of being committed, for their votes in favor of the amendment showed clearly that they were mentally unbalanced. He asked only that Galvão be delivered to him, for this Councilman had exhibited exceptional mental equilibrium, not only in his objection to the amendment but even more in the calm that he had maintained in the face of unreasonable opposition and abuse on the part of his colleagues. The Council immediately granted the request.

Under the new theory a few acts or statements by a person could not establish his abnormality: a long examination and a thorough study of his history were necessary. Father Lopes, for example, was not taken to the Green House until thirty days after the passage of the ordinance. In the case of the druggist's wife fifty days of study were required. Crispim Soares raged about the streets, telling everybody that he would tear the tyrant's ears off. One of the men to whom he spoke—a fellow who, as everyone knew, had an aversion for Bacamarte—ran and warned the psychiatrist. Bacamarte thanked him warmly and locked him up in recognition of his rectitude and his good will even toward someone he disliked, signs of perfect mental equilibrium.

"This is a very unusual case," said the doctor to Dona Evarista.

By the time Crispim Soares arrived at the psychiatrist's house, sorrow had overcome his anger. He did not tear Bacamarte's ears off. The psychiatrist tried to comfort his old friend. He told him that his wife might be suffering from a cerebral lesion, that there was a fair chance of recovery, and that meanwhile he must of course keep her confined. The psychiatrist considered it desirable, however, for Soares to spend a good deal of time with her, for the druggist's guile and intellectual dishonesty might help to overcome the moral superiority that the doctor found in his patient.

"There is no reason," he said, "why you and your wife should not eat lunch and dinner together every day at the Green House. You may even stay with her at night."

Simão Bacamarte's words placed the druggist in a new dilemma. He wanted to be with his wife, but at the same time he dreaded returning to the Green House. He remained undecided for several minutes. Then Dona Evarista released him from the dilemma: she promised to visit his wife frequently and to bear messages between the two. Crispim Soares kissed her hands in gratitude. His pusillanimous egoism struck the psychiatrist as almost sublime.

Although it took Bacamarte almost half a year to find eighteen patients for the Green House, he did not relax his efforts to discover the insane. He went from street to street, from house to house, observing, inquiring, taking notes. And when he committed someone to the asylum, it was with the same sense of accomplishment with which he had formerly committed dozens at a time. This very disproportion confirmed his new theory. At last the truth about mental illness was definitely known. One day Bacamarte committed the Circuit Judge to the Green House, after weeks of detailed study of the man's acts and thorough interrogation of his friends, who included all the important people of Itaguai.

More than once the psychiatrist was on the point of sending someone to the Green House, only to discover a serious shortcoming at the last moment. In the case of the lawyer Salustiano, for example, he thought he had found so perfect a combination of intellectual and moral qualities that it would be dangerous to leave the man at large. He told one of his agents to bring the man in, but the agent, who had known many lawyers, suspected that he might really be sane and persuaded Bacamarte to authorize a little experiment. The agent had a close friend who was charged with having falsified a will. He advised this friend to engage Salustiano as his lawyer.

"Do you really think he'll take the case?"

"Sure he will. Confess everything to him. He'll get you off."

The agent's friend went to the lawyer, admitted that he had falsified the will, and begged him to accept the case. Salustiano did not turn the man away. He studied the charges and supporting evidence. In court he argued at great length, proving conclusively that the will was genuine. After a verdict of acquittal the defendant received the estate under the terms of the will. To this experiment both he and the learned counselor owed their freedom.

Very little escapes the comprehension of a man of genuine insight. For some time Simão Bacamarte had noted the wisdom, patience, and dedication of the agent who devised the experiment. Consequently he determined to commit him to the Green House, in which he gave him one of the choicest cubicles.

The patients were segregated into classes. In one gallery lived only those whose outstanding moral quality was modesty. The notably tolerant occupied another gallery, and still others were set aside for the truthful, the guileless, the loyal, the magnanimous, the wise. Naturally, the friends and relatives of the madmen railed against the new theory. Some even tried to persuade the Town Council to cancel the authorization it had given Bacamarte. The Councilmen, however, remembered with bitterness the word of their former colleague Galvão; they did not wish to see him back in their midst, and so they refused. Simão Bacamarte sent a message to the Council, not thanking it but congratulating it on this act of personal spite.

Some of the important people of Itaguai then went secretly to the barber Porfírio. They promised to support him with men, money, and influence if he would lead another movement against the psychiatrist and the Town Council. He replied that ambition had once led him to violent transgression of the law but that he now recognized the folly of such conduct; that the Council, in its wisdom, had authorized the psychiatrist to conduct his new experiment for a year; that anybody who objected should wait till the end of the year and then, if the Council insisted on renewing the authorization, should petition the Viceroy; that he would not recommend recourse again to a method that had done no good and had caused several deaths and other casualties, which would be an eternal burden on his conscience.

The psychiatrist listened with immense interest when one of his secret agents told him what Porfírio had said. Two days later the barber was locked up in the Green House. "You're damned if you do and you're damned if you don't," observed the new patient.

At the end of the year allowed for verification of the new theory, the Town Council authorized the psychiatrist to continue his work for another six months in order to experiment with methods of therapy. The result of this additional experimentation is so significant that it merits ten chapters, but I shall content myself with one. It will provide the reader with an inspiring example of scientific objectivity and selflessness.

13. PLUS ULTRA

However diligent and perceptive he may have been in the discovery of madmen, Simão Bacamarte outdid himself when he undertook to cure them. All the chroniclers agree that he brought about the most amazing recoveries.

It is indeed hard to imagine a more rational system of therapy. Having divided the patients into classes according to their predominant moral qualities, the doctor now proceeded to break down those qualities. He applied a remedy in each case to inculcate exactly the opposite characteristic, selecting the specific medicine and dose best suited to the patient's age, personality, and social position.

The cases of modesty may serve as examples. In some, a wig, a fine coat, or a cane would suffice to restore reason to the madman. In more difficult cases the psychiatrist resorted to diamonds, honorary degrees, and the like. The illness of one modest lunatic, a poet, resisted every sort of therapy. Bacamarte had almost given up, when an idea occurred to him: he would have the crier with the noisemaker proclaim the patient to be as great as Garcão or Pindar.

"It was like a miracle," said the poet's mother to one of her friends. "My boy is entirely well now. A miracle . . ."

Another patient, also in the modest class, seemed incurable. The specific remedy used for the poet would not work, for this patient was not a writer; indeed, he could barely sign his name. But Dr. Bacamarte proved equal to the challenge. He decided to have the patient made Secretary to the Itaguai branch of the Royal Academy. The Secretary and the President of each branch were appointed by the Crown. They enjoyed the privileges of being addressed as Excellency and of wearing a gold medallion. The government at Lisbon refused Bacamarte's request at first; but after the psychiatrist explained that he did not ask the appointment as a real honor for his patient but merely as a therapeutic device to cure a difficult case, and after the Minister of Overseas Possessions (a cousin of the patient) intervened, the government finally granted the request. The consequent cure was hailed as another miracle.

"Wonderful, really wonderful!" said everybody upon seeing the healthy, prideful expression on the faces of the two ex-madmen.

Bacamarte's method was ultimately successful in every case, although in a few the patient's dominant quality proved impregnable. In these cases the psychiatrist won out by attacking at another point, like a good military strategist.

By the end of five months all the patients had been cured. The Green House was empty. Councilman Galvão, so cruelly afflicted with fairness and moderation, had the good fortune to lose an uncle; I say good fortune, for the uncle's will was ambiguous and Galvão obtained a favorable interpretation of it by bribing two judges. With customary integrity, the doctor admitted that the cure had been effected not by him but by nature's *vis medicatrix*. It was quite otherwise in the case of Father Lopes. Bacamarte knew that the priest was utterly ignorant of Greek, and therefore asked him to make a critical analysis of the Septuagint. Father Lopes accepted the task. In two months he had written a book on the subject and was released from the Green House. As for the druggist's wife, she remained there only a short time.

"Why doesn't Crispim come to visit me?" she asked every day.

They gave her various answers and finally told her the plain truth. The worthy matron could not contain her shame and indignation. Her explosions of wrath included such expressions as "rat," "coward," and "he even cheats on prescriptions." Simão Bacamarte remarked that, whether or not these characterizations of her husband were true, they clearly established the lady's return to sanity. He promptly released her.

If you think the psychiatrist was radiant with happiness on seeing the last guest leave the Green House, you apparently do not yet understand the man. *Plus ultra*[7] was his motto. For him the discovery of the true theory of mental illness was not enough, nor was the establishment in Itaguaí of the reign of reason with the total elimination of psychological abnormality. *Plus ultra!* Something told him that his new theory bore within itself a better, newer theory.

"Let us see," he said to himself, "if I can discover the ultimate, underlying truth."

He paced the length of the immense room, past bookcase after bookcase—the largest library in His Majesty's overseas possessions. A gold-embroidered, damask dressing-gown (a gift from a university) enveloped the regal and austere body of the illustrious physician. The extensive top of his head, which the incessant cogitations of the scientist had rendered bald, was covered by a wig. His feet, neither dainty nor gross but perfectly proportioned to his body, were encased in a pair of ordinary shoes with plain brass buckles. Note the distinction: only those elements that bore some relationship to his work as a scientist were in any sense luxurious; the rest was simple and temperate.

And so the psychiatrist walked up and down his vast library, lost in thought, alien to everything but the dark problem of psychopathology. Suddenly he stopped. Standing before a window, with his left elbow resting on his open right hand and his chin on his closed left hand, he asked himself:

7. Further beyond, to an extreme (Latin).

"Were they all really insane? Did I really cure them? Or is not mental imbalance so natural and inherent that it was bound to assert itself with or without my help?"

He soon arrived at this conclusion: the apparently well-balanced minds that he had just "cured" had really been unbalanced all the time, just like the obviously sane minds of the rest of the people. Their apparent illness was superficial and transient.

The psychiatrist contemplated his new doctrine with mixed feelings. He was happy because, after such long study, experimentation, and struggle, he could at last affirm the ultimate truth: there never were and never would be any madmen in Itaguaí or anywhere else. But he was unhappy because a doubt assailed him. In the field of psychiatry a generalization so broad, so absolute, was almost inevitably erroneous. If he could find just one undeniably well balanced, virtuous, insane man, the new theory would be acceptable—not as an absolute, exceptionless principle, which was inadmissible, but as a general rule applicable to all but the most extraordinary cases.

According to the chroniclers, this difficulty constituted the most dreadful of the spiritual tempests through which the courageous Bacamarte passed in the course of his stormy professional life. But tempests terrify only the weak. After twenty minutes a gentle but radiant dawn dispelled the darkness from the face of the psychiatrist.

"Of course. That's it, of course."

What Simão Bacamarte meant was that he had found in himself the perfect, undeniable case of insanity. He possessed wisdom, patience, tolerance, truthfulness, loyalty, and moral fortitude—all the qualities that go to make an utter madman.

But then he questioned his own self-observation. Surely he must be imperfect in some way. To ascertain the truth about himself he convoked a gathering of his friends and questioned them. He begged them to answer with absolute frankness. They all agreed that he had not been mistaken.

"No defects?"

"None at all," they replied in chorus.

"No vices?"

"None."

"Perfect in every respect?"

"In every respect."

"No, impossible!" cried the psychiatrist. "I cannot believe that I am so far superior to my fellow men. You are letting yourselves be influenced by your affection for me."

His friends insisted. The psychiatrist hesitated, but Father Lopes made it difficult for him not to accept their judgment.

"Do you know why you are reluctant to recognize in yourself the lofty qualities which we all see so clearly?" said the priest. "It is because you have an additional quality that enhances all the others: modesty."

Simão Bacamarte bowed his head. He was both sad and happy, but more happy than sad. He immediately committed himself to the Green House. His wife and his friends begged him not to. They told him he was perfectly sane. They wept, they pleaded. All in vain.

"This is a matter of science, of a new doctrine," he said, "and I am the first instance of its application. I embody both theory and practice."

"Simão! Simão, my love!" cried his wife. Her face was bathed in tears.

But the doctor, his eyes alight with scientific conviction, gently pushed her away. He entered the Green House, shut the door behind him, and set about the business of curing himself. The chroniclers state, however, that he died seventeen months later as insane as ever. Some even venture the opinion that he was the only madman (in the vulgar or non-Bacamartian sense) ever committed to the asylum. But this opinion should not be taken seriously. It was based on remarks attributed to Father Lopes— doubtless erroneously, for, as everybody knew, the priest liked and admired the psychiatrist. In any case, the people of Itaguai buried the mortal remains of Simão Bacamarte with great pomp and solemnity.

Charlotte Perkins Gilman
1860–1935

One of the leading intellectuals of the early American women's movement, Charlotte Perkins Gilman was forgotten for several decades in the mid-twentieth century, then rediscovered in the 1970s by feminists who found virtues in her fiction that had been less obvious to earlier readers. Thus *Herland* (1915), one of Gilman's three utopian novels, has become a landmark in the imagining of alternative sexual relationships. "The Yellow Wallpaper" (1892), with its extraordinary analysis of "normal" marriage and the pathologizing of feminine emotion as "hysterical," has acquired the status of an unquestioned literary classic.

Born in 1860 in Connecticut, Gilman was raised by her mother at the edge of poverty after her father abandoned the family. As soon as she was old enough, she began contributing to the family finances. She studied art and in 1884 married a fellow artist. The birth of a daughter one year later left her in a state of severe depression. Gilman consulted the prominent Dr. S. Weir Mitchell, mentioned by name in "The Yellow Wallpaper," and underwent his so-called "rest cure," which involved total bed rest, confinement, and isolation. Echoing much of the (male) medical opinion of the day, Mitchell advised Gilman after the cure to devote herself entirely to her child and domestic duties—in his view, the proper role for a woman—and avoid all intellectual and artistic work. Unable to follow this advice, Gilman chose instead a trial separation from her husband and a trip to California. Her health was restored, and she and her husband were amicably divorced. A second marriage in 1900 endured until her husband died in 1934, a year before her own death.

During this period, Gilman worked happily and productively as a writer and lecturer on behalf of both women's rights and the political reforms advocated by Edward Bellamy, whose influential utopian novel *Looking Backward* had appeared in 1888. In 1898 Gilman won international fame with *Women and Economics;* inspired in part by the newly developing social sciences, this pioneering work of what is now called interdisciplinary research explored the historical reasons for women's subordination. Her emphasis on the economic dimension of sexual inequality, or how women's status is determined by the fact that their labor inside the family is unpaid, led her to propose a radical solution: cooking, cleaning, and child care should henceforth be managed by paid professionals, thus leaving women free to choose if they desired to work outside the home. Gilman's sympathy for professionalism sheds an interesting light on the critique of professional medicine that many readers have found in "The Yellow Wallpaper." She elaborated and championed this analysis in a series of further books and in seven years of work on a periodical called *The Forerunner,* which she founded and for which she did virtually all the work of writing and editing.

While suggesting that even loving marriage is too often a punishing form of solitary confinement for women, that every husband in a sense plays the role of doctor, "The Yellow Wallpaper" is also an allegory of the situation of the woman writer. The protagonist is forbidden to exercise her craft on the grounds that it is harmful for her, and she finds allegories of her own situation in what she has access to, the furnishings of the room. But Gilman's premise of the narrator-as-mad(wo)man, shared with such rough contemporaries as Tolstoy and Lu Xun, lends itself to a multiplicity of interpretations.

The Yellow Wallpaper

It is very seldom that mere ordinary people like John and myself secure ancestral halls for the summer.

A colonial mansion, a hereditary estate, I would say a haunted house, and reach the height of romantic felicity—but that would be asking too much of fate!

Still I will proudly declare that there is something queer about it.

Else, why should it be let so cheaply? And why have stood so long untenanted?

John laughs at me, of course, but one expects that in marriage.

John is practical in the extreme. He has no patience with faith, an intense horror of superstition, and he scoffs openly at any talk of things not to be felt and seen and put down in figures.

John is a physician, and *perhaps*—(I would not say it to a living soul, of course, but this is dead paper and a great relief to my mind)—*perhaps* that is one reason I do not get well faster.

You see he does not believe I am sick!

And what can one do?

If a physician of high standing, and one's own husband, assures friends and relatives that there is really nothing the matter with one but temporary nervous depression—a slight hysterical tendency—what is one to do?

My brother is also a physician, and also of high standing, and he says the same thing.

So I take phosphates or phosphites—whichever it is, and tonics, and journeys, and air, and exercise, and am absolutely forbidden to "work" until I am well again.

Personally, I disagree with their ideas.

Personally, I believe that congenial work, with excitement and change, would do me good.

But what is one to do?

I did write for a while in spite of them; but it *does* exhaust me a good deal—having to be so sly about it, or else meet with heavy opposition.

I sometimes fancy that in my condition if I had less opposition and more society and stimulus—but John says the very worst thing I can do is to think about my condition, and I confess it always makes me feel bad.

So I will let it alone and talk about the house.

The most beautiful place! It is quite alone, standing well back from the road, quite three miles from the village. It makes me think of English places that you read about, for there are hedges and walls and gates that lock, and lots of separate little houses for the gardeners and people.

There is a *delicious* garden! I never saw such a garden—large and shady, full of box-bordered paths, and lined with long grape-covered arbors with seats under them.

There were greenhouses, too, but they are all broken now.

There was some legal trouble, I believe, something about the heirs and coheirs; anyhow, the place has been empty for years.

That spoils my ghostliness, I am afraid, but I don't care—there is something strange about the house—I can feel it.

I even said so to John one moonlight evening, but he said what I felt was a *draught,* and shut the window.

I get unreasonably angry with John sometimes. I'm sure I never used to be so sensitive. I think it is due to this nervous condition.

But John says if I feel so, I shall neglect proper self-control; so I take pains to control myself—before him, at least, and that makes me very tired.

I don't like our room a bit. I wanted one downstairs that opened on the piazza and had roses all over the window, and such pretty old-fashioned chintz hangings! but John would not hear of it.

He said there was only one window and not room for two beds, and no near room for him if he took another.

He is very careful and loving, and hardly lets me stir without special direction.

I have a schedule prescription for each hour in the day; he takes all care from me, and so I feel basely ungrateful not to value it more.

He said we came here solely on my account, that I was to have perfect rest and all the air I could get. "Your exercise depends on your strength, my dear," said he, "and your food somewhat on your appetite; but air you can absorb all the time." So we took the nursery at the top of the house.

It is a big, airy room, the whole floor nearly, with windows that look all ways, and air and sunshine galore. It was nursery first and then playroom and gymnasium, I should judge; for the windows are barred for little children, and there are rings and things in the walls.

The paint and paper look as if a boys' school had used it. It is stripped off—the paper—in great patches all around the head of my bed, about as far as I can reach, and in a great place on the other side of the room low down. I never saw a worse paper in my life.

One of those sprawling flamboyant patterns committing every artistic sin.

It is dull enough to confuse the eye in following, pronounced enough to constantly irritate and provoke study, and when you follow the lame uncertain curves for a little distance they suddenly commit suicide—plunge off at outrageous angles, destroy themselves in unheard of contradictions.

The color is repellent, almost revolting; a smouldering unclean yellow, strangely faded by the slow-turning sunlight.

It is a dull yet lurid orange in some places, a sickly sulphur tint in others.

No wonder the children hated it! I should hate it myself if I had to live in this room long.

There comes John, and I must put this away,—he hates to have me write a word.

We have been here two weeks, and I haven't felt like writing before, since that first day.

I am sitting by the window now, up in this atrocious nursery, and there is nothing to hinder my writing as much as I please, save lack of strength.

John is away all day, and even some nights when his cases are serious.

I am glad my case is not serious!

But these nervous troubles are dreadfully depressing.

John does not know how much I really suffer. He knows there is no *reason* to suffer, and that satisfies him.

Of course it is only nervousness. It does weigh on me so not to do my duty in any way!

I meant to be such a help to John, such a real rest and comfort, and here I am a comparative burden already!

Nobody would believe what an effort it is to do what little I am able,—to dress and entertain, and order things.

It is fortunate Mary is so good with the baby. Such a dear baby!

And yet I *cannot* be with him, it makes me so nervous.

I suppose John never was nervous in his life. He laughs at me so about this wallpaper!

At first he meant to repaper the room, but afterwards he said that I was letting it get the better of me, and that nothing was worse for a nervous patient than to give way to such fancies.

He said that after the wallpaper was changed it would be the heavy bedstead, and then the barred windows, and then that gate at the head of the stairs, and so on.

"You know the place is doing you good," he said, "and really, dear, I don't care to renovate the house just for a three months' rental."

"Then do let us go downstairs," I said, "there are such pretty rooms there."

Then he took me in his arms and called me a blessed little goose, and said he would go down to the cellar, if I wished, and have it whitewashed into the bargain.

But he is right enough about the beds and windows and things.

It is an airy and comfortable room as any one need wish, and, of course, I would not be so silly as to make him uncomfortable just for a whim.

I'm really getting quite fond of the big room, all but that horrid paper.

Out of one window I can see the garden, those mysterious deepshaded arbors, the riotous old-fashioned flowers, and bushes and gnarly trees.

Out of another I get a lovely view of the bay and a little private wharf belonging to the estate. There is a beautiful shaded lane that runs down there from the house. I always fancy I see people walking in these numerous paths and arbors, but John has cautioned me not to give way to fancy in the least. He says that with my imaginative power and habit of story-making, a nervous weakness like mine is sure to lead to all manner of excited fancies, and that I ought to use my will and good sense to check the tendency. So I try.

I think sometimes that if I were only well enough to write a little it would relieve the press of ideas and rest me.

But I find I get pretty tired when I try.

It is so discouraging not to have any advice and companionship about my work. When I get really well, John says we will ask Cousin Henry and Julia down for a long visit; but he says he would as soon put fireworks in my pillow-case as to let me have those stimulating people about now.

I wish I could get well faster.

But I must not think about that. This paper looks to me as if it *knew* what a vicious influence it had!

There is a recurrent spot where the pattern lolls like a broken neck and two bulbous eyes stare at you upside down.

I get positively angry with the impertinence of it and the everlastingness. Up and down and sideways they crawl, and those absurd, unblinking eyes are everywhere. There is one place where two breaths didn't match, and the eyes go all up and down the line, one a little higher than the other.

I never saw so much expression in an inanimate thing before, and we all know how much expression they have! I used to lie awake as a child and get more entertainment and terror out of blank walls and plain furniture than most children could find in a toy-store.

I remember what a kindly wink the knobs of our big, old bureau used to have, and there was one chair that always seemed like a strong friend.

I used to feel that if any of the other things looked too fierce I could always hop into that chair and be safe.

The furniture in this room is no worse than inharmonious, however, for we had to bring it all from downstairs. I suppose when this was used as a playroom they had to take the nursery things out, and no wonder! I never saw such ravages as the children have made here.

The wallpaper, as I said before, is torn off in spots, and it sticketh closer than a brother—they must have had perseverance as well as hatred.

Then the floor is scratched and gouged and splintered, the plaster itself is dug out here and there, and this great heavy bed which is all we found in the room, looks as if it had been through the wars.

But I don't mind it a bit—only the paper.

There comes John's sister. Such a dear girl as she is, and so careful of me! I must not let her find me writing.

She is a perfect and enthusiastic housekeeper, and hopes for no better profession. I verily believe she thinks it is the writing which made me sick!

But I can write when she is out, and see her a long way off from these windows.

There is one that commands the road, a lovely shaded winding road, and one that just looks off over the country. A lovely country, too, full of great elms and velvet meadows.

This wallpaper has a kind of sub-pattern in a different shade, a particularly irritating one, for you can only see it in certain lights, and not clearly then.

But in the places where it isn't faded and where the sun is just so—I can see a strange, provoking, formless sort of figure, that seems to skulk about behind that silly and conspicuous front design.

There's sister on the stairs!

Well, the Fourth of July is over! The people are all gone and I am tired out. John thought it might do me good to see a little company, so we just had Mother and Nellie and the children down for a week.

Of course I didn't do a thing. Jennie sees to everything now.

But it tired me all the same.

John says if I don't pick up faster he shall send me to Weir Mitchell in the fall.

But I don't want to go there at all. I had a friend who was in his hands once, and she says he is just like John and my brother, only more so!

Besides, it is such an undertaking to go so far.

I don't feel as if it was worthwhile to turn my hand over for anything, and I'm getting dreadfully fretful and querulous.

I cry at nothing, and cry most of the time.

Of course I don't when John is here, or anybody else, but when I am alone.

And I am alone a good deal just now. John is kept in town very often by serious cases, and Jennie is good and lets me alone when I want her to.

So I walk a little in the garden or down that lovely lane, sit on the porch under the roses, and lie down up here a good deal.

I'm getting really fond of the room in spite of the wallpaper. Perhaps *because* of the wallpaper.

It dwells in my mind so!

I lie here on this great immovable bed—it is nailed down, I believe—and follow that pattern about by the hour. It is as good as gymnastics, I assure you. I start, we'll say, at the bottom, down in the corner over there where it has not been touched, and I determine for the thousandth time that I *will* follow that pointless pattern to some sort of a conclusion.

I know a little of the principle of design, and I know this thing was not arranged on any laws of radiation, or alternation, or repetition, or symmetry, or anything else that I ever heard of.

It is repeated, of course, by the breadths, but not otherwise.

Looked at in one way each breadth stands alone, the bloated curves and flourishes—a kind of "debased Romanesque" with *delirium tremens*—go waddling up and down in isolated columns of fatuity.

But, on the other hand, they connect diagonally, and the sprawling outlines run off in great slanting waves of optic horror, like a lot of wallowing seaweeds in full chase.

The whole thing goes horizontally, too, at least it seems so, and I exhaust myself in trying to distinguish the order of its going in that direction.

They have used a horizontal breadth for a frieze, and that adds wonderfully to the confusion.

There is one end of the room where it is almost intact, and there, when the crosslights fade and the low sun shines directly upon it, I can almost fancy radiation after all,—the interminable grotesques seem to form around a common centre and rush off in headlong plunges of equal distraction.

It makes me tired to follow it. I will take a nap I guess.

I don't know why I should write this.

I don't want to.

I don't feel able.

And I know John would think it absurd. But I *must* say what I feel and think in some way—it is such a relief!

But the effort is getting to be greater than the relief.

Half the time now I am awfully lazy, and lie down ever so much.

John says I mustn't lose my strength, and has me take cod liver oil and lots of tonics and things, to say nothing of ale and wine and rare meat.

Dear John! He loves me very dearly, and hates to have me sick. I tried to have a real earnest reasonable talk with him the other day, and tell him how I wish he would let me go and make a visit to Cousin Henry and Julia.

But he said I wasn't able to go, nor able to stand it after I got there; and I did not make out a very good case for myself, for I was crying before I had finished.

It is getting to be a great effort for me to think straight. Just this nervous weakness I suppose.

And dear John gathered me up in his arms, and just carried me upstairs and laid me on the bed, and sat by me and read to me till it tired my head.

He said I was his darling and his comfort and all he had, and that I must take care of myself for his sake, and keep well.

He says no one but myself can help me out of it, that I must use my will and self-control and not let any silly fancies run away with me.

There's one comfort, the baby is well and happy, and does not have to occupy this nursery with the horrid wallpaper.

If we had not used it, that blessed child would have! What a fortunate escape! Why, I wouldn't have a child of mine, an impressionable little thing, live in such a room for worlds.

I never thought of it before, but it is lucky that John kept me here after all, I can stand it so much easier than a baby, you see.

Of course I never mention it to them any more—I am too wise,—but I keep watch of it all the same.

There are things in that paper that nobody knows but me, or ever will.

Behind that outside pattern the dim shapes get clearer every day.

It is always the same shape, only very numerous.

And it is like a woman stooping down and creeping about behind that pattern. I don't like it a bit. I wonder—I begin to think—I wish John would take me away from here!

It is so hard to talk with John about my case, because he is so wise, and because he loves me so.

But I tried it last night.

It was moonlight. The moon shines in all around just as the sun does.

I hate to see it sometimes, it creeps so slowly, and always comes in by one window or another.

John was asleep and I hated to waken him, so I kept still and watched the moonlight on that undulating wallpaper till I felt creepy.

The faint figure behind seemed to shake the pattern, just as if she wanted to get out.

I got up softly and went to feel and see if the paper *did* move, and when I came back John was awake.

"What is it, little girl?" he said. "Don't go walking about like that—you'll get cold."

I thought it was a good time to talk, so I told him that I really was not gaining here, and that I wished he would take me away.

"Why darling!" said he, "our lease will be up in three weeks, and I can't see how to leave before.

"The repairs are not done at home, and I cannot possibly leave town just now. Of course if you were in any danger, I could and would, but you really are better, dear, whether you can see it or not. I am a doctor, dear, and I know. You are gaining flesh and color, your appetite is better, I feel really much easier about you."

"I don't weigh a bit more," said I, "nor as much; and my appetite may be better in the evening when you are here, but it is worse in the morning when you are away!"

"Bless her little heart!" said he with a big hug, "she shall be as sick as she pleases! But now let's improve the shining hours by going to sleep, and talk about it in the morning!"

"And you won't go away?" I asked gloomily.

"Why, how can I, dear? It is only three weeks more and then we will take a nice little trip of a few days while Jennie is getting the house ready. Really dear you are better!"

"Better in body perhaps—" I began, and stopped short, for he sat up straight and looked at me with such a stern, reproachful look that I could not say another word.

"My darling," said he, "I beg of you, for my sake and for our child's sake, as well as for your own, that you will never for one instant let that idea enter your mind! There is nothing so dangerous, so fascinating, to a temperament like yours. It is a false and foolish fancy. Can you not trust me as a physician when I tell you so?"

So of course I said no more on that score, and we went to sleep before long. He thought I was asleep first, but I wasn't, and lay there for hours trying to decide whether that front pattern and the back pattern really did move together or separately.

On a pattern like this, by daylight, there is a lack of sequence, a defiance of law, that is a constant irritant to a normal mind.

The color is hideous enough, and unreliable enough, and infuriating enough, but the pattern is torturing.

You think you have mastered it, but just as you get well underway in following, it turns a back-somersault and there you are. It slaps you in the face, knocks you down, and tramples upon you. It is like a bad dream.

The outside pattern is a florid arabesque, reminding one of a fungus. If you can imagine a toadstool in joints, an interminable string of toadstools, budding and sprouting in endless convolutions—why, that is something like it.

That is, sometimes!

There is one marked peculiarity about this paper, a thing nobody seems to notice but myself, and that is that it changes as the light changes.

When the sun shoots in through the east window—I always watch for that first long, straight ray—it changes so quickly that I never can quite believe it.

That is why I watch it always.

By moonlight—the moon shines in all night when there is a moon—I wouldn't know it was the same paper.

At night in any kind of light, in twilight, candle light, lamplight, and worst of all by moonlight, it becomes bars! The outside pattern I mean, and the woman behind it is as plain as can be.

I didn't realize for a long time what the thing was that showed behind, that dim sub-pattern, but now I am quite sure it is a woman.

By daylight she is subdued, quiet. I fancy it is the pattern that keeps her so still. It is so puzzling. It keeps me quiet by the hour.

I lie down ever so much now. John says it is good for me, and to sleep all I can.

Indeed he started the habit by making me lie down for an hour after each meal.

It is a very bad habit I am convinced, for you see I don't sleep.

And that cultivates deceit, for I don't tell them I'm awake—O no!

The fact is I am getting a little afraid of John.

He seems very queer sometimes, and even Jennie has an inexplicable look.

It strikes me occasionally, just as a scientific hypothesis,—that perhaps it is the paper!

I have watched John when he did not know I was looking, and come into the room suddenly on the most innocent excuses, and I've caught him several times *looking at the paper!* And Jennie too. I caught Jennie with her hand on it once.

She didn't know I was in the room, and when I asked her in a quiet, a very quiet voice, with the most restrained manner possible, what she was doing with the paper—she turned around as if she had been caught stealing, and looked quite angry—asked me why I should frighten her so!

Then she said that the paper stained everything it touched, that she had found yellow smooches on all my clothes and John's, and she wished we would be more careful!

Did not that sound innocent? But I know she was studying that pattern, and I am determined that nobody shall find it out but myself!

Life is very much more exciting now than it used to be. You see I have something more to expect, to look forward to, to watch. I really do eat better, and am more quiet than I was.

John is so pleased to see me improve! He laughed a little the other day, and said I seemed to be flourishing in spite of my wallpaper.

I turned it off with a laugh. I had no intention of telling him it was *because* of the wallpaper—he would make fun of me. He might even want to take me away.

I don't want to leave now until I have found it out. There is a week more, and I think that will be enough.

I'm feeling ever so much better! I don't sleep much at night, for it is so interesting to watch developments; but I sleep a good deal in the daytime.

In the daytime it is tiresome and perplexing.

There are always new shoots on the fungus, and new shades of yellow all over it. I cannot keep count of them, though I have tried conscientiously.

It is the strangest yellow, that wallpaper! It makes me think of all the yellow things I ever saw—not beautiful ones like buttercups, but old foul, bad yellow things.

But there is something else about that paper—the smell! I noticed it the moment we came into the room, but with so much air and sun it was not bad. Now we have had a week of fog and rain, and whether the windows are open or not, the smell is here.

It creeps all over the house.

I find it hovering in the dining-room, skulking in the parlor, hiding in the hall, lying in wait for me on the stairs.

It gets into my hair.

Even when I go to ride, if I turn my head suddenly and surprise it—there is that smell!

Such a peculiar odor, too! I have spent hours in trying to analyze it, to find what it smelled like.

It is not bad—at first, and very gentle, but quite the subtlest, most enduring odor I ever met.

In this damp weather it is awful, I wake up in the night and find it hanging over me.

It used to disturb me at first. I thought seriously of burning the house—to reach the smell.

But now I am used to it. The only thing I can think of that it is like is the *color* of the paper! A yellow smell.

There is a very funny mark on this wall, low down, near the mopboard. A streak that runs round the room. It goes behind every piece of furniture, except the bed, a long, straight, even *smooch,* as if it had been rubbed over and over.

I wonder how it was done and who did it, and what they did it for. Round and round and round—round and round and round—it makes me dizzy!

I really have discovered something at last.

Through watching so much at night, when it changes so, I have finally found out.

The front pattern *does* move—and no wonder! The woman behind shakes it!

Sometimes I think there are a great many women behind, and sometimes only one, and she crawls around fast, and her crawling shakes it all over.

Then in the very bright spots she keeps still, and in the very shady spots she just takes hold of the bars and shakes them hard.

And she is all the time trying to climb through. But nobody could climb through that pattern—it strangles so; I think that is why it has so many heads.

They get through, and then the pattern strangles them off and turns them upside down, and makes their eyes white!

If those heads were covered or taken off it would not be half so bad.

I think that woman gets out in the daytime!

And I'll tell you why—privately—I've seen her!

I can see her out of every one of my windows!

It is the same woman, I know, for she is always creeping, and most women do not creep by daylight.

I see her on that long road under the trees, creeping along, and when a carriage comes she hides under the blackberry vines.

I don't blame her a bit. It must be very humiliating to be caught creeping by daylight!

I always lock the door when I creep by daylight. I can't do it at night, for I know John would suspect something at once.

And John is so queer now, that I don't want to irritate him. I wish he would take another room! Besides, I don't want anybody to get that woman out at night but myself.

I often wonder if I could see her out of all the windows at once.

But, turn as fast as I can, I can only see out of one at one time.

And though I always see her, she *may* be able to creep faster than I can turn!

I have watched her sometimes away off in the open country, creeping as fast as a cloud shadow in a high wind.

If only that top pattern could be gotten off from the under one! I mean to try it, little by little.

I have found out another funny thing, but I shan't tell it this time! It does not do to trust people too much.

There are only two more days to get this paper off, and I believe John is beginning to notice. I don't like the look in his eyes.

And I heard him ask Jennie a lot of professional questions about me. She had a very good report to give.

She said I slept a good deal in the daytime.

John knows I don't sleep very well at night, for all I'm so quiet!

He asked me all sorts of questions, too, and pretended to be very loving and kind.

As if I couldn't see through him!

Still, I don't wonder he acts so, sleeping under this paper for three months.

It only interests me, but I feel sure John and Jennie are secretly affected by it.

Hurrah! This is the last day, but it is enough. John is to stay in town over night, and won't be out until this evening.

Jennie wanted to sleep with me—the sly thing! but I told her I should undoubtedly rest better for a night all alone.

That was clever, for really I wasn't alone a bit! As soon as it was moonlight and that poor thing began to crawl and shake the pattern, I got up and ran to help her.

I pulled and she shook, I shook and she pulled, and before morning we had peeled off yards of that paper.

A strip about as high as my head and half around the room.

And then when the sun came and that awful pattern began to laugh at me, I declared I would finish it to-day!

We go away to-morrow, and they are moving all my furniture down again to leave things as they were before.

Jennie looked at the wall in amazement, but I told her merrily that I did it out of pure spite at the vicious thing.

She laughed and said she wouldn't mind doing it herself, but I must not get tired. How she betrayed herself that time!

But I am here, and no person touches this paper but me,—not *alive!*

She tried to get me out of the room—it was too patent! But I said it was so quiet and empty and clean now that I believed I would lie down again and sleep all I could; and not to wake me even for dinner—I would call when I woke.

So now she is gone, and the servants are gone, and the things are gone, and there is nothing left but that great bedstead nailed down, with the canvas mattress we found on it.

We shall sleep downstairs to-night, and take the boat home to-morrow.

I quite enjoy the room, now it is bare again.

How those children did tear about here!

This bedstead is fairly gnawed!

But I must get to work.

I have locked the door and thrown the key down into the front path.

I don't want to go out, and I don't want to have anybody come in, till John comes. I want to astonish him.

I've got a rope up here that even Jennie did not find. If that woman does get out, and tries to get away, I can tie her!

But I forgot I could not reach far without anything to stand on!

This bed will *not* move!

I tried to lift and push it until I was lame, and then I got so angry I bit off a little piece at one corner—but it hurt my teeth.

Then I peeled off all the paper I could reach standing on the floor. It sticks horribly and the pattern just enjoys it! All those strangled heads and bulbous eyes and waddling fungus growths just shriek with derision!

I am getting angry enough to do something desperate. To jump out of the window would be admirable exercise, but the bars are too strong even to try.

Besides I wouldn't do it. Of course not. I know well enough that a step like that is improper and might be misconstrued.

I don't like to *look* out of the windows even—there are so many of those creeping women, and they creep so fast.

I wonder if they all come out of that wallpaper as I did?

But I am securely fastened now by my well-hidden rope—you don't get *me* out in the road there!

I suppose I shall have to get back behind the pattern when it comes night, and that is hard!

It is so pleasant to be out in this great room and creep around as I please!

I don't want to go outside. I won't, even if Jennie asks me to.

For outside you have to creep on the ground, and everything is green instead of yellow.

But here I can creep smoothly on the floor, and my shoulder just fits in that long smooch around the wall, so I cannot lose my way.

Why there's John at the door!

It is no use, young man, you can't open it!

How he does call and pound!

Now he's crying for an axe.

It would be a shame to break down that beautiful door!

"John dear!" said I in the gentlest voice, "the key is down by the front steps, under a plantain leaf!"

That silenced him for a few moments.

Then he said—very quietly indeed, "Open the door, my darling!"

"I can't," said I. "The key is down by the front door under a plantain leaf!"

And then I said it again, several times, very gently and slowly, and said it so often that he had to go and see, and he got it of course, and came in. He stopped short by the door.

"What is the matter?" he cried. "For God's sake, what are you doing!"

I kept on creeping just the same, but I looked at him over my shoulder.

"I've got out at last," said I, "in spite of you and Jane. And I've pulled off most of the paper, so you can't put me back!"

Now why should that man have fainted? But he did, and right across my path by the wall, so that I had to creep over him every time!

⊶ ⊷⊱⊰⊶ ⊷

Rubén Darío
1867–1916

It has been said that for Latin Americans, the Nicaraguan poet Rubén Darío *was* modernism—so much so that some think modernism should be called "rubenismo." The point may be exaggerated; there were certainly precursors who like Darío learned about poetic form from the French Parnassians and Symbolists and were less eager to confront their society than to escape from it. But Darío, who first used the term *modernismo* (in 1887), is unquestionably the movement's towering figure and one of the greatest poets in the Spanish language.

Born in Metapa, Nicaragua (later renamed Ciudad Darío), Darío began renaming things early. At birth, he was named Felix Ruben Garcia Sarmiento, but he took for himself the old family name, Darío. He began reading at the age of three and by twelve was already publishing poems. In 1882, in an attempt to secure a scholarship to study in Europe, Darío read his poetry to conservative Nicaraguan authorities. He was refused the scholarship; his poems were considered too liberal and officials feared a European education would further encourage his antireligious sentiments. Yet Darío found ways to travel extensively both in Europe and in Latin America, working as a journalist and a diplomat, and he turned his varied experience to good use. In Chile Darío was confronted with racial prejudice due to his dark complexion. His proud identification with his Indian ancestors was to become a distinguishing mark of Latin American modernism. In Europe, modernists could think of themselves (whether correctly or not) as making a radical break with tradition. In Latin America, modernism was just as much a way of joining themselves to that tradition, which was much further away, and this blending could only happen if it recovered its different historical experience, remembered its roots in non-European identity, and reconstructed bridges to the continent's pre-Columbian past.

Darío was named Nicaragua's Ambassador to France in 1903. But his poetic output was by no means arrested. Among his greatest works are *Azul, Prosas Profanas, Cantos de Vida y Esperanza,* and *El Canto Errante.* His poetry was immediately and fabulously influential all over the Spanish-speaking world and beyond. In 1933 Pablo Neruda and Federico García Lorca, perhaps the two greatest twentieth-century poets in the Spanish language, joined in a dialogue to celebrate Darío's unique and lasting achievement.

European aestheticism, or art for art's sake, is certainly a major ingredient in the brilliantly intricate imagery and subdued emotion of Darío's verse. But his personal experience of history also counted for a great deal. He covered the Spanish-American War (1899) for the Argentine newspaper *La Nacion,* looking at it largely from the Spanish side. And his 1904 poem "To Roosevelt" shows that even the most unpolitical of Latin American poets could not help protesting against bullying by his powerful neighbor to the north.

PRONUNCIATION:
   Rubén Darío: rue-BEN da-REE-oh

First, a look . . .[1]

First, a look;
then the fiery touch
of hands; and then
   the rushing blood
5   and the overwhelming kiss.
Later, night and pleasure; later, the flight
   of that spineless cheat
   with another victim to choose.
You do well to weep, but it's too late!
10   Now you know! Didn't I tell you?

Walt Whitman

In his iron land lives an old man of renown,
comely as a patriarch, hallowed and assured.
Upon the Olympic furrow of his brow
he bears dominion and mastery of a noble allure.
5   His soul appears to mirror infinity;
worthy of a mantle are his weary shoulders;
and with a harp carved from age-old oak,
like some new prophet he sings his song.
This priest, who breathes a sigh divine,
10   announces in the future a better time:
"Soar!" he says to the eagle; to the sailor, "Sail!";
and "Work!" to the hearty laborer.
And so the poet makes his way
with the lofty look of an emperor!

To Roosevelt[1]

It would take a voice from the Bible or a verse from Walt Whitman
to get through to you, Hunter!

1. Translated by Alberto Acereda and Will Derusha.
1. U.S. President Theodore Roosevelt supported a 1903 revolution in Panama that resulted in the annexation by the United States of territory for the Panama Canal.

Darío's poem was written in 1904, after Roosevelt proclaimed a corollary to the Monroe Doctrine justifying the use of the U.S. military to "police" Latin America.

Primitive and modern, simple and complicated,
one part Washington and four parts Nimrod!
5 You're the United States,
you're the future invader
of the guileless America of indigenous blood
that still prays to Jesus Christ and still speaks in Spanish.

You're a strong and splendid specimen of your kind;
10 you're cultured, you're skillful; you're the opposite of Tolstoy.
And breaking horses or slaying tigers,
you're an Alexander-Nebuchadnezzar.
(You're a Professor of Energy,
as the madmen of today put it.)

15 You think that life is a conflagration,
that progress is an eruption,
that where you put your bullet
you set the future.

                                        No.

The United States is powerful and big.
20 When it shudders, a deep earthquake
runs down the enormous vertebrae of the Andes.
If you cry out, it's heard like the roaring of a lion.
Once Hugo[2] said to Grant: "The stars are yours."
(The Argentine sun, now dawning, has hardly begun to shine,
25 and the Chilean star is rising . . .) You're rich.
You combine the worship of Hercules with the worship of Mammon;
and lighting the way for easy conquest,
Liberty raises her torch in New York.

Yet this America of ours, which has had poets
30 since the olden days of Netzahualcoyotl,[3]
which preserves the footprints of great Bacchus,
which once learned the Panic[4] alphabet;
which consulted the stars, which knew the Atlantis
whose name comes down to us loud and clear in Plato,
35 which from the first moments of life, so long ago,
has lived on light, on fire, on perfume, on love,
the America of the great Montezuma, of the Inca,
the fragrant America of Christopher Columbus,
Catholic America, Spanish America,
40 the America where the noble Cuauhtemoc[5] said:
"This is no bed of roses"; that America
which shakes with hurricanes and lives on love;
men with Saxon eyes and barbarous souls, it lives.

---

2. Victor Hugo (1802–1885), French poet and novelist. Ulysses S. Grant (1822–1885) fought in the Mexican War, led Union armies in the Civil War, and then served as president for two terms.
3. King of Texcoco (died c. 1472), one of the "triple al-

liance" dominated by the Aztecs; also widely (often erroneously) credited as a major Aztec poet.
4. Having to do with Pan, fertility deity in Greek mythology.
5. Last Aztec emperor (c. 1495–1522).

And dreams. And loves, and quivers, and is the daughter of the Sun.
45   Beware. Spanish America lives!
There are a thousand cubs set loose from the Spanish Lion.
For God's sake, one would need to be, Roosevelt,
a terrifying Sharpshooter and a mighty Hunter
to hold us in your ferrous claws.

50   And, even accounting for everything, you lack one thing: God!

I Pursue a form . . .

I pursue a form that my style does not find,
a bud of thought that seeks to be a rose;
it announces itself with a kiss that alights on my lips
in the impossible embrace of the Venus de Milo.

5   Green palms adorn the white peristyle;
the stars have predicted for me the vision of the Goddess;
and the light reposes in my soul as the bird
of the moon reposes on a tranquil lake.

And I find nothing but the word that gets away,
10   the melodic initiation that flows from the flute,
and the ship of sleep that sails into space;

and under the window of my Sleeping Beauty,
the continuous sob of the fountain's jet
and the great white swan's neck questioning me.

What sign do you give . . .?

What sign do you give, O Swan, with your curving neck
when the sad and wandering dreamers pass?
Why so silent from being white and being beautiful,
tyrannical to the waters and impassive to the flowers?

5   I greet you now as in Latin verses
Publius Ovid Naso[1] greeted you in years gone by.
The same nightingales sing the same trills,
and in different languages it is the same song.

To you my language should not be foreign.
10   Perhaps you saw Garcilaso[2] at some point . . .
I am a son of America, I am a grandson of Spain . . .
Quevedo was able to speak to you in verse in Aranjuez . . .

Swans, may the fans of your cool wings
give to pallid brows their purest caresses
15   and may your white picturesque figures
drive the dark ideas from our sad minds.

---

1. Roman poet (43 B.C.–17 C.E.).

2. Garcilaso de la Vega (1503–1536), first great poet of Spanish Golden Age.

Septentrional[3] mists fill us with sorrows,
our roses are killed off, our palm trees used up,
there is scarecely a dream for our heads,
20   and we are beggars of our poor souls.

They preach war to us with ferocious eagles,
gyrfalcons of bygone days return to the fists,
yet the glories of the old sickles do not shine,
there are no Rodrigos nor Jaimes, no Alfonsos nor Nuños.

25   At a loss for the vital spirit which great things give,
what will we poets do, but seek out your lakes?
For lack of laurels, roses are very sweet,
and for lack of victories, let's seek out adulation.

Spanish America, like Spain as a whole,
30   is set in the East of its fatal destiny;
I question the Sphinx that awaits the future
with the question mark of your divine neck.

Will we be handed over to the wild barbarians?
So many millions of men, will we be speaking English?
35   Are there no worthy nobles nor manly knights anymore?
Will we be silent now only to weep later?

I have raised my cry, Swans, among you
who were the faithful in the face of disappointment,
while I hear a stampede of American colts
40   and the final agony of a senile lion . . .

. . . And a black swan said: "Night foretells the day."
And a white one: "The dawn is immortal! The dawn
is immortal!" O lands of sun and of harmony,
Pandora's box still holds Hope!

[END OF OTHER AMERICAS]

----- ✢ -----

Henrik Ibsen
1828–1906

In 1850, when Henrik Ibsen began writing, theater was largely a form of entertainment, a sort
of doll's house where stock figures and neatly contrived plots were expected to provide an
evening's innocent amusement. By 1899, when his last play was published, it had become an
adult art form comparable to poetry and the novel, shocking and disorienting, giving more
strenuous and instructive kinds of pleasure. With the twenty-five plays he wrote in that half

---

3. Northern (a deliberately archaic term).

century, Ibsen did more than any other single dramatist to bring about this upheaval. The transformation we see in Nora in *A Doll's House* bears a family resemblance to the transformation Ibsen brought to the theater itself.

Born in a small Norwegian town in 1828, Ibsen grew up (like many other nineteenth-century writers, including Dickens and Melville) facing a failure of paternal authority. His father, who had been a prosperous merchant, went bankrupt when Ibsen was a small child, leaving his eldest son to fend for himself in a state of poverty made more bitter by the memory of better days. Ibsen's sense of injustice expressed itself in poems to the European revolutionaries of 1848. Apprenticed to a pharmacist in a small town fifty miles from home, he became involved with a local servant ten years older than himself, got her pregnant, and spent fourteen years paying child support. He had dreams of becoming a doctor, but while studying at night to enter the university in Christiana (now Oslo), he gave them up to join a small theater in Bergen. There he contributed to a radical journal that was suppressed, learned the dramatist's craft, and collected local ballads and legends. Romantic nationalism was in fashion, and for good reason. Norway, which had won its independence from Denmark in 1814, was now united with the more powerful Sweden (it would not become fully independent until 1905), and it still had no national theater. Nor did it have national agreement on its language; it was during these same years that the philologist Ivar Aasen, traveling around the rural west of the country to collect dialects, fashioned a *landsmål* or "national language" to compete with the Dano-Norwegian, or *bokmål,* spoken by eastern urbanites. Of the 145 plays produced in Bergen during Ibsen's years of apprenticeship there, over half were translated from French. What was demanded was a generic, blandly international "well-made play," with a complicated plot involving confidential documents, babies identified by birthmarks, poisoned goblets quaffed by the wrong party, and other devices that had little to do with everyday Norwegian life.

Ibsen married Susannah Thoresen, the daughter of a pastor, in 1858. The couple traveled to Rome on a scholarship in 1864, and it was there that Ibsen wrote *Brand* (1866) and *Peer Gynt* (1867), a play inhabited by trolls and other materials of Nordic legend. These plays established his reputation as his country's first national dramatist. Apart from two short visits to Norway, however, Ibsen spent the next quarter century living in Italy and Germany. Like his admirer James Joyce (who learned Norwegian in order to read his hero in the original), Ibsen was that strange sort of exile, a national poet who felt obliged to examine his homeland from a distance. He became friends with the Danish critic Georg Brandes, author of *Main Currents of Nineteenth-Century Literature* (1872) and translator of John Stuart Mill's *On the Subjection of Women* (in 1869, the same year it came out in English), and Brandes helped turn Ibsen away from verse and toward the realistic wrestling with modern topics for which he was soon to become famous. It's been said that all the poetry Ibsen wrote after 1875 could be put on a single sheet of paper.

Ibsen's treatment of the emancipation of women in *A Doll's House* (1879) marks his full mastery of this new realistic mode. First performed in Copenhagen, Denmark, *A Doll's House* created an immediate sensation. Many found it almost unthinkable that Ibsen should endorse a woman who pays so little heed to her sacred duty as a wife and mother and so much to her own development as an individual. Ten years later, when the play was first presented in London, mainstream reviewers found it morally loathsome; one compared it to a view of an open sewer.

Plays like *A Doll's House*, *Ghosts* (1881), and *An Enemy of the People* (1882) are sometimes described as "naturalist" rather than realist, perhaps because they set their characters in the midst of the large historical processes that define the modern moment and fatally determine the outcome. It was this topical or "problem-play" side of Ibsen that George Bernard Shaw defended in *The Quintessence of Ibsenism* (1891). But *Hedda Gabler* (1890), *The Master Builder* (1892), and *When We Dead Awaken* (1899) returned to a less realistic mode, refashioning the theatrical parable so as to explore high individual aspiration, outside the conventions of society, as Ibsen had already done in *Peer Gynt*. These plays were taken by many to herald the new literary tendency of Symbolism. Older than the other major playwrights of the 1880s and 1890s, the Swedish August Strindberg and the Russian Anton Chekhov, Ibsen nonetheless continued to keep pace with them, and at times to set the pace for them. His last plays were written in Norway, to which he had returned in 1891, and he died there in 1906.

Shocking as *A Doll's House* was to its first audiences, it had an ambiguous relation to the feminism of the time. From the perspective of the two women who had the most direct influence on *A Doll's House,* what is striking is Ibsen's complex and contradictory relations to their cause. Camilla Collett, a pioneering Norwegian novelist and campaigner for women's rights, visited the Ibsens in Germany in the 1870s and, though Ibsen later acknowledged his debt to her, was unimpressed with the playwright's views on the woman question. Laura Kieler wrote a fictional sequel to Ibsen's *Brand* called *Brand's Daughters* (1869) when she was only twenty. It was Kieler's own life story that Ibsen retold in *A Doll's House,* though with changes. When Kieler was attacked as a result of Ibsen's stage portrait of her, she begged him to declare in public that she had acted honorably. He refused. One of his greatest virtues as a dramatist was his ability to separate himself off from unattractive aspects of his personality and put them into his characters.

A Doll's House is after all a well-made play. Like the romantic melodramas Ibsen helped put on in Bergen, it has stock characters (the flighty woman, the heavy insensitive husband, the faithful friend), guilty secrets, sealed lips, and fateful documents. But all these familiar stereotypes are reversed and revalued. After learning to see Nora as a stereotype of silly, childish, thoughtless femininity, we are suddenly asked to reinterpret this stereotype as a piece of theater that for various reasons Nora herself has been staging. In the person of Dr. Rank, we are offered tantalizing hints of the convention by which a rich old gentleman leaves money to the needy heroine and magically resolves all difficulties. Yet instead of the magical denouement that audiences had come to expect, Ibsen offers us, of all things, a serious discussion. We are asked to find the same emotional intensity in ideas about marriage and freedom that we had learned to expect from the discovery of long-lost brothers and sudden inheritances.

Freedom was, of course, more than an issue of sexual justice to Ibsen. Given his mixed feelings about the women's movement, it seems probable that he could make such a strong theatrical statement on Nora's behalf only because in his eyes she was not just a woman, but a figure for his own aspirations as an individual and an artist. Nora's story stood for the artist's defiance of conventional morality and the wishes of those around them, the sacrifice of children in exchange for individual self-realization. It was a defiance and a sacrifice about which he remained ambivalent. In his original notes for the play, Ibsen described it as "a tragedy of modern times." The notes suggest that he knew Nora would have to pay a large price for her liberation, that the story did not end (though this is perhaps the most famous ending in the history of the modern theater) with the slamming of the door.

A Doll's House

A C T   1 [1]

Characters

TORVALD HELMER
NORA, *his wife*
DOCTOR RANK
MRS. LINDSEN
NILS KROGSTAD
THE HELMERS' THREE CHILDREN
ANNA, *their nurse*
A MAID-SERVANT (Ellen)
A PORTER

1. Translated by William Archer.

The action passes in Helmer's house (an apartment) in Christiania.

A room, comfortably and tastefully, but not expensively, furnished. In the back, on the right, a door leads to the hall; on the left another door leads to Helmer's study. Between the two doors a pianoforte. In the middle of the left wall a door, and nearer the front a window. Near the window a round table with arm-chairs and a small sofa. In the right wall, somewhat to the back, a door, and against the same wall, further forward, a procelain stove; in front of it a couple of arm-chairs and a rocking-chair. Between the stove and the side-door a small table. Engravings on the walls. A what-not with china and bric-à-brac. A small bookcase filled with handsomely bound books. Carpet. A fire in the stove. It is a winter day.

A bell rings in the hall outside. Presently the outer door of the flat is heard to open. Then Nora enters, humming gaily. She is in outdoor dress, and carries several parcels, which she lays on the right-hand table. She leaves the door into the hall open, and a Porter is seen outside, carrying a Christmas-tree and a basket, which he gives to the Maid-servant who has opened the door.

NORA: Hide the Christmas-tree carefully, Ellen; the children must on no account see it before this evening, when it's lighted up. [*To the Porter, taking out her purse.*] How much?

PORTER: Fifty öre.[2]

NORA: There is a crown. No, keep the change.

[*The Porter thanks her and goes. Nora shuts the door. She continues smiling in quiet glee as she takes off her outdoor things. Taking from her pocket a bag of macaroons, she eats one or two. Then she goes on tip-toe to her husband's door and listens.*]

NORA: Yes; he is at home.

[*She begins humming again, crossing to the table on the right.*]

HELMER [*in his room*]: Is that my lark twittering there?

NORA [*busy opening some of her parcels*]: Yes, it is.

HELMER: Is it the squirrel frisking around?

NORA: Yes!

HELMER: When did the squirrel get home?

NORA: Just this minute. [*Hides the bag of macaroons in her pocket and wipes her mouth.*] Come here, Torvald, and see what I've been buying.

HELMER: Don't interrupt me. [*A little later he opens the door and looks in, pen in hand.*] Buying, did you say? What! All that? Has my little spend-thrift been making the money fly again?

NORA: Why, Torvald, surely we can afford to launch out a little now. It's the first Christmas we haven't had to pinch.

HELMER: Come come; we can't afford to squander money.

NORA: Oh yes, Torvald, do let us squander a little, now—just the least little bit! You know you'll soon be earning heaps of money.

HELMER: Yes, from New Year's Day. But there's a whole quarter before my first salary is due.

2. A hundred öre equal one crown (*krone*), equivalent to a few dollars today.

NORA: Never mind; we can borrow in the meantime.

HELMER: Nora! [*He goes up to her and takes her playfully by the ear.*] Still my little featherbrain! Supposing I borrowed a thousand crowns to-day, and you made ducks and drakes of them during Christmas week, and then on New Year's Eve a tile blew off the roof and knocked my brains out—

NORA [*laying her hand on his mouth*]: Hush! How can you talk so horridly?

HELMER: But supposing it were to happen—what then?

NORA: If anything so dreadful happened, it would be all the same to me whether I was in debt or not.

HELMER: But what about the creditors?

NORA: They! Who cares for them? They're only strangers.

HELMER: Nora, Nora! What a woman you are! But seriously, Nora, you know my principles on these points. No debts! No borrowing! Home life ceases to be free and beautiful as soon as it is founded on borrowing and debt. We two have held out bravely till now, and we are not going to give in at the last.

NORA [*going to the fireplace*]: Very well—as you please, Torvald.

HELMER [*following her*]: Come come; my little lark mustn't droop her wings like that. What? Is my squirrel in the sulks? [*Takes out his purse.*] Nora, what do you think I have here?

NORA [*turning round quickly*]: Money!

HELMER: There! [*Gives her some notes.*] Of course, I know all sorts of things are wanted at Christmas.

NORA [*counting*]: Ten, twenty, thirty, forty. Oh, thank you, thank you, Torvald! This will go a long way.

HELMER: I should hope so.

NORA: Yes, indeed; a long way! But come here, and let me show you all I've been buying. And so cheap! Look, here's a new suit for Ivar, and a little sword. Here are a horse and a trumpet for Bob. And here are a doll and a cradle for Emmy. They're only common; but they're good enough for her to pull to pieces. And dress-stuffs and kerchiefs for the servants. I ought to have got something better for old Anna.

HELMER: And what's in that other parcel?

NORA [*crying out*]: No, Torvald, you're not to see that until this evening!

HELMER: Oh! Ah! But now tell me, you little spendthrift, have you thought of anything for yourself?

NORA: For myself! Oh, I don't want anything.

HELMER: Nonsense! Just tell me something sensible you would like to have.

NORA: No, really I don't know of anything—Well, listen, Torvald—

HELMER: Well?

NORA [*playing with his coat-buttons, without looking him in the face*]: If you really want to give me something, you might, you know—you might—

HELMER: Well? Out with it!

NORA [*quickly*]: You might give me money, Torvald. Only just what you think you can spare; then I can buy something with it later on.

HELMER: But, Nora—

NORA: Oh, please do, dear Torvald, please do! I should hang the money in lovely gilt paper on the Christmas-tree. Wouldn't that be fun?

HELMER: What do they call the birds that are always making the money fly?

NORA: Yes, I know—spendthrifts, of course. But please do as I ask you, Torvald. Then I shall have time to think what I want most. Isn't that very sensible, now?

HELMER [*smiling*]: Certainly; that is to say, if you really kept the money I gave you, and really spent it on something for yourself. But it all goes in housekeeping, and for all manner of useless things, and then I have to pay up again.

NORA: But, Torvald—

HELMER: Can you deny it, Nora dear? [*He puts his arm round her.*] It's a sweet little lark, but it gets through a lot of money. No one would believe how much it costs a man to keep such a little bird as you.

NORA: For shame! How can you say so? Why, I save as much as ever I can.

HELMER [*laughing*]: Very true—as much as you can—but that's precisely nothing.

NORA [*hums and smiles with covert glee*]: H'm! It you only knew, Torvald, what expenses we larks and squirrels have.

HELMER: You're a strange little being! Just like your father—always on the look-out for all the money you can lay your hands on; but the moment you have it, it seems to slip through your fingers; you never know what becomes of it. Well, one must take you as you are. It's in the blood. Yes, Nora, that sort of thing is hereditary.

NORA: I wish I had inherited many of papa's qualities.

HELMER: And I don't wish you anything but just what you are—my own, sweet little song-bird. But I say—it strikes me you look so—so—what shall I call it?—so suspicious to-day—

NORA: Do I?

HELMER: You do, indeed. Look me full in the face.

NORA [*looking at him*]: Well?

HELMER [*threatening with his finger*]: Hasn't the little sweet-tooth been playing pranks to-day?

NORA: No; how can you think such a thing!

HELMER: Didn't she just look in at the confectioner's?

NORA: No, Torvald; really—

HELMER: Not to sip a little jelly?

NORA: No; certainly not.

HELMER: Hasn't she even nibbled a macaroon or two?

NORA: No, Torvald, indeed, indeed!

HELMER: Well, well, well; of course I'm only joking.

NORA [*goes to the table on the right*]: I shouldn't think of doing what you disapprove of.

HELMER: No, I'm sure of that; and, besides, you've given me your word—[*Going towards her.*] Well, keep your little Christmas secrets to yourself, Nora darling. The Christmas-tree will bring them all to light, I daresay.

NORA: Have you remembered to invite Doctor Rank?

HELMER: No. But it's not necessary; he'll come as a matter of course. Besides, I shall ask him when he looks in to-day. I've ordered some capital wine. Nora, you can't think how I look forward to this evening.

NORA: And I too. How the children will enjoy themselves, Torvald!

HELMER: Ah, it's glorious to feel that one has an assured position and ample means. Isn't it delightful to think of?

NORA: Oh, it's wonderful!

HELMER: Do you remember last Christmas? For three whole weeks beforehand you shut yourself up every evening till long past midnight to make flowers for the Christmas-tree, and all sorts of other marvels that were to have astonished us. I was never so bored in my life.

NORA: I didn't bore myself at all.

HELMER [*smiling*]: But it came to little enough in the end, Nora.

NORA: Oh, are you going to tease me about that again? How could I help the cat getting in and pulling it all to pieces?

HELMER: To be sure you couldn't, my poor little Nora. You did your best to give us all pleasure, and that's the main point. But, all the same, it's a good thing the hard times are over.

NORA: Oh, isn't it wonderful?

HELMER: Now I needn't sit here boring myself all alone; and you needn't tire your blessed eyes and your delicate little fingers—

NORA [*clapping her hands*]: No, I needn't, need I, Torvald? Oh, how wonderful it is to think of? [*takes his arm*] And now I'll tell you how I think we ought to manage, Torvald. As soon as Christmas is over—[*The hall-door bell rings.*] Oh, there's a ring! [*Arranging the room.*] That's somebody come to call. How tiresome!

HELMER: I'm "not at home" to callers; remember that.

ELLEN [*in the doorway*]: A lady to see you, ma'am.

NORA: Show her in.

ELLEN [*to Helmer*]: And the doctor has just come, sir.

HELMER: Has he gone into my study?

ELLEN: Yes, sir.

[*Helmer goes into his study. Ellen ushers in Mrs. Linden, in travelling costume, and goes out, closing the door.*]

MRS. LINDEN [*embarrassed and hesitating*]: How do you do, Nora?

NORA [*doubtfully*]: How do you do?

MRS. LINDEN: I see you don't recognise me.

NORA: No, I don't think—oh yes!—I believe—[*Suddenly brightening.*] What, Christina! Is it really you?

MRS. LINDEN: Yes; really I!

NORA: Christina! And to think I didn't know you! But how could I—[*More softly.*] How changed you are, Christina!

MRS. LINDEN: Yes, no doubt. In nine or ten years—

NORA: Is it really so long since we met? Yes, so it is. Oh, the last eight years have been a happy time, I can tell you. And now you have come to town? All that long journey in mid-winter! How brave of you!

MRS. LINDEN: I arrived by this morning's steamer.

NORA: To have a merry Christmas, of course. Oh, how delightful! Yes, we will have a merry Christmas. Do take your things off. Aren't you frozen? [*Helping her.*] There; now we'll sit cosily by the fire. No, you take the arm-chair; I shall sit in this rocking-chair. [*Seizes her hands.*] Yes, now I can see the dear old face again. It was only at the first glance—But you're a little paler, Christina—and perhaps a little thinner.

MRS. LINDEN: And much, much older, Nora.

NORA: Yes, perhaps a little older—not much—ever so little. [*She suddenly checks herself; seriously.*] Oh, what a thoughtless wretch I am! Here I sit chattering on, and—Dear, dear Christina, can you forgive me!

MRS. LINDEN: What do you mean, Nora?

NORA [*softly*]: Poor Christina! I forgot; you are a widow.

MRS. LINDEN: Yes; my husband died three years ago.

NORA: I know, I know; I saw it in the papers. Oh, believe me, Christina, I did mean to write to you; but I kept putting it off, and something always came in the way.

MRS. LINDEN: I can quite understand that, Nora, dear.

NORA: No, Christina; it was horrid of me. Oh, you poor darling! how much you must have gone through!—And he left you nothing?

MRS. LINDEN: Nothing.

NORA: And no children?

MRS. LINDEN: None.

NORA: Nothing, nothing at all?

MRS. LINDEN: Not even a sorrow or a longing to dwell upon.

NORA [looking at her incredulously]: My dear Christina, how is that possible?

MRS. LINDEN [smiling sadly and stroking her hair]: Oh, it happens so sometimes, Nora.

NORA: So utterly alone! How dreadful that must be! I have three of the loveliest children. I can't show them to you just now; they're out with their nurse. But now you must tell me everything.

MRS. LINDEN: No, no; I want you to tell me—

NORA: No, you must begin; I won't be egotistical to-day. To-day I'll think only of you. Oh! but I must tell you one thing—perhaps you've heard of our great stroke of fortune?

MRS. LINDEN: No. What is it?

NORA: Only think! my husband has been made manager of the Joint Stock Bank.

MRS. LINDEN: Your husband! Oh, how fortunate!

NORA: Yes; isn't it? A lawyer's position is so uncertain, you see, especially when he won't touch any business that's the least bit—shady, as of course Torvald never would; and there I quite agree with him. Oh! you can imagine how glad we are. He is to enter on his new position at the New Year, and then he'll have a large salary, and percentages. In future we shall be able to live quite differently—just as we please, in fact. Oh, Christina, I feel so lighthearted and happy! It's delightful to have lots of money, and no need to worry about things, isn't it?

MRS. LINDEN: Yes; at any rate it must be delightful to have what you need.

NORA: No, not only what you need, but heaps of money—heaps!

MRS. LINDEN [smiling]: Nora, Nora, haven't you learnt reason yet? In our schooldays you were a shocking little spendthrift.

NORA [quietly smiling]: Yes; that's what Torvald says I am still. [Holding up her forefinger.] But "Nora, Nora" is not so silly as you all think. Oh! I haven't had the chance to be much of a spendthrift. We have both had to work.

MRS. LINDEN: You, too?

NORA: Yes, light fancy work: crochet, and embroidery, and things of that sort; [Carelessly] and other work too. You know, of course, that Torvald left the Government service when we were married. He had little chance of promotion, and of course he required to make more money. But in the first year after our marriage he overworked himself terribly. He had to undertake all sorts of extra work, you know, and to slave early and late. He couldn't stand it, and fell dangerously ill. Then the doctors declared he must go to the South.

MRS. LINDEN: You spent a whole year in Italy, didn't you?

NORA: Yes, we did. It wasn't easy to manage, I can tell you. It was just after Ivar's birth. But of course we had to go. Oh, it was a wonderful, delicious journey! And it saved Torvald's life. But it cost a frightful lot of money, Christina.

MRS. LINDEN: So I should think.

NORA: Twelve hundred dollars! Four thousand eight hundred crowns! Isn't that a lot of money?

MRS. LINDEN: How lucky you had the money to spend

NORA: We got it from father, you must know.

MRS. LINDEN: Ah, I see. He died just about that time, didn't he?

NORA: Yes, Christina, just then. And only think! I couldn't go and nurse him! I was expecting little Ivar's birth daily; and then I had my poor sick Torvald to attend to. Dear, kind old father! I never saw him again, Christina. Oh! that's the hardest thing I have had to bear since my marriage.

MRS. LINDEN: I know how fond you were of him. But then you went to Italy?

NORA: Yes; you see, we had the money, and the doctors said we must lose no time. We started a month later.

MRS. LINDEN: And your husband came back completely cured.

NORA: Sound as a bell.

MRS. LINDEN: But—the doctor?

NORA: What do you mean?

MRS. LINDEN: I thought as I came in your servant announced the doctor—

NORA: Oh, yes; Doctor Rank. But he doesn't come professionally. He is our best friend, and never lets a day pass without looking in. No, Torvald hasn't had an hour's illness since that time. And the children are so healthy and well, and so am I. [*Jumps up and claps her hands.*] Oh, Christina, Christina, what a wonderful thing it is to live and to be happy!—Oh, but it's really too horrid of me! Here am I talking about nothing but my own concerns. [*Seats herself upon a footstool close to Christina, and lays her arms on her friend's lap.*] Oh, don't be angry with me! Now tell me, is it really true that you didn't love your husband? What made you marry him, then?

MRS. LINDEN: My mother was still alive, you see, bedridden and helpless; and then I had my two younger brothers to think of. I didn't think it would be right for me to refuse him.

NORA: Perhaps it wouldn't have been. I suppose he was rich then?

MRS. LINDEN: Very well off, I believe. But his business was uncertain. It fell to pieces at his death, and there was nothing left.

NORA: And then—?

MRS. LINDEN: Then I had to fight my way by keeping a shop, a little school, anything I could turn my hand to. The last three years have been one long struggle for me. But now it is over, Nora. My poor mother no longer needs me; she is at rest. And the boys are in business, and can look after themselves.

NORA: How free your life must feel!

MRS. LINDEN: No, Nora; only inexpressibly empty. No one to live for! [*Stands up restlessly.*] That's why I could not bear to stay any longer in that out-of-the-way corner. Here it must be easier to find something to take one up—to occupy one's thoughts. If I could only get some settled employment—some office work.

NORA: But, Christina, that's such drudgery, and you look worn out already. It would be ever so much better for you to go to some watering-place and rest.

MRS. LINDEN [*going to the window*]: I have no father to give me the money, Nora.

NORA [*rising*]: Oh, don't be vexed with me.

MRS. LINDEN [*going to her*]: My dear Nora, don't you be vexed with me. The worst of a position like mine is that it makes one so bitter. You have no one to work for, yet you have to be always on the strain. You must live; and so you become selfish.

When I heard of the happy change in your fortunes—can you believe it?—I was glad for my own sake more than for yours.

NORA: How do you mean? Ah, I see! You think Torvald can perhaps do something for you.

MRS. LINDEN: Yes; I thought so.

NORA: And so he shall, Christina. Just you leave it all to me. I shall lead up to it beautifully!—I shall think of some delightful plan to put him in a good humour! Oh, I should so love to help you.

MRS. LINDEN: How good of you, Nora, to stand by me so warmly! Doubly good in you, who know so little of the troubles and burdens of life.

NORA: I? I know so little of—?

MRS. LINDEN [*smiling*]: Oh, well—a little fancy-work, and so forth.—You're a child, Nora.

NORA [*tosses her head and paces the room*]: Oh, come, you mustn't be so patronising!

MRS. LINDEN: No?

NORA: You're like the rest. You all think I'm fit for nothing really serious—

MRS. LINDEN: Well, well—

NORA: You think I've had no troubles in this weary world.

MRS. LINDEN: My dear Nora, you've just told me all your troubles.

NORA: Pooh—those trifles! [*Softly.*] I haven't told you the great thing.

MRS. LINDEN: The great thing? What do you mean?

NORA: I know you look down upon me, Christina; but you have no right to. You are proud of having worked so hard and so long for your mother.

MRS. LINDEN: I am sure I don't look down upon any one; but it's true I am both proud and glad when I remember that I was able to keep my mother's last days free from care.

NORA: And you're proud to think of what you have done for your brothers, too.

MRS. LINDEN: Have I not the right to be?

NORA: Yes, indeed. But now let me tell you, Christina—I, too, have something to be proud and glad of.

MRS. LINDEN: I don't doubt it. But what do you mean?

NORA: Hush! Not so loud. Only think, if Torvald were to hear! He mustn't—not for worlds! No one must know about it, Christina—no one but you.

MRS. LINDEN: Why, what can it be?

NORA: Come over here. [*Draws her down beside her on the sofa.*] Yes, Christina—I, too, have something to be proud and glad of. I saved Torvald's life.

MRS. LINDEN: Saved his life? How?

NORA: I told you about our going to Italy. Torvald would have died but for that.

MRS. LINDEN: Well—and your father gave you the money.

NORA [*smiling*]: Yes, so Torvald and every one believes; but—

MRS. LINDEN: But—?

NORA: Papa didn't give us one penny. It was *I* that found the money.

MRS. LINDEN: You? All that money?

NORA: Twelve hundred dollars. Four thousand eight hundred crowns. What do you say to that?

MRS. LINDEN: My dear Nora, how did you manage it? Did you win it in the lottery?

NORA [*contemptuously*]: In the lottery? Pooh! Any one could have done that!

MRS. LINDEN: Then wherever did you get it from?

NORA [*hums and smiles mysteriously*]: H'm; tra-la-la-la.

MRS. LINDEN: Of course you couldn't borrow it.

NORA: No? Why not?

MRS. LINDEN: Why, a wife can't borrow without her husband's consent.

NORA [*tossing her head*]: Oh! when the wife has some idea of business, and knows how to set about things—

MRS. LINDEN: But, Nora, I don't understand—

NORA: Well, you needn't. I never said I borrowed the money. There are many ways I may have got it. [*Throws herself back on the sofa.*] I may have got it from some admirer. When one is so—attractive as I am—

MRS. LINDEN: You're too silly, Nora.

NORA: Now I'm sure you're dying of curiosity, Christina—

MRS. LINDEN: Listen to me, Nora dear: haven't you been a little rash?

NORA [*sitting upright again*]: Is it rash to save one's husband's life?

MRS. LINDEN: I think it was rash of you, without his knowledge—

NORA: But it would have been fatal for him to know! Can't you understand that? He wasn't even to suspect how ill he was. The doctors came to me privately and told me his life was in danger—that nothing could save him but a winter in the South. Do you think I didn't try diplomacy first? I told him how I longed to have a trip abroad, like other young wives; I wept and prayed; I said he ought to think of my condition, and not to thwart me; and then I hinted that he could borrow the money. But then, Christina, he got almost angry. He said I was frivolous, and that it was his duty as a husband not to yield to my whims and fancies—so he called them. Very well, thought I, but saved you must be; and then I found the way to do it.

MRS. LINDEN: And did your husband never learn from your father that the money was not from him?

NORA: No; never. Papa died at that very time. I meant to have told him all about it, and begged him to say nothing. But he was so ill—unhappily, it wasn't necessary.

MRS. LINDEN: And you have never confessed to your husband?

NORA: Good heavens! What can you be thinking of? Tell him, when he has such a loathing of debt! And besides—how painful and humiliating it would be for Torvald, with his manly self-respect, to know that he owed anything to me! It would utterly upset the relation between us; our beautiful, happy home would never again be what it is.

MRS. LINDEN: Will you never tell him?

NORA [*thoughtfully, half-smiling*]: Yes, some time, perhaps—many, many years hence, when I'm—not so pretty. You mustn't laugh at me! Of course I mean when Torvald is not so much in love with me as he is now; when it doesn't amuse him any longer to see me dancing about, and dressing up and acting. Then it might be well to have something in reserve. [*Breaking off.*] Nonsense! nonsense! That time will never come. Now, what do you say to my grand secret, Christina? Am I fit for nothing now? You may believe it has cost me a lot of anxiety. It has been no joke to meet my engagements punctually. You must know, Christina, that in business there are things called instalments, and quarterly interest, that are terribly hard to provide for. So I've had to pinch a little here and there, wherever I could. I couldn't save much out of the housekeeping, for, of course. Torvald had to live well. And I couldn't let the children go about badly dressed; all I got for them, I spent on them, the blessed darlings!

MRS. LINDEN: Poor Nora! So it had to come out of your own pocket-money.

NORA: Yes, of course. After all, the whole thing was my doing. When Torvald gave me money for clothes, and so on, I never spent more than half of it; I always bought the simplest and cheapest things. It's a mercy that everything suits me so well—Torvald never had any suspicions. But it was often very hard, Christina dear. For it's nice to be beautifully dressed—now, isn't it?

MRS. LINDEN: Indeed it is.

NORA: Well, and besides that, I made money in other ways. Last winter I was so lucky—I got a heap of copying to do. I shut myself up every evening and wrote far into the night. Oh, sometimes I was so tired, so tired. And yet it was splendid to work in that way and earn money. I almost felt as if I was a man.

MRS. LINDEN: Then how much have you been able to pay off?

NORA: Well, I can't precisely say. It's difficult to keep that sort of business clear. I only know that I've paid everything I could scrape together. Sometimes I really didn't know where to turn. [Smiles.] Then I used to sit here and pretend that a rich old gentleman was in love with me—

MRS. LINDEN: What! What gentleman?

NORA: Oh, nobody!—that he was dead now, and that when his will was opened, there stood in large letters: "Pay over at once everything of which I die possessed to that charming person, Mrs. Nora Helmer."

MRS. LINDEN: But, my dear Nora—what gentleman do you mean?

NORA: Oh, dear, can't you understand? There wasn't any old gentleman: it was only what I used to dream and dream when I was at my wits' end for money. But it doesn't matter now—the tiresome old creature may stay where he is for me. I care nothing for him or his will; for now my troubles are over. [Springing up.] Oh, Christina, how glorious it is to think of! Free from all anxiety! Free, quite free. To be able to play and romp about with the children; to have things tasteful and pretty in the house, exactly as Torvald likes it! And then the spring will soon be here, with the great blue sky. Perhaps then we shall have a little holiday. Perhaps I shall see the sea again. Oh, what a wonderful thing it is to live and to be happy!

[The hall-door bell rings.]

MRS. LINDEN [rising]: There's a ring. Perhaps I had better go.

NORA: No; do stay. No one will come here. It's sure to be some one for Torvald.

ELLEN [in the doorway]: If you please, ma'am, there's a gentleman to speak to Mr. Helmer.

NORA: Who is the gentleman?

KROGSTAD [in the doorway]: It is I, Mrs. Helmer.

[Mrs. Linden starts and turns away to the window.]

NORA [goes a step towards him, anxiously, speaking low]: You? What is it? What do you want with my husband?

KROGSTAD: Bank business—in a way. I hold a small post in the Joint Stock Bank, and your husband is to be our new chief, I hear.

NORA: Then it is—?

KROGSTAD: Only tiresome business, Mrs. Helmer; nothing more.

NORA: Then will you please go to his study.

[Krogstad goes. She bows indifferently while she closes the door into the hall. Then she goes to the stove and looks to the fire.]

MRS. LINDEN: Nora—who was that man?

NORA: A Mr. Krogstad—a lawyer.

MRS. LINDEN: Then it was really he?

NORA: Do you know him?

MRS. LINDEN: I used to know him—many years ago. He was in a lawyer's office in our town.

NORA: Yes, so he was.

MRS. LINDEN: How he has changed!

NORA: I believe his marriage was unhappy.

MRS. LINDEN: And he is a widower now?

NORA: With a lot of children. There! Now it will burn up.

[*She closes the stove, and pushes the rocking-chair a little aside.*]

MRS. LINDEN: His business is not of the most creditable, they say?

NORA: Isn't it? I daresay not. I don't know. But don't let us think of business—it's so tiresome.

[*Dr. Rank comes out of Helmer's room.*]

RANK [*still in the doorway*]: No, no; I'm in your way. I shall go and have a chat with your wife. [*Shuts the door and sees Mrs. Linden.*] Oh, I beg your pardon. I'm in the way here too.

NORA: No, not in the least. [*Introduces them.*] Doctor Rank—Mrs. Linden.

RANK: Oh, indeed; I've often heard Mrs. Linden's name; I think I passed you on the stairs as I came up.

MRS. LINDEN: Yes; I go so very slowly. Stairs try me so much.

RANK: Ah—you are not very strong?

MRS. LINDEN: Only overworked.

RANK: Nothing more? Then no doubt you've come to town to find rest in a round of dissipation?

MRS. LINDEN: I have come to look for employment.

RANK: Is that an approved remedy for overwork?

MRS. LINDEN: One must live, Doctor Rank.

RANK: Yes, that seems to be the general opinion.

NORA: Come, Doctor Rank—you want to live yourself.

RANK: To be sure I do. However wretched I may be, I want to drag on as long as possible. All my patients, too, have the same mania. And it's the same with people whose complaint is moral. At this very moment Helmer is talking to just such a moral incurable—

MRS. LINDEN [*softly*]: Ah!

NORA: Whom do you mean?

RANK: Oh, a fellow named Krogstad, a man you know nothing about—corrupt to the very core of his character. But even he began by announcing, as a matter of vast importance, that he must live.

NORA: Indeed? And what did he want with Torvald?

RANK: I haven't an idea; I only gathered that it was some bank business.

NORA: I didn't know that Krog—that this Mr. Krogstad had anything to do with the Bank?

RANK: Yes. He has got some sort of place there. [*To Mrs. Linden.*] I don't know whether, in your part of the country, you have people who go grubbing and sniffing around in search of moral rottenness—and then, when they have found a "case," don't rest till they have got their man into some good position, where they can keep a watch upon him. Men with a clean bill of health they leave out in the cold.

MRS. LINDEN: Well, I suppose the—delicate characters require most care.

RANK [*shrugs his shoulders*]: There we have it! It's that notion that makes society a hospital.

[*Nora. deep in her own thoughts, breaks into half-stifled laughter and claps her hands.*]

RANK: Why do you laugh at that? Have you any idea what "society" is?

NORA: What do I care for your tiresome society? I was laughing at something else— something excessively amusing. Tell me, Doctor Rank, are all the employees at the Bank dependent on Torvald now?

RANK: Is that what strikes you as excessively amusing?

NORA [*smiles and hums*]: Never mind, never mind! [*Walks about the room.*] Yes, it is funny to think that we—that Torvald has such power over so many people. [*Takes the bag from her pocket.*] Doctor Rank, will you have a macaroon?

RANK: What!—macaroons! I thought they were contraband here.

NORA: Yes; but Christina brought me these.

MRS. LINDEN: What! I—?

NORA: Oh, well! Don't be frightened. You couldn't possibly know that Torvald had forbidden them. The fact is, he's afraid of me spoiling my teeth. But, oh bother, just for once!—That's for you, Doctor Rank! [*Puts a macaroon into his mouth.*] And you too, Christina. And I'll have one while we're about it—only a tiny one, or at most two. [*Walks about again.*] Oh dear, I am happy! There's only one thing in the world I really want.

RANK: Well; what's that?

NORA: There's something I should so like to say—in Torvald's hearing.

RANK: Then why don't you say it?

NORA: Because I daren't, it's so ugly.

MRS. LINDEN: Ugly?

RANK: In that case you'd better not. But to us you might—What is it you would so like to say in Helmer's hearing?

NORA: I should so love to say "Damn it all!"

RANK: Are you out of your mind?

MRS. LINDEN: Good gracious, Nora—!

RANK: Say it—there he is!

NORA [*hides the macaroons*]: Hush—sh—sh

[*Helmer comes out of his room, hat in hand, with his overcoat on his arm.*]

NORA [*going to him*]: Well, Torvald dear, have you got rid of him?

HELMER: Yes; he has just gone.

NORA: Let me introduce you—this is Christina, who has come to town—

HELMER: Christina? Pardon me, I don't know—

NORA: Mrs. Linden, Torvald dear—Christina Linden.

HELMER [*to Mrs. Linden*]: Indeed! A school-friend of my wife's, no doubt?

MRS. LINDEN: Yes; we knew each other as girls.

NORA: And only think! she has taken this long journey on purpose to speak to you.

HELMER: To speak to me!

MRS. LINDEN: Well, not quite—

NORA: You see, Christina is tremendously clever at office work, and she's so anxious to work under a first-rate man of business in order to learn still more—

HELMER [to Mrs. Linden]: Very sensible indeed.

NORA: And when she heard you were appointed manager—it was telegraphed, you know—she started off at once, and—Torvald, dear, for my sake, you must do something for Christina. Now, can't you?

HELMER: It's not impossible. I presume Mrs. Linden is a widow?

MRS. LINDEN: Yes.

HELMER: And you have already had some experience of business?

MRS. LINDEN: A good deal.

HELMER: Well, then, it's very likely I may be able to find a place for you.

NORA [clapping her hands]: There now! There now!

HELMER: You have come at a fortunate moment, Mrs. Linden.

MRS. LINDEN: Oh, how can I thank you—?

HELMER [smiling]: There is no occasion. [Puts on his overcoat.] But for the present you must excuse me—

RANK: Wait; I am going with you.

[Fetches his fur coat from the hall and warms it at the fire.]

NORA: Don't be long, Torvald dear.

HELMER: Only an hour; not more.

NORA: Are you going too, Christina?

MRS. LINDEN [putting on her walking things]: Yes; I must set about looking for lodgings.

HELMER: Then perhaps we can go together?

NORA [helping her]: What a pity we haven't a spare room for you; but it's impossible—

MRS. LINDEN: I shouldn't think of troubling you. Goodbye, dear Nora, and thank you for all your kindness.

NORA: Good-bye for the present. Of course, you'll come back this evening. And you, too, Doctor Rank. What! If you're well enough? Of course you'll be well enough. Only wrap up warmly. [They go out, talking, into the hall. Outside on the stairs are heard children's voices.] There they are! There they are! [She runs to the outer door and opens it. The nurse, Anna, enters the hall with the children.] Come in! Come in! [Stoops down and kisses the children.] Oh, my sweet darlings! Do you see them, Christina? Aren't they lovely?

RANK: Don't let us stand here chattering in the draught.

HELMER: Come, Mrs. Linden; only mothers can stand such a temperature.

[Dr. Rank, Helmer, and Mrs. Linden go down the stairs; Anna enters the room with the children; Nora also, shutting the door.

NORA: How fresh and bright you look! And what red cheeks you've got! Like apples and roses. [The children chatter to her during what follows.] Have you had great fun? That's splendid! Oh, really! You've been giving Emmy and Bob a ride on your sledge!—both at once, only think! Why, you're quite a man, Ivar. Oh, give her to me a little, Anna. My sweet little dolly! [Takes the smallest from the nurse and dances with her.] Yes, yes; mother will dance with Bob too. What! Did you have a game of snowballs? Oh, I wish I'd been there. No; leave them, Anna; I'll take their things off. Oh, yes, let me do it; it's such fun. Go to the nursery; you look frozen. You'll find some hot coffee on the stove.

[The Nurse goes into the room on the left. Nora takes off the children's things and throws them down anywhere, while the children talk all together.]

Really! A big dog ran after you? But he didn't bite you? No; dogs don't bite dear little dolly children. Don't peep into those parcels, Ivar. What is it? Wouldn't you like to know? Take care—it'll bite! What? Shall we have a game? What shall we play at? Hide-and-seek? Yes, let's play hide-and-seek. Bob shall hide first. Am I to? Yes, let me hide first.

[*She and the children play, with laughter and shouting, in the room and the adjacent one to the right. At last Nora hides under the table; the children come rushing in, look for her, but cannot find her, hear her half-choked laughter, rush to the table, lift up the cover and see her. Loud shouts. She creeps out, as though to frighten them. Fresh shouts. Meanwhile there has been a knock at the door leading into the hall. No one has heard it. Now the door is half opened and Krogstad appears. He waits a little; the game is renewed.*]

KROGSTAD: I beg your pardon, Mrs. Helmer—

NORA [*with a suppressed cry, turns round and half jumps up*]: Ah! What do you want?

KROGSTAD: Excuse me; the outer door was ajar—somebody must have forgotten to shut it—

NORA [*standing up*]: My husband is not at home, Mr. Krogstad.

KROGSTAD: I know it.

NORA: Then what do you want here?

KROGSTAD: To say a few words to you.

NORA: To me? [*To the children, softly.*] Go in to Anna. What? No, the strange man won't hurt mamma. When he's gone we'll go on playing. [*She leads the children into the left-hand room, and shuts the door behind them. Uneasy, in suspense.*] It is to me you wish to speak?

KROGSTAD: Yes, to you.

NORA: To-day? But it's not the first yet—

KROGSTAD: No, to-day is Christmas Eve. It will depend upon yourself whether you have a merry Christmas.

NORA: What do you want? I'm not ready to-day—

KROGSTAD: Never mind that just now. I have come about another matter. You have a minute to spare?

NORA: Oh, yes, I suppose so; although—

KROGSTAD: Good. I was sitting in the restaurant opposite, and I saw your husband go down the street—

NORA: Well?

KROGSTAD: —with a lady.

NORA: What then?

KROGSTAD: May I ask if the lady was a Mrs. Linden?

NORA: Yes.

KROGSTAD: Who has just come to town?

NORA: Yes. To-day.

KROGSTAD: I believe she is an intimate friend of yours.

NORA: Certainly. But I don't understand—

KROGSTAD: I used to know her too.

NORA: I know you did.

KROGSTAD: Ah! You know all about it. I thought as much. Now, frankly, is Mrs. Linden to have a place in the Bank?

NORA: How dare you catechise me in this way, Mr. Krogstad—you, a subordinate of my husband's? But since you ask, you shall know. Yes, Mrs. Linden is to be employed. And it is I who recommended her, Mr. Krogstad. Now you know.

KROGSTAD: Then my guess was right.

NORA [walking up and down]: You see one has a wee bit of influence, after all. It doesn't follow because one's only a woman—When people are in a subordinate position, Mr. Krogstad, they ought really to be careful how they offend anybody who—h'm—

KROGSTAD: —who has influence?

NORA: Exactly.

KROGSTAD [taking another tone]: Mrs. Helmer, will you have the kindness to employ your influence on my behalf?

NORA: What? How do you mean?

KROGSTAD: Will you be so good as to see that I retain my subordinate position in the Bank?

NORA: What do you mean? Who wants to take it from you?

KROGSTAD: Oh, you needn't pretend ignorance. I can very well understand that it cannot be pleasant for your friend to meet me; and I can also understand now for whose sake I am to be hounded out.

NORA: But I assure you—

KROGSTAD: Come, come, now, once for all: there is time yet, and I advise you to use your influence to prevent it.

NORA: But, Mr. Krogstad, I have no influence—absolutely none.

KROGSTAD: None? I thought you said a moment ago—

NORA: Of course, not in that sense. I! How can you imagine that I should have any such influence over my husband?

KROGSTAD: Oh, I know your husband from our college days. I don't think he is any more inflexible than other husbands.

NORA: If you talk disrespectfully of my husband, I must request you to leave the house.

KROGSTAD: You are bold, madam.

NORA: I am afraid of you no longer. When New Year's Day is over, I shall soon be out of the whole business.

KROGSTAD [controlling himself]: Listen to me, Mrs. Helmer. If need be, I shall fight as though for my life to keep my little place in the Bank.

NORA: Yes, so it seems.

KROGSTAD: It's not only for the salary: that is what I care least about. It's something else—Well, I had better make a clean breast of it. Of course, you know, like every one else, that some years ago I—got into trouble.

NORA: I think I've heard something of the sort.

KROGSTAD: The matter never came into court; but from that moment all paths were barred to me. Then I took up the business you know about. I had to turn my hand to something; and I don't think I've been one of the worst. But now I must get clear of it all. My sons are growing up; for their sake I must try to recover my character as well as I can. This place in the Bank was the first step; and now your husband wants to kick me off the ladder, back into the mire.

NORA: But I assure you, Mr. Krogstad, I haven't the least power to help you.

KROGSTAD: That is because you have not the will; but I can compel you.

NORA: You won't tell my husband that I owe you money?

KROGSTAD: H'm; suppose I were to?

NORA: It would be shameful of you. [*With tears in her voice.*] The secret that is my joy and my pride—that he should learn it in such an ugly, coarse way—and from you. It would involve me in all sorts of unpleasantness—

KROGSTAD: Only unpleasantness?

NORA [*hotly*]: But just do it. It's you that will come off worst, for then my husband will see what a bad man you are, and then you certainly won't keep your place.

KROGSTAD: I asked whether it was only domestic unpleasantness you feared?

NORA: If my husband gets to know about it, he will, of course pay you off at once, and then we shall have nothing more to do with you.

KROGSTAD [*coming a pace nearer*]: Listen, Mrs. Helmer: either your memory is defective, or you don't know much about business. I must make the position a little clearer to you.

NORA: How so?

KROGSTAD: When your husband was ill, you came to me to borrow twelve hundred dollars.

NORA: I knew of nobody else.

KROGSTAD: I promised to find you the money—

NORA: And you did find it.

KROGSTAD: I promised to find you the money, on certain conditions. You were so much taken up at the time about your husband's illness, and so eager to have the wherewithal for your journey, that you probably did not give much thought to the details. Allow me to remind you of them. I promised to find you the amount in exchange for a note of hand, which I drew up.

NORA: Yes, and I signed it.

KROGSTAD: Quite right. But then I added a few lines, making your father security for the debt. Your father was to sign this.

NORA: Was to—? He did sign it!

KROGSTAD: I had left the date blank. That is to say, your father was himself to date his signature. Do you recollect that?

NORA: Yes, I believe—

KROGSTAD: Then I gave you the paper to send to your father, by post. Is not that so?

NORA: Yes.

KROGSTAD: And of course you did so at once; for within five or six days you brought me back the document with your father's signature; and I handed you the money.

NORA: Well? Have I not made my payments punctually?

KROGSTAD: Fairly—yes. But to return to the point: You were in great trouble at the time, Mrs. Helmer.

NORA: I was indeed!

KROGSTAD: Your father was very ill, I believe?

NORA: He was on his death-bed.

KROGSTAD: And died soon after?

NORA: Yes.

KROGSTAD: Tell me, Mrs. Helmer: do you happen to recollect the day of his death? The day of the month, I mean?

NORA: Father died on the 29th of September.

KROGSTAD: Quite correct. I have made inquiries. And here comes in the remarkable point—[*produces a paper*] which I cannot explain.

NORA: What remarkable point? I don't know—

KROGSTAD: The remarkable point, madam, that your father signed this paper three days after his death!

NORA: What! I don't understand—

KROGSTAD: Your father died on the 29th of September. But look here: he has dated his signature October 2nd! Is not that remarkable, Mrs. Helmer? [*Nora is silent.*] Can you explain it? [*Nora continues silent.*] It is noteworthy, too, that the words "October 2nd" and the year are not in your father's handwriting, but in one which I believe I know. Well, this may be explained; your father may have forgotten to date his signature, and somebody may have added the date at random, before the fact of your father's death was known. There is nothing wrong in that. Everything depends on the signature. Of course it is genuine, Mrs. Helmer? It was really your father himself who wrote his name here?

NORA [*after a short silence, throws her head back and looks defiantly at him*]: No, it was not. *I* wrote father's name.

KROGSTAD: Ah!—Are you aware, madam, that that is a dangerous admission?

NORA: How so? You will soon get your money.

KROGSTAD: May I ask you one more question? Why did you not send the paper to your father?

NORA: It was impossible. Father was ill. If I had asked him for his signature, I should have had to tell him why I wanted the money; but he was so ill I really could not tell him that my husband's life was in danger. It was impossible.

KROGSTAD: Then it would have been better to have given up your tour.

NORA: No, I couldn't do that; my husband's life depended on that journey. I couldn't give it up.

KROGSTAD: And did it never occur to you that you were playing me false?

NORA: That was nothing to me. I didn't care in the least about you. I couldn't endure you for all the cruel difficulties you made, although you knew how ill my husband was.

KROGSTAD: Mrs. Helmer, you evidently do not realise what you have been guilty of. But I can assure you it was nothing more and nothing worse that made me an outcast from society.

NORA: You! You want me to believe that you did a brave thing to save your wife's life?

KROGSTAD: The law takes no account of motives.

NORA: Then it must be a very bad law.

KROGSTAD: Bad or not, if I produce this document in court, you will be condemned according to law.

NORA: I don't believe that. Do you mean to tell me that a daughter has no right to spare her dying father trouble and anxiety?—that a wife has no right to save her husband's life? I don't know much about the law, but I'm sure you'll find, somewhere or another, that that is allowed. And you don't know that—you, a lawyer! You must be a bad one, Mr. Krogstad.

KROGSTAD: Possibly. But business—such business as ours—I do understand. You believe that? Very well; now, do as you please. But this I may tell you, that if I am flung into the gutter a second time, you shall keep me company.

[*Bows and goes out through hall.*]

NORA [*stands a while thinking, then tosses her head*]: Oh nonsense! He wants to frighten me. I'm not so foolish as that. [*Begins folding the children's clothes. Pauses.*] But—? No, it's impossible! Why, I did it for love!

CHILDREN [*at the door, left*]: Mamma, the strange man has gone now.

NORA: Yes, yes, I know. But don't tell anyone about the strange man. Do you hear? Not even papa!

CHILDREN: No, mamma; and now will you play with us again?

NORA: No, no; not now.

CHILDREN: Oh, do, mamma; you know you promised.

NORA: Yes, but I can't just now. Run to the nursery; I have so much to do. Run along, run along, and be good, my darlings! [*She pushes them gently into the inner room, and closes the door behind them. Sits on the sofa, embroiders a few stitches, but soon pauses.*] No! [*Throws down the work, rises, goes to the hall door and calls out.*] Ellen, bring in the Christmas-tree! [*Goes to table, left, and opens the drawer; again pauses.*] No, it's quite impossible!

ELLEN [*with Christmas-tree*]: Where shall I stand it, ma'am?

NORA: There, in the middle of the room.

ELLEN: Shall I bring in anything else?

NORA: No, thank you, I have all I want.

[*Ellen, having put down the tree, goes out.*]

NORA [*busy dressing the tree*]: There must be a candle here—and flowers there.— That horrible man! Nonsense, nonsense! there's nothing to be afraid of. The Christmas-tree shall be beautiful. I'll do everything to please you, Torvald; I'll sing and dance, and—

[*Enter Helmer by the hall door, with a bundle of documents.*]

NORA: Oh! You're back already?

HELMER: Yes. Has anybody been here.

NORA: Here? No.

HELMER: That's odd. I saw Krogstad come out of the house.

NORA: Did you? Oh, yes, by-the-bye, he was here for a minute.

HELMER: Nora, I can see by your manner that he has been begging you to put in a good word for him.

NORA: Yes.

HELMER: And you were to do it as if of your own accord? You were to say nothing to me of his having been here. Didn't he suggest that, too?

NORA: Yes, Torvald; but—

HELMER: Nora, Nora! And you could condescend to that! To speak to such a man, to make him a promise! And then to tell me an untruth about it!

NORA: An untruth!

HELMER: Didn't you say that nobody had been here? [*Threatens with his finger.*] My little bird must never do that again! A song-bird must sing clear and true; no false notes. [*Puts his arm round her.*] That's so, isn't it? Yes, I was sure of it. [*Lets her go.*] And now we'll say no more about it. [*Sits down before the fire.*] Oh, how cosy and quiet it is here!

[*Glances into his documents.*]

NORA [*busy with the tree, after a short silence*]: Torvald!

HELMER: Yes.

NORA: I'm looking forward so much to the Stenborgs' fancy ball the day after to-morrow.

HELMER: And I'm on tenterhooks to see what surprise you have in store for me.

NORA: Oh, it's too tiresome!

HELMER: What is?

NORA: I can't think of anything good. Everything seems so foolish and meaningless.

HELMER: Has little Nora made that discovery?

NORA [behind his chair, with her arms on the back]: Are you very busy, Torvald?

HELMER: Well—

NORA: What papers are those?

HELMER: Bank business.

NORA: Already!

HELMER: I have got the retiring manager to let me make some necessary changes in the staff and the organization. I can do this during Christmas week. I want to have everything straight by the New Year.

NORA: Then that's why that poor Krogstad—

HELMER: H'm.

NORA [still leaning over the chair-back and slowly stroking his hair]: If you hadn't been so very busy, I should have asked you a great, great favour, Torvald.

HELMER: What can it be? Out with it.

NORA: Nobody has such perfect taste as you; and I should so love to look well at the fancy ball. Torvald, dear, couldn't you take me in hand, and settle what I'm to be, and arrange my costume for me?

HELMER: Aha! So my willful little woman is at a loss, and making signals of distress.

NORA: Yes, please, Torvald. I can't get on without your help.

HELMER: Well, well, I'll think it over, and we'll soon hit upon something.

NORA: Oh, how good that is of you! [Goes to the tree again; pause.] How well the red flowers show.—Tell me, was it anything so very dreadful this Krogstad got into trouble about?

HELMER: Forgery, that's all. Don't you know what that means?

NORA: Mayn't he have been driven to it by need?

HELMER: Yes; or, like so many others, he may have done it in pure heedlessness. I am not so hard-hearted as to condemn a man absolutely for a single fault.

NORA: No, surely not, Torvald!

HELMER: Many a man can retrieve his character, if he owns his crime and takes the punishment.

NORA: Punishment—?

HELMER: But Krogstad didn't do that. He evaded the law by means of tricks and subterfuges; and that is what has morally ruined him.

NORA: Do you think that—?

HELMER: Just think how a man with a thing of that sort on his conscience must be always lying and canting and shamming. Think of the mask he must wear even towards those who stand nearest him—towards his own wife and children. The effect on the children—that's the most terrible part of it, Nora.

NORA: Why?

HELMER: Because in such an atmosphere of lies home life is poisoned and contaminated in every fibre. Every breath the children draw contains some germ of evil.

NORA [closer behind him]: Are you sure of that?

HELMER: As a lawyer, my dear, I have seen it often enough. Nearly all cases of early corruption may be traced to lying mothers.

NORA: Why—mothers?

HELMER: It generally comes from the mother's side; but of course the father's influence may act in the same way. Every lawyer knows it too well. And here has this Krogstad been poisoning his own children for years past by a life of lies and hypocrisy—that is why I call him morally ruined. [*Holds out both hands to her.*] So my sweet little Nora must promise not to plead his cause. Shake hands upon it. Come, come, what's this? Give me your hand. That's right. Then it's a bargain. I assure you it would have been impossible for me to work with him. It gives me a positive sense of physical discomfort to come in contact with such people.

[*Nora draws her hand away, and moves to the other side of the Christmas-tree.*]

NORA: How warm it is here. And I have so much to do.

HELMER [*rises and gathers up his papers*]: Yes, and I must try to get some of these papers looked through before dinner. And I shall think over your costume too. Perhaps I may even find something to hang in gilt paper on the Christmas-tree. [*Lays his hand on her head.*] My precious little song-bird!

[*He goes into his room and shuts the door.*]

NORA [*softly, after a pause*]: It can't be. It's impossible. It must be impossible!

ANNA [*at the door, left*]: The little ones are begging so prettily to come to mamma.

NORA: No, no, no; don't let them come to me! Keep them with you, Anna.

ANNA: Very well, ma'am.

[*Shuts the door.*]

NORA [*pale with terror*]: Corrupt my children!—Poison my home! [*Short pause. She throws back her head.*] It's not true! It can never, never be true!

ACT 2

The same room. In the corner, beside the piano, stands the Christmas-tree, stripped, and with the candles burnt out. Nora's outdoor things lie on the sofa.

Nora, alone, is walking about restlessly. At last she stops by the sofa, and takes up her cloak.

NORA [*dropping the cloak*]: There's somebody coming! [*Goes to the hall door and listens.*] Nobody; of course nobody will come to-day, Christmas-day; nor tomorrow either. But perhaps——[*Opens the door and looks out.*]—No, nothing in the letter box; quite empty. [*Comes forward.*] Stuff and nonsense! Of course he won't really do anything. Such a thing couldn't happen. It's impossible! Why, I have three little children.

[*Anna enters from the left, with a large cardboard box.*]

ANNA: I've found the box with the fancy dress at last.

NORA: Thanks; put it down on the table.

ANNA [*does so*]: But I'm afraid it's very much out of order.

NORA: Oh, I wish I could tear it into a hundred thousand pieces!

ANNA: Oh, no. It can easily be put to rights—just a little patience.

NORA: I shall go and get Mrs. Linden to help me.

ANNA: Going out again? In such weather as this! You'll catch cold, ma'am, and be ill.

NORA: Worse things might happen.—What are the children doing?

ANNA: They're playing with their Christmas presents, poor little dears; but—

NORA: Do they often ask for me?

ANNA: You see they've been so used to having their mamma with them.

NORA: Yes; but, Anna, I can't have them so much with me in future.

ANNA: Well, little children get used to anything.

NORA: Do you think they do? Do you believe they would forget their mother if she went quite away?

ANNA: Gracious me! Quite away?

NORA: Tell me, Anna—I've so often wondered about it—how could you bring yourself to give your child up to strangers?

ANNA: I had to when I came to nurse my little Miss Nora.

NORA: But how could you make up your mind to it?

ANNA: When I had the chance of such a good place? A poor girl who's been in trouble must take what comes. That wicked man did nothing for me.

NORA: But your daughter must have forgotten you.

ANNA: Oh, no, ma'am, that she hasn't. She wrote to me both when she was confirmed and when she was married.

NORA [embracing her]: Dear old Anna—you were a good mother to me when I was little.

ANNA: My poor little Nora had no mother but me.

NORA: And if my little ones had nobody else, I'm sure you would—Nonsense, nonsense! [Opens the box.] Go in to the children. Now I must—You'll see how lovely I shall be to-morrow.

ANNA: I'm sure there will be no one at the ball so lovely as my Miss Nora.

[She goes into the room on the left.]

NORA [takes the costume out of the box, but soon throws it down again]: Oh, if I dared go out. If only nobody would come. If only nothing would happen here in the meantime. Rubbish; nobody is coming. Only not to think. What a delicious muff! Beautiful gloves, beautiful gloves! To forget—to forget! One, two, three, four, five, six—[With a scream.] Ah, there they come.

[Goes towards the door, then stands irresolute.]

[Mrs. Linden enters from the hall, where she has taken off her things.]

NORA: Oh, it's you, Christina. There's nobody else there? I'm so glad you have come.

MRS. LINDEN: I hear you called at my lodgings.

NORA: Yes, I was just passing. There's something you must help me with. Let us sit here on the sofa—so. To-morrow evening there's to be a fancy ball at Consul Stenborg's overhead, and Torvald wants me to appear as a Neapolitan fisher-girl, and dance the tarantella; I learned it at Capri.

MRS. LINDEN: I see—quite a performance.

NORA: Yes, Torvald wishes it. Look, this is the costume; Torvald had it made for me in Italy. But now it's all so torn, I don't know—

MRS. LINDEN: Oh, we shall soon set that to rights. It's only the trimming that has come loose here and there. Have you a needle and thread? Ah, here's the very thing.

NORA: Oh, how kind of you.

MRS. LINDEN [*sewing*]: So you're to be in costume to-morrow, Nora? I'll tell you what—I shall come in for a moment to see you in all your glory. But I've quite forgotten to thank you for the pleasant evening yesterday.

NORA [*rises and walks across the room*]: Oh, yesterday, it didn't seem so pleasant as usual.—You should have come to town a little sooner, Christina.—Torvald has certainly the art of making home bright and beautiful.

MRS. LINDEN: You, too, I should think, or you wouldn't be your father's daughter. But tell me—is Doctor Rank always so depressed as he was last evening?

NORA: No, yesterday it was particularly noticeable. You see, he suffers from a dreadful illness. He has spinal consumption, poor fellow. They say his father was a horrible man, who kept mistresses and all sorts of things—so the son has been sickly from his childhood, you understand.

MRS. LINDEN [*lets her sewing fall into her lap*]: Why, my darling Nora, how do you come to know such things?

NORA [*moving about the room*]: Oh, when one has three children, one sometimes has visits from women who are half—half doctors—and they talk of one thing and another.

MRS. LINDEN [*goes on sewing; a short pause*]: Does Doctor Rank come here every day?

NORA: Every day of his life. He has been Torvald's most intimate friend from boyhood, and he's a good friend of mine, too. Doctor Rank is quite one of the family.

MRS. LINDEN: But tell me—is he quite sincere? I mean, isn't he rather given to flattering people?

NORA: No, quite the contrary. Why should you think so?

MRS. LINDEN: When you introduced us yesterday he said he had often heard my name; but I noticed afterwards that your husband had no notion who I was. How could Doctor Rank—?

NORA: He was quite right, Christina. You see, Torvald loves me so indescribably, he wants to have me all to himself, as he says. When we were first married, he was almost jealous if I even mentioned any of my old friends at home; so naturally I gave up doing it. But I often talk of the old times to Doctor Rank, for he likes to hear about them.

MRS. LINDEN: Listen to me, Nora! You are still a child in many ways. I am older than you, and have had more experience. I'll tell you something? You ought to get clear of all this with Doctor Rank.

NORA: Get clear of what?

MRS. LINDEN: The whole affair, I should say. You were talking yesterday of a rich admirer who was to find you money—

NORA: Yes, one who never existed, worse luck. What then?

MRS. LINDEN: Has Doctor Rank money?

NORA: Yes, he has.

MRS. LINDEN: And nobody to provide for?

NORA: Nobody. But—?

MRS. LINDEN: And he comes here every day?

NORA: Yes, I told you so.

MRS. LINDEN: I should have thought he would have had better taste.

NORA: I don't understand you a bit.

MRS. LINDEN: Don't pretend, Nora. Do you suppose I can't guess who lent you the twelve hundred dollars?

NORA: Are you out of your senses? How can you think such a thing? A friend who comes here every day! Why, the position would be unbearable!

MRS. LINDEN: Then it really is not he?

NORA: No, I assure you. It never for a moment occurred to me——Besides, at that time he had nothing to lend; he came into his property afterwards.

MRS. LINDEN: Well, I believe that was lucky for you, Nora, dear.

NORA: No, really, it would never have struck me to ask Doctor Rank—And yet, I'm certain that if I did—

MRS. LINDEN: But of course you never would.

NORA: Of course not. It's inconceivable that it should ever be necessary. But I'm quite sure that if I spoke to Doctor Rank—

MRS. LINDEN: Behind your husband's back?

NORA: I must get clear of the other thing; that's behind his back too. I must get clear of that.

MRS. LINDEN: Yes, yes, I told you so yesterday; but—

NORA [*walking up and down*]: A man can manage these things much better than a woman.

MRS. LINDEN: One's own husband, yes.

NORA: Nonsense. [*Stands still.*] When everything is paid, one gets back the paper.

MRS. LINDEN: Of course.

NORA: And can tear it into a hundred thousand pieces, and burn it up, the nasty, filthy thing!

MRS. LINDEN [*looks at her fixedly, lays down her work, and rises slowly*]: Nora, you are hiding something from me.

NORA: Can you see it in my face?

MRS. LINDEN: Something has happened since yesterday morning. Nora, what is it?

NORA [*going towards her*]: Christina—! [*Listens.*] Hush! There's Torvald coming home. Do you mind going into the nursery for the present? Torvald can't bear to see dressmaking going on. Get Anna to help you.

MRS. LINDEN [*gathers some of the things together*]: Very well; but I shan't go away until you have told me all about it.

[*She goes out to the left, as Helmer enters from the hall.*]

NORA [*runs to meet him*]: Oh, how I've been longing for you to come, Torvald, dear!

HELMER: Was that the dressmaker—?

NORA: No, Christina. She's helping me with my costume. You'll see how nice I shall look.

HELMER: Yes, wasn't that a happy thought of mine?

NORA: Splendid! But isn't it good of me, too, to have given in to you about the tarantella?

HELMER [*takes her under the chin*]: Good of you! To give in to your own husband? Well, well, you little madcap, I know you don't mean it. But I won't disturb you. I daresay you want to be "trying on."

NORA: And you are going to work, I suppose?

HELMER: Yes. [*Shows her a bundle of papers.*] Look here. I've just come from the Bank—

[*Goes towards his room.*]

NORA: Torvald.

HELMER [*stopping*]: Yes?

NORA: If your little squirrel were to beg you for something so prettily—

HELMER: Well?

NORA: Would you do it?

HELMER: I must know first what it is.

NORA: The squirrel would skip about and play all sorts of tricks if you would only be nice and kind.

HELMER: Come, then, out with it.

NORA: Your lark would twitter from morning till night—

HELMER: Oh, that she does in any case.

NORA: I'll be an elf and dance in the moonlight for you, Torvald.

HELMER: Nora—you can't mean what you were hinting at this morning?

NORA [*coming nearer*]: Yes, Torvald, I beg and implore you!

HELMER: Have you really the courage to begin that again?

NORA: Yes, yes; for my sake, you must let Krogstad keep his place in the Bank.

HELMER: My dear Nora, it's his place I intend for Mrs. Linden.

NORA: Yes, that's so good of you. But instead of Krogstad, you could dismiss some other clerk.

HELMER: Why, this is incredible obstinacy! Because you have thoughtlessly promised to put in a word for him, I am to—!

NORA: It's not that, Torvald. It's for your own sake. This man writes for the most scurrilous newspapers; you said so yourself. He can do you no end of harm. I'm so terribly afraid of him—

HELMER: Ah, I understand; it's old recollections that are frightening you.

NORA: What do you mean?

HELMER: Of course you're thinking of your father.

NORA: Yes—yes, of course. Only think of the shameful slanders wicked people used to write about father. I believe they would have got him dismissed if you hadn't been sent to look into the thing, and been kind to him, and helped him.

HELMER: My little Nora, between your father and me there is all the difference in the world. Your father was not altogether unimpeachable. I am; and I hope to remain so.

NORA: Oh, no one knows what wicked men may hit upon. We could live so quietly and happily now, in our cosy, peaceful home, you and I and the children, Torvald! That's why I beg and implore you—

HELMER: And it is just by pleading his cause that you make it impossible for me to keep him. It's already known at the Bank that I intend to dismiss Krogstad. If it were now reported that the new manager let himself be turned round his wife's little finger—

NORA: What then?

HELMER: Oh, nothing, so long as a wilful woman can have her way—! I am to make myself a laughing-stock to the whole staff, and set people saying that I am open to all sorts of outside influence? Take my word for it, I should soon feel the consequences. And besides—there is one thing that makes Krogstad impossible for me to work with—

NORA: What thing?

HELMER: I could perhaps have overlooked his moral failings at a pinch—

NORA: Yes, couldn't you, Torvald?

HELMER: And I hear he is good at his work. But the fact is, he was a college chum of mine—there was one of those rash friendships between us that one so often repents of later. I may as well confess it at once—he calls me by my Christian name; and he is tactless enough to do it even when others are present. He delights in putting on airs of familiarity—Torvald here, Torvald there! I assure you it's most painful to me. He would make my position at the Bank perfectly unendurable.

NORA: Torvald, surely you're not serious?

HELMER: No? Why not?

NORA: That's such a petty reason.

HELMER: What! Petty! Do you consider me petty!

NORA: No, on the contrary, Torvald, dear; and that's just why—

HELMER: Never mind; you call my motives petty; then I must be petty too. Petty! Very well!—Now we'll put an end to this, once for all. [*Goes to the door into the hall and calls.*] Ellen!

NORA: What do you want?

HELMER [*searching among his papers*]: To settle the thing. [*Ellen enters.*] Here; take this letter; give it to a messenger. See that he takes it at once. The address is on it. Here's the money.

ELLEN: Very well, sir. [*Goes with the letter.*]

HELMER [*putting his papers together*]: There, Madam Obstinacy.

NORA [*breathless*]: Torvald—what was in the letter?

HELMER: Krogstad's dismissal.

NORA: Call it back again, Torvald! There's still time. Oh, Torvald, call it back again! For my sake, for your own, for the children's sake! Do you hear, Torvald? Do it! You don't know what that letter may bring upon us all.

HELMER: Too late.

NORA: Yes, too late.

HELMER: My dear Nora, I forgive your anxiety, though it's anything but flattering to me. Why should you suppose that *I* would be afraid of a wretched scribbler's spite? But I forgive you all the same, for it's a proof of your great love for me. [*Takes her in his arms.*] That's as it should be, my own dear Nora. Let what will happen—when it comes to the pinch, I shall have strength and courage enough. You shall see: my shoulders are broad enough to bear the whole burden.

NORA [*terror-struck*]: What do you mean by that?

HELMER: The whole burden, I say—

NORA [*with decision*]: That you shall never, never do!

HELMER: Very well; then we'll share it, Nora, as man and wife. That is how it should be. [*Petting her.*] Are you satisfied now? Come, come, come, don't look like a scared dove. It's all nothing—foolish fancies.—Now you ought to play the tarantella through and practise with the tambourine. I shall sit in my inner room and shut both doors, so that I shall hear nothing. You can make as much noise as you please. [*Turns round in doorway.*] And when Rank comes, just tell him where I'm to be found.

[*He nods to her, and goes with his papers into his room, closing the door.*]

NORA [*bewildered with terror, stands as though rooted to the ground, and whispers*]: He would do it. Yes, he would do it. He would do it, in spite of all the world.—No, never that, never, never! Anything rather than that! Oh, for some way of escape! What shall I do—! [*Hall bell rings.*] Doctor Rank—! —Anything, anything, rather than—!

[*Nora draws her hands over her face, pulls herself together, goes to the door and opens it. Rank stands outside hanging up his fur coat. During what follows it begins to grow dark.*]

NORA: Good-afternoon, Doctor Rank. I knew you by your ring. But you mustn't go to Torvald now. I believe he's busy.

RANK: And you? [*Enters and closes the door.*]

NORA: Oh, you know very well, I have always time for you.

RANK: Thank you. I shall avail myself of your kindness as long as I can.

NORA: What do you mean? As long as you can?

RANK: Yes. Does that frighten you?

NORA: I think it's an odd expression. Do you expect anything to happen?

RANK: Something I have long been prepared for; but I didn't think it would come so soon.

NORA [*catching at his arm*]: What have you discovered? Doctor Rank, you must tell me!

RANK [*sitting down by the stove*]: I am running down hill. There's no help for it.

NORA [*drank a long breath of relief*]: It's you—?

RANK: Who else should it be?—Why lie to one's self? I am the most wretched of all my patients, Mrs. Helmer. In these last days I have been auditing my life-account— bankrupt! Perhaps before a month is over, I shall lie rotting in the churchyard.

NORA: Oh! What an ugly way to talk.

RANK: The thing itself is so confoundedly ugly, you see. But the worst of it is, so many other ugly things have to be gone through first. There is only one last inves- tigation to be made, and when that is over I shall know pretty certainly when the break-up will begin. There's one thing I want to say to you: Helmer's delicate na- ture shrinks so from all that is horrible: I will not have him in my sick-room—

NORA: But, Doctor Rank—

RANK: I won't have him, I say—not on any account. I shall lock my door against him.—As soon as I am quite certain of the worst, I shall send you my visiting-card with a black cross on it; and then you will know that the final horror has begun.

NORA: Why, you're perfectly unreasonable to-day; and I did so want you to be in a re- ally good humour.

RANK: With death staring me in the face?—And to suffer thus for another's sin! Where's the justice of it? And in one way or another you can trace in every family some such inexorable retribution—

NORA [*stopping her ears*]: Nonsense, nonsense! Now, cheer up!

RANK: Well, after all, the whole thing's only worth laughing at. My poor innocent spine must do penance for my father's wild oats.

NORA [*at table, left*]: I suppose he was too fond of asparagus and Strasbourg pâté, wasn't he?

RANK: Yes; and truffles.

NORA: Yes, truffles, to be sure. And oysters, I believe?

RANK: Yes, oysters; oysters, of course.

NORA: And then all the port and champagne! It's sad that all these good things should attack the spine.

RANK: Especially when the luckless spine attacked never had any good of them.

NORA: Ah, yes, that's the worst of it.

RANK [*looks at her searchingly*]: H'm—

NORA [*a moment later*]: Why did you smile?

RANK: No; it was you that laughed.

NORA: No; it was you that smiled, Doctor Rank.

RANK [*standing up*]: I see you're deeper than I thought.

NORA: I'm in such a crazy mood to-day.

RANK: So it seems.

NORA [*with her hands on his shoulders*]: Dear, dear Doctor Rank, death shall not take you away from Torvald and me.

RANK: Oh, you'll easily get over the loss. The absent are soon forgotten.

NORA [*looks at him anxiously*]: Do you think so?

RANK: People make fresh ties, and then—

NORA: Who make fresh ties?

RANK: You and Helmer will, when I am gone. You yourself are taking time by the forelock, it seems to me. What was that Mrs. Linden doing here yesterday?

NORA: Oh!—you're surely not jealous of poor Christina?

RANK: Yes, I am. She will be my successor in this house. When I am out of the way, this woman will, perhaps—

NORA: Hush! Not so loud! She's in there.

RANK: Today as well? You see!

NORA: Only to put my costume in order—dear me, how unreasonable you are! [*Sits on sofa.*] Now, do be good, Doctor Rank! Tomorrow you shall see how beautifully I shall dance; and then you may fancy that I'm doing it all to please you—and of course Torvald as well. [*Takes various things out of box.*] Doctor Rank, sit down here, and I'll show you something.

RANK [*sitting*]: What is it?

NORA: Look here. Look!

RANK: Silk stockings.

NORA: Flesh-coloured. Aren't they lovely? It's so dark here now; but to-morrow— No, no, no; you must only look at the feet. Oh, well, I suppose you may look at the rest too.

RANK: H'm—

NORA: What are you looking so critical about? Do you think they won't fit me?

RANK: I can't possibly give any competent opinion on that point.

NORA [*looking at him a moment*]: For shame! [*Hits him lightly on the ear with the stockings.*] Take that. [*Rolls them up again.*]

RANK: And what other wonders am I to see?

NORA: You shan't see anything more; for you don't behave nicely.

[*She hums a little and searches among the things.*]

RANK [*after a short silence*]: When I sit here gossiping with you, I can't imagine—I simply cannot conceive—what would have become of me if I had never entered this house.

NORA [*smiling*]: Yes, I think you do feel at home with us.

RANK [*more softly—looking straight before him*]: And now to have to leave it all—

NORA: Nonsense. You sha'n't leave us.

RANK [*in the same tone*]: And not to be able to leave behind the slightest token of gratitude; scarcely even a passing regret—nothing but an empty place, that can be filled by the first comer.

NORA: And if I were to ask you for—? No—

RANK: For what?

NORA: For a great proof of your friendship.

RANK: Yes—yes?

NORA: I mean—for a very, very great service—

RANK: Would you really, for once, make me so happy?

NORA: Oh, you don't know what it is.

RANK: Then tell me.

NORA: No, I really can't, Doctor Rank. It's far, far too much—not only a service, but help and advice, besides—

RANK: So much the better. I can't think what you can mean. But go on. Don't you trust me?

NORA: As I trust no one else. I know you are my best and truest friend. So I will tell you. Well, then, Doctor Rank, there is something you must help me to prevent. You know how deeply, how wonderfully Torvald loves me; he wouldn't hesitate a moment to give his very life for my sake.

RANK [*bending towards her*]: Nora—do you think he is the only one who—?

NORA [*with a slight start*]: Who—?

RANK: Who would gladly give his life for you?

NORA [*sadly*]: Oh!

RANK: I have sworn that you shall know it before I—go. I shall never find a better opportunity.—Yes, Nora, now I have told you; and now you know that you can trust me as you can no one else.

NORA [*standing up; simply and calmly*]: Let me pass, please.

RANK [*makes way for her, but remains sitting*]: Nora—

NORA [*in the doorway*]: Ellen, bring the lamp. [*crosses to the stove*] Oh dear, Doctor Rank, that was too bad of you.

RANK [*rising*]: That I have loved you as deeply as—anyone else? Was that too bad of me?

NORA: No, but that you should have told me so. It was so unnecessary—

RANK: What do you mean? Did you know—?

[*Ellen enters with the lamp; sets it on the table and goes out again.*]

RANK: Nora—Mrs. Helmer—I ask you, did you know?

NORA: Oh, how can I tell what I knew or didn't know? I really can't say—How could you be so clumsy, Doctor Rank? It was all so nice!

RANK: Well, at any rate, you know now that I am at your service, body and soul. And now, go on.

NORA [*looking at him*]: Go on—now?

RANK: I beg you to tell me what you want.

NORA: I can tell you nothing now.

RANK: Yes, yes! You mustn't punish me in that way. Let me do for you whatever a man can.

NORA: You can do nothing for me now.—Besides, I really want no help. You shall see it was only my fancy. Yes, it must be so. Of course! [*Sits in the rocking-chair, looks at him and smiles.*] You are a nice person, Doctor Rank! Aren't you ashamed of yourself, now that the lamp is on the table?

RANK: No; not exactly. But perhaps I ought to go—for ever.

NORA: No, indeed you mustn't. Of course you must come and go as you've always done. You know very well that Torvald can't do without you.

RANK: Yes, but you?

NORA: Oh, you know I always like to have you here.

RANK: That is just what led me astray. You are a riddle to me. It has often seemed to me as if you liked being with me almost as much as being with Helmer.

NORA: Yes; don't you see? There are people one loves, and others one likes to talk to.

RANK: Yes—there's something in that.

NORA: When I was a girl, of course I loved papa best. But it always delighted me to steal into the servants' room. In the first place they never lectured me, and in the second it was such fun to hear them talk.

RANK: Ah, I see; then it's their place I have taken?

NORA [*jumps up and hurries towards him*]: Oh, my dear Doctor Rank, I don't mean that. But you understand, with Torvald it's the same as with papa—

[*Ellen enters from the hall.*]

ELLEN: Please, ma'am—[*Whispers to Nora, and gives her a card.*]

NORA [*glancing at card*]: Ah! [*Puts it in her pocket.*]

RANK: Anything wrong?

NORA: No, no, not in the least. It's only—it's my new costume—

RANK: Your costume! Why, it's there.

NORA: Oh, that one, yes. But this is another that—I have ordered it—Torvald mustn't know—

RANK: Aha! So that's the great secret.

NORA: Yes, of course. Please go to him; he's in the inner room. Do keep him while I—

RANK: Don't be alarmed; he sha'n't escape.

[*Goes into Helmer's room.*]

NORA [*to Ellen*]: Is he waiting in the kitchen?

ELLEN: Yes, he came up the back stair—

NORA: Didn't you tell him I was engaged?

ELLEN: Yes, but it was no use.

NORA: He won't go away?

ELLEN: No, ma'am, not until he has spoken to you.

NORA: Then let him come in; but quietly. And, Ellen—say nothing about it; it's a surprise for my husband.

ELLEN: Oh, yes, ma'am, I understand. [*She goes out.*]

NORA: It is coming! The dreadful thing is coming, after all. No, no, no, it can never be; it shall not!

[*She goes to Helmer's door and slips the bolt. Ellen opens the hall door for Krogstad, and shuts it after him. He wears a travelling-coat, high boots, and a fur cap.*]

NORA [*goes towards him*]: Speak softly; my husband is at home.

KROGSTAD: All right. That's nothing to me.

NORA: What do you want?

KROGSTAD: A little information.

NORA: Be quick, then. What is it?

KROGSTAD: You know I have got my dismissal.

NORA: I couldn't prevent it, Mr. Krogstad. I fought for you to the last, but it was of no use.

KROGSTAD: Does your husband care for you so little? He knows what I can bring upon you, and yet he dares—

NORA: How could you think I should tell him?

KROGSTAD: Well, as a matter of fact, I didn't think it. It wasn't like my friend Torvald Helmer to show so much courage—

NORA: Mr. Krogstad, be good enough to speak respectfully of my husband.

KROGSTAD: Certainly, with all due respect. But since you are so anxious to keep the matter secret, I suppose you are a little clearer than yesterday as to what you have done.

NORA: Clearer than you could ever make me.

KROGSTAD: Yes, such a bad lawyer as I—

NORA: What is it you want?

KROGSTAD: Only to see how you are getting on, Mrs. Helmer. I've been thinking about you all day. Even a mere money-lender, a gutter-journalist, a—in short, a creature like me—has a little bit of what people call feeling.

NORA: Then show it; think of my little children.

KROGSTAD: Did you and your husband think of mine? But enough of that. I only wanted to tell you that you needn't take this matter too seriously. I shall not lodge any information, for the present.

NORA: No, surely not. I knew you wouldn't.

KROGSTAD: The whole thing can be settled quite amicably. Nobody need know. It can remain among us three.

NORA: My husband must never know.

KROGSTAD: How can you prevent it? Can you pay off the balance?

NORA: No, not at once.

KROGSTAD: Or have you any means of raising the money in the next few days?

NORA: None—that I will make use of.

KROGSTAD: And if you had, it would not help you now. If you offered me ever so much money down, you should not get back your I.O.U.

NORA: Tell me what you want to do with it.

KROGSTAD: I only want to keep it—to have it in my possession. No outsider shall hear anything of it. So, if you have any desperate scheme in your head—

NORA: What if I have?

KROGSTAD: If you should think of leaving your husband and children—

NORA: What if I do?

KROGSTAD: Or if you should think of—something worse—

NORA: How do you know that?

KROGSTAD: Put all that out of your head.

NORA: How did you know what I had in my mind?

KROGSTAD: Most of us think of that at first. I thought of it, too; but I hadn't the courage—

NORA [tonelessly]: Nor I.

KROGSTAD [relieved]: No, one hasn't. You haven't the courage either, have you?

NORA: I haven't, I haven't.

KROGSTAD: Besides, it would be very foolish.—Just one domestic storm, and it's all over. I have a letter in my pocket for your husband—

NORA: Telling him everything?

KROGSTAD: Sparing you as much as possible.

NORA [*quickly*]: He must never read that letter. Tear it up. I will manage to get the money somehow—

KROGSTAD: Pardon me, Mrs. Helmer, but I believe I told you—

NORA: Oh, I'm not talking about the money I owe you. Tell me how much you demand from my husband—I will get it.

KROGSTAD: I demand no money from your husband.

NORA: What do you demand then?

KROGSTAD: I will tell you. I want to regain my footing in the world. I want to rise; and your husband shall help me to do it. For the last eighteen months my record has been spotless; I have been in bitter need all the time; but I was content to fight my way up, step by step. Now, I've been thrust down again, and I will not be satisfied with merely being reinstated as a matter of grace. I want to rise, I tell you. I must get into the Bank again, in a higher position than before. Your husband shall create a place on purpose for me—

NORA: He will never do that!

KROGSTAD: He will do it; I know him—he won't dare to show fight! And when he and I are together there, you shall soon see! Before a year is out I shall be the manager's right hand. It won't be Torvald Helmer, but Nils Krogstad, that manages the Joint Stock Bank.

NORA: That shall never be.

KROGSTAD: Perhaps you will—?

NORA: Now I have the courage for it.

KROGSTAD: Oh, you don't frighten me! A sensitive, petted creature like you——

NORA: You shall see, you shall see!

KROGSTAD: Under the ice, perhaps? Down into the cold, black water? And next spring to come up again, ugly, hairless, unrecognisable—

NORA: You can't terrify me.

KROGSTAD: Nor you me. People don't do that sort of thing, Mrs. Helmer. And, after all, what would be the use of it? I have your husband in my pocket, all the same.

NORA: Afterwards? When I am no longer—?

KROGSTAD: You forget, your reputation remains in my hands! [*Nora stands speechless and looks at him.*] Well, now you are prepared. Do nothing foolish. As soon as Helmer has received my letter, I shall expect to hear from him. And remember that it is your husband himself who has forced me back again into such paths. That I will never forgive him. Good-bye, Mrs. Helmer.

[*Goes out through the hall. Nora hurries to the door, opens it a little, and listens.*]

NORA: He's going. He's not putting the letter into the box. No, no, it would be impossible! [*Opens the door further and further.*] What's that. He's standing still; not going down stairs. Has he changed his mind? Is he—? [*A letter falls into the box. Krogstad's footsteps are heard gradually receding down the stair. Nora utters a suppressed shriek, and rushes forward towards the sofa-table; pause.*] In the letter-box! [*Slips shrinkingly up to the hall door.*] There it lies.—Torvald, Torvald—now we are lost!

[*Mrs. Linden enters from the left with the costume.*]

MRS. LINDEN: There, I think it's all right now. Shall we just try it on?

NORA [*hoarsely and softly*]: Christina, come here.

MRS. LINDEN [*throws down the dress on the sofa*]: What's the matter? You look quite distracted.

NORA: Come here. Do you see that letter? There, see—through the glass of the letter-box.

MRS. LINDEN: Yes, yes, I see it.

NORA: That latter is from Krogstad—

MRS. LINDEN: Nora—it was Krogstad who lent you the money?

NORA: Yes; and now Torvald will know everything.

MRS. LINDEN: Believe me, Nora, it's the best thing for both of you.

NORA: You don't know all yet. I have forged a name——

MRS. LINDEN: Good heavens!

NORA: Now, listen to me, Christina; you shall bear me witness—

MRS. LINDEN: How "witness"? What am I to—?

NORA: If I should go out of my mind—it might easily happen—

MRS. LINDEN: Nora!

NORA: Or if anything else should happen to me—so that I couldn't be here—!

MRS. LINDEN: Nora, Nora, you're quite beside yourself!

NORA: In case any one wanted to take it all upon himself—the whole blame—you understand—

MRS. LINDEN: Yes, yes; but how can you think—?

NORA: You shall bear witness that it's not true, Christina. I'm not out of my mind at all; I know quite well what I'm saying; and I tell you nobody else knew anything about it; I did the whole thing, I myself. Remember that.

MRS. LINDEN: I shall remember. But I don't understand what you mean—

NORA: Oh, how should you? It's the miracle coming to pass.

MRS. LINDEN: The miracle?

NORA: Yes, the miracle. But it's so terrible, Christina; it mustn't happen for all the world.

MRS. LINDEN: I shall go straight to Krogstad and talk to him.

NORA: Don't; he'll do you some harm.

MRS. LINDEN: Once he would have done anything for me.

NORA: He?

MRS. LINDEN: Where does he live?

NORA: Oh, how can I tell—? Yes—[*Feels in her pocket.*] Here's his card. But the letter, the letter—!

HELMER [*knocking outside*]: Nora!

NORA [*shrieks in terror*]: Oh, what is it? What do you want?

HELMER: Well, well, don't be frightened. We're not coming in; you've bolted the door. Are you trying on your dress?

NORA: Yes, yes, I'm trying it on. It suits me so well, Torvald.

MRS. LINDEN [*who has read the card*]: Why, he lives close by here.

NORA: Yes, but it's no use now. We are lost. The letter is there in the box.

MRS. LINDEN: And your husband has the key?

NORA: Always.

MRS. LINDEN: Krogstad must demand his letter back, unread. He must find some pretext—

NORA: But this is the very time when Torvald generally—

MRS. LINDEN: Prevent him. Keep him occupied. I shall come back as quickly as I can.

[*She goes out hastily by the hall door.*]

NORA [*opens Helmer's door and peeps in*]: Torvald!

HELMER: Well, may one come into one's own room again at last? Come, Rank, we'll have a look—[*in the doorway*] But how's this?

NORA: What, Torvald dear?

HELMER: Rank led me to expect a grand transformation.

RANK [*in the doorway*]: So I understood. I suppose I was mistaken.

NORA: No, no one shall see me in my glory till tomorrow evening.

HELMER: Why, Nora dear, you look so tired. Have you been practising too hard?

NORA: No, I haven't practised at all yet.

HELMER: But you'll have to—

NORA: Oh, yes, I must, I must! But, Torvald, I can't get on at all without your help. I've forgotten everything.

HELMER: Oh, we shall soon freshen it up again.

NORA: Yes, do help me, Torvald. You must promise me—Oh, I'm so nervous about it. Before so many people—This evening you must give yourself up entirely to me. You mustn't do a stroke of work; you mustn't even touch a pen. Do promise, Torvald dear!

HELMER: I promise. All this evening I shall be your slave. Little helpless thing—! But, by-the-bye, I must just—[*Going to hall door.*]

NORA: What do you want there?

HELMER: Only to see if there are any letters.

NORA: No, no, don't do that, Torvald.

HELMER: Why not?

NORA: Torvald, I beg you not to. There are none there.

HELMER: Let me just see.[*Is going.*]

[*Nora, at the piano, plays the first bars of the tarantella.*]

HELMER [*at the door, stops*]: Aha!

NORA: I can't dance to-morrow if I don't rehearse with you first.

HELMER [*going to her*]: Are you really so nervous, dear Nora?

NORA: Yes, dreadfully! Let me rehearse at once. We have time before dinner. Oh, do sit down and play for me, Torvald dear; direct me and put me right, as you used to do.

HELMER: With all the pleasure in life, since you wish it.

[*Sits at piano. Nora snatches the tambourine out of the box, and hurriedly drapes herself in a long parti-coloured shawl; then, with a bound, stands in the middle of the floor.*]

NORA: Now play for me! Now I'll dance!

[*Helmer plays and Nora dances. Rank stands at the piano behind Helmer and looks on.*]

HELMER [*playing*]: Slower! Slower!

NORA: Can't do it slower!

HELMER: Not so violently, Nora.

NORA: I must! I must!

HELMER [*stops*]: No, no, Nora—that will never do.

NORA [*laughs and swings her tambourine*]: Didn't I tell you so!

RANK: Let me play for her.

HELMER [*rising*]: Yes, do—then I can direct her better.

[*Rank sits down to the piano and plays; Nora dances more and more wildly. Helmer stands by the stove and addresses frequent corrections to her; she seems not to hear. Her hair breaks loose, and falls over her shoulders. She does not notice it, but goes on dancing. Mrs. Linden enters and stands spellbound in the doorway.*]

MRS. LINDEN: Ah—!

NORA [*dancing*]: We're having such fun here, Christina!

HELMER: Why, Nora, dear, you're dancing as if it were a matter of life and death.

NORA: So it is.

HELMER: Rank, stop! This is the merest madness, Stop, I say!

[*Rank stops playing, and Nora comes to a sudden standstill.*]

HELMER [*going towards her*]: I couldn't have believed it. You've positively forgotten all I taught you.

NORA [*throws the tambourine away*]: You see for yourself.

HELMER: You really do want teaching.

NORA: Yes, you see how much I need it. You must practise with me up to the last moment. Will you promise me, Torvald?

HELMER: Certainly, certainly.

NORA: Neither today nor tomorrow must you think of anything but me. You mustn't open a single letter—mustn't look at the letter-box.

HELMER: Ah, you're still afraid of that man—

NORA: Oh, yes, yes, I am.

HELMER: Nora, I can see it in your face—there's a letter from him in the box.

NORA: I don't know, I believe so. But you're not to read anything now; nothing ugly must come between us until all is over.

RANK [*softly, to Helmer*]: You mustn't contradict her.

HELMER [*putting his arm around her*]: The child shall have her own way. But tomorrow night, when the dance is over—

NORA: Then you shall be free.

[*Ellen appears in the doorway, right.*]

ELLEN: Dinner is on the table, ma'am.

NORA: We'll have some champagne, Ellen.

ELLEN: Yes, ma'am.

[*Goes out.*]

HELMER: Dear me! Quite a banquet.

NORA: Yes, and we'll keep it up till morning [*Calling out.*] And macaroons, Ellen—plenty—just this once.

HELMER [*seizing her hand.*]: Come, come, don't let us have this wild excitement! Be my own little lark again.

NORA: Oh yes, I will. But now go into the dining-room; and you, too, Doctor Rank. Christina, you must help me to do up my hair.

RANK [*softly, as they go*]: There's nothing in the wind? Nothing—I mean—?

HELMER: Oh no, nothing of the kind. It's merely this babyish anxiety I was telling you about.

[*They go out to the right.*]

NORA: Well?

MRS. LINDEN: He's gone out of town.

NORA: I saw it in your face.

MRS. LINDEN: He comes back tomorrow evening. I left a note for him.

NORA: You shouldn't have done that. Things must take their course. After all, there's something glorious in waiting for the miracle.

MRS. LINDEN: What is it you're waiting for?

NORA: Oh, you can't understand. Go to them in the dining-room; I shall come in a moment.

[*Mrs. Linden goes into the dining-room. Nora stands for a moment as though collecting her thoughts; then looks at her watch.*]

NORA: Five. Seven hours till midnight. Then twenty-four hours till the next midnight. Then the tarantella will be over. Twenty-four and seven? Thirty-one hours to live.

[*Helmer appears at the door, right.*]

HELMER: What has become of my little lark?

NORA [*runs to him with open arms*]: Here she is!

ACT 3

The same room. The table, with the chairs around it, in the middle. A lighted lamp on the table. The door to the hall stands open. Dance music is heard from the floor above.

Mrs. Linden sits by the table and absently turns the pages of a book. She tries to read, but seems unable to fix her attention; she frequently listens and looks anxiously towards the hall door.

MRS. LINDEN [*looks at her watch*]: Not here yet; and the time is nearly up. If only he hasn't—[*listens again*] Ah, there he is. [*She goes into the hall and cautiously opens the outer door; soft footsteps are heard on the stairs; she whispers.*] Come in; there is no one here.

KROGSTAD [*in the doorway*]: I found a note from you at my house. What does it mean?

MRS. LINDEN: I must speak to you.

KROGSTAD: Indeed? And in this house?

MRS. LINDEN: I could not see you at my rooms. They have no separate entrance. Come in; we are quite alone. The servants are asleep, and the Helmers are at the ball upstairs.

KROGSTAD [*coming into the room*]: Ah! So the Helmers are dancing this evening? Really?

MRS. LINDEN: Yes. Why not?

KROGSTAD: Quite right. Why not?

MRS. LINDEN: And now let us talk a little.

KROGSTAD: Have we two anything to say to each other?

MRS. LINDEN: A great deal.

KROGSTAD: I should not have thought so.

MRS. LINDEN: Because you have never really understood me.

KROGSTAD: What was there to understand? The most natural thing in the world—a heartless woman throws a man over when a better match offers.

MRS. LINDEN: Do you really think me so heartless? Do you think I broke with you lightly?

KROGSTAD: Did you not?

MRS. LINDEN: Do you really think so?

KROGSTAD: If not, why did you write me that letter?

MRS. LINDEN: Was it not best? Since I had to break with you, was it not right that I should try to put an end to all that you felt for me?

KROGSTAD [*clenching his hands together*]: So that was it? And all this—for the sake of money!

MRS. LINDEN: You ought not to forget that I had a helpless mother and two little brothers. We could not wait for you, Nils, as your prospects then stood.

KROGSTAD: Perhaps not; but you had no right to cast me off for the sake of others, whoever the others might be.

MRS. LINDEN: I don't know. I have often asked myself whether I had the right.

KROGSTAD [*more softly*]: When I had lost you, I seemed to have no firm ground left under my feet. Look at me now. I am a shipwrecked man clinging to a spar.

MRS. LINDEN: Rescue may be at hand.

KROGSTAD: It was at hand; but then you came and stood in the way.

MRS. LINDEN: Without my knowledge, Nils. I did not know till today that it was you I was to replace in the Bank.

KROGSTAD: Well, I take your word for it. But now that you do know, do you mean to give way?

MRS. LINDEN: No, for that would not help you in the least.

KROGSTAD: Oh, help, help—! I should do it whether or no.

MRS. LINDEN: I have learnt prudence. Life and bitter necessity have schooled me.

KROGSTAD: And life has taught me not to trust fine speeches.

MRS. LINDEN: Then life has taught you a very sensible thing. But deeds you will trust?

KROGSTAD: What do you mean?

MRS. LINDEN: You said you were a shipwrecked man, clinging to a spar.

KROGSTAD: I have good reason to say so.

MRS. LINDEN: I too am shipwrecked, and clinging to a spar. I have no one to mourn for, no one to care for.

KROGSTAD: You made your own choice.

MRS. LINDEN: No choice was left me.

KROGSTAD: Well, what then?

MRS. LINDEN: Nils, how if we two shipwrecked people could join hands?

KROGSTAD: What!

MRS. LINDEN: Two on a raft have a better chance than if each clings to a separate spar.

KROGSTAD: Christina!

MRS. LINDEN: What do you think brought me to town?

KROGSTAD: Had you any thought of me?

MRS. LINDEN: I must have work or I can't bear to live. All my life, as long as I can remember, I have worked; work has been my one great joy. Now I stand quite alone in the world, aimless and forlorn. There is no happiness in working for one self. Nils, give me somebody and something to work for.

KROGSTAD: I cannot believe in all this. It is simply a woman's romantic craving for self-sacrifice.

MRS. LINDEN: Have you ever found me romantic?

KROGSTAD: Would you really—? Tell me: do you know all my past?

MRS. LINDEN: Yes.

KROGSTAD: And do you know what people say of me?

MRS. LINDEN: Did you not say just now that with me you could have been another man?

KROGSTAD: I am sure of it.

MRS. LINDEN: Is it too late?

KROGSTAD: Christina, do you know what you are doing? Yes, you do; I see it in your face. Have you the courage then—?

MRS. LINDEN: I need some one to be a mother to, and your children need a mother. You need me, and I—I need you. Nils, I believe in your better self. With you I fear nothing.

KROGSTAD [seizing her hands]: Thank you—thank you, Christina. Now I shall make others see me as you do.—Ah, I forgot—

MRS. LINDEN [listening]: Hush! The tarantella! Go! go!

KROGSTAD: Why? What is it?

MRS. LINDEN: Don't you hear the dancing overhead? As soon as that is over they will be here.

KROGSTAD: Oh yes, I shall go. Nothing will come of this, after all. Of course, you don't know the step I have taken against the Helmers.

MRS. LINDEN: Yes, Nils, I do know.

KROGSTAD: And yet you have the courage to—?

MRS. LINDEN: I know to what lengths despair can drive a man.

KROGSTAD: Oh, if I could only undo it!

MRS. LINDEN: You could. Your letter is still in the box.

KROGSTAD: Are you sure?

MRS. LINDEN: Yes; but—

KROGSTAD [looking to her searchingly]: Is that what it all means? You want to save your friend at any price. Say it out—is that your idea?

MRS. LINDEN: Nils, a woman who has once sold herself for the sake of others, does not do so again.

KROGSTAD: I shall demand my letter back again.

MRS. LINDEN: No, no.

KROGSTAD: Yes, of course. I shall wait till Helmer comes; I shall tell him to give it back to me—that it's only about my dismissal—that I don't want it read—

MRS. LINDEN: No, Nils, you must not recall the letter.

KROGSTAD: But tell me, wasn't that just why you got me to come here?

MRS. LINDEN: Yes, in my first alarm. But a day has passed since then, and in that day I have seen incredible things in this house. Helmer must know everything; there must be an end to this unhappy secret. These two must come to a full understanding. They must have done with all these shifts and subterfuges.

KROGSTAD: Very well, if you like to risk it. But one thing I can do, and at once—

MRS. LINDEN [listening]: Make haste! Go, go! The dance is over; we're not safe another moment.

KROGSTAD: I shall wait for you in the street.

MRS. LINDEN: Yes, do; you must see me home.

KROGSTAD: I never was so happy in all my life!

[Krogstad goes out by the outer door. The door between the room and the hall remains open.]

MRS. LINDEN [*arranging the room and getting her outdoor things together*]: What a change! What a change! To have some one to work for, to live for; a home to make happy! Well, it shall not be my fault if I fail.—I wish they would come.— [*Listens.*] Ah, here they are! I must get my things on.

[*Takes bonnet and cloak. Helmer's and Nora's voices are heard outside, a key is turned in the lock, and Helmer drags Nora almost by force into the hall. She wears the Italian costume with a large black shawl over it. He is in evening dress and wears a black domino,[3] open.*]

NORA [*struggling with him in the doorway*]: No, no, no! I won't go in! I want to go upstairs again; I don't want to leave so early!

HELMER: But, my dearest girl—!

NORA: Oh, please, please, Torvald, I beseech you—only one hour more!

HELMER: Not one minute more, Nora dear; you know what we agreed. Come, come in; you're catching cold here.

[*He leads her gently into the room in spite of her resistance.*]

MRS. LINDEN: Good evening.

NORA: Christina!

HELMER: What, Mrs. Linden! You here so late?

MRS. LINDEN: Yes, I ought to apologise. I did so want to see Nora in her costume.

NORA: Have you been sitting here waiting for me?

MRS. LINDEN: Yes; unfortunately, I came too late. You had gone upstairs already, and I felt I couldn't go away without seeing you.

HELMER [*taking Nora's shawl off*]: Well, then, just look at her! I assure you she's worth it. Isn't she lovely, Mrs. Linden?

MRS LINDEN: Yes, I must say—

HELMER: Isn't she exquisite? Every one said so. But she's dreadfully obstinate, dear little creature. What's to be done with her? Just think, I had almost to force her away.

NORA: Oh, Torvald, you'll be sorry some day that you didn't let me stay, if only for one half-hour more.

HELMER: There! You hear her, Mrs. Linden? She dances her tarantella with wild applause, and well she deserved it, I must say—though there was, perhaps, a little too much nature in her rendering of the idea—more than was, strictly speaking, artistic. But never mind—the point is, she made a great success, a tremendous success. Was I to let her remain after that—to weaken the impression? Not if I know it. I took my sweet little Capri girl—my capricious little Capri girl, I might say—under my arm; a rapid turn round the room, a curtsey to all sides, and—as they say in novels—the lovely apparition vanished! An exit should always be effective, Mrs. Linden; but I can't get Nora to see it. By Jove! it's warm here. [*Throws his domino on a chair and opens the door to his room.*] What! No light there? Oh, of course. Excuse me—

[*Goes in and lights candles.*]

NORA [*whispers breathlessly*]: Well?

MRS. LINDEN [*softly*]: I've spoken to him.

NORA: And—?

3. A hooded robe with a mask for the eyes.

MRS. LINDEN: Nora—you must tell your husband everything—

NORA [*tonelessly*]: I knew it!

MRS. LINDEN: You have nothing to fear from Krogstad; but you must speak out.

NORA: I shall not speak!

MRS. LINDEN: Then the letter will.

NORA: Thank you, Christina. Now I know what I have to do. Hush—!

HELMER [*coming back*]: Well, Mrs. Linden, have you admired her?

MRS. LINDEN: Yes; and now I must say good-night.

HELMER: What, already? Does this knitting belong to you?

MRS. LINDEN [*takes it*]: Yes, thanks; I was nearly forgetting it.

HELMER: Then you do knit?

MRS. LINDEN: Yes.

HELMER: Do you know, you ought to embroider instead?

MRS. LINDEN: Indeed! Why?

HELMER: Because it's so much prettier. Look now! You hold the embroidery in the left hand, so, and then work the needle with the right hand, in a long, graceful curve—don't you?

MRS. LINDEN: Yes, I suppose so.

HELMER: But knitting is always ugly. Just look—your arms close to your sides, and the needles going up and down—there's something Chinese about it.—They really gave us splendid champagne tonight.

MRS. LINDEN: Well, good-night, Nora, and don't be obstinate any more.

HELMER: Well said, Mrs. Linden!

MRS. LINDEN: Good-night, Mr. Helmer.

HELMER [*accompanying her to the door*]: Good-night, good-night; I hope you'll get safely home. I should be glad to—but you have such a short way to go. Good-night, good-night. [*She goes; Helmer shuts the door after her and comes forward again.*] At last we've got rid of her; she's a terrible bore.

NORA: Aren't you very tired, Torvald?

HELMER: No, not in the least.

NORA: Nor sleepy?

HELMER: Not a bit. I feel particularly lively. But you? You do look tired and sleepy.

NORA: Yes, very tired. I shall soon sleep now.

HELMER: There, you see. I was right, after all, not to let you stay longer.

NORA: Oh, everything you do is right.

HELMER [*kissing her forehead*]: Now my lark is speaking like a reasonable being. Did you notice how jolly Rank was this evening?

NORA: Indeed? Was he? I had no chance of speaking to him.

HELMER: Nor I, much; but I haven't seen him in such good spirits for a long time. [*Looks at Nora a little, then comes nearer her.*] It's splendid to be back in our own home, to be quite alone together!—Oh, you enchanting creature!

NORA: Don't look at me in that way, Torvald.

HELMER: I am not to look at my dearest treasure?—at all the loveliness that is mine, mine only, wholly and entirely mine?

NORA [*goes to the other side of the table*]: You mustn't say these things to me this evening.

HELMER [*following*]: I see you have the tarantella still in your blood—and that makes you all the more enticing. Listen! the other people are going now. [*More softly.*] Nora—soon the whole house will be still.

NORA: Yes, I hope so.

HELMER: Yes, don't you, Nora darling? When we are among strangers, do you know why I speak so little to you, and keep so far away, and only steal a glance at you now and then—do you know why I do it? Because I am fancying that we love each other in secret, that I am secretly betrothed to you, and that no one dreams that there is anything between us.

NORA: Yes, yes, yes. I know all your thoughts are with me.

HELMER: And then, when the time comes to go, and I put the shawl about your smooth, soft shoulders, and this glorious neck of yours, I imagine you are my bride, that our marriage is just over, that I am bringing you for the first time to my home—that I am alone with you for the first time—quite alone with you, in your trembling love-liness! All this evening I have been longing for you, and you only. When I watched you swaying and whirling in the tarantella—my blood boiled—I could endure it no longer; and that's why I made you come home with me so early—

NORA: Go now, Torvald! Go away from me. I won't have all this.

HELMER: What do you mean? Ah, I see you're teasing me, little Nora! Won't—won't! Am I not your husband—?

[*A knock at the outer door.*]

NORA [*starts*]: Did you hear—?

HELMER [*going towards the hall*]: Who's there?

RANK [*outside*]: It is I; may I come in for a moment?

HELMER [*in a low tone, annoyed*]: Oh! what can he want just now? [*Aloud.*] Wait a moment. [*Opens door.*] Come, it's nice of you to look in.

RANK: I thought I heard your voice, and that put it into my head. [*Looks round.*] Ah, this dear old place! How cosy you two are here!

HELMER: You seemed to find it pleasant enough upstairs, too.

RANK: Exceedingly. Why not? Why shouldn't one take one's share of everything in this world? All one can, at least, and as long as one can. The wine was splendid—

HELMER: Especially the champagne.

RANK: Did you notice it? It's incredible the quantity I contrived to get down.

NORA: Torvald drank plenty of champagne, too.

RANK: Did he?

NORA: Yes, and it always puts him in such spirits.

RANK: Well, why shouldn't one have a jolly evening after a well-spent day?

HELMER: Well-spent! Well, I haven't much to boast of in that respect.

RANK [*slapping him on the shoulder*]: But I have, don't you see?

NORA: I suppose you have been engaged in a scientific investigation, Doctor Rank?

RANK: Quite right.

HELMER: Bless me! Little Nora talking about scientific investigations!

NORA: Am I to congratulate you on the result?

RANK: By all means.

NORA: It was good then?

RANK: The best possible, both for doctor and patient—certainty.

NORA [*quickly and searchingly*]: Certainty?

RANK: Absolute certainty. Wasn't I right to enjoy myself after that?

NORA: Yes, quite right, Doctor Rank.

HELMER: And so say I, provided you don't have to pay for it tomorrow.

RANK: Well, in this life nothing is to be had for nothing.

NORA: Doctor Rank—I'm sure you are very fond of masquerades?

RANK: Yes, when there are plenty of amusing disguises—

NORA: Tell me, what shall we two be at our next masquerade?

HELMER: Little featherbrain! Thinking of your next already!

RANK: We two? I'll tell you. You must go as a good fairy.

HELMER: Ah, but what costume would indicate that?

RANK: She has simply to wear her everyday dress.

HELMER: Capital! But don't you know what you will be yourself?

RANK: Yes, my dear friend, I am perfectly clear upon that point.

HELMER: Well?

RANK: At the next masquerade I shall be invisible.

HELMER: What a comical idea!

RANK: There's a big black hat—haven't you heard of the invisible hat? It comes down all over you, and then no one can see you.

HELMER [*with a suppressed smile*]: No, you're right there.

RANK: But I'm quite forgetting what I came for, Helmer, give me a cigar—one of the dark Havanas.

HELMER: With the greatest pleasure. [*Hands cigar-case.*]

RANK [*takes one and cuts the end off*]: Thank you.

NORA [*striking a wax match*]: Let me give you a light.

RANK: A thousand thanks.

[*She holds the match. He lights his cigar at it.*]

RANK: And now, good-bye!

HELMER: Good-bye, good-bye, my dear fellow.

NORA: Sleep well, Doctor Rank.

RANK: Thanks for the wish.

NORA: Wish me the same.

RANK: You? Very well, since you ask me—Sleep well. And thanks for the light.

[*He nods to them both and goes out.*]

HELMER [*in an undertone*]: He's been drinking a good deal.

NORA [*absently*]: I daresay. [*Helmer takes his bunch of keys from his pocket and goes into the hall.*] Torvald, what are you doing there?

HELMER: I must empty the letter-box; it's quite full; there will be no room for the newspapers tomorrow morning.

NORA: Are you going to work tonight?

HELMER: You know very well I am not.—Why, how is this? Some one has been at the lock.

NORA: The lock—?

HELMER: I'm sure of it. What does it mean? I can't think that the servants—? Here's a broken hair-pin. Nora, it's one of yours.

NORA [*quickly*]: It must have been the children—

HELMER: Then you must break them of such tricks.—There! At last I've got it open. [*Takes contents out and calls into the kitchen.*] Ellen!—Ellen, just put the hall door lamp out.

[*He returns with letters in his hand, and shuts the inner door.*]

HELMER: Just see how they've accumulated. [*Turning them over.*] Why, what's this?

NORA [*at the window*]: The letter! Oh no, no, Torvald!

HELMER: Two visiting-cards—from Rank.

NORA: From Doctor Rank?

HELMER [*looking at them*]: Doctor Rank. They were on the top. He must just have put them in.

NORA: Is there anything on them?

HELMER: There's a black cross over the name. Look at it. What an unpleasant idea! It looks just as if he were announcing his own death.

NORA: So he is.

HELMER: What! Do you know anything? Has he told you anything?

NORA: Yes. These cards mean that he has taken his last leave of us. He is going to shut himself up and die.

HELMER: Poor fellow! Of course. I knew we couldn't hope to keep him long. But so soon—! And to go and creep into his lair like a wounded animal—

NORA: When we must go, it is best to go silently. Don't you think so, Torvald?

HELMER [*walking up and down*]: He had so grown into our lives, I can't realise that he is gone. He and his sufferings and his loneliness formed a sort of cloudy background to the sunshine of our happiness.—Well, perhaps it's best as it is—at any rate for him. [*Stands still.*] And perhaps for us, too, Nora. Now we two are thrown entirely upon each other. [*Takes her in his arms.*] My darling wife! I feel as if I could never hold you close enough. Do you know, Nora, I often wish some danger might threaten you, that I might risk body and soul, and everything, everything, for your dear sake.

NORA [*tears herself from him and says firmly*]: Now you shall read your letters, Torvald.

HELMER: No, no; not tonight. I want to be with you, my sweet wife.

NORA: With the thought of your dying friend—?

HELMER: You are right. This has shaken us both. Unloveliness has come between us—thoughts of death and decay. We must seek to cast them off. Till then—we will remain apart.

NORA [*her arms round his neck*]: Torvald! Good-night! good-night!

HELMER [*kissing her forehead*]: Good-night, my little song-bird. Sleep well, Nora. Now I shall go and read my letters.

[*He goes with the letters in his hand into his room and shuts the door.*]

NORA [*with wild eyes, gropes about her, seizes Helmer's domino, throws it round her, and whispers quickly, hoarsely, and brokenly*]: Never to see him again. Never, never, never. [*Throws her shawl over her head.*] Never to see the children again. Never, never.—Oh that black, icy water! Oh that bottomless—! If it were only over! Now he has it; he's reading it. Oh, no, no, no, not yet. Torvald, good-bye—! Good-bye, my little ones—!

[*She is rushing out by the hall; at the same moment Helmer flings his door open, and stands there with an open letter in his hand*]

HELMER: Nora!

NORA [*shrieks*]: Ah—!

HELMER: What is this? Do you know what is in this letter?

NORA: Yes, I know. Let me go! Let me pass!

HELMER [*holds her back*]: Where do you want to go?

NORA [*tries to break away from him*]: You shall not save me, Torvald.

HELMER [*falling back*]: True! Is what he writes true? No, no, it is impossible that this can be true.

NORA: It is true. I have loved you beyond all else in the world.

HELMER: Pshaw—no silly evasions!

NORA [*a step nearer him*]: Torvald—!

HELMER: Wretched woman—what have you done?

NORA: Let me go—you shall not save me! You shall not take my guilt upon yourself!

HELMER: I don't want any melodramatic airs. [*Locks the outer door.*] Here you shall stay and give an account of yourself. Do you understand what you have done? Answer! Do you understand it?

NORA [*looks at him fixedly, and says with a stiffening expression*]: Yes; now I begin fully to understand it.

HELMER [*walking up and down*]: Oh! what an awful awakening! During all these eight years—she who was my pride and my joy—a hypocrite, a liar—worse, worse—a criminal. Oh, the unfathomable hideousness of it all! Ugh! Ugh!

[*Nora says nothing, and continues to look fixedly at him.*]

HELMER: I ought to have known how it would be. I ought to have foreseen it. All your father's want of principle—be silent!—all your father's want of principle you have inherited—no religion, no morality, no sense of duty. How I am punished for screening him! I did it for your sake; and you reward me like this.

NORA: Yes—like this.

HELMER: You have destroyed my whole happiness. You have ruined my future. Oh, it's frightful to think of! I am in the power of a scoundrel; he can do whatever he pleases with me, demand whatever he chooses; he can domineer over me as much as he likes, and I must submit. And all this disaster and ruin is brought upon me by an unprincipled woman!

NORA: When I am out of the world, you will be free.

HELMER: Oh, no fine phrases. Your father, too, was always ready with them. What good would it do me, if you were "out of the world," as you say? No good whatever! He can publish the story all the same; I might even be suspected of collusion. People will think I was at the bottom of it all and egged you on. And for all this I have you to thank—you whom I have done nothing but pet and spoil during our whole married life. Do you understand now what you have done to me?

NORA [*with cold calmness*]: Yes.

HELMER: The thing is so incredible, I can't grasp it. But we must come to an understanding. Take that shawl off. Take it off, I say! I must try to pacify him in one way or another—the matter must be hushed up, cost what it may.—As for you and me, we must make no outward change in our way of life—no outward change, you understand. Of course, you will continue to live here. But the children cannot be left in your care. I dare not trust them to you.—Oh, to have to say this to one I have loved so tenderly—whom I still—! But that must be a thing of the past. Henceforward there can be no question of happiness, but merely of saving the ruins, the shreds, the show—[*A ring; Helmer starts.*] What's that? So late! Can it be the worst? Can he—? Hide yourself, Nora; say you are ill.

[*Nora stands motionless. Helmer goes to the door and opens it.*]

ELLEN [*half dressed, in the hall*]: Here is a letter for you, ma'am.

HELMER: Give it to me. [*Seizes the letter and shuts the door.*] Yes, from him. You
shall not have it. I shall read it.

NORA: Read it!

HELMER [*by the lamp*]: I have hardly the courage to. We may both be lost, both you
and I. Ah! I must know. [*Hastily tears the letter open; reads a few lines, looks at
an enclosure; with a cry of joy.*] Nora!

[*Nora looks inquiringly at him.*]

HELMER: Nora!—Oh! I must read it again.—Yes, yes, it is so. I am saved! Nora, I
am saved!

NORA: And I?

HELMER: You too, of course; we are both saved, both of us. Look here—he sends you
back your promissory note. He writes that he regrets and apologises that a happy
turn in his life—Oh, what matter what he writes. We are saved, Nora! No one can
harm you. Oh, Nora, Nora—; but first to get rid of this hateful thing. I'll just see—
[*Glances at the I.O.U.*] No, I will not look at it; the whole thing shall be nothing
but a dream to me. [*Tears the I.O.U. and both letters in pieces. Throws them into
the fire and watches them burn.*] There! it's gone!—He said that ever since Christmas Eve—Oh, Nora, they must have been three terrible days for you!

NORA: I have fought a hard fight for the last three days.

HELMER: And in your agony you saw no other outlet but—No; we won't think of that
horror. We will only rejoice and repeat—it's over, all over! Don't you hear, Nora?
You don't seem able to grasp it. Yes, it's over. What is this set look on your face?
Oh, my poor Nora, I understand you cannot believe that I have forgiven you. But I
have, Nora; I swear it. I have forgiven everything. I know that what you did was all
for love of me.

NORA: That is true.

HELMER: You loved me as a wife should love her husband. It was only the means that,
in your inexperience, you misjudged. But do you think I love you the less because
you cannot do without guidance? No, no. Only lean on me; I will counsel you, and
guide you. I should be no true man if this very womanly helplessness did not make
you doubly dear in my eyes. You mustn't dwell upon the hard things I said in my
first moment of terror, when the world seemed to be tumbling about my ears. I
have forgiven you, Nora—I swear I have forgiven you.

NORA: I thank you for your forgiveness.

[*Goes out, to the right.*]

HELMER: No, stay—! [*Looking through the doorway.*] What are you going to do?

NORA [*inside*]: To take off my masquerade dress.

HELMER [*in the doorway*]: Yes, do, dear. Try to calm down, and recover your balance,
my scared little song-bird. You may rest secure. I have broad wings to shield you.
[*Walking up and down near the door.*] Oh, how lovely—how cosy our home is,
Nora! Here you are safe; here I can shelter you like a hunted dove whom I have
saved from the claws of the hawk. I shall soon bring your poor beating heart to
rest; believe me, Nora, very soon. Tomorrow all this will seem quite different—
everything will be as before. I shall not need to tell you again that I forgive you;
you will feel for yourself that it is true. How could you think I could find it in my
heart to drive you away, or even so much as to reproach you? Oh, you don't know
a true man's heart, Nora. There is something indescribably sweet and soothing to a

man in having forgiven his wife—honestly forgiven her, from the bottom of his heart. She becomes his property in a double sense. She is as though born again; she has become, so to speak, at once his wife and his child. That is what you shall henceforth be to me, my bewildered, helpless darling. Don't be troubled about anything, Nora; only open your heart to me, and I will be both will and conscience to you. [*Nora enters in everyday dress.*] Why, what's this? Not gone to bed? You have changed your dress?

NORA: Yes, Torvald; now I have changed my dress.

HELMER: But why now, so late—?

NORA: I shall not sleep to-night.

HELMER: But, Nora dear—

NORA [*looking at her watch*]: It's not so late yet. Sit down, Torvald; you and I have much to say to each other.[*She sits at one side of the table.*]

HELMER: Nora—what does this mean? Your cold, set face—

NORA: Sit down. It will take some time. I have much to talk over with you.

[*Helmer sits at the other side of the table.*]

HELMER: You alarm me, Nora. I don't understand you.

NORA: No, that is just it. You don't understand me; and I have never understood you—till tonight. No, don't interrupt. Only listen to what I say.—We must come to a final settlement, Torvald.

HELMER: How do you mean?

NORA [*after a short silence*]: Does not one thing strike you as we sit here?

HELMER: What should strike me?

NORA: We have been married eight years. Does it not strike you that this is the first time we two, you and I, man and wife, have talked together seriously?

HELMER: Seriously! What do you call seriously?

NORA: During eight whole years, and more—ever since the day we first met—we have never exchanged one serious word about serious things.

HELMER: Was I always to trouble you with the cares you could not help me to bear?

NORA: I am not talking of cares. I say that we have never yet set ourselves seriously to get to the bottom of anything.

HELMER: Why, my dearest Nora, what have you to do with serious things?

NORA: There we have it! You have never understood me.—I have had great injustice done me, Torvald; first by father, and then by you.

HELMER: What! By your father and me?—By us, who have loved you more than all the world?

NORA [*shaking her head*]: You have never loved me. You only thought it amusing to be in love with me.

HELMER: Why, Nora, what a thing to say!

NORA: Yes, it is so, Torvald. While I was at home with father, he used to tell me all his opinions, and I held the same opinions. If I had others, I said nothing about them, because he wouldn't have liked it. He used to call me his doll-child, and played with me as I played with my dolls. Then I came to live in your house—

HELMER: What an expression to use about our marriage!

NORA [*undisturbed*]: I mean I passed from father's hands into yours. You arranged everything according to your taste; and I got the same tastes as you; or I pretended to—I don't know which—both ways, perhaps; sometimes one and sometimes the other. When I look back on it now, I seem to have been living here like a beggar, from hand to mouth. I lived by performing tricks for you, Torvald. But you would have it so. You and father have done me a great wrong. It is your fault that my life has come to nothing.

HELMER: Why, Nora, how unreasonable and ungrateful you are! Have you not been happy here?

NORA: No, never. I thought I was; but I never was.

HELMER: Not—not happy!

NORA: No; only merry. And you have always been so kind to me. But our house has been nothing but a play-room. Here I have been your doll-wife, just as at home I used to be papa's doll-child. And the children, in their turn, have been my dolls. I thought it fun when you played with me, just as the children did when I played with them. That has been our marriage, Torvald.

HELMER: There is some truth in what you say, exaggerated and overstrained though it be. But henceforth it shall be different. Play-time is over; now comes the time for education.

NORA: Whose education? Mine, or the children's?

HELMER: Both, my dear Nora.

NORA: Oh, Torvald, you are not the man to teach me to be a fit wife for you.

HELMER: And you can say that?

NORA: And I—how have I prepared myself to educate the children?

HELMER: Nora!

NORA: Did you not say yourself, a few minutes ago, you dared not trust them to me?

HELMER: In the excitement of the moment! Why should you dwell upon that?

NORA: No—you were perfectly right. That problem is beyond me. There is another to be solved first—I must try to educate myself. You are not the man to help me in that. I must set about it alone. And that is why I am leaving you.

HELMER [jumping up]: What—do you mean to say—?

NORA: I must stand quite alone if I am ever to know myself and my surroundings; so I cannot stay with you.

HELMER: Nora! Nora!

NORA: I am going at once. I daresay Christina will take me in for tonight—

HELMER: You are mad! I shall not allow it! I forbid it!

NORA: It is of no use your forbidding me anything now. I shall take with me what belongs to me. From you I will accept nothing, either now or afterwards.

HELMER: What madness this is!

NORA: Tomorrow I shall go home—I mean to what was my home. It will be easier for me to find some opening there.

HELMER: Oh, in your blind inexperience—

NORA: I must try to gain experience, Torvald.

HELMER: To forsake your home, your husband, and your children! And you don't consider what the world will say.

NORA: I can pay no heed to that. I only know that I must do it.

HELMER: This is monstrous! Can you forsake your holiest duties in this way?

NORA: What do you consider my holiest duties?

HELMER: Do I need to tell you that? Your duties to your husband and your children.

NORA: I have other duties equally sacred.

HELMER: Impossible! What duties do you mean?

NORA: My duties towards myself.

HELMER: Before all else you are a wife and a mother.

NORA: That I no longer believe. I believe that before all else I am a human being, just as much as you are—or at least that I should try to become one. I know that most people agree with you, Torvald, and that they say so in books. But henceforth I can't be satisfied with what most people say, and what is in books. I must think things out for myself, and try to get clear about them.

HELMER: Are you not clear about your place in your own home? Have you not an infallible guide in questions like these? Have you not religion?

NORA: Oh, Torvald, I don't really know what religion is.

HELMER: What do you mean?

NORA: I know nothing but what Pastor Hansen told me when I was confirmed. He explained that religion was this and that. When I get away from all this and stand alone, I will look into that matter too. I will see whether what he taught me is right, or, at any rate, whether it is right for me.

HELMER: Oh, this is unheard of! And from so young a woman! But if religion cannot keep you right, let me appeal to your conscience—for I suppose you have some moral feeling? Or, answer me: perhaps you have none?

NORA: Well, Torvald, it's not easy to say. I really don't know—I am all at sea about these things. I only know that I think quite differently from you about them. I hear, too, that the laws are different from what I thought; but I can't believe that they can be right. It appears that a woman has no right to spare her dying father, or to save her husband's life! I don't believe that.

HELMER: You talk like a child. You don't understand the society in which you live.

NORA: No, I do not. But now I shall try to learn. I must make up my mind which is right—society or I.

HELMER: Nora, you are ill; you are feverish; I almost think you are out of your senses.

NORA: I have never felt so much clearness and certainty as tonight.

HELMER: You are clear and certain enough to forsake husband and children?

NORA: Yes, I am.

HELMER: Then there is only one explanation possible.

NORA: What is that?

HELMER: You no longer love me.

NORA: No; that is just it.

HELMER: Nora!—Can you say so!

NORA: Oh, I'm so sorry, Torvald; for you've always been so kind to me. But I can't help it. I do not love you any longer.

HELMER [*mastering himself with difficulty*]: Are you clear and certain on this point too?

NORA: Yes, quite. That is why I will not stay here any longer.

HELMER: And can you also make clear to me how I have forfeited your love?

NORA: Yes, I can. It was this evening, when the miracle did not happen; for then I saw you were not the man I had imagined.

HELMER: Explain yourself more clearly; I don't understand.

NORA: I have waited so patiently all these eight years; for of course, I saw clearly enough that miracles don't happen every day. When this crushing blow threatened me, I said to myself so confidently, "Now comes the miracle!" When Krogstad's letter lay in the box, it never for a moment occurred to me that you would think of submitting to that man's conditions. I was convinced that you would say to him, "Make it known to all the world"; and that then—

HELMER: Well? When I had given my own wife's name up to disgrace and shame—?

NORA: Then I firmly believed that you would come forward, take everything upon yourself, and say, "I am the guilty one."

HELMER: Nora—!

NORA: You mean I would never have accepted such a sacrifice? No, certainly not. But what would my assertions have been worth in opposition to yours?—That was the miracle that I hoped for and dreaded. And it was to hinder that that I wanted to die.

HELMER: I would gladly work for you day and night, Nora—bear sorrow and want for your sake. But no man sacrifices his honour, even for one he loves.

NORA: Millions of women have done so.

HELMER: Oh, you think and talk like a silly child.

NORA: Very likely. But you neither think nor talk like the man I can share my life with. When your terror was over—not for what threatened me, but for yourself—when there was nothing more to fear—then it seemed to you as though nothing had happened. I was your lark again, your doll, just as before—whom you would take twice as much care of in future, because she was so weak and fragile. [*Stands up.*] Torvald—in that moment it burst upon me that I had been living here these eight years with a strange man, and had borne him three children.—Oh, I can't bear to think of it! I could tear myself to pieces!

HELMER [*sadly*]: I see it, I see it; an abyss has opened between us.—But, Nora, can it never be filled up?

NORA: As I now am, I am no wife for you.

HELMER: I have strength to become another man.

NORA: Perhaps—when your doll is taken away from you.

HELMER: To part—to part from you! No, Nora, no; I can't grasp the thought.

NORA [*going out, right*]: All the more reason why is has to be. [*She reenters with her coat and a traveling-bag, which she puts on a chair by the table.*]

HELMER: Nora, Nora, not now! Wait until tomorrow.

NORA: I can't spend the night in a strange man's room.

HELMER: But couldn't we live here like brother and sister—

NORA: You know very well how long that would last. [*Throws her shawl over her shoulders.*] Good-bye, Torvald. I won't look in on the children. I know they're in better hands than mine. The way I am now, I'm no use to them.

HELMER: But someday, Nora—someday—?

NORA: How can I tell? I haven't the least idea what'll become of me.

HELMER: But you're my wife, now and wherever you go.

NORA: Listen, Torvald—when a wife deserts her husband's house, as I am doing, I have heard that in the eyes of the law he is free from all duties toward her. At any rate, I release you from all duties. You must not feel yourself bound, any more than I shall. There must be perfect freedom on both sides. There, I give you back your ring. Give me mine.

HELMER: That too?

NORA: That too.

HELMER: Here it is.

NORA: Very well. Now it is all over. I lay the keys here. The servants know about everything in the house—better than I do. Tomorrow, when I have started, Christina will come to pack up the things I brought with me from home. I will have them sent after me.

HELMER: All over! All over! Nora, will you never think of me again?

NORA: Oh, I shall often think of you, and the children, and this house.

HELMER: May I write to you, Nora?

NORA: No—never. You must not.

HELMER: But I must send you—

NORA: Nothing, nothing.

HELMER: I must help you if you need it.

NORA: No, I say. I take nothing from strangers.

HELMER: Nora—can I never be more than a stranger to you?

NORA [taking her traveling-bag]: Oh, Torvald, then the miracle of miracles would have to happen—

HELMER: What is the miracle of miracles?

NORA: Both of us would have to change so that—Oh, Torvald, I no longer believe in miracles.

HELMER: But I will believe. Tell me! We must so change that—?

NORA: That communion between us shall be a marriage. Good-bye. [She goes out by the hall door.]

HELMER [sinks into a chair by the door with his face in his hands]: Nora! Nora! [He looks around and rises.] Empty. She is gone. [A hope springs up in him.] Ah! The miracle of miracles—?!

[From below is heard the reverberation of a heavy door closing.]

THE END

Higuchi Ichiyo
1872–1896

In her short, meteoric career, Higuchi Ichiyo established herself as one of the pioneering fiction writers of the Meiji era—the period of major reform in Japan under the emperor Meiji (r. 1868–1912). Her family both benefitted and suffered from the period's dramatic social and cultural changes. Her parents came from prosperous provincial peasant stock; seeking to move up in society, they had come to the city of Edo in 1857, a decade before the new emperor renamed the city Tokyo and established it as the capital of modern Japan. Her father gained a foothold in the municipal bureaucracy, received promotions, and began to speculate in real estate. He was able to see to it that his second daughter, Natsuko, received an excellent classical education once she began early on to exhibit a precocious love of literature. In her adolescence, though, the budding poet was kept out of school for several years by her mother, who felt she should be learning housekeeping rather than Chinese verse forms. She persisted in reading and in attending poetry groups, and at age nineteen set her sights on becoming a professional writer—an exceptional goal for a woman of her time and place. She took the lofty pen name of Ichiyo, "One Leaf," a term associated with the contemplative founder of Zen Buddhism.

By this point, her family fortunes had sharply declined. Her father had been edged out in a reorganization of the city bureaucracy, and then invested in a disastrously unsuccessful carting business, started up with some unreliable associates without proper funding or organization. His spirits and health declined after Ichiyo's beloved older brother, Sentaro, died of consumption (tuberculosis), and he himself died not long thereafter, probably of consumption as well. In 1890 Ichiyo and her mother and sister had to begin taking in laundry and sewing to get by, and

Ichiyo worked as a housemaid for her poetry teacher. Even so, she refused to abandon her literary dreams, shifting her focus from poetry to prose after a friend published a successful novel. She found a mentor in a commercial novelist named Nakarai Tosui, and began to write stories, though she could never accommodate herself to the breezy, casual style favored by Tosui and the popular magazines that serialized his work.

Until the late 1880s fiction in modern Japan had been considered light entertainment at best, though as Western novels began to be translated after 1868, a new vogue arose for European realism and the cool scientific objectivity of Naturalism. Ichiyo, however, was obsessed with classic women's writing of the medieval Heian period, especially Murasaki's *Tale of Genji* and the *Pillow Book* of the court lady Sei Shōnagon (see Volume B for both writers). Ichiyo's writing gained resonance from her reading of the great seventeenth-century prose writer Ihara Saikaku, whose *Life of a Sensuous Woman* (see Volume D) had inaugurated a new realism in stories of love and of economic struggles among the nascent middle class. As Ichiyo's stories began to achieve publication in literary journals, her fellow writers saw in her a compelling fusion of old and new. Reviewing Ichiyo's novella *Child's Play,* a prominent novelist, Mori Ogai, wrote that "What is extraordinary about *Child's Play* is that the characters are not those beastlike creatures one so often encounters in Ibsen or Zola, whose techniques the so-called naturalists have tried imitating to the utmost. They are real, human individuals that we laugh and cry with. . . . I do not hesitate to confer on Ichiyo the title of a true poet."

Ichiyo was indeed bringing the eye of a poet to the highly prosaic surroundings of Tokyo's seedy commercial district. In 1893 she and her mother and sister had opened a small stationery shop on the edge of the downtown "pleasure district," and here she came to know the street waifs and the second-rank courtesans or geishas whom she would treat with a deeply sympathetic, unjudgmental irony in her stories. The store failed after nine months, whereupon Ichiyo returned to housework, while her mother and sister worked as seamstresses for low-ranking geishas. Her fiction progressed by leaps and bounds over the next two years, and in 1896 she had stories published monthly in leading journals. Autograph-seekers began to appear at the tiny house she shared with her mother and sister, and she was offered contracts that would have secured her as Japan's first woman writer to fully support herself by her writing. By this time, however, she was seriously ill with consumption; she died in November, at the age of twenty-four.

"Separate Ways" was her last completed story, and it encapsulates all of her major themes, in the intense but fragile friendship between a street urchin and a young woman caught in the marginal life of a seamstress. In its clear observation, its understated eloquence, and its avoidance of melodrama, "Separate Ways" can be compared to the short stories of Chekhov (page 937) and Tagore (page 949), as well as to the stories that James Joyce and Premchand would be writing a decade later (see Volume F). Its haunting portrayal of a pivotal moment in two lives makes "Separate Ways" a consummate tragedy of everyday life.

PRONUNCIATIONS:

Higuchi Ichiyo: he-gou-chee ee-chee-yo
Okyo: oh-k'yoh
Kichizo: key-chee-zoh

Separate Ways[1]

There was someone outside, tapping at her window.

"Okyō? Are you home?"

"Who is it? I'm already in bed," she lied. "Come back in the morning."

"I don't care if you are in bed. Open up! It's me—Kichizō, from the umbrella shop."

---

1. Translated by Robert Lyons Danly.

"What a bothersome boy you are. Why do you come so late at night? I suppose you want some rice cakes again," she chuckled. "Just a minute. I'm coming."

Okyō, a stylish woman in her early twenties, put her sewing down and hurried into the front hall. Her abundant hair was tied back simply—she was too busy to fuss with it—and over her kimono she wore a long apron and a jacket. She opened the lattice, then the storm door.

"Sorry," Kichizō said as he barged in.

Dwarf, they called him. He was a pugnacious little one. He was sixteen, and he worked as an apprentice at the umbrella shop, but to look at him one would think he was eleven or twelve. He had spindly shoulders and a small face. He was a bright-looking boy, but so short that people teased him and dubbed him "Dwarf."

"Pardon me." He went right for the brazier.

"You won't find enough fire in there to toast any of your rice cakes. Go get some charcoal from the cinder box in the kitchen. You can heat the cakes yourself. I've got to get this done tonight." She took up her sewing again. "The owner of the pawnshop on the corner ordered it to wear on New Year's."

"Hmm. What a waste, on that old baldie. Why don't I wear it first?"

"Don't be ridiculous. Don't you know what they say? 'He who wears another's clothes will never get anywhere in life.' You're a hopeless one, you are. You shouldn't say such things."

"I never did expect to be successful. I'll wear anybody's clothes—it's all the same to me. Remember what you promised once? When your luck changes, you said you'd make me a good kimono. Will you really?" He wasn't joking now.

"If only I could sew you a nice kimono, it would be a happy day. I'd gladly do it. But look at me. I don't have enough money to dress myself properly. I'm sewing to support myself. These aren't gifts I'm making." She smiled at him. "It's a dream, that promise."

"That's all right. I'm not asking for it now. Wait until some good luck comes. At least say you will. Don't you want to make me happy? That would be a sight, though, wouldn't it?" The boy had a wistful smile on his face. "Me dressed up in a fancy kimono!"

"And if you succeed first, Kichizō, promise me you'll do the same. That's a pledge I'd like to see come true."

"Don't count on it. I'm not going to succeed."

"How do you know?"

"I know, that's all. Even if someone came along and insisted on helping me, I'd still rather stay where I am. Oiling umbrellas suits me fine. I was born to wear a plain kimono with workman's sleeves and a short band around my waist. To me, all 'good luck' means is squeezing a little money from the change when I'm sent to buy persimmon juice.[2] If I hit the target someday, shooting arrows through a bamboo pole, that's about all the good luck I can hope for. But someone like you, from a good family—why, fortune will come to greet you in a carriage. I don't mean a man's going to come and take you for his mistress, or something. Don't get the wrong idea." He toyed with the fire in the brazier and sighed over his fate.

"It won't be a fine carriage that comes for me. I'll be going to hell in a handcart." Okyō leaned against her yardstick and turned to Kichizō. "I've had so many troubles on my mind, sometimes it feels as if my heart's on fire."

2. Used in waterproofing umbrellas.

Kichizō went to fetch the charcoal from the kitchen, as he always did.

"Aren't you going to have any rice cakes?"

Okyō shook her head. "No thank you."

"Then I'll go ahead. That old tightwad at the umbrella shop is always complaining. He doesn't know how to treat people properly. I was sorry when the old woman died. *She* was never like that. These new people! I don't talk to any of them. Okyō, what do you think of Hanji at the shop? He's a mean one, isn't he? He's so stuck-up. He's the owner's son, but, you know, I still can't think of him as a future boss. Whenever I have the chance, I like to pick a fight and cut him down to size." Kichizō set the rice cakes on the wire net above the brazier. "Oh, it's hot!" he shouted, blowing on his fingers. "I wonder why it is—you seem almost like a sister to me, Okyō. Are you sure you never had a younger brother?"

"I was an only child. I never had any brothers or sisters."

"So there really is no connection between us. Boy, I'd sure be glad if someone like you would come and tell me she was my sister. I'd hug her so tight . . . After that, I wouldn't care if I died. What was I, born from a piece of wood? I've never run into anyone who was a relative of mine. You don't know how many times I've thought about it: if I'm never, ever going to meet anyone from my own family, I'd be better off dying right now. Wouldn't I? But it's odd. I still want to go on living. I have this funny dream. The few people who've been the least bit kind to me all of a sudden turn out to be my mother and father and my brother and sister. And then I think, I want to live a little longer. Maybe if I wait another year, someone will tell me the truth. So I go on oiling umbrellas, even if it doesn't interest me a bit. Do you suppose there's anyone in the world as strange as I am? I don't have a mother or a father, Okyō. How could a child be born without either parent? It makes me pretty odd." He tapped at the rice cakes and decided they were done.

"Don't you have some kind of proof of your identity? A charm with your name on it, for instance? There must be something you have, some clue to your family's whereabouts."

"Nothing. My friends used to tease me. They said I was left underneath a bridge when I was born, so I'd be taken for a beggar's baby. It may be true. Who knows? I may be the child of a tramp. One of those men who pass by in rags every day could be a kinsman. That old crippled lady with one eye who comes begging every morning— for all I know, she could be my mother. I used to wear a lion's mask and do acrobatics in the street," he said dejectedly, "before I worked at the umbrella shop. Okyō, if I were a beggar's boy, you wouldn't have been so nice to me, would you? You wouldn't have given me a second look."

"You shouldn't joke like that, Kichizō. I don't know what kind of people your parents were, but it makes no difference to me. These silly things you're saying— you're not yourself tonight. If I were you, I wouldn't let it bother me. Even if I were the child of an outcast. I'd make something of myself, whether I had any parents or not, no matter who my brothers were. Why are you whining around so?"

"I don't know," he said, staring at the floor. "There's something wrong with me. I don't seem to have any get-up-and-go."

She was dead now, but in the last generation the old woman Omatsu, fat as a *sumō* wrestler, had made a tidy fortune at the umbrella shop. It was a winter's night six years before that she had picked up Kichizō, performing his tumbler's act along the road, as she was returning from a pilgrimage.

"It's all right," she had assured him. "If the master gives us any trouble, we'll worry about it when the time comes. I'll tell him what a poor boy you are, how your companions abandoned you when your feet were too sore to go on walking. Don't worry about it. No one will raise an eyebrow. There's always room for a child or two. Who's going to care if we spread out a few boards for you to sleep on in the kitchen, and give you a little bit to eat? There's no risk in that. Why, even with a formal apprenticeship boys have been known to disappear. It doesn't prevent them from running off with things that don't belong to them. There are all kinds of people in this world. You know what they say: 'You don't know a horse till you ride it.' How can we tell whether we can use you in the shop if we don't give you a try? But listen, if you don't want to go back to that slum of yours, you're going to have to work hard. And learn how things are done. You'll have to make up your mind: this is where your home is. You're going to have to work, you know."

And work he did. Today, by himself, Kichizō could treat as many umbrellas as three adults, humming a tune as he went about his business. Seeing this, people would praise the dead lady's foresight: "Granny knew what she was doing."

The old woman, to whom he owed so much, had been dead two years now, and the present owners of the shop and their son Hanji were hard for Kichizō to take. But what was he to do? Even if he didn't like them, he had nowhere else to go. Had not his anger and resentment at them caused his very bones and muscles to contract? "Dwarf! Dwarf!" everybody taunted him. "Eating fish on the anniversary of your parents' death! It serves you right that you're so short. Round and round we go—look at him! The tiny monk who'll never grow!"[3]

In his work, he could take revenge on the sniveling bullies, and he was perfectly ready to answer them with a clenched fist. But his valor sometimes left him. He didn't even know the date of his parents' death, he had no way to observe the yearly abstinences. It made him miserable, and he would throw himself down underneath the umbrellas drying in the yard and push his face against the ground to stifle his tears.

The boy was a little fireball. He had a violence about him that frightened the entire neighborhood. The sleeves of his plain kimono would swing as he flailed his arms, and the smell of oil from the umbrellas followed him through every season. There was no one to calm his temper, and he suffered all the more. If anyone were to show Kichizō a moment's kindness, he knew that he would cling to him and find it hard ever to let go.

In the spring Okyō the seamstress had moved into the neighborhood. With her quick wit, she was soon friendly with everyone. Her landlord was the owner of the umbrella shop, and so she was especially cordial to the members of the shop. "Bring over your mending any time, boys. I don't care what condition it's in. There are so many people at your house, the mistress won't have time to tend to it. I'm always sewing anyway, one more stitch is nothing. Come and visit when you have time. I get lonely living by myself. I like people who speak their minds, and that rambunctious Kichizō—he's one of my favorites. Listen, the next time you lose your temper," she would tell him, "instead of hitting the little white dog at the rice shop, come over to my place. I'll give you my mallet, and you can take out your anger on the fulling block.[4] That way, people won't be so upset with you. And you'll be helping me—it'll do us both good."

In no time Kichizō began to make himself at home. It was "Okyō, this" and "Okyō, that" until he had given the other workmen at the shop something new to tease

---

3. Paraphrasing a children's song, in which a young monk eats instead of fasting on the anniversary of his parents' death, and is punished by not growing to adult size.

4. Cloth could be cleaned and thickened by beating ("fulling").

him about. "Why, he's the mirror image of the great Chōemon!" they would laugh. "At the River Katsura, Ohan will have to carry *him*!⁵ Can't you see the little runt perched on top of her sash for the ride across the river? What a farce!"

Kichizō was not without retort. "If you're so manly, why don't you ever visit Okyō? Which one of you can tell me each day what sweets she's put in the cookie jar? Take the pawnbroker with the bald spot. He's head over heels in love with her, always ordering sewing from her and coming round on one pretext or another, sending her aprons and neckpieces and sashes—trying to win her over. But she's never given him the time of day. Let alone treat him the way she does me! Kichizō from the umbrella shop—*I'm* the one who can go there any hour of the night, and when she hears it's me, she'll open the door in her nightgown. 'You haven't come to see me all day. Did something happen? I've been worried about you.' That's how she greets me. Who else gets treated that way? 'Hulking men are like big trees: not always good supports.' Size has nothing to do with it. Look at how the tiny peppercorn is prized."

"Listen to him!" they would yell, pelting Kichizō across the back.

But all he did was smile nonchalantly. "Thank you very much." If only he had a little height, no one would dare to tease him. As it was, the disdain he showed them was dismissed as nothing more than the impertinence of a little fool. He was the butt of all their jokes and the gossip they exchanged over tobacco.

On the night of the thirtieth of December, Kichizō was returning home. He had been up the hill to call on a customer with apologies for the late filling of an order. On his way back now he kept his arms folded across his chest and walked briskly, kicking a stone with the tip of his sandal. It rolled to the left and then to the right, and finally Kichizō kicked it into a ditch, chuckling aloud to himself. There was no one around to hear him. The moon above shone brightly on the white winter roads, but the boy was oblivious to the cold. He felt invigorated. He thought he would stop by Okyō's on the way home. As he crossed over to the back street, he was suddenly startled: someone appeared from behind him and covered his eyes. Whoever it was, the person could not keep from laughing.

"Who is it? Come on, who is it?" When he touched the hands held over his eyes, he knew who it was. "Ah, Okyō! I can tell by your snaky fingers. You shouldn't scare people."

Kichizō freed himself and Okyō laughed. "Oh, too bad! I've been discovered."

Over her usual jacket she was wearing a hood that came down almost to her eyes. She looked smart tonight, Kichizō thought as he surveyed her appearance. "Where've you been? I thought you told me you were too busy even to eat the next few days." The boy did not hide his suspicion. "Were you taking something to a customer?"

"I went to make some of my New Year's calls early," she said innocently.

"You're lying. No one receives greetings on the thirtieth. Where did you go? To your relatives?"

"As a matter of fact, I *am* going to a relative's—to live with a relative I hardly know. Tomorrow I'll be moving. It's so sudden, it probably surprises you. It *is* unexpected, even I feel a little startled. Anyway, you should be happy for me. It's not a bad thing that's happened."

5. In a popular puppet play of the time, a merchant named Choemon becomes responsible for a girl after her father's death; in one scene, he carries her on his back across a river.

"Really? You're not teasing, are you? You shouldn't scare me like this. If you went away, what would I do for fun? Don't ever joke about such things. You and your nonsense!" He shook his head at her.

"I'm not joking. It's just as you said once—good luck has come riding in a fancy carriage. So I can't very well stay on in a back tenement, can I? Now I'll be able to sew you that kimono, Kichizō."

"I don't want it. When you say 'Good luck has come,' you mean you're going off some place worthless. That's what Hanji said the other day. 'You know Okyō the seamstress?' he said. 'Her uncle—the one who gives rubdowns over by the vegetable market—he's helped her find a new position. She's going into service with some rich family. Or so they say. But it sounds fishy to me—she's too old to learn sewing from some housewife. Somebody's going to set her up. I'm sure of it. She'll be wearing tasseled coats the next time we see her, la-de-da, and her hair all done up in ringlets, like a kept woman. You wait. With a face like hers, you don't think she's about to spend her whole life sewing, do you?' That's what he said. I told him he was full of it, and we had a big fight. But you *are* going to do it, aren't you? You're going off to be someone's mistress!"

"It's not that I want to. I don't have much choice. I suppose I won't be able to see you any more, Kichizō, will I?"

With these few words, Kichizō withered. "I don't know, maybe it's a step up for you, but don't do it. It's not as if you can't make a living with your sewing. The only one you have to feed is yourself. When you're good at your work, why give it up for something so stupid? It's disgusting of you. Don't go through with it. It's not too late to change your mind." The boy was unyielding in his notion of integrity.

"Oh, dear," Okyō sighed. She stopped walking. "Kichizō, I'm sick of all this washing and sewing. Anything would be better. I'm tired of these drab clothes. I'd like to wear a crepe kimono, too, for a change—even if it is tainted."

They were bold words, and yet it didn't sound as if she herself fully comprehended them. "Anyway," she laughed, "come home with me. Hurry up now."

"What! I'm too disgusted. You go ahead," he said, but his long, sad shadow followed after her.

Soon they came to their street. Okyō stopped beneath the window where Kichizō always tapped for her. "Every night you come and knock at this window. After tomorrow night," she sighed, "I won't be able to hear your voice calling any more. How terrible the world is."

"It's not the world. It's you."

Okyō went in first and lit a lamp. "Kichizō, come get warm," she called when she had the fire in the brazier going.

He stood by the pillar. "No, thanks."

"Aren't you chilly? It won't do to catch a cold."

"I don't care." He looked down at the floor as he spoke. "Leave me alone."

"What's the matter with you? You're acting funny. Is it something I said? If it is, please tell me. When you stand around with a long face like that and won't talk to me, it makes me worry."

"You don't have to worry about anything. This is Kichizō from the umbrella shop you're talking to. I don't need any woman to take care of me." He rubbed his back against the pillar. "How pointless everything turns out. What a life! People are friendly, and then they disappear. It's always the ones I like. Granny at the umbrella shop, and Kinu, the one with short hair, at the dyer's shop. First Granny dies of palsy.

Then Kinu goes and throws herself into the well behind the dyer's—she didn't want to marry. Now you're going off. I'm always disappointed in the end. Why should I be surprised, I suppose? What am I but a boy who oils umbrellas? So what if I do the work of a hundred men? I'm not going to win any prizes for it. Morning and night, the only title I ever hear is 'Dwarf' . . . 'Dwarf'! I wonder if I'll ever get any taller. 'All things come to him who waits,' they say, but I wait and wait, and all I get is more unhappiness. Just the day before yesterday I had a fight with Hanji over you. Ha! I was so sure he was wrong. I told him you were the last person rotten enough to go off and do that kind of thing. Not five days have passed, and I have to eat crow. How could I have thought of you as a sister? You, with all your lies and tricks, and your selfishness. This is the last you'll ever see of me. Ever. Thanks for your kindness. Go on and do what you want. From now on, I won't have anything to do with anyone. It's not worth it. Good-by, Okyo."

He went to the front door and began to put his sandals on.

"Kichizō! You're wrong. I'm leaving here, but I'm not abandoning *you*. You're like my little brother. How can you turn on me?" From behind, she hugged him with all her might. "You're too impatient. You jump to conclusions."

"You mean you're not going to be someone's mistress?" Kichizō turned around.

"It's not the sort of thing anybody wants to do. But it's been decided. You can't change things."

He stared at her with tears in his eyes.

"Take your hands off me, Okyō."

Liu E
1857–1909

Written during the waning years of the Qing dynasty, *The Travels of Lao Ts'an* offers a much-admired glimpse into the complexities of China's transition into the modern age. Its author, Liu E (also known as Liu Tieyun) bridged aspects of both old and new in his background, interests, and experiences. The son of a minor official, he received a broad and eclectic education that included literature, philosophy, music, mathematics, medicine, and other sciences, but he chose not to follow his father's footsteps and did not sit for the civil service examination that would qualify him for government office. Instead, he spent most of his life launching commercial and industrial ventures that ranged from tobacco and print shops to railways, streetcars and coal mines, cotton and silk mills, a steel refinery, waterworks, and traditional Chinese medicine. All came to naught, largely owing to a temperament given to impulsiveness, indiscretion, and the inability to avoid being misunderstood. From 1890 to 1893 he worked as adviser to the governor of Shandong Province on flood control and wrote several books on river conservancy and on mathematics. An avid collector of art and archeological artifacts, he is also credited with having first recognized the importance of oracle bones for an understanding of early Chinese civilization. Less successful in conveying his own intentions clearly, he became a victim of trumped-up charges of sedition because of his links with foreign interests; in 1908 he was arrested and banished to Xinjiang (Chinese Turkestan), where he soon died.

The Travels of Lao Ts'an (Lao Can in the newer system for spelling Chinese names) was written between 1903 and 1904 while Liu E was living in Shanghai. Rambling and episodic in structure and published in serial form, the twenty-chapter novel is clearly based on the author's own peripatetic experiences; it has been praised for both its detailed descriptions of landscape and its political and social critique. The allegorical dream recounted in its first chapter vividly depicts the tensions generated by China's confrontation with Western modernity. Unlike the revolutionaries whose Boxer Rebellion in 1900 sought to expel foreign influence from the country but only succeeded in subjecting it to a humiliating defeat, Liu E appreciated the potential contributions Western thinking and technology could offer. At the same time, however, he both refused to reject the value of traditional civilization wholesale and yet recognized the weakness and corruption that were sustained by many of its practices. The extent of the nation's quandary is captured in the closing lines of his preface to the novel: "The game of chess is finished. We are getting old. How can we not weep?"

from The Travels of Lao Ts'an[1]

Chapter 1

The land does not hold back the water; every year comes disaster;
The wind beats up the waves; everywhere is danger.

The Story tells that outside the East Gate of Tengchoufu, in Shantung, there is a big hill called P'englai Hill,[2] and on this hill a pavilion called the P'englai Pavilion. It is most imposing with its "painted roof-tree flying like a cloud" and its "bead screens rolled up like rain."[3] To the west it overlooks the houses in the town, with mist hanging over ten thousand homes; to the east it overlooks the waves of the sea, undulating for a thousand li. It is a regular custom for the gentlemen of the town to take wine cups and wine with them to the pavilion and spend the night there, to be ready the next morning before it is light to watch the sun come up out of the sea.

However, no more of this for the present.

It is further told that there was once a traveler called Lao Ts'an. His family name was T'ieh, his *ming* was of one character, Ying, and his *hao,* Pu-ts'an.[4] He chose Ts'an as his *hao* because he liked the story of the monk Lan Ts'an roasting taros.[5] Since he was a pleasant sort of person, people deferred to his wish and began to call him Lao Ts'an, which eventually became a regular nickname. He was a Chiangnan man. By the time he was thirty he had studied quite a lot of prose and poetry, but because he was not good at writing eight-legged essays,[6] he had taken no degrees and therefore nobody wanted him as a tutor. He was too old to learn a business and therefore did not attempt it. His father had been an official of the third or fourth rank but was too stubbornly honest to make money for himself, and after twenty years of office-holding he could only afford to travel home by selling his official clothes! How do you suppose he could have anything to give his son?

Since Lao Ts'an had nothing from his family and no definite occupation, he began to see cold and hunger staring him in the face. Just when he was at his wits' end,

1. Translated by Harold Shadick.
2. The First Qin Emperor (r. 221–209 B.C.E.) was said to have launched an expedition from this spot over the eastern sea in search of elixirs of immortality.
3. From a poem by Wang Bo (647–675) composed at a feast at this pavilion.
4. A *ming* was a person's given name, and a *hao,* or style, a formal nickname selected later by himself or his friends. Pu-ts'an (Bucan) means "repairing leftovers," probably

referring to the profession of medicine. Lao ("old") is a familiar means of address for a man.
5. This 8th-century monk, who was lazy (Lan) and fond of eating leftovers (Ts'an), was said to have given half a taro he was roasting to a famous statesman and told him to be prime minister for ten years.
6. Essays written in a rigid style of eight sections required for the civil service examinations in late imperial China.

Heaven took pity on him, for along came a Taoist priest, shaking a string of bells, who said that he had been taught by a wonderful healer and could treat a hundred diseases. He said that when people met him and asked him to heal their diseases he had a hundred cures to every hundred treatments. So Lao Ts'an made obeisance to him as his teacher, learned the patter, and from that time on went about shaking a string of bells and filling his bowl of gruel by curing diseases. Thus he wandered about by river and lake for twenty years.

When our story begins, he had just come to an old Shantung town called Ch'iench'eng, where there was a great house belonging to a man whose family name was Huang (Yellow) and whose *ming* was Jui-ho. This man suffered from a strange disease which caused his whole body to fester in such a way that every year several open sores appeared, and if one year these were healed, the next year several more would appear elsewhere. Now for many years no one had been found who could cure this disease. It broke out every summer and subsided after the autumn equinox.

Lao Ts'an arrived at this place in the spring, and the major-domo of the Huang household asked him if he had a cure for the disease. He said, "I have many cures; the only thing is that you may not do as I tell you. This year I will apply a mild treatment to try my skill. But if you want to prevent the disease from ever breaking out again, this too is not difficult; all we need do is to follow the ancients whose methods hit the target every time. For other diseases we follow the directions handed down from Shen Nung and Huang Ti, but in the case of this disease we need the method of the great Yü.[7] Later, in the Han period, there was a certain Wang Ching[8] who inherited his knowledge, but after that nobody seems to have known his method. Fortunately I now have some understanding of it."

The Huang household therefore pressed him to stay in the house and to give his treatment. Strange to say, although this year there was a certain amount of festering, not one open sore appeared, and this made the household very happy.

After the autumn equinox the state of the disease was no longer serious, and everybody was delighted because for the first time in more than ten years Mr. Huang had had no open sores. The family therefore engaged a theatrical company to sing operas for three days in thanksgiving to the spirits. They also built up an artificial hill of chrysanthemums in the courtyard of the west reception hall. One day there was a feast, the next a banquet, all very gay and noisy.

On the day when our story begins Lao Ts'an had finished his noon meal, and having drunk two cups of wine more than usual, felt tired and went to his room, where he lay down on the couch to rest. He had just closed his eyes when suddenly two men walked in, one called Wen Chang-po, the other Te Hui-sheng.[9] These two men were old friends of his. They said, "What are you doing at this time of, day, hiding away in your room?" Lao Ts'an quickly got up and offered them seats saying, "I have been feasting so hard these two days that I needed a change." They said, "We are going to Tengchoufu to see the famous view from the P'englai Pavilion and have come especially to invite you. We have already hired a cart. Put your things together quickly and we will go right away."

Lao Ts'an's baggage did not amount to much—not more than a few old books and some instruments—so that packing was easy, and in a short time the three men

---

7. Ancient culture heroes associated with agriculture, medicine, and flood control.
8. A Han dynasty official known for his mastery of astronomy, mathematics, the *Book of Changes*, and flood control.
9. Wen Chang-po means "Leader in Literary Composition." Te Hui-sheng means "Student of Morals and Wisdom" [translator's note].

were getting into the cart. After an uneventful journey they soon reached Tengchou and there found lodging beside the P'englai Pavilion. Here they settled and prepared to enjoy the phantasmagoria of a "market in the sea" and the magic of "mirage towers."[1]

The next day Lao Ts'an said to his two friends Wen and Te, "Everyone says the sunrise is worth seeing. Why shouldn't we stay up to see it instead of sleeping? What do you say?" They answered, "If you are so inclined, we will certainly keep you company."

Although autumn is that time of year when day and night are about equal in length, the misty light that appears before sunrise and lingers after sunset makes the night seem shorter. The three friends opened two bottles of wine, took out the food they had brought with them, and, what with drinking and talking, before they were aware of it the east had gradually become bright. Actually it was still a long time before sunrise; the effect was due to the diffusion of the light through the air.

The three friends continued to talk for a while. Then Te Hui-sheng said, "It's nearly time now. Why don't we go and wait upstairs?" Wen Chang-po said, "The wind is whistling so, and there is such an expanse of windows upstairs that I'm afraid it will be much colder than this room. We'd better put on extra clothes."

They all followed this advice and taking telescopes and rugs went up the zigzag staircase at the back. When they entered the pavilion, they sat at a table by a window and looked out toward the east. All they could see were white waves like mountains stretching away without end. To the northeast were several flecks of blue mist. The nearest was Long Hill Island; farther off were Big Bamboo, Great Black, and other islands. Around the pavilion the wind rushed and roared until the whole building seemed to be shaking. The clouds in the sky were piled up, one layer upon another. In the north was one big bank of cloud that floated to the middle of the sky and pressed down upon the clouds that were already there, and then began to crowd more and more upon a layer of cloud in the east until the pressure seemed insufferable. The whole spectacle was most ominous. A little later the sky became a shining strip of red.

Hui-sheng said, "Brother Ts'an, judging from the look of things the actual rising of the sun will be invisible." Lao Ts'an said, "The winds of heaven and the waters of the sea are sufficient to move me; even if we do not see the sunrise the journey will not have been in vain."

Chang-po meanwhile had been looking through his telescope. Now he exclaimed, "Look! There is a black shadow in the east that keeps rising and falling with the waves; it must be a steamship passing." They all took their telescopes and looked in that direction. After a while they said, "Yes! Look! There is a fine black thread on the horizon. It must be a ship."

They all watched for a while until the ship had passed out of sight. Hui-sheng continued to hold up his telescope and looked intently to right and left. Suddenly he cried, "Ayah! Ayah! Look at that sailing boat among the great waves. It must be in danger." The others said, "Where?" Hui-sheng said, "Look toward the northeast. Isn't that line of snow-white foam Long Hill Island? The boat is on this side of the island and is gradually coming nearer." The other two looked through their telescopes and both exclaimed, "Ayah! Ayah! It certainly is in terrible danger. Luckily it's coming in this direction. It has only twenty or thirty li to go before it reaches the shore."

After about an hour the boat was so near that by looking closely through their telescopes the three men could see that it was a fairly large boat, about twenty-three

---

1. A group of rocky islands off the coast created famous mirages.

or twenty-four chang long. The captain was sitting on the poop, and below the poop were four men in charge of the helm. There were six masts with old sails and two new masts, one with a completely new sail and the other with a rather worn one, in all eight masts. The ship was very heavily loaded; the hold must have contained many kinds of cargo. Countless people, men and women, were sitting on the deck without any awning or other covering to protect them from the weather—just like the people in third-class cars on the railway from Tientsin to Peking. The north wind blew in their faces; foam splashed over them; they were wet and cold, hungry and afraid. They all had the appearance of people with no means of livelihood. Beside each of the eight masts were two men to look after the rigging. At the prow and on the deck were a number of men dressed like sailors.

It was a great ship, twenty-three or twenty-four chang long, but there were many places in which it was damaged. On the east side was a gash about three chang long, into which the waves were pouring with nothing to stop them. Farther to the east was another bad place about a chang long through which the water was seeping more gradually. No part of the ship was free from scars. The eight men looking after the sails were doing their duty faithfully, but each one looked after his own sail as though each of the eight was on a separate boat: they were not working together at all. The other seamen were running about aimlessly among the groups of men and women; it was impossible at first to tell what they were trying to do. Looking carefully through the telescope, you discovered that they were searching the men and women for any food they might be carrying and also stripping them of the clothes that they wore.

Chang-po looked intently and finally couldn't help crying out wildly, "The damnable blackguards! Just look, the boat is going to capsize any moment, and they don't even make a show of trying to reach the shore, but spend their time maltreating decent people. It's outrageous!" Hui-sheng said, "Brother Chang, don't get excited; the ship is not more than seven or eight li away from us; when it reaches land, we will go on board and try to make them stop, that's all."

While he was speaking, they saw several people on the boat killed and thrown into the sea. The helm was put about, and the ship went off toward the east. Chang-po was so angry that he stamped his feet and shouted, "A shipload of perfectly good people! All those lives! For no reason at all being killed at the hands of this crowd of navigators! What injustice!" He thought for a while and then said, "Fortunately there are lots of fishing boats at the bottom of our hill. Why don't we sail out in one of them, kill some of that crew, and replace the others? That would mean the salvation of a whole shipload of people. What a meritorious act! What satisfaction!" Hui-sheng said, "Although it might be satisfying to do this, still it would be very rash, and I'm afraid not safe. What does Brother Ts'an think?"

Lao Ts'an smiled at Chang-po and said, "Brother Chang, your plan is excellent, only I wonder how many companies of soldiers you are going to take with you." Chang-po answered angrily, "How can Brother Ts'an be so blind! At this very moment the lives of these people are in the balance. In this emergency we three should go to rescue them without delay. Where are there any companies of soldiers to take with us?" Lao Ts'an said, "In that case, since the crew of that ship is not less than two hundred men, if we three try to kill them won't we only go to our own deaths and accomplish nothing? What does your wisdom think of that?"

Chang-po thought for a while and decided that Lao Ts'an's reasoning was sound; then he said, "According to you, what should we do? Helplessly watch them die?"

Lao Ts'an answered, "As I see it the crew have not done wrong intentionally; there are two reasons why they have brought the ship to this intolerable pass. What two reasons? The first is that they are accustomed to sailing on the 'Pacific' Ocean and can only live through 'pacific' days. When the wind is still and the waves are quiet, the conditions of navigation make it possible to take things easy. But they were not prepared for today's big wind and heavy sea and therefore are bungling and botching everything. The second reason is that they do not have a compass. When the sky is clear, they can follow traditional methods, and when they can see the sun, moon, and stars they don't make serious mistakes in their course. This might be called 'depending on heaven for your food.' Who could have told that they would run into this overcast weather with the sun, moon, and stars covered up by clouds, leaving them nothing to steer by? It is not that in their hearts they do not want to do the right thing, but since they cannot distinguish north, south, east, and west, the farther they go, the more mistakes they make. As to our present plan, if we take Brother Chang's suggestion to follow them in a fishing boat, we can certainly catch them, because their boat is heavy and ours will be light. If when we have reached them we give them a compass, they will then have a direction to follow and will be able to keep their course. If we also instruct the captain in the difference between navigating in calm and stormy weather and they follow our words, why shouldn't they quickly reach the shore?" Hui-sheng said, "What Lao Ts'an has suggested is the very thing! Let us carry it out quickly; otherwise the shipload of people will certainly be doomed."

The three men descended from the pavilion and told the servants to watch their baggage. They took nothing with them except a reliable compass, a sextant, and several other nautical instruments. At the foot of the hill they found the mooring place of the fishing boats. They chose a light, quick boat, hoisted the sail, and set out in pursuit of the ship. Luckily the wind was blowing from the north so that whether the boat went east or west there was a thwart wind and the sail could be used to the full.

After a short time they were not far from the big boat. The three men continued to watch carefully through their telescopes. When they were a little more than ten chang away, they could hear what the people on the boat were saying. They were surprised to find that while the members of the crew were searching the passengers another man was making an impassioned speech in a loud voice.

They only heard him say, "You have all paid your fares to travel on this boat. In fact, the boat is your own inherited property which has now been brought to the verge of destruction by the crew. All in your families, young and old, are on this boat. Are you all going to wait to be killed? Are you not going to find a way of saving the situation? You deserve to be killed, you herd of slaves!"

The passengers at whom he was railing said nothing at first. Then a number of men got up and said, "What you have said is what we all in our hearts want to say but cannot. Today we have been awakened by you and are truly ashamed of ourselves and truly grateful to you. We only ask you, 'What are we to do?'"

The man then said, "You must know that nowadays nothing can be done without money. If you will all contribute some money, we will give our energy and lifeblood for you and will lay the foundations of a freedom which is eternal and secure. What do you say to this?" The passengers all clapped their hands and shouted with satisfaction.

Chang-po hearing this from the distance said to his two companions, "We didn't know there was a splendid hero like this on the boat. If we had known earlier, we needn't have come." Hui-sheng said, "Let us lower part of our sails for the time being. We don't need to catch up with the ship. We'll just watch what he does. If he really has a sound scheme, then we can very well go back." Lao Ts'an said, "Brother Hui is right. In my poor opinion this man is probably not the sort who will really do anything. He will merely use a few fine-sounding phrases to cheat people of their money—that's all!"

The three then lowered their sails and slowly trailed after the big boat. They saw the people on the boat collect quite a lot of money and hand it over to the speaker. Then they watched to see what he would do. Who could have known that when the speaker had taken the money he would seek out a place where the crowd could not touch him, stand there, and shout to them loudly, "You lot of spineless creatures! Cold-blooded animals! Are you still not going to attack those helmsmen?" And further, "Why don't you take those seamen and kill them one by one?"

Sure enough, some inexperienced young men, trusting his word, went to attack the helmsmen, while others went to upbraid the captain; they were all slaughtered by the sailors and thrown into the sea.

The speaker again began to shout down at them, "Why don't you organize yourselves? If all you passengers on the boat act together, won't you get the better of them?"

But an old and experienced man among the passengers cried out, "Good people! On no account act in this wild way! If you do this, the ship will sink while you are still struggling. I'm certain no good will come of it."

When Hui-sheng heard this he said to Chang-po, "After all, this hero was out to make money for himself while telling others to shed their blood." Lao Ts'an said, "Fortunately there are still a few respectable and responsible men; otherwise the ship would founder even sooner."

When he had spoken, the three men put on full sail and very soon were close to the big boat. Their poleman pulled them alongside with his hook, and the three then climbed up and approached the poop. Bowing very low, they took out their compass and sextant and presented them. The helmsmen looked at them and asked them politely, "How do you use these things? What are they for?"

They were about to reply when suddenly among the lower ranks of seamen arose a howl, "Captain! Captain! Whatever you do don't be tricked by these men. They've got a foreign compass. They must be traitors sent by the foreign devils! They must be Catholics! They have already sold our ship to the foreign devils, and that's why they have this compass. We beg you to bind these men and kill them to avoid further trouble. If you talk with them any more or use their compass, it will be like accepting a deposit from the foreign devils, and they will come to claim our ship."

This outburst aroused everybody on the ship. Even the great speech-making hero cried out, "These are traitors who want to sell the ship! Kill them! Kill them!"

When the captain and the helmsmen heard the clamor, they hesitated. A helmsman who was the captain's uncle said, "Your intentions are very honest, but it is difficult to go against the anger of the mob. You had better go away quickly."

With tears in their eyes the three men hurriedly returned to their little boat. The anger of the crowd on the big ship did not abate, and when they saw the three men getting into their boat, they picked up broken timbers and planks damaged by the waves and hurled them at the small boat. Just think! How could a tiny fishing boat bear up against several hundred men using all their force to destroy it? In a short time the fishing boat was broken to bits and began to sink to the bottom of the sea.

If you don't know what happened to the three men, then hear the next chapter tell.

from *Chapter 2*

At the foot of Mount Li the traces of an ancient emperor;
By the side of Lake Ming the song of a beautiful girl.

It has been told how the fishing boat Lao Ts'an was in was damaged by the mob and sank with him into the depths of the sea. He realized that there was no hope for his life. All he could do was to close his eyes and wait. He felt like a leaf falling from a tree, fluttering to and fro. In a short time he had sunk to the bottom. He could hear a voice at his side calling to him, "Wake up, Sir! It is already dark. The food has been ready in the dining hall for quite a long time." Lao Ts'an opened his eyes in great confusion, stared around him, and said, "Ay! After all it was but a dream." * * *

from *Chapter 3*

The next day, feeling that he had done enough sightseeing, he took his string of bells and roamed up and down the crowded streets. Just past the Governor's Yamen[2] he noticed at the entrance to a lane on the west a middle-class house with the main gate facing south. On a board by the gate were three characters, "Mr. Kao's Residence." At the gate stood a man with a long, thin face wearing a brownish-purple padded gown of fine *lo.* He was holding a foreign white brass "carriage-and-pair" water pipe[3] in his two hands. His face bore a melancholy look. Seeing Lao Ts'an he cried out, "Sir! Sir! Can you treat disorders of the throat?" Lao Ts'an answered, "I know something about them." The man then said, "Please come in." Entering the gate they made a turn to the west to a three-*chien*[4] reception room, tolerably well furnished. On both sides there were scrolls, mostly from the brush of famous living men. In the middle hung a single scroll, a painting of a man who looked like Lieh Tzu riding the wind,[5] his clothing, hat, and sash blowing in the gale, the brush strokes most powerful. Above were four characters: "Great wind, powerful wind," also excellently written.

They sat down and exchanged names. The man turned out to be from Kiangsu. His *hao* was Shao-yin, and he held the position of secretary in the provincial government. He said, "I have a concubine who has suffered from ulcerated throat for five days. Today she cannot even swallow a drop of water. Please, doctor, tell me whether there is any hope or not." Lao Ts'an answered, "I can't say anything until I have seen the patient."

Mr. Kao then ordered a servant, "Go to the women's quarters and warn them that a doctor has come for an examination." They then went together through the inner gate to a three-*chien* building. When they had entered the middle room, a maidservant lifted up the *lientzu* [curtain] on the door of the west room, saying, "Please come in." They went into the room where, in the northwest corner, was a big bed, hung with printed grass-linen curtains. There was an oblong table against the west wall by the head of the bed, and at the side of the bed were two stools.

Mr. Kao gave Lao Ts'an the stool to the west, and a hand was stretched out from behind the curtain. The maidservant brought several books and piled them up under the hand. He felt one hand, then the other. Lao Ts'an said, "The pulse in both hands is deep, quick, and taut, showing that the fever is stopped up by the chill and can't get out. The longer this goes on, the more serious it is. Please let me see the throat."

---

2. Administrative office.
3. A pipe with two bowls, which allowed a smoker to choose between different tobaccos.
4. A *chien/jian* was the distance between two beams, and the standard way of measuring rooms.
5. A Daoist philosopher who was said by fellow Daoist Zhuangzi to be able to ride the wind.

Mr. Kao then lifted the curtain. The woman was about twenty years of age. Her face was flushed, yet she appeared to be quite exhausted. Mr. Kao gently raised her up toward the light of the window.

Lao Ts'an bent his head to look: the pale red swellings in the throat were about to meet. When he had looked, he said to Mr. Kao, "This attack was not so serious to begin with—only a little internal heat. But because a doctor has used bitter, cold medicine to check it, the heat could not come out. Besides, the patient is inclined to be moody, and the disorder was originally caused by the repression of her feelings. Even now two doses of pungent and cool diaphoretic will set it right." He took a bottle of medicine and a tube out of his bag and blew some medicine into her throat. Returning to the reception room he drew up a prescription for a medicine called "Infusion of licorice and kikio root with additional flavors." The ingredients were eight in number: licorice, kikio root, burdock, ground ivy, *fang-feng,* peppermint, magnolia, and talcum, while fresh lotus stems formed the adjuvant. When he had written the prescription he gave it to Mr. Kao.

Mr. Kao said, "That's splendid. But how many doses do we give her?" Lao Ts'an said, "Two doses today. Tomorrow I will come to examine her again." Mr. Kao further asked, "Please tell me what your fee is." Lao Ts'an answered, "As I go about practicing my mystery I have no fixed charges. If I cure your concubine's sickness, then when I am hungry you may give me a bowl of rice or when I can't walk you may help with my travel expenses, and I shall be satisfied." Mr. Kao answered, "Since you say this, I will recompense you for everything when she is recovered. Where is your inn, so that if there should be a change I can send a man to fetch you?" Lao Ts'an said, "The Promotion Inn, on Treasury Street." Having said this he left.

From that time on they came every day to fetch him. In a few days the disease began to abate, and the patient returned to normal. Mr. Kao was overjoyed. He gave Lao Ts'an eight ounces of silver in token of thanks and honored him with a wine feast at the North Pillar Restaurant to which he invited his colleagues in the secretariat with the idea of making known Lao Ts'an's skill. One thing led to another until after a while not a day passed without a sedan chair coming for him from the officials and their aides.

One day a feast was given at the North Pillar Restaurant, this time by an expectant *taot'ai.*[6] The man sitting in an upper seat on the right side of the table said, "Yü Tso-ch'en[7] is going to fill the vacancy at Ts'aochoufu." The man at a lower seat on the left side, next to Lao Ts'an, said, "His place on the waiting list is very low. How can he fill the vacancy?"

The man on the right said, "He is so successful in dealing with bandits that in less than a year 'the thing dropped on the road is not picked up.'[8] The Governor considers him quite exceptional. The day before yesterday somebody said to him, 'I was traveling through a certain village near Ts'aochoufu when I saw with my own eyes a blue cloth bundle lying beside the road. No one had dared to pick it up, so I asked the inhabitants: "Whose bundle is this? Why does nobody pick it up?" A native of the place said, "Somebody we don't know put it here last night." I asked, "Why don't any of you take it away?" They all laughed and shook their heads saying, "We want all the members of our family to remain alive, thank you!" From this we see that "the thing

6. Regional official.
7. His name resembles that of a notorious late Qing official who encouraged the Boxer rebels.

8. From the biography of Confucius in Sima Qian's *Grand Scribe's Records,* indicating his beneficial influence as local official.

dropped on the road is not picked up," and the ancient writer was not deceiving us, for what he wrote has actually been achieved today!' When the Governor heard this, he was delighted and is planning to send up a special memorial commending him."

The guest on the left said, "Tso-ch'en is certainly very efficient, but he is much too cruel. In less than a year he has choked to death more than two thousand people in his cages.[9] Do you suppose none of these were unjustly treated?"

Another guest said, "There certainly have been cases of injustice. That goes without saying. What nobody knows is the proportion of those not unjustly condemned."

A man on the right said, "Tyrannical government often looks well on the surface. You all remember that year when Flay-the-Skin Ch'ang was at Yenchoufu. Didn't the same thing happen there? It went on until everybody looked askance at the tyrant."

Another said, "Tso-ch'en's tyranny is indeed oppressive, but the people of Ts'aochou are certainly a bad lot! The year I was administering Ts'aochou scarcely a day passed without a case of banditry. I organized a band of two hundred gendarmes, but they were like a cat who couldn't catch mice—absolutely useless. Of all those who were arrested as bandits by the constables in the various *hsien* [districts], those who were not honest country people were men compelled by the bandits to watch their horses and mules. Out of a hundred men arrested scarcely any were real bandits. But now thanks to the thunder and whirlwind methods of Yü Tso-ch'en, banditry has entirely ceased. All this makes me feel thoroughly ashamed!"

The man on the left said, "All the same, from my stupid point of view, it would be better not to kill so many people. This man may have a great name for a while, but I fear that what he will reap in the future will be too terrible for words." When he had said this, everybody exclaimed, "We have had enough wine. May we have the rice!" After the rice they separated.

A day later Lao Ts'an was sitting idly in his inn in the afternoon when suddenly a blue felt sedan chair stopped at the door and a man came in calling out, "Is Mr. T'ieh at home?"

Lao Ts'an looked out; it was none other than Kao Shao-yin. He quickly went out to welcome him, saying, "At home! At home! Please come in; only the place is very poor; you demean yourself too much in coming." Shao-yin said, "You are much too polite," and came through the inner gate. They then entered Lao Ts'an's quarters. He had a two-*chien* room facing east. At the south end was a brick *k'ang* [bed] on which bedding was spread out. At the north end were a square table and two chairs. To the west were two small bamboo chests. On the table were several books, a small ink slab, some brushes, and a box of seal ink.

Lao Ts'an made Shao-yin sit in the place of honor. Shao-yin began to pick up the books and look at them carefully. Suddenly he said with great surprise, "This is a Sung period Chang Chün-fang wood-block edition of *Chuang Tzu*. Where did it come from? No copy of this book has been seen for a long time. Neither Chi Ts'ang-wei nor Huang P'i-lieh ever came across one.[1] It counts as a rare treasure!" Lao Ts'an said, "They're just a few old books left me by my father. They're not worth selling, so I

---

9. The cage was an unauthorized instrument of torture consisting of a rectangular frame of upright wood slats, so high that the victim, whose neck was held in a small hole in a flat board which formed the top, was only able to touch the ground on tiptoe. When he could no longer remain on his toes the whole weight of his body rested on his neck and he was slowly choked to death [Translator's note].

1. Chang Chün-fang edited a major compendium of Daoist texts in the early 11th century. Chi (b. 1630) and Huang (1763–1825) were well-known book collectors.

carry them around with me in my traveling case to pass the time with when I am bored, instead of novels. Nothing worth mentioning." He turned over another. It was a volume of T'ao's poems in the writing of Su Tung-p'o, the original impression of Mao Tzu-chin's wood-block edition.[2]

Shao-yin sighed in admiration and then asked, "Since you come from such a scholarly family, why don't you find a position in the official world instead of following this thankless trade? 'Wealth and honor' may be 'floating clouds,'[3] but aren't you a bit too high-minded?"

Lao Ts'an sighed. "Your Honor's referring to me as 'high-minded' is truly too much of a compliment. It is not that I have no ambition for official life, but simply because my nature is too free and easy and doesn't fit the times, and because, as the saying is, 'the higher the climb, the greater the fall.' My intention in not climbing high is to make sure that I fall lightly."

Shao-yin said, "Last night I was at an informal dinner in the yamen, and the Governor was saying, 'In our provincial government we have a great deal of talent; all the gifted men we have heard of have been invited to join us.' Mr. Yao Yün, who was sitting with us, said, 'At this very moment there is a man in the city whom the Governor has not invited.' The Governor asked eagerly, 'Who is it?' Mr. Yao Yün reported on your scholarship, your character, your thorough understanding of men and affairs, until the Governor began to fiddle with his ears and stroke his cheeks, he was so pleased. He then told me to send you an official letter without delay. But I answered him, 'I'm afraid that won't do. This man is neither on the waiting list for an office, nor is he seeking office, and I don't even know whether he has any rank or degree. So it would be hard to write him an official letter.' The Governor said, 'In that case send an ordinary invitation.' I said, 'If you were to call him in to treat sickness, he would come instantly, but if you are inviting him into the administration I don't know whether he will want to come or not. It is better to sound him out first.' The Governor said, 'Very good. Go tomorrow to see what he says and bring him here to visit me.' This is why I have come today especially to find out whether or not you will come with me to the yamen to visit the Governor." Lao Ts'an said, "There is no reason why I shouldn't, except that to see the Governor I ought to wear an official cap and belt. I am not in the habit of wearing them, but if I may go in ordinary clothes then it's all right." Shao-yin answered, "Of course ordinary clothes will do. Let us wait a while and then go together. You can sit in my room, and when the Governor comes out of his living quarters in the afternoon, we can talk to him in his office." With this he ordered a chair.

Wearing his ordinary clothes, Lao Ts'an went with Kao Shao-yin to the Provincial Yamen. Now this Shantung Provincial Yamen was formerly the palace of Prince Ch'i of the Ming dynasty, and many parts of it still keep the old names. They reached the third hall, called the Entrance to the Palace. To one side was Kao Shao-yin's office; opposite it was the room where the Governor signed official documents.

They went into Shao-yin's office and in less than half an hour saw the Governor come forth. His figure was majestic and his features kind and open. When Kao Shao-yin saw him, he immediately went forward to welcome him and said a few words in a

2. The Song dynasty scholar-statesman Su Shi (Dongpo, 1036–1101) much admired the poetry of Tao Qian (365–427), which he both copied out and wrote responses to. Mao (1599–1659) was a famous editor, collector, and reprinter of old books.

3. From the *Analects,* 7.15, where Confucius declares his satisfaction with coarse rice to eat, water to drink, and his elbow for a pillow, with "wealth and honor acquired unrighteously but as floating clouds."

low voice. All you could hear was Governor Chuang[4] saying again and again, "Please come over. Please come over." Then a minor official ran across and called out, "The Governor invites Mr. T'ieh to come."

Lao Ts'an hurriedly walked over and stood face to face with Governor Chuang. Chuang said, "Long have I admired you." Then he stretched out his hand and with a slight bow said, "Please come in." An attendant was already lifting up the soft *lientzu* over the door.

Lao Ts'an went into the room and made a low bow, his hands clasped together. The Governor gave him the seat of honor on the redwood *k'ang*. Shao-yin took the opposite seat, and a square stool was placed between the two. The Governor sat down there and began the conversation, "I have heard that Mr. Pu-ts'an's scholarship and knowledge of public administration are both far above the average. I am an unschooled person, but by Imperial Grace I have been appointed to take charge of this territory. In other provinces it is sufficient to put heart and soul into the work of administration, but in my province there is in addition the river work, which is certainly difficult to manage. The only thing I can do is to call in every man of unusual ability I hear of. It's a case of 'many minds, greater gain.' If anyone has a thorough grasp of certain problems and can give advice about them, it is of course greatly appreciated."

Lao Ts'an answered, "Every voice testifies to the fame of the Governor's rule: that goes without saying. However I have heard it rumored that in the matter of the river work, all the plans are based on Chia Jang's 'Three Methods'[5] and follow the principle that you must not struggle with the river for land." The Governor said, "You are quite right. Just consider: in Honan the river is very wide; but here it is very narrow." Lao Ts'an said, "The important thing is not that when the river is narrow there is no room for the water, for this only happens during the month or so when the river is in flood. The rest of the time, the current being weak, the silt is easily deposited. You must know that Chia Jang was only a good essayist. He had had no experience in river work. Less than a hundred years after Chia Jang a certain Wang Ching appeared. His method of river control was derived in a direct line from that of the Great Yü. He emphasized the 'curbing' which is referred to in the expression 'Yü curbed the flood waters.' This directly opposed Chia Jang's views. After Wang Ching had directed flood control, there was no river disaster for over a thousand years. P'an Chi-hsün of the Ming period and Chin Wenhsiang[6] of the present dynasty both followed his doctrine to some extent and as a result enjoyed great fame. I take it the Governor knows this." The Governor asked, "What method did Wang Ching use?" Lao Ts'an answered, "He developed it from the two words 'united' and 'divided' in the passage which reads 'It divided and became nine rivers; these united again to form the "meeting" river.'[7] The *History of the Later Han Dynasty* only tells how he 'built a water gate every ten li and regulated the flow of water from one to the other.' As to the details of the method, they cannot be dealt with completely in a short conversation. If you permit, I will later prepare a memorandum and offer it for your consideration. How would that be?"

---

4. He is modeled on the Governor of Shandong Province, who had a reputation for building roads, dikes and factories, and under whom the author served.
5. An official who served under the Han emperor Ai (r. 6 B.C.E.–1 C.E.) and wrote a memorial to the throne outlining three methods of flood control, with increasing degrees of artificial constraint on the waters and thus of chances of failure.
6. Both men authored several works on flood control.
7. From an obscure passage in the classic *Book of Documents*. The quotation that follows is from the biography of Wang in the *History of the Former Han Dynasty*.

Governor Chuang was so pleased that he said to Kao Shao-yin, "Tell them to prepare that three-*chien* south study as quickly as possible and we will invite Mr. T'ieh to move into the yamen to live so that he can give advice at any time." Lao Ts'an said, "The Governor's great kindness overwhelms me. But I have a relative living in Ts'aochoufu and I'm thinking of paying him a visit. Besides, having heard rumors about Prefect Yü's administration, I want to go and find out what sort of a man he really is. When I come back from Ts'aochou I will hope to profit further by the Governor's wisdom." The Governor's expression showed that he was very disappointed. The talk finished, Lao Ts'an excused himself, and he and Shao-yin left the yamen and went their several ways. * * *

from *Chapter 4*

Arrived at Lok'ou, Lao Ts'an hired a small boat with the understanding that he was to be taken upstream to Tungchiak'ou, the landing place for Ts'aochoufu. He advanced two strings of cash for the boatmen to buy some fuel and rice with. Luckily that day there was a southeast wind, the sail was hoisted, and they were blown along. They sailed until the sun was about to sink behind the hills, and when they had reached the town of Ch'ihohsien, they threw out the anchor and stopped for the night. The second day they stopped at P'ingyin, the third at Shouchang, and the fourth day they reached Tungchiak'ou where, as usual, they spent the night on the boat. At daybreak Lao Ts'an paid for the boat and had his luggage carried to an inn where he took a room.

Now this Tungchiak'ou is on the main road from Ts'aochoufu to Tamingfu, so there are a great many inns there. Lao Ts'an's inn was called The Old Inn of the Second Tung Brother. The innkeeper's name was Tung; he was more than sixty years old, and everybody called him Lao Tung. There was only one servingman, called Wang the Third.

Lao Ts'an settled in the inn. Originally he had planned to hire a cart and go directly to Ts'aochoufu, but since he wanted to find out about Yü Hsien's administration while on the road, he decided to stop here for a time in order to begin his investigations.

By the time the sun was up, even the latest risers among the guests in the inn had all left. The inn servant was sweeping out the rooms and the innkeeper had already made up his accounts and was sitting idly at the door. Lao Ts'an also sat down on a long bench at the door and said to Lao Tung, "I am told that the prefect in this *fu* [prefecture] is very good at handling cases of banditry; what is the true state of affairs?"

Lao Tung sighed and said, "Prefect Yü is no doubt an honest official and he certainly exerts himself in handling such cases; only his method is altogether too cruel. At first he arrested a number of bandits, but soon the bandits caught on to him, and then the tables were turned and he became the bandits' tool!" "What do you mean by that?" said Lao Ts'an. Lao Tung said, "In the southwest corner of this district there is a village called Yüchiat'un, containing about two hundred families. In this village there was a rich man called Yü Chao-tung who had two sons and a daughter. The two sons had both married, and there are two grandchildren. The daughter is also married.

"This family was living in peace and comfort when without warning calamity came to their door. Last year in the autumn they were robbed by bandits. Actually only a few clothes and pieces of jewelry were stolen, not worth more than a few hundred strings of cash. The family reported the robbery and Prefect Yü's energetic handling of the case ended in the capture of two fellows connected with the bandits. The stolen goods which were recovered were only a few pieces of cotton clothing but the bandit leaders had long before escaped where no one could find them.

"Who would have thought that because of this business the bandits would nurse a grudge? This year in the spring they robbed a house in the *fu* city. For several days Prefect Yü moved heaven and earth to find them but didn't catch a single man. After some days another house was robbed, and after the robbery they openly set fire to the place. Just think! How could Prefect Yü put up with that? Naturally he called out a troop of mounted men to go in pursuit.

"After the bandits had committed the robbery, they left the city carrying lighted torches and with rifles in their hands. No one dared to stop them. Outside the east gate they struck north some ten li or more and then the torches were put out. Prefect Yü called together his mounted men and went out on the street. The headman of the neighborhood and the watchman told him exactly what had happened. The mounted troop then left the city in pursuit. In the far distance they could still see the torches of the bandits. They followed for twenty or thirty li and again saw the torches in front of them, and heard two or three rifle shots.

"When Prefect Yü heard the shots, how could he not be angry? He was very brave to begin with, and having twenty or thirty mounted men under him, all armed with rifles, what was there to be afraid of? So he started off in pursuit. When the torches could not be seen, there were still the rifle shots. When it was almost light, he saw that they were not far from their quarry. By that time they had come to this Yüchiat'un. They went past Yüchiat'un still in full pursuit, but there were neither shots nor torches.

"Prefect Yü thought for a bit and said, 'There is no sense in going any farther; the bandits must be in this village.' Immediately they reined in their horses and went back to the village. In the middle of the main street was a Temple of Kuan Ti, and here they dismounted. He then gave orders to his troop, sending eight men east, south, west, and north, two to watch on each side and not let anybody go out. He also called out the headman and elders of the village.

"By this time it was already broad daylight and Prefect Yü himself led his troopers on foot from the south end of the village to the north in a house to house search. They searched for a long time but found no traces of the bandits. Then they searched from east to west, and when they came to the Yü Chao-tung house they discovered three shot guns, several knives, and ten or more staves.

"Prefect Yü was very angry and said, 'The bandits must be in this house.' He sat in the main hall, called the headman and asked, 'Whose house is this?' The headman answered, 'This family's name is Yü. The old man is called Yü Chao-tung; there are two sons, the elder called Yü Hsüeh-shih, the second Yü Hsüeh-li. They are all Collegians by purchase.'[8]

"Right away Prefect Yü ordered the father and two sons to be brought before him. Just think! How could any villager see a big official from the *fu* come in, and very angry at that, and not be afraid? Led into the hall, the three knelt down, already trembling, quite unable to speak.

"Prefect Yü said, 'What daring! Where have you hidden the bandits?' The old man was so frightened that he couldn't get a word out. The second son had studied in the *fu* city for two years and seen something of the world and so had a little more assurance. Still kneeling, he straightened his back, and looking up answered, 'My fam-

8. Either awarded by merit or (as here) available for purchase, the title of Collegian of the National Academy provided an alternative starting point for a career to the civil service examination. The sons' given names mean "Studies *The Book of Songs*" and "Studies *The Book of Rites*."

ily have always been honest people and had no dealings with bandits; how could we dare to hide robbers?'

"Prefect Yü said, 'If you have no connection with the bandits, where do these arms come from?' Yü Hsüeh-li replied, 'Last year after we were robbed, bandits kept coming to our village. We therefore bought several staves and had some of our tenants and farm laborers take turns at guarding the house. Since the bandits all have rifles, while there is no place where we can buy rifles in the country—not that we'd dare buy them—we bought two or three guns from some bird hunters. We fire a couple of shots in the evening to frighten away the bandits.'

"Prefect Yü barked out, 'All lies! What honest people would dare to buy firearms; your family are certainly bandits!' Then he called out, 'Come forward!' The men under his command replied in unison like a clap of thunder: *'Tsa!'*

"'Send men to watch the front and back gates and search the house thoroughly,' said Prefect Yü. The mounted soldiers then came to search the house, beginning with the main building. Clothes presses, wardrobes, chests of drawers—they ransacked everything. Pieces of jewelry that were light in weight and valuable were tucked away in the soldiers' belts. They searched for a long time but still discovered no unlawful articles. Who would have thought that later in the search in the northwest corner where there was a tumble-down two-*chien* building for farm implements they would discover a cloth bundle containing seven or eight pieces of clothing, including three or four of old silk? The soldiers took it to the main hall and reported: 'We found this bundle in an inside storeroom. It doesn't look like their own clothing. Please examine it, Your Excellency!'

"Prefect Yü looked, knit his brows, fixed his eyes on these things and said, 'These clothes look to me like those that were stolen from that house in the city the day before yesterday; we will take them to the yamen and compare them with the statement of that theft!' He then pointed to the clothes and said to old Yü and his sons, 'Tell me where these clothes came from.' They exchanged furtive glances. None could reply. Again it was Yü Hsüeh-li who at last said, 'Truly we don't know where these clothes come from!'

"Prefect Yü then got up and said, 'Twelve soldiers are to stay here and, with the headman, to bring Yü and his sons to the city to be tried.' With this he went out. His followers brought his horse. He mounted and with the remainder of the troop set out for the city.

"And now the Yü father and sons, along with the members of their family, fell on each other's necks and wept bitterly. The twelve soldiers said, 'We have ridden all through the night and are very hungry. Hurry up and get us something to eat. Quick! Everybody knows the Prefect's temper. The longer we delay the worse it will be!' The headman too, all flustered, went to have a word with his family and get his things ready, telling the Yü family to order several carts to take them all into the city. They entered the city just after the second watch had struck.[9]

"Now Yü Hsüeh-li's wife was the daughter of the *Chü-Jen* [Provincial Graduate] Wu in the city. Seeing her husband with his father and elder brother taken under arrest to the city, she was filled with anxiety. She consulted her sister-in-law, saying, 'They have all three been arrested. They must have somebody in the city to help them. I

---

9. Around 11 P.M. There were five watches in the night beginning around 9 P.M., with each lasting about two hours.

think you had better look after the family, while I quickly follow them to town and ask my father to find some way of helping. What do you think?' Her sister-in-law answered, 'That's good; that's very good; I was just thinking that there ought to be someone in the city to help them. Our farm overseers are all country fellows. Even if we sent some of them to the city they'd be like simpletons, quite useless.'

"Saying this, Mrs. Yü got her things ready, chose a 'flying' cart with two animals, and hurried to the city. When she saw her father she began to sob aloud. It was just about the first watch, so she was some ten li ahead of the father and sons.

"Through her tears Mrs. Yü told her father of the sudden calamity. When Wu *Chü-Jen* heard it, he shook all over and still trembling said, 'To offend this "Baneful Star" is a most dangerous matter! I'll go right away and see what can be done!' He hastily put on his clothes and went to the *fu* yamen to ask for an interview. The gate-keeper went in but came out again saying, 'His Honor says he is about to try a case of banditry. He cannot see anybody, no matter who it is.'

"The *Chü-Jen* Wu was well acquainted with the secretary for criminal cases, and he quickly went in to see him and told him all about this case of injustice. The secretary said, 'If this case were in another's hands, certainly nothing would come of it. But up to now this superior of mine has not conducted cases according to legal precedent. If it comes down to my office I guarantee there will be no trouble. But I am afraid it will not come down. In that case nothing can be done.'

"The *Chü-Jen* Wu bowed several times in succession, commended his case again and again, and went out. Then he went to the east gate to wait for his son-in-law and the father and brother to arrive. After a short time the cart guarded by soldiers came. Wu *Chü-Jen* rushed forward and saw the three of them looking almost dead. Yü Chao-tung caught sight of him; he only said, 'Kinsman, save us!' and a flood of tears streamed down his face.

"Wu *Chü-Jen* was just about to speak when one of the mounted guards shouted, 'His Excellency has been sitting in the court waiting for a long time. Already four or five detachments of soldiers have been sent to urge us on! Hurry up!' The cart could not stop any longer, so Wu *Chü-Jen* followed it saying, 'Kinsmen, set your hearts at rest! I'll go through fire and water to help you.'

"As he spoke they reached the yamen gate. He saw a great many runners come out to urge them saying, 'Take them into the court without delay!' Then came several attendants who made the Yü father and sons fast with iron chains, led them in, and made them kneel. Prefect Yü handed down the statement of the theft and asked, 'Have you got anything more to say?' The Yü father and sons had no sooner got out the words, 'Not guilty!' then the gavel struck the table and there was a roar: 'Caught redhanded with stolen goods and yet they cry "Not guilty!" Stand them in the cages! Go!' The attendants to left and right half-pulled, half-dragged them out." * * *

from *Chapter 5*

A devoted wife determines to die faithful;
A village-dweller unexpectedly meets disaster.

When Lao Tung reached this point in his story, Lao Ts'an asked, "Wouldn't that mean that the whole family, father and two sons, were choked to death in the cages?" Lao Tung said, "Of course! When Wu *Chü-Jen* went to the yamen to ask for an interview, his daughter, Yü Hsüeh-li's wife, went with him as far as the gate. She sat waiting in the Prolonging Life Medicine Shop to hear the news. She heard that since the

Prefect had refused to see her father, he had gone into the yamen to ask the secretary's help. She then knew that things were not going well and immediately sent someone to ask the headman of the yamen runners[1] to come to her.

"The headman's name was Ch'en Jen-mei. He was well known in Ts'aochoufu as a capable officer. Mrs. Yü had him come, told him her wrongs, and entreated him to work on her behalf in the yamen. When Ch'en Jen-mei heard the story, he shook his head several times and said, 'This is a trick played by the bandits to get their revenge. Your family had both night watchmen and guards; how did you let the bandits bring stolen goods into a building in your house and know nothing about it? Why, it's the height of stupidity!'

"Mrs. Yü then pulled a pair of gold bracelets off her wrists and gave them to headman Ch'en saying, 'No matter what you have to do, I only ask you to do your best! If the lives of these three men can be saved, I am willing to spend any amount of money! I am not afraid to sell every bit of land and property we possess. Even if our whole family has to beg for food, we will do it!'

"Headman Ch'en said, 'I'll go and see what I can do for you, Mrs. Yü. Don't be too happy if I succeed; don't blame me if I fail. Whatever strength I have I'll use— that's all. The three of them will probably arrive sometime soon. His Excellency has already taken his seat in the hall of justice and is waiting. I'll go right away to do what I can for you!' With this he took his leave and went back to the guard room. He took the gold bracelets and put them on the table in the middle of the hall and said, 'My comrades! The charge brought against the Yü family today is clearly unjust. If any of you has a plan to propose, let us think it over together. If we can save these three lives, in the first place it will be a good deed; in the second place, we can each win several ounces of silver. If anyone of you can think up a good plan, this pair of bracelets is his!' They all answered, 'How can we plan in advance! We must wait and see what happens before we can decide what to do.' The first thing they did was to go and tell their comrades who were already on duty in the hall to keep their eyes open for a chance to do something.

"By this time the three men of the Yü family had already been taken to the hall, Prefect Yü had ordered them to be put in the cages, and the attendants had half-dragged, half-pulled the three of them away.

"At this point the chief guard for the day came to the front of the magistrate's table, went down on one knee, and said, 'I beg to report to Your Excellency that there are no cages vacant today. Will Your Excellency please give instructions.' When Prefect Yü heard this he said angrily, 'Nonsense! I do not remember having put anyone in these two days. How can there be none empty?' The guard answered, 'There are only twelve cages. They were filled in three days. Will Your Excellency please check in the register?'

"The Prefect checked the list, moving his finger down the register and saying, 'One, two, three; yesterday there were three. One, two, three, four, five; the day before yesterday there were five. One, two, three, four; the day before that there were four. There are none empty; yes, you are quite right.' The attendant again asked, 'For today shall we put these in the jail? Tomorrow there are bound to be several dead. When there are vacancies in the cages, we can put these into their places. Is that all right? Will Your Excellency please decide?'

---

1. Head of one of three companies of menial attendants in the local administrative office.

"Prefect Yü frowned and said, 'How I hate these creatures! If we put them in the jail, won't that mean that they will live a day longer? That won't do at all! Go and take down those four who were put in three days ago. Bring them here for me to see.'

"The attendant went and had the four men taken down and brought into the hall. The Prefect himself came down from his table. He felt the noses of the four men with his fingers and said, 'There is still a little life!' He went back, sat down and said, 'Give each one two thousand blows; we'll see whether they'll die or not!' When they had received not more than twenty or thirty blows each, all four were dead.

"The attendants could do nothing but take the Yü father and sons, and put them in the cages. But they put three thick bricks under their feet, so that for three or four days they wouldn't die. They thought hard, but none of the suggestions that were made were of any use.

"This Mrs. Yü truly was a good and virtuous wife! Every day she came to the cages to make them drink some ginseng infusion. Having made them drink, she would go home and weep, then go to solicit help. I don't know how many thousand resounding kowtows she performed, but in spite of it all there was nobody who could move Prefect Yü's oxlike nature. Yü Chao-tung, who was after all a good many years older, died on the third day. By the fourth day Yü Hsüeh-shih was almost finished too. Mrs. Yü took away the body of Yü Chao-tung and with her own eyes saw it prepared for burial. She then changed into mourning clothes, and charged her father with the last rites of her brother-in-law and husband. Then she knelt at the yamen gate and cried her eyes out in front of Yü Hsüeh-li. Finally she said to her husband, 'You come slowly; I will go down first to prepare a dwelling for you!' With that she pulled a little sharp-edged knife out of her sleeve: one cut across her throat, and she breathed her last!

"Now the headman of the yamen runners, Ch'en Jen-mei, saw this and said, 'Men! This Mrs. Yü's courage and faithfulness are worthy of an Imperial Testimonial.[2] I think if Yü Hsüeh-li is taken out right away, he can still live. How would it be to make this an occasion to plead that mercy be shown him?' They all answered, 'Well said.'

"Headman Ch'en immediately went in to look for the clerk of the court and told him about Mrs. Yü's courage and devotion. He further said, "The people are full of sympathy for this faithful wife who has killed herself for the sake of her husband. Couldn't you beg His Excellency to have her husband set free and thus give rest to this brave wife's soul?' The clerk of the court replied, 'What you say is quite reasonable. I will go in immediately.' He picked up his official hat, put it on, and went in to see the Prefect, to whom he told how faithful and brave Mrs. Yü had been and how the people begged him to be merciful.

"Prefect Yü laughed and said, 'You're a fine lot! So you've suddenly become softhearted! You can be softhearted to Yü Hsüeh-li, but you can't be softhearted towards your own master! Whether this man is unjustly punished or not, if I release him he certainly won't rest content, and in the future even my position will be endangered. The proverb says right: "To cut down weeds you must get rid of the root." That applies here. Besides, this Yü woman is especially hateful. She is convinced that I have wronged her whole family! If she weren't a woman, although she's dead, I would

---

2. A posthumous testimonial of merit (originally a banner; later a memorial arch or other monument) conferred by the Emperor upon faithful widows and loyal officials [Translator's note].

give her a couple of thousand blows to give vent to my anger! Go and announce that if anyone comes again to ask mercy for the Yü family I shall take it as proof that he has accepted a bribe. No one needs to come in to appeal. I shall simply take the pleader and stand him in a cage too—and that will be the end of it!' The clerk of the court went out and repeated the words of the Prefect to Ch'en Jen-mei. They all sighed and then dispersed.

"Mr. Wu had already prepared coffins and brought them for the burial. By the evening Yü Hsüeh-shih and Yü Hsüeh-li had died one after the other. The four coffins of the one family were all placed in the Temple of the Goddess of Mercy outside the west gate. When I went into the city this spring I saw them."

Lao Ts'an said, "What happened to the Yü family afterwards? Didn't they try to avenge the wrong?" Lao Tung said: "How could they do that! When an ordinary person is wronged by an official, what can he do but endure it? If an appeal is made, the rule is that the case is returned to the original court for trial so that it would be back in his hands again. Wouldn't that just give him another life to dispose of?

"Now Yü Chao-tung's son-in-law was a *Hsiu-Ts'ai* [Licentiate]. After the death of the four, Yü Hsüeh-shih's wife also went to the city to discuss whether they should make an appeal. But a certain old man who knew the world said, 'It's no good! It's no good! Who do you expect to send? If an outsider goes, they will say, "The matter is not his concern," and he will get a bad name as a busybody; if you say send the elder daughter-in-law, don't forget that the two grandchildren are still small and that the great property of the family is entirely her responsibility. If anything should happen to her, the family property will be divided among all the clan, and then who will protect and bring up the two little children? It might mean the end of incense-burning in the Yü family.' Others said, 'Certainly the elder Mrs. Yü cannot go, but surely there is no reason why the son-in-law shouldn't go!' The son-in-law said, 'It is certainly possible for me to go, only it won't help the main issue but rather will mean another corpse for the cages. Just think. The Governor will certainly send the case back to the original court for trial. Although he will delegate a deputy to be present at the trial, "official protects official." They will confront us again with somebody's statement of theft and some clothes. Even if we say, "Those were hidden by the bandits" they will say, "Did you see the bandits bring them in? What evidence have you got?" Then, of course, we shall have nothing to say. He is an official; we are ordinary people. He has the statement of the theft as evidence; we have nothing to rely on; we have no proofs. Tell me, can we win this case, or can we not?' All of them thought a while, but there was nothing they could do, so they dropped the matter.

"Afterwards I heard tell that when the bandits who had concealed the things learned what had happened, they were all filled with remorse and said, 'At the start we hated them for reporting their loss and causing the death of our two comrades. So we used the method of "killing with a borrowed knife," hoping their family would suffer several months at the hands of the law, and certainly lose one or two thousand strings of cash. Who could have known it would become as serious as the loss of four lives! We certainly didn't have that much hatred for their family!'"

Lao Tung finished the story, then added: "Just think, Your Honor! Wasn't I right in saying that Prefect Yü has become the bandits' tool?"

"Then who was it heard what the bandits said?" Lao Ts'an asked. Lao Tung replied, "Ch'en Jen-mei and his men having struck a snag when they tried to do something, and having seen the members of the Yü family die such a pitiful death, and also having received a pair of gold bracelets for doing nothing, were troubled in their hearts. They were all moved with righteous anger, and made a united effort to solve the mystery of the case. Besides, there were some bold fellows in the district who hated this band of robbers for acting too viciously, and so, before a month had passed, five or six of them were captured. Three or four, who had been involved in other cases, were choked to death; two or three, who were only concerned in the case of concealing stolen goods in the Yü house, were all released by Prefect Yü."

Lao Ts'an said, "This ruthless official Yü Hsien certainly arouses a man's hatred! Has he conducted other cases in the same way?" Lao Tung replied, "Lots of them. Be patient and I will tell Your Honor about them. Even in our own village here, there was a case, also a case of injustice. It was nothing much—it only involved one or two lives. I will tell you about it."

Just as he was going to tell the story, his servingman, Wang the Third, was heard calling out, "Master! What are you up to? We are all waiting for you to deal out the flour for the meal! Your windbag must have sprung a leak! Won't you ever finish talking?"

When Lao Tung heard this, he got up and went in to deal out the flour. Several wheelbarrows then arrived one after another, and guests began coming into the inn for a snack. Lao Tung was called hither and thither and had no more time for gossip.

When they had all eaten, Lao Tung was still bustling about, reckoning up the bills at each table and looking after his business. Lao Ts'an had nothing to do, so he went for a stroll down the street. Leaving the inn he walked twenty or thirty steps east to where there was a small shop selling oil, salt, and other provisions.

Lao Ts'an went in to buy two packets of Ch'ao tobacco flavored with orchid seeds and took the chance to sit down. Looking at the man behind the counter, he judged that he was something over fifty years of age. He asked him, "Your honorable name?" "My name is Wang," said the man; "I'm a native of this place. Your honorable name, Sir?" Lao Ts'an said, "My name is T'ieh—I'm a Chiangnan man." "Chiangnan is certainly a fine place," said the man; "'Above are the halls of heaven; below Su and Hang.'[3] Not like this hell of ours here!" Lao Ts'an said: "You have hills, you have water, you grow rice and you grow wheat. How is it different from Chiangnan?" The man sighed and answered, "It is difficult to tell in a word!" and said no more.

Lao Ts'an asked, "Your Prefect Yü here, is he all right?" The man answered, "He's an honest official! A good official! At the gate of his yamen are twelve cages which are usually full; it's a rare day when one or two are vacant!"

While they were talking, a middle-aged woman with a rough bowl in her hand came out from the back of the shop to look for something among the shelves. Noticing a man on the other side of the counter, she gave one glance at him and continued her search.

Lao Ts'an said, "How can there be so many bandits?" The man replied, "Who knows?" Lao Ts'an said, "Surely most of them must be unjustly condemned." The man answered, "Injustice! No, there's no injustice!" Lao Ts'an said, "I hear that if he happens to see a man who doesn't please his eye, he simply puts him in a cage and chokes him to death; or if somebody talks unwisely and falls into his hands, he's a dead man too. Is this true?" The man said, "No! Never!"

But Lao Ts'an noticed that as the man answered, his face began to turn gray, and his eyes reddened. When he heard the words, "if somebody talks unwisely," tears

3. Chiangnan (Jiangnan) means literally "south of the Yangzi," or southeastern China. Suzhou and Hangzhou are two cities in the region famous for their beauty.

filled his eyes, though they did not fall. The woman who had come in to get things looked round and could no longer restrain the tears which rolled down her face. She stopped in her search, and carrying her bowl in one hand, and covering her eyes with her sleeve with the other, ran out through the back door. When she had reached the courtyard, she began to sob, *ju-ju.*

Lao Ts'an wanted to question the man further, but by his grief-stricken face he knew that he must be weighed down by some wrong or injustice of which he dared not speak, so he merely made a few meaningless remarks and went away.

He returned to his inn and went to sit for a while in his own room, where he read a few pages of a book. When Lao Tung was no longer busy, he wandered out to find him and have another chat. He told Lao Tung what he had seen in the little general store and asked him what it was all about.

Lao Tung said: "This man's name is Wang. There are only the two of them, man and wife, and they were not married until he was thirty. His wife is ten years younger than he. After marriage they had one son, who was twenty-one years old this year. They buy the rougher articles they sell in their shop at our village fair, but for the better-grade articles, this son of theirs always went to the city. This spring, when their son was in the *fu* city he must have had one or two cups of wine too many and let his tongue run away with him, for outside somebody's shop, he started to carry on about Prefect Yü, what a fool he was, how he took pleasure in treating people unjustly. This was overheard by some of Prefect Yü's spies, and he was dragged off to the yamen. The Prefect took his seat and railed at him, 'You thing, you! So you start rumors to disturb the people! What next?' He was then stood in a cage, and in less than two days choked to death. The middle-aged woman Your Honor saw just now is the wife of this man Wang. She is now more than forty. They had only this one son, not another soul in the world. Your mention of Prefect Yü couldn't help hurting her!"

Lao Ts'an said, "This Yü Hsien! Death wouldn't expiate all his crimes! How is it that his reputation in the provincial capital is so great? It truly is an astonishing thing! If I had power, this man would certainly be put to death!" Lao Tung said, "Your Honor had better watch what he says! While Your Honor is here, it doesn't matter if you talk freely. But in the city don't talk like this. It will cost you your life!"

Lao Ts'an said, "Thank you for your kind warning; I will be careful." That night, after supper, he had a good sleep. The next day he took his leave of Lao Tung, got on his cart, and set out.

Anton Chekhov
1860–1904

"All I wanted was to say honestly to people: 'Have a look at yourselves and see how bad and dreary your lives are!' The important thing is that people should realize that, for when they do, they will most certainly create another and better life for themselves. I will not live to see it, but I know that it will be quite different, quite unlike our present life. And so long as this different life does not exist, I shall go on saying to people again and again: 'Please, understand that your life is bad and dreary!'"

A doctor whose own life was weighed down and then cut short at the age of forty-four by tuberculosis, Chekhov was by all accounts anything but dreary himself. Born in southern Russia, son of a merchant and grandson of a freed serf, Chekhov came to Moscow in 1879 to study medicine, receiving his degree in 1884. A lover of games, banter, comic nicknames, vaudeville, and French farce, he began to write jokes and comic sketches for journals to help support himself and his family while he was in school. In time, he wrote a number of hilarious one-act plays for the Moscow stage and hundreds of comic stories. The longer plays that made him famous, masterpieces of the world theater like *The Seagull* (1897), *Uncle Vanya* (1899), *The Three Sisters* (1901), and *The Cherry Orchard* (1904), are often described as tragedies, but Chekhov quarreled with the tragic style in which they were staged by the great director Constantin Stanislavsky, insisting that they were really comedies. The plots alone can't decide this question; as Virginia Woolf once remarked, Chekhov's endings seem "as if a tune had stopped short without the expected chords to close it." Everything depends on the perspective.

The perspective that has come to be called "Chekhovian" is usually characterized by understatement and concealed meaning, scenes of autumn and twilight when things are winding down rather than starting up, prematurely aging heroes who hope for very little and don't know what they want, or perhaps don't even really want what they think they want. Overpowering desire is not Chekhov's trademark effect. What matters is less the actions taken and their consequences than how we look at those actions, whether taken or not. In its outlines, "The Lady with the Dog" might be described as a story about the abrupt and awesome power of passionate love. In its sentence-by-sentence texture, however, it seems easily distracted by other, more mundane matters. Something like the threat of ultimate dreariness seems to hang over even the happiest moments. Can love save us from the hopelessness of everyday banality? Or is love too a farce, nothing but more of that banality? It's as if Chekhov wants us to ask but refuses any conclusive answer.

The Lady with the Dog[1]

1

It was said that a new person had appeared on the sea-front: a lady with a little dog. Dmitri Dmitritch Gurov, who had by then been a fortnight at Yalta, and so was fairly at home there, had begun to take an interest in new arrivals. Sitting in Verney's pavilion, he saw, walking on the sea-front, a fair-haired young lady of medium height, wearing a *béret;* a white Pomeranian dog was running behind her.

And afterwards he met her in the public gardens and in the square several times a day. She was walking alone, always wearing the same *béret,* and always with the same white dog; no one knew who she was, and every one called her simply "the lady with the dog."

"If she is here alone without a husband or friends, it wouldn't be amiss to make her acquaintance," Gurov reflected.

He was under forty, but he had a daughter already twelve years old, and two sons at school. He had been married young, when he was a student in his second year, and by now his wife seemed half as old again as he. She was a tall, erect woman with dark eyebrows, staid and dignified, and, as she said of herself, intellectual. She read a

1. Translated by Constance Garnett.

great deal, used phonetic spelling,[2] called her husband, not Dmitri, but Dimitri, and he secretly considered her unintelligent, narrow, inelegant, was afraid of her, and did not like to be at home. He had begun being unfaithful to her long ago—had been unfaithful to her often, and, probably on that account, almost always spoke ill of women, and when they were talked about in his presence, used to call them "the lower race."

It seemed to him that he had been so schooled by bitter experience that he might call them what he liked, and yet he could not get on for two days together without "the lower race." In the society of men he was bored and not himself, with them he was cold and uncommunicative; but when he was in the company of women he felt free, and knew what to say to them and how to behave; and he was at ease with them even when he was silent. In his appearance, in his character, in his whole nature, there was something attractive and elusive which allured women and disposed them in his favour; he knew that, and some force seemed to draw him, too, to them.

Experience often repeated, truly bitter experience, had taught him long ago that with decent people, especially Moscow people—always slow to move and irresolute—every intimacy, which at first so agreeably diversifies life and appears a light and charming adventure, inevitably grows into a regular problem of extreme intricacy, and in the long run the situation becomes unbearable. But at every fresh meeting with an interesting woman this experience seemed to slip out of his memory, and he was eager for life, and everything seemed simple and amusing.

One evening he was dining in the gardens, and the lady in the *béret* came up slowly to take the next table. Her expression, her gait, her dress, and the way she did her hair told him that she was a lady, that she was married, that she was in Yalta for the first time and alone, and that she was dull there. . . . The stories told of the immorality in such places as Yalta are to a great extent untrue; he despised them, and knew that such stories were for the most part made up by persons who would themselves have been glad to sin if they had been able; but when the lady sat down at the next table three paces from him, he remembered these tales of easy conquests, of trips to the mountains, and the tempting thought of a swift, fleeting love affair, a romance with an unknown woman, whose name he did not know, suddenly took possession of him.

He beckoned coaxingly to the Pomeranian, and when the dog came up to him he shook his finger at it. The Pomeranian growled: Gurov shook his finger at it again.

The lady looked at him and at once dropped her eyes.

"He doesn't bite," she said, and blushed.

"May I give him a bone?" he asked; and when she nodded he asked courteously, "Have you been long in Yalta?"

"Five days."

"And I have already dragged out a fortnight here."

There was a brief silence.

"Time goes fast, and yet it is so dull here!" she said, not looking at him.

"That's only the fashion to say it is dull here. A provincial will live in Belyov or Zhidra and not be dull, and when he comes here it's 'Oh, the dulness! Oh, the dust!' One would think he came from Grenada."

---

2. Literally, "omitted the 'hard sign,'" a characteristic of a progressive intellectual (this anticipated the reform of the Russian alphabet).

She laughed. Then both continued eating in silence, like strangers, but after dinner they walked side by side; and there sprang up between them the light jesting conversation of people who are free and satisfied, to whom it does not matter where they go or what they talk about. They walked and talked of the strange light on the sea: the water was of a soft warm lilac hue, and there was a golden streak from the moon upon it. They talked of how sultry it was after a hot day. Gurov told her that he came from Moscow, that he had taken his degree in Arts, but had a post in a bank; that he had trained as an opera-singer, but had given it up, that he owned two houses in Moscow. . . . And from her he learnt that she had grown up in Petersburg, but had lived in S—— since her marriage two years before, that she was staying another month in Yalta, and that her husband, who needed a holiday too, might perhaps come and fetch her. She was not sure whether her husband had a post in a Crown Department or under the Provincial Council—and was amused by her own ignorance. And Gurov learnt, too, that she was called Anna Sergeyevna.

Afterwards he thought about her in his room at the hotel—thought she would certainly meet him next day; it would be sure to happen. As he got into bed he thought how lately she had been a girl at school, doing lessons like his own daughter; he recalled the diffidence, the angularity, that was still manifest in her laugh and her manner of talking with a stranger. This must have been the first time in her life she had been alone in surroundings in which she was followed, looked at, and spoken to merely from a secret motive which she could hardly fail to guess. He recalled her slender, delicate neck, her lovely grey eyes.

"There's something pathetic about her, anyway," he thought, and fell asleep.

2

A week had passed since they had made acquaintance. It was a holiday. It was sultry indoors, while in the street the wind whirled the dust round and round, and blew people's hats off. It was a thirsty day, and Gurov often went into the pavilion, and pressed Anna Sergeyevna to have syrup and water or an ice. One did not know what to do with oneself.

In the evening when the wind had dropped a little, they went out on the groyne[3] to see the steamer come in. There were a great many people walking about the harbour; they had gathered to welcome some one, bringing bouquets. And two peculiarities of a well-dressed Yalta crowd were very conspicuous: the elderly ladies were dressed like young ones, and there were great numbers of generals.

Owing to the roughness of the sea, the steamer arrived late, after the sun had set, and it was a long time turning about before it reached the groyne. Anna Sergeyevna looked through her lorgnette at the steamer and the passengers as though looking for acquaintances, and when she turned to Gurov her eyes were shining. She talked a great deal and asked disconnected questions, forgetting next moment what she had asked; then she dropped her lorgnette in the crush.

The festive crowd began to disperse; it was too dark to see people's faces. The wind had completely dropped, but Gurov and Anna Sergeyevna still stood as though waiting to see some one else come from the steamer. Anna Sergeyevna was silent now, and sniffed the flowers without looking at Gurov.

"The weather is better this evening," he said. "Where shall we go now? Shall we drive somewhere?"

3. Pier.

She made no answer.

Then he looked at her intently, and all at once put his arm round her and kissed her on the lips, and breathed in the moisture and the fragrance of the flowers; and he immediately looked round him, anxiously wondering whether any one had seen them.

"Let us go to your hotel," he said softly. And both walked quickly.

The room was close and smelt of the scent she had bought at the Japanese shop. Gurov looked at her and thought: "What different people one meets in the world!" From the past he preserved memories of careless, good-natured women, who loved cheerfully and were grateful to him for the happiness he gave them, however brief it might be; and of women like his wife who loved without any genuine feeling, with superfluous phrases, affectedly, hysterically, with an expression that suggested that it as not love nor passion, but something more significant; and of two or three others, very beautiful, cold women, on whose faces he had caught a glimpse of a rapacious expression—an obstinate desire to snatch from life more than it could give, and these were capricious, unreflecting, domineering, unintelligent women not in their first youth, and when Gurov grew cold to them their beauty excited his hatred, and the lace on their linen seemed to him like scales.

But in this case there was still the diffidence, the angularity of inexperienced youth, an awkward feeling; and there was a sense of consternation as though some one had suddenly knocked at the door. The attitude of Anna Sergeyevna—"the lady with the dog" —to what had happened was somehow peculiar, very grave, as though it were her fall—so it seemed, and it was strange and inappropriate. Her face dropped and faded, and on both sides of it her long hair hung down mournfully; she mused in a dejected attitude like "the woman who was a sinner" in an old-fashioned picture.

"It's wrong," she said. "You will be the first to despise me now."

There was a water-melon on the table. Gurov cut himself a slice and began eating it without haste. There followed at least half an hour of silence.

Anna Sergeyevna was touching; there was about her the purity of a good, simple woman who had seen little of life. The solitary candle burning on the table threw a faint light on her face, yet it was clear that she was very unhappy.

"How could I despise you?" asked Gurov. "You don't know what you are saying."

"God forgive me," she said, and her eyes filled with tears. "It's awful."

"You seem to feel you need to be forgiven."

"Forgiven? No. I am a bad, low woman; I despise myself and don't attempt to justify myself. It's not my husband but myself I have deceived. And not only just now; I have been deceiving myself for a long time. My husband may be a good, honest man, but he is a flunkey! I don't know what he does there, what his work is, but I know he is a flunkey! I was twenty when I was married to him. I have been tormented by curiosity; I wanted something better. 'There must be a different sort of life,' I said to myself. I wanted to live! To live, to live! . . . I was fired by curiosity . . . you don't understand it, but, I swear to God, I could not control myself; something happened to me: I could not be restrained. I told my husband I was ill, and came here. . . . And here I have been walking about as though I were dazed, like a mad creature; . . . and now I have become a vulgar, contemptible woman whom any one may despise."

Gurov felt bored already, listening to her. He was irritated by the naive tone, by this remorse, so unexpected and inopportune; but for the tears in her eyes, he might have thought she was jesting or playing a part.

"I don't understand," he said softly. "What is it you want?"

She hid her face on his breast and pressed close to him.

"Believe me, believe me, I beseech you . . ." she said. "I love a pure, honest life, and sin is loathsome to me. I don't know what I am doing. Simple people say: 'The Evil One has beguiled me.' And I may say of myself now that the Evil One has beguiled me."

"Hush, hush! . . ." he muttered.

He looked at her fixed, scared eyes, kissed her, talked softly and affectionately, and by degrees she was comforted, and her gaiety returned; they both began laughing.

Afterwards when they went out there was not a soul on the sea-front. The town with its cypresses had quite a deathlike air, but the sea still broke noisily on the shore; a single barge was rocking on the waves, and a lantern was blinking sleepily on it.

They found a cab and drove to Oreanda.

"I found out your surname in the hall just now: it was written on the board—Von Diderits," said Gurov. "Is your husband a German?"

"No; I believe his grandfather was a German, but he is an Orthodox Russian himself."

At Oreanda they sat on a seat not far from the church, looked down at the sea, and were silent. Yalta was hardly visible through the morning mist; white clouds stood motionless on the mountain-tops. The leaves did not stir on the trees, grasshoppers chirruped, and the monotonous hollow sound of the sea rising up from below, spoke of the peace, of the eternal sleep awaiting us. So it must have sounded when there was no Yalta, no Oreanda here; so it sounds now, and it will sound as indifferently and monotonously when we are all no more. And in this constancy, in this complete indifference to the life and death of each of us, there lies hid, perhaps, a pledge of our eternal salvation, of the unceasing movement of life upon earth, of unceasing progress towards perfection. Sitting Beside a young woman who in the dawn seemed so lovely, soothed and spellbound in these magical surroundings—the sea, mountains, clouds, the open sky—Gurov thought how in reality everything is beautiful in this world when one reflects: everything except what we think or do ourselves when we forget our human dignity and the higher aims of our existence.

A man walked up to them—probably a keeper—looked at them and walked away. And this detail seemed mysterious and beautiful, too. They saw a steamer come from Theodosia, with its lights out in the glow of dawn.

"There is dew on the grass," said Anna Sergeyevna, after a silence.

"Yes. It's time to go home."

They went back to the town.

Then they met every day at twelve o'clock on the sea-front, lunched and dined together, went for walks, admired the sea. She complained that she slept badly, that her heart throbbed violently; asked the same questions, troubled now by jealousy and now by the fear that he did not respect her sufficiently. And often in the square or gardens, when there was no one near them, he suddenly drew her to him and kissed her passionately. Complete idleness, these kisses in broad daylight while he looked round in dread of some one's seeing them, the heat, the smell of the sea, and the continual passing to and fro before him of idle, well-dressed, well-fed people, made a new man of him; he told Anna Sergeyevna how beautiful she was, how fascinating. He was impatiently passionate, he would not move a step away from her, while she was often pensive and continually urged him to confess that he did not respect her, did not love her in the least, and thought of her as nothing but a common woman. Rather late almost every evening they drove somewhere out of town, to Oreanda or to the waterfall; and the expedition was always a success, the scenery invariably impressed them as grand and beautiful.

They were expecting her husband to come, but a letter came from him, saying that there was something wrong with his eyes, and he entreated his wife to come home as quickly as possible. Anna Sergeyevna made haste to go.

"It's a good thing I am going away," she said to Gurov. "It's the finger of destiny!"

She went by coach and he went with her. They were driving the whole day. When she had got into a compartment of the express, and when the second bell had rung, she said:

"Let me look at you once more . . . look at you once again. That's right."

She did not shed tears, but was so sad that she seemed ill, and her face was quivering.

"I shall remember you . . . think of you," she said. "God be with you; be happy. Don't remember evil against me. We are parting forever—it must be so, for we ought never to have met. Well, God be with you."

The train moved off rapidly, its lights soon vanished from sight, and a minute later there was no sound of it, as though everything had conspired together to end as quickly as possible that sweet delirium, that madness. Left alone on the platform, and gazing into the dark distance, Gurov listened to the chirrup of the grasshoppers and the hum of the telegraph wires, feeling as though he had only just waked up. And he thought, musing, that there had been another episode or adventure in his life, and it, too, was at an end, and nothing was left of it but a memory. . . . He was moved, sad, and conscious of a slight remorse. This young woman whom he would never meet again had not been happy with him; he was genuinely warm and affectionate with her, but yet in his manner, his tone, and his caresses there had been a shade of light irony, the coarse condescension of a happy man who was, besides, almost twice her age. All the time she had called him kind, exceptional, lofty; obviously he had seemed to her different from what he really was, so he had unintentionally deceived her. . . .

Here at the station was already a scent of autumn; it was a cold evening.

"It's time for me to go north," thought Gurov as he left the platform. "High time!"

3

At home in Moscow everything was in its winter routine; the stoves were heated, and in the morning it was still dark when the children were having breakfast and getting ready for school, and the nurse would light the lamp for a short time. The frosts had begun already. When the first snow has fallen, on the first day of sledge-driving it is pleasant to see the white earth, the white roofs, to draw soft, delicious breath, and the season brings back the days of one's youth. The old limes and birches, white with hoar-frost, have a good-natured expression; they are nearer to one's heart than cypresses and palms, and near them one doesn't want to be thinking of the sea and the mountains.

Gurov was Moscow born; he arrived in Moscow on a fine frosty day, and when he put on his fur coat and warm gloves, and walked along Petrovka, and when on Saturday evening he heard the ringing of the bells, his recent trip and the places he had seen lost all charm for him. Little by little he became absorbed in Moscow life, greedily read three newspapers a day, and declared he did not read the Moscow papers on principle! He already felt a longing to go to restaurants, clubs, dinner-parties, anniversary celebrations, and he felt flattered at entertaining distinguished lawyers and artists, and at playing cards with a professor at the doctors' club. He could already eat a whole plateful of salt fish and cabbage. . . .

In another month, he fancied, the image of Anna Sergeyevna would be shrouded in a mist in his memory, and only from time to time would visit him in his dreams with a touching smile as others did. But more than a month passed, real winter had come, and everything was still clear in his memory as though he had parted with Anna Sergeyevna only the day before. And his memories glowed more and more vividly. When in the evening stillness he heard from his study the voices of his children, preparing their lessons, or when he listened to a song or the organ at the restaurant, or the storm howled in the chimney, suddenly everything would rise up in his memory: what had happened on the groyne, and the early morning with the mist on the mountains, and the steamer coming from Theodosia, and the kisses. He would pace a long time about his room, remembering it all and smiling; then his memories passed into dreams, and in his fancy the past was mingled with what was to come. Anna Sergeyevna did not visit him in dreams, but followed him about everywhere like a shadow and haunted him. When he shut his eyes he saw her as though she were living before him, and she seemed to him lovelier, younger, tenderer than she was; and he imagined himself finer than he had been in Yalta. In the evenings she peeped out at him from the bookcase, from the fireplace, from the corner—he heard her breathing, the caressing rustle of her dress. In the street he watched the women, looking for some one like her.

He was tormented by an intense desire to confide his memories to some one. But in his home it was impossible to talk of his love, and he had no one outside; he could not talk to his tenants nor to any one at the bank. And what had he to talk of? Had he been in love, then? Had there been anything beautiful, poetical, or edifying or simply interesting in his relations with Anna Sergeyevna? And there was nothing for him but to talk vaguely of love, of woman, and no one guessed what it meant; only his wife twitched her black eyebrows, and said: "The part of a lady-killer does not suit you all, Dimitri."

One evening, coming out of the doctors' club with an official with whom he had been playing cards, he could not resist saying:

"If only you knew what a fascinating woman I made the acquaintance of in Yalta!"

The official got into his sledge and was driving away, but turned suddenly and shouted:

"Dmitri Dmitritch!"

"What?"

"You were right this evening: the sturgeon was a bit too strong!"

These words, so ordinary, for some reason moved Gurov to indignation, and struck him as degrading and unclean. What savage manners, what people! What senseless nights, what uninteresting, uneventful days! The rage for card-playing, the gluttony, the drunkenness, the continual talk always about the same thing. Useless pursuits and conversations always about the same things absorb the better part of one's time, the better part of one's strength, and in the end there is left a life grovelling and curtailed, worthless and trivial, and there is no escaping or getting away from it—just as though one were in a madhouse or a prison.

Gurov did not sleep all night, and was filled with indignation. And he had a headache all next day. And the next night he slept badly; he sat up in bed, thinking, or paced up and down his room. He was sick of his children, sick of the bank; he had no desire to go anywhere or to talk of anything.

In the holidays in December he prepared for a journey, and told his wife he was going to Petersburg to do something in the interests of a young friend—and he set off for S——. What for? He did not very well know himself. He wanted to see Anna Sergeyevna and to talk with her—to arrange a meeting, if possible.

He reached S—— in the morning, and took the best room at the hotel, in which the floor was covered with grey army cloth, and on the table was an inkstand, grey with dust and adorned with a figure on horseback, with its hat in its hand and its head broken off. The hotel porter gave him the necessary information; Von Diderits lived in a house of his own in Old Gontcharny Street—it was not far from the hotel: he was rich and lived in good style, and had his own horses; every one in the town knew him. The porter pronounced the name "Dridirits."

Gurov went without haste to Old Gontcharny Street and found the house. Just opposite the house stretched a long grey fence adorned with nails.

"One would run away from a fence like that," thought Gurov, looking from the fence to the windows of the house and back again.

He considered: to-day was a holiday, and the husband would probably be at home. And in any case it would be tactless to go into the house and upset her. If he were to send her a note it might fall into her husband's hands, and then it might ruin everything. The best thing was to trust to chance. And he kept walking up and down the street by the fence, waiting for the chance. He saw a beggar go in at the gate and dogs fly at him; then an hour later he heard a piano, and the sounds were faint and indistinct. Probably it was Anna Sergeyevna playing. The front door suddenly opened, and an old woman came out, followed by the familiar white Pomeranian. Gurov was on the point of calling to the dog, but his heart began beating violently, and in his excitement he could not remember the dog's name.

He walked up and down, and loathed the grey fence more and more, and by now he thought irritably that Anna Sergeyevna had forgotten him, and was perhaps already amusing herself with some one else, and that that was very natural in a young woman who had nothing to look at from morning till night but that confounded fence. He went back to his hotel room and sat for a long while on the sofa, not knowing what to do, then he had dinner and a long nap.

"How stupid and worrying it is!" he thought when he woke and looked at the dark windows: it was already evening. "Here I've had a good sleep for some reason. What shall I do in the night?"

He sat on the bed, which was covered by a cheap grey blanket, such as one sees in hospitals, and he taunted himself in his vexation:

"So much for the lady with the dog . . . so much for the adventure. . . . You're in a nice fix. . . ."

That morning at the station a poster in large letters had caught his eye. "The Geisha"[4] was to be performed for the first time. He thought of this and went to the theatre.

"It's quite possible she may go to the first performance," he thought.

The theatre was full. As in all provincial theatres, there was a fog above the chandelier, the gallery was noisy and restless; in the front row the local dandies were standing up before the beginning of the performance, with their hands behind them; in the Governor's box the Governor's daughter, wearing a boa, was sitting in the front seat, while the Governor himself lurked modestly behind the curtain with only his hands visible; the orchestra was a long time tuning up; the stage curtain swayed. All the time the audience were coming in and taking their seats Gurov looked at them eagerly.

Anna Sergeyevna, too, came in. She sat down in the third row, and when Gurov looked at her his heart contracted, and he understood clearly that for him there was in

---

4. An 1896 operetta by the Englishman Sidney Jones.

the whole world no creature so near, so precious, and so important to him; she, this little woman, in no way remarkable, lost in a provincial crowd, with a vulgar lorgnette[5] in her hand, filled his whole life now, was his sorrow and his joy, the one happiness that he now desired for himself, and to the sounds of the inferior orchestra, of the wretched provincial violins, he thought how lovely she was. He thought and dreamed.

A young man with small side-whiskers, tall and stooping, came in with Anna Sergeyevna and sat down beside her; he bent his head at every step and seemed to be continually bowing. Most likely this was the husband whom at Yalta, in a rush of bitter feeling, she had called a flunkey. And there really was in his long figure, his side-whiskers, and the small bald patch on his head, something of the flunkey's obsequiousness; his smile was sugary, and in his buttonhole there was some badge of distinction like the number on a waiter.

During the first interval the husband went away to smoke; she remained alone in her stall. Gurov, who was sitting in the stalls, too, went up to her and said in a trembling voice, with a forced smile:

"Good-evening."

She glanced at him and turned pale, then glanced again with horror, unable to believe her eyes, and tightly gripped the fan and the lorgnette in her hands, evidently struggling with herself not to faint. Both were silent. She was sitting, he was standing, frightened by her confusion and not venturing to sit down beside her. The violins and the flute began tuning up. He felt suddenly frightened; it seemed as though all the people in the boxes were looking at them. She got up and went quickly to the door; he followed her, and both walked senselessly along passages, and up and down stairs, and figures in legal, scholastic, and civil service uniforms, all wearing badges, flitted before their eyes. They caught glimpses of ladies, of fur coats hanging on pegs; the draughts blew on them, bringing a smell of stale tobacco. And Gurov, whose heart was beating violently, thought:

"Oh, heavens! Why are these people here and this orchestra! . . ."

And at that instant he recalled how when he had seen Anna Sergeyevna off at the station he had thought that everything was over and they would never meet again. But how far they were still from the end!

On the narrow, gloomy staircase over which was written, "To the Amphitheatre," she stopped.

"How you have frightened me!" she said, breathing hard, still pale and overwhelmed. "Oh, how you have frightened me! I am half dead. Why have you come? Why?"

"But do understand, Anna, do understand . . ." he said hastily in a low voice. "I entreat you to understand . . ."

She looked at him with dread, with entreaty, with love; she looked at him intently, to keep his features more distinctly in her memory.

"I m so unhappy," she went on, not heeding him. "I have thought of nothing but you all the time; I live only in the thought of you. And I wanted to forget, to forget you; but why, oh why, have you come?"

On the landing above them two schoolboys were smoking and looking down, but that was nothing to Gurov; he drew Anna Sergeyevna to him, and began kissing her face, her cheeks, and her hands.

---

5. A pair of eyeglasses with a short handle.

"What are you doing, what are you doing!" she cried in horror, pushing him away. "We are mad. Go away to-day; go away at once . . . I beseech you by all that is sacred, I implore you. . . . There are people coming this way!"

Some one was coming up the stairs.

"You must go away," Ann Sergeyevna went on in a whisper. "Do you hear, Dmitri Dmitritch? I will come and see you in Moscow. I have never been happy; I am miserable now, and I never, never shall be happy, never! Don't make me suffer still more! I swear I'll come to Moscow. But now let us part. My precious, good, dear one, we must part!"

She pressed his hand and began rapidly going downstairs, looking round at him, and from her eyes he could see that she really was unhappy. Gurov stood for a little while, listened, then, when all sound had died away, he found his coat and left the theatre.

4

And Anna Sergeyevna began coming to see him in Moscow. Once in two or three months she left S——, telling her husband that she was going to consult a doctor about an internal complaint—and her husband believed her, and did not believe her. In Moscow she stayed at the Slaviansky Bazaar hotel, and at once sent a man in a red cap to Gurov. Gurov went to see her, and no one in Moscow knew of it.

Once he was going to see her in this way on a winter morning (the messenger had come the evening before when he was out). With him walked his daughter, whom he wanted to take to school: it was on the way. Snow was falling in big wet flakes.

"It's three degrees above freezing-point, and yet it is snowing," said Gurov to his daughter. "The thaw is only on the surface of the earth; there is quite a different temperature at a greater height in the atmosphere."

"And why are there no thunderstorms in the winter, father?"

He explained that, too. He talked, thinking all the while that he was going to see *her,* and no living soul knew of it, and probably never would know. He had two lives: one, open, seen and known by all who cared to know, full of relative truth and of relative falsehood, exactly like the lives of his friends and acquaintances; and another life running its course in secret. And through some strange, perhaps accidental, conjunction of circumstances, everything that was essential, of interest and of value to him, everything in which he was sincere and did not deceive himself, everything that made the kernel of his life, was hidden from other people; and all that was false in him, the sheath in which he hid himself to conceal the truth—such, for instance, as his work in the bank, his discussions at the club, his "lower race," his presence with his wife at anniversary festivities—all that was open. And he judged of others by himself, not believing in what he saw, and always believing that every man had his real, most interesting life under the cover of secrecy and under the cover of night. All personal life rested on secrecy, and possibly it was partly on that account that civilized man was so nervously anxious that personal privacy should be respected.

After leaving his daughter at school, Gurov went on to the Slaviansky Bazaar. He took off his fur coat below, went upstairs, and softly knocked at the door. Anna Sergeyevna, wearing his favourite grey dress, exhausted by the journey and the suspense, had been expecting him since the evening before. She was pale; she looked at him, and did not smile, and he had hardly come in when she fell on his breast. Their kiss was slow and prolonged, as though they had not met for two years.

"Well, how are you getting on there?" he asked. "What news?"

"Wait; I'll tell you directly . . . I can't talk."

She could not speak; she was crying. She turned away from him, and pressed her handkerchief to her eyes.

"Let her have her cry out. I'll sit down and wait," he thought, and he sat down in an arm-chair.

Then he rang and asked for tea to be brought him, and while he drank his tea she remained standing at the window with her back to him. She was crying from emotion, from the miserable consciousness that their life was so hard for them; they could only meet in secret, hiding themselves from people, like thieves! Was not their life shattered?

"Come, do stop!" he said.

It was evident to him that this love of their would not soon be over, that he could not see the end of it. Anna Sergeyevna grew more and more attached to him. She adored him, and it was unthinkable to say to her that it was bound to have an end some day; besides, she would not have believed it!

He went up to her and took her by the shoulders to say something affectionate and cheering, and at that moment he saw himself in the looking-glass.

His hair was already beginning to turn grey. And it seemed strange to him that he had grown so much older, so much plainer during the last few years. The shoulders on which his hands rested were warm and quivering. He felt compassion for this life, still so warm and lovely, but probably already not far from beginning to fade and wither like his own. Why did she love him so much? He always seemed to women different form what he was, and they loved in him not himself, but the man created by their imagination, whom they had been eagerly seeking all their lives; and afterwards, when they noticed their mistake, they loved him all the same. And not one of them had been happy with him. Time passed, he had made their acquaintance, got on with them, parted, but he had never once loved; it was anything you like, but not love.

And only now when his head was grey he had fallen properly, really in love—for the first time in his life.

Anna Sergeyevna and he loved each other like people very close and akin, like husband and wife, like tender friends; it seemed to them that fate itself had meant them for one another, and they could not understand why he had a wife and she a husband; and it was as though they were a pair of birds of passage, caught and forced to live in different cages. They forgave each other for what they were ashamed of in their past, they forgave everything in the present, and felt that this love of theirs had changed them both.

In moments of depression in the past he had comforted himself with any arguments that came into his mind, but now he no longer cared for arguments; he felt profound compassion, he wanted to be sincere and tender. . . .

"Don't cry, my darling," he said "You've had your cry; that's enough . . . Let us talk now, let us think of some plan."

Then they spent a long while taking counsel together, talked of how to avoid the necessity for secrecy, for deception, for living in different towns and not seeing each other for long at a time. How could they be free from this intolerable bondage?

"How? How?" he asked, clutching his head. "How?"

And it seemed as though in a little while the solution would be found, and then a new and splendid life would begin; and it was clear to both of them that they had still a long, long road before them, and that the most complicated and difficult part of it was only just beginning.

Rabindranath Tagore
1861–1941

In the course of a long and immensely distinguished life, the Bengali writer Rabindranath Tagore was a leading figure in the Indian nationalist movement, an antagonist and intimate of Gandhi, the composer of India's national anthem along with many other popular songs, an educational reformer, and winner of the Nobel Prize for Literature. Born in Calcutta three years after Britain took over the government of India, he died six years before national independence in 1947. It is difficult to describe his life and achievements without linking them at every point with the emergence of modern India.

Tagore's father, the son of one of India's richest men, was a noted religious thinker, and Tagore was encouraged to begin publishing at the age of nineteen in a journal run by his family. The foremost Bengali writer of the day, Bankim Chandra Chatterji (1838–1894), acclaimed his youthful poems. He benefited as well from the example of the Bengali reformer Ram Mohan Roy (1772–1833), who offered an early synthesis of European enlightenment with brilliantly reinterpreted Hindu tradition. Roy helped inspire Tagore's lifelong struggle to eliminate prejudice against women, foreigners, and non-Hindus. The Bengali poems of *Gitanjali* (translated into English in 1912) captured the imagination of W. B. Yeats, Ezra Pound, André Gide, and then the Nobel Prize committee, which gave Tagore its prize for literature in 1913. He was knighted in 1915. Tagore's lectures against the dangers of militaristic nationalism, delivered in the midst of World War I, gave grave offense to many British readers, as did his decision to return his knighthood in protest against the Amritsar massacre by the British army in 1919. Still, his international celebrity continued to grow.

An early leader in the movement for India's national liberation, Tagore was the first to call Gandhi "Mahatma," or "Great Soul." No less generous to one who frequently disagreed with him, Gandhi spoke of Tagore as the "Great Sentinel." Repelled by the violence and coercion spawned by Gandhi's Swaraj or self-rule campaign, Tagore withdrew from it in 1921. This withdrawal is the background to his best-known novel, *The Home and the World,* in which a cosmopolitan landowner and his nationalist rival struggle for the affections of the landowner's wife. To some, Tagore's stubborn faith in the unity of mankind has seemed idealistic. To others his life remains a practical inspiration.

PRONUNCIATION:
Rabindranath Tagore: rah-BIN-dra-nath tah-GORE

The Conclusion[1]

1

Apurba Krishna had just passed his BA examination in Calcutta and was returning to his village. On the way his boat had to cross a small river. Later in the year, after the close of the rainy season, it would have been almost dry. Now at the end of Shraban, the monsoon month, it had reached the edge of the village and was lapping at the ruins of the bamboo grove. But after days and days of heavy rain, the sun shone in a cloudless sky.

---

1. Translated by Krishna Dutta and Andrew Robinson.

Apurba's thoughts as he sat in the boat were brimming too. Had we access to the pictures in his young mind we would have seen them dancing like the sun's rays on the wind-ruffled water.

The boat drew up at the usual ghat.[2] From the riverbank Apurba could see the tiled roof of his house through a gap in the trees. No one there knew of his arrival, and so no one had come to meet him. The boatman offered a hand with the luggage, but Apurba refused it and stepped gaily ashore. His feet touched the mud of the ghat, and he fell over, luggage and all. At that instant a melodious peal of high-pitched laughter came from somewhere and startled the birds in a nearby peepul tree.

Extremely embarrassed, Apurba quickly recovered his balance and looked about him. On top of a pile of bricks in course of being unloaded for the local money-lender, a girl sat doubled up with giggles. Apurba recognized her as Mrinmayi, daughter of their recently arrived neighbours. He knew they had previously lived by a big river some distance away, but when the river had swallowed their land they had settled in the village two or three years ago.

Apurba knew much about this girl's reputation. The men of the village referred to her affectionately as Pagli—"Madcap"—but their wives were in a constant state of alarm at her wayward behaviour. All her playmates were boys, and she had vast scorn for girls her own age. In the ranks of biddable children she was regarded as a scourge.

Being her father's favourite made her all the more unruly. Her mother never stopped grumbling about it to her friends. Yet because the father loved Mrinmayi, her tears would have hurt him deeply if he had been at home. That fact, and natural deference to her absent husband, kept the mother from imposing too strict a discipline.

Mrinmayi was dark complexioned with wavy hair that straggled over her shoulders. Her expression was boyish. Her enormous black eyes held no shame or fear, and not the slightest coyness. She was tall, well built, healthy, strong—but of an age people found hard to estimate; otherwise they would have criticized her parents because she was still unmarried. If the boat of some distant zamindar[3] arrived at the ghat, the villagers became impressively alert. As if at a signal, the women pulled their veils down to the tips of their noses, thus concealing their faces like curtains on a stage. But Mrinmayi would arrive holding a naked child to her chest, her unbound hair hanging free. She would stand like a young doe gazing inquisitively in a land where there was neither hunter nor danger. Eventually she would return to her boy playmates and give them elaborate descriptions of the new arrival's manners and mores.

Our Apurba had set eyes on this untamed creature several times during holidays at home, and had occasionally thought of her in a casual way, and sometimes in a not-so-casual way. In the course of life one sees a great many faces, but only a few become fixed in the mind, not for their external appeal but for some other quality—a transparency perhaps. Most faces do not give away much of the personality; but the transparent face—the face in a thousand—clearly reveals the mystery behind it and immediately impresses itself on the mind. Mrinmayi's face was one of these. Her eyes held all the wilful femininity of a nimble, unfettered fawn. It was a face that, once seen, was not easy to forget.

Of course its melodious laughter, however charming it might have been to others, sounded rather painful to the unlucky Apurba. Hastily handing the suitcase to the boatman, he set off red-faced towards home.

---

2. Broad riverside stairway.   3. Tax collector.

And so the scene was beautifully set, with the riverbank, the shady trees, the bird-song, the morning sun, the joy of being twenty—no need to mention a pile of bricks: but as for the person sitting on top of them, she bestowed grace even on that dull and solid heap. How cruel of fate to have turned poetry into farce at the first entrance of the first act.

2

The peal of laughter from that pile was still echoing in Apurba's ears when he picked up his mud-smeared case and chadar,[4] took the path beneath the trees, and arrived at his house. His widowed mother was ecstatic at his unexpected arrival. She sent out at once for rice pudding, curds and *rui* fish and caused a bit of a flurry in the neighbourhood. Once the meal was over she introduced the subject of marriage. Apurba had expected it. He had already received many proposals, and in keeping with the slogan of the day had obstinately insisted "BA pass before bride." But now he was a BA, and his mother had been expectant for so long that he knew further excuses would be useless. He said, "Very well, first let me see the girl. Then I'll decide."

His mother said, "I've seen her. You needn't give it a thought."

Apurba was quite prepared to give it a thought himself and said, "Bride must be seen before marriage." His mother thought she had never heard anything so outrageous, but she consented.

That night, after Apurba had put out the lamp and lain down to sleep in his solitary bed, he caught a sound from beyond the patter of midnight rain and the stillness of the village, the sound of sweet high-pitched laughter. His morning downfall bothered him very much, and he pondered how to rectify the impression he had created. The girl doesn't know that I, Apurba Krishna, am an erudite fellow, he thought, who has spent long periods in Calcutta—not a village bumpkin to be dismissed with a laugh because of a trifling slip in some mud.

The next day Apurba had to inspect the potential bride. She was not far away; the family lived in a neighbouring village. He dressed with some care. Discarding his usual dhoti and chadar, he wore a long silk *chapkan,* a puggree[5] on his head, and his best varnished shoes, and set out at dawn with a silk umbrella in his hand.

The instant he entered the prospective father-in-law's house, he was received with pomp and circumstance. In due time a trembling creature, painted and polished, tinsel round the bun in her hair, and wrapped in a fine colourful sari, was produced before him. She was led silently to a corner, where she remained with her head bent almost to her knees and an elderly maidservant at her back to give her courage. Her small brother Rakhal now concentrated his total attention upon this latest intruder into the family and scrutinized its puggree, gold watch-chain and newly sprouted beard. After stroking this last a few times, Apurba finally asked with a solemn air, "What have you read?" The dumb-founded ornamented bundle made no response. After a few more questions and some encouraging prods in the ribs from the maid, the girl blurted out in a faint voice, "*Charupath*-Volume-Two-Grammar-Volume-One-Descriptive-Geography-Arithmetic-History-of-India." Simultaneously there came a sudden series of repeated thuds outside the room, and a moment later Mrinmayi raced

4. Long shawl.   5. Turban.

breathlessly into the room with her hair flying. Without so much as a glance at Apurba Krishna, she grabbed the brother of the bride-to-be by the hand and began to pull him out of the room. But Rakhal refused to cooperate, so absorbing was the situation indoors. The maid did her best to retrieve this by berating Mrinmayi as sharply as propriety permitted. Apurba Krishna meanwhile preserved his own dignity as best he could by sitting bolt upright in his lofty turban and fiddling with the watch-chain across his stomach. When Mrinmayi finally grasped that she could not distract Rakhal, she slapped him loudly on the back, whipped the veil off the girl's head, and dashed out like a whirlwind. The maid growled in fury, and Rakhal tittered at the sudden sight of his sister minus her precious veil. The slap on the back he did not object to at all, for such exchanges often took place between them. Mrinmayi's hair, for instance, once hung halfway down her back, rather than to her shoulders. One day Rakhal had sneaked up behind her and snipped off a handful with a pair of scissors. She had grabbed the scissors from him in anger and finished the job with a few slashes. Waves of hair had fallen to the ground and lain there like clusters of black grapes. This was the system of discipline between them.

The inspection session fell silent and did not endure much longer. Somehow the girl uncurled herself, regained a perpendicular position and returned to the inner rooms escorted by the old maid. Apurba, still stroking his sparse moustache, rose as solemnly as possible and prepared to depart. But when he reached the door he saw that his new pair of varnished shoes had vanished, and no one could find them. Everyone in the house was frightfully put out and hurled endless reproaches in the direction of the culprit. Eventually a desperate Apurba borrowed an old, torn and flapping pair of slippers belonging to the master of the house. With this additional touch to his fancy *chapkan* and puggree, he very gingerly set out along the village path.

By the edge of a pond, at a deserted point on the path, the high-pitched laughter caught him again. It was as if some fun-loving nymph in the forest had seen the slippers and could not suppress her giggles. While Apurba stood hesitating, she emerged brazenly, placed his new pair of shoes on the path, and was about to take to her heels when Apurba managed to grab both her hands and capture her.

Twisting and turning, Mrinmayi tried to free herself but could not. A stray sunbeam slanted through the trees on to her full, mischievous face. Like a curious traveller stooping to see the sunlit bed of a moving stream through clear water, Apurba gravely gazed on Mrinmayi's upturned face with its sparkling eyes, very gradually loosened his grip on his prisoner, and released her. If he had struck her in anger Mrinmayi would not have been at all surprised, but this gentle sentence of punishment in this empty glade quite baffled her.

The whole sky seemed to ring with laughter like the sound of celestial ankle bells. Lost in thought Apurba Krishna plodded home.

3

All day Apurba made up excuses for not joining his mother in the inner rooms. He had an invitation elsewhere; he ate there. The fact is—though it may be hard to swallow—that even someone as erudite, serious minded and original as Apurba was remarkably eager to regain his lost dignity in the eyes of this simple village girl. What did it matter if she had momentarily reduced him to a laughing-stock, then ignored him in favour of some ignoramus named Rakhal? Must he prove to her that he reviewed books for a magazine called *Visvadip* and carried in his suitcase cologne, shoes, Rubini's camphor, coloured letter paper, and a book on how to play the harmonium, not to mention a notebook awaiting future publication like the dawn in the womb of night? Nevertheless, whatever common sense might say, Mr Apurba Krishna Ray was definitely unprepared to admit defeat at the hands of this flighty rustic girl.

When he appeared in the inner rooms that evening, his mother asked, "Well Apu, you saw the girl. Do you approve?"

Somewhat awkwardly Apurba replied, "I saw the girl, Mother, and there was one I liked."

Astounded, his mother said, "You saw *girls?*"

Then, after much shilly-shallying, he revealed that he had selected Mrinmayi, daughter of their neighbour. What a choice after so much education and study!

At first Apurba was considerably abashed, but he was no longer so when his mother began to object vehemently. He sat there insisting doggedly that he would marry no one but Mrinmayi. The more he thought of the dolled-up kind of girl, the more repulsive became the idea of marrying one.

Battle was joined between them, in the form of tiffs, sulks, fasts and sleepless nights, and after two or three days Apurba was victorious. His mother managed to convince herself that Mrinmayi was still immature, that her own mother had been unable to bring her up properly, but that if taken in hand after marriage Mrinmayi's nature would change. Gradually, she came to believe that the girl had a pretty face. It was when she thought of the girl's cropped hair that her heart filled with despair. Yet even that, she hoped, if tied up firmly and thoroughly soaked in oil, might in time respond to treatment.

To the village people Apurba's choice of bride quickly became labelled *apurba*—original. Many of them rather liked "Pagli Mrinmayi," but not, it had to be said, as a possible daughter-in-law.

Her father, Ishan Majumdar, was informed. He was a clerk in a steamship company, responsible for the correct loading and unloading of goods and the sale of tickets from a decrepit tin-roofed hut at a distant riverside station. When he heard the news, he shed tears of sorrow and joy, mingled in proportions unknown. He petitioned his boss, a head-office sahib, for leave of absence to attend his daughter's wedding. The sahib considered this insufficient grounds and turned down the request. Then, expecting a week's holiday at Puja time, Ishan wrote home to postpone the wedding. But Apurba's mother said, "The auspicious days fall in the present month, the wedding cannot be put off." Twice rejected, the distressed father protested no more and went back to weighing goods and selling tickets.

Whereupon Mrinmayi's mother and all the older women of the village assembled and began to instruct Mrinmayi day and night in her future duties. Their stern prohibitions against playfulness and frolicking around, loud laughter, gossip with boys, and eating when hungry succeeded in making marriage sound like a nightmare. An alarmed Mrinmayi thought she had been sentenced to life imprisonment with hanging at the end of it. Like an unbroken pony she stiffened her neck, reared back, and said, "I'm not going to get married."

4

Nevertheless, she did.

Then her lessons began. Overnight, Mrinmayi's world contracted to the confines of her mother-in-law's inner rooms. Her mother-in-law began the task of correcting her. Assuming a minatory expression, she said, "Look, dear, you are not a little girl any longer. We don't tolerate disgraceful manners in our house." Mrinmayi did not grasp what she meant. If my manners are not tolerated here, I'd better go elsewhere, she thought. That afternoon she went missing. A thorough search was launched. Finally the traitor Rakhal led them to her secret hideout, the abandoned old chariot of the village deity Radha Kanta under a banyan tree. It is easy to imagine how the mother-in-law and willing well-wishers set upon the girl.

That night the clouds gathered and rain began with a pattering sound. Apurba Krishna edged a little closer to Mrinmayi as she lay in bed and whispered in her ear, "Mrinmayi, don't you love me?"

"No!" she said violently, "I will never ever love you!" And then she unleashed all her rage and humiliation on Apurba's head like a thunderbolt.

In a wounded voice he said, "Why, what have I done?"

"Why did you marry me?"

A satisfactory counter to this accusation was tricky. But then and there Apurba decided he must win her over.

The next day the mother-in-law saw all the signs of rebellion and locked Mrinmayi in. At first and for some time she fluttered about the room like a newly captured bird. When she could not escape she shredded the bedsheets with her teeth in futile anger and then, lying prone on the floor, pined for her father and wept.

In time someone slowly came and sat beside her. Affectionately he tried to lift her hair off the floor and away from her face. Mrinmayi shook her head vigorously and threw off the hand. Then Apurba bent down to her and said softly, "I've opened the door. Come, let's get away to the back garden." But Mrinmayi's head shook vehemently and said, "No." Apurba tried to lift her chin and said, "Just look who's here." Rakhal, bewildered at seeing Mrinmayi prostrate on the floor, stood at the door. Without looking up she pushed away Apurba's hand. "Rakhal's come to play with you. Won't you go with him?" In a voice loud with irritation she repeated "No!" Rakhal realized he had chosen the wrong moment and fled with a sigh of relief. Apurba sat on in silence. Mrinmayi wept and wept, until she exhausted herself and fell asleep. Apurba tiptoed out and fastened the door behind him.

The next day she received a letter from her father. He grieved over his inability to attend his darling's marriage, and he sent the newly-weds his heartfelt blessings. Mrinmayi went to her mother-in-law and said, "I want to go to my father." The astonished woman exploded at this outlandish request. "Who knows where her father lives, and she wants to go to him! A fantastic notion!" Mrinmayi went away without replying. She went to her room, bolted the door, and in utter hopelessness began to pray to her father as if to God: "Father, come and take me away. I have no one here. I'll die if I stay here."

In the dead of night, while her husband slept, Mrinmayi very carefully opened the door and left the house. Clouds passed over now and then, but the paths were plain in the moonlight. How to choose one leading to her father was beyond her. She assumed that if she followed the route of the mail runner it would take her to any address in the world. She set off on this familiar path. After walking quite a way she grew weary, and night was nearly over. As a few birds uncertain of the time began to give tentative chirps, she found herself on a riverbank in a place like a large market. She paused to think, and then recognized the "jham jham' sound of the mail runner's ankle bells. Then he himself appeared, out of breath, with the mail bag on his shoulder. Mrinmayi rushed up to him and begged, "I want to go to my father at Kushiganj. Will you take me?"

"I don't know where Kushiganj is." With barely a pause for breath he roused the boatman on the mail boat tied up at the ghat, and the boat cast off. He was not allowed to take time to answer questions.

By and by the market awoke. Mrinmayi went down to the ghat and called to another boatman, "Will you take me to Kushiganj?" Before he could reply, someone in the next boat called out, "So it's you, Minu Ma? What are you doing here?" Bursting with impatience she called back, "Banamali, I'm going to my father at Kushiganj. Can you take me in your boat?" Banamali was a boatman from their village and knew this wilful girl very well. "You're going to your father? That's good. Come on, I'll take you." Mrinmayi jumped in.

The boatman cast off. The clouds descended and a torrential downpour began. The boat tossed in a current swollen with the rains of the month of Bhadra. Mrinmayi was overwhelmed with fatigue. She spread the loose end of her sari, lay down, and went tamely to sleep, rocked by the river like a baby in mother nature's arms.

She awoke in her bed in her married home. Seeing her eyes open the maid began to scold. This brought the mother-in-law and a stream of harsh words. Mrinmayi, wide-eyed, stared at her. But when she made a dig at Mrinmayi's father's bad training, Mrinmayi got up, went to the next room, and bolted the door.

Apurba forsook his usual timidity, went to his mother and said, "What harm is there in sending her to her father for a few days?"

His mother turned on him: "She's bewitched!" and then she took up an old theme: with so many girls to choose from, why had he brought home this bone-burning good-for-nothing?

5

All day the downpour continued, and the atmosphere indoors was equally foul. That night, in the early hours, Apurba woke Mrinmayi and said, "Do you want to go to your father?" Suddenly alert, she clutched his hand and said simply, "Yes!" Apurba whispered, "Come then. We'll escape very quietly. I've arranged a boat."

Mrinmayi looked at her husband with profound gratitude. She got up quickly, dressed, and prepared to leave. Apurba left a note to allay his mother's anxiety, and the two of them stepped out. In the dark, without a soul or a sound nearby, she first put her hand in her husband's of her own free will; the tingle of her excitement thrilled his every nerve.

The boat moved out into the night. In spite of her ecstasy Mrinmayi fell asleep almost at once. The next day, what freedom what delight! On both banks were so many villages, markets, fields of grain, forests, other boats passing back and forth. Soon she was plying her husband with a thousand questions about the tiniest and most trivial of sights. What is in that boat? Where have those people come from? What is the name of this place? Questions whose answers could not be found in any of Apurba's college books or extracted from his Calcutta experience. His friends there would have been embarrassed to know that he answered every one of them and that most of his replies did not tally with the truth. He asserted, for instance, that a boat carrying sesame carried linseed, and he called a magistrate's court a zamindar's warehouse and confused the town of Panchberia with that of Rainagar. His wrong replies did not impede in the slightest the satisfaction in the heart of his trustful questioner.

The following evening they reached Kushiganj. In a tin-roofed hut half lit by an oily old lantern Ishan Chandra sat bare-chested on a stool, bent over a huge leather-bound account book resting on a small desk. The newly-weds entered and Mrinmayi said, "Father!" in a tone of voice quite alien to that room. Ishan wept. He could not think what to say or what to do. His daughter and son-in-law were standing in his hut like the princess and prince of an empire, and all he could offer them for thrones were some bales of jute. He was absolutely disoriented. And what about food? As a poor clerk he cooked his own dal[6] and rice—but this was a joyous occasion. Mrinmayi said, "Father, today we'll all cook." Apurba agreed with alacrity.

The room was without space, servants and food, but joy sprang in abundance from the constricted circumstances of poverty, as a fountain gushes with increased force from a tiny aperture.

Three days went by. Twice the river steamer appeared on schedule with many passengers and much hubbub; but by evening the riverbank had emptied, and then the three of them were at liberty once more. They cooked together, making mistakes, and ended up with meals not quite what they had intended, which Mrinmayi, now the devoted wife, served to son-in-law and father-in-law, while they teased her about a thousand shortcomings in her household arrangements and she jingled her bangles in pretended pique. At last Apurba said they really had to leave. Though Mrinmayi pleaded with him for a few more days, her father said, "Better not."

On the last day he hugged his daughter, stroked her head, and said in a choked voice, "Darling, you must be a Lakshmi[7] to brighten your husband's home. Let no one find fault with my Minu." A sobbing Mrinmayi bade farewell and departed with her husband. Ishan turned and went back to his hut, now twice as cramped and cheerless, and resumed weighing goods, day after day, month after month.

6

When this guilty couple returned home, Apurba's mother wore a long face and said nothing. She blamed no one, and they did not try to exonerate themselves. Unspoken reproof and reproach sat sternly upon the house like a stone. At last the atmosphere became unbearable, and Apurba said, "Mother, college has opened, and I had better return to start my law degree."

His mother said indifferently, "What will you do with your wife?"

"She'll stay here."

"No son, it won't work. You must take her with you." She did not employ the usual affectionate form of address.

Apurba in a mortified tone said, "All right." He began to prepare. On the night before his departure he came to bed and found Mrinmayi in tears. Sorrowfully he asked, "I suppose you don't want to go with me to Calcutta?"

"No."

"Don't you love me?" There was no answer. Sometimes an answer comes easily, but other times the psychology of it is so complex that a shy girl can only keep silent. Apurba asked, "Will you mind leaving Rakhal?"

"Yes," said Mrinmayi without hesitation.

6. Lentils.   7. Celestial maiden.

A pang of jealousy as piercing as the point of a needle passed through this Bachelor of Arts at the thought of the boy Rakhal. He said, "I won't be able to return for a long time."

No reply.

"I think it could even be two years or more."

"When you return, bring a Rogers three-bladed knife for Rakhal," Mrinmayi ordered.

Apurba, who had been reclining against a bolster, rose a little at this and said, "So you really do want to stay here."

"Yes, I'll go and stay with my mother."

Apurba sighed and said, "All right, that's that. I won't come back until you write me a letter. Does that make you very happy?"

Mrinmayi felt that this question did not require a reply and dropped off to sleep. But Apurba did not sleep. He propped himself up with a pillow and remained alert.

Late at night the moon rose, and moonlight fell across the bed. Apurba looked at Mrinmayi and thought he saw a fairy princess put to sleep by the touch of a silver wand. If he could only find a wand of gold he could awaken her and exchange a garland of love. But he knew that such a wand would only bring him heartache instead of happiness, while the silver wand had turned her into a blissfully sleeping beauty.

At dawn he woke her and said, "Mrinmayi, it's time for me to go. Let me take you to your mother's house." She got out of bed and stood there, and Apurba took her hands. "I want you to grant me a wish. I have helped you many times. Now that I am going will you give me a reward?"

Mrinmayi was puzzled. "What?"

"Give me one loving kiss."

Apurba's ridiculous request and earnest voice made Mrinmayi burst into laughter. Then she pulled a long face and prepared to kiss him. She came close and could not, giggled and began to laugh again. Twice she tried, and at last gave up, muffling her hilarity with her sari. Apurba pulled her ears as a punishment but made a stern vow: he must not lower his dignity by snatching his reward by force. It must come spontaneously, as a sacred offering—or not at all.

Mrinmayi laughed no more. They set out together for her mother's house in the hush of early morning. When he returned he said to his own mother, "I thought it over and decided to take her to her mother. Having a wife with me in Calcutta would restrict my studies. She'd have no company there. You don't seem to want her here, so I left her with her own mother." In deep resentment, mother and son parted.

7

In her mother's house Mrinmayi found that she could not settle to anything. The entire house seemed to have altered. Time dragged. What to do, where to go, whom to see, she could not decide. It was as if the house and the village had been obliterated by a total eclipse of the sun at midday. And another thing: the desire to go to Calcutta that overwhelmed her now—where had that been last night? Only a day ago, she had had no conception that the life she loved could completely lose its savour. Today, like a mature leaf ready to detach itself from a tree, she effortlessly rejected her former existence.

There is a tale told of a swordsmith so skilled he could make a weapon keen enough to slice a man in two without his feeling a thing; only when he moved would the two parts divide. Mrinmayi was unaware when the Creator's sword severed her childhood from her youth. She looked around her, astonished and bruised, and saw herself anew. Her bedroom in her old home was no longer familiar. The girl who had lived there had disappeared. Now all her memorable moments gathered around another house, another room, another bed.

No one saw Mrinmayi out of doors any more. No one heard her peals of laughter. Rakhal was afraid even to look at her. Games together were out of the question. She said to her mother, "Take me back to my mother-in-law's house."

There Apurba's mother had been grieving, remembering her son's face at farewell. She agonized over his going away angry and leaving his wife with her own mother. Then the mournful Mrinmayi, veiled with due respect, came to touch her mother-in-law's feet. No wonder the old woman wept, embraced the younger, and in a moment was reconciled. Then the mother-in-law looked into the newly married girl's face and was amazed. The Mrinmayi she had known was no more. Could ordinary beings be so transformed? Such an enormous change would require enormous strength. The mother-in-law had intended to correct Mrinmayi's faults one by one, but an invisible Rectifier had taken charge of her and in one fell swoop had moulded her anew. Now Mrinmayi could understand her mother-in-law, and her mother-in-law Mrinmayi. They intertwined as one household like the branches and twigs of a tree.

A profound sense of womanhood filled every fibre of Mrinmayi and made her feel as tender as heartache. Tears of contrition welled up in her like the inky-black rain-clouds that herald the monsoon. They cast deep shadows beneath her eyelashes. She kept thinking to herself: I didn't know my own mind. You could see that. So why didn't you make it up for me? Why didn't you punish me? I didn't want to go to Calcutta with you and behaved like a witch. Why didn't you make me go? You shouldn't have taken any notice of me and my obstinacy.

She thought of that morning when Apurba had captured her on the lonely road by the pond, had said nothing, only looked at her. She saw the path, the spot beneath the trees, the morning sunbeams, the expression in his eyes and all of a sudden she sensed their full meaning. The half-kiss she had given him before he went away now tormented her like a thirsty bird in the desert darting forward and hesitating before a mirage. Over and over again she thought: I wish I'd done that then, I wish I'd said that, if only it had been like that!

Apurba was similarly despairing. He was telling himself: Mrinmayi has never seen my best self. While Mrinmayi was asking herself: what must he think of me? What must he take me for? A difficult, thoughtless, silly girl, not a mature woman capable of returning his love from an unquenchable heart. She felt sick with shame and remorse and began to repay all her debts to Apurba with kisses and caresses on his pillow.

When he had gone away he had said, "If you don't write, I won't come home." When she remembered that, she shut the door and began a letter on the gold-bordered coloured paper that he had given her. Very carefully she drew some lines and then, after smudging her fingers, without bothering to address her husband with a formal salutation she wrote: "Why don't you write to me? How are you?" and "You come home." What more could she say? Everything worth saying had surely been said, but not perhaps with quite the flair for expression to which humans are accustomed. Mrinmayi understood that and racked her brain for ways to put some new words together. "Now write me a letter, and write how you are and come home, mother is well, Bishu and Puti are well, yesterday our black cow had a calf." With this she ended the letter. She put it in an envelope and in drops of love inscribed each letter: Shrijukta Babu Apurba Krishna Ray. But even so much love could not make the lines straight, the letters neatly formed, the spelling faultless. And on an envelope, besides the name, something else is required. This Mrinmayi did not know. To keep the letter private she gave it to a trusted maid for posting. Needless to say, nothing came of it. Apurba did not come home.

8

His mother knew he had a holiday, yet Apurba had not returned. She and Mrinmayi assumed that he was still angry, and when Mrinmayi thought of her letter she was overcome with shame. It had conveyed nothing she really wanted to say, and Apurba would think her even more immature and even less worthy of his efforts. She was transfixed with anxiety. Again and again she asked the maid, "That letter, did you post it?" A thousand times the maid reassured her, "Yes, I dropped it into the box my-self. The master should have got it days ago."

A day eventually came when Apurba's mother called Mrinmayi and told her, "Daughter, Apu has been gone a long time, so I am thinking of going to Calcutta to see him. Will you come?" Mrinmayi nodded in agreement, went to her room, shut the door, fell on the bed, embraced the pillow and shook with silent laughter. Then all her pent-up emotion spilled out and she became serious, gloomy and apprehensive. Finally she started to cry.

With no prior warning these two repentant women set out for Calcutta to plead with Apurba for absolution. There they stayed at the home of his married sister.

That evening Apurba, who had given up hope of a letter from Mrinmayi, broke his vow and sat down to write to her. No words came. He groped for one to convey mingled love and hurt. Not finding it, he became contemptuous of his mother tongue. Just then a note arrived from his brother-in-law: "Mother is here. Come at once and have your meal with us. All is well." In spite of this assurance, Apurba went along in a mood of gloomy apprehension. As he entered his sister's house he promptly asked, "Mother, is everything all right?"

"Everything is perfectly all right. You didn't come home for the holiday, so I have come to fetch you."

"You needn't have troubled," Apurba said. "You know I have to prepare for the law exams . . ." And so on.

When it was time to eat his sister asked, "*Dada,* why isn't your wife with you?"

"My studies, you know . . ." her brother said solemnly.

His brother-in-law laughed. "All these feeble excuses! You were afraid of us."

The sister said, "You look ferocious enough to frighten any young person."

The banter continued, but Apurba remained downcast. Nothing made him feel happier. All he could think was that since his mother had come, Mrinmayi could easily have come too if she had wished. Perhaps his mother had tried but been turned down. It was hardly something he felt he could question her about: one must simply accept that all human intercourse, in fact all creation, was a maze of deception and error.

After the meal a blustery wind arose and heavy rain came down. Apurba's sister proposed, "*Dada,* do stay with us tonight."

"No, I must get back. I have to work."

"What can you achieve at this hour?" asked his brother-in-law. "Stay. You're not obliged to anyone. Why worry?"

After more urging Apurba acquiesced. His sister said, "*Dada,* you look tired. Don't stay up. Go to bed." That was Apurba's wish as well. He wanted to be alone in bed in the dark and away from all this chatter. At the bedroom door he saw that the room was dark. His sister said, "That wind has blown out your lamp. Shall I bring another?"

"No need. I sleep without a lamp." His sister left.

Apurba began to feel his way towards the bed. He was about to climb into it when with a sudden sound of bangles, a soft arm took him in its embrace, and a pair of lips like a flowering bud smothered him with a flood of passionate kisses that left no space to express surprise. He was startled only for a moment. Then he knew that the half-kiss interrupted by fits of laughter was at long last being concluded among uninhibited tears.

BIBLIOGRAPHY

The Nineteenth Century

General Background • Meyer H. Abrams, *The Mirror and the Lamp: Romantic Theory and the Critical Tradition*, 1953. • Meyer H. Abrams, *Natural Supernaturalism: Tradition and Revolution in Romantic Literature*, 1971. • Nancy Armstrong, *Desire and Domestic Fiction: A Political History of the Novel*, 1987. • Marshall Brown, *The Shape of German Romanticism*, 1979. • J. W. Burrow, *Evolution and Social Theory*, 1970. • Marilyn Butler, *Romantics, Rebels, and Reactionaries: English Literature and Its Background, 1760–1830*, 1981. • Linda Colley, *Britons: Forging the Nation, 1707–1837*, 1992. • Albert Cook, *Thresholds: Studies in the Romantic Experience*, 1985. • Stuart Curran, *Poetic Form and British Romanticism*, 1986. • Sandra M. Gilbert and Susan Gubar, *The Madwoman in the Attic: The Woman Writer and the Nineteenth-Century Imagination*, 1979. • Vesna Goldsworthy, *Inventing Ruritania: The Imperialism of the Imagination* 1998. • Catherine Hall, *Civilising Subjects: Metropole and Colony in the English Imagination 1830–1867*, 2002. • E. J. Hobsbawm, *The Age of Capital, 1848–1875*, 1975. • E. J. Hobsbawm, *The Age of Empire, 1875–1914*, 1987. • Everett Knight, *A Theory of the Classical Novel*, 1970. • Georges Lefebvre, *The Coming of the French Revolution 1789*, trans. R. R. Palmer, 1947. • Jerome J. McGann, *The Romantic Ideology: A Critical Investigation*, 1983. • Ellen Moers, *Literary Women*, 1976. • Franco Moretti, *Atlas of the European Novel, 1800–1900*, 1998. • Karl Polányi, *The Great Transformation: The Political and Economic Origins of Our Time*, 1944. • Charles Rosen, *The Romantic Generation*, 1995. • Kristin Ross, *The Emergence of Social Space: Rimbaud and the Paris Commune*, 1988. • Wolfgang Schivelbusch, *Disenchanted Night: The Industrialization of Light in the Nineteenth Century*, 1983. • Wolfgang Schivelbusch, *The Railway Journey: The Industrialization of Time and Space in the Nineteenth Century*, 1977. • Malini Schueller, *U.S. Orientalisms: Race, Nation, and Gender in Literature 1790–1890*, 1998. • Jean Starobinski, *1789: The Emblems of Reason*, trans. Bar-

bara Bray, 1982. • Alan Trachtenberg, *The Incorporation of America: Culture and Society in the Gilded Age*, 1982. • Gauri Viswanathan, *Masks of Conquest: Literary Study and British Rule in India*, 1989. • Susan J. Wolfson, *Formal Charges: The Shaping of Poetry in British Romanticism*, 1997.

Crosscurrents: The Folk and Their Tales • Isabel Crouch, ed., *Proceedings of Seminar / Conference on Oral Tradition*, 1984. • Alan Dundes, *Interpreting Folklore*, 1980. • Alan Dundes, *The Morphology of North American Indian Folktales*, 1962. • Donald Haase, "Yours, Mine, or Ours? Perrault, the Brothers Grimm, and the Ownership of Fairy Tales," in *The Classic Fairy Tales: Texts, Criticism*, ed. Maria M. Tatar, 1998. • Arlene Hirschfelder, ed., *Native Heritage*, 1995. • Bengt Holbek, *Interpretation of Fairy Tales*, 1987. • Vicki K. Janik, ed., *Fools and Jesters in Literature, Art, and History: A Bio-Bibliographical Sourcebook*, 1998. • Claude Lévi-Strauss. "The Structural Study of Myth," in *Structural Anthropology*, 1963. Claude Lévi-Strauss. Introduction to a Science of Mythology, 4 vols. , 1969–1978. • Max Lüthi, *The European Folktale: Form and Nature*, 1982. • James M. McGlathery, *Fairy Tale Romance*, 1991. • Teresa Pijoan, *Ways of Indian Magic: Stories*, 1985. • Vladimir Propp, *Morphology of the Folktale*, trans. Laurence Scott, 1958. • Evelyn Dahl Reed, *Coyote Tales from the Indian Pueblos*, 1988. • Lutz Röhrich, *Folktales and Reality*, 1979. • Lewis C. Seifert. *Fairy Tales, Sexuality, and Gender in France, 1690–1715: Nostalgic Utopias*, 1996. • Brian Swann and Arnold Krupat, eds., *Recovering the Word: Essays on Native American Literature*, 1987. • Maria Tatar, *Off with Their Heads! Fairy Tales and the Culture of Childhood*, 1992. • Stith Thomson, *The Folktale*, 1946. • Dorothea E. von Mücke, *The Seduction of the Occult and the Rise of the Fantastic Tale*, 2003. • Marina Warner, *From the Beast to the Blonde: On Fairy Tales and Their Tellers*, 1994. • Jack Zipes, *When Dreams Come True: Classic Fairy Tales and Their Tradition*, 1999.

Perspectives: The National Poet • Benedict Anderson, *Imagined Communities: Reflections on the Origin and Spread of Nationalism*, 1991. • Jonathan Arac, "Narrative Forms" in *The Cambridge Guide to American Literature*, vol. 2, ed. Sacvan Bercovich, 1995. • Christophe Bataille, *Annam*, 1996. • Louis Coutelle, *A Greek Diptych: Dionysios Solomos and Alexandros Papadiamantis*, 1986. • Nguyen Du, *Tale of Kieu: A Bilingual Edition of Truyen Kieu*, trans. Huynh Sanh, 1983. www.vietspring.org/literature/kieu.html • Betsy Erkkila and Jay Grossman, *Breaking Bounds: Whitman and American Cultural Studies*, 1996. • Gunther Eyck, *The Voice of Nations: European National Anthems and Their Authors*, 1995. • Ed Folsom, ed., *Whitman East and West: New Contexts for Reading Walt Whitman*, 2002. • Peter Uwe Hohendahl, *Building a National Literature: The Case of Germany 1830–1870*, 1989. • Edmund Keeley and Peter Bien, eds., *Modern Greek Writers*, 1972. • Lloyd Kramer, *Nationalism and Political Cultures in Europe and America, 1775–1865*. • Vassilis Lambropoulos, *Literature as a National Institution*, 1988. • Waclaw Lednicki, *Adam Mickiewicz in World Literature* 1956. • Peter Mackridge, *Dionysios Solomos*, 1989. • Clark Mills and Jan Lechan, *Adam Mickiewicz, Selected Poems*, 1956. • Clark Mills, ed., *Adam Mickiewicz, New Selected Poems*, 1957. • Michael Moon, ed., *Walt Whitman: Leaves of Grass and Other Writings*, 2002. • Brian Porter, *When Nationalism Began to Hate: Imagining Modern Politics in Nineteenth-Century Poland*, 2000. • Doris Sommer, *Proceed with Caution, When Engaged by Minority Writing in the Americas*, 1999.

Perspectives: Occidentalism • James G. Carrier, ed., *Occidentalism: Images of the West*, 1995. • Yasunosuke Fukukita, ed., *Japan's Innate Virility: Selections from Okakura and Nitobe*, 1943. • Oscar Handlin and Lilian Handlin, eds., *From the Outer World*, 1997. • Elaine Yee Lin Ho, "The Chinese Traveller in the West," *Mattoid* vols. 52–53, 1998. p. 316–33. • Dinkar Kowshik, *Okakura, the Rising Sun of Japanese Renaissance*, 1988. • Noriko Muraj, "Okakura's Way of Tea: Representing Chanoyu in Early Twentieth-Century America," *Review of Japanese Culture and Society* vol. 14, December 2002, pp. 60–77. • Edward Said, *Orientalism*, 1978. • Rudolphus Teeuwen, ed., *Crossings: Travel, Art, Literature, Politics*, 2001. • Chiang Yee, *A Chinese Childhood*, 1952. • Chiang Yee, *The Silent Traveller in London*, 1938.

Perspectives: On the Colonial Frontier • Asuncion Lopez Bantug, *Indio Bravo: The Story of José Rizal*, 1997. • Thomas M. Barrett, *At the Edge of Empire: The Terek Cossacks and the North Caucasus Frontier, 1700–1860*, 1999. • Charles Eastman (Ohiyesa), *Indian Boyhood*, 1930. • Peter Holquist, "From Estate to Ethnos: The Changing Nature of Cossack Identity in the Twentieth Century," in *Russia at a Crossroads: History, Memory, and Political Practice*, ed. Nurit Schliefman, 1998. • E. San Juan, *Rizal in Our Time: Essays in Interpretation*, 1997. • Joseph Joel Keith, *Aloha, Polyneisa: Hawaiian Poems*, 1967. • Laurence Kelly, *Lermontov: Tragedy in the Caucasus*, 2003. • Arnold Krupat, *For Those Who Come After: A Study of Native American Autobiography*, 1985. • Susan Layton, *Russian Literature and Empire: Conquest of the Caucasus from Pushkin to Tolstoy*, 1994. • Patricia Limerick, *The Legacy of Conquest: The Unbroken Past of the American West*, 1987. • Patricia Limerick, "The Adventures of the Frontier in the Twentieth Century," in *The Frontier in American Culture: Essays by Richard White and Patricia Nelson Limerick*, ed. James Grossman, 1994. • G. Patrick March, *Eastern Destiny: Russia in Asia and the North Pacific*, 1996. • Pat Namaka Bacon and Nathan Napoka, eds., *Na Mele Welo: Songs of Our Heritage*, 1995. • Alfeo Nudas, *Was Rizal Happy?*, 1993. • Jon Kamakawiwoole Osorio, *Dismembering Lahui: A History of the Hawaiian Nation to 1887*, 2002. • W. S. Penn, *Feathering Custer*, 2001. • Mary Kawena Pukui, ed., *Olelo no'eau: Hawaiian Proverbs and Poetical Sayings*, 1983. • Floro Quibuyen, *A Nation Aborted: Rizal, American Hegemony, and Philippine Nationalism*, 1999. • Richard W. Slatta, *Comparing Cowboys and Frontiers: New Perspectives on the History of the Americas*, 1997. • Richard W. Slatta, *Gauchos and the Vanishing Frontier*, 1992. • Domingo Sarmiento, *Facundo, Or Civilization and Barbarism*, 1998. • Ilan Stavans, *Mutual Impressions: Writers from the Americas Reading One Another*, 1999. • David J. Weber and Jane M. Rausch eds. *Where Cultures Meet: Frontiers in Latin American History*, 1994. • Richard Wilson, *Ohiyesa: Charles Eastman, Santee Sioux*, 1983.

Perspectives: Romantic Nature • John Barrell, *The Idea of Landscape and the Sense of Place, 1730–1840: An Approach to the Poetry of John Clare*, 1972. • Jonathan Bate, *Romantic Ecology: Wordsworth and the Environmental Tradition*, 1991. • Lawrence Buell, *The Environmental Imagination: Thoreau, Nature Writing, and the Formation of American Culture*, 1995. • Stanley Cavell, *The Senses of Walden*, 1981. • F. O. Matthiessen, *American Renaissance: Art and Expression in the Age of Emerson and Whitman*, 1941. • James McIntosh, *Thoreau as Romantic Naturalist: His Shifting Stance Toward Nature*, 1974. • Perry Miller, *Errand into the Wilderness*, 1956. • Raimonda Modiano, *Coleridge and the Concept of Nature*, 1985. • Jean Starobinski, *Jean-Jacques Rousseau: Transparency and Obstruction*, trans. Arthur Goldhammer, 1988. • Raymond Williams, *The Country and the City*, 1973.

Other Americas • Caleb Crain, *American Sympathy: Men, Friendship, and Literature in the New Nation*, 2001. • Ann Douglas, *The Feminization of American Culture*, 1998. • John R. Maitino and David R. Peck, eds., *Teaching American Ethnic Literatures: Nineteen Essays*, 1996. • Doris Sommer, *The Places of History: Regionalism Revisited in Latin America*, 1999. • Ilan Stavans, *Mutual Impressions: Writers from the Americas Reading One Another*, 1999.

The Romantic Fantastic • Roland Barthes, *S/Z: An Essay*, trans. Richard Miller, 1974. • Terry Castle, *The Female Thermometer*, 1995. • Sigmund Freud, "The 'Uncanny,'" in *On Creativity and the Unconscious*, 1958. Geoffrey Galt Harpham, *On the Grotesque*, 1982. • Fredric Jameson, *The Political Unconscious: Narrative as a Socially Symbolic Act*, 1981. • Paul Magnuson, *Coleridge's Nightmare Poetry*, 1974. • Tobin Siebers, *The Romantic Fantastic*, 1980. • Marianne Thalmann, *The Literary Sign Language of German Romanticism*, trans. Harold A. Basilius, 1972. • Tzvetan Todorov, *The Fantastic: A Structural Approach to a Literary Genre*, trans. Richard Howard, 1973.

Charles Baudelaire • Robert Baldick, trans., *Pages from the Goncourt Journals*, 1962. • *Charles Baudelaire: Les fleurs du mal: The Complete Text of "The Flowers of Evil,"* Richard Howard, trans., 1982. • *Charles Baudelaire: Selected Writings on Art and Literature*, trans. P. E. Charvet, 1992. • Walter Benjamin, *Charles Baudelaire: A Lyric Poet in the Era of High Capitalism*, trans. Harry Zohn, 1973. • Leo Bersani, *Baudelaire and Freud*, 1977. • Keith Bosley, trans., *Mallarmé: The Poems: A Bilingual Edition*. New York: Penguin, 1977. • David Carrier, *High Art: Charles Baudelaire and the Origins of Modernist Painting*, 1996. • A. E. Carter, *Charles Baudelaire*, 1977. • Carol Clark and Robert Sykes, eds. *Baudelaire in English*, 1997. • T. J. Clark, *The Absolute Bourgeois: Artists and Politics in France, 1848–1851*, 1999. • T. J. Clark, *The Painting of Modern Life: Paris in the Art of Manet and His Followers*, 1999. • Arthur Rimbaud, *Complete Works, Selected Letters*, trans., Wallace Fowlie, 1966. • J. A. Hiddleston, *Baudelaire and the Art of Memory*, 1999. • J. A. Hiddleston, *Baudelaire and Le spleen de Paris*, 1987. • Louise Boe Hyslop, *Charles Baudelaire Revisited*, 1992. • Edward K. Kaplan, *Baudelaire's Prose Poems: The Esthetic, the Ethical, and the Religious in "The Parisian Prowler,"* 1990. • Edward K. Kaplan, trans., *The Parisian Prowler: Le spleen de Paris: petits poèmes en prose*, 1997. • F. W. Leakey, *Baudelaire and Nature*, 1969. • F. W. Leakey, *Baudelaire, Les fleurs du mal*, 1992. • Rosemary Lloyd, *Baudelaire's World*, 2002. • Elissa Marder, *Dead Time: Temporal Disorders in the Wake of Modernity (Baudelaire and Flaubert)*, 2001. • Derek Joseph Mossop, *Baudelaire's Tragic Hero: A Study of the Architecture of "Les fleurs du mal,"* 1961. • Henri Peyre, *Baudelaire: A Collection of Critical Essays*, 1962. • Claude Pichois, *Baudelaire*, trans. Graham Robb, 1989. • *Approaches to Teaching Baudelaire's "Flowers of Evil,"* 2000. *Correspondence/Charles Baudelaire*, 2 vols. 1973. • Claude Pichois, ed. Charles Baudelaire *Oeuvres complètes*, 2 vols., 1993. • Laurence M. Porter, *The Crisis of French Symbolism*, 1990. • Georges Poulet, *Exploding Poetry: Baudelaire/Rimbaud*, Trans. Francoise Meltzer, 1984. • Sonya Stephens, *Baudelaire's Prose Poems: The Practice and Politics of Irony*, 1999. • William J. Thompson, *Understanding "Les fleurs du mal": Critical Readings*, 1997. • Nathaniel Wing, *The Limits of Narrative: Essays on Baudelaire, Flaubert, Rimbaud, and Mallarmé*, 1986.

Elizabeth Barrett Browning • Kathleen Blake, "Elizabeth Barrett Browning and Wordsworth:

The Romantic Poet as a Woman," *Victorian Poetry* vol. 24, 1986, pp. 387–398. • Helen Cooper, *Elizabeth Barrett Browning, Woman and Artist*, 1988. • Deirdre David, *Intellectual Women and Victorian Patriarchy: Harriet Martineau, Elizabeth Barrett Browning, George Eliot*, 1987. • Angela Leighton, *Elizabeth Barrett Browning*, 1986. • Dorothy Mermin, *Elizabeth Barrett Browning: The Origins of a New Poetry*, 1989. • Marjorie Stone, *Elizabeth Barrett Browning*, 1995. • Gardner B. Taplin, *The Life of Elizabeth Barrett Browning*, 1957. • Virginia Woolf, "Aurora Leigh," in *The Second Common Reader*, 1932.

Anton Chekhov • Harold Bloom, ed., *Anton Chekhov: Modern Critical Views*, 1999. • John Coope, *Doctor Chekhov: A Study in Literature and Medicine*, 1997. • Vera Gottlieb and Paul Allain, eds., *The Cambridge Companion to Chekhov*, 2000. • Ronald Hingley, *Chekhov: A Biographical and Critical Study*, 1966. • V.B. Kataev, *If Only We Could Know: An Interpretation of Anton Chekhov*, 2002. • Virginia Llewellyn Smith, *Anton Chekhov and "The Lady with the Dog,"* 1973. • Janet Malcolm, *Reading Chekhov: A Critical Journey*, 2001. • Donald Rayfield, *Anton Chekhov: A Life*, 1998. • Donald Rayfield, *Understanding Chekhov*, 1999.

Rubén Darío • Keith Ellis, *Critical Approaches to Rubén Darío*, 1974. • Miguel Gonzalez-Gerth and George Schade, *Rubén Darío Centennial Studies*, 1970. • Rosemary LoDato, *Beyond the Glitter*, 1999.

Emily Dickinson • Paula Bennett, *My Life, A Loaded Gun: Female Creativity and Feminist Poetics*, 1986. • Sharon Cameron, *Lyric Time: Dickinson and the Limits of Genre*, 1979. • Joanne Diehl, *Dickinson and the Romantic Imagination*, 1981. • Judith Farr, *Emily Dickinson: A Collection of Critical Essays*, 1996. • Judith Farr, *The Passion of Emily Dickinson*, 1992. • Alfred Habegger, *My Wars Are Laid Away in Books: The Life of Emily Dickinson*, 2001. • Gary Lee Stonum, *The Dickinson Sublime*, 1990. • Robert Weisbuch, *Emily Dickinson's Poetry*, 1975.

Frederick Douglass • William Andrews, *Critical Essays on Frederick Douglass*, 1991. • Harold Bloom, ed., *Frederick Douglass's Narrative of the Life of Frederick Douglass*, 1988. • Nathan

Huggins, *Slave and Citizen: The Life of Frederick Douglass*, 1980. • Waldo E. Martin, Jr. *The Mind of Frederick Douglass*, 1984. • William McFeely, *Frederick Douglass*, 1991.

Fyodor Dostoevsky • Mikhail Bakhtin, *Problems of Dostoevky's Poetics* • Donald Fanger, *Dostoevsky and Romantic Realism*, 1965. • Joseph Frank, *Dostoevsky*, 5 vols., 1983–2002. • Joseph Frank, ed., *Selected Letters of Fyodor Dostoevsky*, 1987. • René Girard, *Resurrection from the Underground: Fyodor Dostoevsky*, 1997. • Frederick Griffiths, *Novel Epics: Gogol, Dostoevsky, and National Narrative*, 1990. • Michael Holquist, *Dostoevsky and the Novel*, 1977. • Michael R. Katz, *Notes from Underground: An Authoritative Translation, Backgrounds, and Sources*, 2001. • Gary Saul Morson, *Narrative Freedom: The Shadows of Time*, 1994. • Victor Terras, *Reading Dostoevsky*, 1998. • Andrew Wachtel, *An Obsession with History*, 1994.

Gustave Flaubert • Julian Barnes, *Flaubert's Parrot*, 1990. • Jonathan Culler, *Flaubert: The Uses of Uncertainty*, 1974. • Peter Eyre, *Chere Maître: The Correspondence of Gustave Flaubert and George Sand*, 2002. • Harry Levin, *The Gates of Horn: A Study of Five French Realists*, 1963. • Herbert Lottman, *Flaubert: A Biography*, 1989. • Franco Moretti, *The Way of the World*. • Laurence Porter, *A Gustave Flaubert Encyclopedia*, 2001. • Francis Steegmuller, *Flaubert in Egypt: A Sensibility on Tour*, 1972. • Richard Terdiman, *Discourse/Counter-Discourse: The Theory and Practice of Symbolic Resistance in Nineteenth-Century France*, 1985. • Geoffrey Wall, *Flaubert: A Life*, 2001.

Ghalib • Aga Shahid Ali, *Call Me Ishmael Tonight: A Book of Ghazals*, 2003. • R. K. Kuldip, *Mirza Ghalib; A Critical Appreciation of Ghalib's Thought and Verse*, 1967. • Daud Rahbar, ed., *Urdu Letters of Mirza Asadu'llah Khan Ghalib*, 1987. • Ralph Russell, Khurshidul Islam, eds., *Ghalib (1787–1869): Life and Letters*, 1994. • Ralph Russell, ed., *Ghalib: The Poet and His Age*, 1972. • Ralph Russell, ed., *The Famous Ghalib*, 2000. • Christopher Shackle, "Classics and the Comparison of Adjacent Literatures: Some Pakistani Perspectives," *Comparative Criticism: An Annual Journal* 21–38 vol. 22, 2000. • Pavan K. Varma, *Ghalib, the Man, the Times*, 1989.

Charlotte Perkins Gilman • Catherine Golden, *The Captive Imagination: A Casebook on "The Yellow Wallpaper,"* 1992. • Joanne Karpinski, ed., *Critical Essays on Charlotte Perkins Gilman,* 1992. • Catherine Golden and Joanna Zangrando, eds., *The Mixed Legacy of Charlotte Perkins Gilman,* 2000. • Jill Rudd and Val Gough, *A Very Different Story: Studies on the Fiction of Charlotte Perkins Gilman,* 1998. • Charlotte Perkins Gilman, *The Living of Charlotte Perkins Gilman: An Autobiography,* 1990. • Ann Lane, *To Herland and Beyond: The Life and Work of Charlotte Perkins Gilman,* 1990.

Johann Wolfgang Goethe • Stuart Atkins, *Goethe's Faust: A Literary Analysis,* 1958. • Marshall Berman, *All That Is Solid Melts into Air: The Experience of Modernity,* 1982. • Nicholas Boyle, *Goethe: The Poet and the Age,* 2 vols., 1991. • Jane K. Brown, *Faust: Theater of the World,* 1992. • Jane K. Brown, *Goethe's Faust: The German Tragedy,* 1986. • Richard Friedenthal, *Goethe: His Life and Times,* 3 vols., 1963. • Ilse Graham, *Goethe: A Portrait of the Artist,* 1977. • Harry G. Haile, *Invitation to Goethe's "Faust,"* 1978. • *Faust,* Cyrus Hamlin, ed., 2001. • Victor Lange, Eric A. Blackall, and Cyrus Hamlin, eds. *Goethe's Collected Works,* 12 vols., 1983–1989. • Franco Moretti, *Modern Epic: The World-System from Goethe to García Marquez,* trans. Quintin Hoare, 1996. • Lesley Sharpe, ed., *The Cambridge Companion to Goethe,* 2002. • Elizabeth M. Wilkinson and Leonard A. Willoughby, *Goethe: Poet and Thinker,* 1962.

George Gordon, Lord Byron • Anne Barton, *Byron: Don Juan,* 1992. • Jerome Christensen, *Lord Byron's Strength: Romantic Writing and Commercial Society,* 1993. • Michale G. Cooke, *The Blind Man Traces the Circle: On the Patterns and Philosophy of Byron's Poetry,* 1969. • Louis Crompton, *Byron and Greek Love,* 1985. • Andrew Elfenbein, *Byron and the Victorians,* 1995. • G. Wilson Knight, *The Burning Oracle,* 1939. • Peter J. Manning, *Byron and His Fictions,* 1978. • Leslie Marchand, *Byron: A Biography,* 3 vols. 1957; abridged and revised in one volume as *Byron: A Portrait,* 1970. • Jerome J. McGann, *Fiery Dust: Byron's Poetic Development,* 1968. • Jerome J. McGann, *Don Juan in Context,* 1976.

Jacob and Wilhelm Grimm • Bruno Bettelheim, *The Uses of Enchantment: The Meaning and Importance of Fairy Tales,* 1977. • Peter Brooks, *Reading for the Plot: Design and Intention in Narrative,* 1984. • Peter Carter, trans., and Peter Richardson, illus., *Grimm's Fairy Tales,* 1997. • Donald Haase, *The Reception of Grimms' Fairy Tales: Responses, Reactions, Revisions,* 1993. • Christa Kamenetsky, *The Brothers Grimm and Their Critics: Folktales and the Quest for Meaning,* 1992. • James M. McGlathery, *Grimms' Fairy Tales: A History of Criticism on a Popular Classic,* 1993. • G. Ronald Murphy, *The Owl, the Raven, and the Dove: The Religious Meaning of the Grimms' Magic Fairy Tales,* 2000. • Maria M. Tatar, "Born Yesterday: Heroes in the Grimms' Fairy Tales," in *Fairy Tales and Society: Illusion, Allusion, and Paradigm,* ed. Ruth B. Bottigheimer, 1986. • Donald Ward, ed. and trans., *The German Legends of the Brothers Grimm,* 1981. • Jack Zipes, *The Brothers Grimm: From Enchanted Forests to the Modern World,* 2003. • Jack Zipes, trans., and John B. Gruelle, illus., *The Complete Fairy Tales of the Brothers Grimm,* 1987.

Henrik Ibsen • Robert Ferguson, *Ibsen: A New Biography,* 1996. • Michael Goldman, *Ibsen: The Dramaturgy of Fear,* 1999. • C. D. Innes, *A Sourcebook on Naturalist Theater,* 2000. • Charles Lyons, *Critical Essays on Henrik Ibsen,* 1987. • Frederick Marker, *Ibsen's Lively Art,* 1989. • James McFarlane, *The Cambridge Companion to Ibsen,* 1994. • Yvonne Shafer, *Approaches to Teaching Ibsen's "A Doll's House,"* 1985. • George Bernard Shaw, *The Quintessence of Ibsenism,* 1994. • Joan Templeton "The Doll House Backlash: Criticism, Feminism, and Ibsen," *PMLA,* vol. 104 (1989), pp. 28–40. • Joan Templeton, *Ibsen's Women,* 1997.

Higuchi Ichiyo • Julie Ann Carson and John Rehm, ed., *In the Pacific Interest: Democracy, Women and the Environment,* 1991. • Robert Lyons Danly, *In the Shade of Spring Leaves: The Life and Writings of Higuchi Ichiyo, a Woman of Letters in Meiji Japan,* 1981. • Margaret Mitsutani, "Higuchi Ichiyo: A Literature of Her Own," *Comparative Literature Studies* vol. 22, 1985. 53–66.

Harriet Jacobs • Yvonne Johnson, *The Voices of African-American Women,* 1998. • Carla Kaplan, *The Erotics of Talk: Women's Writing and Feminist Paradigms,* 1996. • Rafia Zafar and Deborah Garfield, eds., *Harriet Jacobs*

and *"Incidents in the Life of a Slave Girl":*
New Critical Essays, 1996.

Liu E • Milena Dolezelova-Velingerova, ed. *The*
Chinese Novel at the Turn of the Century,
1980. • Liu E, *The Travels of Lao Ts'an,*
Harold Shadick, trans. 1952. • David Der-wei
Wang, *Fin-de-Siècle Splendor: Repressed*
Modernities in Late Qing Fiction, 1894–1911,
1997. • H. Y. Yang and G. M. Tayler, *Mr.*
Derelict by Liu Ngo, 1948. • Liu E, *The Trav-*
els of Lao Can, Xianyi and Gladys Yang,
trans. 1983.

Joaquim María Machado de Assis • Piers Armstrong, *Third World Literary Fortunes: Brazil-*
ian Culture and Its International Reception,
1999. • Earl Fitz, *Machado de Assis,* 1989.
• Richard Graham, *Machado de Assis: Reflec-*
tions on a Brazilian Master Writer 1999.
• Jose Raimundo Maia Neto, *Machado de As-*
sis, the Brazilian Pyrrhonian, 1994 • Maria
Luisa Nunes, *The Craft of an Absolute Winner,*
1989. • Roberto Schwartz, *A Master on the*
Periphery of Capitalism: Machado de Assis,
2001.

Herman Melville • Elizabeth Hardwick, *Herman*
Melville, 2000. • Robert S. Levine, ed., *The*
Cambridge Companion to Herman Melville,
1998. • Hershel Parker, *Herman Melville: A*
Biography, 1996–2002. • Carl Rollyson,
Herman Melville A to Z, 2001. • Geoffrey
Sanborn, *The Sign of the Cannibal: Melville*
and the Making of a Postcolonial Reader,
1998.

Hathali Nez and Washington Matthews
• Raymond J. Demallie, ed., *The Sixth Grand-*
father: Black Elk's Teachings Given to John
G. Neihardt, 1984. • Virginia Faulkner and
Frederick C. Luebke, ed., *Vision and Refuge:*
Essays on the Literature of the Great Plains,
1982. • Stanley A. Fishler, *In the Beginning: A*
Navaho Creation Myth, 1953. • Clyde Holler,
ed., *The Black Elk Reader,* 2000. • Brian Hol-
loway, *Interpreting the Legacy: John Neihardt*
and "Black Elk Speaks," 2003. • Lauren D.
Linford, *Navajo Places: History, Legend, and*
Landscape, 2000. • Sheila Moon, *A Magic*
Dwells: A Poetic and Psychological Study of
the Navaho Emergence Myth, 1970. • Gladys
Amanda Reichard, *Navaho Religion: A Study*
of Symbolism, 1990.

Benedikte Naubert • Jeannine Blackwell, "Frac-
tured Fairy Tales: German Women Authors
and the Grimm Tradition," *The Germanic Re-*
view, vol. 62, 1987. 162–174. • Jeannine
Blackwell and Susanne Zantop, *Bitter Heal-*
ing: German Women Writers, 1700–1830,
1990. • Marianne Henn, Paola Mayer, and
Anita Runge, eds., *Neue Volksmärchen der*
Deutschen, 2001. • Shawn C. Jarvis, "The
Vanished Woman of Great Influence:
Benedikte Naubert's Legacy and German
Women's Fairy Tales," in *In the Shadow of*
Olympus: German Women Writers Around
1800, ed. Katherine R. Goodman and Edith
Waldstein, 1992.

Charles Perrault • Jacques Barchilon and Peter
Flinders, *Charles Perrault,* 1981. • A. E. Johnson, trans., and Gustave Doré, illus., *Perrault's*
Fairy Tales, 1994. • Philip Lewis, *Seeing*
Through the Mother Goose Tales: Visual
Turns in the Writings of Charles Perrault,
1996. • Charles Perrault, *Memoirs of My Life,*
ed. and trans. Jeanne Morgan Zarucchi, 1989.
• *The Complete Fairy Tales of Charles Per-*
rault, Neil Philip, ed., Neil Philip and Nico-
letta Simborowski, trans., and Sally Holmes,
illus., 1993. • Jack Zipes, trans. and ed.
Beauties, Beasts, and Enchantment: Classic
French Fairy Tales, 1989.

Alexander Pushkin • John Bayley, *Pushkin: A*
Comparative Commentary, 1971. • J. Douglas
Clayton, *Ice and Flame: Pushkin's "Eugene*
Onegin," 1985. • D. S. Mirsky, *Pushkin,* 1926.
• Alexander Pushkin, *Eugene Onegin,* trans.
Vladimir Nabokov, 4 vols., 1964. • Gary
Rosenshield, *Pushkin and the Genres of Mad-*
ness: The Masterpieces of 1833, 2003.

Rabindranath Tagore • Ayuiba Abu Sayida,
Modernism and Tagore, 1995. • Carol A.
Breckenridge and Peter van der Veer, eds.,
Orientalism and the Postcolonial Predicament:
Perspectives on South Asia, 1993. • K. Chan-
drasekharan, *Tagore: A Master Spirit,* 1961.
• Bhabatosh Chatterjee, *Rabindranath Tagore*
and Modern Sensibility, 1996. • Rimi B. Chat-
terjee, "Canon Without Consensus: Ra-
bindranath Tagore and *The Oxford Book of Ben-*
gali Verse," *Book History,* vol. 4, 2001.
• Shyamal Chattopadhyaya, *Art and the Abyss:*
Six Essays in Interpretation of Tagore, 1977.
• Krishna Dutta, *Rabindranath Tagore: The*

Myriad-Minded Man, 1995. ● Krishna Dutta and Andrew Robinson, ed., *Purabi: A Miscellany Memory of Rabindranath Tagore 1941–1991,* 1991. ● Rabindranath Tagore: *Selected Letters of Rabindranath Tagore,* Krishna Dutta and Andrew Robinson, eds., 1997. ● Rabindranath Tagore: *Rabindranath Tagore: An Anthology,* Krishna Dutta and Andrew Robinson, eds., 1997. ● Mahatma Gandhi, *The Mahatma and the Poet: Letters and Debates Between Gandhi and Tagore, 1915–1941,* 1997. ● Krishna Kripalani, *Tagore: A Life,* 1971. ● Sudhirkumara Nandi, *Art and Aesthetics of Rabindranath Tagore,* 1999. ● Ashis Nandy, *The Illegitimacy of Nationalism: Rabindranath Tagore and the Politics of Self,* 1994. ● Rabindranath Tagore, *Selected Writings on Literature and Language,* 2001.

Leo Tolstoy ● John Bayley, *Leo Tolstoy,* 1997. ● Italo Calvino, *Why Read the Classics?* 1999. ● Henry Gifford, *Tolstoy,* 1982. ● Georg Lukács, *Studies in European Realism,* 1964. ● Donna Orwin, ed., *The Cambridge Companion to Tolstoy,* 2002. ● William Rowe, *Leo Tolstoy,* 1986. ● George Steiner, *Tolstoy or Dostoevsky?* 1996 ● Raymond Williams, *Modern Tragedy,* 2001. ● A. N. Wilson, *Tolstoy,* 1988.

Mark Twain ● Harold Bloom, ed. *Mark Twain,* 1986. ● Everett Emerson, *Mark Twain: A Literary Life,* 1999. ● Wilma Garcia, *Mothers and Others: Myths of the Female in the Works of Melville, Twain, and Hemingway,* 1984. ● Elizabeth McMahan, ed., *Critical Approaches to Mark Twain's Short Stories,* 1981. ● Peter Messent, *The Short Works of Mark Twain; A Critical Study,* 2001. ● Brian S. Stern, *Mark Twain's Theory of Sexual Morality,* 1996. ● Eric J. Sundquist, ed., *Mark Twain: A Collection of Critical Essays,* 1994.

William Wordsworth ● James Averill, *Wordsworth and the Poetry of Human Suffering,* 1979. ● Alan Bewell, *Wordsworth and the Enlightenment,* 1989. ● David Bromwich, *Disowned by Memory,* 1998. ● Marshall Brown, *Preromanticism,* 1991. ● James Chandler, *Wordsworth's Second Nature: A Study of the Poetry and Politics,* 1984. ● Steven Gill, *Wordsworth: A Life,* 1989. ● Geoffrey Hartman, *The Unremarkable Wordsworth,* 1987. ● Geoffrey Hartman, *Wordsworth's Poetry: 1787–1814,* 1971. ● Mary Jacobus, *Romanticism, Writing, and Sexual Difference: Essays on The Prelude,* 1989. ● Kenneth Johnston, *Wordsworth and "The Recluse,"* 1984. ● Marjorie Levinson, *Wordsworth's Great Period Poems,* 1986. ● Herbert Lindenberger, *On Wordsworth's "Prelude,"* 1963. ● Alan Liu, *Wordsworth: The Sense of History,* 1989. ● Gene W. Ruoff, *Wordsworth and Coleridge,* 1989. ● David Simpson, *Wordsworth and the Figurings of the Real,* 1982. ● David Simpson, *Wordsworth's Historical Imagination: The Poetry of Displacement,* 1987.

CREDITS

969

Nguyen Du: "Reading Hsiao-Ching" from *A Thousand Years of Vietnamese Poetry,* edited by Nguyen Ngoc Bich. Copyright © 1962, 1967, 1968, 1969, 1970, 1971, 1972, 1974 by Asia Society, Inc. Reprinted courtesy of the Asia Society, New York.

Nguyen Du: From *The Tale of Kieu, A Bilingual Edition of Truyen Kieu,* translated by Huynh Sanh Thong. Copyright © 1983 by Yale University Press. Reprinted by permission of the publisher.

Pancatantra: "The Turtle and the Geese" from *The World's Classics: Pancatantra, The Book of India's Folk Wisdom,* translated by Patrick Olivelle. Copyright © 1997 by Patrick Olivelle. Reprinted by permission of Oxford University Press.

Perrault, Charles: "Donkey-Skin," from *Beauties, Beasts and Enchantment,* translated by Jack Zipes, copyright © 1989 by Jack Zipes. Used by permission of Dutton Signet, a division of Penguin Putnam, Inc.

Pushkin, Alexander: From *Eugene Onegin: A Novel in Verse* by Alexander Pushkin, translated with an introduction and notes by James E. Falen. Copyright © 1990, 1995 by James E. Falen. Reprinted by permission of Oxford University Press.

Pushkin, Alexander: "I Visited Again" from *The Poems, Prose and Plays of Alexander Pushkin* by Alexander Pushkin, edited by Avrahm Yarmolinsky, copyright © 1936 and renewed 1964 by Random House, Inc. Used by permission of Random House, Inc.

Pushkin, Alexander: "The Bronze Horseman," from *Narrative Poems by Alexander Pushkin and Michael Lermontov,* translated by Charles Johnston. Copyright © 1984 by Charles Johnston. Reprinted by permission of the Charles Johnston Estate.

Rimbaud, Arthur: "Vowels," "City," and "Departure" from *Rimbaud Complete Works, Selected Letters,* translated by Wallace Fowlie. Copyright © 1966 by The University of Chicago Press. All rights reserved. Reprinted by permission.

Rizal, José: "A Gathering" from *Noli Me Tangere,* by José Rizal, translated by Ma. Soledad Lacson-Locsin, edited by Raul L. Locsin. Copyright © 1997 School of Hawaiian, Asian & Pacific Studies. Reprinted by permission of University of Hawai'i Press, Honolulu.

Rousseau, Jean-Jacques: "Fifth Walk" from *Reveries Of The Solitary Walker,* by Jean-Jacques Rousseau, translated by Peter France. Translation copyright © 1979 by Peter France. Reproduced by permission of Penguin Books, Ltd.

Sarmiento, Domingo: From *Facundo* by Domingo F. Sarmiento: introduction by Ilan Stavans, translated by Mary Mann. Copyright © 1998 by Ilan Stavans. Used by permission of Penguin, a division of Penguin Putnam, Inc.

Solomos, Dionysios: "The Free Besieged-Fragments, Draft III," from *Faith and Motherland: Collected Poems,* by Dionysios Solomos, translated by Mariops Byron Raizis, edited by Theofanis G. Stavrou. Reprinted by permission.

Tagore, Rabindranath: "Conclusion" from *Rabindranath Tagore An Anthology,* edited by Krishna Dutta and Andrew Robinson. Copyright © 1997 by Krishna Dutta and Andrew Robinson. Reprinted by permission of St. Martin's Press, LLC.

Tieck, Ludwig: "Fair-haired Eckbert," by Ludwig Tieck, translated by Thomas Carlyle, from *German Literary Fairy Tales,* Vol. 30 German Library, edited by Frank G. Ryder and Robert M. Browning. Reprinted by permission of The Continuum International Publishing Corp.

Tolstoy, Leo: "After the Ball," from *Short Masterpieces by Tolstoy,* translated by Margaret Wettlin, Introduction copyright © 1963 by F. D. Reeve. Used by permission of Dell Publishing, a division of Random House, Inc.

ILLUSTRATION CREDITS

Cover image: Detail from *Cowlitz Mother and Child,* c. 1848, oil on canvas, by Paul Kane Caw-Wacham. Montreal Museum of Fine Arts, purchased with William Gilman Cheney Bequest. Photo by Denis Farley, The Montreal Museum of Fine Arts. Inside front cover image: Copyright © Corbis. Page xxvi: Public domain. Page 8: *The Vampire* by Walter Crane, from *Fables Less and Less Fabulous.* Private collection. Page 10: Public domain. Page 12 (top left): The Granger Collection, New York. Page 12 (top right): Title page from *Sense and Sensibility* by Jane Austen, 1856 edition. Private collection. Page 12 (bottom left): S. P. Avery Collection. Miriam and Ira D. Wallach Division of Art, Prints, and Photographs. The New York Public Library. Astor, Lenox, and Tilden Foundations. Page 12 (bottom right): Fair Street Pictures. Page 25: The Bodleian Library, Oxford. Page 97: Hamburg Kunsthalle, Hamburg, Germany/The Bridgeman Art Library. Page 160: Leeds Museums and Galleries (City Art Gallery) U.K./The Bridgeman Art Library. Page 304: Staedelsches Kunstinstitut, Frankfurt am Main, Germany. © Kavaler/Art Resource, New York. Page 375: Public domain. Page 432: Oasis-Collection particuliére/Photos12.com. Page 515: From *The Silent Traveller in London,* published by Interlink Books, an imprint of Interlink Publishing Group, Inc. Text copyright © Chiang Yee, 1938. Reprinted by permission. Page 601: Public domain.

FONTS CREDIT

The EuroSlavic, AfroRoman, Macron, TransIndic, Semitic Transliterator, and ANSEL fonts used to publish this work are available from Linguist's Software, Inc., P.O. Box 580, Edmonds, WA 98020-0580 USA, tel (425) 775-1130, www.linguistsoftware.com.

INDEX